# ANACALYPSIS

BY

## GODFREY HIGGINS, ESQ

## VOL. I

D1636790

## A&B PUBLISHERS GROUP

**Brooklyn, New York**

**11201**

# ANACALYPSIS

AN

ATTEMPT TO DRAW ASIDE THE VEIL

OF

## THE SAITIC ISIS

or

AN INQUIRY INTO THE ORIGIN

OF

# LANGUAGES NATIONS AND RELIGIONS

BY

## GODFREY HIGGINS, ESQ

F.S.A F.R.R.A S I A T. S O C., F.R.A S T S.,
OF SKELLOW GRANGE NEAR DONCASTER
RES VERBIS ET VERBA ACCENDUNT LUMINA REBUS

COVER DESIGN: A&B PUBLISHERS GROUP
COVER ILLUSTRATION: SUBLIME VISUALS
All Rights Reserved

PRINTED IN CANADA

ISBN 1-881316-18-1 SET
ISBN 13: 978-1-881316-16-9 VOL. I
ISBN 10: 1-881316-16-5 VOL. I
ISBN 1-881316-17-3 VOL. II

First Published in 1836
Reprinted 1992, 2007
by

A&B PUBLISHERS GROUP
Brooklyn, New York, 11201
(718)783-7808

# PREFACE.

It is a common practice with authors to place their portraits in the first page of their books. I am not very vain of my personal appearance, and, therefore, I shall not present the reader with my likeness. But, that I may not appear to censure others by my omission, and for some other reasons which any person possessing a very moderate share of discernment will soon perceive, I think it right to draw my own portrait with the pen, instead of employing an artist to do it with the pencil, and to inform my reader, in a few words, who and what I am, in what circumstances I am placed, and why I undertook such a laborious task as this work has proved.

Respecting my rank or situation in life it is only necessary to state, that my father was a gentleman of small, though independent fortune, of an old and respectable family in Yorkshire. He had two children, a son (myself) and a daughter. After the usual school education, I was sent to Trinity Hall, Cambridge, as a pensioner, and thence to the Temple. As I was expected to pay the fees out of the small allowance which my father made me, I never had any money to spare for that purpose, and I never either took a degree or was called to the bar.

When I was about twenty-seven years of age my father died, and I inherited his house and estate at Skellow Grange, near Doncaster. After some time I married. I continued there till the threatened invasion of Napoleon induced me, along with most of my neighbours, to enter the third West-York militia, of which, in due time, I was made a major. In the performance of my military duty in the neighbourhood of Harwich, I caught a very bad fever, from the effects of which I never entirely recovered. This caused me to resign my commission and return home. I shortly afterward became a magistrate for the West Riding of my native county. The illness above alluded to induced me to turn my attention, more than I had formerly done, to serious matters, and determined me to enter upon a very careful investigation of the evidence upon which our religion was founded. This, at last, led me to extend my inquiry into the origin of all religions, and this again led to an inquiry into the origin of nations and languages; and ultimately I came to a resolution to devote six hours a day to this pursuit for ten years. Instead of *six* hours daily for *ten* years, I believe I have, upon the average, applied myself to it for nearly *ten* hours daily for almost *twenty* years. In the first *ten* years of my search I may fairly say, I found nothing which I sought for; in the latter part of the *twenty*, the quantity of matter has so crowded in upon me, that I scarcely know how to dispose of it.

When I began these inquiries I found it necessary to endeavour to recover the scholastic learning which, from long neglect, I had almost forgotten: but many years of industry are not necessary for this purpose, as far, at least as is useful. The critical knowledge of the Greek and Latin languages, highly ornamental and desirable as it is, certainly is not, in general, necessary for the acquisition of what, in my opinion, may be properly called *real learning*.   The ancient poetry and composition are beautiful, but a critical knowledge of them was not my object.   The odes of Pindar and the poems of Homer are very fine; but Varro, Macrobius, and Cicero *De Natura Deorum*, were more congenial to my pursuits.   The languages were valuable to me only as a key to unlock the secrets of antiquity.   I beg my reader, therefore, not to expect any of that kind of learning, which would enable a person to rival Porson in filling up the Lacunæ of a Greek play, or in restoring the famous Digamma to its proper place.

But if I had neglected the study of Greek and Latin, I had applied myself to the study of such works as those of Euclid, and of Locke *on the Understanding*, the tendency of which is to form the mind to a habit of investigation and close reasoning and thinking, and in a peculiar manner to fit it for such inquiries as mine; for want of which habit, a person may possess a considerable knowledge of the Classics, while his mind may be almost incapable of comprehending the demonstration of a common proposition in geometry.   In short, we see proofs every day, that a person may be very well skilled in Greek and Latin, while in intellect he may rank little higher than a ploughboy.

Along with the study of the principles of law, whilst at the Temple, I had applied myself also to the acquisition of the art of sifting and appreciating the value of different kinds of evidence, the latter of which is perhaps the most important and the most neglected of all the branches of education.   I had also applied myself to what was of infinitely more consequence than all the former branches of study, and in difficulty almost equal to them altogether, namely, to the *unlearning* of the nonsense taught me in youth.

Literary works at the present day have generally one or both of two objects in view, namely, *money* and *present popularity*.   But I can conscientiously say, that neither of these has been my leading object.   I have become, to a certain extent, literary, because by letters alone could I make known to mankind what I considered discoveries the most important to its future welfare; and no publication has ever been written by me except under the influence of this motive.

When I say that I have not written this work for fame, it must not be understood that I affect to be insensible to the approbation of the great and good: far from it.   But if I had my choice, I would rather rank with Epictetus than with Horace, with Cato or Brutus than with Gibbon or Sir Walter Scott.   Had either present popularity or profit been my object, I had spared the priests; for, in Britain, we are a priest-ridden race: but though I had died a little richer, I had deserved contempt for my meanness.

My learning has been acquired since I turned forty years of age, for the sole purpose of being enabled to pursue these researches into the antiquities of nations, which, I very early became convinced, were generally unknown or misunderstood.   But though I do not pretend to deep classical learning, yet perhaps I may not be guilty of any very inexcusable vanity in saying, that I find myself now, on the score of learning, after twenty years of industry, in many respects very differently circumstanced in relation to persons whom I was accustomed formerly to look up to as learned, from what I was at the beginning of my inquiries; and that now I sometimes find myself qualified to teach those by whom I was at first very willing to be taught, but whom I do not always find disposed to learn, nor to be *untaught* the nonsense which they learned in their youth.

In my search I soon found that it was impossible to look upon the histories of ancient empires, or upon the history of the ancient mythologies, except as pleasing or amusing fables, fit only for the nursery or the fashionable drawing-room table, but totally below the notice of a philosopher. This consideration caused my search into their origin; indefatigable labour for many years has produced the result,—the discovery which I believe I have made, and which in this work I make known to my countrymen.

I am convinced that a taste for deep learning among us is fast declining;* and in this I believe I shall be supported by the booksellers, which is one reason why I have only printed two hundred copies of this work: but I have reason to think the case different in France and Germany; and on this account I have sometimes thought of publishing editions in the languages of those countries. But whether I shall wait till these editions be ready, and till my second volume be finished, before I make public the first, I have not yet determined; nor, indeed, have I determined whether or not I shall publish these editions. This must depend upon the foreign booksellers.

If, like some learned persons, I had commenced my inquiries by believing certain dogmas, and determining that I would never believe any other; or if, like the Rev. Mr. Faber, I had in early life sworn that I believed them, and that I would never believe any other, and that all my comfort in my future life depended upon my *professed* continuance in this belief, I should have had much less trouble, because I should have known what I was to prove; but my story is very different. When I began this inquiry, I was anxious for truth, suspicious of being deceived, but determined to examine every thing as impartially as was in my power, to the very bottom. This soon led me to the discovery, that I must go to much more distant sources for the origin of things than was usual; and, by degrees, my system began to form itself. But not having the least idea in the beginning what it would be in the end, it kept continually improving, in some respects changing, and I often found it necessary to read again and again the same books, for *want of an index*, from beginning to end, in search of facts passed hastily over in the first or second reading, and then thought of little or no consequence, but which I afterwards found most important for the elucidation of truth. On this account the labour in planting the seed has been to me great beyond credibility, but I hope the produce of the harvest will bear to it a due proportion.

I very early found that it was not only necessary to recover and improve the little Greek and Latin which I had learned at school, but I soon found my inquiries stopped by my ignorance of the Oriental languages, from which I discovered that ours was derived, and by which it became evident to me that the origin of all our ancient mythoses was concealed. I therefore determined to apply myself to the study of one of them; and, after much consideration and doubt whether I should choose the Hebrew, the Arabic,

---

* Of this a more decisive proof need not be given than the failure of the Rev. Dr. Valpy's Classical Journal, a work looked up to as an honour to our country by all learned foreigners, which was given up, as well from want of contributors as from want of subscribers.

or the Sanscrit, I fixed upon the first, in the selection of which, for many reasons, which will appear hereafter, I consider myself peculiarly fortunate.

For some time my progress was very slow,—my studies were much interrupted by public business; and, for almost two years together, by a successful attempt into which I was led, in the performance of my duty as a justice of the peace, to reform some most shocking abuses in the York Lunatic Asylum.

In my study of Hebrew, also, a considerable time, I may say, was wasted on the Masoretic points, which at last I found were a mere invention of the modern Jews, and not of the smallest use.*

During this process, I also found it was very desirable that I should consult many works in the libraries of Italy and France, as well as examine the remains of antiquity in those countries, and my reader will soon see that, without having availed myself of this assistance, I should never have been able to make the discoveries of which he will have been apprized. The benefit which I derived from the examination of the works of the ancients, in my two journeys to Rome, and one to Naples, at last produced a wish to examine the antiquities of more Oriental climes, and a plan was laid for travelling in search OF WISDOM to the East;—the origin and defeat of this plan I have detailed in the preface to my Celtic Druids. I am now turned sixty; the eye grows dim, and the cholera and plague prevail in the East; yet I have not entirely given up the hope of going as far as Egypt: but what I have finished of my work must first be printed. Could I but ensure myself a strong probability of health and the retention of my faculties, for *ten*, or, I think, even for *seven* years, I should not hesitate on a journey to Samarkand, to examine the library of manuscripts there, which was probably collected by Ulug-Beig. If the strictest attention to diet and habits the most temperate may be expected to prolong health, I may not be very unreasonable in looking forwards for five or six years; and I hope my reader will believe me when I assure him, that the strongest incentive which I feel for pursuing this course of life is the confident hope and expectation of the great discoveries which I am certain I could make, if I could once penetrate into the East, and see things there with my own eyes.

In a very early stage of my investigation, my attention was drawn to the ancient Druidical and Cyclopæan buildings scattered over the world, in almost all nations, which I soon became convinced were the works of a great nation, of whom we had no history, who must have been the first inventors of the religious mythoses and the art of writing; and, in short, that what I sought must be found among them. My book, called the CELTIC DRUIDS, which I published in the year 1827, was the effect of this conviction, and is, in fact, the foundation on which this work is built, and without a perusal

---

* It may be necessary to inform some persons who may read this book, that, in the dark ages, the Jews, in order to fix the pronunciation and the meaning of their Hebrew to their own fancy at the time, invented a system called the Masoretic Points, which they substituted in place of the vowels, leaving the latter in the text; but, where they could not make them stand for consonants and thus form new syllables, leaving them silent and without meaning. The belief in the antiquity of this system has now become with them a point of faith; *of course here the use of reason ends.* On this account I shall add to the appendix to this volume a small tract that I formerly published on this subject, which I doubt not will satisfy reasoning individuals.

of it, this work will, notwithstanding my utmost care, scarcely be understood. It might very well have formed a first volume to this, and I now regret that I did not so arrange it.

I think it right to state here, what I beg my reader will never forget, that in my explanations of words and etymologies I proceed upon the principle of considering all the different systems of letters, Sanscrit excepted, to have formed originally but one alphabet, only varied in forms, and the different written languages but one language, and that they are all mere dialects of one another. This I consider that *I have proved* in my CELTIC DRUIDS, and it will be proved over and over again in the course of the following work.

Numerous are the analyses of the ancient mythology, but yet I believe the world is by no means satisfied with the result of them. There is yet a great blank. That the ancient mythoses have a system for their basis, is generally believed; indeed, I think this is what no one can doubt. But, whether I have discovered the principles on which they are founded, and have given the real explanation of them, others must judge.

The following work is similar to the solution of a difficult problem in the mathematics, only to be understood by a consecutive perusal of the whole—only to be understood after close attention, after an induction of consequences from a long chain of reasoning, every step of which, like a problem in Euclid, must be borne in mind. The reader must not expect that the secrets which the ancients took so much pains to conceal, and which they involved in the most intricate of labyrinths, are to be learned without difficulty. But though attention is required, he may be assured that, with a moderate share of it, there is nothing which may not be understood. But instead of making a consecutive perusal of the work, many of my readers will go to the Index and look for particular words, and form a judgment from the etymological explanation of them, without attending to the context or the arguments in other parts of the volume, or to the reasoning which renders such explanation probable, and thus they will be led to decide against it and its conclusions and consider them absurd. All this I expect, and of it I have no right to complain, unless I have a right to complain that a profound subject is attended with difficulties, or that superficial people are not deep thinkers, or that the nature of the human animal is not of a different construction from what I know it to be. The same lot befel the works of General Vallancey, which contain more profound and correct learning on the origin of nations and languages than all the books which were ever written. But who reads them? Not our little bits of antiquarians of the present day, who make a splashing on the surface, but never go to the bottom. A few trumpery and tawdry daubs on an old church-wall serve them to fill volumes. It is the same with most of our Orientalists. The foolish corruptions of the present day are blazoned forth in grand folios [1] as the works of the Buddhists or Brahmins ; when, in fact, they are nothing but what may be called the new religion of their descendants, who may be correctly said to have lost, as they, indeed, admit they have done, the old

---

[1] Vide the works, for instance, published by Akerman.

religions, and formed new ones which are suitable to their present state—that is, a state equal to that of the Hottentots of Africa.

Hebrew scholars have been accused of undue partiality to what is sneeringly called their *favourite language* by such as do not understand it: and this will probably be repeated towards me. In self-defence, I can only say, that in my search for the origin of ancient science, I constantly found myself impeded by my ignorance of the Hebrew; and, in order to remove this impediment, I applied myself to the study of it. I very early discovered that no translation of the ancient book of Genesis, either by Jew or Christian, could be depended on. Every one has the prejudices instilled into him in his youth to combat, or his prejudged dogma to support. But I can most truly say, that I do not lie open to the latter charge; for there is scarcely a single opinion maintained in the following work which I held when I began it. Almost all the latter part of my life has been spent in unlearning the nonsense I learned in my youth. These considerations I flatter myself will be sufficient to screen me from the sneers of such gentlemen as suppose all learning worth having is to be found in the Latin and Greek languages; especially when, in the latter part of this work, they find that I have come to the conclusion, that the Hebrew language, or that language of which Hebrew, Chaldee, and Arabic are only dialects, was probably the earliest of the written languages now known to us.

When I affirm that I think the old synagogue Hebrew the oldest written language, *the philosopher* will instantly turn away and say, "Oh ! I see this is only the old devoteeism." He may be assured he will find himself mistaken. I believe that I found my opinion on evidence equally free from modern Christian or ancient Jewish prejudice. I attribute the preservation of these old tracts (the books of Genesis) from the destruction which has overtaken all other sacred books of the priests of the respective temples of the world, to the fortunate circumstance that they were made public by Ptolemy Philadelphus. Natural causes, without any miracle, have produced a natural effect, and thus we have these interesting remains, and have them, too, in consequence of a religious dogma having operated, nearly uncorrupted, in *their general language*, by modern Jewish and Masoretic nonsense. In the SYNAGOGUE books we have, most fortunately, several tracts in a language older than any language, as now written, in the world, not excepting the beautiful and almost perfect Sanscrit. And this I think I shall prove in the course of the work. That my reader may not run away with a mistaken inference from what I now say, I beg to observe, that I pay not the least attention to the generally received ancient chronologies.

In order to arrive at what I believe to be the truth, I have often been obliged to enter into very abstruse and difficult examinations of the meaning of Hebrew words; but they are generally words which have undergone the most elaborate discussion, by very great scholars, and have been the subjects of controversy. This has been a great advantage to me, as by this means I have been enabled to see every thing which could be said on the respective points in dispute, and my conclusions may be considered as the summing up of the evidence on both sides. As the results of my inquiries will sometimes depend upon the meaning of the words, the subjects of these discussions, I have found it necessary to enter, in several instances, into a close and critical examination of their meaning, as I have just said; in which, without care and patience, the reader unlearned in Hebrew will not be able to follow me. But yet I flatter myself that if he will pass over a very few examples of this kind, which he finds too difficult, and go to the conclusion drawn from them, he will, in almost every instance, be able to understand the argument. If, as I believe, the foundations of the ancient mythoses are only to be discovered in the most ancient roots of the languages of the world, it is not likely that such an inquiry into them could be dispensed with.

The letters of the old Synagogue Hebrew language are nearly the same as the English, only in a different form. They are so near that they almost all of them may be read as English, as any person may see in Sect. 46, p. 10, by a very little consideration of the table of letters, and the numbers which they denote. In order that an unlearned reader may understand the etymological conclusions, nearly throughout the whole work every Hebrew word is followed by correspondent letters in English italics, so that a person who does not understand the Hebrew may understand them almost as well as a person who does. Half an hour's study of the table of letters, and attention to this observation, I am convinced is all that is necessary.

In great numbers of places, authors will be found quoted as authority, but whose authority my reader may be inclined to dispute. In every case, evidence of this kind must go for no more than it is worth. It is like interested evidence, which is worth something in every case, though, perhaps, very little. But in many cases, an author of little authority, quoted by me as evidence in favour of my hypothesis, will be found to have come to his conclusion, perhaps, when advocating doctrines directly in opposition to mine, or in absolute ignorance of my theory. In such cases, his evidence, from the circumstance, acquires credibility which it would not otherwise possess: and if numerous instances of evidence of this kind unite upon any one point, to the existence of any otherwise doubtful fact, the highest probability of its truth may be justly inferred. If a fact of the nature here treated of be found to be supported by other facts, and to dovetail into other parts of my system, or to remove its difficulties, its probability will be again increased. Thus it appears that there will be a very great variety in the evidence in favour of different parts of the system, which can only be correctly judged of by a consecutive perusal of the whole. And, above all things, my reader must always bear in mind, that he is in search of a system, the meaning of which its professors and those initiated into its mysteries have constantly endeavoured in all ages and nations to conceal, and the proofs of the existence of which, the most influential body of men in the world, the priests, have endeavoured, and yet endeavour, by every honest and dishonest means in their power, to destroy.

The following work will be said to be a theory: it is given as a theory. But what is a Theory? Darwin says, "To theorise is to think." The peculiar nature of the subject

*b* 2

precludes me from founding my thinkings or reasonings on facts deduced by experiment, like the modern natural philosopher; but I endeavour to do this as far as is in my power. I found them on the records of facts, and on quotations from ancient authors, and on the deductions which were made by writers without any reference to my theory or system. A casual observation, or notice of a fact, is often met with in an author which he considers of little or no consequence, but which, from that very circumstance, is the more valued by me, because it is the more likely to be true.

This book is intended for those only who think that the different mythoses and histories are yet involved in darkness and confusion : and it is an attempt to elucidate the grounds on which the former were founded, and from which they have risen to their present state. It is evident that, if I have succeeded, and if I have discovered the original principles, although, perhaps, trifling circumstances or matters may be erroneously stated, yet new discoveries will every day add new proofs to my system, till it will be established past all dispute. If, on the contrary, I be wrong, new discoveries will soon expose my errors, and, like all preceding theories, my theory will die away, as they are dying away, and it will be forgotten.

I have just said that this work is a theory, and professes, in a great measure, to arrive at probabilities only. I am of opinion that, if ancient authors had attended more to the latter, we should have been better informed than we now are upon every thing relating to the antiquities of nations. The positive assertions, false in themselves, yet not meant to mislead, but only to express the opinions of some authors, together with the intentional falsities of others, have accumulated an immense mass of absurdities, which have rendered all ancient history worse than a riddle. Had the persons first named only stated their opinion that a thing was probable, but which, in composition, it is exceedingly difficult to do, as I have constantly found, their successors would not have been misled by their want of sense or judgment. Every succeeding generation has added to the mass of nonsense, until the enormity is beginning to cure itself, and to prove that the whole, as a system, is false : it is beginning to convince most persons that some new system must be had recourse to, if one can be devised, which may at least have the good quality of containing within itself the *possibility* of being true, a quality which the present *old* system most certainly wants. Now I flatter myself that my *new* system, notwithstanding many errors which it may contain, will possess this quality; and if I produce a sufficient number of known facts that support it, for the existence of which it accounts, and without which system their existence cannot be accounted for, I contend that I shall render it very probable that my system is true. The whole force of this observation will not be understood till the reader comes to the advanced part of my next volume, wherein I shall treat upon the system of the philosophic Niebuhr respecting the history of the ancient Romans.

Of whatever credulity my reader may be disposed to accuse me, in some respects, there will be no room for any charge of this kind, on account of the legends of bards or monks, or the forgeries of the Christian priests of the middle ages ; as, for fear of being imposed on by them, I believe I have carried my caution to excess, and have omitted to use materials, in the use of which I should have been perfectly justified. For example I may name the works of Mr. Davies, of Wales, and General Vallancey, both of which contain abundance of matter which supports my doctrines; but even of these, I have used such parts only as I thought could not well be the produce of the frauds of the priests or bards. I endeavour, as far as lies in my power, to regulate my belief according to what I know is the rule of evidence in a British court of law. Perhaps it may be said, that if I am not credulous in this respect of the monks and priests, I am in respect of the ancient monuments. But these ancient unsculptured stones or names of places, are not like the priests, though with many exceptions in all sects, regular, systematic liars, lying *from interest*, and boldly defending the practice on principle—a practice brought down from Plato, and continued to our own day. Witness the late restoration of the annual farce of the liquefaction of the blood of St. Januarius, and the fraudulent title to what is called the Apostles' Creed in our Liturgy.

Some years ago a fraud was attempted by a Brahmin on Sir William Jones and Major Wilford. These two gentlemen being totally void of any suspicion were deceived, but in a very little time the latter detected the fraud, and instantly published it to the world in the most candid and honourable manner. This has afforded a handle to certain persons, who dread discoveries from India, to run down every thing which Wilford wrote, not only up to that time, but in a long and industrious life afterward. I have been careful, in quoting from his works, to avoid what may have been fraudulent; but so far from thinking that Wilford's general credit is injured, I think it was rather improved by the manner in which he came forward and announced the fraud practised on him. There was no imputation of excessive credulity previously cast upon him, and I consider it likely that this instance made him more cautious than most others against impostures in future. I cannot help suspecting, that this fraud was the cause of much true and curious matter being rendered useless.

It has been said, that the more a person inquires, the less he generally believes. This is true; and arises from the fact that he soon discovers that great numbers of the priests, in every age and of every religion, have been guilty of frauds to support their systems, to an extent of which he could have had no idea until he made the inquiry. Many worthy and excellent men among our priests have been angry with me, because I have not more pointedly excepted the ORDER in the British empire from the general condemnation expressed in my CELTIC DRUIDS, though I there expressly stated that I *did* except many individuals. The fraudulent title of the Apostles' Creed, which I have just named, would alone justify me.

The following rational account of the corruption of religion is given by the cool and philosophical Basnage:[1] " Divines complain that the people have always a violent pro-
" pensity to sensible objects and idolatry; and I do not deny it; but in the mean time

---

[1] Bk. iii. ch. xix. p. 217.

" divines of all ages have been more to blame than the people, since they conducted
" them to the adoration of creatures : that they might be able to discourse longer, and to
" distinguish themselves from the crowd, they have disguised religion with obscure
" terms, emblems and symbols, as if they were alive ; as if they were persons ; and have
" dressed them up like men and women. This has trained up and encouraged the peo-
" ple in their carnal notions. They thought that they might devote themselves to
" the symbols, which were furnished with a wondrous efficacy, and treated of more than
" the Deity himself. Whereas they ought to give the people the simplest ideas of
" God, and talk soberly of him : they embellish, they enrich, and magnify their ideas of
" him, and this is what has corrupted religion in all ages, as is manifest from the in-
" stance of the Egyptians. By veiling religion under pretence of procuring it respect,
" they have buried and destroyed it."

Though the labour which I have gone through in the production of this volume of my
work has been very great, yet it has been sweetened by many circumstances, but by
none so much as the conviction, that in laying open to public view the secret of the
mythoses of antiquity, I was performing one of the works the most valuable to my fellow-creatures which was ever completed,—that it was striking the hardest blow that ever
vas struck at the tyranny of the sacerdotal order,—that I was doing more than any man
had ever done before to disabuse and enlighten mankind, and to liberate them from the
shackles of prejudice in which they were bound.

Another thing which sweetened the labour was, the perpetual making of new discoveries,—the whole was a most successful voyage of discovery.

No doubt, in order to prevent females from reading the following work, it will be accused of indecency. Although I have taken as much care as was in my power to remove any good grounds for the charge, it is certainly open to it, in the same way as are
many works on comparative anatomy. But these, in fact, are indecent only to persons of
indecent and filthy imaginations—to such persons as a late Lord Mayor of London, who
ordered the Savoyard statue-dealers out of the city, until they clothed their Venus de
Medicis with drapery.

In all cases brevity, as far as clearness of expression would admit, has been my object ;
and I can safely say, though the reason for many passages may not be obvious to a reader who has not deeply meditated on the subject as I have done, yet I believe scarcely
one is inserted in the book which has not appeared to me at the time to be necessary to
elucidate some subject which was to follow.

It has been observed, that persons who write a bad style, generally affect to despise a
good one. Now whatever may be thought of mine, I beg to observe, that I regret it is
not better ; I wish I had been more attentive to it in early life ; but I must freely confess,
that my mind has been turned to the discovery of truth almost to the entire neglect of
style.

I fear some repetitions will be found which would not have occurred had I been better
skilled in the art of book-making ; but in many cases I do not know how they could

have been avoided, as a new consequence will often be shewn to flow from a statement formerly made for a different purpose. However, I justify myself by the example of the learned and popular Bryant, who says,

" As my researches are deep and remote, I shall sometimes take the liberty of repeat-
" ing what has preceded, that the truths which I maintain may more readily be perceived.
" We are oftentimes, by the importunity of a persevering writer, teazed into an unsatis-
" factory compliance and yield a painful assent : but upon closing the book, our scruples
" return ; and we lapse at once into doubt and darkness. It has, therefore, been my
" rule to bring vouchers for every thing which I maintain ; and though I might, upon
" the renewal of my argument, refer to another volume and a distant page ; yet I many
" times choose to repeat my evidence, and bring it again under immediate inspection.
" And if I do not scruple labour and expense, I hope the reader will not be disgusted by
" this seeming redundancy in my arrangement. What I now present to the public,
" contains matter of great moment, and should I be found in the right, it will afford a
" sure basis for a future history of the world. None can well judge either of the labour
" or utility of the work, but those who have been conversant in the writings of chrono-
" logers and other learned men upon these subjects, and seen the difficulties with which
" they are embarrassed. Great undoubtedly must have been the learning and perspicacity
" of many who have preceded me. Yet it may possibly be found at the close, that a
" feeble arm has effected what those prodigies in science have overlooked."[1]

I conceive the notice which I have taken of my former work cannot be considered impertinent, as it is, indeed, the foundation on which this is built. The original habitation of the first man, and the merging of nearly all ancient written languages into one system, containing sixteen letters, which in that work I have shewn and proved, pave the way for the more important doctrines that will be here developed, and form an essential part of it. The whole taken together, will, I trust, draw aside the veil which has hitherto covered the early history of man,—the veil, in fact, of Queen Isis, which she, I hope erroneously, boasted should never be withdrawn. If, in this undertaking, it prove that I have spent many years, and bestowed much labour and money in vain, and have failed, Mr. Faber may then have to comfort himself that his failure is not the last. I think it no vanity to believe that I have succeeded better than he has done, because I have come to the task with the benefit of the accumulated labours of Mr. Faber, and of all my predecessors. So that if there be merit in the work, to them, in a great degree, it must be attributed. I have the benefit both of their learning and of their errors.

In the fifth book a number of astronomical calculations are made. But every thing like scientific parade and the use of technical terms, to which learned men are generally very partial, are studiously avoided ; and I apprehend that even the little knowledge of astronomy which any well-educated school-girl may possess, will be sufficient for understanding these calculations. Close attention to the argument will doubtless be re-

---

Bryant, Anal. Pref. p. vii.

quired; but, with less than this, my reader will not expect to solve the problem which has hitherto set at defiance the learning and talent of all scientific inquirers.   When my reader comes to this part of my work he will find, that to make my calculations come right, I have constantly been obliged to make a peculiar use of the number 2160, and in many cases to deduct it.   For this he will find no *quite satisfactory* reason given.   But though I could not account for it, the coincidence of numbers was so remarkable, that I was quite certain there could, in the fact, be no mistake.   In the second volume this will be satisfactorily accounted for; and I flatter myself it will be found to form, not a blemish, but the apex, necessary to complete the whole building.

How I may be treated by the critics on this work, I know not; but I cannot help smiling when I consider that the priests have objected to admit my former book, *the Celtic Druids*, into libraries, because it was antichristian; and it has been attacked by Deists, because it was superfluously religious.   The learned deist, the Rev. R. Taylor, has designated me as *the religious* Mr. Higgins.   But God be thanked, the time is come at last, when a person may philosophise without fear of the stake.   No doubt the priests will claim the merit of this liberality.   It is impossible, however, not to observe what has been indiscreetly confessed by them a thousand times, and admitted as often both in parliament and elsewhere by their supporters, that persecution has ceased, not because the priests wished to encourage free discussion, but because it is at last found, from the example of Mr. Carlile and others, that the practice of persecution, at this day, only operates to the dissemination of opinion, not to the secreting of it.   In short, that the remedy of persecution is worse than the disease it is meant to cure.

On the subject of criticism Cleland has justly observed, " The judging of a work, not " by the general worth of it, but by the exceptions, is the scandal of criticism and the " nuisance of literature; a judgment that can dishonour none but him who makes it." [1] In most cases where I have known the characters of the priests who have lost their temper, and taken personal offence at what I have said against the order, in that work, I have thought I could discover a reason for it which *they* did not assign.   As the subjects there treated of may be considered to be continued here, the objections of my opponents will be found to be refuted without the odious appearance of a polemical dispute.   As for those attacks which were evidently made by the priests merely for the purpose, as far as possible, of preventing their followers from reading the *Celtic Druids*, and not for the purpose of refuting that work, they are of no consequence.   Although it was published in great haste, I am happy to have it in my power to state, that no error of any importance has been pointed out, some few overlooked-errors of the press excepted.   Various attacks upon it are characterized by the obvious vexation and anger of my opponents, rather than by argument.   But the attack of one gentleman I think it right to notice.

The Rev. Hugh James Rose, B. D., Christian Advocate of Cambridge, has honoured

---

[1] Preface to Specimen, p. xi.

it with his notice; but it is gratifying to me to be able to say, that except one proverbial expression, *in toto cœlo* PERHAPS, improperly used, and a mistake in writing Plato for Herodotus, and Herodotus for Plato, which, in a great part of the impression, was corrected with the pen, and in all was ordered to be so corrected with it, before the book left the printer's, and a mistake in writing παρ' εξοχην instead of κατ' εξοχην, he has not found any other fault, though I think he has shewn no want of inclination. With respect to the latter error, as I certainly never discovered the *gross* and *shocking* inadvertency until a great part of this work was printed, I should not be at all surprised if somewhere, as I wrote for Greek παρ' εξοχην instead of κατ' εξοχην, I should have written for French *kat'* excellence instead of *par* excellence.

A writer in the Bishop's review accuses me of being in *a rage* with priests. I flatter myself I am never in a rage with any thing; but, I never have scrupled and never shall scruple to express my detestation of an order which exists directly in opposition to the commands of Jesus Christ—which in no case is of use to mankind, but which has produced more demoralisation and misery in the world than all other causes put together. With this conviction it would be base in me to withhold my opinion, and not even the fear of the auto-da-fé shall prevent me from expressing it.

As long as the art of writing and reading was a secret confined to a few select persons, priests might be thought to be wanted to say the prayers for the ignorant; but as most persons can read now, they are no longer necessary; and the prayer which Jesus Christ taught is so very short and simple, that no person, above the class of an idiot, can be in any difficulty about it; and there can be little doubt that Jesus Christ taught that simple and short form that priests might no longer be necessary.

Matthew vi. 5, 6, 7, 9, makes Jesus say, " When thou prayest, thou shalt not be as the " Hypocrites, for they love to pray standing in the synagogues" [they go in great form to church and have their pew made with high walls and lined with crimson cloth], " and in " the corners of the streets, that they may be seen of men;" [attend Bible and Missionary meetings;] " verily they have their reward. But thou, when thou prayest, enter " into thy closet, and when thou hast shut thy door, pray to thy Father which is in " secret, and thy Father which seeth in secret, shall reward thee openly. But when ye " pray, use not vain repetitions as the heathen do, for they think that they shall be heard " for their much speaking. After this manner, therefore, pray ye," &c.

Here priesthoods and priests, *vipers* as Jesus often called them, are expressly forbidden. *In giving directions what a person is to do when he prays*, he directly countermands every other mode of proceeding. In strict keeping with this, not a single word of his can be pointed out in any one of the gospels, which can be construed into even a toleration of priests; and in the *vain repetitions* liturgies are evidently implied.

In the prayer which Jesus gave, he gave a liturgy and directions for the use of it, and no human being who has learned to repeat this prayer can ever want any priest or other apparatus.

Had Jesus considered any symbol or confession of faith necessary, he would have

c

given one.  As he has not given one, and as he did take upon himself to legislate
in the case, on every principle of sound reasoning it must be held, that he did not think
a belief in this or in that *faith*, as it is called, (which his profound wisdom well knew
never can be a merit or demerit,) was necessary to salvation.  This justifies its name,
*the poor man's religion.*  The poor man's whole duty to God is contained in this prayer,
and the whole moral part of his duty to *man* is contained in the direction to every one
to do to his neighbour as he would wish his neighbour to do to him.  Its founder left
nothing in writing, because the poor man's religion does not require it.

This great simplicity makes the pure, unadulterated Christian religion the most beautiful religion that ever existed.  Restore it to this pure and simple state, and ninety-
nine out of every hundred of all the philosophers in the world will be its friends, instead
of its enemies.  In the accounts which we read of Jesus's preaching, he is made to say,
that if they believed on him they should be saved.  In order to find some pretext for
*their own nonsense*, the priests, by a gross, fraudulent mistranslation, have made *him talk
nonsense* and say, if ye believe ON ME, instead of IN ME, or *in my words*, ye shall
be saved.  On this they found the necessity of faith in their dogmas.  Some persons
will think this a merely *trifling* critical emendation ; but so far is it from being trifling,
that it is of the very greatest importance, and on it some most important doctrines
depend.  All this tends to support the doctrines of the celebrated Christian philosopher
Ammonius Saccas, of which I shall have much to say in the following work.

But it is necessary to observe, that this simple view of the religion leaves *untouched*
every dogma of every sect.  It shews that the religion damns no person for an opinion.
It leaves every one to enjoy his own opinions.  It censures or condemns the opinions of
no one ; but I fear that it will be liked almost by no one, because it prevents every one
from condemning the opinion of his neighbour.  If Jesus can be said to have established
any rite, it will be found in the adoption of the *very ancient* ceremony of the Eucharistia,
the most beautiful of all the religious ceremonies ever established, and of which I shall
often have to treat in the course of my work.  Jesus Christ was put to death, if the four
gospel histories can be believed, merely for teaching what I have no doubt he did teach,
that Temples, Priests, Mysteries, and Cabala, were all unnecessary.  Mohamed, by abo-
lishing priests, liturgies, and symbols, and by substituting a simple hymn in praise of the
Creator, was a much more consistent Christian than the modern Paulite ; and this, and
nothing but this, was the religion of Mohamed.  The Koran was none of his.

The priest to whom I lately alluded has called me misosierist.  This he may do as
long as he pleases.[1]  How is it possible for a person who, like me, is a sincere friend of
religion, not to be indignant at an order which has, by its frauds, rendered the history of
all religions, and of every thing connected with them, doubtful—by frauds systematically
practised in all ages, and continued even to the present day, and in our own country ?

---

[1] My work called *The Celtic Druids* has never been noticed in any way which can be called *a review*, except in the
fifth and sixth numbers of the Southern Review of North America, printed at Charleston.  In that periodical it is
reviewed by a very learned man, with whom I first became acquainted in consequence of his critique.

I consider that when the Bishop's review called me a misosierist, it paid me the greatest of compliments. To be called a misosierist is the same as to be called Philanthropist. I am proud of the epithet.

I have been accused of being fond of paradox. The word *paradox* means, *beyond common opinion*. When common opinion tells me to believe that God, the Supreme First Cause, walked in the garden, or that he, as Júpiter, carried Io away on his back to Crete, I am not afraid of being paradoxical or doing wrong in adopting the opinion of all the first fathers of the church, and in seeking some meaning which the original words do not literally possess.

If the priests can refute the doctrines which I teach, they will not lose a moment in doing it; if they cannot, they will have recourse to turning selected passages and parts of arguments into ridicule. To this they are welcome. I shall rejoice in the proof of my victory.

I have come to one resolution—never to attempt to vindicate myself from any unfounded charge of ignorance or misquotation in this book; but, only to notice such real errors in the work, as may be pointed out, and to correct them, of whatever kind they may be.

Like my learned friend Eusebe de Salverte, I shall be accused of rationalism.[1] I, beforehand, plead guilty to the charge. I can be of no religion which does not appear to be consistent with sound reason, and I cannot stoop, with the advocates of priestcraft and idiotism, to lend my hand to continue the degradation of my fellow-creatures. Since the priests and their abettors have thought proper to convert the exercise of the highest gift of God to man *reason* into a term of reproach—rationalism—I know not how to return the compliment, though I do not like to render *evil* for evil, better than by designating their attempted opposition to reason, *idiotism*.

To guard myself against being accused of the disgusting practice of using abusive epithets, I beg that the term *devotee*, which will often occur, as of course it conveys no meaning against any one's moral character, may not be considered to mean a bigot, but merely a person very much, or rather more than usually religious, which is its true and correct meaning. I leave the use of abusive language, such as *infidel*, to persons who, feeling that their arguments are weak, try to strengthen them by violence.

In the execution of this work I have endeavoured to place myself above all religions and sects, and to take a bird's-eye view of them all; and, as I have favoured none, I know I shall be favoured by none. A few and very few persons, those persons who are really philosophers *will* read it. The generality of mankind will read no further than to that part where it begins to touch their own prejudices or their own religion; then they will throw it down. It is very seldom indeed that a religious person is capable of reasoning respecting matters connected with his religion. This is the cause why, on this subject, no two persons scarcely ever agree. And I beg my reader to recollect, that if he take the opinion of a religious person on any matter connected with such a work as this, as

---

[1] Foreign Quarterly Review, No. XII.

there are numbers of religions, the chances are very great, that in some part it must have attacked the religion of the person whose opinion he takes ; whence it follows, that the chances are in proportion to the whole numbers of religions which exist to one, that he depends on a prejudiced person, and is deceived. All this will operate against the the book ; but how can I expect any better ?—for the immediate effect of my theory, if universally received, would be, to render obsolete nine-tenths of all the literature of the world, and to overthrow almost every prevailing system of history, chronology, and religion. But founding my opinion on a thorough conviction that I have solved the great problem and have discovered the long-lost truths of antiquity which have been so long sought for in vain, I feel no doubt that the time will come when my discovery will be adopted, when the errors in the work or in the system will be corrected, and the truth it contains will be duly appreciated, and that, if I have succeeded in developing the origin of religions, nations, and languages, it will by degrees make its way. Besides, the schoolmaster is abroad. Tempora mutantur, et veritas prævalebit.

I shall be found frequently to express *a suspicion ;* as for instance, *I have a suspicion,* or *I have a strong suspicion.* I think it right to apprize my reader, that when I use these words, I really mean that *I suspect* or *conjecture*, and that however numerous may be the proofs which I produce, I yet admit a doubt, and by no means intend to place the credit of my work upon the absolute truth of the doctrines so doubtfully advanced by me. Of course among such an innumerable number of references contained in the notes, errors would have been found, even if my eyes had not begun to fail me, and to verify them it is impossible to travel again over all the libraries from Glasgow to Naples. I shall be thankful for any corrections.

In many places the explanations of words will be found to be given in numbers. This has been generally treated by the learned with contempt. I think it right to give notice to the reader, that before this work is finished, this *buffoonery*, as it has been called by those who did not understand it, and who were too idle or too proud to inquire what could be the cause that the *most learned of the ancients* used such a practice, will be found of the very first importance, and to be any thing but buffoonery.

It is also necessary to observe, that if an observation or notice of an ancient custom should sometimes appear, which may be thought to be introduced without good cause, it is not therefore to be concluded that all persons will be of that opinion. I think it right to warn my reader, that there are more passages than one in the book, which are of that nature, which will be perfectly understood by my masonic friends, but which my engagements prevent my explaining to the world at large.

My masonic friends will find their craft very often referred to. I believe, however, that they will not find any of their secrets betrayed ; but I trust they will find it proved, that their art is the remains of a very fine ancient system, or, perhaps, more properly, a branch of the fine and beautiful system of WISDOM which, in this work, I have developed.

In the latter part of the work many facts are stated and observations made which ought to have had a place in the earlier parts of it ; this arose from the fact, that when I commenced printing, I thought I had finished my first volume: but, as it proceeded, I continued my researches, and in consequence met with many new circumstances tending to complete or strengthen my system. Was I to leave them unnoticed? This would have been a kind of infanticide. Their late introduction may injure the work ; but my object is not to make a book, but to develop great truths, respecting ancient Language, Religion, and the Origin of Nations.

Sometimes a quotation will be found to contain bad grammar, as for instance, in Book X. Chapter VI. Sect. 11, pp. 716, 717 ; but I have thought it better to leave it as I found it, than run the risk of making an author say what he did not intend, by my correction. Schoolmasters think such things of consequence. They are certainly better avoided. It is a common practice of our scholars to endeavour to tie down inquirers to the niceties which the old languages acquired when they had arrived at their highest state of perfection, prohibiting any licence, and making no allowance for their uncertain state before grammars or lexicons were written. For instance, Buddha and Buda, between which they now make some very nice distinctions ; saying, one is the Planet Mercury, and the other is Wisdom, a distinction adopted evidently in later times. This is the counterpart of the Sun and the planet Mercury of the Greeks, both of which, I shall shew, meant the Sun and the Planet also. The same is the case with the Greek words Ερως and Ερος, one of which I shall be told means *hero* and the other Love ; but which I shall prove must have been originally the same, and each must have had both meanings, before the later Greeks fixed the meaning of every word in their language. These puny criticisms are calculated for nothing but the concealment of truth, and are founded upon a total forgetfulness or ignorance of the principles or history of all languages. This will be discussed much at large in my second volume, but I have thought it right thus slightly to notice it here, in order to assuage the anger of those small critics, in the mean time.

I think it right to make an observation upon an effect of prejudice, which has operated for the concealment of truth in modern times more than almost any other cause whatever, and it is this : it constantly happens that circumstances are met with, to all appearance closely connected with the history of the Jews, and yet in places so remote from Judea, and so unconnected with it, that our inquirers have not been able to admit even the possibility of any connexion having existed between them ; and, in order that they might not expose themselves to ridicule for what has appeared even to themselves to be absurd credulity, they have, without any dishonest motive, disguised and corrupted words without number. Thus we find, instead of Solomon,[1] Soleimon and Suleimon; instead of David, Daoud, and, as the learned Dr. Dorn calls it, Davudze; and instead of Jacob, *Yucoob*, when the name was clearly meant, in the original, to be what we call Jacob.

---

[1] It is true that, properly speaking, neither person ought to have been called Solomon ; but, as the same name of a person was originally meant in both cases, they ought both to be represented by the same letters.

In a similar manner, in Hamilton's Gazetteer, the word which, in old maps, is properly called Adoni, is changed by him into Adavani, and Salem into Chelam. Vide Book x. Chap. vii. Sec. 8, p. 758.

Another evil consequence has arisen out of this union of ignorance and prejudice, which is, that many works, because they contain passages relating to matters which have been thought to be comparatively modern, have hastily been decided to be modern forgeries, and cast away. The force of this argument my reader cannot now estimate, but he will understand it as he advances in the work; on this account the question respecting the genuineness of almost every writing which has been deemed spurious deserves reconsideration. Now I would produce, as examples of this, some of the books of the Apocrypha, and, for one, the book of *Jesus, the son of Sirach*. Something which has caused them to be thought modern, will be found respecting this personage in my next volume. The fact, as my reader will see, is rather a proof of the genuineness of that book at least. The effect of this prejudice has been totally to prevent any approximation towards the truth. The discoveries which I have made have been effected by pursuing a course diametrically opposite. If not merely as much care had been taken to discover the truth as has been taken to conceal it, but only a *fair* and *impartial care* had been taken, the true character of the ancient histories and mythologies would have been discovered long since. This I beg my reader always to bear in mind. It is of the very first importance. When I began my inquiries, I was the dupe of this superstition. This is an example of the many things which I have stated that I found so difficult to unlearn.

For a very long time, and during the writing of the greater part of my work, I abstained from the practice of many etymologists, of exchanging one letter for another, that is, the letter of one organ for another of the same organ; such, for instance, as Pada for Vada, (p. 759,) or Beda for Veda, in order that I might not give an opportunity to captious objectors to say of me, as they have said of others, that by this means I could make out what I pleased. From a thorough conviction that this has operated as a very great obstacle to the discovery of truth, I have used it rather more freely in the latter part of the work, but by no means so much as the cause of truth required of me. The practice of confining the use of a language while in its *infancy* to the strict rules to which it became tied when in its *maturity*, is perfectly absurd, and can only tend to the secreting of truth. The practice of indiscriminately changing *ad libitum* a letter of one organ for another of the same organ, under the sanction of a grammatical rule,—for instance, that B and V are permutable, cannot be justified. It cannot, however, be denied, that they are often so changed; but every case must stand upon its own merits. The circumstances attending it must be its justification.

I have no doubt that the professed Oriental scholars will nearly all unite to run down my work. The moment I name Irish literature and several other subjects, they will curl up the corner of the lip, as they have often done before. Oriental scholars are no ways different from the remainder of mankind, and it is not likely that they should receive with pleasure the rude shock which this work will give to many of their prejudices. It is not likely that they will hear with pleasure, that in all their researches into the history of antiquity they have been in the wrong track. All this is natural, and I find no fault with it—it is what I ought to expect,—it is what has happened in almost every case where an individual has attacked old prejudices. Was it not the case with Locke ? Was it not the case with Newton ? some of whose best works did not go to a second edition in less than thirty years ! If these *master minds* were so treated, would it not be absurd in *me* to hope to escape without illiberal attacks or censures ? But there is one thing of which I must complain in Orientalists,—they always appear to speak on the subjects to which they have directed their studies with authority, as if they did not admit of any doubt. But if a person will carefully attend to them, he will find, nevertheless, that scarcely any two of them agree on a single point.

I must also make another observation which I fear will give offence. Some of them, I think, prize too highly the knowledge of the ancient Oriental dead languages,— they seem to think that these once acquired, all wisdom is acquired also as a necessary consequence. They seem to forget that the knowledge of these languages is of no other value than as a key to unlock the treasuries of antiquity. I wish to recall this to their recollection, and to remind them of the story of the Chameleon, that *others can see as well as themselves.* In making these observations, I hope they will not consider that I wish to depreciate their Oriental learning ; far from it. I think it has not been so much appreciated as it deserves by their countrymen, and though I think they cannot pretend to compete in learning with the Jesuits or the priests of the *propaganda,* whose whole lives were spent in the acquisition of Oriental learning, and almost in nothing else ; yet I think that the proficiency which great numbers of them have made in the learning of the East, in the midst of the performance of numerous arduous labours of civil or military life, is above all praise, and has laid their countrymen under the greatest obligation to them.

Before I conclude, I feel myself bound to acknowledge my obligations to my Printer, Mr. Smallfield, not only for his punctuality and attention, but for many orthographical and other suggestions, which have greatly improved the work. It would have been still more worthy of the reader's perusal, if, like the monks in their works, I could have called a brotherhood to my assistance, or if, like Mr. Bryant,[1] I could have had a learned and confidential friend to advise and assist me.

After having spent many years upon this work, I have long doubted, as I have already intimated, whether I should make it public or not. I will not deny that I feel cowardly. I flatter myself that I am esteemed by many valuable friends, some of whom I may probably lose by my publication. What shall I gain by it ? Nothing.—Posthumous fame ? Perhaps so. Is this worth having ? Pliny and Cicero so thought. Is the work worth publishing ? I flatter myself the answer may be *in the affirmative.* Is it calculated to do good ? Is it calculated to reduce the power and influence of priests,

---

[1] Vide his Preface to the third Volume of the 4to edition.

and to enlighten mankind? It surely is. The discussion alone, supposing I am mistaken, must tend to elicit and to establish truth ; and truth is good. Supposing that I believe the publication to be for the good of mankind, am I justified in suppressing it? In this case, am I doing to the rest of mankind as I would wish them to do to me? A sentiment of the great and good Epictetus is so appropriate to my situation and circumstances, that I think I cannot do better than conclude with his words, except, indeed, it be humbly to imitate their author, and to endeavour, as far as lies in me, to profit by his example.

" If you resolve to make wisdom and virtue the study and business of your life, you " must be sure to arm yourself beforehand against all the inconveniences and discourage " ments that are likely to attend this resolution. I imagine that you will meet with " many scoffs and much derision ; and that people will upbraid you with turning phi " losopher all on the sudden. But be not you affected or supercilious ; only stick close " to whatever you are in your judgment convinced is right and becoming : and consider " this as your proper station, assigned you by God, which you must not quit on any " terms. And remember, that if you persevere in goodness, those very men who derided " you at first will afterward turn your admirers. But if you give way to their re " proaches, and are vanquished by them, you will then render yourself doubly and most " deservedly ridiculous." (Stanhope.) Yes, indeed, I am resolved I will endeavour to imitate thee, immortal slave, and will repeat the words of the modern poet,

> " Steadfast and true to Virtue's sacred laws,
> " Unmoved by vulgar censure or applause,
> " Let the world talk, my friends ; that world, we know,
> " Which calls us *guilty*, cannot make us so.
> " With truth and justice support Nature's plan,
> " Defend the cause, or quit the name of man."

GODFREY HIGGINS.

*SKELLOW GRANGE, NEAR DONCASTER,*
    *May* 1, 1833.

# CONTENTS.

---

## PRELIMINARY OBSERVATIONS.

*d*

## CHAPTER IV.

## CHAPTER V.

## BOOK III. CHAPTER I.

## CHAPTER II.

## CHAPTER III.

## BOOK IV. CHAPTER I.

## CHAPTER II.

## BOOK V. CHAPTER I.

## CHAPTER II.

## CHAPTER VI.

## CHAPTER VII.

## CHAPTER VIII.

## CHAPTER IX.

# CORRIGENDA ET ERRATA.

Page 3, line 6 from the bottom, for 'Bishop D'Oyly,' read *Rev. Dr. D'Oyly*.

7, line 6, for 'XXVIIII.,' read XXVIII.

», bottom line, dele the words 'the first sixteen, perhaps.'

15, bottom line but one, for 'elliptic,' read *circular*.

17, line 33, for 'Tripods,' read *Quipuses*; and in last line but one, for 'Astles,' read *Astle*.

18, line 7 from the bottom, after the second word 'been,' insert *an emblem of*; and, after the word 'fact,' insert the word *of*.

20, in line 5, for 'Kurnec,' read *Carnac*.

22, line 41, expunge the first word *sixteen*.

24, line 22, for 'Sarpendon,' read *Sarpedon*.

25, line 26, after 'merriment,' insert the word *which*.

29, line 28, dele the *inverted commas* after 'sciri.'

30, in the bottom of *note* line, insert VI. after IV.

41, second line from bottom, for 'Crishna,' read *Cristna*.

48, line 31, for 'Aphrodita,' read *Aphrodite*.

54, line 1, for 'Ludim,' read *Lubim*.

60, line 6 from the bottom, for 'Hails,' read *Hales*.

70, line 17, after אדני insert *Adni*.

73, last but one of *note*, after 'qui,' insert *est*.

74, line 5, for 'from the,' read *from a*.

75, line 21, after 'Bologna,' insert *my fig. No. 22.*

77, line 15, for 'where,' read *when*; and in line 29, for 'Versions,' read *version*.

78, line 17, for 'samim,' read *smim*.

78, note 3, for 'Cabala,' read *Kebla*.

91, line 6, for 'though,' read *and*.

96, line 10, from the bottom, for 'this,' read *his*.

101, line 10, for 'Monsani,' read *Mossoni*.

111, line 11, for 'Ame,' read *Ilme*; and in line 6 from bottom, dele *privately*.

120, line 6, dele *such*; and, line 7, for the first 'as,' read *which*.

135, line 32, and in several other places, for 'παρ'εξοχην,' read και' εξοχην.

157, line 20, after Guatama, add, *He taught his master as Jesus taught Zaccheus. Alph. Tib. pp. 33, 34.*

162, line 31, before 'All,' read *almost*.

166, line 15, for 'Lubere,' read *Loubere*.

175, line 5 from the bottom, for 'Manwantara,' read *Manwantara*.

176, line 19, for 'double,' read *doubled*.

181, line 23, in 'Nonnins,' dele *i*.

188, in note 1, for '708,' read 608; and for '725,' read 625.

192, line 18, insert a comma after 'thee;' and for 'eads,' read *invokes*.

201, line 23, before 'Melchisedek,' insert *that*: and, after it, *was thought*.

226, line 24, for 'twelfth,' read *tenth*.

230, in note 1, before 'plates,' read *my*.

231, line 3, after 'gereutis,' insert, *see Fig. 14.*

236, line 9, for יגחמני' inhmni,' read יגהמנו *inhmnu; (See Univers. Hist. Vol. 1. p. 350.)* And in line 14, for 'מני mni,' read מנו *mnu*.

241, note 5, line 2, for 'Psychologist,' read *Physiologist*.

252, note 1, line 5, for 'Ani,' read *Ain*.

253, line 26, for second 'of,' read *to*.

255, line 16, for 'chapter,' read *book*.

258, line 25, change 'o in,' to *o into*.

269, line 17, insert Note 5 in the text.

Page 274, line 13, for 'and,' read *had*; and, in line 26, interchange *Pra* and *Bra*.

285, line 32, for 'depend,' read *depends*.

289, line 3 from bottom, after 'utility,' insert a comma.

296, line 1, for 'Cab,' read *Gab*.

304, line 1, for 'Dyonyg,' read *Dyonys*.

310, in inscription of Isis, for 'θνηθων,' read θνητων; and in note 2, for 'fig. 18,' read *fig. 19*.

319, line 18, for 'Dyonisius,' read *Dionysus*.

329, line 10, for 'translating the LXX. into Greek,' read, *translating the Hebrew into the Greek LXX*.

335, line 29, for 'fig. 20,' read *fig. 21*.

348, line 40, for 'fig. 23,' read *fig. 24*.

363, line 35, for 'Laeshmi,' read *Laeshmi*.

399, line 1, for 'Chap. I. Sect. 1,' read 'Chap. II. Sect. 2.

400, line 23, after 'witness,' insert *He says that*.

407, line 26, for 'and,' read *or*.

411, line 28, for 'Adam,' read *Noah*.

415, line 24, for 'Judia,' read *India*.

420, line 27, for 'tombs,' read *icons*.

423, line 13, *leave out all the words relating to the temple*.

424, lines 35 and 37, for 'Mr.,' read *Major* Rennell.

433, line 3, for 'credibility,' read *rationality*.

445, line 35, for 'full,' read *new*.

446, lines 9 and 10, dele the parenthesis.

450, note, line 2, for 'these,' read *their*.

460, note 4, for 'XPE,' read XPΣ.

482, line 1 of Chapter II., for 'chapter,' read *book*.

519, the parenthesis in lines 15 and 16, is the author's, not Col. Tod's.

524, line 31, for 'Baillie,' read *Bailly*.

535, line 36, dele 'were,' and add *were named* after 'it.'

540, line 21, for 'Greek,' read *Latin*.

541, for '584,' read 544

545, line 5 from the bottom, put the word 'only' after Josephus.

590, line 1, and in several other places, for 'Gebelen,' read *Gebelin*.

593, dele the last clause of note 1.

595, line 7, for 'Eeudra,' read *Eendra*.

602, line 5, for 'they,' read *the latter*.

603, line 3 from bottom, for 'Yahandi,' read *Yahudh*.

614, line 10, after the second 'they,' add the word *may*.

619, line 1, for 'biber,' read *Bible*.

625, line 13, for 'Genesa,' read *Ganesa*.

639, line 17 from the bottom, insert a comma after *Yuthia*

642, line 1, for 'Fish or,' read *or Fish*.

644, line 3, dele 'who were.'

668, line 1, for 'Goguet,' read *Bouchet*.

679, line 4 from the bottom, for 'if Bishop Marsh says the,' read *if, as Bishop Marsh says, the*, &c.

683, bottom line, note, for 'Aries,' read *Pisces*.

692, line 20, for 'and,' after priests, read *of*.

704, line 4 from the bottom, for 'then,' read *three*.

719, in the head line, for 'Section 3,' read *Section 12*.

720, line 27, for 'and by,' read *with*; and in line 29, for 'Nabli,' read *Nabhi*.

737, line 4 from the bottom, for 'Pentateuch,' read *Genesis*.

750, line 14, dele *Goguet*.

776, lines 15 and 16, read the passage thus: *The sixteen-letter of the Tamuls may have been*; and in line 16, for 'the,' read *their*.

# ADDITIONAL ERRATA, &c.

Page 45, line 33, for ' Ζευς κεφαλε,' read Ζευς κεφαλη.
line 36, for ' απανlον,' read απανlων.
49, line 17, for ' Makenzie Beverley,' read *Mackenzie Beverley.*
74, line 17, for ' let premières,' read *les prèmières.*
85, at the bottom, for ' vous enfans,' read *vos enfans.*
119, line 29, for ' κλειζεται,' read κληιζεται.
143, line 33, for ' in mémoire,' read *en mémoire.*
145, line 4, for remarkable,' read *remarquable.*
line 5, dele the comma after ' l'on puisse.'
line 8, for ' tout a fait,' read *tout-à-fait.*
for ' verrons,' read *venons.*
160, line 7, for ' dévoilé,' read *dévoilée.*
162, line 20, for ' se retrouvé,' read *se retrouve.*
line 21, for ' pourions,' read *pourrions.*
190, line 24, for ' aurium,' read *aurum.*
line 29, for ' que,' read *quam.*
192, line 9, for ' arratri,' read *aratri.*
199, line 17, for ' duriatiou,' read *duratiun.*
202, line 29, for ' spaciis,' read *spatiis.*
255, line 7, for, ' incidiaberis,' read *insidiaberis.*
312, line 33, for ' au Vierge,' read *à la Vierge.*
315, line 7, for ' ascendunt,' read *ascendit.*
320, line 15, for ' ipsiis,' read *ipsis.*
356, in note 5, for ' Reserches,' read *Recherches.*
359, line 22, for ' faite' and ' même,' read *faite* and *mène.*
370, line 4, for ' cernit,' read *cernitur.*
397, line 17, for ' qui,' read *que.*
458, line 6, for, ' in Indian,' read *in India.*
492, line 8, for ' Teutzel,' read *Treuttel.*
496, line 3, for ' Richard Makenzie Beverley,' read *Robert Mackenzie Beverley.*

Page 500, line 14, for ' But Βαινω means *to carry*,' read *to be carried?*
504, line 5, for ' εψυχωθαι,' read εψυχωσθαι.
line 6, for ' Poteta' and ' ventus,' read *Poeta* and *ventis.*
line 24, for ' germs,' read *germes.*
line 25, for ' fussit,' ' matérial,' and ' germs,' read *suffit, matériel,* and *germes.*
542, line 8, for ' præteria,' read *præterea.*
line 11, for ' ille,' read *illi.*
545, line 14, for ' recepi,' read *recipi.*
564, line 31, for ' Christiaus,' read *Christian priests.*
588, line 3 of note 2, for ' esemplo,' read *esempii.*
591, line 18, for ' peut-être,' read *peut être.*
607, line 10, for ' n'as,' read *n'a.*
613, last line but one, for ' raproché,' read *rapproché.*
616, line 11 from the bottom, for ' impiaquæ,' read *impiaque.*
650, line 14, for ' poëms,' read *poëmes.*
661, line 5, for ' lie,' read *lié.*
line 7, for ' example special,' read *exemple spécial.*
line 8, for ' members,' read *membres.*
701, line 19, for ' special toutes les sects,' read *spécial toutes les sectes.*
792, line 17, for ' habouring,' read *harbouring.*
806, line 1, for ' se vertus,' read *ses vertus.*
line 7, for ' universe,' read *univers.*
line 16 and 20, for ' matérial,' read *matériel.*
line 6 from the bottom, for ' j'cu,' read *j'en.*
line 20, for, ' mainstains,' read *maintains.*
814, line 31, for ' en profunditaté,' read *in profunditate.*

⁂ SEE THE PLATES AT THE END OF VOLUME II.

# PRELIMINARY OBSERVATIONS.

## CHAPTER I.

1. IN the following preliminary observations, I have repeated much of what may be found in my work, entitled THE CELTIC DRUIDS, but it is so much enlarged, and I hope improved, by additional evidence in its support, that I have found it impossible to avoid the repetition to do justice to my subject. Therefore I hope it will be excused: more particularly as I consider that the removal of all doubt respecting the antiquity of the 16 or Cadmean letter system is necessary, several very important consequences being drawn from it, which have an intimate relation to the docrines developed in the following work.

2. In an inquiry into the origin of nations, or into the early history of mankind, one of the very first objects which offers itself to our attention is the invention of letters and numbers. Of this we have no actual information to which the least attention can be paid; for I suppose no one listens to such stories as those of their invention by Hermes or Mercury in Egypt, or Hercules in Gaul; it is therefore evident that to theory, and to theory alone, we must have recourse for the solution of the difficulty. A bare probability is the utmost at which we can ever expect to arrive in the investigation of this very interesting subject.

3. There is no likelihood that man would be endowed with these sciences at his creation; therefore it follows as a matter of course, that we must suppose the knowledge of them to have been the result of his own ingenuity, and of the gradual development of his faculties. This being admitted, it surely becomes a matter of great curiosity to ascertain the probable line of conduct, and the gradual steps which he would pursue for their acquisition.

4. After he had arrived at the art of speaking with a tolerable degree of ease and fluency, without being conscious that he was reasoning about it, he would probably begin to turn his thoughts to a mode of recording or perpetuating some few of the observations which he would make on surrounding objects, for the want of which he would find himself put to inconvenience. This I think was the origin of Arithmetic. He would probably very early make an attempt to count a few of the things around him, which interested him the most, perhaps his children; and his ten fingers would be his first reckoners; and thus by them he would be led to the decimal instead of the more useful octagonal calculation which he might have adopted; that is, stopping at 8 instead of 10. Thus, 8 + 1, 8 + 2, 8 + 3, instead of 10 + 1 or 11; 10 + 2 or 12; 10 + 3 or 13. There is nothing natural in the decimal arithmetic; it is all artificial, and must have arisen from the number of the fingers; which, indeed, supply an easy solution to the whole enigma. Man would begin by taking a few little stones, at first in number five, the number of fingers on one hand. This would produce the first idea of numbers. After a little time he would increase them to ten. He would, by placing them in order, and making them into several parcels, by degrees acquire a clear idea of ten numbers. He would divide them into two, and compare them with one another and with the fingers on each hand, and he would observe their equality; and thus by varying his parcels in different ways, he would begin to do what we call calculate, and acquire the idea of what we call a calculation. To these heaps or parcels of stones, and operations by means of them, he would give names; and I suppose that he called each of the stones a calculus, and the operation a calculation.

5. The ancient Etruscans have been allowed by most writers on the antiquities of nations, to have been among the oldest civilized people of whom we have any information. In my Essay on *the Celtic Druids*, I have shewn that their

language, or that of the Latins, which was in fact their language in a later time, was the same as the Sanscrit of India. This I have proved not merely by the uncertain mode of shewing that their words are similar, but by the construction of the language. The absolute identity of the modes of comparison of the adjective, and of the verb impersonal, which is my proof I have made use of, cannot have been the effect of accident. The words which I have used above for the first calculation, and for the instruments used in its performance, *calculus*[1] and *calculation*, are Latin, the language of the descendants of the Etruscans, and thus may have been readily derived from the earliest people of the world, whether Asiatic or European. I name this to shew that there is no objection to the names merely because they are the names of a modern language.

6. During the time that man was making this calculation, his attention would be turned to the Sun and Moon. The latter he would perceive to increase and decrease ; and after many moons he would begin to think it was what we call periodical ; and though he had not the name of period, he would soon have the idea in a doubtful way, and with his calculi he would begin a calculation. He would deposit one every day for twenty-eight days, being nearly the time one moon lived, and is the mean between the time of her revolution round the earth, twenty-nine days twelve hours and forty-four minutes, and the time she takes to go round her orbit, twenty-seven days, seven hours and forty-three minutes. Any thing like accuracy of observation it would be absurd to expect from our incipient astronomer. After a few months' observation he would acquire a perfect idea of a period of twenty-eight days, and thus he would be induced to increase his arithmetic to twenty-eight calculi. He would now try all kinds of experiments with these calculi. He would first divide them into two parts of equal number. He would then divide them again, each into two parts, and he would perceive that the two were equal, and that the four were equal, and that the four heaps made up the whole twenty-eight. He would now certainly discover (if he had not discovered before) the art of adding, and the art of dividing, in a rude way, by means of these calculi, probably at first without giving names to these operations. He would also try to divide one of the four parcels of calculi into which the Moon's age was divided still lower, but here for the first time he would find a difficulty. He could halve them or divide them into even parcels no lower than seven, and here begin the first cycle of seven days, or the week. This is not an arbitrary division, but one perfectly natural, an effect which must take place, or result from the process which I have pointed out, and which appears to have taken place in almost every nation that has learned the art of arithmetic. From the utmost bounds of the East, to the Ultima Thule, the septenary cycle may be discovered. By this time, which would probably be long after his creation, man would have learned a little geometry. From the shell of the egg, or the nut, he would have found out how to make an awkward, ill-formed circle, or to make a line in the sand with his finger, which would meet at both ends. The spider, or experiment, would certainly have taught him to make angles, though probably he knew nothing of their properties.

7. A very careful inquiry was made by Dr. Parsons some years ago into the arithmetical systems of the different nations of America, which in these matters might be said to be yet in a state of infancy, and a result was found which confirms my theory in a very remarkable manner. It appears, from his information, that they must either have brought the system with them when they arrived in America from the Old World, or have been led to adopt it by the same natural impulse and process which I have pointed out.

8. The ten fingers with one nation must have operated the same as with the other. They all, according to their several languages, give names to each unit, from one to ten, which is their determinate number, and proceed to add an unit to the ten ; thus, ten *one*, ten *two*, ten *three*, &c., till they amount to two tens, to which sum they give a peculiar name, and so on to three tens, four tens, and till it comes to ten times ten, or to any number of tens. This is also practised among the Malays, and indeed all over the East : but to this among the Americans there is one curious exception, and that is, the practice of the Caribbeans. *They* make their determinate period at five, and add one to the name of each of these fives, till they complete ten, and they then add two fives, which bring them to twenty, beyond which they do not go. They have no words to express ten or twenty, but a periphrasis is made use of. From this account of Dr. Parsons', it seems pretty clear that these Americans cannot have brought their figures and system of notation with them from the Old World, but must have invented them ; because if they had brought it, they would have all brought the decimal system, and some of them would not have stopped at the quinquennial, as it appears the Caribbees did. If they had come away after the invention of letters, they would have brought letters with them : if after the invention of figures, but before letters, they would all have had the decimal notation. From this it follows, that they must have migrated either before the invention of letters or figures, or, being ignorant persons, they did not bring the art with them. If this latter were the case, then the mode of invention according to my theory must have taken place entirely and to its full extent with the Americans, (which proves my assumed natural process in the discovery

---

[1] In the same way we have *annus* and *annulus*, *circus* and *circulus*.

to be correct,) and in part, though not to the full extent, with the Caribbees ; but the same *natural* process must have influenced both, which proves that my theory is rational and probable, and really has a principle of human nature for its foundation. I think the fact of the Caribbees having proceeded by the same route, but having only gone part of the way, is a strong circumstance to confirm my hypothesis.

9. The natives of Java have the quinary system, or calculation by fives. And it is remarkable that the word *lima*, which means *five*, means also the *hand*. It appears from Mr. Crawford, that in early times they had only the quinary system, which by degrees they improved to the denary.

10. In support of the idea which I have suggested above relative to the period of twenty-eight days, several circumstances or historical facts of the earliest nations of whom we have any account, may be cited. The almost *universal adoption* of the septenary cycle, which as a *religious ordinance* was certainly not known to the Israelites before the time of Moses, can in no other way be accounted for, and is in itself not of trifling moment. When man advanced in astronomical science, and parcelled the path of the moon in the heavens into divisions, he did not choose for this purpose twenty-nine or twenty-seven, but twenty-eight; and, accordingly, this was the number of mansions of the moon into which the Lunar Zodiac was divided by the astrologers of Egypt, of Arabia, of Chaldea, and of India. It was not, in my opinion, until a late date, comparatively speaking, that the mansions in India were more correctly divided into twenty-seven; but I do not state this as a fact, because I think it is not clearly made out which of the two Indian divisions, twenty-seven or twenty-eight, with which we meet, was the most ancient. If it were twenty-seven, I should consider this as a circumstance strongly tending to support the doctrine of Bailly, advocated by me in my CELTIC DRUIDS, that a highly civilized nation had formerly existed, of which the learning of India and Egypt was a remnant. I think, from various circumstances which will be noticed in the following work, the reader will be induced to believe that the Indian division was originally the same as those of the Chaldees and Arabians. All the three Zodiacs differ in the figures on them in such a manner as to make it likely that they are not copies from one another, but that they have each given their own figures to the divisions previously made into twenty-eight, from some common source. A learned astronomer, Mr. BENTLEY, in his work lately published, called *Ancient and Modern Hindoo Astronomy*,[1] states them to have been originally *twenty-eight*.

11. The Chinese also have a Lunar Zodiac divided into twenty-eight parts or mansions, and seven classes, four of which are assigned to each of the seven planets. But they do not, like the Hindoos, the Chaldees, and the Arabians, give them the forms of animals.[2] Here is evidently the same system, which so completely accords with my theory of the first lunar observations of uncivilized or infant man. And the circumstance of their Zodiac being without the forms of animals seems to confirm my idea, that the Hindoo, the Chaldean, the Arabic, and Egyptian Zodiacs, must have been drawn from some common source which originally was without them. There must have been some common reason for all these different nations adopting a Zodiac of twenty-eight divisions. I know not any so probable as the supposed length of the Moon's period. The animals in those Zodiacs are many of them natives of low latitudes : for instance, the elephant of Africa and India—which shews where the persons lived who gave them these animals. The Solar Zodiac, which has not the elephant, shews that it is not the produce of any nation where the elephant was indigenous. If the elephant and camel had been natives of the country where the Solar Zodiac was invented, they would not have been left out, to substitute goats or sheep. The modern astronomer, Mr. Bentley, was told by a learned Mohamedan, that the Lunar Zodiacs originally came from a country north of Persia and north-west of China—*the evident birth-place of the Solar Zodiac*.[3]

12. My opinion on this subject is confirmed by that of the learned Professor Playfair, who says, " It is also to the " phases of the Moon that we are to ascribe the common division of time into weeks, or portions of seven days, which " seems to have prevailed almost over the whole earth."[4]

13. It has been observed by Bishop Doyly, in an attack upon Sir W. Drummond, that the Zodiac is not of Indian extraction, but of Greek, because the animals of which it is composed are not natives of India.[5] The argument seems fair; for it is not credible that the elephant should have been omitted in an Indian composition. The same argument applies to Egypt and the remainder of Africa. But this is by no means a proof that it is the invention of the Greeks. The climate of Samarcand, in Tartary, is the same as that of Greece, and as I consider that the latter is quite out of the question, I maintain that it tends strongly to confirm my hypothesis.

---

[1] P. 5.    [2] Encyclop. Brit.    [3] Bentley on Hind. Ast., p. 251.    [4] Trans. Roy. Soc. Edin. Vol. II. p. 140.

[5] The whimsical sign called Capricorn, in the Indian Zodiac, is an entire goat and an entire fish ; in the Greek and Egyptian, the two are united and form one animal. It has been observed, that this is itself a presumptive proof that the Indian is the older of the two. And the Indian name, as noticed by Mons. Dupuis, (Tome III. p. 332,) is, as he has justly observed, probably taken from a primeval language whence both the Greek and Indian have been formed.

14. The Bishop says,[1] "The first astronomers were not calculators, but observers. Now the Moon is *seen* in the " Zodiac, and her place is obvious to the eye of the most rude observer : the Sun is not *seen* in it, and its place is only "known by comparison and calculation. Thus the division of the Zodiac with respect to the Moon was probably "among the earlier results of attention to the heavenly appearances, and its division with respect to the Sun among "the results comparatively later." This is probable ; but it seems to follow that it could not have been invented by the Greeks till they were far advanced in science ; and if this be admitted, it seems absolutely incompatible with the ignorance of the Greek authors of its origin. Their fabulous nonsense clearly proves their ignorance, but Phornutus and other authors admit it. In several passages, Bishop Doyly[2] states quite enough to prove that the Zodiac could be invented neither by the Chaldeans, by whom he always means the Babylonians, nor by the Egyptians, nor the Greeks. It is absolutely certain that the inventors of the Neros and the Metonic cycle must have been infinitely more learned than any of these three at any period of their histories before the birth of Christ. It is also proved from the number of the pillars in the Druidical circles of Britain, that the builders of them must have been acquainted with those cycles. The Phenniche and Phan, noticed in Chap. V. sect. xiv. Chap. VI. sect. xxv. of the Celtic Druids, and the note on it, Appendix, p. 307, prove that the Irish were acquainted with these cycles.

15. It has been observed by Bishop Doyly,[3] "That we may rest assured that the duodecimal division of the Zodiac "was formed in correspondence with the twelve lunations of the year. Since the Sun completed one apparent period "while the Moon completed twelve periods, the distribution of the Zodiac into twelve parts, so as to afford one man- "sion for the Sun during each of the twelve revolutions of the Moon, was by far the most obvious and natural." This is remarkably confirmed by what I have just now observed, and by the well-known historical fact that the Indians, the Chinese, Persians, Arabians, Egyptians, and Copts, had a lunar Zodiac divided into twenty-eight parts, called the mansions of the Moon, from immediate reference to the Moon's motion through the several days of her period. The universality of this division is a proof of its extreme antiquity.[4]

16. Again the Bishop says, "As has been already mentioned, the appointment of the twelve signs of the Zodiac was "probably a result of some advanced state of astronomy : men must then have been not merely observers of the "heavenly appearances, but must have begun to calculate and compare with some degree of science. Now we have "every reason to know that many nations, the Chaldeans and Egyptians especially, were diligent observers in astro- "nomy from very early times. They partitioned out the sphere into many constellations ; noted the risings and "settings of the stars ; kept accounts of the eclipses, &c. ; and, in many instances, determined the calendar with sur- "prising exactness, considering the means which they employed. But then these means were such as to shew that "they had made little or no advance in the science of astronomy, properly so called. Lalande mentions a number of "particulars respecting the early efforts of the Chaldeans and Egyptians in astronomy, which seem to prove decidedly "that they had made no progress beyond rude observation, although they certainly accomplished, in this manner, "more than could have been supposed. Among other things, he mentions,[5] that the Chaldæans ascertained the dura- "tion of the year by the very artificial method of measuring the length of a shadow of a raised pole. The Egyptians "too, settled their years merely by observing the risings and settings of stars.[6] He thinks the latter have been unduly "celebrated for astronomical knowledge, because we hear of them only from the Greeks, who were comparatively "ignorant. He expressly calls the astronomy of the Egyptians very moderate, 600 years B.C."[7] All this shews that the science of the Babylonians and Egyptians was but the débris of former systems, lost at that time by them, as it is known to have been in later times lost by the Hindoos.

17. Hyde gives the following account of the lunar mansions among the Arabians : "The stars or asterisms they "most usually foretold the weather by, were those they call Anwâ, or the Houses of the Moon. These are twenty-eight "in number, and divide the Zodiac into as many parts, through one of which the moon passes every night : as some "of them set in the morning, others rise opposite to them, which happens every thirteenth night." To these the Arabs ascribe great power.[8]

18. All these superstitions appear to us very foolish, but yet we retain some of them. How many Englishmen believe that the Moon regulates the weather, or rather how few disbelieve it ! A moment's reflection ought to teach them, that if the moon had any influence, it would be exerted regularly and periodically, like that upon the tides. But

---

[1] Remarks on Œd. Jud. p. 189.          [2] Ibid. p. 191.          [3] Ibid. p. 190.
[4] Sir W. Jones's Works, Vol. I. p. 330 ; Hyde on the Tables of Ulug. Beg. ; Bailly's Astron. Anc. pp. 109, 126, 476, 475, 491 ; Goguet, Vol. II. p. 401.
[5] See Lalande's Astron., Vol. I. p. 89.          [6] Ib. 93.          [7] Ib p. 102 ; Doyly, p. 192.
[8] Hyde in Not. ad Tabulas Stellar. ; Ulugh Beigh, p. 5 ; Sale's Prel. Disc., p. 41.

our prejudices, like those of the Arabian, will not permit us to see the folly of our own superstitions. Over each day and month the Persians and Arabians, as well as all the followers of the Magi or Magians, believed that a genius or angel presided, giving to each day or month the name of one of them. They had the same names as those of the Jews,—Gabriel, Michael, &c. The Jews say they took them from the Persians.

19. If my reader possess my Celtic Druids, I beg him to turn to the first chapter, section VI., and consider what is there said respecting the Lunar Cycle of twenty-eight days, and what is said afterward respecting the antiquity of the Chaldeans or Culdees, the priests of the first of the nations of the world, with their 360 crosses in Iona, their Metonic Cycles, &c., and the information afforded by Mr. Maurice in his Observations on the Ruins of Babylon, p. 29, that the Chaldeans of Babylon had a LUNAR ZODIAC consisting of twenty-eight mansions or houses, in which her orb was supposed to reside during the twenty-eight nights of her revolution, and I think he must be struck with the surprising manner in which my theory is supported by circumstances.

20. Plutarch, in his Treatise *de Iside et Osiride*,[1] states, that the division of Osiris into fourteen parts was a mythological mode of expression for the different phases of the moon during the increase and decrease of that orb. Mr. Maurice observes, that this " manifestly alludes to the different degrees of light which appear in the moon, and to the " number of days in which she performs her course round the earth."[2]

21. Porphyry distinctly notices the period of twenty-eight days with the Egyptians,[3] which he also observes was a Lunar period.

22. A traveller of the ancients, of the name of *Jambulus*, who visited Palibothra, and who resided seven years in one of the oriental islands, supposed to be Sumatra, states, that the inhabitants of it had an alphabet consisting of twenty-eight letters, divided into seven classes, each of four letters. There were seven original characters which, after undergoing four different variations each, constituted these seven classes. I think it is very difficult not to believe that the origin of the Chinese Lunar Zodiac and of these twenty-eight letters was the same, namely, the supposed length of the Lunar revolution. The island of Sumatra was, for many reasons, probably peopled from China.[4]

23. The Burmas keep four Sabbaths at the four phases of the moon, which shews the cycle of twenty-eight days.[5]

24. Astrologers had also in India another Lunar division. Mr. Colebrooke says, " Astrologers also reckon twenty-" eight *yogas*, which correspond to the twenty-eight nacshatras or divisions of the moon's path."[6] These different astronomical systems are among the oldest of the records of the world which we possess, and come nearest to the time when the science of letters and arithmetic must have been discovered, and tend strongly to support my theory of man's division of time into weeks, and the formation of his first arithmetic from the moon's age.

25. During the time that man was making his observations on the motions of the Moon, he would also be trying many experiments on his newly-discovered circle. He would divide it into two, then into four; thus he would make radii. Whilst he was doing this, he would begin to observe that the Sun was like the Moon, in the circumstance that it was periodical; that it changed continually, and continually returned to what it was before, producing summer and winter, spring and autumn; that after it had blessed him for a certain time with warmth and comfort, and the supply of fruits necessary for his subsistence, it gradually withdrew; but that in a certain number of days it returned, as the Moon had always returned, nearly to its former situation. He would do as he had done with respect to the Moon, collect calculi, and deposit one for every day; and he would find that there were, as he supposed, three hundred and sixty days in a period of the Sun's revolution. About this time, probably, he would hit upon the comparison of his period constantly returning into itself with his circle—the Sun's endless period with his endless circle. He would deposit his calculi about the circumference of his circle. He would divide it by means of these calculi into two parts. He would then halve them cross-ways, thus making four pieces or segments of circles, each having ninety stones. He would halve the nineties, but he could go no lower with halving, than making his ninety into two; therefore after many experiments he would divide his ninety into three divisions, placed in the circumference of the circle, or into thirties: each thirty again he would divide into three, and he would find each little division to contain ten calculi, the exact number of his fingers, and the most important number in his arithmetic, and the whole number would equal the days of a supposed solar revolution—three hundred and sixty days. By this time he must have made considerable progress in arithmetic and geometry. He must have learned the four common rules of the former, and how to make a square, a right-angled triangle, a correct circle, and other useful knowledge in these sciences. To all this there is nothing which can be objected, except it be the assumption, that he would reckon the Sun's period at three hundred and sixty days. But we are justified in assuming this from the well-known fact, that the ancients, even within the reach of history, actually believed the year to consist of only three hundred and sixty days.

[1] P. 93.   [2] Hist. Hind. Vol. I. p. 135.   [3] De Abstin. Lib. iv.; Taylor, p. 145.
[4] Asiat. Res. Vol. X. p. 151.   [5] Ibid. Vol. VI. p. 297.   [6] Ibid. Vol. VIII. p. 366.

26. From the circumstances here pointed out, I suppose it to have happened, that the circle became divided into 360 parts or degrees. Philosophers, or perhaps I should say astrologers, now began to exercise all their ingenuity on the circle. They first divided it into two parts of 180 degrees each ; then into four of 90 degrees each ; then each 90 into three ; and they observed that there were in all twelve of these, which afterward had the names of animals and other things given to them, came at length to be called signs of the Zodiac, and to be supposed to exercise great influence on the destinies of mankind. They then divided each of the 12 into three parts, called Decans, and these decans again into two, called Dodecans ; then there would be

A Circle consisting of 360 degrees,

2 Semicircles of . . . 180 degrees each,

4 Quadrants of . . . 90 degrees each,

12 Signs of . . . . . . 30 degrees each,

36 Decans of . . . . 10 degrees each, or 24 parts of 15 degrees each, and each 15 into 3 fives or Dodecans, and 72 Dodecans of . . 5 degrees each.

27. In a way somewhat analogous to this, they would probably proceed with the division of the year. As it consisted of the same number of days as the circle of degrees, they divided it into halves and quarters, then into twelve months,[1] and these months into thirty days each ; and as each day answered to one degree of the circle, or to each calculus laid in its circumference, and each degree of the circle was divided into sixty minutes, and each minute into sixty seconds, the day was originally divided in the same manner, as Bailly shews. Of this our sixty minutes and sixty seconds are a remnant.

28. The following, I believe, was the most ancient division of time :

| 1 Year | . . . . | 12 Months | . . . . | 1 Circle | . . . . | 12 Signs |
|---|---|---|---|---|---|---|
| 1 Month | . . . | 30 Days | . . . . . | 1 Sign | . . . . | 30 Degrees |
| 1 Day | . . . . | 60 Hours | . . . . | 1 Degree | . . . | 60 Hours |
| 1 Hour | . . . | 60 Minutes | . . . . | 1 Hour | . . . | 60 Minutes |
| 1 Minute | . . . | 60 Seconds | . . . . | 1 Minute | . . . | 60 Seconds. |

29. About the time this was going on, it would be found that the Moon made thirteen lunations in a year, of twenty-eight days each, instead of twelve only of thirty : from this they would get their Lunar year much nearer the truth than their Solar one. They would have thirteen months of four weeks each. They would also soon discover that the planetary bodies were seven ; and after they had become versed in the science of astrology, they allotted one to each of the days of the week ; a practice which we know prevailed over the whole of the Old World. A long course of years probably passed after this, before they discovered the great Zodiacal or precessional year of 25,920 years. In agreement with the preceding division, and for other analogical reasons connected with the Solar and Lunar years above-named, and with a secret science now beginning to arise, called Astrology, they divided it by sixty, and thus obtained the number 432—the base of the great Indian cycles. When they had arrived at this point they must have been extremely learned, and had probably corrected innumerable early errors, and invented the famous cycles called the Neros, the Saros, the Vans, &c.

30. In another way they obtained the same result. It seems to have been a great object with the ancient astrologers to reduce these periods to the lowest point to which it was possible to reduce them, without having recourse to fractions ; and this might perhaps take place before fractions were invented. Thus we find the dodecan, *five*, was the lowest to which they could come. This, therefore, for several reasons, became a sacred number. In each of the twelve signs of the Zodiac of thirty degrees each, they found there were six of these dodecans of five degrees, and that there were of course 6 × 12=72, and 72 × 6=432, in the whole circle, forming again the base of their most famous cycle. It was chiefly for these reasons that the two numbers *five* and *six* became sacred, and the foundations of cycles of a very peculiar kind, and of which I shall have occasion to treat much at large in the course of this work.

31. After man had made some progress, by means of his calculi, in the art of arithmetic, he would begin to wish for an increased means of perpetuating his ideas, or recording them for his own use, or for that of his children. At first, I conceive, he would begin by taking the same course with right lines marked on a stone, or on the inner rind of a tree, which he had adopted with his calculi. He would make a right line for one, two lines for two, and so on until he got five, the limit of one hand. He here made a stop, and marked it by two lines, meeting at the bottom thus, V : after this he began anew for his second series thus, V and I or VI, and so on till he came to VIIII, the end of the

---

[1] What induced the ancient Egyptians and Chaldees to throw two signs into one, and thus make only eleven, it is now perhaps impossible to determine.

second series, and he then made two fives thus, $\overset{\vee}{\wedge}$X, or ten.  This was with him a most important number, and became in process of time of the greatest importance also, as we shall hereafter find, in the concerns of mankind.  It was called the perfect, or complete number, evidently from completing the number of the fingers of the hands.  When man began to follow up his arithmetic to his number of twenty-eight, he proceeded with this as he had done with his calculi and number ten, and added units thus, XI, XII, &c., until he arrived at twenty, and then he wrote two tens thus, XX.  After this he again proceeded in the same way till he arrived at his XXVIIII.  Nothing can be more simple than this, and this is what we find among the Latins, the same nation in which we found our calculi, and the Etruscans, and it is what (except with respect to the X) was used, according to General Vallancey,[1] by the ancient Irish, among whom indeed, if any where, we may expect to find the first traces of civilized man.  How the X came to be varied, or its use left off by the Irish, I know not; but it was probably from a religious motive similar to that which made the Hebrews substitute a letter for their Jod, of which more hereafter.

32. General Vallancey observes, That from the X all nations began a new reckoning, because it is the number of fingers on both hands, which were the original intruments of numbering : hence יד (id) iod in Hebrew means both the *hand* and the number *ten ;*[2] and in the same manner the word *lamb* means *hand* and *ten* with the Buddhists of Tartary, whose first arithmetic stopped at ten ; and *lima* means *hand* and *five* with the Malays, whose first arithmetic stopped at five.  We can scarcely believe that this coincidence of practice is the effect of accident.

33. Among the Hebrews the name of the perfect number, i.e. ten, was Jod or I, their name of God.  Among the Arabs, it was Ya, the ancient Indian name of God (as in the course of this work I shall prove), and among the Greeks it was I or EI, the same as the Hebrew name of God.  By the Etruscans, whatever might be its name, it was described by the X or T, and for the sake of an astrological meaning I have no doubt the Greeks contrived that the X should stand for 600.  But relative to this I shall have much to say hereafter.

34. In the Chinese language the twenty-fourth radical, the Shih, is in the shape of the cross thus +, and means ten.  It also means *complete, perfect, perfectly good.*[3]  Thus the same system is universally found.

35. What I have said respecting the origin of numbers, and the importance which I have attached to them, must not be considered merely a theory, totally without support from history, for the historical accounts of most nations shew us that the superstitious regard to numbers was carried to almost an inconceivable length.  I think the doctrines of Pythagoras may be considered as among the oldest of any which we find in the Western world, and whatever they were, thus much we know, that they were all founded on numbers.  We also know that the astronomical system which is confessed to have been obtained by him in the East was the true one, in its great features—the revolving motions of the planets; then have we not reason to believe that these very numbers, which we find recurring every where in the Eastern and Western systems, were the same ?  We find the numbers five and six continually recurring in both systems, as the basis of the sacred 60, 360, 3600, and 432, 4320, &c.  Then how can we doubt that they became *sacred* for the reasons which I have given ?  There must have been some cause for the effect, and what other can be assigned than that which I have supposed ?

36. We will now return to our incipient astronomers' twenty-eight calculi.

37. I feel little doubt that the system I have here developed was the origin of arithmetic, that it preceded the art of writing, and was its cause or precursor.  It led the way to this most useful discovery.  Mr. Bryant supports my opinion so far as to allow that the use of arithmetic must have been known long before letters.

38. After man had found by this combination of right lines the art of writing down the few limited ideas appertaining to these twenty-eight signs for numbering the days, he would begin to entertain the desire of extending the art of writing to other objects.  For this purpose he would naturally try to use these same right lines.  This experiment we have in full view in the Irish Oghams, and it is particularly exemplified in an Irish inscription called the Callan inscription, which is given in the Celtic Druids, in the second table of Alphabets.  The total unfitness of this kind of writing for the conveyance of complicated chains of reasoning, or indeed of ideas generally, is there exhibited.  Dr. Aikin says, " fifteen lines are required to express the first five letters of this alphabet, and this may be translated in five dif- " ferent ways ; consequently nothing can be more uncertain than its true meaning."  Here I think we find the origin of the Ogham writing and of the Northern Runes.  Thus these simple lines at angles would constitute the first letters or figures or signs used by mankind for the conveyance of ideas.  This is confirmed by the result of our researches into the earliest inscriptions and letters on ancient monuments.

39. The Oghams, or secret alphabets, of the Irish, all consist of right lines, and the ancient Runes of the same ; and it would be very easy to select several complete alphabets, consisting of nothing but right lines, at various angles, from

---

[1] Collect. de Reb. Hib. No. XII. p. 571.  [2] Vall. Col. Vol. V. p. 177.  [3] Morrison's Chinese Dict. p. 299.

the letters on the oldest Greek and Etruscan coins.   The old Runes were inscribed on sticks or staves of wood, cut or shaved so as to expose three plain surfaces, and on these the right-lined letters were engraved with a stylus.   These are what are alluded to by Aulus Gellius,[1] when he states the laws of Solon to have been engraved *axibus ligneis*, which have been mistranslated *table* or *board*.   These two Latin words will bear no such construction.[2]   They mean the staves or stems of trees used by the ancient Druids, as well as by the Greeks.   And on them were inscribed the letters of the Ionian Greeks, which Herodotus says were originally composed of right lines.[3]

40.  The inscribed stems were in part the origin of a vast variety of interesting allegories respecting trees, letters, and science, particularly among the Arabians and a numerous class of oriental philosophers called Gnostics.

41.  The Greek system of notation is nearly the same as the Latin.   The numbers are as follow : I, II, III, IIII, II, III, IIII, IIII, IIIII, Δ, ΔI, ΔII, ΔIII, ΔIIII, ΔII, ΔΔ 20, ΔΔI 21, ΔΔII 25, ΔΔΔ 30, &c.   The principle is evidently the same, and all the letters consist of right lines easily made axibus ligneis ; and though the ten, the sacred number, does not consist of an X, it does of an equilateral triangle, Δ, which I have no doubt was adopted for a mysterious reason, hereafter pointed out.

42.  Pliny the Elder says, that the Ionian letters were the oldest of Greece, and that the most ancient Grecian letters were the same as the Etruscan ; and as he produces the example of an ancient inscription to justify his assertion, it seems more worthy of attention than most of the idle, gossiping stories which he has collected together.   We have just now seen that the most ancient of the Greek and Italian alphabets have a strong tendency to the right-lined practice.   Now the question very naturally arises, who were, and whence came the Ionians ?   This is a question which it is very easy to ask, but very difficult to answer,—a question which will be most intimately connected in the answer with some very abstruse and profound oriental doctrines into which I must enter in the course of the following work, and which will require much previous investigation.   I shall, therefore, beg to suspend it for the present, but the reader will please to bear it in mind.

43.  My reader is not to suppose that I imagine the process of the invention of letters took place literally by one pair of persons as I have here represented.   What is meant is only to shew generally the nature of the process.   The steps by which the result was obtained it is not possible, in the nature of things, to describe with accuracy.   Various persons would from time to time be employed, or perhaps a society, on whom the natural causes which I have pointed out, or other causes similarly natural, would operate to produce the effect ; for example, the number of the fingers of the hand creating the first class of numbers, the two hands the second class, &c.

44.  From General Vallancey I learn a fact which strongly confirms my theory.   He says, " The Phœnicians had nu-" merals before they had letters.   Their first numerals were similar to the Irish Ogham, marks consisting of straight, " perpendicular lines, from one to nine, thus : I, II, III, IV, &c.   *Ten* was marked with an horizontal line — ; and " these they retained after they had adopted the Chaldean alphabetic numerals."[4]—" There cannot be a stronger proof " that numerals preceded letters, than the Hebrew word ספר *Spr, sepher,* which properly signifies to number, to " cipher : numeration, numbering : but after numerals were applied as literary characters, the same word denoted, as it " does at this day, a scribe, a letter, a book, a literary character."[5]   Bates says, the word *sepher* has all the senses of the Latin *calculus*.   Mr. Hammer, of Vienna, found in Egypt an Arabic manuscript which is written in Arabic words, but in a character which is evidently the same as the tree Ogham of Ireland.   See Plate I. Fig. I.   The word Ogham or Agham is Indian, and means secret or mysterious.

45.  From various circumstances it is not improbable that these right-lined figures had originally the names of trees.   In the infant state of society, so large a number of letters or signs for an alphabet as twenty-eight, would be rather an incumbrance than an advantage.   It would take a long time for man to discover the advantage of a correct sign for every vocal sound which he was capable of uttering, and he probably made a selection of sixteen of them : the first sixteen, perhaps.   In our names of numbers there is not now the least appearance of the names of the letters or trees :

---

[1] The words of Gellius are, *In Legibus Solonis, illis antiquissimis, quæ Athenis, axibus ligneis incisæ erant.*   Some learned men, not understanding the nature of the ancient staves on which letters were accustomed to be inscribed, have wished to substitute *assibus* for *axibus.*   Had they succeeded, they would have completely changed the sense of the author, and have concealed the interesting fact, that the ancient Irish and the Greeks used the same mode of writing.   The emendations of Editors have done infinite mischief to science.   I have no objection to emendations suggested in notes, but scarcely ever ought they to be carried into the text.   By emendations, as *authentic records,* the Old and New Testaments have, in innumerable instances, been rendered doubtful as to their real meaning.

[2] See Celtic Druids, Chap. I. Sect. xxxi.                    [3] Ibid. Sect. xxxi. xxxii.
[4] Vall. Col. Vol. V. pp. 183—186.                          [5] Ibid. p. 175.

and the names of many of our numbers may be found in almost all languages. So that if they ever had the names of trees, a change must have taken place at a very early period.

46. The first notice which we have of letters being called by the names of trees is found in one of the alphabets of the ancient Irish, called the Beth-luis-nion. It consists of the seventeen letters in the table, in column No. 4, in the order in which they stand in the Irish grammar, with the meaning of each placed opposite to it:

| 1 | 2 | 3 | 4 | 5 | 6 | 7 |
|---|---|---|---|---|---|---|
| ℛ | B | Boibel | | B | Beith | Birch |
| ⊥ | L | Loth | | L | Luis | Quicken |
| x | F | Foran | | N | Nuin | Ash |
| ⸂ | S | Salia | x | F | Fearan | Alder |
| ⋔ | N | Neaigadon | ⟨ | S | Suil | Willow * |
| ⸒ | D | Daibhoith | ⟩ | D | Duir | Oak |
| ✢ | T | Teilmon | ⟨ | T | Tinne | Furze * |
| ⸝ | C | Casi | ⊆ | C | Coll | Hazel |
| ⸜ | M | Moiria | ⊆ | M | Muin | Vine |
| ⸞ | G | Gath | ⅂ | G | Gort | Ivy |
| | P | | — | P | Poth | Dwarf Elder * |
| 𝟿 | R | Ruibe | ⁊⟍ | R | Ruis | Elder |
| 𝒜 | A | Acab | ⟍L⟋ | A | Ailim | Elm |
| X | O | Ose | ⟋⟍⟍ | O | On, or Oir | Spindle |
| ⋎ | U | Ura | ⋀V | U | Ux | White-thorn or Heath |
| ⸦ | E | Esu | ⋎⋏ | E | Eactha or Eadha | Aspen |
| ⸭ | J | Jaichim | ⟍⟋ | J | Jodha | Yew |

Column No. 1 is another Irish alphabet, of which the letters had a different shape and different names, but it was in number the same.

47. In the following Table the column No. 1 contains the names of the letters of the ancient Samaritan and Hebrew or Chaldee alphabets. No. 2 contains the Samaritan letters. No. 3, the Hebrew or Chaldee letters used after the Babylonish captivity. No. 4 contains the Hebrew or Chaldee final letters, opposite to their powers of notation. No. 5 contains the powers of notation of the Samaritan, the Chaldee, and the Greek letters. No. 6 contains the Greek letters. In No. 7, the asterisks shew the letters first brought to Greece from Phœnicia by Cadmus. No. 8 contains the name of the Greek letters. No. 9 contains the Celtic Irish letters in English characters, placed opposite to the letters in the other alphabets to which they correspond. No. 10 contains the names of the Celtic Irish letters; and No. 11, their meanings.

---

* Logan, Scottish Gael, Vol. II. p. 390.

## ALPHABETS.

| 1 | 2 | 3 | 4 | 5 | 6 | 7 | 8 | 9 | 10 | 11 |
|---|---|---|---|---|---|---|---|---|---|---|
| Aleph | ࠀ | א | | 1 | Α α | • | Alpha | A | Ailm | Elm tree |
| Beth | ࠁ | ב | | 2 | Β β | • | Beta | B | Beth | Birch |
| Gimel | ࠂ | ג | | 3 | Γ γ | • | Gamma | G | Gort | Ivy |
| Daleth | ࠃ | ד | | 4 | Δ δ | • | Delta | D | Duir | Oak |
| He | ࠄ | ה | | 5 | Ε ε | • | Epsilon | E | Eadha | Aspen |
| Vau | ࠅ | ו | | 6 | Ϝ | • | Digamma | Fv | Fearn | Alder |
| Zain | ࠆ | ז | | 7 | Ζ ζ | | Zeta | | | |
| Heth | ࠇ | ח | | 8 | Η η | | Eta | | | |
| Teth | ࠈ | ט | | 9 | Θ ϑ θ | | Theta | | | |
| Jod | ࠉ | י | | 10 | Ι ι | • | Iota | I | Jodha | Yew |
| Caph | ࠊ | כ | ך | 20 | Κ κ | • | Kappa | C | Coll | Hazle |
| Lamed | ࠋ | ל | | 30 | Λ λ | • | Lambda | L | Luis | Quicken |
| Mem | ࠌ | מ | ם | 40 | Μ μ | • | Mu | M | Muin | Vine |
| Nun | ࠍ | נ | ן | 50 | Ν ν | • | Nu | N | Nuin | Ash |
| Samech | ࠎ | ס | | 60 | Ξ ξ | | Xi | | | |
| Oin | ࠏ | ע | | 70 | Ο ο | • | Omicron | O | Oir | Spindle |
| Pe | ࠐ | פ | ף | 80 | Π π | • | Pi | P | Pieth Bhog | Dwarf elder |
| Tzaddi | ࠑ | צ | ץ | 90 | ϛ | | Episemon bau | | | |
| Koph | ࠒ | ק | | 100 | | | Επισημον ϐαυ | | | |
| | | | | 100 | Ρ ρ | • | Rho | R | Ruis | Elder |
| Resh | ࠓ | ר | | 200 | | | | | | |
| | | | | 200 | Σ σ | • | Sigma | S | Suil | Willow |
| Shin | ࠔ | ש | | 300 | | | | | | |
| | | | | 300 | Τ τ | • | Tau | T | Teine | Furze |
| Tau | ࠕ | ת | | 400 | | | | | | |
| | | | | 400 | Υ υ | • | Upsilon | U | Uath* Heath aspirate | White-thorn |
| | | Initials. | Finals. | | | | | | | |
| Caph | K | כ | ך | 500 | Φ φ | | Phi | | | |
| Mem | M | מ | ם | 600 | Χ χ | | Chi | | | |
| Nun | N | נ | ן | 700 | Ψ ψ | | Psi | | | |
| Pe | P | פ | ף | 800 | Ω ω | | Omega | | | |
| Tzaddi | Z | צ | ץ | 900 | ϡ | | Sanpi | | | |

* No doubt the Tau or Teine ought to be the last letter, but the Uath has been obliged to be put here instead of at the sixth place, to make room for the Digamma, an anomaly, in the Greek language, not understood.

48. In the treatise called THE CELTIC DRUIDS, I have proved, by a great variety of circumstantial and positive evidence, that the sixteen or seventeen letter-alphabet here given of the Irish, in its principle or system, was the same as those of the ancient Samaritan, the Phœnician, the Hebrew or Chaldee, the Persian, the Etruscan, the Greek, and the Latin. I have shewn that, however numerous the letters of these languages may be at this day, different learned men, without any intercourse with one another, or any idea that an universal system prevailed among them, have reduced them to, or proved that they were originally, only sixteen or seventeen in number. And these are, in all of them, the very same letters, as is ascertained by their having the powers of notation in a manner so similar as to put the identity of the principle or system out of all question.

49. Bishop Burgess, in his Introduction to the Arabic Language, without having the least idea of the general system which I have pointed out, has confirmed it in a very remarkable manner.[1] He has shewn that the Arabic had originally only seventeen letters, including the Digamma. The near approximation of the powers of notation, and the similarity of the names of the letters, shew that they are the same as the Irish, the Greek, and the Hebrew.

| Arabic | | Hebrew | | Greek | | Irish |
|---|---|---|---|---|---|---|
| 1 | Alef | Aleph | | Alpha | 1 | Ailim. |
| 2 | Ba | Beth | | Beta | 2 | Beth. |
| 3 | Gim | Gimel | | Gamma | 3 | Gort. |
| 4 | Dal | Daleth | | Delta | 4 | Duir. |
| 200 | Ra | Resh | | Ro | 100 | Ruis. |
| 300 | Shin | Shin | | Sigma | 200 | Suil. |
| 90 | Sad | Tzadi | | | | |
| 400 | Ta | Tau | | Tau | 300 | Teine. |
| 70 | Ain | Oin | | Omicron | 70 | Oir. |
| 80 | Fa | Pe | | Pi | 80 | Pieth-Bhog. |
| 20 | Caf | Caph | | Kappa | 20 | Coll. |
| 30 | Lam | Lamed | | Lambda | 30 | Luis. |
| 40 | Mim | Mem | | Mu or Mui | 40 | Muin. |
| 50 | Nun | Nun | | Nu or Nui | 50 | Nuin. |
| 6 | Wau | Vau | | F, formerly Vau, pronounced U, then V, afterwards DIGAMMA | 6 | Fearn. |
| 5 | Ha | He | | Epsilon | 5 | Eadha. |
| 10 | Ya | Yod | | Iota | 10 | Jodha. |
| | | | | Upsilon | | Uath. |

50. The Shin, Shin, and Sigma, I have substituted for the Sin, Samech, and Xi, which are in the Bishop's table, and which is evidently a mistake, the Greek X. being one of the new, and not one of the Cadmean or *ancient* Greek letters. This mistake is a most fortunate circumstance, because it proves that the Bishop did not know the principle of these alphabets which I have been explaining, and therefore cannot be suspected of having made his original letters to suit it. And it also renders it impossible for any one to say, that he has been contriving his seventeen primary letters to make them suitable to the Irish, whose letters he probably looked on with too much contempt to have considered them even for a single moment. This adds very materially to the value of his opinion.

51. The powers of notation are the same in all the ancient alphabets, with their increased number of letters, *till they get to the nineteenth letter, Ra or Resh,* when a variation takes place, which I have shewn probably arose in after times from the coming into use of the Greek Digamma.[2]

52. The following is the table of the Arabian system of numbers given by Bishop Burgess:

| Alif | 1 | | Ya | 10 | 10 | Kaf | 100 | 19 |
|---|---|---|---|---|---|---|---|---|
| Ba | 2 | | Caf | 20 | 11 | Ra | 200 | 20 |
| Gim | 3 | | Lam | 30 | 12 | Shin | 300 | 21 |
| Dal | 4 | | Mim | 40 | 13 | Ta | 400 | 22 |
| Ha | 5 | | Nun | 50 | 14 | Tha | 500 | 23 |
| Wav | 6 | | Sin | 60 | 15 | Rha | 600 | 24 |
| Za | 7 | | Ain | 70 | 16 | Dhal | 700 | 25 |
| Hha | 8 | | Fe | 80 | 17 | Dad | 800 | 26 |
| Ta | 9 | 9 | Sad | 90 | 18 | Da | 900 | 27 |
| | | | | | | Ghain | 1000 | 28 |

---

[1] See Celtic Druids, Ch. VI. Sect. xxvi.          [2] See Ibid.

53. Here, I think, is as triumphant a proof of the truth of the system as can well be desired.   Here is the exact number of the Calculi 28, and here they are interwoven into the decimal calculation in a very wonderful manner; the 1000 exactly answering to the number of 28 figures.   If I be told that the present Arabic alphabet is, comparatively speaking, modern, I reply, however the forms of its letters may have been changed by the Califs, the principle, the system, is evidently ancient, both of the letters and figures.   No one can for a moment believe that they *invented a new alphabet* and system of notation which, by mere accident, coincided with all the old systems of the world; the idea is ridiculous; it involves a contradiction in terms.

54. Some persons have pretended that the Irish selected their letters from the Latin and Greek.   How came they to select the identical letters which Cadmus brought to Greece, and no others?   This at once disposes of this pretence, and proves to a certainty, that, if the Irish received their letters from Greece, they must have received them before the time of Homer; if from Syria, before the time of Moses, whose Pentateuch contains twenty-two letters.   This carries back Irish literature to a time surprisingly ancient.

55. The alphabets of ancient nations have attracted the attention of several learned men at different times and places, and they have endeavoured, with very great care, to ascertain the original number of letters in those alphabets.   Nearly all their investigations have terminated in demonstrating the same facts, viz. that the different systems of letters agree within one; that they all amount to sixteen or to seventeen letters; that they have a striking similarity in their names; and that the correspondent letters have the same numerical powers; and, from incidental circumstances, it is very evident that the learned men to whom I allude, Morton, Chishull, Burgess, &c., have had no intention of making the different alphabets systematically agree with one another.   This I have most clearly proved in my essay on The Celtic Druids, to which, for the complete proof of the truth of these assertions, I must refer.

56. I now beg my reader to refer back to page 5, to the account given by the ancient traveller *Jambulus* of the alphabet of Sumatra, and I think when he has read it with attention he will be obliged to believe that it must have been the same in system as the Arabic, and both to have come from the first system of notation founded on the supposed age of the Moon; and I also beg him to consider the tree alphabet found in the Arabic language by professor Hammer in Egypt; in fact, an Arabic treatise written in an Irish Ogham letter.   Before I finish I shall trace these Arabians to the borders of China.

57. The Sanscrit alphabet consists of not less than fifty letters, but the number of simple articulations may be reduced to twenty-eight, (the number of the Arabic and of my first numbers,) five vowels and twenty-three consonants.   May not the original twenty-eight numerals have been adopted by the Indians for their letters, and sixteen only of them selected by the Arabs?   And may not this have been the reason why the difference between the Arabic and Sanscrit appears to be greater than that between the Sanscrit and all the other Western languages? if indeed there be this difference, a fact which I very much doubt.

58. Though I am ignorant of the Sanscrit language, a close attention to great numbers of its proper names had made me strongly suspect that its system of letters was originally the same as that of the Western nations.   The following two passages which I have discovered will shew that I had good grounds for my suspicion.   Colonel Wilford says, " The Sanscrit alphabet, after striking off the double letters, and such as are used to express sounds peculiar to that " language, has a surprising affinity with the old alphabets used in Europe, and they seem to have been originally the " same."[1]   In another place Col. Wilford says, " I have observed that gradual state of decay in the Sanscrit language " through the dialects in use in the Eastern parts of India down to the lowest, in which last, though all the words are " Sanscrit more or less corrupted, the grammatical part is poor and deficient, exactly like that of our modern language " in Europe, whilst that of the higher dialects of that country is at least equal to that of the Latin language.   From " such a state of degradation no language can recover itself: all the refinements of civilization and learning will never " retrieve the use of a lost case or mood.   The improvements consist only in borrowing words from other languages " and in framing new ones occasionally.   This is the remark of an eminent modern writer, and experience shews that " he is perfectly right.   Even the Sanscrit alphabet, when stripped of its double letters, and of those peculiar to that " language, is the Pelasgic, and every letter is to be found in that, or the other ancient alphabets, which obtained " formerly all over Europe, and I am now preparing a short essay on that interesting subject."[2]

59. This is confirmed by Col. Van Kennedy, who says, " In all essential respects, the Greek, Latin, and Sanscrit " alphabetical systems are similar."[3]

60 In The Celtic Druids I have pointed out a very curious circumstance of a Sanscrit sentence being found a Eleusis.   This is confirmed by an observation of Col. Van Kennedy's, that there are 339 Sanscrit words in the poem of Homer.[4]   I shall resume the subject of the Sanscrit language hereafter.

[1] Asiat. Res. Vol. X. p. 152.    [2] Ibid. Vol. VIII. 8vo, p. 265.    [3] Res. into the Orig. of Lang., p. 131.    [4] Ibid. p. 209.

61. If more than sixteen or seventeen letters be found in the Amiclean or Eugubean inscriptions, I think they prove, either that these inscriptions are forgeries, or that their date has been mistaken. For after the detection of the frauds of the rascals *Ennius* and *Fourmont*, I think they cannot be permitted to overturn the positive assertion of Pliny, that Cadmus brought only sixteen letters, supported as the assertion is by the varieties of authorities and reasonings which have given, and the independent examination and opinions of learned modern inquirers, that all these languages are educeable to sixteen letters. Before the conclusion of this work the reader will find, that consequences of the most important nature follow the reduction of the different written languages to one system, consisting of that number of letters.

62. The decimal system of which the last table (Sect. 52) consists, has every appearance of being founded on the original simple twenty-eight units. After civilization had advanced, a higher notation than the twenty-eight would be wanted, and the Arabians appear to have adopted the decimal system, keeping as near as possible to the ancient twenty-eight letters, as a close examination will prove; for what is the 20 but two *tens*, the 30 but *three* tens, the 100 but *ten* tens, the 1000 but *one hundred* tens? Perhaps it may be said, that the coincidence of the decimal numbers to the twenty-eight calculi is accidental. But is it accidental that the powers of notation in the Arabic, Hebrew, Greek, and Irish letters are the same till they come to nineteen; that is, similar in eighteen instances in succession? It is a very singular ACCIDENT that in each of the eighteen cases the letters and numbers should agree in the different languages. It is also a most fortunate *accident* which should cause the elements of the Irish names of letters, the Muin, Nuin, &c., as I shall now shew, to be found in the Arabic. By a careful comparison of the names of the different letters in the Irish Beth-luis-nion, with the Samaritan, Hebrew, and Greek, it will appear almost certain that they have all been called after the trees which now grow in the latitude of England, or else that the trees have been named after them.[1] But it is proper to observe, that great allowance ought to be made for the change necessarily arising from the lapse of perhaps thousands of years. It seems to me impossible to doubt the original identity of the Samaritan, the Greek, and the Hebrew letters; and how wonderfully are they changed! Then if we do not find the English names of trees differ more from the Irish names of letters, than the names of the Greek, Hebrew, and Samaritan letters, than the alphabets differ from each other, we shall have a similarity as great as, perhaps greater than, can be expected. It is not at all probable that the similarity should continue till this time in all the letters: very few will be sufficient to establish the fact, if they only possess a sufficient degree of similarity. The Arabic system of notation or arithmetic, which is so intimately connected with their system of letters, is believed, by all Orientalists, to have come from India. I trust I shall be able to prove that they came together from India.

63. The Aleph, Alpha, and Ailm, are not strikingly similar; but there is a very obvious resemblance between the words Ailm and Elm; the first letter of the word Ailm being pronounced as we pronounce the A in our A, B, C, or in the word *able*.

64. The Beth or Beith of the Samaritan and Hebrew is the identical Beth or Beith, the Birch-tree of the Irish. Pliny calls Betulla the Birch, a Gaulish tree. In one of the dialects of Britain, the Welsh, it is called Bedw.

65. In the next three names of letters, the similarity is lost, except that they begin with the same consonants.

66. The Digamma forms an exception to all rules.

67. The Jod, or Iod or Iota, and Iodha and Yew, are all clearly the same, or as near as can be expected. This will be immediately found on pronouncing the Y in the word Yew by itself, instantly followed by the other letters.

68. The name of this tree is, as I have shewn in my Celtic Druids, one of the names of Jehovah, *Ieu*. It is considered by our country people to be in its wood the most durable of all trees.

69. There is nothing more which is striking till we come to the Mem, Mu, Muin, vine. The *vine* may have readily come from the word Muin—the letter M being dropped for some unknown cause; or the M may have been prefixed to the Vin, and be what Hebrew grammarians call *formative*; or it may have been prefixed for a reason which will be given hereafter.

70. The Nun is the Nu and Nuin without difficulty, though it has no relation to the Ash in sound or in letters. Yet the Nun of the Hebrew is evidently the same as the Irish tree Nuin.

71. The Oin and the Irish Oir have a similarity, but have no relation to the Spindle or the Oir, except in the first letter of the latter name.

72. The Samaritan and Hebrew Resh is the Irish Ruis.

73. The Shin and Tau are only similar in the first letters to the Suil and Teine.

74. The similarity, it is true, is not found in many of the sixteen letters, but there is sufficient similarity to prove

---

[1] It has been observed in the CELTIC DRUIDS, that the vine which is found among the trees in this alphabet is neither of Indian nor of British origin; for though it grows in both, it is common in neither; but it is indigenous in the same latitude in the country which I suppose was the birth-place of the human race, that is, between 45 and 50 degrees of North latitude, where all the other trees of this alphabet are to be found.

that the Irish have not merely culled letters out of the Roman alphabet and given them the names of trees: for although the examples of similarities are now become oddly and unsystematically arranged, yet their present situation can have arisen from nothing but an original identity, destroyed by various accidents.  If the Ailm have nothing to do with the Aleph, it is evidently the same as the English Elm; and if the Beth or Beith has little or nothing to do with the English Birch, it is evidently identical with the Hebrew Beth.  How came an Irish tree to bear the name of a Hebrew letter?  Thus again, the Jod, Iod, Iota, Jodha, and Yew, are *all* nearly allied, and the Jod and Jodha identical.  Again, how came this Irish name of a tree and a letter of their alphabet to be the same as the Hebrew name of this letter?  Can any one look at the Greek Mu, the Irish Muin, and the English vine, and not be convinced (all the other letters and circumstances considered) that they are the same?  Vine is evidently the three last letters of the Irish *Muin.*

75. The Irish name of the Ash, Nuin, is the same as the Hebrew and Samaritan *Nun* and the Greek *Nu*.

76. Lastly, the Samaritan and Hebrew Resh is unquestionably the Irish *Ruis*, the Elder.  Again I ask, how came these Hebrew letters to bear the name of Irish trees?  Did the Irish literati understand Hebrew several thousand years ago, and call their trees after Hebrew and Samaritan letters on purpose to puzzle the learned men of the present day?  There is no way of accounting for these extraordinary coincidences and circumstances except by supposing an original alphabet called after trees, and changed by accident in long periods of time.  Bigots may ridicule this, but they cannot refute it.

77. It is a singular circumstance, that though the Irish names of letters, for instance the Mem or Muin, and the Beith, are the Irish names of trees, they are not the *known* Hebrew names of trees.  It is impossible to believe that the Asiatics *by accident* called their sixteen letters after the Irish names of trees.  I think it is pretty clear that the Hebrew letters, and of course the Greek or Cadmean taken from them, were originally called after the Beth-luis-nion of the Irish, *or after some language whence that was taken.*

78. The ancient Rabbis had a tradition, that the names of the Hebrew letters had the meaning of the names of different trees, and General Vallancey attempts to specify them.  But he does not seem to have succeeded.  His information is taken from the old Jewish writers, who appear to give rather what they surmise than what they found in the synagogue copies of the Pentateuch.  But their opinion is very important indeed, as a record of an old tradition.  It seems that the Rabbis had received a tradition that the names of their letters had the meaning of the names of trees, which they wished, but wished in vain, to *verify*.

79. The General quotes the authority of Bayer, " that each of the Chaldean or Hebrew letters derives its name " from some tree or shrub; as ב *Beth*, a thorn; ד *Daleth*, a vine; ה *He*, the pomegranate; ו *Vau*, the palm; י *Jod*, " ivy; ט *Teth*, the mulberry-tree; ס *Samech*, the apple-tree; פ *Pe*, the cedar; ר *Resh*, the pine," &c.[1]

80. There is, as I have said, the strongest probability that the art of figuring or of arithmetic took precedence of the art of writing.  The figures would evidently be the first wanted, and probably, in the way I have stated, the names of trees were given to them.  The Mexicans had the knowledge of figures—the decimal calculation, but not of letters: the natives of Otaheite had the same.[2]  From the use of the first ten or fifteen figures for numbers of the calculi, a transition to letters would not be very difficult, and probably took place and gave them their names of leaves.  And I think it very probable that (what is commonly called) the accidental discovery of letters, may have been the original cause of the Old World having attained so superior a state of refinement and civilization—notwithstanding some persons may think this a cause too small for so large an effect.  It would, I conceive, operate by geometrical progression.

81. From all these considerations, there is a strong probability that the first alphabet was denoted by the names of trees; and, from a passage of Virgil's, one might be induced to believe that the leaves themselves were actually used:

> Arrived at Cumæ, when you view the flood
> Of black Avernus, and the sounding wood,
> The mad prophetic Sibyl you shall find
> Dark in a cave, and on a rock reclined.
> She sings the fates, and in her frantic fits
> The notes and names, inscribed TO LEAVES COMMITS.
> What she commits to leaves, in order laid,
> Before the cavern's entrance are display'd.
> Unmoved they lie: but if a blast of wind
> Without, or vapours issue from behind,
> The leaves are borne aloft in liquid air;
> And she resumes no more her museful care,

---

[1] Pref. and Prospect. for an Irish Dict. by Gen. Vallancey; Davies' Cel. Res., p. 305.          [2] Astle, p. 182.

Nor gathers from the rocks her scatter'd verse,
Nor sets in order what the winds disperse.
Thus many, not succeeding, most upbraid
The madness of the visionary maid,
And with loud curses leave the mystic shade.
Æn. Lib. iii. ver. 445.

But, oh! commit not thy prophetic mind
To flitting leaves, the sport of every wind,
Lest they disperse in air our empty fate :
Write not, but, what the powers ordain, relate.
Lib. vi. l. 116—120.

82. I think if any sense is to be made of this poetical description, we must understand that each leaf had or was a letter.

——————— foliisque notas et nomina mandat.
Quæcumque in foliis descripsit carmina virgo,
Digerit in numerum, atque antro seclusa relinquit :
Illa manent immota locis, neque ab ordine cedunt :
Verum eadem verso tenuis cum cardine ventus
Impulit et teneras turbavit janua frondes,
Nunquam deinde cavo volitantia prendere saxo,
Nec revocare situs, aut jungere carmina, curat :
Inconsulti abeunt, sedemque odere Sibyllæ.

It seems pretty clear that if whole words had been written, each word upon a leaf, and these words in verse, the inquirer might easily have put them together. From this it may fairly be inferred, that if letters were written at all, there could only have been one on each leaf.

83. In the religious rites of a people I should expect to find the earliest of their habits and customs, and the above passage relating to this Celtic Sibyl can mean nothing except that the leaves themselves were used either as letters (each leaf standing for a letter) or the names of letters, each written on a leaf which the wind might easily blow away. But it is probable that the leaves themselves may have been used, and that this practice may have been derived from the letters having the names of trees, and may have been adopted for the sake of mystery, which we know was greatly affected in all the old religions. The way in which this passage is connected by Virgil, a native of Cisalpine Gaul, with the Celtic or Cimmerian Sibyl of Cuma, where he died and was buried, *and the misletoe of the Druids*, carries it back to a period antecedent to any ancient Italian history which we possess. I cannot help believing that it has a close connexion with the Irish practice of calling their letters after the names of trees.[1]

84. There have been authors who have wasted their time in inquiries into the mode in which the inventor of the alphabet proceeded to divide the letters into dentals, labials, and palatines. There surely never was any such proceeding. The invention was the effect of unforeseen circumstance—what we call accident; and when I consider the proofs, so numerous and clear, of the existence of the oldest people of whom we have any records, the Indian Buddhists in Ireland, and that in that country their oldest alphabet has the names of trees, I cannot be shaken in my opinion that the trees first gave names to letters, and that the theory I have pointed out is the most probable.

85. I suspect that, some how or other, our practice of calling the parts of our books *leaves* came from this custom. The bark of the Irish birch-tree, the Papyrus, or the *roll* of skin, had no leaves.

86. From Mr. Davies I learn that the Welsh bards had a similar alphabet to that of the Irish. He says, "The Anti-
" quarians claim an alphabet of their own, which, in all its essential points, agrees with that of the bards in Britain.
" 1 It was Druidical. 2. It was a magical alphabet, and used by those Druids in their divinations and their decisions
" by lot. 3. It consisted of the same radical sixteen letters which formed the basis of the Druidical alphabet in Britain.
" 4. Each of these letters received its name from some tree or plant of a certain species, regarded as being, in some
" view or other, descriptive of its power, and these names are still retained.

87. " So far the doctrine of the British Druids is exactly recognized in the *Western island*. The same identical system
" is completely ascertained and preserved. Yet there are circumstances which point out a very ancient and remote
" period for the separation of these alphabets from each other " Mr. Davies then observes, that " among other things
" the order of the letters is different." He says, there are three kinds of writing; and adds, " The third, which is said

---

[1] If it were consistent with the object of this dissertation, I think I could prove by strong circumstantial evidence, that Virgil was initiated into the order of Druids or Chaldeans or Culdees. I am not the first person who has held this opinion. I believe it was held by the great ROGER BACON, but being too profound for his ignorant compeers, like the circular orbits of Pythagoras, it was turned into ridicule.

" to be *(no doubt)* the remains of an old *magical* alphabet, is called *Beth-luis-nion na Ogma*, or the alphabet of *magical* " or *mysterious letters;* the first *three* of which are *Beth, Luis, Nion*, whence it is named." [1]    In my CELTIC DRUIDS I have maintained that our islands were peopled by two swarms from a common Eastern hive, one coming by Gaul, the other in ships through the straits of Gibraltar.   This account of the appearance of the two alphabets of Ireland and Britain seems to support *my system*.

88.   I am quite of opinion that the Welsh are right ; but that not only *their* letters, but all letters, were once magical and astrological, and known only to the sacred caste of priests for many generations.   I am of opinion that our common playing cards once formed an astrological instrument of the same kind.

89.   The Greek, the Hebrew, and the Arabic systems are evidently the same, though in their latter letters, from some unknown cause, a change takes place, and the powers of notation vary ; but they do not vary till they get to the nineteenth letter, as observed above, where the hundreds begin ; and in the mode of variation after it takes place the same system is continued.   From all this I am inclined to think, that the old Arabic language, which I shall shew is really Hebrew, as all the roots of Hebrew and Chaldee words are found in it, was a language before the present Hebrew, Greek, Sanscrit, and Deva Nagari letters were invented ; that the first SYSTEM of arithmetic was that now possessed by the Arabians, *though not invented by them in their present country at least ;* and that the inventors of the first alphabet made it of right lines and lines joined at angles, and called its component parts after certain names of numbers, which, at that time, probably, in the first lost language, had the names of trees ; and that from this came all the allegories of Gnosticism, respecting the trees in the Garden of Eden, held by the Valentinians, Basilideans, Bardesanians, &c., allegories which have been acknowledged by very learned men to have been the produce of a very ancient oriental system, in existence long previous to the birth of Christ—such as that of the tree bearing twelve sorts of fruit, one in each month, &c., &c.   The alphabet was the wood or the forest—the tree was the system—the upright stem, the אלף Alpha, the Chaldee name for the trunk of a tree (as I am informed by General VALLANCEY).—The words were the branches—the letters were the leaves growing out of the stem or branches—and the fruits were the doctrines and knowledge of good and evil, learned by means of receiving these doctrines from letters.   In this manner a prodigious number of allegories were invented.   In the old Irish, the words *wood* and *alphabet* are described by the same letters— *Aos,* which also signify both a tree and knowledge.

90.   Taliesin, a Welsh bard of the sixth century, has written a poem on the battle of the trees, which is yet in existence, and in which he compares the words in the secret letters of the Welsh to twigs or branches of trees.   The subject is the battle between good and evil, light and darkness, Oromasdes and Arimanius   Mr. Davies thinks this is an allusion to the original system. [2]

91.   Apollonius Rhodius says, that when Orpheus played on the lyre, the trees of Pieria came down from the hills to the Thracian coast, and ranged themselves in due order at Zona. [3]   This is a Grecian allegory, of the same kind, perhaps copied from the Orientals.   Virgil has given an account of an elm-tree, which Æneas found growing at the side of the road to the infernal regions, loaded with dreams.   This tree had the name of the elm, the first letter of the alphabet, the alpha, the trunk which bears all the rest, loaded with every kind of science and learning :

> Full in the midst of this infernal road
> An elm displays her dusky arms abroad :
> The god of sleep there hides his heavy head ;
> And empty dreams on every leaf are spread.

92.   The following extract from a work of a Chaldean Rabbi is given by Kircher : Arbor magna in medio Paradisi, cujus rami, *dictiones,* ulterius in ramos parvos et folia, quæ sunt *literæ,* extenduntur : the great tree in the garden of Eden, whose leaves were letters, and whose branches were words.

93.   It is agreed by all authors that the Druids pretended to perform various operations by means of sticks, sprigs, or branches of trees, which are commonly called magical.   Some account of this may be seen in Tacitus *de Moribus Germanorum.*   But, in fact, all the old native authors are full of these accounts : and it is impossible to read or consider them for a moment, without seeing the extraordinary similarity of the practice to that of Jacob with respect to the sheep of Laban, named in Gen. xxx. 37.   The rod of Moses, and that of Auron throwing out sprouts, &c., afford additional instances of similarity

94.   The letters of these magical alphabets, all which answered to the leaves of trees, were engraved on the surface of the rods, or sticks, cut square or triangular, to which the straight and simple form of the letters was peculiarly favourable.   Hence the letters and the alphabets came to be considered magical, and the whole system of writing compared to a tree bearing leaves and fruits.   And hence, also, came the celebrated *Sortes Virgilianæ,* which had this

---

[1] Celtic Res. p. 275.          [2] Ibid., p. 274.          [3] Argonau*, Lib. i. ver. 29.

name from the belief that Virgil was a Chaldean magician or astrologer. He was of the order of men who were banished by Marcus Aurelius, under the name of Mathematici and Chaldei, of whom I shall have much to say hereafter.

95. From these leaf letters, or letters having the names of trees, and from the right-lined letters inscribed on the boles of trees, the ancients, particularly the Arabians, invented their almost innumerable allegories, an account of which, much more detailed than I think it necessary to give, may be found in the fifth volume of Gen. Vallancey's *Collectanea Hibernica*.

96. On this subject General Vallancey observes, " And hence the Sephiroth-tree, or tree of numbers, of the Caba-
" listical Jews: and this tree contained ten names, viz corona, sapientia, prudentia, clementia, gravitas, ornatus, tri-
" umphus, confessio laudis, fundamentum, regnum. The number ten seems to have been fixed on because, as relating
" to numerals, ten was called perfection, as from thence all nations began to count anew. For this reason the Egyptians
" expressed the number ten by the word *mid*, that is, perfection; and the Irish call it *deag*, a word of like meaning:
" and for this reason the Chaldeans formed the word *jod*, or number ten, by an equilateral triangle thus Δ,[1] which was
" the symbol of perfection with the Egyptians. The Egyptians doubled the triangle thus X, and then it became a cross
" of St. Andrew, or the letter X or ten, that is, *perfection*, being the perfect number, or the number of figures on both
" hands: hence it stood for ten with the Egyptians, Chinese, Phœnicians, Romans, &c., and is so used with us at this
" day. The Mexicans also use the same figure in their secular calendars. The Tartars call it *lama*, from the Scythian
" *lamh*, a hand, synonymous to the *jod* of the Chaldeans, and thus it became the *name of a cross*, and of the high priest
" of the Tartars; and with the Irish, *luam* signifies the head of the church, an abbot, &c. Ce qu'il y a de remarkable
" c'est que le grand prêtre des Tartares port le nom de *lama* qui, en langue Tartare, signifie *la croix*: et les *Bogdoi* qui
" conquirent la Chine en 1644, et qui sont soumis au *dalai-lama* dans les choses de la religion, ont toujours des *croix*
" sur eux, qu'ils appellent aussi *lamas*."[2]

97. It has been observed by General Vallancey, that " it seems natural and universal to man to have entertained
" the idea of numbering from his fingers, and it does not appear extraordinary that, when man led an agrestic life, (as
" the Chaldeans and Scythians, the parents of numerals, did,) and had occasion to carry numbers higher than the fin-
" gers on his hands, that, before he had assigned arbitrary marks for numbers, he should have adopted the names of
" trees—objects immediately surrounding him, some of which grew more luxuriantly than others—and that having
" invented an arbitrary mark for such a number, he should give it the name of the tree which stood for it: and thus,
" having formed a numerical alphabet, these numerals at length became letters, as I have shewn in the preceding pages,
" still bearing the original names."[3]

98. I think it very probable that from the use of leaves as letters, the hieroglyphics may have taken their rise. Suppose letters in the shape of the leaves of trees to have been made of thin laminæ of gold or tin, and strung on a cord,
something like the tripods of the ancient Peruvians, a magical letter would thus be invented which could be deciphered
by none but those who understood the secret; and it might be made extremely complicated by the addition of leaves
not in the alphabet, or by the forms of other things, between the words or real letters, which would not, to the initiated,
increase the difficulty of reading it, but rather the contrary, and at the same time would render it perfectly unintelligible
to those not initiated. After some time these leaf letters would be drawn on plain surfaces, and again, with a little
more experience, all other kinds of objects would be added to increase the difficulty and mystery, until the leaves would
be lost sight of altogether, and the hieroglyphics come to what we find them.

99. Much has been said respecting the picture-writing of the Mexicans, sent to Cortes, by the Emperor's messengers.
They made drawings of the horses, ships, &c., because they had never seen such objects before, and of course their
language could convey no idea of them. But this had no resemblance, in reality, to the Egyptian hieroglyphics.
The intention of the ancient hieroglyphics was to enable one person to convey to another information relating to
something already known to both, and of which, therefore, they possessed an idea common to both. But the
pictures of Mexico were intended, by the persons drawing them, to convey a new idea respecting something wholly
unknown to the beholder, for whose use they were intended, and of which, consequently, he had never formed an
idea before.

100. Mr. Astles, on the Origin and Progress of Writing, supports my opinion that hieroglyphics were not the origin
of writing.[4] " The subject of this chapter (Origin of Letters) hath engaged the attention and perplexed the sagacity

---

[1] I know not where Gen. Vallancey got his triangle for the Chaldaic ten, but the triangle was the ten of the Greeks.
[2] Voyage de la Chine, par Avril, Liv. iii. p. 194.    [3] Vall. Col. Heb. Vol. V. p. 187.
[4] Ch. ii. p. 10.

" of many able and judicious persons for many centuries: some of the most respectable writers have reasoned upon
" erroneous principles, and, by their works, have obscured the true path which might have led to the discovery of
" letters. Mons. Fourmont, Bishop Warburton, and Mons. Gebelin, have endeavoured to shew that alphabets were
" originally made up of hierolplyhic characters; but it will presently appear that the letters of an alphabet were essen-
" tially different from the characteristic marks deduced from hieroglyphics, which last are marks for things and ideas,
" in the same manner as the ancient and modern characters of the Chinese; whereas the former are only marks for
" sounds; and though we should allow it an easy transition from the Egyptian hieroglyphics to the characteristic
" marks of the Chinese, which have been demonstrated by Du Halde and others to be perfectly hieroglyphic, yet it
" doth not follow that the invention of an alphabet must naturally succeed these marks. It is true there is a sufficient
" resemblance between the Mexican picture-writing, the Egyptian hieroglyphics, and the Chinese characters; but these
" are foreign to alphabetic letters, and, in reality, do not bear the least relation to them."

101. From a consideration of certain historical facts which cannot be denied, I think I can shew that hieroglyphics
did not precede the invention of letters, as has been generally imagined.

102. It has been observed by almost every philosopher who has visited the pyramids of Egypt, that they are placed
exactly to face the four cardinal points of the compass, from which astronomers know that their builders must have
possessed a very considerable skill in the science of astronomy. This affords a strong presumption that the art of
writing must have been known to their builders; they can scarcely be believed to have possessed so much science as
the fact seems to require, without it. Now, in the next place, it may be observed, that there is not on any one of the
larger pyramids the least appearance of any thing like a hieroglyphic. This fact, combined with the evident knowledge
possessed by their builders of astronomy, justifies the presumption that they were built before hieroglyphical writing
was known, though perhaps after our mode of writing was discovered. Though the two facts may not be considered
to amount to a decisive proof, I maintain that taken together they afford strong presumptive evidence. On the subject
of hieroglyphics,

103. Mr. Maurice says, " Before we quit the pyramids, I must be permitted to make one reflection. On no part
" of the three great pyramids, internal or external, does there appear the least sign of those hieroglyphic sculptures
" which so conspicuously and so totally cover the temples, the obelisks, and colossal statues, of Upper Egypt. This
" exhibits demonstrative proof, that at the period of the construction of those masses, that kind of hieroglyphic
" decoration was not invented, for, had that sacerdotal character been then formed, they would undoubtedly not have
" been destitute of them." [1]

104. Some of the smaller pyramids have been built out of the ruins or stones of temples on which have been
hieroglyphics. This shews these particular pyramids to be of modern date. No doubt they have been tombs. All
our churches are tombs; but they are also places of worship.

105. After the celebrated Mr. Belzoni and Lieut.-Col. Fitzclarence had with great labour obtained admission to the
inner chamber of the second in size of the pyramids, Mr. Belzoni discovered, from an inscription, that it had been
opened before by one of the Califs. It appeared that the contents of the sarcophagus which he discovered had been
thrown out, and were lying on the floor at its side. He preserved part of them, which were bones, and brought them
to England, never letting them go out of his own possession. These were carefully and publicly examined by several
of the first natural philosophers in London, who, to their great surprise, discovered that they were the remains of an
animal of the Beeve kind.[2] Respecting these facts there never has been any dispute. They are perfectly notorious;
and neither Mr. Belzoni, nor the natural philosophers, had any theory, interest, or system, to influence their judgments
respecting them. Part of the bones may yet be seen, where I have seen them, at the house of Lieut.-Colonel
Fitzclarence.

106. I suppose no one will doubt that these were the bones of an exemplar of the famous God Apis, on which some
foolish and absurd priest-ridden king must have been weak enough to lavish such immense labour and treasure. This Bull
Apis has been proved by many philosophers to have been the Bull of the Zodiac; in fact, the Sun, when he entered
the sign of the Bull in the Zodiac, at the vernal equinox, concerning which I shall shortly make some observations,
and of which I shall have much to say in the following work. This being, for the sake of argument, at the present
moment admitted, it follows that the Zodiac must have been invented before one of its signs, the Bull, can have become
the object of adoration.

107. Now I think no person can believe that the Zodiac, with its various signs, and divided and subdivided as
it necessarily is into many parts, was invented before writing. Then it seems to follow, if this be admitted, that

---

[1] Maur. Ant. Hind. Vol. III. p. 95.          Class. Journal, Vol. XXI. p. 16.

the art of writing must have been known before the pyramids, the burial-place of the Bull, were built; and as the hieroglyphics were not invented till after the building of the pyramids, it seems to follow, that they were not invented till after the invention of writing, consequently that they were not, as it has generally been thought, the origin of writing.

108. The intimate relations between India and Egypt, in some ancient period, cannot possibly be doubted. But what is the reason that there are no hieroglyphics in India? The days of the week are dedicated in each to the same Gods. The adoration of the Bull of the Zodiac or the Sun, in the sign Taurus, is common to both. The same Zodiac is, with a trifling variation, also common to both. Then how came they not both to have hieroglyphics, if hieroglyphics were invented before writing, or figures in arithmetic?

109. I conclude that this connexion or intercourse (which will be proved over and over again in the course of the following work) must have existed before the invention of hieroglyphics, and must also, in a great measure, have ceased before their invention, because, if the contrary had been the case, hieroglyphics would, in some degree, have been common to the two countries. When the religion went from one to the other, the hieroglyphical system, if in existence, would have gone also. From which it almost necessarily follows, that hieroglyphics are, comparatively speaking, a modern invention.

110. In their endeavours to prove that hieroglyphics were the originals or parents of letters and writing, philosophers have done every thing which ingenuity could devise to establish the fact; but I think their arguments are founded upon no sufficient data, and therefore have always appeared to me unsatisfactory. For my theory I have a great number of facts and circumstances which cannot be disputed, and I think my arguments founded upon them are sound.[1]

111. From the whole investigation there can be no doubt, whether the leaf alphabets were the origin of hieroglyphics or not, that the latter were invented after the discovery of the art of writing, and were a secret and sacred system invented for the purpose of concealing certain religious or historical truths from the vulgar eye.

112. Before I quit this subject I think it proper to recall my reader's attention to the observation, that whether Egypt was colonized from India or India from Egypt, it is very clear that the intercourse of colonization must have ceased before hieroglyphics were invented, or they would certainly have been found among the priests in both countries. And it is also probable that they were invented after Moses and the Hebrew tribe left Egypt, or we should have found some notice of them in the books of Moses—the Pentateuch. I only say *it is probable;* but it is by no means certain.

113. M. Denon[2] has given a description of a painting in one of the tombs of the kings of Thebes, in which, among other things, is described the sacrifice of a child, and he has these words: " Incense is offered to him in honour of these " victories; a priest writes his annals, and consigns them to sacred memorial. It is, therefore, proved, that the ancient " Egyptians had written books: the famous *Thoth* was then a book, and not inscribed tablets sculptured on walls, as has " been often supposed. I could not help flattering myself that I was the first to make so important a discovery: but I " was much more delighted when, some hours after, I was assured of the proof of the discovery by the possession of a " manuscript itself, which I found in the hand of a fine mummy that was brought to me. In its right hand, and resting " on the left arm, was a roll of papyrus, on which was the manuscript." And here, with respect to this MS., end Mons. Denon's observations; not another word of what became of the papyrus, or of the language or letters in which it was written. But in plate LV. a short description is given of a manuscript found upon a papyrus which, I suppose, is meant for it. Nothing can be made out from it except that it reads from right to left. In plate LVI. is a copy of another manuscript equally unintelligible, which was found upon a papyrus in a mummy.

114. In consequence of the attempts of Mr. Bankes to prove, from the style of building of the temples, confirmed by the explanations of M. Champollion, that many of the hieroglyphics on them relate to the Roman emperors, these manuscripts cannot be made use of to prove the antiquity of letters; but they prove that letters were known before the hieroglyphics on the temples, in which these mummies were found used, or, that hieroglyphics were continued in use after the invention of the art of writing, and along with it. I have no doubt that some of the buildings in Egypt were erected by the Roman emperors, that many others of them were partly their work, and that still more of them were erected by the monarchs of Egypt after the time of Cambyses. But the sepulchres, and many parts of the temples of Thebes and other temples of Upper Egypt, I have no doubt existed before Cambyses's time, and escaped his fury.

115. I have *no doubt* that the churches of Notre Dame and St. Denis, at Paris, were both the workmanship of the

---

[1] The text of the Bible itself proves that letters were well known in the time of Moses, therefore the author does not attempt to refute the arguments of those who pretend that he was the inventor of them.

[2] Vol. III. Chap. xx. Aik. Trans. p. 70.

middle ages, but I think that the Zodiac on the former, and the Mosaic pavement found in the latter, of a Bacchanal filling a wine vessel, were the works of an age long prior.

116. My view of the subject is considerably strengthened by an observation of Belzoni's, I think, that some of the smaller pyramids have been built with stones, the ruins of old temples, on which are hieroglyphics broken and worked into them. And Mons. Denon found in the bases of some of the oldest pillars at Medinet Abou, near Thebes, Kurnec, numerous hieroglyphics. On which he asks, " How many preceding ages of civilization would it require to be able to " erect such buildings? How many ages again, before these would have fallen into ruins, and served as materials for " the foundations of other temples, which themselves have existed for so many centuries?" The questions are interesting : but it would not require a long period for the buildings to have decayed, if the decay were produced by the violent hand of a Cambyses. On the subject of the Origin of Letters, I must refer my reader to the first chapter of THE CELTIC DRUIDS, where it is treated of at large.

# CHAPTER II.

## ETYMOLOGY AND ITS USE.

1. A LITTLE time ago two systems of Etymology were published, one by the Rev. Mr. Whiter, of Cambridge, and the other by Mr. James Gilchrist. The former called his work Etymologicon Universale. It is very large, and was printed by the University of Cambridge, at its press. The object is to prove that ALL the words of every language may be traced back to the word Earth.[1]  Great learning and ingenuity are displayed, and incredible labour must have been bestowed on the production. The work of the latter gentleman, entitled Philosophic Etymology, is not so large, and in its doctrine is directly in opposition to the former. Mr. Gilchrist contends, that CL, CR, LC, or RC, is the primary simple word of written language, and that all the copiæ verborum are merely varieties and combinations of that one simple word, or rather sign.

2. He says, "There is nothing arbitrary about language. All the dialects, as Hebrew, Celtic, Greek, Latin, &c., are " essentially but one language. They have such diversities as may be termed idioms ; but with all their circumstantial " varieties, they have substantial uniformity : they proceed on the same principles, and have the same origin. The " philosophic grammar and lexicography of one, is in reality that of all."[2]  In this I perfectly agree with Mr. Gilchrist : I also agree with him that there is a wide difference between a scholar and a philosopher, but I cannot think with him that men in the first instance conversed wholly by looking, not by listening ; and that the different modifications of sound, emitted from the mouth, were a subsequent step of improvement and conveniency, not contemplated when the mouth was first applied to curiologic signs ; which application of the mouth was not anticipated when these signs were first employed, and which signs were not contemplated when hieroglyphics were invented : that thus, in the use of signs, men were led on step by step from hieroglyphics or picture-writing to curiologics, an abridged form of the preceding ; from curiologics engraved or drawn on any substance, to the expression of them by the mouth ; and from the expression of them by the mouth to the eye, to the expression of them by sound to the ear, enabling men to converse in the dark as well as in the light. If I understand Mr. Gilchrist, he supposes both hieroglyphics and letters to have been invented before speech. This does, indeed, surprise me very much. On reflecting on the first situation of man, I cannot help believing that he would not perceive his mate many minutes before he would utter some kind of a sound or sounds, which would soon grow into monosyllabic words.

3. I lay it down as a principle, that there were no such persons as Aborigines (as this word is often used)—that man did not rise into existence by accident, or without cause : but that he was the effect of a cause, a creation, or formation by a Being possessing power. This admitted, I consider that he must have acquired his knowledge of speech either by experience, or have such knowledge of it given to him by his Creator, as would enable him to communicate his ideas to his mate, and that in each case his Creator gave him the power of using his voice at the same time that he gave him the power of using his teeth and other organs. And if I admit the former, that man acquired by experience the

---

[1] See his Prelim. Diss. p. 77.          [2] Phil. Etymol. p. xx.

use of speech, which of course every philosopher will do, I must think that both Mr. Whiter and Mr. Gilchrist go to causes far too scientific to account for it. Speech would be very much the effect of circumstance—there would not be any thing like system in its first formation.

4. Mr. Gilchrist's idea that the first letters arose from *curved* lines, seems to me not only not to be so probable as that of *right* lines, which I have unfolded above, but it seems to me to be actually against all the *early* and, what is more, *well*-founded historical facts which we possess. For the fact *of the oldest letters and figures which we possess consisting of right lines* does not depend, alone, on the relations of writers, but upon their existing at this day on old coins and stones : in which latter fact, therefore, we cannot be deceived. I think my theory *as rational* as Mr. Gilchrist's ; in addition to which, I have the evidence of the oldest inscriptions, and, as I have shewn, analogy also, on my side ; for the higher we ascend the more *right-lined* the alphabets become.

5. As I have just now said, if I understand Mr. Gilchrist aright,[1] he maintains that hieroglyphics were invented before letter-writing. We know of only one nation, the Egyptians, among whom hieroglyphics ever existed, and I think I have proved that they were not invented by that nation till after letters were in use. I make no account of the Mexican paintings, for our information respecting them is too scanty to draw any conclusions from them ; and that part of our information which we do possess, namely, the painting of Cortes's ships and horses, is against hieroglyphics being the origin of letters, rather than in favour of it ; because, as I have observed above, these drawings were not to convey ideas of known things, but ideas of unknown things—new things, and new ideas.

6. The plan or theory proposed by Mr. Whiter and Mr. Gilchrist, of resolving all words into one, or nearly into one, seems to me to be not only contrary to the analogy of nature, but to clog their philological researches with insuperable and unnecessary difficulties. Let us for a moment consider man to have newly started into existence, by what means does not signify, and to exist alone. I will suppose this to have happened in a beautiful valley in upper Tibet, about latitude 35, at the vernal equinox, a fig-tree growing near him, bearing its early crop of fruit. The olfactory nerves, I think, would speedily draw him to the tree ; he would take of the fruit, and what is vulgarly called instinct would teach him to put it into his mouth and to eat it. Before he ate the fig, he would have become master of several ideas ; but as he would have had no occasion to communicate them, he probably would not have made any effort at speech.

7. We will now suppose this being, in the state of about twenty years of age, to awake and find a beautiful young woman close to him and touching him. Instinct would again begin to move him ; love would ensue and its consequences, and very speedily afterward the wish to communicate happiness ; for it is all a mistake that man is born to *evil* as the smoke flies upwards. He is born to good, and all his NATURAL tendencies are to good, though he possesses passions and is a fallible being, from which circumstances partial evil has naturally arisen. Much time would not elapse before he would, in order to communicate happiness, wish to call the attention of his mate to something—perhaps to partake with him of some fruit—and, to awaken this attention, an attempt to speak or make a sound would be made ; after this, another and another attempt ; and thus a few monosyllabic words would be formed, such as were easiest made by the organs of speech, and thus from this kind of process the first language would arise. It would probably consist of arbitrary sounds, not formed in any way from one another or from one word ; and had Mr. Gilchrist tried to trace all language to these primitive words, he would, I think, have perfectly succeeded.

8. But after some time a second race of original words would have arisen, which would a little increase the first language, and which must not be neglected. The voice of love would have been heard, and would not have been heard in vain. A child would make its appearance, and would have a little language of its own, which would never be lost, which would grow with its growth, strengthen with its strength, and which we actually find yet existing in every language on earth—exemplified in the words Ma, Mater, Moder, Muder, Pa, Pater, Fater, Fader, &c., &c. ; and thus from these two sources came to be formed the first original language. It would probably consist of monosyllabic roots, which would be very simple : and to these, I think, all language may be reduced.[2]

9. It is necessary to guard myself from being misunderstood in what I have said above, that the language of the eyes was not the *first* language, because I believe that it was ; but what I mean is, that this language would last but for a very short time—a very few hours, perhaps only a few minutes. The first man and his mate, surrounded as M. Cuvier has shewn that they probably were, by animals, formed long before, young and old, in every state, and, like these animals, possessing animal sensations, and being, in addition, imitative creatures, would in a very few hours, perhaps minutes, perform all the animal functions, exercise all the animal powers, do as other animals did : and until they

---

[1] Philosophic Etymol. p. 33.

[2] I wish Mr. Gilchrist had undertaken the task of so reducing them, for no man is better qualified. Had he and Mr. Whiter attempted to re-form or re-discover the ancient first language or collection of words, and their systems had been left unfinished, other learned men would have continued them, perhaps, till they had been completed.

had thus exercised these powers, perhaps the eyes, the most eloquent eyes, would continue to be the medium of the communication of ideas; but eloquent as they are, they would not continue to be so much longer; for an attempt to emit sound would be made, and thus would arise the first words.

10. I beg my reader to attend to the beings of the animal creation. He cannot suppose man, though inferior to them in many respects, to be much inferior to them in those which we are considering. How long is it before the dove or the partridge learns to call its mate with the voice of love, or its young about it, when it has found a nest of ants? Has man any language more significant than that which these birds possess? When the hen chucks her first chickens around her, can any language be more intelligible?[1] and she has no profound philosophers to make grammars for her, or divines to write creeds for her. Can the animal man be supposed to have been worse endowed than these fowls? I think not. Grant but these advantages of the animals around him, and it is all which I ask for my system, and I think it must be established.

11. If these philosophers had undertaken to prove that all languages might be resolved into one, consisting of a certain number of monosyllables or roots, they would have undertaken to prove what I am persuaded is perfectly true; and they would, I doubt not, have succeeded in their undertaking. But I think neither of their theories tenable. If their theories had been well founded, the abilities which they have displayed would not have failed to establish them. But though I think they have both failed, I beg to be understood not to have any wish to detract from their merit. Nor do I wish to enter into controversy with either of them. I should not have noticed their treatises but that I felt it would be a great reflection on myself to let it be supposed that I was ignorant of them.

12. I now take my leave of these two gentlemen, to whom, with Bacon, Hobbes, Locke, and Tooke, we are all under great obligation. I enter not more into their systems, because my object and theirs is different. Their systems are only auxiliary to mine. I feel perfectly confident that it will not be long before some ingenious man, with the assistance of Mr. Tooke, Mr. Whiter, and Mr. Gilchrist, will, upon the foundation which I have laid, erect the edifice of the true philosophy of grammar. If in this I am mistaken, I shall be only like hundreds of my predecessors.

13. Perhaps it will be said that my system depends too much on the explanation of words. The observation does not cause me much uneasiness. For if my system be founded in the truth, it must shew itself in the words of all languages, in an infinite variety of ways; in which case the observation will never do it any injury, or be able to prevent its reception when it comes to be known. If it be not true, it will fall, as others have done before it, whether depending on explanation of words, etymology, or not. As among the ancient Greeks and Romans, and the modern Europeans, we have a great number of systems, in like manner there was the same variety among the Orientalists; but I feel confident I shall be able to shew that they all flowed from one fountain; that one refined and beautiful system was not only the foundation, but that, however varied the systems which branched from it might be, yet in many respects the parent, the original, is every where to be seen, even in the Western systems of the present day.

14. It will probably also be objected by those who wish not to discover truth, but to throw discredit upon this work, that I often make etymological deductions in one word from two languages. This would have been more plausible if I had not first proved, most *unquestionably*, (as I believe,) the intimate *connexion*—indeed, I feel I am quite justified in saying the absolute *identity*, of the Western and Oriental languages in a very remote period. And this observation will apply to all the languages in which the sixteen-letter system has obtained. It is impossible to doubt that one original language has extended over all the old world, which is the reason that we find Hebrew and Hindoo words in Britain, and words of the most remote countries and climates intermixed, in a manner in no other way to be accounted sixteen for. All the sixteen-letter languages are but dialects of an original language.

15. But my practice of explaining words from what are at this day two languages, will be objected to by enemies of inquiry, because it has a tendency to discover hidden truths. But if there have been one language upon which several have been founded or built, what is so natural as that the roots of a compound word should be found in several of them? Suppose two colonies emigrated, the one to Europe and the other to Africa, from Chaldea, and that each carried a certain word; this word might change, by being compounded with other words, in both cases, so as to become in each case a new word. Is it not evident that the roots of the word may reasonably be sought in either or both the new languages?

16. In etymological inquiries a mere corruption no doubt may sometimes be admitted; but this must be done with great caution, and when there is strong extra evidence to support it. For proof of this, our own language affords innumerable examples. Of this kind of corruption I need to produce only one instance from our Liturgy—*prevent us* in all our doings. Here we have not a change in one or two radicals only, but in a whole word. Again in the Latin word *hostis*.

---

[1] The common barn-door hen has at least two clear and distinct words, one which she *commonly* uses to her chickens, and another when she calls them to her on having discovered any unexpected hoard of food.

17. Etymology may be considered in another point of view. What is a written word but an effect—an effect arising from an unknown cause? What we want is, to find the cause—to ascertain if there were one original written language —by what steps any given word descended from that first parent to its present state. In many cases this may be difficult, in others it may be impossible to make it out; but is there not the same difficulty with translations? Does not one word often mean several different and often opposite things? There is scarcely a word in Parkhurst's Hebrew Lexicon which has not four or five different meanings; and how do we proceed to find out which, in any case, is the one intended, but by comparing it with the context? Most words may be derived from several others, but the variety or uncertainty, great as I admit it is, is generally not greater than in mere translations.

18. Sir William Jones says, "I beg leave, as a philologer, to enter my protest against conjectural etymology in his- " torical researches, and principally against the licentiousness of etymologists in transposing and inserting letters, in " substituting at pleasure any consonant for another of the same order, and in totally disregarding the vowels." I most heartily join in the protest, though I think etymology the grand and only telescope by means of which we can discover the objects of far distant and remote antiquity. But Sir William afterward says, "When we find, indeed, the " same words, letter for letter, and in a sense precisely the same, in different languages, we can scarce hesitate in " allowing them a common origin."[1] To shew how little he attended to his own sound and sensible remarks respecting the changing of letters, in a page or two preceding he had been observing, that the word Moses ought to have been Musah, not Moses. It is written in the Hebrew משה *Mse*. I cannot admit this to be either Musah or Moses. If, in compliance with modern authority, I admit the *u* to be supplied, I cannot admit the ה *e*, the fifth letter, to be changed into א *a*, the first, and the letter ה *h*, without authority, to be added. I have shewn in my *Celtic Druids*, that the Hebrew system of letters is the same as the English and Greek; and when it is desired to write the Hebrew letters משה *Mse* in the English characters, the same letters which the order and the power of notation shew to be identical, ought to be used, and no others. The practice of substituting one consonant for another can very seldom be admitted; it can be subjected to no rule, but in every instance where such a liberty is taken each case must stand upon its own merits, and be left to the judgment of the reader. I do not mean to say that a letter may never be changed, but it ought never to be changed except for a very good reason; and when it is so changed, the doctrine to be deduced from it will stand on a much worse foundation than if it had not been so changed. But after all, the practice of changing letters cannot possibly be denied. For instance, do we not see sovereigns in India sometimes called Nawab, and sometimes Nabob—the w and b interchanged; and so on in other cases?

19. But uncertain as the nature of etymological science is supposed to be in researches into the early learning of the world, it is the best fountain from which we can draw. Let those of a different opinion pursue their own plan, and continue to believe the histories of Greece that Cadmus founded Thebes by means of men raised from sowing the teeth of serpents; or that Jupiter, in the form of a Bull, ran away with Europa from her father Agenor, by whom he had three sons—Minos, Sarpendon, and Radamanthus, who were really all living persons.

20. As reason cannot be made effectual against etymology, the power of ridicule has been applied, and it has had the success it will always have against truth—it will fail. A pickled cucumber has been derived from Jeremiah King (e. g. Jeremiah King—Jer. King—Girkin). Now this is very good, and whenever similar licences are taken under the same or similar circumstances as this, the result deserves nothing but ridicule, and the persons who depend upon such deductions are really ridiculous. Forced allegories are equally ridiculous; and pray what are our orthodox impugners of etymology better in their literal explanations of the Old-Testament writings? What shall I say to the wrestling of God with Jacob and wounding him in the thigh? What of his ineffectual attempt to kill Moses at an inn? These gentlemen run down etymology in order that they may open the door to their literal meanings. But the truth is, the abuse of either is ridiculous, as every thing must be when not kept within the bounds of sense and reason. And with respect to etymology, however uncertain it may be, it is the only instrument left us for the investigation of ancient science, *all others having failed us*, and the certainty of facts discovered by its agency will depend upon the reason and probability which the etymological deduction will possess, in every individual case; and of each case the reader must be the judge. But the real truth is, that etymology is not run down because it is not calculated to discover truth, but because it is calculated to discover *too much* truth.

21. Very certain I am that if we are not willing to receive the learning of the ancients through the medium of etymology, and a comparison of the words of one language with another, we must remain in ignorance. The early historical accounts are all little better than fables. Every word, in every language, has, no doubt, originally had a meaning, whether a nation has it by inheritance, by importation, or by composition. It is evident, then, if we can find out the original meaning of the words which stand for the names of objects, great discoveries may be expected.

---

[1] Asiat. Res. Vol. III. 4to. p. 489.

22. I repeat, the science of etymology is the standing *but* for the shafts of every fool.   If a witling be so foolish that he can ridicule nothing else, he can succeed against etymology.   The true and secret reason of the opposition to etymology is, that the priests knowing it is by its aid only that ancient science can be discovered, have exerted every nerve to prejudice the minds of youth against it.   After all, what is it but the science of explaining the meaning of words ? Its uncertainty every one must admit.   But in this it is only like the words of all languages, in almost every one of which every noun has a great number of meanings.   On the meaning of the words, as selected judiciously or injudiciously, depends the value of the translation, which is, of course, sometimes sense, sometimes nonsense.   But, I think, one is scarcely less doubtful, or subject to fewer mistakes, than the other.   Are there not at least two meanings given to almost every important text of the Bible ?   The same is the case with etymological deductions.[1]   The devotee, as in duty bound, will take the construction of his priest, the philosopher of his reason.   And when an etymologist finds out a new derivation, we are as much obliged to him as we are to a lexicographer when he discovers a new meaning in a word which has been before overlooked.

23. The first word of Genesis may furnish an example of what I mean.   We have great authorities to justify the rendering of the word either by *wisdom* or *beginning*, or both.   And it must be for the reader to decide whether it has one or the other, or both—the double meaning.

24. When a translator finds a word with several meanings, than which nothing is more common, it is his duty to compare it with the context and to consider all the circumstances under which it is placed, and his prudence and judgment are displayed, or his want of them, in the selection which he makes.   It is precisely the same with etymology. There is no argument which can be brought against etymology which may not be advanced with equal force against translations.   In the course of the following work I shall have occasion to return to this subject several times.

---

# CHAPTER III.

### ORIGIN OF THE ADORATION OF THE BULL, AND OF THE PHALLIC AND VERNAL FESTIVALS.

1. The Rev. Mr. Maurice, in his *learned* work on the Antiquities of India, has shewn, in a way which it is impossible to contradict, that the May-day festival and the May-pole of Great Britain, with its garlands, &c , known to us all, are the remains of an ancient festival of Egypt and India, and probably of Phœnicia, when these nations, in countries very distant, and from times very remote, have all, with one consent, celebrated the entrance of the sun into the sign of Taurus, at the vernal equinox ; but which, in consequence of the astronomical phenomenon, no longer disputed, of the precession of the equinoxes, is removed far in the year from its original situation.   This festival, it appears from a letter in the *Asiatic Researches*,[2] from Colonel Pearce, is celebrated in India on the first of May, in honour of Bhavani (a personification of vernal nature, the Dea Syria of Chaldea, and the Venus Urania of Persia).   A May-pole is erected, hung with garlands, around which the young people dance, precisely the same as in England.   The object of the festival, I think with Mr. Maurice, cannot be disputed ; and that its date is coeval with the time when the equinox actually took place on the first of May.   To account for these facts consistently with received chronology, he says, " When " the reader calls to mind what has already been observed, that owing to the precession of the equinoxes, after the rate " of seventy-two years to a degree, a total alteration has taken place through all the signs of the ecliptic, insomuch that " those stars which formerly were in Aries have now got into Taurus, and those of Taurus into Gemini : and when he " considers also the difference before mentioned, occasioned by the reform of the calendar, he will not wonder at the " disagreement that exists in respect to the exact period of the year on which the great festivals were anciently kept, " and that on which, in imitation of primeval customs, they are celebrated by the moderns.   Now the vernal equinox, " after the rate of that precession, certainly could not have coincided with the first of May less than four thousand years " before Christ, which nearly marks the æra of the creation, which, according to the best and wisest chronologers,

---

[1] I beg my reader to look in Mr. Whiter's *Etymologicon* for the meaning of *argo*.   It has scores of meanings, some as opposite as the poles.

[2] Vol. II. p. 333.

" **began at the vernal** equinox, when all nature was gay and smiling, and the earth arrayed in its loveliest verdure, and
" not, **as others have imagined,** at the dreary autumnal equinox, when that nature must necessarily have its beauty
" declining, and that earth its verdure decaying. *I have little doubt, therefore, that May-day, or at least the day on*
" *which the Sun entered Taurus, has been immemorially kept as a sacred festival from the creation of the earth and man,*
" and was originally intended as a memorial of that auspicious period and that momentous event." He afterwards
adds, " on the general devotion of the ancients to the worship of the BULL, I have had frequent occasion to remark,
" and more particularly in the Indian history, by their devotion to it at that period,

$$\text{———— aperit cum cornibus annum}$$
Taurus,

" ' When the Bull with his horns opened the Vernal year.' I observed that all nations seem anciently to have vied
" with each other in celebrating that blissful epoch ; and that the moment the sun entered the sign Taurus, were dis-
" played the signals of triumph and the incentives to passion : that memorials of the universal festivity indulged at that
" season are to be found in the records and customs of people otherwise the most opposite in manners and most remote
" in situation. I could not avoid considering the circumstance as a strong additional proof, that mankind originally
" descended from one great family, and proceeded to the several regions in which they finally settled, from one com-
" mon and central spot : that the Apis, or Sacred Bull of Egypt, was only the symbol of the sun in the vigour of vernal
" youth ; and that the Bull of Japan, breaking with his horn the mundane egg, was evidently connected with the same
" bovine species of superstition, founded on the mixture of astronomy and mythology."[1]

2. Mr. Maurice in a previous part of his work had shewn that the May-day festival was established to celebrate the
generative powers of nature, called by the ancient Greeks φαλλοφερος—that φαλλος, in Greek, signifies a pole, and that
from this comes our May-pole.

3. After the equinox (in consequence of the revolution of the pole of the equator round the pole of the ecliptic)
ceased to be in Taurus, and took place in Aries, the equinoctial festivals were changed to the first of April, and were
celebrated on that day equally in England and India : in the former, every thing but the practice of making April
fools has ceased ; but in the latter, the festival is observed as well as the custom of making April fools ; that is, the
custom of sending persons upon ridiculous and false errands to create sport and merriment, is one part of the rites of
the festival. In India this is called the *Nuurutz* and the *Huli*[2] festival. This vernal festival was celebrated on the day
the ancient Persian year began, which was on the day the sun entered into the sign of Aries ; and Mr. Maurice says,
" The ancient Persian coins, stamped with the head of a ram, which, according to D'Ancarville, were offered to
" Gemshid, the founder of Persepolis, and first reformer of the solar year amongst the Persians, are an additional
" demonstration of the high antiquity of this festival." When Sir Thomas Roe was ambassador at Delhi, this festival
was celebrated by the Mogul with astonishing magnificence and splendour : it has the name of Naurutz both in India
and Persia, and was celebrated in both alike.[3] And in the ambassador's travels the writer acquaints us, " That some
" of their body being deputed to congratulate the Schah on the first day of the year, they found him at the palace of
" Ispahan, sitting at a banquet, and having near him the *Minatzim*, or astrologer, who rose up ever and anon, and
" taking his astrolobe went to observe the sun ; and at the very moment of the sun's reaching the equator, he published
" aloud the new year, the commencement of which was celebrated by the firing of great guns both from the castle and
" the city walls, and by the sound of all kinds of instruments."

4. It is not only in Persia and India that this worship of the Bull is to be found ; there is no part of the old world,
from the extremest East to the West, where the remains of it are not to be found.[4]

5. The reader will observe in the whole of the above quotations from Mr. Maurice the style of the Christian apologist,
who is endeavouring to account for a disagreeable circumstance which he cannot deny, and to shew that it is not
inconsistent with his religious system. He will see that it is the evidence of an unwilling witness, and on this account
evidence of the greatest importance. The learning and talent of Mr. Maurice are unquestionable, and it cannot for a
moment be doubted, that he would have denied the fact if he could have done it honestly. But in the teeth of the
most clear evidence of its existence *that* was absolutely impossible. I do not, however, mean to insinuate that he was
dishonest enough to have attempted it if he could have done so with a chance of success, for I believe no book was
ever more honestly written. The reality, close connexion, and object, of the Tauric and Phallic worship, have been so
clearly and fully proved by D'Ancarville, Payne Knight, Maurice, Parkhurst in his Hebrew Lexicon, Bryant, Faber,
Dupuis, Drummond, and many others, that there is no room left for a moment's doubt. It would therefore only be an

---

[1] Maurice's Ind. Ant. Vol. VI. pp. 91—93.
[2] The word Huli, I apprehend, is derived from, or is the same as, the ancient Celtic word Yule.
[3] Ind. Ant. Vol. VI. p. 76.    [4] Celtic Druids, Chap. v. Sect. ii.

idle waste of time to attempt to prove it.    I could only repeat an immense mass of facts, now well known, from these authors, without adding any thing new.    I have therefore determined not to attempt it, but to trust that any reader who may not have studied this subject, will depend upon the irreproachable testimony of Mr. Maurice.    If he be not satisfied, he may consult the works above-named, where he will find much instruction, if not amusement.    For these reasons I hope I shall be excused going into the proof of the antiquity of the Phallic and Tauric festivals, although their ancient existence is of the very first importance to my system.—My system, in fact, is founded upon them, and upon them I rest my foot as upon a foundation from which I am convinced nothing can remove me.    The fact that the May-day festivals of India and Britain are admitted to have been instituted to celebrate the entrance of the sun into the sign Taurus at the vernal equinox, overthrows all our learned men's systems of chronology, root and branch; it leaves scarcely a wreck behind, and will enable me nearly to explain the origin and meaning of all the Mythoses of antiquity, and, indeed, of almost all those of modern times also.

# ANACALYPSIS.

---

## BOOK I.

### CHAPTER I.

AGE OF THE WORLD.—FLOOD.—PLANETS AND DAYS OF THE WEEK.—THE MOON.

1. On looking back into antiquity, the circle of vision terminates in a thick and impenetrable mist. No end can be distinguished. There seems reason to believe that this is an effect of that cause, whatever it may be, which first produced and gave law to the revolving motions of the planets, or other phenomena of nature, and therefore cannot be impugned, perhaps ought not to regretted. At all events, if this obscurity be regretted, it is pretty evident that there is little hope of its being removed. But in endeavouring to stretch our eye to the imaginary end of the prospect, to the supposed termination of the hitherto to us unbounded space, it is unavoidably arrested on its way by a variety of objects, of a very surprising appearance; and it is into their nature that I propose to inquire. When I look around me, on whatever side I cast my eyes, I see the ruins of a former world—proofs innumerable of a long-extended period of time. Perhaps among all the philosophers no one has demonstrated this so clearly as Mons. Cuvier. I apprehend these assertions are so well known and established that it is unnecessary to dwell upon them.

The great age of the world must be admitted; but the great age of man is a different thing. The latter may admit of doubt, and it is man with whom, in the following treatise, I propose to concern myself, and not his habitation. On man, his folly, his weakness, and, I am sorry I must add, his wickedness, I propose to treat: his habitation I leave to the geologists.

In the most early history of mankind I find all nations endeavouring to indulge a contemptible vanity, by tracing their origin to the most remote periods; and, for the gratification of this vanity, inventing fables of every description. Of this weakness they have all, in reality, been guilty; but the inhabitants of the oriental countries occupy rather a more prominent place than those of the western world; and I believe it will not be denied that, in the investigation of subjects connected with the first race of men, they are entitled on every account to claim a precedence. If, since the creation of man, a general deluge have taken place, their country was certainly the situation where he was preserved: therefore to the eastern climes I apply myself for his early history, and this naturally leads me into an inquiry into their ancient records and traditions.

2. All nations have a tradition of the destruction of the world by a flood,[1] and of the preservation of man from its effects. Here are two questions. Of the affirmative of the former no person

---

[1] The nature of this flood I shall discuss in a future chapter.—June, 1830.

B 2

who uses his eyes can doubt. **But the latter is in a different predicament.** A question may arise whether man existed before the flood above spoken of, or not. If the universality of a tradition of a fact of this nature would prove its truth, there would be scarcely room for doubt, and the previous creation of man would be established. But I think in the course of the following inquiry we shall find that universal tradition of a fact of this kind is not enough by itself for its establishment. It appears to me that the question of the existence of the human race previous to the flood will not much interfere with my inquiries, but will, if it be admitted, only oblige me to reason upon the idea that certain facts took place before it, and that the effects arising from them were not affected by it.

If I speak of persons or facts before the deluge, and it should be determined that the human species did not exist before that event, then the form of speech applied erroneously to the antediluvians must be held to apply to the earliest created of the post-diluvians; and this seems to me to be the only inconvenience which can arise from it. I shall therefore admit, for the sake of argument, that an universal flood took place, and that it happened *after* the creation of man.

Much difference of opinion has arisen upon the question whether the flood to which I have alluded was universal or not. The ancient records upon which Christians found their religion, as generally construed, maintain the affirmative; but no one who gives even a very slight degree of consideration to the circumstances of the Americas, can deny that probability leans the contrary way. It is a very difficult question, but I do not consider that it has much concern with the object of this work.

Though it be the most probable, if man were created before the last general deluge, that a portion of the human race was saved along with the animals in the new, as well as a portion in the old world, yet it is equally probable that one family, or at most only a very small number of persons, were saved in the latter.

The strongest argument against the descent of the present human race from one pair has hitherto been found in the peculiar character of the Negro. But it is now admitted, I believe, that Mr. Lawrence has removed that difficulty, and has proved that man is one genus and one species, and that those who were taken by some philosophers for different species are only varieties. I shall assume this as a fact, and reason upon it accordingly. If there were any persons saved from the deluge except those before spoken of, who were found near the Caspian Sea, they do not appear to have made any great figure in the world, or to have increased so as to form any great nations. They must, I think, soon have merged and been lost in the prevailing numbers of the oriental nation. But I know not in history any probable tradition or circumstance, the existence of the Negro excepted, which should lead us to suppose that there ever were such persons. If they did exist, I think they must have been situated in China. It is possible that they may have been in that country, but it is a bare possibility, unsupported by any facts or circumstances known to us. No doubt the Chinese are entitled to what they claim—a descent from very remote antiquity. But it is acknowledged that one of their despots destroyed all their authentic and official records, in consequence of which little or no dependence can be placed upon the stories which they relate, of transactions which took place any length of time previous to that event.

The cautious way in which I reason above respecting the universal nature of the flood, and the conditional style of argument which I adopt in treating the question of man's creation before or after it, no doubt will give offence to a certain class of persons who always go to another class, called priests, for permission to believe, without using their own understandings. I am sorry that I should offend these good people, but as I cannot oblige them by taking for granted the truth of alleged facts, the truth or falsity of which is, at least in part, the object of this work, it is clearly not fit, as it is not intended, for their perusal.

3. Of the formation of our planetary system, and particularly of our world and of man, a vast variety of accounts were given by the different philosophers of Greece and Rome, a very fair description of which may be met with in the first volume of the Universal History, and in Stanley's History of Philosophy. Many of these cosmogonists have been highly celebrated for their wisdom ; and yet, unless we suppose their theories to have been in a great degree allegorical, or to have contained some secret meaning, they exhibit an inconceivable mass of nonsense. But some of them, for instance that of Sanchoniathon, so largely discussed by Bishop Cumberland, are clearly allegorical : of course all such must be excepted from this condemnation.

If a person will apply his mind without prejudice to a consideration of the characters and doctrines of the ancient cosmogonists of the western part of the world, he must agree with me that they exhibit an extraordinary mixture of sense and nonsense, wisdom and folly—views of the creation, and its cause or causes, the most profound and beautiful, mixed with the most puerile conceits—conceits and fancies below the understanding of a plough-boy. How is this to be accounted for ? The fact cannot be denied. Of the sayings of the wise men, there was not one, probably, more wise than that of the celebrated Γνωθι σεαυτον, *Know thyself*, and probably there was not one to which so little regard has been paid. It is to the want of attention to this principle that I attribute most of the absurdities with which the wise and learned, perhaps in all ages, may be reproached. Man has forgotten or been ignorant that his faculties are limited. He has failed to mark the line of demarcation, beyond which his knowledge could not extend. Instead of applying his mind to objects cognizable by his senses, he has attempted subjects above the reach of the human mind, and has lost and bewildered himself in the mazes of metaphysics. He has not known or has not attended to what has been so clearly proved by Locke, that no idea can be received except through the medium of the senses. He has endeavoured to form ideas without attending to this principle, and, as might well be expected, he has run into the greatest absurdities, the necessary consequence of such imprudence. Very well the profound and learned Thomas Burnet says,[1] " Sapientia prima est stultitia caruisse ;" " primusque ad veritatem gradus præcavere errores." Again he says, " Sapientis enim est, non tantum ea quæ sciri possunt, scire : *sed etiam quæ sciri " non possunt, discernere et discriminare.*"[2]

It must not be understood from what I have said, that I wish to put a stop to all metaphysical researches ; far from it. But I do certainly wish to controul them, to keep them within due bounds, and to mark well the point beyond which, from the nature of our organization, we cannot proceed. Perhaps it may not be possible to fix the exact point beyond which the mind of man can never go, but it may be possible to say without doubt, of some certain point, beyond this he has not yet advanced. By this cautious mode of proceeding, though we may *pretend* to *less* knowledge, we may in fact *possess more.*

For these various reasons I shall pass over, without notice, the different theories of the formation of the world by the sages of Greece and Rome. In general they seem to me to deserve no notice, to be below the slightest consideration of a person of common understanding. As a curious record of what some of the wise men of antiquity were, they are interesting and worthy of preservation : as a rational exposé of the origin of things, they are nothing.

Among the subjects to which I allude as being above the reach of the human understanding are Liberty and Necessity, the Eternity of Matter, and several other similar subjects.

4. Our information of the historical transactions which it is supposed took place previous to the catastrophe,[3] and its attendant flood, which destroyed the ancient world, is very small. Mons.

---

[1] Arch. Phil. cap. vii.      [2] Ibid. p. 95.

[3] This catastrophe has been thought by many of the moderns to have arisen from a change of the direction of the

Bailly has observed, that the famous cycle of the Neros, and the cycle of seven days, or the week, from their peculiar circumstances, must probably have been of antediluvian invention. No persons could have invented the Neros who had not arrived at much greater perfection in astronomy than we know was the state of the most ancient of the Assyrians, Egyptians, or Greeks. The earliest of these nations supposed the year to have consisted of 360 days only, when the inventors of the Neros must have known its length to within a few seconds of time—a fact observed by Mons. Bailly to be a decisive proof that science was formerly brought to perfection, and therefore, consequently, must have been afterward lost. There are indeed among the Hindoos proofs innumerable that a very profound knowledge of the sciences was brought by their ancestors from the upper countries of India, the Himmalah mountains, Thibet or Cashmir. These were, I apprehend, the first descendants of the persons who lived after the deluge. But this science has long been forgotten by their degenerate successors, the present race of Brahmins. The ancient Hindoos might be acquainted with the Neros, but I think it probable that Josephus was correct in saying it is of antediluvian discovery; that is, that it was discovered previous to the time allotted for the deluge. And it is a curious circumstance that we receive this tradition from the people among whom we find the apparently antediluvian part of the book, or the first tract of the book, called Genesis, about which I shall have much more to observe in the course of this work.

The other cycle just now named, of the seven days or the week, is also supposed by Bailly to be, from its universal reception, of equal antiquity. There is no country of the old world in which it is not found, which, with the reasons which I will now proceed to state, pretty well justify Mons. Bailly in his supposition.

5. In my Preliminary Observations, and in my treatise on *The Celtic Druids*, I have pointed out the process by which the planetary bodies were called after the days of the week, or the days of the week after them. I have there stated that the septennial cycle would probably be among the earliest of. what would be called the scientific discoveries which the primeval races of men would make.

Throughout all the nations of the ancient world, the planets are to be found appropriated to the days of the week. The seven-day cycle, with each day named after a planet, and universally the same day allotted to the same planet in all the nations of the world, constitute the first proof, and leave no room to doubt that one system must have prevailed over the whole. Here are the origin and the reason of all judicial astrology, as well as the foundation upon which much of the Heathen mythology was built. The two were closely and intimately connected.

It is the object of this work to trace the steps by which, from the earliest time and small beginnings, this system grew to a vast and towering height, covering the world with gigantic monuments and beautiful temples, enabling one part of mankind, by means of the fears and ignorance of the other part, to trample it in the dust.

Uncivilized man is by nature the most timid of animals, and in that state the most defenceless. The storm, the thunder, the lightning, or the eclipse, fills him with terror. He is alarmed and trembles at every thing which he does not understand, and that is almost every thing that he sees or hears.

If a person will place himself in the situation of an early observer of the heavenly bodies, and consider how they must have appeared to him in his state of ignorance, he will at once perceive that it was scarcely possible that he could avoid mistaking them for animated or intelli-

---

earth's axis, and a simultaneous, or perhaps consequent, change of the length of the year from 360 to 365 days. The change of the axis was believed among the ancients by Plato, Anaxagoras, Empedocles, Diogenes, Leucippus, and Democritus. Vide book ii. ch. iv. of THOMAS BURNET's *Archæologia Philosophica*.

gent beings. To us, with our prejudices of education, it is difficult to form a correct idea of what his sensations must have been, on his first discovering the five planets to be different from the other stars, and to possess a locomotive quality, apparently to him subject to no rule or order. But we know what happened; he supposed them animated, and to this day they are still supposed to be so, by the greatest part of the world. Even in enlightened England judicial astrologers are to be found.

I suppose that after man first discovered the twenty-eight day cycle, and the year of 360 days, he would begin to perceive that certain stars, larger than the rest, and shining with a steady and not a scintillating light, were in perpetual motion. They would appear to him, unskilled in astronomy, to be endowed with life and great activity, and to possess a power of voluntary motion, going and coming in the expanse at pleasure. These were the planets. A long time would pass before their number could be ascertained, and a still longer before it could be discovered that their motions were periodical. The different systems of the ancient philosophers of Greece and other countries, from their errors and imperfections, prove that this must have been the state of the case. During this period of ignorance and fear arose the opinion, that they influenced the lot of man, or governed this sublunary world; and very naturally arose the opinion that they were intelligent beings. And as they appeared to be constantly advancing towards and receding from the sun, the parent of life and comfort to the world, they were believed to be his ministers and messengers. As they began in some instances to be observed to return, or be visible in the same part of the heavens, they would naturally be supposed by the terrified barbarian to have duties to perform; and when the very ancient book of Job[1] represents the morning stars to have sung together, and all the sons of God to have shouted for joy, it probably does not mean to use merely a figurative expression, but nearly the literal purport of the language.

In contemplating the host of heaven, men could not fail soon to observe that the fixed stars were in a particular manner connected with the seasons—that certain groups of them regularly returned at the time experience taught them it was necessary to commence their seed-time or their harvest; but that the planets, though in some degree apparently connected with the seasons, were by no means so intimately and uniformly connected with them as the stars. This would be a consequence which would arise from the long periods of some of the planets—Saturn, for instance. These long periods of some of the planets would cause the shortness of the periods of others of them to be overlooked, and would, no doubt, have the effect of delaying the time when their periodical revolutions would be discovered; perhaps for a very long time : and, in the interim, the opinion that they were intelligent agents would be gaining ground, and receiving the strengthening seal of superstition; and, if a priesthood had arisen, the fiat of orthodoxy.

From these causes we find that, though in judicial astrology or magic the stars have a great influence, yet that a great distinction is made between them and the planetary bodies; and I think that, by a minute examination of the remaining astrological nonsense which exists, the distinction would be found to be justified, and the probability of the history here given confirmed.

As it has been observed, though the connexion between the planets and the seasons was not so intimate as that between the latter and the stars, yet still there was often an apparent connexion, and some of the planets would be observed to appear when particular seasons arrived, and thus after a certain time they were thought to be beneficent or malevolent, as circumstances appeared to justify the observers' conclusions.

6. Of the different histories of the creation, that contained in the book, or collection of books,

---

[1] Chap. xxxviii. ver. 7.

called Genesis, has been in the Western parts of the world the most celebrated, and the nonsense which has been written respecting it, may fairly vie with the nonsense, a little time ago alluded to, of the ancient learned men of Greece and Rome.

This book professes to commence with a history of the creation, and in our vulgar translation it says, " *In the beginning God created the heavens and the earth.*" But I conceive for the word *heavens* the word *planets* ought to be substituted. The original for the word *heavens* is of great consequence. Parkhurst admits that it has the meaning of *placers* or *disposers*. In fact, it means the planets as distinguished from the fixed stars, and is the foundation, as I have said, and as we shall find, upon which all judicial astrology, and perhaps much of the Heathen mythology, was built.

After man came to distinguish the planets from the stars, and had allotted them to the respective days of the week, he proceeded to give them names, and they were literally the Dewtahs of India, the Archangels of the Persians and Jews, and the most ancient of the Gods of the Greeks and Romans, among the vulgar of whom each planet had a name, and was allotted to, or thought to be, a God.

The following are the names of the Gods allotted to each day : Sunday to the Sun, Monday to the Moon, Tuesday to Mars, Wednesday to Mercury, Thursday to Jupiter, Friday to Venus, and Saturday to Saturn : and it is worthy of observation, that neither Bacchus nor Hercules is among them ; on which I shall have an observation to make in a future part of this work. In almost every page we shall have to make some reference to judicial astrology, which took its rise from the planetary bodies.

The Sun, I think I shall shew, was unquestionably the first object of the worship of all nations. Contemporaneously with him or after him succeeded, for the reasons which I have given, the planets. About the time that the collection of planets became an object of adoration, the Zodiac was probably marked out from among the fixed stars, as we find it in the earliest superstitions of the astrologers. Indeed, the worship of the equinoctial sun in the sign Taurus, the remains of which are yet found in our May-day festivals, carries it back at least for 4,500 years before Christ. How much further back the system may be traced, I pretend not to say.

7. After the sun and planets it seems, on first view, probable that the moon would occupy the next place in the idolatrous veneration of the different nations ; but I am inclined to think that this was not the case. Indeed, I very much doubt whether ever he or she, for it was of both genders, was an object of adoration at all in the very early periods. I think it would be discovered so soon that its motions were periodical, that there would be scarcely any time for the error to happen ; for I cannot conceive it possible that it should have been thought to be an intelligent being after once its periodical nature was discovered.

This doctrine respecting the Moon will be thought paradoxical and absurd, and I shall be asked what I make of the goddess Isis. I reply, that it is the inconsistencies, contradictions, and manifest ignorance of the ancients respecting this goddess, which induce me to think that the Moon never was an object of worship in early times ; and that it never became an object of adoration till comparatively modern times, when the knowledge of the ancient mysteries was lost, and not only the knowledge of the mysteries, but the knowledge of the religion itself, or at least of its origin and meaning, were lost. The least attention to the treatises of Plato, Phornutus, Cicero, Porphyry, and, in short, of every one of the ancient writers on the subject of the religion, must convince any unprejudiced person that they either were all completely in the dark, or pretended to be so. After the canaille got to worshipping onions, crocodiles, &c., &c., &c., no doubt

---

¹ *Celtic Druids*, p. 291.

the moon came in for a share of their adoration ; but all the accounts of it are full of inconsistency and contradiction : for this reason I think it was of late invention, and that Isis was not originally the moon, but the mother of the gods. Many other reasons for this opinion will be given in the course of the work, when I come to treat of Isis and the Moon.

---

## CHAPTER II.

FIRST GOD OF THE ANCIENTS.—THE SUN.—DOUBLE NATURE OF THE DEITY.—METEMPSYCHOSIS AND RENEWAL OF WORLDS.—MORAL EVIL.—ETERNITY OF MATTER.—BUDDHA—GENESIS.

1. I SHALL now proceed to shew, in a way which I think I may safely say cannot be refuted, that all the Gods of antiquity resolved themselves into the solar fire, sometimes itself as God, or sometimes as emblem or shekinah of that higher principle, known by the name of the creative Being or God. But first I must make a few observations on his nature, as it was supposed to exist by the ancient philosophers.

On the nature of this Being or God the ancient oriental philosophers entertained opinions which took their rise from a very profound and recondite course of reasoning, (but yet, when once put in train, a very obvious one,) which arose out of the relation which man and the creation around him were observed by them to bear, to their supposed cause—opinions which, though apparently well known to the early philosophers of all nations, seem to have been little regarded or esteemed in later times, even if known to them, by the mass of mankind. But still they were opinions which, in a great degree, influenced the conduct of the world in succeeding ages ; and though founded in truth or wisdom, in their abuse they became the causes of great evils to the human race.

The opinions here alluded to are of so profound a nature, that they seem to bespeak a state of the human mind much superior to any thing to be met with in what we have been accustomed to consider or call ancient times. From their philosophical truth and universal reception in the world, I am strongly inclined to refer them to the authors of the Neros, or to that enlightened race, supposed by Mons. Bailly to have formerly existed, and to have been saved from a great catastrophe on the Himmalah mountains. This is confirmed by an observation which the reader will make in the sequel, that these doctrines have been like all the other doctrines of antiquity, gradually corrupted—incarnated, if I may be permitted to compose a word for the occasion.

Sublime philosophical truths or attributes have become clothed with bodies and converted into living creatures. Perhaps this might take its origin from a wish in those professing them to conceal them from the vulgar eye, but the cause being forgotten, all ranks in society at last came to understand them in the literal sense, their real character being lost; or perhaps this incarnation might arise from a gradual falling away of mankind from a high state of civilization, at which it must have arrived when those doctrines were discovered, into a state of ignorance,—the produce of revolutions, or perhaps merely of the great law of change which in all nature seems to be eternally in operation.

2. The human animal. like all other animals, is in his mode of existence very much the child of accident, circumstance, habit: as he is moulded in his youth he generally continues. This is in nothing, perhaps, better exemplified than in the use of his right hand. From being carried in

F

the right arm of his nurse, his right hand is set at liberty for action and use, while his left is at rest: the habit of using the right hand in preference to the left is thus acquired and never forgotten. A similar observation applies to the mind. To natural causes leading men to peculiar trains or habits of thinking or using the mind, may be traced all the recondite theories which we find among the early races of man. If to causes of this kind they are not to be ascribed, I should be glad to know where their origins are to be looked for. If they be not in these causes to be found, we must account for them by inventing a history of the adventures of some imagined human being, after the manner of the Greeks and many others, whose priests never had a difficulty, always having a fable ready for the amusement of their credulous votaries.

In opposition to this, I, perhaps, may be asked, why the inhabitants of the new world have not arrived at the high degree of civilization,—at the same results, as the inhabitants of the old? The answer is, Accident or circumstances being at first different, they have been led to a different train of acting or thinking; and if they branched off from the parent stock in very early times, accident or circumstances being after their separation different, are quite sufficient to account for the difference of the results. It seems probable, that from their knowledge of figures and their ignorance of letters, they must have branched off in a very remote period. Although the peculiar circumstance, that few or none of the animals of the old world were found in the new one, or of the animals of the new one in the old, seems to shew a separate formation of the animal creation; yet the identity of many of the religious rites and ceremonies of the inhabitants of the two worlds, and other circumstances pointed out by Mr. Faber and different writers, seem to bespeak only one formation or creation of man.

The rise of the doctrine respecting the nature of God named above, is said to be lost in the most remote antiquity. This may be true; but perhaps a little consideration will enable us to point out the natural cause from which, as I have observed, it had its origin. Like the discovery of figures or arithmetic, the septennial cycle, &c., it probably arose among the first philosophers or searchers after wisdom, from their reflecting upon the objects which presented themselves to their observation.

3. That the sun was the first object of the adoration of mankind, I apprehend, is a fact, which I shall be able to place beyond the reach of reasonable doubt. An absolute proof of this fact the circumstances of the case put it out of our power to produce; but it is supported by reason and common sense, and by the traditions of all nations, when carefully examined to their foundations. The allegorical accounts or mythoses[1] of different countries, the inventions of an advanced state of society, inasmuch as they are really only allegorical accounts or mythoses, operate nothing against this doctrine.

When, after ages of ignorance and error, man became in some degree civilized, and he turned his mind to a close contemplation of the fountain of light and life—of the celestial fire—he would observe among the earliest discoveries which he would make, that by its powerful agency all nature was called into action; that to its return in the spring season the animal and vegetable creation were indebted for their increase as well as for their existence. It is probable that for this reason chiefly the sun, in early times, was believed to be the creator, and became the first object of adoration. This seems to be only a natural effect of such a cause. After some time it would

---

[1] This is nothing against the Mosaic account, because it is allowed by all philosophers, as well as most of the early Jews and Christian fathers, to contain a mythos or an allegory—by Philo, Josephus, Papias, Pantænus, Irenæus, Clemens Alex., Origen, the two Gregories of Nyssa and Nazianzen, Jerome, Ambrose, Spencer de Legibus Hebræorum, Alexander Geddes, the Romish translator of the Bible, in the Preface and Critical Remarks, p. 49. See also Marsh's Lectures, &c., &c. Of this I shall say more hereafter.

be discovered that this powerful and beneficent agent, the solar fire, was the most potent destroyer, and hence would arise the first idea of a Creator and Destroyer united in the same person. But much time would not elapse before it must have been observed, that the destruction caused by this powerful being was destruction only in appearance, that destruction was only reproduction in another form—regeneration; that if he appeared sometimes to destroy, he constantly repaired the injury which he seemed to occasion—and that, without his light and heat, every thing would dwindle away into a cold, inert, unprolific mass.[1] Thus at once, in the same being, became concentrated, the creating, the preserving, and the destroying powers,—the latter of the three being, at the same time, both the destroyer and regenerator. Hence, by a very natural and obvious train of reasoning, arose the creator, the preserver, and the destroyer—in India, *Brahma*, *Vishnu*, and *Siva*; in Persia, *Oromasdes*, *Mithra*, and *Arimanius*; in Egypt, *Osiris*, *Neith*, and *Typhon*: in each case *Three Persons and one God*. And *thus* arose the TRIMURTI, or the celebrated Trinity. On this Mr. Payne Knight says, "The hypostatical division and essential unity of the " Deity is one of the most remarkable parts of this system, and the farthest removed from " common sense and reason: and yet this is perfectly reasonable and consistent, if considered " together with the rest of it, for the emanations and personifications were only figurative abstrac- " tions of particular modes of action and existence, of which the primary cause and original essence " still continued one and the same. The three hypostases being thus only one being, each " hypostasis is occasionally taken for all, as is the case in the passage of Apuleius before cited, " where Isis describes herself as the universal deity.'"[2]

The sun himself, in his corporeal and visible form of a globe of fire, I do not doubt was, for a long time, the sole trinity. And it would not be till after ages of speculation and philosophizing that man would raise his mind to a more pure trinity, or to a trinity of abstractions,—a trinity which would probably never have existed in his imagination if he had not first had the more gross corpo- real igneous trinity, with its effects, for its prototype, to lead him to the more refined and sublime doctrine, in which the corporeal and igneous trinity gave way among philosophers to one of a more refined kind; or to a system of abstractions, or of attributes, or of emanations, from a superior being, the creator and preserver of the sun himself.

It has been said in reply to this, Then this fundamental doctrine on which, in fact, all the future religion and philosophy of the world was built, you attribute to accident! The word accident means, by us unseen or unknown cause; but I suppose, that when an intelligent Being was esta- blishing the present order of the universe, he must know how the unseen cause or accident which he provided would operate,—this accident or unseen cause being only a link in a chain, the first link of which begins, and the last of which ends, in God.

That the sublime doctrine of emanations, or abstractions as it was called, above alluded to, prevailed among the oriental nations, cannot be doubted; but yet there may be a doubt whether they were ever entirely free from an opinion that the creative Deity consisted of a certain very refined substance, similar, if not the same, as the magnetic, galvanic, or electric fluid. This was the opinion of all the early Christian fathers, as well, I think, as of the Grecians. But still, I think, certain philosophers arose above this kind of materialism, among whom must have been the Buddhists and Brahmins of India; but of this we shall see more in the sequel. We shall find this a most difficult question to decide.

---

[1] Described in Genesis by the words חֹהוּ וּבֹהוּ *tëu-u-bëu*, which mean a mass of matter effete, unproductive, unpro- lific, ungenerating, and itself devoid of the beautiful forms of the animal, vegetable, and mineral kingdoms,—the mud or Ἰλυς of Sanchoniathon. The words of our Bible, as here used, *without form and void*, have not any meaning.

[2] Knight, p. 163.

4. The Trinity described above, and consisting of abstractions or emanations from the divine nature, will be found exemplified in the following work in a vast variety of ways; but in all, the first principle will be found at the bottom of them. I know nothing in the works of the ancient philosophers which can be brought against them except a passage or two of Plato, and one of Numenius, according to Proclus.

Plato says, " When, therefore, that God, who is a perpetually reasoning divinity, cogitated " about the god who was destined to subsist at some certain period of time, he produced his body " smooth and equable ; and every way from the middle even and whole, and perfect from the " composition of perfect bodies." [1]

Again Plato says, " And on all these accounts he rendered the universe a happy God." [2] Again he says, " But he fabricated the earth, the common nourisher of our existence ; which being " conglobed about the pole, extended through the universe, is the guardian and artificer of night " and day, and is the first and most ancient of the gods which are *generated* within the heavens. " But the harmonious progressions of these divinities, their concussions with each other, the revo- " lutions and advancing motions of their circles, how they are situated with relation to each other " in their conjunctions and oppositions, whether direct among themselves or retrograde, at what " times and in what manner they become concealed, and, again emerging to our view, cause " terror, and exhibit tokens of future events to such as are able to discover their signification ; of " all this to attempt an explanation, without suspecting the resemblances of these divinities, " would be a fruitless employment. But of this enough, and let this be the end of our discourse " concerning the nature of the visible and *generated* gods." [3]

How from these passages any ingenuity can make out that Plato maintained a trinity of the Sun, the Moon, and the Earth, as the Supreme God or the Creator, I do not know, and I should not have thought of noticing them if I had not seen an attempt lately made in a work not yet published, to depreciate the sublime doctrines of the ancients by deducing from these passages that consequence.

The other passage is of Numenius the Pythagorean, recorded by Proclus, who says that he taught, that the world was the third God, ὁ γαρ κοσμος κατ᾽ αυτον ὁ τριτος εστι Θεος. [4]

This is evidently nothing but the hearsay of hearsay evidence, and can only shew that these doctrines, like all the other mythoses, had become lost or doubtful to the Greeks. The latter quotation of this obscure author will be found undeserving of attention, when placed in opposition to the immense mass of evidence which will be produced in this work. And as for the passage of Plato, I think few persons will allow it to have any weight, when in like manner every construction of it is found to be directly in opposition to his other doctrines, as my reader will soon see. [5]

5. The doctrine as developed above by me, is said to be too refined for the first race of men. Beautifully refined it certainly is : but my reader will recollect that I do not suppose that man arrived at these results till after many generations of ignorance, and till after probably almost innumerable essays of absurdity and folly. But I think if the matter be well considered, the Pan-

---

[1] Plato's Tim., Taylor, p. 483.     [2] Ibid. p. 484.     [3] Ibid. p. 499, 500.
[4] Comment. in Tim. of Plat. II. 93.

[5] In the seventh chapter of the 2nd book of Arch. Phil. by Thomas Burnet, who was among the very first of modern philosophers, may be seen an elaborate and satisfactory proof that the ancient philosophers constantly held two doctrines, one for the learned, and one for the vulgar. He supports his proofs by an example from Jamblicus and Laertius, relative to some notions of Pythagoras, which accorded with the vulgar opinion of the Heavens, but which were contrary to his REAL opinions. He has completely justified the ancients from the attempts of certain of the moderns to fix upon them their simulated opinions. The fate of Socrates furnishes an admirable example of what would happen to those who in ancient times taught true doctrines to the vulgar, or attempted to draw aside the veil of Isis.

theistic scheme (for it is a part of a pantheism) of making the earth the creator of all, will require much more refinement of mind than the doctrine of attributing the creation to the sun. The first is an actual refinement run into corruption, similar to Bishop Berkley's doctrine,—refinement, indeed, carried to a vicious excess, carried to such an excess as to return to barbarism ; similar, for instance, to what took place in the latter ages of Greece and Rome in the fine arts, when the beautiful Ionic and Corinthian orders of architecture were deserted for the Composite.

We may venture, I think, to presume that adoration must first have arisen either from fear or admiration ; in fact, from feeling. As an object of feeling, the sun instantly offers himself. The effect arising from the daily experience of his beneficence, does not seem to be of such a nature as to wear away by use, as is the case with most feelings of this kind. He obtrudes himself on our notice in every way. But what is there in the earth on which we tread, and which is nothing without the sun, which should induce the half-civilized man to suppose it an active agent—to suppose that it created itself ? He would instantly see that it was, *in itself*, to all appearance תהו *tëu*, ובהו *uböu*,[1] an inert, dead, unprolific mass. And it must, I think, have required an exertion of metaphysical subtlety, infinitely greater than my trinity must have required, to arrive at a pantheism so completely removed from the common apprehension of the human understanding. In my oriental theory, every thing is natural and seductive ; in the other, every thing is unnatural and repulsive.

My learned friend who advocates this degrading scheme of Pantheism against my sublime and intellectual theory, acknowledges what cannot be denied, that the doctrines held in these two passages of Numenius and Plato, are directly at variance with their philosophy as laid down in all their other works. Under these circumstances, I think I may safely dismiss them without further observation, as passages misunderstood, or contrivances to conceal their real opinions.

6. Of equal or nearly equal date, and almost equally disseminated throughout the world with the doctrine of the Trinity, was that of the Hermaphroditic or Androgynous character of the Deity. Man could not help observing and meditating upon the difference of the sexes. He was conscious that he himself was the highest in rank of all creatures of which he had any knowledge, and he very properly and very naturally, as far as was in his power, made God after the being of highest rank known to him, after himself ; thus it might be said, that in his own image, in idea, made he his God. But of what sex was this God ? To make him neuter, supposing man to have become grammarian enough to have invented a neuter gender, was to degrade him to the rank of a stone. To make him female was evidently more analogous to the general productive and prolific characters of the author of the visible creation. To make him masculine, was still more analogous to man's own person, and to his superiority over the female, the weaker vessel ; but still this was attended with many objections. From a consideration of all these circumstances, an union of the two was adopted, and he was represented as being Androgynous.

Notwithstanding what I have said in my last paragraph respecting the degradation of making God of the neuter gender, I am of opinion that had a neuter gender been known it would have been applied to the Deity, and for that reason would have been accounted, of the three genders, the most honourable. For this, among other reasons, if I find any very ancient language which has not a neuter gender, I shall be disposed to consider it to be probably among the very oldest of the languages of the world. This observation will be of importance hereafter.

7. Of all the different attributes of the Creator, or faculties conferred by him on his creature, there is no one so striking or so interesting to a reflecting person as that of the generative power.

---

[1] Gen. chap. i.

This is the most incomprehensible and mysterious of the powers of nature. When all the adjuncts or accidents of every kind so interesting to the passions and feelings of man are considered, it is not wonderful that this subject should be found in some way or other to have a place among the first of the human superstitions. Thus every where we find it accompanying the triune God, called Trimurti or Trinity, just described, under the very significant form of the single obelisk or stone-pillar, denominated the Lingham or Phallus,[1] and the equally significant Yoni or Cteis, the female organ of generation : sometimes single, often in conjunction. The origin of the worship of this object is discussed at large in my *Celtic Druids*, and will be found in the index by reference to the words Phallus, Linga, Lithoi.

8. The next step after man had once convinced himself of the existence of a God would be, I think, to discover the doctrine of the immortality of the soul. Long before he arrived at this point, he must have observed, and often attempted to account for, the existence of moral evil. How to reconcile this apparent blot in the creation to the beneficence of an all-powerful Creator, would be a matter of great difficulty : he had probably recourse to the only contrivance which was open to him, a contrivance to which he seems to have been driven by a wise dispensation of Providence, the doctrine of a future state of existence, where the ills of this world would find a remedy, and the accounts of good and evil be balanced ; where the good man would receive his reward, and the bad one his punishment. This seems to me to be the probable result of the contemplation of the existence of evil by the profound primeval oriental philosophers, who first invented the doctrine of the Trinity.

9. Other considerations would lend their assistance to produce the same result. After man had discovered the doctrine of the immortality of the soul, the metempsychosis followed the doctrine of the reproduction or regeneration by the third person of the triune God, by a very natural process, as the doctrine of the triune God had before arisen by an easy process from the consideration by man of the qualities of the beings around him. Everywhere, throughout all nature, the law that destruction was reproduction appeared to prevail. This united to the natural fondness for immortality, of which every human being is conscious, led to the conclusion, that man, the élite of the creation, could not be excepted from the general rule; that he did but die to live again, to be regenerated; a consciousness of his own frailty gradually caused a belief, that he was regenerate in some human body or the body of some animal as a punishment for his offences, until by repeated penances of this kind, his soul had paid the forfeit of the crimes of its first incarnation, had become purified from all stain, and in a state finally to be absorbed into the celestial influence, or united to the substance of the Creator. As it happens in every sublunary concern, the law of change corrupted these simple principles in a variety of ways ; and we find the destroyer made into a demon or devil, at war with the Preserver or with the Creator. Hence arose the doctrine of the two principles opposed to each other, of Oromasdes and Arimanius in perpetual war, typified by the higher and lower hemisphere of the earth, of winter and summer, of light and darkness, as we shall find developed in a variety of ways. What could be so natural as to allot to the destroyer the lower hemisphere of cold and darkness, of winter, misery, and famine ? What so natural as to allot to the beneficent Preserver the upper hemisphere of genial warmth, of summer, happiness, and plenty ? Hence came the festivals of the equinoxes and of the solstices, much of the complicated machinery of the heathen mythology, and of judicial astrology.

From similar trains of reasoning arose the opinion that every thing in nature, even the world itself, was subject to periodical changes, to alternate destructions and renovations—an opinion,

---

[1] Religion de l'Antiquité, par Cruizer, Notes, Introd. p. 525.

perhaps, for sublimity not to be equalled in the history of the different philosophical systems of the world, the only doctrine which seemed, in the opinion of the ancients, to be capable of reconciling the existence of evil with the goodness of God.

10. A little time ago I said, that the first philosophers could not account for the existence of moral evil without the doctrine of the immortality of the soul. I am induced to make another observation upon this subject before I leave it. In the modern Christian system, this difficulty has been overcome, as most theological difficulties usually are, among devotees, by a story. In this case by a story of a serpent and a fruit tree, of which I shall not here give my opinion, except that, like most of the remainder of Genesis, it was anciently held to have an allegorical meaning, and, secondly, that I cannot do Moses the injustice of supposing that he, like the modern priests, could have meant it, at least by the higher classes of his followers, to be believed *literally*.

Moral evil is a relative term; its correlative is moral good. Without evil there is no good; without good there is no evil. There is no such thing known to us as good or evil *per se*. Here I must come to Mr. Locke's fine principle, so often quoted by me in my former book, the truth of which has been universally acknowledged, and to which, in their reasoning, all men seem to agree in forgetting to pay attention,—that we know nothing except through the medium of our senses, which is experience. We have no experience of moral good or of moral evil except as relative and correlative to one another; therefore, we are with respect to them as we are with respect to God. Though guided by experience we confidently believe their existence in this qualified form, yet of their nature, independent of one another, we can know nothing. God having created man subject to one, he could not, without changing his nature, exclude the other. All this the ancients seem to have known; and, in order to account for and remove several difficulties, they availed themselves of the metempsychosis, a renewal of worlds, and the final absorption of the soul or the thinking principle into the Divine substance, from which it was supposed to have emanated, and where it was supposed to enjoy that absolute and uncorrelative beatitude, of which man can form no idea. This doctrine is very sublime, and is such as we may reasonably expect from the school where Pythagoras studied;[1] but I do not mean to say that it removes all difficulties, or is itself free from difficulty. But absolute perfection can be expected only by priests who can call to their aid apples of knowledge. Philosophers must content themselves with something less. Of the great variety of sects or religions in the world there is not one, if the priests of each may be believed, in which any serious difficulties of this kind are found.

11. Modern divines, a very sensitive race, have been much shocked with the doctrine of the ancients, that nothing could be created from nothing, *ex nihilo nihil fit*. This is a subject well deserving consideration. The question arises how did the ancients acquire the knowledge of the truth of this proposition. Had they any positive experience that matter was *not* made from nothing? I think they had not. Then how could they have any knowledge on the subject? As they had received no knowledge through the medium of the senses, that is from experience, it was rash and unphilosophical to come to any conclusion.

The ancients may have reasoned from analogy. They may have said, Our experience teaches that every thing which we perceive has pre-existed before the moment we perceive it, therefore it is fair to conclude that it must always have existed. A most hasty conclusion. All that

---

[1] Carmel, close to the residence of Melchizedek, where was the temple of Iao, without image. See Jamblicus, chap. iii., Taylor's translation. When I formed the table of additional errata to my Celtic Druids, I had forgotten where I found the fact here named relating to the residence of Pythagoras, which caused the expression of the doubt which may be seen there respecting it.

they could fairly conclude was, that, for any thing which they knew to the contrary, it *may* have existed from eternity, not that it *must* have existed. But this amounts not to knowledge.

Are the modern priests any wiser than the ancient philosophers ? Have they any knowledge from experience of matter having ever been created from nothing ? I think they have not.[1] Then how can they conclude that it was created from nothing ? They cannot know any thing about it ; they are in perfect ignorance.

If matter *have* always existed, I think we may conclude that it will always exist. But if it *have not* always existed, will it always continue to exist? I think we may conclude it to be probable that it will. For if it have not always existed it must have been created (as I will assume) by God. God would not create any thing which was not good. He will not destroy any thing that is good. He is not changeable or repents what he has done: therefore he will not destroy the matter which he has created. From which we may conclude, that the change of form which we see daily taking place is periodical ; at least there is in favour of this what the Jesuits would call a probable opinion ; and this brings us to the alternate creations and destructions of the ancients. A learned philosopher says, " The bold and magnificent idea of a creation from nothing was reserved for the more " vigorous faith and more enlightened minds of the moderns, who seek no authority to confirm " their belief ; for as that which is self-evident admits of no proof, so that which is in itself impos- " sible admits of no refutation."[2]

This doctrine of the renewal of worlds, held by the ancient philosophers, has received a great accession of probability from the astronomical discoveries of La Place, who has demonstrated, that certain motions of the planetary bodies which appeared to Newton to be irregular, and to portend at some future period the destruction of the solar system, are all periodical, and that after certain immensely elongated cycles are finished, every thing returns again to its former situation. The ancient philosophers of the East had a knowledge of this doctrine, the general nature of which they might have acquired by reasoning similar to the above, or by the same means by which they acquired a knowledge of the Neros.

This is not inconsistent with the doctrine of a future judgment and a state of reward and punishment in another world. Why should not the soul transmigrate, and after the day of judgment (a figure) live again in the next world in some new body ? Here are all the leading doctrines of the ancients. I see nothing in them absurd—nothing contrary to the moral attributes of God —and nothing contrary even to the doctrines of Jesus of Nazareth. It has been thought that the doctrine of the pre-existence of souls may be found in the New Testament.

Many of the early fathers of the Christians held the doctrine of the Metempsychosis, which they defended on several texts of the New Testament.[3] It was an opinion which had a very general circulation both in the East and in the West. It was held by the Pharisees or Persees, as they ought to be called, among the Jews ; and among the Christians by Origen,[4] Chalcidius, (if he were a Christian,) Synesius, and by the Simonians, Basilidians, Valentiniens, Marcionites, and the Gnostics in general. It was held by the Chinese, and, among the most learned of the Greeks, by Plato and Pythagoras. Thus this doctrine was believed by nearly all the great and good of every religion, and of every nation and age ; and though the present race has not the smallest information more than its ancestors on this subject, yet the doctrine has not now a single votary in the Western part of the world. The Metempsychosis was believed by the celebrated Christian apologist, Soame Jenyns, perhaps the only believer in it of the moderns in the Western parts.

---

[1] The book of Genesis, when properly translated, says nothing on the subject.
[2] Knight, p. 131.     [3] Beausobre, *Hist. Manich.* L. vii. c. v. p. 491.     [4] Ib. p. 492.

The following observations tend not only to throw light on the doctrine of the Indians, the earliest philosophers of whom we have any genuine records, but they also shew that their doctrine is identically the same as that of certain individuals of the Western philosophers, who, recorded traditions inform us, actually travelled in very remote ages to the country of the Brahmins to learn it.

" Pythagoras, returning from his Eastern travels to Greece, taught the doctrine of the
" Metempsychosis, and the existence of a Supreme Being, by whom the universe was created, and
" by whose providence it is preserved ; that the souls of mankind are emanations of that Being.
" Socrates, the wisest of the ancient philosophers, seems to have believed that the soul existed
" before the body ; and that death relieves it from those seeming contrarieties to which it is
" subject, by its union with our material part. Plato (in conformity to the opinions of the learned
" Hindoos) asserted, that God infused into matter a portion of his divine spirit, which animates
" and moves it : that mankind have two souls of separate and different natures—the one cor-
" ruptible, the other immortal : that the latter is a portion of the Divine Spirit : that the mortal
" soul ceases to exist with the life of the body ; but the divine soul, no longer clogged by its union
" with matter, continues its existence, either in a state of happiness or punishment : that the souls
" of the virtuous return, after death, into the source whence they flowed ; while the souls of the
" wicked, after being for a certain time confined to a place destined for their reception, are sent
" back to earth to animate other bodies. Aristotle supposed the souls of mankind to be portions
" or emanations of the divine spirit ; which at death quit the body, and, like a drop of water falling
" into the ocean, are absorbed into the divinity. Zeno, the founder of the Stoic sect, taught that
" throughout nature there are two eternal qualities ; the one active, the other passive : that the
" former is a pure and subtle æther, the divine spirit ; and that the latter is in itself entirely inert,
" until united with the active principle. That the divine spirit, acting upon matter, produced
" fire, air, water, earth : that the divine spirit is the efficient principle, and that all nature is moved
" and conducted by it. He believed also that the soul of man, being a portion of the *universal*
" *soul*, returns after death to its first source. The opinion of the soul being an emanation of the
" divinity, *which is believed by the Hindoos*, and was professed by Greeks, seems likewise to have
" been adopted by the early Christians. Macrobius observes, Animarum originem emanare de
" cœlo, inter recte philosophantes indubitatæ constant esse fidei. SAINT JUSTIN says, the soul is
" incorruptible, because it EMANATES from God ; and his disciple Tatianus, the Assyrian, observes,
" that man having received a portion of the divinity, is immortal as God is. Such was the
" system of the ancient philosophers, Pythagoreans, Brachmans, and some sects of the Chris-
" tians." [1]

Thus from trains of reasoning similar to what I have briefly described, and from natural causes, I think arose all the ancient doctrines and mythologies.

12. The oldest philosophy or mythology of which we have any certain history, is that of the Buddha of the Eastern nations, in which are to be found the various doctrines to which I have just alluded. From the Metempsychosis arose the repugnance among the Buddhists to the slaughter of animals,—a necessary consequence of this doctrine uncorrupted and sincerely believed. From this circumstance in the first book of Genesis, or book of Wisdom, which is probably a work of the Buddhists, the slaughter of animals is prohibited or not allowed. After a time the mild doctrines of Buddha came to be changed or corrupted and superseded by those of Crishna. Hence in the second book of Genesis, or the book of the Generations, or Re-generations [2] of the planetary

---

[1] Forbes, Orient. Mem. Vol. III. Ch. xxxiii. p. 261.       [2] Parkhurst, in voce, ילר *ild.*

bodies, which is, I think, a Brahmin work, they are allowed to be used for sacrifice. In the third book, or the book of the Generations, or Re-generations[1] of the race of man, the Adam, they are first allowed to be eaten as food.

How long a time would elapse before man would arrive at the point I here contemplate—the knowledge of the doctrines which I have described—must evidently depend, in a great measure, upon the degree of perfection in which he was turned out from the hand of his Creator. On this point we are and we must remain in ignorance. I argue upon the supposition that man was created with only sufficient information for his comfortable existence, and, therefore, I must be considered to use merely a conditional argument. If any person think it more probable that man was turned out of his Creator's hand in a state of perfection, I have no objection to this; but my reasoning does not apply to him. If he will condescend to reason with me, he must conditionally admit my premises.

13. It is not to be supposed, that I imagine these profound philosophical results respecting the Trinity, &c., to have been arrived at by the half civilized or infant man all at once—in a day, a week, or a year. No, indeed! many generations, perhaps thousands of years may have elapsed before he arrived at this point; and I think the discovery of several of them in every part of the world, new as well as old, justifies the inference that they were the doctrines of a race, in a high state of civilization, either immediately succeeding or before the flood, which has so evidently left its traces everywhere around us. Before these profound results were arrived at, innumerable attempts must have been made to discover the origin of things. Probably every kind of absurdity imaginable may have been indulged in. All this we may readily suppose, but of its truth we cannot arrive at absolute certainty. At the same time, for any thing we know to the contrary, man may have been created in such a state as easily to have arrived at these conclusions. It is scarcely possible for us at this day to be able to appreciate the advantages which the first races of mankind would possess, in not having their minds poisoned, : d their understandings darkened, and enervated by the prejudices of education. Every part of modern education seems to be contrived for the purpose of enfeebling the mind of man. The nurse begins with hobgoblins and ghosts, which are followed up by the priests with devils and the eternal torments of hell. How few are the men who can entirely free themselves from these and similar delusions in endless variety instilled into the infant mind!

A learned philosopher has said, " It is surprising that so few should have perceived how " destructive of intellect, the prevailing classical system of education is; or rather that so few " should have had courage to avow their conviction respecting classical absurdity and idolatry. " Except Bacon and Hobbes, I know not that any authors of high rank have ventured to question " the importance or utility of the learning which has so long stunned the world with the noise of " its pretensions; but sure it does not require the solid learning or philosophic sagacity of a " Bacon or a Hobbes to perceive the ignorance, nonsense, folly, and *dwarfifying* tendency of the " kind of learning which has been so much boasted of by brainless pedants."

All the doctrines which I have stated above, are well known to have been those of the most ancient nations; the theory of the origin of those doctrines is my own. But I beg leave to observe, that whether the theory of their origin be thought probable or not, the fact of the existence of the doctrines will be proved beyond dispute in a great variety of ways; and it is on the fact of their existence that the argument of this work is founded. The truth or falsity of the theory of their origin will not affect the argument. But of such persons as shall dispute the mode

---

[1] These are the names which the books give to themselves.

above described, by which the ancients are held to have arrived at their knowledge, I request the statement of a more rational theory.

I shall now proceed to shew, that the doctrines which I have here laid down were disseminated among all nations, and first that the Sun or solar fire was the sole object of the worship of all nations either as God himself, or as emblem or shekinah of the Supreme Being.

---

# CHAPTER III.

THE SUN THE FIRST OBJECT OF ADORATION OF ALL NATIONS.—THE GODS NOT DECEASED HEROES.— THE CHINESE HAVE ONLY ONE GOD.—HINDOO GODDESSES.—TOLERATION AND CHANGE IN RELIGIONS.

1. On the first view of the mythological systems of the Gentiles, the multitude of their gods appears to be infinite, and the confusion inextricable. But if a person will only consider the following chapters carefully, and without prejudice, he will probably discover a system which, in some degree, will unravel their intricacies, will reconcile their apparent contradictions, will explain the general meaning of their mysteries, and will shew the reason why, among the various religions in later times, toleration so universally prevailed. But yet it is not intended to attempt, as some persons have done, a complete development of the minutiæ of the mysteries, or to exhibit a perfect system attended with an explanation of the ceremonies and practices which the Heathens adopted in the secret recesses of their temples, which they guarded from the prying eye of the vulgar with the greatest care and the most sacred oaths ; and which have long since been buried amidst the ruins of the finest buildings of antiquity—lamentable sacrifices to the zeal, bigotry, and fury of the Iconoclasts, or of the professors of Christianity.

Few persons have exhibited more learning or ingenuity on the subject of the ancient worship than Mr. Bryant and M. Dupuis : and whatever opinion people may entertain of different parts of their works, or of some of their hypotheses, yet they can scarcely refuse assent to their general assertions, that all the religions of antiquity, at least in their origin, are found to centre in the worship of the Sun, either as God the Creator himself, or as the seat of, or as the emblem of Creator.

Socrates, Pythagoras, Plato, Zoroaster or Zeradust, &c., and all those initiated in the most secret mysteries, acknowledged one supreme God, the Lord and First Cause of all. And perhaps, though it can never be *certainly* known, those who only received the lesser mysteries,[1] might confine their worship to the sun and the host of heaven ; but it was only the vulgar and ignorant who bent the knee to the stone, wood, or metal idols of the gods, perhaps only a *little more* numerous than the images of the Christian saints.

2. It has until lately been the general opinion, that the gods of the ancients were nothing but the heroes or the benefactors of mankind, living in very illiterate and remote ages, to whom a grateful posterity paid divine honours. This appears at first sight to be probable ; and as it has

---

[1] An interesting account of the mysteries of the Heathens will be found in Part II. of Vol. II. of Dupuis's History of all Religions.

served the purpose of the Christian priests, to enable them to run down the religion of the ancients, and, in exposing its absurdities, to contrast it disadvantageously with their own, it has been, and continues to be, sedulously inculcated, in every public and private seminary. The generality of schoolmasters know no better; they teach what they have learned and what they believe. But, as this rank of men increase in talent and learning, this is gradually wearing away.

Although the pretended worship of Heroes appears at first sight plausible, very little depth of thought or learning is requisite to discover that it has not much foundation in truth. It was not in the infant state of society, that men were worshiped; it was not, on the contrary, until they arrived at a very high and advanced state of civilization. It was not Moses, Zoroaster, Confucius, Socrates, Solon, Lycurgus, Plato, Pythagoras, or Numa, that were objects of worship; the benefactors of mankind in all ages have been oftener persecuted than worshiped. No, divine honours (if such they can be called) were reserved for Alexander of Macedon, the drunkard, for Augustus Cæsar, the hypocrite, or Heliogabalus, the lunatic. A species of civil adoration, despised by all persons of common understanding, and essentially different from the worship of the Supreme Being, was paid to them. It was the vice of the moment, and soon passed away. How absurd to suppose that the elegant and enlightened Athenian philosopher could worship Hercules, because he killed a lion or cleaned a stable! Or Bacchus, because he made wine or got drunk! Besides, these deified heroes can hardly be called Gods in any sense. They were more like the Christian Saints. Thus we have Divus Augustus, and Divus Paulus, and Divus Petrus. Their nature has been altogether misunderstood; it will afterward be explained.

3. After a life of the most painful and laborious research, Mr. Bryant's opinion is, that all the various religions terminated in the worship of the Sun. He commences his work by shewing, from a great variety of etymological proofs, that all the names of the Deities were derived or compounded from some word which originally meant the Sun. Notwithstanding the ridicule which has been thrown upon etymological inquiries, in consequence of the want of fixed rules, or of the absurd length to which some persons have carried them, yet I am quite certain it must, in a great measure, be from etymology at last that we must recover the lost learning of antiquity.

Macrobius[1] says, that in Thrace they worship the Sun or Solis Liber, calling him Sebadius; and from the Orphic poetry we learn that all the Gods were one:

'Εις Ζευς, εις Αϊδης, εις 'Ηλιος, εις Διονυσος,
εις Θεος εν παντεσσι. [2]

Diodorus Siculus says, that it was the belief of the ancients that Osiris, Serapis, Dionusos, Pluto, Jupiter, and Pan, were all one. [3]

Ausonius represents all the deities to be included under the term Dionusos. [4]

Sometimes Pan [5] was called the God of all, sometimes Jupiter. [6]

Nonnus also states, that all the different Gods, whatever might be their names, Hercules, Ammon, Apollo, or Mithra, centred in the Sun.

Mr. Selden says, whether they be called Osiris, or Omphis, or Nilus, or Siris, or by any other name, they all centre in the Sun, the most ancient deity of the nations. [7]

Basnage[8] says, that Osiris, that famous God of the Egyptians, was the Sun, or rather the Sun was the emblem of the beneficent God Osiris.

---

[1] Sat. L. i. 18.          [2] Orphic Fragm. iv. p. 364, Gesner, Ed.          [3] L. i. p. 23.
[4] Auson. Epigram. 30; Bryant, Vol. I. p. 310, 4to.          [5] 4 Orp. Hym. x. p. 200, Gesner.
[6] Euphorion.          [7] Selden de Diis Syriis, p. 77.          [8] B. iii. Ch. xviii. Sect. xxii.

Serapis was another name for the Sun. Remisius gives an inscription to Jupiter the Sun, *the invincible Serapis.*

Mithras was likewise the Sun, or rather was but a different name, which the Persians bestowed on the Egyptian Osiris.

Harpocrates also represented the Sun. It is true, he was also the God of Silence ; he put his finger upon his mouth, because the Sun was worshiped with a reverential silence, and thence came the Sigè of the Basilidians, who had their origin from Egypt. [1]

By the Syrians the Sun and Heat were called חמה *hme,* Chamha ; [2] and by the Persians Hama. [3] Thus the temple to which Alexander so madly marched in the desert, was called the temple of the Sun or of Ammon. Mr. Bryant shews that Ham was esteemed the Zeus of Greece, and the Jupiter of Latium.

Αμμας ὁ Ζευς Αριϛοτελει. [4]

Αμμον γαρ Αιγυπτιοι καλεσσι τον Δια. [5]

Ham, sub Jovis nomine, in Africa cultus.[6]

Ζευ Λιβυης Αμμον, κιρα τη φορε κεκλυθι Μαντι.[7]

Mr. Bryant says, " The worship of Ham, or the Sun, as it was the most ancient, so it was the " most universal of any in the world. It was at first the prevailing religion of Greece ; and was " propagated over all the sea-coast of Europe, from whence it extended itself into the inland pro- " vinces. It was established in Gaul and Britain ; and was the original religion of this island, " which the Druids in after times adopted." [8]

This Ham was nothing but a Greek corruption of a very celebrated Indian word, formed of the three *letters* A-U M, of which I shall have much to say hereafter.

Virgil gives the conduct of the year to Liber or Bacchus, [9] though it was generally thought to be in the care of Apollo. It also appears from the Scholia in Horace,[10] that Apollo and Dionusos were the same. In fact, they were all three the same, the Sun.

Ἡλιε παγγενετωρ παναιολε χρυσεοφεγγες. [11]

4. It is allowed that the grand mysteries of the Grecian religion were brought by way of Thrace from Assyria, Persia, Egypt, or other Eastern parts, by a person of the name of Orpheus, or at least that it came from those parts, whoever brought it into Greece. And in the doctrines attributed to this philosopher, we may reasonably expect to find the ground-works of the religion, in fact, the religion unadulterated by the folly of the populace, and the craft of the priests. And here we shall find a pure and excellent religion.

Proclus says of the religion, Ζευς κεφαλε, Ζευς μεσσα· Διος δ᾽εκ παντα τετυκται—Jove is the head and middle of all things ; all things were made out of Jove.

According to Timotheus, in Cedrenus, Orpheus asserted the existence of an eternal, incomprehensible Being, Δημιεργον απαντον, και αυτε τε αιθερος, και παντων των επ᾽ αυτον τον αιθερα, the Creator of all things, even of the æther itself, and of all things below that æther. According to him, this Δημιεργος is called ΦΩΣ, ΒΟΥΛΗ, ΖΩΗ, Light, Counsel, Life. And Suidas says, that these three names express one and the same power, ταυτα τα τρια ονοματα μιαν δυναμιν απεφηνατο : and Timotheus concludes his account by affirming that Orpheus, in

---

[1] Basnage, B. iii. Ch. xviii.           [2] Selden de Diis Syriis Syntag. II. C. viii. p. 247.
[3] Gale's Court of the Gentiles, Vol. I. Ch. xi. p. 72.           [4] Hesychius.           [5] Herodotus, L. ii. C. xlii.
[6] Bochart, Geog. Sac. L. i. C. i. p. 5.           [7] Pind. Pyth. Ode iv. 28, Schol.
[8] Bryant, Vol. I. 4to. p. 284.           [9] Georg. L. i. v. 6.           [10] Lib. ii. Ode xix.
[11] Orphic Fragm. in. Macrob. Sat. L. i. C. xxiii.

his book, declared, δια των αυτων ονοματων μιας Θεοτητος τα παντα εγενετο, και αυτος εςι τα παντα : That all things were made by one Godhead, in three names, and this God is all things.

Proclus gives us the following as one of the verses of Orpheus :

Ζευς βασιλευς, Ζευς αυτος απαντων αρχιγενεθλος·
'Εν κρατος, ἱις δαιμων γενετο μεγας αρχος απαντων.

Jupiter is the king, Jupiter himself is the original source of all things ; there is one power, one god, and one great ruler over all.[1]　But we have seen that Jupiter and all the other Gods were but names for the Sun ; therefore it follows that the Sun, either as emblem or as God himself, was the object of universal adoration.

The Heathens, even in the later days of their idolatry, were not so gross in their notions, but that they believed there was only one supreme God.　They did, indeed, worship a multitude of deities, but they supposed all but one, to be subordinate deities.　They always had a notion of one deity superior to all the powers of heaven, and all the other deities were conceived to have different offices or ministrations under him—being appointed to preside over elements, over cities, over countries, and to dispense victory to armies, health, life, and other blessings to their favourites, if permitted by the Supreme Power.　Hesiod supposes one God to be the Father of the other deities ;

—— Θεων Πατηρ ηδε και Ανδρων·

and Homer, in many passages of the Iliad, represents one Supreme Deity as presiding over all the others ;[2] and the most celebrated of their philosophers always endeavoured to assert this theology.[3]

5. Dr. Shuckford has shewn that the Egyptians originally worshiped the Supreme God, under the name of Cneph, affirming him to be without beginning or end.　Philo Biblius says, that they represented him by the figure of a serpent with the head of a hawk, in the middle of a circle—certainly a very mythological emblem ; but then he represents them to have given to this Being all the attributes of the Supreme God the Creator, incorruptible and eternal.　Porphyry calls him τον Δημιεργον, the Maker or Creator of the universe.[4]

The opinion entertained by Porphyry may be judged of from the following extract :

" We will sacrifice," says he, " but in a manner that is proper, bringing choice victims with the
" choicest of our faculties ; burning and offering to God, who, as a wise man observed, is above
" all—nothing sensual : for nothing is joined to matter, which is not impure ; and, therefore,
" incongruous to a nature free from the contagion belonging to matter ; for which reason, neither
" speech, which is produced by the voice, nor even internal or mental language, if it be infected
" with any disorder of the mind, is proper to be offered to God ; but we worship God with an
" unspotted silence, and the most pure thoughts of his nature."[5]

---

[1] Maurice, Ind. Ant. Vol. IV. p. 704.

[2] Vide Iliad, vii. ver. 202, viii. vers. 5—28, &c.　See also Virgil, Æn., ii. ver. 777.

—— non hæc sine numine Divûm
Eveniunt : non te huic comitem asportare Creüsam
Fas, aut ille sinit superi regnator Olympi.

Jupiter is here supposed to be the numen divûm, and his will to be the fas or fate, which no one might contradict : Fatum est, says Cicero, non id quod superstitiosè sed quod physicè dictum causa æterna rerum. De Divin. L. i. C. xxxv.　Deum—interdum necessitatem appellant, quia nihil aliter possit atque ab eo constitutem sit.　Id. Academ. Quæst. L. iv. C. xliv.

[3] Cic. in lib. de Nat. Deorum, in Acad. Quæst. L. i. C. vii., Ibid. C. xxxiv. ; Plato de Legib. L. x. in Phil. in Cratyl. &c. ; Aristot. L. de Mundo, C vi. ; Plutarch de Placit. Philos. L. i. ; Id. in lib. de E. I. apud Delphos, p. 393.　See Shuckford, B. ix. Vol. II. p. 394.

[4] Plut. de Iside and Osiride, p. 359 ; and Euseb. Præp. Evan. L. i. C. x. ; Shuckford Con. B. v. p. 312.

[5] Val. Col. Vol. III. p. 466.

Shuckford says, " But if we look into Italy we not only find in general that the writers of their " antiquities[1] remark, that their ancient deities were of a different sort from those of Greece, but " according to Plutarch,[2] Numa, the second King of Rome, made express orders against the use of " images in the worship of the Deity; nay, he says further, that the first 170 years after the " building of the city, the Romans used no images, but thought the Deity invisible, and reputed " it unlawful to make representations of him from things of an inferior nature; so that, according " to this account, Rome being built about A. M. 3256,[3] the inhabitants were not greatly corrupted " in their religion, even so late as A. M. 3426, which falls when Nebuchadnezzar was King of " Babylon, and about 169 years after the time where I am to end this work. It is remarkable " that Plutarch does not represent Numa as correcting or refining the ancient idolatry of Italy; " but expresses, that this people never had these grosser deities, either before or for the " first 170 years of their city; so that it is more than probable, that Greece was not thus cor- " rupted when the Pelasgi removed from thence into Italy: and further, that the Trojans were " not such idolaters at the destruction of their city, because, according to this account, Æneas " neither brought with him images into Italy, nor such Gods as were worshiped by the adoration " of images; and, therefore, Pausanias,[4] who imagined that Æneas carried the Palladium into " Italy, was as much mistaken as the men of Argus, who affirmed themselves to have it in their. " city.[5] The times of Numa are about 200 years after Homer, and very probably the idolatry so " much celebrated in his writings might by this time begin to appear in Italy, and thereby " occasion Numa to make laws and constitutions against it."[6]

After the above observations, Shuckford goes on to assert, in a style rather democratical for a Doctor of Divinity, that the first corruptions of religion were begun by kings and rulers of nations! And he produces several examples to support his assertion, which are not much in point. If he had said, that these corruptions had been produced by the knavery of his own order, the priests, working upon the timidity and weakness of timid and weak kings, and making them its tools, he would have been perfectly correct. For this is the mode by which half the miseries of mankind have been produced by this pernicious order of men. And when he says that the inhabitants of *Italy* were not greatly corrupted, he goes too far; he ought to have confined his observations to the Romans. But perhaps to them only he alluded.

6. The Chinese, with all their apparent idolatry, had only one God.

Speaking of the religion of the Chinese, Sir W. Jones[7] says, " Of the religious opinions enter- " tained by Confucius and his followers, we may glean a general notion from the fragments of " their works, translated by Couplet: they professed a firm belief in the Supreme God, and gave " a demonstration of his being and of his providence, from the exquisite beauty and perfection of " the celestial bodies, and the wonderful order of nature in the whole fabric of the visible world. " From this belief they deduced a system of ethics, which the philosopher sums up in a few words " at the close of the Lunyn. He" (says Confucius) " who shall be fully persuaded that the " Lord of Heaven governs the universe, who shall in all things choose moderation, who shall " perfectly know his own species, and so act among them, that his life and manners may conform " to his knowledge of God and man, may be truly said to discharge all the duties of a sage, and to " be exalted above the common herd of the human race!"

Marco Paulo[8] informs us, that in his time the Chinese paid their adoration to a tablet fixed against the wall in their houses, upon which was inscribed the name of the high, celestial, and

---

[1] Dionys. Haliear., Lib. vii.   [2] In Numa, and Clem. Alexand. Stromat. Lib. i.   [3] Usher's Annals.
[4] In Corinthiacis.   [5] Ibid.   [6] Shuckford Con. B. v. p. 352, 8vo. Ed.
[7] Diss. VII. p. 227.   [8] B. ii. Ch. xxvi. Ed. of W. Marsden, 4to.

supreme God; to whose honour they burnt incense, but of whom they had no image. The words, Mr. Marsden says, which were on the tablet were three, *tien,* heaven; *hoang-tien,* supreme heaven; and *Shang-ti,* sovereign Lord. De Guignes tells us, that the word *tien* stands indifferently for the visible heaven and the Supreme Deity.[1] Marco Paulo tells us, that from the God whose name was on the tablet the Chinese only petition for two things, *sound intellect* and *health of body,* but that they had another God, of whom they had a statue or idol called *Natigai,* who was the God of all terrestrial things; in fact, God, the Creator of this world, (inferior or subordinate to the Supreme Being,) from whom they petition for fine weather, or whatever else they want,—a sort of Mediator. Here is evidently a striking similarity to the doctrines of some of the early Christian heretics.

It seems pretty clear from this account, that originally, and probably at this time also, like all the ancients of the West in the midst of their degrading idolatry, they yet acknowledged one Supreme God, with many subordinate agents, precisely the same as the Heathens of Greece and Rome, and modern Christians, under the names of inferior gods, angels, demons, saints, &c. In fact they were Deists.

7. In addition to the authorities which have been produced to prove that the whole of the different Gods of antiquity resolve themselves at last, when properly examined, into different names of the God Sol, it would be easy, if it were necessary, to produce as many more from every quarter of the world; but what, it may be asked, will you do with the Goddesses? The reader shall now see; and first from the learned and Rev. Mr. Maurice.

" Whoever will read the Geeta with attention will perceive in that small tract the outlines of " nearly all the various systems of theology in Asia. That curious and ancient doctrine of the " Creator being both male and female, mentioned in a preceding page to be designated in Indian " temples by a very indecent exhibition of the masculine and feminine organs of generation in " union, occurs in the following passages : ' I am the *father* and *mother* of this world; I plant myself " upon my own nature, and create again and again this assemblage of beings ; I am generation " and dissolution, the place where all things are deposited, and the inexhaustible seed of all " nature ; I am the beginning, the middle, and the end of all things.' " In another part he more directly says, " The great Brahme is the womb of all those various forms which are conceived in " every natural womb, and I am the father that soweth the seed.' "[2] Herodotus informs us that the Persian Mithras was the same with the Assyrian Venus Mylitta or Urania, and the Arabian Alitta.[3] Mr. Cudworth shews that this must have been the Aphrodita Urania, by which was meant the creating Deity. It is well known that the Venus Aphrodite was a Phœnician Deity, worshiped particularly at Citium, and was of both the male and female gender,—the Venus Genitrix.

Proclus describes Jupiter, in one of the Orphic Hymns, to be both male and female, αρρενοθηλυν, Hermaphroditic. And Bishop Synesius adopts it in a Christian hymn.[4] The Priapus of the Etruscans was both male and female. (See Table LVIII. of Gorius.) He has the membrum virile, with the female breasts.

Damascius, treating of the fecundity of the Divine Nature, cites Orpheus as teaching, that the Deity was at once both male and female, αρσενοθηλυν αυτην υπεςησατο, προς ενδειξιν των παντων γεννητικης σσιας, to shew the generative power by which all things were formed. Proclus, upon the Timæus of Plato, cites the following :

Ζευς αρσην γενετο, Ζευς αμβροτος επλετο νυμφη·

Jupiter is a man ; Jupiter is also an immortal maid. And in the same commentary, and the same page, we read that all things were contained εν γαςερι Ζηνος, in the womb of Jupiter.

[1] Tom. II. p. 350.　　[2] Maurice Ind. Ant. Vol. IV. p. 705.　　[3] Hyde de Rel. Pers. Cap. iii. p. 95.　　[4] Ubi sup. p. 304.

8. Manichæus, according to Theodoret, said, in his allegorical language, " That a male-virgin " gave light and life to Eve," that is, created her. And the Pseudo-Mercurius Trismegistus in Pæmander said, that God being male and female, (αρρενοθηλυς ων,) because he is light and life, engendered by the word another intelligence, which was the Creator. The male-virgin, Theodoret says, was called Joel, or Ιωηλ, which Beausobre thinks was " EL, God, and Joha, life-making, " vivifying, life-giving, or the generating God." (So far my friend Beverley.) But which was probably merely the יהו Ieu, אל al, or God Iao, of which we shall treat hereafter. Again, Mr. Beverley says, " In Genesis it is written, ' God said, Let us create man after our own image and " likeness.' This, then, ought in strictness of language to be a male and female God, or else it " would not be after the likeness proposed."

" The male-virgin of the Orientals is, I know, considered the same by Plato as his Ἑϛια, or " Vesta, whom he calls the soul of the body of the universe. This Hestia, by the way, is in my " view a Sanscrit lady, whose name I take to have been EST, or she that is, or exists, having " the same meaning as the great name of the Jewish Deity. Est is shewn in the Celtic Druids to " be a Sanscrit word, and I do not doubt of this her derivation. The A terminal is added by the " Greek idiom to denote a female, as they hated an indeclinable proper name, such as HEST or " EST would have been." Extract from a letter from Makenzie Beverley, Esq.[1]

Apuleius makes the mother of the Gods of the masculine gender, and represents her describing herself as called Minerva at Athens, Venus at Cyprus, Diana at Crete, Proserpine in Sicily, Ceres at Eleusis: in other places, Juno, Bellona, Hecate, Isis, &c.;[2] and if any doubt could remain, the philosopher Porphyry, than whom probably no one was better skilled in these matters, removes it by acknowledging that Vesta, Rhea, Ceres, Themis, Priapus, Proserpine, Bacchus, Attis, Adonis, Silenus, and the Satyrs, were all the same.[3]

Valerius Soranus calls Jupiter the mother of the Gods:

> Jupiter omnipotens, Regum Rex ipse Deûmque
> Progenitor, Genetrixque Deûm ; Deus et idem.

Synesius speaks of him in the same manner :

> Συ Πατηρ, συ δ'εσσι Μητηρ,
> Συ δ'αρσην, συ δε θηλυς.[4]

The like character is also given to the ancient deity Μητις, or Divine Wisdom, by which the world was framed :

> Μητις-ερμηνευεται, Βαλη, Φως, Ζωοδοτηρ.[5]
> Αρσην μεν και θηλυς εφυς, πολυωνυμε Μητι.[6]

And in two of the Orphic Fragments all that has been said above seems to be comprehended. This Deity, like the others, is said to be of two genders, and to be also the Sun.[7]

Μητις, Mr. Bryant says, is a masculine name for a feminine deity,[8] and means Divine Wisdom. I suspect it was a corruption of the Maia or Mia of India.

In Cyprus, Venus is represented with a beard, and called Aphrodite.[9]

Calvus, the poet, calls her masculine, as does also Macrobius.[10]

---

[1] The A at the end of the word EST may be the Chaldee emphatic article; then Vesta would be the EST or the Self-existent.
[2] Apuleii Metamorph. L. ii. p. 241.     [3] Porphyry ap. Eusebium, Evan. Præp. L. iii. C. xi.
[4] Bryant, Anal. Vol. I. p. 315.     [5] Orpheus, Eusebii Chronicon.     [6] Orphic Hymn, xxxi. 10, p. 224.
[7] Bryant, Vol. I. p. 204. Ed. 4to.     [8] Bryant, Anal. Vol. II. p. 25.
[9] Hesychius Servius upon Virgil's Æneid, L. ii. 632.     [10] Satur. L. iii. C. viii.

Jupiter is called feminine, and the genetrixque Deûm,[1] by Augustine.

The Orphic verses make the Moon both male and female.[2]

9. The following extract from Sir W. Jones's Dissertation on the Gods of Greece and India, will, perhaps, be of some weight with the very large class of mankind, who prefer authority to reason ; and may serve to justify or excuse the opinions here expressed, by shewing them that they are neither new nor unsupported : " We must not be surprised at finding, on a close examination, " that the characters of all the Pagan Deities, male and female, melt into each other, and at last " into one or two ; for it seems a well founded opinion, that the whole crowd of Gods and God- " desses in ancient Rome and modern Vâránes, mean only the powers of nature, and principally " those of the *Sun*, expressed in a variety of ways, and by a multitude of fanciful names."

In a future part of this work I shall have much more to say of the Goddesses or the female generative power, which became divided from the male, and in consequence was the cause of great wars and miseries to the Eastern parts of the world, and of the rise of a number of sects in the Western, which have not been at all understood.

Thus, we see, there is in fact an end of all the multitude of the Heathen Gods and Goddesses, so disguised in the Pantheons and books of various kinds, which the priests have published from time to time to instil into the minds of their pupils—that the ancient Heathen philosophers and legislators were the slaves of the most degrading superstition ; that they believed such nonsense as the metamorphoses described by Ovid, or the loves of Jupiter, Venus, &c., &c. That the rabble were the victims of a degrading superstition, I have no doubt. This was produced by the knavery of the ancient priests, and it is in order to reproduce this effect that the modern priests have misrepresented the doctrines of their predecessors. By vilifying and running down the religion of the ancients, they have thought they could persuade their votaries that their new religion was *necessary* for the good of mankind : a religion which, in consequence of their corruptions, has been found to be in practice much worse and more injurious to the interests of society than the old one. For, from these corruptions the Christian religion—the religion of purity and truth when uncorrupted—*has not brought peace but a sword.*

After the astrologers had parcelled out the heavens into the forms of animals, &c., and the annual path of the Sun had become divided into twelve parts, each part designated by some animal, or other figure, or known emblem, it is not surprising that they should have become the objects of adoration. This M. Dupuis has shewn,[3] was the origin of the Arabian and Egyptian adoration of animals, birds, &c. Hence, in the natural progress of events, the adoration of images arose among the Heathens and Christians.

10. The same tolerating spirit generally prevailed among the votaries of the Heathen Gods of the *Western world*, which we find among the Christian saints. For though in some few instances the devotees in Egypt quarrelled about their Gods, as in some few instances the natives of Christian towns have quarrelled about their Divi or tutelar saints, yet these petty wars never created much mischief.[4] They were evidently no ways dangerous to the emoluments of the priests, and therefore they were not attended with very important consequences.

A great part of the uncertainty and apparent contradictions which we meet with in the history of the religions of antiquity, evidently arises from the inattention of the writers to the changes which long periods of time produce.

It is directly contrary to the law of nature for any thing to remain stationary. The law of

---

[1] August. de Civit. Dei, L. iv. C. xi. and L. vii. C. ix.                    [2] Hymn viii. 4.
[3] Ch. i. Rel. Univ.
[4] See Mosheim, who shews that the religious wars of the Egyptians were not like those of the Christians.

perpetual motion is universal; we know of no such thing as absolute rest. Causes over which man has no controul overturn and change his wisest institutions. Monuments of folly and of wisdom, all, all crumble into dust. The Pyramids of Egypt, and the codes of the Medes or of Napoleon, all will pass away and be forgotten.

M. Dupuis, in his first chapter, has shewn that probably all nations first worshiped, as we are told the Persians did, without altars or temples, in groves and high places. After a certain number of years, in Persia, came temples and idols, with all their abuses ; and these, in their turn, were changed or abolished, and the worship of the Sun restored, or perhaps the worship of the Sun only as emblem of the Creator. This was probably the change said to have been effected by Zoroaster.

The Israelites at the *exodus* had evidently run into the worship of Apis the Bull, or the Golden Calf of Egypt, which it was the object of Moses to abolish, and in the place thereof to substitute the worship of one God—*Iao*, Jehovah—which, in fact, was only the Sun or the Solar Fire, yet not the Sun, as Creator, but as emblem of or the shekinah of the Divinity. The Canaanites, according to the Mosaic account, were not idolaters in the time of Abraham; but it is implied that they became so in the long space between the time he lived and that of Moses. The Assyrians seem to have become idolaters early, and not, as the Persians, to have had any reformer like Zoroaster or Moses, but to have continued till the Iconoclasts, Cyrus and Darius, reformed them with fire and sword; as their successor Cambyses soon afterward did the Egyptians. The observations made on the universality of the solar worship, contain but very little of what might be said respecting it; but yet enough is said to establish the fact. If the reader wish for more, his curiosity will be amply repaid by a perusal of Mr. Bryant's Analysis of the Heathen Mythology. He may also read the fourth chapter of Cudworth's Intellectual System, which is a most masterly performance.

---

# CHAPTER IV.

TWO ANCIENT ETHIOPIAS.—GREAT BLACK NATION IN ASIA.—THE BUDDHA OF INDIA A NEGRO.—THE ARABIANS WERE CUSHITES.—MEMNON.—SHEPHERD KINGS.—HINDOOS AND EGYPTIANS SIMILAR.— SYRIA PEOPLED FROM INDIA.

1. In taking a survey of the human inhabitants of the world, we find two classes, distinguished from each other by a clear and definite line of demarkation, the *black* and *white* colours of their skins. This distinguishing mark we discover to have existed in ages the most remote. If we suppose them all to have descended from one pair, the question arises, Was that pair *black* or *white?* If I were at present to say that I thought them black, I should be accused of a fondness for paradox, and I should find as few persons to agree with me, as the African negroes do when they tell Europeans that the Devil is *white.* (And yet no one, except a West-India planter, will deny that the poor Africans have reason on their side.) However, I say not that they were *black,* but I shall, in the course of this work, produce a number of extraordinary facts, which will be quite sufficient to prove, that a black race, in very early times, had more influence over the affairs of the world than has been lately suspected; and I think I shall shew, by some very striking circumstances yet existing, that the effects of this influence have not entirely passed away.

2. It was the opinion of *Sir William Jones*, that a great nation of Blacks[1] formerly possessed the dominion of Asia, and held the seat of empire at Sidon.[2] These must have been the people called by Mr. Maurice Cushites or Cuthites, described in Genesis; and the opinion that they were Blacks is corroborated by the translators of the Pentateuch, called the Seventy, constantly rendering the word *Cush* by Ethiopia. It is very certain that, if this opinion be well founded, we must go for the time when this empire flourished to a period anterior to all our regular histories. It can only be known to have existed from accidental circumstances, which have escaped amidst the ruins of empires and the wrecks of time.

Of this nation we have no account; but it must have flourished after the deluge. And, as our regular chronological systems fill up the time between the flood and what is called known, undoubted history; if it be allowed to have existed, its existence will of course prove that no dependence can be placed on the early parts of that history. It will shew that all the early chronology is false; for the story of this empire is not told. It is certain that its existence can only be known from insulated circumstances, collected from various quarters, and combining to establish the fact. But if I succeed in collecting a sufficient number to carry conviction to an impartial mind, the empire must be allowed to have existed.

3. The religion of Buddha, of India, is well known to have been very ancient. In the most ancient temples scattered throughout Asia, where his worship is yet continued, he is found *black as jet*, with the flat face, thick lips, and curly hair of the Negro. Several statues of him may be met with in the Museum of the East-India Company. There are two exemplars of him brooding on the face of the deep, upon a coiled serpent. To what time are we to allot this Negro? He will be proved to have been prior to the god called Cristna. He must have been prior to or contemporaneous with the black empire, supposed by Sir William Jones to have flourished at Sidon. The religion of this Negro God is found, by the ruins of his temples and other circumstances, to have been spread over an immense extent of country, even to the remotest parts of Britain, and to have been professed by devotees inconceivably numerous. I very much doubt whether Christianity *at this day* is professed by more persons than yet profess the religion of Buddha. Of this I shall say more hereafter.

4. When several cities, countries, or rivers, at great distances from each other, are found to be called by the same name, the coincidence cannot be attributed to accident, but some specific cause for such an effect must be looked for. Thus we have several cities call Heliopolis, or the city of the Sun; the reason for which is sufficiently obvious. Thus, again, there were several Alexandrias; and on close examination we find two Ethiopias alluded to in ancient history—one above the higher or southern part of Egypt, and the other somewhere to the east of it, and, as it has been thought, in Arabia. The people of this latter are called Cushim in the Hebrew text of the Old Testament, and Ethiopians by the text of the Septuagint, or the Seventy. That they cannot have been the Ethiopians of Africa is evident from a single passage,[3] where they are said to have invaded Judah in the days of Asa, under Zerah, their king or leader. But the Lord smote the Cushim; and Asa and the people that were with him pursued them unto Gerar; and the Ethiopians were overthrown, and they (i. e. Asa and his people) smote all the cities round about Gerar, &c. Whence it plainly follows, that the Cushim here mentioned, were such as inhabited the parts adjoining to Gerar, and consequently not any part of the African Ethiopia, but Arabia.

---

[1] I do not use the word Negro, because they MAY not have been *Negroes* though *Blacks*, though it is probable that they were so; and I wish the distinction to be remembered.

[2] But why should not Babylon have been the place?          [3] 2 Chron. xiv. 9—15.

When it is said that Asa smote the Cushites or Ethiopians, in number a million of soldiers, as far as Gerar, and despoiled all the cities round about, it is absurd to suppose that the Gerar in the lot of the tribe of Simeon is meant.   The expression all the cities and the million of men cannot apply to the little town of that tribe.   Probably the city in Wilkinson's Atlas, in the *Tabula Orientalis*, at the side of the Persian gulf, which is called Gerra, is the city meant by the word Gerar; and, that Saba was near where it is placed by Dr. Stukeley, or somewhere in the Peninsula, now called Arabia.

In 2 Chron. xxi. 16, it is said, *And of the Arabians that were near the Ethiopians*.   This again shews that the Ethiopians were in the Peninsula, or bordered on it to the eastwards.   They could not have lived to the west, because the whole land of Egypt lay between them, if they went by land; and the Red Sea lay between the two nations westwards.

In Habakkuk iii. 7, the words Midian and Cushan are used as synonymes: *I saw the tents of Cushan in affliction : the curtains of the land of Midian did tremble.*

It is said in Numbers xii. 1, " *And Miriam and Aaron spake against Moses, because of the Ethiopian woman whom he had married;* for he had married an Ethiopian woman."  כשית *cusit*.   It appears that this Ethiopian woman was the daughter of Jethro, priest of Midian, near Horeb, in Arabia.[1]

5. Dr. Wells has justly observed, that the Cush spoken of in scripture is evidently Arabia, from Numbers xii. 1, just cited; and that it is also certain, from Exod. ii. 15—21, that the wife of Moses was a Midianitish woman; and it is proved that Midian or Madian was in Arabia, from Exod. iii. 1, &c.: consequently the Cush here spoken of, and called Ethiopia, must necessarily mean Arabia.   He also proves, from Ezek. xxix. 10, that when God says he " will make the land " desolate from the tower of Syene to the borders of Ethiopia," *Cush,* he cannot mean an African Cush, because he evidently means from one boundary of Egypt to the other : and as Syene is the southern boundary between the African Ethiopia and Egypt, it cannot possibly be that he speaks of the former, but of the other end of Egypt, which is Arabia.

The circumstance of the translators of the Septuagint version of the Pentateuch having rendered the word Cush by the word Ethiopia, is a very decisive proof that the theory of two Ethiopias is well founded.   Let the translators have been who they may, it is totally impossible to believe that they could be so ignorant as to suppose that the African Ethiopia could border on the Euphrates, or that the Cushites could be African Ethiopians.

From all the accounts which modern travellers give of the country above Syene, there does not appear, either from ruins or any other circumstance, reason to believe that it was ever occupied by a nation strong enough to fight the battles and make the great figure in the world which we know the people called Cushites or Ethiopians did at different times.   The valley of the Nile is very narrow, not capable of containing a great and powerful people.   Sheba and Saba were either one or two cities of the Cushites or Ethiopians, and Pliny says, that the Sabæans extended from the Red Sea to the Persian Gulf, thus giving them the whole of Arabia; one part of which, it is well known, is called from its fertility of soil and salubrity of climate, Felix, or The Happy.

---

[1] Vide Exod. ch. ii. and iii.   It is not to be supposed that this great tribe of Israelites had not laws before those given on Sinai.   It is perfectly clear that great numbers of those in Leviticus were only re-enactments of old laws or customs.   The marriage of Moses with an Ethiopian woman, against which Miriam and Aaron spoke, was a breach of the law, and the children were illegitimate.   This was the reason why Aaron succeeded to the priestly office, instead of the sons of Moses.   This also furnishes an answer to what a learned author has written about the disinterested conduct of Moses proving his divine mission.   The conduct of Moses, in this instance, proves nothing, and all the labour of the learned gentleman has been thrown away.   But Moses had two wives, both Ethiopians—one of Meroe, called Tharbis, and the other of Midian, in Arabia.  Josephus' Antiq. L. ii. ch. x.

Dr. Wells states, that the Ethiopians of Africa alone are commonly called *Ludim,* both by ancient and modern writers.[1]

But the country east of the Euphrates was called Cush, as well as the country west of it; thus giving the capital of Persia, Susan or Susiana, which was said to be built by Memnon, to the Cushites or Ethiopians, as well as Arabia.

Mr. Frey, in his vocabulary, gives the word כוש, *cus,* as a word whose meaning is unknown; but the Septuagint tells us it meant *black.* Mr. Hyde shews, that it was a common thing for the Chaldeans to substitute the Tau for the Shin, thus כות *cut,* for כוש *cus.* Thus, in their dialect, the Cuthites were the same as the Cushites.

If my reader will examine all the remaining passages of the Old Testament, not cited by me, where the words Ethiopia and Ethiopians are used, he will see that many of them can by no possibility relate to the African Ethiopia.

6. Eusebius[2] states the Ethiopians to have come and settled in Egypt, in the time of Amenophis. According to this account, as well as to the account given by Philostratus,[3] there was no such country as Ethiopia beyond Egypt until this invasion. According to Eusebius these people came from the river Indus, and planted themselves to the south of Egypt, in the country called from them Ethiopia. The circumstance named by Eusebius that they came from the Indus, at all events, implies that they came from the East, and not from the South, and would induce a person to suspect them of having crossed the Red Sea from Arabia: they must either have done this, or have come round the northern end of the Red Sea by the Isthmus of Suez; but they certainly could not have come from the present Ethiopia.

But there are several passages in ancient writers which prove that Eusebius is right in saying, not only that they came from the East, but from a very distant or very eastern part.

Herodotus[4] says, that there were two Ethiopian nations, one in India, the other in Egypt. He derived his information from the Egyptian priests, a race of people who must have known the truth; and there seems no reason either for them or Herodotus to have mis-stated the fact.

Philostratus[5] says, that the Gymnosophists of Ethiopia, who settled near the sources of the Nile, descended from the Bramins of India, having been driven thence for the murder of their king.[6] This, Philostratus says, he learnt from an ancient Brahmin, called Jarchas.

Another ancient writer, Eustathius, also states, that the Ethiopians came from India. These concurring accounts can scarcely be doubted; and here may be discovered the mode and time also when great numbers of ancient rites and ceremonies might be imported from India into Egypt: for, that there was a most intimate relation between them in very ancient times cannot be doubted; indeed, it is not doubted. The only question has been, whether Egypt borrowed from India, or India from Egypt. All probability is clearly, for a thousand reasons, in favour of the superior antiquity of India, as Bailly and many other learned men have shewn—a probability which seems to be reduced to a certainty by Herodotus, the Egyptians themselves, and the other authors just now quoted. There is not a particle of proof, from any historical records known to the author, that any colony ever passed from Egypt to India, but there is, we see, direct, positive historical evidence, of the Indians having come to Africa. No attention can be paid to the idle stories of the conquest of India by Bacchus, who was merely an imaginary personage, in short, the God Sol.

Dr. Shuckford gives an opinion that Homer and Herodotus are both right, and that there were two Ethiopias, and that the Africans came from India.[7]

---

[1] Wells, Vol. I. p. 200.      [2] In Chron. ad Num. 402.      [3] In vita Apollon. Tyanei.
[4] L. vii. C. lxx.      [5] Vita Apoll. C. vi.      [6] Crawford, Res. Vol. II. p. 193.      [7] B. ix. p. 334.

7. The Bishop of Avranches thinks he has found three provinces of the name of *Chus;* Ethiopia, Arabia, and Susiana.[1] There were three Ethiopias, that is, countries of Blacks, not three *Chusses;* and this is perfectly consistent with what M. Bochart[2] has maintained, that Ethiopia (of Africa) is not named Chus in any place of scripture; and this is also consistent with what is said by both Homer and Herodotus.[3] The bishop shews clearly, that the ancient Susiana is the modern *Chuzestan* or Elam, of which Susa was the capital. The famous Memnon, probably the Sun, was said to be the son of Aurora. But Eschylus informs us, that Cissiene was the mother of Memnon, and to him the foundation of Susa is attributed; and its citadel was called Memnonium, and itself the city of Memnon. This is the Memnon who was said to have been sent to the siege of Troy, and to have been slain by Achilles; and who was also said, by the ancient authors, to be an Ethiopian or a Black. It seems the Egyptians suppose that this Memnon was their king Amenophis. The Ethiopians are stated by Herodotus to have come from the Indus; according to what modern chronologers deduce from his words, about the year 1615 B. C., about four hundred years after the birth of Abraham, in (1996,) and about a hundred years before Moses rebelled against the Egyptians and brought the Israelites out of Egypt. Palaces were shewn which belonged to this Memnon at Thebes and other places in Egypt, as well as at Susa, which from him were called in both places Memnoniums; and to him was erected the famous statue at Thebes, which is alleged to have given out a sound when first struck by the rays of the morning sun. Bishop Huet thinks, (probably very correctly,) that this statue was made in imitation of similar things which the Jewish traveller Rabbi Benjamin found, in the country where the descendants of Chus adore the sun; and this he shews to be the country of which we speak. It lies about Bussora, where the Sabeans are found in the greatest numbers, and who are the people of whom he speaks.

The bishop thinks this Memnon cannot have been Amenophis, because he lived very many years before the siege of Troy, in which he is said to have been an actor. It seems to me to be as absurd to look to Homer or Virgil for the chronology of *historical facts,* as to Shakespeare, Milton, or any other epic poet. These poems *may* state facts, but nothing of a historical or chronological kind can be received without some collateral evidence in confirmation. It never was supposed to be incumbent on any epic poet to tie himself down to mere historical matters of fact. And wherever it is evident, either from the admission of a later historical author or from any other circumstance, that he is relating facts from the works of the poets without any other authority, he can be as little depended upon as they can.

The bishop has shewn that the accounts of modern authors, George Syncellus, Suidas, Pausanias, Dionysius *Periegites,* &c., &c., are full of contradictions; that they are obliged to suppose two Memnons. All this arises from these persons treating the poem of Homer as a history, instead of a poem. *We shall never have an ancient history worthy of the perusal of men of common sense, till we cease treating poems as history, and send back such personages as Hercules, Theseus, Bacchus, &c., to the heavens, whence their history is taken, and whence they never descended to the earth.*

It is not meant to be asserted that these epic poems may not be of great use to a historian. It is only meant to protest against their being held as authority by themselves, when opposed either to other histories or to known chronology. This case of Memnon is in point. Homer wanted a hero to fill up his poem; and, without any regard to date, or any thing wrong in so doing, he accommodated the history to his poem, making use of Amenophis or Memnon, or the religious tradition whichever it was, as he thought proper. These poems may also be of great

---

[1] Diss. on Parod. Ch. xiii.　　　　[2] Phaleg. L. iv. C. ii.

[3] Homer, Odyss. á; Herod. Polymn. Cap. lxix. lxx.; also Steph. in ʽΟμηρίται.

use as evidence of the customs and manners of the times, both of when they were written and previously, and very often of dry unconnected facts which may turn out to be of consequence. Thus Virgil makes Memnon *black*,[1] as does also Pindar.[2] That Pindar and Virgil were right, the features of the bust of Memnon in the British Museum prove, for they are evidently those of the Negro.

8. It is probable that the Memnon here spoken of, if there ever were such a man, was the leader of the Shepherds, who are stated by Manetho and other historians to have come from the East, and to have conquered Egypt. The learned Dr. Shuckford thinks, that the troubles caused in Egypt by the shepherd kings appear to have happened about the time the Jews left it under Moses. He places these events between the death of Joseph and the birth of Moses.[3] And he supposes that the Jews left the country in consequence of the oppressions of these shepherd kings. It is very clear that much confusion has arisen in this part of ancient history from these eastern shepherds having been confounded with the Israelites, and also from facts relating to the one having been attributed to the other. Josephus takes the different accounts to relate to the same people. This is attended with great difficulty. The shepherds are said by Manetho, after a severe struggle with the old inhabitants, to have taken refuge in a city called Avaris or Abaris,[4] where they were a long time besieged, and whence at last they departed, two hundred and forty thousand in number, together with their wives and children, (in consequence of a capitulation,) into the deserts of Syria.

If there were two races of people who have been confounded together, one of which came from India and overran Arabia, Palestine, and Egypt, and brought thence its religion to the Egyptians, and was in colour black, it must have come in a very remote period. This may have been the race of shepherd kings, of whom Josephus speaks when he says, they oppressed the Israelites : but the assertion of Josephus can hardly have been true, for they must have been expelled long before the Israelites came. The second race were the Arabian shepherd tribe called captives, who, after being settled some time in the land of Goshen, were driven or went out into the open country of Arabia. They at last, under the command of Joshua, conquered Palestine, and finally settled there. Bishop Cumberland has proved that there was a dynasty of Phenician shepherd kings, who were driven out three hundred years before Moses. These seem to have been the black or Ethiopian, Phenician Memnonites. They may have exactly answered to this description, but to his date of three hundred years I pay no attention, further than that it was a great length of time.

Josephus says that the copies of Manetho differed, that in one the Shepherds were called *Captives*, not *kings*, and that he thinks this is more agreeable to ancient history; that Manetho also says, the nation called Shepherds were likewise called Captives in their sacred books; and that after they were driven out of Egypt, they journied through the wilderness of Syria, and built a city in Judea, which they called Jerusalem.[5]

Josephus[6] says, that Manetho was an Egyptian by birth, but that he understood Greek, in which he wrote his history, translating it from the old Egyptian records.

If the author understand Mr. Faber rightly in his Horæ Mosaicæ,[7] he is of opinion that these

---

[1] Æneid, Lib. i.      [2] Olymp. Od. ii.; vide Diss. of Bishop Huet, ch. xiii. p. 185.

[3] Shuckford, Conn. pp. 233, 234.

[4] We read of a person coming from the Hyperboreans to Greece, in the time of Pythagoras, called Abaris or Avaris. Josephus also tells us that the city in the Saite Nomos, (Seth-roite,) i. e. *Goshen*, where the oriental Shepherds resided, was called Avaris. Now I suspect that this man was called from the Hebrew word עבהר *ober*, as was also the name of the city, and that they both meant stranger or foreigner : the same as the tribe of Abraham, in Syria.

[5] Jos. vers. Apion, B. i. § xiv., Whiston, p. 291.      [6] Ut sup. § xiv.      [7] Ch. ii. Sect. xi. p. 23.

Shepherd Captives were the Israelites. The accounts of these two tribes of people are confused, as may naturally be expected, but there are certainly many striking traits of resemblance between them. Mr. Shuckford, with whom in this Mr. Volney agrees, thinks there were two races of Shepherd kings, and in this opinion he coincides with most of the ancients; but most certainly, in his treatise against Apion, Josephus only names one.[1] We shall have much to say hereafter respecting these shepherds, under the name of Palli.

The only objection which occurs against Amenophis or Memnon being the leader of the Hindoo race who first came from the Indus to Egypt is, that according to our ideas of his chronology, he could scarcely be sufficiently early to agree with the known historical records of India. But our chronology is in so very vague and uncertain a state, that very little dependance can be placed upon it. And it will never be any better till learned men search for the truth and fairly state it, instead of sacrificing it to the idle legends or allegories of the priests, which cannot by any possible ingenuity be made consistent even with themselves.

Mr. Wilsford, in his treatise on Egypt and the Nile, in the Asiatic Researches, informs us, that many very ancient statues of the God Buddha in India have crisp, curly hair, with flat noses and thick lips; and adds, " nor can it be reasonably doubted, that a race of Negroes formerly had power " and pre-eminence in India."

This is confirmed by Mr. Maurice, who says, " The figures in the Hindoo caverns are of a very " different character from the present race of Hindoos : their countenances are broad and full, the " nose flat, and the lips, particularly the under lip, remarkably thick." [2] This is again confirmed by Colonel Fitzclarence in the journal of his journey from India. And Maurice, in the first volume of his Indian Antiquities, states, that the figures in the caves in India and in the temples in Egypt, are absolutely the same as given by Bruce, Niebuhr, &c.

Justin states, that the Phœnicians being obliged to leave their native country in the East, they settled first near the Assyrian Lake, which is the Persian Gulf; and Maurice says, " We find an " extensive district, named Palestine, to the east of the Euphrates and Tigris. The word Pales-" tine seems derived from Pallisthan, the seat of the Pallis or Shepherds." [3] *Palli*, in India, means *Shepherd.*

This confirms Sir William Jones's opinion, in a striking manner, respecting a *black* race having reigned at Sidon.

9. It seems to me that great numbers of circumstances are producible, and will be produced in the following work, to prove that the mythology, &c., &c., of Egypt were derived from India, but which persons who are of a different opinion endeavour to explain away, as inconclusive proofs. They, however, produce few or no circumstances tending towards the proof of the *contrary*, viz. that India borrowed from Egypt, to enable the friends of the superior antiquity of India, in their turn, to explain away or disprove.

It is a well-known fact that our Hindoo soldiers when they arrived in Egypt, in the late war, recognized the Gods of their country in the ancient temples, particularly their God Cristna.

The striking similarity, indeed identity, of the style of architecture and the ornaments of the ancient Egytian and Hindoo temples, Mr. Maurice has proved[4] beyond all doubt. He says, " Travellers, who have visited Egypt in periods far more recent than those in which the above-" cited authors journeyed thither, confirm the truth of their relation, in regard both to the number " and extent of the excavations, the beauty of the sculptures, and their similitude to those carved " in the caverns of India. The final result, therefore, of this extended investigation is, that, in

---

[1] Jos. vers. Apion, C. i. § xiv. B. i.    [3] Maurice, Hind. Ant. Vol. II. pp. 374—376.
[2] Maurice, Hist. Vol. II. p. 146.    [4] Antiquities of Hindostan, Vol. I. Sect. viii.

I

" the remotest periods, there has existed a most intimate connexion between the two nations, and
" that colonies emigrating from Egypt to India, or from India to Egypt, transported their deities
" into the country in which they respectively took up their abode." This testimony of the Rev.
Mr. Maurice's is fully confirmed by Sir W. Jones, who says,

" The remains of architecture and sculpture in India, which I mention here as mere monuments
" of antiquity, not as specimens of ancient art, seem to prove an early connexion between this
" country and Africa : the pyramids of Egypt, the colossal statues described by Pausanias and
" others, the Sphinx, and the Hermes Canis, which last bears a great resemblance to the Varáhá-
" vatar, or the incarnation of Vishnou in the form of a Boar, indicate the style and mythology
" of the same indefatigable workmen who formed the vast excavations of Canara, the various
" temples and images of Buddha, and the idols which are continually dug up at Gayá, or in its
" vicinity. The letters on many of those monuments appear, as I have before intimated, partly
" of Indian, and partly of Abyssinian or Ethiopic, origin : and all these indubitable facts may
" induce no ill-founded opinion, that Ethiopia and Hindostan were peopled or colonized by the
" same extraordinary race ; in confirmation of which it may be added, that the mountaineers of
" Bengal and Bahar, can hardly be distinguished in some of their features, particularly their lips
" and noses, from the modern Abyssinians, whom the Arabs call the children of Cush : and the
" ancient Hindus, according to Strabo, differed in nothing from the Africans but in the straight-
" ness and smoothness of their hair, while that of the others was crisp or woolly ; a difference
" proceeding chiefly, if not entirely, from the respective humidity or dryness of their atmospheres :
" hence the people who *received the first light* of the rising sun, according to the limited knowledge
" of the ancients, are said by Apuleius to be the Arii and Ethiopians, by which he clearly meant
" certain nations of India; where we frequently see figures of Buddha with curled hair, apparently
" designed for a representation of it in its natural state." [1]

Again, Sir W. Jones says, " Mr. Bruce and Mr. Bryant have proved that the Greeks gave the
" appellation of Indians to the nations of Africa, and to the people among whom we now live." [2] I
shall account for this in the following work.

Mons. de Guignes maintains, that the inhabitants of Egypt, in very old times, had unquestionably a common origin with the old natives of India, as is fully proved by their ancient monuments, and the affinity of their languages and institutions, both political and religious. [3]

Many circumstances confirming the above, particularly with respect to the language, will be
pointed out hereafter.

10. It is curious to observe the ingenuity exercised by Sir W. Jones to get over obstacles which
oppose themselves to his theological creed, which he has previously determined nothing *shall*
persuade him to disbelieve. He says, " We are told that the Phenicians, like the Hindus, adored
" the Sun, and asserted water to be the first of created things; *nor can we doubt that Syria,*
" *Samaria, and Phenice,* or the long strip of land on the shore of the Mediterranean, *were*
" *anciently peopled by a branch of the Indian stock,* but were afterwards inhabited by that race
" which, for the present, we call Arabian." Here we see he admits that the ancient Phœnicians
were Hindoos : he then goes on to observe, that " In all three *the oldest religion* was the Assyrian,
" as it is called by Selden, and the Samaritan letters appear to have been the same at first with
" those of Phenice." [4] Now, with respect to which was the oldest religion, as their religions
were all, at the bottom, precisely the same, viz. the worship of the Sun, there is as strong a
probability that the earliest occupiers of the land, the Hindoos, were the founders of the solar
worship, as the contrary.

[1] Diss. III.-on Hind., by Sir W. Jones, p. 111.
[2] Jones's Eighth An. Diss. Asiatic Res.
[3] Diss. VII. of Sir W. Jones on the Chinese, p. 220.
[4] Sir W. Jones's Eighth An. Diss.

When the various circumstances and testimonies which have been detailed are taken into consideration, there can be scarcely any doubt left on the mind of the reader, that, by the word Ethiopia, two different countries have been meant. This seems to be perfectly clear. And it is probable that by an Ethiopian, a *negro*, correctly speaking, may have been meant, not merely a *black* person; and it seems probable that the following may have been the real fact, viz. that a race either of Negroes or Blacks, but probably of the former, came from India to the West, occupying or conquering and forming a kingdom on the two banks of the Euphrates, the eastern Ethiopia alluded to in Numbers, chap. xii.; that they advanced forwards occupying Syria, Phœnicia, Arabia, and Egypt; that they, or some tribe of them, were the shepherd kings of Egypt; that after a time the natives of Egypt rose against them and expelled part of them into Abyssinia or Ethiopia, another part of them into Idumea or Syria, or Arabia, and another part into the African desert of Lybia, where they were called Lubim.

The time at which these people came to the West was certainly long previous to the exodus of the Israelites from Egypt; but how long previous to that event must remain doubtful. No system of chronology can be admitted as evidence; every known system is attended with too many difficulties. Perhaps chronology may be allowed to instruct us, in relation to facts, as to which preceded or followed, but certainly nothing more. No chronological date can be depended on previous to the capture of Babylon by Cyrus: whether we can depend upon it quite so far back seems to admit of doubt.

Part of the ancient monuments of Egypt may have been executed by these people. The memnoniums found in Persia and in Egypt leave little room to doubt this. In favour of this hypothesis all ancient sacred and profane historical accounts agree; and poetical works of imagination cannot be admitted to compete as evidence with the works of serious historians like Herodotus. This hypothesis likewise reconciles all the accounts which at first appear discordant, but which no other will do. It is also confirmed by a considerable quantity of circumstantial evidence. It is, therefore, presumed by the writer, he may safely assume in his forthcoming discussions, that there were two Ethiopias, one to the East of the Red Sea, the other to the West of it; and that a very great nation of *blacks* from India, did rule over almost all Asia in a very remote æra, in fact beyond the reach of history or any of our records.

This and what has been observed respecting judicial astrology will be retained in recollection by my reader; they will both be found of great importance in our future inquiries. In my Essay on *The Celtic Druids*, I have shewn, that a great nation called Celtæ, of whom the Druids were the priests, spread themselves almost over the whole earth, and are to be traced in their rude gigantic monuments from India to the extremity of Britain. Who these can have been but the early individuals of the *black* nation of whom we have been treating I know not, and in this opinion I am not singular. The learned Maurice says, "Cuthites, i. e. Celts, built the great temples in India "and Britain, and excavated the caves of the former."[1] And the learned Mathematician, Reuben Burrow, has no hesitation in pronouncing Stonehenge to be a temple of the black, curly-headed Buddha.

I shall leave the further consideration of this *black* nation for the present. I shall not detain my reader with any of the numerous systems of the Hindoos, the Persians, the Chaldeans, Egyptians, or other nations, except in those particular instances which immediately relate to the object of this work,—in the course of which I shall often have occasion to recur to what I have here said, and shall also have opportunities of supporting it by additional evidence.

---

[1] Maurice, Hist. Hind. Vol. II. p. 249.

# BOOK II.

## CHAPTER I.

1. THE religion and ancient philosophy of the Chaldeans, by whom are meant the Assyrians, as given by Stanley,[1] at first view exhibit a scene of the utmost confusion. This may be attributed in part to the circumstance, that it is not the history of their religion and philosophy at any one particular æra, but that it is extended over a space of several thousand years, during which, perhaps, they might undergo many changes. To this circumstance authors have not paid sufficient attention; so that what may have been accurately described in the time of *Herodotus* may have been much changed in the time of *Porphyry*. Thus different authors appear to write in contradiction to each other, though each may have written what was strictly true at the time of which he was writing.

Under the name of the country of the Chaldeans several states have at different periods been included. It has been the same with respect to Persia. When an author speaks of Persia, sometimes Persia only is meant, sometimes Bactria, sometimes Media, sometimes all three; and Assyria is very often included with them. Here is another source of difficulty and confusion.

After the conquest of Babylon and its dependent states, the empire founded by its conquerors, the Persians, was often called, by writers of the Western part of the world, the Assyrian or Chaldean empire. In all these states or kingdoms the religion of the Persians prevailed; and the use of the indiscriminate terms, Persian, Assyrian, and Chaldean, by Porphyry, Plutarch, &c., when treating of that empire, has been the cause of much of the uncertainty respecting what was the religion of the Persians and Assyrians. Thus, when one historian says, the Chaldeans, meaning the Assyrians, worshiped the idol Moloch; and another says, they worshiped fire, as the emblem of the Deity; they are probably both correct: one assertion is true before the time of Cyrus, the other afterward.

Although it may not be possible to make out a connected and complete system, yet it will be no difficult matter to shew, that, at one particular time, the worship of the Assyrians, Chaldeans, Persians, Babylonians, was that of one Supreme God; that the Sun was worshiped as an emblem only of the divinity, and that the religions of Abraham, of the children of Israel, and of these Eastern nations were originally the same. The Christian divines, who have observed the identity, of course maintain that the other nations copied from Moses, or the natives of Palestine, i. e. that several great and mighty empires, copied from a small and insignificant province. No doubt this is possible: whether probable or not must be left to the judgment of the reader, after he has well considered all the circumstances detailed in the following work.

2. The very interesting and ancient book of Genesis, on which the modern system of the

---

[1] Part XIX.

reformed Christian religion is chiefly founded, has always been held to be the production of Moses. But it requires very little discernment to perceive, that it is a collection of treatises, probably of different nations. The first ends with the third verse of the second chapter—the second with the last verse of the fourth.

In the first verse of the first book, the ALEIM, which will be proved to be the Trinity, being in the plural number, are said by Wisdom to have formed, from matter previously existing, the שמים smim, or planetary bodies, which were believed by the Magi to be the rulers or directors of the affairs of men. This opinion I shall examine by and by. From this it is evident, that this is in fact a Persian, or still more Eastern, mythos.

The use of animals for food being clearly not allowed to man, in chap. i. vers. 29, 30, is a circumstance which bespeaks the book of Buddhist origin. It is probably either the parent of the Buddhist religion, or its offspring. And it is different from the next book, which begins at the fourth verse of the second chapter, and ends with the last verse of the fourth ; because, *among other reasons* in it, the creation is said to have been performed by a different person from that named in the first,—by Jehovah Aleim, instead of Aleim. Again, in the first book, man and woman are created at the same time ; in the second, they are created at different times. Again, in the first book, the fruit of ALL the trees is given to the man ; in the second, this is contradicted, by one tree being expressly forbidden. These are in fact two different accounts of the creation.

The beginning of the fifth chapter, or third tract, seems to be a repetition of the first, to connect it with the history of the flood. The world is described as being made by God, (Aleim,) and not as in the second by Jehovah or the God Jehovah or Jehovah Aleim ; and, as in the first, the man and woman are made at one time, and not, as in the second, at different times. The account of the birth of Seth, given in the twenty-fifth verse of the fourth chapter, and the repetition of the same event in the third verse of the fifth chapter, or the beginning of the third tract, are a clear proof that these tracts are by different persons ; or, at least, are separate and distinct works. The reason why the name of Seth is given here, and not the names of any of the later of Adam's children, is evidently to connect Adam with Noah and the flood, the object of the third tract. The permission, in the third tract, to eat animals implying that it was not given before, is strictly in keeping with the denial of it in the first.

The histories of the creation, both in the first and in the second book of Genesis, in the sacred books of the Persians, and in those of the Chaldeans, are evidently different versions of the same story. The Chaldeans state the world to have been created not in six days, but in six periods of time—the lengths of the periods not being fixed. The Persians, also, divide the time into six periods.

In the second book, a very well-known account is given of the origin of evil, which is an affair most closely interwoven with every part of the Christian system, but it is in fact nothing more than an oriental mythos, which may have been taken from the history of the ancient Brahmins, in whose books the principal incidents are to be found ; and, in order to put this matter out of doubt, it will only be necessary to turn to the plates, to Figs. 2, 3, 4, taken from icons in the very oldest of the caves of Hindostan, excavated, as it is universally agreed, long prior to the Christian æra. The reader will find the first to be the seed of the woman bruising the serpent's head ; the second, the serpent biting the foot of her seed, the Hindoo God Cristna, the second person of their trinity ; and the third, the spirit of God brooding over the face of the waters. The history in Genesis is here so closely depicted that it is impossible to doubt the identity of the two.

Among the Persians and all the oriental nations it has been observed, that the Creator or God was adored under a triple form—in fact in the form of a trinity. In India, this was Bramah,

Cristna or Vishnu, and Siva; in Persia, it was Oromasdes, Mithra, and Arhimanius; in each case the Creator, the Preserver, and the Destroyer.

I shall now proceed to shew that, in this particular, the religion of Abraham and the Israelites was accordant with all the others.

3. But before I proceed, I must point out an example of very blameable disingenuousness in every translation of the Bible which I have seen. In the original, God is called by a variety of names, often the same as that which the Heathens gave to their Gods. To disguise this, the translators have availed themselves of a contrivance adopted by the Jews in rendering the Hebrew into Greek, which is to render the word יהוה *Ieue,* and several of the other names by which God is called in the Bible, by the word Κυριος or Lord, which signifies one having authority, the sovereign. In this the Jews were justified by the commandment, which forbids the use of the name *Ieue.* But not so the Christians, who do not admit the true and evident meaning adopted by the Jews—*Thou shalt not take the name of Ieue, thy God, in vain.* And, therefore, they have no right, when pretending to give a translation, to call God by any other name than that in the original, whether it be *Adonis,* or *Ie,* or *Ieue,* or any other. This the reader will immediately see is of the first importance in obtaining a correct understanding of the book. The fact of the names of God being disguised in all[1] the translations tends to prove that no dependence can be placed on any of them. The fact shews very clearly the temper or state of mind with which the translators have undertaken their task. God is called by several names. How is the reader of a translation to discover this, if he find them all rendered by one name? He is evidently deceived. It is no justification of a translator, to say it is of little consequence. Little or great, he has no right to exercise any discretion of this kind. When he finds God called Adonai, he has no business to call him Jehovah or Elohim.

4. The fact that Abraham worshiped several Gods, who were, in reality, the same as those of the Persians, namely, the creator, the preserver, and the destroyer, has been long asserted, and the assertion has been very unpalatable both to Jews and many Christians; and to obviate or disguise what they could not account for, they have had recourse, in numerous instances, to the mistranslation of the original, as will presently be shewn.

The following texts will clearly prove this assertion. The Rev. Dr. Shuckford pointed out the fact long ago; so that this is nothing new.

In the second book of Genesis the creation is described not to have been made by Aleim, or the Aleim, but by a God of a double name—יהוה אלהים *Ieue Aleim;* which the priests have translated Lord God. By using the word Lord, their object evidently is to conceal from their readers several difficulties which arise afterward respecting the names of God and this word, and which shew clearly that the books of the Pentateuch are the writings of different persons.

Dr. Shuckford has observed, that in Genesis xii. 7, 8, Abraham did not call upon the name of the Lord as we improperly translate it; but invoked God in the name of the Lord (i. e. Ieue) whom he worshiped, and who appeared to him; and that this was the same God to whom Jacob prayed when he vowed that the Lord should be his God.[2] Again, in Gen. xxviii. 21, 22, יהיה יהוה לי לאלהים erit Dominus mihi in Deum; and he called the place בית אלהים *(Bit aleim),* Domus Dei. Again, Shuckford says,[3] that in Gen. xxvi. 25, Isaac invoked God as Abraham did in the name of this Lord, יהוה *Ieue* or Jehovah. On this he observes, " It is very evident that Abraham " and his descendants worshiped not only the true and living God, but they invoked him in the " name of the Lord, and they worshiped the Lord in whose name they invoked, so that two per- " sons were the object of their worship, God and this Lord : and the Scripture has distinguished

---

[1] At least I have never seen an exception.        [2] Shuckford, Book vii. pp. 130, 131.        [3] Book vii. p. 130.

" these two persons from one another by this circumstance, that *God no man hath seen at any*
" *time nor can see,*[1] but the Lord whom Abraham and his descendants worshiped was the person
" who appeared to them."[2]

In the above I need not remind my reader that he must insert the name of *Ieue* or *Jehovah* for
the name of Lord.

Chapter xxi. verse 33, is wrong translated : when properly rendered it represents Abraham to
have invoked *(in the name of Jehovah )* the everlasting God.[3] That is, to have invoked the everlasting God, or to have prayed to him in the name of Jehovah—precisely as the Christians do at
this day, who invoke God in the name of Jesus—who invoke the first person of the Trinity in the
name of the second.

The words of this text are, ויקרא-שם בשם יהוה אל עולם et *invocavit ibi in nomine* Ieue *Deum
æternum.*

The foregoing observations of Dr. Shuckford's are confirmed by the following texts :

Gen. xxxi. 42, " Except the God of my father, the God of Abraham, and the fear of Isaac," &c.

Gen. xxxi. 53, " The Gods of Abraham, and the Gods of Nahor, the Gods of their father, judge
betwixt us, אלהי.אביהם. Dii patris eorum, that is, the Gods of Terah, the great-grandfather of
both Jacob and Laban. It appears that they went back to the time when there could be no dispute
about their Gods. They sought for Gods that should be received by them both, and these were
the Gods of Terah. Laban was an idolater, (or at least of a different sect or religion—Rachel stole
his Gods,) Jacob was not ; and in consequence of the difference in their religion, there was a
difficulty in finding an oath that should be binding on both.

In Gen. xxxv. 1, it is said, *And* (אלהים *Aleim) God said unto Jacob, Arise, go up to Bethel, and
dwell there ; and make there an altar unto God* (לאל L ᴀ L) *that appeared unto thee, when thou fleddest
from the face of Esau thy brother.* If two Gods at least, or a plurality in the Godhead, had not
been acknowledged by the author of Genesis, the words would have been, *and make there an altar
unto me, that,* &c. ; or, *unto me, because I appeared,* &c.

Genesis xlix. 25, מאל אביך ויעזרך ואת שדי ויברכך, a Deo tui patris et adjuvabit te ; et omnipo-
tente benedicet tibi. By the God (Al) of thy father *also* he[4] will help thee, and the Saddai (Sdi)
*also* shall bless thee with blessings, &c.

It is worthy of observation, that there is a marked distinction between the *Al* of his father who
will help him, and the *Saddi* who will bless him. Here are two evidently clear and distinct Gods,
and neither of them the destroyer or the evil principle.

*Even by the God* (אל *Al) of thy father, who shall help thee : and by the Almighty,* שרי *omnipo-
tente, who shall bless thee with blessings of heaven above, blessings of the deep that lieth under,
blessings of the breasts and of the womb.* The *Sdi* or *Saddi* are here very remarkable ; they seem
to have been peculiarly Gods of the blessings of this world.

Deut. vi. 4, יהוה אלהינו יהוה אחד. This, Mr. Hails has correctly observed, ought to be rendered Jehovah our Gods is one Jehovah.

The doctrine of a plurality, shewn above in the Pentateuch, is confirmed in the later books of the
Jews.

Isaiah xlviii. 16, ועתה אדני יהוה שלחני ורוחו. Et nunc Adonai Ieue misit me et spiritus ejus :
And now the Lord (Adonai) Jehovah, hath sent me and his spirit.

---

[1] Exod. xxxiii. 20.      [2] Gen. xii. 11 ; Shuckford, Book ix. p. 378, Ed. 3, also p. 400.
[3] Shuckford, Con. Book v. p. 292.      [4] The mighty one named in the former verse, the אביר *Abir.*

Again Isaiah li. 22, כה-אמר אדניך יהוה ואלהיך יריב עמו. Thus thy Adonai Jehovah spoke, and thy Aleim reprimanded his people. Sic dixit tuus Adoni Ieue, et tuus Aleim litigabit suo populo.

Two persons of the Trinity are evident in·these texts. The third is found in the serpent, which tempted Eve in its evil character, and in its character of regenerator, healer, or preserver, in the brasen serpent set up by Moses, in the wilderness, to be adored by the Israelites, and to which they offered incense from his time through all the reigns of David and Solomon, to the time of Hezekiah, the name of which was Nehushtan.[1]   Numbers xxi. 8, 9; 2 Kings xviii. 4. The destroyer or evil spirit may also probably be found in the *Aub* named Lev. xx. 27; Deut. xviii. 11.

There are many expressions in the Pentateuch besides those already given, which cannot be accounted for without a plurality of Gods or the Trinity, a doctrine which was not peculiar to Abraham and his descendants, but was common to all the nations of the ancient world from India to Thule, as I have before observed, under the triple title of creator, preserver, and destroyer—Brama, Vishnu, and Siva, among the Hindoos; Oromasdes, Mithra, and Arhimanius, among the Persians.

We shall see in the next chapter, that the Trinity will be found in the word Aleim of the first verse of Genesis, which will tend to support what I have asserted, viz. that it is an Indian book.

---

## CHAPTER II.

On the word ALEIM or jewish trinity.—SADDAI ADONIS.—TRINITY OF THE RABBIS.—MEANING OF THE WORDS AL AND EL.

1. Perhaps there is no word in any language about which more has been written than the word Aleim; or, as modern Jews corruptly call it, Elohim.[2]   But all its difficulties are at once removed by considering it as a representation of the united Godhead, the Trinity in Unity, the three Persons and one God. It is not very unlike the word Septuagint—of which we sometimes say, *it* gives a word such or such a sense, at other times *they* give such a sense, &c. A folio would be required to contain all that has been said respecting this word. The author believes that there is no instance in which it is not satisfactorily explained by considering it, as above suggested, as the representation of the Trinity.

The root אל *al*, the root of the word Aleim, as a verb, or in its verbal form, means to mediate, to interpose for protection, to preserve;[3]  and, as a noun, a mediator, an interposer. In its feminine it has two forms, אלה *ale*, and אלוה *alue*. In its plural masculine it makes אלים *alim*, in its plural feminine אלהים *aleim*. In forming its plural feminine in ים *im*, it makes an exception to the general Hebrew rule, which makes the plural masculine in ים *im*. But though an exception, it is by no means singular. It is like that made by עזים *ozim*, she-goats, דבים *dbim*, she-bears, &c.[4]  In the second example in its feminine form, it drops the *u* or *vau*, according to a common practice of the Hebrew language.

---

[1] This has been observed by Mr. Maurice, Hind. Ant. Vol. III. p. 209.
[2] In the Synagogue copies it is always Aleim.
[3] Parkhurst in voce.          [4] Parkhurst's Grammar, p. 8.

A controversy took place about the middle of the last century between one Dr. Sharpe and several other divines upon the word Aleim. The Doctor was pretty much of my opinion. He says, " If there is no reason to doubt, as I think there is none, that אלה *ale* and אלוה *alue* are the " same word, only the *vau* is suppressed in the one, and expressed in the other, why may not " אלהים *aleim* be the plural of one as well as of the other ? If it be said it cannot be the plural " of אלוה *alue*, because it is wrote without the *vau ;* I answer, that קרבים *qrbim*, רחקים *rhqim*, " גברים *gbrim*, גדלים *gdlim*, &c., are frequently wrote without the vau : are they not, therefore, " the plurals of קרוב *qrub*," &c. ? Again, he says,

" When, therefore, Mr. Moody tells us that אלהים *aleim* may be the plural masculine of אלה " *ale*, as אדנים *adnim*, and אדני *adni*, are also plurals of אדון *adun*, Lord, so may אלהים *aleim* and " אלהי *alei* be plural of אלוה *Alue*, God." [1]

In the course of the controversy it seems to be admitted by all parties, that the word has the meaning of mediator or interposer for protection, and this is very important.

I cannot quite agree with Mr. Moody, because, according to the genius of the Hebrew language, it is much more in character for אלהים *aleim* to be the plural feminine of אלה *ale*, a feminine noun, than the plural masculine ; and for אלים *alim* to be the plural masculine, of the masculine noun אל *al*.

But it does not seem to have ever occurred to any of those gentlemen, that the words in question, אלה *ale*, or אלוה *alue*, and אל *al*, might be one the masculine, and the two others the feminine, of the same word—like God and Goddess. They never seem to have thought that the God of the Hebrews could be of any sex but their own, and, therefore, never once gave a thought to the question. The observation of Mr. Moody is very just, if אלה *ale* be a masculine noun. But it is much more according to the genius of the language that it should be feminine. If אלה *ale* be masculine, it is an exception. I beg the reader to observe, that the Arabians, from whose language the word al properly comes, have the word for the Sun, in the *feminine,* and that for the moon, in the *masculine* gender ; and this accounts for the word being in the feminine plural. From the androgynous character of the Creator, the noun of multitude, Aleim, by which we shall now see that he was described, probably was of the common gender : that is, either of one gender or the other, as it might happen.

From the plural of this word, אל *al*, was also formed a noun of multitude used in the first verse of Genesis : exactly like our word *people*, in Latin *populus*, or our words nation, flock, and congregation. Thus it is said, ברא אלהים *bara aleim, Aleim formed the earth ;* as we say, the nation consumes, a flock strays, or the congregation sings psalms, or a triune divinity, or a trinity blesses or forms. It is used with the emphatic article : " Their cry came up to THE Gods," האלהים *e-aleim*. In the same way we say, wolves got to THE sheep, or THE flock, or THE congregation sing or sings. Being a noun of multitude, according to the genius of the language, the verb may be either in the singular or plural number.

Parkhurst says, that " the word *Al* means God, the Heavens, Leaders, Assistance, Defence, " and Interposition ; or, to interpose for protection." He adds, " that אלל *All*, with the ל *l* doubled, has the meaning, in an excessive degree, of *vile*; the denouncing of a curse : *nought,* " *nothing, res nihili.*" Mr. Whiter [2] says, that it has the same meaning in Arabic, and that AL AL, also means Deus optimus maximus. Thus we have the idea of creating, preserving, and destroying.

The meaning of mediator, preserver, or intervener, joined to its character of a noun of multitude, at once identifies it with the Trinity of the Gentiles. Christians will be annoyed to find their God

---

[1] Sharpe, on Aleim, pp. 179, 180.     [2] Etymol. Univ. Vol. I. p. 512.

K

called by the same name with that of the Heathen Gods; but this is only what took place when he was called שדי *Sdi*, Saddi, Saddim, or אדני *adni*, Adonai, or Adonis, אדון *adun*, or בעל *bol*, Baal: so that there is nothing unusual in this.

The Jews have made out that God is called by upwards of thirty names in the Bible; many of them used by the Gentiles, probably before they fell into idolatry.

The word אל *àl*, meaning preserver; of course, when the words יהוה ה אלהים *ieue-e-aleim* are used, they mean *Ieue the preserver*, or the *self-existent preserver*—the word *Ieue*, as we shall afterward find, meaning self-existent.

When the אלהים *aleim* is considered as a noun of multitude, all the difficulties, I think, are removed.

It seems not unlikely that by the different modes of writing the word אל *al*, a distinction of sexes should originally have been intended to be expressed. The Heathen divinities, Ashtaroth and Baal-zebub, were both called Aleim. [1] And the Venus Aphrodite, Urania, &c., were of both genders. The God Mithra, the Saviour, was both male and female. Several exemplars of him, in his female character, as killing the bull, may be seen in the Townly Collection, in the British Museum. By the word Aleim the Heathen Gods were often meant, but they all resolved themselves at last into the Sun, as triune God, or as emblem of the three powers—the Creator, the Preserver, and the Destroyer—three Persons but one God—he being both *male and female*. Without doubt Parkhurst and the divines in the controversy with Dr. Sharpe, do not give, till after much research, as meanings of the verb אל *al, to mediate, to interpose, or intervene;* and of the noun *the mediator, interposer, or intervener.* But here we evidently have the preserver or saviour. At first it might be expected that the gender of the word *Aleim* and of the other forms from its root would be determined by the genders of the words which ought to agree with it: but from the extraordinary uncertain state of this language nothing can be deduced from them—as we find nouns feminine and plural joined to verbs masculine and singular (Gen. i. 14); and nouns of multitude, though singular, having a verb plural—and, though feminine, having a verb masculine (Gen. xli. 57). But all this tends, I think, to strengthen an observation I shall have occasion to make hereafter, that the Hebrew language shews many marks of almost primeval rudeness or simplicity; and, that the Aleim, the root whence the Christian Trinity sprung, is the real trinity of the ancients—the old doctrine revived. Nothing could be desired more in favour of my system than that the word *Aleim* should mean preserver, or intervener, or mediator.

At first it seems very extraordinary that the word אל *al* or אלה *ale*, the name of the beneficent Creator, should have the meaning of curse. The difficulty arises from an ill-understood connexion between the Creator, Preserver, and Destroyer—the Creator being the Destroyer, and the Destroyer the Creator. But in this my theory is beautifully supported.

2. It appears that in these old books, God is called by names which are sometimes singular, sometimes plural, sometimes masculine, and sometimes feminine. But though he be occasionally of each gender, for he must be of the masculine or feminine gender, because the old language has no neuter; he is not called by any name which conveys the idea of Goddess or a feminine nature, as separable from himself. My idea is very abstruse and difficult to explain. He is, in fact, in every case Androgynous; for in no case which I have produced is a term used exclusively belonging to one sex or the other. He is never called Baaltes, or Asteroth, or Queen of Heaven. On this subject I shall have much to say hereafter.

Many Christians no doubt, will be much alarmed and shocked at the idea of the word *ale* being of the feminine gender. But why should not the Hebrew language have a feminine to the word

---

[1] Sharpe, p. 224.

אל *al*, as the English have a feminine to the word God, in.Goddess, or the Romans in the words Deus and Dea ? And why should not God be of the feminine gender as easily as of the masculine ? Who knows what gender God is of? Who at this day is so foolish as to fancy that God is of any gender ? We have seen that all the Gods of the Gentiles were, of both genders. We find God called *Al*, *Ale*, *Alue*, *Alim*, and *Aleim*—more frequently *Aleim* than any other name. It must be observed, that God nowhere calls himself by any of those names, as he does by the name יה *Ie* or *Jah*, or יהוה *Ieue*, which is the only name by which he has ever denominated himself. Dr. Shuckford, on Genesis xxvi. 25, makes Ieue,[1] mean Preserver or Mediator.

The God Baal was both masculine and feminine, and the God of the Jews was once called Baal. The learned Kircher[2] says, " Vides igitur dictas Veneris Uraniam, Nephtem, et Momemphitam, " nihil aliud esse quam Isidem, quod et vaccæ cultis satis superque demonstrat proprius Isidi " certe hanc eandem quoque esse, quæ in historia Thobiæ Dea Baal dicitur quæ vacca colebatur ; " sic enim habetur, C. i. 5, Εθυὸν τη Βααλ τη δαμαλει. Scilicet faciebant sacra τη Βααλ " juvencæ seu vaccæ, quod et alio loco videlicet L. iii. Reg. C. xix. ubi Baal legitur feminino " genere ; Ουκ εκαμψαν γονατα τη Βααλ—non incurvaverunt genu Baali. Hesychius autem " Βηλθης inquit, ἡ Ἡρα ἡ Αφροδιτη, Belthes, Juno sive Venus, est cuicum juvencam sacrificârint " Phœnices, veresimile est, eandem esse cum Venere Ægyptia, seu Iside, seu Astarthe Assyrio- " rum, sicut enim Baal est Jupiter, sic Baalis seu Belthis est Juno, seu Venus, cui parallela sunt, " Adonis seu Thamus, et Venus seu Astaroth ; (quorum ille Baal Assyriorum hæc eorum Beltis " est ;) quibus respondent Osiris et Isis, Jupiter et Juno seu Venus Ægyptiorum ; eternum " secuti בעל שמים *Baal samim* est Jupiter Olympius, ita שמים בעלת *Baalet samaim* est Juno " Olympia, scilicet, Domina cœli seu Regina : quemadmodum Jerem. vii. 44, eam vocant Septua- " ginta Interpretes, quod nomen Isidi et Astarthi et Junoni Venerive proprie convenit : uti ex " variis antiquarum inscriptionum monumentis apud Janum Gruterum videre est."[3]

Parkhurst says,[4] " *But* AL *or* EL *was the very name the Heathens gave to their God Sol, their Lord or Ruler of the hosts of heaven.*"

The word Aleim אלהים has been derived from the Arabic word *Allah* God, by many learned men ; but Mr. Bellamy says this cannot be admitted.; for the Hebrew is not the derived, but the primitive language. Thus the inquiry into the real origin or meaning of this curious and important word, and of the language altogether, is at once cut short by a dogmatical assertion. This learned Hebraist takes it for granted from his theological dogma, that the two tribes of Israel are the favourites of God, exclusive of the ten other tribes—that the language of the former must be the original of all other languages ; and then he makes every thing bend to this dogma. This is the mode which learned Christians generally adopt in their inquiries ; and for this reason no dependance can be placed upon them : and this is the reason also why, in their inquiries, they seldom arrive at the truth. The Alah, articulo emphatico alalah (Calassio) of the Arabians, is evidently the אל *Al* of the Chaldees or Jews ; whether one language be derived from the other I shall not give an opinion at present: but Bishop Marsh, no mean authority as all will admit, speaking of the Arabic,[5] says, " Its importance, therefore, to the interpretation of Hebrew is apparent.

---

[1] Which means self-existent. Vide Celtic Druids, Ch. v. Sect. xxxvii. and xxxviii.

[2] Œd. Æg. Synt. iv. Cap. xiii. Vol. I. p. 319.

[3] Proserpine, in Greek Περσεφονη, was styled by Orpheus, (in his Hymn Εις Περσεφονην,) Ζωη και Θανατος, both Life and Death He says of her—φερεις γαρ αιει και παντα φονευεις, Thou both *producest* and *destroyest* all things. Porphyry and Eusebius say, she said of herself, " I am called of a *three-fold* nature, and *three-headed.*" Parkhurst, p. 347.

[4] Lex. p. 20.   [5] Lecture XIV. p. 28.

" It serves, indeed, as a key to that language ; for it is not only allied to the Hebrew, but is at the
" same time so copious, as to *contain the roots of almost all the words in the Hebrew Bible.*" If this
be true, it is evident that the Arabian *language* may be of the greatest use in the translating of the
Scriptures ; though the Arabian version of them, in consequence of its having been made from the
Greek Septuagint or some other Greek version, (if such be the fact,) instead of the original, may
be of no great value.   And if I understand his Lordship rightly, and it be true, that the Arabic
contains the roots of the Hebrew, it must be a more ancient language than the Hebrew.   But,
after all, if the two languages be dialects of the same, it is nonsense to talk of one being derived
from the other.

In the first verse of Genesis the word Aleim is found without any particle before it, and, therefore, ought to be literally translated *Gods formed* ; but in the second chapter of Exodus and 23d
verse, the emphatic article ה *e* is found, and therefore it ought to be translated, that " their cry
" came up to THE Gods," or THE Aleim.   In the same manner the first verse of the third chapter
ought to have *the mountain of the Gods*, or *of the Aleim, even to Horeb*, instead of *the mountain of
God*.   Mr. Bellamy has observed that we cannot say Gods he created, but we can say Gods or
Aleim created ; and the fact, as we see above, of the word Aleim being sometimes preceded by
the emphatic article ה *e* shews, that where it is omitted the English article ought to be omitted,
and where it is added the English article ought to be added.

Perhaps the word Septuagint may be more similar to the word Aleim.   But if there be no idiom
in our language, or the Latin, or the Greek, *exactly similar* to the Hebrew, this is no way
surprising.

3.  Persons who have not given much consideration to these subjects will be apt to wonder that
any people should be found to offer adoration to the evil principle ; but they do not consider that,
in all these recondite systems, the evil principle, or the destroyer, or Lord of Death, was at the
same time the regenerator.   He could not destroy, but to reproduce.   And it was probably not
till this principle began to be forgotten, that the evil being, *per se*, arose ; for in some nations this
effect seems to have taken place.   Thus Baal-Zebub is in Iberno Celtic, Baal *Lord*, and Zab *Death*,
Lord of Death ; but he is also called *Aleim*, the same as the God of the Israelites ; [1] and this is
right, because he was one of the Trimurti or Trinity.

If I be correct respecting the word Aleim being feminine, we here see the Lord of Death of the
feminine gender ; but the Goddess Ashtaroth or Astarte, the Eoster of the Germans, [2] was also
called Aleim. [3]   Here again Aleim is feminine, which shews that I am right in making Aleim the
plural *feminine*.   Thus we have distinctly found Aleim the Creator, (Gen. i. 1,) Aleim the Preserver, and Aleim the Destroyer, and this not by inference, but literally expressed.   We have also
the Apis or Bull of Egypt expressly called Aleim, and its plurality admitted on authority not
easily disputed.   Aaron says, אלה אלהיך *ale aleik, these are thy Aleim who brought thee out of the
land of Egypt.* [4]

Mr. Maurice says, [5] Moses himself uses this word Elohim, with verbs and adjectives in the
plural.   Of this usage Dr. Allix enumerates two, among many other glaring instances, that might
be brought from the Pentateuch ; the former in Genesis xx. 13, Quando errare *fecerunt* me Deus ;
the latter in Gen. xxxv. 7, Quia ibi *revelati sunt* ad eum Deus ; and by other writers in various
parts of the Old Testament.   But particularly he brings in evidence the following texts : Job
xxxv. 10 ; Josh. xxiv. 19 ; Psa. cxix. 1.

The 26th verse of the first chapter of Genesis completely establishes the plurality of the word

---

[1] Sharpe, p. 224.                          [2] See Ancient Universal History, Vol. II. pp. 334—346.
[3] Sharpe, p. 224.            [4] Parkhurst, p. 81.            [5] Ind. Ant. Vol. IV. p 81.

Aleim. *And then said Aleim,* WE *will make man in* OUR *image according to* OUR *likeness.* To rebut this argument it is said, that this is nothing but a dignified form of speech adopted by all kings in speaking to their subjects, to give themselves dignity and importance, and on this account attributed to God. This is reasoning from effect to cause, instead of from cause to effect. The oriental sovereigns, puffed up with pride and vanity, not only imitated the language of God in the sacred book; but they also went farther, and made their base slaves prostrate themselves before them in the same posture as they used in addressing their God. In this argument God is made to use incorrect language in order that he may imitate and liken himself to the vainest and most contemptible of human beings. We have no knowledge that God ever imitated these wretches; we do know that *they* affected to imitate and liken themselves to Him. This verse proves his plurality : the next, again, proves his unity : for there the word *bara* is used—whence it is apparent that the word has both a singular and plural meaning.

On the 22d verse of the third chapter of Genesis, my worthy and excellent old friend, Dr. A. Geddes, Vicar Apostolic of the Roman See in London, says,[1] " *Lo! Adam—or man—is become* " *like one of us.* If there be any passage in the Old Testament which countenances a plurality of " persons in the Godhead ; or, to speak more properly, a plurality of Gods, it is this passage. " He does not simply say, *like us ;* but like *one of us* כאחד ממנו. This can hardly be explained as " we have explained נעשה *Let us make,* and I confess it has always appeared to me to imply a " plurality of Gods, in some sense or other. It is well known that the *Lord* or *Jehovah,* is called " in the Hebrew Scriptures, ' The God of Gods.' He is also represented as a Sovereign sitting " on his throne, attended by all the heavenly host ;" in Job called *the sons of God.* Again he says, " Wherever Jehovah is present, whether on Sinai or Sion, there he is attended by twenty " thousand angels, of the Cherubic order. When he appeared to Jacob, at Bethel, he was " attended by angels, and again when he wrestled with the same patriarch."

The first verse of the twelfth chapter of Ecclesiastes is strongly in favour of the plurality of Aleim—Remember thy Creators, not Creator—זכר את בוראיך. But many copies have the word בוראך and others בראו without the י. " But," as Parkhurst observes, " it is very easy to account " for the transcribers dropping the plural י I, in their copies, though very difficult to assign a " reason why any of them should insert it, unless they found it in their originals."[2] The Trinitarian Christians have triumphed greatly over the other Christian sects and the Jews, in consequence of the plurality of the Aleim expressed in the texts cited above. It appears that they have justice on their side.

There would have been no difficulty, with the word Aleim, if some persons had not thought that the plurality of Aleim favoured the doctrine of the Christian Trinity, and others that the contrary effect was to be produced by making Aleim a noun singular. But whatever sect it may favour or oppose, I am clearly of opinion that it conveys the idea of plurality, just as much as the phrase Populus laudavit Deum, or, in English, The Congregation sings.

4. It has already been observed that the God of the Jews was also called by a very remarkable name שדי אל *al sdi.* The proper name *Sdi* is constantly translated *God Almighty.*[3]

In Gen. xlix. 25, שדי *Sdi* is put for the *Almighty,* (as it is translated,) not only without the word אל *al* preceding it, as usual, but in opposition to it.

In Deut. xxxii. 17, the Israelites are said to have sacrificed to שדים *sdim* and not to אלה *ale*—as it is translated in our version, " to devils and not to God," אלהים לא ידעום *eos noverunt non diis, to Gods whom they did not know.* Here is a marked distinction between the Sadim and the Aleim.

---

[1] Crit. Rem. Gen. iii., pp. 48, 49.        [2] Parkhurst, Lex. p. 82.

[3] Gen. xxviii. 3, xxxv. 11, xliii. 14, xlviii. 3 ; Exod. vi. 3.

Here is *Ale* in the singular number, God; *Aleim* in the plural number, Gods: and here is *Sadim*, the plural number of another name of the Deity, which is both of the masculine and feminine gender.

In Gen. xiv. 3, the kings are said to have *combined*, " *in the vale of Siddim, which is the salt* " *sea.*" This shews that the Gods called Saddai were known and acknowledged, by the Canaanites, before the time of Abraham. This word Siddim is the plural of the word used, in various places, as the name of the true God—both by itself as *Saddi* and *El* Saddi. In Exodus vi. 3, the Israelites are ordered to call God *Ieue* ; but before that time he had been only known to their fathers as *Al Saddi*, God Almighty.

Now, at last, what does this word *Sadi, Saddim,* or *Shaddai,* שדי *Sdi,* really mean ? Mr. Parkhurst tells us, it means *all-bountiful—the pourer forth of blessings ;* among the Heathen, the *Dea Multimammia ;* in fact, the Diana of Ephesus, the Urania of Persia, *the Jove of Greece,* called by Orpheus the mother of the Gods, each male as well as female—the Venus Aphrodite ; in short, the genial powers of nature. [1] And I maintain, that it means also the figure which is often found in collections of ancient statues, most beautifully executed, and called the *Hermaphrodite.* See Gallery of Naples and of Paris.

The God of the Jews is also often known by the name of Adonai אדני [2] But this is nothing but the God of the Syrians, Adonis or the Sun, the worship of whom is reprobated under the name of *Tammuz,* in Ezekiel viii. 14.

From these different examples it is evident that the God of the Jews had several names, and that these were often the names of the Heathen Gods also. All this has a strong tendency to shew that the Jewish and Gentile systems were, at the bottom, the same.

Why we call God masculine I know not, nor do I apprehend can any good reason be given. Surely the ancients, who described him as of both genders, or of the doubtful gender, were more reasonable. Here we see that the God of the Jews is called שדי *Sdi,* and that this Sdi is the Dea *Multimammia,* who is also in other places made to be the same as the אל *al* or אלה *ale.* Therefore it seems to follow, that the Gods of the Israelites and of the Gentiles were in their originals the same. And I think by and by my reader will see evident proof, that the religion of Moses was but a sect of that of the Gentiles ; or, if he like it better, that the religion of the Gentiles was but a sect of the religion of Jehovah, *Ieue,* or of Moses.

It may be here observed that these names of God of two genders are almost all in the old tracts, which I suppose to have been productions of the Buddhists or Brahmins of India, for which I shall give more reasons presently.

5. From what I may call the almost bigoted attachment of the modern Jews to the unity of God, it cannot for a moment be supposed, that they would forge any thing tending to the proof of the Trinity of the Christians ; therefore, if we can believe father Kircher, the following fact furnishes a very extraordinary addition to the proofs already given, that the Jews received a trinity like all the other oriental nations. It was the custom among them, to describe their God Jehovah or Ieue, by three jods and a cross in a circle, thus : (⁖). Certainly a more striking illustration of the doctrine I have been teaching can scarcely be conceived : and it is very curious that it should be found accompanied with the cross, which the learned father, not understanding, calls the Mazoretic *Chametz.* This mistake seems to remove all suspicion of Christian forgery ; for I can hardly believe that if the Christian priests had forged this symbol, the learned Father would not have availed himself of it to support the adoration of the Cross, as well as of the Trinity. The

---

[1] Parkhurst, Lex. pp. 720, 721.    [2] Vide Parkhurst, p. 141 and p. 788.

the jods were also disposed in the form of a crown, thus ⸮⸮⸮, to signify the mystical name of Jehovah or Ieue. The reader may refer to the Œdipus Ægyp. Vol. II. Cap. ii. pp. 114, 115, where he will find the authorities at length, and where, among the reasons given by the father to prove the Christian Trinity, is proof enough of that of the Jews. He will find also an observation of Galatinus's that the three letters יהי ieu were the symbol of Jehovah, an observation made by me in the Celtic Druids, [1] though for a different reason, and accounted for in a different manner; but the fact is admitted. The cross here seems to be united to the Trinity—but more of this hereafter.

Dr. Alix, on Gen. i. 10, says, that the Cabalists constantly added the letter jod, being the first letter of the word *Ieue* to the word Aleim *for the sake of a mystery*. The Rabbi Bechai says, it is to shew that there is a divinity in each person included in the word. [2] This is, no doubt, part of the Cabala, or esoteric religion of the Jews. Maimonides says, the vulgar Jews were forbidden to read the history of the creation, for *fear* it should lead them into idolatry; [3] probably for fear they should worship the Trimurti of India, or the Trinity of Persia. The fear evidently shews, that the fearful persons thought there was a plurality in Genesis.

6. It is a very common practice with the priests not always to translate a word, but sometimes to leave it in the original, and sometimes to translate it as it may suit their purpose: sometimes one, sometimes the other. Thus they use the word *Messiah* or *Anointed* as they find it best serves their object. Thus, again, it is with the word EL, in numerous places. For instance, in Gen. xxviii. 19, *And he called the name of the place Beth-el,* instead of *he called the place The House of the Sun.* The word Beth means *House,* and El *Sun.* [4]

" Ai was situated between Bith-Avon (read Bith-On) and Bith-El; and these were temples of " the Sun, under his different titles of On and El." [5]

Speaking of the word Jabneel, Sir W. Drummond says, " El, in the composition of these " Canaanite names does not signify Deus but Sol." [6] This confirms what I have before observed from Parkhurst.

" Thus Kabzeel, literally means The Congregation of the Sun." [7]

" Messiah-El a manifest corruption of the word Messiah—The Anointed of El, or the Sun. [8]

" Carmel, The Vine of El, or of the Sun." [9]

" Migdal-El Horem, The Station of the Burning Sun." [10]

" Amraphel, Ammon, or the Sun in Aries, here denominated Amraphel, Agnus Mirabilis." [11]

" El-tolad signifies the Sun, or The God of Generation." [12]

In all the above-named examples the word El ought to be written Al. In the original it is אל *Al;* and this word means the God Mithra, the Sun, as the Preserver or Saviour.

---

[1] Ch. v. Sect. xxxviii.　　　[2] Maur. Ind. Ant. Vol. IV. p. 86.　　　[3] Ibid. p. 89,
[4] See Œdip. Jud. p. 250.　　　[5] Ibid. p. 221.　　　[6] Ibid. p. 270.
[7] Ibid. p. 272.　　　[8] Ibid. p. 280.　　　[9] Ibid. p. 334.　　　[10] Ibid. 338.
[11] Ibid. p. 76.　　　[12] Ibid. p. 286.

## CHAPTER III.

ESDRAS AND THE ANCIENT JEWISH CABALA.—EMANATIONS, WHAT.—MEANING OF THE WORD BERASIT.—
SEPHIROTHS AND EMANATIONS CONTINUED.—ORIGIN OF TIME.—PLANETS OR SAMIM.—OBSERVATIONS
ON THE PRECEDING SECTIONS.

1. As all the ancient Heathen nations had their mysteries or secret doctrines, which the priests carefully kept from the knowledge of the vulgar, and which they only communicated to a select number of persons whom they thought they could safely trust; and as the Jewish religion was anciently the same as the Persian, it will not be thought extraordinary, that, like the Persian, it should have its secret doctrines. So we find it had its Cabala, which, though guarded like all ancient mysteries, with the most anxious care, and the most solemn oaths, and what is still worse, almost lost amidst the confusion of civil brawls, cannot be entirely hidden from the prying curiosity of the Moderns. In defiance of all its concealment and mischances, enough escapes to prove that it was fundamentally the same as that of the Persian Magi; and thus adds one more proof of the identity of the religions of Abraham and of Zoroaster.

The doctrine here alluded to was a secret one—more perfect, the Jews maintain, than that delivered in the Pentateuch; and they also maintain, that it was given by God, on Mount Sinai, to Moses *verbally* and not written, and that this is the doctrine described in the fourth book of Esdras, ch. xiv. 6, 26, and 45, thus:

*These words shalt thou declare, and these shalt thou hide.*

*And when thou hast done, some things shalt thou publish, and some things shalt thou shew secretly to the* WISE.

*. . . . the Highest spake, saying, The first that thou hast written publish openly, that the worthy and the unworthy may read it : but keep the seventy last, that thou mayest deliver them only to such as be* WISE *among the people. For in them is the spring of understanding, the fountain of* WISDOM.

Now, though the book of Esdras be no authority in argument with a Protestant Christian for any point of doctrine, it may be considered authority in such a case as this. If the Jews had had no secret doctrine, the writer never would have stated such a fact, in the face of all his country-men, who must have known its truth or falsity. No doubt, whatever might be pretended, the real reason of the Cabala being unwritten, was concealment. But the Jews assert that, from the promulgation of the law on Mount Sinai, it was handed down, pure as at first delivered. In the same way they maintain, that their written law has come to us unadulterated, without a single error. One assertion may be judged of by the other. For, of the tradition delivered by memory, one question need only be asked : What became of it, when priests, kings, and people, were all such idolaters, viz. before and during the early part of the reign of the good King Josiah, that the law was completely forgotten—not even known to exist in the world ? To obviate this difficulty, in part, the fourth book of Esdras was probably written.

2. The following passage may serve, at present, as an outline of what was the general nature of the Cabala:

" The similarity, or rather the coincidence, of the Cabalistic, Alexandrian, and Oriental philo-
" sophy, will be sufficiently evinced by briefly stating the common tenets in which these different
" systems agreed ; they are as follow : All things are derived by emanation from one principle :
" and this principle is God. From him a substantial power immediately proceeds, which is the

" image of God, and the source of all subsequent emanations. This second principle sends forth,
" by the energy of emanation, other natures, which are more or less perfect, according to their
" different degrees of distance, in the scale of emanation, from the First Source of existence, and
" which constitute different worlds, or orders of being, all united to the eternal power from which
" they proceed. Matter is nothing more than the most remote effect of the emanative energy of
" the Deity. The material world receives its form from the immediate agency of powers far
" beneath the First Source of being. Evil is the necessary effect of the imperfection of matter.
" Human souls are distant emanations from Deity, and after they are liberated from their
" material vehicles, will return, through various stages of purification, to the fountain whence
" they first proceeded." [1]

From this extract the reader will see the nature of the oriental doctrine of emanations, which,
as here given in most, though not in all, respects, coincides with the oriental philosophy: [2] and
the honest translation given by the Septuagint of Deut. xxxiii. 2—*he shined forth from Paran with
thousands of saints, and having his angels on his right hand,* [3] proves that the Cabala was as old or
older than Moses.

The ancient Persians believed, that the Supreme Being was surrounded with angels, or what
they called Æons or Emanations, from the divine substance. This was also the opinion of the
Manicheans, and of almost all the Gnostic sects of Christians. As might be expected, in the
particulars of this complicated system, among the different professors of it a great variety of
opinions arose; but all, at the bottom, evidently of the same nature. These oriental sects were
very much in the habit of using figurative language, under which they concealed their metaphysical doctrines from the eyes of the vulgar. This gave their enemies the opportunity, by construing them literally, of representing them as wonderfully absurd. All these doctrines were also
closely connected with judicial astrology. To the further consideration of the above-cited text I
shall return by and by.

3. Perhaps in the languages of the world no two words have been of greater importance than the
first two in the book of Genesis, ראשית ב B-RASIT; (for they are properly *two* not *one* word;)
and great difference of opinion has arisen, among learned men, respecting the meaning of them.
Grotius renders them, *when first;* Simeon, *before;* Tertullian, *in power;* Rabbi Bechai and
Castalio, *in order before all;* Onkelos, the Septuagint, Jonathan ben Uzziel, and the modern
translators, *in the beginning.*

But the official or accredited and admitted authority of the Jewish religion, the JERUSALEM
TARGUM, renders them BY WISDOM.

It may be observed that the Targum of Jerusalem is, or was formerly, the received orthodox
authority of the Jews: the other Targums are only the opinions of individuals, and in this
rendering, the Jewish Cabala and the doctrine of the ancient Gnostics are evident; and, it is, as I
shall now shew, to conceal *this* that Christians have suppressed its true meaning. To the celebrated and learned Beausobre I am indebted for the most important discovery of the secret doctrine
contained in this word. He says, " The Jews, instead of translating Berasit by the words *in the
" beginning*, translate it by *the Principle* (par le Principe) *active and immediate of all things*, God
" *made*, &c., that is to say, according to the Targum of Jerusalem, BY WISDOM, (PAR LA SA-
" GESSE,) God made, &c." [4]

---

[1] Dr Rees' Encyclopedia, art. Cabala.
[2] See Hist. Phil. Enfield, Vol. II. Ch. iii.; Phil. Trans. No. CCI. p. 800; Burnet's Archæol. Lib. i. Cap. vii.
[3] See Beausobre, Liv. ix.
[4] " Il y a encore une réflexion à faire sur cette matière. Elle roule sur l'explication du mot Rasit, qui à la tête
" de la Genèse, et qui, si l'on en croit d'anciens Interprètes Juifs, ne signifie pas *le commencement*, mais *le Principe*

Beausobre also informs us, Maimonides maintains, that this is the only LITERAL and TRUE meaning of the word. And Maimonides is generally allowed to have been one of the most learned of modern Jews. (He lived in the twelfth century.) Beausobre further says, that CHALCIDIUS, METHODIUS, ORIGEN, and CLEMENS ALEXANDRINUS, a most formidable phalanx of authorities, give it this sense. The latter quotes a sentence as authority from the work of St. Peter's now lost. Beausobre gives us as the expression of Clemens, " This is what St. Peter says, who has very " well understood this word : ' God has made the heaven and the earth by the Principle. (Dieu " ' a fait le Ciel et la Terre dans le Principe.) This principle is that which is called Wisdom by " ' all the prophets.' " [1] Here is evidently the doctrine of the Magi or of Emanations.

Of this quotation from Peter, by Clemens, the Christian divine will perhaps say, It is spurious. I deny his right to say any such thing. He has no right to assume that Peter never wrote any letters but the two in our canon ; or that Clemens is either mistaken or guilty of fraud in this instance, without some proof.

The following passage of Beausobre's shews that St. Augustine coincided in opinion with the other fathers whom I have cited on the meaning of the word ראשית Rasit : " Car si par Reschit " on entend le Principe actif de la création, et non pas le commencement, alors Moïse n'a plus dit " que le Ciel et la Terre furent let premières des œuvres de Dieu. Il a dit seulement, que Dieu " créa le ciel et la terre par le Principe, qui est son Fils. Ce n'est pas l'époque, c'est l'auteur " immédiat de la création qu'il enseigne. Je tiens encore cette pensée de St. Augustin. Les " anges, dit il, ont été faits avant le Firmament, et même avant ce qu'est rapporté par Moïse, " Dieu fit le ciel et la terre par le Principe ; car ce mot de Principe ne veut pas dire, que le ciel et " la terre furent faits avant toutes choses, puisque Dieu avoit déjà fait les anges auparavant ; il " veut dire, que Dieu a fait toutes choses par SAGESSE, qui est son Verbe, et que l'Écriture a " nommée le Principe." [2]

By Wisdom, I have no doubt, was the secret, if not the avowed, meaning of the words ; and I also feel little doubt that, in the course of this work, I shall prove that the word Αρχη used by the Seventy and by Philo had the same meaning. But the fact that the LXX. give Αρχη as the rendering of Berasit, which is shewn to have the meaning of WISDOM by the authorities cited above, is of itself quite enough to justify the assertion that one of the meanings of the word Αρχη was WISDOM, and in any common case it would be so received by all Lexicographers.

WISDOM is one of the three first of the Eight Emanations which formed the eternal and ever-happy Octoade of the oriental philosophers, and of the ten Sephiroth of the Jewish Cabala. See Parkhurst's Hebrew Lexicon, p. 668, and also his Greek one in voce Αρχη, where the reader will find that, with all his care, he cannot disguise the fact that ראש ras means wisdom. See also Beausobre, [3] where, at large, may be found the opinions of the greatest part of the most learned of the Fathers and Rabbis on the first verse of Genesis.

The Jerusalem Targum, as already stated, is the orthodox explanation of the Jews : it used to be read in their synagogues, and the following is its rendering of this celebrated text, which com-

---

" actif et immediat de toutes choses. Ainsi au lieu de traduire, Au commencement Dieu fit le Ciel et la Terre, ils " traduisoient, Dieu fit le Ciel et la Terre PAR LE PRINCIPE, c'est à-dire, selon l'explication du Targum de Jerusalem, " PAR LA SAGESSE : Maimonide soutient, que cette explication est la seule LITTÉRALE ET VERITABLE. Elle passa " d'abord chez les Chrétiens. On la trouve non seulement dans Chalcidius, qui marque qu'elle venoit des Hébreux, " mais dans Méthodius, dans Origène, et dans Clement d'Alexandrie, plus ancien que l'un et l'autre." Beausobre, Hist. Manich. Liv. vi. Ch. i. p. 290.

[1] Beausobre, Hist. Manich. Liv. vi. Ch. i. p. 290.  [2] Hist. Manich. Liv. vi. Ch. i. p. 291.

[3] Hist. Manich. Liv. v. Ch. iii. and Liv. vi. Ch. i.

pletely justifies that which I have given of it : בחכמה ברא אלוה יתשמיא וית ארצא In sapientia creavit Deus cœlum et terram. [1]

It is said in Proverbs viii. 22, " Jehovah possessed me," *wisdom*, ראשית *rasit* ; but not בראשית *b-rasit*, which it ought to be, to justify our vulgar translation, which is, " The Lord possessed me " IN *the beginning.*" The particle ב *b*, the sign of the ablative case, is wanting ; but it is interpolated in our translation, to justify the rendering, because it would be nonsense to say the Lord possessed me, *the beginning.* [2]

The Targum of Jerusalem says that God made man by his Word, or Λογος, Gen. i. 26. So says Jonathan, Es. xlv. 12 ; and in Gen. i. 27, he says, that the Λογος created man after his image. See Allix's Judgment of the Jewish Church, p. 131. From this I think Dr. Allix's assertion is correct, that the Targum considered the ראשית *rasit*, and the Λογος to be identical.

And it seems to me to be impossible to form an excuse for Parkhurst, as his slight observation in his Greek Lexicon shews that he was not ignorant. Surely supposing that he thought those authorities given above to be mistaken, he ought, in common honesty, to have noticed them, according to his practice with other words, in similar cases.

4. According to the Jewish Cabala a number of Sephiroths, being Emanations, issued or flowed from God—of which the chief was *Wisdom:* In Genesis it is said, by *Wisdom* God created or formed, &c. Picus, of Mirandula, confirms my rendering, and says, " This *Wisdom* is the *Son.*" [3] Whether the Son or not, this is evidently the first emanation, MINERVA—the Goddess of *Wisdom* emanating or issuing from the head of Jove, (or Iao or Jehovah,) as described on an Etruscan brass plate in the Cabinet of Antiquities at Bologna. [4] This is known to be Etruscan, from the names being on the arms of the Gods in Etruscan letters, which proves it older than the Romans, or probably than the Grecians of Homer.

M. Basnage says, " Moses Nachmanides advanced three Sephiroths above all the rest ; *they* " *have never been seen by any one ; there is not any defect in them nor any disunion.* If any one " should add another to them, he would deserve death. There is, therefore, nothing but a dispute " about words : you call three *lights* what Christians call Father, Son, and Holy Ghost. That " first eternal number is the Father: the WISDOM by which God created the heavens is the Son : " and Prudence or Understanding, which makes the third number of the Cabalists, is the Christian " Holy Ghost." [5]

5. The word *Rasit*, as we might expect, is found in the Arabic language, and means, as our Lexicographers, who are the same class of persons that made our Hebrew Lexicons, tell us, *head*, *chief*—and is used as a term of honour applied to great persons : for instance, Aaron-al-raschid. Al is the emphatic article. Abd-al-raschid, i. e. Abdallah-al-raschid, &c.

For a long time I flattered myself that I might set down Parkhurst as one of the very few Polemics, with whose works I was acquainted, against whom I could not bring a charge of pious fraud, but the way in which he has treated the first word of Genesis puts it out of my power. It seems to me impossible to believe that this learned man could be ignorant of the construction which had been given to the word ראשית *rasit.*

Again, I repeat, it is impossible to acquit Parkhurst of disingenuousness in suppressing, in his Hebrew Lexicon, the opinions held respecting the meaning of this word by CLEMENS ALEXANDRINUS, CHALCIDIUS, METHODIUS, ORIGEN, ST. AUGUSTINE, MAIMONIDES, and by the authors of

---

[1] Kircher, Œd. Ægypt. Syntag. II. Cap. vii.  
[3] Kircher, Œd. Egypt. Syntag. II. Cap. vii.  
[6] Book iv. Ch. v. Sect. vii.  
[2] Vide Parkhurst, p. 668.  
[4] A copy of the plate may be seen in Montfaucon.

the Targum of Jerusalem, the accredited exposition of the Jewish church, and in the slight and casual way in which he has expressed a disapprobation of the rendering of the Targum, in his Greek Lexicon. It is really not to be believed that he and the other modern Lexicographers— Bates, Taylor, Calassio, &c., should have been ignorant, for I believe they all suppress the rendering. It ought to serve as a warning to all inquirers that they never can be too much on their guard. How true is the dictum of Bacon, that every thing connected with religion is to be viewed with suspicion !

*Wisdom* was the first emanation from the Divine power, the protogonos, the beginning of all things, the Rasit of Genesis, the Buddha of India, the Logos of Plato and St. John, as I shall prove. Wisdom was the beginning of creation. *Wisdom* was the primary, and *beginning* the secondary, meaning of the word. Of its rendering in the LXX., by the word Ἀϱχη, I shall treat presently at great length. The fact was, Parkhurst saw that if the word had the meaning of *Wisdom* it would instantly establish the doctrine of Emanations ; and if he had given, as he ought to have done, the authority of the Jerusalem Targum and of Maimonides, no person would have hesitated for a moment to prefer it to his sophistry. But as the doctrine of emanations must, at all events, be kept out of sight, he suppressed the authorities.

The meaning of *wisdom*, which the word *Ras* bore, I can scarcely doubt was, in fact, secret, sacred, and mystical ; and in the course of the following work my reader will perceive, that wherever a certain mythos, which will be explained, was concerned, two clear and distinct meanings of the words will be found : one for the initiated, and one for the people. This is of the first importance to be remembered. If the ancients really had a secret system it was a practice which could not well be dispensed with, and innumerable proofs of it will be given ; but among them there will not be found one more important, nor more striking, than that of the word ראש *ras* or בראשית *b-rasit*. To the reconsideration of the meaning of this word I shall many times have occasion to revert. I shall now return to the text of Deuteronomy, from which I have digressed.

That the angels are in fact emanations from the Divine substance, according to the Mosaic system, is proved from Deut. xxxiii. 2. Moses says, according to the Septuagint, *The Lord is come from Sinai : he has appeared to us from Seir ; he shined forth from Paran with thousands of saints, and having his* ANGELS ON HIS RIGHT HAND. But M. Beausobre[1] has shewn, (and which Parkhurst, p. 149, in voce, דת *dt*, confirms,) that the Hebrew word אשדת *asdt*, which the Septuagint translates *angels*, means *effusions*, that is, *emanations*, from the Divine substance. According to Moses and the Seventy translators, therefore, the Angels were Emanations from the Divine substance. Thus we see here that the doctrines of the Persians and that of the Jews, and we shall see afterward, of the Gnostic and Manichean Christians, were in reality the same.

The fact has been established that the Septuagint copy which we now possess is really a copy of that spoken of by Philo and the Evangelists, though in many places corrupted, so that no more need be said about it. But if any one be disposed to dispute this passage of the LXX., it may be observed to him, that the probability is strongly in favour of its being genuine.

It is not a disputed text. It is found in these words in the ancient Italic version, which was made from the Septuagint, [2] which shews that it was there in a very early period, and it did not flatter the prejudice or support the interest either of the modern Jews or the ruling power of the Christians to corrupt it, but the contrary. As M. Beausobre properly observes, if the question

---

[1] Hist. Manich. Liv. ix. Ch. ii.

[2] Qui avoit été fait sur les LXX. Beausobre, Hist. Manich. Liv. ix. Ch. ii. p. 621 ; and Sim. Hist. Crit. du V. Test. Liv. ii. Ch. xi.

be decided by authority, the authority of the Septuagint is vastly preferable to that of the Masorets, who lived many ages after the makers of the Septuagint. And, as he says, if reason be admitted to decide it, a person inclined to favour the system of emanations, would urge, in the first place, that אשדת *asdt* is a Hebrew word, one entire word, which cannot be divided; and that it is evident from the Septuagint, that the ancient Hebrews did not divide it. Secondly, he would say, that *Dat*, which signifies *law, commandment*, is not a Hebrew but a Median[1] word, which the Hebrews took from the Medes, and is not to be found in any of their books, but such as were written after the captivity; so that there is no reason to suppose it had been used by Moses in Deuteronomy. Thirdly, he would say, that the fire of the law, or the law of fire, as our English has it, is unnatural; and that although it is said the law was given from the middle of the fire, there is nothing to shew that it was from the right hand of God. In fine, he would urge that the explanation of the LXX. is much more natural. God comes with thousands of saints, and the angels, the principal angels, those who are named Emanations were at his right hand. These proofs would have been invincible in the first ages of Christianity, where the version of the Septuagint was considered to be inspired, and had much greater authority given to it than to the Hebrew.

In many of Dr. Kennicot's Hebrew codices, the word אשדת *adst*, is written in one word, but not in all: it is likewise the same in three of the Samaritan; and in two of the latter it is written אשדרת *asdut*. The following are the words of the Septuagint:

Κυριος εκ Σινα ηκει, και επεφανεν εκ Σηειρ ημιν, και κατεσπευσεν εξ ορες Φαραν, συν μυριασι Καδης · εκ δεξιων αυτη Αγγελοι μετ᾽ αυτε.[2]

Nothing can be more absurd than the vulgar translation, which is made from a copy in which the words have been divided by the Masorets. But it was necessary to risk any absurdity, rather than let the fact be discovered that the word meant angels or emanations, which would so strongly tend to confirm the doctrine of the Gnostics, and also prove that the religions of Moses and the Persians were the same. M. Beausobre has satisfactorily explained the contrivance of the Masorets to disguise the truth by dividing the word *Asdt* אשדת, or, as he calls it, *Eschdot*, into two, Esch-Dot. And his observations respecting the authority of the Italic versions and the Septuagint, written so many centuries before the time of the Masorets, when the language was a living one, is conclusive on the subject. The very fact of adopting the use of the points, is a proof either that the language was lost or nearly so, or that some contrivance, after the time of Jerom, was thought necessary by the Jews, to give to the unpointed text such meaning as they thought proper.

6. But to return to the word Berasit, or more properly the word ראשית *Rasit*, the particle ב *beth* being separated from it. A curious question has arisen among Christian philosophers, whether Time was in existence before the creation here spoken of, or the beginning, if it be so translated.

The word cannot mean the beginning of creation, according to the Mosaic account, because the context proves that there were created beings before the creation of our world—for instance, the angels or cherubim who guarded the gate of paradise after the fall.[3]

In common language, the words, *In the beginning*, mean some little time after a thing has begun; but this idea cannot be applied to the creation. The expression cannot be applied to any period of time *after* the universe began to exist, and it cannot be applied to any period *before* it began to exist. If the words *at first* be used, they are only different words for precisely the same

---

[1] He says he owes this remark to Mons. de la Croze, à qui je serois bien fâché de la dérober.

[2] Deut. xxxiii. 2, LXX. juxt. Exemp. Vatic.; Beausobre, Hist. Manich. Liv. ix. Ch. ii. p. 621.

[3] See St. Agustine above, in section 3 and Job xxxviii. 7.

idéa. The translators of the Septuagint and Onkelos are undoubtedly entitled to high respect. In this case, however, they advocate an untenable opinion, if they both do advocate the meaning of *beginning*, because our system was not the first of created things ; and they make the divine penman say what was not true—in fact, to contradict himself in what follows. But if we adopt the explanation of the Jerusalem Targum and of the other learned Jews, and of the earliest of the fathers of the church, there is nothing in it inconsistent with the context ; but, on the contrary, it is strictly in accordance with it, and with the general system of oriental philosophy, on which the whole Mosaic system was founded.

I think the author of Genesis had more philosophy than to write about the *beginning* of the world. I cannot see any reason why so much anxiety should be shewn, by some modern translators, to construe this word as meaning *beginning*. I see clearly enough why others of them should do so, and why the ancient translators did it. They had a preconceived dogma to support, their partiality to which blinded their judgment, and of philosophy they did not possess much. However, it cannot be denied that, either in a primary or secondary sense, the word means *wisdom* as well as *beginning*, and, therefore, its sense here must be gathered from the context.

I will now return to the word *Samim*, as I promised in the early part of this book.

7. The two words called in the first chapter of Genesis השמים *e-samim*, the heavens, ought to be translated *the planets*. In that work the sun, and moon, and the earth, are said to be formed, and also separately from them the samim or planets ; and afterward the stars also. Dr. Parkhurst has very properly explained the word to mean *disposers*. They are described in the Chaldean Oracles as a septenary of living beings. By the ancients they were thought to have, under their special care, the affairs of men. Philo was of this opinion, and even Maimonides declares, that they are endued with life, knowledge, and understanding ; that they acknowledge and praise their Creator. On this opinion of the nature of the planets, all judicial astrology, magic, was founded—a science, I believe, almost as generally held by the ancients, as the being of a God is by the moderns.[1]

Phornutus, Περι Ουρανε,[2] says, " For the ancients took those for Gods whom they found to " move in a certain regular manner, thinking them to be the causers of the changes of the air and " the *conservation of the universe*. These, then, are Gods (Θεοι) which are the disposers (Θετηϛες) " and formers of all things."

The word עיטמיא *itsmia* is used by the Targum of Jerusalem for the word שמים את *at smim* of Genesis, and I think fully justifies my rendering of that word by *planets* instead of the word *heavens*. It comes from the root שם *sm*, which signifies to fix, to enact, *pono, sancior*—and means *placers, fixers, enactors*.

With respect to the שמים *smim*, Parkhurst is driven to a ridiculous shift, similar to the case of the first word ראשית *rasit*. It was necessary to conceal the truth from his Christian reader, but this was very difficult without laying himself open to a charge of pious fraud. In this instance he will be supported by the Jews, because *at this day* neither Jews nor Christians will like to admit that the very foundation of their religions is laid in judicial astrology. But such I affirm is the fact, as any one may at once see, by impartially considering what Parkhurst has unwillingly been obliged to allow in his Lexicon. He does not admit that the singular of the word means *a* disposer or placer, or *the* disposer or *placer*, but he takes the plural and calls them the disposer*s* or placer*s*. And, shutting his eyes to the planetary bodies and to the word רקיע *rqio*, which means the space, air, or firmament, and which can have no other meaning, he calls the שמים *smim*, *the firmament*, and says it is the disposers. It is absurd to speak of the air, or space, or firmament, in the plural ; and that Parkhurst must have known. In some author (I yet believe somewhere in

---

[1] See Faber, Vol. II. p. 226.        [2] Ap. Parkhurst, in voce שם *sm*, p. 745.

Parkhurst) I found the שמים *smim*, called *the disposers of the affairs of men*, and by mistake, if it were a mistake, I quoted it as from Parkhurst in my Celtic Druids. It is of little consequence where I got the quotation, as the fact itself is true. The planets in ancient times were always taken to be the superintendants and regulators of the affairs of mankind, and this is the meaning of Genesis. This idea, too, was the foundation of all judicial astrology : which is as visible as the noonday sun in every part of the Old and New Testament. The word רקיע *rqio* means the firmament or ethereal space ; the word כבב *ccb* means a star : and though the word שמים *smim* sometimes means stars, as we call the planets *stars*, yet its primary meaning is *the disposers* or *planets*. Originally the fixed stars were not regarded as disposers.

For proof that the word שמים *smim* means *placers* or *disposers*, see Hutchinson, " Of the " Trinity of the Gentiles,"[1] and Moses's Principia.[2] They shew that the essential meaning of the word שמים *smim* is disposers or placers of other things. If they were not to dispose or place the affairs or conduct of men, pray what were they to place ? Were they to dispose of the affairs of beasts, or of themselves? They were the צבא *Zba*, or Heavenly Host, and I have no doubt the original word was confined to the wandering stars, whatever it might be afterward. Parkhurst and Hutchinson shew great unwillingness to allow that they mean disposers, but they are both obliged to confess it, and in this confession, admit, in fact, the foundation of judicial astrology.

It is very certain that the ancient philosophers knew the difference between the stars and planets, as well as the moderns. This is the only place where the formation of the planets is named ; the formation of the sun, moon, and stars, is described in the 14th verse. As I have just said, השמים *esmim* does not mean the vast expanse, because this is afterward described in the 6th verse by the word רקיע *rqio*.

In the eighth verse the word *rqio* is used. In our translation it is said, he called the expanse heavens. But before the word רקיע *rqio* the particle ל *l*, the sign of the dative case is written, which shews that a word is understood to make sense. Thus, And he called the שמם *smim*, in the *rqio* or expanse, planets. This merely means, and he gave to the *smim* the name which they now bear, of smim. This explanation of mine is justified by the Jerusalem Targum, in its use of the word יתשמיא *itsmia*, placers.

Persons are apt to regard with contempt the opinion, that the planetary bodies are animated or rational beings. But let it not be forgotten that the really great Kepler believed our globe to be endowed with living faculties ; that it possessed instinct and volition—an hypothesis which Mons. Patrin has supported with great ingenuity.[3] Among those who believed that the planets were intelligent beings, were Philo, Origen, and Maimonides.[4]

The first verse of Genesis betrays the Persian or Oriental philosophy in almost every word. The first word *rasit* ראשית or *wisdom* refers to one, or probably to the chief, of the emanations from the Deity. This is allowed by most of the early fathers, who see in it the second person of the Trinity. The word בארא *bara* in the singular number, followed by אלהים *Aleim* in the plural, or a noun of multitude, refers to the Trinity, three Persons and one God ; and does not mean that the Aleim created, but that it formed, εποιησεν, fecit, as the Septuagint says, out of matter previously existing. On the question of the eternity of matter it is perfectly neutral : it gives no opinion. The word השמם *esmim* in the Hebrew, and ושמין *esmin* in the Chaldee, do not mean the heavens or heavenly bodies generally, but the planets only, the disposers, as Dr. Parkhurst, after the Magi, calls them.

This is all perfectly consistent, and in good keeping, with what we know of the Jewish Cabala.

---

[1] In voce, p. 20.     [2] Part II. p. 56.
[3] Vide Jameson's Cuvier, p. 45, and Nouveau Dict. d'Histoire Naturelle.     [4] Faber, Pag. Idol. Vol. I. p. 32.

And it is surely only reasonable to expect, that there should be something like consistency between this verse and the Cabala, which we know was founded, in some degree, perhaps entirely, upon it.

The conduct of Christian expositors, with respect to the words שמים *smim* and ראשית *rasit*, has been as unfair as possible. They have misrepresented the meaning of them in order to prevent the true astrological character of the book from being seen. But, that the first does mean *disposers*, the word *heavens* making nonsense, and the words relating to the stars, in the 16th verse, shewing that they cannot be meant, put it beyond a question. My reader may, therefore, form a pretty good judgment how much Parkhurst can be depended upon for the meaning of the second, from the striking fact that, though he has filled several columns with observations relating to the opinions of different expositors, he could not find room for the words, *the opinion of the Synagogue is, that the word means* WISDOM, *or the Jerusalem Targum says it means* WISDOM. But it was necessary to conceal from the English reader, as already stated, the countenance it gives to judicial astrology and the doctrine of emanations.

Indeed, I think the doctrine of Emanations in the Jewish system cannot be denied. This Mr. Maurice unequivocally admits : " The Father is the great fountain of the divinity ; the Son and " the Holy Spirit are EMANATIONS from that fountain." Again, " The Christian Trinity is a " Trinity of subsistences, or persons joined by an indissoluble union." [1] The reader will please to recollect that *hypostasis* means subsistence, which is a Greek word—ὑποςασις, from ὑπο *sub*, and ιςημι, *stó, existo.*

In the formation of an opinion respecting the real meaning of such texts as these, the prudent inquirer will consider the general character of the context; and, in order that he may be the better enabled to do this, I request him to suspend his judgment till he sees the observations which will be made in the remainder of this work.

Whatever trifling differences or incongruities may be discovered between them, the following conclusions are inevitable, viz. that the religion of Abraham and that of the Magi, were in reality the same ; that they both contained the doctrine of the Trinity ; and that the oriental historians who state this fact, state only what is true.

Dr. Shuckford gives other reasons to shew that the religions of Abraham and of the Persians were the same. He states, that Dr. Hyde was of his opinion, and thus concludes : " The first " religion, therefore, of the Persians, was the worship of the true God, and they continued in it " for some time after Abraham was expelled Chaldæa, having the same faith and worship as " Abraham had, except only in those points concerning which he received instruction after his " going into Haran and into Canaan." [2]

8. I must now beg my reader to review what has been said respecting the celebrated name of God, *Al,* Ale, Aleim; and to observe that this was in all the Western Asiatic nations the name both of God and of the Sun. This is confirmed by Sir W. Drummond and Mr. Parkhurst, as the reader has seen, and by the names given by the Greeks to places which they conquered. Thus : בית אל *Bit Al,* House of the Sun, became Heliopolis. I beg my reader also to recollect that when the Aleim appeared it was generally in the form of fire, thus he appeared to Moses in the bush. Fire was, in a particular manner, held sacred by the Jews and Persians ; a sacred fire was always burning in the temple of Jerusalem. From all this, and much more which the reader will find presently, he will see that though most undoubtedly the Sun was not the object of the adoration of Moses, it is very evident that it had been closely allied to it. In the time of Moses, not the sun, but the higher principle thought to reside in the sun, perhaps the Creator of the sun himself, had

---

[1] Maurice, Ind. Ant. Vol. IV. p. 49.　　　　　　[2] Shuckford, Book v. p. 308, Ed.

become the object of adoration, by the Gentiles if not by Moses (but of the latter it may be matter of doubt) ; and it is probable that it had arisen as I have supposed and described in my last book.

Thus if a person was to say, that the God of Moses resolved himself at last into the Sun, he would not be correct; but he would be very near it. The object of this observation will be seen hereafter.

I must also beg my reader's attention to the observation at the end of Chapter II. Sect. 4, of this book relating to the word EL, as used by Sir W. Drummond. In the Asiatic language, the first letter of the word is the first letter of the alphabet and not the fifth, as here written by Sir William, and this shews the importance of my system of reducing the alphabets to their originals : for here, most assuredly, this name of the Sun is the same as the Hebrew name of God. But by the mistake of Sir William this most important fact is concealed. No doubt dialectic variations in language will take place [1] between neighbouring countries, which occasion difficulties, and for which allowance must be made : but, by not attending to my rule, we increase them, and create them, where they are not otherwise to be found.

But we do not merely increase *difficulties*, we disguise and conceal absolute *facts*. Thus it is a fact that the Sun and the God of Moses had the same names ; that is, that the God of Moses was called by the same word which meant Sun, in the Asiatic language : but by miscalling one of them *El* instead of Al, the fact is concealed, and it is an important fact, and will lead to important results.

We must also recollect, that when I translate the first word of Genesis by the word *Wisdom*, I am giving no new theory of my own, but only the orthodox exposition of the Jewish religion, as witnessed in the Jerusalem Targum, read in their synagogues, supported by the authorities of the most eminent of the Jewish Rabbis, Maimonides, &c., and the most learned of the Christian fathers, Clemens, Origen, &c. All this is of importance to be remembered, because a great consequence will be deduced from this word *Wisdom*. It was, as it were, the foundation on which a mighty structure was erected.

It was by what may be called a peculiar Hypostasis, denominated *Wisdom*, that the *higher principle* operated when it formed the world. This is surely quite sufficient to shew its great importance—an importance which we shall see demonstrated hereafter, when I treat of the celebrated Buddha of India.

------

## CHAPTER IV.

WHY CYRUS RESTORED THE TEMPLE.—MELCHIZEDEK.—ABRAHAM, WHAT HE WAS.—ABRAHAM THE FATHER OF THE PERSIANS.—DANIEL.—BOOK OF ESTHER, PERSIAN.— ZOROASTER.— VARIATION BETWEEN PERSIANS AND ISRAELITES.—SACRIFICES.—RELIGION OF ZOROASTER.—RELIGION OF ZOROASTER CONTINUED.— ZENDAVESTA.—OBSERVATIONS ON THE RELIGION OF JEWS AND PERSIANS.—ALL ANCIENT RELIGIONS ASTROLOGICAL.

1. FROM the striking similarity between the religion of Moses and that of the Persians, it is not difficult to see the reason why Cyrus, Darius, and the Persians, restored the temples of Jerusalem

------

[1] With the Syrians the A changed into the O.

and Gerizim, when they destroyed the temples of the idolaters in Egypt and other places, which, in fact, they did wherever they came. It appears probable that the temple on Gerizim was built or restored within a few years of the same time with that at Jerusalem : and for the same reason —because the religion was that of the Persians, with such little difference as distance of country or some peculiar local circumstances in length of time might produce.

In Genesis xiv. 20, we read, that when Abraham returned from the pursuit of the five kings who were smitten by him as far as Hobah and Damascus, he received gifts from Melchizedek, King of Salem, and paid him tithes of all he had taken from his enemies. The situation of this Salem has been much disputed, and concerning it I shall have much to say hereafter : but it was evidently somewhere West of the Jordan, in the country of the Canaanites. Now this king and priest is said to have been a priest of the most high God. And as the Canaanites *were then in the land,* (Gen. xii. 6,) or were then its inhabitants, it is evident that he could be no other than their priest. There is nothing in the sacred history which militates against this in the slightest degree. It is quite absurd to suppose that there should be priests without a people, and there were no others besides the Canaanites. There is no expression which would induce us to believe that they were idolaters in the time of Abraham. The covenants and treaties of friendship which Abraham entered into with them, raise a strong presumption that they could not then have been so wicked as they are represented to have been in the time of Moses, five hundred years afterward. As the history supplies no evidence that the Canaanites were idolaters in the time of Abraham, the fact of a priest of the true God, and this priest a king, being in the midst of them, almost proves that they were not idolaters. The conduct of Abimelech, (Genesis xx.,) in restoring Sarah to her husband, as soon as he found her to be a married woman, and his reproof of Abraham for his deceit, shew, whatever his religion might be, that his morality was at least as good as that of the father of the faithful. But several circumstances named in the context, prove him of the same religion.

Dr. Shuckford not only agrees with me that Abraham and the Canaanites were of the same religion, and that Melchizedek was their priest, but he also shews that Abimelech and the Philistines were at that time of the same religion.[1] He also gives some reason to suppose that the Egyptians were the same.[2]

The circumstance that the old inhabitants of Palestine (Palli-stan) were of the same religion as the tribe which came with Abraham, will be seen by and by to be of consequence. This can scarcely be accounted for, except we suppose them to have come from the same country from which he came.

Joseph could hardly have married a daughter of the priest Potiphar, if he had been an idolater. And it is curious that he was priest of On or Heliopolis, a place which will be found to be of great importance in the following observations. Shuckford says,

" Melchizedec, the King of Salem, was a priest of the most high God, and he received and " entertained Abraham as a true servant and particular favourite of that God, whose priest he " himself was; *blessed* (said he) *be Abraham,* servant of the most high God, possessor of heaven " and earth."[3]

Respecting the rites or ceremonies performed by this priest, few particulars are known. It appears his votaries paid him tithes. Abraham, we have seen, paid him tithes of all the plunder which he took from the five kings whom he had defeated. This contribution is enforced in the religion of the ancient Persians, and also in the religious ordinances of the Jews. It is very singular that the exact *tenth* should be found in all the three religions to be paid. It might be asked,

---

[1] Book v. pp. 309, 310.        [2] Ibid. pp. 312, 313.        [3] Gen. xiv. 19 ; Shuckford, Book v. p. 310.

If they were not the *same* religions, how came they all to fix upon the exact number of ten, and not the number of eight or twelve? There is nothing in the number, that should lead their adherents to it, rather than to any other. The second of the rites of Melchizedek's religion which is known, is the offering or sacrifice of bread and wine, about which more will be said hereafter.

It is not possible to determine from *Genesis* where the Salem was of which Melchizedek was priest. (I pay no attention to the *partisan Josephus*.) Taking advantage of this uncertainty the Christians have settled it to be Jerusalem. But it happens in this case that a Heathen author removes the difficulty. Eupolemus states that Abraham received gifts from Melchizedek in the Holy City of Hargarizim, or of Mount Gerizim. Har, in the ancient language, signifies mount. This proves that there was a place holy to the Lord upon Gerizim, long before Joshua's time, whatever the Jews may allege to the contrary against the Samaritans.

There is much reason to believe that this Melchizedek was the priest of the Temple of Jove, Jupiter, or Iao, without image, spoken of by the Greeks, to which Pythagoras and Plato are said to have resorted for study; the place where Joshua placed his unhewn stones. The mountain Carmel, probably, extended over a considerable extent of country. Hargerizim was probably looked on as a mount of Carmel, as Mount Blanc is a mount of the Alps.

Melchizedek (Gen. xiv. 19) ought to be written מלכי־צדק *mlki-zdq*, and means literally *Kings of Justice;* but it is evidently a proper name. The proper translation is, " And Melchizedek, " king of peace, brought forth bread and wine, because he (*was*, understood) priest to the most " high God. And he blessed him (or he bestowed his benediction upon him, first addressing a " prayer to God) and said, Blessed be Abram, by the most high God, possessor of heaven and " earth; (he then addresses Abraham;) and blessed be the most high God who hath delivered " thine enemies into thine hand," &c. I cannot conceive how any person who comes to the consideration of this text with an impartial and candid mind can find any difficulty.

When David and the priests removed the holy place from Gerizim to the city of the Jebusites, they then, perhaps, first called it *Jerusalem ;* and to justify themselves against the charges of the Samaritans, they corrupted the text in Joshua, as some of the most eminent Protestant divines are obliged to allow, substituting Ebal for Gerizim, and Gerizim for Ebal. The whole is a description of the sacrifice of bread and wine, repeated by Jesus Christ a few hours previous to his crucifixion : the same, probably, as was offered by Pythagoras at the shrine of the bloodless Apollo. It was sometimes celebrated with wine, sometimes with water. The English priests, in the time of Edward the Sixth, not knowing what to make of it, ordered it in the rubric to be celebrated with both, mixing them together. It is still continued by the Jews at their pascal feast, and is altogether, when unaccompanied by nonsense not belonging to it, the most beautiful religious ceremony that ever was invented. It is found in the Buddhist rites of Persia before they were corrupted, in the rites of Abraham, of Pythagoras, and, in a future page I shall shew, of the ancient Italians, and of Jesus Ναζωραιος, the Nazarite, of the city of Nazarites, or of Nazareth. Of this city of Nazareth it might be said, that it was nothing, in fact, but a suburb of the sacred city *which God had chosen to place his name there.* (Deut. xii. 5—14.) It was a convent of Essenian Monks, or Carmelites, for all monks were Carmelites before the fifth century after Christ. If Pythagoras were one of them, in this very place, it is probable that he took the vows, *Tria vota substantialia,* Poverty, Chastity, and Obedience, still taken by the Buddhists in India, and Carmelites in Rome. These constituted the companies of prophets named in 1 Sam. xix. 20, and I see no reason why Jesus may not have been the head of the order, though I admit we have no proof of it; but of this more hereafter.

Melchizedek could not be king of the city of Jerusalem in the time of Abraham, because it was not built; tor it was in the *thicket* in this place, Mount Moriah, where he found the ram fast by the horns, when he prepared to sacrifice his son Isaac. It therefore follows, that the city of the Jebusites must have been built between the time fixed for the sacrifice by Abraham, and the time of David; or rather, perhaps, between the time of Moses and of David; and for this to have been effected, there was a space of about five hundred years. By building an altar here it might be made a holy place, and thus a city might be drawn to it. If there had been a city here in the time of Abraham, the history would have said, that he went to the *town* to sacrifice, not to the *mount*. The whole context implies that there was no town.

2. It is very clear that Abraham is represented in the history as a rich and powerful shepherd king, what we should now call an Arab or Tartar chieftain, constantly migrating with his tribe from place to place to seek pasture for his flocks and herds. He probably never remained long in one situation, but dwelt in the mountains in summer, and in the plains in winter. How formidable, and indeed ruinous, wandering tribes of this description have been in later times to the Romans and other civilized nations is well known. And though the distance from Canaan to Persia is considerable, it is not greater than migratory shepherd tribes often pass, and by no means equal to Abraham's journey which we learn from Genesis that he did take from Haran, in the upper part of Mesopotamia, to Egypt. Terah, the father of Abraham, seems to have been of the same migratory character, for he removed from Ur in Chaldea, to Haran in Mesopotamia—no little distance. (Gen. xi. 31.)

Palestine is now nearly in the same situation in which it was in the time of Abraham. The nomade tribes under the patriarchal government of their Sheiks, ramble about the country, sometimes attacking the towns, sometimes making treaties and confederacies with them.

When I speak of Abraham I mean the tribe which became known by the name of Israelites. Whether there was such a man as Abraham, and whether the tribe did not come from much more eastern countries, will be discussed hereafter.

It appears that Abraham attacked the confederate kings, and drove them before him, (Gen. xiv. 15,) and that the war raged (ver. 6) from near Damascus to Mount Seir: from which it is evident, that it must have been a very great one. When, therefore, it is said that Abraham divided his 318 trained servants against the confederate kings, the literal meaning cannot be intended. Some very learned persons have supposed, that the whole of this account is an astronomical allegory, and every one must confess that this is not destitute of probability. But allowing all that Sir W. Drummond has said to be true, it is still evident from the terms used, such as Damascus, Mount Seir, &c., &c., the names of places must have been used in the allegory (and if the names of *places* be used, why should not the names of *persons?*) by way of accommodation: and whether it be all allegory or not, the argument will not be affected, because it is only here undertaken to produce such probable proofs that the worship of Abraham and his family and that of the Persians were the same, as that no unprejudiced person can refuse his assent to them.

Dr. Hyde [1] not being able to account for the great similarity, which could not be denied, between the religion of Moses and of Zoroaster, (without any authority,) supposes, that the latter was a slave or servant in the family of Daniel or of Ezra, at Babylon, during the captivity; and that he was by birth a Jew. This ridiculous fancy is supported by Prideaux; [2] but as it is completely laughed down by Maurice, [3] no more need be said about it, except merely that the similarity, indeed identity, of the two religions being clearly seen by the learned doctor, it was neces-

---

[1] Hist. Rel. Vet. Pers. Chap. xxiv. p. 314.　　　[2] Con. Vol. I. p. 213.　　　[3] Ind. Ant. Vol. II. p. 118.

sary to find some plausible reason for it. Dr. Hyde observed also, that a marked similarity was to be found between Abraham and the Brahma of the Hindoos, but I reserve that point for another chapter.

3. The Persians also claim Ibrahim, i. e. Abraham, for their founder, as well as the Jews. Thus we see that according to all ancient history the Persians, the Jews, and the Arabians, are descendants of Abraham.

But Abraham was not merely the founder of the Persians, but various authors assert, that he was a great Magician, at the head of the Magi, that is, he was at the head of the priesthood, as our king is, and as the Persian kings always were, and as the Roman Emperors found it necessary to become in later days : no doubt a sound and wise policy. His descendants, Jacob for instance, continued to occupy the same station. The standards of the tribes of the Israelites, the ornaments of the Temple, the pillars *Joachim* and *Boaz*, the latter with its orrery or sphere at the top of it, the Urim and Thummim, in short, the whole of the Jewish system betrays judicial astrology, or, in other words, magic, in every part. The Magi of Persia were only the order of priests—Magi in Persia, Clergymen in England. It must not be supposed that the word Magus or Magi, conveyed the vulgar idea attached to modern Magicians, persons dealing with the devil, to work mischief. They probably became objects of detestation to the Christians in the eastern nations from opposing their religion, and in consequence were run down by them, and held up to public odium, in the same way as philosophers are now endeavoured to be, and not without some success. To be versed in *magic* is something horrid, not to be reasoned about. It is to be as bad as Voltaire, or as Lord Byron.

There can be no doubt that judicial astrology, or the knowledge of future events by the study of the stars, was received and practised by all the ancient Jews, Persians, and many of the Christians, particularly the Gnostics and Manicheans. The persons now spoken of, thought that the planets were the signs, that is, gave information of future events, not that they were the causes of them [1] —not that the events were controlled by them : for between these two there is a great difference. Eusebius tells us, on the authority of Eupolemus, that Abraham was an astrologer, and that he taught the science to the priests of *Heliopolis* or *On*. This was a fact universally asserted by the historians of the East. Origen was a believer in this science as qualified above ; and M. Beausobre observes, it is thus that he explained what Jacob says in the prayer of Joseph : *He has read in the tables of heaven all that will happen to you, and to your children.* [2]

4. When the Jews were carried away to Babylon, Daniel is said to have been one of the prisoners, and to have risen to a very high situation at the court of the great king ; and in fact to have become almost his prime minister. (Dan. ii. 48.) On the taking of the city, he appears to have been a principal performer : he was occupied in explaining the meaning of the writing on the wall at the very moment that the city was stormed. After the success of the Persians, we find him again in great power with the new king, who was of his own sect or religion, and as bitter against idolaters as himself. We also find that the Jews were again almost immediately restored to their country.

If Daniel opened the gates of Babylon to admit the enemy, certainly of all men he must have been the best qualified to tell Belshazzar that his city was taken. If he were a Jew, he had been carried away and reduced to slavery by the enemy of his country, and under all the circumstances,

---

[1] It is not meant to say that, at a very early period, the planets were not believed to be the active agents of a superior power : they probably were.

[2] " Il a lu dans les tables du ciel, tout ce qui doit vous arriver, et à vous enfans.".— Beausobre, Hist. Manich. Liv. vii. ch. i. p. 429.

if he made the restoration of his countrymen the price of what in him can hardly be called his treason, very few people will be found to condemn him.

There can be no doubt, but that if the story of Daniel had been met with in a history of the Chinese or the Hindoos, or of any nation where religious prejudice had not beclouded the understanding, all historians would have instantly seen, that the Assyrian despot was justly punished for his egregious folly, in making a slave, whose country he had ruined, one of his prime ministers, and for entrusting him with the command of his capital when besieged by his enemies—by persons professing the same religion as his minister. Upon any other theory, how are we to account for Daniel's being, soon after the capture of Babylon, found to be among the ministers of its conqueror?

I suspect that Daniel was a Chaldee or Culdee or Brahmin priest—a priest of the same order of which, in former times, Melchizedek had been a priest.

The gratification of that spirit which induced Darius, Cyrus, and their successors, to wage a war of extermination wherever they came against the temples, &c., of idolaters, would probably greatly aid Daniel in pleading the cause of his country. But it is worthy of observation that, although the temples, altars, and priests, were restored, both in Judæa and Samaria, yet the country was kept in a state of vassalage to the Persian kings. They had no more kings in Judæa or Samaria, till long after the destruction of the Persian empire by Alexander. [1]

5. Perhaps in the Old Testament there is not a more curious book than that of Esther. It is the only remaining genuine specimen of the ancient chronicles of Persia.

The object of putting this book into the canon of the Jews is to record, for their use, the origin of their feast of Purim. Michaelis is of opinion, from the style of the writing and other circumstances, that the last sixteen verses of this book were added at Jerusalem. This seems very probable. It is pretty clear, from this book, that the religion of Persia in the time of Ahasuerus, as he is named in scripture, had begun to fall into idolatry; and that it was reformed by Mordecai, who slew seventy-five thousand of the idolaters, and restored it to its former state, when it must have been in all its great features like that of the Jews, if not identically the same. A very ingenious writer in the old Monthly Magazine,[2] supposes, " that Ezra was the only Zoroaster, and " that the twenty-one books of Zertusht were the twenty-one books of our Hebrew Bible; with " the exception, indeed, that the canon of Ezra could not include Nehemiah, who flourished after " the death of Ezra, or the extant book of Daniel, which dates from Judas Maccabeus, or the Ec- " clesiastes, which is posterior to Philo: and that it did include the book of Enoch, now retained " only in the Abyssinian canon."

6. No person who has carefully examined will deny, I think, that all the accounts which we have of Zoroaster are full of inconsistencies and contradictions. Plato says, he lived before him 6000 years. Hyde or Prideaux and others, make him contemporary with Darius Hystaspes, or Daniel. By some he is made a Jew; this opinion arose from the observation of the similarity of many of his doctrines to those of the Jews. Now, what is the meaning of the complicated word

---

[1] Cyrus is described as a Messiah or Saviour. He restored the temple, but not the empire. He saved the priests, though he kept the country in slavery; therefore, he was a Messiah, a holy one of God. This is natural enough, and gives us the clue to all the Jewish sacred books. They were the writings of the priests and prophets or monks, not of the nation. An established priesthood generally cares nothing for the nation; it only cares for itself. Though the nation be kept in slavery, if the tithes and altars be restored, all is well; and its conquerors are Saviours, Messiahs. When Alexander conquered Palestine and arrived at Jerusalem, (if he ever did arrive there,) we are told, that the high priest went out to meet him with the keys of the city,—thus renouncing the race of Messiahs who had formerly restored his temple and religion. And in this *treachery* the pious *Rollin* sees great merit: thus what weak people miscal religion obscures the understandings of the best of men.

[2] No. CCCLXXXV. Aug. 1823.

Zoroaster, or Zoradust ?  Of the latter I can make nothing ; but of the former, which is the name by which he was generally called in ancient times, Mr. Faber (I think) has made *Astre, Zur,* or *Syr.*  Here is the star or celestial body *Syr* or *Sur,* which we shall presently find, is, without any great violence, the celestial body, the Bull or the Sun.  Hence we arrive at an incarnation of the Deity, of the Sun, or of Taurus—a renewed incarnation.  This accounts for the antiquity assigned to him by Plato, and for the finding of him again under Darius Hystaspes.  In short, he is a doctrine, or a doctrine taught by a person.  He was the founder of the Magi, who were priests of the religion of the Sun, or of that Being of whom the Sun was the visible form or emblem.

Dr. Hyde, after allowing that the religion of the Persians was originally the same with that of Abraham, and that it fell into Sabiism, says, he thinks that it was reformed by him.  He adds, that the ancient accounts call it the religion of Ibrahim or Abraham.  The idea of its reformation by Abraham, seems to be without any proof.  However, we may safely admit that it consisted in the worship of the one true God, or of the sun, merely as an emblem ; and, that it was really reformed and brought back to this point, from which it had deviated, by some great man, whether he were Abraham or Zoroaster ; as that of the Jews was, from the worship of Apis or the Calf, by Moses.  Hyde says, they had a true account of the creation of the world, [1] meaning hereby the account in Genesis.  This may be very true if the religion of the Jews came from Persia, and was, in fact, identically the same.  How, indeed, could it be essentially different, if, as Dr. Hyde believed, they both worshiped the same God, with nearly the same ceremonies ? [2]

There can be no doubt that the Persians and Assyrians had their religion originally from the same source ; but that the latter, in the time of Cyrus, had degenerated into idolatry, from which the former were at that time free.  This greater purity was probably owing to the reformation which is related by several authors to have been effected by Zoroaster, by whom it had been brought back to its first principles.  It had probably degenerated before his time as much as that of the Assyrians.  The authorities in proof of the fact of some one having reformed the Persian religion, are so decided as to make it almost unquestionable.

7. Notwithstanding the general similarity between the two religions, there are several particulars in which they so pointedly differ, after the time of Moses, that unless the reason of the difference could be shewn, they might be thought to invalidate the argument already adduced.  But as we happen to know, in most cases, the precise reasons for the difference, this very discrepancy rather tends to confirm than to weaken the argument, as they are, in fact, for particular reasons, excep- tions to a general rule.

When it is said that the religions of the descendants of Abraham and of the Persians were the same, considerable allowance must be made for the peculiar circumstances in which they were then placed, and in which they are viewed by us.  We see them in records or histories, whose dates are acknowledged to be long after the time of Abraham, written by persons, strangers, probably, to the religion and language of both these nations.  The Persians have a sacred book, called *Sohfi Ibrahim,* or the book of Abraham, but which ought to be called *the book of the* wisdom *of Abraham.* [3]  The Jews also have a sacred book, called the book of Moses, and the first of which, known to us under the name of Genesis, is called by them רואשית *rasit,* or *the book of wisdom.*  Now, supposing them to have been the same in the time of Abraham, we may reasonably suppose considerable changes and additions would be made, [4] to both religions in the space of five or six hundred years, merely from the natural effects of time : but besides this,

---

[1] Rel. Vet. Pers. Cap. iii.           [2] See Shuckford, Book v. p. 309.
[3] Sohfi is nothing but a word represented by the Greek Σοφια, and by the *Sophoun* of the Arabians
[4] Shuckford, Book v.

we know that they both underwent a great change, one by Zóroaster and the other by Moses, who reformed or formed them anew. The two chiefs or reformers resided at a great distance from each other, and unless they had had some communication it is evident that in their reforms they would not establish the same rites and ceremonies. This may account for several ordinances being found in the law of Moses which are not found in the law of Zoroaster, and *vice versá.*

After the migration of Moses and his tribes from Egypt, before he undertook the invasion of the beautiful country of Palestine, he spent many years in rambling about the deserts or uncultivated pasture lands bordering on the Northern end of the Red Sea, and Arabia Petræa. The settled natives of these countries were sunk into the grossest and most degrading idolatry and super-stition, much worse than even that of the Assyrians, or that of the Persians, before it was reformed by Zoroaster. In order to prevent his people from being contaminated by this example, Maimo-nides informs us, *on the authority of the old Jewish authors,* that Moses made many of his laws in direct opposition to the customs of these people. And for this same reason we are told, in Exodus, that he punished the alliance of his people with any of the natives of these countries, with the most horrible severity : a policy, though sufficiently cruel and unjust, as exercised by him in several cases, certainly wisely contrived for the object he had in view.

The observance of the Sabbath on the *seventh* instead of the *first* day of the week, and in its extreme degree of strictness, was ordained effectually to separate the Jews from the neighbouring nations :[1] and experience has shewn that nothing could have been better contrived for that purpose.

The learned Maimonides says, " they [the Arabians] worshiped the sun at his rising ; for which " reason, as our Rabbins expressly teach in Gemara, Abraham our father designed the West for " the place of the Sanctum Sanctorum, when he worshiped in the mountain Moriah. Of this ido-" latry they interpret what the Prophet Ezekiel saith of the men with their backs toward the " temple of the Lord and their faces toward the East, worshiping the Sun toward the East." (Ezek. viii. 16.) Perhaps a better knowledge of the Arabian superstitions might enable us to account for many other of the ordinances of Moses, which appear to us unmeaning and absurd.[2] In this instance of adoration toward the rising Sun, we see that the religion of the Magi had become corrupted by the Arabians, and that in order to avoid this very corruption, and preserve the worship of one God, (which was the great object of Moses, that to which all the forms and ordi-nances of discipline, both of the Magi and Moses, were subservient,) he established a law directly in opposition to that whence his religion had originally sprung. For the Persians always wor-shiped turning their faces to the East, which the Jews considered an abomination, and uniformly turned to the West when they prayed. And certainly this would be against the author's hypo-thesis, if we did not know exactly the reason for it.

Though Maimonides says that Abraham designed the *West* for the place of adoration, he does not say that he ordered it ; if he had, it would have been mentioned in the Pentateuch. It seems much more likely to have been ordered by Moses, for the same reason that he made the several laws as observed above, in opposition to the corruptions of the Persians or Arabians ; but it might be adopted by Moses for the same reason also that he adopted very many other religious rites of the Egyptians,[3] who sometimes worshiped towards the West, as well as Jews.

---

[1] See my Horæ Sabbaticæ, in the British Museum.

[2] Vide Stanley's Hist. Phil. Chal. Part xix. Ch. ii. pp. 38, 801, 4to.

[3] Perhaps it was not ordained by either Moses or Abraham, as no directions relating to it are to be found in the Pentateuch, but by the builders of the temple, in which the Sacred part, or Cabala, was placed in the West. Beaus. Hist. Manich. Vol. II. Liv. vi. Ch. viii. p. 385 ; Windet de vit. Func. Stat. Sect. vii. p. 77 ; Pirke, Eliez. p. ii. ; Porph. de Ant. Nymp. p. 268.

The third chapter and twenty-fourth verse of Genesis informs us, that a tabernacle was erected to the East of Eden. This tends to prove that this book was of Persian origin, and of a date previous to the time when the Exodus was written ; and that the people whose sacred book it was originally worshiped towards the East. See Parkhurst,[1] who shews that there were tabernacles before that erected by Moses. He also shews that at a time not long after the Exodus the idolaters had the same things.

There can be no doubt that when ignorant fanatics, like the early fathers, Papias, Hegisippus, &c., were travelling, as we know that they did, to find out the true doctrines of the gospel, they would make the traditions bend in some respects to their preconceived notions. Thus the Jewish sects of Nazarenes and Ebionites kept the Sabbath, and other Jewish rites ; and thus, men like Justin, converts from Heathenism, who had no predilection for Judaism, abolished them. Hence we find, at a very early period of the Christian era, the advocates of these opposite opinions persecuting one another, each calling the other *heretic*. The converts from Heathenism, taking their traditions from the Persian fountain, abolished the Sabbath, but adopted the custom of turning to the East in prayer, and the celebration of the Dies Solis or Sunday; as well as some other days, as will afterward be shewn, sacred among the Heathens to that luminary. It is curious to observe the care shewn in every part of the Gospels and the Epistles of the orthodox to discourage the pharasaical observance of the Sabbath, so much and so inconsistently cried up by modern Puritans. Whenever the commandments are ordered to be kept, the injunction is always followed by an explanation of what commandments are meant, and the Sabbath in every instance is omitted.

8. Learned men have exercised great ingenuity in their endeavours to discover the origin and reason of sacrifices, (a rite common to both Jews and Heathens,) in which they have found great difficulty. They have sought at the bottom of the well what was swimming on the surface. The origin of sacrifice was evidently a gift to the priest, or the cunning man, or the Magus or Druid, [2] to induce him to intercede with some unknown being, to protect the timid or pardon the guilty ; a trick invented by the rogues to enable them to cheat the fools ; a contrivance of the idle possessing brains to live upon the labour of those without them. The sacrifice, whatever it might be in its origin, soon became a feast, in which the priest and his votary were partakers; and if, in some instances, the body of the victim was burnt, for the sake of deluding the multitude, with a show of disinterestedness on the part of the priest, even then, that he might not lose all, he reserved to himself the skin. See Lev. vii. 8.

But it was in very few instances that the flesh was really burnt, even in burnt-offerings. Deut, xii. 2: *And thou shalt* OFFER *thy* BURNT-OFFERINGS, *the flesh and the blood, upon the altar of the* LORD *thy God : and the blood of thy sacrifices shall be poured out upon the altar of the* LORD *thy God, and thou shalt* EAT *the flesh :* not *burn* it. At first the sacrifice was a feast between the priest and devotee, but the former very soon contrived to keep it all for himself; and it is evident from Pliny's letter to Trajan, that when there was more than the priest could consume, he sent the overplus to market for sale.

It is difficult to account for the very general reception of the practice of sacrifice, it being found among almost all nations. The following is the account given of it by the Rev. Mr. Faber:

" Throughout the whole world we find a notion prevalent, that the Gods could only be appeased
" by bloody sacrifices. Now this idea is so thoroughly arbitrary, there being no obvious and
" necessary connexion, in the way of cause and effect, between slaughtering a man or a beast, and
" recovering of the divine favour by the slaughterer, that its very universality involves the neces-
" sity of concluding that all nations have borrowed it from some common source. It is in vain to

---

[1] Lex. p. 634.     [2] Druid is a Celtic word and has the meaning of *Absolver from Sin.*

N

" say, that there is nothing so strange, but that an unrestrained superstition might have excogi-
" tated it. This solution does by no means meet the difficulty. If sacrifice had been in use only
" among the inhabitants of a *single* country, or among those of some few neighbouring countries,
" who might reasonably be supposed to have much mutual intercourse; no fair objection could be
" made to the answer. But what we have to account for is, the universality of the practice; and
" such a solution plainly does not account for such a circumstance; I mean not merely the exist-
" ence of sacrifice, but its *universality*. An apparently irrational notion, struck out by a wild
" fanatic in one country and forthwith adopted by his fellow-citizens, (for such is the hypothesis
" requisite to the present solution,) is yet found to be equally prevalent in all countries. There-
" fore if we acquiesce in this solution, we are bound to believe, either that all nations, however
" remote from each other, borrowed from that of the original inventor; or that by a most marvel-
" lous subversion of the whole system of calculating chances, a great number of fanatics, severally
" appearing in every country upon the face of the earth, without any mutual communication,
" strangely hit upon the self-same arbitrary and inexplicable mode of propitiating the Deity. It
" is difficult to say which of the two suppositions is the most improbable. The solution therefore
" does not satisfactorily account for the fact of the *universality*. Nor can the fact, I will be bold to
" say, be satisfactorily accounted for, except by the supposition, that no one nation borrowed the
" rite from another nation, but that all alike received it from a common origin of most remote
" antiquity."

Such is the account given of this disgusting practice. Very well has the Rev. Mr. Faber
described it, *as apparently an irrational notion struck out by a wild fanatic,—an arbitrary and
inexplicable mode hit upon by fanatics of propitiating the Deity.* As he justly says, *why should that
righteous man* (meaning Abel) *have imagined that he could please the Deity, by slaying a firstling
lamb, and by burning it upon an altar? What connexion is there betwixt the means and the end?
Abel could not but have known, that God, as a merciful God, took no pleasure in the sufferings of
the lamb. How, then, are we to account for his attempting to please such a God, by what abstractedly
is an act of cruelty?* [1] Very true, indeed, Reverend Sir, an act of cruelty, as a type of an infinitely
greater act of cruelty and injustice, in the murder, by the Creator, of his only Son, by the hands
of the Jews : an act not only of injustice and cruelty to the sufferer, but an act of equal cruelty
and injustice to the perpetrators of the murder, whose eyes and understandings were blinded lest
they should see and not execute the murder—and lest they should repent *and their sins be forgiven them.* What strange beings men, in all ages, have made their Gods ! ! !

I cannot ascribe such things to *my* God. This may be *will* worship ; but belief is not in my
power. I am obliged to believe it more probable that men may lie, that priests may be guilty of
selfish fraud, than that the wise and beneficent Creator can direct such irrational, fanatical, cruel
proceedings, to use Mr. Faber's words. The doctrine of the Atonement, with its concomitant
dogmas, is so subversive of all morality, and is so contrary to the moral attributes of God, that it is
totally incredible : as the Rev. Dr. Sykes justly observes of actions contrary to the moral attributes
of God, that they are incredible even if supported by miracles themselves. However, I am happy
to say that belief in this doctrine is no part of the faith declared by Jesus Christ to be necessary to
salvation—no part in short of his gospel, though it may be of the gospel of Bishop Magee.

That in later times the practice of sacrifice was very general cannot be denied ; but I think a
time may be perceived when it did not exist, even among the Western nations. We read that it
was not always pratised at Delphi. Tradition states that in the earliest time no bloody sacrifice
took place there, and among the Buddhists, who are the oldest religionists of whom we have any

---

[1] See Faber, Pagan Idol. B. ii. Ch. viii. pp. 466, 482.

sacred traditions, and to whom the first book of Genesis probably belongs, no bloody sacrifices ever prevailed. With Cristna, Hercules, and the worshipers of the Sun in Aries, they probably arose. The second book of Genesis I think came from the last. No doubt the practice took its rise in the Western parts of the world, (after the sun entered Aries,) even among the followers of the Tauric worship, and was carried to a frightful extent. But the prevalence of the practice, as stated by Mr. Faber, is exaggerated. It never was practised by the followers of Buddha, though they have constituted, perhaps, a majority of the inhabitants of the world.

I believe the history of Cain and Abel is an allegory of the followers of Cristna, to justify their sacrifice of the firstling of the flock—of the Yajna or Lamb in opposition to the Buddhist offering of bread and wine or water, made by Cain and practised by Melchizedek.

9. Dr. Shuckford has satisfactorily shewn that the sacrifices and ceremonies of purification of the Heathens, and of Abraham and his family and descendants, were in fact all identical, with such trifling changes as distance of countries and length of time might be expected to produce. [1] Moses can hardly be said to have copied many of his institutions from the Gentiles. The Israelites had them probably before the time of Moses. The prohibition of marrying out of the tribe was one of these. The custom was evidently established by Abraham, Isaac, and Jacob, with their wives.—But to return to my subject.

How many Zoroasters there were, or whether more than one, it is difficult to determine; but one of them was thought by Hyde, as we have already shewn, to have lived in the time of Darius Hystaspes; but whether he really lived then or not is of no consequence, except that the account given of him shews what the religion of the Persians at that time was. Sir W. Drummond thinks he really lived much earlier, as does also Mr. Moyle. [2] He is said to have been deeply skilled in the Eastern learning, and also in the Jewish Scriptures. Indeed, so striking is the similarity between his doctrines and those of Moses, that Dean Prideaux is almost obliged to make a Jew of him: and this he really was, in religion. But why he should abuse him, and call him many hard names it is difficult to understand. He does not appear to have formed a new religion, but only to have reformed or improved that which he found.

The following is Dean Prideaux's account of the religion of Zoroaster: " The chief reformation " which he made in the Magian religion was in the first principle of it; for whereas before they " had held the being of two first causes, the first light, or the good god, who was the author of all " good; and the other darkness, or the evil god, who was the author of all evil; and that of the " mixture of those two, as they were in a continued struggle with each other, all things were " made; he introduced a principle superior to them both, one supreme God who created both " light and darkness, and out of these two, according to the alone pleasure of his own will, made " all things else that are, according to what is said in the 45th chapter of Isaiah, ver. 5—7.—In " sum, his doctrine, as to this particular, was, that there was one Supreme Being, independant " and self-existing from all eternity; that under him there were two angels, one the angel of light, " who is the author and director of all good; and the other the angel of darkness, who is the author " and director of all evil; and that these two, out of the mixture of light and darkness, made all " things that are; and that they are in a perpetual struggle with each other; and that where the " angel of light prevails, there the most is good, and where the angel of darkness prevails, there " the most is evil; that this struggle shall continue to the end of the world; that then there shall " be a general resurrection, and a day of judgment, wherein just retribution shall be rendered to " all according to their works: after which, the angel of darkness and his disciples shall go into a

---

[1] Shuckford, Con. Book v. p. 314.

[2] Pliny mentions a Zoroaster who lived sex millibus annorum ante Platonis mortem. Maurice, Vol. II. p. 124.

" world of their own, where they shall suffer in everlasting darkness the punishment of their evil
" deeds; and the angel of light, and his disciples, shall also go into a world of their own, where they
" shall receive in everlasting light the reward due unto their good deeds : and that after this they
" shall remain separated for ever, and light and darkness be no more mixed together to all eternity.
" And all this the remainder of that sect which is now in Persia and India, do, without any varia-
" tion, after so many ages, still hold even to this day.  And how consonant this is to the truth
" is plain enough to be understood without a comment.  And whereas he taught that God origi-
" nally created the good angel only, and that the other followed only by the defect of good, this
" plainly shews, that he was not unacquainted with the revolt of the fallen angels, and the en-
" trance of evil into the world that way, but had been thoroughly instructed how that God at first
" created all his angels good, as he also did man, and that they that are now evil became such
" wholly through their own fault, in falling from that state which God first placed them in.  All
" which plainly shews the author of this doctrine to have been well versed in the sacred writing
" of the Jewish religion, out of which it manifestly appears to have been all taken." [1]

Another reformation which Zoroaster is said to have introduced, was, the building of temples,
for before his time the altars were all erected upon hills and high places in the open air.  Upon
those the sacred fire was kept burning, but to which they denied that they offered adoration, but
only to God in the fire. [2]  It is said that Zoroaster pretended to have been taken up into heaven,
and to have heard God speak from the midst of a flame of fire ; that, therefore, fire is the truest
shekinah of the Divine presence ; and that the sun is the most perfect fire—for which reason he
ordered them to direct their worship towards the sun, which they called Mithra.  He pretended
to have brought fire from heaven along with him, which was never permitted to go out.  It was
fed with clean wood, and it was deemed a great crime to blow upon it, or to rekindle it except
from the sun or the sacred fire in some other temple.  Thus the Jews had their shekinah or sacred
fire in which God dwelt, and which came down from heaven upon their altar of burnt-offerings :
and Nadab and Abihu were punished with death for offering incense to God with other fire.  The
Jews used clean peeled wood for the fire, and, like the Persians, would not permit it to be blown
upon with the mouth.

To feed the sacred fire with unhallowed fuel, was punishable with death ; to blow upon it the
same.  But though it was thus treated with the most profound veneration, as a part of the glorious
luminary of heaven, it was not worshiped ; though the Lord Jehovah, who shrouded himself in
the sacred fire, or took up his residence in the sun, was worshiped.  Thus God upon Sinai or
Horeb, or in the bush, appeared in a flame of fire to Moses, who fell down on his face to it.  Yet
the text means to represent that he worshiped God, not fire.

A very ingenious and learned critic, [3] in his controversy with Dean Prideaux, has maintained,
that the Persians destroyed the temples in Egypt, because they disapproved the worshiping of
God in temples, when the whole earth was his temple ; and that they had only *two* Principles
and never acknowledged a *third*, superior to the Good and Evil ones, till about the time of the
Christian æra.  He seems to be mistaken in both these respects.  The fact that the Persians had
no closed temples in the time of Herodotus, may be very true, and cannot well be disputed, as he
affirms it : but notwithstanding this, it is plain that though they did not choose to have temples
of their own, they had no objection to the temple-worship of others ; because if they had, they
would not have restored the temples of the Jews and Samaritans at Jerusalem and Gerizim.  This

---

[1] Prid. Con. Part I. Lib. iv. p. 267.  8vo.
[2] These are nothing but the Hill-altars of the Canaanites, (of which we often read in the Old Testament,) the ancient
circles of the Druids, which I have lately discovered are as common in India, Persia, and Syria, as in Britain.
[3] Moyle, Works, Vol. II.

fact proves that their enmity was against the temples of idolaters, not against those of the true God, nor against temples merely as temples. For the same reasons the pious Theodosius destroyed the temples at Alexandria; but he had no objection to temple-worship, or worship in buildings.

The Israelites had no temple till the time of Solomon, but they had circles of stone pillars at Gerizim and Gilgal, exactly the same as those at the Buddhist temple of Stonehenge.

10. Zoroaster retired to a cavern where he wrote his book, and which was ornamented on the roof with the constellations and the signs of the Zodiac; whence came the custom among his followers of retiring to caves which they called Mithriatic caves, to perform their devotions, in which the mysteries of their religion were performed. Many of these caves of stupendous size and magnificence exist at this day in the neighbourhood of Balck, and in different parts of upper India and Persia.

They had several orders of priests like our parochial priests and bishops, and at the head of them an Archimagus or Archpriest, the same as the Pope or the High Priest of the Jews : the word Magus, in the Persian language, only meant priest: and they did not forget that most useful Jewish rite, the taking of tithes and oblations. At stated times the priests read part of their sacred writings to the people. The priests were all of the same family or tribe, as among the Jews.

Dr. Pococke and Hyde acknowledge that many things in their sacred books are the same as those in the Pentateuch, and in other parts of the Bible. Of course they easily account for this by the assertion, that they were taken from the Jews. But the fact of the identity is not denied: which copied from the other is not *now* the question. All that it is necessary to shew is, that they were the same. They contain many of the Psalms, called by the Jews and Christians, absurdly enough, *the Psalms of David,* and nearly the same account of Adam and Eve, the deluge, &c. The creation is stated, as already mentioned, to have taken place in *six* periods, which together make up a year; and Abraham, Joseph, Moses, and Solomon, are all spoken of in the same manner as in the Jewish Scriptures. In these books are inculcated similar observances about beasts, clean and unclean,—the same care to avoid pollution, external and internal,—the same purifyings, washings, &c., &c. Zoroaster called his book *the book of Abraham,* because he pretended that, by his own reformation, he had only brought back the religion to the state in which it was in the time of Abraham. [1] Can any one, after this, doubt the identity of the two religions? If they were not the same, what would make them so?

The Zendavesta which we have, and which was translated by Anquetil Du Perron, is said, by Sir W. Jones, to be spurious; but it is admitted by the best authors to agree with the ancient one, at least "in its tenets and the terms of religion." [2] Upon the question of its genuineness it is not necessary to give an opinion. Probably Sir W. Jones would find anachronisms in it, such as have been pointed out in the Old Testament. These would be quite sufficient to prove to him the spuriousness of the Zend, though not of the Pentateuch. The fact is, they both stand exactly upon the same grounds with respect to genuineness. [3]

Much might have been spared which has been said respecting the *fire worshipers* of Persia. It is very probable that, in some degree, the charge of worshiping fire may be substantiated against them, in the same way as the worship of saints, images, and relics, in some parts of Christendom may certainly be proved to have existed; but it is equally as unjust to call the Persians *fire*

[1] Prid. Con. Part. I. Book iv. pp. 278, &c., 8vo.   [2] Marsh's Mic. Ch. iv. Sect. ix. p. 161.
[3] Marsh's Mic. Vol. IV. p. 288, Vol. I. p. 433.

*worshipers,* as it is to call the Christians *idolaters.* The religion of Persia became corrupted, and so did the Christian. Zoroaster reformed one, Luther, &c., the other.

If we are to credit the history, the religion of Abraham's descendants by Sarah, became also corrupted whilst they were in Egypt; and was restored to its original state, at least in all its great and leading features, by Moses. That they were addicted to the idolatry of Egypt is evident from their setting up for themselves *a golden calf,* the image of the God Apis, in less than three months after their escape into the desert of Sinai.

The religion of Abraham was that of the Persians, and whether he were a real or a fictitious personage (a matter of doubt) both the religions must have been derived from the same source. If Abraham really did live, then the evidence both Jewish and Persian shews that he was the founder of both nations. If he were an *allegorical personage,* the similarity of the religions shews them to have had the same origin. Why should not his family by his wife Keturah, as historians affirm they did, have conquered Persia, as his family by Sarah conquered Canaan ? Both worshiped the solar fire, [1] as an emblem of their God, of God the Preserver and Saviour—of that God with whom Abraham made a covenant; the same Jehovah or Lord who Jacob (Gen. xxviii. 21) vowed should be his God, if he brought him back to his father's house in peace ; the same God worshiped by the brother of Abraham, Nahor, in the land of Ur of the Chaldees, (Gen. xi. 29, xxxi. 53,) and of whom it is written, " My Lord said unto thy Lord, sit thee at my right hand, till I make thine enemies thy footstool." Ps. cx. 1 ; Matt. xxii. 44 ; Mark. xii. 36 ; Luke xx. 42, 43 ; Acts ii. 34, 35.

11. Now perhaps perverseness, bigotry, and ill-temper, will observe, Then you take Abraham and Moses for nothing but Persian magicians and idolaters. I do no such thing. The God of Abraham, of Melchizedek, of the Brahmins, and of the Persians, originally, or about the time of Abraham, was *one,* precisely *the same*—the oriental divine Triad or Trinity, *three* Persons and *one* God. Why Abraham left his country and came into Canaan may be doubtful : but it is not unlikely that he emigrated because the priests had corrupted the religion, as they always corrupt it when they can ; and, that he came into Canaan because he there found his religion in a state of purity, and a priest of the most high God, Melchizedek, at whose altar he could sacrifice, and to whom he could pay his tithes. And it is not unlikely, that he and his family or tribe might have been banished from their country at the time they left it, for endeavouring to oppose the corruption of the priests,—to enlighten or reform their countrymen. Indeed some authors have actually said, and before I conclude this work I shall prove, that this was the case. It is probable, as the Bible says, that the descendants of Abraham, if there were such a man, were induced to take refuge in Egypt for some reason or other ; probably, as stated, by famine ; that after residing in Egypt for some time, two hundred years or upwards, they were beginning to fall into the idolatrous practices of the people among whom they dwelt, and by whom also endeavours were made to enslave them ; that to prevent this or to stop its progress, after a severe struggle, they left Egypt, and betook themselves to the desert, under the command of Moses, who was both the restorer or reformer of their religion, and their leader and legislator ; that, after various wars with other Arab tribes, or settled nations, on whose territories they encroached when in search of pasturage, for they had then no country of their own, they at last succeeded in conquering Canaan—where they finally established themselves—though not completely till the time of David. This country they always occupied along with remnants of the ancient Canaanites, till about the

---

[1] Ireneus says, God is *fire* ; Origen, *a subtle fire* ; Tertullian, *a body.* In the Acts of the council of Elvira it is forbidden to light candles in the cemeteries, for fear of disturbing the souls of the saints. A great dispute took place in Egypt among the monks on the question, whether God was corporeal or incorporeal.

time of Jesus Christ, (in the same way as the Turks have occupied Greece,) when they were finally expelled from it by the Romans, and their tribe dispersed. The country then became partly occupied by Roman colonies, and partly by the remains of the old idolatrous Canaanites, the worshipers of Adonis, Venus, &c., &c. The Jews occupied Canaan, as the Moriscoes occupied Spain. They never completely mixed or amalgamated with the old inhabitans, who continued in slavery or subjection. Every page almost of the Jewish history shews that the Canaanites continued, and had temples. During what is called the time of the Judges it is evident that an almost incessant warfare was carried on between the old inhabitants and the Israelites. The Jebusites possessed, in spite of the latter, the fortress of the city of Jerusalem, until the time of David, who took it by storm ; and the city of Tyre, with its king, set even the power of Solomon at defiance, and never was taken by the Israelites at all.

The difference between the religion of Moses and that of the surrounding nations, consisted merely in this : the latter had become corrupted by the priests, who had set up images in allegorical representation of the heavenly bodies or Zodiacal signs, which in long periods of time the people came to consider as representations of real deities. The true and secret meaning of these emblems, the priests, that is the initiated, took the greatest pains to keep from the people. The king and priest were generally united in the same person : and when it was otherwise, the former was generally the mere tool and slave of the latter. But in either case, the sole object of the initiated was, as it yet is, to keep the people in a state of debasement, that they might be more easily ruled. Thus did the Magi in *ancient* and thus do the chief priests in *modern* times wallow in wealth on the labour of the rest of mankind.

If we may judge of the state of Egypt and Canaan, and the countries in the neighbourhood of Canaan, from the collection of ancient tracts or traditionary histories, called the Jewish canon, we must allow that they had become, in matters of religion, sunk to the very lowest state of debasement. The sacrifices and rites of Baal and Moloch, and the idolatry of Tyre, Sidon, &c., were of the most horrible kind. The priests in almost all ages have found that the more gloomy and horrible a religion is, the better it has suited their purpose. We have this account of the state of the religion, not only from the history of the Jews, but from that of the Gentiles, therefore it can scarcely be disputed. It was to keep his people from falling into this degraded state, that Moses framed many of his laws. To the original religions of these nations, before their degradation, he could have had no objection ; or else he would never have adopted so many of their astronomical and astrological emblems : nay, have even gone so far as to call his God by the same names.

Though the adoption of the astronomical and astrological emblems of the Magi and the Egyptians may be no proof of the wisdom or sagacity of Moses, they are sufficiently clear proofs of the identity of his religion with the religion of the Magi, &c., before their corruption. What are we to make of the brazen serpent set up by Moses in the wilderness, and worshiped by the Israelites till the time of Hezekiah ? What of the Cherubim under the wings of which the God of the Jews dwelt ? These Cherubim had the faces of the beings which were in the four cardinal points of the Zodiac, when the Bull was the equinoctial sign, viz. the ox, the lion, the man, and the eagle. [1] These were clearly astrological.

12. Every ancient religion, without exception, had Cabala or secret doctrines : and the same fate attended them all. In order that they might not be revealed or discovered, they were not written, but only handed down by tradition ; and in the revolutions of centuries and the violent convulsions of empires they were forgotten. Scraps of the old traditions were then collected, and mixed with new inventions of the priests, having the double object in view, of ruling the people and of concealing their own ignorance.

---

[1] See a picture of them in Parkhurst's Hebrew Lexicon in voce, ברכ *krb*. See also Jurieu, Rel. Vet. Vol. I. Part. II. Cap. i.

The twelve signs of the Zodiac for the standards of the twelve tribes of Israel, the scorpion or typhon, the devil or the emblem of destruction, being changed for the eagle by the tribe of Dan, to whom it was allotted ; the ark, an exact copy of the ark of Osiris, set afloat in the Nile every year, and supposed to sail to Biblos, in Palestine ; the pillars Joachim and Boaz ; the festival of the Passover at the vernal equinox, an exact copy of the Egyptian festival at the same time ; almost all the ornaments of the temple, altar, priest, &c., all these are clearly astrological. The secret meaning of all these emblems, and of most parts of the books of the Pentateuch, of Joshua and Judges, (almost the whole of which was astrological, that is, magical allegory,) was what in old times, in part at least, constituted the Jewish Cabala, and was studiously kept from the knowledge of the vulgar. There is no reason to believe that the Cabala of the modern Jews has any similitude to that of the ancients. The childish nonsense of the modern Cabalists, it would indeed be very absurd to attribute to the sages, who, on Carmel, taught Pythagoras the true system of the planetary bodies—or to Elias, whose knowledge of chemistry, perhaps, taught him to out-manœuvre the priests of Baal.

On the subject of the reason why Abraham or his tribe left his or its home, I shall have much more to say in the course of this work, when I flatter myself that *that*, and many other things on which I slightly touch here, will be accounted for.

## CHAPTER V.

### CHARACTER OF THE OLD TESTAMENT.—NATURE OF THE ALLEGORY IN GENESIS.

1. The reader will now perhaps ask, What in the result is the truth respecting the Old Testament ? It is very difficult to answer this question in a few words. Is it the produce of deep learning and profound wisdom, hidden under the veil of allegory, or is it the mere literal history of transactions of past events, as believed by the Christians and modern Jews ? It is probably both : a collection of tracts mixed up with traditions, histories or rumours of events, collected together by the priests of an ignorant, uncivilized race of shepherds, intermixed also with the allegories and fictions in which the ancient philosophers of the eastern nations veiled their learning from the eyes of the vulgar. The Pentateuch is evidently a collection of different mythological histories of the creation, and of the transactions of Moses, the chief of a tribe of wandering Arabs, who was believed to have brought this tribe from the borders of Egypt and to have conquered Palestine : and there is little doubt that it contains a considerable portion of truth. The priests of the hilly part of Judea, after the tribes had united under one government, wanting something whereon to found their system, collected from all quarters the different parts, connecting them together as well as they could, though very unskilfully. And this was probably not all done at once, but by degrees, without any regular preconcerted design. The only part of it which shews any thing like a regular system, is the invariable tendency evident in every page to support the power of the priests or prophets. And this may perhaps be attributed more to a natural effect, arising from the manufacture of the work by priests, than to design.

The treatises in the Pentateuch are put together, or connected with one another, in so very awkward and unskilful a manner, that they would have passed as the work of one person with none but such uncivilized barbarians as the Jews, if they had related to any of the common concerns of life, and *where the reasoning faculty of the human mind could be brought into fair action;* but in matters connected with religion this has never been done, and never will be done: reason has nothing to do with the religion of the generality of mankind.

To this the priests will reply, The circumstances which mark identity in the religions of the Jews and Gentiles we do not deny; the Heathens copied almost all their superstitions from Moses and the Prophets; and probably to multitudes of believers this will be very satisfactory: this satisfaction may naturally be expected to be enjoyed by such persons; reason does not operate with them. To them it is of no consequence, that those heathenish superstitions which are alleged to have been copied from Moses, were in existence hundreds, perhaps thousands, of years before Moses was born or thought of.

That many parts of the books of the Jews are allegorical, cannot be for a moment doubted, and, as was said before, no doubt the true knowledge of these allegories constituted their first Cabala, and the learning of their priests. But as they are evidently made up of loose, unconnected accounts, very often different accounts of the same history or allegory, it is not possible that any complete and regular system should be made out of them. For instance, Genesis contains two histories of the creation; Deuteronomy a history of the promulgation of the law by Moses, different from that given in Exodus, which was evidently written by a different author from that of Genesis. This view of the Jewish writings does not militate against parts of them being the produce of the profound wisdom of the oriental philosophers, which was probably the case, as maintained by M. Dupuis. A person may readily believe that the first book of Genesis was written by an ancient philosopher, whose descendants may have taught Pythagoras (perhaps on Carmel) the demonstration, that the square of the hypothenuse is equal to the square of the two sides of a right-angled triangle. From these circumstances it has followed, that in every part of these writings we meet with a strange mixture of oriental learning, and, to outward appearance, nonsensical and degrading puerilities and superstitions, which in all ages have perplexed the understandings of those persons who have endeavoured to use them on these subjects. No *reasoning* being could believe them literally, no ingenuity could make out of them, taken collectively, a consistent allegory.

But as far as concerns the generality or industrious class of the Jews and modern Christians, they are taken literally. In this sense they were and are yet received. Whether the later Jewish collectors of them into one code understood the allegorical meaning of any of them, remains doubtful; probably they might in part. But it is equally, if not more, probable, that they would care very little whether they understood them or not, so long as they assisted them in establishing their temple, their tithes, and their order. Perhaps after these objects were secured, they would amuse themselves in their leisure hours, like our own priests and bishops, in endeavouring by explanations to make order out of disorder, sense out of nonsense. Hence arose their modern Cabala. And as they were generally men of the meanest capacities, though perhaps men understanding several languages, the modern Cabala is just what might be expected.

The modern and Romish religion being partly founded upon that of the Jews, which was founded upon writings thus connected together, it is not surprising that, like its parent, it should be difficult or impossible to make out a complete system, to fit into or account for every part of it.

2. M. Dupuis, in the first chapter of his third volume, has made many curious observations on the book of Genesis, tending to prove that it was an allegory descriptive of the mythology of the oriental nations in the neighbourhood of Palestine. That it was allegorical was held by the most learned of the ancient fathers of the church, such as Clemens Alexandrinus and Origen, as it had been by the most learned of the Jews, such as Philo, Josephus, &c., so that its allegorical nature may perhaps be safely assumed, notwithstanding the nonsense of modern devotees.

o

The following extract from the work of Maimonides, called More Nevochim,[1] exhibits a fair example of the policy of the ancient philosophers : " Taken to the letter, this work (Genesis) gives " the most absurd and extravagant ideas of the Divinity. . Whoever shall find the true sense of it " ought to take care not to divulge it. This is a maxim which all our sages repeat to us, and " above all respecting the meaning of the work of the six days. If a person should discover the " meaning of it, either by himself or with the aid of another, then he ought to be silent : or if he " speak of it, he ought to speak of it but obscurely, and in an enigmatical manner as I do myself ; " leaving the rest to be guessed by those who can understand me."[2]

Although it is clear from the works of Philo and others, that the learned in all ancient times acknowledged an allegorical sense in the accounts of Genesis ; it is equally clear from the works of that learned man, that in his time its meaning was in a great degree lost. The most celebrated of the Christian fathers equally admitted it to be allegorical, but the moderns have a difficulty to contend with, unknown to them and to the Jews. To admit the accounts in Genesis to be literal, would be to admit facts directly contrary to the moral attributes of God. Fanatical as the ancient fathers were, their fanaticism had not blinded them, as it has blinded the moderns, so far as to admit this. But if the story of the garden of Eden, the trees of knowledge and of life, the talking serpent, and the sin of Adam and Eve were allegorical, redemption by the atonement from the consequences of his allegorical fault could not but be equally allegorical. This, it is evident, instantly overthrows the whole of the present orthodox or fashionable scheme of the atonement—a doctrine not known in the early ages of the religion, but picked up in the same quarter whence several other doctrines of modern Christianity will be found to have been derived. If the history of the fall be allegorical, we repeat, that the allegorical nature of the redemption seems to follow as a necessary consequence.

In reasoning from cause to effect, this seems to be a necessary consequence. From this difficulty arose a great mass of contradictions and absurdities. It is impossible to deny, that it has always been a part of the modern corrupt Christian religion, that an evil spirit rebelled against God, and that he having drawn other beings of his own description into the same evil course, was, for this conduct, expelled along with them from heaven, into a place of darkness and intense torment. This nonsense, which is no part of the religion of Jesus the Nazarite, came from the same quarter as the atonement. We shall find them both in India.

It is quite impossible, that the doctrine of the fallen angels can be taken from the Pentateuch ; for not a word of the kind is to be met with there : but it is the identical doctrine of the Brahmins and later Magi. The Devil is the Mahasoor of the Brahmins, and the Ahriman of the Magi ; the fallen angels are the Onderah and Dewtahs of the Brahmins, and the Dowzakh and Dews of the Magi. The vulgar Jews and Christians finding the story of the serpent, did not know how to account for it, and in consequence went to the Persians for an explanation. They could not have gone to a better place, for the second book of Genesis, with its serpent biting the foot of the woman's seed, is nothing but a part of a Hindoo-Persian history, of which the story of the fallen angels, &c., is a continuation.

In several places in this chapter, the reader will have observed that I have used an expression of doubt respecting the existence of Abraham. This I have done because I feel that in inquiries of this kind a person can scarcely ever be too careful. And after reading the works of Sir William Drummond, Mons. Dupuis, &c., suspicion cannot be entirely banished. Besides, I wish not to take any thing for granted ; particularly the questions under examination, and this question will be amply discussed hereafter. I think it is perfectly clear that magical or astrological theories or

---

[1] Pars II. Cap. xxix.　　　　　　[2] Dupuis, sur tous les Cultes, Vol III. p. 9, 4to.

doctrines were connected with every part of the Mosaic system. It is impossible to separate or conceal them ; they are connected with the numbers, the names of cities, and of men,—in short, with every thing : but this no more proves that there were not such men as Abraham, Moses, Joshua, &c., than it proves that there were not such cities and places as Damascus, Hobah, Gilgal, Gerizim, Bethel, Jericho, &c. The existence of the cities and places, having astronomical names, is clear. There is nothing in these astrological allusions against the existence of the men, any more than there is against the existence of the cities : and those have gone much too far who, *for no other reason,* have run away with the opinion that there were not such men. Their premises will not warrant their conclusions.

# BOOK III.

## CHAPTER I.

ORPHIC AND MITHRAITIC TRINITY SIMILAR TO THAT OF THE CHRISTIANS.—SIR WILLIAM JONES ON THE RELIGION OF PERSIA.— PERSIAN OROMASDES, MITHRA, ARIMANIUS. — OPINIONS OF HERODOTUS, PORPHYRY, STRABO, JULIAN, ON THE ABOVE.—HYDE AND BEAUSOBRE RESPECTING TIMES OF PYTHAGORAS AND ZOROASTER.—FOLLOWERS OF ZOROASTER, NOT YET EXTINCT—WORSHIP FIRE.—THE VEDAS DESCRIBE THE PERSIAN RELIGION TO HAVE COME FROM UPPER INDIA.—MAURICE ON THE HINDOO TRINITY.

1. In the former part of this work, in treating of the Trimurti or Trinity, it was found scarcely possible to avoid anticipating part of what was intended to form the subject of the present book, but the author flatters himself, that the apparent repetition will not be found useless or uninteresting.

Having proved the absolute identity of the religions of the family of Abraham and of the Persians, in this book will be shewn a similar identity between several of the dogmas of the Romish and Protestant Christians, generally accounted of the greatest importance, particularly the Trinity and similar dogmas of the religions of Orpheus and Mithra, or the Sun, held by the Persian Magi : of the latter of which Zeradust was either the great prophet or founder, or the reformer. It is very possible that the moral doctrines of two races of people, totally unconnected, may be the same, or nearly so, because the true principles of morals must be the same : there can be only one true morality ; and each, without any connexion, may originally discover the truth. But it is evidently impossible that such artificial regulations and peculiar opinions, as will be pointed out, could have been adopted by two races of people without some very intimate connexion existing between them. Justin Martyr observed the striking similitude, and very easily explained it. He says, the evil spirits, or demons, introduced the Christian ceremonies into the religion of Mithra. Though this explanation of ceremonies and doctrines, existing long anterior to Christianity, might be satisfactory to the ancient and venerable fathers of the church, it will hardly prove so to modern philosophers. It cannot be expected, that the author should go through the whole of the ceremonies of each religion, and shew that in every individual instance they exactly agreed. The unceasing exertions of Christian priests to conceal the truth, and the change, arising from various other causes, which we know always takes place in long periods of time, in every religion, and indeed in every sublunary concern, render such an expectation unreasonable and absurd ; but it is presumed that the circumstances which will now be pointed out, in addition to what has already been stated, will leave no doubt on the mind of any reasonable and unprejudiced person, that the religions under consideration were originally the same.

In contemplating the different, and often contradictory, circumstances of the religion of the ancient Persians, it is impossible not to observe the striking similarity both of its doctrines, and discipline or practices, to those of their Eastern neighbours of India, on one side; and their Western neighbours, the Christians of Europe, on the other. That religion appears to have been a connecting link in the chain, and probably in this point of view it will be regarded by every unprejudiced person, when all the circumstances relating to it are taken into consideration. Like almost all the ancient systems of theology, its origin is lost in the most remote antiquity. Its foundation is generally attributed to a sage of the name of Zoroaster, but in order to reconcile the accounts given of him with any thing like consistency, or with one another, several persons of this name must be supposed to have lived.

2. Treating of the religion of Persia, Sir W. Jones says, " The primeval religion of Iran, if we " may rely on the authorities adduced by Monsani Fâní, was that which Newton calls the oldest " (and it may justly be called the noblest) of all religions ; a firm belief that ' one Supreme God " ' made the world by his power, and continually governed it by his providence; a pious fear, " ' love, and adoration of him; and due reverence for parents and aged persons; a fraternal " ' affection for the whole human species; and a compassionate tenderness even for the brute " ' creation.' " [1]

Firdausi, speaking of the prostration of Cyrus and his paternal grandfather before the blazing altar, says, " Think not that they were adorers of fire, for that element was only an exalted object, " on the lustre of which they fixed their eyes ; they humbled themselves a whole week before " God; and if thy understanding be ever so little exerted, thou must acknowledge thy dependance " on the Being supremely pure." [2]

However bigoted my Christian reader may be, he will hardly deny that there is here the picture of a beautiful religion. On this subject Mr. Maurice says, " The reader has already been " informed that the first object of the idolatry of the ancient world was the Sun. The beauty, " the lustre, and vivifying warmth of that planet, early enticed the human heart from the adoration " of that Being who formed its glowing sphere and all the host of heaven. The Sun, however, " was not solely adored for its own intrinsic lustre and beauty ; it was probably venerated by the " devout ancients as the most magnificent emblem of the Shechinah which the universe afforded. " Hence the Persians, among whom the true religion for a long time flourished uncorrupted, " according to Dr. Hyde, in a passage before referred to, asserted, that the *throne* of God was " seated in the sun. In Egypt, however, under the appellation of Osiris, the sun was not less " venerated, than under the denomination of Mithra, in Persia." [3]

3. The first dogma of the religion of Zoroaster clearly was, the existence of one Supreme, Omnipotent God. In this it not only coincides with the Hindoo and the Christian, but with all other religions ; in this, therefore, there is not any thing particular : but on further inquiry it appears that this great First Cause, called Ormusd or Oromasdes, was a being like the Gods of the Hindoos and of the Christians, consisting of *three* persons. The triplicate Deity of the Hindoos of three persons and one God, Bramha the Creator, Vishnu or Cristna, of whom I shall soon treat, the Saviour or Preserver, and Siva the Destroyer ; and yet this was all *one* God, in his different capacities. In the same manner the Supreme God of the Persians consisted of three persons, Oromasdes the Creator, Mithra the Saviour, Mediator, or Preserver, and Ahriman the Destroyer. The Christians had also their Gods, consisting of *three* persons and *one* God, the Father, Son, and Holy Ghost. Psellus informs us, Oromasdes and Mithras were frequently used by the Magi for the τὸ Θεῖον, or *whole Deity* in general, and Plethro adds a *third*, called Arimanius, which is confirmed by Plutarch, who says, " That Zoroaster made a threefold distribution of

[1] Sir W. Jones on the Persians, Diss. VI. p. 197.    [2] Ib. p. 201.    [3] Maurice, Ind. Ant. Vol. IV. p. 605.

" things, and that he assigned the first and highest rank of them to Oromasdes, who, in the oracles,
" is called the Father; the lowest to Arimanes; and the middle to Mithras, who, in the same
" oracles, is called the second mind. Whereupon he observes, how great an agreement there
" was betwixt the Zoroastrian and the Platonic Trinity, they differing in a manner only in
" words." [1]

" And, indeed, from that which Plutarch affirms, that the Persians, from their God Mithras,
" called any Mediator, or middle betwixt two, Mithras, it may be more reasonably concluded,
" that Mithras, according to the Persian theology, was properly the middle hypostasis, of that
" triplasian, or triplicated deity of theirs, than that he should be a middle, self-existent God, or
" Mediator, betwixt two adversary Gods, unmade, one good, and the other evil, as Plutarch would
" suppose." [2]     If it were now needful, we might make it still further evident that Zoroaster,
" notwithstanding the multitude of Gods worshiped by him, was an asserter of one Supreme,
" from his own description of God, extant in Eusebius: *God is the first incorruptible, eternal,*
" *indivisible, most unlike to every thing, the head or leader of all good; unbribable, the best of the*
" *good, the wisest of the wise; He is also the Father of law and justice, self-taught, perfect, and*
" *the only inventor of the natural holy.*—Eusebius tells us that the Zoroastrian description of God
" was contained *verbatim* in a book, entitled *A Holy Collection of the Persian Monuments:* as
" also, that Ostanes (himself a famous Magician and admirer of Zoroaster) had recorded the very
" same of him in his Octateuchon." [3]

4. Porphyry, in his treatise, *de Antro Nympharum*, says, " Zoroaster first of all, as Eubolus
" testifieth, in the mountains adjoining to Persia, consecrated a native orbicular cave, adorned
" with flowers and watered with fountains, to the honour of Mithras, the maker and father of all
" things; this cave being an image or symbol to him of the whole world which was made by
" Mithras; which testimony of Eubolus is the more to be valued because, as Porphyrius else-
" where informs us, he wrote the history of Mithras at large in many books,—from whence it may
" be presumed that he had thoroughly furnished himself with the knowledge of what belonged to
" the Persian religion. Wherefore, from the authority of Eubolus, we may well conclude also,
" that notwithstanding the Sun was generally worshiped by the Persians as a God, yet Zoroaster
" and the ancient Magi, who were best initiated in Mithraick mysteries, asserted another Deity,
" superior to the Sun, for the true Mithras, such as was the maker and father of all things, or of
" the whole world, whereof the Sun is a part. However, these also looked upon the Sun as the
" most lively image of the Deity in which it was worshiped by them, as they likewise worshiped·
" the same Deity symbolically in fire, as Maximus Tyrius informeth us; agreeable to which is that
" in the Magic oracles; *All things are the offsprings of one fire;* that is, of one Supreme Deity.
" And Julian, the Emperor, was such a devout Sun worshiper as this, who acknowledged, besides
" the Sun, another incorporeal deity, transcendant to it." [4]     The first kind of things (according
" to Zoroaster) is eternal, the Supreme God. In the first place (saith Eusebius) they conceive
" that God the Father and King ought to be ranked. This the Delphian Oracle (cited by Por-
" phyrius) confirms:—Chaldees and Jews wise only, worshiping purely a self-begotten God and
" King.

" This is that principle of which the author of the Chaldaic Summary saith, *They conceive there*
" *is one principle of all things, and declare that is one and good.*

" God (as Pythagoras learnt of the Magi, who term him Oromasdes) *in his body resembles light;*
" *in his soul truth.*"

---

[1] Cudworth, Book i. Ch. iv. p. 289.     [2] Ib. p. 290.     [3] Ib. p. 293.     [4] Ib. p. 287.

In the same sense the Chaldeans likewise termed God a fire; for *Ur*, in Chaldee, signifying both light and fire, they took light and fire promiscuously.[1] " The name and image whereby they " represented the Supreme God was that of Bel, as appears by the prohibition given by God him- " self not to call him so any more. ' Thou shalt call me no longer Baali :' Bel with the Chal- " deans is the same as Baal with the Phenicians, both derived from the Hebrew Baal." [2]

" They who first translated the Eastern learning into Greek for the most part interpret this Bel " by the word Ζευς, Jupiter. So Herodotus, Diodorus, Hesychius, and others : Berosus (saith Eusebius) was priest of Belus, whom they " interpret (Διa) Jupiter."[3]

From the worship of the one Supreme God, (in Assyria,) they very early fell off to the worship of numbers of gods, dæmons, angels, planets, stars, &c. They had twelve principal Gods for the twelve signs of the Zodiac, to each of which they dedicated a month.[4] The identity of the name Baali among the Chaldeans and the Israelites, as observed by Stanley, raises a strong presumption, that all these religions were fundamentally the same, with only such greater or less adventitious variations as circumstances produced.

Sir W. Jones informs us that the letters Mihr in the Persian language denote the sun, [5] and he also informs us, that the letters Mihira denote the sun in the Hindoo language.[6] Now it is pretty clear that these two words are precisely the same : and are in fact nothing but the word Mithra *the sun.*

5. Dr. Hyde thought that Zoroaster and Pythagoras were contemporaries, but Mr. Stanley was of opinion this was not the fact, but that the latter lived several generations after the former. This subject has been well discussed by M. Beausobre,[7] who has undertaken to shew that they might have lived at the same time, and that there is nothing in the chronology to render it improbable.

It appears that the question respecting Pythagoras and Zoroaster was simply, whether they, or either of them, admitted a first moving, uncreated cause, superior to and independent of any other, or whether they admitted two equal, co-eternal beings, the authors of good and evil. The meaning of the expressions used by these great philosophers must always remain a subject of very considerable doubt. It seems surprising that such men as Stanley and Beausobre should pretend to reduce to a certainty that which, from peculiar circumstances, must always be involved in difficulty. In the first place, the line between the *unity* and *duality*, as explained, is so fine, that in our native language, which we understand, it is difficult to distinguish it ; then how much more difficult must it be in a foreign and dead language ! Besides, we have it not in the language of the philosophers themselves, but retailed to us in a language foreign to that in which it was delivered, and that also by foreigners, living many years after their deaths. After all the ingenuity displayed by M. Beausobre, who has exhausted the subject, considerable doubt must always remain upon this point, whether the two principles professed by the philosophers were identically the same or not. But yet one thing seems certain, all accounts tending to confirm the fact, that the principles were both derived from the same school, situated on the East of the Euphrates ; and, that they are, in fact, so nearly the same, that no one can tell with absolute certainty wherein they differ. No one can doubt that the doctrines of Pythagoras and those of Zoroaster, as maintained when the former was at Babylon after its conquest by Cyrus, were, as it has been already remarked, the same or nearly so ; nor can any one doubt that Pythagoras was either the fellow-labourer and assistant of Zoroaster, or a pupil of his school.

---

[1] Stanley, Hist. Phil. Part xv. Ch. i. p. 765.     [2] Ibid. p. 784.     [3] Ibid.     [4] Ibid. Ch. vii.
[5] Diss. I. on the Gods of Greece, Italy, and India.     [6] Supplement Ess. on Ind. Chron.
[7] Liv. i. Ch. iii. p. 31.

Manes lived long after both of them ; and if it should be contended that he differed from them in any very abstruse speculative point, this will not be admitted as a proof that he did not draw his doctrine from their fountain, when it is known that it came from the East of the Euphrates, and when it is evidently the same in almost every other particular.

6. The ancient followers of Zoroaster are not yet extinct. There is " a colony of them settled " in Bombay, an island belonging to the English, where they are allowed, without any molesta- " tion, the full freedom and exercise of their religion. They are a poor, harmless sort of people, " zealous in their superstition, rigorous in their morals, and exact in their dealings, professing the " worship of one God only, and the belief of a resurrection and a future judgment, and utterly de- " testing all idolatry, although reckoned by the Mahometans the most guilty of it ; for although " they perform their worship before fire and towards the rising sun, yet they utterly deny that " they worship either of them. They hold that more of God is in these his creatures than in any " other, and that therefore they worship God towards them, as being in their opinion the truest " Shekinah of the Divine presence among us, as darkness is that of the devil's : and as to Zoroas- " tres, they still have him in the same veneration, as the Jews have Moses ; looking on him as " the great prophet of God, by whom he sent his law, and communicated his will unto them." [1] Thus it appears that if the Jews have preserved their religion for the last two thousand years, in order to fulfil a miracle or prophecy, the Persians have preserved the same religion without any miracle or prophecy whatever. And it must not be said, that this is confined to one little spot, for they are, like the Jews, dispersed all over Asia.

Although there is the most indisputable evidence, that the Magi, who were the priests of Persia, acknowledged one Supreme Being, called Oromasdes, yet they certainly worshiped the sun under the name of Mithra, the second person of their Trinity. They are said to have done this as only to an emblem or symbol—the seat and throne—of the Supreme Being. But it probably soon came to pass that the Supreme Being was forgotten, and that his image only was adored by the people. The Persian Magi have always denied that they worshiped *fire* in any other sense than as an emblem of the Supreme Being, but it is extremely difficult to ascertain the exact truth ; and the difficulty is increased by the circumstance that most ancient philosophers, and, in fact, almost all the early Christian fathers, held the opinion that God consisted of a subtile, ethereal, igneous fluid, which pervaded all nature—that God was *fire*. Thus, as I have before remarked, he appeared to Moses in the burning bush, and again upon Sinai.

All the Oriental and Grecian writers agree in ascribing to the Persians the worship of one Supreme God : they only differ as to the time when this first began to take place. Much more attention is due to the ancient Oriental, than to the Grecian, histories of Persia, and they all represent the worship of one Supreme God as having begun very early, and this is confirmed, in a considerable degree, by the rebuilding of the Temple of Jerusalem by Cyrus. There is no doubt that the Persian religion was reformed, or improved by some one, that the capital of the empire of the Magi was at one time at Balch, and that it was from this place their religion spread both into India and the West. It was in the neighbourhood of that city, where the first orbicular caves, of which we have heard so much, were excavated, long before the time of Cyrus.

Mr. Maurice says, " But it is now necessary that we should once more direct our attention " towards Persia. The profound reverence, before noticed, to have been equally entertained by " the Magi of Persia and the Brachmans of India, for the solar orb and for fire, forms a most " striking and prominent feature of resemblance between the religion of Zoroaster and that of " Brahma.

---

[1] Prid. Con. Part i. Book iv. p. 285. 8vo.        [2] Maur. Ind. Ant. V. II. p. 116.

7. The Vedas are supposed by the Brahmins to have existed from the most remote antiquity. The *words* are Sanscrit and the *letters* Nagari. [1] On this subject Sir W. Jones says, " That the " Vedas were actually written before the flood, I shall never believe." Sir William, in his first Dissertation, makes many professions of disinterestedness, of a mind perfectly free from prejudice; but the author must be excused by his friends for observing, that the declaration of his firm resolution not to believe a plain historical fact, " *I shall never* believe," gives us very little reason to hope for a fair and candid examinatian of any question, which shall in any way concern the truth or falsity of the doctrines he had previously determined to receive or reject. As might be expected, the result of this pious determination may be seen in almost every page of his works. The author finds no fault with the declaration; it is a mark of candour and sincerity, and it has had two good effects: it has secured to Sir William the praise of the priesthood; and it has put the philosophical inquirer upon his guard. But it would have been a great advantage if so learned a man, and a man possessing so powerful an understanding, as Sir William Jones, could have been induced to examine the subject without prejudice or partiality, or any predetermination to believe either one thing or another. After this declaration of Sir William's, every thing which he admits in opposition to his favourite dogma, must be taken as the evidence of an unwilling witness.

The Vedas are four very voluminous books, which contain the code of laws of Brahma. Mr. Dow supposes them to have been written 4887 years before the year 1769. Sir W. Jones informs us that the principal worship inculcated in them, is that of the solar fire; and, in the discourse on the Literature of the Hindoos, he acquaints us, that " The author of the Dabistan describes a " race of old Persian sages, [2] who appear, from the whole of his account, to have been Hindoos; " that the book of Menu, said to be written in a celestial dialect, and alluded to by the author, " means the Vedas, written in the Devanagari character, and that as Zeratusht was only a re- " former, in India may be discovered the true source of the Persian religion. [3] This is rendered " extremely probable by the wonderful similarity of the caves, as well as the doctrines, of the two " countries. The principal temple of the Magi in the time of Darius Hystaspes was at Balch, the " capital of Bactria, the most Eastern province of Persia, situated on the North-west frontiers of " India and very near to where the religion of Bramha is yet in its greatest purity, and where the " most ancient and famous temples and caverns of the Hindoos were situate." [4] As we know very well that there are no caves in the Western or Southern part of Persia answering to the description above, we are under the necessity of referring what is said here and in the quotation in Section 4, from Porphyry, to the great caves of the Buddhists and the Brahmins in the Northern parts of India and Northern Thibet. This proves their existence in the reputed time of Zoroaster.

8. Mr. Maurice says, " Of exquisite workmanship, and of stupendous antiquity—antiquity to " which neither the page of history nor human traditions can ascend—that magnificent piece of " sculpture so often alluded to in the cavern of Elephanta decidedly establishes the solemn fact, " that, from the remotest æras, the Indian nations have adored a *Triune Deity*. There the " traveller with awe and astonishment beholds, carved out of the solid rock, in the most conspi- " cuous part of the most ancient and venerable temple of the world, a bust, expanding in breadth " near twenty feet, and no less than eighteen feet in altitude, by which amazing proportion, as " well as its gorgeous decorations, it is known to be the image of the grand presiding Deity of " that hallowed retreat: he beholds, I say, a bust composed of three heads united to one body,

---

[1] Jones, Diss. VI. on the Persians, p. 185.　　[2] A Sage is a sagax, or sagacious or wise man, a sophi.
[3] Asiat. Res. Vol. I. p. 349.
[4] Hyde, Hist. Rel. Vet. Pers. Cap. xxiv. p. 320; Maurice, Ind. Ant, Vol. II. pp, 120, 126.

P

" adorned with the oldest symbols of the Indian theology, and thus expressly fabricated, according
" to the unanimous confession of the sacred sacerdotal tribe of India, to indicate the *Creator*, the
" *Preserver*, and the *Regenerator* of mankind." [1]

To destroy, according to the Vedantas of India and the Sufis of Persia, that is, the σοφοι or
wise men of Persia, is only to regenerate and reproduce in another form; and in this doctrine
they are supported by many philosophers of our European schools. We may safely affirm, that
we have *no experience* of the actual destruction,—the *annihilation* of any substance whatever.
On this account it is that Mahadeva of India, the destroyer, is always said to preside over generation, is represented riding upon a bull, the emblem of the sun, when the vernal equinox took place
in that sign, and when he triumphed in his youthful strength over the powers of hell and darkness : and near him generally stands the gigantic Lingham or Phallus, the emblem of the creative
power. From this Indian deity came, through the medium of Egypt and Persia, the Grecian
mythos of Jupiter Genitor, with the Bull of Europa, and his extraordinary title of Lapis—a title
probably given to him on account of the stone pillar with which his statue is mostly accompanied,
and the object of which is generally rendered unquestionable by the peculiar form of its summit or
upper part. In India and Europe this God is represented as holding his court on the top of lofty
mountains. In India they are called mountains of the Moon or Chandrasichara ; in the Western
countries Olympuses. He is called Trilochan and has three eyes. Pausanias tells us that Zeus
was called Triophthalmos, and that, previous to the taking of Troy, he was represented with three
eyes. As Mr. Forbes [2] says, the identity of the two Gods falls little short of being demonstrated.

In the Museum of the Asiatic Society is an Indian painting of a Cristna seated on a lotus with
three eyes—emblems of the Trinity.

---

## CHAPTER II.

THE WORD OM.—OMPHE, OMPHALOS.—OLYMPUS, AMMON, DELPHI.—DIGRESSION CONCERNING THE WORD
ON.—SUBJECT OF AMMON RENEWED.—HAM THE SON OF NOAH, AND AMMON THE SUN IN ARIES.—
NIEBUHR ON THE OMBRICI OF ITALY : SEVERAL REMARKABLE SYNONYMES.—ON THE SPIRIT OR RUH,
THE DOVE.—PRIESTLEY'S OPINION.—SUBJECT OF THE PERSIAN AND HINDOO TRINITY RESUMED.

1. MR. HASTINGS, one of the most early and liberal patrons of Sanscrit literature in India, in a
letter to Nathaniel Smith, Esq., has remarked how accurately many of the leading principles of the
pure, unadulterated doctrines of Bramha correspond with those of the Christian system. In the
Geeta, (one of the most ancient of the Hindoo books,) indeed, some passages, surprisingly consonant, occur concerning the sublime nature and attributes of God, as well as concerning the properties and functions of the soul. Thus, where the Deity, in the form of Cristna, addresses Arjun :
" I am the Creator of all things, and all things proceed from me,"—" I am the beginning, the
" middle, and the end of all things ; I am time : I am all-grasping death, and I am the resurrec-
" tion : I am the mystic figure OM ! I am generation and dissolution." Arjun in pious ecstacy
" exclaims, " Reverence ! reverence ! be unto thee, a thousand times repeated ! again and again
" reverence ! O thou who art all in all ! infinite in thy power and thy glory ! Thou art the father

---

[1] Maurice, Ind. Ant. Vol. IV. p. 736.          [2] Mem. Orien. Vol. III. Ch. xxxv. p. 444.

" of all things animate and inanimate! there is none like unto thee."[1] In our future investigations we shall find this mystic figure OM of the greatest importance; for which reason I shall now inquire into the meaning of this celebrated, *not-to-be-spoken* word.

" In the Geeta, Arjun is informed by Creeshna, that ' God is in the fire of the altar, and that " ' the devout, with offerings, direct their worship unto God in the fire.' ' I am the fire, I am the " ' victim.' (P. 80.) The divinity is frequently characterized in that book, as in other Sanscreet " compositions, by the word OM, that mystic emblem of the Deity in India." The ancient Brahmins, as well as the Buddhists, of India, regarded this word with the same kind of veneration as the Jews did the word IEUE, which they never pronounced except on certain very solemn occasions. This is what is meant by the fourth commandment, which we render, " Thou shalt not " take the name of the Lord thy God" (but which ought to be *Ieue thy God )* " in vain." As a pious Jew will not utter the word Ieue, so a pious Hindoo will not utter the word Om. It is the duty of the Jews and Hindoos to meditate on the respective words in silence, and with the most profound veneration.

The word Om is always prefixed in pronouncing the words which represent the seven superior worlds, as if to shew that these seven worlds are manifestations of the power signified by that word. In an old Purana we find the following passage: " All the rites ordained in the Vedas, the " sacrifices to the fire, and all other solemn purifications, shall pass away; but that which shall " never pass away is the word *Om*—for it is the symbol of the Lord of all things." M. Dubois adds, that he thinks it can only mean the true God. (P. 155.)—The sacred monosyllable is generally spelled OM: but, being triliteral, it seems better expressed by A U M or A O M or A W M, it being formed of the three Sanscrit letters that are best so represented. The first letter stands for the Creator, the second for the Preserver, and the third for the Destroyer.[2]

Sir W. Jones informs us that the names of Brahma, Veeshnu, and Seeva, coalesce and form the mystical word Om, which he says signifies neither more nor less than the solar fire.[3] Here I apprehend we have the identical word used by the ancient Egyptians and their neighbours for the Sun, Ammon.

2. The Hindoo word Om, I think, will be found in the celebrated Greek word Oμφη, which I will now examine, before I proceed with the subject of this chapter, as it will often be found to meet us in our investigations.

In the Greek, Oμφη signifies divina vox, responsum à Deo datum consulenti. Φη or φι by itself, according to Scapula, has no meaning, but is merely a paragogic syllable, as is also the word Oμ;[4] but φη is the root of φαω, to speak or pronounce, and of φημι, to say. I therefore go to the parent language, the Hebrew, and I find the word φη or φι, פה pe or פ pi, to be a noun in regimine, and to mean an opening, a mouth, a measure of capacity. Then the literal meaning will be, the mouth, or the opening, of Om. This is not far from the *divina vox* of the Greek. Hesychius, also Suidas in voce, interprets the word OMΦ to be θεια κληδων, the sacred voice, the holy sound—and hence arose the ομφαλος, or *place of Omphe.* But its real meaning is still further unravelled by explaining it as OM ΦH, the enunciation of the mysterious OM of Hindoo theology, the sacred triliteral AUM, but often written as it is pronounced, OM. The Greeks

---

[1] Maurice, Ind. Ant.   [2] Moore's Pantheon, pp. 413, 414.

[3] Jones, Asiat. Res.

[4] This assertion of Scapula only shews what he had better have confessed, that he knew nothing about it. There are not, I am of opinion, any paragogic syllables, that is, syllables without meaning, in any of the old languages.

often call the oracles, or places where the oracles were delivered, the ομφαλοι, or, as it is interpreted, *the navels* of the earth. These ομφαλοι της γης, (so Euripides, in Medea, calls Delphi,) are by the scholiasts said to be the navels or centres of the earth ; now, as Delphi could not be considered the centre by the Greeks, and as they had many ομφαλοι or centres, it is evident that the true meaning of the word was unknown to them.

The Jews consider Jerusalem to be the navel of the earth.[1]

The above etymon of the word does not quite meet all the circumstances, does not quite satisfy me—unless we consider this MYSTIC WORD to have had more meanings than one. We have seen that ομφαλος meant a navel. It is the name given to Delphi : and Delphi, as Mr. Faber has observed, has the meaning of the female organ of generation, called in India *Yoni*, the Os Minxæ. Jones says, ΟΜΦΗ Oracle, ΔΕΛΦΥΣ—Matrix, womb. In one of the plates in Moore's Hindoo Pantheon, Brahma is seen rising from the navel of Brahme-Maia with the umbilical cord uncut : this justifies the last rendering of Jones, *Matrix*. Closely allied to ομφη seems to be the word ομφαλη, or ομφαλος. I find φαλη or φαλος to mean Phallus or Linga, the *membrum virile*, constantly used for the generative power. Then ομφαλη will mean the generative power Ομ, or the generative power of Om. I find the oracle or Divina vox at Delphi called Omphalos, and the word Delphi or Δελφυς means the female generative power; and in front of the temple at Delphi, in fact constituting a part of the religious edifice, was a large Phallus or Linga, anointed every day with oil. This, all taken together, shews very clearly that Omphale means the oracle of the generative (androgynous) power of Om. But it might also come from the sacred word Ομ φαλος—BENIGNUS—the benignant Om. In the religious ceremonies at Delphi a boat of immense size was carried about in processions ; it was shaped like a lunar crescent, pointed alike at each end : it was called an Omphalos or Umbilicus, or the ship ARGO. Of this Argo I shall have very much to say hereafter. My reader will please to recollect that the os minxæ or Δελφυς is called by the name of the ship Argo. The Aum of India, as might well be expected, is found in Persia, under the name of Hom, and particularly in the mountains of Persia, amongst the Arii, before they are said to have migrated, under Djemchid, to the South. As usual, we get to the North-east, for the origin of things.[2]

Bacchus was called Omestes, explained *the devourer*. This is in fact the Om-Esta,[3] of Persia. " Ista-char, or Esta-char, is the place or temple of Ista or Esta, who was the Hestia 'Εϛια of " the Greeks, and Vesta of the Romans." This Persian ista or esta, is the Latin ista and est, *he* or *she is ;* it is also Sanscrit, and means the same as the *Jah* of the Hebrews. Bacchus, at Chios and Tenedos, was also called Omadius. This is correctly the God, or the holy Om.

3. Mr. Bryant connects the word Olympus with the Omphe. He observes, that wherever there was an Olympus, of which there were a great number, there was also an Omphi or Ompi, and that the word came from the Hebrew Har-al-ompi, *(Har* means *mount,)* which al-ompi was changed by the Greeks into Ολυμπος Olympus.[4] The word means the mount of the God Omphi, according to Bryant's exposition ; but more correctly, I think, the mount of the Phi, or the prophetic voice or oracle of the God Om : whence *tri-om-phe* chaunted in the mysteries at Rome, the triple Omphe. Mr. Bryant's etymon completely fails in accounting for the syllable Om. He probably did not know of the Hindoo Aum, Om. In his work cited above may be found

---

[1] Basnage, Hist. Jud. B. iii. Ch. xiv. p. 194.      [2] Creuzer, notes, p. 686.

[3] Bryant, Anal. Vol. I. p. 227.      [4] Ibid. p. 239.

many very learned and curious observations respecting the word Om and its connexion with various places.   He shews that the meaning of the Oμϕι was totally unknown to the Greeks.

From Parkhurst, (in voce שר sr, p. 771,) it is pretty clear that the omphalos had both the meaning of beeve and umbilicus, and that it had also the same meaning as שר sr.

Amon is the Om of India, and On or אן an of the Hebrews.   Strabo calls the temple of Jupiter Ammon, Ἱερον Ομανϰ.   Bryant[1] says, המה eme is called Hom.[2]   Gale says, " In the Persian lan-" guage Hama means the sun."[3]   These are all evidently the Om of India, variously translated.

The word Am, Om, or Um, occurs in many languages, but it has generally a meaning some way connected with the idea of a circle or cycle, as ambire, ambages, or circum.   This is particularly the case in all the Northern languages.   I need not name again the Umbilicus, nor the way in which this seems to be connected with the idea conveyed by the Greek word Δελϕυς.   Nonnus says, that the Babylonian Bel and the Lybian Hammon were, εν Ἑλλαδι, ΔΕΛΦΟΣ Απολλος.

An attentive perusal of what Jamieson has said, in his *Hermes Scythicus*, (pp. 6, 7,) on the word Am, Om, Um, will satisfy the reader that there is a strong probability that the radical meaning of this word is cycle or circle.   The importance of this will be seen hereafter.

It would be going too far to quote Dr. Daniel Clarke as an authority in support of my explanation of the word Ammon, but I will give a note of his in the seventh chapter of his Travels in Egypt, and leave the reader to judge for himself: " Plane ridiculum est, velle. *Ammonis* nomen " petere à Græcis : cùm Ægyptii ipsi Αμουν appellent, teste Herodoto.[4]   The name of the Su-" preme Being among the Brahmins of India is the first syllable only of this word pronounced " AM."   Again,[5] " Sol superùs et clarus est AMMON."[6]   The ancients had a precious stone called Ombria.   It was supposed to have descended from heaven.[7]   The place of its nativity seems to connect it with the mysterious Om.   The Roman nurses used the letter M, pronounced Mu, as a charm against witchcraft, and from the effects of the evil eye—from being fascinated by the God Fascinus, who had the figure of the membrum virile, and was worn about the necks of women and children, like the Agnus Deis worn by Romish Christians.   The latter, I have no doubt, borrowed the custom from the Gentiles.[8]

4. Various derivations are given of the word ON, but they are all unsatisfactory.   It is written in the Old Testament in two ways, און aun and אן an.   It is usually rendered in English by the word *On*.   This word is supposed to mean the sun, and the Greeks translated it by the word ʼηλιος or sol.   But I think it only stood for the sun as emblem of the procreative power of nature.   Thus, in Genesis xlix. 3, *Reuben, thou art my firstborn, my might, and the beginning of* MY STRENGTH : principium roboris mei :[9] אוני auni, ראשית u-rasit.   It meant the beginning or the first exercise of his pro-creative power.   Again, in Deut. xxi. 17, the words אנו ראשית rasit anu, refer to the firstborn, and have the same meaning : *For he is the beginning of his strength ; the right of the firstborn is his.*   Again, in Psalm lxxviii. 51, we find it having the same meaning : *And smote all the firstborn in Egypt: the* CHIEF OF THEIR STRENGTH *in the tabernacles of Ham :* אונים aunim ראשית rasit : Primitias omnis laboris eorum, in tabernaculis Cham.[10]   In the hundred and fifth Psalm and the thirty-sixth verse, it has the same meaning.

It was from Oenuphis, a priest of On, that Pythagoras is said to have learnt the system of the heavenly bodies moving round the sun in unceasing revolutions.   The priests of this temple were esteemed the first in Egypt.[11]

---

[1] Heathen Myth. p. 3.          [2] Ibid.          [3] Gale's Court of the Gentiles, Vol. I. ch. xi. p. 72.
[4] Vossius de Orig. &c., Idolat. Tom. i. Lib. ii. Cap. ii. p. 362, Amst. 1642.          [5] Ibid. p. 282.
[6] Jablonski, Panth. Ægyp.          [7] Plin. Hist. Nat. Lib. xxxvii. Cap. x.          [8] Vide Ibid. Lib. xxviii. Cap. iv.
[9] Ar. Montanus.          [10] Vulg.          [11] See Plut. de Is. et Osir.

Ænon or עין oinn, where John baptized, was called by a figure of speech only Ænon, or the fountain of the sun. The literal meaning was, The Fountain of the Generative Power.

Mr. Faber, speaking of the calves set up by Jeroboam, says, " that they were, in their use and " application, designed to be images of the two sacred bulls which were the living representations " of Osiris and Isis, is both very naturally asserted by St. Jerome, and may be collected even " from Scripture itself. Hosea styles the idols of Jeroboam *the calves of Beth-Aven:* and imme- " diately afterwards speaks of the high places of the God Aven, whom he denominates *the sin of* " *Israel*. Now we are told, that when Jeroboam instituted the worship of the calves, he likewise " made high places in which their priests might officiate. The high places, therefore, of the " calves are the high places of Aven ; the temple of Aven is the temple of the calves ; and Aven, " the sin of Israel, is the same as at least one of the calves, which are also peculiarly described as " being the sin of Israel. But the God, whose name by the Masoretic punctuation is pronounced " *Aven*, is no other than the Egyptian deity Aun or On : for the very God whose worship Hosea " identifies with that of the calves, is he of whom Potipherah is said to have been the priest : the " two appellations, which our translators variously express, Aven and On, consisting in the He- " brew of the self-same letters. *On,* however, or Aun, was the Egyptian title of the sun, whence " *the city of On* was expressed by the Greeks *Heliopolis ;* and the sun was astronomically the " same as the Tauric God Osiris : consequently On and Osiris are one deity. Hence it is evident, " that the worship of Jeroboam's calves being substantially the worship of On or Osiris, the calves " themselves must have been venerated, agreeably to the just supposition of Jerome, as the repre- " sentatives of Apis and Nevis." [1] The calves were probably emblematical of the Sun in his male and female character—Baal and Baaltis.

5. We have seen that Strabo says, the temple of Ammon was called ἱερον Ομανε, and we have also seen, that the first syllable of the word אם *am* was no other than the celebrated Hindoo word Aum, which designated the Brahmin Trinity, the Creator, the Preserver, and the Destroyer. These three letters, Sir W. Jones tells us, as stated above, coalesce and form the mystic word OM. In the Geeta, Cristna thus addresses Arjun : " I am generation and DISSOLUTION." It was from the last idea that Heliopolis, or the city of On, was called in some of the old versions of the Bible *the city of destruction*. Here are evidently the Creator and the Destroyer. Mr. Strauss says, that Bethaven means *place of unworthiness*. [2]

The word אם *am* in the Hebrew not only signifies might, strength, power, firmness, solidity, truth, but it means also *mother*, as in Genesis ii. 24, and *love*, whence the Latin Amo, mamma. If the word be taken to mean strength, then Amon will mean (the first syllable *am* being in regi- mine) the temple of *the strength of the generative* or *creative power*, or the temple of the mighty procreative power. If the word *am* mean mother, then a still more recondite idea will be implied, viz. the mother generative power, or the maternal generative power : perhaps the Urania of Persia, or the Venus Aphrodite of Crete and Greece, or the Jupiter Genetrix, of the masculine and femi- nine gender, or the Brahme-Maia of India, or the Alma Venus of Lucretius. And the city of On or Heliopolis will be the *city of the Sun* or *city of the procreative powers of nature*, of which the Sun was always the emblem. [3]

I have proved in my Celtic Druids, Ch. ii. Sect. xxiv. that the old Latin was Sanscrit, and I may affirm, that the Alma of Lucretius is of Oriental, not Grecian, origin. The Greeks knew not the word Alma. This word, I think, means *Al* the preserver, and *ma* mother : it will then mean, the preserving mother Venus. I think in this case no one can doubt that the עלמה *olma* of the

---

[1] Pagan Idol. Vol. I. p. 437.      [2] Hos. x. 5 ; Amos iv. 4 ; Helon's Pilgrimage, B. iv. Ch. i.
[3] Drummond, Origines, B. i. Ch. iv. p. 47.

Phœnicians, and the עלמה olme of the Hebrews, which both mean *Virgin*, or young woman, were the same as the Latin *Alma*. The Om or Aum of India is evidently the Omh of the Irish Druids, which means *He who is*.[1] It is a very curious circumstance that in almost all etymologies, when probed to the bottom, the Celtic language is found along with the Hebrew.

There was in Syria or Canaan a place called *Ammon*, the natives of which were always at enmity with the Israelites. This was spelt עמון omun in the Hebrew, and by the Greeks was called Heliopolis. This seems to shew that it was dedicated to the same God as the Αμον of Egypt.

This word is used in the writings of the Hindoos precisely as we use the word Amen, which I have no doubt, both in its meaning and use, comes from this word.

6. The name of the son of Noah was חם *Hm*, called Ham. The name of the solar orb was חמה *Ame* the feminine of חם *Hm*. It appears to me that, from misapprehension, the *Ham* of Noah has been confounded with the *Ham*, or *Hm* or *Om* of Egypt—the Jupiter *Ammon* or *Amon*, the God with the Ram's head, adored at the ιερον Ομανε. The word חם *Hm*, the patriarch, and the word חמה *Hme*, the Sun, being the same, were the cause of the mistake. Suppose the LXX. meant to say that Egypt was given to *Ham*, it by no means follows that this was the *Ham* or *Am* of the temples of the Sol Generator. As we have another much more probable way of accounting for the *Om* of the temple than that of supposing the deification of a man living a thousand miles from the temple of the Oasis, I think we are bound to take it. But if the history of the flood was a sacred mythos, the two words might have the same meaning without being copied from one another. I know no reason for believing that the son of Noah was deified—a mere fancy of modern priests ; but I have many reasons for believing that Amon was the Sun as the generating power, first in Taurus, then in Aries. " Belus, Kronos, Apis, were solar symbols, and Nonnus " ranks Amon with these :

Βηλος επ' Ευφρηταο, Λιβυς κεκλημενος Αμμον,
Απις εφυς Νειλωος, Αραψ Κρονος, Ασσυριος Ζευς.

" Amon was clearly understood by the mythologists to represent the Sun in Aries."[2] Sir W. Drummond has given many other satisfactory reasons for Amon being the Sun : then how absurd is it to go any farther ! All difficulties are easily explained by attending to the circumstance of the fundamental doctrine, that, in fact, all the Gods resolve themselves into the Sun, either as God or as emblem of the Triune Androgynous Being.

Wilkinson, in his Atlas, has placed on the Eastern shore of Arabia, on a river named Lar, a town called Omanum, which was also called Om. Here a moderately fertile imagination may perhaps find a second or third Ammon—and thus several Ammons, several Heliopolises, several Memmons, &c., &c.[3] Some important words are connected with or derived from the word Om. Mr. Niebuhr says, " The Umbri were a powerful people previous to the Etruscans."[4] He also says, that the Greeks detected in the name of these people, which they pronounced Ombrici, an allusion to *a very remote antiquity*. The reader will not be surprised that I should go to the East for the origin of the Om-brici and of Om-brica, and consequently of our Umber—North-umberland and C-umberland.

7. Mr. Niebuhr does not pretend to explain the meaning of the word Italia, but he informs us that the ancient Greeks referred it to Heracleian traditions, and to a Greek word Ιταλος or Ιτϵλος,[5] signifying a BULL. This recalls our attention in a very singular manner to the most ancient superstition. Pliny[6] says, " The people of Umbria are supposed, of all Italy, to be of greatest

---

[1] Maurice, Hist. of Hind. Vol. II. p. 171, ed. 4to.　　　[2] Drum. Orig. B. iv. p. 330.
[3] Ib. B. iii. Ch. iii. p. 360.　　　[4] Ch. vi.　　　[5] Ch. i. p. 31.　　　[6] Nat. Hist. Lib. iii. Cap. xiv.

" antiquity, as whom men think to have been of the Greeks named Ombri, for that, in the general " deluge of the country by rain, they only remained alive." I think it does not require a very fertile imagination to discover here traces of the flood, the first race of men, and the sacred mysterious Om. Br or Pr, in the Eastern language, means sacred and creative,[1] and Omberland will mean, The Land of the Sacred Om.

Thus we have several clear and distinct meanings of Ομφαλος. It was mitis, begnignus. It was the *male* generative power, as Φαλλος. As Omphale, it was the *female* generative power, the wife of Hercules, and the navel of the Earth or Nabbi. It was also the prophetic voice of the benignant Om. We shall see by and bye how it came to have all these different meanings. Before we conclude this work, we shall find a similar variety arising from other names connected with this subject, and in particular it should be recollected that we have found the Indian Creeshna or Cristna calling himself Om.

I cannot help suspecting that the ancients often adopted an extraordinary play upon words—a kind of punning. Thus, שר *Sr*, is the root of Osiris, who changed himself into a bull. He is the Sun. :Surya is the Sun, and is the favourite God of Japan, where the celebrated Bull breaks the mundane egg. שור *Sur*, is a beeve, as Taurus, at the vernal equinox, the leader of the heavenly hosts. שרר *Srr*, means ruler, or absolute director or Lord.

*Brahme* is the Sun, the same as Surya. *Brahma* sprung from the navel of Brahme. The Greeks call the oracles ομφαλοι, or navels of the earth. *Srr* has the same meaning as ομφαλος —and *Sr* means *funis umbilicalis*.

Ομφη means an oracle. The oracle was the spirit of the God, the sanctus spiritus, and came from the ομφαλος. It founded Delphi in the form of a black Dove. A Dove is always the emblem the Holy Spirit. יונה *Iune*, is Hebrew for Dove. This is the Yoni of India, the Os Minxæ, the matrix. At Delphi the response came from a fissure or crack in the mountain, the Yoni of the earth. This was the emblem of the רוח *ruh* or Holy Ghost, the third person of the Trinity.

8. In Psalm xxxiii. 6, it is said, " By the word of Ieue were the שמים *smim* heavens made ; " and all the host of them by the רוח *ruh* breath of his mouth." Again, ver. 9, " For he *spake*, " and it was done ; he *commanded*, and it stood fast."

The third person was the Destroyer, or, in his good capacity, the Regenerator. The dove was the emblem of the Regenerator. When a person was baptized, he was regenerated or born again. A Dove descended on to the head of Jesus at his baptism. Devotees profess to be born again by the Holy Ghost—Sanctus Spiritus. We read of an Evil Spirit and of a Holy Spirit ; one is the third person in his *destroying* capacity, the other in his *regenerating* capacity. We read in the Acts of the Apostles (ch. xvi. 16) of a spirit of Python or a Pythonic spirit, an evil spirit. Python, or the spirit of Python, was the destroyer. But at Delphi he was also Apollo, who was said to be the Sun in Heaven, Bacchus on Earth, and Apollo in Hell.

M. Dubois has observed, (p. 293,) that the Prana or Principle of Life, of the Hindoos, is the *breath of life* by which the Creator animated the clay, and man became a living soul." Gen. ii. 7.

The Holy Spirit or Ghost was sometimes *masculine*, sometimes *feminine*. As the third person of the Trinity, it was as well known to the ancient Gentiles as to the moderns, as it will hereafter be shewn.

Origen expressly makes the Holy Ghost *female*. He says, παιδισκη δε κυριας τ8 αγι8 Πνευματος ή ψυχη—" The soul is maiden to her mistress the Holy Ghost.[2]

---

[1] Loubere, Hist. Siam.
[2] Porson against Travis ; Class. Jour. No. LXXVI., Dec. 1828, p. 207.

I believe by almost all the ancients, both Jews and Gentiles, the Supreme Being was thought to be material, and to consist of a very refined igneous fluid; more like the galvanic or electric fire than any thing with which I am acquainted. This was also the opinion of most of the ancient Christian fathers. This was called the anima as feminine, or spiritus as masculine—and was the רוח *ruh* of the second verse of Genesis, which Parkhurst calls breath or air in motion, (Isaiah xi. 4,) an *incorporeal substance*, and the Holy Spirit. From this comes the expression *to inspire*, or *holy inspiration*. The word Ghost means spiritus or anima. This was often confounded with the igneous fluid of which God was supposed to consist; whence came the baptism by fire and the Holy Ghost. (Matt. iii. 11.) These were absurd refinements of religious metaphysicians, which necessarily arose from their attempts to define *that* of which they had not the means of forming an idea. I should be equally as absurd, if I were to attempt to reconcile their inconsistencies. In the above examples of the different names for the Holy Ghost, a singular mixture of genders is observable. We see the active principle, *fire*, the Creator and the Preserver, and also the Destroyer, identified with the Holy Ghost of the Christians, in the united form of the Dove and of Fire settling on the apostles. Here we have most clearly the Holy Ghost identified with the Destroyer, Fire.

The Dove is the admitted emblem of the female procreative power. It always accompanies Venus. Hence in Sanscrit the female organ of generation is called Yoni. The Hebrew name is יונה *iune*. Evidently the same. The wife of Jove, the Creator, very naturally bears the name of the female procreative power, Juno. It is unnecessary to point out the close relation of the passion of love to the procreative power. There can scarcely be a doubt that the Dove was called after the Yoni, or the Yoni after the Dove, probably from its salacious qualities. And as creation was destruction, and the creative the destructive power, it came to be the emblem of the destructive as well as of the creative power. As the רוח *ruh* or spiritus was the passive cause (brooding on the face of the waters) by which all things sprung into life, the Dove became the emblem of the *ruh* or *Spirit* or Holy Ghost, the third person, and consequently the Destroyer. In the foundation of the Grecian Oracles, the places peculiarly filled with the Holy Spirit or Ghost, or inspiration, the Dove was the principal agent. The intimate relation between all these things, and their dependance on one another, I think, cannot possibly be disputed. We have in the New Testament several notices of the Holy Ghost or the sanctus spiritus, קדיש *qdis*, רוח *ruh*, πνευμα άγιον, ψυχη κοσμυ, or anima mundi, or alma Venus. It descended, as before remarked, upon Jesus at his baptism, in the form of a Dove, and according to Justin Martyr, a fire was lighted in the moment of its decent in the river Jordan. It is also said to have come with a sound as of a rushing mighty wind, but to have been visible as a tongue of fire, settling on each apostle, as described Acts ii. 2, 3. Here we have the רוח *ruh* or *air in motion*, according to Parkhurst's explanation, which brooded on the face of the deep, an active agent in the creation; and we have *fire* the *Destroyer*— the baptism of water, wind, and fire—the baptism of the Etruscans. [1] John says, " I indeed baptize you with water, but one shall come, who shall baptize you with the Holy Ghost and with " fire." (Luke iii. 16.) All this is part of the Romish Esoteric religion of Jesus, which, like other religions, has been lost; a few fragments only now remaining; unless it be privately concealed in the recesses of the Vatican.

8. We may see very clearly from the nonsense of Lactantius that my idea is correct. He says, the Son of God is the sermo or ratio (the speech or reason) of God; also, that the other angels are the breath of God, *spiritus Dei*. But *sermo* (speech) is breath emitted, together with a voice expressive of something.[2] I shall, perhaps, be asked by a disciple of the philosophic Priestley

---

[1] Vide Gorius's Etruscan Monuments.　　　　[2] Priestley, Cor. Christ. Sect. ii.

how I conceive the soul to be connected with or related to the body—to matter. I reply, I know not. I only know that God is good, and that this goodness cannot exist without a state of reward and punishment hereafter to mankind. This makes me certain that, in some way or other, man will exist after death: but *how* the Deity has not given me faculties to comprehend. And if I wanted a proof of this latter proposition, I have only to go for it to the unsatisfactory nature of the Doctor's Disquisitions on Matter and Spirit, from which I think any unprejudiced person must see that he has involved himself in inextricable difficulties, from not attending to Mr. Locke's doctrine, and from attempting that which is beyond the reach of the human understanding.

If my reader will pay a little attention to what passes in his own mind, he will soon see, that when he talks of Spirit or Ghost, he generally has no idea of any thing. This is one of the subjects of which he can acquire no knowledge or idea through the medium of the senses. Therefore, as might be expected, a great confusion of terms prevails. In the foregoing examination, the truth of what I have said will be instantly apparent. The terms betray, in their origin, the grossest materialism. I think the reader must now see that if the *spirit of God* mean any thing, it is a mere figure of speech, and means that God has so modelled his law of creation, that the patient shall have a good disposition, or a good spirit. And if it be said that he has a spirit of prophecy or of foretelling future events, I reply, the expression may as well be, that he has a flesh to foretell as a spirit to foretell. If God have ever given a person a knowledge of what will happen at a future time, this has no more to do with the spirit or the air in motion, than with the flesh. Jesus said, the gates of hell should never prevail against his religion. According to your accounts, Christian doctors, they have prevailed and continue to prevail. But I say, No. They have not prevailed, and never will prevail; the pure, unadulterated doctrines of Jesus will stand for ever. They have only prevailed against the corruptions with which you have loaded his religion. The fine morality and the unity of God, which you would have destroyed, can never really be destroyed, though your idols, your relics, your saints, and your mother of God, will all pass away, like yesterday's shadow of a cloud on the mountain.

9. It is now time to return to the Persians.

After enumerating various other instances to prove the existence of an Indian Trinity, Mr. Maurice says, " Degraded infinitely, I must repeat it, beneath the Christian, as are the characters " of the Hindoo Trinity, yet in our whole research throughout Asia there has not hitherto occurred " so direct and unequivocal a designation of a Trinity in Unity as that sculptured in the Ele- " phanta cavern : nor is there any more decided avowal of the doctrine itself any where to be met " with than in the following passages of the Bhagvat Geeta. In that most ancient and authentic " book, the supreme Veeshnu thus speaks concerning himself and his divine properties : ' I am " ' the holy one, worthy to be known.' He immediately adds, ' I am the *mystic (triliteral)* figure " ' Om ; the *Reig*, the *Yagush*, and the *Saman Vedas*.' [1] Here we see that Veeshnu speaks ex- " pressly of his *unity*, and yet in the same sense declares he is the mystic figure A. U. M., which " three letters the reader has been informed, from Sir W. Jones, coalesce and form the Sanscreet " word OM." A little after, in the same page, Mr. Maurice tells us, that the figure which stands for the word OM of the Brahmins, is designated by the combination of three letters, which Dr. Wilkins has shewn to stand, the *first* for the *Creator*, the *second* for the *Preserver*, and the *third* for the *Destroyer*. [2]

M. Sonnerat also states that the Hindoos adore *three* principal deities, Brouma, Chiven, and Vichenou, who are still but one. [3]

---

[1] Geeta, p. 80.        [2] Maurice, Ind. Ant. Vol. IV. pp. 744, 745.        [3] Ibid. p. 747.

M. Sonnerat also gives a passage from a Sanscrit Pooraun,[1] in which it is stated that it is God alone who created the universe by his *productive* power, who maintains it by his *all-preserving* power, and who will destroy it by his *destructive* power, and that it is this God who is represented under the name of *three Gods*, who are called *Trimourti*.[2] Mr. Forster[3] says, " One circumstance which forcibly struck my attention was the Hindoo belief of a Trinity; the " persons are *Sree Mun Narrain*, the *Maha Letchimy*, a beautiful woman, and a *Serpent*. These " persons are by the Hindoos supposed to be wholly indivisible; the *one* is *three*, and the *three* " are *one*." Mr. Maurice then states that the Sree Mun Narrain, as Mr. Forster writes it, is Narayen the Supreme God : the beautiful woman is the Imma of the Hebrews, and that the union of the sexes is perfectly consistent with that ancient doctrine maintained in the Geeta, and propagated by Orpheus, that the Deity is both male and female.[4]

Mr. Maurice, in his Indian Antiquities, says, " This notion of three persons in the Deity was " diffused amongst all the nations of the earth, established at once in regions so distant as Japan " and Peru, immemorially acknowledged throughout the whole extent of Egypt and India, and " flourishing with equal vigour amidst the snowy mountains of Thibet, and the vast deserts of " Siberia."

## CHAPTER III.

ISRAEL WORSLEY'S ACCOUNT OF ANCIENT TRINITIES.—OPINION OF DR. PRITCHARD AND OTHERS ON THE
TRINITIES.—OPINION OF MAURICE AND OTHERS ON THE TRINITIES. — THE CHRISTIAN TRINITY—ITS
ORIGIN.—MACROBIUS ON THE TRINITY.—PHILO'S TRINITY OF THE JEWS.—FABER'S ACCOUNT OF THE
UNIVERSAL BELIEF OF THE TRINITY.—OBSERVATIONS ON THE DOCTRINE THAT DESTRUCTION IS ONLY
REGENERATION.

1. Mr. WORSLEY says, " This doctrine was of very great antiquity, and generally received by " all the Gothic and Celtic nations. These philosophers taught, that the Supreme God, Teut or " Woden, was the active principle, the soul of the world, which, uniting itself to matter, had " thereby put it into a condition to produce intelligences or inferior gods and men. This the " poets express by saying that Odin espoused Frea, or the Lady, by way of eminence. Yet they " allowed a great difference between these two principles. The Supreme was eternal, whereas " matter was his work, and of course had a beginning. All this was expressed by the phrase, " Earth is the daughter and wife of the universal Father. From this mystical union was born the " God Thor-Asa Thor, the Lord Thor. He was the firstborn of the Supreme, the greatest of " the intelligences, that were born of the union of the two principles. The characters given him " correspond much with those which the Romans gave to their Jupiter. He, too, was the thun- " derer, and to him was devoted the fifth day, Thor's-dag; in German and Dutch, Donder dag,

---

[1] Voyages, Vol. I. p. 259.     [2] Ibid. p. 749.     [3] Sketches of Hindoo Mythology, p. 12.
[4] Maurice, Ind. Ant. Vol. IV. p. 750.

" thunder day. The common oaths of these people mark the same origin. They swear by *donder*
" *and blexen*, thunder and lightning. Friday took its name from Frea, Frea's-dag ; as Wednesday
" did from Woden, Woden's-dag. Tuis was the name which the old Saxons gave to the son of
" the Supreme, whence Tuesday. Thor, being the firstborn, was called the eldest of the sons :
" he is made a middle divinity, a mediator between God and man. Such, too, was the Persians'
" God : for Thor was venerated also as the intelligence that animated the sun and fire. The Per-
" sians declared that the most illustrious of all the intelligences was that which they worshiped
" under the symbol of fire. They called him Mithras, or the mediator God. The Scythians called
" him Goeto-Syrus, the Good Star. All the Celtic nations were accustomed to worship the sun,
" either as distinguished from Thor, or as his symbol. It was their custom to celebrate a feast at
" the winter solstice, when that great luminary began to return again to this part of the Heavens.
" They called it Yuule, from Heoul, Helios, the sun, which to this day signifies the sun in the
" language of Bretagne and Cornwall : whence the French word Noel.

" How great a resemblance may be seen between the expressions which have been stated above,
" relative to these ancient Trinities, and those of some Christian worshipers, who imagine that
" the Father begat the Son—according to some in time, according to others from eternity—and
" that from these two sprang or proceeded the Holy Ghost !" [1]

According to Israel Worsley, [2] " It was Justin Martyr, a Christian convert from the Platonic
" school, who, about the middle of the second century, first promulgated the opinion, that the Son
" of God was the second principle in the Deity, and the creator of all material things. He is the
" earliest writer to whom this opinion can be traced. He ascribes his knowledge of it, not to the
" Scriptures, but to the special favour of God." *But Justin is the very earliest admitted genuine
Christian writer whom we have*, not supposed to be inspired, and it seems that he did not attribute
the knowledge of his doctrine to the gospel histories. The reason of this will be explained hereafter.

Mr. Worsley then proceeds to state that " Modern theologians have defined the three Hypos-
" tases in the Godhead with great precision, though in very different words : but the fathers of
" the Trinitarian Church were neither so positive nor so free from doubt and uncertainty, nor
" were they agreed in their opinions upon it. The very councils were agitated ; nor is that which
" is now declared essential to salvation, the ancient Trinity. They who thought the Word an
" attribute of the Father, which assumed a personality at the beginning of the creation, called this
" the generation of the Son ; regarding him still as inferior to the Father, whom they called *the*
" *God* by way of eminence, while, after the example of the old Heathens, they called the Son
" God. This notion of descent implied inferiority, and on that ground was objected to, and the
" Nicene Council, in 325, issued a corrected and improved symbol ; and Christ, instead of only
" Son, was styled God of God, and very God of very God. But even here the equality of the Son
" was not established, the Father by whom he was begotten being regarded as the great fountain
" of life. The investment of wisdom with a personality still implied a time when he was begotten,
" and consequently a time when he was not. From this dilemma an escape was in process of
" time provided by the hypothesis of an eternal generation ; a notion which is self-contradictory.
" The Nicene Fathers, however, did not venture on the term Trinity ; for they had no intention
" of raising their pre-existent Christ to an equality with the Father : and as to the Holy Spirit,
" this was considered as of subordinate rank, and the clauses respecting its procession and being
" worshiped together with the Father and the Son, were not added till the year 381, at the Council
" of Constantinople." [3] I give no opinion on the statement of Mr. Worsley, as it is not my inten-

---

[1] Israel Worsley's Enquiry, p. 42.          [2] Ibid. p. 54.          [3] Ibid. p. 63.

tion to enter into a controversy as to what the Trinity is, but only to give an historical account of it.

2. Dr. Pritchard, in his Analysis of Egyptian Mythology, (p. 271,) describes the Egyptians to have a Trinity consisting of the *generative*, the *destructive*, and the *preserving* power. Isis answers to Seeva. Iswara, or " LORD," is the epithet of Siva, or Seeva. Osiris, or Ysiris, as Hellanicus wrote the Egyptian name, was the God at whose birth a voice was heard to declare, " that the " Lord of all nature sprang forth to light." Dr. Pritchard again says, (p. 262,) " The oldest " doctrine of the Eastern schools is the system of emanations and the metempsychosis." These two were also essentially the doctrine of the Magi, and of the Jews, more particularly of the sect of the Pharisees, or, as they ought to be called, of the Persees. [1] פרס *Prs*, [2] Mr. Maurice [3] observes, that the doctrines of *Original Sin* and that man *is a fallen creature*, are to be found both in the religion of Brahma and Christ, and that it is from this, that the pious austerities and works of supererogation by the Fakirs and Yogees of the former are derived. The doctrine of the Metempsychosis was held by most of the very early fathers, and by all the Gnostic sects, at one time, beyond all doubt, the largest part of the Christian world. Beausobre thought that the transmigration of souls was to be met with in the New Testament. He says, [4] " We find some " traces of this notion even in the New Testament, as in St. Luke xvi. 23, where there is an ac- " count of the abode of departed souls, conformable to the Grecian philosophy; and in St. John " ix. 2, where we find allusion to the pre-existence and transmigration of souls." The works of supererogation and purgatory of the Romish Church both come from this source. A celebrated modern apologist for Christianity believed the metempsychosis.

The God Oromasdes was undoubtedly the Supreme God of the Persians, but yet the religion was generally known by the name of the religion of Mithra, the Mediator or Saviour.

In the same way in India the worship of the *first* person in their Trinity is lost or absorbed in that of the *second*, few or no temples being found dedicated to Brahma; so among the Christians, the worship of the *Father* is lost in that of the *Son*, the Mediator and Saviour. We have abundance of churches dedicated to the second and third persons in the Trinity, and to saints, and to the Mother of God, but none to the Father. [5] We find Jesus constantly called *a Son*, or as (according to the Unitarians) the Trinitarians choose to mistranslate the Greek, *the Son* of God. In the same way, Plato informs us, that Zoroaster was said to be " the son of Oromasdes or Ormis- " das, which was the name the Persians gave to the Supreme God"—therefore he was *the Son of God*. [6]

Jesus Christ is called the Son of God : no doubt very justly, if the Evangelist John be right, for he says, (ch. i. ver. 12,) that every one who receives the gospel, every one, in fact, who believes in God the Creator, has power to become a Son of God. Ormusd, in Boundehesch, says, " My " name is the principle (le principe) and the centre of all things : my name is, He who is, who is " all, and who preserves all." [7]

As the Jews had their sacred writings to which they looked with profound respect, so had the Persians : and so they continue to have them to this day. Mr. Moyle [8] has endeavoured to discredit the genuineness of these writings, by stating " that they contain facts and doctrines mani- " festly taken from the gospels." It is probable that these writings are no more the writings of

---

[1] The Pharisees were merely Parsees, (the Jews pronounced P like PH or F,) persons who intermingled Magian notions (acquired during the captivity) with the law of Moses: hence a peculiar propriety in *child of fire*, υἱον γεεννης, Matt. xxiii. 15; Sup. to Palæromaica, pp. 63, 100.

[2] Parkhurst in Voce, p. 594; Beaus. Int. pp. 16, 132.    [3] Ind. Ant. Vol. V. p. 195.    [4] Int. p. 16.

[5] See Maur. Ind. Ant. Vol. V. p. 87.    [6] Cud. B. i. Ch. iv. p. 287.

[7] Notes to Creuzer's Religions de l'Antiquité, by Guigniault, p. 670.    [8] Works, Vol. II. p. 57.

Zoroaster, or of a man who lived five or six hundred or a thousand years before Cyrus, than that the Jewish Pentateuch is the writing of Moses.  Yet they are probably partly his or his compilation, in the same way that the Pentateuch is partly the production or the compilation of Moses.  Though these books may not be the writing of Zoroaster, they are the received sacred books of the Magi, the same as the books of the Pentateuch are of the Jews, and their genuineness is entitled to equal respect.  It was, perhaps, on account of these matters, that Dr. Hyde's translations of the Persian works never went to press.

3.  The doctrine of the Trinity is first to be met with to the North-east of the Indus, and it may be traced Westwards to the Greek and Latin nations; but the two latter seem almost to have lost sight of it as a national or vulgar doctrine; indeed, among the multitude in them, nothing half so rational is to be found.  It seems to have been confined to the philosophers, such as Plato —but whether as a secret doctrine or mystery may admit of doubt.

Whether the doctrine of the Trinity formed a part of the Christian religion has been disputed almost from its earliest period, by a great variety of sects, with a degree of bitterness and animosity hardly to be equalled in the history of the world.  If the question had been of vital importance to the religion, or, which is of equal consequence in the estimation of too many, had involved the continuance of the hierarchy or tithing system, instead of being merely an idle speculation, its truth or falsity could not have been contested with greater virulence.  Several considerable sects affirm, that it was introduced by some of the early fathers from the school of Plato : this others as strongly deny.  Mr. Maurice, who being a Churchman is, of course, on the Trinitarian side, candidly allows that it existed in the doctrines of the Jews, and of all the other Asiatic nations from the most remote antiquity.  But so far from seeing any difficulty in this, he concludes from it, that it must have been revealed by God to Adam, or to Noah, or to Abraham, or to somebody else, and from thence he most triumphantly concludes that it is true.  The antiquity of the doctrine he has clearly proved.  His conclusion is another affair.  If it be satisfactory to his mind, it is all well; a worthy and good man is made happy at very little expense.  In Chapter II. Mr. Maurice has brought together a vast variety of facts to prove that the doctrine of the Trinity was generally held by the Gentiles, but they all at last shew its origin to have been the Egyptian Mithraitic or Hindoo school.  From this source the Trinity sprang : a doctrine which it is seen may be traced to very remote periods of time, indeed long prior to the time fixed for the existence of the Jews, or probably of Noah : and it passed to them through the medium of the Persians and Egyptians, as it did also to the Greeks : and from them all it passed to the Christians in a later day.  As it might have been supposed, it is found not to be altogether, but yet fundamentally, the same, and in fact to possess much more similarity than might have been expected from the eternal law of change to which it was subject, during the time it was travelling through various climates, nations, and languages, for hundreds, indeed thousands, of years.  However, in all the great essential parts it is the same.  There are the Father, the Creator—the Son, the Preserver or Saviour—and the evil principle or the devil—in his bad character the destroyer, *in his good one the regenerator ;* the same three persons as in the Christian Trinity—except that the ignorant monks of the dark ages, not understanding there fined doctrine of the Eternity of Matter, and, that *destruction* was only *reproduction*, divided the third person into *two*—the Destroyer and Regenerator, and thereby, in fact, formed *four* Gods—the Father, the Son, the Holy Ghost, and the Devil.

4.  The immediate origin of the complete and correct Christian Trinity, of that peculiar doctrine on which all orthodox persons seem to think their happiness in this life, as well as in that which is to come, actually depends, will now be exhibited on the unquestionable authority of a most unwilling witness, of one of the most learned and orthodox of its priests—the Rev. Mr. Maurice.  Speaking of the Trinity in the oracles of Zoroaster, he says, " Since, exclusive of the error of

" placing PRINCIPLES for HYPOSTASES, [1] which was natural enough to an unenlightened Pagan, it is
" impossible for language to be more explicit upon the subject of a divine Triad, or more confor-
" mable to the language of Christian theologers.

Οτε πατρικη μονας εστι,<br>
Ταναη εστι μονας η δυο γεννα.

" ' Where the *paternal monad* is, that paternal monad amplifies itself, and generates a duality.'
" The word πατρικη, or paternal, here at once discovers to us the two first hypostases, since it
" is a relative term, and plainly indicates a Son. The paternal monad produces a duality, not by
" an act of creation, but by generation, which is exactly consonant to the language of Christianity.
" After declaring that the duad, thus generated, καθηται, *sits* by the monad, and, shining forth
" with intellectual beams, governs all things, that remarkable and often-cited passage occurs :

Παντι γαρ εν κοσμω λαμπει τριας<br>
'Ης μονας αρχει.

" ' For a triad of Deity shines forth throughout the whole world, of which a monad is the head.' " [2]
Thus, after describing the PATERNAL MONAD, as he calls it, he describes a DUALITY, and it is
certainly very remarkable that this DUALITY is not produced by creation or emanation, but by
GENERATION ; and is said to SIT by the side of the MONAD, and to govern all things. It is impossible after reading this, not to recollect the words of our creed, in which this doctrine is clearly
expressed : " Begotten of his Father." " Begotten not made." " He sitteth on the right hand
" of the Father." " And shall come again, to judge both the quick and the dead."

Mr. Maurice then adds, " In the very next section of these oracles, remarkable for its singular
" title of ΠΑΤΗΡ και ΝΟΥΣ, or the Father and the Mind, that Father is expressly said ' to
" ' perfect all things, and deliver them over to Νω δευτερω,' the second Mind ; which, as I have
" observed in the early pages of this dissertation, has been considered as allusive to the character
" of the mediatorial and all-preserving Mithra ; but could only originate in theological conceptions
" of a purer nature, and be descriptive of the office and character of a higher MEDIATOR, even the
" eternal ΛΟΓΟΣ. The whole of the passage runs thus :

Παντα γαρ εξετιλεσσε ΠΑΤΗΡ, και ΝΩ παρεδωκε<br>
ΔΕΥΤΕΡΩ, ον πρωτον κλειζεται παν γενος ανδρων.

" ' That SECOND MIND,' it is added, ' whom the nations of men commonly take for the first.'
" This is, doubtless, very strongly in favour of the two superior persons in the Trinity."
Mr. Maurice goes on to shew that the term *second mind* is used, and is allusive to the *all-preserving Mithra*. He then adds, " The following passage, cited by Proclus from these oracles, is
" not less indubitably decisive in regard to the *third* sacred hypostasis, than the preceding pas-
" sages in regard to the *second :*

" Μετα δε πατρικας Διανοιας Ψυχη εγω ναιω<br>
" Θερμη, ψυχωσα τα παντα.

" That is, ' In order next to the paternal Mind I Psyche dwell warm, animating all things.'
" Thus, after observing in the first section, the Triad or το θειον, the whole Godhead collectively
" displayed, we here have each distinct HYPOSTASIS separately and clearly brought before our view."

---

[1] This almost alone proves that these were not copies from the Christian doctrines. According to the authors cited
both by Kircher and Stanley, these oracles were originally written in the Chaldee language, and were translated into
Greek. Maurice, Ind. Ant. Vol. IV. p. 258.
[2] Maur. Ind. Ant. Vol. IV. p. 259.

And thus, by this learned priest, [1] not by me, the whole correct Christian Trinity, with its various HYPOSTASES, is shewn to have existed in the religion of Mithra and the Magi, ages before Christ was born.

There is now no resource left to the priests, but to declare these oracles of Zoroaster spurious, which Bishop Synesius, in the fourth century, called *holy oracles*. [2] But Mr. Maurice provides against this, by informing his reader, that he has only availed himself of such passages in these oracles as have been quoted by such men as Porphyry, Damascius, and other Greek writers unfavourable to Christianity, and such as have a marked similitude to the ancient tenets of India, Persia, and Egypt; [3] and which, therefore, cannot be modern forgeries. The existence in these oracles of such passages as have been cited, is, the author believes, the only circumstance on which the priests have determined that they are spurious. They have said, These passages must have been extracted from the gospel histories, therefore the books containing them must be spurious. It never once occurred to them, that the gospel histories might copy from the oracles, or that they might have both drawn from a common source. And it also never occurred to them, that the fact of their quotation by old authors proves that they must have existed before the gospels. In pointing out this circumstance Mr. Maurice has really great merit for his candour and honesty. I believe there are very few priests who would not have found an excuse to themselves, for omitting to point out the conclusive and damning fact.

Plutarch [4] says, " Zoroaster is said to have made a *threefold* distribution of things : to have " assigned the first and highest rank to Oromasdes, who, *in the oracles*, is called the Father; " the lowest to Ahrimanes; and the middle to Mithras; who, in the *same oracles*, is called " τον δευτερον Νῦν, the second Mind." As Mr. Maurice says, [5] Plutarch, born in the first century, cannot have copied this from a Christian forgery. Besides, he expressly says it is taken from the oracles—herein going very far to confirm the genuineness of the oracles; indeed, he actually does confirm it, in those parts where the quotations are found.

This doctrine of the oracles is substantially the same as that of Plato. It was taken from the Hymns of Orpheus, which we now possess, and which Mr. Parkhurst allows are the very same that were revered by the ancient Greeks as his, and, as such, were used in their solemn ceremonies. He proves this by a passage from Demosthenes. [6] In the Pythagorean and Platonic remains, written long anterior to the Christian æra, all the dogmas of Christianity are to be found. Witness the Δημιεργος or Ζευς Βασιλευς ; the δευτερος Θεος, or second God; δευτερος Νῦς, or second Mind; the Μιθρας μεσιτης, or mediatorial Mithra; and γεννητος Θεος, or generated God, begotten not made. Again, the ψυχη κοσμε, or soul of the world; i. e. the רוח ruh or spiritus, of Osiris and Brahma, *in loto arbore sedentem super aquam*, brooding on the waters of the deep ; the θειος Λογος, or divine Word, verbum, which Jesus announced to his mother that he was, immediately on his birth, as recorded in the Gospel of his Infancy. [7]

Upon the Logos, Bishop Marsh, in his Michaelis, says, " Since, therefore, St. John has adopted " several other terms which were used by the Gnostics, we must conclude that he derived also " the term Λογος from the same source. If it be further asked, Whence did the Gnostics derive " this use of the expression, ' WORD' ? I answer, that they derived it most probably from the " Oriental or Zoroastrian philosophy, from which was borrowed a considerable part of the Mani- " chean doctrines. In the Zendavesta, we meet with a being called ' *the Word*,' who was not

---

[1] Maurice, Ind. Ant. Vol. IV. p. 267.          [2] Ibid. p. 262.          [3] Ibid. p. 291.

[4] De Iside et Osiride, p. 370.          [5] Vol. IV. p. 367.

[6] See his note in voce שם *sm*, XI.          [7] Maur. Ind. Scep. Conf. pp. 53 and 139.

" only prior in existence, but gave birth to Ormuzd, the creator of good; and to Ahriman, the
" creator of evil. It is true, that the work which we have at present under the title of Zendavesta,
' is not the ancient and genuine Zendavesta ; yet it certainly contains many ancient and genuine
" Zoroastrian doctrines. It is said, likewise, that the Indian philosophers have their Λογος,
·" which, according to their doctrines, is the same as the Μονογενης."

In reply to this, attempts will be made to shew that the Λογος of John is different from the
Oriental Logos : all mere idle, unmeaning verbiage, fit only for those described by Eusebius, who
wish to be deceived : the doctrines as well as the terms are *originally* the same, in defiance of the
ingenuity of well-meaning devotees to hide from themselves the sources whence they are derived.
The variation is not greater than might be expected from change of place, of language, and lapse
of time.

Eusebius acknowledges that the doctrines of the Christians, as described in the first chapter of
John, are perfectly accordant with those of the Platonists, who accede to every thing in it, until
they come to the sentence, *Et verbum caro factum est.* This seems to be almost the only point
in which the two systems differed. The philosophers could not bring themselves to believe that
the Logos, in the gross and literal sense of the Christians, quitted the bosom of God, to undergo
the sorrowful and degrading events attributed to him. This appeared to them to be a degradation
of the Deity. Eusebius allows, what cannot be denied, that this doctrine existed long anterior to
Plato ; and that it also made part of the dogmas of Philo and other Hebrew doctors. He might
have added also, had he known it, of the priests of Egypt, and of the philosophers of India.

The origin of the *verbum caro factum est,* we shall presently find in the East. It was not new,
but probably as old as the remainder of the system. Its grossness well enough suited such men
as Justin, Papias, and Ireneus.[1]   For the same reason that it suited them, it was not suitable to
such men as Plato and Porphyry.

In the doctrines of the Hindoos and Persians, as it has already been stated, the third person in
the Trinity is called both the Destroyer and the Regenerator. Although in the Christian Trinity
the *Destroyer* is lost sight of, yet the *Regenerator* is found in the Holy Ghost. The neophite is
said to be regenerate, or born again, by means of this holy spiritus or mind. Plutarch says, that
Mithras or Oromasdes was frequently taken for the το θειον, or whole deity, and that Mithras is
often called the second mind. " Whereupon he observes, how great an agreement there was
" betwixt the Zoroastrian and the Platonic Trinity, they differing in a manner only in words !" [2]
This second mind is evidently the Holy Ghost of the Christians, so accurately described above in
the oracles of Zoroaster, the רוח *ruh* of the second verse of Genesis, which moved, or more correctly brooded, (see Fry's Dictionary,) upon the face of the waters. This, in sacred writ, is often
called יהוה רוח *Ieue ruh,* or אלהים רוח *Aleim ruh.* The words Ieue and Aleim not being in regimine,
which would make it the Spirit of Aleim, or of Jehovah, but being in the nominative case, they
make it the *Ieue ruh* or *Aleim ruh.*

The figure in the Hindoo caves (whose date cannot be denied to be long anterior to the time of
Moses) of the second person, Cristna, having his foot bitten by the serpent, whose head he is
bruising, proves the origin of Genesis.

There can be no longer any reasonable doubt that it came from India, and as the Christian Trinity is to be found in its first chapter, it raises, without further evidence, a strong presumption

---

[1] These, the early fathers of Christianity, believed, that persons were raised from the dead *sæpissime ;* that Jesus
would come, before that generation passed away, to reign upon earth for a thousand years ; and, that girls were frequently pregnant by demons.

[2] Cudworth, Book i. Ch. iv. p. 289.

that, that also came from India. By the word אלהים *Aleim*, the το Θειον, or whole Deity, or Christian Trinity, is meant. By the word ראשית *rasit*, the *first* Emanation or Æon, Wisdom or the Logos is meant, and by the word רוח *ruh*, the Spirit of God, the *second* mind, the second emanation, the *third* person in the Trinity is meant—forming altogether the whole Godhead, *three* persons and *one* God.

5. Macrobius, in his Commentary on the Dream of Scipio, (a work of Cicero's,) which he explains by the great principles of the philosophy of the Pythagoreans and Platonists, has given in the clearest manner, in his account of the Trinity of the Gentiles, a description of the Triad or Trinity of the orthodox,—the triple distinction of God the Father, of his Logos, and of the Spiritus, with a filiation similar to that which exists in the theology of the Christians, and an idea of their unity inseparable from that of the Creator. It seems, in reading it, as if we were listening to a Christian Doctor, who was teaching us how the Spiritus proceeds, and the Son is engendered from the Father, and how they both remain eternally attached to the Paternal unity, notwithstanding their action on the intellectual and visible world. The following is in substance what Macrobius says.[1] This learned theologian distinguishes first, after Plato, the God Supreme, the first God, whom he calls with the Greek philosophers τ' Αγαθον, *the Good*, par excellence, the First Cause. He places afterward his *Logos*, *his intelligence*, which he calls *Mens* in Latin, and Νꙋς in Greek,[2] which contains the original ideas of things, or *the* ideas—intelligence born and produced from the Supreme God. He adds, that they are above the human reason, and cannot be comprehended but by images and similitudes. Thus, above the corporeal being or matter, either celestial or terrestrial, he establishes the divinity, of which he distinguishes three degrees, Deus, Mens, and Spiritus. God, says he, has engendered from himself by the superabundant fecundity of his Majesty, *Mens* or Mind, with the Greeks Νꙋς or Λογος. Macrobius then describes an immense graduated chain of beings, commencing with the First Cause, to be born or produced from itself. He says that the three first links of this immense chain are the Father, his *Logos*, Νꙋς, *Mens*, and *Anima* or *Spiritus Mundi* ; or, in the Christian phraseology, the Father, Son, and Holy Spirit, the principles of all things, and placed above all created beings. After this he goes on to explain, in exact Christian style of language, the manner in which the Spirit *proceeds*, and in which the Son is *begotten—engendered* by the Father. If a trifling difference can be discovered between the doctrine of the Pagan Macrobius and that of the orthodox Christian, it is not so great as that which may be met with between the doctrines or opinions of different sects of even orthodox Christians upon this subject. Surely a greater resemblance need not be desired between the Platonic and Christian Trinities.

Upon the Trinity of Plato, M. Dupuis observes, that all these abstract ideas, and these subdivisions of the first *Unity*, are not new ; that Plato is not the author of them ; that Parmenides before him had described them ; that they existed long anterior to Plato ; that this philosopher had learned them in Egypt and the schools of the East, as they might be seen in the writings of Mercury Trismegistus and Jamblicus, which contain a summary of the theology of the Egyptians, and a similar theory of abstractions. Marsilius Ficinus has well observed, that the system of three principles of the theology of Zoroaster and the Platonicians, had the greatest similarity with those of the Christians, and that the latter philosophy was founded upon the former. He might have said, that it was not only *similar*, but in reality the same. The curious reader will do well to consult the beautiful and luminous essay of M. Dupuis, *Sur tous les Cultes*, on this subject ; he will find himself amply repaid for his trouble.

---

[1] Macrob. Som. Scip. Lib. i. Cap. ii.—vi.        [2] Heb. *Rasit*, Wisdom.

For proofs that the Grecians worshiped a Trinity in Unity, the reader may consult the Classical Journal, Vol. IV. p. 89. It is there shewn that their Trinity was the JUPITER (that is, the Iao) MACHINATOR.

Speaking of the doctrine of the Chaldeans, Thomas Burnet says,[1] " In prima ordine est Su-" prema TRIAS. Sic philosophatur Psellus." Though he gives no account of what this Trias consisted, there is not much room to doubt that it was the Hindoo, Zoroastrian, Platonic Triad.

Mercury was called Triceps ; Bacchus Triambus ; Diana Triformis ; and Hecate Tergemina.

Tergeminamque Hecatem, tria virginis ora Dianæ.[2]

ΣΩΤΕΙΡΑ occurs as a title of Diana on the brass coins of Agathocles.[3]

Plutarch[4] says, διο και Μιθρην Περσαι τον Μεσιτην ονομαζυσι. Orpheus also calls Bacchus Μισης Mediator, the same as Mithra of the Persians.[5] Proserpine had three heads ; the Triglaf of the Vandals had also three heads ; and Mithras was called Τριπλασιος.

The Trimurti was the Trimighty of the Saxons, the Trimégas of the Greeks, and the Ter-magnus of the Latins.[6] The Trinity is equally found amongst the Druids of Ireland in their Taulac Fen Molloch.[7]

Navarette, in his account of China,[8] says, " This sect (of Foe) has another idol they call " SANPAO. It consists of *three*, equal in all respects. This, which has been represented as an " image of the most blessed Trinity, is exactly the same with that which is on the high altar of " the monastery of the Trinitarians at Madrid. If any Chinese whatsoever saw it, he would say " the SAN PAO of his country was worshiped in these parts."[9]

I must now beg my reader to turn to Book I. Chapter II. Sect. 4, and read what I have there said respecting the material or Pantheistic Trinity, endeavoured to be fixed upon Plato and the Orphic and Oriental philosophers, and I think he must be perfectly satisfied of the improbability that the persons who held the refined and beautiful system which I have developed, could ever have entertained a belief that the Sun, the Moon, and the Earth, were the creators or formers of themselves.

6. As the whole, or nearly the whole, of the ceremonies of the Jews were borrowed from their Gentile neighbours, it would be very extraordinary if their most important doctrine of the Trinity had not been found in the Jewish religion. I shall, therefore, add several more authorities to those already laid before my reader, in Book II. Ch. II. Sect. 5, and particularly that of the celebrated Philo.

Mr. Maurice[10] says, that the first three sephiroth of the Jewish cabala consist of *first* the Omnipotent Father; *second* Divine Wisdom; and *third* the *Binah* or Heavenly Intelligence, whence the Egyptians had their *CNEPH*, and Plato his Νυς δημιυργος. But this demiourgos is supposed to be the Creator, as we have before seen that he must necessarily be, if he be the Destroyer. Thus some of the early Christians confounding these fine metaphysical distinctions, and at a loss how to account for the origin of evil, supposed the world to be created by a wicked demiourgos. The confusion arising from the description of *three* in *one*, and *one* in *three*—the community of Persons and unity of Essence—the admitted mysterious nature of the Trinity, and the difficulty, by means of common language, of explaining and of reconciling things apparently irreconcilable, may nevertheless be easily accounted for. On the subject of the Destroyer Mr.

---

[1] Cap. iv. p. 29.     [2] Æneid, iv. 511 ; Maur. Hind. Ant. Vol. IV. p. 238 ; Parkhurst, p. 347.
[3] Payne Knight, Essay, Gr. Al. Sect. v. p. 105.     [4] De Iside et Osiride, p. 43.
[5] Stukeley, Palæog. Sac. No. I. p. 54.     [6] D'Ancarville, p. 95.     [7] See Celtic Druids, Ch. v. Sect. xix.
[8] Book ii. Ch. x., and Book vi. Ch. xi.     [9] Parkhurst, p. 348.
[10] Hind. Ant. Vol. IV. pp. 183, 184.

Maurice says,[1] " I must again repeat, that it would be, in the highest degree, absurd to continue
" to affix the name of Destroyer, to their third hypostasis in the triad,[2] when it is notorious, that
" the Brahmins deny that any thing can be destroyed, and insist that a change alone, in the form
" of objects and their mode of existence, takes place. One feature, therefore, in that character,
" hostile to our system, upon strict examination, vanishes." He then shews, from the Sephir
Jetzirah, that the three superior sephiroths of the Jewish cabala were invariably considered by
the *ancient Jews* in a very different light from the other seven; that the first three were regarded
as PERSONALITIES, but the last seven only as *attributes*.[3]

Rabbi Simeon Ben Jochai[4] says, " Come and see the mystery of the word Elohim: there are
" *three degrees,* and each degree by itself alone, and yet, notwithstanding, they are all one, and
" *joined together* in one, and cannot be divided from each other." This completely justifies
what I have formerly said, respecting the words אל *al* and אלהים *aleim,* having a reference to the
Trinity.

Priestley says, " But Philo, the Jew, went before the Christians in the personification of the
" Logos, and in this mode of interpreting what is said of it in the Old Testament. For he calls
" this divine word a second God, and sometimes attributes the creation of the world to this second
" God, thinking it below the majesty of the great God himself. He also calls this personified
" attribute of God his πρωτογονος, or his firstborn, and the image of God. He says that he is
" neither unbegotten, like God, nor begotten, as we are, but the middle between the two extremes.
" We also find that the Chaldee paraphrasts of the Old Testament often render *the word of God,*
" as if it were a being distinct from God, or some angel who bore the name of God, and acted by
" deputation from him." [5]

In reply to this I shall be told that Philo Platonized or was a Platonist. To be sure he was;
because recondite, cabalistic, esoteric Judaism, was the same as Platonism. It would have been
as correct, probably, to have said that Plato Hebraized: for as it is evident that the Israelites
held the doctrine of the Trinity, where was it so likely for him to obtain it as from them ? Philo
was a Jew of elevated rank, great learning, and the highest respectability; the very man to whom
we have a right to look for the real doctrines, both esoteric and exoteric of the Israelites: and we
find him maintaining all the doctrines of the Platonic and Oriental Trinity—doctrines held by the
nearest neighbours of the Jews, both on the East and West, and from whom Mr. Spencer has
shewn, that they took almost all their rites and ceremonies. I contend, therefore, that the doctrines
taught by Philo afford the strongest presumption that these were also the doctrines of the Jews.

Of Orpheus, who is said to have brought the knowledge of the Trinity into Greece, very little
is known. But Damascius, Περι Αρχων, giving an account of the Orphic theology, among other
things acquaints us, that Orpheus introduced τριμορφον Θεον, a Triform Deity.[6] This was the
Platonic philosophy above described.

Of this person Mr. Payne Knight[7] says, " The history of Orpheus is so confused, and
" obscured by fable, that it is impossible to obtain any certain information concerning him. He
" appears to have been a Thrasian, and to have introduced his philosophy and religion into Greece;
" viz. plurality of worlds, and the true solar system; nor could he have gained this knowledge
" from any people of which history has preserved any memorial: for we know of none among
" whom science had made such a progress, that a truth so remote from common observation, and
" so contradictory to the evidence of unimproved sense, would not have been rejected, as it was

---

[1] Vol. IV. p. 388.                    [2] He here alludes to the Hindoos.                    [3] Maur. Ind. Ant. Vol. IV. p. 182.
[4] Comment. on the 6th Sec. of Leviticus.                    [5] Priestley, Cor. Christ. Sect. ii.
[6] Maur. Ind. Ant. Vol. IV. p. 336.                    [7] On Priapus, vide note, p. 33.

" by all the sects of Greek philosophers, except the Pythagoreans, who rather revered it as an
" article of faith, than understood it as a discovery of science.

" Thrace was certainly inhabited by a civilized nation at some remote period ; for when Philip
" of Macedon opened the gold mines in that country, he found that they had been worked before
" with great expense and ingenuity, by A PEOPLE WELL VERSED IN MECHANICS, OF WHOM NO
" MEMORIALS WHATEVER ARE EXTANT." I think memorials of these people may be found in
the Pyramids, Stonehenge, the walls of Tyryns, and the Treasury of Messina.

7. The following extract from Mr. Faber's work on the Origin of Heathen Idolatry, exhibits a
pretty fair proof how very general was the ancient doctrine of the Trinity among the Gentiles :—
" Among the Hindoos we have the triad of Brama-Vistnou-Siva, springing from the monad
" Brahm : and it is acknowledged, that these personages appear upon earth at the commencement
" of every new world, in the human form of Menu and his three sons. Among the votaries of
" Buddha we find the self-triplicated Buddha declared to be the same as the Hindoo Trimurti.
" Among the Buddhic sect of the Jainists, we have the triple Jina, in whom the Trimurti is
" similarly declared to be incarnate. Among the Chinese, who worship Buddha under the name of
" Fo, we still find this God mysteriously multiplied into three persons, corresponding with the
" three sons of Fo-hi, who is evidently Noah. Among the Tartars of the house of Japhet, who
" carried off into their Northern settlements the same ancient worship, we find evident traces of a
" similar opinion in the figure of the triple God seated on the Lotos, as exhibited on the famous
" Siberian medal in the imperial collection at Petersburgh : and if such a mode of representation
" required to be elucidated, we should have the exposition furnished us in the doctrine of the
" Jakuthi Tartars, who, according to Strahremberg, are the most numerous people of Siberia :
" for these idolaters worship a triplicated deity under the three denominations of Artugon, and
" Schugo-tangon, and Tangara. This Tartar god is the same even in appellation with the Tanga
" Tanga of the Peruvians : who, like the other tribes of America, seem plainly to have crossed
" over from the North-eastern extremity of Siberia. Agreeably to the mystical notion so familiar
" to the Hindoos, that the self-triplicated great Father yet remained but one in essence, the
" Peruvians supposed their Tanga-tanga to be one in three, and three in one : and in consequence
" of the union of Hero worship with the astronomical and material systems of idolatry, they vene-
" rated the sun and the air, each under three images and three names. The same opinions
" equally prevailed throughout the nations which lie to the West of Hindostan. Thus the
" Persians had their Ormusd, Mithras, [1] and Ahriman : or, as the matter was sometimes repre-
" sented, their self-triplicating Mithras. The Syrians had their Monimus, Aziz and Ares. The
" Egyptians had their Emeph, Eicton, and Phtha. The Greeks and Romans had their Jupiter,
" Neptune, and Pluto ; three in number though one in essence, and all springing from Cronus, a
" fourth, yet older God. The Canaanites had their Baal-Spalisha or self-triplicated Baal. The
" Goths had their Odin, Vile, and Ve : who are described as the three sons of Bura, the offspring
" of the mysterious cow. And the Celts had their three bulls, venerated as the living symbols of
" the triple Hu or Menu. To the same class we must ascribe the triads of the Orphic and
" Pythagorean and Platonic schools : each of which must again be identified with the imperial
" triad of the old Chaldaic or Babylonian philosophy. This last, according to the account which is
" given of it by Damascius, was a triad shining throughout the whole world, over which presides a
" Monad." [2]

---

[1] Voss., de Orig. et Prog. Idol. Lib. ii. Cap. ix., says, that the word Mither, in Persian, means Lord, that Mithras
is derived from Mither. A Mediator is called Mithras in Persian. Mithras also means *love, pity.*

[2] Book vi. Ch. ii. p. 470.

Again he says, " To the great Triad of the Gentiles, thus springing from a Monad, was ascribed " the creation of the world, or rather its renovation after each intervening deluge. It was likewise " supposed to be the governing power and the intellectual soul of the universe. In short, all the " attributes of Deity were profanely ascribed to it. This has led many to imagine that the " Pagans did fundamentally worship the true God, and that even from the most remote antiquity " they venerated the Trinity in Unity." [1]

Thus it is evident, from the Rev. Mr. Faber's admission, that a Being called a Trinity, three persons and one God, was worshiped by all the ancient nations of the earth. He very properly says *to the same class we must ascribe the triads of the Orphic, Pythagorean, and Platonic schools.*

The school of Plato has been generally looked to for the origin of the Christian Trinity, but, as we have seen, it would be more correct to look to the oracles of Zoroaster. Christianity may have drawn from Platonism, but there can be no doubt that Plato had drawn from the oracles of the East. The Second Mind, or the Regenerator, correctly the Holy Ghost, was in the oracles of Zoroaster, and will be shewn to have been in the baptismal service of the Magi. And " the many" to whom Mr. Faber alludes, as believing that the Gentiles venerated the Trinity in Unity, believed what was perfectly true. There can be no doubt that the Heathens adored the Trinity before the Christians, and did not copy it from Christianity. If either copied, the Christians must have copied from their Heathen predecessors. But all this has a strong tendency to prove, that what Ammonius Saccas said was true, namely, that the religions of the Christians and the Gentiles were the same, when stripped of the meretricious ornaments with which the craft of priests had loaded them.

8. Before I quit the subject of the Persian doctrines it may not be irrelevant again to observe, that the ancient philosophers, meditating upon the nature of the universe, and confining their theories and systems to the knowledge which they derived from experience or through the medium of their senses, the only mode by which knowledge or ideas can be acquired, discovered that they had no experience of the destruction of matter; that when it appears to the superficial observer to be destroyed, it has only changed its mode of existence; that what we call destruction, is only reproduction or regeneration. On this account it is that we always find the Destroyer united with the Creator, and also with the Preserver or Saviour, as one person. Upon this curious philosophical and very true principle, an infinite variety of fictions have been invented, by the sportive genius of poets, or the craft of priests. But the simple philosophical principle was at the bottom of them all; and it was that only which philosophers believed. God only knows whither the vanity of the moderns has carried them, or will carry them; but the ancients confined their wisdom or knowledge, in this instance at least, within the compass of their ideas—the limit of real knowledge; and as, in their present state of existence, they could not receive the idea of the annihilation of matter through the medium of the senses, they could not form an idea of it at all; and consequently could not receive as an article of faith that of which they must necessarily remain in profound ignorance. Matter might be created from nothing, or it might not be created; their senses told them it existed; but to them it was unknown whether it had ever not existed; and they did not pretend to decide, as an article of faith, the question—for in its very nature it was not possible to decide it by human means. Not so the wise Christian: he and his priest laugh at the ignorance of the ancient philosopher; and at once declare that matter *was* created; and that they have a perfect idea respecting its creation, which they can by no possibility have received from experience, or through the medium of the senses. With the ancient philosopher the Author confesses his ignorance. The Oriental philosopher, who penned the first verse of

---

[1] Book vi. Ch. ii. p. 471.

Genesis, was too wise to give an opinion upon the subject. He merely says, " God formed (or re-formed) the earth ;" the question of its creation *from nothing*, or *its eternity,* he did not touch.

Thus the reader sees that from the caves of Upper India, Persia, and Egypt, the doctrine of the Christian Trinity was undoubtedly drawn. But though these countries were the places where this doctrine flourished many ages before Christianity ; yet it has been supposed that it was from the Platonists of Greece, who had learned it from these three nations, that the Christians immediately drew their doctrine. And if the keen eye of a modern Thomas Aquinas should discover some. minute metaphysical variation between the ancient and modern systems, this will only be what we may expect to arise from the lapse of ages, and the difficulty of conveying ideas, so very abstruse, from one language into another. Nor will it be very surprising if the profound doctrines of philosophers, like Plato and Pythagoras, should happen to have been misunderstood by such philosophers as Papias and Ireneus. And if this should prove to have been the fact, the philosopher of the present day may not think the modern deviation any improvement upon the system.

I shall add no more at present on the subject of the Trinity or Cabala. I shall return to it very often; and it will not be till I come nearly to the end of this volume of my work, that I shall unfold the whole of what I have to disclose on this subject; when several apparent inconsistencies will be reconciled.

# BOOK IV.

## CHAPTER I.

PROPER MODE OF VIEWING THE RELIGION.—LIFE OF CRISTNA.—SUBJECT CONTINUED. MATUREA.—SIR
W. JONES'S EXPLANATION OF THE CIRCUMSTANCES, AND MR. MAURICE'S ADMISSIONS. — REFLEC-
TIONS ON THE ABOVE.—SOLEMN CONSIDERATIONS OF MR. MAURICE'S IN EXPLANATION.—DIGRESSION
ON THE BLACK COLOUR OF ANCIENT GODS; OF THE ETYMOLOGY OF THE NILE AND OSIRIS.—SUBJECT
CONTINUED.—CHRIST BLACK, AN ANSWER TO A SOLEMN CONSIDERATION.—OTHER SOLEMN CONSIDE-
RATIONS.—OBSERVATIONS ON MR. MAURICE'S SOLEMN CONSIDERATIONS.—MR. MAURICE'S PAMPHLETS.
—BACK RECKONINGS. MATUREA.—BRYANT AND DR. A. CLARKE ON THIS MYTHOS.

1. Having shewn that the Hindoos and Persians had certain of the leading articles of what is
usually called the Christian religion, some thousands of years, probably, before the time assigned
to Jesus,—the actual history of the birth and life of the Second Person of the Trinity, or of the
Saviour of the Romish or modern Christian religion, will now be given; from which it will
be evident to the reader whence most of the corruptions in the histories of the gospel of Jesus
have been derived.

When a person takes a view of the whole of what has constituted the Christian system, at any
period of the time during which it has existed, if he mean to form a correct idea of it, he must not
confine his observation to any one or two of the divisions of which it consists at the time of his
survey, but he must take, as it were, a bird's eye view of it. He must bring all its numerous
subdivisions within the field of his telescopic vision. No doubt each of them will dispute the propriety of this, because there is not one of them, however small and contemptible it may be, which
will not maintain that *it* is the sole and true religion, all the others being merely heresies or corruptions. To this, however, the philosopher, inquiring only for the truth, will pay no attention:
each is an integral part, and the union of the whole forms the religion of that day; though it is
very possible that it may differ essentially from that taught by Jesus, or from the religion of the
present day.

If a person be disposed to dispute the doctrine here laid down, I would beg to ask him what he
would do if he undertook to make a survey of the religion of India. Would he consider
only the religion of the followers of Vishnu; or of that of the followers of Cali; or of that of the
followers of Buddha? No: he would consider each of these as parts of the grand whole; all derived from one common source; and reason upon them accordingly. In the same manner he will
consider the sects of Christians, when he takes a philosophical view of the religion. In carrying
this intention into effect, I shall, of course, often have occasion to notice the writings of Christians
of former times, but which are now little known. Of this kind are what are called the Apocryphal
Gospels. This being the correct mode of viewing the religion, it seems evident that if a general
corruption have pervaded all its sects, we must not expect to find the cause or origin of this cor-

ruption applicable to *one* sect only; but, on the contrary, we shall find it apply in a very considerable degree to the whole of them.

It will not apply alone to the gospel of Paul, or of Montanus, or of Marcion, or of the Egyptians, but it will apply to them all indiscriminately, orthodox and heterodox, without any partiality to any one of them. But it cannot be reasonably expected that the exact place should be pointed out where every one of the facts stated in the whole of the numerous gospels, or histories of the religion, came from. The only question will be, whether sufficient be pointed out to convince the mind of the impartial reader of the identity of the systems, or of the truth of the proposition meant to be established.

It will now be shewn, in the first place, that from the history of the second person of the Indian Trinity, many of the particulars of the gospel histories of the Christians have been compiled.

The book called the Bhagavat Geeta, which contains the life of Cristna, is allowed to be one of the most distinguished of the puranas, for its sublimity and beauty. It lays claim to nearly the highest antiquity that any Indian composition can boast: and the Rev. Mr. Maurice, a very competent judge, allows, that there is ample evidence to prove that it actually existed nearly four thousand years ago. Sir William Jones says, "That the name of Chrishna, and the general outline " of his story, were long anterior to the birth of our Saviour, and probably to the time of Homer, " we know very certainly." In fact, the sculptures on the walls of the most ancient temples,— temples by no one ever doubted to be long anterior to the Christian æra—as well as written works equally old, prove, beyond the possibility of doubt, the superior antiquity of the history of Cristna, to that of Jesus. The authority of the unwilling witness, Sir W. Jones, without attempting any other proof of this fact, is enough. But in the course of this work many other corroborating circumstances will be produced, which, independently of his authority, will put the matter beyond question.

2. These observations being premised respecting the Bhagavat Geeta, we will now consider some of the leading facts which are stated in it relating to the God Cristna, Crisna, or Chrishna. [1] These we shall find are copies of the Christian gospel histories, or the Christian gospel histories are copies from them, or they have both been copied from an older mythos.

In the first place, the Cristna of India is always represented as a Saviour or Preserver of mankind, precisely the same as Jesus Christ. While he is thus described as a Saviour, he is also represented to be really the Supreme Being, taking upon himself the state of man : that is, to have become *incarnate in the flesh*, to save the human race, precisely as Jesus is said to have done, by the professors of the orthodox Christian faith. This is the *Verbum caro factum est* of St. John, to which I alluded in Book III. Chap. III. Sect. 4.

As soon as Cristna was born, he was saluted with a chorus of Deutas or Devatas or Angels, with divine hymns, just as it is related of Jesus in the orthodox Gospel of Luke, ch. ii. 13, 14. He was cradled among shepherds, to whom were first made known the stupendous feats which stamped his character with marks of the divinity. The circumstances here detailed, though not literally the same as those related of Jesus, are so nearly the same, that it is evident the one account has been taken from the other. The reader will remember the verse of the gospel history, *And there were shepherds tending their flocks by night.* Luke ii. 8.

Soon after Cristna's birth, he was carried away by night and concealed in a region remote from his natal place, for fear of *a tyrant* whose destroyer it was foretold he would become; and who had, for that reason, ordered all the male children born at that period to be slain. This story is

---

[1] Sir W. Jones always spells the name of this celebrated person Chrishna.

8

the subject of an immense sculpture in the cave at Elephanta,[1] where the tyrant is represented destroying the children. The date of this sculpture is lost in the most remote antiquity. It must, at the very *latest* period, be fixed at least many *hundred* years previous to the birth of Jesus Christ, as we shall presently see. But with much greater probability *thousands* instead of *hundreds* of years might be assigned to its existence. Cristna was, by the *male* line, of royal descent, though he was actually born in a state the most abject and humiliating—in a dungeon—as Jesus was descended from King David and was born in a cave, used as a stable. The moment Cristna was born, the whole room was splendidly illuminated, and the countenances of his father and mother emitted rays of glory. According to the *Evangelium Infantiæ* " Spelunca repleta erat luminibus, " lucernarum et candelarum fulgorum excedentibus, et *solari luce* majoribus." Cristna could speak as soon as he was born, and comforted his mother, as did the infant Jesus, according to the same gospel history. As Jesus was preceded and assisted by his kinsman, John, so Cristna was preceded by his elder brother, Ram, who was born a little time before him, and assisted him in purifying the world, polluted with demons and monsters. Ram was nourished and brought up by the same foster parents as Cristna. Thus the Gospel of James[2] states, that the prophecy of Zachariah and the supernatural pregnancy of his wife being notorious, Herod suspected that John might be the expected Messiah, and commanded him to be delivered up, in order that he might murder him ; but Elizabeth had sent him into the wilderness to his cousin, by which means he escaped. Cristna descended into Hades or Hell, and returned to Vaicontha, his proper paradise. One of his epithets was that of *a good shepherd,* which we know was that of Jesus. After his death, like Jesus Christ, he ascended into heaven. [3] From the glory described above, in the Evangelium Infantiæ, we see the reason why, in all pictures of the Nativity, the light is made to arise from the body of the infant, and why the father and mother are often depicted with glories round their heads.

3. After the birth of Cristna, the Indian prophet Nared, Σοφος, having heard of his fame, visited his father and mother at Gokul, examined the stars, &c., and declared him to be of celestial descent. As Mr. Maurice observes, here is a close imitation of the Magi guided by his star and visiting the Infant in Bethlehem. Cristna was said to have been born at Mathura, (pronounced Mattra,) on the river Jumna, where many of his miracles were performed, *and in which at this day he is held in higher veneration than in any other place in Hindostan.* Mr. Maurice says, " The " Arabic edition of the Evangelium Infantiæ records Matarea, near Hermopolis, in Egypt, to " have been the place where the Infant Saviour resided during his absence from the land of Judæa, " and until Herod died. At this place Jesus is reported to have wrought many miracles ; and, " among others, to have produced in that arid region a fountain of fresh water, the only one in " Egypt. Hinc ad Sycamorum illam urbem digressi sunt, quæ hodie Matarea vocatur ; et produxit " Dominus Jesus fontem in Matarea, in quo Diva Maria (*Cristna's mother has also the epithet* " DEVA *prefixed to her name)* tunicam ejus lavit. Ex sudore autem, qui à Domino Jesu defluxit, " balsamum in illâ regione provenit." [4]

M. Savary says, that at a little distance from Heliopolis is the small village of Matarea, so called because it has a fresh-water spring, the only one in Egypt. This spring has been rendered famous by tradition, which relates that the holy family fleeing from Herod came hither ; that the

---

[1] Maur. Ind. Ant. Vol. II. p. 149.            [2] Protevangelium Jacobi, p. 23, apud Fabric., p. 25.

[3] Maur. Ind. Ant.

[4] Evangelium Infan. Arab. et Lat. p. 71, ed. Syke, 1697 ; Maur. Hist. Vol. II. p. 318 ; Jones on the Canon, Vol. II. Part III. Ch. xxii.

Virgin bathed the holy child Jesus in this fountain ; and that much balsam was formerly produced in the neighbourhood.[1]

Eusebius and Athanasius state, that when Joseph and Mary arrived in Egypt, they took up their abode in a city of the Thebais, in which was a superb temple of Serapis. On their going into the temple, all the statues fell flat on their faces to the Infant Saviour. This story is also told by the Evangelium Infantiæ.[2]

After Cristna came to man's estate, one of his first miracles was the cure of a leper. Matthew (in ch. viii. ver. 3) states an early miracle performed by Jesus to have been exactly similar, viz. the cure of a leper. Upon another occasion a woman poured on the head of Cristna a box of ointment, for which he cured her of her ailment. Thus, in like manner, a woman came and anointed the head of Jesus. Matt. xxi. 7.

At a certain time Cristna taking a walk with the other cowherds with whom he was brought up, they chose him for their king, and every one had a place under him assigned to him. Nearly the same story is related of Jesus and his playfellows. At another time, the Infant Jesus declaring himself to be *the good shepherd,* turned all his young companions into sheep ; but afterward, at the solicitation of their parents, restored them to their proper form. This is the counterpart of a story of the creation, by Cristna, of new sheep and new cow-boys, when Brahma, to try his divinity, had stolen those which belonged to Nanda's, his father's, farm.[3] To shew his humility and meekness, he condescended to wash the feet of the Brahmins, as Jesus did those of his disciples. John xiii. 5, &c.

Cristna had a dreadful combat with the serpent Calinaga,[4] which had poisoned all the cowherds. In the Apocryphal Gospel above alluded to, the infant Saviour had a remarkable adventure with a serpent, which had poisoned one of his companions.[5]

Cristna was sent to a tutor to be instructed, and he instantly astonished him by his profound learning. In the Gospel of the Infancy it is related, that Jesus was sent to Zaccheus to be taught, and, in like manner, he astonished *him* with his great learning. This also must remind the reader of the disputation in the temple with the Jewish doctors. (Luke ii. 46, 47.) Cristna desired his mother to look into his mouth and she saw all the nations of the world painted in it. The Virgin saw the same in the mouth of Jesus.[6] Mr. Maurice observes that the Gospel of the Infancy is alluded to by Ireneus,[7] which shews that it was among the earliest of the ancient gospel histories.

Finally, Cristna was put to death by being *crucified ;* he descended into hell, and afterward ascended into heaven. For further particulars, see Maurice's Ind. Ant. Vol. II. pp. 149, &c. The descent into hades or hell, and the ascent into paradise or heaven, is stated by Mr. Maurice; the crucifixion is not stated by him ; but my authority for the assertion I shall adduce presently.

It is impossible for any one to deny the close connexion between the histories of Jesus and of Cristna. We now come to the most important point—how such connexion is to be rendered consistent with the existence of the whole of the Christian system as at present expounded by our priests,—how the priests are to explain it away,—how those men who are so unfortunate as to feel themselves obliged to yield to such *conclusive* evidence can be proved to be what the Rev. Mr. Maurice, in true orthodox strain, calls *impious infidels.*

[1] Savary's Travels in Egypt, Vol. I. p. 126.
[2] Vide Euseb. Demon. Evang. Lib. vi. Cap. xx. ; Athan. de Incarnat. Verbi, Vol. I. p. 89.
[3] Maurice, Hist. Hind. Vol. II. p. 322.
[4] *Cali* is now the Goddess of a sect in opposition to that of Cristna, and *Naga* means serpent. It is evidently the same as the old English word for serpent—*Hag.*
[5] Hist. Hind. Vol. II. p. 322.       [6] Maur. Bram. Fraud Exposed, p. 114.
[7] Adv. Heres. Lib. i. Cap. xvii. p. 104, ed. fol. 1596.

4. The mode in which Sir W. Jones gets over the difficulty is very easy. Without pretending that he has any variation of manuscripts, or other authority, to justify him, but merely because he finds the facts to be inconsistent with the existence of the whole of the present Christian system, as he chooses to expound it, he asserts the passages containing them to be interpolations from spurious gospels ; but, unfortunately for his credit, this, for many reasons, will not obviate the difficulty. It is evident that much of the history is the same as the *orthodox* gospels, as well as of those called *spurious*.

In reference to the opinion of Sir W. Jones, Mr. Maurice says, " For, however happy and " ingenious, as it certainly is, may be the conjecture of Sir W. Jones concerning the interpolation " of the Bramin records from the Apocryphal Gospels, it still affords but a partial explanation of " the difficulty. Many of the Mythological sculptures of Hindostan that relate to the events in " the history of this Avatar, more immediately interesting to the Christian world, being of an age " undoubtedly anterior to the Christian æra, while those sculptures remain unanswerable testi- " monies of the facts recorded, the assertion, unaided by these collateral proofs, rather strengthens " than obviates the objection of the Sceptic. Thus the sculptured figures, copied by Sonnerat, " from one of the oldest pagodas, and engraved in this volume, the one of which represents " Chreeshna dancing on the crushed head of the serpent ; and the other, the same personage en- " tangled in its enormous folds, to mark the arduousness of the contest, while the enraged reptile " is seen biting his foot, together with the history of the fact annexed, could never derive their " origin from any information contained in the Spurious Gospels."

Again, Mr. Maurice says, " To return to the more particular consideration of these parts of the " life of Chreeshna, which are above alluded to by Sir William Jones, which have been paralleled " with some of the leading events in the life of our blessed Saviour, and are, in fact, considered by " him as interpolations from the spurious Gospels ; I mean more particularly his miraculous birth " at midnight ; the chorus of Devatas that saluted with hymns the divine infant as soon as born ; " his being cradled amongst shepherds, to whom were first made known those stupendous feats " that stamped his character with divinity ; his being carried away by night, and concealed in a " region remote from the scene of his birth,[1] from fear of the tyrant Cansa, whose destroyer it " was predicted he would prove, and who, therefore, ordered all the male children born at that " period to be slain: his battle, in his infancy, with the dire, envenomed serpent Calija,[2] and " crushing his head with his foot ; his miracles in succeeding years ; his raising the dead ; his de- " scending to Hades ; and his return to Vaicontha, the proper paradise of Veeshnu," &c., &c., &c.

5. Upon the plea of interpolation, which Sir W. Jones has used to account for the extraordinary similarity in the lives of Jesus and of Cristna, and which Mr. Maurice has allowed, *happy and ingenious as it is !* to be altogether unsatisfactory ; it may be asked, what could induce the Brah- mins, the most proud, conceited and bigoted of mankind, to interpolate their ancient books ; to insert in them extracts from the gospel histories, or sacred books of people very nearly total strangers to them ; very few in numbers, and looked on by them with such contempt, that they would neither eat, drink, nor associate with them (which, if they had done, they would have been contaminated, and ruined by becoming outcasts from their order) ;—people who came as beggars and wanderers soliciting a place of refuge ? It cannot be pretended that the Brahmins wished to make converts ; for this is directly contrary to their faith and practice. The books in which these interpolations are found, were obtained from them with the greatest difficulty ;

---

[1] And Mr. Maurice might have added, called Mattra or Maturea, the same name as the place to which Christ was carried, according to Christian tradition, as we have already shewn.

[2] Calija, this is another name for the Calinaga, explained in note p. 131.

they have every appearance of very great antiquity; and are found concealed in the recesses of their temples, evidently built many centuries before the Christian æra. And though the books in which they are found are scarce, yet they are sufficiently numerous, and spread over a sufficient extent of country, to render it impossible to interpolate them all, if they had been so disposed. Upon the impossibility of interpolating the old Hindoo books, I shall treat at large hereafter.

But how is the figure in the cave at Elephanta to be acounted for; that *prominent* and *ferocious* figure, as Mr. Maurice calls it, surrounded by slaughtered infants, and holding a drawn sword? If it were only a representation of the evil principle, how came he only to destroy infants; and, as I learn from Mr. Forbes's Oriental Memoirs,[1] those infants, *boys?* He is surrounded by a crowd of figures of men and women, evidently supplicating for the children. This group of figures has been called the Judgment of Solomon; as Mr. Forbes justly says, very absurdly. But, at the same time he admits, that there are many things in these caves which bear a resemblance to prominent features in the Old Testament. Over the head of the principal figure in this group, are to be seen the mitre, the crosier, and the cross—true Christian emblems.

Again Mr. Maurice says, " All these circumstances of similarity are certainly very surprising, " and, upon any other hypothesis than that offered by Sir W. Jones, at first sight, seem very " difficult to be solved. But should that solution, from the allowed antiquity of the name of " Chrisna, and the general outline of his story, confessedly anterior to the birth of Christ, and " probably as old as Homer, as well as the apparent reluctance of the haughty, self-conceited " Brahmin to borrow any part of his creed, or rituals, or legends, from foreigners visiting India, " not be admitted by some of my readers as satisfactory, I have to request their attention to the " following particulars, which they will peruse with all the solemn consideration due to a question " of such high moment."

We will now attend with SOLEMN CONSIDERATION to these particulars, offering such observa- as occur upon each, as they come in order.

But, gentle reader, if you please, we will, as we go along with the Reverend Gentleman, not forget what Lord Shaftsbury so shrewdly observed, *that solemnity is of the essence of imposture.*

" And first with respect to the name of Christna, (for so it must be written to bear the asserted " analogy to the name of Christ,) Mr. Volney, after two or three pages of unparalleled impiety, in " which he resolves the whole life, death, and resurrection, of the Messiah, into an ingenious " allegory, allusive to the growth, decline, and renovation of the solar heat during its annual " revolution; and after asserting that, by the Virgin, his mother, is meant the celestial sign Virgo, " in the bosom of which, at the summer solstice, the sun anciently appeared to the Persian Magi " to rise, and was thus depicted in their astrological pictures, as well as in the Mithraitic caverns; " after thus impiously attempting to mythologize away the grand fundamental doctrines of the " Christian code, our Infidel author adds, that the sun was sometimes called Chris, or Conservator, " that is, the Saviour; and hence, he observes, the Hindoo god Chris-en or Christna, and the " Christian Chris-tos, the son of Mary. Now, whatever ingenuity there may be displayed in the " former part of this curious investigation, into which I cannot now enter, I can confidently " affirm, there is not a syllable of truth in the orthographical derivation; for Chrisna, nor " Chris-en, nor Christna, (as to serve a worthless cause, subversive of civil society, he artfully " perverts the word,) has not the least approach in signification to the Greek word Christos, " anointed, in allusion to the kingly office of the Hebrew Messiah; since this appellative simply " signifies, as we shall presently demonstrate, *black* or *dark blue*, and was conferred on the Indian " God solely on account of his *black complexion.* It has, therefore, no more connexion with the

---

[1] Vol. III. Ch. xxxv. p. 447.

" name of our blessed Saviour, supposed by this writer to be derived from it, than the humble
" Mary of Bethlehem has with the Isis of Egypt, the original Virgo of the Zodiac : or Joseph, as
" there asserted, has with the obsolete constellation of præsepe Jovis, or stable of Jove, as, in his
" rage for derivation, he ridiculously asserts."

Now, upon the observation of Mr. Maurice, relating to the celestial Virgin, and the Virgin
Mary, the reader is requested to suspend his judgment till he comes to my chapter where she is
expressly treated of. With respect to the remainder of his observation on the *colour* of the
Cristna of India, it is replied, that of all the circumstances connected with this subject, there is not
one so curious and striking as this ; nor one so worthy of the attention of the reader. And
though, at first, he may think the Author, in what he is going to say, respecting the *black* colour,
is deviating from the subject, he will in the end find nothing but what is closely connected with it,
and necessary for its elucidation.

7. On the first view, it seems rather an extraordinary circumstance that the statues of the Gods
of the ancients should be represented of a black colour ; or that they should have been made of a
stone as nearly black as it could be obtained. Where the stone could not be obtained quite black,
a stone was often used similar to our blue slate, of a very dark blue colour ; the drapery of the
statue often being of a different, light-coloured stone. It is evident that the intention was to
represent a black complexion ; of this there can be no doubt. The marble statues of Roman
Emperors are often found with the fleshy part black, and the drapery of white or some other
colour.

Eusebius informs us, on the authority of Porphyry, " That the Egyptians acknowledged one
" intellectual Author or Creator of the world, under the name of Cneph ; and that they worshiped
" him in a statue of human form and *dark blue complexion*." Plutarch informs us, " That Cneph
" was worshiped by the inhabitants of the Thebaid ; who refused to contribute any part towards
" the maintenance of the sacred animals, because they acknowledged no mortal God, and adored
" none but him whom they called Cneph, an uncreated and immortal being." The temple of
" Cneph, or Cnuphis, was in the island of Elephantine, on the confines of Egypt and Ethiopia. [1]

In the Evangelical Preparation of Eusebius, [2] is a passage which pretty well proves that the
worship of Vishnu or Cristna was held in Egypt, under the name of Kneph : Τον Δημιουργον
Κηφ, οἱ Αιγυπτιοι προσαγορευϑσιν, την χροιαν εκ καονϑ μελανος, εχοντα κρατϑντα ζωνην
και σκηπτρον (λεγϑσιν). " The Egyptians, it is said, represented the Demiurgos Kneph, as of
a blue colour, bordering on black, with a girdle and a sceptre." [3]

Mr. Maurice [4] has observed that the Cneph of Egypt, and the statue of Narayen, in the great
reservoir of Catmandu, are both formed of black marble. Dr. Buchanan states the statue of Juggernaut to be of wood, painted black, with red lips.

Mr. Maurice says, " That Osiris, too, the black divinity of Egypt, and Chreeshna, the sable
" shepherd-God of Mathura, have the striking similitude of character, intimated by Mr. Wilford,
" cannot be disputed, any more than that Chreeshna, from his rites continuing so universally to
" flourish over India, from such remote periods down to the present day, was the prototype, and
" Osiris the mythological copy. Both are renowned legislators and conquerors, contending
" equally with physical and spiritual foes : both are denominated *the Sun ;* both descend to the
" shades and raise the dead." [5]

Again he says, " Now it is not a little remarkable that a dark blue tint, approaching to black,
" as his name signifies, was the complexion of Chreeshna, who is considered by the Hindoos not

---

[1] Pritchard's Anal. of Egypt, Mythol. p. 171.      [2] Lib. iii. p. 115.      [3] Class. Journ. No. XXIX. p. 122.
[4] Ant. Ind. Vol. I. Sect. viii.          [5] Hist. Hind. Vol. II. p. 477.

" so much an avatar, as the person of the great Veeshnu himself, in a human form." [1] That is, he was incarnate, or in the flesh, as Jesus was said to be.

For reasons which the reader will soon see, I am inclined to think that Osiris was not the copy of Cristna, but of the earlier God, Buddha.

That by Osiris was meant the Sun, it is now allowed by every writer who has treated on the antiquities of Egypt. Mr. Maurice, as the reader sees, states him to have been black, and that the Mnevis, or sacred bull, of Heliopolis, the symbol of Osiris, was also black. Osiris is allowed, also, to be the Seeva of India, [2] one of the three persons of the Indian God—Bramha, Vishnu or Cristna, and Seeva, of whom the bull of the Zodiac was the symbol.

It is curious to observe the number of trifling circumstances which constantly occur to prove the identity of the Hindoos and Egyptians, or rather the Ethiopians. The word Nile, in the Indian language, means *black*. Dupuis [3] says, " Nilo in Indian signifies black, and it ought " to signify the same in Egyptian; since, whenever the Arabs, the Hebrews, the Greeks, " and the Latins, have wished to translate the word Nil, they have always made use of a word " which in their language signifies black. The Hebrews call it *Sichor ;* the Ethiopians, *Nuchul ;* " the ancient Latins, *Melo ;* the Greeks, *Melas*—all names signifying *black*. The word or name " *Nilos*, then, in Egyptian, presents the same idea as the word Nilo in Indian." But the name of Nile was a modern one, (comparatively speaking,) a translation of the ancient name of this river, which was Siri. Speaking of the word Nile, Tzetzes says, το δε Νειλος νεον εςι. [4]

Selden [5] says, " Sit Osiris, sit Omphis, Nilus, Siris, sive quodcunque aliud ab Hierophantis " usurpatum nomen, ad unum tandem solem antiquissimum gentium Numen redeunt omnia." He says again, " Osiris certe non solum idem Deus erat cum Nilo, verum ipsa nomina Nili et " Osiridis, sublato primo elemento, sunt synonyma. Nam lingua prophetarum שחר schichor est " Nilus, ut doctissimi interpretum volunt, quod שחר schichori, lingua Æthiopica (ita monet " illustrissimus Scaliger filius) prolatum—in Σειϱις aut Σιϱις Græca scriptione, transmigravit." See also Parkhurst's Lex. שחר pp. 728, 729.

The word Osiris may be a Greek word, composed by the Greeks from their own emphatic article O, and the Hebrew word שחר shr, written with their customary termination Οσιρις. The meaning of the Hebrew word is black. And one meaning of the Greek is evidently *the black*, or *the black God*. This is confirmed by Plutarch, in his treatise de Iside et Osiride.

The Nile was often called יאר *iar*, which is the Hebrew word for river, and was probably the Egyptian one also. It was simply *the river* παϱ' εξοχην. It was never called Neilos by the Egyptians, but by the Greeks, and that only from the time of Hesiod, in whose writings it is first so called. This pretty nearly proves it a translated name. [6] If the author be right in this conjecture, the reason is evident why this word sets etymological inquiries at defiance. Sir W. Jones says, Nila means *blue ;* but this blue is probably derived from the colour of the stone—a dark blue, meant originally to describe *black*. The Nile was called Αιγυπτος *Ægyptus*, before the country had that name. This last name also defies the etymologists. But it was probably an Eastern word mangled by the Greeks, who mangled every thing. It will be explained hereafter.

M. De Lambre tells us, from Censorinus, that the Egytians called the year of 365 days by the word Νειλος, *Neilos*. And he observes that, in the Greek notation, the letters of which this word is composed denote 365. Sir W. Drummond calls this buffoonery, and asks if M. De Lambre has

---

[1] Maurice, Hist. Hind. Vol. I. p. 66, 4to. ; also Ant. Ind. Vol. III. p. 375.  [2] Maurice, Ant. Ind.
[3] Vol. III. p. 351.  [4] Drummond, Ess. Zod. pp. 106 and 112.
[5] De Diis Syriis, De Vitulo Aureo, Syntag. i. Cap. iv.  [6] Vide Drummond's Orig. B. iv. Ch. ii.

forgot that the Egyptians did not speak Greek. To which it may be answered, that the polite and learned among them did speak Greek, after the time of Alexander. It is overlooked by Sir William, that this name (as he acknowledges) νεον εστι, is modern. It is probable that the Greeks found the *ancient* Egyptian name to signify *black*, and the letters of it to denote or to signify the year of 365 days. But as they could not in their language give it a term which would signify both, and as they understood why it was called 365 or the year, but did not understand why it was called black, they adopted the former, and called it Νειλος.

The ancient name, as we have said, was Sir, or Siri, the same as O-sir, or Osiris, who was always black; after whom it was called, and by whom was meant the sun. Thus it was called the river of the sun, or the river sun, or the river of Osiris—as we say, the river of the Amazons, or the river Amazon. And this river flowed from the land of the sun and moon. It arose in the mountains of the moon, and flowed through the land of Sir, perhaps the land of Siriad, where Josephus was told that columns had been placed which were built before the flood—κατα την γην Συριαδα. Manetho, 300 years before Josephus, says, these columns stood εν τη γη Συριαδικη, and from them Josephus took his history, which was inscribed on them in the sacred language and in hieroglyphical characters, a language and character evidently both unknown to him. These columns were probably the Egyptian monuments—Pyramids, or *Obelisks*, which had escaped the destruction of Cambyses, perhaps because they were only historical and not religious, or perhaps because they were linghams, to which the Persians might not object—but the knowledge of whose characters was at that time lost amidst the universal destruction of priests and temples, and which has never been really known since, though the new priests would not be willing to confess their ignorance. Query, שור *sur* אי *ia* די *di*, The holy land of Sur?

The river Nile in Sanscreet books is often called Crishna. [1]

שר *sr*, is the origin or root of Ósiris, and means a leader, regulator, ruler, or director. The ninth of the meanings given to it by Parkhurst in the form שור *sur*, is that of Beeve.

The modern words Sir, Mon-sieur, Mon-seignor, are all derived from the Hebrew word שר *Sr*, or Lord, as we translate it, which was an epithet of the sun in all the eastern countries. This is the same as the Iswara of India, which means Lord. [2] The Bull of the Zodiac, or the sun, also had a name very similar to this, whence probably it came to be applied to the animal; or at least they had the same names. See Parkhurst in voce שור *sur*.

Mr. Maurice says, [3] Persæ Συρη Deum vocant. Surya is the name of the solar divinity of India. It is also the name of Osiris. Mr. Bryant says, Οσειριν προσαγορευσσι και Συριον. [4] As the God of the Egyptians went by several names, as Apis, Serapis, Cnepb, Osiris, &c., so did the God of the Hindoos. The word *sable* or *black* was one of their epithets. Thus *Christ* is, in like manner, an epithet of Jesus. He is called Jesus the Christ, *the. Anointed*.

8. As the reader has seen above, and also in my Celtic Druids, I have derived Osiris from the word *Sr*, and the Greek emphatic article O. This derivation is justified by Porphyry. But Hellanicus informs us, that it was sometimes written Υσιρις. Now, as Isis was the wife of Osiris, may it not have come from the Hebrew word ישע *iso*, to save, and שר *sr*, or שור *sur*? Osiris was the Sun, so was Surya in India and Persia: for, as we have seen, Persæ Surê Deum vocant. Syria was the land of the Sun. The Sun was called Lord and Saviour; so was Mithra. The Bull was the emblem of the Sun—of Mithra, called Lord, and of the God in the land where Surya or the Sun, with seven heads, was adored, and in Japan, where he breaks the mundane egg with his

---

[1] Maurice, Bram. Fraud Exposed, p. 80.      [2] See Pictet, p. 16.

[3] Ant. Ind. Vol. II. p. 203.      [4] Ibid. p. 221.

horn. The Bull was the body into which Osiris transmigrated after his death; and, lastly, the Hebrew name for bull is שור *sur.* Orpheus has a hymn to the Lord Bull. Iswara of India or Osiris, is the husband of Isi or of Isis ; and Surya is Buddha. Can all these coincidences be the effect of accident ?

" Osiris, or Isiris, as Sanchoniathon calls him, is also the same name with Mizraim, when the " servile letter M is left out." [1] The reason of the monogram M being prefixed to this, and to many other words, will be shewn by and by.

I have some suspicion that *O-siris* is a Greek corruption ; that the name ought, as already mentioned, to be what it is called by Hellanicus, *Ysiris* or *Isiris,* and that it is derived from, or rather I should say is the same as, *Iswara* of India. Iswara and Isi are the same as Osiris and Isis—the male and female procreative powers of nature.

" Iswara, in Sanscrit, signifies Lord, and in that sense is applied by the Bramans to each of " their three principal deities, or rather to each of the forms in which they teach the people to " adore Brahm, or the GREAT ONE . . . . Brahma, Vishnu, and Mahadeva, say the *Puranics,* " were brothers : and the Egyptian triad, or Osiris, Horus, and Typhon, were brought forth by " the same parent." [2]

Syria was called Suria. Eusebius says the Egyptians called Osiris, Surius, and that, in Persia, *Surē* was the old name of the sun. [3]

In the sol-lunar legends of the Hindoos, the Sun is, as we have seen, sometimes male and sometimes female. The Moon is also of both sexes, and is called *Isa* and *Isi.* [4] Deus Lunus was common to several nations of the ancient world. [5]

The peculiar mode in which the Hindoos identify their three great Gods with the solar orb, is a curious specimen of the physical refinements of ancient mythology. *At night and in the West, the Sun is Vishnu : he is Brama in the East and in the morning :* and from noon to evening, he is Siva. [6]

The adoration of a black stone is a very singular superstition. Like many other superstitions this also came from India. Buddha was adored as a square black stone ; so was Mercury ; so was the Roman Terminus. The famous Pessinuntian stone, brought to Rome, was square and black. The sacred black stone at Mecca many of my readers are acquainted with, and George the Fourth did very wisely to be crowned on the square stone, nearer black than any other colour, of Scotia and Ireland.

In Montfaucon, a black Isis and Orus are described in the printing, but not in the plate. I suspect many of Montfaucon's figures ought to be black, which are not so described. [7]

Pausanias states the Thespians to have had a temple and statue to Jupiter the Saviour, and a statue to Love, consisting only of a rude stone ; and a temple to Venus Melainis, or *the black.* [8]

Ammon was founded by Black doves, Ατρε-Ιωνες. One of them flew from Ammon to Dodona and founded it. [9]

At Corinth there was a black Venus. [10]

In my search into the origin of ancient Druids, I continually found, at last, that my labours terminated with something *black.* Thus the oracles at Dodona, and of Apollo at Delphi, were founded by BLACK doves. Doves are not often, I believe never really, black.

---

[1] Cumberland, Orig. Gen. p. 100.   [2] Asiat. Res. Vol. III. p. 371 ; Moore's Pantheon, p. 44.
[3] Maur. Ind. Ant. Vol. VI. p. 39.   [4] Moore's Pantheon, pp. 289, 290.   [5] Ibid. p. 291.
[6] Faber, Or. Idol. B. iv. Ch. i.   [7] Montf. Exp. Vol. II. Plate XXXVII. Fig. 5.
[8] Pausanias, Lib. ix. Cap. xxvi. xxvii.   [9] Nimrod, p. 276.   [10] Ibid. p. 400.

T

Osiris and his Bull were black; all the Gods and Goddesses of Greece were black: at least this was the case with Jupiter, Bacchus, Hercules, Apollo, Ammon.

The Goddesses Venus, Isis, Hecati, Diana, Juno, Metis, Ceres, Cybile, are black. The Multimammia is black in the Campidoglio at Rome, and in Montfaucon, Antiquity explained.

The Linghams in India, anointed with oil, are black: a black stone was adored in numbers of places in India.

It has already been observed that, in the galleries, we constantly see busts and statues of the Roman Emperors, made of two kinds of stone; the human part of the statue of *black* stone, the drapery *white* or *coloured*. When they are thus described, I suppose they are meant to be represented as priests of the sun; this was probably confined to the celebration of the Isiac or Egyptian ceremonies.

9. On the colour of the Gods of the ancients, and of the identity of them all with the God Sol, and with the Cristna of India, nothing more need be said. The reader has already seen the striking marks of similarity in the history of Cristna and the stories related of Jesus in the Romish and heretical books. He probably will not think that their effect is destroyed, as Mr. Maurice flatters himself, by the word Cristna in the Indian language signifying black, and the God being of that colour, when he is informed, of what Mr. Maurice was probably ignorant, that in all the Romish countries of Europe, in France, Italy, Germany, &c., the God Christ, as well as his mother, are described in their old pictures and statues to be black. The infant God in the arms of his black mother, his eyes and drapery white, is himself perfectly black. If the reader doubt my word, he may go to the cathedral at Moulins—to the famous chapel of the Virgin at Loretto—to the church of the Annunciata—the church of St. Lazaro, or the church of St. Stephen at Genoa—to St. Francisco at Pisa—to the church at Brixen, in the Tyrol, and to that at Padua—to the church of St. Theodore, at Munich, in the two last of which the whiteness of the eyes and teeth, and the studied redness of the lips, are very observable;—to a church and to the cathedral at Augsburg, where are a black virgin and child as large as life:—to Rome, to the Borghese chapel Maria Maggiore—to the Pantheon—to a small chapel of St. Peter's, on the right-hand side on entering, near the door; and, in fact, to almost innumerable other churches, in countries professing the Romish religion.

There is scarcely an old church in Italy where some remains of the worship of the BLACK VIRGIN and BLACK CHILD are not to be met with. Very often the black figures have given way to white ones, and in these cases the black ones, as being held sacred, were put into retired places in the churches, but were not destroyed, but are yet to be found there. In many cases the images are painted all over and look like bronze, often with coloured aprons or napkins round the loins or other parts; but pictures in great numbers are to be seen, where the white of the eyes and of the teeth, and the lips a little tinged with red, like the black figures in the Museum of the India Company, shew that there is no imitation of bronze. In many instances these images and pictures are shaded, not all one colour, of very dark brown, so dark as to look like black. They are generally esteemed by the rabble with the most profound veneration. The toes are often white, the brown or black paint being kissed away by the devotees, and the white wood left. No doubt in many places, when the priests have new-painted the images, they have coloured the eyes, teeth, &c., in order that they might not shock the feelings of devotees by a too sudden change from black to white, and in order, at the same time, that they might furnish a decent pretence for their blackness, viz. that they are an imitation of bronze: but the number that are left with white teeth, &c., let out the secret.

When the circumstance has been named to the Romish priests, they have endeavoured to disguise the fact, by pretending that the child had become black by the smoke of the candles; but it was black where the smoke of a candle never came: and, besides, how came the candles not to blacken the white of the eyes, the teeth, and the shirt, and how came they to redden the lips ? The mother is, the author believes, always black, when the child is. Their real blackness is not to be questioned for a moment.

If the author had wished to invent a circumstance to corroborate the assertion, that the Romish Christ of Europe is the Cristna of India, how could he have desired any thing more striking than the fact of the black Virgin and Child being so common in the Romish countries of Europe ? A black virgin and child among the white Germans, Swiss, French, and Italians ! ! !

The Romish Cristna is black in India, black in Europe, and black he must remain—like the ancient Gods of Greece, as we have just seen. But, after all, what was he but their Jupiter, the second person of their Trimurti or Trinity, the Logos of Parmenides and Plato, an incarnation or emanation of the solar power ?

I must now request my reader to turn back to the first chapter, and to reconsider what I have said respecting the two Ethiopias and the existence of a *black* nation in a very remote period. When he has done this, the circumstance of the black God of India being called *Cristna*, and the God of Italy, *Christ*, being also black, must appear worthy of deep consideration. Is it possible, that this coincidence can have been the effect of accident ? In our endeavours to recover the lost science of former ages, it is necessary that we should avail ourselves of rays of light scattered in places the most remote, and that we should endeavour to re-collect them into a focus, so that, by this means, we may procure as strong a light as possible : collect as industriously as we may, our light will not be too strong. [1]

I think I need say no more in answer to Mr. Maurice's shouts of triumph over those whom he insultingly calls *impious infidels*, respecting the name of Cristna having the meaning of black. I will now proceed to his other *solemn considerations*.

10. The second particular to which Mr. Maurice desires the attention of his reader, is in the following terms : " 2d, Let it, in the next place, be considered that Chreeshna, so far from being " the son of a virgin, is declared to have had a father and mother in the flesh, and to have been " the *eighth* child of Devaci and Vasudeva. How inconceivably different this from the sanctity " of the immaculate conception of Christ !"

I answer, that respecting their *births* they differ ; but what has this to do with the points wherein they agree ? No one ever said they agreed in every minute particular. Yet I think, with respect to their humanity, the agreement continues. I always understood that Jesus was held by the Romish and Protestant Churches to have become incarnate ; *that the word* was made flesh. [2] That is, that Jesus was of the same kind of flesh, at least as his mother, and also as his brothers, Joses, James, &c. [3] If he were not of the flesh of his mother, what was he before the umbilical cord was cut ?

It does not appear from the histories, which we have yet obtained, that the immaculate concep-

---

[1] But though the Bull of *Osiris* was black, the Bull of *Europa* was white. The story states that Jupiter fell in love with a daughter of Agenor, king of Phœnicia, and Telephassa, and in order to obtain the object of his affections he changed himself into a white bull. After he had seduced the nymph to play with him and caress him in his pasture for some time, at last he persuaded her to mount him, when he fled with her to Crete, where he succeeded in his wishes, and by her he had Minos, Sarpedon, and Rhadamanthus. Is it necessary for me to point out to the reader in this pretty allegory the peopling of Europe from Phœnicia, and the allusion in the colour of the Bull, viz. *white*, to the fair complexions of the Europeans ? An ingenious explanation of this allegory may be seen in Drummond's Origines, Vol. III. p. 84.

[2] John, ch. i. ver. 14.

[3] I look with perfect contempt on the ridiculous trash which has been put forth to shew that the brothers of Jesus, described in the Gospels, did not mean *brothers*, but *cousins !*

tion has been taken from the history of Cristna. However, we shall find hereafter, that, in all probability, it came from the same quarter of the world.

Mr. Maurice observes, 3dly, " That it has been, from the earliest periods, the savage custom " of the despots of Asia, for the sake of extirpating one dreaded object, to massacre all the males " born in a particular district, and the history of Moses himself exhibits a glaring proof how " anciently, and how relentlessly it was practised." The story of Moses, Pharaoh, and the order to murder the boys of the Israelites, will be shewn hereafter to have a certain mystical meaning much closer to the Indian Mythoses, particularly to that of the God Cristna, than Mr. Maurice would have liked, had he known it.

4th. " In his contest with the great serpent, Calija, circumstances occur which, since the story " is, in great part, *mythological*, irresistibly impel me to believe that, in that, as in many other " portions of this surprising legend, there is a reference intended to some traditional accounts, " descended down to the Indians from the patriarchs, and current in Asia, of the *fall of man*, and " the consequent well-known denunciation against the serpentine tempter." This like the last particular proves nothing.

5th. " In regard to the numerous miracles wrought by Chreeshna, it should be remembered, that " miracles are never wanting to the decoration of an Indian romance ; they are, in fact, the life " and soul of the vast machine ; nor is it at all a subject of wonder that the dead should be raised " to life, in a history expressly intended, like all other sacred fables of Indian fabrication, for the " propagation and support of the whimsical doctrine of the Metempsychosis. The above is the " most satisfactory reply in my power to give to such determined sceptics as Mr. Volney."

11. The reasons of Mr. Maurice to account for the history of Cristna are so weak, that they evidently do not deserve a moment's consideration ; and, as well as Sir W. Jones's HAPPY AND INGENIOUS theory of interpolation, are only named in order that the Author may not be accused of suppressing them ; that the reader may see how learned divines explain these matters ; and that he may hear both sides. Mr. Maurice's jeer upon miracles never being wanting to an Indian romance, is rather hard upon such of his friends as believe, or affect to believe, histories or romances where miracles are the very life and soul of the *machine*, to use his own expression ; which, in fact, consist of miracles from one end to the other ; and he seems to have forgotten that most of the early orthodox fathers believed in the Metempsychosis.

The reader will please to recollect that the circumstances related of Cristna come to us very unwillingly from the orthodox *Jones* and *Maurice ;* whether any others of consequence would be found, if we had a translation of the whole Vedas, is as yet uncertain. Without any reflection on these gentlemen, it may be permitted us to say, that circumstances which did not appear important to them, might on these subjects appear of great consequence to others.

Sir William Jones strives to deceive himself into a belief, that all the cycles or statements of the different astronomical events related in the Hindoo books are the produce of modern back-calculations. Those books are brought from different nations of India, so remote and numerous, that it is *almost impossible* to suppose them all to be the effect of artifice ; and, when united to the evident extreme antiquity of the Zodiacs, and some of the monuments of both India and Egypt, *quite impossible*. All this he did for fear his faith in the chronology of the Bible, which he did not know how to reconcile to that of the Indians, should be shaken. His incredulity is so great as to be absolutely ridiculous credulity. What a lamentable figure it exhibits of the weakness of mind, and the effect of early prejudice and partial education, in one of the greatest and very best of men !

In the same way that he finds a pretext to disguise to himself the consequences which follow from the great antiquity of the Indian temples, books, and astronomy, he finds an equally satisfactory reason for disguising the evident identity of the history of Cristna, or as he is sometimes called Heri-Cristna, with Christ, *(Heri* means Saviour,) by the idle pretence, as we have seen, that the Brahmins, some way or other, have got copies of part of the Apocryphal Gospels, from which they have taken the history of the birth, life, and adventures, of Cristna—these gospels being written some time, of course, after the birth of Jesus Christ. How wonderfully absurd to suppose that all the ancient emblems and idols of Cristna in the temples and caves, scattered over every part of India, and absolutely identified with them in point of antiquity, can have been copied from the Gospels about the time of Jesus! How wonderfully absurd to suppose that the Brahmins, and people of this widely-extended empire, should condescend to copy from the real or cast-away spurious Gospels, of a sect at that time almost entirely unknown even in their own country, and many thousand miles distant from these Brahmins!

12. After Mr. Maurice discovered that the truths which had been permitted to appear in the Asiatic Researches, and in his History of Hindostan and Antiquities of India, had been observed by the philosophers, he published a couple of pamphlets, the intention of which was to remedy the mischief which he had done. But they contain very little more than what he had said before. When the reader observes that the Brahminical histories not only apply to the New Testament and the Apocryphal Gospel histories, but that the Jewish histories of the creation and fall of man, as translated, not by the Romish Church only, but by Protestants, are also closely interwoven with them, he will not easily be persuaded that they are copies of these Gospels. The battle of the infant Cristna with the serpent is considered as the greatest as well as the first of all his wonderful actions. This is evidently the evil principle, the tempter of Eve, described in the sphere: it is evidently the greatest of the victories of the Romish Jesus as well as of Cristna. It is the conquests of Hercules and of Bacchus, when in their cradles. If the Brahmins had been merely interpolating from the Gospels, they would not have troubled themselves with the Old Testament.

When a person considers the vast wealth and power which are put into danger by these Indian manuscripts; the practice by Christian priests of interpolating and erasing, for the last two thousand years; the well-known forgeries practised upon Mr. Wilsford by a Brahmin; and the large export make to India of orthodox and missionary priests; he will not be surprised if some copies of the books should make their appearance wanting certain particulars in the life of Cristna: but this will hardly now be noticed by the philosophical inquirer; particularly as the figures in the temples cannot be *interpolated*, nor very easily erased. No doubt this observation is calculated to give pain to honourable men among the priests; but they cannot be responsible, as they cannot controul their coadjutors, too many of whom have in all ages lost sight of honesty and integrity, in things of this kind.

The Hindoos, far from labouring to make proselytes to their religion, do not admit into it those who have been born in and professed any other faith. They say that, provided men perform their moral duties in abstaining from ill, and in doing good to the utmost of their ability, it is but of little importance under what forms they worship God; that things suitable to one people may be unfit for another; and that to suppose that God prefers any one particular religion to the exclusion of others, and yet leaves numbers of his creatures ignorant of his will, is to accuse him of injustice, or to question his omnipotence.[1] I wish our priests would attend to the sound wisdom and benevolence of these people, called by our missionaries *ignorant and benighted.*

13. In reply to the observation of such persons as have contended that the Hindoos have made use of back-reckoning, Mr. Craufurd pertinently observes, " That to be able to do so, implies a

---

[1] Craufurd's Researches, Ch. ii. p. 158.

" more accurate practice in astronomy than the Hindūs seem to possess ; for it is evident that
" their knowledge in science and learning, instead of being improved, has greatly declined from what
" it appears to have been in the remote ages of their history.   And, besides, for what purpose
" should they take such pains ?   It may possibly be answered, from the vanity of wishing to
" prove the superior antiquity of their learning to that of other nations.   We confess that the
" observation, unsupported by other proofs, appears to us unworthy of men of learning, whom we
" should expect to find resting their arguments on scientific proofs only." [1]

No doubt it is extremely difficult to arrive, on this subject, at mathematical certainty or proof,
but yet it may probably be safely concluded that, if preconceived notions respecting danger to the
literal meaning of the Mosaic text had not stood in the way, no difficulty would have been
found in admitting the sufficiency of the evidence of the Hindoo antiquity.   It strongly calls to
recollection the struggle and outcry made against Walton and others for asserting that the
Mazoretic points, in the Hebrew language, were of modern adoption.   As long as the discovery
was supposed to endanger the religion, the proofs were pronounced to be altogether insufficient ;
but as soon as it had been shewn that the religion was in no danger, the truth of the new theory
was almost universally admitted.   Exactly similar would be the case of the Hindoo astronomical
periods if it could be shewn that religion was not implicated in the question.   The author has no
doubt of the side of the question which any unprejudiced person will take, who will carefully read
over the works of Playfair, and the Edinburgh Review, upon this subject, and Craufurd's Researches, and his Sketches. [2]

However, there is a passage in Arrian, which proves that one of the great leading facts, which
forms a point of striking similarity between the Cristna of India and the Christ of Europe, was
not taken from the Gospels after Jesus's death, but was actually a story relating to Cristna, in
existence in the time of Alexander the Great.   The reader has seen already all the curious circumstances narrated in the Gospel histories, and by Athanasius and Eusebius, respecting the city of
Matarea in Egypt, to which place Jesus fled from Herod.   He has also seen that it was at Mathura
of India, where the holy family of Cristna resided in his infancy.   In a future part of this work
I shall shew, that Hercules and Bacchus are both the same, the Sun—one in Taurus, the
other in Aries.   Then the following passage from the Edinburgh Review, of the article Asiatic
Researches, Vol. XV. p. 185, will prove most clearly, and beyond all doubt, that the history of
Cristna, his residence at Matarea, &c., cannot have been copied from the histories in the spurious
Gospels ; but must have been older than the time of Alexander the Great.

" Arrian (Ch. viii.) proceeds to relate that Hercules was fifteen centuries later than Bacchus.
" We have already seen that Bacchus was Siva ; and Megasthenes distinctly points out what
" Indian divinity is meant by Hercules.   ' He was chiefly adored (says Arrian) by the Suraseni,
" ' who possess two large cities, Methora and Clissobora.   The Jobares, a navigable river, flows
" ' through their territories.'   Now Herichrisna, the chief of the Suraseni, was born in the metro-
" polis of their country, Mathura :  and the river Jamuna flows through the territory of the
" Suraseni, Mathura being situated on its banks, and called by Ptolemy, Matura Deorum ; which
" can only be accounted for by its being the birth-place of Christna ;" in fact, of the triplicate
God Brahma, Cristna, and Seeva, three in one and one in three—the Creator, the Preserver or
Saviour, and the Destroyer or Regenerator.   The great city of Mathura or Methora, and the river

---

[1] Craufurd's Res. Ch. viii. p. 17.
[2] Edinb. Review, Vol. XV. p. 414, Vol. X. p. 469, also Vol. XVI. pp. 390, 391 ; see also Trans. Royal Soc. of
Edinburgh, Vol. II. pp. 155, 160, 169, 185, Vol. IV. pp. 83, 103.

Jobares or Jumna, could not be called after the city or river in Egypt in accommodation to the Christian story.

The statue of Cristna in the temple of Mathura is black, and the temple is built in the form of a cross,[1] and stands due East and West. "It is evident the Hindoos must have known the "use of the Gnomon at a very remote period. Their religion commands that the four sides of "their temples should correspond with the four cardinal points of the Heavens, and they are all "so constructed."[2]

It is to be regretted that Arrian has not given a more detailed account; but in the fact which he gives of Heri-Cristna, Hercules or the Sun, being worshiped at Mathura, called by Ptolemy Matura Deorum, there is quite enough to satisfy any person who chooses to use his understanding, of the antiquity of the history.[3]

Mr. Bryant says, "It is remarkable that among some Oriental languages Matarea signifies the "sun. This may be proved from the Malayan language, expressed Mataharii, and Matta-harri, "and Mattowraye, and Matta'ree, and from that of the Sumatrans at Acheen. It seems to be a "compound of Matta and Ree, the ancient Egyptian word for the Sun, which is still retained in "the Coptic, and, with the aspirate, is rendered Phree." This Phree is, I doubt not, the Coptic ΦPH, explained in my Celtic Druids,[4] to mean the number 608, of which I shall have much to say hereafter.

Strabo[5] says, that close to Heliopolis was a city called Cercesura. This name and the Cercasorum of Herodotus, are, I do not doubt, corruptions of Clissobora.

In the Classical Journal will be found an attempt, by Dr. Adam Clarke, to invalidate what Mr. Maurice has said respecting Cristna treading on the serpent's head, and, in return, the serpent biting his heel. He seems to have rendered it doubtful whether there were pictures, or icons, of the serpent biting the heel, but the biting of the foot, I think, is admitted by the learned Doctor. It is of little consequence : but the reader must observe that, since gentlemen of the Doctor's warmth of temper and zeal have considered this to be inimical to their system, the same cause which prevents our finding any icons or pictures of Wittoba, (of which my reader will be informed shortly,) probably prevents our finding exemplars of the biting serpent. It seems perfectly in keeping with the remainder of the system, particularly with the doctrine of Original Sin, which is known to be one of the Hindoo tenets, and for this and other reasons, I confess I believe Mr. Maurice, although I thereby become, according to the Doctor's expression, an Infidel and a viper. The following passage is from Sonnerat, and I think it must be regarded as fully justifying Mr. Maurice : C'est in mémoire de cet évènement que dans les temples de Vichnou, dédiés à cette incarnation, on représente Quichena le corps entortillé d'une couleuvre capelle, qui lui mord le pied, tandis qu'il est peint, dans un autre tableau, dansant sur la tête de cette même couleuvre. Ses sectateurs ont ordinairement ces deux tableaux dans leurs maisons.[6]

Dr. Clarke says, "I have proved, and so might any man, that no serpent, in the common sense "of the term, can be intended in the third chapter of Genesis ; that all the circumstances of the "case, as detailed by the inspired penman, are in total hostility to the common mode of interpre-"tation, and that some other method should be found out."[7] I partly agree with the Doctor ; but

---

[1] Maur. Ind. Ant. Vol. II. p. 355.                         [2] Cranfurd's Res. Vol. II. p. 18.

[3] Many of the Brahmins, declare that there is no need to send missionaries to convert them ; that it would better become us to convert ourselves, by throwing off the corruptions of our religion, which is only a branch or sect of theirs ; that our Jesus is their Cristna, and that he ought to be black.

[4] Ap. p. 308.               [5] Lib. xvii.            [6] Voyage aux Ind. Vol. I. pp. 168, 169, see plates, fig. 5, 6.

[7] Class. Jour., No. VI. June, 1811, p. 440.

beg leave to add, that without deserving to be called Viper or Infidel, I have as much right to consider the whole as *an allegory*, as he has to consider the serpent to be an *ape.* But here is the Doctor not believing according to the orthodox faith. Then, on his own shewing, he must be both Infidel and Viper. But God forbid that it should be meted to this Protestant heretic, as he metes to others.

The observation which Dr. Clarke has made is extremely valuable, that in the drawings of Sonnerat the serpent is not biting the HEEL of Cristna, but the side of the foot. This clearly shews that they are not servile copies of one another; but records of a mythos substantially the same. Had the Hindoos copied from the Bible, they would have made the serpent bite the heel, whether it were of the mother or of the son. If the author of Genesis copied from the Hindoo, in making the serpent bite the heel, he substantially, and to all intents and purposes, made him bite the foot. But the two accounts are not mutually convertible one for the other. This story of Cristna and the serpent biting his foot, is of itself alone sufficient to prove, that the mythos of Cristna is not taken from the Romish or Greek religion of Jesus Christ, because in it the mother, not the son, bruises the serpent : Ipsa contaret caput tuum, &c.[1]

In a future chapter, I shall take an opportunity of saying much more on the subject of the Indian Hercules.

---

## CHAPTER II.

1. IN compliance with the rule which I have laid down for the regulation of my conduct, critically to examine every thing relating in any degree to my subject with the most impartial severity, nothing to suppress, and nothing of importance to add, without stating the authority on which I receive it,—I now present my reader with two very extraordinary histories relating to the crucifixion. I say, *fiat veritas ruat cœlum.* Nothing can injure the cause of religious truth, except, indeed, it be the falsities, suppressions, pious frauds, and want of candour of the priests, and of its weak and ill-judging friends. The pious frauds of the priests of all religions, imperiously demand of the philosophizing critic the most severe and suspicious examination. And whether the priests of the modern British church are to form an exception, will be a subject of inquiry in the second part of this work. In the work of Mons. Guigniaut[2] is the following passage :

" On raconte fort diversement la mort de Crichna. Une tradition remarquable et avérée le fait
" périr sur un bois fatal (un arbre), ou il fut cloué d'un coup de flèche, et du haut duquel il prédit
" les maux qui allaient fondre sur la terre, dans le Cali-youga.[3] En effet, trente ou trente-six ans
" après, commença cet age de crimes, et de misères. Une autre tradition ajoute que le corps de

---

[1] Vulgate.                    [2] Vol. I. p. 208.
[3] The word Yug or Youga is evidently the same word as the English word *age*, both having the same meaning. Paul, Sist. B. pp. 149, et sq. ; vide Sonnerat, I. pp. 169, et sq. ; Polier, II. pp. 144, 162, et sq.

l'homme-dieu fut change en un tronc de *tchandana* ou sandal; et qu'ayant été jeté dans l'Yamouna, près de Mathoura, il passa de là dans les eaux saintes du Gange, qui le portèrent sur la côte d'Orissa: il y est encore adoré à Djagannatha ou Jagrenat, lieu fameux par les pélerinages, comme le symbole de réproduction èt de la vie.[1] Il est certainment fort remarkable, quelques variantes que l'on puisse, découvrir dans les différens récits, de voir Siva et Crichna réunis à Djagannatha, nom qui signifie *le pays du maître du monde*, en sous-entendant Kchetra; car, par lui-même, ce nom est une epithète de Crichna. La Mythologie Egyptienne nous offrira une tradition sur le corps d'Osiris, toute a fait analogue à la dernière que nous verrons de rapporter.[2]

The first part of the above-cited passage respecting the nailing of Cristna to the fatal tree, and his prediction of the future evils of the world, is very remarkable, particularly when coupled with the following recital:

Mr. Moore describes an Avatar called Wittoba, who has his foot pierced. After stating the reason why he cannot account for it, he says, " A man who was in the habit of bringing me Hin-" doo deities, pictures, &c., once brought me two images exactly alike: one of them is engraved " in plate 98, and the subject of it will be at once seen by the most transient glance. Affecting " indifference, I inquired of my Pundit what Deva it was: he examined it attentively, and, after " turning it about for some time, returned it to me, professing his ignorance of what Avatar it " could immediately relate to, but supposed, by the hole in the foot, that it might be Wittoba; " adding, that it was impossible to recollect the almost innumerable Avataras described in the " *Puranas*.

" The subject of plate 98 is evidently the crucifixion; and, by the style of workmanship, is " clearly of European origin, as is proved also by its being in duplicate."[3]

This incarnation of Vishnu or CRISTNA is called Wittoba or Ballaji. He has a splendid temple erected to him at Punderpoor. Little respecting this incarnation is known. A story of him is detailed by Mr. Moore, which he observes reminds him of the doctrine *of turning the unsmote cheek to an assailant.* This God is represented by Moore with a hole on the top of one foot just above the toes, where the nail of a person crucified might be supposed to be placed. And, in another print, he is represented exactly in the form of a Romish crucifix, but not fixed to a piece of wood, though the legs and feet are put together in the usual way, with a nail-hole in the latter. There appears to be a glory over it coming *from* above. Generally the glory shines from the figure. It has a pointed Parthian coronet instead of a crown of thorns. I apprehend this is totally unusual in our crucifixes. When I recollect the crucifix on the fire tower in Scotland, (Celtic Druids, plate 24,) with the Lamb on one side, and *the Elephant* on the other, and all the circumstances attending this Avatar, I am induced to suspect I have been too hasty in determining that the fire tower was modern because it had the effigy of a crucified man upon it, and relating to this we shall find something very curious hereafter.

All the Avatars or incarnations of Vishnu are painted with Ethiopian or Parthian coronets.[4] Now, in Moore's Pantheon, the Avatar of Wittoba is thus painted; but Christ on the cross, though often described with a glory, I believe is never described with the Coronet. This proves that the figure described in Moore's Pantheon is not a Portuguese crucifix. Vide plates, fig. 7.

2. Mr. Moore endeavours to prove that this crucifix cannot be Hindoo, because there are duplicates of it from the same mould, and he contends that the Hindoos can only make one cast from

---

[1] Voy. Langlès. Monum., I., p. 186, *conf.* pp. 127, et. sq.

[2] Religions de L'Antiquitié, Du Dr. Fréderic Creuzer, par J. D. Guigniaut. Paris, Treuttel et Wurtz, Rue de Bourbon, No. 17. 1825.

[3] Moore's Ind. Pantheon, pp. 98, 416, 420.   [4] Jones, Asiatic Res. Vol. I. p. 260. 4to.

one mould, the mould-being made of clay. But he ought to have deposited the two specimens where they could have been examined, to ascertain that they were duplicates. Besides, how does he know that the Hindoos, who are so ingenious, had not the very simple art of making casts from the brass figure, as well as clay moulds from the one of wax? Nothing could be more easy. The crucified body without the cross of wood reminds me that some of the ancient sects of heretics held Jesus to have been crucified in the clouds.

Montfaucon says, " What can be the reason that, in the most common medals, some thousands " of which might be got up, we never can find two struck with the same die, though the impres- " sion and inscription be still the same? This is so constantly true, that whenever we find two " medals which appear to be struck with the same die, we always suspect one is a modern piece " coined from the other, and upon strict examination find it always is so." [1]

I very much suspect that it is from some story now unknown, *or kept out of sight,* relating to this Avatar, that the ancient heretics alluded to before obtained their tradition of Jesus having been crucified in the clouds. The temple at Punderpoor deserves to be searched, although the result of this search would give but little satisfaction, unless it were made by a person of a very different character from that of our missionaries. The argument respecting the duplicates on which Mr. Moore places his chief dependence to prove it Christian, at once falls to the ground when it is known that the assertion is not true : duplicates of brass idols, or at least copies so near that it is very difficult to distingush them, or to say that they are not duplicates from the same mould coarsely and unskilfully made, may be seen at the Museum at the India House; and also in that of the Asiatic Society in Grafton Street, where there are what I believe to be dupli- cates of figures from the same mould. I therefore think it must remain a Wittoba. But the reader has seen what I have found in Montfaucon, and he must judge for himself.

That nothing more is known respecting this Avatar, I cannot help suspecting may be attributed to the same kind of feeling which induced Mr. Moore's friend to wish him to remove this print from his book. The innumerable pious frauds of which Christian priests stand convicted, and the principle of the expediency of fraud admitted to have existed by Mosheim, are a perfect justifica- tion of my suspicions respecting the concealment of the history of this Avatar: especially as I can find no Wittobas in any of the collections. I repeat, I cannot help suspecting, that it is from this Avatar of Cristna that the sect of Christian heretics got their Christ crucified in the *clouds.*

Long after the above was written, I accidentally looked into Moore's Pantheon, at the British Museum, where it appears that the copy is an earlier impression than the former which I had consulted : and I discovered something which Mr. Moore has apparently not dared to tell us, viz. that in several of the icons of Wittoba, there are marks of holes in both feet, and in others, of holes in the hands. In the first copy which I consulted, the marks are very faint, so as to be scarcely visible. In figures 4 and 5 of plate 11, the figures have nail-holes in both feet. Fig. 3 has a hole in one hand. Fig. 6 has on his side the mark of a foot, and a little lower in the side a round hole; to his collar or shirt hangs the ornament or emblem of *a heart,* which we generally see in the Romish pictures of Christ; on his head he has an Yoni-Linga. In plate 12, and in plate 97, he has a round mark in the palm of the hand. Of this last, Mr. Moore says, " This cast is in " five pieces : the back lifts out of sockets in the pedestal, and admits the figures to slide back- " wards out of the grooves in which they are fitted : it is then seen that the seven-headed *Naga* " (cobra), joined to the figure, continues his scaly length down Ballaji's back, and making two " convolutions under him forms his seat: a second shorter snake, also part of the figure, pro-

---

[1] Ant. Exp. Supplement, Vol. III. B. v. p. 329.

" trudes its head, and makes a seat for Ballaji's right foot, and terminates with the other snake " behind him.    Unless this refer to the same legend as Crishna crushing Kaliya, I know not its " allusion."[1]

Figure 1, plate 91, of Moore's Pantheon, is a Hanuman, but it is remarkable that it has a hole in one foot, a nail through the other, a round nail mark in the palm of one hand and on the knuckle of the other, and is ornamented with doves and a five-headed Cobra snake.

It is unfortunate, perhaps it has been thought prudent, that the originals are not in the Museum to be examined.   But it is pretty clear that the Romish and Protestant crucifixion of Jesus must have been taken from the Avatar of Ballaji, or the Avatar of Ballaji from it, or both from a common mythos.

In this Avatar the first verse of Genesis appears to be closely connected with the crucifixion and the doctrine of the Atonement.   The seven-headed Cobra, in one instance, and the foot on the head of the serpent in others, unite him with Surya and Buddha.   Some of these figures have glories at the back of them.   In Calmet's Fragments, Cristna has the glory.   Some of the marks on the hands I should not have suspected to be nail-marks, if they had not been accompanied with the other circumstances : for the reader will see that they are double circles.   The nail-holes may have been ornamented for the sake of doing them honour, from the same feeling which makes the disgraceful cross itself an emblem of honour.   I have seen many Buddhas perfectly naked, with a small lotus flower in the palms of the hands and on the centre of the soles of the feet.   The mark in the side is worthy of observation and is unexplained.   I confess it seems to me to be very suspicious, that the icons of Wittoba are no where to be seen in the collections of our societies.

Mr. Moore gives an account of an influence endeavoured to be exercised upon him, to induce him not to publish the print, for fear of giving offence.   If it were nothing but a common crucifix, why should it give offence ?

3. It cannot and will not be denied, that these circumstances make this Avatar and its temples at Terputty, in the Carnatic, and Punderpoor near Poonah, the most interesting to the Christian world of any in India.   Pilgrimages are made to the former, particularly from Guzerat.   Why have not some of our numerous missionaries examined them ?   Will any person believe that they have not ?   Why is not the account of the search in the published transactions of the Missionary Society ?   There is plenty of nonsense in their works about Juggernaut and his temple.   Was it suppressed for the same reason that the father of Ecclesiastical History, Eusebius, admits that he suppressed matters relating to the Christians, and among the rest, I suppose, the murder of Crispus, by his father Constantine, viz. that it was not of good report ?   It would be absurd to deny that I believe this to be the fact.   When Mr. Moore wrote, Terputty was in the possession of the English, who made a profit of £15,000 a year of the temple.   The silence itself of our literati and missionaries speaks volumes.

Mr. Moore (p. 415) says, " In Sanscrit this Avatara is named Vinkatyeish ; in the Carnatic " dialect, Terpati ; in the Telinga country and language, Vinkatramna Govinda ; in Guzerat and " to the westward, Ta'khur, or Thakhur, as well as Ballaji : the latter name obtains in the neigh- " bourhood of Poona, and generally through the Mahratta country."   The name of Terpati, or as he elsewhere calls him Tripati, identifies him with the ancient Trinity.   This word is almost correctly Latin, but this a person who has read Sect. XXV. of Chap. II. and Ap. p. 304, of my CELTIC DRUIDS, will not be surprised at.   Pati or Peti is the Pali[2] word for father.   And what does Wittoba's other name Ballaji look like but Baal-jah, בעל‎ Bol, יה‎ Ie, or יה‎ Iie ?   Whenever the languages of India come to be understood, I am satisfied that Colonel Wilford's opinion will be

---

[1] P. 416.        [2] We shall find in the end that the Pali language was originally the same as the Tamul.

proved well founded, and that they will be discovered at the bottom to be derived from the same root as the sixteen-letter system of the Phœnicians, Hebrews, &c., &c., and their Gods the same. The circumstance of Ballaji treading on the head of the serpent shews that he is, as the Brahmins say, an Avatar of Cristna. I shall be accused of illiberality in what I am going to say, but I must and will speak the truth. Belief is not (at least with me) a matter of choice, it is a matter of necessity, and suspicion is the same—and I must say, if I speak honestly, that after the circumstances of concealment for so many years stated above, I shall not believe that there is not something more in the Avatar of Wittoba if his temples be not searched by persons well known to be of a sceptical disposition. And even then, who knows that the most important matters may not have already been removed? It is lamentable to think that the lies and frauds of the unprincipled part of the priesthood, and generally the ruling part, have rendered certainty upon these subjects almost unattainable: however, it comes to this, that it is perfectly absurd to look for *certainty*, or to blame any one for an opinion. The fact of the God treading on the head of the serpent is a decisive proof, both in his case and in that of Cristna, that this cannot have been taken from the Romish or Greek writings, or the spurious Gospel histories; because the sects whose writings they are, ALL make the woman, not the *seed* of the woman, bruise the serpent's head. The modern Protestant churches translate the Hebrew in Genesis by the word *ipse ;* the ancient Romish church, by the word *ipsa ;* the latter, to support the adoration of the Virgin, the Maia ; the former, to support their oriental doctrine of the *Atonement,* which never was held by the latter. I believe the seed of the woman bruising the serpent's head was never heard of in Europe till modern times, notwithstanding some various readings may be quoted. The Brahmins surely must have been deeply read in the modern scholastic divinity, to have understood and to have made the distinction between the Romish and Protestant schools! They must, indeed, have had a MAGEE on the Atonement. The mode in which all the different particulars relating to the serpent, Osiris, &c., are involved with one another, seems to render it impossible to suppose that the history relating to Cristna can have been copied from the gospel histories. The seed of the woman crushing the serpent's head is intimately connected with the voyage of the God from Muttra to the temple of Jaggernaut,—evidently the same mythos as the voyage of Osiris to Byblos. Of the seed of the woman crushing the serpent's head, or of the descent into hell, similar to that of Cristna, there is not a word in the orthodox gospel histories.

4. I shall presently make some observations on the celebrated Hercules, and I shall shew that he is the same as Cristna, a supposed incarnation of the Sun in Aries. On this God the very celebrated and learned divine Parkhurst makes the following observation :[1] " But the labours of Her-
" cules seem to have had a still higher view, and to have been originally designed as emblematic
" memorials of what the real Son of God, and Saviour of the world, was to do and suffer for our
" sakes,

Νοσων θελκτηρια παντα κωμιζων,—

" *bringing a cure for all our ills,* as the Orphic hymn speaks of Hercules."

Here Mr. Parkhurst proceeds as a Christian priest, who is honest and a believer in his religion, ought to do. This is very different from denying a fact or concealing it. The *design,* of the labours of Hercules here supposed, having nothing to do with the antiquity of nations, does not in any way interfere with my inquiry. For my own part I feel that whether I approve the reason assigned or not, Mr. Parkhurst and other Christians of his school have as much right to their opinion as I have to mine ; and, for entertaining such opinion, ought not to be censured by me or any one. My object is facts—and, if I could avoid it, I would never touch a dogma at all.

---

[1] In voce עז *oz,* III. p. 520.

I am extremely glad to find such a reason given, because it liberates me from a painful situation; for it is evident, that if Hercules were Cristna or Buddha, they must have been types or symbols of Christ if Hercules were : and if this be the religion which I contend that I am justified in taking from Parkhurst, how absurd is it to suppress the facts respecting Cristna ! For, 'it is evident the nearer and closer they are to the history of Jesus Christ, the more perfect is the type or emblem ; and upon this ground the complaint of the philosopher against the religion will be, not that these histories are similar, but that in certain cases they are *not* similar. He will say, this cannot be a type or emblem, because it is not the same. Thus the frauds of the priests in suppressing facts will recoil upon themselves. And when we perceive that the Hindoo Gods were supposed to be crucified, it will be impossible to resist a belief, that the particulars of that crucifixion have been suppressed. To suppose that Buddha and Cristna are said in the Hindoo books to be crucified, and yet that there are no particulars of such crucifixion detailed, is quite incredible. The argument of Mr. Parkhurst is very different from that of Mr. Maurice, and I hail it with delight, because it at once sets my hands at liberty, and shews that in future the defenders of the religion must bring forth, not suppress, ancient histories. This shews the folly of the disingenuous proceedings of our priests with respect to Hindoo learning.

For a long time I endeavoured to find some reason or meaning for the story of the crown of thorns, so unlike any thing in history but itself, but in which the prejudices of our education prevent our seeing any absurdity. I have at last come to an opinion, which I know will be scouted by every one who has not very closely attended to the extreme ignorance of the first professors of Christianity, and it is this, that the idea of the thorns has been taken from the pointed Parthian coronet of Wittoba or Balaji. Not understanding it, and too much blinded by their zeal to allow themselves time to think, as in many other instances, they have run away with the first impression which struck them. If I were not well acquainted with the meanness of understanding of these devotees, I should not certainly harbour this opinion, but it is not more absurd than many other of their superstitions.

5. In many of the most ancient temples of India, the Bull, as an object of adoration, makes a most conspicuous figure. A gigantic image of one protrudes from the front of the temple of the *Great Creator*, called in the language of the country, Jaggernaut, in Orissa. This is the Bull of the Zodiac,—the emblem of the sun when the equinox took place in the first degree of the sign of the Zodiac, Taurus. In consequence of the precession of the equinoxes, the sun at the vernal equinox left Taurus, and took place in Aries, which it has left also for a great number of years, and it now takes place in Aquarius. Thus it keeps receding about *one degree* in 72 years, and about a whole *sign* in 2160 years. According to this calculation, it is about 2500 years by the true Zodiac, before the time of Christ, since it was in the first degree of Aries, and about 4660 before the time of Christ, since it was in the same degree of Taurus. M. Dupuis has demonstrated that the labours of Hercules are nothing but a history of the passage of the sun through the signs of the Zodiac ; [1] and that Hercules is the sun in Aries or the Ram, Bacchus the sun in Taurus or the Bull. From this it follows that the worship of Jaggernaut must have been instituted, and his temple probably built, near 6500 years ago, and that the temple and worship of Cristna, or the Indian Hercules, must have taken place at least, but probably about, 2160 years later. This brings the date of Cristna to about 2500 years before Christ. When Arrian says that the Indian Hercules was fifteen hundred years after Bacchus, it appears that he had learnt a part of the truth, probably from the tradition of the country. The great length of time between the two was known by tradition, but the *reason* of it was unknown. But I think we may see the truth

---

[1] In the sphere, Hercules treads on the serpent's head. See Dupuis.

through the mist. The adoration of the Bull of the Zodiac is to be met with every where throughout the world, in the most opposite climes. The examples of it are innumerable and incontrovertible; they admit of no dispute.

6. The reader will not fail to recollect that in our observations on the Cristna of India, some difference between him and Jesus Christ, relating to the immaculate conception, was observed by Mr. Maurice, and laid hold of by him as a point on which he could turn into ridicule the idea of the identity of the two histories of Cristna and Jesus. The life of Pythagoras will shew us where the Christians may have got the particulars which differ from the history of Cristna. The early fathers travelling for information, which was the case with Papias, Hegesippus, Justin, &c., mixed the traditions relating to Pythagoras, which they found spread all over the East, with those relating to the Indian Cristna, and from the *two* formed their own system. Pythagoras himself having drawn many of his doctrines, &c., from the Indian school, the commixture could scarcely be avoided. Thus we find the few peculiarities respecting the birth of Jesus, such as the immaculate conception, wherein the history of Jesus differs from that of Cristna, exactly copied from the life of Pythagoras. And the circumstances relating to the immaculate conception by the mother of Pythagoras, I have no doubt were taken from the history of Buddha, as I shall shew in my next chapter, and from the virgin of the celestial sphere—herself of Oriental origin. Thus from a number of loose traditions at last came to be formed, by very ignorant and credulous persons, the complete history of the Jesus Christ of the Romish Church, *as we now have it*. I think no person, however great his credulity may be, will believe that the identity of the immaculate conceptions of Jesus and Pythagoras can be attributed to accident. The circumstances are of so peculiar a nature that it is absolutely impossible. With this system the fact pointed out by the Unitarians is perfectly consistent, that the first two chapters of Matthew and of Luke, which contain the history of the immaculate conception, are of a different school from the remainder of the history.

The first striking circumstance in which the history of Pythagoras agrees with the history of Jesus is, that they were natives of nearly the same country; the former being born at Sidon, the latter at Bethlehem, both in Syria. The father of Pythagoras, as well as the father of Jesus, was prophetically informed that his wife should bring forth a son, who should be a benefactor to mankind. They were both born when their mothers were from home on journeys: Joseph and his wife having gone up to Bethlehem to be taxed, and the father of Pythagoras having travelled from Samos, his residence, to Sidon, about his mercantile concerns. Pythais, the mother of Pythagoras, had a connexion with an Apolloniacal spectre, or ghost, of the God Apollo, or God Sol, (of course this must have been a *holy* ghost, and here we have THE *Holy Ghost*,) which afterward appeared to her husband, and told him that he must have no connexion with his wife during her pregnancy—a story evidently the same as that relating to Joseph and Mary. From these peculiar circumstances, Pythagoras was known by the same identical title as Jesus, namely, *the Son of God*; and was supposed by the multitude to be under the influence of Divine inspiration.

When young, he was of a very grave deportment, and was celebrated for his philosophical appearance and wisdom. He wore his hair long, after the manner of the Nazarites, whence he was called the long-haired Samian. And I have no doubt that he was a Nazarite for the term of his natural life, and the person called his daughter was only a person figuratively so called.

He spent many years of his youth in Egypt, where he was instructed in the secret learning of the priests, as Jesus, in the Apocryphal Gospels, is said to have been, and was carried thence to Babylon by Cambyses, the iconoclast and restorer of the Jewish religion and temple, where he was initiated into the doctrines of the Persian Magi. Thence he went to India, where he learned the doctrines of the Brahmins. Before he went to Egypt he spent some time at Sidon, Tyre, and

Biblos, learning the secret mysteries of all these places. Whilst in this country he chiefly dwelt in a temple on Mount Carmel; probably in the temple of Jove, *in which there was no image.* After his return from India, he is stated to have travelled about the world, to Egypt, Syria, Greece, Italy, &c., preaching reformation of manners to these different nations, and leaving among them numbers of proselytes. He was generally favoured by the people, but as generally persecuted by the governments; which almost always persecute real philanthropists. Here are certainly some circumstances in this history very like those in the histories of Jesus.

The stories told of the mother of Pythagoras having had connexion with an Apolloniacal spectre, is not the only one of the kind: the same story is told of Plato, who was said to be born of Parectonia, without connexion with his father Ariston, but by a connexion with Apollo. On this ground the really very learned Origen defends the immaculate conception, assigning, also, in confirmation of the fact, the example of Vultures, (Vautours,) who propagate without the male. What a striking proof that a person may possess the greatest learning, and yet be in understanding the weakest of mankind!

It seems to be quite impossible for any person of understanding to believe, that the coincidence of these histories of Plato [1] and Pythagoras, with that of Jesus, can be the effect of accident. Then how can they be accounted for otherwise than by supposing that in their respective orders of time they were all copies of one another? How the priests are to explain away these circumstances I cannot imagine, ingenious as they are. They cannot say that Jamblicus, knowing the history of Christ, attributed it to the philosophers, because he quotes for his authorities Epimenides, Xenocrates, and Olimpiodorus, who all lived long previous to the birth of Christ.

In my next chapter all these sacred predicted births will be shewn to be supposed renewed incarnations of portions of the Holy Spirit or Ghost. And here I must observe, that these miraculous facts, charged to the account of Plato and Pythagoras, by no means prove that these men did not exist, nor can such facts, charged to Jesus, if disbelieved, justify an Unbeliever in drawing a conclusion that he never existed.

---

[1] Vide Olimpiodorus's Life of Plato.

# BOOK V.

## CHAPTER I.

1. The time is now arrived when it becomes proper to enter upon an examination of the doctrines of the celebrated Buddha of India, which were the foundations of all the mythoses of the Western nations, as well as of those which we have seen of Cristna ; and from these two were supplied most of the superstitions which became engrafted into the religion of Jesus Christ.

I shall now shew, that Buddha and Cristna were only renewed incarnations of the same Being, and that Being the Solar power, or a principle symbolized by the Sun—a principle made by the sun visible to the eyes of mortals : and particularly exhibiting himself in his glory at the vernal equinox, in the heavenly constellation known by the name of Taurus, as BUDDHA, and subsequently in that of Aries, as CRISTNA.

But I must previously make one observation to guard my reader against mistake.

There is a style of writing or speaking, adopted by our orientalists from inadvertency or inattention to its consequences, which has a great tendency to mislead the reader. They take up a book in Ceylon or Pegu, perhaps, to learn from it the doctrines of Buddha or of Cristna ; they read this book, and then tell us that these are the doctrines of Buddha, never considering that this book may contain only the doctrines of an obscure sect of Buddhists. Suppose a Brahmin were to come to England, and to take up a book of Johanna Southcote's, or of Brothers', or of Calvin's; how much would he misrepresent the religion of Jesus if he represented it as he found it there ! Except in a few leading particulars, it is as difficult to say what is at present the religion of Buddha, as it is to decide what is the religion of Christ. Again, if any one would say what the religion of Christ is at this day, in any particular country, it would be very different from what the religion of Christ was *four* hundred, or even *two* hundred, years ago. We have no service *now* in our Liturgy for casting out devils. And it is the same with Buddhism and Vishnuism. My search is to find the spring-head whence all the minor streams of Buddhism have sprung. A description of the rivulets flowing from it and which have become muddy in their progress, however interesting to some persons, is not my object; nor is it to my taste to spend my time upon such nonsensical matters, which can have no other effect than to disguise the original of the religion, and to gratify evil passions, by depreciating the religion of our neighbour. If his religion have sunk into the most degraded state, as in Ceylon, the more the pity. It shall not be my task to expose the foolish puerilities, into which our unfortunate fellow-subjects, now unable to defend themselves, have fallen ; but to shew the truth that, fallen as they are, they once possessed a religion refined and beautiful.

M. Creuzer[1] says, "There is not in all history and antiquity perhaps a question at the same " time more important and more difficult than that concerning Buddha." He then acknowledges that by his name, his ASTRONOMICAL character, and close connexion, not only with the mythology and philosophy of the Brahmins, but with a great number of other religions, this personage, truly mysterious, seems to lose himself in the night of time, and to attach himself by a secret bond to every thing which is obscure in the East and in the West. I apprehend the reason of the difficulty is to be found, in a great degree, in the fact, that our accounts are taken from the Brahmins who have modelled or corrupted the history to suit their own purposes. I am of opinion that the Buddhists were worshipers of the sun in Taurus, the Bacchus of the Greeks ; that they were the builders of the temple of Jaggernaut, in front of which the Bull projects ; and that they were expelled from Lower India when the Indian Hercules, Cristna, succeeded to the Indian Bacchus. That is, when the sun no longer rose at the equinox in the sign *Taurus*, but in the sign *Aries*. This is, I believe, the solution of the grand enigma which M. Creuzer says we are not able entirely to solve, and this I will now endeavour to prove.

2. " Buddha is variously pronounced and expressed *Boudh, Bod, Bot, But, Bad, Budd, Bud-*
" *dou, Boutta, Bota, Budso, Pot, Pout, Pota, Poti,* and *Pouti.* The Siamese make the final T or
" D quiescent, and sound the word *Po ;* whence the Chinese still further vary it to Pho or Fo. In
" the Talmudic dialect the name is pronounced *Poden* or *Pooden ;* whence the city, which once
" contained the temple of Sumnaut or Suman-nath, is called *Patten-Sumnaut.* The broad sound
" of the *U* or *Ou* or *Oo,* passes in the variation *Patten* into *A,* pronounced *Ah* or *Au ;* and in a
" similar manner, when the *P* is sounded *B,* we meet with *Bad, Bat,* and *Bhat.* All these are in
" fact no more than a ringing of changes on the cognate letters *B* and *P, T* and *D.* Another of
" his names is Saman, which is varied into *Somon, Somono, Samana, Suman-Nath,* and *Sarmuna.*
" From this was borrowed the sectarian appellation of *Samaneans,* or *Sarmaneans.* A third is
" *Gautama,* which is indifferently expressed *Gautameh, Godama, Godam, Codam, Cadam, Cardam,*
" and *Cardama.* This perpetually occurs in composition with the last, as *Somono-Codom* or *Sa-*
" *mana-Gautama.* A fourth is *Saca, Sacya, Siaka, Shaka, Xaca, Xaca-Muni* or *Xaca-Menu,*
" and *Kia,* which is the uncompounded form of *Sa-Kia.* A fifth is *Dherma,* or *Dharma,* or
" *Dherma-rajah.* A sixth is *Hermias, Her-Moye,* or *Heri-Maya.* A seventh is *Datta, Dat-*
" *Atreya, That-Dalna, Date, Tat* or *Tot, Deva-Tat* or *Deva-Twasta.* An eighth is *Jain, Jina,*
" *Chin, Jain-Deo, Chin-Deo,* or *Jain-Eswar.* A ninth is *Arhan.* A tenth is *Mahi-Man, Mai-*
" *Man,* or (if *Om* be added) *Mai-Man-Om.* An eleventh is *Min-Eswara,* formed by the same
" title *Min* or *Man* or *Menu* joined to *Eswara.* A twelfth is *Gomat* or *Gomat-Eswara.* A thir-
" teenth, when he is considered as *Eswara* or *Siva,* is *Ma-Esa* or *Har-Esa ;* that is to say, the
" great *Esa* or the *Lord Esa.* A fourteenth is *Dagon* or *Dagun,* or *Dak-Po.* A fifteenth is
" *Tara-Nath.* And a sixteenth is *Arca-Bandhu* or *Kinsman of the Sun.*"[2]

Again. " *Wod* or *Vod* is a mere variation of *Bod ;* and *Woden* is simply the Tamulic mode of
" pronouncing Buddha : for in that mode of enunciation, *Buddha* is expressed *Pooden* or *Poden ;*
" and Poden is undoubtedly the same word as *Voden* or *Woden.*"[3] This etymology is assented to by Sir W. Jones, if it were not, as I believe it was, originally proposed by him. Woden was the

[1] Religions de l' Antiquité, Vol. I. p. 285, ed. de Mons. Guigniaut.
[2] Faber, Pag. Idol. B. iv. Chap. v. p. 351.     [3] Ib. p. 355.

x

God of the Scuths or Goths and Scandinavians, and said to be the inventor of their letters; as Hermes was the supposed inventor of the letters of the Egyptians.   This, among other circumstances, tends to prove that the religion of the Celts and Scuths of the West was Buddhism. The Celtic Teutates is the Gothic Teut or Tuisto, Buddhas titles of *Tat, Datta,* or *Twashta. Taranis* is *Tara-Nath.   Hesus* of Gaul is, *Esa, Mu-Hesa,* and *Har-Esa.*   But those are by the Latin writers called Mercury.[1]

My reader will observe that I have given from Mr. Faber sixteen different names of Buddha, by which he undertakes to prove that he was known at different times and in different places.   Mr. Faber enters at great length into the discussion of each, and proves his case, in almost every instance, in a way which cannot reasonably be disputed.   I do not think it necessary to follow him, but shall take those names upon his authority.   He makes it evident that Buddhism extended almost to every part of the old world : but we must remember that the British Taranis, and the Gothic Woden, were both names of Buddha.   In my Celtic Druids I have shewn that the worship of Buddha is every where to be found—in Wales, Scotland, and Ireland.[2]   Hu, the great God of the Welsh, is called Buddwas ;[3]   and they call their God Budd, the God of victory, the king who rises in light and ascends the sky.[4]

In Scotland, the country people frighten their children by telling them, that *old Bud* or the *old man* will take them.   In India, one of the meanings of the word Buddha is *old man.*

3. In this inquiry it seems of the first consequence to ascertain the meaning of the word *Buddha.* From the examination of the accounts of the different authors, this celebrated word appears to have the same meaning as the first word of Genesis, that is, WISDOM, or *extremely wise,* or *wise in a high degree.*[5]   M. Creuzer gives it *savant, sage, intelligence, excellente,* et *supérieure.*   He says, it allies itself or is closely allied to the understanding, mind, *intelligence* unique, and supreme of God.

This is confirmed by Mr. Ward, the missionary, who tells us, that Buddha is the Deity of WISDOM, as was the Minerva of Greece.   When devotees pray for wisdom to their king, they say, May Buddha give thee wisdom.[6]

The etymology of the word Buddha seems to be unknown to the Hindoos, which favours the idea of a date previous to any of the present known languages.   In the Pali, of Ceylon, it means *universal knowledge* or *holiness.*[7]

The word Buddha has been thought, by some Hindoo authors, to be a general name for a philosopher ; by others it has been supposed to be a generic word, like Deva, but applicable to a sage or philosopher ;  but still it is allowed to mean, *excellence,* WISDOM, *virtue, sanctity.*

In Sanscrit we have, Sanskrit Root, *Budh,* to know, to be aware ;  *Budhyati,* he knows, is aware ; *Bodhayāmi,* I inform, I teach.

*Buddhi,* wisdom ;  *Buddha,* sage, wise ;  *Bodha,* WISDOM.[8]

ברא *bda* in the Hebrew means, to devise of himself alone ;  or I should say, to think or theorise. In Arabic it means, to begin to produce, or to devise something new.

Two facts seem to be universally agreed upon by all persons who have written respecting Buddha.   The first is, that at last he is always found to resolve himself into the sun, either as the

---

[1] Faber, Orig. Pag. Idol     [2] Celtic Druids, pp. 197, 306, &c.     [3] Davies, Celtic Myth. p. 118.
[4] Ib. p. 116.     [5] Moore's Pantheon, p. 234.     [6] Ward's Hist. of Hind. p. 452.
[7] Asiat. Res. Vol. XVII. p. 33.
[8] Some of our Indian scholars make a distinction between Buddha, and Budd, the Planet Mercury.   I can no more admit this, than I can admit that the God Mercury was not the Sun ;  though I know that Mercury is the name of a Planet, and that the planet is not the Sun.   The cases are exactly similar.

sun, or as the higher principle of which the sun is the image or emblem, or of which the sun is the residence. The second is, that the word Buddha means WISDOM. Now, we cannot believe that this WISDOM would be called by so singular a name as Buddha, without a cause.

It has been observed by several philologers that the letters B D, B T, universally convey the idea either of former or of creator. But Genesis says the world was formed by WISDOM. Wisdom was the Buddha or former of the world: thus WISDOM, I conceive, became called Bud. Wisdom was the first emanation, so was Buddha. Wisdom was the Logos by which the world was formed; but Buddha was the Creator: thus the Logos and Budd are identical, the same second person of the Trinity.

Rasit, or WISDOM, was contemporaneous with the commencement of creation—it was the beginning of things, and the beginning was WISDOM, the Logos.

The beginning, as the word Rasit is explained by our version, is contradictory to the context, because the existence of space, of time, of created angelic beings, is implied, before the moment which gave birth to the mundane system. This will not be thought to be too refined for the inventors of the Trinity,—the Creator, Preserver and Destroyer. I shall shew that Logos, Bud, and Rasit, were only names in different languages for the same idea.

Mr. Whiter says, " Through the whole compass of language the element B D denotes Being : " hence we have the great Deity worshiped all over the East—Budda." [1] Then Buddha will mean the existent or *self-existent wisdom*, self-existent as an integral part of the Trinity. He then informs us that, in Persian, *Bud-en Bud*, signifies *to be*. The same as *Is, est, existo*. Bud is clearly the *I am that I am* of our Bible; or, in the original, which has no present tense, the *I shall be*, or the *I have been;* or what, perhaps, this celebrated text may mean, THAT WHICH I HAVE BEEN, I SHALL BE—Eternity, past and future.

4. Mr. Crawfurd says, oriental scholars have for some time suspected that the religions of Brahma and Buddha are essentially the same, the one being nothing but a modification of the other. [2] This we shall find hereafter confirmed.

The following is the speech of Arjoon respecting Vishnu as Cristna—Thou art all in all. Thou art thyself numerous Avatars. Thy Hyagrive Avatar killed Madhu, the Ditya, on the back of a tortoise. In thy Comma Avatar did the Devites place the solid orb of the earth, while from the water of the milky ocean, by the churning staff of mount Meru, they obtained the immortal Amrita of their desires. Hirinakassah, who had carried the earth down to Patal, did thy Varaha Avatar slay and bring up the earth on the tusks of the boar: and Prahland, whom Hirinakassah tormented for his zeal towards thee, did thy Narasing Avatar place in tranquillity. In thy dwarf or Bahmen Avatar thou didst place Bali in the mighty monarchy of Patal. Thou art that mighty Parasa Rama, who cut down the entire jungle, the residence of the Reeshees:[3] and thou art Ram the Potent slayer of Ravar. O supreme Bhagavat, thou art the Buddha Avatar who shall tranquillize and give ease to Devaties, human creatures, and Dityes. [4]

I think I could scarcely have wished for a more complete proof of the truth of my doctrine of the renewal of the Avatars, than the above. It shews, in fact, that both Buddha and Cristna are nothing but renewed incarnations in each cycle.

The ancient identity of the worship of Buddha and of Cristna, receives a strong confirmation

---

[1] Etymol. Univ. Vol. I. p. 310.      [2] Hist. Ind. Arch. Vol. II. p. 222.

[3] I apprehend the Reeshees, or Rishees, when the word is applied to men, are the Ras-shees—the φιλοσοφοι. They are said to have been seven in number, and the Pleiades were dedicated to them. But I shall return to this subject hereafter.

[4] Camb. Key, Vol. II. p. 294.

from the fact, that the Buddhists have TEN incarnations of Buddha, the same as the followers of Cristna, and, what is remarkable, called by the same names. [1] Mr. Ward says, " Vishnu had ten " incarnations, and Buddha had the same number." [2] These ten incarnations, thus noticed by this missionary, we shall find of the very first importance in our future disquisitions.

The Rev. Mr. Maurice has given a very long and particular account of these ten grand Avatars or incarnations, of the God of the Hindoos. The accounts of the Brahmins consist, to outward appearance, of a great number of idle and absurd fables, not worth repetition. The only fact worthy of notice *here* is, that Buddha was universally allowed to be the first of the incarnations; that Cristna was of later date; and that, at the æra of the birth of Christ, eight of them had appeared on the earth, and that other two were expected to follow before the end of the Cali-Yug, or of the present age. But the Brahmins held that 3101 years of it had expired at the period of the birth of Christ, according to our reckoning.

Between the Brahmins and the Buddhists there exists the greatest conceivable enmity: the former accusing the latter of being Atheists, and schismatics from their sect. They will hold no communication with them, believing themselves to be made unclean, and to require purification, should they step within even the *shadow* of a Buddhist. Much in the same way the Buddhists consider the Brahmins. The ancient histories of the Hindoos are full of accounts of terrible wars between the different sectaries, which probably lasted, with the intermissions usual in such cases, for many generations, and extended their influence over the whole world; and we shall see in the course of this work, that, in their results, they continue to exercise an influence over the destinies of mankind.

Buddha is allowed by his enemies, the Brahmins, to have been an avatar. Then here is *divine wisdom* incarnate, of whom the Bull of the Zodiac was the emblem. *Here* he is the Protogonos or first-begotten, the God or Goddess Μητις of the Greeks, being, perhaps, both male and female. He is at once described as divine wisdom, the Sun, and Taurus. This is the first Buddha or incarnation of wisdom, by many of the Brahmins often confounded with a person of the same name, supposed to have lived at a later day. In fact, Buddha or the wise, if the word were not merely the name of a doctrine, seems to have been an appellation taken by several persons, or one person incarnate at several periods, and from this circumstance much confusion has arisen. But I think we may take every thing which the Brahmins say of the first Buddha to his advantage, as the received doctrine of his followers. They hate all Buddhists too much to say any thing in his favour which they think untrue.

5. The mother of Buddha was MAIA, who was also the mother of Mercury, a fact of the first importance. Of this Maia or Maja the mother of Mercury, Mr. Davies [3] says, " The universal " genius of nature, which discriminated all things, according to their various kinds or species—the " same, perhaps, as the Meth of the Ægyptians, and the Μητις of the Orphic bards, which was of " all kinds, and the author of all things.—Και Μητις πρωτος γενετωρ. Orph. Frag." To this Mr. Whiter adds, " To these terms belong the well-known deities Budda and Amida. The Fo of " the Chinese is acknowledged to be the Fod or Budda of the Eastern world, and the Mercury of " the Greeks." He then gives the following passage from Barrow's Travels: " The Budha of " the Hindūs was the son of Maya, and one of his epithets is Amita. The Fo of China was the " son of Mo-ya, and one of his epithets is *Om-e-to;* and in Japan, whose natives are of Chinese " origin, the same God *Fo* is worshiped under the name of Amida. I could neither collect from " any of the Chinese what the literal meaning was of *Om-e-to,* nor could I decipher the characters " under which it was written."

---

[1] Ward's India, p. 387.    [2] Transac. Asiat. Soc. Vol. I. p. 427.    [3] Apud Whiter, Etymol. Univ. p. 103.

I think there can be no difficulty in finding here the Maia in the Mo-ya, nor the *Om-e-to* in the *Am-i-da* and *Am-i-ta*. Nor, in the first syllable of the three last, the letters A, U, M, coalescing and forming the word OM. The Μητις is well known to mean divine wisdom, and we have seen above, that it is πρωτος γενετωρ or first mother of all. [1] The first of the Æons of all nations was *wisdom.* Is Am-i-da, ׳ד di ה e עם om ?

The followers of Buddha teach that he descended from a celestial mansion into the womb of Maha-Maya, spouse of Soutadanna, king of Megaddha on the north of Hindostan, and member of the family of Sakya Sa-kia, [2] the most illustrious of the caste of Brahmins. His mother, who had conceived him, (BY A RAY OF LIGHT, according to *De Guignes*,) sans souillure, without defilement, that is, *the conception was immaculate*, brought him into the world after *ten months* without pain. He was born at the foot of a tree, and he did not touch the earth, Brahma having sought him to receive him in a vase of gold, and Gods, or kings the incarnations of Gods, assisted at his birth. The Mounis [3] and Pundits (prophets and *wise men)* recognized in this marvellous infant all the characters of the divinity, and he had scarcely seen the day before he was hailed Devata-Deva, God of Gods. Buddha, before he was called by the name Buddha or WISDOM, very early made incredible progress in the sciences. His beauty, as well as his *wisdom*, was more than human; and when he went abroad, crowds assembled to admire him. After a certain time he left the palace of his father, and retired into the desert, where he commenced his divine mission. There he ordained himself priest, and shaved his head with his own hands, i. e. adopted the tonsure. He there changed his name to Guatama.

After various trials, he came out of them all triumphant; and after certain *temptations or penitences,* to which he submitted in the desert, were finished, he declared to his disciples that the time was come to announce to the world the light of the true faith, the Gods themselves descending from heaven to invite him to propagate his doctrines. He is described by his followers as a *God of pity*, the *guardian or saviour of mankind*, the *anchor of salvation*, and he was charged to prepare the world for the day of judgment.

Amara thus addresses him: " Thou art the Lord of all things, the Deity who overcomest the " sins of the Cali-Yug, the guardian of the universe, the emblem of mercy towards those who " serve thee—OM: the possessor of all things in vital form. THOU ART BRAHMA, VISHNU, AND " MAHESA: thou art the Lord of the universe: thou art the proper form of all things, moveable " and immoveable, the possessor of the whole, and thus I adore thee. Reverence be unto thee, " the bestower of salvation.— . . . . I adore thee, who art celebrated by a thousand names, and " under various forms, *in the shape of* BUDDHA *the* GOD *of mercy.* Be propitious, O most high " God." [4]

Buddha was often said not only to have been born of a virgin, but to have been born, as some of the heretics maintained Jesus Christ was born, *from the side of his mother*. [5] He was also said to have had no father. This evidently alludes to his being the son of the androgynous

---

[1] Jupiter took Μητις *Metis,* to wife: and as soon as he found her pregnant, he devoured her: in consequence of which HE became pregnant, and out of his head was born Pallas or Minerva. Now μητις means DIVINE WISDOM. That this is an allegory closely connected with the doctrine of Buddha (wisdom), and of the ראשית *rasit,* or wisdom of Genesis, the first emanation of the Jews, I think no one will doubt, though it may be difficult to explain its details.

[2] If we look back to Section 2, we shall see that Mr. Faber states Sa-kia to be a name of Buddha. This Xaca or Saka is the origin, as I shall shew, of the name of our Saxon ancestors.

[3] Mounis are nothing but Menus or wise men, like the Minoses of Crete, &c., Rashees of India, and Sophis of Persia.

[4] Moore's Pantheon, pp. 23, 33, 39.    [5] And as Maui was said to be born.

*Brahme-Maia.*[1] This I suppose to be described in the prints in Moore's Pantheon, where Buddha is rising from the navel of Brahme-Maia, with the umbilical cord uncut.

Mons. De Guignes[2] states that Fo, or Buddha, was brought forth not from the matrix, but *from the right side,* of a virgin, *whom a ray of light had impregnated.* The Manichæans held that this was the case with Jesus Christ, and by this single fact, without the necessity for any other, they identify themselves with the Buddhists.

St. Jerom says,[3] Apud Gymnosophistas Indiæ, quasi per manus, hujus opinionis auctoritas traditur, quod Buddam, principem dogmatis eorum, *è latere suo virgo generavit.*

We see here that the followers of Buddha are called Gymnosophists. It has been observed that the Meroe of Ethiopia was a Meru. This is confirmed by an observation of Heliodorus, that the priests of Meroe were of a humane character, and were *called Gymnosophists.*[4]

When we treat of some doctrines held by a gentleman of the name of Bentley, I must beg my reader to recollect that in the account of Jerom, the Mythos of Buddha, the same as that of Cristna, was known to him in the fourth century, and therefore cannot have been invented to oppose Christianity, about the sixth century, or to deceive Mohammed Akbar in the sixteenth.

Jayadeva thus addresses Buddha: " Thou blamest (O wonderful) the whole *Veda* when thou " seest, O kind-hearted! the slaughter of cattle prescribed for sacrifice—O Kesava! assuming " the body of Buddha. Be victorious, O Heri! lord of the universe."[5] It may be observed that Heri means *Saviour.*

There was a Goddess called Jayadevi, i. e. the Goddess Jaya.[6]

6. Buddha as well as Cristna means shepherd. Thus, he was the *good shepherd.* M. Guigniaut says, there is a third Guatama, the founder of the philosophy Nyaya. I ask, may not this be the philosophy of a certain sect, which in its ceremonies chaunts in honour of Cristna the word IEYE, in fact, the name of the Hebrew God *Ieue,* or *Jehovah* as we disguise it?[7] We know that names of persons in passing from one language into another, have often been surprisingly changed or disguised; but there is in reality no change here; it is the identical name.

This is one of thousands of instances where the identity of the Eastern and the Western names is not perceptible, unless recourse be had to the sixteen-letter system, which I have exhibited in my Celtic Druids; and here I must stop to make an observation on the identity of languages. I do not consider the identity of common names, though it is not to be neglected, as of half so much consequence as the identity of proper names. I think no person who has made himself master of my doctrine respecting the ancient system of sixteen original letters, can help seeing here the identity of the IEYE and the *Ieue* of the Hebrews, nor can at the same time help seeing its great importance, in diving to the bottom of the ancient mythologies. The two words are identical; but write the Hebrew word in the common way *Jehovah,* and the truth is instantly lost. It matters not how they are pronounced in modern times; when they were originally written with the same letters, they must have been the same in sound.—Iaya-dèva is said to have been a very celebrated poet, but we see he had the name of one of the Hindoo Deities. From the practice of calling their distinguished personages by the names of their Gods and Goddesses, the confusion in their history is irremediable. Iayadevi was the wife of Jina, one of the incarnations of Vishnu.[8]

---

[1] Ratramn. de Nat. Christ. Cap. iii. ap. Fab. Pag. Idol. B. iv. Ch. v. p. 432.
[2] Hist. des Huns, Tome I. Part ii. p. 224.     [3] Hieron. in Jovinianum.
[4] De Paw, Recherches sur les Egyptians, Vol. II.     [5] Moore's Pantheon, p. 234.
[6] Moore's Pantheon, p. 235, and Asiatic Res. Vol. III. art. 13, also Vol. IX.
[7] See Maur. Hist. Hind. Vol. II. p. 339, ed. 4to.     [8] Moore's Panth. p. 235.

One cannot reflect for a moment upon the histories of the different Avatars of India, without being struck with the apparent contradiction of one part to the other. Thus Cristna is the Sun, yet he is Apollo. He is Bala Rama, and yet Bala Cristna. He is also Narayana floating on the waters. Again, he is Vishnu himself, and an incarnation of Vishnu. He is also Parvati, the Indian Venus. In short, he is every incarnation. All this is precisely as it ought to be, if my theory be correct. He is an Avatar or renewed incarnation, in every case, of the sun, or of that higher principle of which the sun is an emblem—of that higher principle which Moses adored when he fell down upon his face to the blazing bush. The adoration of the solar fire, as the emblem of the First Great Cause, is the master-key to unlock every door, to lay open every mystery.

Buddha may be seen in the India House with a glory round his head. This I consider of great consequence. The glory round the head of Jesus Christ is always descriptive of his character, as an incarnation of that Higher Power of which the sun is himself the emblem, or the manifestation.

There were thousands of incarnations, but those were all portions of the divinity. Emanations, perhaps they may be called, in vulgar language, from the Divine Mind, inspired into a human being. But Cristna, as the Brahmins hold, was one of the three persons of their Trinity, Vishnu himself incarnated; he was the second person of their Trinity, become man. Inspired or inspirated might be said to be the same as *incarnated ;* this was exactly the same as the Christian doctrine. We have many inspired persons, but Jesus is held to be God himself incarnated—the Logos, one of the three, incarnated.—To return to my subject.

Buddha passed his infancy in innocent sports ; and yet he is often described as an artificer. In his manhood he had severe contests with wicked spirits, and finally he was put to death, we shall find, by *crucifixion,* [1] descended into hell, and re-ascended into heaven. The present sect of the Brahmins hold Buddha to have been a wicked impostor ; therefore, we need not expect them to say any thing favourable of him ; but I can entertain no doubt that he was the same kind of incarnation as Cristna.

In my *Celtic Druids* I have observed, that the word Creeshna, of the old Irish, means the Sun. Now, in the Collectanea of Ouseley, [2] we find Budh, Buth, Both, fire, the sun ; *Buide lachd,* the great fire of the Druids. We also find in Vallancey's ancient Irish history, that they brought over from the East the worship of *Budh-dearg,* or king Budh, *who was* OF THE FAMILY OF SACA-SA, or *bonus Saca.* In the Hindoo Chronology there is a Buddha Muni, who descended in the family of Sacya: and one of his titles was *Arca-bandu,* or Kinsman of the Sun. If my reader will look back a little, and observe that the Hindoo Budhh was of the family of SAKYA, he will, I think, believe with me that here we have the Hindoo Buddha in Ireland. It is impossible to be denied. How contemptible does it make our learned priests appear, who affect to despise facts of this kind, and to consider the learning wherein they are contained, beneath their notice ! But they do *not* despise them ; they hate them and fear them. They feel conscious that they prove a state of the world once to have existed, which shakes to their foundations numbers of their non-sensical dogmas, and, with them, their gorgeous hierarchies.

In the above extract General Vallancey calls *Saca*-SA, bonus Saca. I dare say it means bonus,

---

[1] Neither in the sixteen volumes of the Transactions of the Asiatic Society of Calcutta, nor in the works of Sir W. Jones, nor in those of Mr. Maurice, nor of Mr. Faber, is there a single word to be met with respecting the crucifixion of Cristna. *How very extraordinary that all the writers in these works should have been ignorant of so striking a fact !* But it was well known in the Conclave, even as early as the time of Jerom.

[2] Vol. III. No. I.

but it means also, I think, the same as the Greek word Σα, from Σαω *to save*, or the Hebrew word יש *iso*, and means *Saviour*.

The Arca-bandhu, above-mentioned, is the same as the word Nau-banda, and has the same meaning, as well as that of *Kinsman of the Sun*, if Arca-bandu have that meaning; ארג *arg*, in Chaldee, means ship. Of the probability of this, we shall be better able to judge hereafter.

M. Matter has made a very correct observation (as we proceed in our inquiries, every new page will produce some additional proofs of its truth); he says, L'Antiquité vraiment dévoilé, nous offrirait peut-être une unité de vues, et une liaison de croyances, que les temps modernes auraient peine à comprendre.[1] This was the doctrine of the learned Ammonias Saccas, of which I shall treat hereafter.

7. The farther back we go in history the more simple we find the icons of the Gods, until at last, in Italy, Greece, and Egypt, we arrivé at a time when there were *no icons* of them. And from this circumstance, which seems to have been applicable to all nations, I draw a conclusion favourable to the superior antiquity of the Buddhist worship. For Buddha is never seen in the *old temples*, where his worship alone prevails, but in one figure, and that of extreme simplicity. And in many temples about Cabul, known to be Buddhist, there are no images at all. In this case they can only be known by tradition.

The stone circles, and the ruins at Dipaldinna,[2] are undoubtedly among the most ancient in India. They are evidently not Brahminical, but Buddhist or Jain. The execution of them may well compete with the works of the most skilful of the Greeks. The drawings which Colonel Mackenzie employed the natives to execute, are very beautifully done, but in many instances a close comparison with the originals at the India House will shew, that they by no means equal them. In these works none of the unnatural monsters, with numerous heads or arms, which we see in the *later* works of the Brahmins or Buddhists, are to be found. These facts seem to shew, that in the most remote periods of Indian history, good taste, as well as skill, prevailed—circum- ε .es which are very worthy of observation.

Though in these drawings, by Col. Mackenzie, of sculptures, at Dipaldinna, near Amrawatty, which are most beautifully executed, no example of a monstrous figure will be found—a figure with three or four heads—yet the Linga and Yoni are every where to be seen as well as the favourite Cobra Capella, shielding or covering its favourite God with its hood.

The images of Buddha can be considered only as figures of incarnations, of a portion of the Supreme Being; in fact, of human beings, filled with divine inspiration; and thus partaking the double quality of God and man. No image of the supreme Brahm himself is ever made; but in place of it, his attributes are arranged, as in the temple of *Gharipuri*, thus:

| BRAMA | POWER | CREATION | MATTER | THE PAST | Earth. |
|-------|-------|----------|--------|----------|--------|
| WISHNU | WISDOM | PRESERVATION | SPIRIT | THE PRESENT | Water. |
| SIVA | JUSTICE | DESTRUCTION | TIME | THE FUTURE | Fire. |

Thus each *triad* was called the Creator. In the last of these divisions we find the Trinity ascribed to Plato, which I have noticed in B. I. Ch. II. Sect. 4. We see here whence the Greeks have obtained it, and as was very common with them, they misunderstood it,[3] and took a mere figurative, or analogical, expression of the doctrine, for the doctrine itself. Probably the Earth, fire, water, might be given to the canaille, by Plato, to deceive them, as it has done some moderns, to whose superstition its grossness was suitable.

---

[1] Matter sur les Gnostiques, Vol. II. p. 205.
[3] Moore's Panth. p. 242.

[2] Mackenzie's Collection in the India House.

8. The figure in the plates numbered 8, descriptive of Buddha or Cristna, is given by Mons. Creuzer. The following is the account given of this plate by Mons. Guigniaut:[1] Crichna 8e avatar ou incarnation de *Vichnou*, sous la figure d'un enfant, allaité par *Devaki*, sa mère, et recevant des offrandes de fruits; près de là est un groupe d'animaux rassemblés dans une espèce d'arche. La tête de l'enfant-dieu, *noir*, comme indique son nom, est ceinte d'une auréole aussi bien que celle de sa mère. *On peut voir encore, dans cette belle peinture, Buddha sur le sein de Maya.*[2]

M. Creuzer observes that the images of Cristna and Buddha are so similar, that it is difficult to distinguish them; and the groupe pictured above is acknowledged by Moore, in his Hindoo Pantheon, to be applicable to Buddha on the knee of his beautiful mother Maya.[3] But yet there is one circumstance of very great importance which is peculiar to Buddha, and forms a discriminating mark between him and Cristna, which is, that he is continually described as a Negro, not only with a black complexion, in which he agrees with Cristna, but with woolly hair and flat face. M. Creuzer observes, that the black Buddha, with frizzled or curled hair, attaches himself at the same time to the three systems into which the religion of India divides itself.

9. Mr. Moore, on his woolly head, says, " Some statues of Buddha certainly exhibit thick " Ethiopian lips;[4] but all woolly hair : there is something mysterious, and unexplained, connected " with the hair of this, and only of this, Indian deity. The fact of so many different tales having " been invented to account for his crisped, woolly head, is alone sufficient to excite suspicion, that " there is something to conceal—something to be ashamed of; more than meets the eye."[5]

The reason why Buddha is a Negro, at least in the very old icons, I trust I shall be able to explain in a satisfactory manner hereafter. The Brahmins form a species of corporation, a sacerdotal aristocracy, possessing great privileges ; but the Buddhists have a regular hierarchy; they form a state within a state, or a spiritual monarchy at the side of a temporal one. " They have their " cloisters, their monastic life, and a religious rule. Their monks form a priesthood numerous and " powerful, and they place their first great founder at their head as the sacred depositary of their " faith, which is transmitted by this spiritual prince, who is supported by the contributions of the " faithful, from generation to generation, similar to that of the Lamas of Thibet." M. Creuzer might have said, not *similar to*, but *identical with* the Lama himself; who, like the Pope of Rome, is God on Earth, at the head of all, a title which the latter formerly assumed. Indeed the close similarity between the two is quite wonderful to those who do not understand it.

The monks and nuns of the Buddhists, here noticed by M. Creuzer, take the three cardinal vows

---

[1] 61, xiii.

[2] Of the two trays which are placed by the figure with the infant, one contains boxes, part of them exactly similar to the frankincense boxes now used in the Romish churches, and others such as might be expected to hold offerings of Myrrh or Gold. The second contains cows, sheep, cattle, and other animals. If my reader has ever seen the exhibition of the nativity in the church of the Ara Cœli at Rome, on Christmas-day, he will recollect the sheep, cows, &c., &c., which stand around the Virgin and Child. It is an exact icon of this picture. Hundreds of pictures of the Mother and Child, almost exact copies of this picture, are to be seen in Italy and many other Romish countries.

[3] Col. Tod says, Dare we attempt to lift the veil from this mystery, and trace from the seat of redemption of lost science its original source? This, I answer my good, learned, and philanthropic friend, I only have done. The allegory of Cristna's Eagle pursuing the Serpent Buddha, and recovering the books of science and religion with which he fled, is an historical fact disguised. True! and its meaning is so clear, it requires no explanation. In the Cave at Gaya, which means the Cave or Gaia or the Earth, it is written—*Heri who is Buddha.* Here the Col. says, that Cristna and Buddha, in characters, are conjoined. This is true, and they mean, Buddha who is Heri, and Heri who is Buddha. —Hist. Rajapoutana, p. 537.

[4] The lips are often tinged with red to shew that the blackness does not arise from the colour of the bronze or stone of which the image is made, but that black is the colour of the God.

[5] Moore's Pantheon, p. 232.

of *poverty, chastity, and obedience,*—the same as the monks and nuns of the European Christians. This singular fact at once proves the identity of the orders in the two communities, and that they must have had a common origin.   I know not any circumstance of consequence in their economy in which they differ.

Maya is called the great mother, the universal mother.   She is called Devi, or the Goddess παρ᾿ εξοχην—the Grand Bhavani, the mother of gods and of men.   She is the mother of the *Trimurti,* or the being called the Creator, Preserver, and Destroyer, whom she conceived by Brahm : and when the Brahmins can get no farther in their mystics, they finish by calling her *Illusion.* Perhaps they had better have said, *Delusion,* which is the very point arrived at by Bishop Berkeley, in his metaphysics.   Plate VI. of Creuzer's work represents Maia receiving the adoration of the other divinities.   On the top of the building appear the Beeve, and, at the side of it, the Yoni and Lingha, in union.   The Burmese make Maria, or Maha-Maria, the mother of their God Somon-Codom, who was Buddha. [1]

10. A certain order of persons called Samaneans are noticed by Porphyry and Clemens Alexandrinus. I do not doubt that these are the Somonokodomites of Siam, and the Buddha called by them their leader—to be the Buddha of Siam, who, as Surya with the seven heads, is the sun and the seven planets.   This Mons. Guigniaut, in his note, by a curious etymological process, has proved. [2]   And that this Buddha was of very remote date is also proved by the fact noticed by Guigniaut, that he is identical with Osiris and the Hermes of Egypt.   " L'Hermes d'Egypte, appelé encore Thoth " ou Thaut, a tous ses charactères, et se retrouvé à la fois dans les cieux, sur la terre, et aux enfers : " l'Hermes ou Mercure des Grecs et des Latins *est fils de Maya comme Buddha.*   Nous pourions " pousser beaucoup plus loin ces rapprochemens." [3]   Learned men have endeavoured to make out several Buddhas as they have done several Herculeses, &c. [4]   They were both very numerous, but at last there was only one of each, and that one the sun.   And from this I account for the striking similarity of many of the facts stated of Buddha and Cristna.   What was suitable to the sun in Taurus, would, for the most part, be suitable to him in Aries, and it was probably about this change that a great war took place between the followers of Buddha and Cristna, when ultimately the Buddists were expelled from Lower India.   This was the war of the Maha-barata.   Maha means *great,* and Barata is the Hebrew ברא *bra* and בראת *brat,* and means Creator or Regenerator. This, I have no doubt, was the meaning of this proper name, in the old language.   What meaning the Brahmins may give to it, in their beautiful, ARTIFICIAL Sanscrit, I do not know.   All the proper names of gods, men, and places, will be found, if we could get to the bottom of them, in the Hebrew.   On this I must request my Sanscrit reader to suspend his judgment till I treat of the Sanscrit language.

Porphyry, in his treatise on *Abstinence,* gives a very good description of the Brahmins and Samaneans, [5] from which it appears that the latter had precisely the same monastic regulations in his time, that they have at this day.

The Hermes of Egypt, or Buddha, was well known to the ancient Canaanites, who had a temple to הרם *erm,* " *The Projector,* by which they seem to have meant the *material spirit,* or rather " *heavens,* considered as *projecting, impelling,* and *pushing forwards,* the planetary bodies in their " courses." [6]   Notwithstanding the nonsense about *material spirit* or *heavens,* the Hermes, or Buddha, is very apparent.

---

[1] La Loubère, P. iii. p. 136.
Hesychius says, that Μαι, μεγα, and Maha, had the meaning of great, and Μαι has the meaning of *great* in modern Coptic.  Asiat. Res. Vol. III. p. 415.
[2] Vol. I. p. 292.                    [3] Ibid.                    [4] See the Desatir, published at Bombay, in 1818.
[5] De Abs. Lib. iv. Sect. xvii.                    [6] Parkhurst, Lex. in voce רמה *rme.*

The different Bu, ddbasCristnas, Ramas, &c., are only different incarnations of the same being. The want of attention to this has caused great and unnecessary confusion.  In the Samaneans and Buddha of Porphyry and Clemens, we have a proof that the doctrines of Buddhism were common in their day.

These Samaneans were great travellers, and makers of proselytes ; and by this means we readily account for the way in which the oriental doctrines came to be mixed up with the history of Jesus, by such collectors of traditions as Papias, Irenæus, &c.  These writers made prize of every idle superstition they found, provided they could, by any means, mix it up with the history and doctrines of Jesus of Nazareth, as I shall abundantly prove in the second part of this work.

" Both Cyril and Clemens Alexandrinus [1] agree in telling us, that the Samaneans were the sa-" cerdotal order both in Bactria and in Persia.   But the Samaneans were the priests of Saman or " Buddha, and it is well known that the sacerdotal class of Bactria and Persia were the Magi : " therefore the Magi and the Samaneans must have been the same, and consequently Buddha, or " Maga, or Saman, must have been venerated in those regions.  With this conclusion, the my-" thologic history of the Zend-avesta will be found in perfect accordance.  The name of the most " ancient Bull, that was united with the first man Key-Umurth, is said to have been *Aboudad*. " But *Aboudad*, like the *Abbuto* of the Japanese, is plainly nothing more than *Ab-Boud-dat*, or " father *Buddh-Datta*." [2]  But this is not the only proof of the Buddhism of the Persians.  According to the Desatir of Moshani, Maha-bad, i. e. the great Buddha, was the first king of Persia and of the whole world, and the same as the triplasian Mithras. [3]

Buddha has his three characters, the same as Brahma, which produced three sects, like those of the Brahmins—that of Buddha or Gautama, that of Jana or Jina, and that of Arhan or Mahiman. [4] I think in the last of these titles may be found the Abriman or the Ma-Ahriman, the destroyer, of Persia.  But Buddha is allowed by the Brahmins to have been an incarnation of Vishnu, or to be identified with Brahma, Vishnu, and Siva, and like them he was venerated under the name OM.

Colonel Franklin (p. 5) says, " The learned Maurice entertains no doubt that the elder Boodh " of India is no other than the elder Hermes Trismegistus of Egypt, and that that original cha-" racter is of antediluvian race ; here then is an analogy amounting almost to positive and irre-" fragable conviction ; for Boodh and Jeyne are known throughout Hindostan, with very little " exception, to be one and the same personage."  In p. 41, Colonel Franklin remarks, that Bacchus agrees in his attributes with the Indian Boodh.  And Mr. Faber observes, " that THOR is " represented as the first-born of the Supreme God, and is styled in the Edda ' the eldest of " Sons.' [5]   He was esteemed in Scandinavia as a middle divinity, a *mediator* between God and " man." [6]

Colonel Franklin (p. 99) speaks of " Jeyne Ishura, or Jeyne the preserver and guardian of " mankind."  Here is the Indian Osiris as preserver, or saviour, from the same root as the Hebrew יש iso, to save.

Buddha in Egypt was called *Hermes Trismegistus ;* Lycophron calls him *Tricephalus*.  This speaks for itself, as we have seen that *Buddha* is identified with *Brahma, Vishnu, and Siva*.

---

[1] Clemens Alexandrinus in particular states that the Samaneans were the priests of the Bactrians.  Strom Lib. i. p. 305; Faber, Pag. Idol. B. iv. Ch. v. p. 235.

[2] Faber, Pag. Idol. B. iv. Ch. v. p. 353.          [3] Ibid.          [4] Ibid. p. 349.

[5] Faber, Horæ Mosaicæ, Vol. I.

[6] Franklin's Res. p. 49.  Brahma is generally in the neuter gender.  But as Vishnu or Narayen he is masculine, as he is also when he is considered as the Creator.  Asiat. Res. Vol. I. pp. 242, 243 ; Collier, Sect. iv.

Mr. Moore says, " Most, if not all, of the Gods of the Hindoo Pantheon, will, on close investi-
" gation, resolve themselves into the three *powers*, and those powers into one Deity, Brahm, typi-
" fied by the sun." [1]   Again, " In Hindu mythology every thing is indeed the Sun." Nothing
can be more true. Mr. Moore adds, " We may here, as usual with all Hindu deities, trace
" Kama's genealogy upwards to the sun, who is Brahm." [2]

It is admitted that Surya is the Sun, and that he is Buddha : hence Buddha is the sun.  He is
described with seven heads.  Here he is the sun, attended by five planets and the moon.  At
other times, he is described sleeping on a coiled serpent with seven heads, overshadowing and
protecting him, his and the serpent's heads making eight.  The first is a mythos probably adopted
before the earth was discovered to be a planet, like the other five, which were only called שמים
*smim*, or disposers, the angels or messengers of God.

11. About the city of Bamiam, in the kingdom of Cabul, are many caves of immense size without
any sculptures.  The formation of these caves is attributed, by tradition, to the Buddhists.  They
are in ancient Persia, not far from Balch.  The city has been of very great size, and has been
compared to Thebes in Egypt.  It is called in Sanscrit Vami-Nagari, or the beautiful city.  The
Buddhist caves, *without image* or sculpture, seem to bespeak the most remote period.  In the
oldest of the caves in India, those of Ellora, Salcette, Elephanta, the sculptures attest the identity
of Buddha with Cristna.  In most of the temples, of which the architecture bespeaks a more recent date, nothing is found relating to Buddha, but he is found in the temple of Jaggernaut, where
there is no distinction of castes or sects.  The date of these temples is generally totally unknown.
The colossal Bull in front of that at Jaggernaut evidently betrays Buddhism.

These circumstances confirm the hypothesis that Buddhism was the first religion, and I shall
hereafter prove that the religion of Cristna was engrafted into it, when the festival was changed
from Taurus to Aries.

Colonel Franklin says, " That as the figures in the caves at Cabul all bear the stamp of an
" Indian origin, we may justly ascribe them to the votaries of Boodh, who has already been identi-
" fied with the Mithras of Persia." [3]

M. Creuzer has observed, that the doctrines of Buddha are said to have come to India from the
north.  Of this I have no doubt.  I think that the place of his birth was in a far higher latitude
than either that of Upper Egypt, or of Lower India—in a latitude where the month of Maia, his
mother, would be the month of flowers and delight.  This would be the case in Northern Thibet,
or in a climate very similar to it, but not in a climate where, in the month of May, all verdure was
withering away by the excess of the heat, and the ground fast reducing to a parched desert.

Buddha is stated by Sir W. Jones to be *Woden*, and not a native of India. [4]   But it is remarkable, that *Woden* is his Tamul name, and the Tamulese are now in South India.  This will be found
of importance hereafter.

Mons. Guigniaut, in his notes on Creuzer, has very justly observed that the earliest notice we
have of the Persian religion has come from the north, from the ancient Aria or Balch, the ancient
Bactriana.  He says, " Nous avons déjà parlé des temples souterrains de Bamiam, à quelque
" distance de Caboul.  Ici la Perse et l'Inde, Hom et Brahma, *Bouddha et Zoroaster, semblent se
" donner la main.*" [5]   The doctrine of Buddha extends throughout China and its tributary nations ;
over the great empires and states of Cochin China, Cambodia, Siam, Pegu, Ava, Asam, Tibet,
Budtan ; many of the Tartar tribes, and, except Hindostan perhaps, generally all parts east of
the Ganges, including vast numbers of large and populous islands. [6]

---

[1] Pantheon, pp. 6, 16.                [4] Ibid. p. 447.                    [3] P. 113.
[4] Asiat. Res. Vol. II. 4to. p. 9.     [5] Creuzer, Vol. I. p. 677.          [6] Moore's Pantheon, p. 240.

The immense extent of country over which Buddhism prevails surely raises a strong presumption, that it was the root, and Cristnism a branch from it. M. Schegel has remarked, that in the temples of Buddha are to be found *all the Pantheon of the idols of India ;* not only their theogony, but their heroical mythology; the same mysticism which teaches man to unite himself by contemplation to the Deity ; and, that the chief difference between the Buddhists and Vishnuites consists in the former forbidding the shedding of blood either for sacrifice or food. But as Schegel justly observes, it is also considered to be a great virtue with the devotees of Vichnu to abstain from these practices. The Buddhists are allowed to have been at one time very numerous on this side the Ganges, but it is said they were exterminated or expelled. They are, however, beginning to reappear in the Djainas. M. Schegel says, " I know not in truth what difference one can " establish between the new sectaries and the Buddhists." [1] In the Transactions of the Asiatic Society [2] it is said, " The princes of the country continued Jains till the prince, in the time of " Pratap, turned to Vishnou." It is added, " the Buddists and Jains are the same."

12. The following copy, in Moore's Hindoo Pantheon, of an inscription which was found in Bengal, the very focus of the country of the Brahmins, is of itself, as its genuineness cannot be disputed, almost enough to prove the original identity of Cristna and Buddha. The address is said to be to the Supreme Being : " Reverence be unto thee in the form of Buddha : reverence be " unto thee, Lord of the earth : reverence be unto thee, an incarnation of the Deity, and the " eternal one : reverence be unto thee, O God ! in the form of the God of mercy : the dispeller " of pain and trouble : the Lord of all things : the Deity who overcomest the sins of the Kali " Yug : the guardian of the universe ; the emblem of mercy toward those who serve thee, OM ! " the possessor of all things in vital form. Thou art Brahma, Vishnu, and Mahesa ; [3] thou art " the Lord of the universe ; thou art the proper form of all things, moveable and immoveable ; " the possessor of the whole, and thus I adore thee ; reverence be unto thee, the bestower of " salvation : reverence be unto thee, (Kesava,) the destroyer of the evil spirit, Kesi.—O *Damor-* " *dara !* shew me favour. Thou art he who resteth upon the face of the milky ocean, and who " lieth upon the serpent Sesha." [4] Again, Mr. Moore says, " In Ceylon, the Singhalese have " traditions respecting Buddha, that, like the legends of Krishna, identify him with his prototype, " Vishnu." I think with Mr. Moore and Major Mahony, that the identity of Buddha and Vishnu is clearly made out. [5]

I have been asked if they be identical, how are we to account for the wars ? I answer, is not the religion of the Protestant and the Papist identical, that is, alike forms of Christianity ? Then, how are we to account for their wars ? As the wars of the West may be accounted for, so may those of the East.

In my last chapter I said, that the word OM was used exactly like our word Amen. In the above prayer is a proof of what I there advanced, with this only difference, that it was not spoken but meditated on, in profound silence, at the end of the distich or the prayer. The worship of Cristna has been proved to have been in existence, at the temple of Mutra or Maturea on the Jumna, in the time of Alexander the Great. This accords with what Mr. Franklin [6] has observed, that the Buddhist statues dug up around the ruins of old temples in *every* part of India, prove that the religion of the country was formerly that of Java, which is that of Buddha. He regrets that they have hitherto been treated with neglect. The name of the island Java, is clearly the

---

[1] In the Museum of the Asiatic Society is a Buddha with a Bull on the pedestal of the image. It is a Djain Buddha. No. X.

[2] P. 532.     [3] Is the Ma-hesa of Mr. Moore the MA or great-*hesus* of Gaul ? I believe so. But, nous verrons.

[4] Pp. 222, 224.     [5] Ib. p. 229.     [6] Researches on Bodhs and Jeynes, Ch. i.

island of Ieua, i. e. יהוה *ieue*. Mr. Franklin makes an observation which is new to me, that the ancient Etrurians had the countenances of Negroes, the same as the images of Buddha in India.[1]   This is very striking, when compared with the proofs which I have given in my CELTIC DRUIDS, Ch. II. Sect. xxv. Ap. p. 304, of the identity of the Sanscrit and the ancient language of Italy.   Cristna having been made out to be the sun, the consequence necessarily follows, that Buddha is the Sun ; and this easily and satisfactorily accounts for the similarity in the history of Cristna and of Buddha.   And all these circumstances are easily accounted for, if Buddha and Cristna were the Sun in Taurus and Aries.   In the quotation above, from Mons. Schegel, the second Hermes Trismegistus is alluded to.   In the sequel I shall shew that these alleged appearances of second persons of the same name were derived from a system of renewed incarnations, and of unceasing revolving cycles.

The elder Buddha being now admitted by all oriental scholars to have long preceded Cristna, I have no occasion to dwell longer on this subject.

## CHAPTER II.

CASSINI.   LUBÈRE.   CYCLES.—ISAIAH'S PROPHECY KNOWN TO THE EGYPTIANS AND THE CELTS OF GAUL.—
MYSTICAL MEANING OF THE LETTER M.—EXPLANATION OF THE ORIENTAL ASTRONOMICAL SYSTEMS.—
SUBJECT CONTINUED.   MR. BENTLEY.   BEROSUS.—MOSAIC AND HINDOO SYSTEMS.   VARIOUS PROPHECIES.
—MARTIANUS CAPELLA.   SUBJECT CONTINUED.

1. THE following observations of the very celebrated astronomer Cassini, made more than a hundred years ago, and extracted from La Loubère's History of Siam, will enable me to elicit several conclusions respecting the famous Neros, of the greatest importance.   As an astronomer, M. Cassini is in the first rank.   No one will deny that his calculations upon *acknowledged* or *admitted facts* are entitled to the highest respect.   I think they will enable me to point out the origin of many of the difficulties respecting Buddha and Cristna, and to explain them.   They will also enable me to shew the mode which was adopted by the early popes and other priests, in fixing the times of several of the most important Christian epochas ; as well as to exhibit the mode in which the Gods Buddha and Cristna have been regenerated.   These circumstances have either been unobserved, or they have been concealed from Europeans.   After a long discussion on the formation of the Siamese astronomical and civil epochas, in which, with profound learning, Cassini explains the process by which they have been formed, he says,

" The first lunisolar period, composed of whole ages, is that of 600 years, which is also com-
" posed of 31 periods of 19, and one of 11 years.   Though the chronologists speak not of this
" period, yet it is one of the ancientest that have been invented.

" Josephus,[2] speaking of the patriarchs that lived before the deluge, says, that ' *God prolonged*
" *their life, as well by reason of their virtue, as to afford them the means to perfect the sciences of*
" *geometry and astronomy, which they had invented: which they could not possibly do, if they had*

---

[1] Researches on Bodhs and Jeynes, p. 149.         [2] Antiq. Jud. Lib. i. Cap. iii.

" *lived less than* 600 *years, because that it is not till after the revolution of six ages, that the great*
" *year is accomplished.*'

" This great year, which is accomplished after six ages, whereof not any other author makes
" mention, can only be a period of lunisolar years, like to that which the Jews always used, and
" to that which the Indians do still make use of. Wherefore we have thought necessary to
" examine what this great year must be, according to the Indian rules.

" By the rules of the first section it is found, then, that in 600 years there are 7200 solar
" months; 7421 lunar months, and $\frac{11}{111}$. Here this little fraction must be neglected; because
" that the lunisolar years do end with the lunar months, being composed of entire lunar months.

" It is found by the rules of Section II., that 7421 lunar months do comprehend 219,146 days,
" 11 hours, 57 minutes, 52 seconds: if, therefore, we compose this period of whole days, it must
" consist of 219,146 days.

" 600 Gregorian years are alternatively of 219,145 days, and 219,146 days: they agree then to
" half a day with a solilunar period of 600 years, calculated according to the Indian rules.

" The second lunisolar period composed of ages, is that of 2300 years, which being joined to
" one of 600, makes a more exact period of 2900 years: and two periods of 2300 years, joined to
" a period of 600 years, do make a lunisolar period of 5200 years, which is the interval of the time
" which is reckoned, according to Eusebius's chronology, from the creation of the world to the
" vulgar Epocha of the years of Jesus Christ.

" These lunisolar periods, and the two epochas of the Indians, which we have examined, do
" point unto us, as with the finger, the admirable epocha of the years of Jesus Christ, which is
" removed from the first of these two Indian Epochas, a period of 600 years, wanting a period of
" 19 years, and which precedes the second by a period of 600 years, and two of 19 years. Thus
" the year of Jesus Christ (which is that of his incarnation and birth, according to the tradition of
" the church, and as Father Grandamy justifies it in his Christian chronology, and Father Riccio-
" lus in his reformed astronomy) is also an astronomical Epocha, in which, according to the mo-
" dern tables, the middle conjunction of the moon with the sun happened the 24th of March, ac-
" cording to the Julian form re-established a little after by Augustus, at one o'clock and a half in
" the morning, at the meridian of Jerusalem, the very day of the middle Equinox, a wednesday,
" which is the day of the creation of these two planets.

" The day following, March 25th, which, according to the ancient tradition of the church, re-
" ported by St. Augustine,[1] was the day of our Lord's incarnation, was likewise the day of the
" first phasis of the moon; and, consequently, it was the first day of the month, according to the
" usage of the Hebrews, and the first day of the sacred year, which, by the divine institution, must
" begin with the first month of the spring, and the first day of a great year, the natural epocha of
" which is the concourse of the middle equinox, and of the middle conjunction of the Moon with
" the Sun.

" This concourse terminates, therefore, the lunisolar periods of the preceding ages, and was an
" epocha from whence began a new order of ages, according to the oracle of the Sibyl, related by
" Virgil in these words (Eclog. iv.):

> Magnus ab integro sæclorum nascitur ordo;
> Jam nova progenies Cœlo dimittitur alto.

" This oracle seems to answer the prophecy of Isaiah, *Parvulus natus est nobis;* (ch. ix. 6 and 7;)
" where this new-born is called God and father of future ages; *Deus fortis, pater futuri sæculi.*

" The interpreters do remark in this prophecy, as a thing mysterious, the extraordinary situation

---

[1] De Trin. Lib. iv. Cap. v.

" of a *Mem* final (which is the numerical character of 600) in this word לסרבה *lmrbe, ad multipli-*
" *candum,* where this *Mem* final is in the second place, there being no other example in the whole
" text of the Holy Scripture where-ever a final letter is placed only at the end of the words.   This
" numerical character of 600 in this situation might allude to the periods of 600 years of the Pa-
" triarchs, which were to terminate at the accomplishment of the prophecy, which is the epocha,
" from whence we do at present compute the years of Jesus Christ." [1]

On this prophecy Mr. Faber says, " In this extraordinary poem, he (Virgil) celebrates the ex-
" pected birth of a wonderful child, who was destined to put an end to the age of iron, and to in-
" troduce a new age of gold, (precisely the idea of Isaiah).

" *The last period sung by the Sibylline prophetess, is now arrived ; and the grand series of ages,*
" THAT SERIES WHICH RECURS AGAIN AND AGAIN IN THE COURSE OF ONE MUNDANE REVOLUTION,
" *begins afresh.   Now the Virgin Astrea returns from heaven ; and the primæval reign of Saturn*
" *recommences ; now a new race descends from the celestial realms of holiness.   Do thou, Lucina,*
" *smile propitious on the birth of a boy, who will bring to a close the present age of iron, and intro-*
" *duce, throughout the whole world, a new age of gold.   Then shall the herds no longer dread the*
" *fury of the lion, nor shall the poison of the serpent any longer be formidable : every venomous ani-*
" *mal and every deleterious plant shall perish together.   The fields shall be yellow with corn, the*
" *grape shall hang in ruddy clusters from the bramble, and honey shall distil spontaneously from the*
" *rugged oak.   The universal globe shall enjoy the blessings of peace, secure under the mild sway of*
" *its new and divine sovereign.*" [2]

Many of our divines have been much astonished at the coincidence between the prophecy of the
heathen Sibyl and that of Isaiah ; the difficulty I flatter myself I shall now be able to remove, by
shewing that it related to the system of cycles, which Mons. Cassini detected in the Siamese manuscript.

I shall now proceed to prove that the period of 600 years, or the Neros alluded to by Cassini,
which has been well described by the most celebrated astronomers as the finest period that ever
was invented, and which Josephus says was handed down from the patriarchs who lived before
the flood, is the foundation of the astronomical periods of the Indians, and is probably the age or
mundane revolution alluded to by Virgil.   On the subject of this fine cycle, and the important
consequences deduced by Mons. Bailly from the knowledge of it by the ancients, my Celtic Druids
may be consulted.   There my reader will see proofs that it was probably the invention of a period
long prior to any thing which we have been accustomed to contemplate as founded on historical
records.

In Sect. III. M. Cassini has shewn that there was among the Siamese a very important epocha
in the year 544 before Christ.   This is the æra fixed for the second Buddha according to the
Brahmins.   He has also pointed out another epocha, 638 years after the birth of Jesus Christ ;
these my reader will please to retain in recollection.   The æra of Buddha is calculated from his
death, that of Christ from his birth, and this should always be remembered.

The following observations shew Mons. Cassini was of opinion, that these Siamese periods had
some connexion with Pythagoras ; he says,

" This Siamese Epocha (of 543 or 544 B. C.) is in the time of Pythagoras, whose dogmata were
" conformable to those which the Indians have at present, and which these people had already in
" the time of Alexander the Great, as Onesicritus, sent by Alexander himself to treat with the In-
" dian philosophers, testified unto them, according to the report of Strabo, Lib. xv." [3]   Cassini

---

[1] La Loubère, Hist. Siam, Tome II. Sect. xxii. and xxiii.           [2] Pagan Idol. Vol. II. p. 10.
[3] La Loub. Cass. Tome II. p. 203.

has shewn [1] why the above-named epocha ought to be 543 and not 544, [2] (his reasons it is not ne-cessary for me to repeat,) then, if we add 543 to the second period 638, we shall have the space of 1181 years between them ; if we add to which the period 19, we shall have exactly 1200, which makes two Neroses. Cassini says, " Between the two Indian epochas there is a period of 1181 " years, which being joined to a period of 19 years, there are two periods of 600 years, which re-" duce the new moons near the equinoxes." [3]

Lalande, in his Astronomie, [4] says, " Si l'on emploie la durée de l'annee que nous connoissons " et le mois Sinodique tel que nous l'avons indiqué ci-devant, c'est-a-dire, des mois de 29 jours " 12 heures 44 min. 3 sec. chacun, on aura 28 heures, 1 min., 42 sec. de trop, dans les sept mille, " quatre cent, vingt-une lunaissons : ainsi la lune retarderoit de plus d'un jour au bout de six " cents ans."

I notice this, here, that a reader learned in astronomy may not suppose me ignorant of it, or that I have overlooked it. In mythological calculations for short periods, small errors like this can be of little consequence. In a future book of this work, I shall shew that, at last, a very im-portant consequence arose from this error ; and I flatter myself that I shall be able, by its means, to explain a part of the ancient mythology, beyond all question the most curious and important of the whole.

2. The prophecy of Isaiah alluded to by Cassini had reference in the first place to a new cycle, which may be called the cycle of Cyrus, because in Isaiah he is described by name. It probably began about the captivity. The date of it professes to be some time before that cycle of 600 years, which cycle preceded the birth of Christ ; which birth ought to be precisely at the end of the cycle above-named, in which the 543 years before Christ are spoken of. It is evident that this prophecy of the cycle of Cyrus would, in a considerable degree, apply to every succeeding cycle of the Neros. In the same manner I shall shew that the prophecies of Cristna and Buddha will be found to apply to their re-appearances.

The prophecy of Isaiah may be said to have been a mystery, an example of judicial astrology. It required no divine inspiration to prove to the initiated, that, at the end of the cycle then run-ning, a new cycle would commence, or that the cycle of the God Cristna, the Sun, would be born again : and this leads us to a discovery which will account for and remove many of the difficulties which our learned men have encountered respecting Buddha and Cristna. It is evident that both of them being the sun, mystically and astrologically speaking, their year was 600 years long, and their birthday on the first year of the 600, on which was a conjunction of sun and moon at the vernal equinox. The day of the first birth of Buddha was at the vernal equinox of that 600 when the sun entered Taurus, of Cristna of that 600 nearest to the time when he entered Aries. The birthdays of both returned every 600 years—when the Phën or Phenishe or Phœnix was con-sumed on the altar of the temple of the sun at Heliopolis, in Egypt, and rose from its ashes to new life. This, I think, seems to have been purely astrological.

At first many persons will be greatly surprised at the assertion, that the passages of Isaiah, ch. vii. 14, viii. 8, are not prophecies of Christ. In order to force the text of Isaiah to serve this

---

[1] Sect. xix. p. 219.      [2] Vide Asiat. Res. Vol. VI. p. 266. 8vo.
[3] The Brahmins were acquainted with the Cycle of 19 years. Crawfurd says, " It is curious to find at Siam the " knowledge of that Cycle, of which the invention was thought to do so much honour to the Athenian astronomer " Meton, and which makes so great a figure in our modern calendars." Researches, Vol. II. p. 18. The Siamese had the Metonic cycle more correctly than Numa, Meton, or Calippus, and the Epact also more correct than the French in the time of Cassini. Cassini, p. 213. M. Bailli observed that the Chinese, the Indians, the Chaldeans, and the Egyptians, all had the same astronomical formulæ for the calculation of eclipses, though the principles of them were forgotten. Faber, Pag. Idol. Vol. I. p. 37.
[4] Tome II. Art. 1570, ed. 3.

z

purpose, Clemens of Alexandria, Bishop Kidder, Dr. Nicholls, Bishop Chandler, Dr. Campbell, and many others, have been obliged to suppose that God inspired the author to use a double sense, and that the predictions related both to the prophet's son, born about the time when these were written, and to Christ, born many hundred years afterward. These learned men do not seem ever to have thought either of the unworthiness of the motive which they attribute to the Deity by this deceit, or of the gross absurdity of making the prophecy of Christ, who was to be born so many hundred years afterward, a sign to the people then living. However, the monstrous absurdity of this double sense has been refuted by Dr. Sykes, Dr. Benson, Bishop Marsh, and others; and Dr. Ekerman, and Dr. George S. Clarke, in his Hebrew Criticism and Poetry, Lond. 1810, maintain that the Old Testament contains no prophecy at all which literally relates to the person of Christ.[1]

Again, Dr. Adam Clarke maintains, that the prophecy of Isaiah—*A virgin* [2] *shall conceive and bear a son, and call his name Immanuel*, does not mean Christ.[3]

Dr. Clarke says, " It is humbly apprehended that the young woman usually called the Virgin is " the same with the prophetess, [4] and Immanuel is to be named by his mother, the same with the " prophet's son, whom he was ordered to name Maher-shalal-hash-baz." [5]

I think no one will deny that Dr. Adam Clarke, the annotator on the Bible, is a very learned man, and he is here an unwilling witness, and he comes to this conclusion in the teeth of all the prejudices of his education, after having read all the laboured attempts of our divines to make the prophecy of Isaiah a prophecy relating to Jesus Christ. I maintain then, that this fairly opens the door to the explanation which I shall now give, and which, I think, will be considered probable, when I shew that many other expressions of Isaiah are the same with the Hindoo doctrines and predictions. At all events, with every person whose understanding is not quite dwarfified by superstition, there is an end of the belief in what has been called the prophecy of Isaiah, as a necessary article of faith. The Hebrew for Immanuel is עמנואל *omnual*, which may certainly be rendered *with us God*. But it might also be rendered by OM OUR GOD, the word Om being the first syllable of the name of Ammon, the surname of Jupiter Ammon, of the Ἱερον Ομανε, and of the Ammonites, ch. viii. 8,—" And the stretching out of his wings shall fill the breadth of thy land, O " Immanuel, or *God with us*," or the land of thee, Om our God—the A. U. M. or Om of India.

I can entertain little doubt that this prophecy was well known to the Gauls or Celts and Druids, long before the time of Christ, as is made sufficiently evident by an inscription VIRGINI PARITURÆ, which was found at Chartres upon a *black* image of Isis. This image was made by one of their kings, and the Rev. M. Langevin says it was existing in his day, about 1792.[6] They are almost the words of Isaiah, and Mons. Langevin says, were inscribed one hundred years before the birth of Christ. Along with the statue of Isis was a boat, which M. Langevin says was the symbol under which this Goddess was adored. This was the Argha of India, of which I shall treat hereafter.

---

[1] Class. Journal, Vol. XXXIII. p. 47.

I beg leave to ask the candid reader, if one can be found, how he can expect unlearned persons to pay any attention to these prophecies, as they are called, when some of the most learned divines, much against their inclinations, are obliged to confess that they are no such thing? One fact, however, this clearly proves, that no man can be expected, by a merciful God, under pain of punishment, to believe subjects involved in so much difficulty.

[2] The word *virgin* here is, in the Hebrew, עלמה *olme*, and is preceded by the emphatic article ה *e*, therefore of course it means THE not A virgin. In the Phœnician, Bochart says, עלמא *olma* signifies virgin. This is evidently the same word, the celestial virgin, the Alma Venus of Lucretius, and the Brahme-Maia of India, or the Virgin Astrea, alluded to by Virgil.

[3] Class. Journ. Vol. IV. p. 169, of No. VI. and No. VII.      [4] Chap. viii. 3.

[5] Class. Journ. Vol. I. p. 637. בו *be* שש *hs* שלל *sll* מחר *mer*. I cannot for a moment believe that the REAL, that is, the secret, meaning of these words is, *prædam acceleravit spolium festinando*.

[6] Recherches Hist. sur Falaise, par Langevin, prêtre.

This prophecy, which our divines have been so eager to make apply to Jesus Christ, was known also to the Egyptians and Greeks, as well as to the Hindoos and Jews. This fact strongly supports my rendering, and that it related to their sacred *Om*.[1]

Singular as my reader may imagine it to be that Isaiah should allude to the Om of India, he will not think it so very paradoxical and singular, when he learns, that the history of Cyrus, who is prophesied of by name by Isaiah, is taken from a passage in the life of Cristna, from some history of whom Herodotus must have copied it. For the particulars of this the reader may refer to Mr. Maurice's History of Hindostan.[2] I beg him to reflect on this extraordinary fact before he proceeds. His utter inability to account for it he must confess.

The connexion noticed by Cassini between the prophecy of Isaiah, the oriental cycles, and the prophecy of the Sibyl in Virgil, has a strong tendency to confirm the explanation which I have given above of the word עמנואל *omnual* or Immanuel, used by Isaiah.

In addition to all this, in the course of the following work, when I treat of the Sibyls, I shall produce many very striking proofs of identity between the doctrines of Isaiah and those of the Orientalists. And I beg my reader to remember, what I have already proved, that all the learned ancients held that the sacred books had two meanings. He will also remember, that almost every thing is closely connected with judicial astrology.

3. The calculation of the age of the world before Christ, according to Eusebius, ending exactly with the Siamese cycle, is very curious. On the birth of Christ the Eastern astrologers, who, according to the two disputed chapters in Matthew and Luke, had calculated his nativity, came to Bethlehem, or the temple of Ceres, where Adonis or Adonai was adored, to make to him the solar offerings, as Isaiah, according to the same disputed chapters, had foretold. All this applies very well to the sun, to Cristna or Buddha, to Jesus of Bethlehem, but has nothing to do with Jesus of Nazareth. When the Irenæuses, Papiases, and early Popes, were intruding the disputed chapters of Matthew and Luke into their canon, they took all the remainder of the story to which these books alluded. The book of Isaiah might probably mislead them.[3]

The book of Isaiah has given much trouble, as already mentioned, to our divines. They have wanted it for a prophecy of Christ, while it *literally expresses* that it alludes to *Cyrus*,[4] and that it was for a sign to the prophet's contemporaries: in consequence, as I have just stated, they have been obliged to have recourse to *a double sense*. No doubt, in one point of view, the double sense is justified, as Isaiah's prediction relating to the cycle next coming would, in a considerable degree, apply to every new revolving cycle, as it arose. As a work of judicial astrology, it is indeed very probable that the prediction had a double sense, for that is strictly in conformity with the spirit of astrology or magic.

Our divines, depending on the very questionable authority of their chronology, will tell me, that Isaiah foretold Cyrus as a Messiah, before he was born. I say nothing of the ease with which these prophecies might be corrupted, a circumstance which we know, either less or more, has happened to every sacred writing in existence: but observe, that the word *Cyrus* is a solar epithet, that in fact it means the sun.[5] Isaiah must have been an unskilful astrologer or Chaldean if he could not

---

[1] See Celtic Druids, Ch. v. Sect. viii. p. 163, note.    [2] Vol. II. p. 478. Ed. 4to.

[3] As usual we find them laying their hands on every thing they found. Thus in Luke ii. 25—38, we have a story of Simeon, and of Anna, the daughter of Phanuel, which is a complete interloper. Why it is here no one can tell; but Phanuel is Phan or Phen-our-god, the cycle of the neros; vide Celtic Druids, App. pp. 307, 308; and of Anna, or the year, we shall see more by and by.

[4] Isaiah xlv. 1—4. The circumstance of Cyrus being *called by his name* is different from every other prophecy.

[5] Cyrus was called Cai Cosroe, the primitive of which is, *Coresh*, a Persian name for the Sun. Maur. Hist. Hind. Vol. II. p. 478.

foretell the time of a new incarnation of the sun. This solar epithet of honour given to the Persian conqueror, and the events of the incarnation, very well agree with the other part in the same prophecy, where OM *our God,* or the Hero or Messiah of the soli-lunar cycle, is foretold. Of the names of the earliest of the ancients we have scarcely one which has not been given on account of some supposed quality, or something in the life, of the bearers, which could only be known (except by divine inspiration) after their deaths. This must have been the case with the name of Cyrus. It was not till after he lived that he would be known to the world to deserve the solar title. I believe the name Pharaoh, of Egypt, was a similar solar title, meaning, in the Coptic, without vowels, $\Phi$ 500, P 100, H 8,=608.

In Usher's Chronology, the famous eclipse of the sun, which caused the battle between the Medes and Lydians to cease, and which was said to have been foretold by Thales, is placed exactly 601 years before Christ. I am well aware that the date of this eclipse has been a subject of much controversy. But the date of it being fixed by Usher, where, according to my theory it ought to be, is striking. In the same year the city of Nineveh is said to have been taken, and the Assyrian empire destroyed, as it was foretold in holy writ, and the Great Cyrus to have been born. These coincidences can scarcely have been the produce of accident. They are all closely connected with the sacred prophecies.

The case of the MEM final in the Hebrew word לםרבה *lmrhe,* the sign of 600, noticed by Cassini, leaves little room to doubt of the allusion. Secrets of this kind constitute sacred mysteries, cabala. I am by no means certain that there is not a secret religion in St. Peter's, not known perhaps to any persons but the Pope and Cardinals. I believe I am at this moment letting out their secrets. I beg leave to ask them if they have not in some of the Adyta of St. Peter's Church, a column or lithos of very *peculiar shape,* on which are ascribed the words Σευς Σωτηρ, or some words of nearly similar meaning? I have not seen it, but I have it on authority which I cannot doubt.

This Mem final was understood by Picus of Mirandula, who maintained that the closed ם Mem in Isaiah, taught us the reasons of the Paraclete coming after the Messiah. He [1] evidently understood that there was a secret concealed under this word of Isaiah. He was a man much celebrated for his learning in the antiquities of the Jews, and thus it appears that my idea, taken from M. Cassini, is no modern thought, but that a similar opinion respecting this word was held four hundred years ago, by a man who, of all others in modern times, was the most likely to understand it. [2] This, I hope, will justify me and Cassini against the charge of being fantastical.

In the celebrated history called The Gospel of the Infancy, which, I think it probable, was originally in Arabic, but of which there are some passages remaining in Greek, Jesus is said to have been sent to a school-master, to whom he explained the mystical meaning of the letters. This gospel was peculiarly the gospel of the Nestorians, and of the Christians of *St. Thomas on the coast of Malabar,* of whom I shall have to speak hereafter. This story is repeated in another Gospel, called the Gospel of St. Thomas, which is in Greek, and, for the reasons which the reader will see, was probably translated from Syriac, Hebrew, or Arabic. When the master taught Jesus the word Aleph, (the mystical meaning of which has been proved to be *the Trinity* by Chardin,) he pronounced the second letter, which is written in the Greek letters, but in the Hebrew language, Μπεϑ *Mpeth,* after which it is said, that he explained to his master the meaning of the prophets. Here we see the mystical ם *Mem,* or 600 of Isaiah, only written in Greek letters.

---

[1] Basnage, Hist. Jews, B. iii. Ch. xxiv. xxv.

[2] I recommend the perusal of the works of Picus to persons disposed to follow up my inquiries.

This was the explanation of the mystery of Isaiah, of the prophets. If the person translating this work from the Hebrew had given to the letters the Greek names *Alpha*, *Beta*, &c., the mystery would not have been contained in them; therefore he gave them in the Hebrew. Mr. J. Jones says, these Gospels were published in the beginning of the second century. They were received by the Manichæans, and the Gnostic sects, particularly that of the Marcosians (probably followers of Marcus). The Gnostics existed, as will be proved, not only before St. Paul, who wrote against them, but also before the Christian æra. [1]

It will be objected here, that in the Mpeth, and in several other instances, the Mem or Muin is not the Mem final, but the common Mem or Muin, which stands only for 40. The objection seems reasonable, but I think a great number of circumstances, which I shall produce in the course of this work, will satisfy my reader, that the mystical use of the M final was transferred to the common M, in the languages which had not an M final, and in which another letter was used for the number 600. I suspect that a regard for the sacred character of the M was the reason why the Greeks, in their language, never permitted a word to end with the letter M. Thus the superstition of the Hebrews caused them to use the Teth ט *t* and Vau ו *v* for 15, instead of the Jod י *i* and He ה *e*, the name of their God. This cannot be attributed to a custom with the Greeks of writing the Hebrew B by MP, because, had not the mystery been alluded to, it would have been written Beta. I am not ignorant that the Greeks wrote the double B by M P, as noticed by Georgius [2] and Dr. Clarke, in his Travels in Greece: but I suspect it arose from this sacred mystic practice getting into use among ignorant, uninitiated people.

When the chief priest placed his hands on the candidate for orders or for initiation into the priesthood, he *Samached* him, that is, he made the mark of the cross, or marked the candidate with the number or sign of 600. [3] This letter in the Hebrew means 60 and 600, (the two famous cycles of the Indians,) the Samach being, in fact, nothing but the M final.

*And Joshua the son of Nun was full of the spirit of* WISDOM; *for Moses* (סמך *smk*) *samached him, laying his hands upon him.* Deut. xxxiv. 9, χειροτονια.

The Mem final—the letter Samach—was adopted for the 600, because the cycles of 60 and 600 are, in reality, the same, or one a part of the other: they would equally serve the purposes of the calendar. If they reckoned by the Neros, there were 10 Neroses in 6000; if the reckoning was made by 60, there were 100 times that number in 6000 years. This we shall understand better presently. This explanation of the Samach completes what I have said respecting the X being the mark for 600, in my *Celtic Druids*, Ch. iv. Sect. ix.

In the Coptic language there is a very peculiar use of the letter M. Ptolomeos is there written Mptolomeos: on which Dr. Young says, "The prefix M of the Copts, which CANNOT BE TRANS-" LATED, is frequently found in the inscription, with the same indifference as to the sense." [4] Thus in the quotation above, from the Gospel of the Infancy, it is not written Beth or Peth, but M-Peth. The M is nothing but a sacred Monogram prefixed, and meaning precisely the same, as the + or X, which is found often prefixed to words and sentences in the writings of the dark ages. It is the Samach.

But M is the sign of the *passive* as well as of the *active* principle, that is, of the Maia. Thus it is the symbol of both; that is, of the Brahme-Maia; and this is the reason why we find this the Monogram of the Virgin upon the pedestal of the Goddess Multimammia, and of the Virgin Mary, with the Bambino, or black Christ, in her arms, as may be seen in many places in Italy.

---

[1] Jones on Canon, Vol. I. pp. 396, 433; Vol. II. p. 232.　　[3] Alp. Tib. Sect. vi.

[2] See *Celtic Druids*, Ch. iv. Sect. ix.

[4] Mus. Crit. Camb. No. VI. p. 172; Rud. of a Dict. of Hieroglyph. Pref.

The Hebrews and the Arabians had the same system of 28 letters for arithmetical figures; but, in order to place this *Mem* or *Muin* in the centre, the former dropped one letter. Thus we have this central letter on the figures of the Virgin, the female generative power; the allusion is plain enough.

The Momphta of Egypt, named by Plutarch, admitted by Kircher to be the passive principle of nature, is evidently nothing but the Om-tha or Om-thas, with the Mem final, the sign of 600, prefixed. The sun was the emblem of the active principle, the moon of the passive principle. Hence she was generally female, often called Isis, to which she was dedicated, and Magna Mater.[1]

The recurrence of the word Om, in the names of places in Egypt, and in Syria,[2] about Mount Sinai, is very remarkable, and raises strong ground for suspicion that it has a relation to the Om of India. We must remember that this Om is the Amen or sacred mystical word of the Bible, of the law given on Sinai.[3] It is also the word Omen—good or bad—which means prophecy.

4. Before I proceed to the following calculation, I must beg to observe, that whether the equinoxes preceded after the rate of 72 years to a degree, or something more or less, was a subject of great debate among the ancient, as it has been among modern, astronomers. But the rate of 72 has been finally determined to be sufficiently near for common mythological purposes, though not correctly true. I must also further premise that our received chronology, that is, Archbishop Usher's, which fixes the creation at 4004 years before Christ, is generally allowed to be in error 4 years, and that it ought to be only 4000. This was done in compliance with a settlement of it by Dionysius Exiguus, who fixed it to the end of the 4713th year of the Julian period. The REAL reason why this is allowed to be too late by our divines is, that it makes Christ to have been born after the death of Herod, who sought to kill him. And the REAL reason why Usher fixed it at 4004, instead of 4000 years, was a wish to avoid the very striking appearance of judicial astrology contained in the latter number.

There was a remarkable eclipse in March 4710 of the Julian period,[4] about the time of Herod's death, and the birth of Christ. This is as it ought to be. The conjunction of the Sun and Moon took place on the birth of Christ. This was exactly 600 years after the birth of Cyrus, who was *the Messiah*, to use the epithet of the Old Testament, who immediately preceded Jesus Christ.

Mr. Fry[5] states, that the year preceding the year 4 B. C., was the year of the nativity. He adds, " We arrive at B. C. 4, the year before which is supposed, by most writers of eminence,

---

[1] Clarke's Travels, Vol. II. p. 318.          [2] Vide Burchardt's Travels.

[3] Some will think this to be paradoxical, and if I did not know that the secret learning of the ancients was in strict keeping with it, I should think so too. But I beg my reader to refer to the history of the Cabala by Basnage, and presuming that he will oblige me in this, I shall push this abstruse speculation a little farther. The 14th, the middle numerical letter in the alphabet is called Muin: this is evidently the *vine*, the Marital tree, sacred to Bacchus, ן" *iin*, with the M prefixed. May not this ם *m* final be a monogram prefixed to the name, long after it came into use? It is found in all the languages. How came Bacchus to be the God of wine? (Bacchus was the sun in Taurus.) Did it arise from the junction of this Mem, as a Monogram or emblem of the sun in Taurus, mystically given to the name of the tree of wine? I know not. Let it be more probably accounted for; first taking into account the ancient mystic doctrines and practices relating to figures. It was from the mystical emblems carried on the signets of the ancients that our modern coats of arms arose. How can any thing be more recondite and mystical than the figures and monograms on the ancient signets? Any one may see an example in Clarke's Travels, Vol. II. pp. 320, 326, ed. 4to. I shall return to the Om or M in the course of this work.

[4] See Asiat. Res. Vol. X. p. 48; Calmet, Chron.; and Encyclop. Britt. art. Chron., p. 754.

[5] Epocha of Daniel's Proph. p. 5.

" to have been the year of the holy nativity." This is the same as Marsham and Hevelius who fix the Christian æra, calculating from the Hebrew, at exactly 4000 years from the creation.

In calculating periods, a variation of several years has arisen from a very natural cause : one author or translator speaks of the tenth year, another uses the same expression, and, without any ill intention, calls it ten years : this, again, is followed by another, who makes the ten years into the eleventh year, and this again into the twelfth. A similar variation is exhibited in the Indian Cali Yug, which is placed 3000, 3001, 3002 years before Christ.

Dr. Hales has given many very satisfactory reasons why the difference of one or two, in chronological calculations, cannot be admitted to impugn them, chiefly on account of the different methods of speaking of the same number, by different persons. It is not necessary to repeat them. [1]

In addition to what Dr. Hales has said, it may, perhaps, be useful to observe, that a difference of 1 in chronological calculations can seldom be reasonably used as an argument against any conclusion to which there is no other objection, in consequence of authors often neglecting to keep distinct the *last* and *first* numbers of series, whence it happens that one unit is counted *twice over*. Colonel Wilford says, " It is also to be observed, that where we put 0 at the beginning of a " chronological list, the Hindoos put 1, as we used to do formerly : and that year should be " rejected in calculations : but this precaution is often neglected, even in Europe." [2]

The Hindoo astronomical accounts having been found to make a great impression on the public mind, an attempt was made in the sixth volume of the Asiatic Researches to remove it, by a gentleman, before noticed, of the name of Bentley. His essay was attacked in the Edinburgh Review, to which he replied in the eighth volume of the above-mentioned work.

He states that there are only three Hindoo systems of astronomy now known. The first is called *Brahma Calpa*, the second *Padma Calpa*, the third *Varaha Calpa*. I shall not trouble my reader with the details, but merely with certain results. Mr. Bentley states (p. 212) the Cali Yug to have commenced 3101 years before Christ. In the Brahma Calpa, (p. 225,) a Maha or great Yug or Calpa consists of 2400 years, which great Yug was divided into four other Yugs ; of course these were 600 years each. The beginning of this 2400 was 3164 years B. C., and it ended 764 years B. C. Here, in the division into four, we have clearly four ages or yugs of 600 years each. I think the Neros cannot be denied here.

In a future page I shall explain how this Brahma Calpa arose, which is unknown to the present Brahmins.

If from 3164 we take 764 and add a Neros 600, we shall have exactly five Neroses between the commencement of the system and the birth of Christ, which commencement we shall afterward see must have been meant, according to this system, for the date of the flood, and of the Cali Yug. I think the four divisions obviously prove, that the sum of 2400 years is only a part of a system consisting of Neroses ; and, as we shall soon see, of the ten incarnations, in reality Neroses, spoken of in the first chapter and fourth section of the present book of this work.

In the next system, the Padma Calpa, a Calpa is called 5000 years ; but the term called Brahma's life consists of 387,600,000 years. Mr. Bentley says, (p. 220,) " By this table it will " appear, that the Satya, or golden age, as we may call it, of the first system, began on the same " year that the third Mauwantara of the second system did ; that is, the year before Christ 3164." Here is evidently the same system ; and being the same, the Neros must be at the bottom, however carefully hidden : I have, therefore, no occasion to add any thing more at present.

In Usher's Chronology, the death of Shem, when he was exactly the age of a Neros or 600 years old, took place 502 years after the flood : this we shall find of consequence. One of the Hindoo

---

[1] Chron. Vol. I. p. 121.     [2] Asiat. Res. Vol. X. p. 161.

systems makes the Cali Yug begin 3098 years B. C.,[1] at which time some Brahmins maintain that the flood happened. This shews the same mythos as that relating to Shem. $98+502=600+3000$ $=3600-600=3000$ or 5 Neroses.

The third or Varaha Calpa has the famous cycle of 4,320,000,000 years for its duration. This system makes the Cali Yug (Mr. Bentley says) begin 3098 years B. C.[2] In the preliminary discourse, (Sect. 26, p. 6,) we have shewn that a dodecan consisted of 5 days, and 72 dodecans of course formed a natural year of 360 days : 360 solar diurnal revolutions formed a natural year. The Sun, or rather that higher principle of which the Sun was the emblem or the Shekinah, was considered to be incarnated every six hundred years. Whilst the sun was in Taurus, the different incarnations, under whatever names they might go, were all considered but as incarnations of Buddha or Taurus. When he got into Aries, they were in like manner considered but as incarnations of Cristna or Aries. And even Buddha and Cristna, as I have before stated, were originally considered the same, and had a thousand names *in common*, constantly repeated in their litanies— a striking proof of identity of origin. Of these Zodiacal divisions, the Hindoos formed another period, which consisted of ten ages or Calpas or Yugs, which they considered the duration of the world: at the end of which, a general renovation of all things would take place. They also reckoned ten Neroses to form a period, each of them keeping a certain relative location to the other, and together to form a cycle.

5. To effect this, they double the precessional period for one sign, viz. 2160 years, thus making 4320, which was a tenth of 43,200, a year of the sun, analogous to the 360 natural days, and produced in the same manner, by multiplying the day of 600 by the dodecans $72=43,200$. They then formed another great year of 432,000, by again multiplying it by 10, which they called a Cali Yug, which was measurable both by the number 2160, the years the equinox preceded in a sign, and by the number 600. They then had the following scheme :

| | |
|---|---:|
| A Cali Yug, or 600 (or a Neros, as I will call it) Age.... | 432,000 |
| [3] A Dwapar, or Duo-par Age......................... | 864,000 |
| A Treta, or tres-par Age............................ | 1,296,000 |
| A Satya, or Satis Age .............................. | 1,728,000 |
| Altogether 10 ages, making a Maha Yug, or Great Age.. | 4,320,000 |

These were all equimultiples of the Cycle of the Neros 600, and of 2160, the twelfth part of the equinoctial precessional cycle : and in all formed ten ages of 432,000 years each.

This is a most important Cycle, and I think we shall here see the reason for the formation of such very long periods by the Hindoos. The Neros or cycle of 600 was originally invented to enable them to regulate the vernal and autumnal Phallic festivals. After some time they discovered that their cycle of 600 no longer answered, but that their festivals returned at a wrong pe-

---

[1] Asiat. Res. Vol. VIII. p. 237.        [2] Ibid.

[3] It is curious to observe that these Sanscrit names are nothing but Latin, except the first : but this will not surprise a person who has read Ch. II. Sect. XXV. of *The Celtic Druids*, where the close affinity of the Latin and Sanscrit is shewn. The first Cali is a mystical word, a little corrupted by its translation from Sanscrit into English, or by its translation from a primeval language. It may be the Chaldee word composed of the letters פלק *klo*. This word I have shewn, in the Celtic Druids, from General Vallancey, meant ק *k*=500 ל *l*=30 ע *o*=70, total 600. It may also be the same as the Greek word καλος, and mean *benignant, beautiful*, the same as Mundus and κοσμος—*Beauty* arising from order ; peculiarly appropriate to the cycle of the Neros of 600. The Yug means age, and really looks, as before intimated, very like our word *age* ; in fact, it is nothing but our word. One is a corruption of the other, but which *is* the *corruption* I do not say. *Klo* is found in the Greek in the word κυκλος, circle or cycle, and *Hericlo* is Hercules, the saviour 600, or the Sun in Aries, when the Cali began. But more of this hereafter.

riod, as the equinox, which once fell on the first of May, now took place on the first of April. This led ultimately to the discovery, that the equinox preceded about 2160 years in each sign, or 25,920 years in the 12 signs; and this induced them to try if they could not form a cycle of the two. On examination, they found that the 600 would not commensurate the 2160 years in a sign, or any number of sums of 2160 less than 10, but that it would with ten, or, that in ten times 2160, or in 21,600 years, the two cycles would agree: yet this artificial cycle would not be enough to include the cycle of 25,920. They, therefore, took two of the periods of 21,600, or 43,200; and, multiplying both by ten, viz. 600×10=6000, and 43,200×10=432,000, they found a period with which the 600 year period, and the 6000 year period, would terminate and form a cycle. Every 432,000 years the three periods would commence anew: thus the three formed a year or cycle, 72 times 6000 making 432,000, and 720 times 600 making 432,000.

Again, to shew this in another way: the year of 360 days, or the circle of 360 degrees, we have seen was divided into dodecans of 5 days, or degrees, each; consequently the degrees or days in a year or circle being multiplied by 72, that is, 72 × 360 gives 25,920, the length of the precessional year. In the same way the Hindoos proceeded with the number 600, which was the number contained in a year of the sun; they multiplied it by 72, and it gave them 43,200: but as the number 600 will not divide equally in 25,920, and they wanted a year or period which would do so, they took ten signs of the Zodiac, or 10 times 2160, the precessional years in a sign, which made 21,600, thus making their Neros year ten periods, to answer to ten signs; then multiplying the 43,200 by 10 they got 432,000: thus, also, they got two years or periods commensurate with each other, and which formed a cycle, viz. 21,600 and 432,000, each divisible—the former by 600, and the latter by 21,600. As the latter gave a quotient of 20, in 20 periods of 21,600 years, or 432,000 years, they would have a cycle which would coincide with the Neros; and which is the least number of the signs of the Zodiac, viz. 10, which would thus form a cycle with the Neros.

Thus a year of the Clo or Cli or Cali Yug, or age, or 600, is ............... 432,000
Then a year of the double Neros, or 1200, will be..... .................... 864,000
Of a triple ditto ................................................ ........ 1,296,000
And of a quadruple ................................................ 1,728,000

And of a year formed of the ten ages or Neroses altogether, or of the 6000 years, 4,320,000

And this long period they probably supposed would include all the cyclical motions of the Sun and Moon, and, perhaps, of the Planets. Whether this was the result of observations some will hesitate to admit. Persons of narrow minds will be astonished at such monstrous cycles; but it is very certain that no period could properly be called the *great year* unless it embraced in its circle every periodical movement or apparent aberration. But their vulgar wonder will perhaps cease when they are told that Mons. La Place has proved, that if the periodical aberrations of the Moon be correctly calculated, the great year must be extended to a greater length even than the 4,320,000 years of the Maha Yug of the Hindoos. And certainly no period can be called a year of our planetary system, which does not take in all the periodical motions of the planetary bodies.

As soon as these ancient astronomers had found that the equinoxes had the motion in antecedentia, or preceded, they would, of course, endeavour to discover the rate of the precession in a given time. It is evident that this would be a work of very great difficulty. The quantity of precession in one year was so small, that they must have been obliged to have recourse to observations in long periods, and it is not very surprising that they should at first have been guided, in part, by theory. The orderly arrangement of nature appeared so striking to the Greeks, as to induce them thus to accou t for the Planets being called *Disposers*, the appellation (as we learn from Herodotus) first

2 A

given to the Gods,—the םימש *smim* of Genesis. From observations taken during the precession through several degrees, the Hindoos were first induced to suppose that the precession took place after the rate of 60 years in a degree, or 1800 in a zodiacal sign, and of 21,600 in a revolution of the whole circle. And Sir W. Jones informs us, from an examination of their periods, that this was the rate at which they reckoned. But they afterwards discovered, as they thought, that this was not true, and that the precession was at the rate of a degree in 60 years and a fraction of a year ; and that thus the precession for a sign was in 1824 years, and for the circle in 21,888 years. During the time this was going on, they discovered, as they thought, the Soli-Lunar period of 608 years, and they endeavoured to make the two cycles go together. For this purpose they took the periods in a zodiacal circle, viz. 12 × 1824 = 21,888, and they found the two cycles of 608 and 21,888 would agree and form a new one, at the end of which both cycles would terminate, and begin anew. Hence came to be formed the sacred 608. But both of them were erroneous.

Among the ancient Romans we find a story of 12 vultures and 12 ages, the meaning of which was certainly unknown ; for the 12 ages of 120 years each will by no means account for all the particulars of the history. But we find among them also the sacred period of 608 years. This arose from the following cause : they came from the East before the supposition that the precession took place a degree in about 60 years, and 1824 years in a sign had been discovered to be erroneous ; and as they supposed the Neros made a correct cycle in 608 years, and believed the precessional cycle to be completed in 21,888 years, they of course made their ages into 12. As both numbers were erroneous, they would not long answer their intended purpose, and their meaning was soon lost, though the sacred periods of twelve ages and of 608 remained.

The equinoxes were believed by Hipparchus and Ptolemy to have preceded after the rate of a degree in 100 years, and of the circle in 36,000 years, thus : 1 deg. : 100 yrs. : : 360 deg. : 36000 yrs , and that then the Αποκαταϛασις or restitution or regeneration of all things would take place. This, I think, was nothing but a remnant of, probably, the most ancient of the Indian mythoses, when the precessional-years in each sign of the Zodiac were supposed to be 3000 in number, and consequently 36,000 in the circle, and 36 seconds in a year. [1] This doctrine of the Greeks is evidently nothing but a theory, and not the result of observation ; for it cannot be believed that erroneous observations should have brought out these peculiar round numbers.

Some time after the arrival of the Sun in Aries, at the Vernal equinox, the Indians probably discovered their mistake, in giving about 60 years to a degree ; that they ought to give 50″ to a year, about 72 years to a degree, and about 2160 years to a sign ; and, that the Luni-Solar cycle, called the Neros, did not require 608 years, but 600 years only, to complete its period. Hence arose the more perfect Neros.

After some time the erroneous Neros of 608 would be lost sight of altogether in the country of its birth, and would be superseded by the more perfect, of 600 years. Hence the old one is only found, as it were, in scraps and detached parts, as in the calculations on chronology, which the reader has seen, and in certain verses of Martianus Capella's, which I shall presently give. But it continued in use among the ignorant devotees in Latium and in Greece, who knew nothing of its meaning, or of the profound astronomy from which it had its origin. As I have just said, I suppose the great Neros of 608 years came to the West before the less and more correct one of 600 was discovered, and, in consequence of the communication between these distant countries being intercepted, the greater one remained, as a sacred number, uncorrected.

Perhaps after some time the Indians found that the equinox did not precede correctly 50″ in a year, or a degree in 72 years ; but 50″ and a fraction, i. e. 50″ 9‴ ¼ in a year, or a degree in 71

---

[1] Costard, Ast. p. 131.

years, eight or nine months, and an entire sign in 2152 or 2153 years. [1] They, therefore, divided the 43,200 by 71; this gave them the number 608 $\frac{3\,2}{7\,1}$, and from this arose the sacred number of their Manwanteras 71. It is evident that the error is so small a fraction, as to amount in practical effect to *nothing* in these long periods; for as, in these religious systems, they calculated in whole numbers, the error did not operate unless it was more than a fraction of the 72 years in one degree.

It is necessary to observe, that few of the numbers respecting the precession are *absolutely* correct: for instance, the number of years for a sign is 2153, instead of 2160; the difference arises from fractions, as I have stated above, and is so small, that it is not worth notice. The following observation of M. Volney's will explain it.

" Edward Barnard discovered from ancient monuments that the Egyptian priests calculated, " as we do, the movement of precession at 50″ 9‴ ¼ in a year: consequently that they knew it " with as much precision as we do at this day.

" According to these principles, which are those of all astronomers, we see that the annual " precession being 50″ and a fraction of about a fourth or a fifth, the consequence is, that an entire " degree is lost, or displaced, in seventy-one years, eight or nine months, and an entire sign in " 2152 or 2153 years." [2]

Again Volney says, " It is, moreover, worthy of remark, that the Egyptians never admitted or " recognized, in their chronology, *the deluge* of the Chaldeans, in the sense in which we understand " it: and this, no doubt, because among the Chaldeans themselves it was only an allegorical " manner of representing the presence of Aquarius in the winter solstitial point, which presence " really took place at the epoch when the vernal equinoctial point was in Taurus: this carries us " back to *the thirty-first* (3100) *or thirty-second* century before our æra, that is, precisely to the " dates laid down by the Indians and Jews." [3]

The observation respecting the Hindoo period of 3100 years before Christ is striking. What he means by the Jews, I do not understand.

Besides the Neros of 600 years, and the great Neros of 608 years, which were both sacred numbers, the ancients had also two other remarkable and sacred numbers—650 and 666. Sir William Jones, I have before observed, has stated that the Hindoos at a very early period must have believed, that the precessional year consisted of 24,000 years. " They computed this motion " (the precession of the equinox) to be at the rate of 54″ a year: so that their annus magnus, or " the times in which the stars complete an entire revolution, was 24,000 years." [4]

I will now try to shew how the above-named sacred numbers arose.

I suppose that at first the Soli-lunar cycle was thought to consist of 666 years; and the great year, caused by the precession of the equinoxes, of 24,000 years. Nothing can be more awkward and intractable than these numbers. 66 years to a degree give 23,760 to the great year, which are too few; and 67 years to a degree give 24,120 to the great year, which are too many to complete a period without fractions: thus, $66 \times 30 \times 12 = 23,760$; $67 \times 30 \times 12 = 24,120$. Nor will 666 divide equally in 24,000, for they leave a remainder of 24. The Luni-solar period of 666 years was abandoned when its incorrectness was perceived. About the same time it was thought to be discovered that the equinox did not precede 24,000 in the great year, but 65 years in a degree, and 23,400 in the great year, the Soli-lunar period was thought to be 650 years. These two periods agree very well, and together form a cycle: $36 \times 650 = 23,400$. Then 650 became a sacred number, and we have it recorded in the number of the stones at Abury. Of this cycle M. Basnage has given an account.

[1] Volney, Res. Vol. II. p. 453.　　[2] Transl. of Volney on Anc. History, Vol. II. p. 453.　　[3] Ibid. p. 455.
[4] Trans. Royal Soc. Edin. Vol. II. p. 141.

If we turn to the *Celtic Druids*, Ch. vi. Sect. xxiii., we shall see the other sacred numbers of the Cycles of India described. Since I wrote that work I have discovered that the sum-total of the pillars discovered by Dr. Stukeley, and confirmed by Sir R. C. Hoare, at Abury, made exactly the sacred Solar number 650. There can therefore be little doubt that they adopted that number of pillars for their temple to record this Cycle.

All these different Neroses form cycles with the then supposed great precessional year, except the number 666. This number, for the reason already assigned, will not form a cycle with 24,000. And it might be on account of this awkwardness that it became a reprobated number—the number of evil, of discord, of the beast in the Revelation. Some persons will probably think these theories fanciful. I should certainly think with them, if I did not bear in mind that all the ancient mythoses were replete with fancies of this kind. Their nonsense respecting sacred numbers is palpable, but the numbers having sacred characters applied to them are not fancies, but historical facts; and, though these fancies are nonsensical in their own nature, they cease to be so when consequences important to the good of mankind depend upon them.

General Vallancey says, " The Saros, according to Berosus, consisted of 6660 days. Syncellus and " Abydenus,[1] tell us, that it was a period of 3600 years; but Suidas, an author contemporary with " Syncellus, says, the Saros was a period of lunar months amounting to 18 years and a half, or " 222 moons. Pliny mentions a period of 223 lunar months, which Dr. Halley thinks is a false " reading, and proposes the amendment by reading 224 months. Sir Isaac Newton makes the " Saros 18 years and 6 intercalary months, which agrees with Suidas; but it is not the simple " Saros, but the tenfold Saros, that makes this number, as will appear from the numerical or celes- " tial alphabet. The word is evidently derived from שׁור *sor*, revolutio, mensura. In the old Irish " it is called Siora."[2] We have seen how the 666 arose, and in its multiplication by *ten*, we have the cycle of 6660, which being founded on an erroneous calculation, was itself erroneous, but it was agreeable to the *principle* of the cycle of 6000 years, as I have already explained.

It is impossible to read the above extract with attention and not to see that the meaning of the cycle or Saros of 666 was unknown, because, in order to make the reckoning by months agree, they must use a fraction, and also, *without any reason whatever*, according to their scheme, multi- ply the number by *ten*. General Vallancey gives the following proof:

|  |  | Proof |  |
|---|---|---|---|
| S—שׁ—300 | | 360 | |
| A—ע— 70 | | 18 | |
| R—ר—200 | | 6480 | |
| V—ו— 6 | | 180 | 6 months |
| S—צ— 90 | | 6660 | |
| 666 | | 222 | |
| 10 | | 30 | |
| 6660 | | 6660 | |

The Irish had a festival called *La Saora*, always kept in the night; and many persons have de- rived Serapis, from Sor or Soros Apis, meaning the entombed Apis; Soros being the name of a stone coffin. All this tends to support my idea, that this number of the beast was only an ex- ploded or heretical cycle. The year of the Apocalypse being calculated at only 360 days, I must maintain is a decisive proof of its extreme antiquity:

---

[1] Al. Polyhistor.  [2] Ouseley, Orient. Coll. Vol. II. No. iii. p. 214.

The cycle of 19, a common number of the Irish stone circles, is called, in the Irish language, *Baise-Bhuidin*.[1] I confess I can read this no other way than *Bud-base* or *Buddhist foundation*—it being the foundation, in one sense, of the famous Neros. The temple in Cornwall, called Biscawoon, said to be a corruption of Baise-bhuidin, contains in its circle 19 stones. The meaning of this can scarcely be doubted.[2]

It is curious to observe how often trifling circumstances keep occurring to support the claim of the Etruscans to be placed among the most ancient of the nations. The cycle of 666 is an example of this kind. It is found with them, as the following passage of Niebuhr proves, but its meaning was lost. "In the year of Rome 666 the Haruspices announced, that the mundane day of the "Etruscan nation was drawing to a close." This cycle has a strong tendency to prove, what no one who looks impartially at the apocalypse of John, and the continual recurrence in it of the numbers contained in the ancient cycles, can doubt, that it is an allegorical mythos, and relates chiefly to them; though perhaps only emblematically.

The Etruscan cosmogony is exactly that of one of the earlier Brahmin systems. It supposes that the author of the creation employed 12,000 years in his work. In the first thousand he made the planets and earth; in the second, the firmament; in the third, the sea and waters; in the fourth, the sun and moon, and also the stars; in the fifth, living creatures; in the sixth, man :— that after they were finished in the six thousand years, they were to last six thousand years, then a new world was to begin, and the same things to go over again.[3] Here is the renewal of the Cycles of Virgil and Juvenal; but as may be expected of a system, if it can be called a system, which has ripened into form, as circumstances favoured, through thousands of years, the length of the period is unknown, a subject of speculation varying in different nations and different times.

Although Nonnius is perfectly in the dark respecting the length of the great year, making it to be 456 years long, yet he accidentally makes a calculation, from various circumstances, that the Phœnix must have made its appearance in the year 608 before Christ, which evidently produces, to that time, one of the Neroses. This I can attribute to nothing but the fact, that one of the periods had been discovered, though not understood. This is the best kind of evidence to establish facts of this nature.

The Irish expressly state the life of the Phenn or Phennische to have lasted 600 years.[4] In Egyptian, *Pheneh* is cyclus, periodus, ævum. (Scaliger.)

Phœnix, Egyptiis astrologiæ symbolum.      Bochart.

Una est quæ reparat seque ipsa reseminat

Ales, Assyrii Phœnica vocant.          Ovid.[5]

If I mistake not, I have pointed out the origin of the Hindoo cycles; and it is probable, that the principle which I have unfolded will account for the various systems which are found among the learned in different parts of India. One system founded on one series of observations would be adopted by the sect of one nation of that widely-extended country, and another of another. And thus have arisen the different systems which we find. The festivals, forms, and ceremonies, (matters of the VERY FIRST importance to devotees in all nations,) depending on the cycles, we need not be surprised that old, incorrect systems should have been continued in different places. And after the religion was divided into sects, the fortunate detectors of the early mistakes, by which they were enabled to keep their own festivals in order, would probably be very unwilling to

---

[1] Ouseley, Orient. Coll. Vol. II. No. iii. p. 213.

[2] Val. Coll. Hib. Vol. VI. p. 383. Vide ch. ii. Sect. i. of this book for Cassini's opinion on the Metonic Cycle.

[3] Universal Hist. Vol. I. Cosmog p. 64.    [4] Vallancey, Vol. VI. p. 379.    [5] Metam. xv. 392.

communicate information of this kind, to those who were considered by them as heretics. Again, it is not at all unlikely, that the correction of festivals should have actually created sects   These are, I think, some of the chief reasons why these systems were concealed, and confined with so much care to a very few persons, and why the knowledge of the principles was forgotten, while the formulæ were continued in use.

I consider that the Hindoo religion was not the produce of premeditation, but like most others of circumstance, of accident—and that it kept pace, in some measure, with the gradual approximation of their astronomy to perfection. And I think it is pretty clear that it must have been fully established some time about the year 3100 B. C., at least not very long after that date. It might, perhaps, be five or six hundred years later, for which time, of course, they must have had recourse to back-reckoning. I think it also probable, that this may, in part, have furnished plausible grounds for much of the nonsense which has been broached on the subject of back-reckonings.

6. Mr. Bentley, notwithstanding he has written so much against the antiquity of Hindoo astronomy, admits (p. 212) that the Cali Yug began 3101 years before Christ; that the Brahma Calpa began 3164 years before Christ; that one of the four ages of the Padma Calpa began precisely at the same time as the Brahma Calpa; and that the third or the Varaha Calpa began 3098 years before Christ. It is very evident that all these systems are the same—and yet the trifling variation shews that they were not contrived for the purpose of deceit or fraud : for, if they had been, they would have been made to agree. They rather seem to shew the result of observations made independently of one another, from some common source. It is very evident from Mr. Bentley's admissions, that the present Brahmins, whatever they may pretend to, do not know much respecting their different systems; and that they have to make them out precisely as they are made out by Europeans—in a considerable degree by conjecture and calculation.

Among other matters, Mr. Bentley, by a long train of reasoning, undertakes to shew the Calpa of 432,000 years to have been invented after the Christian æra. The following table will demonstrate how little his kind of proof can be depended on, because it shews, that this cycle was known long before that æra commenced.

The following is the description of the Chaldean kings given by Berosus, which again proves the system of very great antiquity. I give along with it the system of Moses.

| Antediluvian patriarchs according to Genesis. | | | Chaldean Antediluvian Kings according to Berosus. | | |
|---|---|---|---|---|---|
| Names. | Ages. | In Years. | Names. | Ages in Sares. | In Years. |
| Adam | | 930 | Alor | 10 | 36,000 |
| Seth | | 912 | Alaspar | 3 | 10,800 |
| Enos | | 905 | Amelon | 13 | 46,800 |
| Cainan | | 910 | Amenon | 12 | 43,200 |
| Mahalaleel | | 862 | Matalar | 18 | 64,800 |
| Jared | | 895 | Daon | 10 | 36,000 |
| Enoch | | 365 | Evidorach | 18 | 64,800 |
| Methuselah | | 969 | Amphis | 10 | 36,000 |
| Lamech | | 777 | Otiartes | 8 | 28,800 |
| Noah | | 950 | Xisuthrus | 18 | 64,800 |
| | | | | 120 | 432,000 |

This proves that one, and the most important, of the immensely-extended cycles of the Hindoos was in existence long before the Christian æra, and of itself entirely overturns Mr. Bentley's doctrine. It also raises a very strong presumption, that the Hindoos and Chaldeans had an intimate connexion in the time of Berosus, for the identity of these large numbers cannot have been the effect of accident.

I will now endeavour to point out the truth of my theory in another way. We will take for granted the truth of the millenary period of 6000 years as an age—the age of iron : the ages are supposed to be in the proportion of 4, 3, 2, 1,—the same as those of the Grecian Hesiod. Now, if we take the last to be 6000 and count backwards, we shall have

| | | |
|---|---:|---:|
| Present Iron age or Cali age | 6,000 | 1 |
| Brass | 12,000 | 2 |
| Silver | 18,000 | 3 |
| Gold | 24,000 | 4 |
| Ten periods | 60,000 | |
| Multiply this by | 72 | |
| | 120,000 | |
| | 420,000 | |

as we formerly multiplied the Dodecans by 72 to compose a common solar
year, and we shall have a year of Brahma or of the whole system ······ 4,320,000

The anonymous author of the Cambridge Key to the Mythology of the Hindoos, endeavours to prove this theory of increasing numbers to apply to the period before the deluge of 900 years. Thus 400, 300, 200, and the last, or tenth, to be that now running. But here his theory completely fails ; because the last period instead of being, as it ought to be, only 100 years, has already extended since the flood, according to his own account, to near 4000 years. If the above scheme be right, if the Cali Yug or the last 6000 began 3100 years B. C., there ought to be 1070 yet to run—as 3100+1830=4930+1070=6000. Here we see we have the famous 6000 of the Hindoos, Jews, Greeks, and Romans, for one extreme, and the famous Maha-Yug or great year for the other—the year when all things were to resolve themselves into the Deity. Though this is a second system, yet it is evidently the same in principle, and the two are in perfect accordance.

Mr. Bentley, in a recent work published after his death, states that he has obtained the Janampatri of Cristna, or the positions of the planets at his birth ; that is, if I understand it rightly, the astrological calculation of his nativity. Now, I think this tends strongly to confirm what the reader has seen from La Loubère. Cassini has shewn that the birth of Christ, as fixed by Eusebius, exactly agreed with an astronomical epoch of the Buddhists of Siam, which is also connected with the Neros or cycle of 600, as the reader has seen. According to the Janampatri, (the genuineness of which I suppose we must admit,) and the Brahmins' and Mr. Bentley's calculation from the Janampatri, (p. 111,) Cristna was born exactly at the end of 600 years (the termination of a Neros) from the time fixed by Eusebius for the birth of Christ and the Buddhist cycle. Thus the fact comes out, that the birth-days fall at the beginning of the different Neroses ; and, I think, from a consideration of the whole of what Cassini, Loubère, and Bentley say, it is clear that this Luni-solar period of 600 must be considered as the year of both Buddha and Cristna. Mr. Bentley says, (p. 61,) "The[1] epoch of Buddha is generally referred to the year 540 or 542 before "Christ." It is impossible not to see here the epoch of Cassini of 543 years before Christ. From these circumstances we may easily account for many difficulties which have been met with

---

[1] The only difference between the æras of Christ and Buddha is, that one is calculated from the birth, the other from the death of the person from whom the cycle is named.

in the histories of Buddha and Cristna, and which have induced Mr. Bentley and others to imagine them of later dates than they are : for it is evident that very nearly the same relative positions of the Sun and Moon would be renewed every fresh cycle or Luni-solar period as it ran its course. Thus, like the Phœnix, they were eternally renewing themselves.

But though the sun and moon would have the same relative positions, the planets would differ in each of these cycles. Hence Mr. Bentley was induced to believe, that Cristna was first born in this last cycle : whereas he was, in fact, born in each of five preceding ones. His first birth was at the egress of Noah or Menu from the ark, which the Hindoos say took place when they suppose the sun entered Aries at the vernal equinox, and which they fix at 3101 years before Christ.

M. Loubère says that the Siamese date their civil year from the *death of Sommono-Collom*, 544 years before Christ. He, however, adds, " But I am persuaded that this epocha has quite another " foundation, which I shall afterwards explain." (P. 8.) This explanation we have already seen ; and it proves that, though he understood the astronomy, he was not aware of the mystery. This epoch, not being like that of Jesus, from his birth or incarnation, but from his death, it seems to me that we shall have another Neros or cycle if we add 56 to the 544, the years of the life of Buddha. This we shall see presently.

M. Bailli professed to have discovered, by calculation, that on the 18th of February, 3102 years before the Christian æra, there was a very remarkable conjunction of the planets and an eclipse of the moon. [1] This is the moment when the Brahmins say their Cali Yug began.

From the epochas and cycles explained by Mons. Cassini we may readily infer the mode which was adopted by Eusebius and the Christian fathers in settling the times of the festivals and of the births, &c., of John and Jesus. It is almost certain that they were indebted to the Sommono Co-domites or Samaneans, noticed by Clemens Alexandrinus, as shewn above. All this dovetails perfectly into the astronomical theories of Mons. Dupuis ; into what the learned Spaniard, Alphonso the Great, said,—that the adventures of Jesus are all depicted in the constellations ; into what Jacob is reported to have said, that the fortunes of his family were read in the stars ; and also into what Isaiah said, that the heavens were a book. This was really believed by some of the Cabalists, who divided the stars into letters. [2]

Itaque hunc in modum intelligi potest, quod in Josephi precatione à Jacobo dicitur ; legit in tabulis cœli quæcunque accident vobis et filiis vestris, quia etiam complicabitur quasi *liber*. [3]

I have sometimes entertained a suspicion, that the speech of Alphonso alluded to the Messiah of each Cycle, and that the Zodiacs of Esne and Dendera are of the nature of perpetual calendars, for one of the cycles of 600, or 608 years.

We must recollect that the likeness between the history of Hercules and Jesus Christ is so close that Mr. Parkhurst has been obliged to admit, that Hercules was a type of *what the Saviour was to do and suffer*. Now M. Dupuis has shewn the life of Hercules in the sphere in a manner which admits not of dispute ; and Hercules, as it has also been shewn, is the Hericlo, the saviour 600.

The commentary on the Surya Siddhanta says, " The *ayanansa* (equinoctial point) moves east-" ward thirty times twenty (= 600) in each Maha Yug", 600. Again, " By the text, the *ayana* " *bhagana* (revolution) is understood to consist of 600 *bhaganas* (periods) in a *Maha Yug ;* but " some persons say the meaning is thirty *bhaganas* only, [4] and accordingly, that there are 30,000 " *bhaganas*." Again, " The *Sacalya Sanhita* states, that the *bhaganas* (revolutions) of the *cranti*

---

[1] Bailli's Astronomie Indienne et Orientale, p. 110, 4to. Ed. 1787.        [2] See Basnage, Hist. Jews, B. iii.

[3] Orig. Comm. in Genes. ; Val. Coll. Hib. Vol. VI. p. 345.        [4] Asiat. Res. Vol. II. p. 267.

" *pata* (point of intersection of the Ecliptic and Equator) in a *Maha Yug* [1] are 600 eastward"
(4,320,000 years). Again, " The *Bhaganas* (revolutions) of the *ayanansa* (equinoctial points) in
" a *Maha Yug* are 600 (4,320,000), the saura [2] years in the same period 4,320,000 : one *bhagana*
" of the *ayanansa* therefore contains 7,200 years." Here the Neros and the origin of the famous
432,000 are very clear, [3] where it is shewn that, according to the Hindoos, the equinoxes have a
libration.

This La Place is said to have demonstrated, but he makes it very small, while they extend it
from the third degree of Pisces to the twenty-seventh of Aries, and from the third of Virgo to the
twenty-seventh of Libra, and back again, in 7200 years.

It is admitted by all the Brahmins that their Cali Yug, or their *fourth period* (at the beginning
of which THEY SAY the vernal equinoctial point was in the first degree of *Aries)* took place or began
3101 years before Christ. [4] The beginning of this fourth period is evidently about the end of the
fifth back from the æra of Christ, which is the time assigned by them to the flood of Noah
when he came out of the ark. These *five,* and the *three* preceding, make eight ages, or Yugs, or
Neroses, which we shall see were known by the initiated in both the Eastern and Western nations.
But I must stop my argument to give a specimen of the uncertainty of ancient chronology.

The following statement will shew how little dependance can be placed upon systems of chronology :

Blair and Usher state the period from the creation to Christ, to be in the Hebrew

| | |
|---|---|
| Version of the Bible | 4004 years |
| The LXX | 5872 |
| The Samaritan | 4700 |
| Josephus states it to be [5] | 4483 |
| And Eusebius | 5200 |

Sir William Drummond, in his treatise on the Zodiacs of Esne and Dendera, gives the following
numbers :

| | | |
|---|---|---|
| Received text | | 4004 |
| Samaritan text | | 4245 |
| Septuagint 2262+3128 | | 5390 |
| Josephus | | 5688 |
| Seder Olam Sutha | | 3751 |
| Maimonides | Jewish Authorities | 4058 |
| Gersom | | 3754 |
| Asiatic Jews | | 4180 |

Sir William Drummond adopts the LXX., and thus divides it—2262 years to the deluge, and
3128 from the deluge to the birth of Christ.

The following numbers are taken from Dr. Hales :

---

[1] The reader will observe that the Yug, or age as it ought to be translated, is of all lengths—from 5 to 5000 years.
Every system, and there is a vast number of systems, has its own yug.

[2] Does the word Saura mean Surya ?         [3] See Asiat. Res. Vol. II. pp. 268—270.

[4] Jones's Asiat. Res. Vol. II. p. 393.

[5] Vide Whiston on Old Testament, p. 214; preface to the 21st volume of Universal History; also Celtic Druids,
p. 148.

|  |  |
|---|---|
| Alphonsus of Castile············· | 6984 years |
| —— Hales ···················· | 5411 |
| Meghasthenes ················· | 5369 |
| Other Indians according to Gentil . | 6204 |
| Arab ···················· | 6174 |
| LXX.—Abulfaraji ············· | 5586 |
| Vatican ··············· | 5270 |
| Alexandrine ········ ⎫ | |
| Abyssinian ·· ········ ⎬ | 5508 |
| Russian ············ ⎭ | |
| Josephus ··················· ⎫ | 5555 |
| ⎬ | 5481 |
| ⎬ | 5402 |
| ⎭ | 4698 |

Samaritan computation :

|  |  |
|---|---|
| Scaliger····················· | 4427 |
| Samaritan text ·············· | 4305 |
| Hebrew text ·················· | 4161 |
| Usher····················· | 4004 |
| Hevelius ⎫ ············ ······ | 4000 |
| Marsham ⎭ | |

The above is quite enough to shew the utter hopelessness of making out a system of chronology; but in Hales's treatise on this subject there may be seen, in addition to this, a list of more than 100 systems, each proved by its author to be the true and perfect system, and varying in their extremes not less than 3000 years. Each author (as he comes in order, finishing with Dr. Hales, as confident as those who have gone before him) succeeds in nothing but in overthrowing the doctrines of his predecessors; but in this he has no difficulty. Can any thing be devised which shall raise a stronger presumption, that a system of chronology never was the leading object of the books ? The whole tends to support the doctrine of *nearly all the learned men of antiquity*, that, like the Mythological histories of the Gentile nations, a secret doctrine was concealed under the garb of history. The same thing is seen in the early history of Rome, in the Iliad, [1] the Æneid, the tragedies of Æschylus, &c., &c.

Mr. Faber says, " There can scarcely be a doubt, I think, that we ought to adopt the longer " scheme of chronology, as it is called, in preference to that curtailed one which appears in the " common Hebrew Pentateuch. I am myself inclined to follow the Seventy in their antediluvian " chronology, and the Samaritan Pentateuch in early postdiluvian chronology." [2]   Thus by taking a little of one and a little of another, *ad libitum*, a system is easily to be formed.

It may be considered certain from the above, that no dependance can be placed on any system of Chronology, and that there is no hope whatever of ascertaining the truth, unless some person shall be able to devise a plan of proceeding different in principle from any thing which has hitherto been adopted. Therefore I think it will be allowed, that I am not to be tied down by any of them as authority.

---

[1] Herodotus says, that when Paris ran away with Helen, he was driven by contrary winds to Tarichea, (probably the Heracleum of Strabo,) and that she was detained by the king of the country, and given up to her husband. Here we have a sober fact stated by the historian. Upon this the sacred Mythos might be founded. Vide Rennel on Geog. Sys. of Her. Vol. II. p. 155 ; Herod. Euterpe, 113, et seq. ed. Belœ.

[2] Pag. Idol. Vol. I. p. 234.

Besides, it must be evident, on a moment's consideration, that it cannot be expected that I should make the cycles, which I shall shew existed, agree with any of them. I do not pretend to do it, though it is possible that, in some instances, I may. My object is merely to shew that the Neros *did exist*, and was the foundation of a system, not that it fitted to any of the systems of chronology—systems which not only disagree with one another, but almost every *one of which is totally inconsistent with itself*, as M. Volney, in his researches, has clearly proved.

The extraordinary exaggerations in numbers of years, and in other matters, have been noticed by the Author of the Cambridge Key to the Chronology of the Hindoos, of both the Hindoos and Jews, and he endeavours to shew that they are written in a species of cipher, and how the former ought to be reduced. These statements, taken by the priests in a literal sense, have caused many persons to doubt the whole history, but they no more prove that the Jewish history is in the great leading articles false, than the lengthened cycles of the Indians, before the year 3100, prove that they had no history, or that they did not exist.

7. I will now shew that the Mosaic system is exactly the same as that of the Brahmins and the Western nations ; I will unfold one part of the esoretic religion. But first I shall avail myself of the statement of several facts of the highest importance, which cannot be disputed, made by Col. Wilford in the Asiatic Researches.[1]

In consequence of certain prodigies which were reported to have been seen at Rome, about the year 119 before Christ, the sacred College of Hetruria was consulted, which declared that the EIGHTH REVOLUTION OF THE WORLD was nearly at an end, and that another, either for the better or the worse, was about to take place.[2]

Juvenal, who lived in the first century, declared that he was living in the *ninth revolution,*[3] or sæculum. This shews that the cycle above alluded to had ended in Juvenal's time, and that a new one had begun : and this ninth revolution consisted evidently of a revolution of more than 100 or 120 years—of several centuries at least.

" Nona ætas agitur, pejoraque sæcula ferri temporibus : quorum sceleri non invenit ipsa Nomen, " et à nullo posuit natura metallo." On this passage Isaac Vossius says, Octo illas ætates credit appellatas à cœli regionibus, quas octo faciebant Pythagorei : nonam vero, de qua hic, à tellure denominatam opinatur : in libello de Sibyle. Orac. Oxoniæ, nuper edito, Cap. v.

This statement of Juvenal's, which no author has ever yet pretended to understand, will now explain itself, and it completes and proves the truth of my whole system. It is of the greatest importance to my theory, as it is evidence, which cannot be disputed, of the fact on which the whole depends. Virgil lived before Christ, Juvenal after him. This is quite enough for my purpose, as we shall soon see.

About sixty years before Christ the Roman empire had been alarmed by prodigies, and also by ancient prophecies, announcing that an emanation of the Deity was going to be born about that time, and that a renovation of the world was to take place.

Previous to this, in the year 63 B. C., the city had been alarmed by a prophecy of one Figulus, that a king or master to the Romans was about to be born, in consequence of which the Senate passed a decree, that no father should bring up a male child born that year : but those among the Senators, whose wives were pregnant, got the decree suppressed.[4] These prophecies were applied to Augustus, who was born 63 years before Christ according to some persons, but 56 according to several writers in the East, such as the author of the Lebtarikh and others. " Hence

---

[1] Vol. X. p. 33.  [3] Ibid. ; Plutarch in Syllam, p. 456.

[2] Satire xiii. v. 28.  [4] See Sup. to Tit. Liv. CII. Decad. Cap. xxxix.

" it is, that Nicolo de Conti, who was in Bengal and other parts of India in the fifteenth century,
" insists that Vicramaditya was the same with Augustus, and that his period was reckoned, from
" the birth of that Emperor, fifty-six years before Christ." Now, it is evident that these fifty-six
years before Christ bring us to the æra of the Buddha of Siam, for the beginning of the new æra,
foretold by the Cumæan Sibyl, as declared by the *Mantuan* or Celtic poet, the Druid of Cisalpine
Gaul, in his fourth eclogue.[1] This, in some old manuscripts seen by Pierius, is entitled *Interpretatio Novi Sæculi*.[2] This Eclogue was evidently a *carmen Sæculare*.

Virgil says,

> The last great age, foretold by sacred rhymes,
> Renews its finished course : Saturnian times
> Roll round again, and *mighty years*, begun
> From their first orb, in radiant circles run.
> The base degenerate iron offspring, (*or the Cali-yuga,*) ends
> A golden progeny (*of the Crita, or golden age*)[3] from heaven descends :
> O chaste LUCINA, speed the mother's pains :
> And haste the glorious birth : thy own Apollo reigns !
> The lovely boy with his auspicious face !
> The son shall lead the life of Gods, and be
> By Gods and heroes seen, and Gods and heroes see.
> Another Typhis shall new seas explore,
> Another Argo land the chiefs upon the Iberian shore :
> Another Helen other wars create,
> And great Achilles urge the Trojan fate.
> O of celestial seed ! O foster son of Jove !
> See, labouring nature calls thee to sustain
> The nodding frame of heaven, and earth, and main :
> See, to their base restored, earth, seas, and air.

Col. Wilford on this passage observes, that these are the very words of Vishnu to the *earth*,
when complaining to it, and begging redress.[4]  Here is the Brahmin periodical regeneration
clearly expressed. And here is an admission by Virgil, that the poem of Homer was a religious
Mythos. All these prophecies, I apprehend, alluded to the renovation of the cycle of the Neros,
then about to take place in its ninth revolution.

I quote these verses here merely to shew that some great personage was expected. The
Ultima Cumæi venit jam carminis Ætas, of Virgil, I shall discuss in a future page, and shew that
it is in accordance with my theory.

Several of the other most celebrated Roman authors have noticed the expectation of the arrival
of some great personage in the first century, so that this could not be a mere *solitary* instance of
Virgil's base adulation in this interesting poem.

Tacitus says, " The generality had a strong persuasion that it was contained in the ancient
" writings of the priests, that AT THAT VERY TIME the East should prevail : and that some one who
" should come out of Judea, should obtain the empire of the world : which ambiguities foretold
" Vespasian and Titus. But the common people, (of the Jews,) according to the usual influence
" of human wishes, appropriated to themselves, by their interpretation, this vast grandeur foretold

---

[1] The æras of the Heroes, or Messiahs, of the cycle, (as the Bible calls Cyrus,) did not always commence on their
births, either in very old or more modern times. Thus Buddha's æra, above-mentioned, was from his death ; Jesus
Christ's is four years after his birth.  Mohamed was born A. D. 708, his æra begins 725.

[2] Vide Dupuis sur tous les Cultes, Vol. III. p. 15?.

[3] We may observe, *and reserve for future consideration*, that Col. Wilford says *the* CRITA *or Golden age* was about
to return. In his observation of the Cali Yug he is wrong.

[4] Asiat. Res. Vol. X. p. 31.

" by the fates, nor could be brought to change their opinion for the true, by all their adversities.[1]
" Suetonius[2] says, There had been for a long time all over the East a constant persuasion that it
" was (recorded) in the fates (books of the fates, decrees, or fortellings), that AT THAT TIME some
" one who should come out of Judea should obtain universal dominion. It appeared by the event,
" that this prediction referred to the Roman Emperor: but the Jews referring it to themselves,
" rebelled."

*Percrebuerat oriente toto constans opinio esse in fatis,*[3] ut eo tempore, Judæi profecti rerum
potirentur. Id de imperio Romano, quantum postea eventu patuit, prædictum, Judæi ad se
habentis, rebellarunt.

Josephus says,[4] " That which chiefly excited them (the Jews) to war, was an *ambiguous pro-*
" *phecy,* which was also found in the *sacred books, that at that time some one,* within their *country,*
" *should arise,* that should obtain *the empire* of the *whole world* (ὡς κατα τον καιρον εκεινον απο
" της χωρας, της αυτων αρξει την οικεμενην). For this they had received by tradition, (ὡς
" οικειον εξελαβον,) that it was spoken of one of their nation: and many wise men, (σοφοι, or
" *Chachams,*) were deceived with the interpretation. But, in truth, Vespasian's empire was
" designed in this prophecy, who was created Emperor (of Rome) in *Judæa.*"[5] The Chachams
above are Hakims, from the Hebrew word חכם *hkm,* wisdom. The accompanying word σοφοι
would have proved it, if it required any proof.

Another prophecy has been noticed by Prideaux[6] of one Julius Marathus, in these words :
Regem populo Romano naturam parturire.[7]

Among the Greeks, the same prophecy is found. The Oracle of Delphi was the depository, according to Plato, of an ancient and SECRET prophecy of the birth of a son of Apollo, who was to
restore the reign of justice and virtue on the earth.[8] This, no doubt, was the son alluded to by
the Sibyl.

Du Halde, in his History of China, informs us, that the Chinese had a prophecy that a holy
person was to appear in the West, and in consequence they sent to the West, which I think would
be Upper India, and that they brought thence the worship of Fo, (i. e. Buddha,) whom they call
Fwe, K-yau, and Shek-ya. This is evidently the *Iaw* of Diodorus, and the *Iau* of Genesis, and
the Sa-kia the name of Buddha.[9]

Now, according to my idea, the Sibyl of Virgil would have no difficulty, as, from her skill in judicial astrology, she would know very well when the Neros would end. Isaiah might easily learn
the same (even if he were not initiated, a thing hardly to be believed) from the Sibyl of Judæa,[10]
perhaps called a *Huldah.* Nothing is so likely as that Augustus should permit his flatterers to
tell the populace that his age exactly suited to the prophecy. Few persons would dare to canvas
this matter too closely ; it was good policy, to strengthen his title to the throne. But respecting
him I shall have much to say hereafter. The Hindoo works, Colonel Wilford informs us, foretell
the coming of Cristna, in the same manner, at the time he is said to have come. Nothing is more
likely. This has been erroneously supposed to prove them spurious. Any astronomer might tell

---

[1] Hist. Cap. xiii.  [2] Frag. apud Calmet, Dict. Vol IV. p. 65; Vespasian, Cap. iv.

[3] I beg my reader to observe the words *fates* and *fatis,* and I think he will see the origin of the unchangeable fates,
i. e. *the true prophets.*

[4] De Bello, Lib. vii. Cap. xxxi.  [5] Apud Calmet, Frag. Vol. IV. p. 65.

[6] Connec. P. ii. B. ix. p. 493, fol.  [7] Suet. in Oct. Cap. xciv.

[8] Plato in Apolog. Socr. et de Repub. Lib. vi. ; A. Clarke's Evidences ; Chatfield on the Hindoos, p. 245.

[9] Vide B. v. Ch. i. § ii.  [10] Named by Pausanias and Ælian. Vide Asiat. Res. Vol. X. p. 30.

it, for it was what had been told for every new age, before it arrived, that a great personage would appear—in fact the presiding genius, Cyrus, or Messiah, of the Cycle.

In addition to all these prophecies, which are in themselves sufficiently striking, there is yet another very celebrated one respecting Zeradusht, which is noticed by Mr. Faber. He maintains, and I think proves, the genuineness of this famous prophecy of Zeradusht, who declared that in the latter day a virgin should conceive and bear a son, and that a star should appear blazing at noon-day. " You, my sons," *exclaimed the seer,* " will perceive its rising before any other na-
" tion. As soon, therefore, as you shall behold the star, follow it whithersoever it shall lead you :
" and adore that mysterious child, offering him your gifts with profound humility. He is the al-
" mighty WORD, which created the heavens." [1] This prophecy, Mr. Faber observes, is found among the Celts of Ireland, ascribed to a person of the name of Zeradusht,[2] a daru or Druid of Bock-hara,[3] *the residence of Zeradusht* (whose mother was called Dagdu, one of the names of the mother of the Gods). He shews by many strong and decisive proofs, that this can be no monkish forgery of the dark ages.

Amongst other arguments against its being a forgery, Professor Lee observes, that the very same prophecy, in the same words, is reported by Abulfaragius to have been found by him in the oriental writings of Persia. This prophecy thus found in the East and in Ireland, and in the Virgini parituræ, of Gaul, before noticed, previous to the Christian æra, is of the very first importance. It cannot have been stolen from the Christian books, but they must have been copied from it, *if either be a copy,* (which yet may not be the fact,) for they are absolutely the same. It cannot have been copied from the Jewish prophets, because there is nothing like it, not a word about *a star at noon* in any of them. This prophecy is alluded to in the gospel of the infancy :
" Ecce ! magi venerunt ex Oriente Hierosolymas, quemadmodum prædixerat Zoradascht, erantque
" cum ipsis munera, aurium, thus, et myrrha." [4]

The star above spoken of, was also known to the Romans. " Chalcidius, a *heathen writer*
" who lived not long after Christ, in a commentary upon the Timæus of Plato, discoursing upon
" portentous appearances of this kind in the heavens, in different ages, particularly speaks of this
" wonderful star, which he observes, presaged neither diseases nor mortality, but the descent of a
" God among men : Stellæ, quam à Chaldæis observatam fuisse testantur, que Deum nuper natum
" muneribus venerati sunt." [5] Nothing can be more clear than that the Romish Christians got their history of the Star and Magi from these Gentile superstitions.

These prophecies have been equally troublesome to the priests and to the philosophers. The divines would have been very glad of them, but the adoption of them carried with it the shocking consequence, that God must have had such bad taste, as to have preferred even the wicked pagans

---

[1] Vol. II. p. 97.

[2] This Zeradusht is no other than the person generally called *Zoroaster* by our old authors. Now I learn from the learned oriental Professor Lee, of Cambridge, that the latter orthography is a complete mistake, and that in all the old oriental authors it is spelt *Zeradusht.* I think this furnishes a very strong proof of the real antiquity and genuineness of the Irish records : for if they had been merely compiled or formed from the works of the Western nations, they would have had the Western mode of spelling the word, and would not have had the Eastern mode, of which they could know nothing. It proves that they had this word direct from the East, and not through the medium of Western reporters.

If I mistake not, another equally striking proof of the same kind may be found in the word Dagdhu, the mother of the Gods. Circumstantial evidence of this kind excels all written evidence whatever. This is worth the whole of the chronicles of Eri. Dagdhu is הוה *ewa* or *eva* גד *dg,* Eve the propagatrix.

[3] Bochara means place of learning.　　　　[4] Jones on the Can. Vol. II. Part iii. Ch. xxii. S. 7.

[5] In Timæum, Platonis, p. 19, apud Hind. Hist. of Maurice, Vol. II. p. 296.

to his own people—his priestly nation—the Pagan prophecies being much clearer than those of the Jews. The philosophers have been annoyed because they clearly foretell a great person to come, and unless they allowed it to be Jesus Christ, they could make nothing of them. The Persians, the Chinese, and the Delphians, could not prophesy of Cæsar, and the close resemblance of the prophecies from all parts of the world, could not be the effect of accident. These matters being premised, we will now compare the calculations made a little time ago, with the periods produced by the precession of the equinoxes. But first it is necessary to recollect, that Julius Cæsar fixed the solstice to the 25th of December, about one in the morning, which brings the Equinox, in the zodiacal circle, to the 25th degree of Pisces.

From the birth of Christ to the beginning of Aries will be—35 degrees, or about······ 2520 years.
From Aries to the beginning of Taurus          30 ················ 2160

In the whole about········· 4680

$$30 \text{ degrees in May, } Taurus.$$
$$30 \text{ degrees in April, } Aries.$$
$$5 \text{ degrees in March, } Pisces$$
$$65 \times 72 = 4680$$

$$8 \times 600 = 4800$$
$$4680$$
$$120$$

This difference is what we might expect, because the two cycles of the precession, and of the Sun and Moon, the Neros would not coincide till the end of 10 signs. For, $2160 \times 8 = 17280 \div$ by 600, leaves a remainder of 480, to which, if we add the difference of 120, it exactly completes the cycle of 600. Then add 120 to the 4680, and it gives us exactly the time for 8 Neroses, 4800. This shews the reason why, in most of the calculations which I shall presently make, the sum of 2160, the years of the precession in one sign, must first be deducted, to make the sums come right.

These results serve to shew that the system must have been made up, or completed, by the Brahmins, some time after the beginning of their Cali Yug. Their attempts to reconcile facts irreconcileable—the 2160 years of the precession from Taurus to Aries, with the three Neroses, and a wish to begin to count the latter from the beginning of the Cali Yug—in short the whole exhibits a system of expedients, or shifts. The coincidence of numbers in my explanation is so extraordinary as to set at defiance the supposition of accident. The system being originally founded in error, as I will presently shew, when the Brahmins discovered the error, they had recourse to such expedients as offered themselves.

8. In the following verses of Martianus Capella, the celebrated Monogram of Christ ΤΗΣ, 608, is described. These very well apply to the Cristna of India, of the Jews, and also of the father of Ecclesiastical history, Eusebius, by whom the Roman church is followed, and by whom, in fact, it was established; and I beg my reader to pay particular attention to the Sacrum nomen et cognomen, the ΤΗΣ in these verses, which are written in Roman letters on our pulpit cloths, in Greek letters on the inside of the roof of the cathedral of St. Alban's, and in every kind of letters on the churches in Italy.[1]

This period of 608, I have just now shewn, was a celebrated cycle with the Hindoos. I shall call it the Great Neros, to distinguish it from that of 600, the Neros of Josephus.

Solem te Latium vocitat, quòd solus honore
Post Patrem sis lucis apex, radiisque sacratum
Bis senis perhibent caput aurea lumina, ferre:

---

[1] For some interesting observations respecting the *crux ansata*, the reader may consult Dr. Daniel Clarke's Travels, Vol. III. ch. iv., and Socrat. Schol. Histor. Eccles., lib. v. cap. xvii.

Quòd totidem menses, totidem quod conficis horas.
Quatuor alipedes dicunt te flectere habenis,
Quòd solus domites, quam dant elementa quadrigam.
Nam tenebras prohibens, retegis quod cerula lucet.[1]
Hinc Phœbum perhibent prodentem occulta futuri ;
Vel quia dissolvis nocturna admissa.  *Isæum*
Te Serapim Nilus, Memphis veneratur Osirim :
Dissona sacra Mitram, Ditemque, ferumque Typhonem :
Atys pulcher item, curvi et puer almus arratri,
Ammon et arentis Libyes, ac Biblius Adon.
Sic vario cunctus te nomine convocat orbis.
Salve vera deûm facies, vultûsque paternæ,
OCTO ET SEXCENTIS NUMERIS, CUI LITERA TRINA
CONFORMAT SACRUM NOMEN, COGNOMEN, ET OMEN.
Da, Pater, æthereos mentis conscendere cœtus :
Astrigerûmque sacro sub nomine noscere cœlum.
Augeat hæc Pater insignis memorandus ubique.[2]

Latium calls thee Sol, because thou alone art in honour, AFTER THE FATHER, the centre of light ; and they affirm that thy sacred head bears a golden brightness in twelve rays, because thou formest that number of months and that number of hours.   They say that thou guidest four winged steeds, because thou alone rulest the chariot of the elements.   For, dispelling the darkness, thou revealest the shining heavens.   Hence they esteem thee, Phœbus, the discoverer of the secrets of the future ; or, because thou preventest nocturnal crimes.   Egypt worships thee as *Isæan* Serapis—and Memphis as Osiris.   Thou art worshiped by different rites as Mithra, Dis, and the cruel Typhon.   Thou art also the beautiful Atys, and the fostering son of the bent plough.   Thou art the Ammon of arid Libya, and the Adonis of Byblos.   Thus under a varied appellation the whole world worships thee.   Hail ! thou true image of the Gods, and of thy father's face !  THOU WHOSE SACRED NAME, SIRNAME, AND *Omen*, THREE LETTERS MAKE TO AGREE WITH THE NUMBER 608.   Grant us, oh Father, to reach *the ethereal intercourse of mind*, and to know the starry heaven under this sacred name.   May the great and universally adorable Father increase these his favours.

For an explanation of the Sacrum Nomen, vide Celtic Druids.[3]

For the reason given above by Colonel Wilford, M. Cassini has shewn that the æra of Buddha ought to be fixed to the year 543, not 544, before Christ.   It is said that the Cali Yug took place 3101 years before Christ.   The era of Buddha, it has been before stated, is calculated from his death.   Now let us count the difference between his death and the beginning of the cycle for his life, and it will be 57.   Take this from the time the Cali Yug has run, and it will give 3101—57 = 3044.   Take from this the time which Christ is placed too late, accordering to Usher, viz. 4 years, and we shall have from the beginning of the Cali Yug 3040.   Divide this by the mystical number of Martianus Capella, the Monogram of Christ, ΥΗΣ, = 608, and we shall have exactly the number of five Yugs, or five great Neroses, between the flood, or the entrance of the Sun into the Hindoo Aries or the beginning of the Cali Yug, and Christ.   This and the three in the preceding 2160 years, the time the Sun took to pass through Taurus, make up the eight.

In the 2160 years there is an excess of 360 years over the three Cycles or Neroses.   This arises from the system having originally commenced, or at least been in existence, when the precession was supposed to be 1800 years in passing through a sign, treated of before in Section 5.   This was probably connected with Enoch's conveyance to heaven, when 360 years of age, (not 365), as his age ought to be.   I shall return to this presently.

If we take from the period of 5,200 stated by Cassini as Eusebius's, (viz. from the creation to the birth of Christ,) the precession for one sign, viz. 2160, we shall leave exactly 3040, which sum is five sacred Christian periods, or great Neroses of 608 each.   Thus : 5 × 608 = 3040 ; which will

---

[1] Quæ cærula lucent ?        [2] Martianus Capella, de Nuptiis Philologiæ, Lib. ii. p. 32.        [3] Ch. iv. Sect. viii.

be the time from the Cali Yug, or the entrance of the sun into Aries, to the birth of Christ, according to Eusebius.[1]

Again, add together 4 cycles of 600 each, and we have ........................... 2400

Then add the æra of the death of Buddha pointed out by Cassini.................... 543

Then add the difference between the æra of his death and the beginning of a Neros, the duration of his life ............................................ .................... 57

And it leaves exactly 5 Neroses ........................................... 3000

The beginning of the Cali Yug is invariable, being 3100 B. C., or 3044 before Vicramaditya.[2] This last 3044+2160=5204, is Eusebius's period, Usher's mistake allowed for.

If in the last calculation we count the æra for the death of Buddha at 544, as uncorrected by Cassini, and take the age of Buddha at 56, exactly the time, according to the Lebtarikh, which Augustus was born before Christ, we shall have 3000 years, or five Neroses from the flood to the birth of Christ.[3]

Wilford says, the Samaritans count 3040 years from the flood to the birth of Christ. From this it appears that they used the Neros of 608 in their calculation.

Again, from the period between the Cali Yug and Christ, 3101 years, take the time between the epoch 543 and Christ, viz. 57, and we have 3044: exactly the time, according to the Samaritan computation, between the birth of Christ and the flood, Usher's error allowed for.

In India there was an æra called the æra of Vicramaditya. Many learned Pundits make him begin to reign 3044 years after the flood, and they add that, after a reign of 56 years, he died in the year 3101, which year 3044 was the first of the Christian æra of the flood, according to the Samaritan computation, Usher's error allowed for; thus completing the cycle, and with three before the flood, make the eight required.[4]

Years of the world to Christ............ 4000
Years from creation to flood ············ 1656
                                         2344
Admitted error in Hebrew, or the }
Samaritan without error········ }   ....   700
                                         3044
Life of Vicramaditya 56 years.......... 56
                                         3100

This shews the Indian and Samaritan to be precisely the same.

There was also an æra of Salivahana, of whom I shall have much to say hereafter. He conquered and killed Vicramaditya. His æra commenced at the death of his enemy, that is, at the birth of Christ. The Samaritans, who give 700 years more between the flood and Christ than the Hebrew and Vulgate, appear to have calculated by the precession of the equinoxes, and to have

---

[1] The Cali Yug begins when the Sun enters Aries at the Vernal Equinox. Jones, Asiat. Res. Vol. II. p. 393. This is the date of the flood according to the Brahmin doctrines.

[2] Asiat. Res. Vol. IX. p. 86.

[3] According to some calculations, Augustus was born 63 years before Christ. (Asiat. Res. Vol. X. p. 33.) Then 5 Yugs or Neroses=3000+638+63=3701—3101=600. This evidently alludes to the second æra of Buddha, of 638 years after Christ, formerly noticed in Section 1.

[4] Asiat. Res. Vol. X. p. 122.

calculated in such a manner, that 65 degrees, and a part of a degree, had passed at the birth of Christ :
$65 \times 72 = 4680$; add for a part of a degree 20 years $= 4700$.  The principle on which the Samaritan
computation is made is pretty clear.

As the Samaritans count[1] 3044 between the flood and Christ, and as they reckon 4700 from the
creation to Christ, they must reckon the same time between the creation and flood as Usher, viz.
1656 years.[2]  The Julian period begins, the 4 years' mistake of Usher allowed for, 4709 or 4710
years before Christ.  This evidently is meant to coincide with the Samaritan system.

All these periods are correct except the Julian period, which comes sufficiently near to prove
very clearly, that what Megasthenes said was true, that the Jews and the Hindoos had the same
system of chronology, and we shall see by and by, in a future book, when I come to treat of the
Jews, the reason of this.

The Greeks and Romans considered the two numbers 608 and 650 as in a particular manner
sacred to Bacchus.  Now, when Eusebius was making out his 5200 by deducting from it the years
of the precession in the sign Taurus, and then calculating five cycles from the beginning of Aries
to Jesus Christ, as the reader has seen, he would naturally inquire, what the other sacred number
650 would do; and he would find, that if multiplied by eight, (the number of cycles stated by Juvenal and Censorinus to have run to Christ,) it would exactly make his number of 5200; so that
one made the cycles from Taurus, the other from Aries,—but both coming to the same thing, eight
cycles in the whole, and the same number of years.  It seems to me to be absolutely impossible,
that the coincidence of these numbers can have been the effect of accident.

The cycle of 600 does not appear to have been known as a sacred number to the Greeks and
Romans, but only to the Jews and oriental nations.  The reason was, because the 608 and 650
came from the East before their error was discovered.  I think I need not have desired any thing
better to confirm, both my theory of the origin of the sacred solar numbers, and of the eight periods
or cycles to the birth of Christ, than that the multiplication of the 650 by eight, should give us the
exact number stated by Eusebius to have passed before the birth of Christ.

The following is surely a singular coincidence of numbers :

| | |
|---|---|
| Usher's age of the world ·············· | 4004 |
| Usher's time of the flood ·············· | 1656 |
| Flood before Christ ····················· | 2348 |
| Add Samaritan correction··············· | 700 |
| | 3048 |
| Add *real* precession for one sign ·········· | 2152 |
| | 5200 |

If we suppose, as is the fact, that the sun left the last degree of Aries, and entered Pisces, about
the year 380 before Christ, and add the years of the commonly reputed precession for the two signs
Aries and Taurus, $2160 + 2160 = 4320$, we shall have exactly the Samaritan computation $4320 +
380 = 4700$.  If this be accident, it is surely a wonderful accident, that should bring all those num-
bers which my theory requires to an exact agreement.

---

[1] Asiat. Res. Vol. V. p. 241.

[2] See Universal History, Vol. I. p. 147, where the Hebrew and Samaritan chronology, before the flood, are reconciled
on the hypothesis of Father Tournemine.  In this reconciliation, I think, will be found the trifling error or difference
before mentioned, of the ten in the Julian period.

I consider this to be very important, because the Samaritan computation not only agrees with the Hindoo in system, but it adopts the error, using its favourite number 72 instead of 71 ; and again, the Hindoo error of 2160 instead of 2152.

Colonel Wilford says, " The year of the death of Vicramarca and that of the manifestation of " Sal'-ba-han, are acknowledged to be but one and the same, and they are obviously so ; according " to the Cumarica-chanda, that remarkable year was the 3101st of the Cali Yuga, and the first of " the Christian æra, thus coinciding also with the Samaritan text, which is a remarkable circum- "'stance."[1]

With respect to the time fixed by Eusebius for the age of the world before Christ, we must re-collect that it is very different from all the others, because at the time when he and his master, Constantine, were settling and establishing the Christian religion—destroying by the agency of Theodoret such gospel histories as they thought wrong, and substituting such as they thought right — they may be fairly supposed to have had information on these subjects, which may very easily have been lost in later times. I think no one will believe that it was by accident, that the number of the years of the Sun's precession in a sign, (2160,) the number of Eusebius, (5200,) and the eight cycles, agreed with the doctrines of Juvenal and Censorinus and the eight Avatars of India.[2]

Every part of this curious mythos betrays marks of a system founded originally in error, but at this day lost, and made out by expedients or doubtful calculations : and when we reflect upon the fact stated by Josephus, that the Jews had a knowledge from their ancestors of the beautiful cycle of the Neros, we need not be surprised that their chronology should shew proofs of their know-ledge of the precession of the equinoxes, as the Samaritan, I think, does. When Josephus says that the Jews had the Neros, he of course means the Israelitish nation, the descendants of Abraham.

# CHAPTER III.

SUBJECT CONTINUED. — TWO CYCLES. JOSHUA STOPS THE SUN AND MOON. — JEWISH INCARNATIONS.— MILLENIUM. PRITCHARD. PLATO.—JEWISH AND CHRISTIAN AUTHORITIES FROM DR. MEDE.—PLUTARCH AND OTHER WESTERN AUTHORS ON THE 600-YEAR CYCLE.— THE HINDOOS HAD DIFFERENT SYSTEMS. —OBSERVATIONS ON PYTHAGORAS, &c.—LA LOUBÈRE ON THE WORD SIAM.

1. As we have the two small cycles 600 and 608, we have in like manner two *systems* of chrono logy depending upon them. The first is Eusebius's. It begins with the egress of Noah from the

---

[1] Asiat. Res. Vol. X. p. 122.

[2] Methodius, Bishop of Tyre, states, that in the year of the world 2100, there was born unto Noah a fourth son, called Ioni-thus. (Nimrod, Vol. I. p. 4.) This has certainly a mythological appearance and looks as if it was meant for the 2160 years, the precessional time between Taurus and Aries. If this 2100 be added to the 3100 years which the Hindoos place between the flood and Christ, it exactly makes up the date fixed on by Eusebius, 5200 years for the age of the world. The word *Ioni*, we know the meaning of, and may not the *Thus* mean *the black ?* for it is often written Ioni-chus. Perhaps it may allude in some way to a schism which took place between the followers of Taurus and the Ioni, which I shall treat of presently, and the followers of the Yoni alone. Other chronicles confirm the existence of this Ioni-thus as a son of Noah. He was a famous astrologer and prophet. " He held the region from the entering in " of Etham to the sea, which region is called Heliochora, because the sun riseth there."

ark. Deducting from his statement of the world's age (i. e. 5200) the years of the precession for the sign Taurus, 2160, and it leaves 3040, equal to 608×5, or five Great Neroses to the birth of Christ. This, as we have before noticed, is the correct Samaritan computation, according to Col. Wilford,[1] the mistake of Usher being allowed for, and correct, according to Marsham and Hevelius.

The second system begins at the birth of Shem. The fourth period ends with the death of Shem, who lived exactly 600 years, and who is said[2] to have died in the year of the flood 502. Then, 502+3101 (the duration of the Cali Yug before Christ)=3603; the Neros, that of Shem, being deducted, it leaves 3003, and then Usher's 4 years for the birth of Christ placed too forward, being also deducted, we have 3000, or five correct Neroses of 600 years each, all but an unit, which we have seen is of no material consequence.

It is a circumstance worthy of observation, that Shem is said by Usher to have died at the 2158th which may be called 2160th year of the world's age. These were the years of the precession in one sign. This, like other coincidences, could scarcely have been the effect of accident. If we add to 2160, five great Neroses or 3040, we shall have the calculation of Eusebius, the man of all others, since the time of Christ, the most likely to understand the machinery of the system. And this again shews why, in these calculations, the time which the equinox preceded in one sign, viz. 2160 years, ought to be deducted.

Thus we have two systems of the Neros, one of 600, and the other of 608 years each.

Hesiod, in his Works and Days, makes out that he is *himself* living in the fifth age, that of Iron, the fourth having just passed away. This evidently alludes to the six millenaries, in the fifth of which he lived. A learned and anonymous author of Cambridge (Key to Chronology of the Hindoos) comparing the chronology of the Hindoos and Jews says, speaking of the Works and Days, " The commencement of the fourth age is, if possible, yet more clearly marked. The three first " ages having consumed 1000, 800, and 600 years, the fourth commences with A. M. 2400—and to " this age is assigned 400 years. Hesiod styles it the age of the Demigods, and represents a part " of it as a time of great virtue, justice, and piety." We may here observe how the ingenious Cantab,[3] who does not in the least understand or even suspect the nature of my theory, stumbles upon my numbers, only mistaking the end of the fourth age, 2400, for its commencement. He thinks Moses answered to Cristna. This alludes to the period which the Samaritans allotted to the bringing of the ark to Shiloh, by Joshua.

It is stated, Joshua x. 12, 13, that he stopped the sun and moon ABOUT a day : *Sun, stand thou still upon Gibeon; and thou, Moon, in the valley of Ajalon—and the Sun hasted not to go down* ABOUT *a whole day. Is not this written in the book of Jasher ?* [4]

The Bible says, "about *a day.*" I shall endeavour to shew *why* and for *how long a time* Joshua stopped it. This stoppage probably continued during the time between the ending of one of Noah's and one of Shem's cycles, viz. 98 years : i. e. 98 + 502 = 600. By this means he brought the two cycles together. 98 years would be more than equal to one degree, or the 360th part of the circle, but not quite to one degree and a half. At that time each degree, or 72 years, represented a day, of the year of 360 days long. Every festival would fall back a day in about 72 years.

The circumstance of the Moon being stopped as well as the Sun, is allusive to the double cycle, of Sun and Moon. It was a throwing back the Luni-solar period. If this were not so, why should

---

[1] Asiat. Res. Vol. V. p. 241, Map.        [2] Universal History.        [3] Vol. II. p. 289.

[4] As our version says, but as Josephus says, *in the writings laid up in the temple.* (See Parkhurst in voce ישר *isr,* and in voce ספר *spr.*) But, as I should say with Parkhurst, *in the emblematical writing ;* and, I should also add, of the Saviour ישר *isr;*—from the word ישע *iso,* to save.

Joshua make use of the expression to stop the Moon? Surely the Sun gave light enough without the Moon! I suppose nobody is so weak now as to take these texts to the letter.

The system of Shem was that of 608 years to a Neros, and when Joshua is said to have stopped the Sun and Moon, he dropped the use of the 608 and adopted the 600. He corrected the Calendar, as Cæsar did in a later day. In all these calculations I look upon the first books of Genesis as Hindoo works, and, for reasons which will hereafter be given upon the Mosaic and Hindoo systems, in their foundations or principles the same. The Mosaic has been shewn to be the same as the Persian, and Sir William Jones has shewn that the old Persian was the same as the Hindoo, which is also proved, by the Desatir of Moshani.

It is admitted that the Neros could not have been invented without a very great degree of astronomical knowledge, or till after very long and correctly recorded astronomical observations. As I have stated, the great Neros was probably the cycle before their increased knowledge enabled them to bring it to perfection, and was carried very early to the West, and is thus found with the Etruscans.

The cycles would require correcting again after several revolutions, and we find Isaiah making the shadow go back ten degrees on the dial of Ahaz. [1] This would mean nothing but a second correction of the Neros, or a correction of some cycle of a planetary body, to make it agree with some other.

In the annals of China, in fact of the Chinese Buddhists, in the reign of the Emperor YAU, (a very striking name, being the name of the God of the Jews,) it is said, that the sun was stopped ten days, that is, probably, ten degrees of Isaiah, [2] a degree answering to a year, 360 degrees and 360 days.

As might well be expected, when Joshua stopped the sun it was observed in India. Mr. Franklin says, " 1575 years before Christ, after the death of Cristna (Boodh the son of Deirca), the sun " stood still to hear the pious ejaculations of Arjoon. This is the great leader of the Jews— " Moses." [3]

The author of the Cambridge Key says, that in the text of the Bible the sun is said to stand still in A. M. 1451, the year in which Moses died. This is the Cali year 1651, in which the sun stood still to hear the pious ejaculations of Arjoon for the death of Cristna. [4] The learned Jesuit Baldæus observes, that every part of the life of Cristna has a near resemblance to the history of Christ : and he goes on to shew that the time when the miracles are supposed to have been performed was during the Dwaparajug, which he admits to have ended 3100 years before the Christian æra. [5] So that, as the Cantab says, *If there is meaning in words the Christian missionary implies that the history of Christ was founded on that of Crishnu.*

After this, in p. 226, Cantab goes on to shew, that it is almost impossible to doubt that the history of Cristna was written long prior to the time of Christ. The same mythos is evident, in all these widely-separated nations. Its full meaning, I have no doubt, will be some day discovered.

The Cali Yug is fixed to about the year 3100 before Christ, in the middle of the *ninth century*, by Albumazar, a famous-Arabian astronomer, who lived at the court of the celebrated Al-Mamun at Balkh. [6] This alone proves that the Hindoo periods are not of modern invention, and is of itself enough to refute all Mr. Bentley's arguments which have been used, and have for their foundation solely his assertion, that the astronomical calculations were forged for the purpose of deceiving Mahmood Akbar in the 16*th century*. George of Trebizond, who died about 1448, says, that the

---

[1] 2 Kings xx. 11; and Isaiah xxviii. 8.     [2] Pref. to the last Vol. of Univers. Hist. p. xiii.
[3] On Buddhists and Jeynes, p. 174.     [4] Vol. II. p. 224.     [5] Ibid.
[6] Vide Asiat. Res. Vol. IX. p. 142; Vol. X. p. 117.

Persians reckoned from the flood to A. D. 632, the æra of Yesdejird, 3733 years. Thus, 632+3101 =3733. This again shews that the Persians had the same system as the Hindoos,[1] and again clearly proves, that these Hindoo calculations cannot have been made to deceive Mahmood Akbar.

2. Noah began a new world, and thus also did Cristna.

In looking back to the Jewish history, I find the flood ended on the day that Noah finished his 600th year, when a new world began. We have already seen that the year of the saviour Cristna was feigned to be 600 years—the duration of the Neros. He was the saviour of India, expressly predicted in the ancient writings of the Brahmins. The saviour of the Jews and of Europe was the same. The Jewish incarnations were the same as those of the Hindoos, as was indeed almost every part of their system. But from the extremely corrupt state of the details of the Hebrew history in the three old versions of it, there is no probability that the cycles should ever be made out correctly according to either of them.

The first cycle began with the sun in Taurus, the creation of the system, and ended with Enoch, who did not die, but who ascended into heaven. I think this speaks for itself.

Enoch is said to have lived 365 years, but it is probable that his life was only 360, the time which it was necessary to intercalate to make up the difference between the three Neroses, and the precession for one sign, 1800+360=2160, when the system of Noah, the correct system, began. In this theory I am supported by evidence (under the circumstance in which we have it) which I call strong. Dr. Shuckford says, " Now if Enoch was 60 years old at *Methusaleh's* birth, according to " Eusebius himself, from Methusaleh's birth to the 180th year of Noah is but 300 years, and con- " sequently Eusebius, to have been consistent with himself, should have made Enoch's age at his " translation 360, but he has made it 365."[2] Dr. Shuckford has some very interesting observations on the different systems of chronology, and professes to have removed or accounted for the difference between the Hebrew and the LXX., with the exception of the very suspicious round sum of 600 years.

As I have just stated, I consider the Mythos of Enoch as an intercalation, to make the periods come right, after the discovery that the precession did not take place in 1800 years, but in 2160; 1800+360=2160. The cyles were like men, and died of old age. The cycle of Enoch not being finished, he was taken up to heaven, but did not die. In every part of this mythos we see proofs that, like most other systems of this kind, it was made up by expedients from time to time, as circumstances called for them. The first errors respecting the true length of the cycles, and their subsequent improvements, rendered this a necessary consequence. The Arabians called Enoch *Edris,* and say that Edris was the same as Elijah, who did not die. And the Arabians and the Jews also had a tradition, that Phinehas, the son of Eleazar, revived in Elijah.[3] Thus the Jewish and Arabian traditions unite Enoch and Elijah, and Elijah and Phinehas, by correct renewed incarnations ; and I suppose every one who reads this will recollect, that the Jews are said to have believed Jesus to be Elijah.[4] Jesus declares that John Baptist came in the SPIRIT and power of Elijah.[5] These circumstances have at least a *strong tendency* to prove, if they do not really prove, that the Hindoo doctrine of renewed incarnation was the esoteric religion of the Jews. When Elijah went up to heaven he left his cloak and prophetic office to Elisha, or to *the Lamb of God.*[6]

The Arabians say that Elijah was the same with Enoch and Phinehas, who was the same with a person called by them Al-Choder. But Al-Choder signifies a Palm-tree. In Sanscrit Al Chod is

---

[1] Asiat. Res. Vol. X. p. 119.          [2] Connec. B. i.          [3] See Hottinger de Mohamedis Genealogiâ.

[4] Mark viii. 28.                        [5] Matt. xi. 10, 14.

[6] In a future page I shall shew, that this cloak is the Pallium of the Romish church, by the investiture with which the Popes infused a portion of the Holy Ghost into their Bishops. Without the investiture there was no bishop.

God,[1] as it is in English. " Thus, then, according to the Arabian traditions, Henoch was the same
" with Elijah, and Elijah with Phinehas. But all these three were the same with Al-Choder, that is,
" ὁ φοῖνιξ, *palma.*" This Al-Choder is said to have flourished at the same time with a certain
*Aphridun* which signified ὁ φοῖνιξ, *avis.*[2] We have not inquired respecting the birth-place of this
celebrated bird. Lucian says what we might expect, that it is an Indian bird, Φοῖνιξ το Ινδιχον
οργεον. But the Irish have it in Phenn, and Phennische.[3]

The *annus magnus* of the ancients was a subject of very general speculation among the Greeks
and Romans, but not one of them seems to have suspected the sacrum nomen, cognomen, et omen,
of Martianus Capella. Several of them admit that by the Phœnix this period was meant, or at
least that its life was the length of the great year. From this I conclude that, as it was well known
to Martianus Capella, it must have been a secret known only to the initiated. Solinus says, it is a
thing well known to all the world, that the grand year terminates at the same time as the life of the
Phœnix.[4] This is confirmed by Manilius and Pliny.[5]

George Syncellus says, that the Phœnix which appeared in Egypt, in the reign of Claudius, had
been seen in the same country 654 years before. On this Larcher says, " This pretended Phœnix
" appeared the seventh year of the reign of Claudius, the year 800 of Rome, and the 47th year of
" our æra. If we take from 800 the sum of 654, which is the duriation of life of this bird, accord-
" ing to this chronographer, we shall have for the time of its *preceding* apparition the year 146 of
" the foundation of Rome, which answers to the year 608 before our æra."[6] It is surely a very
extraordinary *accident* that should make the learned Larcher's calculation exactly agree with the
term of one of the great Neroses, which this bird's name means; and also, that the other term
147 of our æra, should, within one year, be the term of the six last whole Neroses of Shem, from the
flood : $6 \times 608 = 3648$. Deduct one Neros, thus, $3648 - 608 = 3040 = 5$ Neroses. We must recollect
that the Neros of Shem, in the time of the flood, was partly before the flood and partly afterward,
so the one spoken of might be said to be either the fifth or the sixth from the flood. Faber says,
" sometimes the Phœnix is said to live 600, sometimes 460, and sometimes 340 years."[7]

We will now return to the cycles. I before stated that I suspected the first ended with the
birth of Enoch. The second ended with the birth of Noah. The third ended with Noah leaving
the ark, when he was 600 years old. The fourth ended about the time of Abraham, and was probably Isaac, whose name may mean *joy, gladness, laughter,* and who was so called because he was
the saviour, not because his mother laughed at God.[8] The word I shall explain in a future page,
when I treat of the Jews. And here it may be observed, that in the conduct of this curious system,
if I correctly develop it, the incarnations ought not to coincide exactly with the beginning of a
cycle ; because, though the priests could regulate the dates of long-past events, they could not so

---

[1] Al-Choder is the Syrian and Rajpoot OD only aspirated, and with the Arabic emphatic article AL. When the Buddhists address the Supreme Being or Buddha, they use the word AD, which means *the first.* This is exactly one meaning
of the first word of Genesis. Here we have *the first* and Wisdom, (Col. Tod,) as in Genesis.—Buddha, Wisdom, is
called Ad, *the first.*

[2] Sir W. Drummond, Class. Journ., Vol. XV. pp. 12, 13.

[3] In the Irish Trinity called Tauloc PHENN Molloch, the Middle, or Saviour, is the Phenn, 600.

[4] Solini Polyhistor. Cap. xxxvi., Ed. Salmas.

[5] Hist. Nat. Lib. x. Cap. ii., and Mem. Acad. Paris, An. 1815, in a treatise by Larcher.                    [6] Ibid.

[7] Orig. Pag. Idol. Vol. I. p. 147.

[8] The exoteric reason given to the devotees of Judea, and, as it appears from their being satisfied with it, suitable to
their understandings, as it has hitherto been to the understandings of the devotees of London ; but the inhabitants of
the latter are fast outgrowing, when literally understood, such nonsense,—at least they are in St. Giles's, whatever they
may be in Lambeth and St. James's.

easily regulate the births or deaths of individuals, entered most carefully in public registers,—facts which must have been remembered by families,—but events, such as the arrival of the ark at Shiloh, would be easily swelled into importance, and regulated also as to its date, to make it suit.   In the course of a very few years the actual date of such an event would be forgotten, and might be advanced or retarded a few years to suit the occasion.   It is evident also, that it is only some events of this kind which could be regulated.   For example the going out of Abraham must be difficult to reconcile, if it were wished, which it probably was not.   This going out I shall by and by explain, and shew its truth.   All this is perfectly consistent if there were such persons as Isaac, &c., the supposed incarnations, as I shall shew there were—persons who had those peculiar names given to them, because they were supposed to be incarnations.   The meaning of the ages of man in the Jewish books, and the lengths of time which events took in passing, I do not understand; but I have no doubt they had a mythological or figurative meaning, or concealed some doctrines.   To suppose that a system of chronology was really meant, is to suppose the writers of the books incapable of adding and subtracting, which any one must be convinced of in a moment by looking into Volney's Researches into Ancient History, where their *arithmetical* inconsistency with one another is shewn.

It was the belief that some great personage would appear in every cycle, as the Sibylline verses prove; but it was evidently impossible to make the birth of great men coincide with the birth of the cycle.   But when it was desirable to found power upon the belief that a living person was the hero of the cycle, it is natural to expect that the attempt should have been made, as was the case with the verses of Virgil and others, as I shall hereafter shew.   This great person is, according to Mr. Parkhurst, the type of a future saviour.

The fifth Jewish cycle might end when the Samaritans say the prophecy of Jacob was verified, that is, when Osee, expressly called the Messiah or Saviour—Joshua or Jesus—brought the ark to Shiloh.   The versions vary more than 200 years respecting the time of Abraham's stay in Canaan and the residence of the Israelites in Egypt; so that the chronology furnishes no objection.   The language of the prophecy of Jacob to Judah, that a Lawgiver should not pass from beneath his feet till Shiloh should come, has been a subject of much dispute.   Dr. Geddes and others maintain, that it is no prophecy, but Christians in general consider it to be one.   The Samaritans insist that it is a prophecy, and that it was fulfilled in the son of *Nun*, Osee, called properly Jesus or the Saviour, and improperly *Joshua*, on his bringing the ark to Shiloh, as remarked above.   Sir William Drummond has shewn, in a most ingenious and convincing manner, in his Œdipus Judaicus, how this prophecy is depicted on the sphere.

The sixth incarnation I will not attempt to name.   The Jews, like the Hindoos, had many saviours or incarnations, or persons who at different times were thought to be inspired, or to be persons in whom a portion of divine wisdom was incarnate.   This makes it difficult to fix upon the right person.   Might not Samson be one of them ?   He was an incarnation, as we shall soon see.

The next cycle must be, I think, that of Elias, (Ἡλιος) or Elijah, יהו אל *al-ieu*, or God the Lord, according to Calmet and Cruden, but I should say, *God the self-existent ;* that is, it means to say, an incarnation or inspiration of Ἡλιος or *the God*, יהו *ieu*, the Iaο of the Greeks, or the solar power. [1]   He left his prophetic power to Elisha, which Cruden and Calmet say means *the Lamb of God.*

It seems from the Hebrew words, when they come to be translated into English, that these

[1] It is curious to observe numbers of churches in Greece dedicated to St. Elias, which have formerly been temples of the sun.

books must have been esoteric, i. e. *secret* writings, known only to the chief priests, probably first exposed to the public eye by Ptolemy Philadelphus, 246 years before Christ, when he caused the Pentateuch to be translated. The explanation made by Ezra of such parts of the book as he thought proper at the gate of the temple, or the reading of it to the good king Josias, militates nothing against this hypothesis. I feel little doubt that the publication of the Jewish writings was forced, *as the Jews say*, by Ptolemy, and to that publication, I think, we are indebted for them ; for, after they were once translated and published, there would be no longer any use in keeping them locked up in the temple, and copies of the original would be multiplied. At the Babylonish captivity they were not destroyed, because the desolation of Palestine happened at two different periods ; so that one part of the people preserved the sacred book in their temple, when all was burnt in the temple of the other. When Cambyses sacked Egypt, all was destroyed in a moment, except the obeliscal pillars, which were left, and some of which are standing yet, particularly the finest of them all at Heliopolis.

Of the Hero of the eighth age it is said in our version, *Thus saith the Lord to his anointed,* HIS MESSIAH, *to Cyrus, whose right hand I have holden to subdue nations.* [1]  Here I beg it may be observed that if persons doubt the existence of Joshua or Abraham, they cannot well doubt the existence of Cyrus. This observation will be found of importance hereafter. The eighth period began about the Babylonish captivity, about 600 years before Christ. The ninth began, as the Siamese say, with Jesus Christ, making in all eight cycles before Christ.

I do not claim to be the first who has observed the renewal of incarnations among the Jews, nor can I deserve the whole of the ridicule which will be lavished by the priests upon the doctrine, because they cannot refute it. I learn from the Classical Journal, [2] that the Rev. Mr. Faber believed MELCHIZEDEK *to be an incarnation of the Son of God.* Mr. Faber says, " It was con-" tended that every *extraordinary* personage, whose office was to reclaim or to punish mankind, " was an avatar or descent of the Godhead." Again, " Adam, and Enoch, and Noah, might in " outward appearance be *different* men, but they were really the *selfsame* divine person who had " been promised as the seed of the woman, successively animating various human bodies." [3] From the black Cristna bruising the head of the serpent, and the circumstances of the two mythoses being so evidently the same, there seems nothing inconsistent in this. The renewed solar incarnation, every 600 years, seems pretty clear. The fact of a renewed incarnation could not escape Mr. Faber ; his mode of accounting for it is a different matter ; but I beg leave to add, that I must not be accused by the priests of being fanciful in this instance, since their great oracle, the very learned Mr. Faber, had stated it previously. Although the author of Nimrod does not appear to have the least idea of what I conceive to be the true system, yet the idea of a cycle in the history of Noah forcibly occurred to him. He says the fourth in order from Noah, with whom this present cycle, or system, of the world commenced. [4]

Col. Franklin, in his treatise on the Jeynes and Buddhists, says, " *First* Bood'h, the self-exist-" ing, *Swayam Bhuva,* whose *outar* or period of time commenced 4002 years before Christ, or, " according to the fictitious calculations of the Hindoos, 3,891,102 : he ended his mortal career " when the three first ages were complete, or, agreeable to the Hindoo computation, during the " commencement of the fourth age." [5]  Here is evidently a proof of the truth of my theory, though concealed under a mythos. Here is the first equinoctial Avatar Buddha, ending when the sun enters Aries, after three Neroses or ages, according to the Brahmins, when Cristna begins.

---

[1] Isaiah xlv. 1.       [2] Vol. XIX. p. 72.       [3] Fab. Orig. Pag. Idol. Vol. III. pp. 612, 613.
[4] Vol. I. p. 7.                  [5] P. 172.

Col. Franklin says, the Avatar ended *during the commencement* of the fourth age.   He was obliged to use this nonsensical mode of expression, because it would not fit to the end of the third or the beginning of the fourth age.   It ended in the middle of the fourth age.   This arises from confounding the equinoctial cycle with the Neros, which Col. Franklin did not understand.   He had a slight glimpse of the two systems of cycles, but did not see that there were two cycles running, but not exactly *pari passu*.

3.  I shall now endeavour to demonstrate the existence of the cycle of 600 or 6000 among the Western nations.   Col. Wilford has shewn that the Buddhas and Brahmins were well known and distinguished from each other by Strabo, Philostratus, Pliny, Porphyry, &c. [1]   The alternate destruction of the world by fire and water was taught by Plato.   In his Timæus he says, that the story of Phäeton's burning the world has reference to a great dissolution of all things on the earth, by fire.   Gale [2] shews that the Jews, as well as Plato, maintained that the world would be destroyed at the end of 6000 years; that then the day of judgment would come : manifestly the Jewish and Christian Millenium.

On this subject Plato says, " When the time of all these things is full, and the change is need-
" ful, and every kind upon the earth is exhausted, each soul having given out all its generations,
" and having shed upon the earth as many seeds as were appointed unto it, then doth the pilot of·
" the universe, abandoning the rudder of the helm, return to his seat of circumspection, and the
" world is turned back by fate and its own innate concupiscence.   At that time also the Gods,
" who act in particular places as colleagues of the supreme Dæmon, being aware of that which is
" coming to pass, dismiss from their care the several parts of the world.   The world itself *being*
" *turned awry*, and falling into collision, and following inversely the course of beginning and end,
" and having a great concussion within itself, makes another destruction of all living things.   But
" in due process of time it is set free from tumult, and confusion, and concussion, and obtaineth a
" calm, and then being set in order, returneth into its pristine course, &c." [3]   Nimrod then
adds, " as we farther learn from Virgil, that the next renovation of the world will be followed by
" the Trojan war—I do not think that more words are necessary in order to evince that the Ilion
" of Homer is the Babel of Moses."   Cicero says, [4]   " Tum efficitur, cum solis et lunæ, et
" quinque errantium ad eundem inter se comparationem confectis omnium spaciis, est facta con-
" versio."   And Clavius, Cap. i., says, " Sphæræ quo tempore quidam volunt omnia quæcunque
" in mundo sunt, eodem ordine esse reditura, quo nunc cernuntur."

The doctrine of the renewal of worlds has been well treated by Dr. Pritchard. [5]   He shews that the dogma was common to several of the early sects of philosophers in Greece; [6] that traces of it are found in the remains of Orpheus ; that it was a favourite Doctrine of the Stoics, and was regarded as one of the peculiar tenets of that school; and that we are indebted chiefly to their writings for what we know of this ancient philosophy.   But although the successive catastrophes are shewn to have been most evidently held by them, yet, from the doctor's account, it is very clear that they were not generally understood ; some philosophers describing the catastrophes to have taken place in one way, some in another; some by water, some by fire, and some by both alternately.   " Seneca, the tragedian, teaches that all created beings are to be destroyed, or re-
" solved into the uncreated essence of the divinity ;" and " Plutarch makes the Stoic Cleanthes
" declare that the moon, the stars, and the sun will perish, and that the celestial ether, which,

---

[1] Asiat. Res. Vol. IX. p. 298.            [2] Court Gent. Vol. I. B. iii. Ch. vii. Sect. iii. v.
[3] Plat. Polit. p. 37. apud Nimrod, Vol. I. p. 511.            [4] De Nat. Deor.
[5] Anal. of Egypt. Myth. p. 178.            [6] See Lipsius de Physiol. Stoic. Dissert. 2.

" according to the Stoics, was the substance of the Deity, will convert all things into its own
" nature, or assimilate them to itself. [1]    And Seneca compares the self-confidence of the phi-
" losopher to the insulated happiness of Jupiter, who, after the world has melted away, and the
" gods are resolved into one essence, when the operations of nature cease, withdraws himself for
" a while into his own thoughts, and reposes in the contemplation of his own perfections." [2]    The
Doctor shews that the same thing was affirmed by Chrysippus, Zeno, and Cleanthes ; and we find
passages similar to the foregoing cited by Cicero, [3] Numenius, [4] Philo Judæus, [5] and many others.
I think in the account given above of Jupiter from Seneca, we cannot help recognising the Hindoo
doctrine—Brahma reposing on the great abyss.  After this, the Doctor goes on to state [6] the
opinions of Numenius, Censorinus, Cassander, &c., as to the alternation from heat to cold, and the
length of the periods, in which they all disagree ; but enough comes out, I think, to shew that they
were all connected " with the revolution of the annus magnus, or great year," and must have
originally come from the East, where the doctrine of the change in the angle which the plane of
the ecliptic makes with the plane of the equator was well understood, [7] and whence it probably came
to the Greeks.    The words of Plato, cited above, *being turned awry*, are allusive to this.  It was
called Λοξιας, unless Λοξιας was applied to the elliptic orbits, of which I have some suspicion.  It
is very certain that if it be true that this change in the angle do take place, something very like
the alternations from heat to cold, and cold to heat, in certain long periods, must happen : and
paradoxical as many of my readers may think me, yet I very much suspect that if the angle do
increase and decrease as just mentioned, and the race of man should so long continue, evils very
like those above described must be experienced.

   " In the Surya-Sidhanta, Meya, the great astronomer, has stated the obliquity of the ecliptic
" in this time at 24°, [8] from whence Mr. S. Davis computed, that supposing the obliquity of the
" ecliptic to have been accurately observed by the ancient Hindus at 24°, and that its decrease
" had been from that time half a second a year, the age or date of the Surya-Sidhanta (in 1789)
" would be 3840 years ; therefore Meya must have lived about the year 1956 of the creation." [9]
It appears from the preceding sentence that Meya's system differs much from the older Puranas.
His begins from the moment the sun enters Aries in the Hindoo sphere, as Mr. Davis says,
" which circumstances alone must form a striking difference between it and the Puranic system." [10]
I am not sufficiently skilled in astronomy to speak POSITIVELY upon the subject, but I should
think that the reduction to nothing of the angle which the ecliptic makes to the equator, that is,
the coincidence of the equator and ecliptic, would necessarily cause some very great changes in the
circumstances of the globe.  The decrease of this angle or obliquity we see was certainly known
by the celebrated Brahmin Meya, who fixes it in his time at 24°.  The knowledge of this change
gave rise, I think, to the allegory or mythos of the flood.  The extraordinary changes which have
taken place at different and remote æras or long intervals, in the crust of our globe, cannot possibly be denied.  It was supposed that these were caused by the change in the angle above alluded
to, and the mythos of the flood and ship fastened to the peak of Naubanda was formed to account
for it to the vulgar.  This was I think confounded with another flood, of which I shall treat
hereafter.

---

[1] Plut.  [2] Seneca, Epist. ix.  [3] De Nat. Deor. Lib. ii.
[4] Apud Euseb. Prep. Evang. Lib. xv.  [5] De Immortal. Mundi.  [6] P. 183.
[7] Mr. Parkhurst has shewn (in voce שמש *ste*, vi. p. 730) that the declination of the plane of the ecliptic to the plane
of the equator was as well known to the ancients of the West as it is to the moderns.
[8] An interesting account of the discovery of this phenomenon may be seen in the preface to Blair's Chronology.
[9] Asiat. Res. Vol. V. 4to, p. 329.  [10] Ibid.

4. The following Jewish and Christian authorities will go far to establish what I have said respecting the above doctrines : Ita enim legitur in Gemara Sanhedrin, Perek CHELEK.   Dixit R. Ketina, *Sex annorum millibus stat mundus, et uno vastabitur : de quo dicitur,* ET EXALTABITUR DOMINUS SOLUS DIE ILLO.   Sequitur paulo post, *Traditio adstipulatur,* R. *Ketinæ : sicut e septenis annis septimus quisque annus remissionis est : ita e septem millibus annorum mundi, septimus millenarius remissiones erit : quemadmodum dicitur,* [1] ET EXALTABITUR DOMINUS SOLUS DIE ILLO. Dicitur item[2] PSALMUS CANTICUM DE DIE SABBATI ; id est, *de die quo tota quies est.* Dicitur etiam [3] NAM MILLE ANNI IN OCULIS TUIS VELUT DIES HESTERNUS.   *Traditio Domús Eliæ : Sex mille annos durat mundus ; bis mille annos inanitas, (seu vastitas* וחת *tueu,) bis mille annis lex : denique bis mille annis dies Christi.* [4]   None of the Fathers have written more clearly respecting the Millenium than Irenæus, and he expressly declares that, after it, the world shall be destroyed by fire, *and that the earth shall be made new after its conflgration.* [5].  Here is the admission of the identical renewal of worlds held by the oriental nations.   Irenæus, [6] Quotquot diebus hic factus est mundus, tot et millenis consummatur. . . . . .   Si enim dies Domini quasi mille anni, in sex autem diebus consummata sunt qua facta sunt : manifestum est, quoniam consummatio isporum sextus millesimus annus est.   Lactantius, [7] Quoniam sex diebus cuncta Dei opera perfecta sunt : per secula sex, id est, annorum sex millia, manere in hoc statu mundum necesse est.   Dies enim magnus Dei nille annorum circulo terminatur. . . . . .'. Et ut Deus sex illos dies in tantis rebus fabricandis laboravit, ita et religio ejus et veritas in his sex millibus aunorum laborare necesse est, malitiâ prævalente et dominante.   Mede's works, [8] where several other Christian authorities may be found.

St. Augustin had an indistinct view of the true system.   He says, that the fifth age is finished, that we are in the sixth, and that the dissolution of all things will happen in the seventh. [9]   He evidently alluded to the thousands, not the Neroses ; and that the world should be burnt and renewed. [10]  Barnabas says, " In six thousand years the Lord shall bring all things to an end."   He makes the seventh thousand the millenium, and the eighth the beginning of the other world.   Ovid quotes the expected conflagration :

> " Esse quoque in fatis reminiscitur affore tempus.
> " Quo mare, quo tellus, correptaque regia cœli
> " Ardeat, et mundi moles operosa laboret." [11]

Nothing astonishes me more than the absolute ignorance displayed in the writings of the ancients, of the true nature of their history, their religious mythology, and, in short, of every thing relating to their antiquities.   At the same time it is evident that there was a secret science possessed somewhere, which must have been guarded by the most solemn oaths.   And though I may be laughed at by those who inquire not deeply into the origin of things for saying it, yet I cannot help suspecting, that there is still a secret doctrine known only in the deep recesses, the crypts, of Thibet, St. Peter's, and the Cremlin.   In the following passage the real or affected ignorance of one of the most learned of the Romans is shewn of what was considered as of the first consequence

---

[1] Isai. ii. 11, 17.                     [2] Psal. xcii.                        [3] Psal. xc.

[4] Capentarius Com. Alcinoum Platonis, p. 322 ; Mede's Works, pp. 535, 894.   In the same page of Mede several other Jewish authorities may be seen for the existence of the 6000-year period.

[5] Floyer's Sibyls, p. 244.          [6] Lib. v. Cap. xxviii.          [7] De Divino Præmio, Lib. vii. Cap. xiv.

[8] P. 893.              [9] Civ. Dei, Lib. xxii. Cap. xxx. ; Ouseley, Orient. Coll. Vol. II. No. ii. p. 119.

[10] Floyer's Sibyls, p. 245.

[11] For prophecies of a Millenium, see Isaiah xxvi. 19, lx. 1, 3, 11, 12, 19, 21, lxv. 17, 18, 19, 25, lxvi. 12, 23 ; Ezekiel xlvii. 12 ; Joel iii. 18, 20 ; Isaiah xxiv. 23, xxv. 7 ; 2 Esdras viii. 52, 53, 54.

In their religion—the time of their festivals. Censorinus says,[1] " How many ages are due unto the
" city of Rome, it is not mine to say; but what I have read in Varro, that will I not withhold. He
" saith in the 18th book of his antiquities, that there was one Vettius, a distinguished Augur at
" Rome, of great genius, and equal to any man in learned disputations ; and that he heard Vettius
" say, that if that was true which historians related, concerning the auguries of Romulus the foun-
" der, and concerning the twelve Vultures, then, as the Roman people had safely passed over their
" 120th year, they would last unto the 1200th."[2]    I construe this to mean, that the Vultures had
relation to two cycles of 60 years each, or to the two of 600 each ; and, as time had shewn that it
did not relate to the former, it must relate to the latter.   Rome was to finish with the 1200th year,
because the world was then to end, as was supposed by the priests, who did not understand their
mythology.

But besides the period announced by their twelve Vultures, the Etruscans had also another ill-
understood system of ten ages, which was the system common· to the Hindoos, the ·Jews, and the
Romans, and this fact adds one more to the numerous proofs of the identity of the two races.

5. Plutarch in Sylla has ᵗtated, that on a certain clear and serene day, a trumpet was heard to
sound which was so loud and clear, that all the world was struck with fear.   On the priests of
Etruria being consulted they declared, that a new age was about to commence, and a new race
of people to arise,—that there had been EIGHT races of people, different in their lives and manners,
—that God has allotted to each race a *fixed period*, which is called the great year,—that when one
period is about to end and another to begin, the heaven or the earth marks it by some great prodigy.   The author of Nimrod[3] observes, that Plutarch gives the account loosely and mistakes the
age then ending, the eighth, for the ultima ætas; *for the correction of which we are indebted to the
invaluable treatise of Censorinus*.   This ultima ætas was the same as the Ultima Ætas Cumæi Car-
·minis of Virgil, which I believe meant, not the last age of the world, but the latter part of the age
or cycle sung of by the prophetess of Cuma,—as we should say, the last end of the cycle of the
Cumæan Sibyl had·arrived.   If it be supposed to allude to the periods of 120 years, I ask, how is it
possible to believe the Romans could be such idiots as to fancy that new Troys, Argonauts, &c.,
would arise every 120 years?   But I shall return to this again.

Although a certain great year was well known to the Romans, yet the nature of it seems, in the
latter times of the commonwealth, to have been lost.[4]   The end of one of these great years, and the
beginning of another, were celebrated with games called Ludi Sæculares.   They were solemnized in
the time of Sylla, when the ninth age was said to have commenced by his supporters, probably for
the sake of flattering him with being the distinguished person foretold.   Nimrod says " Sylla was
" born in the year of Rome, 616,[5] but it is uncertain in what year the Sæcular games were cele-
" brated, whether in 605, in 608, or in 628.   It was a matter of the most occult science and ponti-
" fical investigation to pronounce on what year each sæculum ended, and *I am not satisfied whether
" the Quindecemviri did not publish the games more than once, when they saw reason to doubt which
" was the true Sibylline year*.   *It was not fixed by law or custom to be an unvarying cycle of* 110
" *years*,

     " **Certus undenos decies per annos**
     " **Orbis,**

" till after the games held by Augustus ; if even then."[6]

---

[1] Cap. xvii. *in fine*.   [2] Nimrod, Vol. III. 496.   [3] Vol. III. pp. 459—462.
[4] For proofs that the Etruscans had lost the true length of the Sæculum, vide Niebuhr, Rom. Hist. Vol. I. pp. 93, &c.,
and p. 164.
[5] Appian, Civil. lib. i. cap. cv.     [6] Sueton. Domit. cap. iv.; Nimrod, Vol. III. p. 462.

The latter part of the above quotation which I have marked with italics, shews that the learned author of Nimrod was not aware that the great year was either the great or little Neros—either 600 or 608 years. His expression respecting the games probably being celebrated in more periods than the 608th year of Rome, in the time of Sylla, seems to shew that they were not then understood, and it seems actually to prove the correctness of the idea also of Nimrod, that all the early Roman history is a Mythos. I consider the fixing of the period by Augustus at 110 years, as a manifest modern contrivance to serve political purposes of the moment. The extreme difficulty and profound pontifical investigation necessary to fix the time of the Ludi Sæculares, admitted by Nimrod, was one of the circumstances which gave weight to the opinion of Figulus, named before, in Chap. II. Sect. 7, because he was considered to be the most learned in dark and mysterious science of any man in Rome.

From a careful consideration of all that has been written on the subject of the Ludi Sæculares, I am quite satisfied that the Romans had no certain knowledge respecting them, which is proved by the circumstance of their having celebrated them at different times, in order that they might hit upon the right time. Another fact, that one of these times was the supposed 608th year from the foundation of Rome, the great Neros, raises a strong presumption that this was originally the religious forgotten period to which they referred. The pretended period of 120 years, as a real period of history, is disposed of by an observation of the only historian of Rome to whom any attention can be paid—Niebuhr—who says,[1] " From the foundation of Rome to the capture, I here find 360 " years, (Rome's fundamental number, twelve times thirty,) and this period as a whole broken into " three parts: one third manifestly occupied by the three first kings, to the year 120 ; the second " by the remaining kings, to the banishment of Tarquin ; the third, the commonwealth. Divisions " so accurate are never afforded by real history. They are a sign which cannot be mistaken, of an " intentional arrangement dependent on the notion of a religious sanctity in numbers." This kind of superstition has every where prevailed and corrupted all history. Mr. Niebuhr's observation, that twelve times thirty make the 360, is true; but why should these numbers have been adopted? I apprehend they, in this case, counted by the cycle of Vrihaspati 60, and they made 6 cycles ; 6 × 60 = 360 : and this was founded on the Indian dodecan 5, which, with them, was called a Lustrum, and which, equally with the 6, formed a base for the cycle of 60, or of 120, or of 600, or of 1200, or of 6000, or of 432,000. By means of the two sacred numbers, 5 and 6, already described in my preliminary observations, (p. 6,) they would always form cycles, which would be commensurate with one another, so as easily to count their time, in order to regulate their festivals.

The ancient Etruscan sacred period was *ten*—that of the Romans (disguised under a story of twelve vultures) was *twelve*—but to make the two come together the twelve periods were made of 120 years each, (10 × 120 = 1200,) this makes up just two Neroses. But probably the Indian system of 432,000 was the secret cycle; for, from the founding of Rome to the building of Constantinople was called 1440 years : 4 × 360 = 1440, and 12 × 360 = 4320 : the same cyclical system. These circumstances, and the evident identity of the Sanscrit and Etruscan written languages, seem to raise a fair presumption, that the sacred cycles were the same in both India and Italy. I repeat that I feel no doubt that the Roman Sæculum of 110 years was, comparatively speaking, a modern invention, when, from the carelessness of the Consuls or Priests, the burning of the sacred books, or some other cause, their ancient measures of time had become lost. Varro states,[2] " In the eighth Sæcu- " lum it was written, that, in the tenth, they were to become extinct." This evidently refers to the 10 Neroses.

The observation of Mons. Niebuhr, respecting the Mythos, is very just, but he might have

[1] Vol. I. ch. xvii. p. 201.        [2] In Censorinum, cap. xvii.; Niebuhr, cap. v. p. 93.

gone a little farther, and have shewn that the Mythos was a correct imitation of that of Troy and of Egypt.

| ROME. | EGYPT. | TROY. |
|---|---|---|
| Romulus, Founder | Vulcan | Dardanus |
| Numa, Legislator | Apollo | Erichton |
| Hostilius, Warrior | Good Fortune | Tros |
| Martius | Serapis | Ilus |
| Tarquin | Pan | Ganymede |
| Servius Tullius | Osiris, Isis | Laomedon, Hesione |
| Tarquin the Superb, banished for the rape, by Sextus. | Typhon the Superb, destroyed by the Gods. | Priam lost the kingdom for the rape of Paris. |

And even the same system may be found in Kemfer's Japan. The whole may be seen drawn out at length by Gebelin.[1] The seven kings reigned 245 years,[2] thirty-five for each on an average, which is incredible. This shews it to be a Mythos.

When the first 600 years from the supposed foundation of the city arrived, and also when the 1200 arrived, the Roman devotees were much alarmed for fear of some great unknown calamity. This all referred to the lost period either of 600 or 608 years. In the later years of the Republic, or in the early years of the Emperors, the sæculum having become quite uncertain both as to its termination and its meaning, a shorter period was fixed on to gratify the people's love of shows, and the vanity of the ruler of the day in the exhibition of them. It is pretty certain that there were several systems in different nations, all arising from the supposed lengths of the Neros, the real length of which being only found out by degrees, they were obliged to make out their system by expedients as well as they were able.

If we take the period of the Trojan war as settled by Usher at 1194 years before Christ, making it very nearly two Neroses, the period with which these cycles in all different countries end, we shall see that the Mythos of Troy was the same as that of Rome. It is perfectly clear that the Romans knew there ought to be a sacred sæculum or age, that the eighth sæculum from the beginning of the world, was running, but the exact length of it, or when it began or ended, they did not know. The Sibylline verses, foretelling a new Troy and a new Argonautic expedition, cannot be construed to allude to a short period of 110 or 120 years : nor can the expression, *a series of ages which recurs again and again in the course of one mundane revolution*, be construed to refer to it. It may be said that Virgil's prophecy by the Sibyl of the age being about to expire will apply to the eighth century from the supposed building of Rome, as well as to the Neros. But this is not the case, because it will not apply to the renewal of Trojan wars, Argonautic Expeditions, &c.

Among all the ancient nations of the world, the opinion was universal, that the planetary bodies were the disposers of the affairs of men. Christians who believe in Transubstantiation, and that their priests have *an unlimited power to forgive sins*, may affect to despise those who have held that opinion, down to Tycho Brahe, or even to our own times ; but their contempt is not becoming, it is absurd. From this error, however, arose the opinion, that the knowledge of future events might be obtained from a correct understanding of the nature of the planetary motions. This was, perhaps, an improvement on the other. It was thought that the future fortunes of every man might be known, from a proper consideration of the state of the planets at

---

[1] Vol. VIII. p. 428.      [2] Ibid.

the moment of his birth. As, of course, these calculations would continually deceive the calculators, it was very natural that endeavours should be made (overlooking the possibility that the
system might be false from the beginning) to ascertain the cause of these failures. This was soon
believed to arise from a want of correctness in the calculation of the planetary motions—a fact
which would speedily be suspected and then ascertained. This produced the utmost exertion of
human ingenuity, to discover the exact length of the periods of the planets: that is, in other
words, to perfect the science of astronomy. In the course of these proceedings it was discovered,
or believed to be discovered, that the motions of the planets were liable to certain aberrations,
which it was thought would bring on ruin to the whole system, at some future day. Perhaps by
reasoning on the character of the Deity they might be induced to believe this to be incorrect, or at
least to doubt it, and this would at last be confirmed by the discovery that what appeared, in some
instances, to be aberrations, were periodical; and this at last produced the *knowledge*, or the belief,
that every aberration was periodical—that the idea of the system containing within itself the seeds
of its own destruction was a mistake. Whether they arrived at the point of calculating the exact
period of every apparent aberration may be doubtful; but it is very clear they believed that the
nearer they got to this point, the nearer to the truth would be the calculation of nativities or of the
fortunes of mankind, made from the planetary motions. Experience would teach them that they
never could be certain they had discovered all the aberrations, and thus they never could be certain
that they had calculated all the periods. They would also perceive that the longer they made their
cycles or periods the nearer they came to the truth. For this reason it was, and it was a sensible
reason, that they adopted the very long periods: for it was evident that, in every one of the
lengthened periods, multiples of 600, the cycle of the Sun and Moon would be included, and with
it would make a cycle. When our priests can discover, or suppose, no other reason for these
lengthened periods than a wish to appear the most ancient of nations, I fear they estimate the
understandings of those who discovered the Neros, by the measure of their own.

I do not pretend to shew how our modern astrologers tell their friends' fortunes, (for, be it observed, these gentlemen never pretend to tell their own, from which defect they sometimes get
hanged,) but the ancients proceeded, as Mons. Dupuis [1] has shewn, on a very ingenious plan, and,
*if their data had been true*, a very certain one. Believing that all nature was cycloidal, or periodical, as Virgil says—every thing will be renewed—new Iliums, new Argonauts, &c.—they supposed
that if they knew in what part of a planet's cycle a thing had formerly happened, they could
ascertain when it would happen again. And though this does not prove the truth of judicial
astrology, it certainly removes much of its absurdity; for, though the reason is false, it is not
foolish. Soon after the discovery of the last of the primary planets, an astrologer called on a friend
of the author's who was well known to be a skilful calculator, and requested him to calculate for
him the periodical motions of the newly-discovered planet; observing, it was probable that the
want of the knowledge and use of its motions was the cause that, in judicial astrology, the predictions so often failed. Here is a beautiful modern exemplification of the ancient reasoning which I
have just given above.

I am always rejoiced when I find my theories supported by learned Christian dignitaries. I
then flatter myself that they cannot be the produce of a too prurient imagination. Bishop Horsley
could not help seeing the truth, that the fourth Eclogue of Virgil referred to the child to whom
the kings of the Magi came to offer presents. In the second volume [2] of Sermons, he has undertaken to prove that this Eclogue is founded on old traditions respecting Jesus Christ, and that he

---

[1] Vol. III. p. 158.          [2] Sermon I.

is the child of whom Virgil makes mention. I suspect this learned Bishop had *at least* a slight knowledge of the esoteric doctrine. On this I shall say more when I treat of the Sibyls; I shall then shew that the bishop is perfectly right.

The period of the great Neros, I think, may be perceived in China.[1] La Loubère has observed, that the Chinese date one of their epochas from 2435 years before Christ, when they say there was a great conjunction of the planets; but this seems to be a mistake: for Cassini has shewn that there was no conjunction of the planets, but one of the Sun and Moon, at that time. This mistake arises from the destruction of their books, which was effected by one of their kings, about 200 years before Christ. Their period of 2435 years before Christ has probably been $608 \times 4 = 2432$. They calculated by a cycle of 60 years; this is evidently the same as the 600, Usher's mistake allowed for.

6. I think it is probable that, by Europeans, several allegories of the Hindoos have been confounded together, and it is exceedingly difficult to separate them. They are known to have had various periods called Yogas or Calpas, and it is not unlikely that their allegories alluded to the renewals of different periods : some to the renewal of all visible nature, the fixed stars included; some to our planetary system, and some only to the renewal of our globe; and to this last, the sæcula or ages of 600 and of 6000 years applied. It has been before observed, that it was anciently thought that the equinoxes preceded only after the rate of 2000, not 2160 years in a sign. This would give 24,000, or 4 times 6000 years, for the length of the great year. Hence might arise their immensely-lengthened cycles, because it would be the same with this great year as with the common year, if intercalations did not take place. It would be more erroneous every common year, till it travelled quite round an immensely-lengthened circle, when it would come to the old point again. Thus there were believed to be regenerations of the starry host, of the planetary host or our solar system, and of this globe. If the angle which the plane of the ecliptic makes with the plane of the equator had decreased gradually and regularly, as it was till very lately believed to do, the two planes would have coincided in about 10 ages, 6000 years; in 10 ages, 6000 years more, the sun would have been situated relatively to the Southern hemisphere, as he is now to the Northern; in 10 ages, 6000 years more, the two planes would coincide again; and, in 10 ages, 6000 more, he would be situated as he is now, after the lapse of about 24,000 or 25,000 years in all. When the Sun arrived at the equator, the 10 ages or 6000 years would end, and the world would be destroyed by fire; when he arrived at the Southern point it would be destroyed by water; and thus alternately, by fire and water, it would be destroyed at the end of every 6000 years or ten Neroses. At first I was surprised that the Indians did not make their Great Year 12 Neroses instead of 10; but a reason, in addition to that which I have formerly given, is here apparent : $12 \times 600 = 7200 \times 4 = 28,800$ instead of 24,000, the first-supposed length of the precessional year. This 6000 years was the age of the world according to the early Christians.

M. La Place professes to have *proved*, that the sum of the variation of the angle made by the plane of the equator with the plane of the ecliptic is only very small, and that the libration, which he admits, is subject to a very short period. Certainly the ruinous state of the strata of the earth might induce a belief that it was not small, but, as the Hindoos believed, very great.

An account is given by Suidas, to which reference has already been made, of the formation of the world as held by the Tuscans, or Etrurians. They supposed that God, the author of the universe, employed twelve thousand years in all his creations, and distributed them into twelve houses : that in the first chiliad, or thousand years, he made the heaven and the earth; in the next the firmament which appears to us, calling it heaven; in the third the sea and all the

---

[1] Hist. Siam. p. 258.

2 B

waters that are in the earth; in the fourth the great lights, the sun and the moon, and also the stars; in the fifth every volatile, reptile, and four-footed animal in the air, earth, and water; in the sixth man. It seems, therefore, according to them, that the first six thousand years were passed before the formation of man, and that mankind are to continue for the other six thousand years, the whole time of consummation being twelve thousand years. For they held, that the world was subject to certain revolutions, wherein it became transformed, and a new age and generation began; of such generations there had been in all, according to them, eight, differing from one another in customs and way of life; each having a duration of a certain number of years assigned them by God, and determined by the period which they called *the great year.*[1] If Suidas can be depended on, and I know no reason to dispute his authority, we have here, among these Italian priests, in the six ages of creation, evident proofs of the identity of their doctrines with those of the Hindoos, the ancient Magi of Persia, and the books of Genesis. And what is more, we have, if Mons. Cuvier can be depended on, proofs that these very ancient philosophical priests all taught the true system of the universe, one of the most abstruse and recondite subjects in nature. To what is this to be attributed? Most clearly either to the learning of the primeval nation, or to revelation. Different persons will entertain different opinions on this subject.

There are few readers who have read my abstruse book thus far, who will be surprised that I should look back to an existent state of the Globe in a very remote period. I allude to a time when the angle which the plane of the ecliptic makes with the plane of the equator was much larger than it is at this moment; the effect of which would be to increase the heat in the polar regions, and render them comfortable places of residence for their inhabitants. This easily accounts for the remains of inhabitants of warm climates being found in those regions, which they probably occupied before the creation of man. Every extraordinary appearance of this kind is easily accounted for, as the effect of that periodical motion of the earth which, *if continued*, will bring the planes of the ecliptic and equator to coincide, and, in process of time, to become at right angles to one another. The circumstance of the animals of the torrid zone being found in the high latitudes near the poles, is itself a decisive proof, to an unprejudiced mind, that the time must have been when, by the passage of the Sun in his ecliptic his line of movement was much nearer the poles than it is now, the northern regions must have possessed a temperate climate. This shews, in a marked manner, the sagacity of the observations of Buffon, Baillie, Gesner, &c., though ridiculed by weak people, that the northern climes were probably the birth-place of man. For though in the *cause* which they assigned for this they might be mistaken, in the *effect* they were correct.

7. The date of Pythagoras's birth has been much disputed by learned men. After what the reader has seen, he will not be surprised to find this great philosopher connected, as has been already noticed from the work of La Loubère, like the Jewish worthies, Augustus Cæsar, and others, with one of the Neroses. And the circumstance that the discovery has much of the nature of accident, or, at least, that it is not made out by me or any person holding my system, adds greatly to the probability of its truth. Dr. Lempriere, after stating the great uncertainty of the date of Pythagoras, says, " that 75 or 85 years of the life of Pythagoras fall within the 142 " years that elapsed between B. C. 608, and B. C. 466." Here 608, the boundary of his period, evidently bring out the cycle of the greater Neros. Whether the date of Christ be quite correct or not, there is no doubt that the learned men, who have at different times endeavoured to fix it,

---

[1] Anonym. apud Suid. in voce Tyrrheni, Univers. Hist. Vol I p. 64.—The Universal History adds, that the Druids also taught the alternate dissolution of the world by water and fire, and its successive renovation. Ibid.

have reasoned upon certain principles, and that they have all had access to the same data whereon to ground their calculations. When, therefore, I find this same number 608 constantly occurring as a number in some way or other connected with their periods, I cannot help believing that it has been used by the persons formerly making the ancient calculations. Thus in this I find 608 years to form one boundary, or to come out as one number. Again, in the inquiry into the proper period from the foundation of Rome, on which the Ludi Sæculares ought to be celebrated in the time of Sylla, I find that the result of the very difficult calculations of one or some of the aruspices employed for the purpose of making the calculations, brings out the number 608 as one of the probable periods on which they ought to be celebrated; and, as I find several other such coincidences with this peculiar number, I cannot help thinking that they tend greatly to confirm my doctrines. It shews that this sacred number was in general use, and it justifies me in believing that it was often used in cases where the direct evidence of its use is only weak, but where analogy of reasoning would induce me to expect to find it.

It is impossible to read Stanley's account of the doctrines of Pythagoras and not to see that, as a complete system, they were totally unknown to the persons who have left us the account of them. One says one thing, another says another. But it is evident, that much the greater part of what they say is *opinion* only; or what they had heard, as being the *opinion* of some one else. This state of uncertainty is the inevitable consequence of abstruse doctrines handed down *by tradition*. Then it follows, that evidence in these cases can amount at last only to probability, never to absolute demonstration. But when the probability is sufficiently strong, faith or belief will follow. And I think in reasoning, I have a right to take any asserted fact and reason upon it, depending for its reception by the reader, upon such evidence, positive, or circumstantial, or rational, as I shall be able to produce. Now I will produce an example of what I mean. We have every reason to believe, that Pythagoras travelled far to the East to acquire knowledge. In looking through the great mass of facts or doctrines charged to him, we find much oriental doctrine intermixed with truth and science, the same as we find at this day among the Brahmins : truth and science very much more correct than that which his successors (whose ignorance or uncertainty respecting him is admitted) knew or taught, mixed with an inconceivable mass of nonsense, of that description of nonsense, too, which his followers particularly patronized, and taught as sense and wisdom. Have we not, then, reason to make a selection, and give Pythagoras credit only for such parts as we find of the wise character to which I have alluded, and throw out all the remainder as the nonsense of his successors? What can be more striking than the fact of his teaching that the planets moved in curved orbits, a fact for the statement of which he got laughed at by his ignorant successors, but a fact which we now know to be well-founded !

All his doctrines, we are told by his followers, were founded on numbers, and they pretend to give us what was meant by these numbers, and choice nonsense they give us,—nonsense very unworthy of the man who taught the 47th proposition of Euclid, and the true planetary system. Then are we to believe them? I reply, no; we ought to believe only such parts as are analogous to the oriental systems, and to good sense. All the remainder must remain *sub judice*. I find very nearly the whole of the doctrine of numbers ascribed to him, by his successors, as nonsensical as their story of his golden thigh, so that I can give no credit to them; and, in consequence, I am obliged to have recourse to the East, and to suppose that when they repeat the admitted fact, that his doctrines were founded on numbers, the oriental numbers, on which the astronomical cycles and periods were founded, must chiefly be meant: such as the Zodiacal divisions, the Neros, the precessional year, &c. And this is confirmed when I read what has been extracted respecting Pythagoras from La Loubère, and when I find them stumbling on the cycle of the great Neros. If Pythagoras were not in some way or other connected with it, it seems surprising that this iden-

2 B 2

tical number preceding the celebrated epocha of Jesus Christ, as shewn by Cassini, should be found by our modern doctors as a boundary line in the way the reader has seen. There must have been some circumstances closely connected with the great Neros in the ancient data on which our modern divines have founded their calculations, to induce them to pitch upon this number. The effect must have a cause: accident will not account for it. The reader must not forget that all the ancients who give us the account of this philosopher, pretend to what they may, are only possessed of shreds and patches of his system. But I have little doubt that out of the shreds and patches left us by his successors, of the real value of which they were perfectly ignorant, a beautiful oriental garment might be manufactured—bearing a close analogy to the purest of what we find in the East, which, in our eyes, at this day, would be beautiful, but which, by his ancient biographers, would, like his planetary orbits, be treated with contempt. Before I conclude what I have to say, at present, respecting this great man, I will make one more observation. It is said, that the Monad, the Duad, the Triad, and the Tetractys, were numbers held in peculiar respect by him. The last is called the perfection of nature. But Dr. Lempriere says, " Every attempt, however, to " unfold the nature of this last mysterious number has hitherto been unsuccessful." This seems wonderful. Surely Dr. Lempriere cannot have understood the Hebrew language, or he would at once have seen that this can be nothing but the Tetragrammaton of the Hebrews—the sacred name יהוה ieue or ieu e—THE self-existent, the I am, often called the name of four letters, or, in other words, the TETRACTYS. This is confirmed by what, according to Aristotle, Pythagoras said of his Triad. " He affirmed that the whole and all things are terminated by three." Here are the three letters of the sacred word, without the emphatic article,—the three signifying I am Jah. Of the Tetractys he says, "Through the superior world is communicated from the Tetractys to the " inferior, LIFE and the being (not accidental, but substantial) of every species." "The Tetractys " is the divine mind communicating." This can be nothing but the Tetragrammaton of the Hebrews. I confess I can entertain no doubt that his Monad, his Duad, his Triad, and his Tetractys, formed the Hindoo Trinity, and the sacred name of four, including the three.

We have already seen that Buddha was born after TEN MONTHS, sans souillure, that is, he was the produce of an *immaculate conception*. This was attributed to many persons among the Gentiles; and whenever any man aspired to obtain supreme power, or to tyrannize over his countrymen, he almost always affected to have had a supernatural birth, in some way or other. This was the origin of the pretended connexion of Alexander's mother, Olympias, with Jupiter. Scipio Africanus was also said to be the son of God. There is no doubt that he aimed at the sovereignty of Rome, but the people were too sharp-sighted for him. A. Gellius says, " The wife of Publius " Scipio was barren for so many years as to create a despair of issue, until one night, when her " husband was absent, she discovered a large serpent in his place, and was informed by soothsay- " ers that she would bear a child. In a few days she perceived signs of conception, and after TEN " MONTHS gave birth to the conqueror of Carthage."[1] Arion was a divine incarnation, begotten by the gods, in the citadel Byrsa, and the Magna Mater brought him forth after TEN MONTHS, μετα δεκα μηνας. Hercules was a TEN MONTHS' child, as were also Meleager, Pelias, Neleus, and Typhon.[2] The child foretold in the fourth eclogue of Virgil was also a ten months' child. Augustus also was the produce, after a ten months' pregnancy, of a mysterious connexion of his mother with a serpent in the temple of Apollo.[3] The ten months' pregnancy of all the persons named above, had probably an astrological allusion to the ten ages. The name of Augustus, given to Octavius, was allusive to his sacred character of presiding dæmon of the Munda, κοσμος or cycle. Solomon, according to the Bible, was also a ten months' child.

---

[1] Aul. Gell. lib. vii cap. i.; Nimrod, Vol. III. p. 449.        [2] Nimrod, ib.        [3] Ibid. p. 458.

Several of the Hindoo incarnations, particularly that of Salivahana and of Guatama, of whom I shall treat by and by, are said, like Scipio, Augustus, Alexander, &c., to have been born after a ten months' pregnancy of their mothers, and also to have been produced by a serpent entwining itself round the body of the mother. The coincidence is too striking to be the effect of accident.[1]

The author of Nimrod has shewn, at great length, that about the time of Augustus, and a considerable time previously, there had been a very general idea prevalent in the world, that a supernatural child would be born, in consequence of a new age which was then about to arise; but the certain time of which was either unknown or a profound secret. All this was connected with the eighth cycle, which I have explained. To these supernatural births I shall return in a future page.

If my reader have gone along with me in the argument, he must have observed that there is a difficulty arising from the blending of the cycle of 600—the Neros and the cycle—and the distinguished personage who was the hero of it. I find it difficult to explain what I mean. Expressions constantly refer to the cycle of 600 years, and to a person, an incarnation of the divine mind. The age and person are confounded. This, it might plausibly be said, operates against my theory, if I could not shew that it was the custom of the ancient mystics thus to confound them. But we have only to look to the words of Virgil in the prophecy of the Sibyl, B. V. Ch. II. Sect. 7, and the quotation from Mr. Faber, and we have a clear example of what I allúde to. The ninth age was to arrive, but a blessed infant also was to arrive with it, to restore the age of gold. The age lasted 600 years, but it did not mean that the child was to live 600 years. The Buddha, the Cristna, the Salivahana of India, each arrived in a period, and they are identified with the period, but they are none of them said to have lived the whole term of 600 years. Cyrus was foretold, and I have shewn that he was born in the eighth age or cycle, but he was not supposed to live to the end of it. I acknowledge this would form a difficulty if it were not obviated by the express words of Virgil, which cannot be disputed. To the objection I reply, that the cycle or age in India and Judæa was used, precisely as it was by the mystics of Virgil. Whatever one meant respecting the child being born, was meant by the other. And this leads to another observation respecting the Messiah of the Jews. We have here express authority from the record itself what a Messiah was— what was meant when a Messiah was foretold. He was a man endowed with a more than usual portion of the divine spirit or nature, and as such was considered to be the presiding genius of the cycle—the αιων των αιωνων—the father of the succeeding ages. We have seen that the word Cyrus meant Sun.

The mother of Cyrus, or of the incarnation of the solar power, had, as we might expect, a very mythological name. She was called MANDA-ne.[2] In the oriental language this would have the same meaning as κοσμος, correctly a cycle. In the same spirit the mother of Constantine was called Helen, her father Coilus. Great mistakes (perhaps intended) have been made in the construing of the word mundus. It has often been construed to mean world, when it meant cycle. It was, I think, one of the words used by the mystics to conceal their doctrine, and to delude the populace.

The results of the calculations made by Cassini are in a very peculiar manner satisfactory. They are totally removed from suspicion of Brahminical forgery, either to please Mohamedan conquerors, or European masters, or sçavans, because they are strictly Buddhist, and have no

---

[1] Trans. Asiat. Soc. Vol. I. p. 431.
[2] This I take to be a word formed of *Munda* and *Anna*.

concern whatever with the followers of Cristna—Siam being far away from the country where the religion of Cristna prevails. The old manuscript which La Loubère sent over to Cassini was not understood by him, but sent to the astronomer for examination. It was not until a hundred years after this manuscript came to Europe, that any of the circumstances relating to Cristna, which the reader has seen from Mr. Maurice, &c., were known: and it is very probable that M. Cassini did not see the consequences which would arise from his calculations.

Mr. Maurice has laboured hard to prove that the Babylonians were the inventors of the Neros. This he does because he fancies it supports the Mosaic system. I shall now shew that it cannot have been invented either by them or by the Egyptians; and I suppose no one will suspect the Greeks of being the inventors of it. And this will compel us to go for it to the ancestors and country of Abraham, if we can only find out who and where they were: this I do not despair of doing in due time.

Respecting the extent of the walls of Babylon we have two histories, one of Herodotus, and the other of Diodorus Siculus, between which there appears at first to be a considerable disagreement. Herodotus states them to be, in his time, 480 furlongs; Diodorus, that they were originally made only 360, *in accordance with the supposed number of days in the year;* that two millions of men were employed to build a furlong a day, by which means they were completed in a year of 360 days.[1] This apparent contradiction Mr. Maurice has reconciled, by shewing from another passage of Berosus, reported by Josephus, that they were lengthened by Nebuchadnezzar, so as to equal those of Nineveh, which were 480 furlongs in extent. From this ignorance of the length of the year I conclude that the builders of Babylon could not be the inventors of the cycle of the Neros; nor could they even have known it. This fact is at once decisive against the whole of Mr. Maurice's theory, that the Babylonians were the inventors of the ancient astronomy. I place my finger on the cycle of the Neros, and unhesitatingly maintain, that the persons acquainted with it could not have believed the year to be only 360 days long.

Mr. Maurice has shewn that the Babylonians were ignorant of the length of the year so late even as the reign of Cyrus, until which time they supposed it to consist of only 360 days. This all tends to confirm Baillie's doctrine, that the Babylonian science is only the débris of an ancient system. The ignorance of the early Egyptians of the true length of the year is as well established as that of the Babylonians. This we learn from Diodorus Siculus, who, among other things, states that the Egyptian priests made 360 libations of milk on the tomb of Osiris, when they bewailed his death, which he says alluded to the days of the *primitive year,* used in the reign of that monarch.[2] I contend also, that the inventors of the Zodiac were in the same state with respect to science as the builders of Babylon, or they would not have divided it into 360 degrees only. Had they known the real length of the year, they would have made some provision for the five days.

Respecting the length of the old year, there is a very curious story in Plutarch, which has been noticed by Sir William Drummond, in his Œdipus Judaicus, p. 103, in the following words:
" The number 318 is very remarkable. Plutarch relates, that a connexion having been discovered
" between Saturn and Rhea, the Sun threatened that the latter should not be delivered of a child
" in any month or year. But Mercury, who was in love with Rhea, having won from the Moon
" at dice the 20th part of each of her annual lunations, composed of them the 5 days, which were
" added to the year, and by which it was augmented from 360 to 365 days. On these 5 days
" Rhea brought forth Osiris, Arueris, Typhon, Isis, and Nephte. Now the old year being com-

---

[1] Berosus, apud Josephus, Antiq. Lib. x. Cap. xi.

[2] Diod. Sic. Lib. xvii. p. 220; Maurice, Observ. on the Ruins of Babylon, p. 39.

" posed of 360 days, the 20th part amounts to 18 days. Let us then take 12 lunations at 28 days
" each, and we shall get a period of 336 days. Deduct a 20th part of the old year of 360 days
" from the 12 lunations at 28 days each, and the remainder will be 318 days. The equation may
" be given as follows : $28 \times 12 - \frac{360}{10} = 318$."

8. In the course of his history, M. La Loubère drops several observations which, when I consider the facts of two islands of Elephanta, two Matureas, the seed of the woman bruising the head
of the serpent in Europe and also in India, &c., &c., seem to me well worthy of notice. I shall
give them in his words and leave them to the reader, but I shall return to them again very often.
Speaking of the name of *Siam*, he says, (p. 6,) " and by the similitude of our language to theirs,
" we ought to say the *Sions*, and not the *Siams*: so when they write in Latin they call them
" *Siones*." Again, (p. 7,) " Nevertheless, Navarete, in his *historical treatises of* the kingdom of
" China, relates, that the name of *Siam*, which he writes *Sian*, comes from these two words *Sien*
" *lo*, without adding their signification or of what language they are." In the same page he says,
" from *Si-yo-thi-ya*,[1] the *Siamese* name of the city of *Siam*, foreigners have made JUDIA."[2] No
doubt at the present moment, my reader will think the facts stated respecting *Sion* and *Judia* of
no consequence, but in a little time, if he read with attention the remainder of this work, he will
find them well worthy of consideration. He will find them, when united to other circumstances,
to be facts to account for which it will be very difficult, upon any of the systems to which we
have been accustomed to give credit. My reader will not forget that we are travelling on mystic
ground ; and that the object of our researches, the secret history of the mythoses of antiquity, is
concealed from our view, not only by the sedulous care and the most sacred oaths of our ancestors, in the most remote ages, but by the jealousy of modern priests interested in preventing the
discovery of truth, and also by the natural effect of time, which is itself almost enough to render
of no avail the most industrious researches. It seems to be a law of nature, that the memory of
man should not reach back beyond a certain very confined boundary. We are endeavouring to
break down, to overstep, this boundary.

When we go to India we find that the Brahmins had eight Avatars complete, and were at or in
the ninth at the birth of Christ.[3] The first was Buddha or the Sun in Taurus, and all the Avatars
must have been, properly speaking, his till the flood, or the Sun entered Aries, when the first
cycle of Cristna and that of Joshua began, according to Col. Wilford. Then, after the last cycle
of Cristna, or the cycle of Cyrus, where his history, in part is found, had ended, perhaps such of
the priests as understood the secret doctrines might wish for, and might attempt to introduce, the
ninth Avatar, but to this the populace, and such of them as had perhaps forgotten or did not
know the secret meaning of their Avatars, would not consent.

It is not improbable that the attempt to introduce a new practice at the end of the periods of
six hundred years should have often been attended with religious wars. It seems to be almost a
necessary consequence, that these should take place. The devotees would, of course, be very
averse, as devotees always are, to part with their old superstition, which the initiated would perceive was becoming obsolete and unsuitable to times and circumstances ; hence might arise several

---

[1] This is evidently a corruption of the word I-oud-ya, the name of the kingdom of Oude, in Upper India ; and this
will be found, when joined to some other matters, to connect the capital of Siam with the city of Oude.

[2] In the city of *Siam* they have a sacred tooth of *Sommona-Codom*, resorted to by many pilgrims. This is the oldest
relic worship which I have met with. They have also a sacred foot of Sommona-Codom, the same as that in Ceylon,
and that named of *Hercules*, in *Scythia*, by *Herodotus*, and that of Jesus in Palestine This is the first sacred foot-
mark I have met with, the last is that of Louis le DÉSIRÉ on the pier at Calais ! ! !—Printed March, 1831.

[3] "Sree Mun Narrain, since the creation of the world, has at nine different periods assumed incarnated forms, either
for the purpose of eradicating some terrestrial evil, or chastising the sins of mankind. According to the Hindoo tradition a *tenth* is yet expected." Forster's Travels. p. 43.

of the religious wars which otherwise seem inexplicable. On this ground they are easily explained : and this circumstance will satisfactorily explain several other equally inexplicable phænomena, as we shall see hereafter. In some parts of India a *ninth* Avatar was believed to have come, called Salivahana ; in others, Ceylon for instance, he was thought to be another Buddha. Respecting this I shall say more hereafter.

Perhaps I shall be told that the incarnations of the Hindoo Gods are innumerable, and extend through millions of ages. This is true : probably to conceal their real periods from the profane eye.[1] But with these I do not meddle, as they do not militate against the existence of *real* cycles and for periods of *true* time. The ten incarnations were the ten revolutions of the Neros or the sacred OM. At the birth of Christ, *eight* had passed as allowed by the Brahmins, and testified of by Virgil, Zoroaster, and the Sibyls. All the mystics expected the world to end in 6000 years ; that was in ten Avatars, Yugs, Calpas, or ages of 600 years each. The Gentiles were in no fear, as they thought there were yet 1200 years to run, while many Christians, taking their uncertain and doubtful calculations from the LXX. and Josephus, expected the end of the world every day. They saw the calculations in these books could not be brought to any certainty ; and, to make the matter worse, they knew not whether their ages were to begin from the *creation* or the *flood.* But the term of 6000 years, for the duration of the world, was the generally received opinion among the early Christians ; and this continues to be the opinion of many of them. The celebrated mystic, Mr. Irving, who lately preached with great éclat to the rabble of St. James's and St. Giles's, in London, has just announced that the Millenium will commence in a very few years.

The reader may probably have observed that, in my inquiries into the various incarnations of Buddha and Cristna, and into the ancient cycles, &c., I have scarcely ever named any thing later than the supposed æra of Jesus Christ. Since that epoch, however, much very interesting matter and most valuable information respecting the last two cycles, and the origin of the Romish religion, *will be* laid before him ; but, after much consideration, I have determined to defer it until I have shewn whence the various rites and ceremonies of that religion, on which I have not yet touched, were derived. I shall also previously explain many other circumstances relating to the ancient mythoses.

---

# CHAPTER IV.

CROSS, THE MEANING OF IT. — JUSTIN AND TERTULLIAN ON THE CROSS. — MONOGRAMS OF CHRIST AND OSIRIS. — CROSS OF EZEKIEL AND OTHERS. — OTHER MONOGRAMS OF CHRIST. — CHRISMON SANCTI AMBROGII. — SACRED NUMBERS IN THE TEMPLES OF BRITAIN. — MITHRA. — JOSEPHUS AND VALLANCEY ON MYSTIC NUMBERS. — INDIAN CIRCLES. — LAMA OF TIBET. — INDRA CRUCIFIED. — JESUITS' ACCOUNT OF TIBET.

1. I WILL now shew how the cycle of 600, or the Neros, was concealed in another system and by another kind of mysticism. I scarcely need remind my reader that the cross has been an emblem used by all Christians, from the earliest ages. In my Celtic Druids he may see many proofs that it was used by the most ancient of the Gentiles, the Egyptians, and the Druids. The meaning of it, as an emblem, has been a matter much disputed. It has generally been thought to be

---

[1] Asiat. Res. Vol. II. p. 114.

emblematic of eternal life. It has also been considered, from a fancied similarity to the membrum virile, to be emblematic of the procreative powers of nature.  The general opinion, I think, seems to have settled upon an union of the two—that it meant *eternally renovating life,* and this seems to agree very well with the nature of a cycle—with the Neros, which eternally renovated itself, and of which it was probably an emblem.  But in my opinion, it is much more probable, that it became the emblem of generation and regeneration, from being the emblem of the cycle, than from any fancied resemblance alluded to above; and that it was the emblem, from being the figure representing the number, of the cycle.

Mr. Payne Knight says, " The male organs of generation are sometimes represented by signs " of the same sort, which might properly be called symbols of symbols.  One of the most remark- " able of these is the cross in the form of the letter T, which thus served as the emblem of " creation and generation." [1]

At first I hastily concluded, that the circle which we often see joined to the cross, was meant merely as a handle, but this, on reflection, I cannot believe.  It is contrary to the genius and character of the ancient mythologists, to use such a lame and unnecessary contrivance.  I am satisfied it was meant, like the cross itself, as an emblem.  In some inscriptions, particularly at the end of one of the oldest with which I am acquainted, from Cyprus, that given in Pococke's description of the East, [2] as a monogram, it is given thus—the cross and ⚵ circle of Venus, or Divine Love.

Cyprus was, in former times, a place of great consequence.  It must be a delightful island. It is about 130 miles long and 60 broad.  In its centre it had its Olympus, now the Mount of the Cross, where, as might be expected, remains to this day a convent of Monks, dedicated to the holy Cross—descended in direct succession, I have no doubt, from the earliest times of Paganism.

The cross was the Egyptian Banner, above which was carried the crest, or device of the Egyptian cities.  It was also used in the same manner by the Persians.  According to oriental traditions, the cross of Calvary and that supposed to be set up by Moses in the Wilderness were made of the wood of the tree of life, in Paradise.  It was carried in the hand of the Horus, the *Mediator* of the Egyptians, the second person in their Trinity, and called *Logos* by the Platonists. Horus was supposed to reign one thousand years.  *He was buried for three days,* he was regenerated, and triumphed over the Egyptian evil principle.  Among the Alchemists the T with a circle and crescent, is the numerical sign of Mercury.  The sign of Venus is a crux ansata, that is, a cross and a circle. [3]

Mr. Maurice describes a statue in Egypt as " bearing a kind of cross in its hand, that is to say, " a PHALLUS, *which, among the Egyptians, was the symbol of fertility.*" [4]  Fertility, that is in other words, the productive, generative power.  On the Egyptian monuments, in the British Museum, may be seen the mystic cross in great numbers of places.  And upon the breast of one of the Mummies in the Museum of the London University, is a cross exactly in this shape, a cross upon a Calvary.

' On Priapus, p. 48.                    ² Vol. I. p. 213, Pl. xxxiii.
³ Monthly Mag. Vol. LVI.              ⁴ Ant. Vol. III. p. 113.

The reader may refer to the thirty-ninth number of the Classical Journal, for some curious and profound observations on the Crux ansata.

2. The sign of the cross is well known to all Romish Christians, among whom it is yet used in every respect as is described by Justin, who has this passage in his Apology: " And whereas " Plato, in his Timæus, philosophizing about the Son of God says, He expressed him upon the " universe in the figure of the letter X, he evidently took the hint from Moses ; for in the " Mosaic writings it is related, that after the Israelites went out of Egypt and were in the desert, " they were set upon and destroyed by venomous beasts, vipers, asps, and all sorts of serpents ; " and that Moses thereupon, by particular inspiration from God, took brass and made the sign of " the cross, and placed it by the holy tabernacle, and declared, that if the people would look upon " that cross, and believe, they should be saved ; upon which he writes, that the serpents died, and " by this means the people were saved."

He presently afterward tells us that Plato said, " The *next power* to the Supreme God was " decussated or figured in the shape of a cross on the universe." These opinions of Plato were taken from the doctrine of Pythagoras relating to numbers, which were extremely mystical, and are certainly not understood. Here we have the SON OF GOD typified by the X, hundreds of years before Christ was born, but this is in keeping with the Platonic Trinity.

It is a certain fact that there is no such passage as that quoted by Justin relating to the cross in the Old or the New Testament. This is merely an example of economical reasoning, or pious fraud, in the first Christian father, not said to be inspired, any of whose entire and undisputed works we possess. The evident object of this fraud was to account for the adoration of the cross, which Justin found practised by his followers, but the cause of which he did not understand.

Tertullian says, that " The Devil signed his soldiers in the forehead, in imitation of the Chris- " tians : Mithra signat illic in frontibus milites suos." [1]    And St. Austin says, that " the cross " and baptism were never parted : semper enim cruci Baptismus jungitur." [2]

The cross was a sacred emblem with the Egyptians. The Ibis was represented with human hands and feet holding the staff of Isis in one hand, and a globe and cross in the other. It is on most of the Egyptian obelisks, and was used as an amulet. Saturn's astrological character was a cross and a ram's-horn. Jupiter also bore a cross, with a horn.

" We have already observed, that the cabalists left these gross symbols to the people, but the " learned and the initiated piercing through these objects, pretended to aspire to the knowledge and " contemplation of the Deity." [3]    Again, " What hideous darkness must involve the Egyptian " history and religion, which were only known by ambiguous signs !  It was impossible but they " must vary in their explication of these signs, and in a long tract of time forget what the ancients " meant by them.  And thus every one made his own conjectures : and the priests taking advan- " tage of the obscurity of the signs, and ignorance of the people, made the best of their own " learning and fancies. Hence necessarily happened two things—one, that religion often changed ; " the other, that the cabalists were in great esteem, because necessary men." [4]

From these quotations it is evident the sign of the cross was a religious symbol common both to Heathens and Christians, and that it was used by the former long before the rise of Christi- anity. [5] The two principal pagodas of India, viz. at Benares and Mathura, are built in the form of crosses. [6] The cross was also a symbol of the British Druids. [7] Mr. Maurice says, " We

---

[1] Tertul. de Præscrip.                        [2] Aug. Temp. Ser. CI ; Reeve's Ap. Vol. I p. 98.

[3] Bas. B. iii. Ch. xix. Sect. xix. xx.        [4] Ibid.

[5] See Justin's Apol. Sect. lxxii. lxxvii. ; Tertullian's Apol. Ch. xvi.        [6] Maur. Ind. Ant. Vol. II. p. 359.

[7] See Borlase, Ant. Cornwall, p. 108 ; Maur. Ind. Ant. Vol. VI. p. 68.

" know that the Druid system of religion, long before the time of Cambyses, had taken deep root " in the British Isles."[1]  " The cross among the Egyptians was an hieroglyphic, importing the " life that is to come."[2]

Mr. Ledwick has observed that the presence of Heathen devices and crosses on the same coin are not unusual, as Christians in those early times were for the most part Semi-pagans.  This is diametrically in opposition to all the doctrines of the Protestants about the early purity of the religion of Christ, and its subsequent corruption by the Romists.  It equally militates against the purity of the Culdees.  In fact it is mere nonsense, for there can be no doubt that the cross was one of the most common of the Gentile symbols, and was adopted by the Christians *like all their other rites and ceremonies* from the Gentiles—and this assertion I will prove, before I finish this work.

Nothing in my opinion can more clearly shew the identity of the two systems of the Christian priests, and of the ancient worshipers of the Sun, than the fact, unquestionably proved, that the sign or monogram used by both was identically the same.  It is absolutely impossible that this can be the effect of accident.

3. The following are monograms of Christ, ☧ ☧ ; but it is unquestionable, that they are also monograms of Jupiter Ammon.  The same character is found upon one of the medals of Decius, the great persecutor of the Christians, with this word upon it, BA☧ATO.[3]  This cipher is also found on the staff of Isis and of Osiris.  There is also existing a medal of Ptolomy, king of Cyrene, having an eagle carrying a thunderbolt, with the monogram of Christ, to signify the oracle of Jupiter Ammon, which was in the neighbourhood of Cyrene, and in the kingdom of Ptolomy.[4]

Basnage says, " Nothing can be more opposite to Jesus Christ than the oracle of Jupiter " Ammom.  And yet the same cipher served the false God as well as the true one ; for we see a " medal of Ptolomy, king of Cyrene, having an eagle carrying a thunder-bolt, with the monogram " of Christ to signify the Oracle of Jupiter Hammon."[5]

Dr. Clarke has given a drawing of a medal, found in the Ruins of Citium, in Cyprus, which he shews is Phœnician, and, therefore, of very great antiquity.  This medal proves that the Lamb, the holy cross, and the rosary, were in use in a very remote period, and that they all went together, long before the time of Jesus of Nazareth.

It is related by Socrates that when the temple of Serapis, at Alexandria, was demolished by one of the Christian emperors in his pious zeal against the demons who inhabited those places, under the names of Gods, that beneath the foundation was discovered the monogram of Christ, and that the Christians made use of the circumstance as an argument in favour of their religion, thereby making many converts.  It is very curious that this unexpected circumstance should have carried conviction (as we learn that it did) to the minds of the philosophers of the falsity of the religion of Christ, and to the minds of the Christians of its truth.  Unquestionably when the Christians held that the digging up of this monogram from under the ruins of the temples was a proof that they should be overthrown by the Cross of Christ, with the Christian Roman Emperor and his legions at their elbow, they would have the best of the argument.  But what was still more to the pur-

---

[1] Ind. Ant. Vol. VI. p. 104; Celtic Druids, by the Author.

[2] Ruffinus, Vol. II. p. 29; Sozomen says the same, Hist. Eccl. Vol. VII. p. 15.

[3] I suspect that this word having been inscribed on a coin is circular, and may either begin or end with the O—that it ought to be OBA☧AT, and that it is a Hebrew word written in Greek letters, meaning *the* Creator, formed from the word ברא *bra* to create.  The X is put in the middle of the word, the same as the Samach or Mem final, in the passage of Isaiah, and for the same reason.

[4] Bas. B. iii. Ch. xxlii. S. iii.        [5] Χρηστηριον, Scaliger in Euseb. Chron., Hist. Jews, B. iii. Ch. xxiii.

pose, the pagan religion was out of fashion.   Reason has hitherto had little or nothing to do with religion.

On this subject of the cross Mr. Maurice says, " Let not the piety of the Catholic Christian be " offended at the preceding assertion, that the cross was one of the most usual symbols among the " hieroglyphics of Egypt and India.   Equally honoured in the Gentile and the Christian world, " this emblem of universal nature, of that world to whose four quarters its diverging radii pointed, " decorated the hands of most of the sculptured images in the former country ; and in the latter " stamped its form upon the most majestic of the shrines of their deities." [1]  I think Mr. Maurice should have said this emblem of the *prolific powers* of nature.   In the cave of Elephanta, in India, over the head of the figure who is destroying the infants, whence the story of Herod and the infants at Bethlehem (which was unknown to all the Jewish, Roman, and Grecian historians) took its origin, may be seen the Mitre, the Crozier, and the Cross ; and, a little in the front of the group, a large Lingam, the emblem of generation, the creative power of nature. [2]

4. Mr. Maurice observes, that in Egypt, as well as in India, the letter T, or in other words, the Cross, or the *Crux Hermis*, was very common, in which form many of the temples of India are built, and those in particular dedicated to Cristna : as for example, those at Matterea or Mattra, and at Benares.   D'Ancarville and the generality of mythologists explain this symbol to refer to the Deity in his creative capacity, in both ancient Egypt and India.   Mr. Bruce frequently met with it in his travels in the higher Egypt and Abyssinia, and it was also very often noticed by Dr. Clarke.   It was commonly called the *crux ansata*, in this form        and was what was referred to in Ezekiel, [3] in the Vulgate, and the *ancient* Septuagint, accord-        ing to Lowth, rendered, " I " will mark them in the forehead with the T or Tau."   It is also        referred to by Tertullian, when he says that the Devil signed his soldiers in the forehead in imitation of the Christians.   It is certainly very remarkable that God should select this Mithraitic symbol for the mark to distinguish the elect from those that were to be slain by the sword of the destroyers.   This may furnish another reason why Christians should moderate their anger against those who used this symbol of the creative power of God. [4]   The Latin Vulgate [5] does in fact read, " You shall mark their forehead " with the letter Thau," i. e. $\tau \alpha \upsilon \ \sigma \eta \mu \epsilon \iota o \nu$, and not as at present in the LXX. $\tau o \ \sigma \eta \mu \epsilon \iota o \nu$. [6]   In the Mazoretic Hebrew it is תו *tau*, which confirms the Vulgate and shews what it was considered to be by the Mazorites of the middle ages.   The cross was much venerated by the cabalists of the early Christians who endeavoured to blend the arcana of Plato and the numerical doctrines of Pythagoras with the mysteries of Christianity.   I have no doubt that it is either the origin of the words Taut and Thoth, names of the Egyptian Gods, or, that these words are the originals from which it came ; and perhaps of the Thor of the Celts, who went into Hell and bruised the head of the great snake.   The monogram of the Scandinavian Mercury was represented by a cross.   The Monogram of the Egyptian Taut is formed by three crosses thus,        united at the feet, and forms, to this day, the jewel of the royal arch among free ma-        sons.   It is the figure        and is X$=$600 H$=$8$=$608.

The Samaritans had, in very early times, the Tau of their alphabet in the form of the Greek Tau, as is clearly proved by their ancient Shekels, on which it is so inscribed. [7]   St. Jerom and Origen

[1] Maurice, Ind. Ant. Vol. I. p. 359.                    [2] Forbes's Oriental Memoirs, Vol. III. Ch. xxxv. p. 448.
[3] Ch. ix. ver. 4.              [4] Maurice, Ind. Ant. Vol. VI. p. 67.                     [5] Ezekiel Ch. ix. ver. 4.
[6] Maurice, Hist. Hind. Vol. I. p. 245.

[7] The reader may find some curious observations on the Crux Ansata in Monthly Magazine, Vol. LVI. No. III. p. 388.

both assert that it was so in Samaritan copies of the Pentateuch in their day. The Celtic language of Wales has it also in the form of a Tau, though a little changed thus, ᴄ. This tends to prove that the Greeks and Celts had their letters from the Samaritans, or early Chaldeans. Might not the Tat or Taut be TT=600, or TTL=650? This will be explained by and by.

On the decad or the number X, the Pythagoreans say, "That ten is a perfect number, even the " most perfect of all numbers, comprehending in it all difference of numbers, all reasons, species, " and proportions. For, if the nature of the universe be defined according to the reasons and pro- " portions of numbers; and that which is produced, and increased, and perfected, proceed accord- " ing to the reasons of numbers; and the decad comprehends every reason of number, and every " proportion and all species; why should not nature itself be termed by the name of ten, X, the " most perfect number?"[1]

The Hexad or number *six* is considered by the Pythagoreans a perfect and sacred number; among many other reasons, because it divides the universe into equal parts.[2] It is called Venus or the mother. It is also perfect, because it is the only number under X, ten, which is whole and equal in its parts. In Hebrew VAU is *six*. Is *vau* mother EVA or EVE? הוא *eua*.

5. The Rabbins say, that when Aaron was made high-priest he was marked on the forehead by Moses with a figure like the Greek χ.[3] This is the Samaching. This letter X in the Greek language meant 600, the number of the Neros. It answered to the Mem final of the Hebrews, found in so peculiar a manner in the middle of the word לסרבה *lmrbe* in Isaiah. We every where meet with X meaning 600, and XH and ΥΗΣ meaning 608, the monograms of Bacchus according to Martianus Capella, in the churches and monuments in Italy dedicated to Jesus Christ; and in this is found a striking proof of what I have said before, in the beginning of this book, respecting the two Neroses; for the use of the X for 600, and the XH and ΥΗΣ for 608, INDISCRIMINATELY AS MONOGRAMS OF CHRIST, connect them altogether, and prove that the two Neroses, the one of 600 and the other 608, had the same origin. This must not be lost sight of, for it is a grand link which connects Christianity with the ancient oriental mythoses, in a manner which cannot be disputed, and most unquestionably proves the truth of the doctrine of Ammonias Saccas, that the two religions are in principle identical. I *do not* know what persons may believe on this subject: but I *do* know that this is evidence, and conclusive evidence.

The T, Tau, was the instrument of death, but it was also (as before mentioned) what Ezekiel ordered the people in Jerusalem to be marked with, who were to be *saved from the destroyer*. It was also the emblem of the Taranis or the Thoth or Teutates or TAT[4] or Hermes or Buddha among the Druids. It was called the *Crux Hermis*. The old Hebrew, the Bastulan, and the Pelasgian, have the letter Tau thus, X; the Etruscan, +X; the Coptic, +; the Punic, XX. It is not unlikely that the Greek priests changed their letters as marks of notation, from the ancient Phœnician or Cadmean, by the introduction of the *episemon bau* or *vau*, to make them suit the mystery contained in the sacred number 608, and the word derived from the Hebrew word *to save* and the sacred cross. Thus the letter X stood for the 600 of the Hebrews, for Ezekiel's sacred mark of salvation, and for the astronomical or astrological cycle.

Nothing can be more common than the letter X in Italy as a monogram of Christ. But we have seen above, from Plato, as quoted by the celebrated Justin Martyr, that it was the emblem

---

[1] Moderatus of Gaza apud Stanley, Hist. Pyth. P. IX. Ch. iv.

[2] In Chapters x. and xiv. of Part IX. of Stanley's History of Philosophy may be seen abundant proofs, that the science of Pythagoras relating to numbers had been then a long time totally lost. For the mystery of letters see Jones on the Canon, Vol. II. p. 425; also Basnage, B. iii. Ch. xxvi. Sect. ii. iii.

[3] Life of Usher, p. 348.          [4] See B. v. Ch. i. Sect. 2.

of the *Son of God*, the Logos, which Son of God is declared over and over again by Justin to be *divine wisdom*, i. e. the same as Buddha.   Whenever proselytes were admitted into the religion of the Bull—of Mithra—they were marked in the forehead with this mark of 600, X.   The initiated were marked with this sign also, when they were admitted into the mysteries of Eleusis.   We constantly see the Tau and the Resh united thus ⊃.   These two letters in the old Samaritan, as found on coins, stand the first for 400, the second ┼ for 200=600.   This is the staff of Osiris.   It is also the monogram of Osiris, and has been adopted by the Christians, and is to be seen in the churches in Italy in thousands of places.   See Basnage, (Lib. iii. Cap. xxiii.,) where several other instances of this kind may be found.   In Addison's Travels in Italy there is an account of a medal, at Rome, of Constantius, with this inscription : In hoc signo Victor eris ☧.   In the Abbey church at Bath, the monogram on the monument of Archdeacon Thomas lately buried is thus : ☧.   This shews how long a superstition will last, after its meaning is quite lost.

Dr. Daniel Clarke has made several striking observations respecting the Crux Ansata.   After repeating the well-known observation of Socrates Scholasticus, that it meant *life to come*, he says, " Kircher's ingenuity had guided him to an explanation of the *crux ansata*, as a *monogram* which " does not militate against the signification thus obtained.   He says, it consisted of the letters " ΦT, denoting *Ptha*, a name of Mercury, Thoth, Taut, or Ptha."   He then observes, that it was often used as a key, and might be the foundation of the numerous allusions in sacred writ, to the keys of Heaven, of Hell, and of Death   In a note, he says, " Sed non erat ullum templum, in " quo non figura *crucis ansatæ*, ut eum eruditi vocant : sæpius vixenda occurreret, hodieque in " ruderibus ac ruinis etiamnum occurrat.   Ejus hæc est species ☧ ....   Crucem vero istam an- " satam, quæ in omnibus Ægyptiorum templis sæpius ficta et picta extabat, quam signa deorum " Ægyptiorum manu tenere solent, quæ partem facit ornatis Sacerdotalis, nihil aliud esse quam " phallum." [1]   " Jamblicus thinks the crux ansata was the name of the Divine Being. ... Some- " times it is represented by a cross fastened to a *circle* as above : in other instances, with the

" letter T only, fixed in this manner ⚲ to a circle." [2] I think few persons will doubt, what old Kircher says is true, that it means ┼ X = 600.

$$P\ Thas \cdots\cdots\cdots\left\{\begin{array}{l} \phi = 500 \\ \theta = 9 \\ a = 1 \\ \varsigma = 90 \end{array}\right\} = 600.$$

And when accompanied by the circle, it is the Linga and Ioni of India united.   The Deity Φθας presided in the kingdom of *Omptha*, *Om-tha*, the cycle *Om*.   Here we have the cycle of 600, the *Om* of Isaiah, the cross of Christ, and the *Om-tha* of Egypt all united.   The Greek numbers must have been once the same as the Hebrew above, and have been changed, as the reader will be convinced in a moment, by considering the two alphabets in my Table of Alphabets, page 10. The Greek Tau was anciently written +. [3]

6. The monogram which constitutes figure 9, I copied from a bad drawing of a stone at the back of the Choir in the Duomo at Milan, lent to me by the Sacristan, who told me that it had been then lately removed, in consequence of a gentleman from Naples having noticed it, and having made a drawing of it.   He had come from Naples on purpose.   I saw it there myself the first time I went to Milan ; when I went again it was gone.   (The church is very discreet.)   The following is the description of it, taken from Nuova Descrizione Del Duomo di Milano, presso

---

[1] Vide Jablonski, Panth. Ægyp I 282.                    [2] Clarke's Travels, Vol. III. p. 107.
[3] Vide Parkhurst's Lexicon in voce T.

Ferdinando Artaria, 1820: " Non lungi da questo monumento si vede incastrata nel muro una
" pietra, la quale, entro a misterioso cerchio contiene scolpito il monogramma ossia l'abbreviatura
" del nome del Salvatore in lettere Greche coll' alfa ed omega dall' una e dall' altra parte, antica-
" mente chiamato il crisma o sia oracolo di S. Ambrogio : Landolfo, scrittore Milanese, assicura
" che questo serviva di primo elemento ai catecumini per iniziarli nei misteri della fide. Sotto
" questa pietra ed agli ornamenti de marmo che vi sono stati posti diutorno, leggesi la iscrizione
" sequente, in parte mascherata da un confessionale :
" CIRCULUS · HIC · SUMMI · CONTINET · NOMINA · REGIS · QUEM · SINE · PRINCIPIO · ET · SINE
" FINE · VIDES · *principium* · *cum* · *fine* · *Tibi* · *designat* A · *et* · Ω nella antica lapida era ag-
" giunto :
" X. · ET · P. CHRISTI · NOMINA · SANCTA · TENET."

In the next page, 30, is a description of the last footstep on Mount Olivet, thus printed :
" Nostro Signore IHV—Cristo." In the Chrismon above are the Etruscan Tau 400 and the Resh
200=600. In my essay on *The Celtic Druids*, (p. 264,) I have shewn an example from Dr.
Clarke of a mixture of the Phœnician and Etruscan letters in a Phœnician inscription in Etruscan
characters.

In this magical device of St. Ambrose, which is a CROSS WITH EIGHT POINTS, here are the Alpha
and Omega, the well-known emblems of eternity, united to the cycle of 600, the X and P, pronounced to be emblems of eternal life. See plates, fig. 9.

The learned Spencer says, " Nomen solis mysticum ad numerum octo et sexcentorum pervenie-
" bat, uti nos docet Martianus Capella. Id autem hoc modo notabatur, XH. Cabalisticus ille
" deorum nomina designandi modus eo antiquior habeatur, quod veri Dei (nempe Christi) nomen
" mysticis numeris expressum, in claro illo ænigmate.[1] Sibyllino reperiamus : quamvis haud
" adeo inter doctos conveniat cuinam Christi nomini vel titulo, numerus ille melius congruat." [2]

The Abbé Pluche says that the Egyptians marked their God Canobus indifferently with a T or a
+. The Vaishnavas of India have also the same sacred Jar, which they also mark with crosses
thus +, and with triangles thus ✡. The vestment of the priests of Horus is covered with these
crosses +.[3] This is the same as the dress of the Lama of Tibet. These are the sectarian marks
of the Jains, +, +.[4] The distinctive badge of the sect of Xaca Japonicus, is this 卍.[5]
The religion of the Jains, Buddha, or Xaca, and Fo, all having been proved the same, we have
here the sign of Fo, identical with the cross of Christ.

In Montfaucon[6] may be seen several medals of Anubis or Noubis, where he is called X and T,
Noubis or Noumis, or in his fig. 10, Anoubis. Again,

In the same[7] is a medal with the letters ΦPH. Φ=500, P=100, H=8,=608. In the same
plate, No. 36, is a young man crowned ; with a cup in one hand, and the letters X on one side of
him, and Θ on the other; this last is an Etruscan letter, which stands for 8, X Θ=608. Another,
not numbered, above 33, exhibits a female nursing a child, with ears of corn in her hand, and the
legend *ωαι, Iao.* She is seated on clouds, a star is at her head, and three ears of corn are rising
from an altar before her. The reading of the Greek letters, from right to left, shews this to be no
produce of *modern* Gnosticism, but to be very ancient.

---

[1] Orac. Sibyl. L. i. p. 171, ed. Par. 1699.

[2] Spencer, Lib. ii. Cap. xiv. p. 365.    [3] See Caylus, Vol. VI. Pl. 7 ; Vall. Col. Vol. VI. p. 185.

[4] See Moore's Ind. Pantheon, pp. 401, 451.    [5] Georgius, Alphab. Tib. Ap. III. p. 725.

[6] Ant. Exp. Vol. II. Pl. 49.    [7] Ibid. Vol. II. Pl. 50, Fig. 14.

It is the common and unsatisfactory way of accounting for the mystical character of medals of this kind, to throw them all aside as the idle superstitions of the Gnostic Christians. But here the style of writing from right to left proves the foregoing to be of a date long prior to Christianity. The idle and unfounded plea of Gnostic Christianity has been of inestimable value to the Christian priesthood, by enabling them to conceal many very important facts, which, in consequence of this plea, cannot be adduced as evidence of ancient doctrines. Were it not for this plea I should fill a book with these facts.

In Dr. Daniel Clarke's Travels, at the head of Chapter XI. of Vol II., will be found a print of the medal of the ancient Phœnicians found at Citium or Cyprus, before named, on one side of which are a ram couchant, and on the other the cross, the rosary, and two letters or figures.

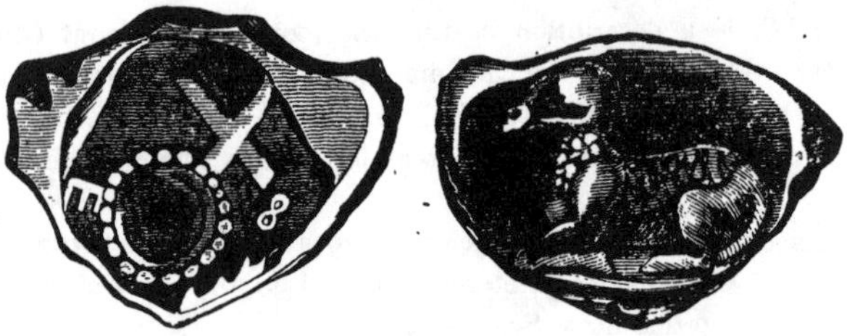

The following are copies, taken most carefully from Mr. Astle's table of the general alphabet of the Etruscans: H ⊟ 8 ⊖ ⊗ ; M ᘻ ΠΓ. I ask, may not these two letters on the medal, connected here with the lamb, the cross, the circle, and the rosary, (the latter found in the hands of most Hindoo Gods,) signify M. 600, H. 8? The letter M, as described on this medal, differs both from the closed and the open Mem of the Hebrews, in shape, but as there is a variety of ways in which the ancient Etruscans formed this letter, we can never be certain that this may not have been a Mem final standing for 600, like that of the Hebrews. The figure for the H is evidently the origin of our 8. And here, as joined with the Mem and connected with all the other circumstances, raises a very strong presumption that the celebrated 608 is meant.[1] When I consider all the collateral circumstances attending this medal, I cannot help thinking that many things are received in which the imagination is more taxed than in this. I affirm nothing except that I wish some one to give me a more rational explanation of the two letters or figures. I beg my reader to recollect we tread on mystic ground.

The votaries of the Roman Church constantly mark themselves with the cross—the emblem of 600. They will say, they do it in commemoration of the sufferings of their Saviour. When I consider the peculiarity of the cycles and epochs in Siam, that of Mr. Bentley, the *Mem* final of Isaiah, his prophecy, that of Zoradusht, of the Sibyl, and of Virgil, and also that of the Druid of Bochara in Ireland, the magical character of the disputed chapters in Luke and Matthew, and the X and IHΣ XH, the monograms of the black Christ, I cannot help believing that they all refer to the same person—Buddha—or the Christ, the black God of the temple of Bethlehem, but not to Jesus of Nazareth; and, in support of this opinion, a thousand other reasons will be given in the course of this work.

I shall now exhibit, in an extract from my Celtic Druids, another example of the mystical numbers 600 and 608, where few persons would expect to find it, viz. in the ancient Druidical temples of Britain. "The most extraordinary peculiarity which the Druidical circles possess, is

---

[1] Ancient Teutonic M, ᙏ.

" that of their agreement in the number of the stones of which they consist with the ancient
" astronomical cycles. The outer circle of Stonehenge consists of 60 stones, the base of the most
" famous of all the cyles of antiquity. The next circle consists of 40 stones, but one on each side
" of the entrance is advanced out of the line, so as to leave 19 stones, a metonic cycle, on each
" side, and the inner, of one metonic cycle, or 19 stones. At Abury we find all the outward
" circles and the avenues make up exactly the 600, the Neros, which Josephus says was known
" before the flood. The outer circles are exactly the number of degrees in each of the 12 parts,
" into which, in my aerial castle-building, I divided the circle, viz. 30, and into which at first the
" year was divided, and the inner, of the number of the divisions of the circle, viz. 12, and of the
" months in the year. We see the last measurement of Stonehenge, taken by Mr. Waltire, makes
" the second circle 40; but for the sake of marking the two cycles of 19 years, two of the stones,
" one on each side of the entrance, have been placed a little within. I think it very likely that
" the outer circle of the *hackpen* of 40 stones was originally formed in the same manner. Surely
" it is not improbable that what is found in one temple should have been originally in the other.
" I also think that the whole number of stones which Stonehenge consisted of was 144, according
" to Mr. Waltire's model, and including along with it three stones which could not be described in
" Mr. Waltire's model for want of room; thus making the sum-total of stones amount exactly to
" the oriental cycle or vau of 144 years.

Outer circle with its coping stones ...................... 60
Inner ........................................... 40
Outer ellipse ......................................... 21
Inner parabola ....................................... 19
Altar ............................................. 1
Three outer stones................................. 3
                                                    ———
                                                    144

 " In this temple the outer circle is the oriental cycle of Vrihaspati, 60. Next outer circle, ex-
" clusive of two entrance stones a little removed inside the line, to mark a separation from the
" others, making two metonic cycles, each 19. The trilithons are seven in number, equal to the
" planets. The inner row is a parabolic curve, and the stones a metonic cycle. Now with re-
" spect to Abury we find the same peculiarity.

" Outer circle........................................... 100 stones
Northern temple outward circle ........................ 30
Inner circle............................................ 12
The cove ............................................. 3
Southern temple, outward circle ....................... 30
Inner circle of the same ............................. 12
Central obelisk ..................................... 1
Ring stone .......................................... 1
Kennet avenue ..................................... 200
Outer circle of the hackpen or serpent's head.......... 40
Inner circle of ditto ............................... 18
Beckhampton avenue.................................. 200
Longstone cove ....................................... 2
Inclosing stone of the serpent's tail .................. 1
                                                    ———
                                        Total  650 stones.

"Of these, the whole number of the OUTSIDE LINES of the structure make 600, viz. 100 + 30
"+ 30 + 200 + 40 + 200 = 600, the cycle of the Neros, alluded to in Chapter II. Section
"XIII. The whole of the smaller circles make 142; 30 + 12 + 30 + 12 + 40 + 18 = 142.
"When I consider all the other circumstances of the attachment of the Druids to cycles, I cannot
"help suspecting that they have been 144, and that there is some mistake." ...... "If all the
"stones of Abury be taken, except the inner circles, you will have the number 608, a very curious
"number, the sacred number of the God Sol, already described in Chap. IV. Sect. VIII., to which
"I beg to refer my reader. If this be the effect of accident, it is an odd accident."

I confess I cannot help considering the discovery of these cycles in the old temples as confirmatory in an extraordinary manner of my system. My theory respecting the Druids being oriental
Buddhists is confirmed by the oriental Neroses of Siam; and my theory of the origin of the oriental doctrines is confirmed by the temples of the West. Circumstances of this kind surpass all
written testimony : there can be no forged interpolations here. The reader has seen that the total
number of stones in the temple of Abury was SIX HUNDRED and FIFTY, as discovered by Stukeley,
and confirmed by Sir R. C. Hoare's later examination. Neither of those gentlemen had any idea
of the importance of the number of the stones, and therefore had no theory to support, which, if
found by me only, might make persons think I was deceived by a prurient imagination. The following is a passage from Basnage's History of the Jews, [1] which I have discovered since I published my Celtic Druids :

"Martianus Capella speaks of two letters, X. and N.; who would not think here was a character
"of Christianity ? Χριϛος Νικα, Christ victorious : but it was a mystical name of the Sun; and
"these two letters designed a certain number he was used to be signified by;" X = 600, N = 50.
But if it did not mean Χριϛος νικα, it meant something very near it, viz. Χρηϛος νικα, as I
shall shew in the twelfth book of this work.

8. The Persian God is often called Mitr. Of course we may expect to find the more perfect Neroses,
or sacred numbers, described by the letters of notation of the later nations, and the ruder Neroses
with the more early, all in fact descriptive of the solar cycle. Thus in Hebrew we have מיתר mitr,
ר 200, ת 400, י 10, מ 40 = 650. This was probably the first way of writing it; the second was Mithras
Μιθρας, written without an E and meaning CCCLX., M 40, I 10, Θ 9, P 100, A 1, Σ 200 = 360;
but afterward, when the length of the year was more perfectly understood, it was as it is commonly found with an e, Meithras. [2] A Mitra Mithridates est, et Mitra quod alii corrupte Misra
scribunt, etiam multi Brahmanes appellantur. [3] Might not the name of the Egyptian Misraim be
a corruption of the word מיתרים mitrim ? If this were the case, it would have had the same name
in the oriental, as Italy had in its, language Itala, a bull. Bishop Cumberland thought that Mitzraim was the word Isiris or Itziris, with the mystic M prefixed, which seems by no means improbable.

The number 650, sacred to the Sun, and found in the temple at Abury in so remarkable a
manner, again confirms my theory. He must have a prurient imagination indeed who can attribute all these coincidences to accident. Why this number 650 came to be sacred to the Sun I
have explained in Chap. ii. Sect. 5.

The following extract will exhibit the metonic cycle in as remarkable a manner as the Neros :
"At Biscawen'unn, near St. Buriens in Cornwall, there is a circular temple consisting of 19
"stones, and a twentieth stone stands in the centre higher than the rest.—I beg my reader to refer
"to the description of the temple at Classerness in the introduction, plate No. 28. There he will

---

[1] B. iii. Chap. xxiii. p. 236.          [2] See Mont. Ant. Exp. Vol. II. p. 226.          [3] Bartolomeus, Sys. Brach. p 2.

" again find the metonic cycle.—Near Clenenney, in North Wales, is a circle containg 38 stones, " two metonic cycles.—Near Keswick is an oval of 40 stones. This I have little doubt is in " number 40, for the same reason as the second circle at Stonehenge, already explained.—Dr. " Borlase says, 'There are *four* circles in the hundred of Penwith, Cornwall, (the most distant " two of which are not eight miles asunder,) which have 19 stones each, a surprising uniformity, " expressing, perhaps, the two principal divisions of the year, the twelve months, and the seven " days of the week. Their names are Boscawen'unn, Rosmodereny, Tregaseal, and Boskednan.' " Here the similarity could not escape Dr. Borlase; but the idea of a cycle never occurred to " him. There is no room to attribute any thing here to imagination."

In the same chapter my reader may see many other examples of astrological numbers in the old temples of the Druids. Before I quit the temple of Abury, I beg leave to suggest whether it may not be probable that the number of the stones of the inner circle of the serpent's head may have been 19 instead of 18; that it may have had a centre stone; and that the Longstone Cove which stands at a little distance may have been considered as part of the temple? This would give, instead of 142 for the number of stones in the inner circles, the number 144, and would not derange any of the other cyclar sums, as my reader will find on experiment. Amidst the intricacy of the modern buildings and old stones, Dr. Stukeley and Sir R. C. Hoare might easily be led into so trifling a mistake. I beg my reader to make this correction, then to take his pencil and try an experiment or two with the different numbers, and he will find how curiously the sums into which I first supposed the great circle to have been divided come out, viz. 12 signs, 36 decans, 72 dodecans, and 360 degrees. All this may be nonsensical enough, but are not all judicial astrology and the ancient mystical doctrines of lucky and unlucky, sacred and profane numbers, nonsensical? It is of no use to say they are nonsensical. Can any one say that even the wisest of the ancients did not entertain these doctrines?

9. What I have said respecting the division of the great circle into 360 degrees, and into decans and dodecans, receives a strong confirmation from the description which Josephus gives of the mystical meaning of the Jewish tabernacle, &c. He says, " And when he ordered twelve loaves " to be set on the table, he denoted the year as distinguished into so many months. By branching " out the candlestick into seventy parts he SECRETLY intimated the *Decani*, or seventy divisions of " the planets; and as to the seven lamps upon the candlesticks, they referred to the course of the " planets, of which that is the number." Again: " And for the twelve stones, whether we under- " stand by them the months, or whether we understand the like number of the signs of that circle " which the Greeks call the Zodiac, we shall not be mistaken in their meaning."[1] The Decani here mentioned must evidently allude to what Sir William Drummond calls *Dodecans*, each of which consists of five degrees; and what is here called 70 must mean 72, for $72 \times 5 = 360$; but $70 \times 5$ would only equal 350, neither the division of the circle, nor of the year which Moses made to consist of 360 days. In his account of the flood the year or circle is divided exactly according to my theory. In his explanation Josephus is confirmed by Philo, another very eminent person, who states the identical doctrine. The expression used here respecting the *seventy* divisions of the *planets*, shews that when the word *seventy* is used, seventy-two must be understood, as it still is, and always was, in some other cases; for example, in that of the version of the seventy, though LXXII. always is meant. It is here evident that though a secret meaning was known to exist, its nature was only a subject of speculation.

---

[1] Antiq. B. iii. Chap. vii. If this tabernacle was not astrological, I should be happy to be informed what would make it so.

That 72 constellations were meant, we also know from Pliny, who says (Lib. ii.), that 1600 stars may be counted in the 72 *constellations*, meaning the 72 divisions of the Zodiac. See the Classical Journal, No. XXXI., where the reader may see satisfactory proofs, given by Sir W. Drummond, of what I have said in my Celtic Druids—that the ancients had the use of the telescope. I shall prove the truth of what is said here of the use of the term 70 for 72, more at large hereafter.

The following passage from the Appendix to my Celtic Druids, pp. 307, 308, will exhibit the two Neroses in Ireland.

" Vallancey says, the Irish have the cycle of the Neros by the name of Phennicshe, which in
" Chaldean numerals make the number as given below, No. 1 ; and he says, if you add רּ H, which
" alters not the pronunciation, it makes up in the Coptic language the Egypt period of 608,
" No. 2.

| No. 1. | | | | No. 2. | | | |
|---|---|---|---|---|---|---|---|
| Ph. | פ | · · · · · · | 80 | Ph. | פ | · · · · · · | 80 |
| E. | ה | · · · · · · | 5 | E. | ה | · · · · · · | 5 |
| N. | ן | · · · · · · | 50 | N. | ן | · · · · · · | 50 |
| N. | ן | · · · · · · | 50 | N. | ן | · · · · · · | 50 |
| I. | י | · · · · · · | 10 | I. | י | · · · · · · | 10 |
| K. | ק | · · · · · · | 100 | K. | ק | · · · · · · | 100 |
| Sh. | ש | · · · · · · | 300 | Sh. | ש | · · · · · · | 300 |
| E. | ה | · · · · · · | 5 | H. | ח | · · · · · · | 8 |
| | | | 600 | E. | ה | · · · · · · | 5 |
| | | | | | | | 608 |

" If my reader will refer back to Chapter V. Sect. XIV., he will find Phanes or Fan amongst
" the Irish Gods. He is a God of fire. He is one of the celebrated ancient triad, the Creator,
" the Preserver, and the Destroyer, and the word meant αιων or æternitas. It is in this respect
" particularly applicable to the idea of a cycle.

$$\begin{array}{ll} \Phi \text{ Ph.} & 500 \\ \text{H E.} & 8 \\ \text{N N.} & 50 \\ \text{N N.} & 50 \\ \hline & 608 \end{array}$$

" From this cycle of 600 came the name of the bird Phœnix, called by the Egyptians Phenn,
" with the well-known story of its going to Egypt to burn itself on the altar of the sun (at Helio-
" polis), and rise again from its ashes, at the end of a certain period." For the word ΦΡΗ *pre*
or *phre*, see Celtic Druids,[1] where the manner in which the mystics concealed various other cycles and objects by means of figures is explained.

In an old Irish Glossary the Phœnix is said to be a bird which lives 600 years or turns of Beal, or the sun, with all the remainder of the history of the burning, &c.[2]

Phanes is called Protogonos, and had the head of a Bull.[3]

In Montfaucon[4] " is an Isis sitting on the Lotus. She hath a Globe on her head with a radiant
" circle round it, which denotes the Sun. The inscription on the reverse hath some affinity with

---

[1] Chap. IV. Sect. VIII.       [2] Ouseley, Coll. Orient. Vol. II. No. iii. p. 203.

[3] Porphyry on Cave of Nymphs, trans. Taylor, p. 190.

[4] Supplement to the Ant. Exp. Pl. LII. Fig. 7, Vol. II., and in my plates, Fig. 10.

" the figure. It is ΙΕΟΥ ΑΡΣΕΝΟΦΡΗ. Ιεʊ is for Ιαω, which is the usual way of the ec-
" clesiastic authors reading the Hebrew word Jehovah ; for in these kinds of words the change or
" transposition of vowels is not regarded. The gem here hath Ιεʊ, and Eusebius hath Ιευω.
" The last syllable in the next word (φϱη which we read phri) signifies, in the Egyptian lan-
" guage, the sun. Therefore the whole word, αϱσενοφϱη, signifies *the sun is male*, if we may be
" allowed to join a Greek word and an Egyptian together. We see here the rays of the sun, but
" they proceed from a woman's head; which particular disagrees with the inscription. Doth
" this signify that Isis, who is taken for the moon, is male ?" [1] Here Isis, whose veil no mortal
shall ever draw aside, the celestial virgin of the sphere, is seated on the self-generating sacred Lotus,
and is called Ιεω or יהו *ieu*, or Jove, and also the solar cycle φϱη : Φ 500, P 100, Η 8=608.
The breasts shew the female sex, the αρσενος shews the male, and united, they shew as usual the
Androgynous deity.

In the Greek and Coptic the famous *Io Sabboe* means 360 :

$$\begin{array}{ll} \text{I} & \dots \ 10 \\ \text{O} & \dots \ 70 \\ \Sigma & \dots 200 \\ \text{A} & \dots \ 1 \\ \text{B} & \dots \ 2 \\ \text{B} & \dots \ 2 \\ \text{O} & \dots \ 70 \\ \text{E} & \dots \ 5 \\ \hline & 360 \ [2] \end{array}$$

This shews that the earliest year in Greece was 360 days only. Thus we find the same ignorance in Greece, and in the book of the deluge of Moses, and in the Apocalypse, as well as in
Egypt: but with the Indians, we find the Metonic cycle and the Neros, which evince a more correct knowledge of the length of the year;.and it was also shewn by the builders of the Metonic
cycles of pillars in Britain.

Whilst on the subject of Druidical circles, I will take the opportunity of stating, that Dr.
Daniel Clarke found a Druidical circle on the top of mount Gargarus, the ancient Ida, where the
Gods of Homer assembled at the siege of Troy. It may be put down as a parallel to Joshua's
Gilgal, (Joshua viii. 30, 31,) on mount Ebal—the Proseucha discovered by Epiphanius. The
Temples of Greece are constantly said to be surrounded with à τέμενος, the meaning of which has
been doubted. Homer [3] says,

Γαργαρον, ενθα δε ὁι τεμενος βωμος τε θυήεις·

Here I think the temenos was the Gilgal of Dr. Clarke. See CELTIC DRUIDS, *passim*. And from
this we may not unreasonably suspect that the τεμενος meant a stone circle; or, at all events,
that a stone circle was a τεμενος.

10. In my Celtic Druids I have given an example of two Cromlehs in India, Plates 39 and 40 ;
and I have given a drawing of another in figure 18 of this work. I have since found that stone
circles, similar to our Stonehenge, Abury, &c., are very common in the Northern parts of India.
The natives can give no account of them.

---

[1] P. 243.　　　[2] Ouseley, Coll. Orient. Vol. II. No. iii. p. 209.　　　[3] Lib. viii. v. 48.

These circles appear to be a remnant of antiquity of a similar species to those of the Puniha-Pandawars, a great number of which are to be seen scattered on the adjacent heights about a mile west of a place called Durnacotta. The stones composing these circles are of a hard blackish granite, very irregular in shape, measuring in general about 3 feet in height, and of the same dimension in thickness. The country people seem ignorant on the subject of these antiquities, and can give no information for what purposes they were designed. It is reported that circles of a similar description are very numerous among the skirts of the hills of Wudlamaun and others in that neighbourhood, that on some of these being opened by the late Rajah, Vassareddy, they were found to contain human bones of a large size, and that in some there were earthern pots curiously placed together containing ashes or charcoal. Similar to the above at Amravutty, on the river Christna or Kistna, is to be seen a mound called Depaldenna.[1]

Drawings of great numbers of these circles may be seen in Mackenzie's manuscripts above-mentioned. I shall give a drawing of only one of them, because, although there is no reason to doubt the general accuracy of the accounts, yet no attempt has been made to ascertain of what numbers of stones these circles originally consisted, which was the only thing that could render them really useful; but which, as was originally the case in England, was thought to be of no consequence. It is, however, remarkable that, in the circle which I have given, fig. 11, as the reader will find on counting them, (allowance being made for one evidently broken,) 19 stones, the number of the Metonic cycle, are found.

11. For the origin of the cross we must go to the Buddhists and to the Lama of Tibet, who takes his name from the cross, called in his language Lamh, which is with his followers an object of profound veneration.[2]

The cross of the Buddhists is represented with leaves and flowers springing from it, and placed upon a mount Calvary, as among the Roman Catholics. They represent it in various ways, but the shaft with the cross bar and the Calvary remain the same. The tree of life and knowledge, or the Jamba tree, in their maps of the world, is always represented in the shape of a cross, eighty-four Yoganas (answering to the eighty-four years of the life of him who was exalted upon the cross) or 423[3] miles high, including the three steps of the Calvary.[4]

12. The celebrated Monk Georgius, in his Tibetinum Alphabetum, p. 203, has given plates (in my figures No. 14 ) of the God Indra nailed to a cross, *with five wounds*. These crosses are to be seen in Nepaul, especially at the corners of roads and on eminences. Indra is said to have been crucified by the keepers of the Hindoo garden of Paradise for having robbed it. The country of Nepaul is evidently the Caucasus where Alexander went to look at the cave of Prometheus, to whom the whole mythos obviously applies. But it is the same as that of Jesus, evidently existing here also, long before the time of Christ. All these crucifixes, &c., &c., must be well known to our Indian travellers. Have the Romish Monks been more honest than our philosophers of Calcutta? It would be absurd to deny that I think *they have*. Ah! old Roger Bacon, how truly hast thou said, " Omnia ad religionem in suspicione habenda" !

Georgius says, " Si ita se res habet, ut existimat Beausobrius, *Indi*, et *Budistæ* quorum religio, " eadem est ac Tibetana, nonnisi a Manichæis nova hæc deliriorum portenta acceperunt. Hæ " namque gentes præsertim in urbe Nepal, Luna XII. *Badr* seu *Bhadon Augusti* mensis, dies

---

[1] See Col. Mackenzie's manuscripts, *India Antiqua Illustrata*, in the Museum in the India-House, No. 9, 1816, 1817, and plates, Fig. 11.

[2] See Celtic Druids, App. pp. 307—312.     [3] This I suppose to be in the original a misprint for 432.

[4] Asiat. Res. Vol. X. p. 123. See my plates, Figures Nos. 12, 13.

" festos auspicaturæ Dei *Indræ*, erigunt ad illius memoriam ubique locorum *cruces* amictas
" *Abrotono*. Earum figuram descriptam habes ad lit. B, Tabula pone sequenti. Nam A effigies
" est ipsius *Indræ crucifixi* signa *Telech* in fronte manibus pedibusque gerentis." [1]

Again, he says, [2] " Est Krishna (quod ut mihi pridem indicaverat P. Cassianus Maceratensis,
" sic nunc uberius in Galliis observatum intelligo a vivo litteratissimo De Guignes) nomen ipsum
" corruptum Christi Servatoris."

And again, speaking of Buddha, Georgius says, [3] " Nam Xaca et Christus nomina sunt æquæ
" significationis apud Tibetanos, quemadmodum apud Sinenses, teste et vindice De Guignesio,
" Christus et Fo : apud Indos vero Christus et Bisnu : Christus et Chrisnu." Buddha is often
seen with a glory, and with a tongue of fire on his head.

Gen. Vallancey, says, " The Tartars call the cross *Lama* from the Scythian *Lamh*, a hand,
" synonymous to the *Jod* of the Chaldeans : and thus it became the *name of a cross*, and of the
" high-priest with the Tartars ; and, with the Irish, *Luam* [5] signifies the head of the church, an
" abbot, &c.

" From this X all nations begin a new reckoning, because it is the number of fingers on both
" hands, which were the original instruments of numbering : hence יד *(id) iod* in Hebrew is the
" hand and the number *ten*, as is Lamh with the Tartars." [6]

Though I have noticed this before, I think it right to repeat it here.

This figure X not only stands for ten, but was considered, as it has been already shewn, a perfect number, i. e. the emblem of perfection, and hence stood for 600—the cycle—which, after
many attempts, was erroneously thought to be perfect.

From the abuse of the original incarnation or divine inspiration, for if they were not identical
they were very nearly allied, arose the Lama of Tibet, now become a mere tool of the Monks, by
means of which their order keeps possession of the sovereign sway. If the circumstances of the
Lama and the Pope be carefully examined, the similarity will be found to be very striking. In
each case the Monks and their Pope have the temporal power in the surrounding territory, and in
each case extensive foreign states admit their spiritual authority. And when in former times the
priests gave the Pope of Italy the epithet of Deus, and elevated him as they yet do, ON THE ALTAR
of St. Peter's, and bending the knee to him, offered him, to use their own words, *adoration*—they
in fact very nearly arrived at *Tibetian* perfection. In each case the head of the empire is called
Papa and Holy Father, and in each case the empire is called that of the Lama, the Lamh, or the
Cross—for Lamh means Cross. Lamh looks very like Lamb. I know not the etymology of our
word Lamb ; but each *empire is that of the Lamb of God upon earth, which taketh away the sins of
the world*. I shall hereafter treat on this point.

But the word Ram, ראם *ram*, in Hebrew means both Bull and Ram. [7] This arose, I suspect,
from the Indian incarnation of Rama, who preceded Cristna. In fact he was the incarnation of
the Neros when the Sun left Taurus and entered Aries ; thus he was incarnate in the signs of both
the Bull and the Ram.

" Boodism," Col. Franklin [8] says, " is known very widely in Asia under the appellation of

---

[1] Alph. Tibet, p. 203.          [2] Ibid. pp. 253—263.          [3] Ibid. p. 364.

[4] See Moore's Pantheon, Pl. 71, 72.

[5] This Luam is evidently a corruption of Lamh or Lamb. The High-priest was an incarnation of the Lamb of the
Zodiac.

[6] Celtic Druids, App. p. 312.          [7] Vide Parkhurst in voce.

[8] Treatise on the Tenets of the Jeynes and Buddhists, p. 186.

" Shamanism: the visible head of which religion, the Dalai Lama, resides in a magnificent palace
" called Putala, or the Holy Mountain, near Lassa, the capital of the extensive region of Thibet.
" He is believed to be animated by a Divine Spirit, and is regarded as the vicegerent of the Deity
" on earth, and by some as the Deity incarnate, and death is nothing more, it is pretended, than
" the transmigration of the spirit into another body, like that of the Bull God Apis in Egypt."
Here is the principle which will unravel all the mysteries of antiquity.

In my Celtic Druids I have proved that the first race of man after the flood came from about
the latitude 45, perhaps Balk or Samarkand, not far from Northern Tibet. The following extract
from the work of the Christian Jesuits will shew that some of the Romish doctrines might have
been copied, and probably were copied by the Persian or Pythagorean school, from a source different from that of modern Christianity. The authority of the Jesuits in this case cannot be disputed, and the doctrines, from their being identified with the Buddhism of Tibet, must have an antiquity far higher than that of the doctrines of Cristna.

13. The close coincidence between the religion of Tibet and that of the Christians, can hardly
be disputed, as the knowledge of it comes to us from several persons who do not appear to have
any interest in trying to deceive. " Father Grebillon observes also with astonishment, that the
" Lamas have the use of holy water, singing in the church service, prayers for the dead, mitres
" worn by the bishops ; and that the Dalai Lama holds the same rank among his Lamas, that the
" Pope does in the Church of Rome : and Father Grueber goes farther; he says, that their religion
" agrees, in every essential point, with the Roman religion, without ever having had any connexion
" with Europeans : for, says he, they celebrate a sacrifice with bread and wine ; they give extreme
" unction ; they bless marriages ; pray for the sick ; make processions ; honour the relics of their
" saints, or rather their idols ; they have monasteries and convents of young women ; they sing in
" their temples like Christian Monks ; they observe several fasts, in the course of the year, and
" mortify their bodies, particularly with the discipline, or whips : they consecrate their bishops,
" and send missionaries, who live in extreme poverty, travelling barefoot even to China. Father
" Grueber says he has seen all this : and Horace de la Pona says, that the religion of Tibet is
" like an image of that of Rome. They believe in one God : a Trinity, but filled with errors ; a
" Paradise, Hell, Purgatory ; but mingled with fables : they make alms, prayers, and sacrifices
" for the dead ; they have convents, wherein they make vows of chastity and poverty ; have con-
" fessors appointed by the grand Lama, and, besides holy water, the cross, chaplets, and other
" practices of Christians." [1]    The above is confirmed by Grueber and D'Orville, the missionaries,
in the account of their Voyage to China.

Whatever Protestants may say to the contrary, this is correct Popish, and also Protestant,
Christianity. The Pope, like the Archbishop of Canterbury, is believed by his consecration,
ordination, or installation, that is, by the ceremony of making him pope or bishop, by the imposition of hands, by the Samach, or by investiture with the Pallium, to have had instilled or inspired
into him a portion of the divine spirit, of the logos, or divine wisdom : thus endowed, as it is
clearly expressed, he has power to remit sins, in the Romish service *on the condition of repentance ;*
in the Protestant (as appears in the service for the ordination of priests) *without a condition.*

The accounts of the Jesuits are, in some instances, confirmed by the Journal of a most
respectable gentleman, sent by Mr. Hastings to Tibet. [2]    Mr. Turner says, that the mysterious
word Aum or Om, is equally sacred with the Buddhists of Thibet, as with the Brahmins of

---

[1] Remains of Japhet, 4to. p. 201.          [2] Turner's Travels in Tibet.

Bengal, under the form of *Oom maunee paimee oom.* The temple at Jaggernaut, and most of the other places in India held sacred by the Brahmins, are equally held sacred by the Buddhists of Tibet.[1] They have monasteries for Monks and Nuns, precisely like those of the Romish Church, in which prayers are chaunted, with music, which never cease night or day for thousands of years, accompanied with occasional processions. They make pilgrimages to the chief holy places in India, the ruined city of Gowr, to Gya, Benares, Mahow, Allahabad, &c., and the rich, like those of the Romish Church, do it by proxy. They say that the Grand Lama has been regenerated at all these places. The principal idol in their temples is called Mahamoonie:[2] the Buddha of Bengal, called Godama or Gautama, in Assam and Ava : Samana in Siam : Amida and Buth in Japan : Fohi in China ; Buddha and Shakamuna, in Bengal and Hindostan : Dherma Raja and Mahamóonie, in Bootan and Tibet. From time immemorial they have had the art of printing, *though it has been limited to their religious works*; and it is still more curious, that it has been done upon blocks similar to the stereotype method, and not by moveable letters, which shews that they have not learnt it from the West; for, when Mr. Turner visited them, the art of printing in that manner was not known in Europe. It is much to be lamented that Mr. Turner did not get copies of, or procure more information respecting, their sacred books, of which he states them to have great numbers in their monasteries.

This account of the Buddhists of Upper India, is confirmed by the account given by Mr. Crawford[3] of the same religionists, in the island of Siam, a thousand miles from them. He says, " The " Siamese have as excellent a morality as the Christians. They have their Talapoins or Monks, " who take the vows of chastity and poverty ; they have auricular confession ; they believe that " the professors of any religion may be saved."

" Agreeably to the prevailing belief in a succession of similar worlds, over each of which pre " sides a Buddha or Menu, the inhabitants of Ceylon suppose that, towards the end of the present " mundane system, there will be long wars, unheard-of crimes, and a portentous diminution of the " length of human life : that a terrible rain will then sweep from the face of the earth all except a " small number of pious persons, who will receive timely notice of the evil, and thus be enabled to " avoid it ; and that the wicked will be changed into beasts, and that ultimately Maitri[4] —Buddha " —will appear and re-establish a new order of things."[5] Here are the metempsychosis and the renewal of worlds.; the exact doctrine, which was noticed before, of Irenæus.

I must now beg my reader to pause a little, and to reflect upon the accounts which he has read in this book respecting the prophecies of Cristna, of Isaiah, of Virgil, of the Sibyls, as reported by Figulus and other Romans, of the prophecy of Zoroaster, and of the Druid of Ireland,—and I would then ask him what he thinks of it. Can he for a moment doubt that all this relates to the renewal of the cycles, and to a succession of incarnations ? The mysterious child, alluded to in the beginning of this book, was a new incarnation of Divine Wisdom, the πρωτογονος, the first emanation, the logos, the solar fire, the sacred, mysterious, never-to-be-spoken OM, the Trimurti, united in the person of Buddha or Cristna,[6] born to be king of the people of Sion, of the country

---

[1] They have the custom of forming Carns by piling heaps of stones over dead bodies, like those of the Western world, pp. 221, 222. Every traveller passing by adds a stone to the heap.

[2] Pp. 306, 307.                    [3] Res. Vol. II. pp. 190, et seq.

[4] I suspect this word *Maitri* is the French *Maître*, the Spanish and Italian *Maéstro*, the Dutch *Meester*, and our *Master*,—all probably derived from the Latin *Magister ;* and the *last* equally with *Maitri* from a common origin.

[5] Fab. Orig. Pag. Idol. Vol. II. p. 339.                    [6] Ibid. p. 43.

2 H

of JUDIA, of the tribe of YUDA,[1] whose language was that of the Baali of Siam and Persia—of the people called Palli, or Pallestini or Philistines—of the black nation of Sir William Jones, and whose name was, with the Greeks, X 600, and XH and ΥΗΣ 608; and Jupiter, Ieu-pati, the Saviour, represented in St. Peter's by the stone image to which I have before alluded, having inscribed on it the words Ζευς Σωτηρ.

---

## CHAPTER V.

### MENU.—SIR WILLIAM JONES ON MENU.

1. IN the Hindoo mythology we meet with a very important personage, called MENU. He is allowed to be identical with Buddha, and with the Sun, and to be surnamed Son of the Self-existent, or, in other words, Son of God. The word Menu signifies *mind* or *understanding*, and is closely connected with the idea of WISDOM. It is, in short, but another epithet for Buddha. This root is closely allied to the root מנר *mnr*, whence comes the Minerva of the Greeks,[2] and the English word man, and the Latin words MENS *mind*, memini *to remember*, and the Sanscrit man or men, *to think*. I am of opinion that the Numa of the Romans, the legislator who had the mystical surname of P-Om-pilius,[3] was a Menu corrupted; read from right to left it is Manu.

Menu, meaning mind, or soul, or spirit, every incarnation was a Menu, or a manifestation of the Divine Mind. This was the same as Divine Wisdom, the πρωτογενος. To this Divine Mind or Wisdom the priests most discreetly attributed their codes of law. Thus Menes in Egypt gave the first laws;[4] and Minos, the son of Jupiter (Iao) and the beautiful Io, was the first legislator of Crete. From the second syllable of the word Menu the Greek word Νοος has been thought to be derived. The heretical Jews worshiped the planetary bodies, under the name of מני *mni*, which means, the disposers or placers in order. In the Hindoo system there are said to have been fourteen Menus, (the last of whom finished with the flood,) or the same person is said to have appeared many times. He is attended by seven companions, who are called Rashees or Rishees, before explained, but evidently the five planets, the earth, and the moon.

2. Menu was maintained by Sir W. Jones to be the נח *nh*, or, as we call him, the Noah of Genesis. This is strongly supported by the fact, that it is said in Genesis viii. 13, " in the six hundred and " first year of Noah's life, in the first month, the first day of the month, the waters were dried " up from the earth." Here is evidently the cycle of the Neros, ending with the drying of the waters, and beginning anew. Here are the ending of one year or life of Menu or Buddha, and the beginning of a new one.

The intimate connexion between Minerva and Buddha, as WISDOM and mind, I need not point out. On this Word or Person Mr. Faber says, " The import of the Greek word *Nous* and of the " Sanscrit Menu is precisely the same : each denotes mind or *intelligence :* and to the latter of

---

[1] Of the tribe of Yuda I shall have much to say hereafter.          [2] See Parkhurst in voce מנר *mnr*.

[3] With *Pi* the Coptic emphatic article, Pi-Om-philius or filius, *the son of Om*.          [4] Maurice, Hist.

" them the Latin *Mens* is evidently very nearly allied : or, to speak more properly, Mens and " Menu, perhaps also our English Mind, are fundamentally one and the same word." [1]

After the Gods, Diodorus makes the first king of Egypt, Menas, or Menes, to reign at Thebes, not at Memphis ; the latter was a modern city compared with the former. Thus Menes is found as first king at Thebes and at Memphis; in Crete, by the name of Minos, and in India as Menu. The Men-des or Pan of Egypt may mean the Divine Mind, [2] in fact, the Holy Mind or Ghost. Menu is also shewn by various writers to be the Sun, and in this respect the same as Buddha. All these Hindoo persons, like the different Gods of the Western nations, resolve themselves at last into the Sun.

Of the Theban kings Eratosthenes says, The first who reigned was *Mines* the Thebinite, the Thebæan, which is by interpretation Dionius : Πρωτος εβασιλευσεν Μινης Θηβινιτης, Θηβαιος, ὁ ἑρμηνευεται Διονιος. The second was called by interpretation Ἑρμογενης *Hermogenes*, i. e. Begotten of Hermes.

Mr. Faber correctly observes, that the Menu of the Hindoos is the Maha-bad or Great Bud of the Buddhists : he has the same history : what applies to the one, with very little variation, applies to the other. [3] There were fourteen Maha-bads, as there were fourteen Menus. In the Desatir of Moshani fourteen Mahabads are treated of. These were the imaginary persons of whom Sir William Jones made a dynasty of kings.

Mr. Faber has very successfully proved that Buddha and Zoroaster, [4] or the star of the Bull, as he explains the word, are the same person, the same as the Menu of the Chusas of Iran. He says, " The early worship, therefore, of Iran, according to the Zendavesta, was the worship of " *Buddha* or *Tat* under the form of a Bull, compounded with the human form." [5]

In Persia they had five Zoroasters : these were but renewed incarnations of the Tauric God. [6]

In short, I believe the word Menu had the same meaning, originally, as Rasit, *Wisdom;* that it was the same as the mount of Meru, and that Meru and Menu were mere dialectic variations. In this I am supported by Mons. La Loubère, who states that Maria and Mania are written and used *indiscriminately* in the Siamese language : and this fact, when it is considered that the whole Eastern mythos was removed to the West, justifies a suspicion that along with the others came the oriental il-avratta, or mount of Meru, and that we have it in the mount now called Baris and Armenia : that is, *Ar* or *Er-Meni-ia*, the country of mount Meru or Meni. The mount Baris is the mount of Nau-banda. Dr. Jones [7] says, Βαρις, a structure of any sort, a boat or barge. The mount of Naubanda, in the Indian language, is said to mean *ship-cabled mount*. To this mount in the flood of Noah the Ark was said to be fastened. The word *Nau* is the Latin *Navis*, and the Greek Ναυς : and the word *band* is a common English word for a cord or cable. [8] The expression mount Meru or Menu, means the mount *of* Meru. In the Hebrew language when a word is in regimine, in many cases it can only be known by the context whether it be in the nominative or genitive case. The words for *mount Meru* and *mount* OF *Meru* would be the same. This, if the Hebrew or any language like the Hebrew were the original language, readily accounts for the names of many places. If Manes, the son of Budwas, *the son of Thomas, of whom we*

---

[1] Faber, Orig. Pag. Idol. Vol. I. p. 40.

[2] In Egypt there was a city called Mendes. The symbol of Mendes was a Goat: the reason of this I shall explain hereafter.

[3] Fab. p. 123.     [4] Ch. iii.     [5] Vol. II. p. 83.     [6] Nimrod, 231.     [7] In Lexicon.

[8] This is a good example of the utility of applying to several languages for the meaning of a word, for I am quite certain no one can doubt the identity of signification in the word *naubanda*.

*shall hereafter have much that is very extraordinary to offer,* were really a man, he had his name from Menu, and when his doctrines were said to be those of Manes, it was meant that they were the doctrines of the INCARNATE WISDOM.

In consequence of the word for moon מן *mn* or Μηνη being the same as the name of the Menu of India, I cannot shew examples of him very clearly in the West, because the two names are so confounded, that it is almost impossible, in most cases, to be certain of *which* the ancient author is treating. But Arrian has observed that the mount Meru was known to the Greeks, and was sacred to Bacchus.[1]

In Genesis v. 29, it is said, that Noah had his name of נח *nh* (ינחמני *inhmnu) because he shall comfort us ;* or, *because he shall cause to rest.* Now, I think these explanations of the name of the Man, the grand point of whose life was the ruin of a world by floods and winds, are both ridiculous, and only prove that the meaning of the word, of this half-lost language, is unknown. Under all the circumstances I have a suspicion that there is here a mistake between the letter He ה *e* and the letter Heth ח *h,* and that the word ינח *inh,* followed by the word מנו MNU, meant, *Menu shall lead or precede.* We have already seen that Noah and Menu were the same. Thus we find that in the Western as well as in the Eastern part of Asia, there was a Menu, and each was saved in an Ark from a flood. The letter ח *h* and the letter ה *e* are often substituted for each other in the Hebrew, as they are in the Greek.

In Gen. ix. 20, Noah is called by Moses איש האדמה *ais eadme,* that is, the husband of the earth. Thus Saturn was the husband of Rhea.[2] I shall have more to say on the meaning of the word *Menu* hereafter.

---

## CHAPTER VI.

HERCULES AND SAMSON THE SAME.—ETYMOLOGY OF SAMSON.—MUTTRA, HERCULES AT.—DRUMMOND ON HERCULES. THE FOXES. — WILFORD ON HERCULES AT MUTTRA. MEANING OF WORD HERCULES.— HERCULES BLACK. CRISTNA IN EGYPT.

1. I SHALL now proceed to exhibit some other circumstances to prove that the God of Western and Eastern Asia was the same. In the particulars of the God Hercules some striking marks of the identity of the two will be found. In his adventures also a number of facts may be perceived, which identify him with the Samson of the Jews and the Cristna of India.

Samson שמשון *smsun,* is explained by Calmet and Cruden to mean *his sun.* This explanation I greatly doubt. Samson answers correctly to the Hindoo incarnation Shama, or Shama-Jaya, which is one of the thousand names of Vishnu, which the Hindoos repeat in their litanies, as is

---

[1] Hist. Ind. pp. 318, 321 ; Diod. Sic. Lib. ii. p. 123 ; Bryant, Anal. Vol. III. p. 196. Menu in India was the supposed author of a celebrated code of laws called the Institutes of Menu, translated into English by the learned Professor Haughton.

[2] Gale, Court Gent. B. iii. Ch. ii.

done by the Romish Christians.[1]　Bal-iswara was the son of this *Shama,* and the *Sem-i-ramis* of Assur, of Scripture.[2]　Several of the early Christian fathers, and along with them Syncellus, acknowledge the identity of Samson and Hercules, who, they say, was copied by the Gentiles from the Bible.　The whole story of Samson, the Philistines, the Lion, Thamnath or Thamnuz, תמנתה *tmnte,* is a mythos : it is explained by Dupuis, sur tous les Cultes, in his dissertation on the labours of Hercules.

Mr. Faber says, " On the sphere he *(Hercules)* is represented in the act of contending with the " serpent, the head of which is placed under his foot : and this serpent, we are told, is that which " guarded the tree with golden fruit in the midst of the garden of the Hesperides.　But the garden " of the Hesperides, as we have already seen, was no other than the garden of Paradise : conse- " quently the serpent of that garden, the head of which is crushed beneath the heel of Hercules, " and which itself is described as encircling with its folds the trunk of the mysterious tree, must " necessarily be a transcript of that serpent whose form was assumed by the tempter of our first " parents.　We may observe the same ancient tradition in the Phœnician fable respecting Ophion " or Ophioneus."[3]　The reader will not dispute the authority of the orthodox Faber.　Would he wish for a more decisive proof that Genesis is a mythos, as the Rev. Dr. Geddes properly calls it ? If he do, let him consult Mons. Dupuis sur tous les Cultes, where Mr. Faber acquired his knowledge, though he wishes to keep M. Dupuis's fine work in the back-ground.

The situation of the foot of the celestial Hercules on the Serpent's head, pretty well identifies him with the Cristna of Genesis and India.　Parkhurst admits that the labours of Hercules are nothing but the passage of the sun through the signs of the Zodiac ; and the circumstances relating to him he adopts as " *emblematic memorials of what the real Saviour was to do and to suffer*"—the name of Hercules being, according to him, " A TITLE OF THE FUTURE SAVIOUR." He could not foresee that the origin of Hercules was to be found (viz. at Maturea or Muttra) in India.[4]

2. The etymology of the name of Samson and his adventures are very closely connected with the solar Hercules.　Sampsa was the name of the Sun.　Among the Arabians Baisampsa was the name of a city of their country, which was the same as Heliopolis or city of the Sun.　Isidore, of Seville, says, that the name of Samson signifies the solar force or power ; that is, he defines it as Macrobius defines Hercules.　Whatever may be the origin of the name, we know that Samson was of the tribe of Dan, or of that which, in the astrological system of the Rabbins, was placed (casée) under Scorpio, or under the sign with which the celestial Hercules rises.　He became amorous of a daughter of Thamnis. תמנתה *tmnte.*[5]　In going to seek her, he encountered a furious lion which, like Hercules, he destroyed.　Syncellus says of him, " In this time lived " Samson, who was called Hercules, by the Greeks.　Some persons maintain, nevertheless," adds he, " that Hercules lived before Samson ; but traits of resemblance exist between them, which " cannot be denied."[6]

It is not surprising that Mr. Parkhurst should be obliged to acknowledge the close connexion between Hercules and Jesus—as the fact of Hercules, in the ancient sphere, treading on the head of the serpent leaves no room for doubt on this subject, and also identifies him with

[1] The practice of calling the God by many names, and repeating them in their Litanies, is still followed in the Romish Church. I counted forty-three names of the black virgin under her image at Loretto. See plates, fig. 15. Cristna has one thousand names ; as time passed on they probably increased.

[2] See Wilford, Asiat. Res. Vol. V. p. 293.　　[3] Faber, Orig. of Pag. Idol. Vol. I. p. 443.

[4] For some interesting observations on this God the reader may consult Parkhurst's Lexicon in voce עז *oz,* p. 520.

[5] Judges xiv. 1.　[6] Dupuis, sur tous les Cultes, Vol. I. pp. 311, 539.

Cristna of India, who is seldom seen without the head of the Cobra beneath his foot: and these two facts at once locate Cristna *before* the Christian æra.

The identity of Cristna and Hercules has been shewn. Christian priests say that the man treading on the head of the serpent is an emblem of Jesus; then here we have the same emblem of Cristna, Hercules, and Jesus. Whether this will prove the identity of the three, I leave to the devotees. It surely proves the identity of the doctrine or mythos of the second book of Genesis, of Greece, and of India. I am not surprised that the Rev. and superstitious Parkhurst should state Hercules to be an emblem of the future Saviour. How could any person who had eyes avoid seeing the identity of the history of the two? However, let me not be abused for first seeing this: it was the pious Parkhurst who discovered it, I only repeat his words, and I have no inclination to dispute his explanation of the mythos.

Col. Wilford says, that Megasthenes reckons fifteen generations between Dionysius and Hercules, by the latter of whom, he observes, we are to understand Cristna and Bala-Rama. He adds, " It appears that, like the spiritual rulers of Tibet, Deo-Naush did not, properly speaking, " die, but his soul shifted its habitation, and got into a new body, whenever the old one was worn " out, either through age or sickness;" Here we have the true system of incarnations and the · metempsychosis. Whether there be in the Hindoo mythos an incarnation called Bala-Rama between Bachus, that is Dionysius, that is Taurus—and Hercules, that is Cristna, that is Aries, or not, is of no consequence. It may have been the fact. It will not affect the general argument. But Bala-Rama is said to be the same as Cristna. The two grand incarnations, whether called Bala-Rama or by whatever other name, were those of Buddha and Cristna. After the equinox began in Taurus, they were all incarnations of Buddha until the sun entered Aries, and after his entrance into Aries, of Cristna; and both were incarnations of Vishnu, or of the Trimurti.

By the word generation, used above, I apprehend is meant century. Then if we admit that Bala-Rama was the incarnation, as I am inclined to believe he was, of the cycle next before Cristna, and if to the 1500 we add 600, his cycle, this would bring us to the year 2100 from the Sun's entrance into Taurus to his entrance into Aries, for the incarnation of his successor, Cristna. Bala-Rama is constantly held, by the present ignorant Brahmins, to be the same as Cristna. This is because he was the next previous incarnation. The nearness of the two, connected also with the fact, that they were in reality renewed incarnations or regenerations of the same person, prevents the Brahmins from seeing the distinction. Besides, he was the same in another sense; he was the Sun in the equinoctial sign Aries, and in the cycle of the Neros,—both running at the same time, and crossing each other in their progress.[1]

3. The old statues of the Gods at the famous Muttra or Maturea have been destroyed by the Mohamedans, and the new ones have been erected in modern form, and in consequence have no resemblance to those described by Megasthenes, but at a place called Bala-deva, about thirteen miles from Muttra, there is a very ancient statue, which minutely answers to his description; it was visited some years ago by the late Lieut. Stewart, who describes it in the following words: " Bala-Rama, or Bala-deva, is respresented *there* with a plough-share in his left hand, with which " he hooked his enemies; and in his right hand a thick cudgel, with which he cleft their sculls; " his shoulders are covered with the skin of a tiger." Captain Wilford adds, " Here I shall ob- " serve, that the ploughshare is always represented very small, and sometimes omitted; and that " it looks exactly like a harpoon with a strong hook or a gaff, as it is usually called by fishermen.

---

[1] The doctrine of regeneration has been actually carried to the letter in India. Mons. D'Ancarville, p. 102, gives an account of a Prince being admitted to the Brahmin caste by being passed through the body of a golden cow. The Brahmins hold that they are the descendants of Brahma, and the Cow or Beeve is the emblem of him.

" My Pundits inform me also, that Bala-Rama is sometimes represented with his shoulders co-
" vered with the skin of a lion." [1]

Our account of Samson and the bone of the Ass is probably some misunderstanding of the text,
or a corruption. I feel little doubt that the gaff and the bone were the same thing, whatever they
were. [2]

On most of the Egyptian monuments a priest is seen with a lituus or crosier of a peculiar shape.
This I take to have been the Hieralpha (described by Kircher) and the ploughshare in the hand of
Bala-Rama, just mentioned. This is confirmed by a passage of Diodorus Siculus respecting the
rites of the priests of Ethiopia and those of the Egyptians ; " The several colleges of priests
" (they say) observe one and the same order and discipline in both nations. For, as many as are
" so consecrated for divine service are wholly devoted to purity and religion, and in both countries
" are shaven alike, and are clothed with the like stoles and attire, and carry a sceptre like unto a
" ploughshare, such as their kings likewise bear, with high-crowned caps tufted at the top,
" wreathed round with serpents called asps : by which is seemed to be signified, that those who
" contrive any thing against the life are as sure to die as if they were stung with the deadly bite
" of an asp." Here I think the lituus, which is seen so often and is called a ploughshare, is
meant. [3]

This image of Bala-Deva is probably that of Cristna. The Hindoos know little about the names
of their Gods. Bala-Deva is but one of the names of Cristna and Buddha.

4. Sir William Drummond says, " I have already observed that Gaza signifies a Goat, and was
" the type of the sun in Capricorn. It will be remembered that the gates of the sun were feigned
" by the ancient astronomers to be in Capricorn and Cancer, from which signs the tropics are
" named. Samson carried away the gates from *Gaza* to *Hebron*, the city of conjunction. Now,
" Count Gebelin tells us that at Cadiz, where Hercules was anciently worshiped, there was a re-
" presentation of him, with a gate on his shoulders. [4] The story of Samson and Delilah may re-
" mind us of Hercules and Omphale.

" לחי *Lehi, lhi*, a Jawbone. It will be remembered that in the first decan of *Leo* an Ass's head
" was represented by the Orientalists. רמת לחי *Rmt Lhi, Ramath Lehi,* means the high place of
" the Jawbone.

" Samson had seven locks of hair (the number of the planetary bodies). The yellow hair of
" Apollo was a symbol of the solar rays : and Samson with his shaven head may mean the sun
" shorn of his beams." [5]

Volney says, " Hercules is the emblem of the sun : the name of Samson signifies the sun :
" Hercules was represented naked, [7] carrying on his shoulders two columns called the Gates of
" Cadiz : Samson is said to have borne off and carried on his shoulders the Gates of Gaza. Her-
" cules is made prisoner by the Egyptians, who want to sacrifice him : but while they are pre-
" paring to slay him, he breaks loose and kills them all. Samson, tied with new ropes by the
" armed men of Judah, is given up to the Philistines, who want to kill him : he unties the ropes
" and kills a thousand Philistines with the Jawbone of an Ass. Hercules (the sun) departing for
" the *Indies*, (or rather Ethiopia,) and conducting his army through the deserts of Lybia, feels a
" burning thirst, and conjures *Ihou*, his father, to succour him in his danger : instantly the ce-
" lestial RAM appears : Hercules follows him, and arrives at a place where the ram scrapes with

---

[1] Asiat. Res. Vol. V. p. 294.      [2] Vide Dr. D. Clarke's Travels, Vol. III. Ch. iv.     [3] B. iii. Ch. l.

[4] Drum. Œd. Jud. p. 361.      [5] Ib. p. 360.      [6] In Arabic Shams-on means The Sun.

[7] See Montfaucon, Ant. Exp. Vol. I. p. 127.

" his foot, and there comes forth a spring of water (that of the Hyads or Eridan).[1]   Samson after
" having killed a thousand Philistines with the jawbone of an ass feels a violent thirst : he be-
" seeches the God *Ihou* to take pity on him : God makes a spring of water to issue from the
" jawbone of an ass."[2]   M. Volney then goes on to shew that the story of the foxes is copied
from the Pagan mythology, and was the subject of a festival in Latium.   The labours of Hercules
are all astronomically explained by Mons. Dupuis in a manner which admits of no dispute.   They
are the history of the annual passage of the sun through the signs of the Zodiac, as may be seen
on the globe, it being corrected to the proper æra and latitude.

The story of the Foxes with the fire-brands[3] is vindicated by Ovid[4] —passages which imply,
though the author himself affirms the contrary, more than a solitary instance of mischief, to justify
a general and annual memorial—and is farther explained by Lycophron's Λαμπουρις and Suidas'
voc. γεωρια.   The Roman festival, *Vulpium combustio*, recurred about the middle of April, when,
as Bochart in his Hieroz. remarks, there was no harvest in Italy.   Hence it must have been imported from a warmer climate.[5]

Bochart (in the Pref. to Histor. de Animal.) says, " In memory of Samson's foxes,[6] there were
" let loose *in the circus at Rome* about the middle of April foxes with firebrands.   Whereunto ap-
" pertains that which the Bœotians, who sprang partly from the Phœnicians, boast of themselves,
" that they could kindle any thing by means of a torch affixed to a fox : and that of Lycophron, a
" Cilician, by whom a fox is termed λαμπερις, from its shining tail : *or from a torch bound to*
" *its tail.*"   The same Bochart tells us, " that the great fish which swallowed up *Jonah*, although
" it be called a whale,[7] yet it was not a whale properly so called, but a dog-fish, called Carcharias.
" Therefore in the Grecian fable Hercules is said to have been swallowed up of a dog, and to have
" lain three days in his entrails.   Which fable sprang from the sacred history, touching *Jonah*
the Hebrew prophet, as is evident to all."[8]

Hesychius says, that by *Cetus* Κητος, which we translate Whale, was meant a large ship, in
bulk like a whale.   Κητος, ειδος νεως· Κητινη πλοιον μεγα ὡς Κητος.   Mr. Bryant[9] says, that
when Andromeda is said to have been carried away by a sea-monster, this was probably only a
ship—perhaps by pirates.

Respecting the Hercules of India, Captain Wilford says, " Diodorus Siculus, speaking of
" Palibothra, affirms that it had been built by the Indian Hercules, who, according to Megasthenes,
" as quoted by Arrian, was worshiped by the Suraseni.   Their chief cities were *Methora* and
" Clisobora : the first is now called Mutra, (in Sanscrit it is called *Mat'hura*,) the other *Mugu-*
" *nagur* by the Musselmans, and Calisa-pura by the Hindus.   The whole country about *Mutra*
" is called *Surasena* to this day, by learned Brahmins.

" The Indian Hercules, according to Cicero, was called Belus.   He is the same as Bala, the
" brother of Crishna, and both are conjointly worshiped at *Mutra ;* indeed, they are considered
" as one Avatar or incarnation of *Vishnu.*   *Bala* is represented as a stout man, with a club in his
" hand.   He is called also *Balarama.*   To decline the word *Bala*, you must begin with *Balas*, which
" I conceive to be an obsolete form, preserved only for the purpose of declension and etymological
" derivation.   The first *a* in *Bala* is pronounced like the first *a* in *America*, in the Eastern parts
" of India : but in the Western parts, and in Benares, it is pronounced exactly like the French *e*

---

[1] Eridan, river of Adonis, from the words ירי רד *ir dn.*          [4] Volney, Res. Vol. I. p. 35.

[3] Judges xv. 4, 5.          [4] Fasti, IV. 681, 707.          [5] Class. Jour. Vol. VI. p. 326.

[6] Ibid.          [7] Matt. xii. 40, and by LXX. *Jonah* ii. 1.          [8] Gale, Court Gent. B. iii. Ch. ix.

[9] Anal. Vol. III p. 550.

" in the pronouns *je*, *me*, &c.; thus the difference between *Balas* and *Belus* is not very great.. " As *Bala* sprung from *Vishnu* or *Heri*, he is certainly *Heri-cula*, *Heri-culas*, and *Hercules*." [1] Here we see the Ball or בעל *Bol*, of Assyria and Ireland, the Bel of Syria and Phœnicia, and the Belinus of Gaul. Cristna is evidently Hercules, and Bala-Rama is the *strong* Bala. Rama is the Greek Ρωμη. To Bel I shall return presently. [2]

It seems here convenient to inquire a little further into the meaning of the word Hercules. This word is admitted to be neither Greek nor Latin; then I think we must look for it to the Barbarians. He is called in the Dionysiacon,[3] 'ΗΡΑΚΛΗΣ. astris amictus, Rex Ignis, Princeps Mundi, Sol, &c. He was called (I learn from Vallancey) EREKOELL, that is ה $e{=}5{+}$ ר $r{=}200$ $+$נ $e=5{+}$ כ $k{=}20{+}y$ $o$ $70{+}$ה $e$ $5{+}$ל $l{=}30{+}$ל $l{=}30{=}365$; or again, E$=5+$P$=100+$K$=20+$E$=5$ $+$Λ$=30+$E$=5+$Σ$=200=365$; or, as 'ΕΡΚΛΕΣ$=360$. In my Celtic Druids [4] I have shewn that this practice of describing persons by letters as numbers was common, (the origin of which I shall endeavour to demonstrate in a future book,) both in writings and in the numbers of pillars in the ancient circular temples, which are equally common in India and Europe.[5] I ask, may not the word Hercules have been derived from *Heri* the *saviour*, and ה $k{=}500{+}$ל $l{=}30{+}y$ $o$ $={=}70{=}600$, which was sacred among the Egyptians under the shape of a cat, and which, in their language, had this name? Their cat mummies may be seen in the British Museum. Then he would be the saviour of the Neros or the ם *Mem* final of Isaiah, the X of Plato. By and by we shall find several other examples of Gods whose names had the meaning of more than one cycle.[6]

As *Hercules* was called *Heri-cules* so *Mercury* was called *Mer-coles*, or *Mer-colis*. The *Mer* I do not understand; the *colis* is the *clo* of the *Chaldees*—the *Cali* of India, and the *Coll* or *Cal* of Ireland. Col. Wilford speaks of a God called *Hara-ja* or *Hara-cula*.[7] Here Heri the saviour and the God *Ie* are identified with Hercules or Cristna.[8]

The word *Heri* in Sanscrit means shepherd as well as saviour. Cristna is called Heri, and Jesus is always called Shepherd. He is the leader of the followers of the Lamb. He is the good shepherd, as was also Cristna. In Ireland a shepherd is called *Sheepheri*, or sheep-aire. See Gen.

---

[1] Asiat. Res. Vol. V. p. 270.

[2] Bryant says, the most considerable mission in Madura is called Aour (אור *Aur*) at this day. (Travels of Jesuits by Lockman, Vol. I. p. 470.) Near it are a city and the river Balasore. Bal is the Chaldean and Syrian Deity, well known. Anal. Vol. III. p. 207.

[3] Lib. xl. p. 683.      [4] Ch. vi. Sect. xxv. p. 245, and Appendix, p. 309.

[5] Vide one of the Metonic cycle plates, fig. 11.

Allowance must be made for *one* stone evidently broken into *two*. A very curious account of a circular temple under a tumulus in the province of Coimbatoor, is given by my particular friend, the learned Psychologist, Sir Anthony Carlisle, in the twenty-first volume of the Transactions of the Society of Antiquaries. He says, " These mounds occur " numerously in the province of Coimbatoor; they are each invariably denoted by a circle of rude stones or masses of " rock, the diameter of the larger areas being often as much as one hundred feet. In one example, the circle was " formed by upright flat obelisks, averaging sixteen feet in height, rude, and without impression of tools. In the " centre of each mound a massive table of unhewn stone forms the roof or cover to four chambers, the sides and septa " being of the same rude, unworked stone, and mortices with tenons apparently ground out by trituration, serve to fix " the roof upon the walls. One of these roofs contained upwards of three hundred cubic feet of Granite, and being " immoveable as a whole, it was divided into four equal divisions by stone-cutters, in order to expose the subjacent " recesses, or chambers." This is, in reality, almost an exact description of the temple and tumulus at New Grange, in Ireland, and its circle of pillars described in my Celtic Druids.

[6] If it be said I have here placed a final *Caph* at the *beginning* of a word, I justify myself by the example of the Mem final in Isaiah, and by the Μπεθ in the Gospel of the Infancy.

[7] Asiat. Res. Vol. VI. p. 514.

[8] In an ancient inscription at Delphi Dr. Clarke found the word 'ΗΡΑΚΛΕΙΟΥ. Ib. p. 196. At the foot of Olympus was a town called Heraclea. Ib. 301.

Vallancey, Ouseley's Col. Orien. p. 315, where he proves that the ryots of India were known in Ireland, and were the Ara-Cottii famed for *linen geer* of Dionysius.

In this case there will be two origins for the name of Hercules; and this is certainly mystical enough. But it must be recollected that we are now in the centre of the land of mystery. Cristna is constantly called Heri-Cristna : this is the *black*. But it may be the beneficent or good saviour, or good Heri; for Cristna may come from some old word, whence came the Greek word Χρησος *bonus*. He was called Creechna in Ireland. 1 have proved that all the very ancient languages are the same, mere dialects, and I will not be fettered in my search after truth either by one language or another. The utility of my endeavour first to prove the identity of the ancient systems of letters and language I hope is obvious. It is no more likely that the *black* Hindoos should call their God the *black* Saviour or Heri, than it is that the *white* French should call Henry Quatre their *white* Henry; but it is as natural for them to call him the *good Saviour*, as for the French to call their king their *good Henry*. It is certain that in Sanscrit *cris* means *black*, and in old Greek χρης means *good;* he may, therefore, have been named from both words. On the subject of the word χρης I shall have much to say hereafter.

Arrian says, on the authority of Megasthenes, that the Indian Hercules had the same habit as the Theban Hercules, and that he had an only daughter called Pandæa.[1] This was precisely the same name as that which was given to the only daughter of Cristna, to whom he left a mighty empire—the Pandæan kingdom.

6. In addition to all the other circumstances of identity between Cristna and Hercules, is the fact that they were both *blacks*. Of Hercules, Homer, in what Nimrod calls his genuine verses, thus speaks :

———— ὁ δ'ερεμνῇ νυκτι γεγεικως
Γυμνον τοξον εχων και επι νευρηφιν οϊστον.

———— BLACK he stood as night,
His bow uncased, his arrow strung for flight.[*]

In B. iv. ch. i. Sect. 13, I have shewn, from Mr. Bryant, that the last syllable in the word *Maturea,* viz. *re,* meant the sun. The first syllable, I suspect, was the Hebrew מטה *mte,* which meant a resting-place, a couch, a bed, a sofa or sopha, (that is, as the Re was a ray of the sun which was Wisdom,) or soph-ia or place of wisdom,—a resting-place of divine wisdom—a Divan, that is, Deva-ana or holy place, where, in the Asiatic courts, is the Sopha on which the king reposes to administer justice. From the same idea I have no doubt it was, that the kings of the Franks, (or as, in a future page, I shall prove them,) the kings of the Sacæ or Saxons, had their Beds of Justice. In the Maturea of India, Cristna spent his youth, after taking refuge there from the tyrant who strove to destroy him. And in the Maturea of Egypt, Jesus Christ is said, as we have before shewn, to have spent his youth, after he took refuge there from the tyrant Herod.

Mr. Maurice has pointed out a passage of Eusebius from which it seems probable that the Cristna in Egypt was well known in his time. He says, " That at Elephantina they adored an-
" other deity in the figure of a man, in a sitting posture, *painted blue,* having the head of a Ram
" with the horns of a Goat encircling a disk. The deity thus described is plainly of astronomical

---

[1] Arr. Hist. Ind. ch. viii.; Creuzer, Vol. II. ch. v. p. 190.

[*] Nimrod, Vol. I. p. 19, Sup. ed. Nimrod is the name given by a very learned devotee to an anonymous work in three volumes octavo, published by Priestley, Holborn. The first volume was suppressed, and then republished. The work abounds with the most profound Greek learning, but falls short, in many places, in consequence of its ingenious author, most unfortunately, not understanding the Oriental languages.

" origin, denoting the power of the sun in Aries. It is, however, exceedingly remarkable that
" Pococke actually found, and on his 48th plate has engraved, an antique colossal statue of a man,
" sitting in the front of this temple with his arms folded before him, and bearing in his hand a
" very singular kind of Lituus or crosier."[1]  I think there can be hardly any doubt that the figure
described by Eusebius was that of Cristna or Buddha.  There was a city in Egypt called Hera-
cleopolis.

It does not appear to me to be more surprising that there should be two Matureas, one in India
and one in Egypt, than that there should be two islands of Elephanta in which the statues of
Cristna should be found, one near Bombay, where the famous cavern is seen, and one in Upper
Egypt.  Every one knows the fact of our Seapoys discovering their favourite God Cristna, when
they arrived in Egypt, during the last war, and which, very naturally, they immediately fell to
worshiping.  This alone at once proves the fallacy of all the deductions which are drawn from the
astronomical calculations and reasonings of Mr. Bentley, on which I will now make some observations, and may serve to shew how little the abstruse and complicated chains of reasoning used by
him can in any case be depended on.  The fact of the God Cristna being found in the ruins of the
old temples at Thebes in Egypt of itself settles the question of its antiquity, for it could not be
put there after the birth of Christ.[2]

We have seen above that the striking similarity between the vulgarly-received Jesus of Nazareth and Hercules cannot be denied by the learned and orthodox Parkhurst, and we have also seen
the mode in which he accounts for it.  I have fairly stated the facts for the consideration of my
reader, who must see at once that if the explanation of Parkhurst be satisfactory for Hercules, the
same explanation will serve for Cristna.  In an honest inquiry into the superstitions of the world,
I could not conceal the circumstances relating to Cristna; and there are many others, which I
shall state.  Of course I cannot condemn any one for being satisfied with Mr. Parkhurst's judgment.  That it is not satisfactory to me, may be readily accounted for from an opinion which I
entertain, that I *can* and *shall* account for the facts in a very different and more satisfactory manner, when I come to that part of my work where I shall undertake to prove that a person usually
called Jesus Christ did live, and that the doctrines which he taught were true.  I must beg my
reader to recollect that in this work I am not writing for the ignorant, nor to gratify the passions
of any class, but that it is the object of my work to develop and unveil the secret history of the
ancient world, which operates influentially upon us ; that it is meant for legislators and philosophers, to enable them the better to determine what is the most expedient course for them to pursue for the good of their fellow-creatures.

---

[1] Ind. Ant. Vol. III. p. 211.

[2] In one of the plates of my Celtic Druids of a round tower in Scotland, the crucified Saviour has a lamb on one
side, and an ELEPHANT on the other.  How came an elephant to be thus found in Scotland?

## CHAPTER. VII.

1. SINCE Bailly, Playfair, and the other learned men have been dead, as might be expected, renewed attempts have been made to shew that the Brahmins' astronomical tables are not the produce of actual observation, but a combination of back reckonings and forgeries. The gentleman of the name of Bentley, of whom I have before spoken, has, by means of the most deeply-learned and profound calculations, published in the Asiatic Researches, endeavoured to shew that the history of Cristna was invented in the year after Christ 600, and that the time of the story was laid about the birth of Christ. The object of this invention he, in his first essays, says, was to prevent the propagation of the Christian religion in India, by a colony which arrived from the West about that time; and in his latter essays he says, the object was to deceive Mohamed Akbar in the 16th century into a belief that they were the oldest of nations.

In these essays, a most inflated and exaggerated account has been given by him, of the forgeries of the Hindoo writings : in answer to which I beg leave to refer to some observations long before written by Mr. Colebrooke, in the Asiatic Researches,[1] where he gives most convincing reasons why the chief part of the Hindoo writings cannot have been forged or materially interpolated. As he justly observes, it would be as fair to conclude that all European books were forged, because there have been forgeries in Europe, as it is, because there have been forgeries in India, to conclude the same thing of them. His argument really shews, that it would be just as easy to forge the gospels *at this day,* as it must have been to forge the Vedas;[2] and the impossibility of the former need not be pointed out.

2. The Vedas of the Brahmins have hitherto been attended with several difficulties. According to the received BRAHMIN tradition, they were originally, after being revealed by Brahma, transmitted by ORAL TRADITION to the time of Vyasa, who collected them and arranged them into books. And this Vyasa, which word it is said means *compiler,* has been thought to be merely an epoch in the history of the literature of India.[3] The number of the Vedas is also a matter of dispute; some making them in number only three, some four, and some add to them the collection of books called the Pouranas, of which they make a fifth Veda. From these circumstances it seems probable that the Brahmin Vedas were first collected or remodelled, after the great division between the followers of Buddha and Cristna. They are said to contain internal evidence of being composed at different times. The Pouranas are eighteen in number; they are also the work of Vyasa. Each has a particular and characteristic name. For instance, one of the lotus, another of the egg of the world, and the LAST is that of Cristna, called Bhagavad—Baga-veda. Now it has been observed that the Brahmins admit that Buddha was the ninth Avatar; then what is the reason that he has no Pourana ? But at the same time that the Brahmins admit him to have been an incarnation or Avatar, they say he was *an impostor,* that he was every thing that is bad, and

---

[1] Vol. VIII. pp. 484—488.

[2] It has been said that Mr. Playfair changed his opinion before he died respecting the antiquity of the Hindoo tables. I have made the most careful inquiry of his friends, and have reason to believe this to be false.

[3] Creuzer, Liv. I. p. 671.

that he lived many ages after Cristna.[1] This appearance of contradiction I shall explain by and by.

In wishing to condemn the whole of the Hindoo writings, because there are, as he says, corruptions in them, Mr. Bentley does not perceive the blow which he is striking at the gospel histories, which contain 30,000 various readings, half of which must be corruptions. He also instances the prophetic style of the Hindoo writings as a mark of corruption. In these cases it is frequently no such thing, not even if a person be designated by name, as the persons, viz. the Buddhas, the Balis, &c., were all the same—re-incarnations, regenerations of the same being, and often called by the same name. I admit that many corruptions and interpolations have taken place; but I maintain that if these are sufficient to condemn the Vedas, the gospels also must be condemned, for they contain various readings or corruptions, some of them of VITAL consequence to the religion. But it is not just to infer of either, that they are not genuine, because the priests have corrupted them.

It is pretty clear that in order to get over the absolute identity of the history of Christ and Cristna, many attempts will be made to shew, that the story of Cristna is an interpolation in the Hindoo books, though they are among the oldest of their records. Mr. Colebrooke observes, that " the former of these (the story of Cristna) is inserted in all the collections of the Upanishads " which" he has " seen."[2] Dr. Pritchard[3] admits, that the history of Cristna, &c., are to be found in all the caves of Ellora, Elephanta, &c., which are known to be the oldest, as he says, by their *flat roofs*, &c. Mr. Colebrooke allows, that the formulas attached to the Vedas for adjusting the periods for celebrating the religious festivals, " were evidently formed in the infancy of astro- " nomical knowledge:" hence he infers that they were written about 200 years after the Pentateuch. But the fair inference is, that as the Vedas, and the caves, and the astronomical observations, and the formulæ, are all closely interwoven with the history of Cristna—that history is of the same early date, and the formulæ at least equally ancient. However, as Dr. Pritchard allows that the formulæ are much older than Christ, it is evident that they cannot have been written to serve any purpose in any way connected with Christianity.

But the stories related of Cristna are most clearly no interpolation; they are intimately blended with, they are, in fact, the ground-work, of the whole system. The system of the Brahmins cannot exist without them. Besides, what is to be said of the sculptures in the caves? Are they interpolations too? What, of the tremendous figure destroying the infant *boys*? What, of the cross-shaped temple in the city of Mathura, allowed by Mr. Maurice to have been once the capital of a great empire?[4] This is most certainly proved by Arrian to have been in existence in the time of Alexander. Was this built to support the apocryphal gospel history? The April festival, in Britain and India, was it founded for the same purpose; or the statue of Hercules and Samson still remaining at Rama-deva? Mr. Maurice acknowledges that the Evangelists must have copied from the Puranas, or the Brahmins from the Evangelists.[5] The reader has seen the reply of Mr. Maurice given in his Antiquities, and must judge for himself. There is nothing in Mr. Maurice's pamphlets but a mere repetition. But in his pamphlets I do not perceive that he makes a single observation on the subject of the figures in the caves. This is prudent; but it settles the question.

---

[1] Dr. Collier observes, that the genuineness of the Vedas is proved by Mr. Ward beyond dispute. (Ward's Account of Hindoos, 4to. edit. Serampore.) By this the Doctor does not mean proved to be free from modern interpolation, but that they are the real Vedas.

[2] Vide Asiat. Res. Vol. VIII. p. 494.      [3] Anal. Egypt. Mythol. p. 261.

[4] Maur. Bram. Fraud Exp.      [5] Ibid. p. 81.

When the small number of the Christians, in comparison with the immense number of Hindoos spread over all India, and using a great variety of dialects, is considered, it seems perfectly incredible, that the system of fraud supposed by Mr. Bentley can have taken place; that for this object the figures in the temples should have been cut out of the rock, or the caves excavated, or the temples themselves erected. Mr. Bentley's effect is out of all proportion to its cause. Cristna, his statues, temples, and books, &c., respecting him, are to be found where a Christian never came. Is it not absurd to suppose that all at once the Brahmins could invent the story of Cristna, and make it dovetail into all their other superstitions—make him form an integral part of their curious Trinity, the actual Trinity of ancient Persia and of Plato—make him also exactly fit into the theological inferences of the modern Christians respecting the meaning of the first chapters of Genesis—make his story exactly agree with the orthodox massacre of the innocents— and, finally, make all this be received as an ancient doctrine and article of faith, by millions of people who must have known very well that it was all perfectly new to them, and that they had never heard of it before![1]  Besides, it is not only the immaculate conception and crucifixion of Cristna which must have been invented to serve Mr. Bentley's purpose; the crucifixion of the God Indra in Nepaul; in fact, the immaculate conception, crucifixion, and resurrection of Buddha, in Nepaul and Tibet, equally with the religion of the Samanæans of Clemens Alexandrinus,[2] and of the Buddha of Porphyry and Jerom, born from the side of his mother, must have been invented. Yes, *all these things* must have been forged.

3. The forgeries of the early Christians are so numerous as to be almost incredible; but they bear no proportion to what, if we are to believe Mr. Bentley, has been taking place in India in modern times. In the history of Buddha, as well as of Cristna, are to be found many of the stories which are supposed to be forged; so that two sects hating one another, and not holding the least communication, must have conspired over all the immense territories east of the Indus, to destroy and to rewrite every old work, to the amount almost of millions; and so completely have they succeeded, that all our missionaries have not, in any of the countries where the Brahmins are to be found, or in which there are only Buddhists, been able to discover a single copy of any of the works uncorrupted with the history of Cristna. Buddha is allowed by Mr. Bentley to have been long previous to Cristna, and he is evidently the same as Cristna, which can only arise from his being the sun in an earlier period. This identity with Mercury and Woden, the Budvar day, the *Maia* mother of Mercury and Buddha, the Maturea in India and Egypt, the two Elephantas with their Cristnas, and the destroying tyrant of the gospel history in that of the Eastern, the Samaneaps of Clemens Alexandrinus, and many other circumstances, unite to prove that something must be wrong in the principle of Mr. Bentley's very learned and abstruse calculations. As I have said before, the fact of Cristna being found in Egypt by the seapoys of itself decides the question. It is of importance to observe, that by far the greatest part of the writings stated by Mr. Bentley to be forgeries, have little or no relation to religion. Those that have, are filled with stories of immensely elongated cycles and complication, for the sake, perhaps, of secrecy; or, perhaps, as our priests say, to produce astonishment in the minds of weak and ignorant persons, and for the gratification of the silly vanity of being thought the most ancient of nations. That this has caused the adoption of their old cycles, which is done by merely adding a few ciphers,

---

[1] See Buckingham's Oriental Herald.

[2] Clemens (Lib. i. p. 305) says, that the Indian Gymnosophists consisted of two sects, the Sarmanæ and the Brachmanes; that there are also some in India who followed the doctrines of Buttæ. He says Hellenicus writes, that there are Hyperboreans beyond the Riphæan mountains, who eat no flesh, but live on fruits, &c. Again, (p. 451,) he says, that the Brackmens neither eat flesh nor drink wine.

may, however unlikely, be true. But this will not account for the destruction of the old works in all the dialects spoken by various sects over all the countries east of the Indus, which existed before a certain period, and the manufacture of almost innumerable new works, *for the use of all these different and hostile sects.*

4. It has been observed by Mr. Colebrooke that the observations of Hindoo astronomers were ever extremely coarse and imperfect, and their practice very inferior to their theory of astronomy. An improved theory, or the hint of it, was borrowed from the West: but they did not learn to make correct observations. They were content, in practice, with a rude approximation.....Again Mr. C. says, " We are not to try their rules by the test of their agreement with accurate observations " at any assignable moment, and thence conclude that the rule and its correct application are " contemporaneous. This has always been the point at issue between Mr. Bentley and me. He " mentioned, in his first essay, that the age of a Hindu astronomical treatise can be so determined " with precision : I have always contended that their practical astronomy has been too loose and " imperfect for the application of that test, except as an *approximation.* In one instance, by the " rigorous use of his test he would have had to pronounce that the work under examination is of " *an age yet to come* (1454 years after A. D. 1799). [1] To avoid so monstrous an absurdity he " rejected this case, and deduced a mean from the other results, varying from 340 to 1105 years" [2] But I think the example of the fallacies to which Mr. Bentley's mode of argument is liable, which the deduction of Mr. Colebrooke in this case has shewn, is quite sufficient to prove that Mr. Bentley's conclusions cannot on any account be permitted to weigh against all the facts and powerful reasons which have been given. Indeed, Mr. Colebrooke's observation seems to me at once to *prove* the fallacy of his rule, notwithstanding that it has been admitted by some very eminent astronomers.

Respecting the manuscripts of India, the missionary Dr. Buchanan says, [3] " The greater part " of *Bengal* manuscripts, owing to the badness of the paper, require to be copied at least once in " ten years, as they will in that climate preserve no longer : and every copiest, it is to be sus- " pected, adds to old books whatever discoveries he makes, relinquishing his immediate reputation " for learning, in order to promote the grand and profitable employment of his sect, the delusion " of the multitude." Or as he probably would say, (in fact as *all priests* would say,) the enlightening of the multitude. I know no reason why the Doctor should be guilty of any deceit here : but if he state the fact fairly we see how completely he justifies what Mr. Colebrooke has said respecting the corrections of the ancient astronomical works by the moderns ; and thus entirely overthrows Mr. Bentley's specious reasonings, from the correctness of the astronomical observations. The fact here stated at once accounts for no old manuscripts being found uncorrected. No man would renew a copy except from the last version.

Mr. Colebrooke seems to consider the adoration of Cristna as Hero-worship ; the same of Menu. This is a great mistake. They are both personifications or incarnations, like Buddha, of Divine Wisdom—from the latter of which came the Hebrew נה *nh*, the Greek Νοος, and the Latin *Mens*, as I have before shewn. I have no doubt that the Buddhists and Brahmins constituted one sect, followers of Brahma, till the Sun entered Aries ; then they divided ; and the Buddhists were driven out of India. But the Buddhists had the renewed incarnations, precisely the same in number as the Brahmins—for the systems were the same; and this accounts for the younger Buddha, after Christ, whom the Brahmins call an impostor. That there were to be ten incarnations in all, was a doctrine admitted by both.

---

[1] See Asiat. Res. Vol. VI. p. 570.      [2] Asiatic Journal, March 1826, p. 365.      [3] Asiat. Res. Vol. VI. p. 174.

When it is considered that the Vyasa, of whom so much has been said, is an imaginary character, that the word means merely a compiler, and that when we say *Vyasa* compiled the Vedas, we ought to say, the compiler compiled them at such or such a time, and, that it is admitted that they were compiled from oral traditions—it does not seem to me probable, that the Brahmins had any fraudulent or dishonest intention in correcting the astronomical parts of them. They contained astronomical facts, in which, in their old books, they discovered errors, and they corrected them. The astronomical tables had no connexion with religion : nor was it possible the Brahmins could foresee that these tables could ever, in London or any where else, at a future day, have any connexion with it. After the Mythos was established about the year B. C. 3101 on the Cycle of the Neros, it stood still ; but the astronomy constantly advanced. The same thing takes place with our astronomical tables, tables of Logarithms, &c., &c. In every new edition errors are corrected.

Mr. Colebrooke[1] after a very careful examination of the credit due to the genuineness of the Vedas, inclines to think the worship of Cristna may have been introduced at or after the time that the persecution took place of the Buddhists and Jains. [2] This I think is the truth, and as far as the fact goes agrees perfectly with my theory, that Cristna is only the Indian Hercules, the Sun in Aries. And this obviates entirely another opinion of Mr. Colebrooke's, and proves that the Hindoos did not deify heroes. [3] The precise time when the struggle took place between the followers of the Sun in Taurus, and those of the Sun in Aries, is doubtful. It *must*, however, have taken place at some time—it may have been a long time—and if they did not then perfectly understand the precession of the equinox, it probably was *a long time after* the Sun entered Aries.

The argument relied on by Mr. Bentley is of an extremely abstruse and difficult nature : and I should say, in opposition to the numerous facts, and the mass of circumstantial evidence in favour of the antiquity of the Hindoo works, will itself serve as an example of the fallacy of the system recommended by him. I know not better how to describe it, than by giving an extract from a paper of Mr. Colebrooke's in the Asiatic Researches. [4] The practice of modernizing books, alluded to by Mr. Colebrooke, seems to harmonize the facts, which cannot be questioned, with the plausible hypothesis of Mr. Bentley, and thus to remove a very great difficulty :

" Without entering at length into any disquisition on this subject, or discussing the accuracy " of the premises, but acceding generally to the position, that the date of a set of astronomical " tables, or of a system for the computation of the places of planets, is deducible from the ascer- " tainment of a time when that system or set of tables gave results nearest to the truth ; and " granting that the date above-mentioned approximates within certain limits to such an ascertain- " ment ; I shall merely observe that, supposing the dates otherwise irreconcilable, still the book " which we now have under the name of Súrya, or Saura, Sidd' hanta, may have been, and " probably was, modernized from a more ancient treatise of the same name, the later work borrow- " ing its title from an earlier performance of a different author. We have an instance of this " practice in the kindred case of the Brahme-sidd' hanta : for we are acquainted with no less than " three astronomical treatises bearing this title: and an equal number of tracts, entitled Vasisht'ha- " sidd' hanta, may be traced in the quotations of authors. This solution of the objection also is " entirely compatible with the tenour of the references to the Saura, which have been yet remarked " in the works of Brahmegupta and Várahamira ; none of them being relative to points that furnish " arguments for concluding the age of the book from internal evidence."

---

[1] Asiat. Res. Vol. VIII. 8vo. pp. 377, 480, 497.       [4] Vide p. 495, ed. Lond. 1808.

[3] Ibid.                    [4] Vol. XII. p. 228.

This passage is of the very first importance; because, as all the arguments against the antiquity of the Hindoo learning have been refuted, so as to leave no question except this of Mr. Bentley's, it shews that this last hold, even if not removed by other arguments and presumptive evidence, is not any longer tenable. And it shews this in the best manner; for it does not shew that Mr. Bentley has been wrong, either in his reasoning or his fact : but it harmonizes both to the assumed assertions of the Hindoos and the other circumstances. This also harmonizes perfectly with the system of renewed incarnations which I have exhibited to the view of the reader; and thus the minute examination, consequent on the controversy, in the end, as it always does conduce, has conduced to the cause of truth. All this also harmonizes perfectly with what has been said in the preliminary observations respecting the great antiquity and the identity of the Tauric festivals in India and Britain.

The undisputed fact noticed above by Mr. Colebrooke of the practice of the Brahmins in modernizing their ancient treatises, at once renders Mr. Bentley's arguments *inconclusive,* and leaves in full force all that Mr. Colebrooke has said respecting the impossibility of forging books to. the extent contemplated by Mr. Bentley, though that would be absolutely necessary to support his system. The quantity of fraud and forgery necessary for deceiving the single despot Mohamed Akbar about the year 1556,[1] according to the theory of Mr. Bentley, unsupported by any authorities, constitutes an effect so out of all proportion to its supposed cause, that it is, I believe, by almost all scientific Europeans of the Hindoo school, looked upon with the most perfect contempt. The observation of Mr. Colebrooke in the last sentence of the quotation above, that the references are to works unconnected with the internal evidence seems conclusive, and I cannot find in Mr. Bentley's answer any thing to afford a satisfactory reply to this. I therefore feel obliged to adopt Mr. Colebrooke's mode of accounting for the apparent difficulties which Mr. Bentley has pointed out. But I apprehend, independently of the other argument, that the circumstance of the old æra of the Cali-yug exactly agreeing with its present date, having been observed by Al Mansor at the court of Balk, as noticed before by me, tends strongly to overthrow all the nonsensical speculations of modern forgery to please Mohamed Akbar.

5. In my Celtic Druids I have said that the renovation of the cycles would account for the appearance of Cristna in one of those of late date. As I have observed before, it may be replied to this, that although the sun and moon would hold the same relative situation to one another in consequence of the precession of the equinoxes, they would not hold the same situations in relation to the planets and fixed stars. It is very clear that this must have been observed by the Hindoo astronomers, in a very little time, if they made any actual observations, and in each cycle, when they renewed their books they would endeavour, as they thought, to correct them. This perfectly agrees with what Mr. Colebrooke has informed us above respecting the Brahma Sidhantha, &c. These tracts, which he notices, have evidently escaped the correction, and serve in a different and distant clime to confirm the profound argument of Michaelis and Bishop Marsh respecting the difficulty of corrupting the gospel histories *in later times.* It is evident that the Brahmins who made the corrections, have not had possession of all the old copies, which, in some retired temple of some of the numerous sects, have probably been copied by a person ignorant of what was done at Benares or Ougein. The Janampatri of Cristna, given by Mr. Bentley for about the year 600 after Christ, was not long before the time when the Mohamedans overran India, and destroyed all the temples and colleges : and from this time probably may be dated the ignorance of the Brahmins, and the cessation of the general correspondence among them, which

---

[1] Vide Bentley on Hindoo Astr. p. 164.

2 K

would be a consequence of the overthrow of their *universal* power, and hence they could no longer attempt to correct astronomical errors. Thus we find their tables most correct, at the time of their conquest, the destruction of their power, and the pollution of their temples and colleges.

These considerations also account for the correction without the imputation of intentional fraud in the Brahmins, to whom (though I do not consider them better than other priests, for all priests, as bodies, will deceive, if they have the power) I do not like to impute fraud, if I can avoid it. These considerations also leave Mr. Bentley's astronomical arguments all their force, and to him all the credit which is justly due for his ingenuity. The greatly exaggerated accounts of Mr. Bentley betray a consciousness of weakness in argument. The doctrine that a renewed incarnation was expected every 600 years, is supported by a great number of facts which cannot be disputed, totally independent of each other, and found in widely-separated countries. For example— the *ten* ages in India and in Europe, *eight* of them nearly finished, and a ninth expected to arrive, when a new saviour was to appear—a new incarnation of the Supreme Being. This supplies a clue to all the difficulties respecting the date of the God with a thousand names. He was born in the time of Joshua, and in the time of Cæsar ; but though he had different names, yet he had the same name. This is similar to the mistake of the Jewish rabble in taking Jesus Christ for an incarnation of Elias, Eλιος, or the God יהו *ieu*, אליהו *alieu*, al-Ieu.

Mr. Bentley has admitted several facts of consequence, which, as he is an opponent to my doctrines, the reader will know how to estimate.

Mr. Bentley has observed, that Hermes was the son of Osiris and Maia, and that Mercury was the son of *Jupiter* and Maia ; that Buddha was also the son of Maia, and was the same as Mercury, and that his name meant WISE or WISDOM. [1] He allows [2] that the image of Siva, is generally accompanied with a Bull *to indicate the commencement of the year from the sign Taurus, or first of May*. He says 'that *Sura* in Sanscrit means light, and *Asura* means darkness. This is evidently the Surya, and שר *sr*, Osiris. Mr. Bentley also shews that the Hindoo mansions of the moon were *originally* 28 not 27 in number. [3] Coming from Mr. Bentley, my opponent, these are all important admissions—strongly supporting my system.

6. Long after I had written the above respecting Mr. Bentley, I found what at once settles the question ; but as I think it extremely desirable, in a case of such importance, that my reader should see the steps by which I have gradually arrived at my conclusions, I shall not expunge what I had previously written.

If any dependence can be placed on Mr. Bentley's own words, he was at last satisfied that the story of Cristna having been copied from that of Jesus Christ, of which I have treated in my Celtic Druids, and also before in this work, was not to be supported. In a letter from him, published by the Rev. J. Marsham, D. D., in his Elements of the Chinese Grammar, is the following passage : " July 4th, 1813, *Krishna was contemporary with Yoodhisht' hira (see the Geeta), and the epoch of Yoodhist' hira's birth was the year 2526 of the Cali Yug of the present astronomers, or about 575 years before the Christian æra.*" The fact of Cristna's living more than 500 years before Christ at once disposes of all the nonsense, both oral and written, about the history of Cristna being copied from that of Christ. The admission also removes the only plausible objection to the whole of my theory, and at once shews that my explanation of the nature of the Janampatri of Cristna is correct. Mr. Bentley's admission opens the door to my theory, that renewed incarnations of the same persons were believed to have taken place, and indeed nearly proves the truth of it respecting them : for we have here one Cristna about 600 years before Christ, and another Cristna about 600 years after him. Here are three persons of the same name in the world, at three very pecu-

---

[1] Pp. 55, 56, 60.      [2] P. 58.      [3] P. 5.

liar epochas—Cristna about 600 B. C., Christ himself at the end of this 600, and Cristna 600 years afterward.

After this, in another letter, (Ib.) Mr. Bentley goes on to shew, by ASTRONOMICAL CALCULA-TIONS AND PROOFS, that he is correct, and that Cristna was certainly, as he had before said, more than 500 years before Christ.

The date of the æra of Yudist'hira is the only fact which materially concerns my argument, this being allowed by Mr. Bentley to be the date of the birth of Cristna. This date, *in his posthumous work*, I find fixed, to use his own words, *decidedly beyond the possibility of doubt*, to the year 575 before Christ. (See pp. 67, 72.) Then the history of Cristna cannot have been copied from that of Christ. I shall return to Mr. Bentley several times in the course of the work.

No doubt the difficulty of coming at the truth in questions of this nature is exceedingly great and almost insuperable. It is very evident that written evidence can scarcely ever be made free from objection, as the controversy between Mr. Colebrooke and Mr. Bentley proves; and I conceive that it can be discovered which side is in the right, only from collateral circumstances, over which neither party engaged can have any controul, and which we learn from persons or writings that cannot by any possibility have any interest in the question. I allude to such evidence respecting the Heri-Cristna at Mutra as is afforded by Arrian, and to such facts as the existence of two Mutras or Matureas. All this goes to prove the great absurdity of believing that God would give a system to his creatures to be believed under pain of damnation, depending on written evidence of this kind. In this case I cannot forget that passion, religious bigotry, and interest, are on one side, and *dis*interested philosophy, and nothing that I can perceive but a love of truth, on the other. When I consider the letters to Dr. Marsham, with the ultra pietism of Mr. Bentley, and all the circumstances relating to his last work, partly written, as I am told, on his death-bed, I confess I feel rather inclined to adopt, of his two opinions, that entertained when he was sound both in body and mind. It is very unwise and generally very unkind, in surviving relatives to publish the death-bed works of their friends. Nothing can be more unsatisfactory than the opinions of persons in this situation.

There can be no doubt now, I think, that the history of Cristna is the history of the equinoctial sun in Aries, and that Buddha was the equinoctial sun in Taurus. Buddha was Bacchus, Cristna was Hercules, in reality, one 2160 years after the other: this nearly agrees with what is said by Arrian, that Hercules was many generations—1500 years—after Bacchus; and that, as Plutarch says, Bacchus and Hercules were modern Gods,[1] that is, they were not so old as the Gods which gave names to the planets. After the sun, I suppose the five planets, the *disposers*, as Moses and the Pelasgi[2] called them, were the objects of adoration, and the foundation of astrology. The signs of the Zodiac, and the festivals at the vernal equinox, followed in due course.

---

[1] Plutarch says, De Iside et Osiride, (Squire, p. 35,) " Osiris and Isis were translated as some say to the rank of ' Gods, as Bacchus and Hercules were in after ages"—thus confirming my idea, that the latter were not the oldest Gods.

[2] Pelasgi, Phœnician Sailors. See Celtic Druids, pp. 258 et seq.

## CHAPTER VIII.

MATUREA.—OBJECTIONS.—MR. SEELEY'S OBSERVATION ON THE SERPENT.—ATONEMENT, ORIGINAL SIN.—
BLACK NATION OF BUDDHISTS IN ASIA.

1. When the identity of the doctrines of Genesis with the story of Cristna is considered, the circumstances of the Egyptian city of Heliopolis or Maturea, the city of the Sun, as I have formerly shewn, are very striking. It was the capital of Goshen, (Goshen means *house of the sun*,) where the Israelites settled under Jacob. It was here the priest Potiphar lived and officiated, to whose daughter Joseph was married. It was here, where a Jewish temple was built by Onias, who was at the head of a sect of schismatical or heretical Jews, whose doctrines we *cannot* know, or on what grounds they maintained that this was the proper place for the temple of Jehovah. But we *do* know that they were hated by the orthodox, as almost always happen to heretics.

Jerusalem, ACCORDING TO THE PENTATEUCH, had no more right to call itself the place chosen *by Jehovah to place his temple there*, than Heliopolis or any other city. This same Heliopolis was the place to which, as has been already shewn, Joseph and Mary fled from Herod, and where Jesus performed great miracles—and, in his time, was called Maturea—the name of the birthplace of Cristna, the Maturea Deorum of Ptolemy. It may be said these things do not *prove* the identity of Jesus and Cristna, and that the story of the former was copied from the latter. This I admit. But though they do not prove the identity of Jesus and Cristna, they prove that the corruptions of the religion of Jesus have been collected from the mythoses of India, which is the object for which they are produced. Before I conclude this work, I shall produce evidence that the man Christ Jesus, to use the words of the gospel histories, was not a man living in India. [1]

I feel a perfect conviction that I have proved that Buddha preceded Cristna, and I am equally convinced that no unprejudiced person can doubt the existence of the worship of Cristna in the reign of Alexander the Great. We have seen that Buddha was the son of Maia, a virgin, in whose womb he was incarnate *sans souillure*, [2] and whose birth was foretold many centuries before it took place. This is the identical history of the immaculate conception of Pythagoras, and in like manner of Jesus, foretold before Jesus was born. Almost immediately afterward we have Buddha and the Samaneans, his priests, noticed by Clemens Alexandrinus, who states Buddha to have been the founder of the sect of the Gymnosophists, in the same manner as the Brahmins were used to attribute their institution to Brahma. [3] Reland says, " *Vehar*, templum Dei primarii " Buddæ βουττα quem Indos ut Deum venerari jam olim notavit Clemens Alexandrinus." [4]

---

[1] "The Antonine Itinerary gives 24 MP. between Heliopolis and Memphis; of which 12 are taken up between Heli-
" opolis and Babylon. The former of these places is universally allowed by travellers to have been at Matarea, where,
" amongst other remains, an obelisk is still standing. Besides the remains at Matarea which are by no means equivocal,
" in respect of the fact which they indicate, there are other circumstances which must be allowed in proof of the posi-
" tion. The fountain at Matarea is named Ani-Schams, or the fountain of the sun. A modern town, situated so near to
" the site of the remains at Matarea, as that the skirts of the two are within a mile and half of each other, is named
" Keliub: which is no doubt the same with Heliopolis, a little changed. The province is also called Keliubie; and an-
" swers to the ancient prefecturate of Heliopolis. The mound of Heliopolis, according to Dr. Pococke, is about a mile
" in length, by half that breadth. The obelisk, now standing, occupies nearly the centre of it." Rennel, Her. p. 495.
[2] An immaculate conception.          [3] Asiat. Res. Vol. I. p. 168.
[4] Strom. Lib. i. p. 223, Dissert. xi. pars tertia, p. 85.

2. Our inquirers into the history of the mythology of the natives of India generally take their accounts from the writings of the followers of Cristna, never recollecting that they are all denied any authority by the greatest part of the immense population of those countries in which Buddhism prevails—a population covering a country ten times as large as that of the Brahmins. In consequence of this, as might be expected, they are merely echoes of the misrepresentations of the Brahmins. But at last enough escapes from their own writings, notwithstanding all the attempts of the Brahmins at concealment, to shew that there was a Buddhism before the time of Cristna; and I never can forget the unexceptionable testimony of Arrian to the Indian Bacchus having long preceded the Indian Hercules.

In the various accounts which different authors have given us respecting Buddha, I perceive but one plausible objection to the theory which I have proposed of his being the Sun in Taurus, as all allow that he *was* the Sun; and that is, the difficulty of accounting for the Cristna of the Brahmins having come to Egypt. That a colony did pass from India to Egypt no one can doubt, and that, too, after the rise of the name and mythos of Cristna. At first to account for this, when the prejudices of the Brahmins against leaving their country or making proselytes is considered, seems difficult. Yet I think there are certain facts, now well known, which will justify us in supposing, that the Brahmins had not always the same objection to leaving their country which they have had for many centuries past. It is very certain that the Sanscrit language, in its present state, is an artificial one, and that it is not the oldest of India. Now, it is equally certain that the mythos did come to Italy; then it must have come previous to the Sanscrit being perfected. The examples of the personal verb, the formation of the degrees of comparison of the adjective, and the identity of the names of numbers, &c., with those of the Latin, which I have given in my *Celtic Druids*, decidedly and incontrovertibly prove the identity of the two languages. I suppose it will not be held that Italy has colonized India. Will any one be absurd enough any longer to maintain that Egypt colonized India, making *two* islands of Elephanta—*two* Matureas, carrying also thither an astronomical mythology, suitable to no part of its own territory, or of that of India, and that India sent back in return a language to Italy and the ΟΜ ΠΑΞ ΚΟΓΞ,[1] in language not *Greek* but *Indian*, to Eleusis?

The fact of the black God Cristna being found in Italy, Germany, Switzerland, and France, is of itself, independent of all other circumstances, sufficient to decide the question. How came the French and Italians to dye their own God *Cristna* black, before they sent icons of him to India? How came his mother to be black?—the black Venus, or Isis the mother, the virgin mother of divine love, of Aur or Horus, the Lux of St. John, the Regina Cœli, treading, in the sphere, on the head of the serpent—all marks of the Jesus of Bethlehem—of the temple of the sun, or of Ceres, but *not of Jesus of Nazareth.*

3. The following observation of Mr. Seely, is alone quite sufficient to determine the question as to which of the two countries, Egypt or India, colonized the other.

Mr. Seely says, " The Cobra capella, or hooded Snake, being unknown in Africa, except as " hieroglyphic, it may be concluded (as also from other arguments), that the Egyptians were the " depositaries, not the inventors, of their mythological attainments."[2] If it be true that there are no snakes of this kind in Africa, though they are very commonly found among the hieroglyphics, I

---

[1] Celtic Druids, Ch. II. Sect. XXVII.

By a *pretended emendation* of the text of Hesychius, a learned German of the orthodox school, of the name of Lobeck, has attempted to overthrow the argument of Col. Wilford respecting these curious words, BUT he is obliged first to emend the text. I prefer the opinions of Creuzer, Schelling, Munter, and Uwarrow, upon this passage, to that of Mr. Lobeck. Vide Foreign Quarterly Review, Jan. 1831, p. 51.

[2] On the Caves of Ellora, p. 216.

can scarcely conceive a more decisive proof, that the Egyptian mythology came from India. From the union of these considerations and *indisputable facts* I conclude, that, in very early times, soon after the sun entered Aries, the Brahmins did not, as at this day, object to travel from their own country; and I think we may find a probable reason for their present dissocial system being adopted. We know that the Buddhists, under the name of Sekhs or Jaines, have been for many centuries endeavouring to convert the Vishnuites, and it was probably to prevent this that their followers were forbidden by the Brahmins to hold any commerce with strangers, or to quit their own country: and that it was thus their rule of seclusion became established. There seems in this to be nothing very improbable. There is no miracle, nothing contrary to the order of nature, required here. Of course, I suppose this to have taken place some time after the change of the equinoctial festival from May to April,—from Taurus to Aries. This change, there is reason to believe, was not made without considerable bloodshed and confusion. But I think wherever it took place, there is now no Buddism, properly so called. I think there is evidence enough to prove that it took place in Egypt, and that Moses adopted it. We read in ancient times of several Brahmins having come into the West. But, according to Mr. Wilford, the difficulty really does not exist; for *he* says, " The Hindoos are not prohibited from visiting foreign countries,—" they are only forbidden to pass certain rivers; but there is no objection to their *ascending round* " *their heads*, so they only do not cross them." [1]    This interpretation has evidently been adopted to evade the law.

4. As we find that most of the other absurd doctrines with which fanatics and priests have loaded the religion of Jesus have come from India, so we also find that, from the same source, has come *original sin*. Mr. Maurice says, " It is the invariable belief of the Brahmins that man is a " fallen creature. Upon this very belief is built the doctrine of the migration of the souls through " various animal bodies, and revolving BOBUNS or planetary spheres." Hence arose all the austerities of the Yogees, Fakirs, and other fanatics, which were carried to an excess that is scarcely credible.

The Rev. Dr. Claudius Buchanan has the following passage: [2] " The chief and distinguishing " doctrines of Scripture may be considered the four following—the Trinity in Unity: the incarna-" tion of the Deity: a vicarious atonement for sin: and the influence of the Divine Spirit on the " mind of man. Now, if we should be able to prove that all these are represented in the systems " of the East, will any man venture to affirm that it happens by chance ?" No, indeed, no man, who is not a fool, will venture to say any such thing. The Doctor then goes on to admit, that the Brahmins must have known of the plural nature of the Aleim, which he calls the ELOHIM, the " Let us make man," of the first chapter of Genesis, the incarnation, the atonement, and the influence of the Holy Spirit,—the doctrine of regeneration or *man twice born.* Thus in having shewn that all these Jewish and Christian doctrines are to be found among the ancient Brahmins, I am supported in the fact by divines of the first eminence. The fact that the doctrines are common to the East and West of the Indus, cannot be disputed, and the only question will be, whether the East copied the doctrines of Christianity from the West, BEFORE the birth of Christ, for they were there BEFORE his birth, or the West copied from the East its ancient doctrines, to the corruption and almost ruin of the beautiful and simple system of their Founder and Saviour.

Original Sin, the foundation of the doctrine of the atonement, was not known to the early Christians, [3] and therefore it is perfectly clear that it cannot have been copied from them. Original

---

[1] Asiat. Res. Vol. VI. p. 533.          [2] Christian Researches in Asia, p. 266.
[3] See Jones on the Canon, Vol. II. p. 348.

Sin entirely depends on the story of the fruit-tree of Genesis being taken in a literal sense. But the ancient fathers of the church understood that it was an allegory; therefore, in their writings, there could be nothing about original sin. The doctrine is not known to the Romish or Greek Churches, and the reason of this is, in addition to what I have stated respecting allegory, that *these churches* make the text say, the woman, not the seed of the woman, shall bruise the serpent's head: " Inimicitias ponam inter te et mulierem, et semen tuum et semen illius : IPSA conteret caput tuum, et tu incidiaberis calcaneo ejus." [1] This decisively proves, when joined with the other circumstances, as I have said before, that the Hindoo doctrines have not been copied from the Christian. It seems probable that the doctrine of the Metempsychosis was gradually super-seded by that of the Atonement in the Christian religion. The former was held by most or all the early Christians, to whom the latter seems to have been unknown. The two appear to me to be totally incompatible. Perhaps we do not find in history any doctrine which has been more perni-cious than that of Original Sin. It is now demoralizing Britain. It caused all the human sacri-fices in ancient times, [2] and actually converted the Jews into a nation of Cannibals, as Lord Kingsborough, in his splendid work on Mexican Antiquities, has proved that they were.

5. The reader will recollect what was said in the first chapter respecting the two Ethiopias—the opinion of Sir W. Jones and Mr. Maurice, that a nation of *blacks* formerly ruled over all Asia, and the other circumstances where the black colour occurred in various ways : and now I think he will be prepared for a few questions, for which I have been from the beginning paving the way : May not this nation have been a nation of *black* Buddhists ? May not the peaceable religion of the curly-headed Buddha have pervaded and kept in peace for many generations, of which we have no history, the whole of Asia? May not the people professing it, have been the Palli or Palles-tini of Mr. Maurice and Sir William Jones, or the shepherd kings or Cushites, of whom so much has been said? Sir W. Jones thought the seat of this empire may have been Sidon. The Grand Lama, or the sovereign priest of this empire, might as easily reside in the neighbourhood of Sidon, as in any other place. And in favour of this opinion, there are many trifling circumstances which may induce a person to think, that Mount Gerizim, the favourite place of Joshua, was, in very remote times, like the capital of the Lama of Thibet, a place of great sanctity. Who was Mel-chizedek ? Was he a Grand Lama ? That Gerizim, not Jerusalem, was his residence, we are told by the disinterested witness Eupolemus, whose evidence also is confirmed by various circum-stances. Why should not a nation have ruled all Asia in peace, as the Chinese have done their empire, for several thousand years ? If these were Jain Buddhists, their propensity to propagate their doctrine, so different from the practice of the Brahmins, easily shews why it was carried to the extremest West, and why it was found in Britain. But if they were the first people, the Celts, for instance, as I believe they were, and their religion the first, it would of course go with them.

" Buddha, the son of Máyá, is considered as the God of Justice ; and the Ox, which is sacred " to him, is termed Dherma. So that this epithet, like that of Buddha, is not confined to any in-" dividual or any race." [3] " On the contrary, we learn from the institutes of Menu, that the very " birth of Brahmins is a constant incarnation of Dherma, God of Justice." Here I think we have a Melchizedek. In the interior of the great temple of Bali, at Maha-bali-pore, is a couch called the bed of Dherma-rajah. [4] This compound word translated, is *Bed of the king of justice* or *Bed of Melchizedek.*

Against a nation, as Sir W. Jones thought, having ruled over all Asia, I see no objection ; and

[1] Vulg.    [2] See Celtic Druids, last chapter.    [3] Camb. Key, Vol. I. p. 216.
[4] Chambers' Asiat. Researches.

if they were Cushite Buddhists attached to their religion in the way we see many oriental nations attached to their religion at this day, I know no reason why their royal high-priests should not have ruled them with justice, and in peace, for many generations, till they were disturbed, perhaps, by the inroads of some northern tribes. During this golden age a most intimate correspondence among the priests of different and remote countries may have been kept up ; and this may account for the transfer of the festival of Taurus to that of Aries, in some countries, in Britain perhaps, without any struggle. When I contemplate what the character of a Buddhist must have been before corruption crept into the religion, I can readily believe any thing which is good of a people professing it. The real, true, conscientious Buddhist, must have been an exact prototype of Jesus Christ, as I shall prove, both in doctrine and practice. It is pretty evident from the Pascal feast, the sacrifice of the Lamb, the change of the beginning of the year to the first of Aries, the anger at Aaron's Bull or Bulls, the going back of the Israelites to the Bulls of Bethavon, בית אן *bit an*, &c., &c., a great part of Moses's object was the change of the festival of the equinox from Taurus to Aries. I cannot help suspecting that in very ancient times a human being was sacrificed at the Pascal festival by some devotees, and that the story of Abraham's sacrifice of Isaac was the mythologic mode of describing the change, either from this worship, or from the offering of the bull or calf, to that of the Lamb, perhaps of both.

The simultaneous existence of the worship of the sun in Taurus with the sun in Aries, is, in most cases, easily accounted for. In general it was not an abolition of an old worship so much as the addition of a new one, which was required to keep the festivals in order. So that in most cases the two would go on amicably together, the prejudices of the followers of the old religion being indulged. Thus we find the festival of Taurus continued along with that of Aries in Britain. In the peninsula of India there appears to have been a severe struggle, and the old religionists were expelled ; but even here some remains of the old or Tauric religion are found : for instance, in the temple at Jaggernaut, and at Mavalipuram or Mahabalipore, the city of the Great Bali, the ruins of which on the coast of Coromandel, near Sadrass, prove it to have been of vast size. In Egypt they appear to have gone on amicably. And we have Osiris, Apis, Serapis, and Jupiter Ammon—Osiris, after his death, regenerated, transmigrated into the body of Apis. Plutarch says that the Bull Apis was an image of the spirit of Osiris. [1]

---

## CHAPTER IX.

BAAL.—SIR W. JONES AND THE DESATIR.—ETYMOLOGY OF THE WORD BAL.—DR. HAGER ON APOLLO.—
CUFA GRASS, SACRIFICE OF.

1. BALA or Bal was one of the names of Buddha. [2] It cannot be modern ; in most ancient times it is every where to be found—in Carthage, Sidon, Tyre, Syria, Assyria—the Baal of the Hebrews. It is impossible to modernize him. The temples with the Bull remaining, and the ruins of the most magnificent city of Maha-bali-pore not quite buried beneath the waves, and the

---

[1] De Is. et Osir.  [2] Wilford, Asiat. Res. Vol. X. p. 134.

figures in the temples prove the antiquity of this crucified God. Captain Wilford has pointed out some very striking traits of resemblance in the temples of Bal or Buddha, in Assyria, India, and Egypt : but this is not surprising, for they were all temples of Apis, the Bull of the Zodiac.

From a great variety of observations it appears to me that the earliest remains of antiquity may be expected to be found in the most remote situations—on the extreme bounds of continents, or in islands, or in places the most distant from the centre of migration. Thus, Syria from upper India ; again, the Ionians on the West of Asia Minor, the British, and still more the Irish. In these situations the migrators from the first hive settled, and removed no more ; and here, in consequence, the earliest habits, customs, and Gods, are found.

In the Indian Archipelago there are an island of Madura, and an island of Bali. In the first, where the Brahmin religion prevails, it is difficult not to recognize a duplicate of the Muttra or Maturea of Cristna, on the Jumna, In the second, Bali, we have the same name as the temples of Maha-Bali-pore, a little to the south of Madras—of the Bali so often connected in upper India with Cristna, of the Baal of Syria, of Han-ni-bal and Asdru-bal of Carthage, of Belinus of Bretagne, and of Baal or Bal-timore, Bal-linasloe, and of the fires of the Baal of Ireland, through which the people yet pass their children, as they did of old time in Asia. The identity of these respective Bals does not depend on identity of names only, but is confirmed by historical and present existing facts and local customs, like that last named. [1]

Of the islands here alluded to Crawford [2] says,

" There are two islands near the east-end of the island of Java called Balli, or Baly, and Ma-
" dura. They have an acient language of their own, which differs entirely from their neighbours':
" the latter is the grand emporium of the Brahmin religion in the Indian Archipelago. It is now
" almost confined to these two islands."

When all the other circumstances are considered, it will not have surprised the reader to find the Hebrew God *Baal*, the bull-headed, among the Hindoo Gods. He is called *Bala-Rama* or *Bala-hadra*. He is the elder brother of Cristna, that is, probably, he preceded Cristna. M. Guigniaut says, Bala.is evidently an incarnation of the sun ; and Mr. Muller remarks, that he is a modification of *Sri-Rama*, and forms the transition or connecting link between *Sri-Rama* and Cristna. This *Sri* is evidently the שר *sr* or Osiris, with the bull of Egypt. This *Sri* is found in the Surya of India, which is no other than Buddha ; as we have seen, it is the oriental word for Bull, שור *sur*, from which perhaps Syria, where the worship of Baal prevailed, had its name. Bali is allowed by the Brahmins to have been an incarnation or Avatar, but he is also said to have been a great tyrant and conquered by Cristna. In the history of this Avatar the rise of Cristnism is described. Vishnu or Cristna at first pretends to be very small, but by degrees increases to a great size, till at last he expels the giant, but leaves him the sovereignty of a gloomy kingdom. [3]

2. Sir W. Jones, in his Sixth Annual Discourse, gives an account of a celebrated Persian work, called the Desatir, written by a person named Moshani Fani, in which is described a dynasty of Persian kings descending from a certain Mahabad who reigned over the whole earth, by whom, he says, the castes were invented ; that fourteen Mahabads or Great Buddhas had appeared or would appear ; and that the first of them left a work called the Desatir, or Regulations, [4] and which was

---

[1] The word Baal or Bal was in fact a title of honour. Dr. Russell observes, " that this same title was conferred by
" the Phœnicians, the Persians, the Syrians, the Phrygians, and even by the remote people of India, on all their sove-
" reigns " The Jews, who passed their children through the fire to Baal, were called pupils of Buddha or Bauddhers.
2 Kings xvii. 17 ; Cambridge Key, Vol. II. p 220.
[2] Hist. Ind. Archipel. Vol. II. p. 97.    [3] Creuzer, Vol. I. p. 187.
[4] Of which we now have a translation, published by Mulla Firuz Bin Kaus, from the Courier press, Bombay, 1818.

received by Mahabad from the Creator. This Maha-Bad is evidently the great Buddha ; [1] and the *Maha-Bul* or *Maha-Beli* the great Baal or Bol of Syria, with the head of a bull, in fact the sun— the whole most clearly an astrological or astronomical mythos or allegory. The Desatir, the work here alluded to, is written in a very *ancient language*, which, it is said, would have been unintelligible without the Persian translation. As a mythos the Mahabadian history of Moshani Fani is very interesting ; as the true account of a dynasty of kings it is nothing. But I think there is great reason to believe that the Desatir is one of the oldest religious works existing, though probably much corrupted by the Mohamedan Moshani. This work confirms what I have said in B. V. Ch. V. S. 2, that Menu and Buddha were identical.

Sir William Jones maintains that Mahabad is the same as the Indian Menu ; that the fourteen Mahabads are the fourteen manifestations of Menu ; that the celestial book of Mahabad is the celestial book of Menu ; and that the four castes of Mahabad are the four castes of Menu. [2] Mahabad and Menu were the same, because both were the sun. But they were probably not the same incarnation. This, however, is of little consequence. [3]

3. To return to the word Baal. The word בעל *bol*, called by us Baal, seems to be an original root. It makes בעלים *Bolim* in its plural. Schleusner says, Βααλ ὁ et ἡ Baal. Nomen Hebraicum indeclinabile ; בעל *bol* quod significat *dominum*. Like the word אל *al* it seems to make both its masculine and feminine in ים *im*. בעל *bol* is also called אלהים *aleim*. It is said by Parkhurst to be equivalent to the Greeek ῾Ο εχων, one having authority. It is also said by him to mean the solar fire. Baal is also called *Lord of heaven*, which may be the meaning of בעל שמין *Bol smin*, translated Lord of heaven. But שמים *smim* or שמין *smin* meant the planets or the disposers. Its most remarkable meaning was that of a Beeve of either gender. It was an idol of the Syrians or Assyrians, often represented as a man with the head of a bull. [4]

In the Hebrew or Chaldee language, we see the word Baal is written בעל *Bol*. The Syrians had constantly the habit of changing the y *o* in the ה *e*, and the *e* into *o* ; thus, with them, on the sea-coast, it was called בחל *Bel*. These sea-coast people were the Pelasgi, who went to Greece, and, from their changing the B into P, probably came the Greek Homeric verb Πελω *I am*. From these Pelasgic sailors of Syria, came the Bel or Belinus into the West. All this confirms Parkhurst's idea of its meaning ὁ εχων, or *one having authority*. From this comes the word Pelorus : Pel-aour, or Bel-aour—Self-existent fire—the son of Isis, the Maia or Great Mother. The true

---

[1] Vide Faber, Pag. Idol. Vol. II. pp. 74—83.      [2] Disc. on Pers. Asiat. Res. Vol. II. p. 59.

[3] Faber, Pag. Idol. Vol III. p. 441.
It is clear to me that the Desatir is a work of Sabean Buddhists, or Buddhists who worshiped, as a kind of mediators, the Planets. With them Hurmusd is Jupiter, or Iao-piter. (P. 74.) The planets are all named and are supposed to have intelligent souls, and are called angels. The stars also are supposed to have intelligent souls. I shall hereafter say more respecting the fourteen Mahabads.

[4] For Bull-worship, see D'Ancarville, Vol. I.
My explanation of the word Pelasgi, in the Celtic Druids, Ch. VI. Sect. XXIX., is of considerable importance, as it removes many obscurities which are caused by these people in ancient history. I am happy to find myself supported in a conclusive manner by Bishop Cumberland, (Origen Gent. p. 295,) who says, " My opinion is, that their name " comes from πελαγιοι, by inserting the letter s, which was usually done in ancient times : and such were the times " when this name was first given. For one example of this, he is called *Masnes* in *Dionysius Halicarnassensis*, who is " *Manes* in *Herodotus.* Again, Casmænæ for Camænæ : Casmillus for Camillus : and Dusmus for Dumus, &c., &c. " For I believe it only signifies that they were strangers that came by sea (πελαγος) to settle more commodiously than " they were before : so they might be adventurers of any tribe, family, or nation : or mixt of many that would agree to " seek their fortune by shipping into another country." Myrsilus, the Lesbian, says, the Tyrrhenians obtained the name of Storks or Pelasgi because they depart and return again. This shews them to be sailors. Niebuhr, Vol. I. p. 69.

God was originally called בעל *Bol*,[1] *Thou shalt no more call me Baali.* He was afterward called יה *ie* or יהוה *ieue*, which meant the Self-existent, and was the root of the word Iαω, or Iao-pater, Jupiter, and in Egypt, with the head of a ram, was called Jupiter Ammon. The followers of Baal were the worshipers of the sun in Taurus : those of Iao of Ammon—of the sun in Aries. From the word בעל *Bol* probably came our word Bull. Here the struggle betwixt the two sects of Taurus and Aries shews itself.

4. The Apollo of the Greeks was nothing but the name of the Israelitish and Syrian Bol בעל *bol*, with the Chaldee emphatic article prefixed and the usual Greek termination.

Dr. Hager says, " Heliopolis, (of Egypt,) or the city of the sun, where the first *obelisks* were " erected, and where the sun was first worshiped. It (Jablonski's Proleg.) seems that the name " of Apollo, or the sun among the Greeks, was likewise derived from *Bel*, otherwise Baal, with an " ain." Then, after some reasoning in which I cannot agree with him, he says, " Thus in the " Greek alphabet, which is derived from the Phœnician, the *o micron* stands exactly in the same " place where the ain (as he miscalls the oin) of the Phœnician stood, whose shape it also has re- " tained. Besides, what in Chaldæa was pronounced like an *a*, in Syria sounded like *o*—as *olaph* " instead of *aleph*, *dolath* instead of *daleth*, &c. If we then join a Greek termination, and prefix " the Phœnician article *Ha*, we have the Apollo of the Greeks and Romans, who had no aspirate " letters, like the modern Greeks and Italians, their descendants, or did not pronounce them. The " same *Bel* was also called *Pul* : which we ought not to wonder at, the ain being a guttural sound, " sometimes approaching to *a*, sometimes to *o*, and sometimes to *u*. Thence we find the different " pronunciations of *Bal, Bol, Pul*, just as *But, Pot*, Fo, in more Eastern countries." [2]

On le voit (Baal or Bel) comme nom du Soleil, says Count de Gebelin, sur des médailles Phéniciennes de Cadiz et de plusieurs autres villes d' Espagne.[3] Hence Baalbek in Syria was called by the Greeks *Heliopolis*, and according to Macrobius Assyrii Heliopoli solem magnâ pompâ coluere sub Jovis Heliopolitani nomine.[4]

The most remarkable of the remains of the Indian Bal or Bala-Rama yet to be found in the West, is the temple of Heliopolis or Balbec in Syria. Jablonski informs us, that Bec and Beth are synonymous. Then this will be the בית *bit* or temple or house of Bal. The remains of the modern temple are very large and magnificent ; but I learn from an intelligent young friend and traveller, that this building is evidently of two dates—that it is a Grecian building, erected upon Cyclopæan foundations. There is one stone upwards of 60 feet long, and 12 feet thick, which is placed in a wall, at least 20 feet from the ground. The Cyclopæan remains prove that this temple was erected in the most remote æra. It is remarkable that, like Stonehenge and Abury, no Roman or Greek writer has noticed it before the time of Augustus. Antoninus is said to have rebuilt the temple, but it must have been on the old foundations. The Greek name Heliopolis proves, if proof were wanting, the meaning of the word Bal.[5]

---

[1] Hosea ii. 16.

[2] Diss. on Babyl. Ant. p. 35. That Bel was the Sun, see Voss. de Idol. ; Vitringa, Comment in Isa. xlvi. ap. Brucker ; Hist. Crit. Philos. ; de Philos. Chaldæor. Lib. ii. Cap. ii. ; Hist. Babyl. ; Univers. Hist. Vol. III. Sect. ii.

[3] Monde Primitif, Vol. IV.     [4] Saturn, Lib. i. ; Hager, Dissert. on Bab. Ant.

[5] In my Celtic Druids, (p. 198,) I have derived Jupiter from Iao-pater. Mr. Sharon Turner (Trans. Soc. Lit.) enables me to go to a more distant fountain, perhaps the fountain-head of the same stream. He says, p. 49, Sanscrit *Matri* mother ; p. 60, Sanscrit *Ipatri* father. Here are most clearly the *Mater* and *Pater* of Italy. But how came the *I* to precede the *Patri?* I think it was the same *I* which I have noticed in my Celtic Druids, Chap. V. Sect. XLII., as the sacred name of the island of Iona, called II in the annals of Ulster, and by which the God Jehovah or יהוה *Ieue* is always called by the Chaldee paraphrases, which confirms what I there said respecting Iona. It is almost impossible to read a page of Sir William Jones's works and not to observe the elements of the word יהוה *ieue* recurring continually

5. The Hindoos have a sacrifice held in very high esteem which, their traditions state, goes back to the most remote æra : this is the sacrifice of a certain species of grass, called Çufa grass. This ancient sacrifice was also in use among the Egyptians. It is noticed by Porphyry *de absti-nentiâ*,[1] in these words : " It seems that the period is of immense antiquity, from which a nation, " the most learned of all others, as Theophrastus says, and who inhabit the most sacred region " made by the Nile, began first, from the Vestal hearth, to sacrifice to the celestial Gods, not " myrrh, or cassia, or the first-fruits of things, mingled with the crocus of frankincense : for " these were assumed many generations afterward, in consequence of error gradually increasing, " when men wanting the necessaries of life offered, with great labour and many tears, some drops " of these, as first-fruits to the Gods. Hence they did not at first sacrifice these, BUT GRASS, " which, as a certain soft wool of prolific nature, they plucked with their hands."

The identity of the two sacrifices of grass assimilates very well with the veneration of the Egyptians and PHŒNICIANS for the cow.[2]

---

## CHAPTER X.

### YAJNA OR PASSOVER.—EIGHT VASUS.

1. IF the religions of Moses and the Hindoos were the same, it was reasonable to expect that we should find the celebrated Egyptian festival of the Passover in both countries, and it is found accordingly. We have it in the most solemn of the religious rites of the Brahmins, the sacrifice of the Yajna or the Lamb.

I have no doubt that, with the Hebrews, this succeeded to the Mithraitic sacrifice of the Bull ; and that it was in celebration of the passage or passover of the equinoctial sun from the Bull to the Ram. This history of the passage of the sun and of the passage of the Israelites from Egypt, affords a very remarkable example of the double meaning of the Hebrew books. The story of the ten plagues of Egypt might be very suitable for the rabble[3] of Jerusalem and London, but the higher classes in the former had, and I should hope in the latter now have, too much sense to believe such degrading accounts of the Deity as the LITERAL meaning of this history exhibits.

---

in the names of Indian Gods. It is, in fact, the יה *ie* Jah of the Chaldees. Father is also, in the Sancrit and Bali languages, *Pita*. The planet Jupiter is called *Vrihaspati* in Sanscrit. From the attributes of this God, Sir W. Jones has shewn him to be the Jupiter of the Latins. This is probably the *Patri* with some other word prefixed, perhaps as a title of honour : and it is probably the way in which *Ie* and *Ye* are used in the names of the Sanscrit Gods. But in the old Bali or Pali, a language much older than the improved Sanscrit, Mr. Turner gives Pati for father.

   [1] Taylor, B. ii. p. 47.

   [2] Ibid. p. 51. For want of a system, Mr. Maurice falls into great mistakes. In page 40 of his Modern History, ed. 4to., he calls Cristna *Bacchus ;* in p. 129, he makes him to be *Hercules ;* and in page 135, he makes him Bali. In one sense he is right, for they are all the sun, but the sun at different epochs. M. Guigniaut has observed, that all the Gods and Goddesses of India return or run into one another. This exactly accords with what the reader has already seen—that all the Gods and Goddesses of the Western world centre in the Sun.

   [3] See Bryant on the Plagues of Egypt.

Rabbi Bechai, in commenting on the twelfth chapter of Exodus, speaks to the following purport : *Scripsit Maimonides, in ratione hujus præcepti, quod proptereà quod sidus Aries in mense Nisan maximè valeret, et hoc sidus fructus germinare faceret, ideo jussit Deus mactare arietem.* Here is a pretty clear avowal on the part of Maimonides, the most learned of the Rabbins, that the paschal lamb was a type of the astronomical Lamb.[1]

Before the time of Moses, the Egyptians fixed the commencement of the year at the vernal equinox. R. A. Seba says, *Incipiebant autem Ægyptii numerare menses ab eo tempore, quo sol ingressus est in initium sideris Arietis*, &c. In the Oriental Chronicle it is said, that the day when the sun entered into Aries, was *solennis ac celeberrimus apud Ægyptios.* But this Ægyptian festival commenced on the very day when the Paschal lamb was separated. *Insuper die mensis decimo,* says R. A. Seba, *ipso illo die quo Ægyptii incipiebant celebrare cultum Arietis, &c., plàcuit Deo ut sumerent agnum, &c.*[2] In this festival the Israelites marked their door-posts, &c., with blood, the Ægyptians marked their goods with red.[3] The Hebrew name was פסח *psh* pesach, which means *transit*. The Lamb itself is also often called Pesech, or the Passover.

In India, the devotees throw red powder on one another at the festival of the Huli or vernal equinox. This red powder, the Hindoos say, is in imitation of the pollen of plants, the principle of fructification, the flower of the plant. Here we arrive at the import of this mystery. A plant which has not this powder, this flower or flour, is useless ; it does not produce seed. I could carry this farther, *sed sat* for the present.[4] This Huli festival is the festival of the vernal equinox ; it is the Yulé ; it is the origin of our word *holy ;* it is Julius, Yulius.

The followers of Vishnu observed the custom, on grand occasions, of sacrificing a ram. This sacrifice was called Yajna; and the fire of the Yajna was called *Yajneswara,* or the God fire. The word " Yajna, M. Dubois says, (p. 316,) is derived from Agni *fire,* as if it were to this God " that the sacrifice was really offered. I need not point out the resemblance between the word " *Agni* and the Latin *Ignis.*" And I suppose *I* need not point out the resemblance of the word Agni to the Latin Agnus, to those who have seen the numerous extraordinary coincidences in the languages of Italy and India, which I have shewn in this work and in my Celtic Druids. Mr. Bentley says, (p. 45,) " Aries or the Ram is to be found in the sign of Agni, who, according to " the fictions of the Hindus, was feigned to ride that animal." It seems to me that the Rev. M. Dubois did not choose to see the *Agnus,* though he could clearly see the *Ignis.*

Agnus is not so properly the Latin word for a lamb as for an animal peculiarly dedicated to God, hostia pura ; therefore similar to the Greek αγνος *purus.* The lamb being the animal peculiarly sacred, thus became called Agnus. This the reader will see confirmed at once by turning to Moore's Hindoo Pantheon, (Plate 80,) where there are three examples of the Agni Avatar ; one is riding on a Ram, the other two have flags in their hands, on which are inscribed the Ram. He may also see the same repeated several times in the plates of M. Creuzer.

In this ceremony of sacrificing the lamb the devotees of India chaunt with a loud voice, *When will it be that the Saviour will be born ! When will it be that the Redeemer will appear !* The Brahmins, though they eat no flesh on any other occasion, at this sacrifice taste the flesh of the animal : and the person offering the sacrifice makes a verbal confession of his sins[5] and receives absolution.[6] On this I need make no observation. Mr. Parkhurst's doctrine of types explains

---

[1] Drum. Œd. Jud. p. 376.   [2] Ibid. p. 378.   [3] Ibid. p. 380.

[4] See a beautiful note, No. 66, in Professor Haughton's Laws of Menu, to which I shall return.

[5] Loubère says, auricular confession is practised by the Siamese.

[6] Travels and Letters of the Jesuits, translated from the French, 1713; London, 1714, pp. 14—23, signed Bouchet.

it to those who admit the doctrine of types. The Hindoos have a sacred fire which never dies, and a sacrifice connected with it, called Oman. [1]  They have also the custom of casting out devils from people possessed, by prayers and ceremonies, [2] which is also practised by the people of Siam. All this is very important.

The first sentence of the Reg-Veda is said to be Agnim-ile, *I sing praise to fire.* Here we are told that Agnim means fire. When we reflect upon the slain lamb, and the call for the Saviour, we must be struck with the scene in the fifth chapter of the Apocalypse, from verse five to ten, where praise is given to the slain Lamb. The identity of the Mythoses cannot be denied.

That the word *agnus* means *lamb* every one knows ; but it will, perhaps, be said, that though it may have this meaning in Latin or Etruscan, it has it not in Sanscrit. To this I reply, if it have not this meaning in the Sanscrit, it must have had it in the old language on which the Sanscrit was built, because it is impossible to consider the way in which we find the Indian language mixed with Latin, and to see the Agni always mounted on a lamb, or in some way or other accompanied by the lamb, and the lamb slain and burnt, without believing that, however it may have changed, it must once have had this meaning. But it probably had both the meaning of the Lamb and of fire—of the *Sun* in Aries. The whole seems to raise a presumption that this Lamb worship was in existence before the artificial Sanscrit was composed, and that the Brahmins have lost the meaning of their mythology as well as of their astronomy. I only wish my reader to cast his eye over the plates of the Agni in Moore and Creuzer, to be convinced of what I say. It is the same with the word Iaya, and several others, which I have pointed out in the course of this work.

It seems to me to be quite impossible for any person who has studied this subject, and considered the Zodiacal Agnus, the Yajna sacrifice, the worship of the lamb in the East and in the West, and the icons of Agni with the Lamb on them, to doubt that the Agnus means lamb : then, to such a person, the proof that the Agnus meant lamb, must carry the conviction, that the original language of the early mythology is lost. This is of great consequence, as it removes the only impediment to my interpretation of the name of the God יהוה *ieue*, which, as I have shewn, is found in all the names of the Gods. I am told that, in the Sanscrit, Massih means alike Aries, fire, and Saviour. This is correctly the משיח *msih* of the Hebrew, the anointed, or Saviour. Thus the Lamb is the Messiah.

I know that my method of rendering many Indian names will be contested by Hindoo scholars, who will *poh, poh* me down,—as we are told by the traveller, *I have seen, Sir, and sure must know!* But I am not to be put down in this way. I tell them that their authority, in many cases, is exactly similar to that which was proffered to me in the case of the sacrifice of the Yajni. I said in a large party of learned Orientalists, that this sacrifice of the God Agni was not that of the God of Fire merely, but that also of the Lamb ; the Aries of the Zodiac. I was *poh, pohed* down, put down with authority : these learned gentlemen said, it had not that meaning in Sanscrit ; but as I persisted, and shewed them that the thing offered in the sacrifice was a Lamb, tasted by Brahmins on that occasion, though *they* never eat flesh at any other time ;—that this God of fire, though always surrounded by a glory, was at the same time *invariably* accompanied by a Lamb, he mostly riding a lamb, they were silenced. The truth was, they had never looked so far. But the fact itself of this meaning of the word being lost in the Sanscrit, tends to prove the modern date of that language. I cannot believe that the Brahmins do not know the meaning of the word Agnus. Their wish for secrecy can be the only reason that I can imagine for the signification of it not being found in

---

[1]  ON the generative power of Om.

[2]  Travels and Letters of the Jesuits, pp. 14—23.          [3] Ibid. p. 29.

their dictionaries. Another example of *lost* signification is in the word Ya, Ya, chaunted in their ceremonies. I shall be told it means only *victory ;* but is not the God Jah, יהוה *ieue* and יה ‌ *ieie*, always called the God of victory ? It has, therefore, both these meanings. What can be more striking than the invocation in both cases of the slain lamb and of the Saviour ?

There is in India a sect or tribe called Agniculas. These I suppose to be followers of the Cycle of the Agni or Igni. It is observed by Ainsworth, that the word Agniculus is not Latin. I think my readers will be satisfied, before I have finished, that the Sanscrit must have been formed upon a great number of other languages.

Yajn-eswara is Janus-osiris, or Lord Janus. Eswara is found united to numbers of words, and seems now to be used as an epithet of honour, like *Lord* with us. The sacrifice of the Ram is the Ram of the Zodiac at the vernal equinox. Thus the adoration of the Ram succeeded to the Bull, (but it did not entirely abolish it,) as in the case of Asteroth of the Sidonians, which had first the head of a Bull, and afterward that of a Ram.

2. I beg my reader to recollect that, in the ancient languages, the V and the I are perpetually confounded and written for one another, and that the Brahmins had eight Vasus,[1] or Gods of the winds, or of air in motion, and that Agni was the NINTH ; Agni, the Lord of fire, carried on the back of a Ram and sacrificed at the vernal equinox. Thus there were eight Vasus, the number of the Cycles B. C., and of the Salivahanas, of whom I shall treat by and by. This Wind was also called Vayu—query יהיה *ieie ?* I cannot help believing that Yasu-vati (query *Jesu-vates ? )* and Ya-du, the tribe of Cristna's ancestors, and Vasus and Vayu and Agni and the Lamb were all closely connected. Cristna is identified with *Vasu-deva* by the orthodox Vaishnavas.[2] Having first considered all the circumstances relating to Cristna, the extraordinary transformations which names undergo in passing from one country to another, and the interchanges of the letters V and I, I beg my reader to consider and compare the two syllables of the name *Vasu* with the word *Jesus,* and I think he will be obliged, with me, to entertain a strong suspicion that there has been some connexion between them. The word *deva* is evidently *deus,* and thus, with *Vasus,* making the God Vasus.

Jadu was the ancestor of Cristna,[3] that is, יה *ie*, יד *di, holy Ie.*

Moore says, " Agni is the Hindu regent or personification of fire." Again, " I will here observe, " that although all the Hindu deities partake more or less remotely of the nature and character of " Surya, or the Sun, and all more or less directly radiate from, or merge in, him, yet no one is, I " think, so intimately identified with him as Vishnu ; whether considered in his own person, or in " the character of his most glorious Avatara of Krishna."[4]

It is evident from a careful perusal of Moore, from pp. 265—272, that the Brahmins did not know what to make of the Vasus or holy air in motion. When Jesus was baptized in the Jordan, (a river having the same name as Padus and the Ganges,) he was filled with the Holy Ghost or air in motion, which descended in the form of a dove, and the Agni, or Lord of fire, appeared in the water.[5]

From the following passage of Porphyry, *de abstinentiâ,* I cannot help thinking the Yajna sacrifice is probably alluded to, which receives considerable confirmation from its connexion with Pythagoras, whose æra was the same as that of Buddha, B. v. Ch. ii. S. i. The *tasting,* but not *eating,* is the identical practice of the Brahmins. " The truth of this may also be perceived from the altar " which is even now preserved about *Delos,* which, because no animal is brought to, or is sacrificed " upon it, is called the altar of the pious. So that the inhabitants not only abstain from sacrificing

---

[1] Moore's Ind. Panth. p. 268.    [2] Colebrooke, Trans. Asiat. Soc. Vol. I. p. 576.    [3] Ibid. p. 538.
[4] Moore's Ind. Panth. pp. 294, 295.    [5] Justin Martyr.

" animals, but they likewise conceive, that those who established are similarly pious with those
" who use the altar.  Hence the Pythagoreans, having adopted this mode of sacrifice, abstained
" from animal food through the whole of life.  But when they distributed to the Gods A CERTAIN
" ANIMAL instead of themselves, *they merely tasted of it,* living in reality without touching other
" animals."[1]  This is the very picture of the Brahmin practice at this day; it tends strongly to
satisfy me of the identity of the Brahmin and Pythagorean systems.  In Book iv. p. 152, of the
same work, Porphyry informs us that in very old times, the sacrificing or indeed the using of the
flesh of animals was not practised either by the Athenians or by the Syrians—the Syrians, that
is the natives of the ancient city of Iona and the Pallistini, the Ionians, of whom I shall speak
presently.  Advancing still eastwards, we find Porphyry giving an account of the Magi from Eubolus, who wrote their history, in which he states that " the first and most learned class of the Magi
" neither eat nor slay any thing animated, but adhere to the *ancient abstinence* from animals."
After this he goes to the Gymnosophists called Samaneans and Brahmins of India, of whom he
gives an account, and from which it appears that they have varied very little from what they were
in his time.  But all these accounts seem to shew signs of the first black Buddhist people, as
eating no animal food—of the Black Pelasgi or Ionians, as coming to Italy and bringing the black
God and his mother along with them.  And they not only brought the black God and his mother,
but they brought his house, the house at Loretto, as I shall shew in its proper place.

---

## CHAPTER XI.

RASIT, OR WISDOM, RESUMED.—SECRET DOCTRINES. — BULL-HEADED AND RAM-HEADED GODS.—DATE OF
THE SYSTEM.  NAMES OF BUDDHA, &c.— IGNORANCE OF THE BRAHMINS AND ANCIENTS. — CREUZER,
HAMMER, GUIGNIAUT, &c.—TREE OF GENESIS AT IPSAMBUL, AND THE SAME IN MONTFAUCON.

1.  THAT the tribe of Israelites did go out from Egypt and conquer Canaan I feel no doubt; but
it is very clear to me that the priests, in their books, have wrapped up the whole in allegory;
that, in fact, as the learned philosophers of the Jews say, these writings had two meanings—one
for the priests, and one for the people.  The former meaning, as might be expected, has been
nearly lost; the latter is still received by *most* Jews and Christians.  What evils have been produced by the system of endeavouring to keep the mass of mankind in ignorance!  The words
בראשית *b-rasit* no doubt had two meanings, one for the priests, and one for the people—*wisdom*
for the former, *beginning* for the latter.  This is strengthened by the fact, that the Jews divided
their Cabala into two parts.  T. Burnet says, Barischith et Merkavah, illic philosophiam naturalem,
hic Metaphysicam intelligi.—In the distribution and system of nomenclature adopted by Joshua
for the land of Canaan, an astrological, or, if my reader like it better, an astronomical system was
adopted of the same kind as that which the Israelites had left in Egypt.  Sir William Drummond
has proved this in his Œdipus Judaicus.  This was in compliance with an order in Deuteronomy

---

[1] Taylor's Trans. B. II. p. 65.

to pull down the altars of the nations they subdued, to cut down their groves, burn their graven images, and to destroy and blot out their names from under heaven. [1]

If divines deny that the word רֵאשִׁית rasit means *wisdom*, and affirm that it only means *beginning*, they forget that they are *moderns* expounding a language which has been dead more than a thousand years, a great part of which the best judges have allowed to be lost, or no longer understood; and that they are deciding against the collected opinion of the divines or priests of the people whose vernacular language it was; in short, against the opinion of their church, held by that church when the language was yet a living one, and therefore must have been well understood. These reasons joined to those which I have before given, and by which I have shewn that the meaning *beginning* as applied to the creation is actually nonsense, fully justify me in maintaining that the word has two meanings, and that it means both *beginning* and *wisdom*. Besides, the reader will not fail to observe, that the meaning *wisdom* is in good keeping with all the cabalistic doctrines which must have been founded upon this verse. The Jewish Sephiroth consisted, as I have already shewn, of ten existences, which answered to the trinity, and to the spirits or emanations of the seven planetary bodies. By some later Jews the first three were said to be Hypostases, the other seven Emanations. Here we have the beginning of our Hypostatical Trinity. The first of the Sephiroth was *corona*, and answered to the Father, or *Brahma;* the second was *wisdom*, Σοφια, the Πρωτογονος and Λογος, and answered to *Vishnu*, the Preserver; the third was *prudentia* or Πνευμα, and answered to *Siva* in his regenerating capacity. I confess it appears to me to be somewhat presumptuous for a modern divine to assert, that a word in an ancient *dead* language, a religious epithet, *has not* the meaning which was given to it by the priests of that people whose language it was, when it was a *living* language, merely because it does not support a modern religion. Like many other words, it had two meanings. In this case the translation of the word רֵאשִׁית *rasit* will rule the word Αρχη.

2. The pretended genealogy of the tenth chapter of Genesis is attended with much difficulty. It reads like a genealogy : it is notoriously a chart of geography. It is exoterically *genealogical*, esoterically *geographical*. I have no doubt that the allotment of the lands by Joshua was astronomical. It was exactly on the same principle as the nomes of Egypt, which every one knows were named astronomically, or rather, perhaps, I should say, astrologically. The double meaning is clear; but probably the exact solution of the whole riddle will never be made out. Most of the names which are given in the tenth chapter of Genesis are found in the mystic work of Ezekiel. The works of all the prophets are mystical. This chapter divides the world into 72 nations. Much ingenuity must have been used to make them agree with the exact number of dodecans into which the great circle was divided. But who, after observing this fact, can help seeing the mystical character of the chapter? Many of the works of the Greeks were equally mystical.

I request any person to read the travels of Pausanias in Greece, and he must be astonished at the puerile nonsense which that good man appears to have believed. But did he believe it? Was not the book written merely for the amusement of devotees, like the *novels* of our evangelical ladies or gentlemen ?—like the Paradise Lost of Milton ? It is evident he knew that there was a *secret* doctrine, for in several passages he admits it in distinct terms.[2] " *But the particulars respecting the* " *pomegranate,* as they belong to a secret discourse, I shall pass by in silence." Again,[3] "that " such of the Greeks as were formerly reckoned wise, designedly concealed their wisdom in ænig- " mas : and I conjecture, that what I have just now related concerning Saturn contains some-

---

[1] Ch. vii. 5, 24, ix. 14.      [2] B. i. Ch. xiv., B i. Ch. xxxvii., B. ii. Ch. xvii.
[3] For the mystical nature of the pomegranate, see Cumberland's Origines Gentium.

" thing of the wisdom of the Greeks. And we should consider things relative to divine concerns
" after this manner."[1] Plutarch undertakes to prove that Osiris and Bacchus are the same, *without recourse to the secret rites, which are not to be divulged.*[2]

Speaking of the statements respecting the Gods in Homer, Maximus Tyrius says, " For every
" one on hearing such things as these concerning Jupiter and Apollo, Thetis and Vulcan, will im-
" mediately consider them as oracular assertions, in which the apparent is different from the latent
" meaning."[3] This is confirmed by Herodotus, who constantly says, when describing things in
Egypt, there is a sacred reason (ιερος λογος) for this, which I shall not give. I suspect that
Cicero, Pausanias, &c., were like Gibbon and Warburton, and many other of our authors, who, for
the sake of the peace of society, pretend to be what they are not, a mischievous device of the
priests, which has done more to retard the improvement of mankind than all other causes put
together.

3. The Greeks have been supposed by some persons to have learnt their mythologies from the
Egyptians. But I have shewn, on the authority of their own writers, that all their OLD oracles
came from the Hyperboreans by way of Thrace. Their Eleusinian mysteries I have also shewn to
have come by the same route, probably from India. I consider Osiris, Bacchus, Astarte with the
Bull's head, Bol or Baal, Mithra, Adonis, Apis, and Buddha, to have been contemporary, or to
have constituted one class. In the same manner I consider Hercules, Cristna, and (Jupiter)
Ammon, and Astarte with the Ram's head, to have been contemporary, or to have formed a
second class. My theory is strikingly confirmed by the fact, which, I believe, has not been noticed
before, that the first class are all ταυροκεφαλοι, or Bull-headed. Buddha is closely allied or connected with the Siamese or Japanese bull, breaking the Mundane egg with his horn, and was partly
*man*, partly *bull*, in Persia, as Mr. Faber has proved ; and therefore I conclude from this, exclusive
of the other reasons given above, that these Gods are nothing but the Sun in the sign of Taurus, at
the vernal equinox : and the other class are all χριοπροσωποι, or Ram-headed, and are in like
manner, for similar reasons, the sun in the sign of Aries, at the vernal equinox. Several of those
which were first *bull*-headed became *ram*-headed in later times. Ammon, for instance. In the histories of the births, deaths, funerals, and resurrections, of all these Gods, a striking similiarity prevails, as I shall shew in a future page ; but yet there are between the two classes some trifling
discrepancies. These discrepancies probably arose from the circumstance that one class refers to
the adventures of the God Sol in the sign of the Bull, the other to those of the God Sol in the sign
of the Ram. It is evident that almost every where civil war arose on the change of the worship from Taurus to Aries. But though this may account for the trifling differences which we find,
yet we may readily suppose that the great points of resemblance, being equally applicable to the
sun in both cases, might remain unaltered.[4]

The adoration of the Bull still continued in most countries after the equinox had receded to
Aries. This was the case in Egypt, where Apis still continued, though Ammon with his sheep's-
head arose—if he did not, as I believe he did, change his *beeve's* head for that of a *ram*. I have
shewn that Ammon meant the generative power of Am, or Aum, or Om : but Am was the Bull

---

[1] B. viii. Ch. viii.    [2] De Iside et Osir. Sect. xxxv. Squire.
[3] Max. Tyr. Ed. Taylor, p. 87, and Dissertation xvi.
[4] In Fig. 3, Plate 36, Vol. II. of the Montf. (Ant. Exp.) is exhibited an Isis sitting, nursing the infant Orus. She
has the head of a cow, but the body of a woman. Plutarch (de Iside et Osir. Ed. Squire, Sect. xxxv. p. 46) says, that
to Bacchus the Greeks gave the face and neck of an Ox. The women of Elis called Bacchus Ox-footed ; the people of
Argos called him Ox-begotten. Porphyry (de Abstin. Sect. xvi.) says, the Greeks united the Ram to Jupiter, but the
horns of a Bull to Bacchus.

Mithra, Buddha—therefore it must have changed. The prayers to the God Bull, of Persia, given by Mr. Faber, are very curious. Asteroth, or Astarte, in Syria, was first represented with the horns and head of a beeve, and in later times with those of a sheep.[1] Thus in India the Bull, the emblem of Buddha, continued to be adored long after Cristna arose, and along with him at some few places.

From Waddington and Hanbury's voyage up the Nile, I think it appears that in Egypt, as in Syria, the emblems of the conjoined Sun and Moon, the Cycle, the Crescent, and the Disk, which are found on the oldest Tauric Monuments, were taken from the Bull, and removed to the Ram.[2] I think the lunette and circle on the head of the Bull, and in later times on the head of the Ram, alluded both to the compound cycle of the Neros, and to the precession, or to the male and female generative powers.

In the temple cave at Ellora, the Bull Nundi, or Nandi, is placed opposite to the Yoni and Lingham, as an emblem of the prolific power. In this temple, on each side of the entrance is a Sphinx, similar to those in Egypt, placed on the outside of the entrance exactly in the same manner.[3]

I have already remarked on the alleged disinclination of the Brahmins to leaving India for the purpose of colonization. I do not think Egypt was first colonized by them as the priests of Cristna, but by Buddhists, the worshipers of the Sun in Taurus. The story and effigies of Buddha are so similar to those of Cristna, that the Seapoys of India, when in Egypt, might very readily mistake one for the other. But the theory of religion, as time advanced, would cause the Ram-headed God to arise in both places, without copying one another; and supposing the icons not exactly the same, they might be near enough to exhibit the same mythos to our seapoy officers and men, who would not be very careful inquirers. Yet every thing tends to confirm what I have before said, that there is reason to believe the first Brahmins were not so averse to communicate with, or to visit foreigners, as are those of a later day : and thus the worship of Cristna may have been brought at a later period to Egypt.

M. Dubois confirms my opinion that the Brahmins came from the north, and that they established their religion on the ruins of that of Buddha. He adds, that he lived in the midst of the Jainas or followers of Buddha, and that they far surpassed the Brahmins in probity and good faith.[4] Herodotus[5] says the Pelasgians learnt the *names* of their Gods from the barbarians ; "that at first they "distinguished them by no name or surname, for they were hitherto unacquainted with either; but "they called them Gods, which by its etymology means disposers, from observing the orderly dis- "position and distribution of the various parts of the universe." It is easy here, I think, to recognize the planets, the disposers, the שמים *smim*, of the first book of Genesis.

4. In all our speculations hitherto, we have reasoned that the facts under consideration must have taken place *before* such or such a time. I think we shall now be able to deduce a very important consequence in an opposite direction. We have seen that the days of the week are, in the most remote corners of the world, called by the names of the same planets, and in the same order, and these planets after the same Gods. The universality of this shews its extreme antiquity— that in all probability it must have been adopted before the human race became divided into nations. But the fact that all these Gods were identified with the Bull of the Zodiac in some way or other, proves that they must have been adopted later than the time when the sun, at the vernal

---

[1] Drummond, Orig., Vol. III. p. 229.        [2] Landseer, Sabæan Res. p. 228.
[3] Seeley's Wonders of Ellora, p. 138. The cave temples in Cabul are 12,000 in number, all dedicated to Buddha. Ibid. p. 139.
[4] Pp. 42, 305, 324, 326, 327, 549, &c.        [5] Euterpe, LII. p. 377.

equinox, entered Taurus by the true Zodiac, which would be about 4700 years before Christ. (A very great French philosopher, Mons. Dupuis, for some other reasons, has thought this time so much too short, that he has been induced to suppose the period ought to be thrown back, to where Taurus would be at the autumnal equinox, about 11,000 years; but, though this might be correct, yet I think sufficient proof of its correctness is not produced.) This consideration seems to offer something like a boundary to our researches; something like a distant view of our journey's end, which I greet with pleasure; for I think we can find no traces of any thing before the Tauric worship commenced. And this brings our chronology to agree, as near as can be expected, with the various systems. The *eight* ages, about the time of Augustus, cannot be doubted. If these were 600 years each—4800, and we add a thousand before the Tauric worship commenced for mankind to arrive at their then state of civilization, we shall not be very much out of the way in our calculations.

The *Disposers,* as Herodotus says the Pelasgi first called their Gods, that is, the שמים *Smim* of Genesis, or the Planets, were in later times all called by names appropriated to the days of the week which were dedicated, by astrologers, to the Gods who were typified by the Bull: Monday to the horned *Isis;* Tuesday to Mercury, the same as Hermes and Osiris; Wednesday to Woden; Fo, Buddha, and Surya; Thursday or Thor-day, or תור *Tur,* (written both Tur and Sur,) or Taurus, or Bull-day, to Jove or Jupiter, who, as a Bull, stole Europa, which shews what he was at first; (the manner in which he is called not merely *Jupiter,* but *Jupiter* with the word *Ammon* added, seems to shew that the two words were not always joined. In Montfaucon's Antiquities [1] may be seen an account of various Jupiters connected with the Tauric worship, which proves that, although he had latterly the head of a Ram, he had originally that of a Bull.) Friday was dedicated to Venus, Ashteroth, or beeve-horned Astarte; Saturday to Saturn, identified by Mr. Faber [2] with Moloch and the *Centaur Cronus* or Taschter; Sunday to the Sun, every where typified by Taurus. All these, I think, must have taken their names after the entrance of the Sun into Taurus; and before this date all history and even mythology fails us. Each of the days and the planets had a monogram, consisting of a *cross* with some form annexed to it; another proof of the great antiquity of the adoration of the cross.

But yet it seems fair to infer, that man must have existed a great number of years before he could have divided the heavens into signs, degrees, &c., &c. How long a time may have been required for this I pretend not to say. It must have depended upon that which we can never know, the exact state in which he was turned out of the hand of his Creator. But I think many generations must have passed before the May-day festivals were established in Britain and India.

Some of the cave-temples of India which are *arched,* are, on that account, supposed to be more modern than those with *flat* roofs; but I think this is a hasty inference. If, indeed, the arch were formed of wedge-shaped stones, like modern arches, this would be probable; but when the curve is merely cut out of the solid granite without any of the architectural knowledge necessary in throwing an arch, I do not think the inference warranted. Mr. Seely says, " Karli and Canarah " are evidently the production of the followers of Buddha." He states, that the arched temple of Vishvacarma at Ellora is also Buddhist; and he adds, " Their whole history is involved in such a " labyrinth of mystery from beginning to end, that there is not the most remote chance, by the " deepest research, of arriving at any satisfactory data." [3] I hope Mr. Seely is mistaken. But in the assertion of the unsatisfactory nature of all the theories hitherto proposed, he is certainly correct.

What I have said respecting the temple of Jaggernaut in Orissa being *Buddhist,* is confirmed by

---

[1] Fig. 8, Plate 11, p. 31.        [2] Pag. Idol. Vol. II. p. 86.        [3] Pp. 186, 194.

one of the flat-roofed cave temples at Ellora being dedicated to him by the name of Jaggernaut, i. e. Creator.[1] The Brahmins not being able to conceal the Buddhist doctrines in some of their temples, without their entire destruction, are obliged to admit a ninth Buddhist Avatar, at the same time that they most absurdly maintain that this Buddha, this ninth Avatar, was an impostor. It is singular enough that the Buddha in the cave at Ellora is called the Lord paramount, the Maha-Maha-Deo,[2] the great great God. At this temple the Brahmin uttered the name BUDDHA without any hesitation, which is what a Brahmin will seldom do.[3] Their ninth Avatar was a Buddha, because he was an incarnation of divine wisdom, perhaps not understood by modern Brahmins. The Brahmins and Buddhists have, as already stated, each the same number of Avatars, and, at the time of Jesus Christ, they both say that eight were gone, and that a ninth then came. The Buddhists say he came among them, and was called Buddha. The Brahmins affirm that he came among them, and was called Salivan, of whom I shall treat hereafter. This is the reason why they allege that the ninth Buddha was an impostor.

It is no small confirmation of the superior antiquity of Buddha, that over *all* India, whether among Bauddhas, Saivas, or Vaishnavahs, the day of Woden, or Wednesday, is called BUDHVAR.[4] In Sanscrit it is Bou-ta vâr, and in the Balic, Van Pout; in the northern nations, Woden's day; the latter having no B, write W,[5] where the reader may also find additional proofs that Mercury or Hermes, Sommonacodom and Buddha, are all the same—with Maia for their Mother.

As I have formerly said, the fact of Buddha giving name to one of the days of the week, Wednesday, fixes him to the very earliest period of which we have any record or probable tradition. He is acknowledged to be the Sun or the Surya, with seven heads, of Siam and Japan and Ceylon; and to be the son of Maia. Thoth and Teutates and Hermes are allowed to be identical, and Hermes is allowed to be Mercury; and Mercury is the God to whom Wednesday is dedicated, and the mother of Mercury is Maia. Sir William Jones clearly proved that the first Buddha was Woden, Mercury, and Fo, and I think, however he may have alarmed himself and his prejudices when he came to see the consequences of his proofs, he never was able to overthrow them.[6] Mr. Faber says, " The Egyptian cosmogony, like the Phœnician, is professedly of the Buddhic school : for the " fullest account which we have of it is contained in a book ascribed to Hermes or Thoth : but " Hermes or Thoth is the same person as Taut, who is said to have drawn up the Phœnician sys- " tem : and Taut again is the same as the Oriental Tat or Buddha."[7]

The Tau, T, is the emblem of Mercury, of Hermes. It is the *crux ansata*, and the *crux Hermis.* It was the last letter of the ancient alphabets, the end or boundary, whence it came to be used as a terminus to districts; but the crux Tau was also the emblem of the generative power, of eternal transmigrating life, and thus was used indiscriminately with the Phallus. It was, in fact, *the phallus.* The Tau is the Thoth, the Teut, the Teutates of the Druids;[8] and Teutates was Mercury, in the Sanscrit called Cod or Somona-cod-om; and in German God. In old German Mercury was called Got. The remains of the crosses are to be found in the highways at the boundaries of the parishes, and every where at cross-road ends in this country. They have precisely the same meaning as the Roman Terminuses, and had the same origin. It is the same with the crosses which have now the crucified Saviour on them, all over the continent, and, being engrafted into Christianity, were thus preserved. Many of them are thousands of years old.

[1] Seely, Wond. of Ellora, p. 218.
[2] Here, in the repetition of the word Maha, we may perceive the Hebrew practice of expressing the superlative degree by a repetition of the adjective.
[3] Seely, Wond. of Ellora, 220.      [4] Moore's Pantheon, p. 240.      [5] See Asiat. Res. Vol. I. pp. 161, 162.
[6] Asiat. Res. Vol. VIII. 8vo. p. 531 ; also Diss. on Chron. of Hind. Asiat. Res. Vol. II.
[7] Pag. Idol. Vol. I. p. 223.                          [8] See Herod. Euterpe, LI. p. 375.

M. Sonnerat thinks Rama is Buddha; " Sir W. Jones is of a very different opinion, and thinks " that Dionysos and Rama were the same person." [1]  They are both right, they all were the Sun : and it is very surprising to me that those gentlemen did not perceive that what applied to one, applied to all three ; with this only exception, perhaps, that one might be the Sun in Taurus, the other the Sun in Aries.  And into the Sun, in his male or female character, all the great Deities of India and the Western world resolve themselves.  I think it not improbable that many images ascribed to Cristna may belong to Buddha—their histories being so very similar.

5. The uncertainty of the real names of the Gods of India has been pointed out by Mr. Seely, who, after stating that he has detected the Brahmins in forgetting names which they had bestowed a day or two before on the same figure, says, "On making inquiries the Brahmins rather confound " than assist in your researches.  Each has his favourite deity and peculiar local name, generally " accompanied with some fanciful theory of his own.  My Brahmin was a native of Poonah; he " was fond of his Wittoba, Ballajee, Lakshmi, and others, and wished them to be paramount in all " the temples.  A different list would have been preferred by a Benares Brahmin ; while a coast " (Coromandel) Brahmin would probably have been for the Buddhist heroes.  If to this discrepancy " we add the numberless host of minor or secondary deities, all with their consorts, giants, sages, " and holy men, the whole wrapped up in impenetrable and mysterious fable, some faint idea may " be entertained of the difficult and abstruse subject of Hindoo mythology."  The description is, I do not doubt, just.  The accounts of the present Brahmins can be little depended on.  Of the minor details of their mythology they are totally ignorant.  After a careful consideration of the work of the father of history, Herodotus, I have no doubt that the generality of priests in his day were as ignorant as the Brahmins in ours.  The Priests, whenever they were ignorant of a fact, coined a fable, which the credulous Greek believed and recorded ; and which the still more absurdly credulous modern Christians continue to believe.  Witness, as one out of many examples, the history of Jupiter and Europa,[2] believed by classical scholars to have been actually a king and queen, to have reigned, had children, &c., &c.

I cannot help thinking that even the oldest of both the Greek and Roman writers, unless I except Homer, were absolutely and perfectly ignorant of the nature of their Gods—whence they came, and of what they consisted.  As the people by degrees emerging from barbarism began to open their eyes, they found them.  They received the Gods from their ancestors, who, having no writers, transmitted their superstitions, but not the histories of their Gods.  Whether the initiated into the mysteries were any wiser seems very doubtful.  But I think it is possible that the only secrets were, the admission of their own ignorance and the maintenance of a doctrine respecting the nature of God (of which I shall treat hereafter) and in substance of the unity of God.  We can hardly suppose that such men as Phornutus, Lucian, and Cicero, were not initiated in the higher mysteries.  Then, if the nature of the Gods had been known in these mysteries, I think we should not have those men writing about them : and, in every sentence, proving that of their real nature they were perfectly ignorant.  If they were not ignorant, they were dishonest.  But this I can scarcely believe.  If they were ignorant I cannot entertain a doubt that Messrs. Dupuis and D'Ancarville were much more likely to discover the secret nature of the Gods than Cicero or Phornutus, Porphyry or Plutarch.  The mistaken vanity which prevented these latter philosophers from looking to the Barbarians for their Gods, tended to keep them in a state of ignorance, in a bondage from which we are free, and, in consequence, are much more likely to discover the truth.

I shall be told *I* have a theory.  This is very true : but how is it possible to make any sense out of the mass of confusion without one ?  And are not facts sufficient collected to found a

---

[1] Seely, p. 176.           [2] Drum. Orig. Vol. III. p. 82.

theory upon? My theory has arisen from a close attention to the facts which transpire from the writings of a vast variety of authors, and is, I think, a theory which will be found to be established by them. I have not first adopted my theory, and then invented my facts to confirm it. The facts have come first, and the theory is the consequence. Whether they be sufficient to support the theory, is the only question. This must be left to the reader. I feel confident that I can explain every thing which appears inconsistent with the theory, unless it be a very few of the histories of the inferiors Gods, which may very well be supposed to have been mistaken or mistated, by the Priests, whose ignorance or deceit is acknowledged.

6. After studying with great attention the very learned and able review of the German authors Creuzer, Hammer, Rhode, Goërres, &c., by Mons. Guigniaut, my opinions founded on the works of Maurice, Bryant, Cudworth, Stanley, &c., are nothing shaken. I am more than ever confirmed in my opinion, that all the Gods of the ancients resolve themselves into one—the Sun, or into the refined or spiritual fire seated in the Sun: and that the Trinity, contended for by Mr. Maurice and Mr. Faber, cannot be disputed. The hypothesis of Mr. Maurice, respecting the great antiquity of the worship of the Bull of the Zodiac, can never be overthrown, until it can be shewn that all our Indian travellers, who tell us of the celebration of our May-day games and April-fool festivals, have deceived us. I place my foot upon the identity and ubiquity of these Tauric, Phallic Games, as upon a rock, from which I feel nothing can remove me. They set at defiance all books and all systems of chronology. Next to them is the reasoning of Mons. Bailly on the septennial cycle, and on that of the Neros. Collectively they form a mass of evidence of the existence of a state of the world in a most remote period, very different from what any of our historians contemplate. In searching into the records of antiquity it is impossible to move a step without meeting with circumstances confirmatory of the Tauric worship, the date of which the known precession of the equinoxes puts out of all dispute. My excellent and learned old acquaintance Mr. Frend would make the cycles Antediluvian, but how are the bull on the front of the temple of Jaggernaut, and hundreds of other similar circumstances, to be accounted for? Was the temple built before the flood? I am very far from wishing to depreciate the learned and meritorious labours of the German scholars to whom I have just alluded, but I feel confident if they had paid a little more attention to the FACTS pointed out in the writings which contain the whimsical theories[1] of our Bryants, Fabers, &c., they would have been more successful in discovering the secret meaning of the ancient Mythoses. Had they attended to what is indisputable —that all the Gods of antiquity resolve themselves into one—the Sun—either as an original object of worship or as the type, or the Epiphania, or Shekinah of the triune male and female Deity, they would have found themselves in their researches relieved from many difficulties.

Protestant priests for some years past have endeavoured to shew that the Mosaic accounts are to be found in India, and generally among the Gentiles. What good this can do them I cannot understand. However, they have certainly succeeded. The labours of the learned Spencer have shewn that there is no rite or ceremony directed in the Pentateuch, of which there is not an exact copy[2] in the rites of Paganism. The Rev. Mr. Faber has proved that the Mythoses, as the Romish Dr. Geddes properly calls them, of the creation and the flood have their exact counter-

---

[1] Though I call them whimsical I mean no disrespect to their authors. The world is much obliged to these gentlemen for their labours.

[2] From this must be excepted some few laws adopted by the Jewish law-giver to make a line of demarcation between his people and the Gentiles—such, for instance, as the Sabbath on the *last* instead of the *first* day of the week, and a few others that are very apparent. The object of Moses was to restrict his law to the Jews as much as possible, to the exclusion of all other nations. The object of the law of Jesus was to restore the worship of Jehovah to all nations,

parts among the wild mythologies of the followers of Buddha and Cristna; and the history of the serpent and tree of life have been lately discovered by Mr. Wilson to be most correctly described on the ruins of the magnificent temple of Ipsambul in Nubia.[1]   So that it is now certain, that all the first three books of Genesis must have come from India: the temple at Ipsambul, as well as the famous Memnon, being the work of the ancient Buddhists—the latter proved most satisfactorily by Mr. Faber.

After what the reader has seen he will not be surprised that I should have been struck most forcibly by an observation which seems casually given by M. Denon in his account of the Temples in Upper Egypt. He does not appear to have been aware of its importance, or, indeed, in a theological point of view, that it had any importance at all. In[2] speaking of a very beautiful small temple of the ancient Egyptians at Philoe, he says, " I found within it some remains of a " domestic scene, which seemed to be that of Joseph and Mary, and it suggested to me the sub- " ject of the flight into Egypt, in a style of the UTMOST TRUTH and interest."

It is said, by late travellers, that the Christians converted the ancient temples of Upper Egypt into churches, and they thus account for the Christian Mythos. But in this case, at Ipsambul, the pretence is totally destitute of foundation, because the figures were in that part of the temple which was buried in sand, and were excavated by Belzoni. No person will believe that the sand was brought here since the Christian æra. But I shall discuss this matter at length presently.

7. In the supplement to Vol. 1. of Montfaucon,[3] is exhibited a tree, on the two sides of which are Jupiter and Minerva. He says, " It was preserved for several centuries in one of the most " ancient churches of France, and passed for an image of terrestrial paradise, to represent the fall " of Adam. The tree bearing fruit, in the middle, passed for that from whence the forbidden fruit " was gathered. The robe on Jupiter's shoulders, the thunderbolt which he has in his hand, the " helmet on Minerva's head, and her habit covering her all over: these particulars might easily . " have undeceived persons moderately versed, I will not say in mythology, but even in the history " of the Bible, that it was a mere conceit. But in those times of simplicity, people did not con- " sider some things very closely. Jupiter holds the thunderbolt raised in his right hand; he has " a robe on, which does not cover his nakedness. Minerva is armed with a helmet and dressed " as usual: the serpent at her feet is the peculiar symbol of Minerva polias of Athens, which " seems to support the opinion of the gentlemen of our academy, that this agate relates to the " worship of Jupiter and Minerva at Athens. The tree, and the vine curling round the tree, the " goat beneath Jupiter's foot, and all the animals pictured about—the horse, the lion, the ox, and " others, seem to denote nature, of which Jupiter is the father. An Hebrew inscription graved " round the gem, appears to be modern; it is in Rabbinical characters, scarcely to be deciphered: " the sense of it is this: *The woman saw that the tree was good for food, and that it was pleasant* " *to the eyes, and a tree to be desired to make one wise.*"[4]

Who can help seeing here a refined allegory? Here is the God Ieo, Jove, ‏יהו‎ *ieu*. Here is Minerva, divine wisdom, which sprung from the head of Jove—the πρωτογονος, the first-begotten, Buddha. Here is the tree of the knowledge of good and evil. Here is the vine with its fruit

---

pure and undefiled as held by Melchizedek. Moses made his Sabbath on the day of Saturn, in opposition to the festival of all other nations, which was on the *dies solis*. The doctrine of the Nazarite of Samaria being intended for the whole world, his followers acted very properly in restoring the festival to the dies solis, on which no doubt it was in the time of Melchizedek, of which religion Jesus was declared to be a priest.

[1] Wilson's Travels; Franklin's Researches on the Jeynes, p. 127.

[2] The English Trans. by Arthur Aikin, 1803, Vol. II. Chap. xiv. p. 169.

[3] Ant. Exp. Plate 5, Fig. 17.          [4] P. 35. See my plates, fig. 16.

united to the elm, which Virgil met with at the side of the road to hell, loaded with science—as the Mem, the 600, was united to the *vin* in the name of the word Muin, the name of the letter which denoted the most sacred of the cycles. The elm is commonly planted in Gaul and Italy for the vine to ascend, and selected as the tree of knowledge, because it was the name of the first letter of the alphabet, or the Aleph of the Hebrews, which meant the trunk of a tree, which was the tree of Virgil, and bore all the remainder. The circumstance of this gem having a Hebrew legend round it is exceedingly curious, and is not to be got quit of by the observation of Montfaucon, the innocent produce of his prejudice and ignorance, that it appears to be *modern*. It was of the same school with the Virgo Paritura, the Bacchus's Wine-cask and Tiger-hunt of St. Denis,[1] the Isis of Notre Dame, and several other matters which I shall adduce in their proper time and place.

In fig. 9 of the 52nd plate of the Supplement to Montfaucon's *Antiquité Expliquée*, there is a representation of Abraham sacrificing Isaac : but Abraham has not a sword or a knife, but a thunderbolt, in his hand. Can any thing be more clear than that the makers of these very ancient gems considered that the story of Abraham covered a mythos ? Vishnu or Cristna is often represented with thunder and lightning in his hand—as in the act of giving the benediction with *three* fingers, and as wearing a triple crown.

---

## CHAPTER XII.

THE EAGLE GARUDA.—SPENCER, FABER, BURNET, CALMET, &c., ON GENESIS AND ITS ALLEGORY.—FA-
BER'S TRINITY OF THE INDIANS AND THE HEBREWS.

1. THE following example of an Eastern mythos, in the West, will be thought not only curious, but will be found, in a future page, to involve some important consequences.

Mr. Moore says, " Sonnerat notices two basso-relievos placed at the entrance of the choir of " Bourdeaux Cathedral : one represents the ascension of our Saviour to heaven on an Eagle : the " other his descent, where he is stopped by Cerberus at the gates of hell, and Pluto is seen at a " distance armed with a trident. In *Hindu* pictures, VICHNU, who is identified with Krishna, is " often seen mounted on the Eagle GARUDA, sometimes with as well as without his consort " Lakshmi.[2] And were a *Hindoo* artist to handle the subject of Krishna's descent to hell, which " I never saw, he would most likely introduce Cerbura, the infernal three-headed dog of their " legends, and Yama, their Pluto, with the *trisula*, or trident : a farther presumption of early in- " tercommunication between the Pagans of the Eastern and Western hemispheres."[3] An account

---

[1] In the church of St. Denis near Paris. See Prel. Obs. Ch I. Sect. 115.
[2] Whence comes the name of Cristna's consort Lakshmi? We will write it as it may be pronounced, and we shall have no farther trouble—L'Akmè. It is not surprising that Wisdom, חכמה *hkme*, should be the wife of Cristna, the incarnation of Vishnu, the second person or the Logos of the Indian trinity; but it is very curious, indeed, that we should find it here in Greek and modern French. If this stood alone, it might be taken for accident, but with its concomitant circumstances, this cannot be admitted. I believe the Lamed of the Hebrew is often used as an emphatic article, as it is in the Arabic, Italian, and French. It is an abbreviation of the Arabic *Al*. Thus we find it in the word Aceldama—*Ac* place of, *al* the, *dama* blood.
[3] Pantheon, p. 214.

2 N

is given by Arrian of a visit of Alexander the Great to the cave of Prometheus [1] on the borders of India.

In addition to what Mr. Moore and M. Sonnerat have said, I beg to observe that Bourdeaux, in whose cathedral this Garuda was discovered by them, is watered by the river Garumna, evidently the Latinised Garuda or the Frenchised Garonne. It is situated in the department of the Gironde. Messrs. Sonnerat and Moore seem to have overlooked the striking names of the river and the department. Respecting Garuda and Prometheus, Colonel Wilford says, " I inquired after Garuda-" sthan and was perfectly understood. They soon pointed it out to me in the Puranas and other " sacred books, and I immediately perceived that it was situated in the vicinity of Cabul, where " the historians of Alexander have placed it, and declare that this hero had the curiosity to go and " see it." [2] He then states how he inquired for the legend relating to Prometheus and the eagle in the books of the Buddhists, where he found it, and from which inquiry he discovered, that the Buddhists had Vedas and many valuable books of their own, different from those of the Brahmins, by which he was induced to retract an opinion hastily given against the Buddhists.[3] The eagle Garuda, as appears from Moore's Pantheon, is intimately blended with the history of Cristna in a variety of ways : and, if I mistake not, forms in the three facts of the Garuda at Bourdeaux on the Garumna, in the Gironde—of Alexander's visit—and of its connexion with the Cristna of India and the Cristna of Europe—a chain of evidence in proof of the intimate connexion between the East and the West; and equally so of the existence of Cristna and his mythos in India long previous to the birth of Jesus of Nazareth ; though perhaps not of Jesus of Bethlehem. And this again overthrows all Mr. Bentley's doctrines, except recourse be had, as I believe it ought to be had, to renewed cycles. Admit the cycles, and Mr. Bentley's alleged proofs are all in my favour.

Prometheus formed the first woman, for the formation of whom he stole fire from heaven, &c., &c. The word Prometheus is the Sanscrit word PRAMATHAH or PRAMATHAS, which comes from PRA-MAT'HA-ISA, which coalescing, according to the rules of Sanscrit grammar, [4] form PRAMA-THESA. Now, Pra is the Siamese Bra, creator or former; Matha is Mati, in the Bali language Mother, and esa is Isa or Iscah or Eve or Isis—the whole meaning, maker of mother Eve or Isis. It is no small confirmation of what I have said, that Prometheus, the name of the Greek God, is Sanscrit ; [5] as is also Deucalion, his son. The latter is Deo-cala-yun or Deo-Cala-Yavana. There is an account of his contest with Cristna, who was driven from Mathura by him, but by whom he was at last, with his Ya-vanas, finally expelled from India. On this I shall say more presently. I am well aware of the forgery practised on Colonel Wilford, but the knavish priest could not forge the image in Bourdeaux Cathedral, nor the passage in Arrian respecting Alexander the Great. I am also well aware, that an elegant, flowery style of writing would have the effect of convincing many readers better than dry facts. People of this description are not worth converting to any opinion, and no opinion of theirs can be worth having. But to persons of critical judgment, who know the value of evidence, a fact of the kind here stated is worth volumes of declamation. The authority of the ancient historians of Alexander, in a case circumstanced like this, cannot be doubted ; nor, in consequence, can the fact that there was a cave of Prometheus in the time of

---

[1] In my account of the cave of Prometheus, I have carefully omitted the parts where Colonel Wilford was deceived by his Pundit.

[2] Asiat. Res. Vol. VI. p. 512.        [3] Ibid.        [4] Ibid. p. 51⁵.

[5] The absolute identity of the Indian mythos at Bourdeaux and the Indian mythos of Prometheus and his Eagle, of whom I shall have much more to say hereafter, will prepare us for the reception of another and a similar mythos at Baieux, in a future page of this work.

Alexander, in Upper India, some one of the numerous cave temples yet remaining, similar to those at Ellora, Elephanta, or Cabul—hereby decidedly proving that the Greek mythology was not brought into India in the time of the Seleucidæ, as a learned and ingenious author has, as a last resource, alleged. This is of the same nature as that of the Hercules at Maturea, as described by Arrian, and noticed before. These are *proofs* not *probabilities*. Trifling as they appear to be at first sight, they are worth volumes of fine reasoning. They are like the Maypole, and April festival in India and in England, and must carry conviction to the mind of every person who knows the value of evidence. Many facts of this kind cannot be expected, but very few, *one* indeed, if it be clear, is enough to prove the truth of the suspected history. It has also been said, that if the books of the Hindoos, the Vedas, &c., had been in existence in the time of the Seleucidæ, the Greek authors would have noticed them. I do not admit that the argument has any weight, when the contempt of the Greeks for the Barbari is considered ; and when it is also considered with what difficulty we have obtained the Brahmin books. It is as inconclusive as the argument of those who maintain that Stonehenge is modern, because the Romans do not notice it. [1]

2. How the proof of the histories in Genesis being intermixed with the mythoses of the Gentiles can be of any service to the defenders of the literal construction of these books, I cannot conceive. It seems to me that if the plagues of Egypt and the history of the flood were found in every parish throughout the world in the most ancient of times, they would not be rendered in their literal meaning in the least degree more credible, not even though supported by the Oracles, the Sibyls, and the affirmations of the priests. Throughout all the world the same system prevailed, nor could any country be properly said to have copied its system from others. It travelled with the aborigines ; with them it flourished, and with them decayed : at first as the religion of Buddha, that is of Brahma or divine wisdom, afterward as the religion of Cristna, another incarnation of the same being or hypostasis.

Mr. Faber [2] says, " The close resemblance of the whole Levitical ceremonial to the ceremonial " in use among the Gentiles has often been observed, and has differently been accounted for. This " resemblance is so close and so perfect, that it is alike absurd to deny its existence, and to as- " cribe it to mere accident. The thing itself is an incontrovertible matter of fact : and it is a fact " which might at first seem to be of so extraordinary a nature, that we are imperiously called on " to account for it." Again, he says, [3] " Spencer has shewn at full length, that there is scarcely " a single outward ordinance of the Mosaical law, which does not minutely correspond with a " parallel outward ordinance of Gentilism.".

If persons will only reflect a little they will perceive that, if every ordinance of the Jews is the same as the ordinances of the Gentiles, the Mythoses must necessarily be the same : that is, that the religions in their chief part must be the same.

Mr. Maurice says, [4] " After all, we must own, with Calmet, that the temple of the great " Jehovah had many decorations similar to those in the hallowed temples of Asia. He was served " there, says the last cited author, with all the pomp and splendour of an Eastern monarch. He " had his table, his perfumes, his throne, his bed-chamber, his offices, his singing-men and his " singing-women."

Mr. Faber states three ways of accounting for these facts. The first is, that the Gentiles copied

---

[1] Since I published my CELTIC DRUIDS, it has been observed to me, that of all the numerous tumuli which surround Stonehenge and which have been opened, though a variety of articles have been found, there has not been the least appearance of any thing Roman or of later people's. Can a more decisive proof be desired, that the bodies were buried before the time of the Romans, and that the tumuli ceased to be cemeteries on their conquest of the island?

[2] Orig. Pag. Idol. Vol. III. p. 624.        [3] Ibid. p. 629.        [4] Ind. Ant. Vol. V. p. 174.

from the Jews. This he easily refutes. The second is, that the Jews copied from the Gentiles. Of this he says, " The second theory, which is precisely the reverse of the first, and which sup- " poses the Levitical ark to be a copy of the ark of Osiris, is wholly unincumbered, indeed, with " chronological difficulties : but it is attended by others, which, perhaps, are scarcely less formi- " dable. Its orignal author was, I believe, the Jew Maimonides : the learned Spencer has drawn " it out, at full length, and has discussed it with wonderful ingenuity : and the mighty Warburton, " without descending to particulars, has given it the honourable sanction of his entire approba- " tion." [1]   He then satisfactorily shews that neither of these schemes is defensible, and under- takes to prove, that all the ceremonial and ritual in principle originated from an old patriarchal religion. And in this I quite concur with him ; though I cannot allow that religion to have con- sisted in the adoration of Noah, his ark, and his family ; the idea of which is to me altogether ri- diculous, too ridiculous to deserve a serious refutation. But by and by I shall shew from what patriarchal religion these Mosaic rites were derived. [2]

Had not Mr. Faber been bound by the prejudices of his education, and by the sacerdotal oaths which he took, whilst almost a boy, and by which he in fact solemnly engaged never to abandon the former, I have no doubt that my present labours would have been unnecessary. No man before him ever came so near the truth. The following is nearly his account of the ancient philosophy, taught in the mysteries, with the exception of a few sentences which I have omitted, and which are inserted by him to make it apply to his ship and old women—to make his ship and old women appear the originals, and the heavenly bodies and the recondite philosophy, the mythological representations under which they were disguised ; instead of the heavenly bodies and the philosophy being the originals, and the ship and old women the mythological representa- tions under which the latter were concealed from the vulgar eye. He has certainly proved the second and third books of Genesis to be Hindoo Mythoses.

As we have seen, it is acknowledged that the Jewish and the Gentile ceremonies are the same. It is also admitted that neither can have been borrowed from the other. We have seen also, that the doctrines are the same. Then is it not reasonable to look for the origin of the one, where you look for the origin of the other ? At first, the same system must have pervaded the whole world. I think I have already proved, that all ancient nations, almost within even the reach of history, had a form of worship without idols. The ancient Latins, the ancient Greeks, the Egyptians, the Pelasgi, the Syrians, who made treaties with Abraham and Isaac, had no names for their Gods. What can this universal religion have been, but that of Buddha or Brahma ?

If it be true that the Pentateuchian system is a mythos, or more properly several detached parts of a mythos, in principle the same as the mythoses of the neighbouring nations, it is no ways surprising that it should have many traits of similarity to them. The reader has seen what I

---

[1] Orig. Pag. Idol. Vol. III. p. 628.

[2] Although our great men can swallow the literal meaning of the first chapter of Genesis now, and find no difficulty in it ; yet the stomachs of the ancients were not quite so capacious. Siracides says, the world was not created day after day, but all at once—*simul* in the Latin Vulgate ; κοινῇ in the LXX. (Eccles. xvi. 1.)   Philo calls it silly, to think that the world was made in the compass of six days.   Lib. Alleg.   St. Augustin also says, it was produced at one time. (De Civ. Dei, Lib. xi. Cap. xxxi. ; Morer. Dial. on the Sabbath, II. p. 107.)   The absurdity of the history those men could not get over, therefore they had recourse to explanations. And although the SAINT, Augustin, could not believe such things, he was canonized ; but if a man doubt *now* he is damned. But the fact was, that all these apparent absurdities had an allegorical meaning, and do not prove, as some persons have imagined, the falsity of the religion ; they only prove that the esoteric religion has not been thrown open to the vulgar. The esoteric religion was a masonic mystery ; I am under no tie, and I will explain to the world what it really was.

have said to have been the foundation, or nearly the foundation, of all the mythoses of antiquity; but he has yet a great deal more to see. It is natural to suppose that in long periods of time, and in different nations and languages, great changes would take place, and that a vast variety of minor systems or mythoses would arise. It is equally natural to expect that a general similarity should nevertheless prevail, or, that in all the different superstructions some traces of the original should be found. As with the systems of *writing*, though they became very different, yet enough (indeed super-abundant) relics of the old first language are apparent in all of the sixteen-letter system, to shew that they are all from one source. From the above-named mythoses, Mr. Faber and Nimrod have selected a great number of similar matters, which have given to their systems a certain degree of plausibility. The ingenuity of Mr. Faber is shewn in annexing the word *Helio* to the word ark, by which means he succeeds in attributing to his imaginary worship of the ship, the real worship of the sun. Divide the words, and what will apply to the sun, is, in general, ridiculous as applied to his ship or to an old man, the exalted father its sailor : and, on the contrary, what will apply to the ship is ridiculous as applied to the sun. But it is impossible to deny, from the facts, the etymologies, and the analogies, pointed out by these learned and ingenious devotees, that it is apparent an universal mythos has prevailed—that the Pentateuch and the Iliad (of which I shall say more hereafter) have originally had the same mythological doctrines for their foundations. These gentlemen taking the allegorical or mythological accounts of the Bible to the letter, have made the mythoses of the Gentiles bend to them. Had they possessed understandings a little more enlarged, their learning and ingenuity would probably have organized the chaos. But what can be expected from persons, however learned, who believe like Nimrod that the old Gentile oracles *really* prophesied,[1] or that the possession of human beings by dæmons once prevailed.[2] Persons who can believe in dæmonology, second sight, witchcraft, and similar nonsense,[3] although very learned and skilful in writing novels, or making pictures, are weak men, undeserving the name of philosophers. They may amuse a few of their sect to-day; posterity will only smile to-morrow.

The philosophy in question taught that matter itself was eternal, but that it was liable to endless changes and modifications; that over it a demiurgic INTELLIGENCE presided, who, when a world was produced out of chaos, manifested himself at the commencement of that world as the great universal father both of men and animals : that, during the existence of the world, every thing in it was undergoing a perpetual change : no real destruction of any substance taking place, but only a transmutation of it : that, at the end of a certain appointed great period, the world was destined to be reduced to its primeval material chaos : that the agent of its dissolution was a flood either of water or of fire : that at this time all its inhabitants perished; and the great father, the Brahme-Mai, from whose soul the soul of every man was excerpted, (i. e. emanated,) and into whose soul the soul of every man must finally be resolved, was left in the solitary majesty of abstracted meditation : that, during the prevalence of the deluge and the reign of chaos, he floated upon the surface of the mighty deep, the being on which he reposed being represented by a ship, a lotus, an egg, the sea-serpent, the navicular leaf, or the lunar crescent : that the two generative powers of nature, the male and female, were then reduced to their simplest principles, and were in a state of mystic conjunction brooding on the surface of the deep. The Brahme-Maia or Great Father was but mystically alone : for he comprehended within his own essence three filial emanations, and was himself conspicuous in eight distinct forms :[4] that at the close of a divine year, the deluge abating,

---

[1] P. 488, of Supp. Edition.    [2] Also Dolphin, p. 405, *ib.*

[3] Vide story of the Ghost seen by the Rev. Mr. Ruddle, &c., &c.! in Nimrod, p. 588, *ib.*

[4] Wonderful to tell, Mr. Faber can see nothing here but Adam, Cain, Abel, and Seth—or Noah, his wife, and Shem,

the Great Father awaked to the reforming of the world out of the chaotic mass; and that he appeared with his three emanations,[1] and in his eight forms,[2] as he had appeared at the commencement of former worlds : that this new world was destined to run the same course as former worlds : that this alternation of destruction and reproduction, was eternal both retrospectively and prospectively: that to destroy was, consequently, nothing more than to create under a new form. [3] This is the doctrine which Mr. Faber supposes was taught in the ancient mysteries, except my leaving out and altering some trifling parts forced in to suit it to his peculiar theory.  But it will not be denied to be on the whole a sublime system.  It has the merit, too, of being, when thus corrected, nearly the true system of the first sages of antiquity.

3. The following account of the Hebrew and Indian Trinities, according to Mr. Faber, is very striking :

" In the preceding citations from the Geeta, we may observe that Vishnou or Crishna is identi-
" fied with Brahm, although one of his three emanations ; and we may also observe, that in the
" single character of Brahm, all the three offices of Brahma, Vishnou, and Siva, are united.  He is
" at once the creator, the preserver, and the destroyer.  He is the primeval Hermaphrodite, or
" the great father and the great mother blended together in one person.  Consequently he is the
" same as the hermaphroditic Siva, in the form which the Hindoos call *Ardha-Nari ;* the same
" also as Brahma and Vishnou, for each of these is similarly an hermaphrodite by an union with
" his proper Sacti or heavenly consort; [4] the same moreover as the Orphic Jupiter and the Egyp-
" tian Osiris ; the same as Adonis, Dionusus, and Atys ; the same, in short, as the compound
" great father in every part of the pagan world."—" Yet this compound great father, as the whole
" of his history shews, is not the true God ; but a being, who has been made to usurp his attri-
" butes.  He is primarily Adam and the Earth, and secondarily Noah and the Ark.  In the former
" case, his three emanations of children, who partake of his nature, and who discharge his pre-
" tended functions, are Cain, Abel, and Seth; in the latter, they are Shem, Ham, and Japhet.
" Accordingly, Brahm himself is declared to be the same as Menu ; and Brahma, Vishnou, and
" Siva, are identified with those three sons of Menu, who appear at the commencement of every
" Manwantara, whose proper human names are said by the Hindoos to be *Sama* and *Cama* and
" *Pra-Japati*, and who transmit to their descendants the sceptre of sovereignty throughout the
" whole duration of their allotted period.

" On this point the Hindoo writers are sufficiently explicit; though by their wild system of
" personal multiplication and repeated Avatarism, they have superinduced a certain degree of con-
" fusion.  The evidence may be summed up in the following manner :

" We are taught on the one hand, that Brahma, Vishnou, and Siva, are essentially but a single
" person ; and this single person is Brahm, who unites in himself the divided attributes of the

---

Ham, and Japhet, and their three wives—in all eight.  He either conceals, or his prejudice has blinded him to the Brahme-Maia, the Supreme Being and his three emanations—Brahma, Vishnu, and Siva—the creator, the preserver, and the destroyer; and the eight planetary bodies, the Sun, the Earth, the Moon, and the five Planets.  I really can hardly bring myself to the belief that he can be so blind.  But he pretty well proves where the mythos of Genesis came from, or on what it was founded.

[1] Powers.  The forming power, the preserving power, and the destroying power; attributes of omnipotence.

[2] The planetary substances having form, his Angels or Messengers, the אמין *amin*.

[3] Orig. Pag. Idol. Vol. III. p. 117.

[4] From this hermaphrodite described by Mr. Faber, probably came the construction of the verse in Genesis, (*so God created man in his own image, in the image of God created he* HIM ; *male and female created he* THEM,) that the first male and female human beings were joined in one body, or were, in some way, Hermaphroditic.  This was the belief of many Jews and Christians in former times.  Here, as usual, we go to India, both for the book and its meaning.

" three; and that the triplicated Brahm is materially the World, astronomically the Sun, and mys-
" tically the great Hermaphrodite, who is equally the father and the mother of the universe. But
" we are told, on the other hand, that Menu-Swayambhuva is conjointly and individually Brahma,
" Vishnou, and Siva; that he had three sons, who sprang in a mortal shape from his body, and
" who named his three daughters; and that these three sons were severally Brahma, Vishnou, and
" Siva.

" Such are the declarations of the Hindoo theologists; and the inference to be drawn from them
" is abundantly obvious. Since Brahma, Vishnou, and Siva, are conjointly Menu-Swayambhuva;
" and since they are also conjointly the imagined supreme God Brahm; it is evident, that Brahm
" and Menu-Swayambhuva must really be the same person. And again, since Brahma, Vishnou,
" and Siva, are severally the three sons of Menu-Swayambhuva; and since they are also three
" supposed emanations from Brahm; it must plainly follow, that the famous triad of Hindoo theo-
" logy, which some have incautiously deemed a corrupt imitation of the Trinity, is really composed
" of the three sons of a mere mortal, who, under the name of Menu, is described as the general
" ancestor of mankind. Brahm then at the head of the Indian triad, is Menu at the head of his
" three sons. But that by the first Menu we are to understand Adam is evident, both from the
" remarkable circumstance of himself and his consort bearing the titles of *Adima* and *Iva*, and from
" the no less remarkable tradition that one of his three sons was murdered by his brother at a sa-
" crifice. Hence it will follow that Brahm, at the head of the Indian triad, is Adam at the head of
" his three sons, Cain, Abel, and Seth." [1]

This may be true, unless the reader should think with me that the profound Hindoo doctrine
does not arise from the history of the men, but that the doctrine is disguised under the allegory of
men to conceal it from the vulgar eye, after the manner of all the other Mythoses of Antiquity.

Again, Mr. Faber says, " Each Menu, however, with his triple offspring, is only the reappearance
" of a former Menu with *his* triple offspring; for, in every such manifestation at the commence-
" ment of each Manwantara, the Hindoo Trimurti or Triad becomes incarnate, by transmigrating
" from the human bodies occupied during a prior incarnation; Brahm or the Unity appearing as
" the paternal Menu of a new age, while the triad of Brahma, Vishnou, and Siva, is exhibited in
" the persons of his three sons. The first Menu, therefore, with his three sons, must be viewed
" as reappearing in the characters of Menu-Satyavrata and his triple offspring—Sama, Cama,
" and Pra-Japati. But the ark-preserved Menu-Satyavrata and his three sons, are certainly
" Noah and his three sons, Shem, Ham, and Japhet. Hence again it will follow, since Menu-
" Satyavrata is only a reappearance of Menu-Adima, and since the triplicated Menu-Adima is the
" same as the triplicated Brahm, that Brahm at the head of the Indian triad is likewise Noah at the
" head of his three sons." [2]

Notwithstanding the nonsense in the above extracts about Brahm being the world, &c., and the
ingenious misrepresentation that Brahm is not the true God, enough transpires to shew that the
mythoses of the Israelites and of the Brahmins are essentially the same. When this is added to
the general character of the history, of the serpent, of the tree of knowledge, &c., &c., and to the
proof which has been given by Sir W. Drummond, in his Œdipus Judaicus, that the names of
the persons and places in Genesis have astronomical meanings, I think no one can hesitate to
agree with the ANCIENT JEWS AND FATHERS OF THE CHRISTIAN CHURCH, that the whole is
allegory. In this I believe few people would differ from me, if a literal interpretation were
not wanted to bolster up those pernicious heresies, Original Sin and the Atonement—the wild
chimeras of insane fanatics, of former times, and held by the moderns through the prejudices of

---

[1] Faber, Orig. Pag. Idol. pp. 117, 118.          [2] Ibid. p. 119.

education. How surprising that a man of learning and talent like Mr. Faber should succeed in persuading himself that the Platos and Ciceros of antiquity, were contemptible enough to adore three or four old women and a rotten ship !

It seems never to have occurred to Mr. Faber, in his attempt to prove that all the profound theories and learning of the Platos, Pythagorases, and Hindoo philosophers, were nothing but figurative representations of his ship and old women, that he might prove the ship and its crew were nothing but an allegorical representation or an incarnation of the theories of the philosophers. However, with great learning and talent, he has certainly rendered this extremely probable, if he have not actually proved it—which, indeed, I think most unprejudiced people will allow that he has done. In this he has shewn that the priests of the Israelites were like those of all other nations, who dressed up or disguised their recondite philosophical doctrines under the representation of human adventures of different kinds, in order the better to secure to themselves dominion over the vulgar—that vulgar who will be in a fury with me for endeavouring to undeceive them.

The similarity of the numbers, in the Mosaic history, with the numbers constantly recurring in the Hindoo systems, seems very striking. Here are Adam and his three sons, and Noah and his three sons, each class answering to Brahm and his three emanations—Brahma, Vishnou, and Siva. There are eight persons in the ark, answering to the sun and seven planetary bodies. But whether the histories of Adam and Noah and their families were taken from the metaphysical and profound theory of the hermaphroditic creator, preserver, and destroyer—the sun presiding over the planetary system ; or, the recondite system was formed, and the sun and planets numbered after him and his family, I leave to every person to judge of as he thinks proper. The pious devotee, to the literal meaning, will, no doubt, take the former. I incline to the latter, which will enable me by and by to prove the truth of Christianity to the philosophers. But I do not mean by Christianity, that of the Pope, putting up the picture of the massacre of St. Bartholomew in his chapel ; or that of Calvin, burning Servetus ; or that of Cranmer, burning Joan Bocher.

The book of Genesis was considered by *most*, if *not all*, of the ancient Jewish philosophers and *Christian fathers* as an allegory. For persons using their understandings, to receive it in a *literal* sense, was impossible : and when we find modern Christians so receiving it, we only find a proof that, with the mass of mankind, reason has nothing to do with religion, and that the power of education is so great, as in most cases to render the understanding useless. In the Jewish religion, as in all other religions, there was an esoteric and an exoteric meaning of its dogmas. One great object of Moses evidently was to destroy idolatry ; he was of the Iconoclastic sect—that was all. He was, in fact, of the Linga sect of the Indians, and of the Persee sect, or of the religion of the Persians. He adored the sacred fire as the emblem of the Supreme Being, precisely after the manner of the Oriental nations, and he reprobated the worship of Adonis, the name equally of the Israelitish and Heathen God, and Astarte, in the shape of a Golden Calf,[1] at Sinai. This was the chief object of his system ; but something more will be pointed out hereafter.

---

[1] In the annunciation of the festival of the golden calf Aaron expresses himself in the following words : Festum Adonai cras. (Selden de Diis Syriis Synt. I. Cap. iv.) In Arabia, where Aaron then was, Bacchus, the Saviour, was adored under the name of Urotalt, and under the title of Adonai or of Adoneus. (Auson. Epig. 29.) Urotalt is evidently the two Latin words *Urus* and *Altus*—the lofty Bull or Beeve. Probably the title of Urania, given to Venus, came from the Urus. The junction of the two, the Venus and the Urus produced God the generator. D'Ancarville, Vol. I. p. 47.

In Jer. xlvi. 15, the LXX render the passage, ὁ Ἄπις, ὁ μοσχος ὁ εκλεκτος σɛ—Apis thy chosen Calf. This is justified by forty-six of Dr. Kennicot's manuscripts, which read אֲבִירֶךָ *abirk* in the singular, and not אֲבִירֶיךָ *abirik* in the plural. Now, as I look upon the LXX as a most valuable gloss, and as being unprejudiced wherever it gives a meaning against the doctrines of the Jews of its own or of later times, I pay much attention to it, particularly when, as here, I find it supported by the various readings.

There is one fact which must, I should think, have been observed by every person conversant with inquiries of the nature of those on which I have been employed, and it is this : all those works, without exception, which we call early histories, are deeply tainted with mythology; so that we have not, in fact, one early real history. Whatever may have been the cause, the effect is, that the early history of every state, like that of Rome, has been made use of as a kind of peg to hang a system of priestcraft or mythos on. The mythos, not the history, is the object of the writer : as might be expected, the *history* bends, not the *mythos*, if they do not fit. Of this the early Roman history is an example. The historians not understanding it have recorded as history the most palpable nonsense. Herodotus is an example of this. His story is the first in Greece which was told for the purposes of history. All former stories were for the purpose of a secret doctrine, desired to be perpetuated in secrecy : first verbally told in verse or rhythm for the assistance of the memory, next written. Such were the works of Hesiod and Homer.

Mr. Faber has clearly proved, as the reader has seen, that the Mosaic accounts of the creation, and of the flood of which I shall treat in my next book, are to be found in the works of the Hindoos; the outlines or great points being evidently the same. Yet the particulars differ sufficiently to induce a suspicion, that they are not copies of each other, but were probably drawn from a common source. The material parts of the history may be true. I believe it, as I believe the history of Tacitus. I believe that Vespasian lived ; but Vespasian's miracles, as related by him, I cannot believe. I believe in a creation ; but I do not believe that God walked in the Garden. I believe in a flood ; but I cannot believe that all the animals of the old, as well as those of the NEW WORLD,[1] were put into one ship. Many other things I believe, and many other things I do not believe ; but it is always a pleasure to me to find (if the doctrines of Jesus alone be the religion of my country) that my faith, though differing from it, in a few trifling and unimportant points, is nevertheless *the same* in its great foundations. If the reader will consult the Transactions of the Asiatic Society of Calcutta, particularly Volume IV., he will find innumerable proofs that the Grecian histories, equally with the Mosaic and Hindoo mythologies, are most of them drawn from the same common fountain, in Upper India, about Balk, Cabul, and Samarkand. The same universal system pervaded the whole, and, no doubt, had its origin in ancient Buddhism.

Many facts stated by Mr. Faber having been taken from the works of Mr. Wilford, before the frauds which one of the Brahmins practised upon him were discovered, it is necessary to read with caution, and exclude the parts in which he might be deceived ; but there is quite enough to satisfy any unprejudiced person, that the books of Genesis are mythoses or parables, the same as those of the Hindoos, and, in short, of all the other nations of antiquity.

That the Mosaic ceremonies were the same as those of the Gentiles, has been proved by Spencer, Faber, and other learned divines, beyond dispute. This being the fact, it does not seem surprising that the doctrines of the two should also partake of the same character, when stripped of the corruptions which the priests and the infirmities of humanity have introduced into them. We see not only the same fundamental Trinity, but we see the same system of concealment under apparently absurd mythoses or allegorical representations,—absurd, indeed, to outward appearance, but probably, if perfectly understood, covering a system of wisdom and truth. But enough escapes to prove that, for our good, as much is known as is necessary. I am of opinion that the object of Jesus was the reform of the Jewish polity, and the restoration of the religion of the Gentiles to that of Abraham and Melchizedek, that is, Buddha; for I am persuaded they were originally the same—the religion of the first Persians, or something very near to it, described by

---

[1] None of which were ever found in the old world.

2 o

Sir W. Jones as being so beautiful. But the discussion of this point belongs to the latter part of my work.

Let the reader look at the print of Cristna bruising the serpent's head, and that also of his brooding on the waters, and then doubt, if he can, that the system of Genesis and that of India were the same. This proves the doctrine, as well as the ritual, to be identical. They are prints of statues cut out of rocks long before the Christian æra. Let him consider the histories of Samson, Hercules, and Bala-Rama, of Buddha and Osiris, Budvar, Hermes, and Fo, and doubt the identity if he can. Then, how is it possible to doubt, that the original mythoses on which these are founded were the same?

On this subject Maimonides says, " Non omnia secundum litteram intelligenda et accipienda " esse quæ dicuntur in opere Bereschet, (Genesis,) sicut VULGUS hominum existimat......sensus " enim illorum pravas vel gignunt cogitationes, imaginationes, et opiniones, de natura Dei, vel " certe fundamenta legis evertunt, hæresimque aliquatenus introducunt." [1]

The learned Spencer says, E superioribus evidens esse censeo, omnis generis arcana sub rituum " Mosaicorum tegmine latuisse. Quod itaque Plutarchus, credulâ temeritate, de religiosis Egyp- " tiorum institutis dixit, de Judæorum sacris et ceremoniis usurpemus. Nihil à ratione dissonum, " fabulosum nihil, nihil superstitionem olens, in eorum sacris constitutum est: sed quædam ethicas " et utiles doctrinas in recessu continentia, alia vero non experta elegantiæ cujusdam historicæ vel " philosophicæ." [2]

The fact that the books of Moses do cover a secret doctrine being here broadly admitted by Spencer, one of the most learned divines of the British Protestant Church, I hope and trust I may stand excused, if I find myself under the necessity of adopting his principle—which, under the words omnis generis, is pretty extensive. This has nothing to do with the question whether the esoteric doctrine, admitted to exist, be or be not rightly understood by me. I only here contend that there was a secret doctrine. What that secret doctrine was, is not the subject of this section.

The following is the opinion of the learned Thomas Burnet, one of the first of Christian philo- sophers: " Sed quid tandem, inquies, omnibus perpensis, de Hebræorum Cabala statuendum erit? " Nil habet arcani sensûs, nil sapientiæ reconditæ; neque olim habuit? Rabbinorum cordatissi- " mus, Moses Maimonides, ait, olim fuisse apud Hebræos de rebus divinis multa mysteria, sed " periisse: vel injuria temporis, et repetitis gentis istius calamitatibus; vel ex eo quod prohibitum " fuit, mysteria divina scriptis consignare. Sed audiamus, si placet, ipsius verba Latinè. Scito " multas egregias sententias, quæ in gente nostra olim fuerunt, de veritate istarum rerum, partim " longinquitate temporis, partim infidelium et stultorum populorum in nos dominatione: partim " etiam quod non cuivis (sicut exposuimus) concessa erant mysteria, periisse, et in oblivionem " devenisse. Nihil enim permissum erat litteris mandare, nisi ea quæ in libros sacros digesta et " relata erant. Nosti enim Talmud ipsum inter nos receptum, olim non fuisse in certum librum " digestum, propter rationem istam, quæ tum passim obtinebat in gente nostra: VERBA QUÆ " DIXI TIBI ORE, NON LICET TIBI SCRIPTO DIVULGARE." Hæc est sententia Maimonidis " de ' occultâ veterique Judæorum sapientiâ." [3] Again he says, " Si veniam damus conjecturis, in illam " opinionem facile descenderem, Antiquam Cabalam Realem (nam verbalis est figmentum huma- " num) tractasse potissimum de rerum originatione, et gradationibus. Sive de modo productionis " aut profluxus rerum a primo ente, et earundem rerum gradibus et descensu a summis ad ima." [4]

---

[1] Maim. More Nevoc. Pars ii. Cap. xxix. p. 273; Beaus. Hist. Manich. Vol. II. p. 451.

[2] Lib. i. Cap. xi. Sect. 3.        [3] Burnet, Archæol. Cap. vii. p. 84.        [4] Ib. p. 85.

Again, " Hæc est rerum et temporum ratio, in historia primi hominis et Paradisi. Quæ cum sin-
" gula mecum revolvo, æquo animo, et in omnem partem flexili, qua ducit ratio et veritatis amor :
" succensere non possum, ex patribus, et authoribus antiquis, illis, qui in symbola, aut PARABOLAS
" aut sermones populares, hæc convertere studuerunt." [1] After this Burnet goes on to exhibit the
opinion of Cicero, Seneca, Zeno, and others, from which it appears that many of the learned Greeks
and Latins held the identical doctrine respecting the absorption of all things into the Deity, and
their periodical renovation and regeneration, with those of the oriental philosophers. I shall say
nothing more at present respecting the esoteric religion of the Jews, or the secret meaning of their
Pentateuch, except, if the modern priests will persist in discarding the opinions of the learned
ancients, both before and after Christ, that these books had an allegorical meaning, and will still
persist in taking them *to the letter*, that the time is rapidly coming, when they will not be received
at all, except by a few persons of very mean understandings—persons who remind me of the very
appropriate speech of the Egyptian priest to Solon : *Vos Græci semper pueri estis : Senex Græcorum est nullus.* And I should say, *Vos* religiosi semper pueri estis : Senex ultra-piorum est
nullus.

---

## CHAPTER XIII.

DISPUTED CHAPTERS OF MATTHEW AND LUKE.—CAUSE OF THE BLACK CURLY-HEAD OF BUDDHA.—GENE-
RAL OBSERVATIONS ON THE MORAL DOCTRINES OF DIFFERENT RELIGIONS.

1. EVERY one knows the violent altercations which have taken place among learned Christians,
almost from the beginning of Christianity, respecting the last eight verses of the *first* and the whole
of the *second* chapter of Matthew—and the whole of the *second*, and all the *first* chapter, except the
first four verses, of Luke. Great numbers of men, of first-rate character for learning and talent,
have declared them and proved them spurious, men who have shewn their sincerity by the resig-
nation of rich livings rather than appear to tolerate them against their consciences. [2] Some interesting questions here naturally suggest themselves. What are those chapters ? Are they mere
forgeries of the orthodox ? Why should the orthodox wish for *an immaculate conception* or *a
divine incarnation ?* They would have been just as rich and powerful without these doctrines. I
cannot think they were mere forgeries. They have no appearance of any such thing. Then what
are they ?

I think they are evidently the effects of the same cause as that which produced the oracles of
Zeradust, the different prophecies which alarmed the Romans, [3] the Sibylline oracles, the
prophecies of Virgil, &c., in the West ; and as that which produced the same species of prophecy
among the Brahmins, named above, of expected saviours—the saviours expected and prayed for in
the Yajna sacrifice, " *When will it be that the Saviour will be born ! when will it be that the Re-
" deemer will appear !*" To deny these heathen prophecies is impossible. I know not how to

---

[1] Burnet, Archæol. p. 400.　　　　[2] Amongst whom were Lindsey, Disney, Jebb, and Frend.
[3] Cited in Chap. II. Sect. 7.

account for them, except by supposing that they alluded to the renovating cycles demonstrated above. With this, the whole Jewish history and the disputed chapters are in perfect keeping. We have seen that all the ceremonies and much of the doctrine of the Jews, indeed the most important part, their Trinity, were exactly the same as those of the Gentiles. And I think if a person will pay but a very little attention, he must see that the incarnation described in these chapters was but the counterpart or repetition of former incarnations, or extraordinary conceptions, such for instance as that of Isaac or Samuel, or Buddha, or Cristna, or Pythagoras—the arrival of the three Magi, with the gifts sacred to the God Sol, or Mithra—the episode of Anna or the year, and Phanuel, or Phan, our God—of John having the power of the God Ieu (Elijah) אליהו *alieu*. All this dovetails very well into the remainder of the Gentile history, and proves these chapters to have a secret meaning, and to refer to the prophecies alluded to above. It all tends to prove the truth, a truth of which I have no doubt, that an identical secret system pervaded the whole world; singular as it may appear, in its universal extension, perhaps, unknown to the world. We have most unquestionably the same prophecy in Ireland, in Greece, in Persia, in Judæa, in Italy, and in India. But we have no reason to believe that any nation had merely copied the prophecy of the other nations. We read in Roman and Greek authors of the eighth age, and the ninth age, but scarcely another word do we meet with about them. So that it seems as if the meaning of these ages had become lost; and this I really believe was the truth. I should set it down as part of the secret mysteries, without any difficulty; but I cannot help believing that the mysteries, the real meaning of the Gods, &c., was actually lost. Cicero, Phornutus, Macrobius, &c., would not have written as they have done had they been understood. A general traditionary opinion had descended from the Buddhists, that the world would be renovated at the close of every ten ages, or ten Neroses, or six thousand years. These were the ages the knowledge of which was almost, but not entirely, lost. The priests and prophets had some slight perception of them, but it was, as through a glass, *darkly*.

2. I must now once more bring back the attention of my reader to the curly-headed, flat-faced, thick-lipped, black-skinned Buddha, almost forgotten. For these singularities we have not yet attempted to give any reasons. This Negro God cannot have been the only *Negro* East of the Indus, without some cause. On this subject credible history is silent. Let us try if we can form a theory.

It will not be denied that the animal, man, is in many respects like most other animals with which we are acquainted, and the philosophers Buffon and Lawrence have proved, that he partakes of the animal character in a much greater degree than was generally admitted in former times. And I think it will scarcely be denied that, like most other animals, he is capable of being improved, as well in person as in mind. I suppose that no one will deny the latter, how much soever the bigots may turn into ridicule the march of intellect, or improvement of the human understanding. Now I suppose, that man was originally a Negro, and that he improved as years advanced and he travelled Westwards, gradually changing, from the jet black of India, through all the intermediate shades of Syria, Italy, France, to the fair white and red of the maid of Holland and Britain. On the burning sands and under the scorching sun of Africa, he would probably stand still, if he did not retrograde. But the latter is most likely to have happened; and, accordingly, we find him an unimproved Negro, mean in understanding, black in colour. We know from experience that by coupling animals of beautiful forms, our animals constantly increase in beauty; indeed, our breeders of sheep, horses, and other domestic animals, know how to give them almost any colour or character they choose. They breed the high-mettled racer, the bold and warlike game-cock, or the sluggish, fattening Leicestershire sheep. The same effect has arisen in the form of man. In the rich soils of India, unfit for pasturage or hunting, but well calculated for the operations of agriculture, distinctions of rich and poor would much sooner arise than among the nomade or wandering tribes ; and as soon as a class became rich, the natural propensity would operate in causing the most handsome of the males, which would be the rich, those who were well fed and lived without labour, to couple with the most handsome of the females. This cause, in long periods of time, constantly acting, produced a great improvement in the human form. The scorching climate kept man black ; but, by degrees, the curly hair, flat face, and thick lips, yielded to the improved appearance of the present race.

Mr. Crawford has observed, that no country has produced a great or civilized race, but a country which, by its fertility, is capable of yielding a supply of *farinaceous* grain of the first quality. This he ingeniously supports by a great many examples.

When the Equinoctial Sun entered Taurus, he found man in India, like the first Buddha, a Negro ; when he entered Aries, he found him black, it is true, but with the aquiline nose and long hair of the handsome Cristna. The God of wood, of stone, of gold, stood still: the man in the space of 2160 years, perhaps of peace and prosperity, had materially improved. Not so the curly-haired man of Africa. Every thing tended to the improvement of the former, every thing to stop the improvement of the latter. In the African Ethiopia he remains a curly-headed black. In Egypt he formerly was so ; as the Memnon, Sphinxes, &c., prove. But in Egypt, where he became rich and civilized, and where good farinaceous food was grown, the same effects, in a great measure, took place as in India: and if he be not quite so black, the mixture of white Europeans, and, comparatively speaking, *white Turks*, will account for the difference. It has been observed, that the figures in the old caves of India are representations of a very different race from the present inhabitants ; that, although the figures possess a graceful elegance of form, yet a remarkable difference may be observed in the countenance, *which is broad and full : the nose flat : the lips, particularly the under lip, remarkably thick,* and the whole very unlike the present natives of Hindostan. [1]    All these circumstances are easily accounted for, by the reasons alleged to account for the singular appearance of the curly-headed Buddha.

I request my reader to reflect with me upon the present state of different parts of the world ;— go to Lower Egypt and look at the tinted natives, and ascend to the torrid zone, and we shall find them to grow darker as we approach the Sun, always, when humanized, described as black. The straight hair grows woolly as we approach the scorched, steril regions of Nubia, and generally the parched sands of Africa, *where no corn grows,* where the tree of the Sun, the *everlasting* [2] Phœnix or Palm tree, is perhaps the only plant on which man depend for the certain production of a scanty subsistence ; the only fruit-bearing tree which raises its head, a majestic head, around the few solitary springs of the parched desert. Let us go to India, and we find the same effect, with this only difference, that in this grain-growing country, this land of ease and luxury, the persons are more handsome, and the hair straight and long. And, above all, let us contemplate the Jewish character, the jet-black hair, and peculiar complexion, verging to the oriental, among the white European followers of Abraham. Let us reflect on all these circumstances ; when my reader has done this, I trust he will think that the solution of the enigma, which I have attempted, is the most probable which has been devised.

The opinion which I have here given, is supported by the ingenious Dr. Pritchard, in his Researches into the Physical History of Man, p. 41. He says, " The perception of beauty is the " chief principle, in every country, which directs men in their marriages. It is very obvious that " this peculiarity in the constitution of man, must have considerable effects on the physical

---

[1] Maur. Ant. Hind. Vol. II. p. 376.    [2] To be explained by and by.

" character of the race, and that it must act as a constant principle of improvement.". . . . . . . .
Again, (p 43,) " The noble families of modern Persia were originally descended from a tribe of
" ugly and bald-headed Mongoles. They have constantly selected for their harams the most
" beautiful females of Circassia. The race has been thus gradually ameliorated, and is said now to
" exhibit fine and comely persons."

I believe that all the Black bambinos of Italy are negroes—not merely blacks; this admitted,
it would prove the very early date of their entrance into Italy.

Dr. Pritchard has successfully proved that the blackness of the skin is not caused by heat alone;
that the Negro is to be found in cold as well as hot climates, and that the change which, in
various instances, has taken place in his complexion, is to be ascribed more to civilization than to
climate. This perfectly agrees with the observation of Mr. Crawford, that man is found improved
in rich and farinaceous, but stationary in *desert* districts. Civilization was the effect of the former
—barbarism of the latter.

Dr. Pritchard[1] has observed, that the Brahmins are, as might be expected, the finest formed
race in India. He has also shewn, in a very satisfactory manner,[2] that the ancient Egyptians,
the masters of Thebes, were Negroes—or, that they were black, with curly heads.

Col. Wilford says, " It cannot reasonably be doubted that a race of Negroes had formerly
" pre-eminence in India."[3]    These were the inhabitants of India in the time of the curly-headed
Buddha, who was succeeded, after 2160 years, by the long-haired Cristna—one an incarnation of
the solar God in Taurus, the other in Aries.

Thus I account for the Negro Buddha, and for the handsome, though black, Cristna.[4]

In aid of this theory, a reconsideration of the foregoing pages will shew, that we have found the
black complexion or something relating to it whenever we have approached to the origin of the
nations. The Alma Mater, the Goddess Multimammia, the founders of the oracles, the Memnons
or first idols, were always black. Venus, Juno, Jupiter, Apollo, Bacchus, Hercules, Asteroth,
Adonis, Horus, Apis, Osiris, Ammon,—in short, all the wood and stone Deities were black. The
images remained as they were first made in very remote times. They were not susceptible of any
improvement; and when for any reason they required renewal they were generally made exactly
after the former sacred pattern. I once saw a man repainting a black God on a house-side in Italy.

3. The shocking state of degradation into which the religion of the Brahmins has sunk, gives a
plausible appearance of truth to the rantings of our Missionaries; but, nevertheless, the religion
of Brahma is no more idolatrous than the religion of the Romish Church. Abul Fazil, a Mahometan author, in the Ayeen Akbery, states, that the opinion that the Hindoos are Polytheists has
no foundation in truth, but that they are worshipers of God, and only of one God. They maintain (with all enlightened followers of the Romish Church), that images are only representations of
the great Being, to which they turn whilst at prayer, in order to prevent their thoughts from
wandering. They hold that " the Being of beings is the only God, eternal, and every where
" present, who comprises every thing; there is no God but HE."[5]    The religions of Brahma and
of Buddha have both become corrupted, but a third has arisen—that of the Sikhs, a reformed
Buddhism, more pure than either of them, and which may perhaps be destined to possess the
sovereignty of India. Certainly nothing but the British can prevent it.[6]

---

[1] P. 390.        [2] Sect. v. p. 376.        [3] Asiat. Res. Vol. III.

[4] It is remarkable that the Abyssinian or Ethiopian has always continued the Indian Sanscrit custom of writing his
letters from left to right, in the syllabic form retaining the vowels. This appears to have been a remnant of the first
Buddhism of India. Much will be said upon this subject by and by, and the reason of the change in the custom of other
nations shewn.

[5] Crawford's Researches, Vol. I. pp. 200—220.                [6] Ibid. Ch. vii. of the Sikhs.

The following is the most celebrated verse of the Vedas, called the Gayatri: " Let us adore the " supremacy of that divine Sun, the Godhead who illuminates all, from whom all proceed, to whom " all must return, whom we invoke to direct our understandings aright in our progress towards " his holy seat." [1] On this Sir William Jones says, " The many panegyrics on the Gayatri, the " Mother, as it is called, of the Vedas, prove the author to have adored, not the visible material " sun, but that *divine and incomparably greater light which illumines all, delights all, from which* " *all proceed, to which all must return, and which alone can irradiate* (not our visual organs merely, " but our souls and) *our intellects.* These may be considered as the words of the most venerable " text in the Indian Scripture." [2] The words in italics mark the words of the Veda text.

If we are to believe our priests, at the same time that nothing can be more pure than our religion, or more charitable than themselves, nothing can be more horrible than the religion or practices of the wicked Heathens. Yet it is worthy of observation, that we curse *sinners* on Ash Wednesday, and our *enemies* whenever we are at war: but when the Athenians in a moment of fury ordered the priestess to curse Alcibiades for having insulted the mysteries, she REFUSED— saying, *she was the priestess of prayers, not of curses.* [3] The passage in Martianus Capella, cited Chap. II. Sect. 8, shews that the Pagans were no more Idolaters than the modern Romans.

One of the most common and triumphant boasts of the Christian priests has been, that no morality could be put in competition with theirs. The following extract, from the eleventh discourse of Sir William Jones to the Asiatic Society, will abundantly prove how slender are the foundations upon which these arrogant pretensions are built. These are the words of the pious president; though they be rather long, their importance will plead their excuse:—" Our divine " religion, the truth of which (if any history be true) is abundantly proved by historical evidence, " has no heed of such aids, as many are willing to give it, by asserting that the wisest men of " this world were ignorant of the two great maxims, that *we must act in respect of others, as we* " *would wish them to act in respect of ourselves;* and that, *instead of returning evil for evil, we* " *should confer benefits even on those who injure us:* but the first rule is implied in a speech of " Lysias, and expressed in distinct phrases by Thales and Pittacus; and I have even seen it word " for word in the original of Confucius, which I carefully compared with the Latin translation. It " has been usual with zealous men, to ridicule and abuse all those who dare on this point to quote " the Chinese philosopher; but instead of supporting their cause, they would shake it, if it could " be shaken by their uncandid asperity,—for they ought to remember, that one great end of reve- " lation, as it is most expressly declared, was not to instruct the wise and few, but the many " and unenlightened. If the conversion, therefore, of the Pandits and Maulavis in this country " shall ever be attempted by Protestant Missionaries, they must beware of asserting, while they " teach the gospel of truth, what those Pandits and Maulavis would know to be false : the former " would cite the beautiful A'ry'a couplet, which was written at least three centuries before our æra, " and which pronounces the duty of a good man, even in the moment of his distraction to consist " *not only in forgiving, but even in a desire of benefiting, his destroyer, as the Sandal tree, in the* " *instant of its overthrow, sheds perfume on the axe which fells it ;* and the latter would triumph in " repeating the verse of Sadi, who represents *a return of good for good as a slight reciprocity,* but " says, the virtuous man *confers benefits on him who has injured him ;* using an Arabic sentence, " and a maxim apparently of the ancient Arabs." Thus we see the essence of the Christian moral doctrine was known at least three hundred years before Jesus was born.

And the following extract will shew that the Mohamedans were as enlightened upon this subject

---

[1] Moore, Panth. p. 410.          [2] Ibid.          [3] Plutarch, apud Payne Knight on Sym. S. lvii. n.

as any of them :—" Nor would the Musselmans fail to recite four distichs of Hafiz, who has
" illustrated that maxim with fanciful but elegant allusions :

> " Learn from yon orient shell to love thy foe,
> " And store with pearls the hand that brings thee woe :
> " Free like yon rock, from base vindictive pride,
> " Imblaze with gems the wrist that rends thy side :
> " Mark, where yon tree rewards the stony show'r,
> " With fruit nectareous, or the balmy flow'r :
> " All nature calls aloud ; *shall man do less,*
> " Than heal the smiter, and the railer bless ?"

" Now there is not a shadow of reason for believing that the poet of Shiraz had borrowed this
" doctrine from the Christians." [1]

In Mr. Maurice's History [2] may be found many moral sentiments identically the same as those
of the Christians.

In order to exalt the credit of the Christian religion, nothing which talent and ingenuity could
contrive has been left untried by divines to depreciate the philosophy of the ancients, and to
blacken the characters of its professors. No doubt among the followers of Socrates, Pythagoras,
Aristotle, Plato, &c., as well as among the followers of Jesus and Mohamed, brawls and squabbles
the most disgraceful have taken place. But it does not appear that better men have been produced by the latter, than by the former. The Antonines and Epictetus are not to be placed below
any men whom modern history can produce : and although we cannot now give a catalogue of illustrious ancient names equal in number to that of the moderns, this by no means proves that such
individuals did not formerly exist. The peculiar circumstances of the case prevent our knowledge
of them, and that principally in consequence of the destruction of their works—an effect arising
from various causes.

The oldest and wisest of the Grecian philosophers taught the very best parts of the Christian
morality, many hundred years before Jesus was born. Pythagoras said, that the best way for a
man to revenge himself of his enemies was to make them friends : and Socrates, whose character
has been vindicated from reproach by Dean Prideaux, [3] says in the Crito, that it is not permitted
to a man who has received an injury to return it by doing another. An able defence of Socrates
may be found in the Travels of Mr. Buckingham to India, published in 1829.

Our treatises on the Christian religion are sufficiently numerous ; but it may be doubted very
much whether they exceed in number those of the ancient philosophers, or even of the modern
Mohamedans. On the philosophy of Plato eight thousand commentaries were said to have been
written. The greatest fault of the ancient philosophers consisted in the affected obscurity with
which they strove to conceal their real doctrines from the public eye. Into this error they all
seem to have fallen ; though in different ways. Many of them concealed their principles under
fables and figurative expressions,—by the literal interpretation of which Christian divines, overlooking the corruptions into which religion had fallen, have very unjustly succeeded in persuading
mankind that their doctrines were both pernicious and contemptible in the highest degree.

The liberal and benign doctrine of the followers of Brahma, in its original purity, can never be
too much praised, and must fill every one with admiration. No doubt in succeeding ages its corrupt and mercenary priests engrafted into it, as we see daily to take place in all religions, and
wherever priests are concerned, doctrines and practices utterly repugnant to the mild spirit of its

---

[1] Jones, 11th Dis. to Asiat. Soc.    [2] Vol. II. Ch. iii.    [3] Vide Moyle's Works, Vol. II. p. 77.

founders. Those founders maintained that all religions come from God, and that all modes of adoring him, when springing from an upright heart, are acceptable to him. Their enlightened followers still affirm that " the Deity is present with the Mahometan in the mosque counting his " beads, and equally in the temple at the adoration of the idols; the intimate of the Musselman " and the friend of the Hindoo; the companion of the Christian, and the confidant of the Jew." They are of opinion that he has many times appeared and been incarnate in the flesh, not only in this world, but in others, for the salvation of his creatures; and that both Christians and Hindoos adore the same God, under different forms. [1]

The fine sentiment here given from the ancient religion of the Brahmins, and on which I fear they did not always act, has been copied by the Christian historians of the gospel; but, either from its mixture with other doctrines of a pernicious nature, or from some other cause, it has unfortunately scarcely ever been acted on : *Then Peter opened his mouth, and said, Of a truth I perceive that* GOD *is no respecter of persons : but in every nation he that feareth him, and worketh righteousness, is accepted with him.* [2]  (Acts x. 34, 35.)  Beautiful as is this sentiment, clear as is the language, and beneficial to mankind as is its tendency, I have found divines who, with a narrowness of mind almost inconceivable, have endeavoured to explain away its plain and obvious sense, and to limit its meaning to countries in which a man may dwell. But how little can such men know of the Divine paternity who need to be told that God will not damn a man because he was a Frenchman, a Dutchman, a Turk, or a Hindoo !

Much fault has been found with the Decalogue, and justly, as a *code* for the whole world. But not justly when it is confined, as it ought to be, to the country of Judæa. By its language, when properly translated, it is strictly confined to the Israelites. And as a code, in its totality, it was never adopted by Jesus Christ. The whole of it is as impossible to be obeyed by the remainder of mankind, as it is to make a circle triangular, or a triangle, the angles of which shall not be equal to two right-angles. Jesus Christ never inculcated it, though part of the moral doctrines which he taught are to be found in it. In this instance, by not understanding or attending to the letter of the old language, priests have mistaken the doctrine both of Moses and of Jesus. They are both correct when properly understood. The Decalogue may be easily defended—but not on the mistaken grounds taken by our priests. I should like to meet a disciple of M. Voltaire on the subject of the *jealous God.*

There is in the Geeta, (p. 81,) a sentiment which is peculiar to the religion of Brahma, and which (at least if the happiness of mankind in this world is to be considered as one object or end of religion) places it above all others. Happy, indeed, would it have been for the world had the Mohamedan and Christian religions contained this most admirable and benevolent doctrine. The Deity speaks—" *They, who serve even other Gods with a firm belief, in doing so, involuntarily* " *worship me. I am he who partaketh of all worship, and I am their reward.*" [3]  How admirable is this sentiment! How superior to the Jewish doctrine of a *jealous* God, improperly adopted by Christians ! and how true ! True, at least, if benevolence, justice, and mercy, are the attributes of the Creator. For the peace and happiness of mankind in this world, it may safely be affirmed that, in all the Jewish, Christian, and Mohamedan religions, there is no dogma of half so much importance, or which has been of the twentieth part of the utility as *this* would have been, had it been taught in those religions. Yet there is a very fine and nearly similar sentiment in the Koran :

---

[1] Maurice, Hist. Ind. 4to. Vol. II. p. 301; see Anathema, 1 Cor. xvi. 22 !!!
[2] This is, indeed, the genuine doctrine of the philosophical Nazarite, Carmelite, or Essenian of Samaria.
[3] Maurice, Ind. Ant. Vol. V. p. 1052.

" If God had pleased, he surely had made you one people : but he hath thought fit to give you " different laws, that he might try you in that which he hath given you respectively. Therefore " strive to excel each other in good works ; unto God shall ye all return, and then will he declare " unto you that concerning which ye have disagreed." [1]   How superior is this to the *faith without works* of our modern and fashionable fanatics ! [2]

Mr. Maurice [3] pours out a torrent of abuse upon M. Volney for having endeavoured to rob him of his immortality, and to destroy the best interests of society by violating the truth of history, &c.   It seems difficult to conceive why M. Volney should wish any one to be robbed of his immortality, or why he should not be very glad to have the hope of it, if he could entertain it on what appeared to him reasonable grounds.   But he, no doubt, felt an utter repugnance to admit such doctrines, or any doctrine, on the mere assertion of priests, paid to support their systems, right or wrong ; who find Cristna a God in Asia, and Jesus in Europe ; who are the regular paid appendages to every arbitrary government, and are as naturally found to belong to it as an exciseman or a soldier.   When Mr. M. rails at Volney for violating the truth of history, he should have shewn distinctly how he violated it : empty railing will not answer any longer : men begin to use their understandings.   And when Mr. Maurice says Volney violated the truth of history in order to destroy the best interests of society, he ought to have said, the best interests of a hired priesthood, whose interests have always been opposed to the best interests, and to the liberty and happiness, of mankind.   But there is no reason to believe that M. Volney ever intentionally violated the truth of history.

If the work which is now presented to the world be executed with any tolerable degree of talent, no doubt the author will be honoured like M. Volney with the abuse of the priests.   It will be said that he has violated the truth of history ; that he hates the religion of Jesus, &c., &c.   That he has violated the truth of history *intentionally* he utterly denies.   He equally denies that he hates the religion of Jesus.   He does hate the hypocrisy of its priests, and the intolerance of their, not *its*, principles—as, on the contrary, he loves the liberality and tolerating spirit of the ancient, uncorrupted religion of the Buddist or Brahmin ; which teaches that God is equally the Father of the devout and sincere Chinese, Brahmin, Christian, and Deist ; which contains no creed inculcating that *except a man believe this or that he cannot be saved ;* a creed whose tendency is to fill the world with war and bloodshed, and to sacrifice, indeed, the best interests of society to those of a corrupt and pernicious order or corporation.

---

[1]  Koran, Ch. v. p. 131.
[2]  On the subject of the Koran, the *Apology for the Life and Character of Mohamed,* by the author of this work, may be consulted.
[3]  Hist. Ind. Vol. II. pp. 499, 501.

# BOOK VI.

## CHAPTER I.

FLOOD OF NOAH.—LEARNING OF GENESIS.—TEXT OF GENESIS.—INLAND SEAS OF ASIA.—THEORY OF A LEARNED CANTAB.—THEORY OF MR. GAB.—RENNEL ON EGYPT.—ORIGIN OF THE DELTA OF EGYPT. —CASPIAN SEA.—PLATO'S ATLANTIS.—GEOLOGICAL FACT IN YORKSHIRE.

1. I now propose to fulfil the promise which I gave in my last book—to make some observations on the flood or floods which have taken place upon our globe. To treat this subject fully would require a volume. I must confine myself to one or two observations, upon a few well-known facts.—I suppose it will not be denied that the history of the flood is an integral part of the Mosaic system; that whether it be allegory or a literal history, the whole book or collection of books called Genesis must go together, and be considered on the same principle : if the first and second tracts be allegory, so likewise must the third.

In almost every part of the world the fossil remains of animals are found,—animals which the researches of Mons. Cuvier have proved must have been deposited at long intervals of time, between which depositions great floods or catastrophes must have taken place.[1] He has shewn the order in which the different classes of living creatures have been formed; and it has been observed, that they have taken place exactly in that order in which they are said to have been formed, in the first book of Genesis, which figuratively describes them as being created in successive days. The observation strikingly illustrates the allegorical principle : for, though it absolutely proves the falsity of the *letter* of the record, it, at the same time, proves the truth of the allegory, as far as we clearly understand it. Now, if man had been formed before the flood, at the same time with the Elks, Elephants, &c., found fossilized, it is not possible to believe that some remains of him would not have been found among them in some part of the earth. " Human bones have " been found indurated and preserved by vitriolic, sparry, and ferrugino s incrustation : these are " modern operations of daily process, but have no relation to the petrefaction incident to the bones " of elephants and other animals confined in the bowels of the earth : in earth undisturbed since " its original formation of consistency, and which bones (in some cases) are indurated to the " hardest agate."[2] The whole world has been ransacked for a specimen; but it has not been found : for the priests have seen that the want of such specimen strikes a death-blow, at their literal interpretation of the text, and at what I must call their modern, mischievous, demoralizing doctrines, depending upon it. This failure alone has brought the matter to this point—either Genesis is *false*, or, it is an allegory or parable ; and to the latter conclusion every enlightened Christian must now come. The creation of the world in six successive days and nights, and the creation of man before the floods which embedded the animals in the strata above alluded to, are assertions, the falsity of which, if taken to the letter, is as well proved as the nature of the case

---

[1] Vide Celtic Druids.        [2] Gent. Mag. Vol. LVIII. A. D. 1788, p. 384.

will admit. Therefore the doctrine of allegory must now be revived—the doctrine of the ancient Jews, and the earliest and most learned fathers of the Christian Church—a doctrine lost in the darkness and debasement of intellect during the middle ages. It is said that the proof of the allegorical signification is only *negative* proof; but it is a very peculiar kind of negative proof; for the fossil elephant is *found*—but in the same strata the positive *absence of the remains of man* is palpable. The history of Noah and the Deluge being the same in India and Western Syria,[1] whatever may be the meaning of the one must be the meaning of the other.

M. Cuvier, after shewing *that there are no human bones in a fossil state*—that is, in a *fossil state properly so called,*[2] goes on to prove that the bones of men and birds, or of very small animals, are as indestructible in their nature as those of Elephants, &c. He concludes, " How- " ever this may have been, the establishment of mankind in those countries in which the fossil " bones of land animals have been found, that is to say, in the greatest part of Europe, Asia, and " America, must necessarily have been posterior not only to the revolutions which covered up " these bones, but also to those other revolutions by which the strata containing the bones have " been laid bare. Hence it clearly appears, that no argument for the antiquity of the human " race in those countries can be founded either upon these fossil bones, or upon the more or less " considerable collections of rocks or earthy materials, by which they are covered."[3]

The way in which M. Cuvier's fear of the priests shews itself here, is very marked. It is true, as he says, that no argument for the antiquity of the human race can be formed from the fossil bones, or collections of rocks by which they are covered; but it is clear that an argument which he keeps back can be formed, and must be formed, *for the contrary*—for its *modern* creation— that is, that it must have been created since the great catastrophe here alluded to took place :[4] and thus, that the third book of Genesis or Mosaic book of the Flood, contains a figurative account like the other two.

2. The history of Genesis conceals, under its allegory, the most profound knowledge of natural philosophy, and the general formation of the world, as proved by the most learned researches of Mons. Cuvier and other Geologists : and this has a strong tendency to support the opinion of the great Bailly, that a profoundly learned race of people existed previous to the formation of any of our systems. In this investigation we must recollect, that M. Cuvier's doctrines are not founded on what are called theories, but on experimental philosophy.

On the existence of living animals M. Cuvier states, that when the Spaniards first penetrated into South America, they did not find it to contain a single quadruped exactly the same with those of Europe, Asia, and Africa. The Puma, the Jaguar, the Tapir, the Capybara, the Lama or Glama, and Vicugua, and the whole tribe of Sapajous, were to them entirely new animals, of which they had not the smallest idea.[5]

Dr. Pritchard says,[6] " The Count de Buffon observed that the animals which inhabit the old

---

[1] In a future page I shall shew that there were two Syrias.

[2] Cuvier, ap. Jameson, pp. 62, 63, 128.                         [3] Ibid. p. 134.

[4] Thus away goes the learned Mr. Faber's Helio-archite hypothesis, that is, his *Sunned-ship* or his *shipped-Sun* worship. It is often very useful when you treat with superficial persons, to use an unintelligible word, like Helio-archite. Similar to this is our word *Heavens* in the first verse of Genesis.

[5] Cuvier ap. Jameson, pp. 62, 63. My reader will often find the expression *before the flood* used. He will recollect I formerly warned him, that he must consider this to mean merely *the earliest known period.* He must not consider it as the giving of an opinion as to the occurrence or non-occurrence of that event, before the creation of the present race of man.

[6] Sect. iii. p. 101.

" world are in general different from those of the new, and that whatever species are found to be
" common to both are such as are able to endure the extreme cold of the Arctic regions, and may
" therefore be supposed to have found a way from one continent to the other, where they approach ,
" very near together, and may probably have been formerly joined." After a careful examination
of this opinion of the Count's, Dr. Pritchard concludes thus : " But as far as accurate knowledge
" extends, the opinion of Buffon and his followers seems to be well founded. It does not appear
" that any one animal was originally common to the warm parts of the old and new world." [1]
Here, again, I think is an end of the universal deluge, taken with all its details, except in the
sense in which most of the other parts of Genesis must be taken; namely, as an allegory, under
which some secret doctrine is concealed : like the expression of God's walking in the garden,
&c., &c., it must be construed figuratively. And I think, for hundreds of reasons given in Mr.
Faber's learned work on Pagan Idolatry, it is evident, that the story of the ark of Noah is the
same as that of the Argha of the oriental Menu, in which the germ of animated nature is supposed
to have floated on the ocean, and to have been thus preserved.

The deductions of Dr. Pritchard and M. Buffon, as stated above, are perfectly legitimate, and
are decisive against the *literal* meaning of the text taken as a whole. I cannot bring myself to
believe that the Doctor can be in earnest, in the sophistry which he uses in page 138, to assuage
the anger of the priests, by pretending to reconcile the deduction to the literal meaning. But he
probably was aware that, if it did not pacify them, the same fate would befal his work which
afterward happened to Mr. Lawrence's. The Doctor's argument is, that God, by a great miracle,
brought every animal to the ark, and carried it back again,—great Elephants, and, of course, the
little mite of the Cheshire-cheese. But, unfortunately for the learned and ingenious Doctor's
scheme, the text does not warrant any such inference. Besides, how came God not to have
completed his work, and to have carried all the animals back again ?—for example, the Horse, the
Cow, the Elephant, and the Camel; and how came he not to leave us some of the animals which
they have, but which we have not ? [2]

That several floods have taken place cannot be doubted; ocular demonstration as well as
tradition prove this. Like what has been called *early history*, the fact was seized on by the priests,
and made subservient to the secret religion which every where prevailed. Thus we have a story
in India, or Eastern, Syria, Mesopotamia or Chaldea, of the germ or seed of all nature preserved
in a ship fastened to the mount of *Nau-band-a*, or the *ship-banded* or *cabled* mount; [3] in Western, [4]
Syria or Mesopotamia or Chaldea, the story of the ark of Noah and his eight sailors. But because
the fact was thus converted into a parable, and used for the purpose of preserving a mythos, and
the same mythos in both countries, it does not therefore follow that there was not a flood.

3. The account of the flood, taken from our common version, is plain and unaffected; and
has probably been misunderstood from its too great simplicity. It is as follows : *And the waters
prevailed exceedingly upon the earth ; and all the high hills that were under the whole heaven were
covered. Fifteen cubits upward did the waters prevail ; and the mountains were covered.* (Gen.
vii. 19, 20.) Now I take the liberty of asking, of what earth, and of what mountains or hills, does
the author speak ? I answer, most clearly not of those of the new, but of those of the old world,
of the height of which we know nothing. All that we know of them is, that there were hills, or

---

[1] Sect. iii. p. 133.

[2] The Ark was a correct parallelogram, square at the ends, 300 cubits long, 50 cubits broad, and 30 cubits deep.
It had no pretensions to the name of a *ship*. As it was like nothing else, perhaps its most appropriate name is Ark.
Origen calculated that it was about *thirty* miles long.

[3] See B. V. Ch. V. Sect. 2.          [4] There were two countries of each of these names.

mounts, or mountains; but we have many reasons for believing that they were not at that time very high: besides, the text certainly implies that they were not *more* than fifteen cubits high, for the water, having risen fifteen cubits, covered them. Now, if we consider the history in this simple point of view, which is the only way the words will fairly bear to be considered, because the whole context relates to the old world, it is by no means improbable that the same convulsion which covered the highest land of the old world with water only fifteen cubits or less than thirty feet deep, might also throw up Mont Blanc and Chimborazo.

But I must make another observation. The text does not say, that the surface of the whole globe was covered. The word הארץ *e-arz* does not necessarily include the whole surface of the globe: for this observation I am indebted to my friend Cooper, the learned Professor of Columbia College, in America. It may mean nothing more than the surface of the old land, and have nothing to do with the Americas, for it often means countries as well as the earth.[1] When a word has clearly two meanings, it is a most unwarrantable proceeding to adopt that which gives an impossible sense, instead of that which is consistent with reason and probability. Professor Cooper observes, " If the acknowledged facts cannot be explained without a miracle, we must " admit the miracle: if they can, we ought not to resort to supernatural interposition, when the " known action of secondary causes will suffice." If this reasoning be adopted, we have nothing in sacred writ respecting the deluge merely, at variance with possibility. For, if the hills of the old world were not very high, there is ten times as much water in the ocean as would cover the land to thirty feet deep; and no one can say, that the cause which forced up Mont Blanc was not powerful enough to cause a proportionate concussion of the waters.

Now, if we consider the history of the flood in this point of view, there is nothing improbable in the destruction having been so great over the world as to have left only a very few persons of one or two nations (the Indians and Chinese perhaps) in such a state as to retain possession of their books and records—whence they might be called the inhabitants of the city of Sephora, that is, the city of letters; Sephor, in Hebrew, meaning a letter, or a cipher or figure of notation. No person has ever pretended to find this city, but it has been thought to be Babylon. At all events, I think I have shewn that when the prejudices of philosophers against the nonsense of devoteeism, and the prejudice of devotees for nonsense, are disposed of, and the text fairly understood and explained, there is nothing implied in the *flood* of Noah impossible or incredible, or that may not rationally be accounted for from natural causes. When I look at Ætna and count the volcanoes burning and worn out, I have no difficulty in believing that what has caused them, may have split the globe in pieces, as we see it has been. So far as this, I think geologists will go with me. I am well aware that there are many phenomena which my theory *will not reach*, but which I think are not in opposition to it, or which do not impugn it, and which must be accounted for from other and additional causes, probably previous deluges. These are not in my province; I leave them to the Geologists, and come to this conclusion merely,—that there was a convulsion or flood, which raised the highest mountains; and, that there may have been other convulsions which destroyed the people of Greece, &c., of which Plato gives us an account. But none of these can have been the flood which buried the Elks, &c., before treated of.

4. When the first of the great convulsions spoken of above had ceased, I suppose that the world was left with the Mediterranean a great lake, overflowing a head or bank at the straits of Gibraltar; covering with water the Delta, or Lower Egypt, if it then existed, the Pontine Marshes of Italy, and many islands and shores of the Mediterranean now dry. The Aral, the Caspian Sea, the Sea of Asoph or Maietis or Mæotis, and the Euxine, were probably one sea, or a series of

---

[1] Gen. x. 5, 20, 31, ii. 11, 12; Deut. vi. 1, 3, 10; Psa cvi. 27, cv. 44, et al.

lakes, exactly like the series of lakes in North America, flowing over the head at Niagara. After a long course of years, the breaking down of the banks which held up these eastern or higher lakes might cause very great local floods, probably those alluded to by Plato,—might cause first the low lands on the banks of the Mediterranean to be flooded, and, at last, by breaking through the barrier at Gibraltar, cause them to be again left dry. All this is within the bounds of possibility, and probability too, if what the traveller Pallas says be true, that the appearance of the surface of the countries between the Aral, the Caspian, and the Sea of Asoph, shews that they have formerly all been connected. In all this we have nothing more than natural effects succeeding to natural causes. [1]

In some author, whose name I have forgotten, I have met with an assertion, that the plain of Troy has certain appearances which indicate that a great flood has formerly swept over it, which may have destroyed the city of Ilion. This may readily account for the general character which the rivers, &c., bear to the account in the poem of Homer, and for the difficulty in minute particulars of making them agree. Although the poem is evidently a sacred mythos, there was probably a true basement on which it was erected, as was the case with the Roman mythos, treated of by Niebuhr.

5. A learned orientalist of Cambridge, in a work called the Cambridge Key to the Chronology of the Hindoos, has made some pertinent observations on the subject of a flood. The work of this gentleman is the best defence of the flood of Noah that I have seen. He shews that an immense flood was believed by all nations to have taken place, and he produces proofs, I think satisfactory, that in all of them certain traditions were nearly the same as to date, and that these traditions place it at or about A. M. 1656, [2] of Usher's Chronology. His great object is to prove that the Mosaic history of the Patriarchs before the flood is real history and not a mythos, and he considers the proof of the existence of a general tradition of a flood, a proof of the truth of Noah's flood with all its details. But there may be a demur to this conclusion, even by persons who may admit most of the premises. Assuredly the circumstances and traditions, so generally found, furnish strong grounds for belief that some great flood did take place since the formation of the world and of man. But the reasons which I have given to prove that man has been created since the universal flood, which buried the last race of fossilized animals, seem to be satisfactory; therefore, the flood of which I now speak must have been of later date, and this later flood is what the priests of all religions have exaggerated into an universal deluge, burying the highest of our present mountains fifteen cubits deep. This flood may have taken place in the period of from about two to three thousand years before Christ. At this time the celebrated city of the great Bali, or Maha-Balipore, near Sadrass, in India, may have been destroyed. Of this city the Cambridge Key [3] says, " The stately palaces, august temples, and stupendous edifices, of this once magnifi-" cent city, are universally believed by every Hindoo, whether learned or unlearned, to have been " destroyed by ' a general deluge brought upon the earth by the immediate mandate of the Supreme " God.' They still shew the chasm in the rock, that forms one of the largest choultrys; and " the divided sculpture but too plainly shews that nothing less than such a convulsion of nature

---

[1] From the relations of *Pallas* and other travellers in the neighbourhood of the Caspian, there are distinct traces of the Aral, the Caspian, the Mæotis or Sea of Asoph, the Euxine, all having been once united. Quarterly Review, No. LXXXVI. p. 447.

[2] We have formerly seen that Hercules succeeded Bacchus about fifteen generations (meaning centuries) or 1500 years. This tradition alludes to the three Neroses before the flood. The Indians fixed the flood at the Cali Yug, and this was the mistaken time between Taurus and Aries.

[3] Vol. I. p. 313.

" could have rent so large a mass of solid stone, leaving the divided sculpture on each side the
" chasm,—evidently denoting that it was carved before the convulsion took place. This is a truth
" too apparent to be denied."

Here we have an argument worthy the consideration of a philosopher, and not far from being
conclusive as to a very great convulsion, if the account given by the Key be not exaggerated. I
wish this Indian scholar had been a little more full, and had told us that he had seen it himself:
for I have a high opinion of his sincerity. It seems to me to be a place more worthy of careful
examination than perhaps any other in the world.

The account given by this gentleman is, in general, confirmed by William Chambers, Esq., in
the first volume of the Asiatic Transactions. [1]

As I have just said, all this tends to prove that there really has been a very great convulsion
since the creation of man, and the foolish exaggerations of priests are not enough to invalidate it,
any more than the mythos spliced on to the history of ancient Rome, as satisfactorily shewn by
Niebuhr, is enough to prove that Rome did not exist. Few persons, except priests of very confined education, now believe the account of the flood literally, as expounded by devotees, but
consider it, as they consider the texts which say that God wrestled with Jacob, and strove to kill
Moses at an inn, *but failed*. The case is very difficult—but I am inclined to look upon the history
of the flood, as Mr. Niebuhr shews that the early history of Rome ought to be considered; and
that it is not a mere fable, but, on the contrary, that it has real history for its foundation—though
disguised by the contrivance of priests to excite astonishment in the minds of their votaries, or
perhaps merely to conceal their secret doctrines.

We are told by Plato, that before the race of people who occupied Greece in his time lived, a
previous race had been destroyed by a great flood. Now, I think it may be possible to find a
probable cause for this effect : but I will previously make a few observations on the Pyramids and
Delta of Egypt, from which I think we may, in our search, gain some assistance.

6. I shall, in the first place, give an extract from the work of a learned priest of the name of
Gab, of the Romish Church, which contains a statement of several curious and unobserved facts.
He says, " But before I draw any further inferences from the discoveries, or perhaps I should say
" revival of facts, (sunk, through the inattention of the learned, into a temporary oblivion,) now
" submitted to their consideration, by one who has little to boast of beyond taste and diligence in
" such a pursuit ; I will hazard the experiment, and see what progress I can make in the investi-
" gation of the antiquity of this interesting monument, this paragon so replete with principles of
" science, the great Pyramid of Giza, or ancient Memphis.

" There appears no convincing reason to conclude the other pyramids to be coeval with this,
" as may be gathered from the sequel of the present discussion. I have before observed, that
" were I to hazard a conjecture of this Pyramid being erected by the Antediluvians, I should
" not want for arguments to bear me out. But if I have deceived myself, and should fail in this
" attempt, still the Pyramid will neither fail, nor suffer any diminution of its beneficent utility in
" assisting in further discoveries.

" It has been a very prevailing, not to say a general, opinion, that the sands which environ the
" Pyramid, and hide a great part of its reclining sides, next to the foundation, have been drifted by
" the winds from other parts of those regions, and lodged in the circuitous strata now seen on
" every side of it. A strange property, surely, must be imagined in those winds, thus invariably
" to combine their efforts to bury this stupendous monument of art, without ever taking back

---

[1] Page 152, Ed. 8vo.

" any part of their deposite. Strange, however, as it appears to me, it has been received by most
" writers and visiters of the Pyramid, which opinion I now shall venture to combat.—At the time
" Herodotus reported the length of the side of the base to be 800 feet, (proved above to be of the
" standard chest, and equal to 583 feet 8 inches of ours,) all will agree that he dug not, like the
" French of late, through the sands, in search of the exact length of the foundations of a pile,
" which he was led to believe to be a sepulchral monument, but only measured on the adventitious
" surface, and that probably to no great exactness, but thought a few feet of no such consequence
" as to spoil the round number of 800, by inserting them.

" Now, if the surface had continued to rise by the incessant arrival of sand; as, about 2000
" years after Herodotus, Mr. Greaves, Professor of Astronomy, most accurately measured the side
" of the base also on the adventitious surface, he must have necessarily found, from 2000 years'
" accumulation of sand against the declining sides, a much less length of side than Herodotus
" records : whereas he made the length 693 feet English, which exceeds it by 110 feet. And
" the learned admit that we may depend on the veracity of Herodotus in such matters as fell
" under his cognizance : and who can deny Mr. Greaves an equal character? This inference,
" then, may fairly be drawn, that the winds in those regions have been imperceptibly stripping
" the sand-covered sides of this Pyramid, for at least 2000 years, instead of increasing the accu-
" mulation. This conclusion, however, rests not entirely on the accuracy of these stated dimen-
" sions. The argument is supported by these further considerations.

" All who have written on the Pyramids, agree in one point, though scarce any two in many
" others, that the sands which cover the surface of the rock, and are accumulated about the sides
" of the Pyramids, are adventitious. But by what agency, is the question? Most have taken it
" for granted, without further investigation, they have been brought by the winds : and indeed we
" read of wonderful effects thus produced in those regions of the earth : as tremendous columns
" of sand, raised by the impetuous whirlwinds, to the great terror of the alarmed travellers : but
" where do we read of these phenomena becoming stationary even for a day? Common obser-
" vation teaches us, that fine sands and pulverized earth are invariably driven by the wind from
" higher grounds and summits, and lodged in vales. All readers and travellers know the surface
" whereon the Pyramid stands, is the summit of an extensive rising ground or covered rock, at
" a sufficient distance from the mountains of Lybia to give the wind free access to the site
" whereon the Pyramid is built. And it is directly contrary to common experience to attribute
" that deposite of sand to the agency of the wind, since the removal of it is rather the natural and
" invariable effect of that agitated element. And that this has been the case with the sands
" deposited about the Pyramid, the greater altitude of them at the time of Herodotus, and the
" less altitude when Mr. Greaves visited the Pyramid, seems to be a proof, wanting nothing but
" accuracy in their statements to be a demonstration : and though no man is infallible, can it be
" reasonable to argue two such reputable characters, as Greaves and Herodotus, could either of
" them, in so short a length, as at most one stadium or furlong, have deviated from the other and
" from truth, by 110 feet?

" But if this deposite of sand is not the effect of the winds, by what agency came it there?
" Not by any extraordinary overflowing of the Nile, from which a sediment might be left : for it
" is known, that river never rose to near the height of that plain of rock, nor are there any kind
" of shell-fish in the Nile : whereas shells and petrified oysters are found in the sands about the
" Pyramids.

" And it must be allowed, when this Pyramid of Giza was built, there were no such depths either
" of sands or of earth upon the rock, as in the time of Herodotus, from the absurdities that would
" follow such a supposition : since the builders must first have dug out their depth of sand equal

" in extent to twelve English acres : and when their work was completed, must be argued to have
" filled in, against the declining sides, to the level of the former surface, and thus have buried a
" considerable part of their own work.

" From these positions, it evidently appears, this Pyramid must have been erected by the
" Antediluvians before the universal deluge, called Noah's flood, and the description given of it in
" Holy Writ will account in a satisfactory manner for the lodgment of sands on the surface of
" that extensive rock.

" It is natural to conclude the heavier particles of sand, when the waters became tranquil,
" would sink first, and the lighter particles, of course, both on account of their texture as well as
" their more exposed situation, would easily pulverize, and be sooner conveyed by the winds to
" distant places, than the ponderous, compressed layers, intermixed with shells and portions of
" loam, which more immediately covered the sides of the Pyramid nearer the rock. Of course
" the reduction of this consolidated mass has been by slow degrees, and its dispersion by the
" winds so imperceptible as to defeat observation." [1]

Herodotus stated the length of the side to be about 600 feet, of our measure about 583 feet ;
Mr. Greaves states it to be 693 feet English, or 110 feet more. The French found the base of
the Pyramid 31 feet below the surface : now, taking the area at eight acres, the builders must
have removed 611,177 cubic yards to lay the foundation. And if Herodotus's account be taken,
of the less height of the Pyramid and increased depth of sand, it would be 3,745,928 yards. The
French found Mr. Greaves's measurement correct.

In addition to the argument of Mr. Gab, upon the excavation to acquire a foundation for the
Pyramids, it may be asked, If they were built on the rock before it was covered with sand from
the desert, how *came* the ROCK itself not to be covered ? Did the winds only begin to blow sand
when the Pyramid began to be built ? During the thousands of years before, was no sand blown ?
This appears to me to form a very strong argument in favour of Mr. Gab's hypothesis, though it
seems to have been overlooked by him.

7. The oases in the deserts are much more exposed than the Pyramids to the drifting of the
sands by the winds, and they are not covered, nor are likely to be so. The ruins of the old
temple of Jupiter Ammon are yet remaining, and the groves of palm trees, and the ruins of temples
around it, would form as effectual obstructions to the free passage of the sands as the Pyramids.
But between the sandy deserts of Lybia and the Pyramids, is a ridge of mountains placed, as if on
purpose to form a barrier against the sands ; and so completely have they answered this purpose,
that, as Major Rennel says, [2] " So little have the sands of Lybia raised the country, that they
" have not even filled up the old bed of the Nile, which runs past the Pyramids, and which is
" easily distinguishable by a hollow and series of lakes, and an old canal. And it appears that
" Giza is several miles from the present Giza, where the Pyramids are." Authors speak of the
Etesian winds as causing this effect. I believe these winds do not blow from West to East, but,
on the contrary, blow mostly up the river from North and North-east to South and South-west. [3]

From the best information which I have been able to acquire, it does not appear that the sand
ever continues for any great length of time higher on one side of the Pyramid than on the other,
but, in fact, as we might expect, it varies with the winds—sometimes higher on one side, sometimes on another.

Ancient Giza was, I think, the sea-port before the Nile changed its bed ; and the change was
probably effected by the inundation of which I shall speak, which at the same time buried the

---

[1] Gab's Finis Pyramidis.　　　　[2] Geog. Syst. of Herod. Vol. II.　　　　[3] Univers. Hist. Vol. I. p. 419.

Pyramids in sand, changed the bed of the river, and, in great part, if not entirely, formed the Delta. The flood which, I shall shew, flowed up Egypt, probably covered a considerable part of Lybia, and carried thither shells similar to those found at the foot of the great Pyramid,· and on the surface of the sand around the temple of Seva or Jupiter Ammon,[1] to which it is not impossible the flood extended. The phenomena noticed by Mr. Gab, I think may be accounted for in the following manner :

I suppose that when the Pyramids at Giza were built, Memphis was the capital, and Giza the sea-port, placed at the end of a gulf or bay. By the breaking of the mounds which formed banks to the Euxine, the Palus Mæotis, the Caspian - and Aral Seas, when they were all in contiguous lakes or in one sea, as I have expressed my persuasion that they formerly were, before the opening of the Darnanelles took place—a sudden, mighty rush of water would be made on to the shores of Athos and Greece, which being stopped directly in front, would be divided, and half of it turned into the bay of Egypt, and over the land of Upper Egypt ; and the other half of it into Thrace,—causing the flood, recorded by Plato, drowning the first race of people on the East shores of Greece, and carrying along with it, in each case, the mass of sand and sea-shells now found around the Pyramids.[2] However this may have been, the petrified oysters and other sea-shells never can have been brought thither by the winds of Libya, nor by the downward annual flowings of the Nile. The former supposition is, upon the face of it, impossible, and the oyster shells are never found except in salt water, and therefore cannot be supposed to have come down the river, but must have gone up it. In the assertion that there are no oysters in the Nile, I have ascertained that Mr. Gab has fallen into a great mistake. There are oysters in the lower part of it, some of which, of course, would be carried up by any great body of water suddenly rushing into the country above Memphis.

If it be not thought possible that a great rush of water coming from the Euxine, against Greece and Negropont, might flow up Egypt, I know of no resource we have, except, perhaps, *the more probable theory* of Mr. Gab, that in the universal deluge, which raised up Mont Blanc and Chimborazo, and which happened since the building of the Pyramids, *and left them perfect and uninjured*, the oyster shells may have been brought down from the mountains of the Moon, for I know no where else that they can have come from.

If we suppose that the strait of Gibraltar was originally closed like the Isthmus of Suez, and that the water flowed over the neck of land, we may readily conceive how Lower Egypt, the Isthmus of Suez, the Pontine Marshes, and many islands, would be left dry, on its breaking down the neck into the Atlantic. Whether the opening increased gradually for a great number of years after its first disruption, or it happened at once, it will readily account for the Pharos of Alexandria having once stood a considerable distance from the land, and for the city of Hadria and the sea-port of Padua, in Italy, being left far inland, where they are now found.

8. Pretty nearly as numerous as the theories of the origin of the Nile and its floods, and as nonsensical, have been the theories of the origin of the Delta of Egypt. Herodotus, Diodorus Siculus, Strabo, and Ptolemy, assert that the Delta of Egypt was once overflowed by the sea.[3] This is perfectly consistent with reason and probability, and with the experience which we have of the formation of deltas at the mouths of other rivers ; and I cannot see why, for its mere formation, we are to seek for any other cause : but this argument does not apply to the question of the *slow* or *speedy* formation of the Delta.

In a discourse recently delivered at Paris, Cuvier declared, that " *we come by a very simple*

---

[1] Vide Rennel, ib. pp. 238, 257.  [2] See Asiat. Journal, Jan. 1828.  [3]. Ency. Britt. art. Phil.

*" calculation to the result, that* 2000 *years before Christ the whole of Lower Egypt had no exist-*
*" ence.* We presume that the learned philosopher does not mean to bind us to the strict letter, or
" we shall find some difficulty, even on the lowest system of chronology, in constructing that
" kingdom of Egypt which Abraham visited, and the city of Zoan (Tanis), where in all probability
" its king resided." [1]

I apprehend there can be no doubt that the flood of the Nile is the effect of the periodical rains,
or the melting of snow in the mountains of Africa, or of both these causes united. For many
generations the river has not deposited annually much sediment, but, for obvious reasons, this can
raise no objection to the supposed formation of the Delta by the deposite from the river, aided by
the North winds blowing into the mouth of it. For though, as appears from Mr. Bruce's account,
all the rivulets by which the Abyssinian Nile is fed, now have stony beds, free from mud ;
yet what Herodotus has said may probably be perfectly true, that the Delta was raised by the
gradual deposition of *mud* brought from the high countries,—because this may have taken place
before the mud was exhausted ; before the hill-sides and the beds of the rivers of the high
country were washed almost clean : since that time no very considerable deposite may have taken
place. The same process is now going on in the lake of Geneva. The Rhone deposits its mud,
and forms islands or lagunes at the top of the lake, and runs out at the bottom as clear as crystal.
At first the sediment would be invisible, until at last it would come near the surface, and the whole
bay would become very shallow, with the exception of one or perhaps two deep gullies : and when
the disruption, to which I have before alluded, took place, and the great mass of water escaped at
Gibraltar, the land which had been gradually forming under the water would be left dry, and the
Delta would shew itself.

When I look at a map, and contemplate the little progress made by the Euphrates and Tigris,
by the Indus, Ganges, and Burrampoutra, in filling up the gulfs at their mouths, and in converting
their bays into promontories; and again at the promontory of the Nile, and the recession of
the sea from the shores of the Mediterranean in various parts, and reflect on what the ingenious
geologist, Mr. Lyal, has said respecting the rate of the formation of Deltas generally, I cannot help thinking that there must have been some *peculiar* cause for the more rapid formation,
or at least exaltation above the sea, of the Delta of Egypt, than mere subsidence of alluvial matter.
And this I attribute to the breaking down of the bank at the straits of Gibraltar, or the widening
of an ancient opening at those straits, or to the lowering, from some other cause, of the waters of
the Mediterranean. For the elevation of the Pontine marshes and other shores and islands of this
sea must be accounted for, which cannot be done by the subsidence of the sediment of any rivers,
because in many cases there are no rivers to deposit sediment. No doubt a strong surface current
sets into the Mediterranean at present from the Atlantic, which makes against my system, but
this may not always have been so, and a deep counter current is generally believed at present to
take place. The ingenious author of the review of Mr. Lyal's fine work on Geology, says, the
latter is an unwarranted hypothesis. I have been told, on the contrary, that it has been ascertained, from actual experiment, by some of our naval officers, to be true. [2]

But, whatever may be the fact with respect to the current at Gibraltar, the truth of which is not
yet, I think, ascertained, I cannot doubt that the water of the Mediterranean, fed by the Danube,
Nile, Rhone, Tiber, Tanais, Dnieper, &c., &c., must have some way of escaping. Evaporation is
not enough to account for the effect. Evaporation must take place in the great Atlantic as well as
the small Mediterranean. If it do not go by the straits of Gibraltar, it must have a subterraneous

---

[1] Quarterly Review, No. LXXXV., May 1830, p. 131 *n.*       [2] Ibid. No. LXXXVI. p. 446.

passage, like the Dead sea and the Caspian. Some time ago I was told by an Indian traveller, that the surface of the Caspian was forty feet below the surface of the Indus at its mouth, and that he supposed the water of this sea escaped by an immense whirlpool which was not far from its South end. On naming this circumstance to another Indian traveller, to Captain E—, whose public duty it is to inquire into matters of this kind, he told me my friend, Col. W—,[1] was mistaken; that he had made a mistake from having a defective barometer; that he had tried it himself with a good instrument made by Troughton, and he found it not forty, but one hundred and forty feet below the Indus. Now this is an extremely interesting fact, and raises the questions, What becomes of the water? Does the water circulate when heated by an equatorial sun, and flow up to the poles and back again, as it flows out and back again in the newly-discovered apparatus for warming buildings?

10. We learn from Plato, and other Greek authors, that, in a very remote æra, a large island in the Atlantic ocean was swallowed up by the sea, and with it numerous nations, at one moment, drowned. This history does not seem improbable, and will, if admitted, account for many coincidences between the natives of the old and new worlds.

Of the size of this Atlantis we know really nothing. It may have been three times as large as Australia, for any thing which we know to the contrary. If we look at the map of the globe, and consider the relative space of its surface which is occupied by land and water, we must at once see, that if there be only an equal quantity of each, there is infinitely more than enough water to cover the land fifteen cubits high, above even the hills of the old world, which might be low. But in addition to this, the space of sea is not merely equal, but is much greater than the space of land.

The first convulsion of which I have spoken is that which made Britain an island, and threw up Mount Blanc and Chimborazo. After that convulsion another might have been caused by the sinking of Atlantis. This may have been caused by that which occasioned the destruction of Mahabali-pore. Another great change in all the islands and shores of the Mediterranean may have taken place when the opening was made at the straits of Gibraltar, and another great change may have taken place when the lakes Aral, Asoph, and Euxine, broke their banks, by which the flood described by Plato may have been first effected, and the Delta of Egypt and the shores of Italy left dry, after it had escaped at the straits. All those different catastrophes probably happened. Of their order, except with respect to the first, I give no opinion.

I think it not at all unlikely that when the Atlantis sunk, the level of the water of the Mediterranean may have been changed, in some way or other, which we cannot discover, though the sinking of the island would have a tendency to raise it. But since the building of Adria, Padua, &c., it seems certainly to have been changed. This is an indisputable fact, which it is of no use to deny. At the time that this happened, the passage which connected the Dead sea with the Red sea, shewn by Burchardt formerly to have existed, and the isthmus of Suez formerly covered with water, may have been both left dry. I shall in a future page give some reasons to prove, that Egypt was not peopled by tribes passing over the isthmus of Suez, but across the Red sea from some place near Mecca.

If ever the rock over which the water rushes at Niagara should suddenly g've way, no doubt a very sensible flood would be experienced in Ireland. In consequence of having a vastly greater space to expand its waters over, this flood, when compared with those in the Mediterranean, would be trifling. On the order of the floods of which I have spoken we must always remain ignorant; but it is probable, I think, that one of them, and perhaps the second spoken of by me, 2500 or 3000

---

years before Christ, caused the destruction of almost the whole of mankind; a few might be saved in ships, and it might happen that among these few might be the possessors of our system of letters. The distressing state in which they may have been left will account, without difficulty, for the loss of the learning which their fathers, as Bailly supposed, possessed. But all these matters are mere theories; of their truth we cannot be certain.

11. I have lately discovered a geological fact of a nature which bears strongly upon this subject. There is in Yorkshire, near the confluence of the rivers Ouse and Trent, within the angle which they make before they unite and form the river Humber, a tract of alluvial country of great riches and fertility, which has formerly been covered with oak and fir timber, the lower parts of which yet remain in the ground fixed as they grew. Sometimes whole trees are found lying on their sides. The firs are mostly a little bent by the weight of the superincumbent soil, but they yet retain their white colour. The oak is generally perfectly black. This country is now defended from the tides by banks maintained at a very great expense; but the fact to which I have alluded is this—the tides now rise at least six feet above the surface of the soil where the remains of these trees are yet found. From the appearance of the trees, it is probable, that after being long covered with water they have rotted off a little above ground, the tops have fallen, and most of them been floated away by the tides and floods, and the bottoms have been by degrees covered with alluvial soil as they are now found.

From this it is quite certain that a great change must have taken place in the relative levels of the land and ocean, because these trees could never have grown in a soil where they were daily flooded with the salt water. What I have stated with respect to the tides and the remains of the trees which I have seen, are facts which cannot be disputed, and I think they shew that a very *great* but *unsuspected* change has taken place, or is taking place, in the relative situations of the land and the sea. Every thing tends to shew, that the surface of the Mediterranean sea, with respect to its shores, has been lowered. The facts stated respecting the trees in Yorkshire PROVE that the Atlantic, with relation to the land of Britain, has been raised, or vice versâ, the land lowered. The district where these trees are found was drained, in the time of Charles II., by one Sir Cornelius Vermuyden, and there does not appear any reason to believe that the relative altitudes of the land and ocean have undergone any perceptible change since that time. Of course, in a country like this, the natives watch every thing relating to those altitudes with great anxiety. The relative levels of the land and tides have lately been ascertained by experienced engineers with very great care.

The bold shores on the east and south-east coast of Britain keep constantly yielding to the washing of the bases of their cliffs by the tides; but the rising within the last century of the large and valuable tract of land called Sunk island, at the mouth of the Humber, proves, that if any change be taking place in the relative altitude of the island and the ocean, the former is now rising, not sinking; but I do not think there is reason to believe that any change is taking place. The whole subject is one of very great curiosity and interest: I shall now leave it to the consideration of my reader, but I shall return to it again in the course of the following pages. For more information on subjects connected with the series of lakes, or the inland seas of Asia, the reader may consult, among the ancients, Strabo, Lib. i.; Pliny, Hist. Nat. Lib. ii. Cap. 90; and Diodorus Siculus: among the moderns, Pallas, Reise, durch Siberien, Book v.; Klaproth's Survey of the Country North of Caucasus; Mons. Choiseul Gouffier, Memoire de Institut. Royal de France, 1815; Dr. Clarke's Travels; and Muller's Univers. Hist. Eng. Trans. Vol. I. p. 33.

## CHAPTER II.

ADORATION OF THE VIRGIN AND CHILD.—CARMELITES ATTACHED TO THE VIRGIN. — VIRGIN OF THE SPHERE. — FESTIVAL OF THE VIRGIN. — GERMAN AND ITALIAN VIRGIN. — MANSIONS OF THE MOON.— MONTFAUCON.— MULTIMAMMIA. — ISIS AND THE MOON.— CELESTIAL VIRGIN OF DUPUIS. — KIRCHER.— JESUS BEN PANTHER.—LUNAR MANSIONS.

1. In the two following chapters I shall repeat, with some important additions, or shall collect into one view, what has been said in a variety of places in the foregoing work, respecting the Queen of Heaven, the Virgin Mary, and her son Iaw; to which I shall also add some observations respecting the famous God Bacchus.

In very ancient as well as modern times, the worship of a female, supposed to be a virgin, with an infant in her arms, has prevailed. This worship has not been confined to one particular place or country, but has spread to nearly every part of the habitable world. In all Romish countries to this day, the Virgin, with the infant Jesus Christ in her arms, is the favourite object of adoration; and it is, as it has been observed before, a decisive proof that the Christ, the good shepherd, the Saviour of the Romish church of Italy, is the same as the person of the same name in India; that he is, like him, described to be black, to be an Ethiopian. It seems that if a person wanted a fact to complete the proof of the identity of the person of Cristna and the Romish Jesus, he could not have invented any thing more striking than this, when all the other circumstances are considered. But though they were both black, I think they had both the name of Crish, or Christ, or Χρης̄ος, from a word in a very ancient language, (the parent both of the Greek and the Sanscrit,) having the meaning of *Benignus*, of which I shall say more hereafter. We will now try to find out who the celebrated virgin, the mother of this person, was.

The Virgin Mary, in most countries where the Roman faith prevails, is called the Queen of Heaven: this is the very epithet given by the ancients to the mother of Bacchus, who was said to be a virgin. The Rev. Dr. Stukeley writes, "Diodorus says Bacchus was born of Jupiter (mean- " ing the Supreme) and Ceres, or as others think, Proserpine."—" Both Ceres and Proserpine " were called Κορη, which is analogous to the Hebrew עלמה *virgo*, παρθενος, LXX., Isaiah vii. 14: " Behold a virgin shall conceive. It signifies eminently *the* virgin. Αθηναιοι Διονυσον τ Διος " και Κορης σεβεσιν. Arrian, Alex. II. The Egyptians called this same person Bacchus, or the " sun-deity, by the name of *Orus*, which is the same as the Greek word Κορος aspirated. The " heathen fables as oft confound Bacchus's mother and wife."

"·Ovid, Fasti iii., makes Libera, the name of Ariadne, Bacchus's pretended wife, whom Cicero, " de Nat. Deor., makes to be Proserpina, Bacchus's mother. The story of this woman being " deserted by a man, and espoused by a God, has somewhat so exceedingly like that passage, " Matt. i. 19, 20, of the blessed virgin's history, that we should wonder at it, did we not see the " parallelism infinite between the sacred and the profane history before us.

" — Ariadne was translated into heaven, as is said of the Virgin, and her nuptial garland was " turned into an heavenly crown: she was made queen of heaven."·

Testis siderese torta corona Deae. Propert. iii. 17.

" — There are many similitudes between the Virgin and the mother of Bacchus in all the old

" fables ; as for instance, Hyginus (Fab. 164) makes Adoneus or Adonis the son of Myrrha.
" Adonis is Bacchus beyond controversy."

> Ogygia me Bacchum vocat
> Osirin Egyptus putat
> Arabica gens Adoneum.     AUSON.

" Adonis is the Hebrew אדני *(Adni)* Adonai, which the Heathens learned from the Arabians—
" one of the sacred names of the Deity.   Mary or Miriam, St. Jerome interprets *Myrrha* MARIS :
" Mariamne is the same appellation of which Ariadne seems a corruption.   Orpheus calls the mo-
: ther[1] of Bacchus, Leucothea, a *sea Goddess.*

" — Nonnus in Dyonyg. calls Sirius star Mœra, Μαιρης.  Hesychius says, Μαιρα κυον το
" ασρον.   Our Sanford hence infers this star to mean Miriam, Moses's sister.   Vossius de Idolal.
" approves of it.   Μαιρα by metathesis is Μαρια."[2]

Thus we see that the Rev. and learned Gentleman, Dr. Stukeley, has clearly made out, that the
story of Mary, the queen of heaven, the mother of אדני *(Adni)* Adonis, *or the Lord,* as our book
always renders this word, with her translation to heaven, &c., was an *old story* long before Jesus
of Nazareth was born.   After this, Stukeley observes, that Ariadne, the queen of heaven, has upon
her head a crown of twelve stars.   This is the case of the queen of heaven in almost every church
on the continent.

2. In the service or liturgy of the Carmelites, which I bought in Dublin at the Carmelite monastery, the Virgin is called STELLA MARIS ; that is, in fact, the star of the sea—" Leucothea"—
Venus rising from the sea.

All monks were Carmelites till the fifth century.[3]  After that time, from different religious motives, new orders branched off from the old one, and became attached to new superstitions : but
the Carmelites always remained, and yet remain, attached in a peculiar manner to the Virgin Mary,
the Regina Stellarum.[4]  The Carmelites were the original monks, Ναζωραιοι, translated from

---

[1] Nurse.          [2] Stukeley, Pal. Sac. No. I. p. 34.          [3] Priestley, Hist. Cor. Vol. II. p. 403.

[4] I am of opinion that a certain class of persons, initiated into the higher mysteries of the ancients, were what are
called *Carmelites Therapeutæ* and *Esseniens,* or that they constituted a part of, or were formed out of, these sects, and
were what we now call *Freemasons.*  They were also called Chaldæi and Mathematici.  I think that the rite of circumcision was originally instituted for the characteristic mark of the fraternity or society.  I doubt its being a religious
community solely.  Abraham brought circumcision from Urr of the Chaldees.  When the Jewish tribe was declared a
priestly tribe it was circumcised, part of the secret rites were thrown open to all, probably the tribe refused any longer
to be excluded from them, and the rite no longer continued the secret symbol.  We read of three hundred and eighteen
servants trained in Abraham's own house.  On these persons, the Apostle, St. Barnabas, the companion of St. Paul, has
the following passage :
  " For the Scripture says, that Abraham circumcised three hundred and eighteen men of his house.  But what, there-
" fore, was the mystery that was made known to him ?  Mark the eighteen and next the three hundred.  For the
" numeral letters of *ten* and *eight* are I H, and these denote Jesus ; and because the cross was that by which we were
" to find grace, therefore he adds, *Three hundred :* the note of which is T *(the figure of his cross).*  Wherefore by two
" letters he signified Jesus, and by the third his cross.  He who has put the engrafted gift of his doctrine within us
" knows that I never taught to any one a more certain truth : but I trust ye are worthy of it."—Epist. Barnabas, Sect.
ix. ed. Wake.
  This epistle of St. Barnabas was formerly read in the Romish churches ; but the Protestants do not allow it to be
genuine.  One reason why Jones contends that it is spurious is, because it says that Abraham circumcised 318 men of
his family, which is not now in the text.  But the Hebrew word which Jones renders circumcised חניכיו *hnikiu,* in one
sense means initiated, and this justifies Barnabas.  In fact, this word *hnikiu* is our initiate.  (Jones on Canon, Pt. III.
ch. xli. p. 449.)  If what I suspect be true, viz. that circumcision was the mark or test of initiation, Barnabas the Apostle
might not understand the full import of the *Greek ;* but he cannot be supposed to have been ignorant of the *Hebrew,*

Meru and Tibet to Mount Carmel, or the mount of *the garden of God*, or *of the sun*, at the foot of Lebanon, or of the mountain of the moon. They were the original monks of Maia or Maria; the others were all offsets from the parent tree, or perhaps they were a species of heretics who arose from the original monkish religious system. This accounts for the Carmelites being, in a peculiar manner, attached to the adoration of the Virgin.

Isidore of Seville says, that the meaning of the word Mary is, One who begins to illuminate— *Maria illuminatrix*. He gives to this virgin, as her mother, a person called Anna, an allegorical name, by which the Romans meant the annual revolution of the sun, which they personified, and for whom they had a festival, under the name of *Anna Perenna*, at the beginning of the year. [1] The Hindoos have the same person as a Goddess under the name of Anna, or Unnu Poorna. [2] Poorna is evidently Perenna, or Poraua. There is extant, in Jones on the Canon, a gospel history called that of *James* or of *Mary*, in which her mother is called Anna, of whom I shall say more presently.

Dr. Pritchard says, " The beneficent form of Bhavani, termed Devi or Anna Purna, is doubtless, " as Sir W. Jones remarked, the Anna Perenna of the Romans." Again, " Anna Purna is, how- " ever, also the counterpart of the Egyptian Isis. She is figured as bent by the weight of her full " breasts, and reminds us of the statues of Isis Multimammia." Again, " Bhavani is invoked by " the name of Ma, as was Demeter among the Greeks by that of Maia." [3] In the passages where the Hebrew word מרים mrim of the Old Testament is translated by the Vulgate, it is rendered Maria, and the LXX. render it Μαριαμ. All this clearly proves that they are the same name. [4]

3. Though there can be no doubt, that the celestial virgin of the sphere was one original source whence the Madonna, Regina Cœli, Θεοτοκος—and Mater Dei, were derived, yet the Goddess Cybele was another. She was equally called the Queen of Heaven and the Mother of the Gods. As devotees now collect alms in the name of the Virgin, so did they in ancient times in the name of Cybele, in which they were protected by a law when begging was not otherwise allowed. The Galli now used in the churches of Italy were anciently used in the worship of Cybele. Our Lady-day, or the day of the blessed Virgin of the Roman Church, was heretofore dedicated to Cybele. " It was called Hilaria," says Macrobius, " on account of the joy occasioned by the arrival of " the equinox." Lampridius also says, that it was a festival dedicated to the Mother of the Gods. A Greek commentator on Dionysius cited by Demster, in his Antiquities, also states, that the Hilaria was a festival in honour of the Mother of the Gods. In the fourth century there existed a sect of Christians called Collyridians, who made offerings of cakes to the Virgin Mary as a Goddess and Queen of Heaven. [5]

The Collyridians are said, by Mr. Sayle, [6] to have come from Arabia. They worshiped the Virgin Mary for God, offering her a sort of twisted cake called collyris, whence the sect had its name. This notion of the divinity of the Virgin Mary was also believed by some persons at the Council of Nice, who said there were two Gods besides the Father, viz. Christ and the Virgin

---

because he was a Jew, and therefore must be supposed to understand the common powers of notation of the letters of his own language. He here makes the Hebrew T stand for 300, which, in my table, appears to stand for 400. The canons of criticism by which Jones pretends to try the genuineness of ancient books, can on no account be admitted.

[1] Dupuis, Vol. III. p. 47, 4to.
A very learned dissertation on the Anna of the Romans, with much very curious information, may be found in Nimrod, Vol. III. p. 47. See also Taylor's Calmet, Vol. IV. p. 68. For the history of *Anna*, the mother of Mary, and of *Joachim*, that is חי *ie*, חכם *hkm*, Jah the wise, Jones on the Canon, Vol. II. p. 145, may be consulted.

[2] Vide Ward's India.          [3] Anal. Egyp. Mythos. p 280.          [4] Exod. xv. 20.
[5] Jortin, Eccles. Rem. Vol. I. 332.          [6] Prem. Dis. to Koran, Sect. ii. p. 45.

Mary; and they were thence named Mariamites.[1]  Others imagined her to be exempt from humanity, and deified; which goes but little beyond the Popish superstition in calling her the Complement of the Trinity, as if it were imperfect without her.

It is very evident that the idea of Mary being the mother of God, and also God himself, in some way or other, arose from the Maia of India, the spouse of Brahme.  Maia was the female generative power, and, as such, the Deity, and the mother of Buddha, or Divine Wisdom or the Logos.  Thus she was the mother of Iao or of IHΣ or of Jesus, and still a part of the Deity.  She was also the רוח *ruh*, and thus it was that this word was feminine in the Hebrew or the Buddist book of Genesis.

4. Samuel and John the Baptist had the same person for their mothers as the Virgin Mary, viz. Anna, or at least persons of the same name, who all produced their sons in their extreme old age.  Samson's mother was delivered of her son in the same way, but her name is not given : but from the similarity in other respects it was probably the same.  All these ladies might very properly be called what, I have no doubt that they were called, PERENNAS or PER-ANNAS; having the same meaning as Per-vetustas.  But this Per-anna, or old year, seems nonsense.  I believe it secretly or mystically alluded to the MIGHTY year celebrated by Virgil, (see B. v. Ch. ii. Sect. 7,) and that it was the period of 608 years, to which it alluded.[2]

The 25th of March was a day of general festivity throughout the ancient Grecian and Roman world, and was called Hilaria.  The Phrygians kept the same holiday and worshiped Atys, the mother of the Gods, with similar rites.  Hence the appointment of this day, Lady-day, to the honour of the mother of Jesus, called by the Catholics, the mother of God.[3]  Here Atys is made a female.  Atys in the Persian means *fire.*  This must be Vesta.  Is it anagrammatically *ysta,* Latin ista ?

In the 15th verse of the third chapter of Genesis God says to the serpent, which had tempted Eve, " I will put enmity between thee and the woman, and between thy seed and her seed : IT " shall bruise thy head, and thou shalt bruise HIS heel."  Here the seed is called IT, and afterward HIS in the masculine gender.  But the Roman Church (as I have before shewn) translates this in the Vulgate IPSA *conteret caput tuum,* by which they cause the woman to bruise the serpent's head, and not, as the Protestants do, the seed of the woman to bruise it.  The Hebrew language having no neuter gender, therefore a *literal* translation must have either *he* or *she.*  Availing themselves of this equivocal or double meaning, they have made this passage serve as a justification of their adoration of the celestial virgin, which they found in Italy and other countries ; and which, of course, in compliance with their much abused traditionary practice, they adopted.

When I first examined this subject, I was of opinion that the adoption of the *ipsa* instead of the *ipse* was the effect of ignorance ; but since I considered the matter more deeply, I have been induced to believe that this rendering was the effect of profound learning, not of ignorance ; and that it was done in order to adopt secretly the adoration of the double principle.  The adoption of the word *ipsa* instead of *ipse* is of very great importance ; as, when combined with the reasoning which the reader has seen respecting the serpent's biting of the foot, and not the heel, of Cristna, it shews most clearly that the Mythos of the East cannot have been copied from that of the West.

In Dr. Géddes's Critical Remarks on this passage may be seen every thing of any consequence which has been said upon the question, whether the Hebrew ought to be rendered by *he* or *she ;* but I am quite certain that the result of unprejudiced examination must be, that it may be ren-

---

[1] Vide Beausobre, Hist. Manich., Vol. I p. 532.

[3] Israel Worsley's Enq. p. 13.

[2] Magnus ab integro sèclorum nascitur ordo.

dered either way. The two words היא *eia* and הוא *eua* Mr. Parkhurst[1] has very correctly shewn are convertible, and both of them have a masculine and also a feminine meaning.

5. In many churches as well as in many places in the streets of Mayence on the Rhine, the Virgin is seen having the child on one arm, and a branch of lilies, the lotus, in the hand of the other arm, standing with one foot upon the head of a serpent, which has a sprig of an apple-tree with an apple on it in its mouth, and its tail twisted about a globe partly enveloped in clouds; therefore evidently a celestial globe. Her other foot is placed in the inside of a crescent. Her head is surrounded with a glory of stars. Can any one doubt that this is the Regina Stellarum of the sphere? The branch of the apple-tree in the mouth of the serpent with the Virgin's foot upon its head, shews pretty clearly who this Virgin of the sphere was—*Ipsa conteret caput tuum.* The circumstance of the Virgin almost always having the lotus or lily,' the sacred plant both of Egypt and India, in her hand (or an angel has it and presents it to her) is very striking. It is found, Sir R. Ker Porter observes,[2] " in Egypt, Palestine, Persia, India, all over the East, and was of old in " the tabernacle and temple of the Israelites. It is also represented in all pictures of the saluta- " tion of Gabriel to the Virgin Mary; and, in fact, has been held in mysterious veneration by " people of all nations and times."

The worship of the *black* Virgin and Child probably came from the East. The *white* one is the Goddess Nurtia or Nortia of the Etruscans.[3] I saw in the palazzo Manfreni, at Venice, in a collec- tion of Etruscan antiquities, some small figures of the Virgin and Child in Bronze, evidently origi- nally from Egypt. In the Museum F. Gorii will be found a print of an Etruscan Virgin and Child; the Goddess Nurtia or Nortia, as he calls her.[4]

There can be no doubt, that the Virgin of the sphere, who treads on the head of the serpent, is the Virgin of the first book of Genesis. This is all explained by Mons. Dupuis.[5] In some of the spheres we see the Virgin with the lotus or lily, in others with ears of ripe corn in her hand. I apprehend the Virgin with the ripe corn was the Virgin of Taurus: and that the birth-place of this mythos will be found in a latitude where corn will be ripe in August or the beginning of September, and this will fix it to a latitude very far from Lower India or Upper Egypt; to about that latitude where May, or the month of Maia, the mother of the God Buddha, would be the leading spring month, in which all nature would be in its most beautiful attire, and this would be at least as high as latitude 45, or North of Samarkand.

The Abbé Pluche admits, what indeed is evident, that Virgo symbolizes the harvest season. But in the plains of Sennaar the harvest season is over several months before the sun passes into that sign.[6]

---

[1] Vide his Hebrew Grammar.          [2] Travels in Persia, VI. p. 628, 4to.

[3] The present church of St. Stephen at Bologna is formed from several Heathen temples which have stood together like those at Tivoli and Ancona. The centre one, of a circular form, has been a temple of Isis. On the side of the church is to be seen an ancient inscription in these words: Dominæ victrici Isidi.

[4] Tab. 4, Ant. Fran. Gorii, Nortia Tuscorum Dea. Summa religione à Volsiniensibus et Volaterranis culta. A statue of a female much covered with drapery, with a child in swaddling clothes in her arms. The head of the mother is broken off, and the complexion of the figures cannot be judged of from the print. She was called the Magna Dea by the Etruscans: on the arm of the mother is an inscription in Etruscan letters. See plates, fig. 17; also Pliny, Lib. xxxvi. Cap. vii.; Livy, Lib. vii.; etiam Festum Pompeium: Juvenalem, Sat. x. v. 74; and the treatise Donianas inscriptiones antiquas Francisci Gorii. Class. I. Num. 149, 150; Tertullian, Apologet. Cap. xxiv. Reinesius states, Class. I. Num. cxxxi., that an inscription was found in the foundation of the Church of S. Reparatæ at Florence in these words—*To the great Goddess Nortia.* See also Cicero, Lib. ii. de Officiis; Martianus Capella, Lib. de Nuptiis Philolog. Cap. ix.

[5] Tome III. p. 90, and his plate, No. 19. In this plate is described the whole horoscope of the birth of Jesus, &c.
[6] Drum. Zod. p. 95.

The Virgin's having generally the *lotus,* but sometimes an *ear of wheat* in her hand, arose from a very profound and mysterious doctrine—connected with the pollen of plants—of which I shall treat hereafter, as already intimated.

6. The signs of the Zodiac are not any of them remarkable for being connected with objects of an Indian nature. The twenty-eight Hindoo lunar mansions and the asterisms are almost all named after objects peculiarly Hindoo. This raises a strong presumption against the solar Zodiac being of Hindoo invention. If the solar Zodiac had been of Hindoo or African growth, the elephant and camel would have been found there. [1]

Mr. Maurice has observed, that the signs of the Zodiac cannot be of Egyptian origin because they are not adapted to the order in which the seasons succeed each other in Egypt. For instance, Virgo with ears of ripened corn in her hand evidently points to the season of harvest— such, in fact, it is when the sun enters into September; but the corn harvest in Egypt is in March. The same argument applies to Aquarius, which denotes the chilling cold rains of winter, when, in reality, the depth of winter is the season of pleasure in Egypt. [2] All the arguments of Mr. Maurice against Egypt being the birthplace of the Zodiacal signs apply with equal force against India. They must, in fact, have all come from a latitude far higher than Egypt, India, or even Chaldæa. Samarkand is the lowest that can be admitted. There being in these Zodiacs no sign of the elephant, the pride of the animal creation both in Africa and India, is a fact alone sufficient to shew that the Zodiac is not an invention of these countries.

Maia, the mother of Mercury, Mr. Davies says, [3] is the universal genius of nature, which discriminated all things, according to their various kinds or species: the same, perhaps, as the Meth of the Egyptians and the Μητις of the Orphic bards, which was of all kinds, and the author of all things—και Μητις πρωτος γενετωρ.

" Sir William Jones was told by a Cashmirian, that Maya herself is the mother of universal " nature, and of all the inferior gods. This exactly agrees with the import of the word among the " Geeks. Maia properly denotes a *grandmother* or *a great mother.*" Hesychius (Lex.) says, Μαια, πατρος και μητρος μητηρ. [4]

We have seen, I think, that it is beyond the possibility of doubt that Buddha and Mercury, sons of Maia, were the same person. This receives a very remarkable confirmation from the fact, that Mercury was always called by the Gentiles the Logos—" The *word* that in the beginning was " God, and that also was a God.". [5] But this Logos we have also shewn to be the *Divine Wisdom,* and he was, according to the Pagan Amelius, the Creator. He says, " And this plainly was " the Λογος by whom all things were made, [6] he being himself eternal, as Heraclitus would say : " and by Jove the same whom the barbarian affirms to have been in the place and dignity of a " principal, and to be with God, and to be God, by whom all things were made, and in whom " every thing that was made has its life and being : who, descending into body, and putting on " flesh, took the appearance of a man, though even then he gave proof of the majesty of his na- " ture : nay, after his dissolution, he was deified again." If this do not prove the identity of Buddha and the Romish Jesus nothing can do it.

Sommona Codom I consider to be admitted as one of the names of Buddha. M. La Loubère says, " His mother, whose name is found in some of their Balie books, was called, as they say, " Maha Maria, which seems to signify the *great Mary,* for *Maha* signifies *great.* But it is found

---

[1] Maur. Ant. Hind. Vol. VII. p. 604.
[3] Apud Whiter, Etym. Univ. p. 103.
[4] R. Taylor, Dieg. pp. 183—185.

[2] Ind. Ant. Vol. I. p. 29.
[4] Fab. Pag. Idol. B. iv. Ch. v. p. 333.
[6] Ibid.

" written *Mania*, as often as Maria. ...... This ceases not to give attention to the missionaries,
" and has, perhaps, given occasion to the Siamese to believe that Jesus being the Son of Mary was
" brother to Sommono-Codom, AND THAT HAVING BEEN CRUCIFIED, he was that wicked brother
" whom they give to Sommono-Codom, under the name of *Thevetat*, and whom they report to be
" punished in hell, with a punishment which PARTICIPATES SOMETHING OF THE CROSS. The
" father of Sommona-Codom was, according to this same Balie book, a king of *Teve-Lanca*, that
" is to say, a king of the famous Ceylon."[1] Cyril of Alexandria calls the Egyptian Mercury
Teutat.[2] Now *Tat* has been shewn to be one of the names of Buddha; and Teve-Lanca is evidently the same as Deve-Lanca, which has been called island Lanca—in the same manner as the
island in the West was called *I* or *Ii*, which it is said means island; but it means also *holy*, or is
the name of God. From all this it follows pretty clearly, that Deve-Lanca, or Teve-Lanca, means
*holy Lanca*, or *Seren-*DIVE, and that *Teve-Tat* means *holy*, or God or Divus Tat : but *Tat* is
Buddha; and, of course, as Tat is the son of Mary, Buddha is the son of Mary. But *Tat*, or
*Deve-Tat*, or *Theve-Tat*, was crucified ! !

The Mercury of Egypt, Teut-tat, is the same as the Gothic Thiod-tat, or, query, Thiod-ad ?[3]
Here we come, perhaps, at the origin of Θεος. Jayadeva describes Buddha as bathing in blood,
or sacrificing his life to wash away the offences of mankind, and thereby to make them partakers
of the kingdom of heaven. On this the author of the Cambridge Key[4] says, " Can a Christian
" doubt that this Buddha was the type of the Saviour of the world ?" This Buddha the Cantab.
supposes to have been Enoch.

The circumstance of Maria being called Mania is worthy of observation. In the old language,
without vowels, MN means moon. Is this one of the reasons why Mary is always represented
with a moon in some way or other—generally standing on it ? If Maria be the same as Maia, and
is the female generative power, we see why she is always connected with the moon. This Mary
is found in the kingdom of *Sion* or Siam in the city of Judia.[5] The mother of the gods was
called Ma in the Phrygian dialect.[6] In the Hebrew and Arabic languages we have the word
Maria מריא *mria*, which means a female beeve, and also a wild dove.[7] The word in the Hebrew
is attended with much difficulty. I suspect it is in some way mystical, and not understood.

Maia the the mother of Mercury was the daughter of Atlas. Virgil calls her Maia or Maja.[8]
Hesiod calls her Μαιη.

$$\text{Ζηνι δ' αρ Ατλαντις Μαιη τεκε κυδιμον Ερμην.}$$

But Pausanias calls her Maera.

$$\text{Μαιρας γυναικος τε Τεγεατε Θυγατερα δε Ατλαντος φασιν ειναι την Μαιραν.}[9]$$

*Wen* is acknowledged to belong to the Celtic terms for a woman, from which the Latin *Venus* is
derived.[10] Then Alma Venus might mean *the mother*, the mother Venus, the Deity-mother woman,
or the female great Deity. This Alma might mean virgin, because the mother Goddess, though a
mother, was always held to be a virgin. From these abstruse, misunderstood doctrines, might
arise the idea of some of the Christian heretics, that Jesus was taken from the side of his mother.

---

1 Part iii. p. 136.    2 In Julian. Vide Anc. Univer. Hist. VI. p. 50; Jameson's Herm. Scyth. p. 130.
3 Hermes Scythicus, Origin of Greeks, p. 131; Univers. Hist. Vol. VI. p. 33.    4 Vol. I. p. 118.
5 La Loubère, pp. 6, 7.    6 Sir William Jones, Asiat. Res. Vol. III. p. 14. 4to.
7 Vide Bochart's Opera, Vol. II. p. 283.    8 Æn. VIII. v. 138.
9 Arcadic. Cap. xlviii. p. 698; Jameson's Hermes Scyth. p. 130.
10 Whiter, Etymol. Univ. p. 757; Davies on the Druids, p. 445.

7. In the fourth plate of the first volume of Montfaucon's Antiquity Explained may be seen several exemplars of the Mother of the Gods. She is called Cybele, and she is on the same monument often joined with Atys. But her most remarkable name is that of Suria. She is loaded in some figures with paps, and on the base of one statue[1] is the word *Suriæ*. On another, *Mater Deor. Mater Suriæ*. This figure is sitting, and is crowned with a mitre of the Romish church, and in appearance is altogether the very picture of the Pope, when seated in his chair, giving his benediction; with the exception that he has not the caduceus, the sistrum, and the emblematic animals with which she is covered. She is evidently the same as Diana or the Multi-mammia, many figures of which may be seen in Montfaucon's 46th plate. But the most remarkable figure is in plate 47, where the text describes her as black, but with long hair, therefore not a Negress. On one of the other figures are the words ΦΥϹΙϹ ΠΑΝΑΙΟΛΟϹ ΠΑΝΤ ΜΗΤ, and on another, Φυϲιϲ παναιολοϲ. None of these figures seem to be of very great antiquity. I have seen many of them in Rome, but it has happened that all which I recollect to have seen have had white drapery, —although the face, hands, and feet, were black. I suspect that this Syrian goddess, or Dea Suriæ, or Syriæ, is of a far more *eastern* origin; that she is closely connected with the Buddhist Syria; that she is a native of Syra-stra, or Syra-strene.[2] In Fig. 11 of the thirtieth plate to the Supplement to Montfaucon's Antiquity Explained, is a tablet, on which are described *three* females. It was found at Metz. The inscription is, *In honorem Domús Divinæ* DIS MAIRABUS *Vicani Vici Pacis: In honour of the divine house, to the Goddesses Mairæ, they of the street of peace.* Montfaucon thinks them deities of the country. These are the three Marys of the Christians, before Christ was born; of course one of them must have been the Gallic *Virgo paritura.* A plate of this and of several other German triads may be seen in the preface to Maurice's Ind. Ant.[3] All the three women who attended Jesus at his death were called Marys,—Mary, the mother of Jesus, Mary, the mother of James, and Mary Salome.[4] In Sanval's History of the Antiquities of Paris, the virgin is called *étoile éclatante de la mer.* He says that St. Denis was the first bishop of Paris: he came thither in the time of the emperor Decius.

8. On a first examination the Goddess Isis will be generallly taken to be the moon, and as such *it* will appear to receive the adoration of its votaries. Osiris, the sun, is said to be her spouse, and also her brother: and Horus, called the πρωτογονος θεος, or first-born, is said to be their son. The name Horus is derived from the Hebrew or Phœnician word אור *aur,* lux, or light: but yet there are some circumstances unaccountable upon this supposition, except the moon was merely adored as an emblem of the Supreme Being. On the front of the temple of Isis at Sais, under the synonyme of Minerva, according to Plutarch, was the following description of her:

$$\text{Ισις εγω ειμι παν}\textcent\text{ο γεγονος, και ον και}$$
$$\text{εσομενον, και το εμον πεπλον}$$
$$\text{ɵδεις των ɵνη}$$
$$\text{ɵων απε}$$
$$\text{καλυ}$$
$$\text{ψε}$$
$$\text{ν.}$$

---

[1] Fig. 3.

[2] Vide my plates, fig. 18, taken from a figure of the Goddess Multimammia, in Montfaucon's 47th plate, cited above.

[3] Vol. V., ed. 8vo.                                   [4] Calmet, Dict. in voce Salome.

I *Isis* am all that has
been, that is or shall
be; no mortal Man
hath ever
me un-
vei-
le-
d.

This cannot apply to the moon. The Indian deity is described to be, All that is, everywhere, always. On many words closely connected with this topic, almost every page of Sir William Drummond's Essay on a Punic Inscription may be consulted.

I am persuaded that there is no subject on which more mistakes have been made than on that of the Goddess Isis, both by ancients and moderns. She has constantly been taken for the moon, which in many countries was masculine. But she is constantly declared to be the same as Ceres, Proserpine, Juno, Venus, and all the other Goddesses; therefore they must all be the moon. This is out of the question. The case I believe to be this;—the planet called the *moon* was dedicated to her in judicial astrology, the same as a planet was dedicated to Venus or Mars. But Venus and Mars were not those planets themselves, though those planets were sacred to them. The inscription in front of her temple at Sais at once proves that she cannot be the moon; it is totally inapplicable to that planet. The mistake of the ancients is only one proof among hundreds, that they had lost the knowledge of the principles of their mythology, or that we do not understand it. I am of opinion that much of the confusion in the ancient systems arose from the neglect, or the ignorance, of the distinction between religion and judicial astrology.

Apuleius makes Isis say, I am nature, the parent of all things, the sovereign of the elements, the primary progeny of time, the most exalted of the deities, the first of the heavenly Gods and Goddesses; whose single deity the whole world venerates in many forms, with various rites, and various names. The Egyptians worship me with proper ceremonies, and call me by my true name, Queen Isis.[2] Isis is called Myrionymus, or Goddess with 10,000 names.[3] Herodotus[4] says, that the Persian Mithra was Venus.

No person who has considered well the character of the temples in India and Egypt, can help being convinced of the identity of their character, and of their being the production of the same race of people; and this race evidently Ethiopian. The Sphinxes have all Ethiopian faces. The bust of Memnon in the British museum is evidently Ethiopian. The worship of the Mother and Child is seen in all parts of the Egyptian religion. It prevails everywhere. It is the worship of Isis and the infant Orus or Osiris. It is the religious rite which was so often prohibited at Rome, but which prevailed in spite of all opposition, as we find from the remaining ruins of its temples. It was perhaps from this country, Egypt, that the worship of the black virgin and child came into Italy, where it still prevails. It was the worship of the mother of the God Iaw, the Saviour; Bacchus in Greece, Adonis in Syria, Cristna in India; coming into Italy through the medium of the two Ethiopias, she was, as the Ethiopians were, *black*, and such she still remains.

Dr. Shuckford[5] has the following curious passage: "We have several representations in the "draughts of the same learned antiquary *(Montfaucon)*, which are said to be Isis, holding or

[1] Basnage, p. 217; Maurice, Ind. Ant. Vol. IV. pp. 682—684.     [2] Metamorph. Lib. xi., Payne Knight, p. 67.
[3] Squire's Plutarch, de Iside et Osir. cap. liii. p. 74.     [4] Clio. Sect. cxxxi.
[5] Con. Book viii. p. 311.

" giving suck to the boy Orus; but it should be remarked, that Orus was not represented by the
" figure of a new-born child: for Plutarch expressly tells us, that a new-born child was the
" Egyptian picture of the sun's rising."[1]    Plutarch and Montfaucon were both right.   Orus
was the sun, and the infant child was the picture of the sun, in his infancy or birth, immediately after the winter solstice—when he began to increase.  Orus, I repeat, is nothing but the
Hebrew word אור aur, lux, light — the very light so often spoken of by St. John, in the first
chapter of his gospel.  Plutarch[2] says, that Osiris means a benevolent and beneficent power, as
does likewise his other name OMPHIS.  In a former book I have taken much pains to discover the
meaning of Omphi.  After all, is it any thing but the OM, with the Coptic emphatic article *Pi* ?

There is no more reason for calling Isis the moon, than the earth.  She was called by all the
following names : Minerva, Venus, Juno, Proserpina, Ceres, Diana, Rhea seu Tellus, Pessinuncia,
Rhamnusia, Bellona, Hecate, Luna, PolymorphusDæmon.[3] But most of these have been shewn to be
in fact all one—the Sun.  Isis, therefore, can be nothing but the sun, or the being whose residence
was the sun.  This being we have seen was both masculine and feminine:  I therefore conclude that Isis was no other than the first cause in its feminine character, as Osiris was the first
cause in the masculine.  The inscriptions cited above, upon the temples of Isis, completely
negative the idea of her being the moon.  From Pausanias[4] we learn that the most ancient statue
of Ceres amongst the Phigalenses was black; and in chap. vi., that at a place called Melangea, in
Arcadia, was a Venus who was black, the reason for which, as given by him, evidently shews that
it was unknown.  At Athens, Minerva Aglaurus, daughter of Cecrops, was *black*, according to
Ovid, in his Metamorphoses.[5]  Jerom observed, that " Juno has her priestesses devoted to one
" husband, Vesta her perpetual virgins, and other idols their priests, also under the vows of
" chastity."[6]  The Latin *Diana* is the contract of *Diva Jana.*[7]  Gale says they styled the moon
" Urania, Juno, Jana, Diana, Venus, &c.; and as the sun was called Jupiter, from יה *(ie,) ja,*
" πατηρ, and Janus from יה *(ie) Jah, the proper name of God ;*[8] so Juno is referred to the moon,
" and comes from יה *(ie) Jah,* the proper name of God, as *Jacchus* from יה *(ie) ja*-chus.  Amongst
" the ancient Romans Jana and Juno were the same."[9]  That the moon was the emblem of the
passive generative power cannot be denied, but this was merely astrological, not religious.  She
was not considered the passive power itself, as the sun was himself considered the active power,—
but merely as the planets were considered:  for though the planet was called Jupiter, as I have
before observed, that *planet* was not considered Lord of heaven, the Great Creator.

Some years ago I was informed, by a friend, since deceased, that he had seen a church (I think)
in the Netherlands, dedicated to the Black Virgin, au Vierge Noire.  I have no doubt of the fact,
though I have forgotten the place.  Here we have the black Venus and Ceres.  To make the
thing complete, we want nothing but a church dedicated to the Black Saviour ; and if we cannot
shew this, there is scarcely a church in Italy where a black bambino may not be seen, which
comes very near it.  If Pausanias had told us that the *infant* Jupiter[10] which he found in Arcadia
had been *black*, we should have had all we required; for he had before told us,[11] that Jupiter had
the title of Saviour, and Statius tells us he was black.[12]

*Heres* signifies the sun, but in the Arabic the meaning of the radical word is *to preserve,* and of

---

[1] Lib. de Iside et Osiride, p. 355.                     [2] De Iside et Osiride, Sect. xlii., Squire.
[3] Kircher, Œd. Egypt. Tom. I. p. 188.     [4] Book viii. ch. v. and ch. xlii.        [5] Nimrod, Vol. III. p. 151.
[6] Priestley, Hist. Cor. Vol. II. p. 386.         [7] Voss. de Idolat. Lib. ii. cap. xxv.         [8] Ib. xxvi.
[9] Clarke's Travels, Vol. II. p. 317. ed. 4to.        [10] Book viii. ch. xxxi.        [11] Book ii. ch. xx.
[12] Asiat. Res. Vol. V. p. 299, ed. 4to.   Vide my plates, fig. 20, from Montfaucon.

*haris*, guardian, *preserver*.[1] This is the name of the Messiah Cyrus, and also of Ceres, for it is only a different way of pronouncing the same word, aspirated or not, *and this makes out a Ceres or Heres of both the masculine and feminine genders*. All this is easily accounted for, on the androgynous principle. Hara-Hara is a name of Maha-Deva, which is *Great God; Heri* means Saviour. When people are in great distress they call on Maha-Deva by the name of Hara-Hara.[2] In Greek, Αμμα *Amma* means at once Mother and Great Mother of all the Earth. Ceres is called Alma Ceres, and among the Trœzenians, *Amœa*.[3] The generative principle is considered to have existed before light, and to be the mother of both gods and men, as the generative source of all things. In this character she is the black Venus of Orpheus,[4] and the black Maia or Maria of Italy, the Regina Cœli, Regina Stellarum, &c. " From the God Maius of the Etruscans, and " his wife Maia, the month of May received its denomination : and at its commencement, when the " sun entered into Taurus, were celebrated in their honour those phallic mysteries, of which the " now almost obsolete May-games are a transcript and a relic."[5] Jupiter, Bacchus, Hercules, Apollo, Æsculapius, had each the appellation of Saviour. They are all indeed the same person— Jehovah. Stukeley[6] allows that the thyrsus of Bacchus is only the rod of Aaron and Moses, called הרזה pinus.[7]

9. M. Dupuis says, the celestial sign of the Virgin and Child was in existence several thousand years before the birth of Christ. The constellation of the celestial Virgin by its ascension above the horizon presided at the birth of the God Sol, or light, and seemed to produce him from her side. Here is the origin of Jesus born from the side of his mother. The Magi, as well as the priests of Egypt, celebrated the birth of the God Sol, or Light, or Day, incarnate in the womb of a virgin, which had produced him without ceasing to be a virgin, and without connexion with man. This was he of whom all the prophets and mystagogues prophesied, saying, "A virgin shall " conceive, and bear a son" (and his name shall be Om-nu-al, Om our God). One may see in the sphere the image of the infant god Day, in the arms of the constellation under which he was born, and all the images of the virgin offered to the veneration of the people represent her, as in the sphere, nursing a mystical infant, who would destroy evil, confound the prince of darkness, regenerate nature, and rule over the universe. On the front of the temple of Isis at Sais was this inscription, below that which I have given above : " The fruit which I have brought forth is the " sun." This Isis, Plutarch says, is the chaste Minerva, who, without fearing to lose her title of virgin, says she is the mother of the sun.[8] This is the same virgin of the constellations whom, Eratosthenes says, the learned of Alexandria call Ceres or Isis, who opened the year and presided at the birth of the god Day. It was in honour of this same virgin, (from whom the Sun emanated, and by whom the god Day or Light was nursed,) that, at Sais, the famous feast of lights was celebrated, and from which our Candlemas, or our feast of the lights of the purification, was taken. Ceres was always called the Holy Virgin.[9]

The Christians have a feast called the Assumption of the Blessed Virgin. In one of the ancient Gospel histories an account is given of the assumption of Mary into heaven, in memory of which event this feast was kept. On this feast M. Dupuis says, " About the eighth month, when the " sun is in his greatest strength, and enters into the eighth sign, the celestial virgin appears to " be absorbed in his fires, and she disappears in the midst of the rays and glory of her son." The Roman calendar of Columella marks at this epoch the death or disappearance of the virgin. The

---

[1] Trans. Asiat. Soc. Vol. II. p. 313.  [2] Asiat. Res. Vol. V. p. 137.  [3] Whiter, Etym. Univ. p. 107.
[4] Orph. Hymn. lxxxiii. 5, ii. 1, 2; Faber, Pag. Idol. Vol. III. p. 49.  [5] Fab. Pag. Idol. Book iv. ch. v. p. 397.
[6] Pal. Sac. I. p. 27.  [7] Ib. p. 28.  [8] Plutarch, de Iside, p. 354; Procl. in Tim. p. 30.
[9] Dupuis, Vol. III. pp. 40, &c , 4to.

sun, it says, passes into the Virgin the 13th before the kalends of September. The Christians place here the assumption, or reunion of the Virgin to her Son. This used to be called the feast of the passage of the Virgin. At the end of three weeks, the birth of the Virgin Mary is fixed. In the ancient Roman Calendar the assumption of the virgin Astrea, or her reunion to her son, took place at the same time as the assumption of the Virgin Mary, and her birth or her disengagement from the solar rays at the same time with the birth of Mary.[1] How is it possible to believe that these extraordinary coincidences are the effect of accident?[2] Every particular necessary to constitute actual identity is found in the two systems, which the reader will find explained at much greater length by M. Dupuis. As the Christians celebrated the decease or assumption of the celestial virgin into heaven, called by them the Virgin Mary, so also they did her impregnation or annunciation; that is, the information communicated to her that she should become pregnant by the holy ghost. " The Pamylia were on the 25th of the month Phamenoth, and on the new moon " of that month the ancient Egyptians celebrated the entrance of Osiris into the moon," or Isis. This, " Plutarch says,[3] is the beginning of the spring......' The moon is impregnated by the " sun.' Nine months after, at the winter solstice, Harpocrates is born.' It is no wonder, there- " fore, that Dupuis[4] compares the Pamylia, a word which in Coptic, according to Jablonski,[5] " means ' *annunciation*,' to the annunciation of the Blessed Virgin, which is marked in our " calendars on the 25th of March, four days after the vernal equinox, and nine months before the birth of Christ."[6]

The identity of the Holy Virgin of the Christians and of that of the Gentiles had been observed before M. Dupuis's time. Albert the Great says,[7] that the sign of the celestial virgin rises above the horizon at the moment in which we fix the birth of the Lord Jesus Christ.—All the mysteries of his divine incarnation, and all the secrets of his miraculous life, from his conception even to his ascension, are traced in the constellations, and figured in the stars which announced them. For a more detailed proof of the assertion of Albert, the reader may consult Dupuis.[8] Bochart[9] says, that Leo X. gave the Virgin Mary the title of Goddess. Pelloutier,[10] as noticed before,[11] has observed, that more than a hundred years before the Christian æra, in the territory of Chartres, among the Gauls, honours were paid to the virgin (VIRGINI PARITURÆ) who was about to give birth to the God of Light. That this was really the Buddhist worship, I have no doubt. The Virgin was the beautiful Maya, the mother of Buddha—the Budwas found in Wales, as noticed in my Celtic Druids.[12]

Adonis, the Syrian God, was the son of Myrrha.[13] This Myrrha was feigned to be changed into a tree of the same name with it, consecrated by the Eastern nations to the sun.[14] This was what was offered by the Magi to Christ at his birth. The trifling, but still striking, coincidences between the worship of the god Sol and the stories of Jesus are innumerable.[15]

Kircher the Jesuit gives an astrological[16] account of the seven planets, of the twelve signs of

---

[1] On the 8th of September in our calendars What can have induced our priests to retain this figment of Heathenism I do not know, and do not think it worth the trouble of inquiring.

[2] Dupuis, Vol. III. p. 48, 4to.     [3] De Iside, cap. xliii.     [4] Tom. I. pp. 375—409, ed. 4to.

[5] Lib. v. cap. vii. sect. v.     [6] Mr. Carlile's Republican, Vol. XII. No. xii. p. 371.     [7] Lib. de Univers.

[8] Vol. III. p. 47, and notes, p. 318, ed. 4to.     [9] Against Veron. p. 815.

[10] Hist. des Celtes, liv. v. p. 15; Dupuis, Vol. III. p. 51.     [11] In Book v. ch. ii. sect. 2.

[12] Ch. v. sect. viii. and xxxvii.     [13] Dupuis, Vol II p. 157, ed. 4to.

[14] Vide Kircher, Œd. Tom. II. Part ii. p. 206.     [15] Dupuis, Vol. II. p. 272, notes, ed. 4to.

[16] The whole of this part of Kircher's work is a development of the judicial astrology of the Egyptians, the Arabians, and the Hebrews, which he shews to have been common to them all.

the Zodiac, of the thirty-six decans into which the twelve signs were divided, and *De* 48 *Asteris-*
*mis, sive mansionibus Deorum* αντιτεχνων : in the latter of which he has the words, *In medio*
*autem horum numinum, Mithram, quem et* Μεσιτην, *hoc est Mediatorem, ponebant, id est, Solem.*
He afterwards has the following heading to a chapter, p. 200: *Dispositio Iconismorum, quâ*
*Egyptii ex mente Avenaris, singulorum signorum dodecutemoria, in tres facies subdiviserunt, singu-*
*lisque faciebus appropriatas imagines attribuerunt ;* in which is this passage :

" 5. Intra Virginis et Libræ mansiones ascendunt aspis magna, quæ et Agathodæmon Ophionius
" dicitur, una cum cratere vini, teste Avenar. Tametsi Indorum astrologi hoc loco arborem
" ponant magnam, in cujus ramis Canis et Ibis existant. Sed audiamus verba authoris : *Ascendit-*
" *que* [1] *ibi arbor magna, in cujus ramis Canis et Ciconia, quæ et Ibis dicitur, et à Philostorgiâ ap-*
" *pellatur Hebræis Rachama* רהכמה *rhkme.* Nihilque hoc aliud, quam stationem Mercurialium
" Numinum indigitabant. Dicunt præterea Ægyptii apud Avenarem, hoc loco poni virginem pul-
" chram, capillorum longitudine spectabilem, duas in manu spicas habentem ; sedet autem in throno,
" et puerum lactat parvulum, nutritque ipsum summâ diligentiâ. Verum cum verba Avenar con-
" sideratione dignissima sint, ea hîc adduco : [2] *In prima, inquit facie virginis, ascendit virgo pul-*
" *chra, longis capillis et duas in manu spicas continet, sedetque supra sedem, et nutrit puerum adhuc*
" *parvulum, et lactat eum, et cibat eum.* Expressiùs multò Albumazar ea in suo in astrologiam
" introductorio describit, quæ verba allegat Stefflerus in Sphæra Procli ; ita autem disserit : *Oritur*
" *in primo virginis decano puella, Arabicè dicta* [3] *Aderenosa, id est, virgo munda, virgo immaculata,*
" *corpore decora, vultu venusta, habitu modesta, crine prolixo, manu duas aristas tenens, supra*
" *solium aulæatum residens, puerum nutriens, ac jure pascens, in loco, cui nomen Hebræa, puerum*
" *dico à quibusdam nationibus nominatum Iesum, significantibus Issa, quem et Græcè Christum*
" *dicunt.* Hæc Albumazar. Ex his manifestè patet, Salvatorem nostrum ex illibata Virgine
" natum indigitari. Oritur ergo hæc virgo IKSUM pascens. Pudeat hic protervos Hebræos, dum
" virginem matrem renuunt, cum tantis ætatibus, tot ante secula Gentiles ista præviderint. Quod
" si Verpus dicat : *Non dicunt hi ipsam virginem pueri illius matrem, sed tantum jure ipsum pas-*
" *centem :* erubescat infelix, quia quæ jure ipsum pascet, non nisi mater est. Simile quid legitur
" apud Sybillam Europæam : *Veniet montes et colles transiliens, et in paupertate regnans cum silentio*
" *dominandi è Virginis vase exiliet.* Ponitur quoque hoc eodem loco ab Ægyptiis figura hominis
" Ταυρομορφθ, id est, figuræ Taurinæ. Ita Avenar." [4]

11. Mr. Faber says, Jesus was not called originally Jesus Christ, but Jescua Hammassiah.
Jescua is the same as Joshua and Jesus, and means Saviour ; and Ham is evidently the Om of
India, (the Ammon,) and Messiah is the *anointed.* It will then be, *The Saviour Om the anointed ;*
precisely as Isaiah had literally foretold : or, reading in the Hebrew mode, *The anointed Om the*
*Saviour.* This was the name of Jesus of Bethlehem. The name of Jesus also was JESUS BEN
PANTHER. Jesus was a very common name with the Jews. Stukeley observes, that the patro-
nymic of Jesus Christ was Panther ; and that Panthers were the nurses and bringers up of
Bacchus ; and adds, " 'Tis remarkable that Panther was the sirname of Joseph's family, our Lord's
" foster-father. Thus the Midrashkoheleth, or gloss, upon Ecclesiastes : ' It happened that a

---

[1] Hebrew text omitted.  [2] Hebrew omitted.  [3] Corruptè.
[4] Kircher, Œdip. Ægypt. Tom. III. cap. v. p. 203. For more particulars upon this subject my reader may consult
Drummond's Œdip. Jud. p. 277 ; also p. 318 of Dupuis' notes, Vol. III. ed. 4to. The Jesuit Riccioli calls this virgin
of the Sphere *Virgo Dei para.* Dupuis, Vol. III. pp. 2, 52, ed. 4to. She had the name of Ceres, whom Hesychius
calls the Holy Virgin. Ibid. Avecenna calls her Isis, the mother of the young Horus, who died and rose from the
dead. Ibid.

" ' serpent bit R. Eleasar ben Damah, and James, a man of the village Secania, came to heal him
" ' in the name of Jesus ben Panther.' This is likewise in the book called Abodazara, where the
" comment upon it says, *This James was a disciple of Jesus the Nazarene.*"

Here, in this accidental notice of Jesus, by these two Jewish works, is a direct and unexceptionable proof of his existence.; it is unexceptionable, because, if it be not the evidence of unwilling
witnesses, it is the evidence of disinterested ones. On this I shall have occasion to say more
hereafter. No one will dispute the piety of Dr. Stukeley. The similarity of the circumstances
related of Jesus and Bacchus could not be denied, and therefore he accounts for it by supposing
that God had revealed to the Heathen part of what was to happen in future. This may be satisfactory to some persons, as it was no doubt to the Doctor. The accidental manner in which, the
assertion is made, that the father of Jesus was called Panther, removes the possibility of accounting for it by attributing it to the malice of the Jews. In a former chapter it has been proved that
Bacchus was mistaken by the Romish priests for Jesus. Here the reader sees that the pious Dr.
Stukeley has proved, as might be expected, that the mother of Bacchus is the same person as the
mother of Jesus, viz. Mary. And as the persons who brought up Jesus were called Panthers, the
name of an animal, so Bacchus was brought up by the same kind of animal, a panther. When
the reader reflects that the whole Roman Christian doctrine is founded, as the Roman Church
admits, on tradition, he will have no difficulty in accounting for the similarity of the systems.
The circumstance of Joseph's family name being supposed to be Panther, is remarkably confirmed
by Epiphanius,[1] who says, that Joseph was the brother of Cleophas, the son of James, sirnamed
Panther. Thus we have the fact both from Jewish and Christian authorities.[2] It is very clear
that Bacchus's Panther must have been copied from that of Jesus or $IH\Sigma$, or that of Jesus from
Bacchus's. I leave the matter with my reader.

The worship of the Virgin was in no sense applicable to Mary the wife of Joseph. If this
worship had been originally derived from her, or instituted in her honour, she would not have
been called a virgin as a distinguishing mark of honour; for she was no more a virgin than any
other woman who had a large family: for such a family, after the birth of Jesus, it cannot be denied
that, according to the Gospel accounts, she had. Therefore why, more than other women, should
she be called a virgin? The truth is, that the worship of the virgin and child, which we find in
all Romish countries, was nothing more than a remnant of the worship of Isis and the god Horus
—the Virgin of the celestial sphere, to whom the epithet virgin, though a mother, was without
absurdity applied.

I know very well what the devotees have said to conceal the fact of the Virgin's family, but it
is all answered at once by the observation, that if James, &c., were the children of Joseph by a
former wife, they were not brothers of Jesus, but half-brothers. They are totally different things.
But what folly there is in all this! Is there any thing wrong in a married woman having a family?

12. It is well known that almost all the oriental nations, the Hindoos, the Persians, the Syrians,
the Arabians, the Egyptians, the Copts, and, I believe, the Jews in their astrology, had a Lunar
Zodiac divided into 28 parts, allusive to the days in the moon's period—called the mansions of the
moon. Over each of these divisions a genius or dæmon presided. There can be no doubt that it
was the same system in all these nations, and probably the doctrines held respecting it may have
been originally the same in each of them, although it may not be possible to demonstrate this
by a rigorous proof: but for the sake of argument I shall consider them the same. The access to

---

[1] Hæres. 78, Antidic. S. vii.       [2] See Jones on the Canon, Vol. II. p. 137.

these mansions was supposed to be by the milky way, as it was called by the Greeks and Romans, who, not understanding it, as usual, invented a story of their own to account for it.[1]

But the original oriental name was the *strawey way*—via straminis seu paleæ—and was thus called from an astronomical allegory of the celestial virgin, who, fleeing from the evil principle Typhon, let fall some of the ears of corn, or corn in the straw, which she carried in one of her hands. This celestial virgin was feigned to be a mother: she is represented in the Indian Zodiac of Sir William Jones with ears of corn in one hand, and the lotus in the other: in Kircher's Zodiac of Hermes, she has corn in both hands. In other planispheres of the Egyptian priests she carries ears of corn in one hand, and the infant Horus in the other. In Roman Catholic countries, she is generally represented with the child in one hand, and the lotus or lily in the other. This milky way is placed immediately under that degree of North latitude, which is called the tropic of Cancer, and the two tropics of Cancer and Capricorn have been called by the astrologers the Gates of Heaven or the Sun;[2] at each of which the sun arrives in his annual progress. The reason why these two lines were called the *gates* was this: they were the boundaries to the North and South, beyond which the sun never extended his course. The space between them might be called the dominion of the sun, and when you passed into the space between them you might be said to pass into his kingdom. The Southern gate is called the tropic of Capricorn, an amphibious animal, half *goat* half *fish*, in our present Zodiacs, but in the most ancient Zodiacs of India, it is described as two entire beings, a goat and a fish.

The Brahmins also call the tropics of Cancer and Capricorn the Gates of the Sun. Kircher, in his Œdipus Egyptiacus,[3] has undertaken to give the names of the dæmons or genii who presided over each of the Lunar mansions, and the meanings of these names. The sincerity of the learned old Jesuit cannot be doubted, though some of his etymologies may. He states that the first is called the gate of the *fish*. This evidently alludes to the Indian sign of Capricorn, and is very satisfactory. The thirteenth is called the station of *love* by the Egyptians or Copts; by the Arabs, the *alzarphet*, or that which takes away cold; and by the Greeks and Romans the *ear of corn*. Of this Cicero says, Spicam illustrem tenens splendenti corpore Virgo. Kircher says, Incipit hæc statio a quarto virginis, et terminatur in decimo octavo gradu ejusdem dodecatemorii Virginis. Genius est Masaiel; statio pacis et unionis conjugalis.

The following passage is from p. 278 of Sir William Drummond's Œdipus Judaicus: " חשמן " *(hsmun)* Heshmon. It is clear that the letters in this name have been transposed, and probably " for a mysterious purpose. In the Onomasticon, the word Heshmon is brought from " משה *(msh)* unxit, and even the English reader will easily see that this is only a transposition " of the radicals in חשמ-ן *(hsm-un)*. The Jews, in fact, pretend that one Messiah משיח *(msih)* " was to be born of the tribe of Judah, and another of the tribe of Ephraim.[4] This *Heshmon* " seems to indicate him who was the anointed of Judah, and who indeed is called Ben-Jehudah, " Judah's son." Let us inquire if there be any astronomical allusion here. " Again," he says, " Immediately on leaving the sign of Leo, the emblem of Judah, the sun passes into the sign " where, as we have already seen, the ancient Persians, Arabians, and Syrians, depicted *Virgo* " with a male infant in her arms. Now I observe, that the Arabians make Messaiel, the pro-

---

[1] It was said to have the name of milky, from its whiteness, which was caused by the accidental spilling on the ground of some of the milk of Juno.

[2] Porphyry, Cave of the Nymphs, Taylor, p. 193.          [3] Vol. III. Cap. x. p. 241.

[4] We see here that one Messiah was to come from the tribe of Judah under the tropic of Capricorn, the other from the tribe of Ephraim, the exactly opposite in the camps of the Hebrews. See Drummond, plate 15, which would place him in the tropic of Cancer. (Can the reader doubt the astrological meaning of all this?)

" tecting genius in the sign of Virgo.[1]  This Messaiel seems a manifest corruption from Messiah-
" El.  It is vain to talk of the Shin being dageshed by the Masorites,.....................
" or of the aspirate being suppressed.  We ourselves suppress the sound of the aspirate in Eve,
" Messiah, and many other words.  Besides, the Syrians certainly often softened the harsh
" aspirate ; and the Arabians may have caught the sound from them.  Mesai-El, then appears to
" be a corruption for משיח-אל (msih-al) Messiah-El—the anointed of El, the male infant, who
" rises in the arms of Virgo, who was called Jesus by the Hebrews, that is, ישע (iuso) the Saviour,
" and was hailed the anointed king or Messiah."

When it is considered that this Heshmon, and the whole of the towns specified in this passage
of Joshua, are part of the allotment given to the tribe of Judah, it can scarcely be doubted that a
close connexion with the Christian Messiah will be found here.  Sir W. Drummond has shewn,
that all the names of the other places which are certainly understood have an allegorical meaning
allusive to the heavenly bodies.  It must also be recollected that these astrological circumstances
preceded the birth of Jesus Christ.

## CHAPTER III.

1. We will now make a few inquiries respecting the celebrated God Bacchus, the son of the
Goddess of whom we have been treating.

Diodorus Siculus acknowledges that some historians maintained that Bacchus never appeared
on earth in a human shape.[2]  Had we but the works of these authors, probably at that time despised, we should see the truth, which their narrow-minded contemporaries were not able to
appreciate.  Diodorus Siculus also says,[3] that the Libyans claim Bacchus, and say that he was
the son of Ammon, a king of Libya, who reigned in a city called Ammon; that, after various
adventures, he returned to Libya, and built a temple to his father Ammon.  The account of
Diodorus is full of contradiction, but the result is, that Bacchus built the temple of Ammon, and
was succeeded by Jupiter; consequently that the Bull worship preceded the Ram-headed Jupiter.
Plutarch[4] says, that Bacchus was the same deity as Osiris, and that he was also the same as the
Εϱως πρωτογονος of Orpheus and Hesiod.  The word Ammon in Greek is often written Αμυν :
this is, when written from right to left, Numa.[5]  It is also written Ομανος.  In Hebrew the word
is written עמון omun, which, if read from left to right, is Numo.  In the last chapter it was noticed
that Osiris was called Om-phi, and that Om-phi might be merely Pi-Om—The Om : Pi being
the Coptic emphatic article.  Plutarch[6] says, Phylarchus taught that Bacchus first brought into

[1] See Kircher's Œdipus, Vol. III. p. 245.      [2] Lib. iii. p. 137.      [3] Ibid. iii.      [4] De Iside et Osiride.
[5] Nothing was more common with the ancients than to transpose the letters of names, or to write in anagrams for
the sake of secresy.
[6] De Iside et Osiride.

Egypt from India the worship of Apis and Osiris. Eusebius has stated that Bacchus came to Egypt from the Indus. In the temples of Diana a festival of Bacchus was celebrated, called *Sacæ*.[1] Of this Saca I shall treat at large hereafter. Bacchus had generally the horns of a bull, though often hidden beneath a crown of ivy or grapes.[2] The Pope is always accompanied by one or two large fans made of feathers. The Buddhist priests of Ceylon always have the same,—as Mr. Robinson says, *the mystic fan of Bacchus*.[3] Bacchus and Hercules were both Saviours, they were both put to death, and rose again the third day, at our time of Easter, or the vernal equinox: so were Osiris and Adonis.

Porphyry[4] says, " Hence, a place near to the equinoctial circle was assigned to Mithra as an " appropriate seat. And on this account he bears the sword of Aries, which is a martial sign. " He is likewise carried in the Bull, which is the sign of Venus ; for Mithra, as well as the Bull, " is the demiurgus and Lord of Generation." Again,[5] he says, " Thus also the Greeks united a " ram to the statue of Jupiter : *but the horns of a bull to that of Bacchus*." Again,[6] " Homer " calls the period and revolution of regeneration in a circle 'Circe, the daughter of the Sun, who " perpetually connects and combines all corruption with generation, and generation with corrup- " tion." Again,[7] " Nymphs, says Hermias,[8] are Goddesses who preside over generation, and are " the attendants of Bacchus, the son of Semele. On this account they are present with water, " that is, they ascend, as it were, and rule over generation. But this Dionysius, or Bacchus, " supplies the regeneration of every sensible nature."

2. Bacchus and Osiris are the same person, and that person has been shewn to be the sun ; and they were both black. But Bacchus was also the Baghis of India, as Sir W. Jones has shewn. Baghi-stan in Persia was the town of Bacchus. · Bacchus was called Dionusos or Dionissus : this is simply Dios-nusos, or the God of the city spoken of by Arrian, on the confines of India—Nysa, the capital of Nysea. He is also the Dios Nysa, a city of Arabia, and Nysa, on the top of a mountain in Greece. He is also Seeva, one of the three persons of the Hindoo Trinity. But Seeva is called Om.[9] Plutarch witnesses that Osiris and Isis were Bacchus and Ceres, and there can be no doubt that they were the Eswara and Isa of India. He is found in the Old Testament under the name IEUE *Nissi* יהוה נסי which, translated from the Greek, would be Dios Nyssos or Dionusos, a name of Bacchus.[10] Indeed, being the Sun, he is naturally enough found every where.

> Ogygia me Bacchum vocant,
> Osirim Ægyptus putat,
> Mysi Phanacem nominant,
> Dionyson Indi existimant,
> Romana Sacra Liberum,
> Arabica gens Adoneum,
> · Lucaniacus Pantheum.

He was also Deo-Naush, or Deva-Nahusha, and Ram or Rama-Deva. He was three times born in India ; and the Greeks call Osiris πρωτογονον, διφυη, and τρίγονον.[11]

Strabo[12] says, " It is for this reason that they give to this God (Bacchus) the name of Mηρο- " τραφης, *Merotraphes*." This means One nourished in Meru, the propriety of which is evident

[1] Strabo, Geog. Lib. xi. ; Pausan., Lib. iii. cap. xvi. ; Hoffman, voc. Anaitis ; Jameson, Herm. Scyth. p. 136.

[2] See Spence, Polymetis, p. 129, folio ed.  [3] Last Days of Heber, p. 43.

[4] In his Cave of the Nymphs, Sect. ii. p. 190, ed. Taylor.  [5] De Abstin., Sect. xv. p. 110.  [6] Ibid. 247.

[7] Ibid. 248.  [8] In Plat. Phædrum.  [9] Malcolm's India, p. 505.  [10] Stukeley, Paleog. Sac. No. I. p. 10.

[11] Maurice, Hist. Vol. II. 133, 4to ; Moore's Pantheon, p. 272.  [12] Lib. xv.

enough to us, since we have acquired the Indian learning. Casaubon proposed to change the word to Μηρορραφης, Merorrhaphes. This shews the danger, in these old authors, of changing a word because we do not understand it. Had the suggestion of the learned Casaubon been adopted, we should have lost the most important fact, that Bacchus was nourished in the celebrated Mount of the Indians.

According to Herodotus,[1] Bacchus was called Iacchus, in the mysteries. Και προκα τε φωνῆς ακϑειν, και οἱ φαινεσϑαι την φωνην ειναι τον μυςικον Ιαχχον·—και την φωνην τῆς ακϑεις, εν ταυτῃ τῃ ὁϱτῃ Ιαχχαζϑσι. Selden and Vossius allow this to be the same as the Jah, or Iαω of Diodorus. Now, from Hamilton[2] I learn that the people of Pegu, in a district called Syrian, give their God the name of KIACK, also of KIACKIACK, *God of Gods*. This is nothing, I think, but the corrupted, or perhaps only aspirated, *Iack* of the mysteries. It answers to the Βαχχεϐαχχος. Casaubon[3] says, " Sed nómen Βαχχεκορος, ut alia item quam plurima, alibi " quam apud Orpheum non legas. Imitatus est eleganter in novanda ea dictione vetustissimam " Bacchi appellationem Βαχχεϐαχχος, quam heroici metri lex non admittebat : ita Liberum " patrem in ipsiis orgiis et mysteriis vocant." Βαχχεϐαχχος, Ὁ Διονυσος οὑτως εχαλειτο εν ταις ϑυσιαις.[4] I ask if Bacchus, in the Æolic dialect, proved above by Herodotus to be Iacchus, be anything but Iacchus ? Pococke[5] says,

BACCHA, grandem, magnum, præclarum, esse denotare.

I have a strong suspicion that the K in the above word Kiack is only the aspirate ; and that the final ck is only the barbarous mode of writing the Hebrew ח h, adopted by most of our grammarians ח ch. This would make the word יה ie, called in the Psalms JAH, into the word Kiach.

Mr. Taylor, in his Diegesis, has called the word Jah, Jack. Those who will persist in miscalling the Hebrew ח h by the letters ch, have no right to complain. According to their practice he is right : but they are wrong, as I have proved in the table of Alphabets, p. 11

Bacchus is said by Orpheus[6] to have slept three years.

Ὁς παρα Περσεφονης-ιεροισι δομοισιν ιαυων
Κοιμιζει ΤΡΙΕΤΗΡΑ χρονον Βαχχηιον αγνον.

This is exactly met by a fact which the natives of Pegu named of their god Kiack, that he was then asleep, and was to sleep 6000 years. This God in Pegu was of immense size, and lay in a temple in a sleeping posture, evidently the Buddha whom we see sleeping in the India House. When, in their ceremonies, the Hindoos call out IETE, IETE, what is this but the ETOE, ETOE of the Bacchantes ?

3. Diodorus Siculus in his second book says, that, after Bacchus had conquered India, his army becoming unhealthy, he retreated to a mount in the north, called Meros, (Μηρον in the accusative case,) where he refreshed them, and that this word Μηρω meaning *thigh* in Greek, the Greeks feigned the story of his being nourished *in a thigh*. Pomponius Mela[7] says, " Urbium " quas incolunt, Nysa est clarissima et maxima : Montium Meros, Jovi sacer : famam hinc præ- " cipuam habent, in illa genitum, in hujus specu Liberum arbitrantur esse nutritum : unde " Græcis autoribus, ut femori Jovis incitum dicerent, aut materia ingessit aut error." Here we have the connexion, or, in fact, identification of Bacchus with the resident of Meru, and here

---

[1] Lib. viii. cap. lxv.      [2] New Account of East Indies, ch. xxxvi. p. 43.      [3] De Poësi Satyr. Græcorum.
[4] Hesychius.      [5] Spec. Hist. Arab. p. 107.      [6] Hymn in Bacchum, No. 52.      [7] Lib. ii. cap. xi.

we have also a very pretty example of the way in which the minor details of the Greek mythologies were made up. The ignorance of the Greeks in their own concerns is inconceivably ridiculous, as well as their absurd credulity. In addition to the above, Philostratus[1] says, "The " inhabitants of India had a tradition that Bacchus was born at *Nysa*, and was brought up in a " cave on Mount *Meros.*" And Diodorus Siculus says, that " when Semiramis marched into India, " she stopped and formed fine gardens at a place in Media called Βαγιςανον, Baghistan," that is, *place of Bacchus.*[2] The story of Pythagoras' shewing his golden thigh to the people in the public assembly in Greece, is well known. When the other accounts of Pythagoras, and his profound philosophy, are considered, this seems a most unaccountable story, and can be regarded only as a fable, or an allusion to something which we do not understand. We have seen that Mount Meru was a type or symbol of the Linga and Ioni. Now I suspect that what Pythagoras shewed to the people was one of the models of Meru, or of the united Linga and Ioni, which we see in such a variety of ways in the museum at the India-house. Of this the rabble made a golden thigh. If impartial philosophers could be found to search for it in India, I doubt not that all, or nearly all, the ancient mythology would be explained; and no small part of that of the Greeks would be found to have arisen from their mistakes. Herodotus says that Jupiter carried Bacchus in his *thigh* to Nyssa. This confirms what I have said, that, in his story, there is some unknown meaning.[3]

We have seen above, that Bacchus was identified with Mount Meru, the residence of Brahm, where he held his court in the sides of the North. But the reader will not forget that Bacchus was called Broumios. This was the Bruma of the Etruscans. In Ovid's *Fasti*, Janus announces that he is the same with Bruma, and that the year began of old with Bruma, and not with the Spring, because Bruma had the first honour. Bruma meant also the winter or the north. All the ancients looked to the north for the seat of the Deity, and I believe in all nations the letters B. R. and P. R. conveyed the idea of Former or Creator. Ovid says,

> Bacchumque vocant, Bromiumque, Dyœumque,
> Ignigenam, Satumque iterum, solumque Bimatrem.
>
> Ovid's Met. Lib. iv.

Here I beg my reader to observe that Bacchus is both *Igni-genam* and *Bi-matrem.* The ignigenam I suppose I need not explain. The poetical expression of Bi-matrem, which I suppose means twice born, alludes to Bacchus in his character of Menu or Noah, and to the mythological fact of his having lived in two worlds, or the life of Noah having continued into the fourth cycle. Noah or Menu lived in two cycles—in the third, and in part of the fourth. He lived also in two worlds—*before* the flood, and *after* the flood; in two ages—in the Cali-yug, and in the age before it. He lived when the sun at the equinox was in two constellations—in Taurus and in Aries : so that on many accounts he might be called twice born, as Bacchus was, according to Ovid.

Diodorus Siculus also reports that, according to some authors, he was twice born. Here the *renewed* incarnation creeps out, as well as the striking similitude to Noah. Bacchus is said, like Noah, to have planted the vine, to have made wine, and to have been the victim of its inebriating quality. M. D'Ancarville[4] shews that the name of Brouma given to Bacchus was Brama, and that Diodorus calls this name indigenous (εγχωριον διαλεκτον). He also shews, in the most satisfactory manner, that Bacchus was brought from India ; that the object of his religion was God the Creator of all things, the generative power of which was represented under the form of the Bull.[5]

---

[1] In Vita Apol. Lib. ii. cap. ix.     [2] Lib. ii.     [3] Herod. Euterp. cap. cxlvi.     [4] P. 98.
[5] Ibid. p. 127.

Strabo says, that Bacchus reigned over all the oriental nations, but that Hercules reigned over only those of the western parts : Περι δε Ἡρακλεης οἱ μεν επι τ' αναντια μονον μεχρι των ἑσπεριων περατων ἱςορϱσιν, οἱ δε εφ' εκατερα. [1] This alludes to the fact, of the truth of which I have no doubt, that the religion of Buddha or Bacchus once extended throughout Ava, China, Tibet, and the islands as well as the peninsula of Hindostan. But the religion of Cristna or Hercules extended only over the peninsula.

4. Bacchus was called ΕΥΟΙ. This is the ΙΕΥΩ, ΙΑΩ, ΙΑΟΥ, or Yahouh, the same as the IE on the temple of the Delphian Apollo. [2] Bacchus was also called a Bull, and a Son of God. When the Prince of Thebes forbade his mysteries, neglected his miracles, and denied his divinity, he put on the appearance of man, and submitted to be bound and led to prison. He was exposed by his grandfather king Cadmus, was preserved in an ark, and nursed in a cavern by Rhea, the mother of God. [3] Bacchus was twice born, was represented at the winter solstice as a little child, born five days before the end of the year. On his birth a blaze of light shone round his cradle. [4] The Romans had a god called *Quirinus ;* he was said to be the brother of Bacchus. His soul emanated from the sun, and was restored to it. He was begotten by the God of armies upon a *virgin* of the blood royal, and exposed by order of the jealous tyrant *Amulius,* and was preserved and educated among shepherds. [5] He was torn to pieces at his death, when he ascended into heaven ; upon which the sun was eclipsed or darkened. [6] Bacchus's death and return to life were annually celebrated by the women of Delphi ; his return was expected by his followers, when he was to be the sovereign of the universe. [7] He was said to sit on the same throne as Apollo. He was three nights in hell, whence he ascended with his mother to heaven, where he made her a goddess. [8] He killed an amphisbæna which bit his leg ; and he, with several other gods, drove down the giants with serpents' feet, who had made war against heaven. [9] The same general character is visible in the mythoses of Hercules and Bacchus. Hercules was called a Saviour: he was the son of Jove by the virgin Prudence. [10] He was called the UNIVERSAL WORD. [11] He was reabsorbed into God. [12] He was said by Orpheus to be self-produced, the generator and ruler of all things, and the father of time. [13]

---

[1] Strabo, Lib. xv. p. 687.

[2] Vide a Dialogue, the taste of which I cannot admire, supplied by a literary friend of mine to Mr. Carlile, for the first number of Vol. XI. of the Republican. I am not at liberty to give his name, but I shall quote his Dialogue by his initials, J. H. As I know him to be a man of deep learning, and have a perfect confidence in his honour, I shall depend upon him for his references, which are almost innumerable, to which the learned may apply for proofs of the assertions.

[3] J. H., Dial. in Rep.   [4] Ibid ; see also the Gospel of the Infancy.   [5] J. H. in Rep.   [6] Ibid.

[7] Ibid.   [8] Ibid.   [9] Ibid.   [10] Julian, Orat. vii. p. 427.

[11] Cornut. de N. D. p. 89; Lucian, Hercul. cap. iv. and v.   [12] Ibid. p. 409.   [13] J. H. in Rep.

# CHAPTER IV.

NAMES OF JESUS AND IAO.—CHIFFLET AND OTHERS ON THESE NAMES.—KIRCHER ON THE NAME IAO.—
NAME IAO.—NAME IAO KNOWN TO THE GENTILES.—YHS, DERIVATION OF IT.—OBSERVATIONS.

1. I will now submit to my reader some observations on the origin of the word Jesus, and the opinions of different learned men both on the word itself, and on various points connected with it. Here will be found several facts repeated in a similar manner to what has taken place with the Queen of heaven, his mother; but I hope the importance of the subject will excuse their being all brought together under one view.

In the ancient books of the Jews we constantly find mention made of the god Jehovah, who ought to be called Jah, or Ieue. This God answered to the person whom the Hindoos designate by the name of Cristna, the second person in their trinity, or their God the saviour or preserver; and was he whom the Persians designated by the name of Mithra, the second person in *their* trinity, and also *their* preserver or saviour; and was he whom the Romish Christians designate by the name of *Jesus*, also the second person in *their* trinity, and *their* saviour or preserver. He is called by the Jews the Lord of hosts, God of Sabaoth: which means God of the stars and constellations. This name with the Greeks, Romans, and Gentiles in general, was understood and meant to designate both the Supreme Being and the Sun, Dominus Sol, the Lord of heaven and the heavenly host.

The God Ιαω, יהוה *ieue*, IHS, Jehovah, was the son of the celestial virgin, which she carries in her arms; the ואר *aur*, Horus, Lux, of the Egyptians;[1] the Lux of St. John. It is from this infant that Jesus took his origin; or at least it is from the ceremonies and worship of this infant, that his religion came to be corrupted into what we have it. This infant is the seed of the woman who, according to Genesis, was to bruise the head of the serpent, which, in return, was to bite his foot or heel, or the foot or heel of her seed, as the figure of the Hindoo Cristna proves.[2] From the traditionary stories of this god Iao, which was feigned annually to be born at the winter solstice, and to be put to death and raised to life on the third day at the vernal equinox, the Romish searchers after the evangelion or gospel, made out their Jesus. The total destruction of every thing at Jerusalem and in Judæa,—buildings, records, every thing—prevented them from coming to any absolute certainty respecting the person who, they were told by tradition, had come to preach the gospel of peace, to be their saviour, in fulfilment of the prophecy which their sect of israelites found in their writings, and who had been put to death by the Jews. From all these circumstances he came to have applied to him the monogram of IHS, and the name of IHΣους, and to him at last all the legendary stories related of the god Iao were attributed. Jesus was commonly called Christ.

" The ineffable name also, which, according to the Masoretic punctuation, is pronounced Jehovah, was anciently pronounced Jaho, Ιαω, or Ιευω,[3] as was also Sabazius or Sabadius,[4] which " is the same word as Sabaoth, one of the scriptural titles of the true God, only adapted to the

---

[1] See Plate 19 of Dupuis, the Celestial Sphere.　　　　　[3] Plates, No. II. and V.

[2] Hieron. Comm. in Psalm viii.; Diod. Sic., Lib. i.; Philo-Bybl. apud Euseb. Prep. Evang. Lib. i. cap. ix.

[4] Mart. Fel. Sat. Lib. i. cap. xviii.

" pronunciation of a more polished language. The Latin name for the Supreme God belongs also
" to the same root; Ιυ-πατηρ, Jupiter, signifying father Ιευ, though written after the ancient
" manner, without the dipthong, which was not in use for many ages after the Greek colonies
" settled in Latium, and introduced the Arcadian alphabet. We find St. Paul likewise acknow-
" ledging that the Jupiter of the poet Aratus was the God whom he adored;[1] and Clemens
" Alexandrinus explains St. Peter's prohibition of worshiping after the manner of the Greeks not
" to mean a prohibition of worshiping the same God, but merely of the corrupt mode in which he
" was then worshiped."[2]

Diodorus Siculus says, that Moses pretended to receive his laws from the God called ΙΑΩ.
This shews that the Greeks considered the name of the Jewish God to be, not Jehovah, but, as I
have stated it, יהו ieu, or Ieo. Ιηιος[3] is one of the names of Apollo: and Nimrod[4] says, ΙΑΩ
means *I heal, I make sound*. It was probably from this the Essenian monks, his followers, in
Egypt and Syria were called Therapeutæ, or physicians of the soul. In the first volume of Asiatic
Researches Sir W. Jones names a female deity called Hygeia, or *health*, and another called Iaso,
whom he calls *remedy*, daughters of Æsculapius. May not this *remedy* mean Preserver? Perhaps
the reader may think that the use of any correct etymology is not to be expected from such
grammarians as Justin, Papias, and Irenæus. The last gives the following derivation of the name
Jesus : " Jesus nomen secundum propriam Hebræorum linguam litterarum est duarum et dimi-
diæ......et secundum antiquam Hebraicam linguam cœlum est.[5] Is it possible to believe that
Irenæus had ever seen the gospel history by Matthew ?

. 2. Chifflet, speaking of Iao in his treatise on coins, says, that except the Christians no other
sect or religion has given this name to the divinity. This is unquestionably a very great mistake.
M. Beausobre says,[6] " Supposing that to be true, it does not follow that these figures belonged to
" the Basilidians ; they might be from some I know not what Gnostic sect, which pretended that
" Iao is the name of an angel. One *must* allow that it is that of Jehovah, which the ancients have
" written and pronounced sometimes Jaho, [7] sometimes Jevo,[8] and sometimes Iaou.[9] But it is
" necessary also to allow, that Iao is one of the names that the Pagans give to the sun. I have
" noticed the oracle of Apollo at Claros, in which Pluto, Jupiter, the sun, and Iao, divide the
" seasons amongst them. These four divinities are at bottom the same.

Εις Ζευς, εις Αδης, εις Ηλιος, εις Διονυσος,

" that is to say, Jupiter, Pluto, the Sun, and Bacchus, are the same. That which is called
" Dyonysus in the last verse is the same which is called Iao in the oracle. It is Bacchus who
" presides over the autumn. Macrobius reports another oracle of Apollo which is couched in
" these terms :

Φραζω τον παντων υπατων θεον εμμεν Ιαω·

" ' I declare to you that Iao is the greatest of the Gods.' It would be doing too much honour to
" the Demon, if one believed that the god called Iao is the Jehovah of Scripture, or the true God.
" This is no other than the sun. Iao, which was a barbarous name, has been changed by the
" Greeks into Ιηιος (Ieios). Macrobius, well instructed in the Pagan theology, affirms, that Iao

---

[1] Acts xvii.    [2] Stromat. Lib. v. ; P. Knight, p. 195.    [3] Scapula.    [4] P. 517.
[5] Iren. contra Hær. lib. ii. cap. xli. ; Dalleus, De Usu Pat. p 243.
[6] Beaus. Hist. Manich. Vol. II. liv. iv. chap. iv. p. 59.    [7] Euseb. Dem. Ev. lib. iv. p. 129.
[8] Euseb. Præp. Evan. lib. i. x.    [9] Clem. Alex. Strom. lib. v. p. 562.

" is the sun, and that Cornelius Labeo had shewn this in a book entitled, ' *Concerning the Oracle*
" ' *of Apollo at Claros.*' "   Speaking of the oracle of Apollo above-named by Macrobius, Dr. Cudworth says,[1] " And the oracle applied this to the sun as the supreme God." Porphyry says, that
Sanchoniathon received information from Hierombalus, a priest of Ιαω.  The Ευοι Βαχχε λεγον-
τες is nothing but the IEUE of the tribe of Judah, in the country of Palestine, miswritten
by the Greeks, who miswrote every thing. "Athenæus IX. gives Bacchus the name of Ιηιος.
" I doubt not but it is the great name of Jehovah, which they learnt from among the Jews : and that
" Evòhe Sabòhe is the Jehovah Sabaoth, Lord of Hosts, in the Scripture ; whence Bacchus was
" called Sabazius likewise.  Diodorus Siculus says expressly, the Jews call God Iao ; and the
" learned universally agree *that* is Jehovah.  Evòhe is but another awkward way of pronouncing
" it."[2]

In almost innumerable places in Italy *very old* paintings may be seen of Christ in various situations, labelled with the words in the middle of the painting, *Deo Soli*.  These words it is evident
have two meanings—To God alone, and To the God Sol.  In most of them there are seen the
attributes of the latter, such as the glory, &c.  The former sense is in no way applicable to Christ,
because as one person of the Trinity he cannot be called *solus*.  These pictures, with their two
meanings, shew an example like the first verse of Genesis, one for the priests, and one for the
people—the *esoteric* and the *exoteric* religion.

I think we may now assume that we have found the origin of the word Jesus.  M. Beausobre
may talk as much as he pleases about honour to the Dæmon, but all his ingenuity will never be
able to overthrow the fair and legitimate consequence which arises from his argument.  He has
clearly proved that the Sun, Iao, and Jesus, were all taken for the same being by the ancients, and
it will require more than the skill of the whole priesthood to disprove it.  But there is another
way of deriving the name of Ιησες more probable than the explanation of M. Beausobre ; though
they both come so nearly to the same thing that they are in fact and substance evidently the same.
On this subject Sir W. Drummond says,

" That the sun rising from the lower to the upper hemisphere should be hailed the Preserver or
" Saviour appears extremely natural : and that by such titles he was known to idolaters can-
" not be doubted.[3]  Joshua literally signifies the preserver or deliverer ; and that this preserver
" or deliverer was no other than the sun in the sign of the ram, or lamb, may be inferred from
" many circumstances.  It will be observed that the LXX. write Ιησους for Joshua, and the lamb
" has always been the type of Ιησους."[4]

Matthew[5] says, that the son of Mary was called Jesus, *because he would save* (i. e. preserve)
*his people from their sins.*[6]  The Jews say in their Talmud, that the name of Jesus was Bar
Panther, but that it was changed into Jesus.  The word Jesus, as was before remarked, is the

---

[1] Book i. chap. iv. p. 285.                     [2] Stukeley, Pal. Sac. No. I. p 21.
[3] " The Sun, according to Pausanias, was worshiped under the name of Saviour, at Eleusis."
[4] Drummond, Œdip. Jud. p. 195.                     [5] Chap. i. verse 21.
[6] We are told in Numbers, (xiii. 16,) that Moses changed the name of Osee to Joshua.

ויקרא משה להושע בן-נון יהושע  *And Moses called Leusu, son of Nun, Ieusu.*  I believe there is in this passage a
correct example of the word לה *le*, being used as the emphatic article, and the correct translation would be, And
Moses called the saviour or guardian or protector, (*who was* understood) the son of Nun, וה *ie* ושע *ueo*: as we should
say, He entitled the protector (who was) the son of Nun, *the Lord Protector*.  It is exactly our practice, our idiom,
and even the very word Lord, according to our translation.  At this time the Hebrew nation was a federative republic
of twelve tribes, under leaders elected by the people, or often by the prophet or priest.  I believe that *ie* became a title
of honour, like Bal and Lord, and, for several reasons which I shall give hereafter, that the word לה *le* or the letter ל *l*,
the *el* or *al* of Arabic, the *le* of France, and the *il* of Italy, was a Hebrew emphatic article.

same as the word Joshua in the Hebrew, and has the same signification. It may be correctly derived either from the Hebrew word יש‎ *iso*, or from the Greek word σαω or σωζω *to save ;* .σοος, *safe.* It may be correctly derived from the Greek as well as the Hebrew, because the Greek is itself derived from the Hebrew. [1] It may be derived also from יה *ie*,[2] the name of the Hebrew God, often rendered Jah, and יש‎ *iso*, saviour ; or Jehovah or Iao saviour.[3] In the old Irish and Etruscan languages the word Aesar means God. In Sanscrit the word Isa, Iswara, means Lord and Saviour. Probably the Greeks understanding that the Hebrew word יה *ie* meant God the Saviour, added a significant termination according to the genius of their language, taken from the word σαω *to save*, and so made of it Iη-σσς, or Iao the Saviour.

3. Kircher informs us, that " the ancient Jews absolutely applied the three first letters of this " name (יהוה) to denote the three superior Sephiroth, and he remarks that, in fact, there are but " three distinct letters in the word, which are Jod, He, and Vau ; the last letter being only a repe- " tition of the second."[4] " This name (says Buxtorf) signifies ENS, EXISTENS A SEIPSO, *ab* " *æterno et in æternum, omnibusque aliis extra se essentiam et existentiam communicans :* the being " existing of necessity from all eternity and to eternity." Again, " Nam, litera JOD ab initio, " characteristica est *futuri :* VAU in medio, participii, temporis *presentis :* HE, in fine, cum " Kametz subscripto, *præteriti*."[5]

In my Celtic Druids[6] I have said, that the יהוה *ieue* of the Israelites was but Iao with the emphatic article, making it *the Iao :* and that it was originally Ieu, not Ieo ; the first three letters of of the word *ieu-e*. In the Bible we constantly meet with the expression *the Aleim*, but in no instance with the expression THE Jehovah. This arises from the expression *ieue* meaning *the ieu*. I have in the Celtic Druids also shewn that the word Abraxas meant 365, the solar period or the sun. This Abraxas is constantly identified on the coins of Chifflet and Kircher with the names of God, Adonai, Sabaoth, &c. Kircher[7] says, " Gnostici natione Ægyptii, religione primum He- " bræi, dum virtutem nominis Dei tetragrammati ex veterum relatione cognoscerent, ad impietatis " suæ complementum, superstitiosa sua nomina passim nomine IAω et CEBAω, quod idem est " ac יהוה *(ieue)* Jehova et שבות *(sbout)* Sabaoth, summa tamen nominum corruptela indigitarunt." But the name of Jesus was sometimes written Ieu. I have observed before, that in the Duomo at Milan, the first time I went to Italy, I found it written thus, IEV—Cristo. In the above passage we see the identity of the Jesus of the Roman Church and the Iao of the ancients proved, not by implication, but by documents produced by the learned Jesuit Kircher. In a few pages later,[8] the learned father adds, " Hujus farinæ fecit quoque quæ lib. ii. cap. xiii. Irenæus de Gnosticorum " impietatibus refert, ubi nomen absconditum Redemptoris sic profantur. *Messian fromagno in* " *scenchaldin mosomeda ecacha saronhepseha Jesu Nazarene :* quorum interpretationem hanc esse " dicunt : *Christi non divido spiritum, cor et supra cœlestem virtutem misericordem fruar nomine* " *tuo Salvator veritatis :* confirmatus autem et redemptus respondet: *Ego redimo animam meam* " *ab hac œone et omnium quœ ab eo sunt in nomine IAO, qui redimit animam meam.* Hujus quo- " que impietatis censenda sunt pleraque lapidibus, gemmis, laminisque metallicis insculpta sine " numero nomina."

Cedrenus says that the Chaldeans adored the light : that they called it intellectual light, and that they described it, or symbolized it, by the two letters α and ω, or αω, by which he meant the extreme terms of the diffusion of matter in the seven planetary bodies, of which the first or the

---

[1] Parkhurst, p. 299, ed. 7.      [2] יה *Ie*, self-existing—existing by his own power.      [3] See Pictet, pp. 6—16.
[4] Maur. Hind. Ant. Vol. IV. p. 196.      [5] Ibid. p. 198.      [6] Chap. v. sect. xxxviii.      [7] Vol. III. p. 416.
[8] P. 469.

moon, answered to the vowel α, and the last, or Saturn, to the vowel ω; and that the letter I described the Sun; and this altogether formed the word Ιαω—the *Panaugria* of the Gnostics, otherwise the universal light distributed in the planets. All this is evidently judicial astrology. St. John says, "and the life was light, and the light was life, and the light was the word: Vita erat lux, et lux erat vita, et lux erat verbum, in Greek *Logos*,[1] where Christ is described in the midst of seven candlesticks, and seven stars in his hand. The Guebres, the Magi, and the Manicheans, all describe God to be an eternal, intelligent, and perfectly pure light. The Manicheans call this, Christ, the son of The Light Eternal, which Plato calls the Sun. The Scriptures and the fathers of the church all call God a sublime light.[2]

4. On the word יהוה *Ieue*, or Jehovah, Mr. Parkhurst, p. 155, has the following observations, which confirm what Beausobre has said upon it. His authority will not be disputed. That this divine name "יהוה *ieue* was well known to the heathen, there can be no doubt. Diodorus Siculus, "lib. i., speaking of those who attributed the framing of their laws to the Gods, says Παρα τοις "Ιουδαιοις Μωσην ιςορουσι τον ΙΑΩ επικαλουμενον Θεον. Among the Jews they report that "Moses did this to the God called Iao. *Varro*, cited by St. Austin, says, Deum Judæorum esse "Jovem, that Jove was the God of the Jews; and from יהו׳ the Etruscans seem plainly to have "had their *Juve* or *Jove*, and the Romans their Jovis or Jovis-Pater, that is, Father Jove, after-"wards corrupted into Jupiter. And, that the idolaters of several nations, Phœnicians, Greeks, "Etruscans, Latins, and Romans, gave the incommunicable name יהוה, with some dialectical varia-"tion to their false Gods, may be seen in an excellent note in the Ancient Universal History."[3] It is rather whimsical that Mr. Parkhurst should state this name of God to be incommunicable, when, in the same sentence, he informs us that it was common to almost all nations. Here seems a manifest and gross contradiction, which, in a note, I will now try to account for.[4]

The truth will sometimes escape from learned sectaries when they very little intend it. The pious Dr. Parkhurst, as we have just seen in his Hebrew Lexicon, proves, from the authority of Diodorus Siculus, Varro, St. Augustin, &c., that the Iao, Jehovah, or יהוה *ieue*, or יה *ie* of the Jews, was the Jove of the Latins and Etruscans. In the next page, and in p. 160, under the word חלל *ell*, he allows that this יה *ie* was the name of Apollo, over the door of the Temple of Delphi. He then admits that this יהוה *ieue* Jehovah is Jesus Christ in the following sentences: "It would be "almost endless to quote all the passages of scripture wherein the name יהוה (*ieue*) is applied to "Christ: let those, therefore, who own the scriptures as the rule of faith, and yet doubt his essen-"tial deity, only compare in the original scriptures (the passages too numerous to insert), and "I think they cannot miss of a scriptural demonstration that Jesus is Jehovah." But we have seen it is admitted that Jehovah is Jove, Apollo, Sol, whence it follows that Jesus is Jove, &c.

---

[1] See Apocalypse, Ch. i.  [2] Dupuis, Vol. III. p. 105, ed 4to.  [3] "Vol. XVII. pp. 274, &c."

[4] The Jews maintain that the fourth command in the decalogue, not to mention the name of God, means not to mention the word *Ieue*. But from considering that it is so often named in their writings, and the manner in which it is named, and ordered to be named in them; as for instance, in Exodus, ch. vi.,—in the decalogue,—and also to Moses by God in the bush, &c., &c.,—that it is directed to be used in such a manner as to carry with it the necessity of constantly repeating it in the performance of the service in their synagogues, and also considering other parts of their Cabala, the prophecy of Isaiah, the names of places, and the identity of Jewish and Heathen doctrines, (of Heathens both East and West of them,) I have been induced to suspect that their secret word was the Indian Om, and not really Ieue. It seems to be nonsense to tell them the word *Ieue* is not to be repeated when it is ordered to be repeated continually. If I be right, the verse of the decalogue might be paraphrased thus: "*Thou shalt not repeat the secret name of thy God Ieue.* This exoteric and esoteric meaning of the passage is in perfect keeping with what we know of the remainder of the Jewish Cabala; but upon this subject I must entreat my reader to suspend his judgment till he has travelled with me over countries the most distant, and times the most remote, in search of this celebrated cabala.

5. The three letters I H S, from the very earliest age of the Romish Christians, have been adopted for the insignia of their religion. We now very commonly see them embroidered in golden letters upon the velvet pulpit cloths of the churches in England, and the clergy say they mean *Jesus Hominum Salvator*. But it is very remarkable, as I have observed in B. v. Ch. ii. S. 8, that these three letters, in the Greek language, are the insignia of Bacchus or the Sun, and stand for the mystical number 608, which is sacred to him; a pretty striking proof of the identity of the two. Of the signs or monograms to express in a short way the names of their gods, used by the Gentiles, perhaps there is no one of them more striking than their celebrated YHS. These letters were anciently placed upon the temples or other buildings sacred to Bacchus or Sol; as they are now by Christians in their churches: and as the Christians, in the very dark ages, when temples, churches, towns, every thing indeed was destroyed; by the unceasing anarchy and civil war which for many ages prevailed, supposed the ruins upon which they were found to have belonged to their religion, they construed them to mean Jesus Hominum Salvator. Thus the ruins proved the truth of the monogram, the monogram the truth of the Christian ruins. Of course every stone or inscription where this is found, is at once, by all Christian antiquarians, settled to be of Christian origin; and this happy accident has converted to Christianity, old stones, temples, and statues innumerable, in almost all nations.

We find the word rendered *Jehovah* in English, for several words which are differently spelt in the Chaldaic Hebrew. In most places it is spelt יהוה *Ieue*, particularly in Exod. vi. 3, where God says, *I appeared unto Abraham, unto Isaac, and unto Jacob, by the name of Al Sadi* אל שדי, *but by my name of* יהוה *Ieue was I not known unto them*. But in other places it is spelt יהיה *Ieie*. In the Hebrew, words are often met with repeated in a peculiar manner, as שבת שבת *sbt, sbt*, sabat, sabat. This has been considered by grammarians merely as an intensitive, or to do honour, to give emphasis to a word, for various purposes, as we write a word in italics. This may have been the case with the word יהיה *Ieie*. No word is more likely to be so distinguished. Whether it were meant as at present written for one word, or two, cannot be known; in the old manuscripts there were no divisions between the words. יה *ie* is often translated by the word Jah:[1] *My strength and my song is Jah. Praise him by his name Jah*. Psalm lxviii. 4. This יה *ie* in the Syriac dialect was יו *io*, and was the Androgynous *Io* whom the Bull Jupiter ran away with.

Mr. Parkhurst has very properly observed, that, from one of those divine names, the Greeks had their Iη Iη in their invocations of the Gods, particularly of Apollo. " And hence ꓱI (written after " the oriental manner from right to left), afterward IE, was inscribed over the great door of the " Temple of Apollo at Delphi."[2] No doubt what Mr. Parkhurst says is true, and from this source came also the Greek *Io triumphe* of Bacchus. The reason why the word ꓱI was written to be read from right to left was, because it had been adopted in a very early time, when the Greek language was read βꭒⲋρoφηδoν, or from right to left, and back again.

The " Devatas of India sing out in transport in honour of Cristna the words JEYE! JEYE!"[3] Here we have the identical name Jehovah.—IEVE יהוה ꓱIꓱI or IEIE. That the word יה[4] translated *Jah* is correctly the word of the Greeks over their temple at Delphi, *My strength and song is Jah, Praise him by his name Jah*, is still more clearly proved from the circumstance that, in the Hebrew and Greek, they are the same letters in order and in numerical power, י I standing for *ten*, and ה E for *five*, in each language. They would not, however, be in exactly the same order, if a letter were not inserted in the Greek for the number *six*, which makes them agree.

---

[1] Exod. xv. 2.          [2] Parkhurst, voce היה, p. 157.          [3] Maurice Hind. Hist. Vol. II. p. 339, ed. 4to.
[4] Exod. xv. 2, and Psalm lxviii. 5.

The followers of Iao, יהוה *ieue*, constantly sung the word *Hallelujah* in his praise. This they did in the temple of Solomon, in the temple of Delphi, and they still continue the same hallelujahs in the temple at Rome. Dr. Parkhurst says, " הללים *elulim* praises,[1] הללויה *(elluie) Praise ye Jah*— " Eng. Marg. *Hallelujah:* and so the LXX. throughout, leaving it untranslated, Αλληλεϊα. It " occurs very frequently at the beginning and end of the Psalms. And from this solemn form of " *praise to God,* which, no doubt, was far prior to the time of David, the ancient Greeks plainly " had their similar acclamation Ελελευ Ιη *(eleleu ie),* with which they both began and ended their " Pæans or Hymns in honour of Apollo, i. e. *The light.*"[2]

Jesus in the gospels is always called Lord, or in the Greek Κυριος. This is the word by which the Hellenistic Jews, in translating the LXX. into Greek, constantly rendered the word יהוה *ieue*. The word Κυριος is derived from the word Κυρω, *to be, exist, subsist;*[3] and is a very excellent word to use for the Hebrew word יה *ie*, which has precisely the same meaning. But this word יה *ie*, as it has been before observed, was the name given to Apollo or the sun at Delphi, who is always called Κυριος, and the day dedicated to him κυριακη, *dies dominica*, or the Lord's-day. From some, or from a combination, of these circumstances, Jesus took the name of Lord, the etymological meaning of which will be explained hereafter. Eupolemus states, that there was a temple of Iao or Jupiter on Carmel, without image, which is confirmed by Tacitus.[4] This was evidently the temple of Melchizedek, of Joshua, and the proseucha discovered by Epiphanius. This, probably, was also the temple where Pythagoras, who sacrificed to the bloodless Apollo at Delos, went to acquire learning, or to be initiated. Numa autem rex Romanorum erat quidem Pythagoreus, ex iis autem quæ à Mose tradita sunt adiutus, prohibuit Romanis ne homini aut animali similem Dei facerent imaginem. Cum itaque centum et septuaginta primis annis templa ædificarent, nullam imaginem, nec affictam, nec depictum fecere. Occulte enim eis indicaret Numa, quod est optimum, non alia ratione quam sola mente ulli, licet attingere.[5]

Alexander autem in libro de symbolis Pythagoreis, refert Pythagoram fuisse discipulum Nazarati Assyrii. Quidum eum existimant Ezechielem, sed non est, ùt ostendetur postea: et vult præterea Pythagoram Gallos audiisse et Brachmanas.[6] I have very little doubt that a considerable part of the ancient idolatry arose from a cause apparently trifling, but yet quite proportionate to the effect. This was the necessary personification of objects by the primeval language which had no neuter gender, as we know was and yet is the case with the synagogue Hebrew; and I doubt not all its cognate dialects, in early times, were the same. " None dare to enter the temple of Serapis, who " did not bear on his breast or forehead the name Jao or J-ha-ho, a name almost equivalent in " sound to that of the Hebrew Jehovah, and probably of identical import; and no name was " uttered in Egypt with more reverence than this of Iao. In the hymn which the hierophant or " guardian of the sanctuary sang to the initiated, this was the first explanation given of the " nature of the Deity: *He is one, and by himself, and to him alone do all things owe their existence.*" Translation from the German of Schiller.[7]

Voltaire, in his commentary on Exodus, tells us, that some critics say the name Jehovah signifies destroyer.[8] The Egyptians pronounced it Jaou, and when they entered into the temple of the Sun they carried a phylactery, on which the name Iaou was written. Sanchoniathon wrote it Jevo.

---

[1] Lev. xix. 24.     [2] Parkhurst's Lexicon, voc. הלל, p. 160, ed. 7.     [3] Ibid. voc. הוה, p. 155, ed. 7.
[4] Vide Diss. III. in Preface to Whiston's Josephus and Tacitus.     [5] Clem. Alex. Strom. Lib. i. p. 304.     [6] Ibid.
[7] Monthly Repository, Vol. XX. pp. 198, 199.
[8] Where Voltaire got his authority for Jehovah meaning *destroyer* the author does not know, but it is probably true, as it is in perfect keeping with the remainder of the picture, and arose from the mistake between the Creator and Destroyer.

Origen and Jerom think it ought to be pronounced Jao. The Samaritans called it Jave. From this name comes the ancient Jovis, (ancient nom. case, see Parkhurst,) Jovispiter—Jupiter with the ancient Tuscans and Latins. The Greeks made from Jehova their Zeus.

The god *Horus* is stated by Dodwell to have the meaning of *destroyer*.

Shuckford says, " The name Jehovah was, I believe, known to be the name of the Supreme " God, in the early ages, in all nations." Again, " Ficinus remarked, that all the several nations " of the world had a name for the Supreme Deity, consisting of four letters only.[1] This I think " was true at first in a different sense· from that in which Ficinus took it: for I question not but " they used the very same word, until the languages of different nations came to have a " more entire disagreement than the confusion at Babel at first caused."[2] He goes on in the same page to observe, that it is said by Philo-Biblius in Eusebius, that the God of the Phœnicians was called *Jevo* or *Jao*. How can any one doubt that this is the Jove, who, according to the report of the Greeks, had a temple in Carmel, where no image was adored ? To this temple, as I have before remarked, Plato and Pythagoras probably withdrew for study.

Adrian Reland, De Nomine Jehovah, says, "It is plain that the Latins formed the name of " their god Jupiter, whom they called Jovis, from the name Jehovah."[3] Mr. Maurice says, " From this word יהוה *Ieue*, the Pagan title of Jao and *Jove* is, with the greatest probability, formed."[4] " In the Indra or Divespiter of India, and his symbol, the vaira or forked bolt, we im- " mediately recognize the *Jupiter Tonans* of the Greeks and Latins. Jupiter conquered the " Titans, Indra the Assoors, with their bolts."[5] Deva, or Deo, was a sacred title.[6] It was pro- phesied that Cristna was to become incarnate in the house of YADU at Mathura, of his mother *Devaci*.[7] The elements of the words *Ie* and *Deus* or *Diva* are evident in these names. Cristna was born in the eighth month, on a Wednesday at midnight, in the house of *Vasudeva*, his father, of *Devaci*, his mother.[8] The same is here again to be found in the word Vasudeva. I cannot entertain a doubt that the Indra of the Brahmins is the Jupiter of the Etruscans and Latins. He is called Dyupeti and Dyupetir.[9] Although various specious derivations of the word Jupiter may be given, yet I think the most probable is, that it is nothing but Peti or Pater יעו *ieu*, or Jupiter: the Ieu shortened into Ju. Mr. Whiston, in a note on Book ii. chap. xii. of Josephus, has ob- served, that the way I write Jehovah by Jao is correct. Even amongst the Chinese *the God* is to be found. In ascending to their fabulous history, they say their first legislator was Yao.[10] In short, it is evident that *all* these derivations are, at the bottom, essentially the same.

6. It is thus proved by fair deduction and logical reasoning on unquestionable authority, that the God יהוה IEUE Jehovah, יה IE or Jah of the Jews, the God ΑΙ, the Apollo of Delphos, the Deus, the Jupiter, Jovis, Jovispiter of the Latins, the god Mithra of the Persians, and all the gods of the Heathens, are identically the same person or being; not merely derivatives from one another, but that they are, with only such trifling apparent differences as may reasonably be expected to arise from the lapse of many ages, and from the inevitable uncertainty of names translated without any definite rule out of one language into another, one and the same; and this same being, *the sun*, or shekinah of the self-existent Being. In short, that Jehovah was the sun; for if Jehovah was Iao, and Iao was the sun, Jehovah must be the sun. Dr. Parkhurst admits that Jesus was Jehovah; but if Jesus was Jehovah, and Jehovah the sun, it follows that Jesus, that is, the Romish Jesus,

---

[1] The Hebrew word for the God of Abraham consisted merely of vowels, but we have put three consonants into our translation of it, *Jehovah*.

[2] Book ix. pp. 388,·391.  [3] Val. Col. Lib. ii. p. 296.  [4] Hind. Ant. Vol. IV. p. 73.
[5] Hist. Hind. Vol. I. pp. 461, 462.  [6] Asiat. Res. Vol. V. p. 288.  [7] Maurice, Hind. Sceptic Refuted, p. 56.
[8] Maurice, Bram. Frauds exp.  [9] Moore's Pantheon, p. 259.  [10] Muller's Hist., Vol. I. p. 320.

but not the Jesus of Nazareth, must be the sun. Perhaps the reverend, pious, and learned doctor would not have been so ready to make this admission, if he had foreseen the consequences to which it would lead. But he was perfectly right; the Jehovah of the Jews is the Jesus of corrupted Christianity, and multitudes of passages in the gospels prove it, or allude to it, as the Doctor truly says—passages which are really genuine parts of these works, as well as many which are misrepresented by accident, many by design, and also many which are forged. The philosophical Unitarians may continue their toils to overturn this doctrine of Dr. Parkhurst, by exposing the false or misunderstood passages in the text; but when they have done their utmost, enough will remain for its support.

The author will not attempt an argument with them; he leaves them to the doughty champions of the church—the Burgesses and the Wranghams, who are never backward to take the field in defence of the favourite doctrine of the Trinity, which is evidently involved in this question. It cannot be said that these doctrines are merely a chimera, an invention of the author's own imagination; almost every assertion which he has made is supported by the authority of some one or other of learned *Christian* divines who have studied the subject most carefully. Jesus being mistaken, by the founders of the Roman church, for the god Sol or the sun, it follows that the rites, ceremonies, and doctrines of the devotees of the god Sol or the sun may be expected to be found in their religion. In the following part of this work it will be shewn that that which may be expected to be found, is really found; and that most of the rites and doctrines of modern Christianity are nothing more than the rites and doctrines of the old religion, collected by devotees of very weak and mean understandings, and applied either to a real, or to an imaginary personage. Which of these two is the truth, it will be the final object of this work to determine.

# BOOK VII.

## CHAPTER I.

IONIANS, ORIGIN OF.—DERIVATION OF IONIAN.—ARGONAUTS.—LINGA AND YONI.—THE ARGHA.

1. It has been a general, but a very erroneous opinion, that there were no religious wars among the ancients. But we read of them in Egypt, and from the inquiries of our countrymen into the habits and manners of the oriental nations of very remote times, we learn that traces yet exist, which cannot be mistaken, of religious wars in India of the very worst description—wars not exceeded in duration or atrocity by any of those in modern Europe, bad as they have been. It also appears that the religions of India became, in very early times, divided into an almost inconceivable number of sects, some of which, after bloody wars, were expelled to the West, under different names. In one of these sects, either driven out or emigrating from India, I think will be found the ancient Ionians. These people are chiefly found in Attica, and on the most Western coast of Asia Minor. The story of the latter being a colony from Athens is not worth a moment's consideration. The vain Athenians found traces of them in Greece and in Asia; then, of course, their national vanity suggested that the Ionians must have come from Athens. It probably never occurred to them that the two remnants might have a common origin. As usual, the Greeks being perfectly ignorant of their origin, in order to account for it they invented a story; and in this case, it was of a king called Ion, from whom it was said that they took their name. It is not improbable that they might have arrived at Athens from the North-east by way of Thrace. But it may be a doubt whether part of them may not have come by sea at a more early period to Argos, and the Argolis, where they are found to have been settled. They were also said to have once dwelt in Achaia, whence the adjoining sea and islands had the name of Ionian. But their principal settlement was in Asia Minor, on the western coast of which they had a very fine country, and twelve states or tribes in a confederacy, which all assembled at stated times to worship at a temple built by them in common, like that of the Jews, a circumstance worthy of attention; it was called Pan-Ionium. We have here a very close resemblance to the Israelitish system. I suspect that the district was called by this name, but that the national temple was at Ephesus, a town which was said to have been built by Amazons, and was certainly *one* of the principal Ionian cities, if not the chief of them. Here was the famous image of the BLACK Di-ana, or Di-jana, or Dia-jana, which was supposed to have descended from heaven.

2. On the derivation of the word Ionian, Dr. Lempriere says, "It is generally thought to come " from the Hebrew *Iavan*, or (if pronounced with the quiescent *vau*) *Ion ;* and in like manner " the Hellenes are thought to be the same with *Elisa*, in the sacred writings, more especially " their country Hellas. Hence Bochart makes *Iavan*, the son of *Japhet*, the ancestor of the " Iones." He had just before observed that Greece was anciently divided between the Hellenes and the Ionians, and that Hellen has the same meaning as Ioni, and both that of the female generative power. They are said by Conon to have descended from a king called Hellen, the son

of Deucalion, one of whose grandsons settled in the Peloponnesus, then called Apia. Thus we find them to descend from a man saved at the flood of Noah, Japeti; and also from Deucalion, said by the Greeks to have been saved from the flood, whose son was called *Hellen*. They are also said to have built a town called Argos, and to have dwelt in a country called Apia, the name of the Egyptian Apis. In their city of Argos the goddess Juno was particularly worshiped; and here Io, the daughter of Jasus, or Ιασος, or Ιησος, was born, with whom Jupiter or the God Iao fell in love; to prevent whose intrigues the bull-eyed[1] Juno set Argus, with a hundred eyes, to watch. Jupiter turned Io into a beautiful heifer; she wandered into Egypt, and, as they say, became the goddess Isis, the wife of the bull-headed Osiris or Apis. Another story says, she was the daughter of Jordanus, a king in Phœnicia; that Jupiter turned himself into a bull; and after persuading her to mount him, swam over the sea with her to Crete, where she brought forth a most celebrated lawgiver, called Minos, who is the same as the lawgiver of India, called Menu, and as the first king and lawgiver of Egypt, Menes. Respecting king Jordanus, that is, the king named after the river Jordan, I shall say more hereafter. I think the reader will agree with me, that all this is sufficiently mystical.

The Hindoo books are full of accounts of the expulsion from India of a class of persons called Yavanas. Now who were these Yavanas; and when expelled, what became of them? To this I think I can produce an unanswerable reply,—the evidence of, *in this case*, an unimpeachable witness. The person in the Pentateuch called *Javan* is thought to have planted Greece; the LXX. were of this opinion, and constantly translate the Hebrew word Javan into Ἑλλας, the country of Hellen, or Greece.[2] When I consider the circumstance of the Yavanas being Greeks, and the fact, that many Greek towns, as I shall presently shew, were called after those in India, I cannot doubt that some at least of the Greek states were colonies from that country. " Javan was called by Moses ן *iun*. Between this name and that of Janus there is thought to be " a great similitude."[3]

Respecting the word Helen, Proclus[4] says, that all the beauty subsisting about generation from the fabrication of things, is signified by Helen: about which there is a perpetual battle of souls, till, the more intellectual having vanquished the more irrational forms of life, they return to the place from whence they originally came. Mr. Taylor, the Platonist, says, that the word Helen signifies *intelligible beauty*, being a certain *vessel* (ἑλενη τις ουσα) attracting to itself intellect.[5]

3. The elegant, polite, and enlightened Greeks, a nation celebrated for wise men, had a history of a voyage called the Argonautic expedition, of a company of heroes, who sailed from Greece in a ship called the Argo, to the kingdom of Colchis, in search of the golden fleece of a Ram. Although the history literally taken is full of the most puerile nonsense and absurd contradictions, it was in substance generally believed; the ancient wise men, as in some similar cases modern ones do, endeavouring to explain the difficulties away. The story is very long and is really so foolish, if understood literally, that I cannot bring myself to repeat it, but it may be found in Dr. Lempriere's Classical Dictionary, gravely told, not disputed, but countenanced, for the instruction of our youth—and a very beautiful thing it is for the purpose. He finishes, instead of expressing any doubt about its having taken place, by observing, that many persons, *the learned no doubt*, consider it as a commercial enterprise, that Dr. Gillies considers it partly as a voyage of instruction for young Greeks, and partly for retaliation for injuries sustained by Greece from strangers; and

---

[1] Homer.     [2] Shuckford, Lib. iii.     [3] Bryant, Anal. Vol. II. p. 251.     [4] In Plat. Polit. p. 398.
[5] Class. Journal, No. XLV. p. 39.

the Leviathan of wise men, the Aleim or God of modern Britain, Sir Isaac Newton, considered it to be an embassy: and so firmly was this talented and silly, wise and foolish,[1] though very good man, convinced of its truth, that he founded upon it a system of chronology. It is probably an astronomical allegory: and from various terms used and incidental circumstances, it is evidently not of Grecian invention, though accommodated by them to their traditions and localities. On this part of the subject Mr. Maurice says, [2]

" Now the mythological history of Canopus is, that he was the pilot of that sacred vessel,
" (meaning the ship Argo,) and was adored as the God of mariners among the Egyptians, who,
" therefore placed him on the rudder, calling him Canobus, from *Cnoub*, the Coptic term for gold—
" in reference to the singular colour and lustre of a star, one of the most brilliant in the southern
" hemisphere. The circumstance of this star not being visible in any of the celebrated cities of
" Greece has already been noticed from the same author, and Dr. Rutherford, in proof that the
" Greeks were not the original inventors of that asterism."

Again, Mr. Maurice says, " Dr. Rutherford, in one of the most ingenious productions on the
" subject of natural philosophy that ever was published, has in the clearest manner evinced that
" the constellations delineated on the sphere, though apparently allusive to the Argonautic expe-
" dition, could not possibly be the fabrication of Chiron, or any other Grecian for that purpose ;
" since the greatest part of the stars in the constellation Argo, and, in particular, Canopus, the
" brightest of them, were not visible in any part of Greece; and no astronomer would be so absurd
" as to delineate constellations to direct the course of a vessel, the principal stars in which 'could
" 'not be seen by the mariners either when they set out or when they came to the end of the
" ' voyage.' "[3]

Here is an end of the Argonautic expedition as a Grecian story ; we will try if we can find it elsewhere.

Of the Argonautic expedition Sir W. Jones says, " That it neither was according to Herodotus,
" nor indeed could have been originally, Grecian, appears even when stripped of its poetical and
" fabulous ornaments, extremely disputable: and I am disposed to believe it was an emigration
" from Africa and Asia, of that adventurous race who had first been established in Chaldæa."[4]

In a little treatise of Mr. Maurice's, called Sanscreet Fragments, published in 1798, is an account of a sage called Agastya, whom he shews to be the star Canopus, the famous steersman or pilot of the Argo of Greece. The circumstance that this star was not visible in Greece, and that it was in this particular manner noticed and said to be a hero, placed in the heavens by the Sanscreet historians, is very remarkable, and pretty well shews that the mythos of the Argonauts is, as we might expect, of Hindoo origin. When we consider how intimately this Argonautic story is blended with all the Greek mythoses—what multitudes of their towns and districts are called from it—the accounts of it in the poems of Homer—and that its stars are not visible in Greece, how can we doubt that all their systems came from the same place whence it came, viz. India ?

Sir W. Jones has observed, that the asterisms of the Greek and Indian hemispheres are so similar, that it is plain the systems are the same, yet that there are such variations as to make it evident they were not copied from one another; whence it follows, that they must have come from a common source.[5]

When the almost infinite variety of ways in which the Argonauts are connected with the mythoses of Greece is considered, it of itself affords a strong probability, amounting very near to a

---

[1] Witness his Essays on the Revelation of St. John. He was the greatest of natural, and the least of moral, philosophers.
[2] Hist. Hind. Vol. II. p. 38.      [3] Ind. Ant.      [4] Supplement to Ind. Chron.
[5] Asiat. Res. Vol. IV. p. 10.

demonstration, that the Grecian mythology came from India. Indeed, I think a probable opinion might be very safely founded upon it alone.[1] Babylon must have been the great connecting link between India and Europe.

4. It now becomes necessary to make a few observations on the Indian Linga and the I, or Yoni, as connected with the celebrated boat of the Hindoos, called *Argha*, which I propose to shew gave rise, among the Greeks, to the fables of the above-named Argo, Argonauts, &c., &c. In the old philosophy of the Hindoos I have shewn that the world was supposed to be destroyed and renewed at the end of certain periods, and this process was supposed to be of immense, if not of eternal, duration. This was a very recondite and philosophical idea, and was partly founded upon the principle that God was perfectly wise, and that he would form or create nothing that was bad, and that as he was not changeable, he would not really finally destroy that which he had made, which was necessarily good: and that consequently what appears to us to be changed must be only periodical, and therefore that a periodical renovation of every thing would take place. At the end of every period the world was supposed to be destroyed. At this moment Brahme or Brahme-Maia, the Creator, was believed to be in a state of repose or inaction in the profundity of the great abyss or firmament: and the male and female generative powers of nature, in conjunction, were said to float or brood on the surface of the firmament or abyss, and in themselves to preserve the germ of animated nature,—of all plants and animated beings. This operation of the two powers is described by the Linga, in the shape of a mast, fixed in the Yoni, in the shape of a boat, floating in the firmament. After this operation has proceeded a certain time, the female generative power begins to act, by feeling the passion of love, the *ερως* of the Greeks, which is described by the sending forth of a dove, and this is the beginning of a new age. Of this Col. Wilford says,[2]

" Satyavrata having built the ark, and the flood increasing, it was made fast to the peak of " Naubandha with a long cable.[3]

5. The mystic Ocean in which the ship Argha floated, is the ethereal space or fluid, the רקיע rqio,[4] called firmament in Gen. i. 7, in which the bodies of the planetary system revolve. The Ark or Argha, the ship, with its mount Meru in the centre by way of mast, may be seen in every temple of India, and requires no explanation. It is the Omphale of Delphi. See the Yoni and Linga, plates, fig. 20.

The Earth was often called the Arga: this was imitated by the mystic Meru. The north pole was the Linga, surrounded by seven dwips or zones rising one above another, and seven seas, or rivers, or waters, and an outward one called Oceanus. In this Oceanus the whole floated. Thus the earth, mother Eartha, became the Argha or Ione, and Meru the pole, the Linga.

---

[1] I ought to have explained to my reader before, that a probable opinion is such a one as a man may entertain, whether it be true or false, without being damned for it. It is the scientific term for a doctrine of the Jesuits, discussed and misrepresented by Pascal in the Provincial Letters. The Jesuits, making allowance for the infirmities of human nature, maintained, that if a person by inquiry of those who were likely to be informed, or by the best means in his power, came to an erroneous conclusion, he would not be subject to condemnation for it. The Calvinists, and those who adopt the Athanasian creed, are of a different opinion; but then they are a more enlightened race than the benighted Jesuits!

[2] Asiat. Res. Vol. VI. p. 524.

[3] Nau-band-a I have explained before (in B. v. chap. v. sect. 2 ). Sati-avrata is composed of the word Sati, meaning Saturn, (which I shall explain hereafter,) and a-vrat, which is the Hebrew emphatic article, and בראת *brat*, and means former or creator, from ברא *bra*, to form or create: and jointly it means mount of Sati the Creator. Thus Il-avrata is the mount of God (il) the Creator. In the Sanscrit the b and v are used indifferently for each other.

[4] From this word *rqio* came the *rack* of Shakspeare. " Shall leave not a *rack* beniad." See title page of the Celtic Druids.

It is quite clear that this mythos must have been formed in the infancy of astronomical science, when the plane of the ecliptic was believed to coincide with the plane of the equator.

" During the flood, Brahma,[1] or the creating power, was asleep at the bottom of the abyss : the " generative powers of nature, both male and female, were reduced to their simplest elements— " the Linga and the Yoni. The latter assumed the shape of the hull of a ship, since typified by " the Argha, whilst the Linga became the mast. (Maha-deva is sometimes represented standing " ing erect in the middle of the Argha, in the room of the mast. Maha-deva means *magnus-deus.*) " In this manner they were wafted over the deep, under the care and protection of Vishnu." (The three in *one,* and one in *three.*) " When the waters had retired, the female power of nature ap- " peared immediately in the character of *Capoteswari,* or the DOVE, and she was soon joined by " her consort *Capoteswara.*"[2] I think he must be very blind who does not see here the duplicate of the Mosaic allegory of a ship and a deluge. The animated world in each case preserved in a boat, or Argha, or Theba, חבה *tbe,* Θιϐη, but in the latter, instead of putting all the live animals into one ship, the germ or principle of generation is substituted.[3]

The Argha is represented by a vessel of copper, by the Brahmins in their sacred rites.[4] It is intended to be a symbol or hieroglyphic of the universal mother. It is very often in the form of an elliptic boat or canoe, having both ends similarly pointed, or biprora, as its name was.[5] In the centre of it is an oval rising, embossed, which represents the Linga. But it is to be seen in the shape described in the plate, repeated in every variety of way, in every temple of India. By this union of the Linga and Yoni, or Ioni, it is intended mystically to represent the two principles of generation—to represent them as one. This boat, as I have already intimated, was the Argo of Greece, the name of the mystic ship in which the Ionians, who lived at Argos, sailed to seek the golden fleece of the Ram. It was also the name of a man, Argos, who is said to have lived at Amphilochium, in the bay of Am-brasius, and it was the invention of *divine wisdom* or Minerva. This Argha was also the cup in which Hercules sailed over the ocean.[6]

In my plates, fig. 21, is an example of the Argha and Linga and Ioni, from a great number in Moore's Hindoo Pantheon, and from Creuzer's plates. The Argha of India was the same as the

---

[1] Brahma is ברא *bra, creator,* and ma, or maha, *great*—that is, great Creator. Vide Book v. chap. i. sect. 10, *n.*

[2] Asiat. Res. Vol. VI. p. 523.

[3] This leads me to digress a moment to make an observation upon the ιλυς or mud of Sanchoniathon, into which the mass of our globe was supposed, not unphilosophically, to have been reduced; a state into which M. Cuvier's researches shew that it has been at least nearly reduced many times. This substance, Genesis says, was תהו *tëu,* ובהו *u-bëu,* incapable of generation or of producing any of those beautiful animal or vegetable forms which we see around us. God communicated to it this faculty, and we know not, and probably never shall know, how far it extended. For any thing we know, he might subject it to certain rules, or endow it with certain properties, which should give it the power, under certain limited circumstances, of what we call self-generation, or self-production. I contend that, if we admit a God, we cannot doubt his possession of this power ; and, as we cannot know that he has not exercised it, we cannot, I think, from equivocal generation, conclude that he does *not exist.* When certain particles of matter, under certain circumstances, come together, they shoot into certain regularly-shaped crystals, always having the same forms, but not animated. Where is the improbability in the Creator having subjected matter to such other rule or law, that when other particles of it come together, under certain peculiar circumstances, certain other forms having the faculty or capability of vivification, the property of animation, to a certain limited extent, should be produced ? For instance, the animalculæ observed to appear in vinegar, in which any vegetable matter is steeped. We are totally ignorant of the means by which the principle of vitality acts upon matter. Then shall we draw positive conclusions merely from our ignorance? Heat applied to an inanimate egg produces what we call life. This egg is matter under a certain modification, fitted, when heat is applied, to produce the effect, *life.* In the same manner, the matter in the vinegar is under such circumstances as are fitted to produce the effect which we see.

[1] Asiat. Res. Vol. VIII. pp. 52, 275.        [5] This was the shape of the ship of the Argonauts.

[6] Asiat. Res. Vol. III. pp. 363, 365.

Patera of the Greeks and Romans, so sacred in the mysteries of Delphi, and every where in those of Apollo. It is called among the Hindoos sometimes Argha, and sometimes Patera, and sometimes Argha-patera. It is also called Pan-patera or Pan-patra. Among the numerous plates in Moore's Pantheon, there is scarcely one in which the Linga and Ioni or Argha are not to be seen, varied in different ways.[1] In the ceremonies of the Hindoos there is no emblem in more universal use. For a full account of it, I must refer my reader to the book itself.

The meaning of the word Argo as applied to the ship Argo, is generally acknowledged to be unknown, and not to be intelligible in the Greek language. Argŏlis is Argo-polis. Argia, the other name of the same place, is Argo-ia; written in Hebrew letters it would be ארגיא *argia*, or ארגאי *argai*, and would mean the place of Argo. This was in Arcadia, which was called the cradle of the Greeks, where also was Delphi. Arcadia is Arca or Arga-dia, the Sacred Arga. The Greeks were called Argives. The mariners of this ship were called Argonautæ. The ship carried a beam on her prow cut in the forest of Dodona, by Minerva, which gave out oracles, and which falling on Jason, the captain of the ship, killed him. Of course it must have been carried upright as a mast, or it could not have fallen down upon him. The ship was built by seven Cyclops, who came from Syria or the country of the Sun, שר *sr*. It conveyed many passengers[2] who at one time carried the ship 150 miles, from the Danube to the Adriatic, on their shoulders. They passed from Greece by way of the river *Tanais* or the *Don* to the ocean. Some authors have said the ship was built by Hercules ; Dr. Lempriere *solemnly assures us* this is false. I therefore place no dependence on it. He seems really to have believed that there once was such a ship.

There was also a town of Acarnania, called Argos Amphilochium,[3] in the bay of Ambracius. It was founded by Amphilochus of Argos, son of Amphiareus son of Apollo. It is at present called Filoquia. Here again we find the words Argo and Amphe or Omphe or Om closely connected. There was also a city in Macedonia called Amphipolis, of which Thucydides gives an explanation, but which was not satisfactory to D'Anville. It had the name of Crysopolis. Its Turkish name is Iamboli or Emboli. It was anciently also called Eion, out of which the Greeks made Iampolis. It is at the mouth of the Strymon, near Palæo-Orphano, and not far from the tomb of Orpheus, near which Dr. Clarke[4] found a medal with a Boustrophedon inscription thus : AM

IΦ.

These names may be considered to be translations of one another. Crysopolis is πολις, Χρησος *benignus*, *mitis*.[5] Iam-boli is polis-om, or om-polis, with the monogram *I* prefixed, as was very common. The Eïon is the on of Egypt and the Delphic ει. But of the meaning of these words we shall see more presently. Col. Leake found an inscription at a village near the Strymon in Macedonia, called at this time Yenikeni, the remains of the ancient Amphipolis.[6] Mr.

---

[1] Panth. p. 388.    [2] Onomacritus makes the passengers by the Argo amount to fifty-two.

[3] I suspect that this is Om-pi-lhkm or Omphi-l'-hkm—town of the wise Omphi, or of the wisdom of Om, or Omphi. If my suspicion be correct, the mystic Om ought to be found wherever the mythos is found. I much suspect that in all these words, even in the word Omphi, the phi, as I have before intimated, is the Coptic emphatic article *Pi*, and that we have sought too deeply for the meaning of this word. I shall be told that Pi is not Greek; but is it not evident that the Greek and Coptic were originally one? Can any thing, therefore, be more likely than that the names given to places should be similar in both of the languages? The Egyptian, however, must have been the oldest: but I shall discuss the question of this language presently.

[4] Travels, Vol. IV. p 401. 4to.

[5] Why not Χρυσος will be explained hereafter.

[6] Walpole's Travels, Vol. II. p. 512. In the same work, p. 516, I find Apollo called ΑΠΛΟΤΝ, in Thessaly. This is, I think, Apollyon.

Bryant has observed that the Greeks new-named many places. For example, Palmyra, for Tadmor ; but that among the natives the ancient names are yet to be found in use, the Greek name being forgotten. I suspect this is the case with Amphipolis and Yeni-keni, and that the former part of this word was a corruption of Yoni. The country about Amphipolis was peculiarly sacred. The river Strymon was anciently called Ioneus.

The Greeks considered Delphi to be the navel of the earth, as the Jews, and even the first Christians, thought that the true navel was Jerusalem ; and the Mohamedans still consider Mecca as the mother and navel, or nabhi. All these notions appear to have arisen from the worship of which we have been treating. The Yoni and Nabhi or navel, are both denominated *Amba* or mother : but Wilford says, the words *Amba, Nabhi,* and *Argha,* have gradually become synonymous ; and as αμβη and *umbo* seem to be derived from *amba* or the circular *argha,* with a boss like a target, so ομφαλος and *umbilicus* apparently spring from the same root : and even the word navel, though originally Gothic, was the same anciently with *Nabhi* in Sanscrit and *Naf* in Persian.[1] This is also the same with the *Nau* in Sanscrit for ship, and *Navis* in Latin. A great umbilicus, carried in the processions both at Delphi and in Egypt, had the form of a boat or Nau. From this Nau the centre part of our churches was called Nave, and built in their present oblong, inconvenient form.

The Protogenos or first Emanation from the divine power—from the head of Jupiter, was Minerva or Divine Wisdom, or the female generative power, of which the Ioni or Argha of India was an emblem. See plates, fig. 22. This was the Rasit of Genesis, the Wisdom or the FIRST principle (or *principe* in French) by which God formed the world. It was the Argo of Greece : it was the Αρχη of the feminine gender, which meant *the first cause, the ruler, the beginning.*[2] Its verb was Αρχω, *to command, to set in order.*[3] The Ionian Pelasgi or Ionian sailors called their gods *disposers* or *placers in order.* Here is the Argha or Argo or Αρχη, the *first* or pre-eminent placer in order, both in time and dignity. The way in which these profound doctrines emanate from one another is striking and beautiful. This shews how the Exoteric meaning of Genesis is *beginning,* and its Esoteric *wisdom.* As I have before observed, if the Greek had merely meant *in the first place,* or *in the beginning,* it would have said πρωτως. The Argha or Ark is called κιβωτος by the LXX. When a Buddha or new Incarnation of *divine wisdom* appeared in Japan he was called Cobotos.[4] Can any one doubt that this was the Argha or κιβωτος of the LXX. ? This shews that the κιβωτος could not mean a ship, but, as I have said before, it had the same meaning as Argha, the female generative power, in opposition to the Linga. As a boat was also the emblem of the female generative power, the two came at length to be confounded.

---

[1] Asiat. Res. Vol. III. p. 367.      [2] See Jones's Lex.

[3] The Hebrew ערד *ord* and the English *order* are the same Saxon words.      [4] Kæmpfer, Japan.

## CHAPTER II.

THE LOTUS.—MAURICE ON THE LOTUS.—PAYNE KNIGHT ON THE SAME.—MOORE ON THE SAME.—
NIMROD ON THE SAME.

1. THE double sex typified by the Argha and its contents is also by the Hindoos represented by the " Nymphæa or Lotus, floating like a boat on the boundless ocean, where the whole plant " signifies both the earth and the two principles of its fecundation. The germ is both Meru and " the Linga : the petals and filaments are the mountains which encircle Meru, and are also a type " of the Yoni : the leaves of the Calyx are the four vast regions to the cardinal points of Meru : " and the leaves of the plant are the Dwipas or isles round the land of Jambu."[1]   As this plant, or the lily, was probably the most celebrated of all the vegetable creation among the mystics of the ancient world, and is to be found in thousands of the most beautiful and sacred paintings of the Christians at this day, I must detain my reader with a few observations respecting it.   This is the more necessary, as it appears that the priests of the Romish Church have lost the meaning of it : at least this is the case with every one of whom I have made inquiry.   But it is like many other very odd things, probably understood in the Vatican, or the crypt of St. Peter's.

2. Maurice says, " Among the different plants which ornament our globe, there is no one which " has received so much honour from man as the Lotos or Lily, in whose consecrated bosom " Brahma was born, and Osiris delighted to float.   This is the sublime, the hallowed, symbol that " eternally occurs in oriental mythology : and in truth not without reason ; for it is itself a lovely " prodigy.   Throughout all the Northern hemisphere it was every where held in profound venera- " tion, and from Savary we learn that that veneration is yet continued among the modern Egyp- " tians."   And we shall find in the sequel, that it still continues to receive the respect, if not the adoration of a great part of the Christian world, unconscious, perhaps, of the original reason of their conduct.

3. The following is the account given of it by Mr. Payne Knight, in his very curious disserta- tion on the Phallic worship :[2]

" The Lotos is the Nelumbo of Linnæus.   This plant grows in the water, and amongst its " broad leaves puts forth a flower, in the centre of which is formed the seed vessel, shaped like a " bell or inverted cone, and punctuated on the top with little cavities or cells, in which the seeds " grow.   The orifices of these cells being too small to let the seeds drop out when ripe they shoot " forth into new plants, in the places where they were formed : the bulb of the vessel serving as " a matrix to nourish them, until they acquire such a degree of magnitude as to burst it open, and " release themselves, after which, like other aquatic weeds, they take root wherever the current " deposits them.   This plant, therefore, being thus productive of itself, and vegetating from its " own matrix, without being fostered in the earth, was naturally adopted as the symbol of the " productive power of the waters, upon which the active spirit of the Creator operated in giving " life and vegetation to matter.   We accordingly find it employed in every part of the northern " hemisphere, where the symbolical religion, *improperly called idolatry*, does or ever did prevail. " The sacred images of the Tartars, Japanese, and Indians, are almost all placed upon it, of which

---

[1] Asiat. Res. Vol. III. p. 364.

[2] Pp. 84—86. This book was never sold, but only given away. A copy is kept in the British Museum, but it is *not in the catalogue*. The care displayed by the trustees in keeping it out of the catalogue, to prevent the minds of the studious gentlemen who frequent that institution from being corrupted is above all praise ! ! !   I have read it in the Museum.

2 x 2

" numerous instances occur in the publication of Kæmpfer, Sonnerat, &c.. The Brahma of India
" is represented sitting upon his Lotos throne, and the figures upon the Isiac table hold the stem
" of this plant surmounted by the seed vessel in one hand, and the CROSS representing the male
" organs of generation in the other: thus signifying the universal power, both active and passive,
" attributed to that Goddess."

Creuzer says,[1] from the peculiar mode in which the sacred Lotus propagates itself by its bean,
came the religious veneration for this seed ; on which Mr. Muller observes, that it was from this
that Pythagoras, who was of the school of the Buddhists, ordered his disciples to hold in veneration and to abstain from beans. See my plates, fig. 23. The Nelumbo Nymphæa is not a
native of Egypt, though seen upon almost all its ancient monuments, but of the North-eastern
parts of Asia.[2] This is the correct and proper plant of the sacred mysteries, but after the original meaning of it had become lost, in modern times, any lily was indiscriminately used, as may
be observed in the Romish pictures of the Virgin, particularly of the annunciation or impregnation, where the ministering angel is always seen to carry in his hand a branch of some kind of
lily.

4. Of the Lotos, Mr. Moore says, " The Nymphæa or Lotos floating on the water, is an emblem
" of the world : the whole plant signifies both the earth, and its two principles of fecundation.
" The stalk originates from the navel of Vishnu, sleeping at the bottom of the ocean,[3] and the
" flower is the cradle of Brahma or mankind. The germ is both Meru and the Linga : the plants
" and filaments are the mountains which encircle Meru, and are also the type of the Yoni : the
" four leaves of the calyx are the four vast dwipas, or countries, toward the four cardinal points.
" Eight external leaves, placed two by two in the intervals, are eight subordinate dwipas or coun-
" tries."[4]

5. Concerning the Lotus of the Hindoos, Nimrod[5] says, " The Lotus is a well-known allegory,
" of which the expanse calyx represents the ship of the Gods floating on the surface of the water,
" and the erect flower arising out of it, the mast thereof : the one was the Galley or Cockboat,
" and the other the mast of Cockayne : but as the ship was Isis or Magna Mater, the female
" principle, and the mast in it the male deity, these parts of the flower came to have certain other
" significations, which seem to have been as well known at Samosata[6] as at Benares." This
plant was also used in the sacred offices of the Jewish religion. In the ornaments of the temple
of Solomon the Lotus or lily is often seen.[7]

Athenæus says that Suson was a Greek word for a Lily, and that the name of the city Susa
meant the city of Lilies.[8] This is very remarkable, as it was the capital of the Cushites or Ethiopians. But the Lotus of the Nile and Ganges was, I believe, dark blue, which sometimes was
the colour of Cristna : but he was as often black as blue. He is perfectly black in the India
House. John Crawford says, " I suppose the Lotos to be here an emblem of Parvati, who, as
" well as Sri, I find has the epithet of Padmi in the nomenclature of the Gods." Again, " A
" Lotos is frequently substituted for the Yoni."[9] This may be seen in thousands of places in
Egypt and India. We will now return to our Ionians and their Argo.

---

[1] Liv. prem. Ch. ii. note, p. 160; Maurice, Ant. Hind. Vol. III. p. 245.

[2] Payne Knight's Inquiry, Sect. 146.    [3] See plates 7 and 8 of Moore's Pantheon.

[4] Asiat. Res. Vol. VIII. p. 308 ; Moore, Hind. Panth. p. 270.    [5] Vol. I. p. 127, Sup. Ed.

[6] Vide Luc. Ver. Hist. Lib. ii. Cap. xlv.

[7] In the North of England children make boats of Walnut shells which they call cock-boats, a remnant of the same
superstition. See Nimrod, Vol. I. p. 441, note.

[8] Nimrod, Vol. I. p. 44.    [9] Asiat. Res. Vol. XIII. p. 359.

# CHAPTER III.

THE LOADSTONE.—HELEN ATHENA.—YAVANAS.—DIVISION OF THE FOLLOWERS OF THE MALE AND
FEMALE PRINCIPLES, AND THEIR REUNION.

1. In my CELTIC DRUIDS I have proved that the loadstone was known to the ancients; and I
think it was used by the priests for the purposes of superstition, for which it was evidently peculiarly calculated.[1] " The Temple of Jupiter Ammon was esteemed of the highest antiquity, and
" we are informed that there was an Omphalus here: and that the Deity was worshiped under
" the form of a navel."[2] Quintus Curtius says, " Id quod pro Deo colitur, non eandem effigiem
"habebat, quam vulgo Diis artifices accommodarunt. Umbilico maxime similis est habitus,
" smaragdo, et gemmis, coagmentatus. Hunc cum responsum petitur, navigio aurato gestant
" sacerdotes, multis argenteis pateris ab utroque navigii latere pendentibus." I think with Scotus
and Hyde that this relates to the compass.[3] I have little doubt that here was the sacred Argha
concealing in it a loadstone or magnet, or carrying it perhaps upright as the mast, by which the
credulous devotees were duped. The Paterae ab utroque latere pendentes were votive offerings.[4]
2. The name of the chief Grecian city of the Ionians, Athena, was the name of the female generative principle, as was also Helena, called by Lycophron the Dove, which is a translation of the
word Pleias, and also of the word Semiramis,[5] and Ion or Ione. The Ionian Athenians claimed
to be called Athenians from Athena, which was the name of Minerva, who was both the female
generative principle and divine wisdom. The Greeks were called Hellenes, which has precisely
the same meaning as Ionians. And they are called Argives from the ship Argo, which was invented by Minerva, who fixed in the prow of it the pole or phallus cut at Dodona, as before

---

[1] Aristotle describes the Mariner's Compass. See Niebuhr, Vol. I. p. 28.
[2] Bryant, Anal. Vol. I. p. 246. [3] Hyde de Relig. Vet. Pers. App. p. 496.
[4] For what I have said in my Celtic Druids on the subject of the Telescope, Gunpowder, the Mariner's Compass,
and other examples of the learning of the ancients, as might well be expected, I have been turned into ridicule by ignorant, narrow-minded persons, whose understandings permit them to see no further either behind or before them than
the length of their noses. However, the doctrine I advocate has been placed above the reach of cavil by Sir W.
Drummond, in the 19th volume of the Classical Journal, p. 297. Among other matters, he there observes, that we are
not to laugh at the powers which the ancients claimed to possess, because we do not possess them ourselves; and he
instances the burning of the Roman ships by the Mirror of Archimedes, which was not believed to be possible till it
was successfully imitated by Buffon: and the hatching of eggs in an oven in Egypt, which was laughed at till imitated
by Reaumur: and which I have been told is now commonly practised in breeding poultry for the London market.
Roger Bacon believed in the possible transmutation of the baser metals into gold, and his reasoning amounted to this—
Since carriages have been moved without the aid of animals—since boats have been impelled through the water without
oars or sails—since men have been transported through the air—since very distant and very minute objects may be
made perfectly clear to vision by means of glasses—and since the effects of thunder have been produced by a few
grains of powder—how can it be contended that the transmutation of metals is impossible? Class. Journ. Vol. XIX.
p. 303. From this most extraordinary exhibition of the words of this most celebrated natural philosopher or alchemist,
or magician, or judicial astrologer, I feel very little doubt that among the ancient priests or astrologers, all these
secrets were known; and that from his books of the occult sciences he came by the information, that these important
secrets were formerly known, though perhaps only known to a very few of the heads of a secret order, guarded as
Masonic secrets, and consequently in later times lost.
[5] Nimrod, Vol. I. p. 451.

noticed. All these names have a direct reference to the female generative power, and had their origin in India. Minerva was both the female generative power and divine wisdom, because wisdom was the first emanation of the Divine Power, and man can conceive no way in which it can become active except by producing ; thus the mystics united the two.

Mr. Bryant says, " The Grecians were, among other titles, styled Hellenes, being the reputed " descendants of Hellen. The name of this personage is of great antiquity : and THE ETYMOLOGY " FOREIGN." Again, " The Hellenes were the same as the Iönim, or Ιωνης, whence Hesychius " very properly mentions Ιωνας, Ἑλληνας. *The Ionians and Hellenes are the same family.* " The same is to be said of the Æolians and Dorians : they were all from one source, being de- " scended from the same ancestors, the *Ionim* of Babylonia and Syria: as the Phœnician women " in Euripides acknowledge :

Κοινον[1] αιμα, κοινα τεκεα
Τας κερασφορε πεφυκεν Ιες.

" The term Hellen was originally a sacred title." [2]

Many states of Asia Minor and other countries were said to have been colonized by Greeks. This, in most instances, arose from mistakes respecting the word Helen. Sometimes they were Hellenes, sometimes Argives, and sometimes Ionians ; but neither ancients nor moderns have suspected the real meaning of these words, and therefore have applied them all to the Greeks—in doing which they have fallen into innumerable inconsistencies. Mr. Bryant has shewn that Jason was as well known in the East as in Greece ; [3] that he was styled Argos, and gave name to a mountain near Ecbatana in Media. All this tends to strengthen the proofs that the Argive, Hel-lenian, or Ionian doctrines came from the East. Mr. Bryant says, [4] " The city Antioch, upon the " Orontes, was called Iönah. Ιωνη ετως εκαλειτο ἡ Αντιοχεια, ἡ επι Δαφνη, ἡν ωκισαν Αργειοι. " *Who these Argeans were that founded this city, Iöna, needs not, I believe, any explanation.*" I think not. And I trust my reader will soon think with me, if he do not think so already.

Jeremiah says, [5] " Arise, and let us go again to our own people and to the land of our nativity, " from the face of the sword of the *Ionim.*" The LXX. translate the last words, Απο προσωπε μαχαιρας Ἑλληνικῆς : and in chap. l. ver. 16, it is translated in the same way. Johannes An-tiochenus calls the Midianites Hellenes. He calls Jethro, father-in-law of Moses, Αρχιερευς των Ἑλληνων. I think, though it is a difficult etymon, that the word must have come from the He-brew לא al the sun, and עין oin a fountain or an eye. [7]

3. Among the Hindoos, the natives of the Western world are called Yavanas. The word Ya-vana is a regular participial form of the Sanscrit root *Yu*,[8] from which root the word Yóni or the female nature is derived. Thus the Yavanas are the same as Yónijas or the Yoni-ans. And here we find the origin of the Ionians, as we might expect, in a religious principle—a principle which, though now almost lost and forgotten, I do not doubt formerly placed one half of mankind in arms against the other, the feuds of the two covering the world, for many generations, with carnage and blood : a feud about the most ridiculous and trifling of nonsense. " The Yavanas " were so named from their obstinate assertion of a superior influence in the Yoni or female, over " the Linga or male nature, in producing perfect offspring." [9] And from this nonsense, almost as

---

| | | |
|---|---|---|
| [1] Phœniss. V. 256. | [2] Anal. Vol. III. p. 383. | [3] Ibid. Vol. II. p. 513. |
| [4] Anal. Vol. III. p. 370. | [5] Steph. Byzant. Ιωνη. | [6] Chap. xlvi. ver. 16. |
| [7] Vide Trans. Roy. Soc. Edinb. Vol. III. p. 140. | | [8] In Syriac Yo or Io both male and female. |
| [9] Asiat. Res. Vol. III. p. 358. | | |

absurd as most of the sectarian doctrines of the Christians, the whole world was involved in war and misery.

In the earliest times of which we have any records, the Brahme-Maia, that is the male and female generative principles in union, or the Linga and the Ioni, were the objects of adoration. After some time the division, which I have just noticed, took place, and a terrible war arose between the followers of the Linga and those of the Ioni, and the latter were at last expelled, with great slaughter, to the West. This war was between the followers of Iswara the *active* generative principle, and the Yónijas the followers of the *passive* generative principle. It was probably the origin of the Greek fable of the war between the Gods and the Giants, or sons of the earth,[1] which we know, from Nonnus, had its origin in India.[2] For a more particular account of this war I refer to the Asiatic Researches.[3] This was the famous war of the Maha-barat, in which the Buddhists were expelled from South India. The Buddhists were particularly attached to the male principle.

4. In this manner the ancient religion became divided into two : the sect which adored the sacred Yoni or female generative principle alone, were called Yavanas,[4] and were expelled from India, and are to be found almost all over the Western world. But we are informed that after some time a reconciliation took place, and the two parties united, and once more returned to the worship of the double principle. This is very important. We shall find traces of it in our researches almost every moment, which will enable us to account for many seemingly inconsistent circumstances. Although various sects went out from India, as one party or other prevailed, the natives of that country now make no distinction, but call them all Yavanas.

From the reunion of the two principles it is that we have the Ioni and Linga united in almost every temple in India, as well as at Delphi, &c., in Greece ; in the former, described by the two objects in union, in the latter, by the stone pillar and orifice in the earth called Omphe, and by the boat, the Argha, with a man in it, carried in procession in their ceremonies. The meaning of the united two, the *self-existent* being, at once both male and female—the *Aleim*, called *Jah* in Genesis, and the IE on the temple at Delphi, the Ieo of Greece, the Iu-piter Genetrix of Latium.

Of the reality of the great wars here noticed, I think there can be no doubt, and if the habits of life of the ancient Indians were in any degree similar to those of the present Afghans, they must in a very remarkable manner have been calculated for easy emigration. The existence of nations in the form of tribes yet continues in North India, and when we look back in Europe to the most remote periods, we every where find traces of it—many indeed yet remaining. In the earliest periods, the population of the world consisted of many tribes, with a few cities, the slow produce of commerce. In modern times, the latter have prevailed; there are *few* tribes, and *many* cities, and the land has become divided and appropriated.

In these doctrines respecting the Ioni I am not singular, for, according to Theodoret, Arnobius, and Clemens Alexandrinus, the Yoni of the Hindoos was the sole object of veneration in the mysteries of Eleusis.[5] In this temple was the celebrated OM ΠΑΞ ΚΟΓΞ. When my friend, Colonel Tod, author of the beautiful history of Rajah-Poutana, was at Pæstum in the neighbourhood of the temple of Ceres, he saw at that place several little images of the Goddess holding in her hand the Linga and Ioni, or mysterious Argha ; and he observed the same on the porch of the temple of Isis at Pompeii. It is probable that in early times the Yoni alone may have been adored

---

[1] Asiat. Res. Vol. III. p. 360.　　[2] Dionys. l. 34, v. 241, ab. Asiat. Res. ibid.　　[3] Vol. III. p. 361.
[4] Asiat. Res. Vol. VI. p. 510.　　[5] Asiat. Res. Vol. III. p. 365.

at Eleusis; but here, as elsewhere, I have no doubt the two sects united. At Eleusis there was a famous vessel called the Mundus Cereris, used in the mysteries. It was probably the Argha of India; it was supposed to contain the male and female organs of generation.

5. Another sect which was expelled from India was called by the name of *Iadavas*. They were said to be descendants of one Yadu,[1] the father of Cristna, to have been persecuted by an enemy of Cristna's, and to have emigrated during his minority.[2] But it is said that after Cristna came of age, he conquered and punished their persecutors. As Cristna certainly was not the female generative power, though the emblem of the two united principles is seen now in all his temples, this story serves to shew that the Iadus were probably in enmity to it also, and this by and by will be found of consequence, for we shall find they continued in this religion in the West. The word Ia-du is evidently the Deus or the Divus *Ia* or *Ie*, the God *Ie*. Of course the descendants of Ya-du are his votaries or followers. Of Ia-du and his descendants, or tribe, I shall treat very much at large presently.

Mount Meru, the Moriah of India, is the primeval emblem of the Linga and the earth, Mother Eartha, is the mysterious Yóni expanded, and open like the Padma or Lotos, which is, as we have seen, with its seed in the centre, an emblem of the same thing. Iswara is called Argha-nát'h'a or the Lord of the broad-shaped vessel; and Osiris or Ysiris, as Hellanicus calls him, was, according to Plutarch, the commander of the Argo, and was represented by the Egyptians, in their processions, in a boat carried on the shoulders of 72 men, and at Delphi in an umbilicus of white marble. I have some suspicion, that the history of the Argonautic expedition is an allegorical description of the war of the two principles, and of their reunion.

<hr />

# CHAPTER IV.

### SHIP OF EGYPT AND GREECE.—DUPUIS ON THE ARGONAUTS.—ARKS AND ARCA.—THEBES, TIBET.

1. In the mysteries of Egypt and Greece a ship was commonly used—this was the Argha. But it has been remarked by Mr. Bryant that this ship was not a common ship, but was of a peculiar construction; was, in fact, a mystic ship.[3] It had both ends alike, was a correct, very much elongated, ellipse, and was called Αμφιπρυμναïς Amphiprum*naus*. Hesychius says, Αμφιπρυμ-να, τα επι σωτηρια πεμπομενα πλοια. That is, *Amphiprumna are used in voyages of salvation.* This alludes to the processions in which these ships were carried about, in the middle of which was placed the phallus. They were sometimes of immense size. " Ælian[4] informs us, that a " Lion was the emblem of this God in Egypt (i. e. Hephaistos) : and in the curious description " which Capella has given us of the mystic ship navigated by seven sailors, we find that a Lion

<hr />

[1] Cristna, called Yadava, was the descendant of Yadu, the son of Yayáti. Asiat. Res. The Iadu of Mr. Maurice ought probably to be written Idv—it would then mean the God *I.*

[2] Asiat. Res. Vol. III. pp. 326, 327.　　　[3] Bryant, Anal. Vol. II. p. 224.　　　[4] Lib. xii.

" was figured on the mast in the midst of the effulgence which shone around. This ship was a " symbol of the Universe—the seven planets were represented by the seven sailors—and the Lion " was the emblem of Phtha, the principle of light and life."[1]  The Hindoos have a stone called Shalgramu, which they worship.  Mr. Ward saw one which had fallen down and broken, by which it appeared to be a shell petrefaction.  The shell in the inside of this stone is that which is called the Argonauta Argo,[2] or the Nautilus, which sets its pretty sail before the wind.  Every Hindoo God almost has one of them in his hand.  How this shell-fish came to have the name of Argo-Argonauta in the West, I know not ; but I have no doubt it has a connexion in some way with the Indian superstition, and that it relates to the Argha.  In the cabinet of the Baptist Missionaries at Bristol, is an Indian one in copper.  I think in the ship Argo, or Nautilus, with its mast supplied by Minerva or divine wisdom, I can perceive a beautiful mythos.  It is really a ship, not of human, but of divine, invention and manufacture.  From a careful consideration of the Argonautic story, I can entertain little doubt that it is a mistaken and misrepresented Indian mythos.  The arguments of Dr. Rutherford, given in Chapter I. Section 3, clearly prove, that it must have had its origin very many degrees to the South of Greece ; and this must have been, I think, where, as I shall presently shew, the Bay of Argo, and the Golden or Holy Chersonesus, that is, South India and Siam, are to be found.  It is probable that the solution of this enigma will be found in the Vedas or Puranas.

I believe, fantastical as my opinion may be thought, that, as I have before stated, our churches were built in the inconvenient oblong form, instead of square or round, in imitation of these ships, and that hence the centres of the churches are called naves.[3]  This was exactly the case of many of the ancient temples from which we have copied ours—if indeed our mysticism and theirs be not the same.  This ship was very often described as a lunar crescent ☽, and was mistaken for the moon, and thus she often became an object of adoration, when in fact she was not meant to be so.  The meaning of the Argo or Argha, or the origin of the Argives, was all entirely unknown to the Greeks.  If the moon were intended, why should her infant state have been always chosen ?  Why is she never worshiped when at full or in the quarters, by her figure in the latter of which on monuments she would be much the best described ?  I suspect she never was an object of adoration till the meaning of the Amphiprumna or Argo was lost.  Besides the moon was very often a male.

There was an order of priests in Greece called Argeiphontes—that is, priests of Argha or Argus.  Their origin or meaning was probably unknown to the Greeks.  The chief of them, at Athens, had the second rank to the Archontes, that is, the second rank of the magistracy.  He wore a crown and had the title of king.[4]

2. Mons. Dupuis thought the Argonautic story merely astronomical.  I must say I cannot *entirely* agree with him.  I believe it was both astronomical and astrological, or magical or alchemical.  It was, in fact, all four, for they were so closely united, and folly and nonsense were so completely mixed up with real science, that it is impossible to separate them.  Sir W. Jones calls it a mixed story.  He says, " This is a mixed fable, which is astronomical in one sense, and che-" mical in another ; but this fable is of Egyptian, not of Grecian, invention.  The position of the " ship Argo in the heavens would render this assertion evident, were we even without the autho-

---

[1] Drummond, Class. Journ. No. XXXIX.

[2] Ward's India, Table of Contents, p. 5 ; Asiat. Res. Vol. VII. p. 240.

[3] These amphiprumna or naves were all prophetic.  I have no doubt that the Hebrew word for prophet, *Nabi*, and these naves, had the same origin.

[4] Montfaucon, Vol. II. p. 6.

" rity of Plutarch for saying, that this constellation is of Egyptian origin. *Canopus*, the great
" star at the helm, is not visible beyond 35 deg. N. lat. Now the chemical sense of the fable, say
" the alchemists, is so clear, that some ancient Greek author, of whom Suidas, according to his
" custom, probably borrowed the language, thus expresses himself : ' *Golden fleece—this is not*
" ' *what it is poetically said to be, but it was a book written on skins, containing the mode of making*
" ' *gold by the aid of chemistry.*' The alchemists have explained what was meant by the dragon,
" and the oxen with brazen feet, which guarded the golden fleece : nor is their explanation with-
" out some show of plausibility : but I wonder that they have neglected to cite a passage in Hesiod
" about Medea, and another passage in Apollonius Rhodius, in which it is said that the ram which
" carried Phrixus was converted into gold by Mercury." [1]

I believe that whatever was meant by the Μηλον of the Argonauts, was also meant by the
Μηλον of the Hesperides. The same mythos is concealed—that the Ionian heresy of the Magna
Mater, and the tree of the knowledge of good and evil, of Paradise, and the allegories of the tree
bearing twelve fruits, &c., &c., are all implicated. In one case, the book or written skin conveyed
the knowledge ; in the other the tree, of which the leaves were letters ; the fruits, the books conveying knowledge, &c.

The doctrine of regeneration is closely connected with the Yoni and its emblem the Dove. In
India are various clefts in the ground or in rocks, (these are all nabi or navels,) into which devotees
go, and from which when they come out they are regenerated or born again. There is a large
stone in Nepaul called Guhya-sthan used for this purpose. Here is a curious mixture of Greek
and English found in India [2] — the stan or stone of Γαια, Gaia the earth. There is a similar
opening in several of the Celtic monuments of the British Isles, and particularly in the rocks at
Brimham, near Harrowgate in Yorkshire, a place formerly much used by the Druids. See Celtic
Druids. If the hole in the stone were too small for the body, as Col. Wilford says, they put a
hand or a leg in, and WITH FAITH *it did as well.* [3] The early Christians called those things *Cunni
Diaboli*, and from the former of these words came the vulgar appellation for the membrum fœmineum in England.

The country of Greece, the Peloponnesus where the Ionians dwelt, was called Apia or the country of Bees, and Archaia. The Athenians had a story, that when they sent out their pretended
colony to Asia Minor, it was preceded by the nine Muses in the form of Melissæ or Bees ; and
the emblem of the generative principle in Egypt, the Bull, was called Apis. That this has some
meaning connected with this subject cannot be doubted. Porphyry *de Abstinentia* [4] says, it was
reported that Apis gave the first laws to the Greeks.

3. Great confusion seems to have taken place respecting the different Arks. The Ark of Noe
or of נח *nh* is called תבה *tbe* (Gen. vi. 14) in the Hebrew ; Κιϐωτος by the LXX ; and *Arca* by
the Vulgate. The Ark of the covenant (Exod. xxv. 10) is called ארון *arun* or ארן *arn*, in the Hebrew ; and by the LXX. and the Vulgate as above. It is very remarkable that the Ark of Noah
should not be called in any one of the three versions by any name which answers to our word
ship—in Hebrew אניה *anie* or אני *ani ;* in Greek ναυς ; in Latin Navis. The Latin word Arca
may be old Etruscan, therefore it cannot be objected to, as an original name of the ark. But
still, I repeat, it is very remarkable, that not one of the three versions should have called it by any

---

[1] Class. Journ. Vol. XIX. p. 301.

[2] In England we have Penis-stone, and Girdle-stone, and Gods-stone, &c., &c., &c. ; in India Garga-stan, and Gher-
ghis-stan, and Aitni-stan, &c., &c., all having the same meaning.

[3] Asiat. Res. Vol. VI. p. 502.    [4] Bk. iii. p. 110, Taylor.

name answering to our word *ship ;* for Arca means *box* and not *ship*. This has certainly a mystical appearance. From the profound secrecy observed respecting the Hebrew Arca, I suspect came the word arcanus. All the ancient nations appear to have had an ark or Argha, in which to conceal something sacred; and in all of them (unless I except that of the Jews) the Yoni and Linga were inclosed.

Now, from the studied avoidance of every thing like a ship, either in the name of the article or in its shape, for it was not shaped at all like any boat that ever was built, being a solid parallelogram, with rectangular ends, (cubits 300 by 50 by 30,) I contend that I am justified in supposing, that it was meant expressly to exclude the idea of a ship. The Argha of the Hindoos is of various shapes,[1] oval, like a boat, having *both ends alike*, that is crescent-shaped, as well as round and square. The name Argha does not mean a boat, but merely the proper name of that variously-shaped structure. The boat Ark of Moses is called תבה *tbe'* in the Hebrew; but in the LXX generally κιβωτος ; but where the infant Moses is preserved on the river, it is called Θιβη in the LXX. This word Θιβη is the name of the city of Thebes, Theba, and both Nimrod and Faber admit that it has the meaning of the female generative power; the Argha and the Ioni. All this tends to shew that the ark and all the other vessels had one mystical meaning, which meaning is plain.[2]

The famous Argha of India, I believe, never means an inclosed box, therefore it is rather forced to fetch the Latin Arca from it; but, in our necessity, we must be obliged to do so, for we have no where else to fetch it from. On this very questionable word *Arca* all Mr. Bryant's and Mr. Faber's etymology turns. The word Argha in India does not answer to our word ship, but is the proper name given to a certain ship or boat, as we name our ships. From the name of a mount, *Naubanda*, I conclude that *Nau* is their name for ship: then it would be the *nau* called *Arga*. In the Chaldee, ארג *arg* meant a ship. In Greece many places are called by words something similar, but not the same, (which Mr. Bryant constantly refers to the Ark—for instance, Αρχυαιοι he calls Arkites,) because there is no such word as αρχος for ship or box in the language ; and the letter X being one of the new letters shews that it is a new word, and must be a corruption of some old word. There is no word known to us to which it can apply but the word Αργος. It will then mean Argives, or followers of the Argha. Thus when we read in Macrobius[3] of the Arkitæ or Architæ, in Syria, we ought to read Αργειοι. These considerations render almost all Mr. Bryant's reasoning respecting these words inconclusive.

If my reader will turn to the table of alphabets, *Prel. Obs.* Sect. 47, he will observe, that the Latin C answers to the Greek Gamma and the Hebrew Gimel, each being the third letter in the respective alphabets; and it is the same in the Arabic and Ethiopian. Then, the identity of all these alphabets being allowed, it seems to follow that the powers of notation in each of them must originally have been the same ; and that the third letters must consequently have been the same, that is, that the C in Latin answered to the G in the other cognate languages. This admitted, the Latin Arca, and the Greek Αρχη, and Hebrew Arga, ארגא *arga*, must have been all the same. Every Greek scholar will allow that the word Αρχη is a most obscure word, in fact a word not understood—like many of the Greek names of the Gods. In early periods, if written at all, it

---

[1] Asiat. Res. Vol. II. p. 364.

[2] The Egyptians had two Gods called Apis and Nevis, Beeves. The first was the male, the second the female, and from this called Neve or Nave—that is, the Argo.

[3] Sat. Lib. i. Cap. xxi.

could not have been written with the X but with some other letter, (because the X, as already remarked, was a *new* letter,) and this letter would, I think, be the gamma or gimel or c.

4. It is a striking circumstance that the two cities of Thebes should be called by the Hebrew word for this ship or box—the word תבה *The* or Θιϐη or Thibe, which answers to the names of several Greek towns—Argos. It is also the name of Tibet, whence came all the sacred concerns of the Hindoos, the cradle, in fact, of the human race. One name of Tibet is also Baltistan, i. e. place of Baltis. In or near Tibet is the mount called Naubanda, or mount of the *ship's cable*, called so, as the Brahmins say, from this ship Argha being simulatively fastened to it when it floated in the ocean, carrying within it the two principles of generation or the germ of animal life, in a state of quiescence and union—before the εϱος [1] or divine love began to act upon the Brahme-Maia who was reposing at the bottom of the profound abyss. After a time divine love began to act, and the creator, Brahm, divided himself into three. *the creating, the preserving, and the destroying powers*, described in our books by Adam and Eve and their three sons, and by Noah and his three sons. This all alludes, I think, to the origin of the sects which became dispersed about the world. [2]

In all ancient towns, we find an elevated place of the nature of a mount called by different names. All these mounts were imitations of the Meru of India. In Greece this was called the Acropolis—place of the Arca, Arca-polis; in Rome, the capitol. In this place the moveable Arca was always kept, and it was itself an Arca. The Capitolium of Rome will be said to have been so called from an imaginary likeness to the head of a man, it being the highest part. This may be true; but it was called *caput* for another reason: it was an icon or model of the Meru, which was itself an icon of the sun and planetary bodies—the sun, the visible sign or icon of the protogonos or Rasit of Moses, Rachid of the Arabians, Αϱχη of Greece, Caput-olium of Latium, and the Arca of Jerusalem. The Arabic and Ethiopic Rachid means head; the same as the Roman Caput the Greek αϱχη, and the Hebrew ראשית *rasit*, and they have all the same mystic allusion. At last, they are all allusions to the protogonos, to divine love—recondite and mystical enough I do not deny; but, I am persuaded, not more mystical than many doctrines; both of the ancients and of modern Christians. I need not remind my reader of the allegorical allusions in our own language to *head* and *wisdom*. A wise man has a good head; he is a long-headed fellow; his mind always resides in the head. Tibe or תבה *the* or Θιϐη or Thebes or the Beeve of the Zodiac, is Tibet, a noun in the feminine form. Georgius has shewn that Ti-bet is Di-bud—Holy Bud; the generative power, divine wisdom, of which the Arga and Ioni were symbols. We have before observed in Book V. Ch. I. Sect. 1, 2, and 3, that the letters B D, B T, are found in almost every country to mean Creator, but we have not seen clearly why. I think we have the reason in the Hebrew טוב *tub* good, the same as Καλος or Cali. This is nothing but the name of Budda, Butta, But, read in the Hebrew, instead of the Indian, fashion—בוט-רי *but-di*. The origin of the word Di or Ti, I shall explain in a future page: but it is רי *di*, Δις, dius, divus.

---

[1] Cupid, called in some mythoses the oldest of the Gods.

[2] To Noah a fourth son was said to be born, called Inachus, the father of the Ionians.

# CHAPTER V.

JANUS.—APHRODITE AND DIANA.—GANESA.—THALES, AND MEANING OF PROPER NAMES.—TWO SYRIAS; TWO MERUS; TWO MORIAHS.—THE GREEKS NEW-NAMED THEIR CONQUESTS. OM.

1. The Romans and Etruscans had a God called *Janus*: of his origin they were perfectly ignorant. He was absolutely unknown in Greece. Of the different circumstances connected with these recondite subjects, there is none more surprising and unaccountable than the complete state of ignorance in which the best-informed persons were of the meaning and origin of their Gods. Janus was not one of what they called their twelve *great* Gods, but he was said to be the father of them all. He had twelve altars erected to him. He held in one hand letters denoting 365, and in the other the keys of heaven, which he opened to the *good* and shut to the *wicked*. The first month of the year, Januarius, was dedicated to him. He was represented sometimes with two, and sometimes with four faces; the reason of which is unknown. He was called Junonius from the Goddess Juno, whose name Mr. Bryant resolves into Juneh, which signifies *a dove*, and is in the Hebrew language יונה *iune*, and is the same as the Yoni or Yuni, the female principle, as observed by Col. Wilford. On his coins are often seen a boat and dove, with a chaplet of olive leaves, or an olive branch. Gale, after observing that Juno was the same as Jana, and that Janus came from יה Jah of the Hebrews, and that Diana was Di-va Jana, or Dea Jana, says also, that she was the same as Astarte or Asteroth of the Sidonians, and had the head of a Bull. He also says, that she was the Belisama of the Hebrews.[1] In Sanscrit Di-Jana is the Goddess Jana. Macrobius tells us, that the *introitus* and *exitus*, the *front* and *back*-door entrances of buildings, were sacred to Janus: on this account he had two faces, he was *bifrons*. Zeno says that Janus was the first who built temples and offered sacred rites in Italy to the Gods, that, therefore, he deserved to be the first to be sacrificed to.[2] He was supposed to open and shut the gates of heaven in the morning and evening, and thus the prayers of men were admitted by his means to the Gods. C. Bassus says, he was represented (bifrons) double-faced, because he was the porter (janitor) of heaven and hell. January was called after him, because it was the gate of the year—the opening of the year. Twelve altars were erected to him, because he presided over the first days of the twelve months. The doors of his temple were shut in time of peace, and open in time of war.

Gale,[3] who wrote more than 150 years ago, and therefore could have no prejudice arising from Hindoo learning, likens Janus to Noah, on account of the " cognation of his name with the He- " brew יין *jain* wine, whereof Noah was the inventor;" and he says the entrance of a house called *janua*, and the month *January*, were sacred to him, because he was, after the flood, the beginner of all things. Again, he says, " others refer the origination (both of name and person) of Janus " to Javan the son of Japhet, the parent of Europeans. For, 1st, יון (*iun*) Javan is much the " same with Janus; 2nd, Thence that of *Horat.* Lib. i. 3, *Japeti Genus.* So Voss. Idol. Lib. ii. " Cap. xvi. Janus's name taken historically is the contract of *Javan.*"

Bochart[4] asserts, that from *Japhet*, mentioned Gen. x. 2, the Grecians refer their first genealogies to *Japetus*, whom they make to be the most ancient man. Thus from *Javan, Japhet's* son,

---

[1] Court Gent. Vol. II. pp. 120, 121.       [2] Mac. Sat. Cap. ix.
[3] Court Gent. Book ii. Chap. vi. Seq.      [4] Phaleg. Lib. iii. Cap. i.

the Grecians derived their *Ionians*. Also from אלישׁה *Alise*, (Elishah,) Javan's son, Gen. x. 4, they had their Hellas.

Jana was the same as Diana, (*i. e.* Di-iana,) or Venus, or Juno, or Lucina, the goddess of parturition, in which capacity she was .called Diana, Di-iana, or the divine *Jana.* Mr. Faber[1] observed, that the Italians had a Goddess called Maia. This was evidently the Maia of India, and answered to the Di-jana; they had also a God called Maius, who answered to the Janus. There was also a God called Aius, and a Goddess called Aia; evidently the same. One with the monogram M prefixed, the other without it.[2] I think in the Jain or Janus and Jana, we have the reunion of the two principles. Some persons have thought that the word *annus* came from the word Janus; and certainly the holding of the number 365 in his hand seems to shew a close connexion between them. And the same may be said of his wife (or mother as I suppose) Annaperenna, and Di-ana or Diva-Iana. From Bryant I learn that the name of this God was often written Jannus, or I-annus. In this latter case the *I* was prefixed as a monogram, as the *M* was above.[3] Mr. Faber says, " Juno herself, indeed, was the same character as Isis or Parvati, in " her varied capacity of the ship Argha, the Yoni and the sacred Dove.[4]

2. In Cyprus, Venus, I believe, was particularly called Ἀφροδίτη. But Dr. Clarke[5] has observed from Tacitus, that *simulacrum Deæ non effigie humana*. From what he says, and from the pateras with the cone in the centre of them, it seems probable that she was here represented by the Linga and Ioni in conjunction—the Meru in the Argha. Juno was called Hera, which is probably the same as Heri in Sanscrit, and means Saviour : she was also called Argiva. A certain Deïone was feigned to be beloved by Apollo. This is the Indian De and Ione.[6] " Diana is " a compound of De läna, and signifies the Goddess Jana. That her name was a feminine from " Janus, we may learn from Macrobius, who quotes Nigidius for his authority. Pronunciavit " Nigidius Apollinem Janum esse, Dianamque Janam. From this läna, with the prefix, was " formed Diana, which I imagine was the same as Dione :" that is, Di-Ione[7] in the Sanscrit. The God Janus was the unknown God of the Romans, whose first legislator was Numa, which, as I have already intimated, I take to be a corruption of the word Menu. According to Cornificius, the name of Janus was probably *Eanus*. But Eanus was undoubtedly the same as the Οἰνας of the Greeks, and the Ionas of the Eastern nations.[9]

" One of the names of Buddha is Jain or Jain-Esa : and it has been clearly shewn by Sir W. " Jones, that the mythology of Italy was substantially the same as that of Hindostan," and I have proved their ancient languages the same. " Such being the case, it seems highly probable that " the oriental Jain ought to be identified with the Western Janus, whose worship, like that of " Suman, the Romans apparently borrowed from the Etruscans or ancient Latins. To this opi- " nion I am equally led by similarity of appellation, and by unity of character. Janus, when the

---

[1] Vol. II. p. 397.

[2] See B. V. Ch. II. S. 3. The M, which is found in a very unaccountable manner in the beginning of Egyptian words, Drummond (Orig. Vol. III. p. 456) calls the *nominal* prefix. He so called it because he did not know what to make of it.

[3] The letters I, M, and X, were constantly prefixed to words as monograms, the reason for which will be explained by and by. The practice is still kept up with the X. See signature to a letter from Bishop Doyle, Morning Chronicle, August 2, 1831.

[4] Pag. Idol. Vol. I. p. 389.        [5] Travels, Vol. II. p. 334, Ed. 4to.

[6] Bryant, Anal. Vol. II. p. 339.        [7] Bryant, Anal. p. 340.

[8] Etymorum libro tertio, Cicero, inquit, non Janum, sed Eanum nominat. Macrob. Sat. Lib. i. Cap. ix. p. 158.

[9] Bryant, Anal. Vol. II. p. 258.

" Latin termination is omitted, is the same as Jain."[1]    Mr. Faber then observes, that, like
Buddha, he stands insulated as it were from the reigning superstition : and his worship appears
rather to have been super-added to it, than to have formed an originally constituent part of it.   Of
this Ovid seems to have been fully conscious when he asks, not unnaturally, in what light he ought
to consider the God Janus, since the theology of the Greeks, which was radically that of the
Romans, acknowledged no such divinity.   Mr. Faber proceeds to observe, that precisely the same
actions are attributed to Janus, which are attributed by the Greeks to Dionusus, and by the
Egyptians to Osiris.   But the Dionusus or Bacchus of the Greeks, Wilford and Jones have
shewn to be the god Deo-naush of India.   Lucian says, Bacchus was born of Semele and also
out of Jupiter's thigh ; that, after he was born, he was taken to Nysa, whence he was called
Dionysius.[2]

Having proved that the Jains were Buddhists, I think it cannot well be doubted that the Etruscans, with their four-faced god, Janus, were anciently descended from that stock.   The extraordinary circumstance that the god Janus was unknown to the Greeks, shews that the first settlers
of Italy did not come from Greece, but confirms, in a remarkable manner, the hypothesis laid
down in my CELTIC DRUIDS, that these countries were peopled by tribes from the North-east.

3.  Sir W. Jones has endeavoured to prove, that the Ganesa of the Hindoos is the Italian Janus.
This seems not unlikely.[3]   Ganesa is called Pollear : this is evidently the polis[4] in the sense of
gate.

Ganesa has almost all the attributes of the Roman or Etruscan Janus.   He opens the year ; he
is the chief and preceptor of the heavenly host.   He has often two heads.   He is the leader of all
enterprises, and his name is inscribed in the beginning of books and on the doors.[5]   I think no
one can doubt that this is the Janus of the Romans, of whom it appears that Cicero knew little or
nothing, except that he was the *oldest of their Gods*.   No doubt he was the Ganesa brought to
Italy by the persons who brought the Indian words given in Ch. II. Sect. XXV. of my Celtic
Druids ; and as there were no historical records, those things not being then invented—nothing
but mere traditions—and our Indian knowledge not being possessed by them, it is not surprising
that they should be ignorant of every thing relating to their origin.[6]

The Heliopolitæ, or inhabitants of On, in Egypt, worshiped the god Gennæus in the form of a
Lion : so Damascius in Photius, in the life of Damascius, τον δε Γεννειον Ἡλιουπολιται τιμωσιν
εν Διος ὑδρυσαμενοι μορφην τινα Λεοντες.[7]   Now is this Gennæus the god Janus or not ?   It is
true the gamma answers not to the Iota of Janus, but the Greeks and Latins made such sad
havock in their rendering of the proper names of one country into those of another, that there is
no answering for any thing.

In general, the meaning of the names of the old hero Gods (as they are called) of Greece, was
unknown to the Greeks *and cannot be ascertained from their language ;* in it, they have no meaning : but many of them are to be found in, and explained by, the oriental languages, in which they
have significant meanings.   This is at once a proof that the mythologies travelled from India to
Greece and not from Greece, or from any country West of the Indus, to India.   It is to me surprising that this decisive argument should have been overlooked.   Of this Prometheus is one ex-

---

[1] Fab. Pag. Idol. Vol. II. p. 369.
[3] See Asiat. Res. Vol. I. p. 226.
[5] Creuzer, Liv. prem. Ch. ii. pp. 166, 167.
[6] Like Janus, Mithra held in his hand two keys.  Vide Montfaucon, Vol. I. p. 232 ; Monthly Mag. Vol. LVI. p. 22.
[7] Mr. Beverley's unpublished book, called Religion Critical, xxxiv.

[2] Dial. between Neptune and Mercury.
[4] Asiat. Res. Vol. VII. p. 343.

ample : Deucalion and Saba,[1] the latter of which means *host* or *congregation*, are others.  Semiramis, whose history, except as a mythos, has always been attended with insuperable difficulties, is another.  She was Sami-Rama.  Col. Wilford says, " Sami-Rama is obviously the Semiramis " of the Western mythologists, whose appellation is derived from the Sanscrit Sami-Râmésí, or " Isi (Isis)."[2]  They are also further identified by the fact that *Capotesi*, or the Dove, was considered a manifestation of Sami-Rama, in India.  And in Assyria, Semiramis was born of a dove, and disappeared at last in the form of a dove.  Besides these, there are many other circumstances which make the identity of the two unquestionable, of which I shall observe more hereafter.

4. The natural philosophy of Sanchoniathon and Mochus *( Query* Moses ?) is said to have been brought into Greece from Phœnicia, by Thales, the founder of the Ionic school of philosophy.  I have a strong suspicion that Thales, who was most certainly a mythological person, was a corruption of the $\Phi \vartheta \alpha \varsigma$ of the Egyptians.  But I state this as a suspicion only.

I have said that there never were such men as Hercules and Bacchus, but that they are merely mythological persons, their histories being, in fact, astronomical allegories.  This I think Mons. Dupuis has most satisfactorily proved.  But I do not mean this rule respecting the mythological personages to be entirely without exception ; because it is very difficult to point out the boundary-line where mythology ends, and history begins ; and on this account it is possible, that some persons having a suspicious appearance may have been real persons.  For the cause of truth, however, we had better mistake in believing too little than too much.  This observation I apply to Thales.  What he was, it is very difficult to make out, as the various fables about his genealogy prove.  I have no doubt that, *generally*, ancient names had a meaning, particularly technical terms or terms of art.  But from this I must except such names as are taken, that is transferred, from ·one language into another.  As this was done by the ancients, as indeed it is yet constantly done by the moderns, without any rule or system, this great class of names will of course form an exception.  As a consequence, whenever, in ancient history, I meet with a word, a rational or probable meaning of which I cannot find, either in its own or any other language, I set it down as unknown, and by no means accept what appears an absurd meaning.  On the subject of language, Nimrod[3] has some very pertinent observations.  " We now make a difference between a name " which is positive and insignificant, like Mr. White and Mr. Brown, (for these names are insig- " nificant *quoad* the individuals,) and a title which has relation and significancy, as William " RUFUS.  But in those early times, when language was analogical and nearly perfect, all appella- " tions were significant, and represented some quality, or some religious symbol, or something of " good omen : and men gave as many names to famous characters, as their fancy, guided by " various circumstances, might chance to dictate : and oftentimes the very same sense, essentially, " was given in different phraseology.  If any one of those could be called the name rather than " the others, it must have been when a name was imposed by divine authority, with a prophetic " import.  Many of the great men recorded in scripture had several appellations, as Solomon, " Lemuel, Jedidiah.  Achilles had two other titles, Liguron and Pyrissous.  We must not there- " fore wonder at finding him called Bellerophon in Glaucus's pedigree, who in some others is " called Memnon, or Theseus or Romulus."

5. That the Ionic philosophy should come from the coast of Phœnicia, from the natives, perhaps, of Antioch, anciently called Iona, or from the Palli or Philistines, the natives of Gaza, (also anciently called Iona,) who were the great enemies of the tribe of Abraham, seems natural enough,

---

[1] Nimrod, Vol. I. p. 393.          [2] Asiat. Res. Vol. IV. p. 368 ; Nimrod, Vol. II. pp. 249—253.
[3] Vol. I. p. 91, Sup. Ed.

and not inconsistent with my theory. For the Pelasgi or sailors may, I think, without any great violence, be supposed to have extended the whole length of the sea-coast of Syria, or Assyria, as it has been said that it was most anciently called, the whole being the country, no doubt, of the same priests, the Culdees or Chaldees of the Ionas, and of Babylon. Now, when I reflect on the singular repetition of names of places in the Eastern part of Asia, and in the Western part of it, the Sions, the Moriahs or Merus, the Rama, near Jerusalem and near Gaza, the Semi-rama-is of Babylon, of India, and of Ascalon, the Hercules of Maturea, and the Hercules or Samson of Gaza, (Iona,) I cannot help suspecting that Syria or Suria is the Western country of the Soors of India, and that Asguria is the Western country of the Assoors, two celebrated and opposed sects of India, the first meaning devotees of Sur, the sun or light; and the other a name of reproach given them by their enemies, meaning a-soor or a-sur, *without light*, darkness, the meaning of the names of the two sects in India, but which we may be well assured the latter never gave to themselves, but only received it from their enemies, their real name being not told to us, or being Suri or Soors. The Assoors of India were a very bad race of people; so were the Carthaginians; and both for the same reason, probably, because we only hear the account from their enemies, who may have destroyed all their records and books, if they had any. It is thought by Gale, that the Assuri were only Suri, with the emphatic article prefixed: this I would readily admit if they were Assuri only in the Greek books, as we English talk about the Arabic Al-koran, which is *The The* Koran; but they are called אשורים *asurim* by the authors of the country, who would never make such a mistake. The poets Dionysius and Apollonius observe, that there were more countries than one called Assyria. Mr. Bryant[1] has shewn, that the word *our* was often written *sour*. Syncellus[2] says, Abraham was born εν τη χωρα των Χαλδαιων εν Σουρ τη πολει.

A treatise, *De Dea Suriæ*, was published by Lucian, which has been much celebrated. It appears that this was meant to convey the idea of a treatise relating to the Goddess of Syria. This is only one of the numerous mistakes of the Greeks. This Goddess was the Goddess Suria, from which Syria took its name, not the Goddess of Syria: though she certainly was the Goddess of that country. My idea that Syria and Assyria were rather *sectarian* than *proper* names of these countries, is confirmed by a passage of Strabo noticed by Mr. Bryant: "Those whom we Gre-"cians name Syrians, are by the Syrians themselves named Armenians and Aramæans."[3]

As we have seen that there were two Elephantas, two Matureas, and two Sions, the reader will not be surprised to find two Moriahs. The *Moriah* of Isaiah and of Abraham, is the *Meru* of the Hindoos, and the *Olympus* of the Greeks.[4] Cruden expounds it *the mount of doctrine*. This is so unsatisfactory as at once to prove that the word is not understood; and the reason of this is, because it is a word of some far more Eastern clime. Of the mountain Moriah, Mr. Faber[5] says, "I greatly doubt whether the name of this hill be Hebrew: with Mr. Wilford, I am much inclined "to believe, that it was a local Meru or imitative Paradisiacal Ararat." In this I quite agree with Mr. Faber. It was nothing but a Meru.[6]

6. It is a well-known fact, that the Greeks gave new names to almost all the towns and countries which they conquered or acquired. If the place had a name whose meaning was known to them, the new title was often a mere translation. But this had all the effect of new names. It might arise from the same superstition as that noticed by me in B. V. Ch. XI. Sect. 1. It is pro-

---

[1] Anal. Anc. Myth. Vol. III. pp. 147, 446, 463, 465.    [2] P. 95.    [3] Bryant, Anal. Vol. III. p. 90.
[4] Al-om-pi.    [5] Orig. Pag. Idol. Vol. III. p. 620.
[6] The Hindoos had in the North of upper India a mountain of the moon. In imitation of this when the Palli or Palestini took possession of Syria, they called the most northern of its mountains Lebanon, which means Moon. See Celtic Druids, App. p. 310.

bable that the ancient names always continued among the natives, and Dr. Clarke has observed, that after the conquest of the countries by the Saracens and Turks, they appear to have retaken their old appellations. This is similar to the observation which I quoted in Chap. I. Sect. V. from Mr. Bryant: and it is a very interesting observation, and will be found to lead to some very important consequences. I shall return to it very often. In the following names of places, the Om of India I think is very apparent. I cannot help suspecting that this OM is, at last, nothing but the monogram M, the numerical symbol of the God of the cycle of 600. Generally speaking, a person will look in vain into the Greek geographers for these Oms, and nobody will doubt that they are ancient and not modern names.[1] " Homs-Emesa; Om Keis-Gadara; Om el Djemal; " Om-Ezzertoun; Om-Haretein; Om-el-Kebour; Om-Waled; Om-'Eddjemal; Om-ba, where " resides the Sheikh or El HAKEM; Om-el-Sheratyth; Tel-Houm, Capernaum; Om-el-Taybe; " Ammon or Philadelphia; Om Djouze; Om-el-Reszasz; Om-Aamed; Om-teda; Biar Om- " shash; Om-megheylan; Omran tribe of; Hom-mar river of; Om-Hash; Om-haye; Om-Had- " jydjein; Omyle; Om-Kheysyr; Om-Shomar; Om-Dhad, places near Sinai," &c., &c.[2]

In or near the island of Meroe, Burckhardt calls a place Senaar, (which I consider a corruption of Shinar,) and he mentions Tuklawi and an island of Argo, and below Assouan, two temples called Hierosyeaminon. In many places, particularly near Mount Sinai, he notices *mountains* called Om; as Om Thoman. Animals also are called Om. And from one passage it appears as if this word had the meaning of Mother. But it is also applied to a village called Om Daoud, evidently *David*. And near Mount Sinai he met with a tribe of Arabs, who paid adoration to a saint called *El Khoudher* (St. George). This is evidently the name of Al Choder, of the ancient Arabs. But how Burckhardt came to know that he was St. George does not appear. Burckhardt says, that, at the period of the Mohamedan conquest, the peninsula of Mount Sinai was inhabited exclusively by the tribe of Oulad Soleiman, or Beni Selman. It is clear that this tribe of sons (Beni) of Solomon, cannot have come, or had their name, from the Mohamedans.

---

# CHAPTER VI.

ID-AVRATTA, MERU AND MEROE.—EDEN AND ITS RIVERS.—WHISTON AND JOSEPHUS ON DITTO.—DELOS.— PLAN OF THE MYSTIC CITY.—HANGING GARDENS AND SEVEN HILLS.—SELEUCUS OF ANTIOCH.—GREEK MYTHOLOGIES.—HOMER.—TROY, ILION.—ULYSSES AND ST. PATRICK.

1. To the work of the learned person under the name of *Nimrod*, I am chiefly indebted for the following observations: they appear to me to confirm the doctrines advanced by me, in a very remarkable manner.

Ilavratta, Id-avratta, or Ararat, or Mount Meru, of the Indians, was surrounded with seven belts of land, and seven seas, and, beyond them, by one much greater, called *the Ocean*. This was exactly in imitation of the earth and the seven planets. The Mount, with its seven belts in the

---

[1] See Bk. V. Chap. II. Sect. 3.          [2] Burckhardt's Travels in the Decapolis or Houran, and to Mount Sinai.

form of an ellipse, was a type of the planets in their elliptic orbits—with the sun, the seat of the generative principle in their centre, all floating in the ocean or firmament. The whole was represented by the Lotus, swimming in the water; by the ship of Noah and its eight sailors ; by the Argha and its mast; and (as we shall soon see) by a tower in each city, or an Argha-polis, or Arco-polis, or acropolis, and seven other hills, and surrounded with seven districts, and one larger than the others, called oceanus, at the outside. On the top of the Mount Meru, called the Mount of Saba, or of the congregation or heavenly host, was the city of Brahmapore ; the place of assembly of the Gods, and it was square, not round or elliptical. There the Gods were said to assemble in consultation, *on the side of the Mount of the North.*

Here we find the seat of God with its seven earths, emblematical of the sun and seven planets. And the Hindoo Sabha, called congregation, meaning the same as Sabaoth, " *Lord God of Sabaoth,*" Lord God of the heavenly host, the starry host. We always end with the sun and heavenly host. And here is also Il-avratta, Id-avratta, *holy* Avratta, or Ararat. The Saba is what we call in the Bible Sabaoth, but in the Hebrew it is the same as the Sanscrit צבא *zba ;* and generally means Lord of the planetary bodies—צבא ה שמים *zba-e-smim,* though, perhaps, the stars may sometimes be included by uninitiated persons. Here is the origin of the Sabæans, which has been much sought for. See Parkhurst in voce.[1]

The learned Dr. Hager says,[2] The number *seven* seems to have been sacred among the *Chaldeans,* in the same way as it was afterward among other nations, in honour of the *seven planets,* over which they believed that *seven angels* or *Cabirian deities,* presided ; and therefore they may have built *seven* towers. In the eighth, says Herodotus, was the temple of Belus. Belus's tower consists of eight stories, a perfect square circuit, 2250 feet.[3] Τον δε Βηλον, ὁν και Δία μεθερμηνευσιν—" Belus whom they interpret Jupiter." That is, the Babylonians interpret.[4] Sanchoniathon says, that Jupiter Belus was the son of Saturn. In Syria is a river Belus, near which is a tomb of Memnon ; and here Hercules was cured of his wounds.[5]

If my reader wish for a short and very clear account of the great learning of the ancient Chaldeans and Egyptians, he may consult a treatise on this subject, published by Sir W. Drummond, in the thirty-first number of the Classical Journal.

The striking similarity between the Meru of India and of Babylon, could not escape Mr. Faber, and, to prove the identity of their designs and objects, he has[6] given a very ingenious paper, which he concludes with the following sentence : " Agreeably to the just opinion of the Hindoo " Theologians, the Pyramid on the banks of the Euphrates, an artificial mountain raised in a flat " country where there are no natural mountains, was *the first erected copy of the holy mount Meru* " *or Ararat.*" I refer my reader to Mr. Faber's essay, which will much please him, if he will make only a reasonable allowance for Mr. Faber's *official* superstition.

Meru, as I have already intimated, is the Ararat of the Hindoos. There has been a considerable difference of opinion respecting the precise situation of Ararat. Most persons have placed it in the high land of Armenia, near the fountains of the Euphrates : but some have supposed that it lay in the mountainous country of Cashgar, to the North of India, and that it was a part of that lofty chain of hills which the Greeks called the Indian Caucasus. The latter of these opinions was

---

[1] Faber, Orig. of Pag. Idol. There was an obelisk in Babylon, according to Diodorus Siculus, (Lib. ii.) erected by Semiramis, 130 feet high. The name of 'Ερμαιος Λοφος (Hesychius) or Hermæ given to the places of the obelisks, shew that they were Buddhist, Hermes being Buddha.

[2] Diss. Babyl. Bricks, p. 27.     [3] Bombay Transactions, Vol. I. p. 137.

[4] Berosus, ap. Scal. Græc. Euseb. p. 6.     [5] Clarke's Travels, Vol. II. p. 395, ed. 4to.

[6] In the Classical Journal, No. XLI.

held by Heylin and Shuckford :[1] and it has lately been revived, with much ingenuity and with the advantage of great local knowledge, by Mr. Wilford.[2]   I cannot help thinking that there were two Ararats.   The hypothesis of the oriental site of Ararat, as maintained in my Celtic Druids, but ridiculed by some pragmatical individuals, is supported both by Heylin and Shuckford.   " Ila-" vratta or Ida-vratta signifies the circle of Ila, the earth, which is called Ida.   The Jews and " Greeks soon forgot the original Meru, and gave that name to some favourite mountain of their " own country : the first to Sion or Moriah.   The Greeks had their Olympus and Mount Ida, " near which was the city of Ilium, Aileyam in Sanscrit, from Ida, whose inhabitants were " Meropes, from Merupa : being of divine origin, or descended from Meru."[3]   Meru is Olympus, of Olympus is Meru.   There are several Olympuses, but only one Meru, though several less sacred mounts, called Splinters of Meru.   This raises a strong presumption that Meru was the original, and, when joined to the consideration that almost all the Greek proper names are Indian, is conclusive as to which is the original and which is the copy.   It is very likely that *vratta* may mean circle, for the divine mind was constantly represented by a circle ; but I believe the derivation of it is בראת *brat*, from ברא *bra*, *to form*.   Ida is the Hebrew ידי *ido*, idea or mind, and the whole is the mount of the creative or *formative mind*.

In most countries, there was a sacred mount, an Olympus, an Athos, or Atlas, or Ida, in short, a Meru—and a sacred city.   In Egypt, Thebes was the city ; and as they could not conveniently have a mount, without, in fact, going out of the valley of the Nile, they had a sacred island, and this was Phylæ or Meroe.   The most sacred oath of the Egyptians was, by the bones of Osiris, buried at Phylæ.   And Diodorus Siculus says, that when the priests of Phylæ thought proper, they sent a command to the king to put *himself to death*, with which command he was obliged to comply.   The first rulers of nations were Priests, Kings *their* generals.

It appears from Diodorus Siculus,[4] that the Babylon of Egypt was built on a hill, which was selected for the purpose—Meru, I can scarcely doubt.   That Meroe was a Meru receives strong confirmation from the fact, that its priests had the same name, Gymnosophists, as the Indian priests of Buddha.[5]   This has been observed before,[6] and is the name given to the Buddhists by Jerome ; and also by Clemens Alexandrinus, who says that Butta was the institutor of them ;[7] and in this my idea or suspicion that the Meroe of Egypt was an imitation of the Hindoo Meru is strongly supported.   Here is evidently an establishment of the oriental priests or sectaries, in imitation of that which had been left.   This adds probability to all the other examples of the same kind already produced in the course of this work, and of which we shall yet see several others.

In the map to Waddington's Travels, at a considerable distance above Assouan will be found an Argo and a Merawe,[8] and the author says, " As far as we could judge, from the granite and " other sculptures remaining at Argo and Djebel el Berkel, that art (sculpture) seems to have " been as well understood, and carried to as high perfection by the sculptors of Meroë, as it was " afterward by their scholars at Thebes and at Memphis."[9]   Now I ask any incredulous reader, whether he do not perceive something worthy of notice in a Meru and an Argo being found

---

[1] Connect, Book II. p. 98.        [2] Faber, Pag. Idol. Vol. I. p. 307.        [3] Wilford, Asiat. Res. Vol. VIII. p. 316.

[4] Lib. i.                          [5] De Paw, Reserches sur les Egyptiens, Vol. II.

[6] Book I. Ch. IV. Sect. 6; also, Book V. Ch. I. Sect. 5.                    [7] Hagar, p. 9.

[8] Mr. Waddington has justly observed, that the accounts of the building of Meroe by Cambyses, as given by Strabo and Diodorus, are not worth notice.

[9] P. 185.

together in Nubia or Ethiopia? I desire him to recollect my observation, that in many instances after the conquerors of a country, the Greeks for instance, had given new names to it, the old inhabitants or their descendants restored the original ones.

2. The Hindoo religion states Mount Merou to be the Garden of Eden or Paradise, out of which went four rivers. These rivers are the Burramputer, or Brahmapouter, the son of Brahma; 2dly, the Ganges, Ganga or river $\varkappa\alpha\tau'\epsilon\xi o\chi\eta\nu$, female or Goddess Ganges, in fact, a generic name for sacred rivers; 3dly, the Indus, Sind, the river *blue* or *black*; and, 4thly, the Oxus, Gihon, or Djihhoun.

These rivers were also called Chaishu, Bhadra, Sita, and Ganga, in the Hindoo language: and the country between two of the rivers was called a douab from duo-aub, like Mesopotamia, from $\mu\epsilon\sigma o\varsigma\ \pi o\tau\alpha\mu o\varsigma$-ia. In like manner, the rivers Euphrates and Tigris were supposed to flow from Ararat and Paradise; but still one of them was thought to be the river Ganges, which flowed underground from India, and appeared at the foot of the Armenian mountains : and they formed, likewise, a Mesopotamia. The Nile also was supposed to be the Euphrates, which, by an underground channel, was conveyed into Africa. In this way is accounted for the apparent absurdity of the Nile being one of the rivers of Paradise. The Ganges was called Padus, one of the names of Buddha, and the same as the Eridanus of Italy. Whether the Euphrates, or the Tigris, or the Nile, was ever called Padus I do not know; but I do know, that Buddha was the sun, and that two of those rivers, the Ganges and the Nile, were called rivers of the sun, as I shall shortly prove to have been the meaning of Eridanus.

Volney, in treating on the four rivers of Paradise, and the fact that Josephus makes one of them to be the Ganges, observes, that the Buddhists' and Brahmins' seven chains of mountains with their seven seas which surround Mount Meru, or the sacred mount of the Gods—the seven planetary bodies with their seven ethereal spaces around them in which they float, are, with the Buddhists, circular; but, with the Brahmins, elliptical. From this he infers the superior antiquity of the Buddhists. The inference is curious and interesting.

3. Mr. Whiston, on the passage where Josephus states the Ganges to be one of the rivers, observes, that upon the face of it an allegorical or esoteric meaning is intended by him—but adds, that what it is he fears it is now impossible to be determined. The record of Josephus, that one of the rivers was the Ganges, can scarcely be supposed to have been made without some traditionary or doctrinal connexion with India. But the passage of Josephus deserves much attention; indeed, more, I believe, than it has hitherto received. Mr. Whiston observes, on the work of creation, that Moses speaks of it *philosophically*, which must mean, according to the words of his preface, ænigmatically or allegorically;[1] and the whole of the work of this *ancient priest* shews the absurdity of the moderns, in construing these allegories or parables to the letter. It is evident that his account of the rivers flowing from Paradise has a secret meaning. Whiston observes, " Moses says farther, that God planted a paradise IN THE EAST, flourishing," &c...... " Now " the Garden was watered by one river which ran *round about the whole* earth, and was parted " into four parts. And Phison, which denotes a multitude, running into India, makes its exit " into the sea, and is by the Greeks called Ganges. Euphrates also, as well as Tigris, goes down " into the Red Sea.[2] Now the name Euphrates, or Phrath, denotes either a dispersion or a " flower : by Tigris or Diglath, is signified what is swift, with narrowness : and Geon runs through " Egypt, and denotes *what arises from the East*, which the Greeks call *Nile*."

---

[1] See Whiston's note on Ch. i. Book i.

[2] Mr. Whiston shews that all the Eastern Sea had the same name, which we call Red Sea.

Josephus knew that the Ganges was the sacred river of the original Ararat or Paradise, and to account for the fact of its being in India, it was feigned to run under ground; but can any circumstance tend more to confirm my hypothesis that the mythos is of oriental birth? If the whole had not originally sprung from the Ganges, how could the Ganges have ever been thought of as one of the rivers? and had not Josephus known this, he would have made the Ganges, if he had noticed it at all, run from Armenia to India. If my reader will turn for a minute to the map, he must either admit an allegory or a secret meaning, or take Josephus for an idiot. But if he will for a moment consider the Hindoo accounts of the river *Oceanus* (the name of the Nile) running round the earth, and again of some of the rivers running under ground, he will see that the account is in reality nothing but a confused copy of the mythos of the Hindoos. It is, in fact, an ænigmatical explanation of an ænigma; and it is evidently a version of the Hindoo history, so couched as to be now evident to us who have the Hindoo mythos as a key, but must have been unintelligible to the Greeks or Romans, who never heard of, or had access to, the books of the Brahmins. That they never heard of these books, will surprise no one who pays the least attention to the vanity which made them despise the learning of the Barbarians, and to the difficulty which we, the *possessors* of India, have had to get the better of the excessive repugnance of the Brahmins to let them be seen by persons not of their own caste or religion.

4. Gale says, " דחלן *dhln*, is often used in the Chaldee paraphrases for the Gentile gods; so Exod. " xx. 23; wherefore the Phœnicians called Delos דחל *Dhl* Deel; that is, the island of the god " Apollo ; [1] or, in the plural, דחלן *dhln* of the gods Diana and Apollo, for the birth of whom this " place was famous. Thence Inopus was called by the Phœnicians אוב *aub* עין *oin* the fountain of " Python, being a river in the same island, *derived by secret passages* under the earth from Nilus, " as supposed, and Cynthus, the mountain of Delos, where Latona brought forth Apollo, from חנט " *hnt, to bring forth;* whence the Phœnician חנטא *hnta*, and the Greek Κυνϑος, ט being put for ϑ, " as in Cadmus's alphabet." [2] The circumstance of the Nile having a subterraneous passage to this famous mountain and temple, is exactly parallel to the Ganges and Nile coming to the Ararat of Armenia; but still more curious and striking is the name of the mountain *Cyn* or *Cunthus*, being exactly the same as the Hindoo name of the goddess of the generative power, *Cunti*, and the name of the membrum fœmineum in Britain. The name of the membrum virile, god of generation, in Hebrew, is אלתולד *altuld, al tolad*. [3] In the north of England, by boys at school, it is called sometimes Tally, at other times Tolly. Is there any one so blind as not to see here the identity of the ancient languages of India, Syria, and Britain?

5. The following description of the city on Meru is given by the author of Nimrod, with a copy of his plan :—" In the sides of the north," that is, at the North Pole, " according to the fictions of " Indian mythology, is the pure and holy land of Ilavratta, and in the centre of that land stands " Brahma-puri, the city of the gods, and in the centre of Brahma-puri rises Mount Meru, their " Olympus. The forms which have been the subject of our discussion have been curiously com- " bined on this occasion. The land of Ilavratta is a perfect circle, but the city Brahma-puri is a " perfect square; and instead of right concentric lines fencing in the central sanctuary, eight cir- " cular towers are placed round the wall." [4] See my plates, fig. 23.

The author of Nimrod has shewn that Babylon was built with the tower in the middle of it, *square*, in imitation of Meru, or the Indian city or their Ararat, surrounded by streets, making seven concentric squares of houses, and seven spaces, and twenty-eight principal streets, (like the

---

[1] Or in Hebrew די-אל di-al.    [2] Boch. Can. Lib. i. Cap. xxiv.; Gale, Court Gent., p. 43.
[3] Drummond Œd. Jud. 285.    [4] Wilford, Asiat. Res. VIII. 285, 376, No. 4, X. 128; Nimrod, Vol. I. p. 257.

seven lands and seas of Meru,) and the eighth, the outward fosse or Oceanus.[1] He has shewn that the tower was formed upon seven towers, one above another, exactly as the Indian priests taught or imagined that the world was formed of belts of land and sea, step above step to the Meru or North pole, in the centre and at the top. Here appears to be a complete jumble of astronomy and mythology. The seven seas and mount of the North, Isaiah's seat of the gods, were theological, the seven planets astrological, and concealed from the vulgar.

Nimrod has shewn, I think pretty clearly, that Meru was surrounded with its paradise. Now we have seen how closely Bacchus was connected with Meru, or this place of Paradise. Diodorus says, that Semiramis made a Garden or a Παραδεισον, at a place in the mountains of Media called Baghistan, or the place of Baghis. Sir W. Jones had no doubt that Baghis was Bacchus.

Ecbatana or Egbatana, in like manner, was built in seven inclosures, one rising above the other; it was in the mountains of Media, and was the summer residence of the kings of Persia, who resided in the winter at Susa, the city of MEMNON who was supposed to have built it. Susa means Lotus or Lily—the city of the Lotus.[2]

On the island of Bali, a small appendage to Java, are the ruins of an ancient temple, in which the mount Meru is exactly copied. It is a square stone building, consisting of seven ranges of wall, each range decreasing as you ascend, till the building terminates in a kind of dome. It occupies the whole of a small hill which is shaped to receive the walls and to accommodate itself to the figure of the whole structure. It contains 310 images of Buddha yet entire. This temple is in the district of Kodu. This Kodu is a corruption of Iodu or Ioud. Of this more hereafter.[3] The Pagoda of Vilnour has seven stories: il y a un huitième étage, says Gentil, qui soutient le faite de la pyramide, mais l'escalier ne même qu' au septième étage.

6. From the supposition that Meru or Ararat stood in the middle of the garden of paradise, came the attachment of all religious to groves or gardens. In imitation of this, the hanging gardens were built at Babylon: rising like the seats of the Amphitheatre at Verona one above another, but oblong in imitation of the elliptic Meru.[4] These raised-up or hanging gardens round the temple of Belus, no doubt were in analogical imitation of the seven belts of land rising above one another around mount Meru, and of the mystic garden of Paradise. In imitation also of Babylon and Meru, the city of Iona,[5] or the Syrian Antioch, was built on seven hills, and was likewise supplied with its sacred groves, called the gardens of Daphne, which were very famous. The gardens of Adonis, at Byblos, in this country, were also very celebrated. Daphne was the name of the bay tree, (sacred to Apollo the HELLENistic deity,) and of the tree of knowledge of the Sibyl.[6] In or near most cities where the adoration of the Magna Mater prevailed, these gardens are to be found. The celebrated garden of delight or Paradise of Daphne, planted by Seleucus at Iona or Antioch, was placed on the site of a former one, which was said to have been planted by Hercules.

7. If, as I think cannot be denied, I have proved or shall prove that one universal religion— that of Buddha or Cristna—pervaded the whole of the old world, the conduct of Seleucus, as I shall presently shew, in the building of his city of Antioch on the ruins of the ancient Iona, in imitation of Babylon, Egbatana, Aia-aia, Mount Meru, &c., &c., will sufficiently demonstrate the reason why we meet with the several Babylons, Troys, Sions, &c.; namely, that it proceeded from a superstitious imitation of the first sacred city. In the old Greek authors a city called Aia-aia is often named. This means *Earth of Earth*, or *Land of Lands*. It is celebrated as the

---

[1] Vol. I. p. 279.  [2] Nimrod, Vol. I. pp. 248, 289.  [3] Asiat. Res. Vol. XIII. p. 161, 4to. ed.
[4] Vide Nimrod, Vol. I. p. 279.  [5] Ibid. Vol. III. p. 382.  [6] Ibid. Vol. I. pp. 249, 287.

residence of king Æetes, of the Orphic Argonauts, and was also the island of Circe and Aurora. It had its central tower, its seven or eight precincts, its garden or τεμενος or grove : but I suppose it is merely mythological, and in reality never did exist. Its remains are no where to be found. [1]

Thebes in Bœotia was called Heptapylos, as Nimrod supposes, from its seven gates in succession, one within the other, which formed it into districts like Babylon ; and, in the centre like all other Greek cities, of course had its acropolis.     And though we have no absolute authority for saying so, it is probable that Thebes in Egypt, that is the city of Theba, of the Heifer or of the Argha, was the same ; for the French scavans clearly made out five of the seven circuits among the ruins.     It was one of the oldest cities of Egypt or of the world. [2]

M. Volney has observed that, in the language of the first observers, the great circle was called *mundus* and *orbis*, the world.     Consequently, to describe the solar year, they said that the world began ; that the world was born in the sign of Taurus or of Aries ; that the world ended in such another sign.     If this explanation be justified by the oriental languages, of which M. Volney was, I believe, a very competent judge, it will remove several difficulties.

Of Troy not much is known, except that it was placed on seven hills.     Near it was the famous Mount Ida or Gargarus, with its Buddhist Gilgal, or stone circle, or τεμενος of Homer, seen and described by Dr. Clarke, where the gods were accustomed *to assemble on the sides of the North.* In my Essay on the *Celtic Druids,* (Ch. VI. Sect. XXI.,) I have given a quotation, with a translation, from Homer, where the chiefs are represented as assembling in counsel, on seats, each at his stone pillar, in a circle.     It is only fair to suppose that the circle of stones found on Gargarus, by Dr. Clarke, were the very stones alluded to by Homer, for they exactly suit to the description ; and, by this fact, afford a remarkable piece of circumstantial evidence, that the poem is not entirely destitute of foundation.

Rome was built upon *seven* hills, with a capitol or acropolis, which was square, and in other respects was an exact imitation of Babylon.     It is worthy of observation that Constantinople also was built, by the Christian Constantine, upon *seven* hills.     These circumstances tend to shew that one secret system was at the bottom of them all.     The oriental trinity is found in each of the cities in different ways ; but, after the observations on the universal prevalence of the trinity which the reader has already seen, it is unnecessary to add more here.     The word Troia or Troy, the district [3] in which the city of Ilion was placed, I have before observed means in Greek and Hebrew *the three places :* or, in English, Tripoly, of which name we have several towns now remaining.

8.  We can with certainty trace back the history of the Greeks till we are lost in absolute barbarism ; and in that state we find them in possession of gods, of whose origin they know nothing, except that the priests in their temples tell them they have learned from their predecessors that they are foreigners, and that they came from the East or the North-east—some say by land, others by sea.     In the earliest periods there were no idols attached to these temples, but in lieu thereof a plain upright obelisk or stone pillar, which was daily anointed with oil.     The God or Gods had then no names.     By degrees they got idols, and gave them names which are universally acknowledged to have come from the East or Egypt.     We examine these temples and Gods now, and we find the earliest ceremonies in a language unknown to the Greeks—the names of the Gods unintelligible, in fact, also in an unknown tongue.     But we find these ceremonies and these names intelligible in the Sanscrit, and the same ceremonies and Gods now in existence in India, the his-

---

[1]  Nimrod, Vol. I. pp. 300, 311, 322.                         [2]  Volney, Res. Anc. Hist. Vol. II. p. 403.

[3]  Nimrod, Vol. I. p. 438.

tories of which all agree in saying, that they were sent in remote times to the West. We find as soon as the Greeks became civilized, that their learned men travelled to the East for knowledge, and that they brought back with them the identical philosophical doctrines taught in India from the most remote antiquity: the Metempsychosis and the Trinity for instance. We are, however, desired to believe, that the whole or the most important of these facts, gods, and doctrines, were learned by the people of the East from those of the West, among whom it is asserted they arose hundreds of years after we know that they were taught by the travelling philosophers. Surely persons who tell us to believe this, must think us very credulous. Nimrod says, " The word " Syrian is oftentimes confounded by the Greeks with Assyrian, but it doth nevertheless denote a " very different country, that between Euphrates and the Mediterranean, famous or infamous for " the Ionian or Hellenic worship, for the lewd groves of Daphne, the mysteries of Hermaphroditus, " and the Dove temples of Hierapolis and Ascalon, at which last Semiramis was fabled to have " been born. This was mere fable, for it only means that that was the country of the Dove. The " Syrians at large bore the appellation of IONIANS and IONITES."[1]

Again, Nimrod says,[2] " From the Semiramis or Dove, the heretical people got the denomina- " tion of Ionic, which, as a sectarian name, may apply to them all: but, as a Gentile name, was " particularly affected by certain of the Pelasgi or Graïcs. The name Ione was borne by the " Syrian city which afterwards took the title of Antiochia, and which, with its Daphne, was a " great type of Babylon: and also by other places. When Alexander of Abonos Teichos sought " to reanimate Paganism BY A SHAM AVATAR OF APOLLO PYTHON, in the form of a serpent which " he called Γλυχ-Ων, he requested of the Emperor that the town might change its name to Iono- " Polis. The name was evidently applicable, and χατ εξοχην, to Babylon, which city was the " Iona vetus of Propertius."

After this, Nimrod endeavours to shew that the Ionians were emigrants from Babylon; that Ionia, in Greece, was founded by one *Caunus*, son of Miletus, son of the second Minos; that the capital of Attica was a type of Babylon, and that it adopted, to an unusual extent, the legends as well of the Diluvian as of the Tauric age; that the Acropolis, with its olive, was the Ark-tower, which, he says, is the meaning of Acro-polis or Acra: to which purpose may be noticed the Smyrnean coin inscribed Ζευς ΑΚΡΑΙΟΣ Σμυρναιων Πανιωνιος. All this evidently alludes to the celebrated Yoni or Argha. The Acropolis was the high-place or the Meru. Again; that not less than seven cities had the name of Athena, who was no other than the female principle in her warlike form, springing from the head of Jupiter Ammon, and supporting her own party with *wisdom* and *power;* that one city was the Minyeian Archomenus, whose citizens manned the Argo;[4] that the emigration of these colonies was the celebrated ἡ Ιωνικη αποικια, and the age in which it happened the Χρονος Ιωνικος—and that Homer was one of these αποικοι, and thence called an Ionian: that there were other colonies besides the Ionians, one of which " bore the " name of Aiol or the whole earth;" (the Æolians;) and others again that of D'Ore, or D'Aour (the Dorians); that the Bacchic pomp,[3] in the Eleusinian mysteries or singing the Iacchus, which he explains as the mysteries of *the son shall come,* (but which I think were the mysteries of *the son of Sol,* ινις 'Ηλιος, Eleus-in,) was in commemoration of these emigrations; that the Iacchus was named Τρι-Ομφ and Τρι-Αμϐ—and that " now when the causes of their connexion have been

---

[1] Tz. Exeg. in Iliad, p. 135; Nimrod, p. 121, Sup. Ed.      [2] Vol. I. Sup. Ed. p. 163.

[3] Bryant explains our word *pomp* from P'ompha. I have before said that the second name of Numa, that of Pom-pilius comes from the same source.

3 A

" long forgotten, the name Iacch is identified with John or Johan, and is said to be a diminutive
" thereof, although exactly of the same length." [1]

It seems probable that Babylon was a great emporium of Ionism, as it advanced to the West. If
the reader cast his eye on the map, he will see that it could scarcely be otherwise. It must have
come, I think, from the North of India, as Persia does not seem to have been much tainted with it,
if at all, for any great length of time. Greece was chiefly divided between the Æolians, Aiolians
or Aiol-Iones and the Ionians, [2] and in this I think may be seen an example of the subdivision of
the religion : the name of Aiol-ians, I believe, means a mixed race or sect,—perhaps a mixture of
the male and female, the Linga and Ioni in opposition to the Ioni alone. The emigrations are
called αποικοι or *the going out* or *leaving the house*. (This is the very expression applied to
Abraham : he is said to have left his father's house.) The Aiolians were the larger sect in Greece,
occupying Bœotia, Thessaly, Eubœa, Locris, &c. [3]

9. The opinion which I entertain, in common with such of the ancients as were most likely to
be well-informed, that the Iliad is a sacred mythos, by no means carries the consequence that
there was *not* such a city as Ilion, or a war and siege of it. I am strongly inclined to believe that
its neighbourhood was a holy place, in a very remote æra. The Druidical circle or Gilgal, found
by Dr. Clarke on the summit of mount Gargarus, in a very striking manner reminds me of the
Proseucha, probably a similar circle, found by Epiphanius on Gerizim. I suspect Olympus, Parnassus, Athos, Ida, Gerizim, and Moriah, were each a Meru or high-place ; a sacred place of the
same universal primary religion, that of Buddha, of which the same distinctive marks in its stone
circles, tumuli, carns, lingas, and Cyclopean buildings, are every where to be found, from India to
Stonehenge and Iona. It is very remarkable that on these mountains, either numbers of monks
or numerous remains of them are always found. Are these remains of the colleges of the prophets, named in the Old Testament, remains of Buddhist monks of Thibet, with the tria vota substantialia ? These three vows completely identify them with Christian Monks — Carmelites.
Lycurgus is said to have found the poems of Homer, being, as the Rev. G. Townsend describes
them, [4] merely a collection of ballads, with their appropriate titles. In the 5th, 6th, and 7th volumes of the Asiatic Researches, the story of the Trojan war is given from Sanscrit authors : its
episodes, like those of Homer, are placed in Egypt : and the traditions of Laius, Labdacus,
Œdipus, and Jason, are all found among the same ancient compositions. When, in addition to
all this, the fact is considered, that the works of Homer are discovered to contain more than 300
Sanscrit words, the true character of the Iliad will be seen ; namely, that it is a *sacred poem*, made
up by Pisistratus, and after him by Aristotle, out of a number of ballads relating to the religion of
the Indians and Greeks. Many of them have been thought to have a reference to events described
in Holy Writ, and this is natural enough if *holy writ* itself be indebted to the East for its events
and doctrines.

The resemblance between the Cristna of Valmic and the Achilles of Homer, proves the identity
of the origin of the two mythoses. Each of them, in mythology, is supposed invulnerable, except
in the right heel : each was killed by an arrow piercing that part : each was the son of the mother
of the God of Love : and the presence of each was indispensable for the overthrow of the enemy. [5]
I can scarcely believe that this identity is accidental.

I should suppose no man was more likely to understand the nature of the poems of Homer than

[1] Nimrod, Vol. I. p. 170, Sup. Ed.          [2] Strabo, Lib. xiii. p. 841 ; Steph. Byzant.
[3] Nimrod, Vol. I. p. 167, Sup. Ed.          [4] Class. Journ. No. XLVII. p. 9.
[5] Key to Chron. Camb. p. 221.

Plato, and the question whether they were to be construed literally or allegorically, and he banished them from his imaginary republic, because youth would not be able to distinguish *what is, from what is not, allegorical.*[1] And Porphyry says, we ought not to doubt that Homer has secretly represented the images of divine things under the concealments of fable.[2] The very name of the Iliad, viz. Rhapsodies, precludes all reasonable expectation of discovering the meaning of the whole of the minute parts of it, for they were known originally to have been loose detached songs, very much in the style of what Ossian's poems are said to have been. Besides, it is evident from Mr. Payne Knight's observation, that it is full of very large interpolations, as he calls them, or at least parts inserted, perhaps by different authors, which are unconnected or awkwardly interwoven with the poem, but which are still necessary to unite the songs. But if the reader consider the history of its collection by Pisistratus, and its revisal by Aristotle and his friends, for the use of Alexander, he must see at once that the expectation of shewing or making a regular system out of it is hopeless. I have no doubt that poetry or rhythm was originally invented for the purpose of assisting the memory to retain the sacred and secret doctrines; that when used in the mysteries, it was set to music, and repeated in the manner of chaunting or recitative.

I think it will not be denied, that the observations of Nimrod respecting the war of Troy are marked with much good sense; but yet there is a difficulty to be found in Greece and many other countries, in the gigantic Cyclopean buildings every where scattered about them. Who were they that built the stone circles, the walls of Tyrins, the cave at Mycenæ, &c., &c.? Great and powerful people must have lived who executed these works, and that before even the fabulous periods of Grecian history. Were they the people who formed the Trojan Mythos? But if they were, they must have lived long before the time assigned for the date of the Trojan war. They were the Cyclopes, as I shall shew; but they had not each only *one* eye.

The opinion which I have expressed respecting the Western names of Gods being found in India is strongly confirmed by Dr. Vincent. On Indian names he says, " Most, if not all, of the " Indian names which occur in classical authors, are capable of being traced to native appellations, " existing at this day among the Hindoos, at least, if not the Moguls."[3]

Col. Franklin[4] has observed the connexion between the Mythoses of the East and West. He says, " The Gods are *Merupa* (Meropes of Homer) and signify in Sanscrit *Lords of Mount Meru,* " the North-pole of the Hindoos, which is a circular spot, and the strong hold of the Gods: it is " called Ila: or, in a derivative form, Ileyam or Ilium. There is a Triad (Troiam) of towers " dedicated to the three Gods. The Trojans are styled divine, and αθανατοι, athanatoi, immor- " tals; they are Meropes and came from the place where the *sun stables his horses.* The Gods " and giants at each renovation of the world fight for the *Amrit* or beverage of immortality (Nec- " tar), and also for the beautiful *Laeshmi* (or Helen): she is called Helena. In Sanscrit all these " derivations, Meropes, for Merupa, Ileyam or Ilium, Troiam or Troia (Troja), Helena or " Helene, are the same, and point to the same thing. The story is told with some variations: " and the Trojan war happened soon after the flood of Deucalion, called in Sanscrit *Deva Cala* " *Yavana,* but to be pronounced Deo Calyun." " All the expressions in the mysteries of Bac- " chus are Erse, according to General Vallancey: Sanscrit, according to Col. Wilford in the 5th " volume of the Asiatic Researches: and Hebrew, according to Parkhurst in his Lexicon: three " singular opinions, which only persuade the unprejudiced reader of their immense antiquity and " their Eastern origin."[5] It is then noticed that Homer refers to a language different from the

[1] Taylor on the Myth. of the Greeks, Class. Journ. No. XLV.　　[2] Ibid. p. 41.
[3] Voyage of Nearchus, 129.　　[4] Researches into the Jains, p. 43.　　[5] Class. Journ. Vol. III. p. 179.

Greek, called *the speech of the Gods.* Mr. Van Kennedy's 300 Sanscrit words, in Homer, I take to be part of the speech of the Gods.

Diodorus, in his preface to his fourth book, says, that many authors, for instance, Ephorus, Callisthenes, and Theopompus, passed over the ancient mythology on account of its difficulty. This proves it unknown.

It is recorded in old traditions, that Homer, in a temple in Egypt, found a poem relative to a war against a city called Troy, near Memphis. The town, I believe, is admitted to have existed.[1] Tatian, in his oration ad Græcos,[2] says, that Metrodorus, of Lampsacus, in his treatise on Homer, made not only the Gods and Goddesses, but the heroes, of the poem, allegorical persons.

It may be a matter of doubt, whether the whole story of the Iliad may not be found in the histories of Joseph and Uriah, the gallantry of David, his marriage with Michal, his banishment, &c.[3]

Maximus Tyrius, as I have noticed in a former chapter, expressly asserts, that the stories of the Gods and Goddesses in Homer are oracular, and have a meaning different from what is apparent at first sight.

It has been said that the celebrated Dr. Bentley wrote a treatise to prove that the Iliad and Odyssey were written by Solomon, king of Israel. But to guard himself from persecution for so singular an opinion, he added, that they were written after the apostacy of this WISE MAN. Lempriere says,[4] that the Bentley manuscript (the treatise was never published) is in the British Museum. A writer in the Times newspaper of April 30th, 1829, p. 5, says the MS. is not there. Its contents were wicked, and have been probably destroyed by the priests in whose hand that establishment is. But it proves one fact,—that Bentley thought he could prove the Mythos of the tribe of Judah and of Homer were the same; and we have just now seen, that there was an Ileyam or Ilium in India; that, in fact, Meru was Ilium. Ilavratta, or the Indian Ararat, was often written *Idavratta.* This is evidently mount Ida.

The system of renewed incarnations is not strongly marked with the Greeks and Romans, but it may occasionally be found: the prophecy of a renewed Trojan war by the Sibyl cannot be mistaken, particularly when we find there were formerly many Troys and Trojan wars, with their ten years' sieges and cities taken. And this leads to the question, who was Homer? He was born at or in Cyprus, Egypt, Lydia, Italy, Lucania, Rome, and Troy. His college or place of education was Chios, Smyrna of Æolis, Colophon, Argos, Athens, Ithaca, Teos, Tenedos, Grynium, and Crete. The Sibyl of Babylon said he stole from her. Lucian of Samosata says he was a Babylonian, called Tigranes:[5] and Proclus,[6] that he was a cosmopolite—καθολυ πασα πολις αντιποιειται του ανδρος, οθεν εικοτως κοσμοπολιτης λεγοιτο. The name consists of two syllables, *Hom* and *er*, or *eer*, which word, Nimrod says, " is indicative of early or beginning time, whether it be THE OPENING " OF A MUNDANE CYCLE, the spring of a year, or the morning of a day."[7] In one word, I know nothing about him; but yet I believe I know as much as any body else. I believe with Bentley or Barnes, it matters not which, that the Iliad is a sacred oriental mythos, accommodated to Grecian circumstances, written, perhaps, by a Solomon, though not the Solomon of Jerusalem, and that *Homer* or *Om-eer* was a Solomon—if the epithet given to the poem do not mean the poems of *Om-heri* the saviour OM. Near Ajemere, in India, is a place called *Ummerghur*, that is, the walled city of *Ummer* or *Omer.* The *Ipthi-genia* of Homer is literally Jeptha's daughter.[8] It

---

[1] Class. Journ. Vol. V. p. 18.     [2] Sect. 37.     [3] See Pope's note on the Iliad, Bk. vi.
[4] Class. Dict. Barker's Ed.     [5] Luc. Ver. Hist. Lib. ii. Cap. xx. Vol. IV. p. 279, ap. Nimrod, p. 545.
[6] De Genere Homeri, Ed. Barnes, ap. Nimrod, Vol. II. p. 544.     [7] Ibid. pp. 514, &c.     [8] R. Taylor, Dieg. p. 21.

is impossible for this identity of name, joined to almost identity of history, to be the effect of accident.

10. It seems desirable to know what was the meaning of the name Troy, and the learned Nimrod explains it as follows : " Tr'oia is the triple oia, and oia means *one* or *unique,* so that Tr'oia " is three in one, the tripolitan and triunal kingdom. Oia was the chief of a Tripolis or of three " cities, belonging together in Libya, near the fertile banks of the Cinyps, which was reported to " flow from the *High-place of the three Graces :* and the said Oia, having survived her two sisters, " still keeps to herself the name of Tripoly.[1] But Troia was the land of the universal *Omphè* or " of all the *Omphès,* according as you will take the word *Pan* distributively or collectively, for in " that country from its first beginnings

Ara pan-omphæo vetus est sacrata Tonanti.—Ovid.

" Omphè is a word for voice or speech, but, like ossa, it is confined to such as proceeds from a " deity, or otherwise in a præternatural way. $O\mu\phi\eta$ $\theta\epsilon\iota\alpha$ $\varkappa\lambda\eta\delta\omega\nu$......Ol-ymp, properly Hol- " ymp, is the *universal voice,* and equivalent to Pan-omphæus......Iphis, in Greek, is a woman " with a familiar spirit. Hence we often find the word *Am-phi* in the name of soothsayers, as " Amphiareus, Amphilochus, Amphion."[2] Troy meant the country of which Ilium or $H\lambda\iota o\nu$ was the capital. There was a Troy in Egypt built by Semiramis.[3]

I have said that there may have been an Ilion. Nimrod has observed, that it would be considered blasphemy to doubt it ; yet with him I must be guilty and doubt. That the wars of Troy related to the Phrygian Troas is certain ; but that the remains of this city should be invisible to the scrutiny of the oldest of those who sought for its foundations is almost incredible. The existence of a mighty monarchy in Greece, and an organized system, ages before the dawn of civilization in that country, he maintains, is utterly fabulous ; and that no means are apparent which could have thrown back into barbarism a country so far advanced, as to give birth to the league of so many nations, to a decennial siege by more than one hundred thousand men, and above all to the artful writings of Homer. Barbarous, by their own accounts, the Greeks were before this war—barbarous for ages after. What then shall we make of this gleam of glory, dividing, as it were, the upper from the lower darkness? It is very extraordinary, that this paltry town should have interested all mankind. Every nation desired it to be believed, that they came from conquered Troy. There was a Troy or Ilion in Phrygia in Asia Minor, one in Epirus, one in Latium, one in Egypt, and one near Venice. Every state almost was founded by its conquered and dispersed refugees. They are found in Epirus, Threspotia, Cyprus, Crete, Venice, Rome, Daunia, Calabria, Sicily, Lisbon, Asturia, Scotland, Wales, Cornwall, Holland, Auvergne, Paris, Sardinia, Cilicia, Pamphylia, Arabia, Macedonia, and Libya. Every people descended from unfortunate Troy. It was a mythos, a sacred history. It was like the ancient history of all nations, a mythos—*tons* of fable mixed up with some *grains* of truth. All nations were alike. There were two Moriahs, two Sions, two Ararats, an African and an European Thebes ; an Asiatic and Egyptian Babylon ; multitudes of Memnoniums, seven cities of Athena, the name of the Goddess, the Magna Mater, the female principle in her warlike form. The Titans fought the Gods ten years ; the Sabeans besieged Babylon ten years ; Rome besieged Veii, the site of which nobody can find,

---

[1] There was a Tripoly in Africa and one in Western Asia, and a Tripetti and Trichinopoly in India—a Tanjore in India, and one in Africa.

[2] Nimrod, Vol. II. p. 443.          [3] Asiat. Res. Vol. III. p. 454.

ten years; Eira in Messenia, and Eiran in Æolia had ten years' wars; and Thebes was besieged by the Epigons for ten years. And all this, grave and wise men call history and believe it true.

How can any one consider these striking circumstances and not see that almost all ancient history and epic poetry are mythological,—the secret doctrines of the priests, disguised in parables, in a thousand forms? Mr. Faber, Mr. Bryant, and Nimrod, have proved this past doubt. Whether they have found the key to the parable or mythos is another matter. The talents and learning of these gentlemen cannot be doubted. If they had not brought minds to the subject bound by a predetermined dogma, which was to be supported, there is very little doubt but that they would have solved the ænigma. But they have failed. Weak and credulous as man has been, he did not mistake a rotten ship and a few old women for his God and Creator. Under the guise of the ship and old women a system is emblematically described. Our priests have taken the emblems for the reality. The lower orders of our priests are as much the dupes as their votaries. The high-priests are wiser. Our priests will be very angry and deny all this. In all nations, in all times, there has been a secret religion : in all nations and in all times, the fact has been denied.

"There is nothing new under the sun," said the wise Solomon, who never uttered a wiser speech; and in its utterance proved that he understood the doctrines of the eternal renewal of worlds; that new Troys, new Argonauts, would arise, as the Sibyl of Virgil subsequently foretold.

11. In the CELTIC DRUIDS, Chap. V. Sect. XLIV., I have said, "Thus there is an end of St. Patrick." I shall not repeat the reasons which I have given for that opinion, which are quite sufficient for its justification. A learned and ingenious gentleman has written a life of St. Patrick, and Nimrod says, " Firstly, and most obviously, the express tradition that St. Patrick's fosse and
" purgatory were the fosse and *necyia* of Ulysses. Ogygia (moreover) was the isle of Calypso, in
" which Ulysses sojourned : and Plutarch informs us that it was situated five days' sail to the
" West of Britannia, and that there were three other islands near it. From the South-east of
" Britain, where the Romans used to land, it would have been a five days' journey to Ireland for
" ancient navigators. The first name of Ulysses, before he came to be styled Ho-dys-cus, was
" *Nanus*, and the first name of St. Patrick was *Nannus*. In Temora, the bardic capital of Ireland,
" *Nani* tumulum lapis obtegit, and it is one of Ireland's thirteen mirabilia. Ulysses, during his
" detention in Aiaia, was king of a host of Swine : and Patrick, during a six years' captivity in
" the hands of King Milcho or Malcho, was employed to keep swine. Ulysses flourished in Babel,
" and St. Patrick was born at Nem-Turris or the *Cælestial Tower* ; the type of Babel in Irish
" mythology is *Tory* island or the isle of *the Tower*. At the time of its expugnation Sru emigrated
" from the East. Rege *Tutane* gestum est prælium campi Turris et expugnata est Troja Tro-
" janorum : but Tutanes is the Teutames, King of Assyria, whose armies Memnon commanded.
" Ulysses the κλωψ δελφινοσημος was the Koiranus (or king) whom a dolphin saved, and whom
" all the Dolphins accompanied from Miletus : his son Telemachus, whom a dolphin saved, was
" the bard Arion; but Arion was King of Miletus in the days of Priam, King of Troy : and as
" Miletus was a considerable haven of Asia Minor in Homer's time, it is the most probable place
" of Ulysses's departure. But a great consent of tradition brings the colonists of Ireland from
" Miletus. Miletus, father of *Ire*, came to Ireland in obedience to a prophecy."[1] The above is a very small part of the similitudes between Ulysses and St. Patrick; but it is enough to confirm what I have said in the *Celtic Druids*, and to blow the whole story of the saint into thin air. I believe that the whole is a Romish fable.

---

[1] Nimrod, Vol. II. p. 63?.

Nimrod[1] afterward goes on at great length to shew how the story of St. Patrick is accommodated to the ancient Homeric Mythos, and Patricius and the Pateræ to the saint; and he particularly notices a famous ship temple, described by General Vallencey in the Archæologia. Now I think it is quite impossible to date this great stone ship after the rise of Christianity. This at once raises the strongest probability, indeed almost *proves*, that the stories of Ulysses King Brute, &c., &c., detailed in the old monkish historians, are not their invention in the dark ages, as they are now considered by all our historians, and as such treated with contempt, but are parts of an universally extended Mythos, brought to the British isles in much earlier times, and as such in a high degree worthy of careful examination. The proof of any part of this Mythos having existed in Ireland or Britain before the time of Christ opens the door for the consideration of all the remainder, and is a point of the greatest importance.

Jeoffrey of Monmouth gives an account of King Brutus, grandson of Æneas, who having killed his father Sylvius in Italy, after many adventures arrived in Britain, which he conquered. He had three sons, LOGRIN, to whom he gave England;[2] CAMBER, to whom he gave Wales, Cambria; and ALBANACT, to whom he gave Scotland, Albania, or Callidonia—Callidei-ánia.

---

## CHAPTER VII.

CASSANDRA.—BABYLONIAN MYTHOS.—CONSTANTINE AND HELENA. ASTROLOGY.—BRYANT ON EARLY HISTORY. —NATIVE COUNTRY OF THE OLIVE AND OF ARARAT.

1. There is existing, in the Greek language, a very dark and obscure poem called Cassandra; purporting to be written by a person named Lycophron, in the time of Ptolomy Philadelphus. It pretends to be chiefly poetical and prophetic effusions delivered by Cassandra, during the Trojan war. For its profound learning it was in the highest estimation with the Greek philosophers. It has been called το σκοτεινον ποιημα, *the dark poem.* This may excuse my inability to explain it. But if the reader be satisfied with me that the Iliad is a sacred poem relating in part to the renewal of the Sacrum Sæculum, he will probably think, that the following lines prove that the prophecies of Cassandra relate to the same subject.

> But when athwart the empty, vaulted heaven
> Six TIMES of years have roll'd, War shall repose
> His lance, obedient to my kinsman's voice,
> Who, rich in spoils of monarchs, shall return
> With friendly looks, and carolings of love,—
> While Peace sits brooding upon seas and land.

It speaks of the Healing or Saviour God *who thus ordained and poured the voice divine* (l. 1607); of the impious railers *who taunt the God of light, scorning his word, and scoffing at his truth.* It calls the different ages Woes.

> One Woe is past! another woe succeeds.

The distribution of these woes seems impenetrably dark, but the last, I think, clearly alludes to the wars of Alexander. As the Sæculum or Neros was confounded by the early Christians

---

[1] Vol. II. p. 637.          [2] Query, Ingli-aria? or, Angli-aria—Onglir—L'Ongir

and Jews with the sæculum of one thousand, and with that of six thousand years; so I think the ages were confused by Lycophron, which arose probably from his having only an obscure and indistinct view of his subject. Like all the other mythologies and mysteries, they were in the West, after the time of Cambyses, only partly understood. Thus, though the Mellenium was the established doctrine of the early Christians, the date of its commencement, though expressly foretold, was yet unknown. I shall shew, in the second part of this work, what was the opinion of the authors of the Gospels and Canonical Epistles. The renewal of the Argonautic Expedition is foretold by Lycophron's Cassandra, exactly as it was afterwards made to be foretold in Virgil by his Sibyl.

> — Again rush forth the famished wolves, and seize
> The fateful fleece, and charm the dragon guard
> To sleep; so bids the single-sandall'd king,
> Who, to Libystian Colchis, won his way, &c.

In the course of the work she says that the Egyptian Sphynx was black; and, what is very extraordinary, she says the same thing of the *White* Sow of Alba Longa, calling her Κελαινή. Jupiter is called Ethiopian or black. I have no doubt that whatever was meant by the prophecy of Virgil's Sibyl, was meant by Cassandra. Nothing can be more dark and mystical than this poem. But I think its general tendency may perhaps be discovered from detached passages like the above. It speaks of a Budean Queen, and compares her to a dove: *dragged like a dove unto the vulture's bed.* This is an evident allusion to Semiramis, the Dove, and to the Promethean cave.

2. The author of Nimrod has bestowed almost incredible labour to prove, that the Mythos of the Trojan war, the early history of Rome, &c., &c.; in short, almost all ancient mythology, came from Babylon, and were close copies of the Babylonian history (say, Babylonian *mythos*). The close similarity between the Gods of India and those of Greece, has been proved over and over by Sir William Jones and others. Then, did they come direct from India? It is difficult to conceive how that could be effected. Nimrod has untied the knot: for Colonel Wilford has shewn,[1] that all the Babylonian Mythoses came from India, its Semi-ramis or Sami-Rama-isi, &c., &c. It is evident, therefore, that from India they came to Babylon or Assyria, thence to Syria and Sidon; thence brought by Cadmus or the Orientals to Greece: hence the duplicates and triplicates of the cities, the ten years' wars, &c. And thus at last the grand truth will be established, that they are all mythoses from the East or North-east of the Indus.

3. I have said, that Mr. Faber, Nimrod, and Niebuhr, have proved that all ancient history is little better than fable. This is true. It is all mythological. By this I do not mean to say that there is not some truth in it; but I mean to say, that there is scarcely one history, perhaps not one, which does not contain more religious fable than truth. They do not appear to have been written for the same purpose as our grave and serious histories; or they were mythoses made up of old traditions. They seem to have been a species of religious novels. Even so late as Constantine, Nimrod has pointed out something very suspicious. He says, " It is to me a matter of " grave suspicion whether the woman, his mother, was really and by her true name *Helena ;* or " whether her name was not purely fictitious, as her parentage from *Coil* or *Uranus,* King of " Britannia. In the church legend, when she dug and found the true cross, she also found a " statue of *Venus.* A most suspicious legend. Venus was daughter of Coilus, *(how,* I need not " say,) and Helena was Venus."[2] This, no doubt, is suspicious enough. Alas! what is to be

---

[1] Asiat. Res. Vol. IV. pp. 378, &c.        [2] Nimrod, Vol. III. p. 150.

believed? Concerning this Lady, I beg my reader to peruse the eighth chapter of Usher's Antiquitates, headed thus: De patria Constantini Magni, et Matris ejus HELENA, variæ et discrepantes Authorum Sententiæ, quam alii Britanniam, alii Galliam, alii Bithyniam, Nonnulli etiam Daciam fuisse volunt. She was said to have produced Constantine at York.[1]

I am quite certain that no one possessing the least candour can deny the mystical character of the story of Helen. Then, what are we to make of it? Are we to disbelieve the story of the churches built by Helena and Constantine? If we are to throw this out, what are we to believe? Where is our incredulity to stop? But can the existence of the suspicious circumstance be denied? It surely cannot.

The explanation of the Helena probably is this: it was desired to make out that her son was a renewed incarnation, and therefore he and she adopted the sacred mythical names. He wished to be thought, and perhaps thought himself, the Paraclete prophesied of by Jesus Christ. This will easily account for his hitherto unaccountable mixture of Heathenism and Christianity.

Sir W. Drummond pointed out the mythological character of the history of Jacob. This was finely ridiculed by a gentleman of the name of Townsend, who undertook, by the same means, to prove the twelve Cæsars to be the twelve signs of the Zodiac, and his success is wonderful; but it all raises the most unpleasant state of uncertainty in my mind, and makes me, after very long consideration, almost to doubt whether we really have one history uncontaminated with judicial astrology. I ask, why have we twelve Cæsars? Why do the learned historians labour to make out twelve? Twelve emperors called after the Celtic God of war, Æsar?

I feel a great difficulty, indeed I may say an impossibility, to bring my mind to believe, that the story of Helena and the twelve Cæsars are not true histories. But I recollect, that only as yesterday, I should have had the same feeling with respect to the early history of Rome. By degrees I began to doubt of Remus, Antius, Camillus, &c., &c., and at last Mr. Niebuhr has dissipated all this trash, and has converted my doubts into conviction. Then am I to doubt the existence of the Cæsars? This is impossible. Then what am I to do? I am obliged to believe, that all true history has been debased and corrupted by judicial astrology and mythology; that all histories are like the Acta sincera of the Christian martyrs, very far from SINCERE. I think no one can deny, that the desire to make out the twelve Cæsars to be twelve, and not eleven or thirteen, is astrological, and I believe that the names given to them, or assumed by them, had astrological meanings; and that it is from this circumstance that Mr. Townsend has been enabled to support his ingenious raillery in apparently a plausible manner. Without its professors intending to do so perhaps, I believe judicial astrology has corrupted almost every ancient history which we possess.

It has been observed that Cæsar was an astrological name. It was in fact the Celtic Æsar, or God of war, taken, as the Hindoo princes take their names, from a favourite God—the God of the country which Cæsar conquered. Gen. Vallancey has observed, that Cæsar did not give the name to the solstitial month, but that he took his name from it. In the old Irish, half June and half July was called Mi-Jul: thence Cæsar's name of Julius.

---

[1] On the ancient Roman road, at the ford over the river Wharf, between Tadcaster and Wetherby, a mile from Thorparch, is a place called St. Helen's Ford, and near it St. Helen's Spring, not far from which, on a mount, formerly stood a curious stone cross. A few years ago this cross, after standing perhaps 1500 years, was carried away, in my Lord Elgin's style, by an Antiquarian Lady of the name of Richardson, who took it to her garden at Gargrave. She is now dead, and it has probably become useful to mend the roads. The spring used to perform miracles, and if we may judge from the votive rags which I have seen hanging on the bushes adjoining, suspended by the persons who have experienced the efficacy of its water, its power still continues.

3 B

CONSTANTINE AND HELENA.

—— " Venerisque ab origine proles
" Julia descendit cœlo, cœlumque replevit,
" Quod regit Augustus socio per signa Tonante,
" Cernit in cœtu Divum, magnumque Quirinum,
" Ille etiam cœlo genitus, cœloque receptus."

MANILIUS.[1]

Augustus was also a mystical name given to their princes by the Egyptians. I suspect Julius was Cæsar's family sacred name, what we call *Christian* name. Cæsar was a name he assumed as conqueror of Gaul, and Augustus was assumed by his successor as prince of Egypt; but we shall understand this better hereafter.

Sir William Drummond has shewn, that the names of most of the places in Joshua are astrological; and General Vallancey has shewn, that Jacob's prophecy is astrological also, and has a direct reference to the Constellations. The particulars may be seen in Ouseley's Orient. Coll. [2] To this, probably, Jacob referred when he bade his children *read in the book of heaven what must be the fate of you and your children.*[3] The meaning of all this is explained by the passage of Virgil, that new wars of Troy and new Argonauts would arise.

It is evident that where we meet with such names as Heliogabalus, connected with such numbers as twelve, or with other numbers which we know are astrological, we may be certain some superstition, probably astrological, is alluded to; thus we may be perfectly assured that both Sir W. Drummond and Mr. Townsend are right, that the names noticed by the latter, such as Lucius, Augustus, Julius, and the number 12, have all astrological allusions. I beg Mr. Townsend to recollect that there is scarcely a name in *very ancient* history, either sacred or profane, which was not an adopted or second name, or a name given with a reference to the supposed quality or office of its owner. I beg him to begin with Abram, and he may end, if he please, with the Saviour and his cousin, John; the latter formed from the oriental word for *dove,* the holy messenger, and the former called Jesus, *because he should save his people.* Matters such as these have made some persons hastily disbelieve, and treat with contempt, all early sacred history. Although Niebuhr has shewn that almost all early Roman history is fable, this does not prove that during the three or four hundred years of Rome's fabulous period, that there was no Rome, that there were no Consuls, no Senates, or no people. It is equally rash to maintain, that there were no wars of Joshua or Judges, because we find the walls of Jericho falling to the sound of Rams' horns, or the mythological history of Hercules as Samson, or of Iphigenia as Jeptha's daughter. At the same time that Mr. Faber and Nimrod have proved the early Jewish history to be in great part the same as the mythology of the nations, they have shewn us, from the history of this mythology, that it is the height of rashness hence to conclude that it is ALL FALSE. It in *no way* differed from the history of other nations; like them it had much fable; like them it had much truth. The very ancient, curious, and interesting records of the Israelites, have never had fair play. One class of readers swallows every thing—the Frogs of Egypt, the Bulls of Bashan, the Giants, and all; the others will swallow nothing; and I am rather surprised that they admit the inhabitants of Duke's Place ever to have had any fathers. Why cannot the Jewish books be examined like the history of Herodotus, by the rules of common sense and reason? But this, I fear, is not likely very soon to happen.

Thucydides, in the beginning of his history, allows, that before the Peloponnesian war, which was waged in the time of Arta-Xerxes and Nehemiah, he could find nothing in which he

---

[1] Ouseley Orient. Coll. Vol. II. No. III. p. 221.   [2] Vol. II. No. IV. pp. 336, &c.   [3] Ibid. p. 103.

could place any confidence. This is confirmed by Bochart, in the preface to his Phaleg, and also by Stillingfleet,[1] and again by Gale.[2]

4. The following is the state of ancient history given by Mr. Bryant, and nothing can be more true:—" Besides, it is evident that most of the deified personages never existed : but were mere " titles of the Deity, the Sun ; as has been in a great measure proved by Macrobius. Nor was " there ever any thing such detriment to ancient history, as the supposing that the Gods of the " Gentile world had been natives of the countries where they were worshiped. They have been " by these means admitted into the annals of times: and it has been the chief study of the " learned to register the legendary stories concerning them : to conciliate absurdities, and to " arrange the whole into a chronological series—a fruitless labour, and inexplicable: for there " are in these fables such inconsistencies and contradictions as no art, nor industry, can remedy. " ........This misled Bishop Cumberland, Usher, Pearson, Petavius, Scaliger, with numberless " other learned men, and among the foremost the great Newton. This extraordinary genius has " greatly impaired the excellent system upon which he proceeded, by admitting these fancied " beings into chronology. We are so imbued in our childhood with notions of Mars, Hercules, " and the rest of the celestial outlaws, that we scarce ever can lay them aside.........It gives " one pain to see men of learning and principle, debating which was the Jupiter who lay with " Semele, and whether it was the same that outwitted Amphitryon. This is not, says a critic, " the Hermes that cut off Argus's head ; but one of later date, who turned Battus into a stone. " I fancy, says another, that this was done when Io was turned into a cow. I am of opinion, " says Abbé Banier, that there was no foundation for the fable of Jupiter's having made the night " on which he lay with Alcmena, longer than others: *at least this event put nothing in nature* " *out of order ; since the day which followed was proportionably shorter, as Plautus remarks.* " Were it not invidious, I could·subjoin names to every article which I have alleged, and produce " numberless instances to the same purpose." Mr. Bryant, after this, goes on to shew that the early fathers believed these Gods to have been men, and then turns the numerous Gods into ridicule ; observing, that a God was always ready on every occasion—five Mercuries, four Vulcans, three Dianas, five Dionususes, forty Herculeses, and three hundred Jupiters. He then asks why Sir Isaac Newton, in his chronological[3] interpretations, chooses to be determined by the story of Jupiter and Europa, rather than by that of Jupiter and Leda.[4] Thus he goes on to shew that the whole, if literally understood, was a mass of falsity and nonsense.

On the account given by Mr. Bryant these questions naturally arise—Has he mended the matter ? Has he satisfactorily removed the difficulty ? I believe nine-tenths of mankind will say No; though he has certainly great merit in clearing the way for others. He was followed by Mr. Faber, and he by Nimrod, who have given as little satisfaction ; and the reason is, because these gentlemen have all set out with begging the question under discussion: then making every thing bend to it—bend to a certain dogma, because they happen to have been born in England, where it was held. It may be reasonably asked of me, What right have you to think that you will succeed any better ? I answer, *I* have no predetermined dogma ; but the chief and most important of my opinions have arisen during my examination, and from it. And in addition I have the assistance of the learning of Mr. Bryant, Mr. Faber, Nimrod, and several others, which gives me, without any merit of my own, a great advantage over them. I have the advantage also of their errors as well as of their learning.

---

[1] Orig. Sac. Book i. Ch. iv.                    [2] Court. of Gent. Book iii. Ch. ii.
[3] Newton's Chronology, p. 151.                   [4] Bryant, Anal. Vol. I. p. 460.

The idea of a reduction of the Western nations to the situation of Tibet, will be turned into ridicule by the priests, who would wish the rest of mankind to believe them to be the most industrious and useful of bees, only working and storing up truths for the good of mankind ; but experience shews that they can never be watched too carefully; and if they do not anew establish their empire of the tenth century, to the printing-press alone their failure must be attributed. However amiable in private life many priests may be, there is scarcely one of them who ever loses sight of the aggrandisement of his order. Look at them in Portugal, Spain, and France ; look at the wicked and unhallowed exertions of the priests of the Protestant sect in Ireland to oppress the followers of the Romish Church, and to rivet and continue their own usurped power. And -however we, the *philosourists,* may flatter ourselves with the effects of the press, it is yet to be proved that it cannot be rendered subservient to the designs of the order. Though the Protestant and Romish sects are at present in opposition, there is no doubt in my mind, that if government were to hold a just and equal hand to both, they would speedily unite. *Then* it is much to be feared, that the liberties of Europe would speedily be destroyed.

5. No doubt the question of the originality of the ancient mythoses is, to the present generation, of the greatest possible importance; as it, in fact, involves the existence of a most terrific system of priest-craft and priest-rule—a system most dangerous to the well-being of all mankind, except the favoured caste—a system which cannot stand still, but which must either soon fall or go on increasing in power till it reduce the remainder of the world to the situation of its parent in Tibet. To resist successfully the artful sophistry of the able men among the priests is a task of the greatest difficulty. The reader must have observed that written evidence can scarcely, in any case, be made conclusive, but fortunately circumstances may ; and I consider that of the olive as an example of these fortunate circumstances. It cannot have been forged, and the recourse which the very able priest, or the priest-ite Nimrod, is obliged to have, as we shall see, to the stale plea of miracle, shews that it is conclusive and incapable of being explained away.

The observation of Nimrod is confirmed in a remarkable manner by Col. Wilford, when treating of the Oriental Ararat, which at once proves where the *third* book of Genesis, or the book of the Flood, came from : " The region about Tuct-Suleiman is the native country of the olive-tree, " and I believe the only one in the world. There are immense forests of it on the high grounds, " for it does not grow in plains. From the saplings, the inhabitants make walking-sticks, and " its wood is used for fuel all over the country ; and as Pliny justly observes, the olive-tree in " the Western parts of India is sterile, at least its fruit is useless, like that of the Oleaster. " According to Tenestalla, an ancient author cited by Pliny, there were no olive-trees in Spain, " Italy, or Africa, in the time of Tarquin the Elder. Before the time of Hesiod, it had been " introduced into Greece : but it took a long time before it was reconciled to the climate, and " its cultivation properly understood : for Hesiod says, that, whoever planted, never lived to eat " of its fruit. The olive-tree was never a native of Armenia ; and the passage of Strabo cited " in support of this opinion, implies only that it was cultivated with success in that country." [1] Of the two Ararats this pretty well proves which is the original, and which the copy.

The argument drawn from the olive is like that of Mr. Seely's respecting the Cobra Capella not being found in Egypt, but which will be soon brought thither, if it should be thought decisive. The Missionaries will not be long in bringing them ; this will be easily effected.

The author of Nimrod is as unwilling a witness as can be imagined to any circumstance that shall remove Ararat from the country between the two seas, and place it to the East of the

---

[1] Asiat. Res. Vol. VI. p. 525.

Caspian: for it at once upsets the whole of his ingenious system, and scatters the fruits of his immense labour into thin air. The observation respecting the olive has not escaped him. The following extract will shew how he surmounts the difficulty : " The olive is not an Armenian " tree: nor, if it had been so, could it have been ταννφυλλος (as Homer supposed) by any " natural means. The transaction is a miracle, (that is, a thing in which the divine power is not " only exercised unaccountably, as it is in all things, but conspicuously, and for a *particular* " purpose, and that purpose an *apparent* one,)[1] and I surmise that it may have been a miracle " of creation, producing a new thing such as the rainbow was,[2] and which had not existed " before. It was a tree of peace and reconciliation, and a pledge that the tree of life should one " day be restored. It was probably removed to Babel, and thence propagated over the world. " Whether plants sprung up, after the flood, from seeds that were preserved in the mud, or by " an original creation, is unknown. The Ambrosia of the Gods, or elixir of immortality, was, " according to one ancient opinion, the oil of olives. Thetis anointed Achilles every day with " Ambrosia, and exposed his body to the action of fire by night, that he might become immortal " and exempt from old age, which the scholiast Apollonius explains by these words, θειοτατω " ελαιω περιεχρις. If this does not mean the oil of olives, it at least alludes to the sanctity of " that ointment."[3]

## CHAPTER VIII.

ROME.—IMAGES NOT ANCIENTLY USED. ORIGIN OF THE NAME ROMA.—LABYRINTH.—OBSERVATIONS ON PROPER NAMES.—HERO GODS ACCOUNTED FOR.—SELEUCUS NICATOR ANTICHRIST.—GENERAL OBSERVA-TIONS.—YAVANAS EXPELLED FROM TOWNS THEY BUILT.

1. A great number of curious circumstances are known respecting the city of Rome—the *eternal city*, which convince me that it was a place of very great consequence, and closely con-nected with the universal mythos which I am endeavouring to develope, long before the time usually allotted to Romulus and the wolf. The following particulars extracted from the work of Nimrod are very striking: " I cannot help suspecting that Roma was, when occupied by the " predecessors of the Tusci and the Ombri, called Rama. Rome herself was supposed by many

---

[1] Though, for a purpose not connected with the question of miracle, and that I may not be accused of unfair quo-tation, I insert this definition, I by no means admit any thing so unphilosophical and confused.

[2] Here Nimrod supposes, as a matter of course, that there was no rainbow before the flood, and that it was the effect of an instant miracle. If there had been rain there must have been a bow. From a former expression it seems he believes that the obliquity of the ecliptic to the equator did not exist, but that it was the effect of miracle, contrary to the doctrine that it is the effect of the periodical revolution of the pole of the equator round the pole of the ecliptic, as the Hindoo philosophers hold. But even if this were so, it ought not to be spoken of as he speaks of it: for it is in that case a natural effect arising from a natural cause. The miracle was the disturbance of the direction of the pole of the earth, not the appearance of the bow.

[3] Nimrod, Vol. I. p. 272.

" authors[1] to have been a city of the Etrurians, during the time anterior to its foundation in the
" year B. C. 752, and subsequent to its abandonment by the ancient aborigines : and the site of
" Rome had been excavated by certain subterraneous passages of extraordinary size and solidity,
" the cloacæ, or rather cluacæ maximæ: operum omnium dictu maximum suffosis montibus
" atque urbe pensili,[2] subterque navigatâ. This work is ascribed by some to the imaginary
" king, Tarquin the ancient : but so inconsistent is Roman mythology, that we find them existing
" as buildings of indefinite antiquity in Romulus's time, when the image of Venus Cluacina (the
" expurgatrix, the warrioress, or the illustrious, for the sense is doubtful) was discovered in
" these gloomy canals. They were not adapted to the shape[3] and ground-plan of Rome, but
" probably were conformable to that of some older city. Fabretti observes,[4] that there are
" several very ancient watercourses at Rome, entirely subterranean, one of which is situated
" between the church of St. Anastasia and that of St. George, and leads directly into the caverns
" of Cloaca Maxima. They were large enough for a waggon loaded with hay[5] to pass, and
" upon one occasion, after they had been neglected, the cleansing of them was contracted for at
" 3000 talents.[6] It has been justly and sagaciously observed, by Dr. Ferguson, that works of
" convenience or cleanliness were rarely undertaken in times of remote antiquity, and if these
" were made with such an intent, they stand alone among those wonderful monuments, whose
" having existed is only credible because they still exist and are visible, and which were all sub-
" servient to the uses of ambition or fanaticism. And we may infer in a more particular manner,
" that the works in question were directed to one or both of these objects from the example of
" the Egyptian Theba Hecatompylos,[7] which was excavated with navigable canals, through
" which the kings used to lead forth their armies, under the city, and unobserved by the inhabi-
" tants. M. Vipsanius Agrippa,[8] in like manner went into the cloacæ with his barge and sailed
" through them into the Tybur."[9]

On the subject of these Cloacinæ Dr. Ferguson[10] says, " These works were, in the midst of
" Roman greatness, and still are, reckoned among the wonders of the world. And yet they are
" said to have been works of the elder Tarquin, a prince whose territory did not extend in any
" direction above sixteen miles : and on this supposition they must have been made to accom-
" modate a city that was calculated chiefly for the reception of cattle, herdsmen, and banditti.
" Rude nations sometimes execute works of great magnitude, as fortresses and temples, for the
" purposes of war and superstition : but seldom palaces : and still more seldom works of mere
" convenience or cleanliness, in which for the most part they are long defective. It is not there-
" fore unreasonable to question the authority of tradition in respect to this singular work of anti-
" quity, which so greatly exceeds what the best-accommodated city of Europe could undertake
" for its own conveniency. And as these works are still entire, and may continue so for thou-
" sands of years, it may be suspected that they were even prior to the settlement of Romulus,
" and may have been the remains of a more ancient city, on the ruins of which the followers of
" Romulus settled, as the Arabs now hut or encamp on the ruins of Palmyra or Balbec. Livy
" owns that the common sewers were not accommodated to the plan of Rome as laid out in his
" time : they were carried across the streets, and past under buildings of the greatest antiquity.
" This derangement he imputes to the hasty rebuilding of the city after its destruction by the

---

[1] Dion. Hal. Arch. Rom. I. Cap. xxix.          [2] Plin. Lib. xxxvi. Cap. xxiv. Sect. 2, p. 698, Franz.
[3] Lib. v Cap. lv.          [4] De aquis Romæ, Dis. III. p. 190, Rom. 1680          [5] Strabo, v. p. 336.
[6] Dion. Hal Lib. iii. Cap. lxxxvii.          [7] Plin. xxxvi. Cap. xx. (or xiv.) p. 688, Franz.
[8] Dion. Cassius, xlix. Cap. xliii.          [9] Nimrod, Vol. I. p. 321.
[10] Hist. Rom. Rep. Vol. I. note, p. 13, 4to.; Liv. Lib. i. Cap. xxxviii.

" Gauls. But haste it is probable would have determined the people to build on their old foun-
" dations : or at least not to change them so much as to cross the directions of former streets."
Nimrod observes upon this,[1] " Dr. Ferguson Has omitted to notice one remarkable passage of
" Lactantius, which shews that the sewers were in existence before the time of Romulus, and an
" object of ignorant veneration to that founder and his colleague. Cloacinæ simulacrum in cloacâ
" maximâ repertum Tatius[2] consecravit, et quia cujus effigies esset ignorabat, ex loco illi nomen
" imposuit. Yet we are to believe, that they were made by the fourth king after Romulus."
After this Nimrod goes on to shew what is extremely probable, that the first Roma, which
would probably be the Roma or Rama of the Ombri, or Osci, was destroyed by a natural convulsion, a volcano.

It is very certain the old traditions agreed that Rome was built on the site of a former city.
The chronicle of Cuma (which Niebuhr calls modern and worthless, but, query ?) says, that the
name of the first city was Valentia, and that this name was synonymous with Roma. Now, there
was a Valentia in Italy, and one in Britain ; there is one in Ireland, and one in Spain. There
was also a Brigantia in England, and there is one yet in Spain. There was Umbri in England,
(North-umberland and river Umber,) and Umbri in Italy. The Hindoo Gods by the same names
are all found in Ireland, as well as the Etruscan. Now, I ask, have these singular names of
people descended from a people from Upper India, speaking the Sancrit language before it was
brought to its present perfection ? How can the singularity be otherwise accounted for ? The
early history of Rome is most certainly a mythos, its real history is absolutely unknown. The
Greeks also, namely Lycophron and Aristotle, state, that there was a city in old time before that
of Romulus, called Roma or Ρώμη.[3]

I suspect with Nimrod, that Rama, so common both in India and in Syria, was the same as
Roma; that it was a noun adjective appellative, and meant, in one sense, *strong*. Thus Bala-
rama, the *powerful* or *potent Bal.* He says, " I believe that Roma is radically the same word as
" Rama, the Romans being Pelasgi, and here we have the vowel E concurrent with A and O, for
" Remus is always in Greek Ρωμος, and the name Romulus, on the contrary, was sometimes
" expressed Remulus. Livy gives me further confirmation by deriving Ram-nenses à Romulo."
Nimrod says, " For the flatterer of Octavius, the pretended Ænead prince, freely owns that
" when Æneas landed, Evander the Arcad,

Evandrus Romanæ conditor arcis,

" was already established at mount Palatine : nay, even he displayed to Æneas the ruins of yet
" an older city. And Antiochus, an authority far elder and graver than Virgil, makes Rome an
" established city in the time of Morges." Nimrod then compares the Cloacæ to the Labyrinths
of Egypt, &c., and the Caves of Ellora, and observes, that these things are inconceivable and
mark an astonishing state of society. This is, indeed, very true, and the history and date of it,
is that of which we are in search.

2. In the course of this work the reader must have observed, that it has been shewn that the
Romans, the Greeks, and the Egyptians, had none of them originally the use of images. This I
believe was when the Buddhist doctrine prevailed, or rather I should say the Buddhist Jaines :
and probably for some time also after that of Cristna had succeeded to it. I think there can be
no doubt that images were used by the Etruscans. This seems to be fairly implied in the order
of Numa, that in the Roman service they should not be used ; for, if they had not been used by

---

[1] Vol. III. p. 76.     [2] Lactant. Lib i. Cap. xx.     [3] Niebuhr's Rom. Hist. Vol. I. p. 151.

some persons, he would never have thought of prohibiting them.   I have said that I suspect
Numa of being a Menu or a Noah, as it is written in the Hebrew a *Nuh* נח.   The tribe of Juda
were strictly followers of the doctrines of Noah or Nuh, and in this respect were correctly
followers of the same doctrine as Numa.   It was from this cause that his city was called by the
Brahmin name of Rama or Roma, or Ρωμη, the name of several cities in Syria and India.   The
words in India, in Greece, and in Latium, having the same meaning, shew them to be the same. [1]

Mr. Heyne in his work entitled Veteris Italiæ Origines Populi et Fabulæ ac Religiones, in the
following passage, has suggested another origin for the name of Rome.   He says, " Quid quod
" satis probabile mihi sit, etsi aliquid pro liquido et explorato in his, quorum nulla fides historica
" est, tradere velle ineptum sit, ipsam fabulam de Romulo et Remo a lupa lactatis a nominis in-
" terpretatione esse profectam : nam a ruma, seu rumi, quod vetus mammæ nomen est, Romæ
" nomen deduxisse nonnullos videmus ; ut alios a virtute ac robore ad Græcum vocem ρώμην.
" Ignoratio originis, a qua nomen urbis ductum esset, hominum animos ad conjecturas convertit,
" quæ postea in narrationes abierant.   Quod si verum est et ex antiquioribus sumptum, quod
" Servius ad lib. 8, 90, et alibi habet, ut Tiberis priscum nomen Rumon fuerit (neque illud
" adeo abhorrens ab antiquissimo aquarum et omnium nomine per Celtas et Græcos vulgato :
" Rha, Rho, Rhu, Rhin, Rhiu, Rhei, (ρέω, ρόος,) non improbabile sit, urbis nomen A FLUMINE
" esse DUCTUM, ET omnia alia, quæ narrantur, pro commentes seriorum ætatum esse habenda."
On this my learned friend who pointed out to me the passage of Heyne observes, that the epithet
of *Roma* or *strength* given to Rome, must have been given after it grew strong.   Of course the
observation falls to the ground when it is known that it was a mystical name, *given from an
ancient mythos or city in the East*, and was itself built on the foundation of an ancient city.   The
following assertion of Atteius settles this question : Atteius asserit Romam ante adventum Evan-
dri diu Valentiam vocitatam. [2]

I cannot answer for the opinions of others, but the fact of these names having the same meaning,
and the numerous other circumstances connected with them, compel me to believe that the
Numa was a Menu, and that the Roman religion was from India.   But we all know that it was
also from Ilium or Troy ; that is, that it was closely connected with the Trojan mythos in some
way or other.   This raises a strong presumption that that of Troy must have been from
the East.   Every thing increases the probability that the Hindoo system once universally prevailed.   All this tends also to add probability to what the reader has seen respecting a city of
Valentia having formerly occupied the site of the present Roma.   If I prove that the early
Roman history is a mythos, I open the door to very latitudinarian researches to discover its
origin.   And for the proof that it is so, I am quite satisfied to depend upon what Niebuhr
has said, supported by the numerous facts pointed out by Nimrod.   Taking Valentia and Roma
to be the same, we find them in England, in Ireland, in Spain, in Italy, in Phrygia, in Syria, (as
Rama,) and in India.   Then, when can these synonymous cities have been built but when or
before the Hindoo Gods Samanaut, Bood, Om, Eswara, &c., &c., [3] came to Ireland, and the
God Jain or Janus to Italy ?   I beg my reader to recollect that however different the Cristnuvites
may be at this day, the Jains and Buddhists are, and always were, great makers of proselytes.

Numa expressly forbade the Romans to have any representation of God in the form of a man
or beast, nor was there any such thing among them for the first 170 years.   And Plutarch adds
to this, that they were Pythagoreans, and shed no blood in their sacrifices, but confined them

---

[1] Hesychius says, Ραμα; Ὁ ὑψιϛος Θεος.        [2] Serv. in Æn. I. 277; Nimrod, Vol. III. p. 110.
[3] Celtic Druids, Ch. V. Sect. XXVI.

to flour and wine. Here is the sacrifice of Melchizedek again; the Buddhist or Mithraitic sacrifice, which I have no doubt extended over the whole world.[1] In the rites of Numa we have also the sacred fire of the Irish St. Bridget, of Moses, of Mithra, and of India, accompanied with an establishment of Nuns or Vestal virgins. Plutarch also informs us, that May was called from the mother of Mercury, and that in the time of Numa the year consisted of 360 days.[2] " Numa ordered fire to be worshiped as the principle of all things: for fire is the most active " thing in nature, and all generation is motion, or at least with motion: all other parts of matter " without warmth lie sluggish and dead, and crave the influence of heat as their life; and when " that comes upon them they immediately acquire some active or passive qualities. And there- " fore Numa consecrated fire, and kept it ever burning, in resemblance of that eternal power " which actuates all things."[3] Again, in the Life of Numa, he says, " Numa built the temple " of Vesta, which was intended as a repository of the holy fire, in an orbicular form, not with a " design to represent the figure of the earth, as if that were Vesta, but the frame of the universe, " in the centre of which the Pythagoreans place the element of fire, and give it the name of " Vesta and Unity: but they do not hold that the earth is immoveable, or that it is situated in " the middle of the world, but that it has a circular motion about the central fire. Nor do they " account the earth among the chief or primary elements. And this they say was the opinion " of Plato, who, in his old age, held that the earth was placed at a distance from the centre, for " that being the principal place was reserved for some more noble and refined body."

The Phliasians had a very holy temple in which there was no image, either openly to be seen or kept in secret.[4]

The Abbé Dubois states, that the Hindoos in the earliest times had no images. As we have found that this was the case in most other nations it was to be expected that it would be the same in India.

3. The ancients had a very curious kind of building, generally subterraneous, called a laby- rinth. The remains of this are found in Wales, where the boys yet amuse themselves with cutting out SEVEN inclosures in the sward, which they call the city Troy. There is a copy of it taken from Nimrod's work,[5] in my plates, figure 25. Pliny names it,[6] and his de- scription agrees with the Welsh plan.[7] This, at first sight, apparently trifling thing, is of the very first importance; because it proves that the traditions respecting Troy, &c., found in the British isles, were not the produce of monkery in the middle ages, but existed in them long before.

The Roman boys were also taught a mazy or complicated dance, called both the Pyrrhic war- dance, and the dance of *the city Troy*. Pliny says that Porsenna built a labyrinth under the city of Clusium, in Etruria, and over it a monument of enormous and incredible dimensions.[8] The Cloacæ Maximæ, under the city of Rome, have by some been thought to be a labyrinth. These labyrinths were sometimes square and sometimes elliptical. The sacred mazy dance was to imitate the complicated motions of the planets,—was in honour of the Gods—that is, of *the dis- posers:* in short, it had the same object as the labyrinths.

The Roman circus was an allegory corresponding to the labyrinth, as the author of Nimrod supposes. The circuits were seven, saith Laurentius Lydus, because the planets are so many. In the centre was *a pyramid on which stood three altars to Saturn, Jove, and Mars,* and below it

---

[1] Vide Plut. Life of Numa.    [2] Ibid.    [3] Plut. Life of Camillus.

[4] Cumb. Orig. Gent. p. 264.    [5] Vol. I. p. 241.    [6] XXXVI. Cap. xix. Sect. ii.

[7] Nimrod, Vol. I. p. 319.    [8] Ibid. p. 319.

three others— to Venus, Hermes, and Luna. The circuits were marked by posts, and the charioteers threaded their way through them guided by the eye and memory. "The water of "*the ocean*, coming from heaven upon mount Meru, is like Amrita, (amber or Ambrosia,) and "from it arises a river which through seven chânnels encircles Meru." [1] The circuits of the circus were called Euripi. An Euripus was a narrow channel of water: ductus aquarum quos illi Nilos et Euripos vocant. [2] The three Gods, on the pyramid, had reference to the three Gods in the capitol, called Συνναιοι, [3] or *the dwellers together*, for these three were the Dii Magni Samothraces—Θεοι μεγαλοι, Θεοι δυνατοι, Θεοι, ΧΡΗΣΤΟΙ. But the Θεοι χρηςοι, though three were all one, and that one the Sun or the higher power of which the Sun was the emblem: and Tertullian says, that the three altars in the circus were sacred—trinis Diis, magnis, potentibus, valentibus: eosdem Samothracas existimant.

The city of Troy also had its labyrinth. The Pergamus, in which Cassandra was kept, was in the shape of a pyramid, and had three altars—to Jove, Apollo, and Minerva; but the Capitolium of Rome and all her sacred things were avowedly but revivals of the religion of Troy. Her founder arrived in Latium,

*Ilium in Italiam portans* victosque Penates.

The seven tracts or channels of the sky, through which the planets move, are called in the Homeric Greek τειρεα—

Αρες ὑπερμενετα . . . . πυραυγεα κικλον ελισσον
αιθερος ἱππαπορος ενι τειρεσιν— [4]

a word which has nothing to do, Nimrod says, with τερας, a portent, but implies merely the common idea *terere iter*, and of τριβος, via trita, or, as the Brahmins say, the paths of the planets. With the teirea agree the euripi of the circus, and the seven main streets which, taking the square as a round, circuit the seven-fold city. [5] These latter are called its αγυιαι, and Apollo Ergates, the architect God, who built the walls of Troy, was therefore called Αγυιεος, and because he traced the walls of the great seven-streeted city or πολις ευρυαγυια in the shape of an exact square, or superficies of a cube, the idol or sculptured form of the God Aguieus was a cube, σχημα τετραγωνον. [6] Orpheus describes the city of Aiaia as consisting of seven circles of walls and towers, one within another; and Gnossus, in Crete, was the alleged site of the Labyrinth of Minos, of which Ariadne possessed the glue. [7] The celebrated fair Rosamond had her underground labyrinth, near Woodstock, and *her bower from which the labyrinth did run.* [8]

In the isle of Lemnos there was a labyrinth of which some remains existed in the time of Pliny. It is very remarkable for having been surrounded with 150 columns, which were revolving cylinders, so movable that a child could spin them round. These are evidently what we call rocking-stones. [9] The maze of complicated circles near Botallek, in Cornwall, described in plate

---

[1] Asiat. Res. VIII. pp. 322, 323, 357.  [2] Cicero de Legibus, Lib. ii. Cap. i.
[3] Serv. in Æn. Lib. ii. ver. 225.  [4] Hom. Hym. Mart. ver. 6, 7.
[5] The Olympian course of Jupiter, at Pisa, was 600 feet long, as were all the running courses of Greece: this was instituted by Hercules. Stanley's Hist. Phil. Part ix. Ch. iii.
[6] Pausan. Lib. viii. Cap. xxxii. Sect. 3.  [7] Nimrod, Vol. I. pp. 247, 315.
[8] Drayton, note A, on Ep. of Ros. p. 81, Ed. London, 1748; Percy's Relics, Vol. III. p. 146.
[9] The Asphodel was called by Theophrastus the Epimenidian plant. The name As-phod-el is the Asian God Phod or Buddha, whose name rings every change upon the vowels, and upon the two variable consonants B. F. P. V. and D. T. Th. Nimrod, sup. Ed. p. 18. This was the plant used to move the celebrated Gigonian rocking-stone, (which I have noticed in my Celtic Druids,) which stood near the Pillars of Hercules, not far from the Straits of Gibraltar.

No. 29, of my Celtic Druids, was also, in some way, allusive to the planetary motions. The labyrinth of the Fair Rosamond could be nothing but an astrological emblem, allusive to the planets.

There are also histories of labyrinths in Egypt, seen by Herodotus; in Andeira; at the Lake of Van; Præneste, &c. The etymology of the word labyrinth is unknown, therefore probably Hindoo or Oriental; but Nimrod has some interesting speculations concerning it. From its form exactly corresponding to the sacred mount, &c., of India, and of the cities formed after its pattern, they probably were meant to be in one sense representations of the paradise, &c., *in inferis*, as we know these sacred matters on earth were supposed to be exactly imitated in the Elysian regions.

I have before observed, that each city had its ten years' war, its conquest and dispersion, I therefore need not here repeat them.

4. No one who has reflected much on the names of Grecian Gods and Mythoses, can deny, that their etymologies are in general most unsatisfactory. This is caused by searching for them no where but in the Greek language. The spoken language of Greece was, like that of all other nations, the child of circumstance. It was composed out of a mixture brought by Celtæ, by Ionians, if they were not the same,—by Pelasgi from Phœnicia,—from the second race of Celtæ, called Scythians,—and perhaps by others; so that it is evident, from the nature of the case, as Plato truly said, recourse ought to be had for, probably, all the old names, to the Barbari. The state of the case, as I have already intimated, is the same with respect to all ancient nations. Their spoken language was a general mixture, and the sixteen letters were common to all, and were used to record this mixture, or heterogeneous compound. This admitted, we see the reason why in etymology we ought not to be bound to any one nation for the origin of words, but why we ought to seek them wherever we can find them. They are exactly like the present English; but who would think of seeking the meaning of all English words in one language?

It addition to these reasons it must not be forgotten, that all the ancient names of towns and persons had a meaning, and, as their early histories were all mythological, this meaning was astrological. Egypt was divided, as every one knows, in its names, with a reference to the heavenly bodies: and, as I have just observed, Sir William Drummond has shewn, that most of the names of the towns and persons recorded in Joshua had an astrological meaning. It is, therefore, reasonable to believe that those which we cannot explain would be shewn to be the same, if our ignorance of their meaning could be removed. The history of every ancient state was a mythos: with such trifling variation as change of place and change of time produced, they were all the same. Such towns as were erected *de novo* were built astrologically, or with a reference to the prevailing mythos: such as arose by degrees were, when their inhabitants became rich, assimilated as far as possible to the prevailing and universal superstition. This, I think, satisfactorily accounts for the mixture of mythology and true history, and it is only by a careful attention to separate the two—an attention which has never yet been properly paid,— that any thing like a rational history can be formed. The learned author of Nimrod could not avoid seeing the universal character of the mythos; but, bound by religious prejudice, he has most absurdly exerted his great learning and talent after the example, and in aid, of Mr. Faber, to make it fit to his own superstition. He assumes that his own mythos is true literally, and as the mythoses are all fundamentally the same,—as a general, generic, or family character runs through the whole,—it is no difficult matter to give a certain degree of plausibility to his scheme. But these gentlemen never perceive that their literal systems involve consequences utterly absurd, and contrary to the moral attributes of God.

The districts of Canaan appear to have been allotted or divided according to astronomical or astrological rules, in the same manner as was practised with the *nomes* of Egypt.  The tenth chapter of Genesis is an example of the same kind—a division of the world into *seventy-two* countries or nations, under the mask of a genealogy.  Every chapter of Genesis exhibits an esoteric and an exoteric religion.  The same persons named in the tenth chapter of Genesis are found in Ezekiel, and also in Job—a sacred book of the Jews, in which the destroyer makes a great figure.

The following passage exhibits a pretty fair example of the mist which superstition sometimes raises before the eyes of men of learning and talent, and also, in no small degree, tends to confirm what Sir W. Drummond says in his Œdipus Judaicus, viz. that the astronomical meaning, which almost all the early names in the book of Joshua contain, prove it to have an allegorical meaning:  " The names of the Patriarchs of the line of Shem had a significancy " prophetic of events which should occur in their lives.  I conceive that Salah flourishing, the " people were sent forth : Heber flourishing, they crossed or transgressed the mighty river " Euphrates or Tigris: Peleg flourishing, mankind were split by the great schism: Rehu " flourishing, the Patriarchal Unity was broken, and the kingdom of Ione, or Babel, erected in " opposition to that of Ninus: and, lastly, Serug flourishing, the confusion of tongues took " place." [1]   When I consider the fact, that the names of the towns and places described in the Jewish books, as well as the names of the persons, have all meanings like those above, I am surprised that any one who knows it should hesitate a moment to admit that an allegory is used —in fact, a mythos described.

Nimrod takes Babylon for his standard, as I have before said, not because it is more convenient or because it was the original, but because he thinks it is necessary to the religion in the belief of which he happens to have been educated; and he is probably unconscious of the fact, and will strenuously deny it, and be very angry with me for stating it.  But no philosopher or unprejudiced person, reading his book, will ever raise any question about it.  In our endeavours to explain the ancient mythoses, great care ought to be taken not to confound two cases which must be, in their nature, extremely difficult to separate,—the ancient mythological or allegorical histories, and the idle stories invented by the Greek or Roman priests of comparatively modern times, to conceal their ignorance,—and this is so very difficult a matter, that our success, exert whatever care we may, must always be attended with considerable doubt.

5.  The account which is constantly given of the attempt of Alexander and others to declare themselves Gods, has never been satisfactory to me.  With Christian priests it has always been a favourite theme, and if they have not striven to disguise the truth, we may safely say they have not taken much pains to discover or explain it.  I have shewn, that in the latter times of the Roman republic an eminent person to be a general benefactor of mankind was expected to arrive along with a new and more happy sæculum.[2]  This was the renewal either of the Neros or of the cycle of 608—ΥΗΣ.  On the beginning of every one of these new ages a person of great merit was supposed to come, endowed with a portion of the Divine Spirit, of the ἅγιον πνευμα or the Ερως, which was the protogenos or first-begotten of the Supreme Being.  It was correctly the new incarnation of the mythologists of India.  It was correctly the Christian inspiration.  The Supreme First Cause was generally believed to overshadow, or, in some other mysterious manner, to impregnate the mother of the favoured person, by which she became pregnant.  This was done

---

[1]  Nimrod, Vol. I. p. 16, Sup. Ed.

[2]  This cycle was what the Romans called *sæculum*, at the end of which the Ludi Sæculares were celebrated—when black victims were sacrificed.  These sacred and unascertained periods were professed to be known only to the keepers of the Sibylline books, from which they were learnt.  Nimrod, Vol. III. p. 191.

in various ways. When any person became very eminent as a benefactor of mankind, his successors generally attributed this inspiration to him; and he was said, by the vulgar, to have a God for his father: but the initiated understood it as first stated, which was a doctrine too refined for the understandings of the populace, and was never confided to them; and which, for the most part, we only know by halves—by collecting trifling facts that have unintentionally escaped from the mysterious adyta of the temples—in which, perhaps, in later times, the whole doctrine was not known, but in great part lost. The periods of the renewal and the actual length of the cycle were unquestionably lost. It is the natural and, I take it, inevitable consequence of all secret doctrines of this kind, unwritten and handed down by tradition, that they should either be lost or become doubtful. It was a knowledge of this natural and inevitable effect, probably, which caused the priests in several countries to commit the doctrines to writing in the guise of ænigmas or allegories or parables, and experience has shewn that this is equally unavailing; or perhaps it is of worse consequence, as the allegory being at length believed to the letter, the secret meaning has not only been forgotten, but the belief of it, or the allowance of its existence, has been denounced as heretical—a crime—and the persons entertaining it, subjects of persecution. This is a great evil, but evil, less or more, is always a necessary consequence of disingenuous and deceitful conduct in man. Plato and Pythagoras, among the Gentiles, were both examples of eminent men supposed to be the produce of divine influence or inspiration, as I have shewn in B. IV. Ch. II. Sect. 6. Their mothers were believed to have been overshadowed or obumbrated by an Apolloniacal spectre, to have been *afflata numine* filled with the קרש רוח *qds ruh*, and to have produced their respective sons without connexion with man. This, in fact, was correctly Hindoo incarnation. All the extraordinary births recorded in the two Testaments, such as those of Samson, Samuel, John Baptist, &c., were examples of the same kind.

Persons wishing to obtain power often attempted to induce a belief that *they* were the effects of this kind of divine interference. This was the case with Alexander the Great,[1] who was feigned to be begotten by Jupiter Ammon in the form of a Dragon. This was the case also with Augustus Cæsar, whose mother fell asleep in the temple of Apollo, and who (when she awaked) saw reason quasi a concubitu maritali purificare se, et statim in corpore ejus extitisse maculam, velut depicti draconis......Augustum natum *mense decimo*, et ob hoc Apollinis filium existimatum.[2] When Scipio Africanus aspired to be the tyrant of his country, a similar story was told of his mother, and of him—but the Romans discovered his object, and he was banished for it,— he failed. His mother was said to have been impregnated by a serpent creeping over her body when she was asleep. In the same manner Anna, the mother of the Virgin Mary, was said, in one of the spurious Gospel-histories, to have been impregnated, when an infant of only three or four years old, by the Holy Ghost, in the form of a serpent, creeping over her body when asleep; the produce of which was Mary, the mother of Jesus. And as Jesus was in like manner the produce of the Holy Ghost, they declared Mary to be both the mother and the daughter of God. The Serpent was the emblem of divine wisdom equally in India, Egypt, and Greece.

An attempt was also made by Sylla to establish himself as the object in honour of whom the Ludi Sæculares were celebrated; but if such were his object, it does not seem to have succeeded. He appears not to have been supported by the priests, and therefore probably gave it up. " Sylla " was born in the year of Rome[3] 616, but it is uncertain what year the Sæcular Games were cele- " brated, whether in 605, in 608, or in 628. It was a matter of the most occult science and pon- " tifical investigation, to pronounce on what year each Sæculum ended, and I am not satisfied

---

[1] Nimrod. Vol. III. pp. 366, &c.        [2] Suet. Octav. Cap. xciv., Nim. Vol. III. p. 458.
[3] Thuscæ Historiæ cit. Censorin. p. 84; Plut. Sylla.

" whether the decemviri did not publish the games more than once, when they saw reason to " doubt which was the true Sibylline year."[1] It is quite clear that these difficulties would not apply to so short a period as 110 or 120 years. The nails driven annually by the consuls with great ceremony, from a time long anterior to that here alluded to, must have readily fixed the time for the celebration of feasts of such short periods.

6. Perhaps in ancient times there never was a more remarkable example of this superstition than that of Seleucus Nicator, who founded the city of Antioch, which was finished by Antiochus, who was called EPIPHANES, perhaps on that account. The original name of this city, situated on the Orontes, was Iona or Iopolis, the city of Io, the beeve *Ie*. (Io was sometimes the name of a male, sometimes of a female; and the Syrians, we are told, were in the habit of changing the Chaldaic א *a* and ת *e* into the *y o*.) It was said to have been built by Triptolemus, i. e. Enyulius or Mars, as a funeral monument to the cow Io, which died there when she fled from Jupiter Picus (Pi-chus THE black); but it was called Antiochia by Seleucus in honour of his son Antiochus Soter.[2] The name of the kings of Antioch sufficiently explain the fact. The *first* was called Soter or the Saviour; the *second*, Theos or the Holy, or the God; the *third*, who finished the city, Epiphanes, or the Manifestation of the Deity to the Gentiles. One of them, in furtherance of this scheme, endeavoured to place his image in the Temple at Jerusalem, but was defeated by the religious zeal of the Jews, to the uninitiated of whom he would appear but as an enemy to their local God Iao or Ieue. To these Jews the secret meaning could not be explained without letting out all the mysteries of the religion to the vulgar. The Seleucidæ governed almost all southern and central Asia, including part of Upper and Lower India, and here they probably learnt anew many of the ancient mysteries then lost to the Western nations. This may have caused Seleucus Nicator to build a magnificent temple in Antioch or Iona to *Jupiter Bottius*, that is Jupiter Buddæus, whose high-priest he called Amphion—Om-phi-on. The Christians are said to have received the name of Christian at Antioch. At first they were every where considered by the Gentiles as Jews, as they really were, and the God of Seleucus was called Antichrist by the Jews. This would be in the Greek language Αντι Χρησος, or an opponent or second Χρησος, meaning against the good or holy one, the holy one of Israel, and this would cause the Christians, the servants of the God of the Jews, to call themselves followers of the Χρησος, or of the good dæmon, the opposite of Antichrist. And from this it was, that Theodoret and other fathers maintained that the city of Antioch was a type of Antichrist. The Antichristian Antioch, *Antichristian* before the birth of Christ, unravels the mystery. Nimrod has most clearly proved, that the Seleucidæ meant to convert the city of Antioch into a sacred place, and to found their empire upon a close connexion between church and state:[3] but he has not observed that Buddha and the grand Lama of Tibet were their model.[4] The grand Lama, successor of Buddha, was at that time probably an efficient monarch, and not reduced to the inanity of the present one by the priests. Jerusalem was set up by the *Antichrist* David, as the Samaritans would call him, in opposition to the old worship on Gerizim,[5] and Antioch was the same, in opposition to Jerusalem. Thus we discover the origin of Antichrist, with whom modern Christians have so long amused or tormented themselves. But of the Χρησος more hereafter. Another reason why they called Antioch by the name of Antichrist was, because the king of it usurped the name of Epiphanes,

---

[1] Nimrod, Vol. I. p. 462, Sup. Ed.

[2] Vide Nimrod, from pp. 370 to 490, Vol. III.

[3] As all politic modern kings do.

[4] The Jupiter Bottius proves this.

[5] According to the first religion of Moses, Gerizim, not Jerusalem, was the place *chosen by God to place his altars there*. The text of Joshua contains satisfactory, internal proof of its corruption by the Jews to favour the claim of Jerusalem, as is admitted by the first Protestant divines.

or the Manifestation of God to the Gentiles, which belonged only to their God. Notwithstanding the destruction of the books at Antioch, under the superintendence of the Apostles, and of the Christian priests, systematically continued to the present day in all other countries, enough has escaped to prove it was the doctrine of the ancient religion, that a saviour should come at the end of the Sæculum.

The system of renewed incarnations seems to offer a strong temptation to ambitious spirits to declare themselves to be emanations of the Deity, as we have seen it was attempted by Alexander the Great and several others. Mr. Upham, in his history of Buddhism,[1] has given an account of a successful attempt of this kind in the kingdom of Ava. From this example it does not seem unlikely that similar attempts, in other places, Ceylon for instance, may have been made. In this way, at the same time that the system of incarnations which I have described, is supported, the absurd and degraded state of Buddhism in Ceylon and other places may be accounted for. Mr. Upham admits, as every one must, a primeval Buddha of great antiquity. His existence he does not attempt to explain, except so far as to admit that he was the Sun. Mr. Upham's is the account of modern Buddhism; with this I do not concern myself, except in some few instances, where the ancient truth hid, under the modern trash, seems to shew itself: as for instance, in the cycles noticed by Loubère and Cassini. From the lapse of time and other circumstances, the view of the Hindoo avatars has become indistinct; yet they are still so visible that almost every Christian who has of late carefully looked into the early history of them, is obliged to admit them. Thus the Rev. Mr. Townsend says,[2] " As this incarnate being was considered as a divine person, and " the son of God, and as Nimrod claimed the authority and titles of the incarnate, it is evident " that his father or his ancestor must, from some cause, have been also considered as divine." I can have no doubt that Mr. Townsend is right, and that Nimrod was Bala-rama, an avatar, probably Maha-Beli,[3] or an avatar of Buddha. Nimrod and Bala-Rama were both grandsons or sons of Menu, i. e. נ Nu. But since these most learned and orthodox gentlemen are obliged to admit the fact, I beg I may not be called fantastical and paradoxical, at least, unless they be coupled with me.

7. It is quite impossible to believe that all the striking marks of similarity between the names of towns, the modes or plans of building them, the names of persons, and the doctrines of the Orientals and the Western nations, can have been the effect of accident; and I can see no other way of accounting for them than by supposing that they were brought by the first race of people who travelled Westwards from India, and who all had, with various sectarian differences, fundamentally the same religion, and gave the same names to their towns as those they had left in their own North-eastern countries. This practice we know has always prevailed among emigrating people, and prevails to this day, and it rationally removes all the difficulties. It cannot be expected that at this late day, amidst the ruins of cities which have almost disappeared, we should find in each all the traits or marks of the system, or a whole system, complete. It is as much as we can expect, if we can find, in each, detached parts of the system: for example, suppose I found the head of a man in Babylon, the leg of a man in Troy, and the hand of a man in Rome; though I did not find a whole man in any of them, I should be obliged to believe that all the towns had formerly been occupied by men. It is the same with the universal system. In every city some of the débris are to be found, quite enough to enable us to judge of the remainder, with as much certainty as we should in the case of the limbs of a man, or of an animal.

An actual example of this kind took place in Ireland: in one place the back-bones of an elk

---

[1] Pp. 110, 111.  [2] Class. Journ. No. XLVIII. p. 236.  [3] Ib. p. 237.

were found, in another thigh-bones, in a third legs, and in another the magnificent antlers, and so on till all the bones of a perfect animal were found. They were collected, put together, and now form that most beautiful and majestic skeleton standing in the Hall of the Institute in Dublin. Does any one doubt that the elk was in former times an inhabitant of these places in Ireland? Just so it is with the mythological system of the ancients, with the adoration of the Sun and the host of heaven, the Lord of Hosts. Every where the same system with, in part, the same ceremonies prevailed, from Iona in Scotland to Iona at Athens, or Iona at Gaza, Iona at Antioch, or the Ioni or Argha in India.

I think it probable that the natives of central Asia, in the times of which we are treating, were nearly in the situation of the Afghans, inhabitants of the same country described by the Hon. Mr. Elphinston at this day.[1] They are in a great measure nomadic and divided into tribes, but yet are more located than the Arabians of the deserts. Wars often take place between them, and one tribe drives out another, who quit their country not in a state of distress and weakness, but of power—compared with the countries into which they come. The celebrated Baber is an example of this; he was expelled from his country about Balk into the South, where he attacked the empire of Delhi and conquered it.

8. In the old books of the Hindoos, as it was before stated, we meet with accounts of great battles which took place between the followers of the Linga and those of the Ioni, and that the latter in very early times were expelled from India under the name of Yavanas. After the sun had left Taurus and entered Aries, or about that time, it is probable that the war above alluded to arose. Whether the question of the precedence of the Linga and Ioni had any connexion with the transit from Taurus to Aries I know not, but the two events appear to have taken place about the same time. The Buddhists or Yavanas were expelled; their priests were Culdees; and they were Jaines. They passed to the West. In their way they built, or their sect prevailed in, the city of Baal, Bal, or Babylon—as Nimrod says, probably the old Iona :

Et quot *Iona* tulit vetus, et quot Achaia formas.[2]

They built, or their sect prevailed in, the city of Coan or Aiaia, if ever there were such cities— the city of Colchis or of the golden fleece, if ever there was such a city, to which the Argonauts are feigned to have sailed—the city of Iona which afterward became Antiochia—and the city of Iona called afterward Gaza, where they were Palli or Philistines, and near to which Jonas was swallowed up by a whale—and the city of Athens, called Athena, (a word having the same meaning as Iona,) with its twelve states and Amphictyonic council. They dwelt in Achaia, they built Argos, they founded Delphi, or the temple of the navel of the earth, where they were called Hellenes and Argives. They founded the state of the Ionians, with its twelve towns in Asia Minor. They built Ilion in Troy, or Troia or Ter-ia, i. e. *country of the Three.* They carried the religion of Osiris and Isis, that is Isi and Is-wara, to Egypt; they took the Deity Janus and Jana or Iana to Italy, where their followers were called Ombri : they founded the city of Valentia or the city of Rama or Roma :—they built Veii or the city of *Uei* (read from right to left Ieu), if ever there was such a city :—they built the temple of Isis, now called Notre Dame or the Queen of Heaven, at Paris ; and, as it might be called, Baghis-stan now St. Dennis, and were called Salarii from their attachment to and practice of the sacred Mazy dance :—they left the Garuda at Bourdeaux :—they founded the most stupendous monument in the world called Carnac,[3] of the same name as the temple of Carnac in Egypt, and the Carnatic in India:—they built Stonehenge, or Ambres-stan, and Abury or Ambrespore :—they founded Oxford on the river

---

[1] Hist. Cabul.          [2] Nimrod, Vol. I. p. 287.          [3] See Celtic Druids.

which they called Isis, and Cambridge on the river Cam, Cham, HAM, Am or Om:—they built Iseur or Oldborough, and called the Yorkshire river by the name OM-ber or Umber or Humber, and called the state, of which Iseur was the capital, Brigantia, the same as the state which they had left behind them in Spain or Iberia, and Valentia a little more to the North, and Valentia in Ireland the same as the Roma and Valencia in Italy and Spain: and finally they founded a college like Oxford or Cambridge or the island of Ii or Iona, or Columba, which remained till the Reformation, when its library, probably the oldest in the world at that time, was dispersed or destroyed.[1] These were the people, Jains or Buddhists, whom, in my Celtic Druids, I have traced from Upper India, from Balk or Samarcand, one part between the 45th and 50th degree of North latitude by Gaul to Britain and Ireland, and another part by sea, through the Pillars of Hercules, to Corunna, and thence to Ireland, under the name of Pelasgi or sailors of Phœnicia.

### APPENDIX TO BOOK VII.

In the history of Brutus and his three sons, noticed at the end of Chapter VI., we have the universal mythos in Britain, in imitation of Adam, Cain, Abel, and Seth—Noah, Shem, Ham, and Japhet. The Welsh game of Troy, noticed by Pliny, in Ch. VII. Sect. 3, proves the Trojan mythos in Britain before the time of the Romans. With this may be classed a medal of the Saviour found in Wales with the Hebrew inscription, in Fig. 26, described by Roland in his Mona Antiqua,[2] which may rank with the Crucifix, the Lamb, and the Elephant, or Ganesa at Brechin,[3] in Scotland; and with a ring having its Ling-ioni, its Bulls and Cobra, found in the same country, exhibited by the Earl of Munster to the Asiatic Society, and described in Volume II. art. xxvi. of their Transactions (vide my plates, Fig. 27); and with the Indian Gods Samnaut, Bood, Om or Aum, Eswara, Cali, Neith or Naut, and Creeshna, in Ireland, described in Chapter V. Section XXVI. of the Celtic Druids; and with the Trimurti of Ireland, Criosan, Biosena, and Sheeva,[4] and with the Culdees or Chaldæans in every part of the British isles.

---

[1] It is known that part of it went to Douay in Flanders.
[2] Plate V. p. 93, add. p. 298.    [3] Vide Celtic Druids, plate 24.    [4] Class. Journal, Vol. III. p. 179.

# BOOK VIII.

## CHAPTER I.

JEWISH PENTATEUCH : PUBLICATION FORCED.—JEWS A HINDOO OR PERSIAN TRIBE.—NAME OF PHŒNICIA AND SYRIA.—REASON OF ABRAHAM'S MIGRATION.—ABARIS, MEANING OF. — YADUS A TRIBE OF JEWS. — GOD CALLED BY GENTILE NAMES, BUT ALWAYS MALE. — DIFFICULTY IN THE METEMPSYCHOSIS. — DR. HYDE SHEWS ABRAHAM TO HAVE BEEN A BRAHMIN.

1. It is scarcely necessary to remind any person who has read the preceding part of this work, of the very extraordinary manner in which the Jews appear to have been, as it were, insulated amidst the surrounding nations. If we may believe the literal sense of the Bible, (for a short time, *the Persians* excepted,) they were always at secret enmity or open war with their neighbours, the Gentiles, or the *idolaters*, as, by way of reproach, they are generally called. By the Greeks they were scarcely noticed; known they certainly were; but probably their doctrines were first made public by the translation of their Pentateuch, in the time of Ptolemy Philadelphus, and its consequent publication, which was so abhorrent to the feelings of the Jews, that a solemn fast to atone for the sin was established on the anniversary of the day that the translation was finished. This fast continues to be observed annually throughout all the world, where there are any of the Jewish nation. Notwithstanding what is said of Jesus reading in the synagogue, which admits of explanation so as not to be adverse to my opinion, I believe that anciently the Pentateuch was kept strictly secret by the Jews, and would probably have been lost like similar works of different temples,—Diana, Eleusis, Delphi, &c.,—had it not been for the translation forced by Ptolemy. In Athens they had a prophetic and a mysterious book, which they called the Testament, to which they believed the safety of the republic was attached. They preserved it with so much care, that among all their writers no one ever dared to make any mention of it; and the little we know of this subject has been collected from the famous oration of Dinarchus against Demosthenes, whom he accuses of having failed in the respect due to this *ineffable* book, so connected with the welfare and safety of the state.[1] Manetho notices a sacred book in the grand Egyptian library of Osymandias, said to be written by Pharoah Supris.[2] This is Pharoah, Σοφος, the Wise. This was probably a similar book to that of the Athenians.

No doubt every division of the universal religion had its secret and sacred writings as well as the Jews, only they were never made public, and thus were lost. To the peculiar circumstance which caused Alexandria to be almost filled with Jews and Samaritans, and to the necessity which Ptolemy found of causing their books to be translated in order that he might know how to decide between them in their squabbles, and to a wish, perhaps, to govern them by their own laws, we are, probably, indebted for our knowledge of the books of the Old Testament. After they were once translated into Greek, there could be no longer any object in concealing the originals.

---

[1] Spinetto on Hierog. p. 123.     [2] Ibid. p. 304.

Of the reality of the translation there can be no doubt ; but whether it was made from the copy of the Samaritans or from that of the Jews cannot be certainly known : against the Samaritans, Josephus is not evidence : but as the Jews allow the Samaritan to be the sacred character, from that it was probably taken : in consequence of the unintentional corruption of the LXX. by Origen, nothing can be deduced by comparison of the versions.

Calmet says, the Samaritans allege that " their translation was preferred before that of the " Jews, and laid up in the library of Alexandria." This seems not improbable. The Samaritan is said to be the sacred language of the Jews by Josephus, who, *in this case*, must be allowed to be an unquestionable authority, because it is evidence against himself and his sect. He says that the Petalon, [1] or gold plate on the forehead of the high priest, had on it " the name of God in " *sacred characters.*" This plate was in existence in the capitol of Rome in the time of Origen, who relates that the letters were Samaritan. Josephus was here the most unwilling of witnesses, consequently his evidence is good, [2] and Origen's is the same.

2. Christians and Jews will find no difficulty in accounting for the insulated state or the singularity of the Jews, to which allusion was made in the last Section. They will say the Israelites were singular because they were the elect of God—God's chosen people. But philosophers will not be so easily satisfied, and perhaps they may reply, that this is an assumption made by the priests of almost every nation in its turn. A wish may also exist on their parts to discover the cause of this singularity combined with the general family likeness which, notwithstanding their peculiarity, may be perceived in their ceremonies and doctrines to those of the other nations. This wished-for cause I shall now proceed to shew may be found in the probable fact, that they were a tribe of Hindoo or Persian nomades or shepherds, for a wandering tribe they certainly were—one of the sects of the Hindoo religion after it divided into two, i. e. those of the Linga and Ioni, or Buddha and Cristna, or perhaps of the sect of the Linga after the separation, but before the reunion of the two. I think this theory will account for most of the difficulties with which we meet, and that there will not be a disagreement from the Hindoo religion, *in its probable original purity,* greater than may be expected to have arisen from the lapse of time, the change of place, revolutions, and other circumstances. I incline to the opinion that it was of the religion of the followers of the Linga after the separation. Thus they were the followers of the God Ie-pati or Iaw, in opposition to the Goddess Parvati or Venus, Astarte or Asteroth, &c. They were the followers of the *male* Io, in opposition to the *female* Io, of Syria ; for the Io, as we have seen, was of both sexes. The Io of Syria, was probably nothing more than the Iη or Iεω of Moses, with the peculiar Syriac dialect, which changed the ε into the ο.

We are told that Terah, the father of Abraham, originally came from an Eastern country called Ur, of the Chaldees or Culdees, to dwell in a district called Mesopotamia. Some time after he had dwelt there, Abraham, or Abram, or Brahma, and his wife Sara or Sarai, or Sara-iswati, left their father's family and came into Canaan. If the letter A be changed, by metathesis, from the end of the word Brahma to the beginning, as is very often practised in the oriental languages, we shall have correctly Abrahm ; or the A might be only the emphatic Chaldee article, making *the Braham* or Brahmin. The word *Iswati,* in the second name, is now said to be merely a term of honour, like *Lady* Sarah. [3] The identity of Abraham and Sara with Brahma and Saraiswati was first pointed out by the Jesuit missionaries.

---

[1] I apprehend that the use of the word Πεταλον here, exhibits a remnant of the first style of writing on leaves. The sacred word must have been written on a golden leaf—folium or עלה *ole.*

[2] Antiq. B. iii. Chap. vii. Sect. 6.   [3] I shall explain it hereafter.

" Mr. Paxton, in his illustrations of the Holy Scriptures, describes the striking similarity of
" manners, habits, and customs, observable between the Israelite and Hindoo nations.  Abraham
" is said to be the son of a Hindoo Rajah, who, abandoning his caste and native land, which was
" Mesopotamia, went to reside .in a foreign country."[1]   This Mesopotamia, as it was intimated
in the last book, must evidently be the country called Doab,[2]. or the Mesopotamia of India, the
same as the Greek, Μεσος ποταμος.  This is probably meant for Matura on the Jumna, in the
country between the Indus and the Ganges.  They came ultimately into a country which they
called Canaan, probably from a place in India, which had the same name, noticed by Dr.
Buchanan.[3]

3. In Isaiah xxx. 4, the city of Maturea, or Heliopolis, is called סנה *hns ;* in the Vulgate,
*Hanes,* and in the LXX. *Heliopolis.*  Mr. Bryant observes that the place called *Hanes* is, by
Stephanus Byzantinus, called Inys or Ινυσσος, and by Herodotus Ιηνισος.  Now it is remarkable
that this was the very city, to which the ΦΗΝ or Φ.hnn or Phœnix, came at the end of every 600
years to burn itself, on the altar of the temple of the sun.  But under the circumstance of the
Hebrews having no letter which answered to the Coptic or Egyptian letter Φ, the word, by them,
may have been rendered by the letter ח *h.*  This must also suppose the Egyptian language, when
the name Phanes was given to the city, to be older than the Syrian of the time of Isaiah.  But
when what I have said and shall say respecting the antiquity of the language of African Ethiopia
is considered, this will be found to be of no consequence.  As Phœnicia was imagined to have had
its name from a hero, Phœnix, so Syria is said to have had its name from a man called Syrus, [4]

---

[1] Franklin on Buddhists and Jeynes, p. 10.

[2] In the Indian language *ab* means river, like aub in Danaub, and *Do* is the Latin duo.  The whole means, in the
Indian language, *country of the two rivers.*  Here in the *do* is a beautiful and incontrovertible example of the necessity
of having recourse to mixed etymology.

[3] Franklin on the Jeynes, p. 3.  ' I have said, in my Celtic Druids, that Canaanites meant *traders.*  I have changed
my opinion on this subject.  They were traders no doubt, but they were called from the Hebrew כנן *knn,* and כין *kin.*
Natura, omnium genetrix, et directrix.  Hence the *Kann* or Diana of the Etruscans, and the כיון *kiun* or round cakes,
in honore Reginæ Cœlorum ; hence the Chann or the Jana of the ancient Romans; as Chiun became Juno.  (Ouseley's Collect. Vol. III. No. II. p. 120.) · It was closely connected with the Chaones or Caones, and had the same
meaning as the Apollo Cunnius.  The Sun God of Egypt is called Kan, by Diodorus Siculus : and Col. Tod has
observed, that the Lotus is equally sacred to the Kan of Egypt and Kaniya of India.  (Hist. Raj. p. 538.)  In
Deuteronomy Moses orders the Israelites to destroy the names of the divinities of the land.  Solomon Jarchi says, this
was done by giving them a contemptible name.  This was the origin of .Babylon—city of Confusion.  In the same
way, and for the same reason, probably, Canaan was a sectarian name of reproach with the Jews.  In Greece Βηλος
(vide Etym. M. in voce) signified Mount Olympus or Heaven, and Βε-Βηλος any place abominated or unholy.  (Nimrod,
p. ii. Sup. Ed.)  Hence *Babylon* perhaps.  The great disorder in ancient history has arisen, in some measure,
from the custom of calling princes by new names—by titles of honour.  This is carried to such an extent in the Birman
empire,. that a native of that country shudders at the idea of calling his prince by his proper name.  (Asiatic Res.)
Nothing can be more clear than that this, or something very similar to it, and equally embarrassing to the historian,
was practised in the East in ancient times.  We find Abraham, Jacob, Joshua, and many others, changed their names ;
and in these cases the text of the history tells us why, or at least when, they changed them ; but what should we have
done if we had not had that information ?  We should then have known these people by their new names at one time,
and by their old ones at another—in fact, not have known them at all.  Thus it may well be supposed to be with Persian
and other names, in the Persian histories, in which it cannot be expected that the explanation can be given.  There must
always have been a great difficulty in distinguishing between father and son in historical accounts, and different nations
had recourse to different expedients.  I have no doubt that judicial astrology had a great influence in this matter, for
it seems to have been a practice in all nations to give children names in reference to their horoscope, or the calculation of their nativity according to the planets, which were sacred names, and were borne in addition to their paternal
names.

[4] Syncellus, p. 150.

one of the earth-born people. But Mr. Bryant[1] says, *Sur, Sour,* whence was formed Συρος, signified the sun. It was the same as Sehor of Egypt, called Σειριος by the Greeks. The city of Ur in Chaldea was sometimes called Sur, and Syncellus says Abraham was born in the city *Sur.* Stephanus says *Sur* was common to many places. From this it seems that Abraham may have come from an oriental Sur or Suria.

But Abraham or the Brahmin came from Ur of the Chaldees, (this may have been the peninsula of Saurastra or of Zoroaster or Sura-stan,) which has been supposed to mean the fire of the Chaldees, alluding to their fire worship. Fire worship, however, was not objected to by Moses, but was continued by him as much as by other nations; for it was adopted by no nations, in their temples, except merely as an emblem of a superior Being. We have seen just now, that Abraham was said by some authors to have come from a place called *Sur* as well as Ur; and Sur meant Beeve or Bull : see Book IV. Chap. I. Sect. 8. All this is consistent, for Sur was called from the Bull, Ur in the old language being the origin of the word Urus or Beeve. After what has been said respecting the identity of the ancient languages of Italy and India, I feel no hesitation in locating Latin words in India. And thus I am led to the conclusion, that Abraham's family may have come away from his country to avoid the adoration of the Bull, as well as that of the Yoni.[2] We have found the Agnus or Aries in the Yajna sacrifice—the Agni construed to mean Fire, the Agnus *Lamb* overlooked. In the same manner we find the word Ur called fire, the meaning of Urus or bull being overlooked. The circumstance of the Agni being only known at this time to mean *fire* is a proof that the Sanscrit language has been changed, and that we ought to go to an older language, its parent, or rather to it before its change. No one, I think, who looks at the word AGNI and considers that, in the Yajna sacrifice or the sacrifice of the Agni, a lamb is slain, and that the Agni always rides a lamb, or if on foot carries a standard bearing a lamb, and the other circumstances pointed out by me in Book V. Chap. X., can doubt that the word Agni has originally meant lamb. I do not think that the least appearance of the worship of the Bull can ever be perceived in the tribe of Abraham until their return from Egypt. But the sacrifice of the Ram is ordained by God in lieu of the human sacrifice of Isaac. There was a district of India called Ur or Urii or Uriana on the Jumna, which we shall find was the place from which Abraham came.

4. Abraham and his family or clan probably left their country on account of what he truly considered the corruption of the religion, viz. the reconciliation or the coalition which the Brahmin books say took place between the followers of the Linga and those of the Ioni. He seems to have been of the sect of the Linga alone. When he first came into Canaan, the natives with their Canaanitish king-priest Melchizedek, were of his religion—that of Brahma and Persia. When his tribe returned from Egypt under the command of Joshua or the Saviour, to which only they had been driven by famine, and where it is evident that they never were comfortable, they found the Canaanites with their *Ionic* cities (Iona at Antioch and Iona at Gaza) had become corrupted, they had fallen into the heresy of Babylon and the Culdees, the measure of their iniquity was full, and they conquered them. The Canaanites forfeited their dominions, and the Israelites seized them, and under the Saviour, the son of Nave, restored the temple of Melchizedek on Gerizim,[3] which was afterward removed by David and Soleiman or Solomon to Jerusalem.

---

[1] Anal. Vol. III. p. 446.     [2] Bulls of Bashan, Calves of Bethel and Dan.

[3] Har-Gerizim, probably, was so called after some sacred Mount in India. Ar, in the old language of Upper India as well as in Hebrew, is constantly applied to sacred mounts, indeed to all mounts—as Ar-buddha. Ar, in Sanscrit, means hill, and Gir *circle.* Azim, in Arabic, means *greatness,* a title of eminence : hence Ar-ger-izim might mean *hill of the great circle.* The great circle consisted of the circle of stones set up by Joshua, and was the Proseucha, the remains of which Epiphanius found on Gerizim, as I have already mentioned. Hebrew names are not uncommon in India : the Baithana of Ptolemy is so clear that it cannot be mistaken. Asiat. Res. Vol. IX. p. 199.

This shews us why the Israelites were a peculiar people in the midst of nations of enemies on every side—hating all nations except the Persians, who, in the time of Cyrus and Ahasuerus, were of their own religion, and who, without minding their domestic feud, restored their temples both on Gerizim and at Jerusalem. The Israelites exhibit several remarkable points of resemblance to the followers of Brahma and Cristna at this day. Their religions are mutually intermixed with many of the rites and ceremonies of their predecessors, the Buddhists. The first book of Genesis is Buddhist; the sacrifice of the Lamb at the vernal equinox or at the passover, is clearly the sacrifice of the Yajna, offered by the followers of Cristna or Brahma. This accounts for the hatred of Moses to the Bull, and his partiality to the Lamb. Jeroboam and the Samaritans fell off to the Bull and the Queen of heaven—into the union—and thus, to the Ioudahites, became heretics.

· I have said above, that Abraham came from India or Persia. It is very possible that the tribe might originally have come from India and have resided a long time in Persia, before it moved forwards into Canaan. It is very possible that great numbers of persons constituted the tribe and came into Syria, and went thence into Egypt, though the history of the family of Abraham only is given. I think this is not contrary to the fair meaning of the history, and removes some difficulties.

Although the ancients of the West do not seem to have known much of the doctrines or sacred books of the Jews, yet Abraham was well known to them; several persons, both Greek and Oriental, having written respecting him. They all agree that he was not a native of Syria, but that he came thither from the East. If we can believe Mr. Faber and the Desatir, which must, I think, be genuine, (however much it may have been corrupted by Moshani in rendering it out of the old language into Persian,) the adoration of the Bull and Buddhism first prevailed in Persia; but this, there is reason to believe, was succeeded by Cristna and the Lamb which might have come in with Gemshid. The ancients would say that from Brahma, who came into Persia, came Brahminism, and the Brahmins, but yet there would have been no Brahma. Thus, when the Israelitish tribe, who were a sect of Brahmins, came into Syria, they would merely say that *Abram* came. The whole history of Abram or Abraham, that is אברם *Abrm* or אברהם *Abrem*, has a most mythological appearance. The reason given for changing his name in Gen. xvii. 5, is very unsatisfactory,[1] and I am induced to think that it looks very like the reason of a person writing and not understanding the meaning of the name; or, which is still more likely, *not choosing* to give the meaning of it, under the change of which some mystery was probably concealed. The word הם *em* means *multitude*, and the word אב *ab* may mean *father*: but אבר *abr* never means father. Now suppose the letter א *a* after the manner of the Chaldee to be emphatic, to mean *the*, and the word ברם *brm* to mean the same as the Brahm of India, whatever that might be: and suppose this בר *br* the first syllable of the Brahme-Maia to mean, as Mr. Whiter says it does mean in all old languages, creator or *former*, giver of forms; then, by adding to it the word הם *em*, we get the meaning given by the author of Genesis, and this in a way in perfect keeping with the remainder of the book, though perhaps mystical enough. I again repeat, that according to the *common idiom* of the Hebrew, Abraham cannot mean *father of a multitude*. Dr. Hales says, that Ab-ram meant "a high "father," and Abraham "a father of a multitude of nations:" from אב *ab* "a father," רב *rb* is Chaldee "great," and הם *em* the abridgment of המון *emun*, "multitude."[2] It has been thought

---

[1] The change made in the name of Abraham was by the addition of the vowel ה *e*, the first name not having a vowel. This is evidently mystical. I have a strong suspicion that, formerly, the vowels were only used when it was necessary to distinguish one word from another which had the *same* consonants, but a different *meaning*. In this case the vowel in one of the words was inserted to distinguish it, as the modern Jews have since done with their points.

[2] Chron. Vol. I. p. 131.

that the word Abraham had the meaning of *stranger*. This will apply to the Brahmins as well as to Abraham, because they are considered to have come into India from the North. The reader must remember that I am supposing Moses to have written many hundred years after the arrival of the tribe from the East, and that, in the course of the events of which I treat, time enough had passed for the languages to have materially changed—an event which we know to have taken place. Then I think there is nothing against our going back to a language common to both for the origin of the word : for the farther back we go, the nearer, of course, all the languages would be to one another.

Let me not be called a wicked atheist for seeing the likeness between Brahma and Abraham ; for what says the Rev. and learned Joseph Hager, D. D.?[1] " As the Indian alphabets are all syllabic, " and every consonant without a vowel annexed is understood to have an ʌ joined to it, there is no " wonder if from *Abraham* was made Brahma ; and thus we see other Persian words in the Sans- " crit having an *a* annexed, as *deva* from *div*, *appa* from *ab*, *deuda* from *deud*," &c.[2] Dr. Hyde says, that Ibrahim or Abraham, by the Persians, is never called otherwise than Ibrahim or *Abraham Zerdusht*,[3] that is evidently Zerdusht the Brahmin. All this I think is confirmed by a fact which we learn from Damascenus, that Abraham first reigned at Damascus ; and Alexander Poly-histor, who lived about ninety years before Christ, and Eupolemus, who lived about 250 years before Christ,[4] say that he came and resided in Egypt at Heliopolis, that is Maturea, and there taught astrology, which he did not profess to have invented, but to have learnt from his ancestors, of course in the East. This is confirmed by Artapanus. It seems not unreasonable to suppose that by means of Abraham, Maturea acquired its Indian name,—the name of the birth-place of Cristna.

5. Mr. Bryant thinks[5] that Abaris in Egypt had its name from the word עבר *obr*. This seems not unlikely : as it was here that the Israelites dwelt, it does not seem improbable that it had its name from them—as I have shewn, in my CELTIC DRUIDS, that they had their name from the word עבר *obr*.

" The city of Abaris was called *Setkron* and *urbs Typhania :* Seth being (as Plutarch assures " us) the Egyptian name of Typhon, the great enemy of their Gods."[6] It seems to me to be dif-ficult to say that Abaris was not the city of Maturea of Abaris, or עברי *obri*, the strangers—of Heliopolis of On, or of destruction, as it was called, or Typhon. The names of this city curiously confirm my doctrines. It was called On, or the city of the generative power of the sun ; it was also called the city of Typhon, or of destruction, because destruction was regeneration ; it was also the city of the Sun, because the sun was both Creator and Destroyer. The sacred books tell us why Abraham went into Egypt, and the Gentile authors find him there, and thus confirm the fact, and the finding this Brahmin and his tribe at Maturea is very striking. All this is confirmed in various ways by Eupolemus, Berosus, Philo, and Josephus, and indirectly also, I think I may say, by Sanchoniathon.[7] When Alexander says that the Heliopolitan priests made use of the astrology of Abraham, it is the same as to say of the astrology of the Brahmins.[8] And when the Greek Orpheus says, that God of old revealed himself to one Chaldæan only, I quite agree with Hornius,[9] that it is probable the person called Abraham is meant, whether he was really a person, or a sect, or a system. I beg leave to observe, en passant, that from Sanchoniathon we have in substance the same Cosmogony for the Phœnicians as is found in Genesis. On this account the genuineness

---

[1] Diss. Bab. Ins. Lond. 1801.
[3] Hyde de Rel. vet. Pers. Cap. ii. et. iii.
[6] Cumb. Orig. Gen. p. 47.
[9] Hist Philos. Lib. ii. Cap. x.

[5] See Paolino's Amarasinha, p. 12; Symes's Embassy to Ava, ch. xiv.
[4] Maurice, Anc. Hist. Vol. I. p. 438.
[7] Gale, Vol. II. Book i. Ch. i. § 8, 9, &c.

[5] Vol. III. p. 238.
[8] Ib. § 9.

of his work has been doubted, but I think without sufficient reason, as the reader must perceive. [1]
Josephus and Plutarch think, that the Phœnician shepherds, said to be driven out of Egypt, were
the Israelites ;-but what Bishop Cumberland has written upon Sanchoniathon's account, has nearly
satisfied me, that these people must have been expelled more than three hundred years before.
The circumstance of these Phœnicians being able to conquer and hold possession of Egypt, shews
that Phœnicia (and, I suppose, of course, its capital Sidon) must have been a very great and powerful state before the time of Abraham. [2] I think these shepherds must have been the Palli, or Philistines, who came from the border of the Ærethrean sea, and at first from the peninsula of Sau-
restrene or Saurastra, which perhaps means *country of Zoroaster.*

6. I will now state another fact, which, coming from the quarter whence we have it, cannot be
disputed on account of any interest or system. The tribe of Cristna had a name, noticed by me
before in Book V. Chap. X. Sect. 2, which is very remarkable. Captain Wilford says, " The
" *Yadus,* his own tribe and nation, were doomed to destruction for their sins, like the descendants
" of YAHUDA or YUDA, which is the true pronunciation of JUDA. [3] They all fell, in general, by
" mutual wounds, a few excepted, who lead through *Iam bu-dwípa,* a miserable and wretched life.
" There are some to be found in *Guzarat,* but they are represented as poor and wretched." [4] Mr.
Maurice says, " The *Yadavas* were the most venerable emigrants from India; they were the
" blameless and pious Ethiopians, [5] whom Homer mentions, and calls the remotest of mankind.
" Part of them, say the old Hindu writers, remained in this country; and hence we read of two
" Ethiopian nations, the Western and the Oriental. Some of them lived far to the East; and
" they are the Yadavas who stayed in India, while others resided far to the West." [6] The fact of
part of the tribe yet remaining in existence, is one of the pieces of circumstantial evidence which
I consider invaluable. It cannot be the produce of forgery, and couples very well with the two
Sions, two Merus, &c., &c. It is on circumstances of this kind that I ground my system. They
surpass all written evidence, for they cannot have been forged. This emigrating tribe of Yadu or
Yuda, we shall find of the first importance, for they were no other than the Jews.

Porphyry, in his book called Περι Ιεδαιων, quoted by Eusebius, [7] makes Saturn to be called
Israel. His words are these : Κρονος τοινυν, ον Φοινικες Ισραηλ προσαγορυσσι. Then he adds,
that the same Saturn had by a nymph called Ανωβρετ, an only son, ον, δια τυτο, Ιευδ εκαλυν,
whom, for this, they call *Ieud,* as he is so called to this day, by the Phœnicians. This only son,
he adds, was sacrificed by his father. Bochart [8] says, " Thus Ieud amongst the Hebrews is יחיד
" *(ihid) Iehid,* which is the epithet given to Isaac, [9] concerning whom it is evident that Porphyry
" writes." Bochart is followed by Stillingfleet, [10] who says, " Abraham is here called by the
" name of his posterity, *Israel, Isaac Jeoud.* So Gen. xxii. 2 : *Take thy son :* יחיד *ihd* is the
" same with the Phœnician Joud." This is again confirmed by Vossius. [11]

There is, I think, no difficulty in finding here the Iudai or tribe of Yuda of the Hindoos long
before the Jews of Western Syria could have taken that name from one of the sons of Jacob,
called Judah,—a name which cannot have been first derived from him, because it is clear that they
had the epithet long before he was born—his grandfather Isaac having borne it.

---

[1] Montfaucon, Vol. II. p. 245, thinks Sanchoniathon a forgery, and doubts of his translator Philo Byblius. But his
reasons seem feeble: it must remain doubtful. The work of Sanchoniathon was thought spurious by Basnage, Hist.
Jews, Book iii. Ch. xxvii. p. 251.

[2] Cum. San. Rem. I. p. 109.      [3] It ought to be יהורה *ieude* or ieu-de, which means *the holy Ieu.*
[4] Asiat. Res. Vol. X. p. 35.      [5] Hist. Hind. Vol. II. p. 262.      [6] Asiat. Res. Vol. III. p. 368.
[7] Præpar. Evang. Lib. i. Cap. ix.      [8] Can. Liv. ii. Ch. ii. fol. 790.      [9] Gen. xxii. 2.
[10] Origin. §. B. iii. C. v.      [11] Vide Gale, Court Gent. Vol. I. Book ii. Ch. i.

Stillingfleet and Bochart observe that חן-עינברת hn-onbrt, αυωβϙετ, means *conceiving by grace*, Respecting the Anobret of Sanchoniathon, Vallancey has given a copy of a very extraordinary Irish MS. with a translation of it, in which an Irish king's wife is said to bring forth a white lamb, whence she was called Uanabhreit, i. e. *bringing forth a white lamb.* This distressed her very much; but she again conceived and brought forth a son, when she was told by the priest that her womb was consecrated, and the lamb must be sacrificed as *her first-born, for her ceanin* (קנין qnin ) *cion-iuda* or *purification of her first-born.* [1] I quite agree with Vallencey that this can be no monkish forgery of the eleventh century. I think it decidedly proves, first, that the Irish did really come from Phœnicia; and, secondly, that Sanchoniathon is not a forgery. But the proper meaning of קנין qnin Cion-Iuda is evidently not what Vallencey gives above, viz. *for the purification of the first-born,* but *for the salvation of Juda of Sion.* The whole story is exceedingly curious. The son she brought forth was called Aodh-Slaine, i. e. *because he was saved from the sacrifice.* I think Aodh-Slaine is the same as יצחק izhk, though it is so much corrupted as scarcely to be discoverable. That the history of the sacrifice is of the nature of a mythos, or fable, or parable, for the purpose of teaching a doctrine is, I think, very clear, and I think the doctrine also is clear. The first object was to abolish *human sacrifices* by the substitution of the Lamb, which Moses afterward did better by a redemption-price; the next object was to inculcate the absolute necessity of obeying without any, even the slightest, doubt or hesitation the orders of God—in other words, the order of the priest.

That we should find the name of Iudai of the sect, in the father of the twelve tribes, is not surprising, and accords well with what I have suggested. The word Jew is a mere Anglicism, and the word Yudi or Iudi is more correctly the Hindoo name, come from where it would. No doubt it might come from the name of a son of Jacob; but still this must have been at second-hand, after the division of the tribes. It is most probable that it came from the tribe of Iudia, as the head of the tribe seems to have been known by that name, as I have before stated, many years before the son of Jacob was born, and who was probably so called after his ancestor. When Porphyry called Isaac by the epithet Ioud, he, perhaps, meant Isaac the Ioud-ite, or Isaac of the tribe of Ioud or Yuda. The name given to Jacob, Israel or שראל isral—notwithstanding Cruden's attempt to explain it by improperly changing one of the letters—is evidently unknown. שר isr is the name of the book of Jasher, which has been construed *the correct book.* As this word gives name to the whole tribe, it is a very important and desirable thing to ascertain its meaning. I expect it will be discovered in the East. But, perhaps, it may only mean the same as ישרון isrun, *an upright person :* then it might be, *the great upright one.*

Bochart, Gale, and many other of our learned men, think the Phœnicians derived their letters, learning, &c., from the Jews. This is easily explained. When the Israelitish tribe arrived in Canaan they found the natives professing their religion in all its first principles. It might be of the Indian religion before the division about the Linga and Yoni took place, or when it partook of both, or before the division had travelled so far westwards. However this might be, the name of *Iona,* borne by the towns of Gaza and Antioch, pretty well shews that it became, if not entirely, yet in a great measure, Ionian afterward. This easily accounts for the idea of Gale and Bochart, to which, without it, there would be opposed the striking fact, that we scarcely know of the Phœnicians from the Jews except as their enemies; and this makes greatly against the Phœnicians having borrowed their learning from them. People are not often willing to learn of their enemies. Abraham is said, by oriental historians, to have brought the knowledge of astronomy to the Cana-

---

[1] Coll. Hib. Vol. IV. p. 430.

anites and Egyptians. It may have been the astronomy of the Brahmins which he brought. It is not unlikely, that though the Egyptians and Phœnicians may have had much knowledge before Abraham, or his sect or tribe, arrived, he may have brought them an increase, and this would be quite enough to authorize his successors to say and to believe, that he was their first instructor. And this theory accounts for the similarity between the writings of Sanchoniathon and the book of Genesis.

Porphyry (lib. iv. adversus Christianos) says, "that Sanchoniathon and Moses gave the like ac-"count of persons and places; and that Sanchoniathon extracted his account, partly out of the "annals of the cities, and partly out of the book reserved in the temple, which he received from "Jerombalus,[1] priest of the God Jeuo, i. e. Jao, or Jehovah."[2] The words of Porphyry are, as given by Eusebius, τα ὑπομνημαῖα παρα Ἱερομβαλε τε ἱερεως τε θεε Ιαω. All this shews that the *fundamental* doctrines of the tribe of Abraham and the Phœnicians were the same, though they themselves might be of different sects. The system established by Moses confirmed the line of separation between them. His great anxiety was to prevent his people from falling into the Tauric and Ionian heresy, the heresy of Babylon, of Iona, ancient Antioch, and of Iona of the Philistines of Gaza, his bitter enemies. To prevent them from relapsing into the worship of the Bull-headed Baal and Baaltis, and Bull-eyed Juno or Asteroth, the queen of heaven, he endeavoured to keep them to the religion professed by Melchizedek, to the worship which Abraham brought, and which his tribe followed at Maturea or Heliopolis of Egypt, to the worship of the Saviour or Messiah, typified by the Lamb of the Zodiac, in India, called the Saviour or Heri-Cristna; in short to the worship of the *Male* generative principle. We have seen that Yadu was said in India to be the father of Cristna.

7. It has often appeared to me an extraordinary circumstance that the God of Moses should be called by the same names as the Gods of the Gentiles—Adonis and Baal, for instance. I have read that the Jews count in the Bible thirty-two names of God; but I believe in no case whatever will he be found by the name of one of their Goddesses. Though he is called Baal, he is not called Baaltis. If I be right, this is easily accounted for. When Abraham arrived in Canaan the Ionian heresy did not prevail, and he had no objection to his God being called after the names of the Gods of the *single* male principle, or perhaps of the *double* principle; but he utterly rejected the Ionism and the idolatry, its general concomitant, into which Canaan or Syria fell, between the time of his tribe going into Egypt and returning, as the Hebrew text says, after upwards of four hundred years. When the tribe left Canaan the Ionic principle might be gaining ground, but not have become the prevailing superstition. When the Jews returned, increased in strength and sword in hand, the name of the towns Iona, shew that Ionism prevailed. As I have stated before, the close similarity between Paganism and Judaism is not only admitted by Mr. Faber, but is descanted on by him at great length; and, after shewing the absolute insufficiency of all theories yet promulgated to account for it, he says, "Judaism and Paganism sprang from a common source; hence their close "resemblance, in many particulars, is nothing more than might have been reasonably antici-"pated."[3]

If it be said that we do not find such clear marks of this resemblance in the books of the Jews as we ought to do, I reply, we every where find the worship of the female generative power reprobated, under the name of Astaroth of the Sidonians, Queen of heaven, בעלהשמים *bolesmim*, and מלכתהשמים *mlktesmim;* and the Male Jou, or Jupiter,[4] extolled. If I be right, it is evidently the

---

[1] Jerombalus is probably Ἱερος-ομφαλος.

[2] Gale, Court of Gent. Book iii. Ch. ii. §. i., Vol. II. Book. i. Ch. iii. § viii.          [3] Orig. Pag. Idol. Vol. I. p. 105.

[4] These were mere dialectic variations, but of the same name.

object of the Israelitish books, to conceal the secret doctrine under an allegorical history; and it is very possible that the real truth might be soon forgotten by the Jews, who contemplated their histories with only the narrow views and eyes of sectaries.[1] In the whole of the Jewish books I cannot discover a single passage indicative of a tendency to tolerate the worship of the Queen of heaven. If ever any thing like an attempt was made, as in the case of Solomon, it was met with the bitterest intolerance on the part of the priests; witness their violence against him for his toleration of the Sidonians; not his adoption of their religion I believe, but only his toleration of it.

With respect to the adoration of the female generative principle, the Israelites and the neighbouring Gentiles seem to have been situated exactly like the Papists and the Protestants. The Israelites adored the Phallus or Linga, as is evident from the stone set up and anointed with oil by Jacob. But no where can an emblem of the female principle be discovered. The festival of the Ram, the Yajna sacrifice, the emblem of the *I am that I am*, or the *I will be what I have been*, in the masculine gender, is apparent in a variety of ways; but no where can any emblem of the female principle be discovered, except as an object of reprobation. The Gentiles adored both; examples of which need not be given. The modern Romists adore the Ram, the Lamb of God, and also the Virgin, the mother of God, the Queen of Heaven, the Regina Stellarum: the Protestants adore the Lamb of God; but they, like the Israelites, can scarcely be found in any case to pay the least respect to the Queen of heaven. At Antioch-ian-Iona, at Delphi, at Rome, both are adored; at Jerusalem and London, only one—the Lamb. The Ioni was and is detested in the last-named places. The fact cannot be denied. Was it the effect of accident, or of a secret religion? Probably the same cause—some cause arising from the character of man in certain classes—which produced the dislike to Ionism or the adoration of the *female* anciently in India, produced the same in our Calvins and Luthers, of the real nature of which they might be themselves unconscious.

It will, perhaps, be objected to this, that there is no more particular account of the distinction in the Scriptures. But the case in this respect is exactly the same as it would be with us, if all the writings of our time were lost except the sacred ones, as were those of the Israelites. But the worship of the Queen of heaven is reprobated many times by the prophets, particularly by Jeremiah, and that in the strongest terms. My reader must recollect that, according to the Hindoo history of the religion, the first worship was paid to a double object, and that the worshipers were afterward divided into those who adored the *male* and those who adored the *female* principle.

It is notorious, that there are in India great numbers of sects divided from each other, like the sects of the Christians; sometimes by important, at other times by trifling and perfectly unimportant, distinctions. With this well-known fact before them, it is perfectly astonishing that our Indian philosophers should expect to find the different astronomical or astrological mythoses explained by one key. There are, probably, great numbers of systems, all having, perhaps, the same kind of foundation, but differing in the superstructure. The system of the *ten* ages, which I have explained, is one; the system of the *fourteen* Manwantaras, is another.

8. I have been told in reply to my arguments in favour of Abraham and his tribe of Iudai being Brahmins, that if it were so, we should find the metempsychosis in Judaism. I am ready to acknowledge that this seems a fair objection; but this tenet may have constituted part of the esoteric doctrine, as alleged by Mr. Maurice,[2] and as some other equally important doctrines appear to have done. For instance, the immortality of the soul is so little apparent in the Penta-

---

[1] I trust I am writing for the eyes of philosophers, taking an enlarged and bird's-eye view of all sects and nations, and as I shall favour none, I shall be favoured by none. A few philosophers are all that I ever expect to read my work.

[2] Ind. Ant. Vol. II. p. 288.

teuch, that many of the most learned Christian divines have denied that it is there at all : a great Bishop has written *twelve* volumes to prove it is not there. And I reply, that whatever caused the concealment of the one, caused the concealment of the other ; or, whatever caused the one to be little apparent caused the other to be little apparent. They are in their nature closely allied. The most learned of the old Jewish Rabbis, and the first and most learned fathers of the church, I suppose, thought that they could see them in the Bible as they maintained both the doctrines ; which they would scarcely have done unless they had thought they had authority for their opinion.

Learned Christian divines have found no small difficulty, in the fact just named, that in the Pentateuch there is not the least appearance of the doctrine of a future life, or of a place of punishment after death. The cause of this is to be found in the circumstance that the Jews secretly held the doctrine of the metempsychosis, and the perpetual renewal of worlds,—doctrines thought to be too sublime for vulgar comprehension. The doctrine of a *hades*, or *hell*, arose in times long after those of Moses, among the Persians, when the doctrine of two principles came to be formed, and the sublime Hindoo *trimurti* was forgotten. It is evident that the doctrine of a hell is quite inconsistent with the metempsychosis. This simple consideration removes all Bishop Warburton's difficulties. At first, when Christianity was unsettled, the transmigration of souls, and the millenium, or renewal of worlds, were received by the Christian fathers ; but as the more modern doctrine of two principles, *good* and *evil*, gained ground, the other declined and was forgotten. The two doctrines were totally incompatible. The failure of the prophecies of the millenium greatly aided in producing this effect ; but of all this I shall treat hereafter. At first the Gnostic and Manichæan doctrines, which possessed much sublimity, were, with a very trifling exception, universal. At that time mankind retrograded rapidly ; and as they became degraded, the degrading doctrines of the Greek and Latin sectaries prevailed, till the world was overrun with Thaumaturgists and Devil-drivers, and all the absurdities which Protestantism has unveiled.

9. The likeness between Abraham and Brahma, and between their wives and histories, was observed by Dr. Hyde. Indeed it is so marked, that to miss observing it is impossible. Of course he supposes that all the immense fabric of Hindoo superstition was derived from the *man* Abraham. In palliation of this absurdity, it must be recollected that in the time of Hyde the nature of the Hindoo history and religion was not at all known ; but seeing the striking similarity between the doctrines of the Hindoos and those of the Christians and Jews, he pronounces that Brahma was Abraham. [1] Postellus, in commentario ad Jezirah, had long before asserted the same thing, and that the Brahmins were the descendants of that patriarch by his wife Keturah, and were so called *quasi Abrahmanes*. This doctrine is supported by the Arabian historians, who contend that Brahma and Abraham, their ancestor, are the same person. [2]

Drs. Hyde and Prideaux, perceiving the likeness between the Persians and Jews, supposed Zoroaster to have been of the Jewish religion. [3] They were certainly so far right, that the two nations were of the same religion. I have already observed, that the Persians generally call Abraham *Ibrahim Zeradust*. Hyde says, Persarum Religio in multis convenit *cum Judaicâ, et magnâ ex parte ab eâ desumpta fuit*. [4] Hyde, in his first chapter, shews that the ancient Persians had a sacred fire, precisely the same as the Jews, from which it did not differ in any respect, and that the reverence to, or adoration of, this fire was exactly the same as that of the Jews to theirs, from which, he says, the Persians copied it. He quotes Ezra vi. 24, to shew that Cyrus consi-

---

[1] Hyde, Hist. Rel. Pers. p. 31.            [2] Maurice, Indian Antiq. Vol. II. p. 293.
[3] Maurice, Ind. Ant. Vol. II. p. 123.      [4] Cap. x. p. 170.

dered the religion of the Jews the same as his own. For proofs of the truth of this theory my reader may refer back to Book II. Chap. IV. It is admitted that Abraham and Brahma are the same; therefore the Hindoos must have come from Abraham, or the Israelites from Brahma. Now, Christian reader, look to the Pentateuch, which you cannot dispute, and you will see the whole history of circumcision, and how and why it was first adopted by Abraham for all his descendants; and if the Brahmins had descended from him, they would certainly have had this rite; but in no part of India is this rite observed by the Brahmins. This at once proves that Abraham came from the Brahmins, if either came from the other.

Sir W. Jones, in his translation of the Institutes of Menu, renders the word *Brahmana* in the sense of Priest. And the Jesuit Robert de Nobilibus, in what have been said to be his *forged* Vedas, calls the high-priest of the Jews and his associates Yúda-Brahmana.[1] That is, the words being in regimine, *Brahmin of the holy Ie.* I suspect that in mystic words like Yúda, the last syllable ending in d and a vowel, always means *holy*, or has the meaning of the Latin *Divus.* The expression of the Jesuit shews, that he considered the word Yúda, to be the same as the name of the tribe of Abraham.

M. Herbelot, Bibliot. Orient. article Behergir, calls Abraham " un Brahman de la secte, ou de " l' ordre, de ceux qui l' on appelle Gioghis (Yoygees)." From the word Yogees our word Jews may probably have come. I beg the reader to pronounce aloud the word Gioghis. The Sanscrit word *Ayudya* becomes in English *Oude*, in Javanese *Nayugya*, and in Dutch, still more barbarously, *Djoyu.*[2] Here we arrive very nearly at the words Jude and Jew, as is apparent on pronouncing the words. And here it is found in the island of Java, the mother or sister of the island of Bali, which contains a place called Madura—the same as the Muttra of Upper India, where the statue of Bala Rama, and Cristna, so often before noticed, is found. The island of Java is the island of Ieue or Jehovah.

## CHAPTER II.

THE DOVE OF THE ASSYRIANS.—BLACK JEWS.—MEGASTHENES' ACCOUNT OF THE JEWS. — SOLYMI OR . SOLOMONS.—JUDAISM SHEWN BY EUSEBIUS TO BE OLDER THAN ABRAHAM.—HELLENISM.—JEWISH MY-THOS IN NUBIA AND INDIA.—HIGH PLACES.

1. We have seen that the dove is, in a peculiar manner, the emblem of the Ioni. With this we find the Jews at almost perpetual war. The Assyrians are constantly described in the Jewish books by the term *sword of the oppressor.* In several places where we find this it ought to be rendered *the sword of the Dove.*[3] This was the emblem, or crest, or coat of arms[4] carried by

---

[1] Asiat. Res. Vol. XIV. p. 58.                [2] Ibid. Vol. XIII. p. 357.

[3] Jer. xxv. 38, xlvi. 16 ; Hosea xi. 11 ; Zeph. iii. 1.

[4] I have a suspicion that the Armorial-bearing called Crest, arose from being originally the sectarian brand or mark to distinguish the followers of the sect which called its divine incarnation, κατ'εξοχην, the Crest or Benignus, as the sect in India called their God *Cristna* or *Cris-en.* In both sacred and profane history we meet with accounts of

the followers of the imaginary, or at least mystical, Semiramis, who was said to have been born at or near the Phillistine Iona,—of the Semirama-isi of India, of whom I shall presently treat. See Col. Wilford's essay on Semiramis.[1] Persons may have different opinions as to the cause of the Dove, or Ca-pot-Eswari becoming the emblem of the female generative power, as also of the Holy Spirit, the third person of the Trinity, but the fact cannot be disputed.

The Chaldeans, or Chasdim, or Culdees, were priests of the Assyrians, and worshipers of the Dove or female generative power, whence they called their sacred isle of the West Iona or Columba, that is, the *female* dove, not the *male* or Columbus. No person who has studied the Romish Hagiographa can doubt of the origin of the bishops *Iona* and *Columba*.

2. The Rev. Dr. Claudius Buchanan, I believe a missionary, some years ago published Travels in India, in which he states, that he found no less than *sixty-five* settlements of BLACK *Jews* in different parts of the peninsula.[2] It is a great pity that these different races of people could not be examined by a philosopher. Dr. Buchanan, who found the Christians of St. Thomas (before they were what he would call *corrupted* by the Romish Church) to have been, and yet to be, correct Lambeth Christians, notwithstanding that they received the Gospel of the Infancy, and were Nestorians, could not be expected to discover much. These *black* Jews are remnants of the sect of the Iadus, who, Col. Wilford informs us, yet remain in Guzerat. I apprehend they were part of the sect of the Linga, who would not unite with, or divided from, the followers of the female principle, the Argha or Ioni, or from those of the double principle, and, on that account, were persecuted and expelled, and from them came the tribe of Abram or the Brahmin. If this were the case, they would not, of course, have all the Mosaic books *in the form* in which we have them, except they received them from the West. And this seems rationally to account for the places in Syria being called by names of places in India. We know how almost all emigrants have given the names of the countries of their births, to their new habitations.

Jeremiah Jones says, " M. La Crose, in a letter dated at Berlin, the 4th of the ides of December, " 1718, supposes it (i. e. the Gospel of the Infancy) written by some person who was a Nestorian ; " because in a Synod, called Diamperana, held by Alexius de Menezes, Archbishop of Goa, in the " diocese of Augamala, in the mountainous country of Malabar, in the year of Christ 1559, he " found it thus condemned : ' The book which is entitled, *Of the Infancy of our Saviour*, or *the* " ' *History of our Lady*, already condemned by the ancient saints, because it contains many " ' blasphemies and heresies, and many fabulous stories without foundation,' &c. Instances of

---

sudden panics, or alarms having seized large bodies of men. That of Brennus the Celt, our barbarian ancestor, was accompanied by a circumstance which appears trifling, but which exhibits a proof of the great antiquity of our practice of bearing devices or coats of arms. Nimrod, Vol. I. p. 178, sup. Ed. says, " The confusion fell upon the army at the " closing in of the evening, and at first a few only were confounded in mind, who imagined they heard the tramp of " horses, and the onset of some enemy. And in a little time this alienation possessed the minds of them all. And " taking up arms, and dividing among themselves, they mutually destroyed one another, no longer understanding their " own native tongue, nor yet recognizing the countenances of each other, NOR THE DEVICES ON THEIR SHIELDS." The Assyrians always carried for their standard or coat of arms *a dove;* the Romans an eagle. On the key-stone over the inner entrance of the Amphitheatre of Verona is a shield bearing a cross, evidently coeval with the building, thus—(✝). See also Nimrod, Vol. II. p. 273.

In Æschylus's tragedy of the Seven Chiefs against Thebes, the shields of six of them are charged with Armorial-bearings, expressive of their characters, and as regular as if they had been marshalled by a herald at arms. Potter says, " The impresses are devised with a fine imagination and wonderful propriety." But he has omitted to remark that even the motto is not wanting. On one was inscribed the words I WILL FIRE THE CITY. The siege of Troy, if it ever took place, was a species of crusade. On the antiquity of armorial-bearings Mons. Gibelin may be consulted.

[1] Asiat. Res. Vol. IV. pp. 370, &c.　　　　　[2] Christ. Res. p. 226, Ed. 1819.

" which are produced in that Synod, the same as are in Dr. Sykes's Gospel; and it is there said, " that it was commonly read among the Nestorians in Malabar."

From an observation which Mr. Jones has made respecting the Marcosians, a branch of the Gnostics, and respecting a passage of Irenæus, already noticed, I think it is unquestionable that the Gospel of the Infancy existed in the second century. There is also existing part of a gospel called the Gospel of St. Thomas, which is evidently taken from the same source as that of the Infancy,[1] and St. Thomas is said to have instructed the Indians. The extract from Jones shews, that if what Buchanan says be true, that the opinions of the Malabar Christians are the same as the present English Protestants, they must have surprisingly changed since the arrival among them of the Portuguese. It seems remarkable, that the Portuguese Papists should have converted these Nestorians into Protestants !

It is to me utterly incredible that any tribe of people, existing as a tribe, should exist *as Mosaic Jews* without the Pentateuch; because the Pentateuch forms their bond of union. It is not only their religious, but it is their civil code, which regulates the decisions of their judges in disputes about the common affairs of life. If they ever were Jews they must once have possessed the Pentateuch, and they must have lost it, which seems incredible, when it must always have been in daily use by the judges. I believe the case to be this, that they were tribes of Joudi or Yadu, which were spared when opposing sects got the better of them in the wars of the Maha-bharat, and were left in a poor and miserable state, without books or literature,—spared, in fact, from mere contempt, being too low to excite fear or anger; that in the course of many generations their origin was forgotten, and meeting with Jews from the West, and comparing notes, they found a near relationship, and accounted for it by supposing that they must have come from Western Syria, in consequence of the revolutions which had taken place there. Their real history, in two thousand years and upwards, might well be forgotten. The ancient civil-religious wars of India are recorded in the books of the Brahmins, but they are totally forgotten among the mass of the people.

From the accounts given by Dr. Buchanan of the *black* tribes, some of them having Pentateuchs, and others not having them; and of those who have them, having obtained them from the white tribes, it seems probable that they are indebted for them solely to the white tribes. This will exactly agree, as might be expected, with my theory, if it should turn out to be true; because the αποικος or *going out* of the tribe of Judi or Ioudi from India, in all probability, must have taken place before Moses lived, and before he partly wrote, and partly compiled or collected, the tracts into what we now call the Pentateuch. In all probability the first books of Genesis were brought from India with the tribe—with Abraham or the Brahmin. .

The more I meditate on the extraordinary fact stated by Buchanan, that there are many *black* tribes of what are called in our language *Jews*, but evidently tribes of Ioudi, in different parts of India, who have not the Pentateuch of Moses, the more extraordinary and important it appears.[2] The Pentateuch is the civil law of the Jews. By what law do these tribes govern themselves ? Is it by tradition ? If they be Jews, they must be descendants of Jacob or Abraham, which branched off before the law was given; and if their law be very similar to that of the present Ioudi, it will prove, what indeed seems pretty clear without it, that Moses adopted, into his written law, many of the old laws which his tribe had before.

Eusebius, in his Chronicon, says, that *Ethiopians* coming from the Indus or black river settled near Egypt. There seems to be nothing improbable in these Ethiopians being the tribe of Jews—

---

[1] Vide J. Jones, Vol. II. Part iii. Ch. xxiv.      [2] Jesus was a Jew, in Italy *black.*

the tribe of Jacob or Israel. I think these Ethiopians did come under Jacob, and did settle in Goshen, and gave the names of Maturea and Avaris to the city in which they dwelt. Avari in Hebrew would be as often written עברי *obri*, or the city of the Hebrews or Foreigners.

It can scarcely be maintained that the places in Egypt which have names connected with the word Judah can have been called, in that early day, from that tribe of the Jews; but if it be, I then ask, how the name of Solomon, which is found in the desert of Solyme, &c., is to be accounted for? Taken together, the two exhibit the general Judæan mythos, independently of the tribe of Jacob or Israel. [1]

Eusebius's assertion, in his Chronicon, (by Scaliger,) that about the year B. C. 1575, a tribe of " Ethiopians came from the river Indus and encamped and settled near Egypt," is but a loose kind of information, and therefore can be little depended on; but as he fixes them to about the time when the Jews are generally supposed to have come, it rather tends to confirm my idea, though I pay little attention to the dates. It is not impossible that, without knowing it, he may allude to the Jewish tribe. But if this evidence be only weak, I will now produce what will not be easily overthrown.

3. Megasthenes, who was sent to India by Seleucus Nicator, about three hundred years before Christ, and whose accounts from new inquiries are every day acquiring additional credit, [2] in a very remarkable manner confirms my hypothesis of the Jews' coming from India. He says, *That they were an Indian tribe or sect* called Kalani, and that their theology has a great resemblance to that of the Indians. [3] The discovery of this passage, after I had written what the reader has read respecting the Jews, gave me no little pleasure, because it ALMOST *proves* the truth of my theory, and is very different from founding my theory upon it. I will now produce another proof, if records by *unwilling witnesses* are proofs, for Josephus is an unwilling witness.

Aristotle gave an account of the Jews that they came from the Indian philosophers, and that they were called by the Indians Calami, and by the Syrians Judæi. [4] I think few persons will doubt that the Calami here are the Calani of Megasthenes, one of the two being miscalled. We have seen a Calani in Ceylon, where we found a Zion, Adam's foot, Mount Ararat, and Columbo, &c., and in Gen. x. 10, and Amos. vi. 2, a Calneh or Calani is also named.

Gale [5] has observed, that the information of Megasthenes is confirmed by Clearchus, the Peripatetic. I think in this question these Grecian authorities constitute good evidence. Thus for my hypothesis we have as good written evidence as can be expected. We will presently try to confirm it by circumstances.

Respecting Megasthenes, Col. Wilford says, " Megasthenes, a man of no ordinary abilities, who " had spent the greatest part of his life in India, in a public character, and was well acquainted " with the chronological systems of the Egytians, Chaldeans and Jews, [6] *made particular inquiries* " *into their history,* and declared, according to Clement of Alexandria, that the Hindoos and Jews " were the only people who had a true idea of the creation of the world, and the beginning of " things." [7] From these circumstances Col. Wilford draws the conclusion, " that there was an " obvious affinity between the chronological systems of the Hindus and the Jews." [8] And they have an obvious tendency to support my theory of the origin of the Jewish tribe.

In a former part of this work, I have noticed the assertion of Megasthenes, that the Jews and

---

[1] In the Map of Antis's Egypt is a hill near Maturea called Tel-el-Ihudieh, or Jewry's hill.

[2] Vide Lempriere's Class. Dict. ed. 1828.       [3] Volney's Researches, Anc. Hist. Vol. II. p. 395.

[4] Josephus adv. Apion, B. I. Sect. 22, p. 214.       [5] Court of Gent. Vol. II. p. 75.

[6] See Asiat. Res. Vol. V. p. 290.       [7] *Ibid.* Vol. X. p. 118.       [8] *Ibid.* p. 242.

Indians were the only people who had a true notion of chronology, and I have also most clearly proved that what he said was true, or, at least, that their chronologies were the same.

If I had desired to invent a piece of evidence in confirmation of what I have said respecting the emigration of the Israelitish tribe from India to Syria, I could not have had any thing better than the following passage from Col. Wilford. The Zohar Manassé, which the reader will find named, cannot, in this case, be disputed as evidence of the ancient, probably the secret or esoteric, opinion of the Jews. The seven earths one above another is a circumstance so totally inapplicable to Jerusalem, and so clearly Hindoo, that the identity of the two cannot be mistaken.

Wilford says, " *Meru* with its three peaks on the summit, and its seven steps, includes and " encompasses really the whole world, according to the notions of the Hindoos and other nations, " previously to their being acquainted with the globular shape of the earth. I mentioned in the " first part that the Jews were acquainted with the seven stages, Zones or Dwipas of the Hindus : " but I have since discovered a curious passage from the Zohar Manassé on the creation, as cited " by Basnage in his history of the Jews. [1] ' There are,' says the author, ' seven earths, whereof one " ' is higher than the other, for Judæa is situated upon the highest earth, and Jerusalem upon the " ' highest mountain of Judæa.' This is the Hill of God, so often mentioned in the Old Testa- " ment, the mount of the congregation where the mighty king sits in the sides of the north, ac- " cording to Isaiah, and there is the city of our God. The *Meru* of the *Hindus* has the name of " *Sabha*, or the congregation, and the Gods are seated upon it in the sides of the north. There " is the holy city of Brahma-puri, where resides Brahma with his court, in the most pure and holy " land of Ilavratta." [2] The Judæa or Ioud-ia and Jerusalem named above, are evidently compared to the North-pole and Mount Meru, which is thus called the place of Ioudi. We shall presently find that, with the Arabians, the Pole-star was called the star of Ioudi. The following passages from the Bible are very striking :

" Beautiful for situation, the joy of the whole earth, is mount Zion, on the sides of the north, the " city of the great king." [3] " The mountain of the house of the Lord shall be established in the top of " the mountains." [4] " Then Solomon began to build the house of the Lord at Jerusalem in mount " Moriah, where the Lord appeared unto David his father." [5] " For thou hast said in thine heart, I " will ascend into heaven, I will exalt my throne above the stars of God : I will sit also upon the " mount of the congregation, in the sides of the north." [6] " I will dwell in the midst of Jerusalem : " and Jerusalem shall be called a city of truth ; and the mountain of the Lord of Hosts, the holy " mountain." [7] When we consider that our Bible is merely the sacred writings of the temple upon this mountain, of Sion or Moriah, or Meru, the exaggeration above is only what we might expect to find in them. Thus the Indians say the same of their Meru. I think it probable that all these mounts were imitative of the Heavenly Jerusalem, described in the last two chapters of the very ancient work called the Apocalypse.

4. I think if my reader will look back to the preceding pages, he will now observe several cir- cumstances, particularly respecting the Solymi, which will tend strongly to confirm an opinion to which I have come after the most patient investigation, that the Israelites were one of the tribes which emigrated from the country of the Afghans or Rajpouts, that is, from the East, to avoid persecution. This is, indeed, in substance the account given by Moses. They were, in fact, a sect which worshiped the male generative principle in opposition to the female. The circum-

---

[1] Eng. Trans p. 247.

[2] Asiat. Res. Vol. X. p. 128, Vol. VIII. 285 ; 2 Chron. iii. 1, Isaiah xiv. 13, Psalm xlviii. 2.

[3] Psalm xlviii. 2.  [4] Micah iv. 1.  [5] 2 Chron. iii. 1.  [6] Isaiah xiv. 13.  [7] Zech. viii. 3.

stances relating to the city of Jerusalem and the Solymi will be found to be very striking, and will shew clearly why we meet with a Mount Sion in India, and with another in Syria. But though I think attachment to the adoration of the Male principle, or at least the double principle, in opposition to the female singly, or to Ionism or Hellenism, was one reason for their emigration, I also think it probable that dislike to the adoration of the Bull was another. If Solomon, of Syria, THE WISE, were a Buddha, one of the fourteen Solymi, or fourteen Menus, or fourteen Maha-bads, all supposed to be incarnations of divine wisdom, we see why he was so celebrated for that virtue. He was the son of the shepherd דוד *dud*,[1] who was the son of ישי *isi*, who was the son of עובד *Oubd*. I think *Dud* was a corruption of *Yud*, as Iacchus became Bacchus, Eioneus Deioneus, Zeus Deus, Zancle Dancle, or Dancle Zancle.[2] ישי *isi*, is the male Isis of India, עובד *Oubd* is (Syriace) *Obad* or A-bad, i. e. the Buddha.

" The Persians had a title, Soliman, equivalent to the Greek Αιολος, and implying *universal* " *cosmocrator*, qu'ils ont cru posséder l'empire universel de toute la terre, and Thamurath aspired " to this rank ; but the divine Argeng, in whose gallery were the statues of the seventy-two Soli- " mans, contended with him for the supremacy. This Argeng was the head of the league of " Αργειοι, and the number 72, is that of the kings subject to the king of kings."[3]

The history of Solomon bears a very mythological appearance, which is much confirmed by a passage in Strabo,[4] who asserts, that both Syria and Phœnicia had their names from India. He says, speaking of the irruption of the Greeks of the Seleucidæ, into India, " These same Greeks " subjugated the country as far as the territory of the Syri and Phanni." Casaubon supposed the Phannon of Strabo to mean Phoinicon, and so corrected it.[5] This shews that there were nations of these names in India, which could not be very far from the peninsula of Sawrastrene or Syrastrene :[6] or perhaps Rajahpoutana or Afghanistan.

The word Rajahpoutana, I think, is Rajah-pout-tana, or three words which mean *the country of the royal Buddha*—Pout being one of the names of Buddha. That Rajah is *royal* I shall shew by and by. Of Afghan I can make nothing; but in the travels of Ibn Batuta there is a place mentioned, near Delhi, called Afghanpoor.

5. The following passage I did not notice till I had written the whole which the reader has seen respecting the tribe of Iudai. I consider this *under these circumstances* as very valuable circumstantial evidence. This kind of coincidence I value more than direct authorities. " Some of the " ancient fathers, from terms ill-understood, divided the first ages into three or more epochas, and " have distinguished them by as many characteristics : Βαρβαρισμος, Barbarismus, which is sup- " posed to have preceded the flood ; Σκυθισμος, Scythismus, of which I have been speaking ; and

---

[1] Ruth iv. 22.

[2] " In Thessaly they have a practice of prefixing a β before the original name, which is pronounced V ; as β' Othry, " for Othrys ; and β' Alos for Alos." (Clarke's Travels, Vol. IV. p. 256, 4to.) *Thebes*, by the natives of Lebadea, is called Thiva. (Ibid. p. 215.) " Thus we have the initial digamma in *wreck*, break, from ῥήσσω." (Ibid. p. 160.) These changes are not greater than *iud* to *dud* or *diud*. Besides David was a man after God's own heart to do his will, and might be called St. David. This would be in the old language *Di-ud*. The word *ad* or *od* is the common name of God or eminent person among the Rajahpoots ; this had the very same import among the old Syrians and Assyrians. *Adodus* is called king of Gods. Cumberland says, " For as Macrobius (Saturnal. I. Cap. xxxi.) hath informed us, " *Adad* signifies among the *Assyrians* the ONE EMINENTLY, and therefore may well be the title of a monarch, or single " sovereign, and of the sun, their deity. Hither belongs also Josephus's observation from the Damascenus, that the " ten successions from *Hadad-ezer* in Syria took all of them the title of *Hadad*." (Origin. Gent. pp. 170, 171, 172, 235, 236.

[3] See Herbelot in voce Soliman ; Nimrod, Vol. III. p. 12.     [4] Vol. IV.

[5] Asiat. Soc. Vol. I. p. 335.     [6] Ibid. 336.

" Ἑλληνισμος, Hellenismus, or the Grecian period; this last must appear as extraordinary as any. " For how was it possible for an Hellenic æra to have existed before the name of Hellas was " known, or the nation in being?" I suppose the reader, after having read what I have said relating to the Ionians, does not require an answer to the question. To this Mr. Bryant adds in a note,—Αι δε των αιρεσεων πασων μητερες τε και σρωκριτοι και ονομαςοι εισιν αὑται, Βαρβαρισμος, Σκυθισμος, Ἑλληνισμος, Ιȣδαϊσμος¹—" In like manner a fourth heresy is supposed to " have arisen, styled JUDAISMUS, BEFORE THE TIME OF EITHER JEWS OR ISRAELITES."² Here the tribe of Yadu, or Judai, or Ioud, of which I have treated, is evident, which these fathers could not help seeing, but of which they could not understand the origin or meaning.

6. The existence of the Ionian or Hellenistic heresy, as well as its antiquity, is clearly recognized by several of the fathers. Eusebius³ says, Σερȣχ, ᾿ςις πρωτος ηρξατο τȣ Ἑλληνισμȣ : Serug was the first who introduced the false worship called Hellenismus. Epiphanius says, ⁴ Ραγαμ γεννα τον Σερȣχ, και ηρξατο εις ανθρωπȣς ἡ ειδολολατρεια τε, και ὁ Ἑλληνισμος— Ragem or Ragan had for his son Seruch, when idolatry and Hellenismus first began among men. Johannes Antiochenus styles the people of Midian, Hellenes, and speaking of Moses, who married the daughter of Jethro, the Cuthite, the chief priest of Midian, he represents the woman⁵ την Θυγατερα Ιοθορ τȣ αρχιερεωϑτων Ἑλληνων, as the daughter of Jother, the high-priest of the Hellenes. The introduction or adoption of Hellenism or Ionism by Serug, several generations before Abraham, is as much in favour of my hypothesis as any thing can be.

Apollodorus⁶ says, Hellen was the firstborn of Deucalion by Pyrrha; though some make him the son of Jove or Dios. There was also a daughter Protogeneia, so named from being the firstborn of women. Manetho⁷ says, that the learning of Egypt was styled Hellenic, from the Hellenic shepherds, and the ancient theology of the country was described in the Hellenic character and language. This theology was said to be derived from Agathodæmon, by Syncellus.⁸ These Hellenic shepherds, I suppose, were the Pallestini or Palli, whom we meet with in many places, and whom, in Syria, we call Philistines. But what were the Hellenic character and language? I do not know. Scarcely any question is more difficult to answer (when all the circumstances are considered); but yet I think it was probably only a sixteen-letter system.

7. Mr. Franklin says, "Another striking instance is recorded by the very intelligent traveller " (Wilson) regarding a representation of the fall of our first parents, sculptured in the magnificent " temple of Ipsambul in Nubia. He says that a very exact representation of Adam and Eve in " the Garden of Eden is to be seen in that cave, and that the serpent climbing round the tree is " especially delineated, and the whole subject of the tempting of our first parents most accurately " exhibited."⁹ How is the fact of the Mythos of the second book of Genesis being found in Nubia, probably a thousand miles above Heliopolis, to be accounted for, except that it came from Upper India with the first Buddhists or Gymnosophists? There they were found by Clemens Alexandrinus, and there they founded a Meru, now called Meroe. The same Mythos is found in India. Col. Tod says, "A drawing, brought by Colonel Coombs, from a sculptured column in a " cave-temple in the South of India, represents the first pair at the foot of the ambrosial tree, and

---

¹ Chron. Paschall. p. 23; Epiphan. Lib. i. p. 9; Euseb. Chron. p. 13.    * Bryant's Anal. Vol. III. p. 151.
³ Chron. p. 13.    ⁴ Hæres. Lib. i. Cap. vi. p. 7.    * Pp. 76, 77.    ⁶ Lib. i. p. 20.
⁷ Ap. Euseb. Chron. p. 6.    * P. 40; Bryant. Anal. Anc. Myth. Vol. III. p. 157.
⁹ On Buddhists and Jeynes, p. 127, Note.

" a serpent entwined among the heavily-laden boughs, presenting to them some of the fruit from
" his mouth.   The tempter appears to be at that part of his discourse, when

> ' ——————————— his words, replete with guile,
> Into her heart too easy entrance won :
> Fixed on the fruit she gazed.'

" This is a curious subject to be engraved on an ancient Pagan temple : if Jain or Buddhist, the
" interest would be considerably enhanced." [1]   No doubt it would be enhanced, but not I think
so much as the Colonel apprehends.   The same mythos, as the Romish Dr. Geddes calls Genesis,
is at the bottom of the religions of Moses, India, and Egypt, with such small variations only as
time and circumstance may be expected to produce.   We will not forget this mythos, when we
treat, in a future book, of the religion of South India.   It is the mythos which we have just now
noticed in Upper Egypt.   In my plates, fig. 27, may be seen a copy of one of the groups of figures
in Montfaucon.   However it may differ, can any one doubt that it is allusive to the Pentateuchian
or Mosaic mythos ?   See also fig. 16.

8. Although Sion or Moriah, or the Syrian Meru, was a high-place, yet we find high-places
every where reprobated in the Old Testament, in the most pointed terms.   This is because they
had become in a peculiar manner dedicated in these countries to the Ionic worship—to Ionism or
Hellenism.   This is proved by the name given them by the LXX.—πορνειον, Lupanar.   This
again confirms what I have said respecting the Jews being attached to the exclusive *male* generative power.   In these places, called πορνεια, they had cells or adyta which the Greeks called
Naïda, where the secret and licentious rites of the Ionic worship were celebrated.   I have before
observed that I suspect that from these places, built of an oblong form in imitation of the Hindoo
Argha or Nav or Kibotos or Tibe, came the naves of our churches, and that their inhabitants were
the Naïdæ ; and if in consequence of the performance of these rites a boy was born, he was considered sacred ; in a peculiar manner dedicated to the priesthood, and educated by them with the
greatest care.   These Naïdæ were nothing more nor less than the dancing girls, who are now
found in the temples of India.   In the temple of Venus at Corinth, a thousand of them were kept.
Calmet says there were dancing girls in the Temple of Jerusalem.   No doubt our prudes will be
angry with me for repeating what Calmet has let out, but for my own part I must freely confess, I
like the girls, with all their sins, better than the nasty Galli.

Throughout all the ancient world the distinction between the followers of the Yoni and Linga
may be seen.   All nations seem to have been Ionians except the Jews and Persians ; and, as the
Jewish or *male* principle prevailed, the other declined.

---

[1] Tod's Hist. Raj. p. 581.

---

## CHAPTER III.

NAMES OF PLACES.—RAJPOUTS, RANNÆ OF PTOLEMY.—INDIAN CHRONOLOGY.—AJIMERE.—MOUNT SION. —SION AND HIEROSOLYMA.—VARIOUS MOUNTS OF SOLYMA: TEMPLES OF SOLOMON.—JERUSALEM: JESULMER.—MEANING OF JERUSALEM.—TEMPLE OF SOLOMON IN CASHMERE.

1. WE will now examine the names of some of the states and cities in India, and in them I think we shall find conclusive proofs of the place where Judaism came from, and probably along with it the first written language.

In India, in very ancient times, there was a state of great power. Its capital was in lat, 26° 48′ N., long. 82° 4′ E., of prodigious extent, being one of the largest of Hindostan, anciently called Ayodhya or Oude. It was, and yet is, a place celebrated for its sanctity, to which Pilgrims resort from all parts of India. The Hindoo history states that it was the seat of power, of a great prince called Dasaratha, the father of Rama, and of Rama, the brother of Cristna. Dasaratha extended his conquests as far as Ceylon, which he subdued. We shall find in a future page, from the similarity of the mythos in South India to that of Oude, reason to believe this story of the conquest to be substantially true. Ayodhia or Iyodhya is nothing but Judia, and Oude, Juda. Iyodhia is Iyo-di-ia—country of the sacred Iou, or Jud. I shall return many times to this etymon.

I feel little doubt that the tribe of Iaoud was expelled from this kingdom, perhaps from Maturea, from which place they took their names. Every difficulty will be removed if we suppose that the religious wars of the sects of the Ioni and Linga were long, and had alternate successes ; and this perfectly agrees with the Hindoo histories, which represent the wars to have been long, and of this description. The cities above-named are situated a little Westward of Tibet. The tribe of Ioud or the Brahmin Abraham, was expelled from or left the Maturea of the kingdom of Oude in India, and, settling at Goshen, or *the house of the Sun* or Heliopolis in Egypt, gave it the name of the place which they had left in India, Maturea. I beg my reader to look back to Book V. Ch. VII. Sect. 1, for all the striking circumstances of connexion, for a vast number of years, between the tribe of Abraham and Heliopolis. Let him also consider what I said just now, respecting this same city of destruction, being called the city of Seth or Typhon, and of Abaris or Avaris, that is, of the Hebrews.

We have seen that the City of Avaris was probably called Abaris, which meant Strangers or Hebrews, and close to it was the mount of Ieudieh. Bryant[1] shews that this Avaris was called Cercasora, which will turn out to be the same as the Calisa-pura in the kingdom of Ioudya or Oude, in India.[2] Thus we shall connect Maturea, Judah, and Abraham together, and, as I have suggested, the doctrines of Cristna or the Lamb.

There is an account of the Hyperborean called *Abaris*, viz. that he came into Greece carrying in his hand the arrow of Apollo, which served him as a passport through all countries. Col. Tod[3] has given an instance of the arrow of a tribe from the kingdom of Oude being made use of as a passport, exactly in the same manner. Coincidences of this kind appear trifling, but they are in reality very important. They render it probable, that the same mythos is in both countries.

Abraham came from Mesopotamia of the Chaldees.[4] This precisely answers to the situation

---

[1] Vol. III. p. 260, 4to.

[3] Hist. Rajapoutana.

[2] Vide Book V. Chap. VI. Sect. 6, of this work.

[4] Acts vii. 2—4.

of Mutra or Maturea on the Jumna. It is the country of the ancient kingdom of Oude between the two rivers Ganges and Indus, and is called Duab or Mesopotamia, as I have before stated. He probably came just before the change of the worship took place, from Taurus to Aries, from Buddha to Cristna.

Let us suppose, for the sake of argument, that a tribe or sect was expelled from India. Is it not natural to expect, that when they settled in a distant country they would give the same names to their new habitations after they had conquered or acquired them, as those places bore which they left? And if this were the case, is it not probable, that though several thousand years may have since passed, the names of the new settlements should be found in the old country? Thus it is: and as this was a sect, or national religion widely extended, and not the inhabitants of a town merely, it happens that we have names of places in the country near the Mediterranean where they settled, which are found in many parts of India, in Siam, Pegu, Tibet, &c.

I beg my reader to refer to the Map which is taken partly from those of Bishop Heber and Col. Tod, and he will find the kingdom of Oude, anciently Ayodhia, in a district called Agra, in which is a city, called anciently Argha[1] or Agra. It was in ruins in the time of Akbar—and was rebuilt by him and called Akberabad. [2] He will also find a place called Daoud-nagur, that is Dud (דוד *dud*) or David-nagur. Nagur means *fort* or *walled town*. There is also a district called Daod-potra, that is, *town of the sons of David*. Thus we have a city of David and a country of the children or sons of David.

Maturea has been before noticed in Egypt and on the Jumna, or Jamuna, or Yamuna. There is also a city in the same country called Joud-poor, or Yuddapoor, or the city of Jud, where Bishop Heber says are the ruins of a magnificent city. This is called by called Col. Tod *Ocde-poor :* it is about lat. 24½, long. 73¾. There are also several other towns of the same name. There is also, in about lat. 26¼, and long. 73, a city called, by Col. Tod, Jodpoor, with a district of the same name. About lat. 27 and long. 76, may be seen a town called Jeipour, with a district of the same name. There is also, about lat. 26, long. 78, a district called Jado-ouwatti. Bishop Heber says, the king of the country of Joud or Jud-poor, is called Malek, that is, in correct Hebrew, the King. [3] . All these places, as well as Delhi and Benares, were included in the kingdom of Oud, or Ayodhia, or Juda. .

There are three places in a triangle between 25 and 30 degrees of latitude, and about 73 of longitude, in the kingdom of Oude or Juda—the first, called Oudipour, or Cheitore, or Meywar, or Midwar; the second, Joodpour, or Yuddapoor; the third, called Ambeer, or Amere, or Joinagur, or Jyenagur, or Jyepour. [4] I need not remind my reader that he must strike off the syllable *pour* or poor, which means place or town, and then he will have the real name. As we may expect from its name Midwar or Medway in English, Oudipore or Cheitore is in the middle of the other two. My reader may smile at this observation, but the farther back he goes, the more numerous he will find these kinds of extraordinary coincidences. They are the words of an universal and very old language. In some of the Northern nations *Day* is called *Var*. This is similar to Midwar and Medway, *Med* or Mid-day.

The river Chelum, or Jalum, or Jhylun, or Behut, or Jenaut[5] has on its West side the country of the Joudis, at the foot of the mountains of Joud. There is also a place or district in this country called Seba or Siba. There is also a tribe called Jajoohahs, which descended from the

---

[1] Heber.

[2] A district of Jerusalem was called Acra: this must have been Arga, as it is not likely that this city should have a quarter called by a Greek name.

[3] Vol. I. p. 368.          [4] See Rennell's Memoir, p. cxxxii.          [5] Rennell, p. 98.

Joudis. Here are the Jews, descended from Judah. In the mountains of Solomon are found a tribe of people called Judoons,[1] (that is, Judæans,) and a place called Gosa, (that is Gaza,) and a people called Jadrauns, and another called Jaujees (Jews).[2] The mountains of Solomon, or Solimaun, have this name in the old books, though they are not commonly known at this time by it.[3] These mountains are higher than the Andes.[4] One of the mounts of the chain is called Suffaid Coh.[5] The Sofees of Persia are called Suffarees.[6] In this country, also, is the city of Enoch, the Anuchta of Ptolemy.

Col. Tod says,[7] the traditions of the Hindoos assert that India was first peopled or colonized by a race called *Yadu*, to which they trace the foundations of the most conspicuous of their ancient cities.[8] The Yadus are in the unpolished dialect pronounced Jadu or Jadoons.[9] The *Eusofzyes*, or tribe of *Joseph*, is also called Jadoons, that is, Judæans.

2. The country of Cheitore or Oudipore belongs to the tribe called Rajpoots, their chief called by the title of Rana. In Ptolemy they are called Rhannæ.[10] They are a most warlike tribe, and, in fact, have never been permanently subdued. They are the warrior tribe noticed by Arrian and Diodorus. Not far from the above is a town called Ajimere, the Gagasmira of Ptolemy.[11] Father Georgius admits the truth of what I have said respecting the names of the Indian places: he says, Regnum Ayiodia alias Avod (meaning Ayodia and Oude) ex depravato nomine Jehuda, seu Jeuda. He then shews that *Giodu,* Giadu, Giadubansi, are all the same as the יהוה *ieude* of the Hebrews, and he gives the following translation of a passage of the Bagavan : " Ipse (Cristna) " salvabit Gentem suam Gioda nempe Pastorum : vitam dabit bonis : interficiet Gigantes : " relinquet Gokul, et Madiapur : agnoscetur ab universo terrarum orbe : et nomen ejus invo- " cabunt omnes, Divinum est vaticinium : nec dubita, haud : sic erit." Of course all with the monk, is clearly copied from the kingdom of Juda, which Herodotus could not find. Is it possible for any proof to be more clear than this, of the truth of the theory advocated by me, of the double mythos in Eastern and Western Syria ?

3. I shall not attempt to enter into the history and chronology of India ; I consider that it is so contaminated with nonsense and fraud, that it is merely soiling paper to transcribe it. The Grecian heroic times are sense compared to it. I will give one specimen, from which a comparison may be made with all the others. Parasu Rama, who lived since the time of Christ, looking down from a hill on the sea-shore, saw some dead Brahmins. These by magic he brought to life, and from them descended the Ranas of Udaya-pur, as Major Wilford calls it, to disguise the true name, the *city of Judea.*[12] This is a fair specimen of the way in which the lost origin of the various tribes is accounted for. Ex uno disce omnes. From this I shall be told that these Rannas are of modern date, but Ptolemy's notice of them, as well as of Gazamera or Ajimere, settles this question. They were kings of one of the very old cities of the tribe of Joudi, miscalled or disguised by the name of Udaya-pur. Col. Tod gives it its proper name and calls it *Ioude,* or Oudipore. The notice of the Rannæ, by Ptolemy, shews that the tribe was in existence before the dispersion of the Jews in the time of Vespasian. In the attempt to discover the truth in questions of this kind, it is very seldom that a proof of a fact can be obtained, but I think it is obtained respecting the Rannæ of Oudipore. They were evidently here in the time of Ptolemy, and they are yet remaining. There can be no shadow of pretence to set up that they have been destroyed by the

---

[1] Elphins. Vol. II. p. 99.          [2] Ib.          [3] Ib. Tab. Vol. I. p. 148.          [4] Ib. p. 155.

[5] Ib. p. 156.          [6] Ib. p. 257.          [7] Trans. Royal Asiat. Soc. Vol. III. pp. 1, 141.

[8] For a sketch of this race see An. Rajastan, Vol. I. p. 85.          [9] Ibid. p. 86.          [10] Rennell, p. 153.

[11] Rennell, p. 145.          [12] Asiat. Res. Vol. IX. p. 238.

Mohamedans, and the city of Oude or Oudi-pore built by Mohamedans, and since that time a new tribe of Rannæ set up. The city of Gagasmera or Ajimere confirms this. The city of Oudepore is very large, and carries on the face of it marks of extreme antiquity. If the antiquity of the city of Oude or Ioudi-pore, and its Rannæ be considered to be proved, and that they existed before the time of Christ, I think it carries with it pretty good presumptive proof, that all the other towns in its neighbourhood having Jewish or Israelitish names are the same. Then, except as I have accounted for it, how is it to be accounted for?

Delhi, was formerly called Indraprest'ha, and was founded by Yoodishtra. The *shtra* is like the *shtra* in Saurasthra, a termination which I do not understand, but it leaves the Yoodi.[1] The most ancient of the cities of this part of India, are Oude or Yodya, and Agra, the latter of which went to decay, and was rebuilt by Akbar.

Col. Tod says a colony of the Yadu dwelt in the mountains called in Rennell's map Ioudes, when they were expelled from Saurastra. No one can deny that these Yadu or Ioudi dwelt, to use a Bible phrase, in the mountains of Juda. These were the Yadus of *Jess-ul-mer*.[2] These Yadus have now got corrupted into Jadoon.[3] Speaking of Jodpoor, the Colonel says, " The " view will give a more correct idea of the ' City of Joda' than any description."[4] Here the doctrine which I teach is unconsciously adopted by Col. Tod. *Iod* means Joda or Juda.

4. In lat. 26, 31 N. long. 74, 28 E., is the city called Ajimere or Gazamere, the Gazamera of Ptolemy adjoining to a large lake. Here is Gaza, of Syria, and the old English word *mere* for a lake. We have Wittlesey *Mere* near Peterborough, Hornsey *Mere* near Kingston-on-Hull, in the kingdom of *Brigantia*, near the river *Umber*. Is all this accidental? Col. Tod says that the word *mer* in the Hindoo language means *hill*. Then it will be the *hill* of Aji. But the expression of Ptolemy shews, that the two words Aji and Gaza are the same. The word which we call Gaza, in the Hebrew is written עזא *oza*. This means Goat, the same as Aje—which tends to prove that the original must have been Aji. The lake of Potsha is close by Ajimere, and the town of Gaza being on the sea, the word *mer* must mean both hill, and the Latin Mare, or Meris, or Mæris, a lake —the Hebrew מרה *mre* or מרר *mrr*.[5]

Col. Tod explains the word Jerusalem to mean Mer-Jesul or Hill of Jessul. The double meaning of the word Mer arises from all these sacred mounts being imitative Merus. Thus they might be all called Mer. Meru, we must recollect, was a hill in a sea, or surrounded by an oceanus. And from this the two came to be confounded. But this will be more clearly shewn presently.

The river anciently called Pontus, in Thrace, is now by the Turks called *Mer*, and the lake into which it runs, Mer-mer: whence I am justified in concluding that the word Mer meant lake, in the old language, before it was changed or translated, by the Greeks, into Pontus.

No one can doubt that Casimere or Cashmere was called from the lake which probably once filled its valley. This again fixes one of the meanings of the word *Mere*.

5. The missionary Dr. Buchanan states his opinion, that the religion of Buddha arose near Tibet. He names a river of Siam, which rises near the frontiers of China, and which is in the Burman empire; and he gives a description of a most holy imaginary mountain in the same empire called Sian.[6] I think it probable that the kingdom of Siam had its name and religion from this country. Here we have the Sion referred to by Loubere, in Book V. Chap. III. Sect. 8. The Siamese, he states to be called Yoo-dă-ya, which, he observes, is nothing but Judæi.

---

[1] Tod's Hist. Raj. p. 87.   [2] Hist. Raj. pp. 61, 62.   [3] Ib. p. 86.   [4] Ib. p. 709.

[5] Littleton, Dic.   [6] Asiat. Res. Vol. VI. p. 242.

Mount Sion is a mystic mount, and came from the Mount Zion of the Burmese empire, or of the kingdom of Siam, or as La Loubère says of the Sions—for there seems to have been a ridge of them, like the ridge of the Alpes. It is the mount of the Gods or of happy beings, [1] in the kingdom of Siam—the mount where the Gods reside, and there were several of these mounts above one another for different orders of beings ; and though I have no authority for the assertion, I have no doubt that they were *on the sides of the North.* In short, Sion meaning the holy mount was Mount Meru. There were seven heavens before the throne of God. The word ציון *ziun*, in Hebrew, correctly means *a stone mount,* and has also the meaning of the stone Carn of the Western nations. Mr. Turner observed the same Carns in Tibet. They are equally found in Iona of the Hebrides. Every person in passing these mounts thinks it an act of piety to add a stone to them. There is also a mystical Zion in Ceylon, where the Samaritan Pentateuch places Mount Ararat. The Cingales' traditions state them to have come from the land of Ava, that is, of Eva.

In the Buddhist doctrines of Ceylon, the Mount Zian, or *triumphing heaven,* makes a great figure. [2] It is called a place of SALVATION. It is evidently like the Mount Zion of the Jews a mystical mount, having in reality the same name. The etymology of the word Sion I reserve to a future book.

The ancient name of Thibet or Tibet was Baltistan ; that is, the place of Balti, or Baaltis, of Syria. [3]

Mr. Faber has shewn, that the city of Sidon, in Syria, where the God Dagon was adored, had its name from an oriental city on the Erythrean Sea called Sidon ; but Trogus says that the Erythrean Sidon was not the original settlement of the Sidonians, *but that they came from a more Eastern part.* [4]

6. The following observations of Nimrod's will pretty well shew us the origin of the famous Mount Moriah or Sion of the Jews. Coming as they do from so good a Greek and Latin scholar, and at the same time from a devotee and unwilling witness, with the impartial inquirer they will command the greatest respect. " Belerophon fought against the female host of the Amazonians. " He fought also with the Solymi, a circumstance which tends to identify him with Memnon, who, " on his way to relieve Troy, met and overthrew

" Αργαλεων Σολυμων ιερον ςρατον. [5]

" Immediately behind Phaselis, of Pamphylia, rose Mount Solymus, and close to it (probably one " of its peaks) Mount OLYMPUS, [6] called also Φοινιχοεις, or *the red.* Also, a Lophos, or conical " hill over Termessus, of Pisidia, was called Σολυμος Λοφος, and hard by it a work of antiquity, " called the rampart of Belorophon or mound : χαραξ. [7]    A mount Solymus was, like Ida to " Jove, the σκοπιη, or seat of speculation, to the Ethiopian Neptune.

Τον δ' εξ Αιϑιοπων ανιων κριων Ενοσιχϑον
Τηλοθεν εκ Σολυμων ορεων ιδεν. [8]

" In fact, it was one of the many names used among the nations for an Olymp, or sacrificial and " oracular high place. In the maritime Syria there was a very famous city of immemorial

---

[1] Asiat. Res. Vol. VI. p. 187.    [2] Upham's History of Buddhism, p. 74.
[3] Lett. Edif. Vol. XV. p. 188.    [4] Orig. Pag. Idol. Vol. III. p. 562.
[5] Qu. Sm. L. ii. ver. 120; Herod. L. i. C. clxxiii. ; Steph. Byz. in voce Milyæ.    [6] Strabo, L. xiv. p. 952.
[7] Vide Strabo, L. xiii. p. 904.    [8] Hom. Od. L. v. ver. 283.

3 G

" sanctity, and containing within its purlieus several mounts dedicated to the mysteries of the
" Syrian or IONIAN religion, especially.the Mount Moriah or Olivet, and the Mount Sion. This
" city, founded by the Jebusite Canaanites, was called Solyma, and, by way of honour, Hiero-
" Solyma. It was taken from its subsequent possessors, the Jews and Benjamites, by Nebuchad-
" nezzar the Great, a prince of the Syrian religion, which heresy he raised to an unexampled pitch
" of splendour: and out of the spoils of Hiero-Solyma he founded a new city, Solyma,[1] in
" Assyria."[2]

Again, Nimrod says, " This place, Hiero-Solyma, was not occupied by the chosen people till
" the time of Joshua,[3] but it was solemnly consecrated to the uses of the Christian worship in
" the days of Abraham, by the symbolical offering of his son : and the same Abraham having
" vanquished a league of kings, met in the neighbourhood, with a personage named Melchisedek,
" king of Salem, who initiated him into the mysteries of the Christian sacrament. Sacrifice,
" with immolation and libation, was appointed for anticipation of an atonement to come : but the
" two latter were thought sufficient for the commemoration thereof when complete........We
" are not told what place it was that was called Salem, but we find the Israelites, when in pos-
" session of Hiero-Solym, invariably calling it Jeru-salem, Behold peace : and Josephus, who was
" ignorant of the nature and character of Melchisedek, and mistook him for some Jebusite
" prince,[4] informs us, that he first gave to the city, Jerusalem, its present name. Here then we
" have the truth : the name Solym was changed to Salem, and Hiero-Solym to Hieru-Salem."[5]

Notwithstanding some nonsense and several mistakes, here are several very important admissions
of Nimrod's, as we shall presently see. What I have said before respecting the change of Salem to
Jerusalem is here confirmed. The meaning of the present name Jerusalem is, according to our
divines, *he shall see peace.* But perhaps, like many other mythic words, it had two meanings.

Nimrod seems to have forgotten that Eupolemus tells us, that Melchizedek lived at Gerizim.[6]
Before I proceed further with the meaning of the word Jerusalem, we must discuss several other
circumstances connected with it.

7. The Solymi are named by Homer, and there were a people noticed of that name in Lycia, in
Asia Minor, a province adjoining to Pisidia. I suspect that they were a sect driven out of India
to the West, and the builders of Jerusalem, or Hiero-Solyma, the Sacred Solyma. I learn from
the author of Nimrod, that Memnon was said to have fought the Solymi,[7] that is, that the sun
fought them. This might mean that they were driven from the East. There were *fourteen* Bads or
Buddhas, or incarnations of divine wisdom under that name. There were also *fourteen* incarnations
of divine wisdom under the name of Menu. And there were *fourteen* Soleimans, all, perhaps,
different names for the same mythos. But in the Jewish books we only read of *one* Menu, and
one Noah, or of *one* Solomon, *the Wise.*

I now beg my reader to reflect upon the fact, of Sanscrit words being found in the Latin and
Greek languages. This done, he will probably not be surprised to find Latin words in India. He
will recollect that the temples or sacred places in Judæa were called בית אל *bit al,* or house of
God, and Solomon built a house to the Lord, by which name of house, the temple of Jerusalem,
in a very pointed manner, was called. Thus, this being premised, the next place which I shall

---

[1] Asin. Quadr. Ap. Steph. Byz. in. voce.      [2] Nimrod, Vol. I. Sup. Ed. p. 96.

[3] Joshua, that is Jesus, that is the Saviour, the son of Nave, that is *of the boat,* or the Argha, or the female generative power : note of the author's, not Nimrod's.

[4] No mistake—note by G, H., not by Nimrod.      [5] Ibid. p. 97.

[6] On this point Josephus is not evidence. He is a partisan.      [7] Vol. I. p. 98.

notice is Tucte Soliman—this, is tectum, or house of Solomon. It is one of the five sacred mounts, Merus or Olympusés or Solymi of India. It is not far from the hills called the mountain or ridge of Solyman. But the Tucte Soleymans, or houses of Soleiman, were not confined to India.

In Morier's Travels in Persia, (see plates, Fig. 28,) may be seen a building, the style of which at once proves its great antiquity. It is called Madré Soleiman. On seven towers of Cyclopean architecture, stands a square house, with pitched roof, formed of large stones projecting one over the other, like the roof of the cave at New Grange, in Ireland, the cave at Mysenæ, the walls of Tyrins, and the temple of Komulmar, described by Col. Tod, in the history of Rajapoutana. The Persians attribute it to Solciman, but modern learned men think they have made out, that it is the tomb of Cyrus. [1] They may please themselves with this fancy; but the style, the traditional name, the seven steps, and the square building at the top, all joined together, pretty well satisfy me that it is a tecte Soleiman. If it had been the tomb of their great Cyrus, it would never have lost its name or designation. I would ask, what has a Madré Soleiman to do in Persia, according to our construction of the text of the Jewish historians? Though the Persians say that Abraham was their ancestor—they do not say his successors, a thousand years afterward, were their ancestors. Then how came they to think of Soleiman as the author of this building? I think it probable, under these circumstances, that this is not the building alluded to by Arrian, Curtius, Pliny, &c., in their account of the visit to it of Alexander the Great, [2] but one of the same nature as the Merus of India. I consider the traditional name of the building, among the ignorant natives, as better authority than Greek historians. For I again ask, how could the name of Solomon come here among the unlearned natives? Persons are struck, at first, with the connexion between Abraham, whom, as just mentioned, the Persians claim for their ancestor, and Solomon. But such persons do not attend to the circumstance of the dates, which shew that, even admitting Abraham to have been the ancestor of the Persians, this gives them no interest whatever in the son of Bathsheba, Abraham's descendant, who never was in Persia, or had any connexion with it.

The Persian romances say, that there were seventy or seventy-two rulers, called Suleiman, before Adam: this has an obvious relation to the seventy-one Manwantaras of the Hindus, [3] and evidently is the same history as the seventy-two Soleimans alluded to before in this work.

Perse-polis, or the city of Perse, in Greek, was called in Persian Tucht-i-Gemsheed; from which we may infer that this fabulous king was the Perseus of the Greeks, who was the Sun. [4]

Thus, Tucht-i-Gemsheed being the same as *city of Gemshid*, we come to the conclusion that Tucht-i-Soleiman is the same as *the city of Soleiman*. Here we arrive at an important truth by recourse to my system of applying to several languages, and going, in fact, to the first system of letters and written language, as far as we can get. No one will doubt the identity of these Tuctis.

Nimrod says, " The Mahabadian line is nothing but the succession of antediluvian patriarchs;" [5] that is, a supposed succession of re-incarnations of Buddha, or the Sun in Taurus. Maha-Bad is Great Bud. He says, *After this line* came Gemshid or Perseus, whose emblem was a Lamb, which is yet common on medals struck in his honour.

A very important observation has been made by Sir R. Ker Porter,—that he found the traits of resemblance striking and numerous, betwixt the ruins of the temples of Persepolis and the description of the temple of Solomon. [6]

---

[1] But query, was not Cyrus a Solomon ?    [2] Vide Hale's Chronology, p. 111.
[3] Asiat. Res. Vol. VI. p. 524, and also Vcl. X. p. 93.    [4] Nimrod, Vol. I. p. 141.
[5] Vol. I. p. 141.    [6] P. 700, Cruezer, p. 676.

In Porter's Travels[1] may be found the description of the remains of a city called *Tackt-i-Soli-mon* of very great and unknown antiquity.  This city of ancient ruins has been thoughtlessly ascribed to the 15th Calif.  Another of these places called *Tuckt-i-Suleiman,* or *the throne of Suliema,* may be found described in Vol. I. p. 485.  Pliny calls this place Pasargada, and says, that here is the tomb of Cyrus, by whom it was built.

If my reader will consult Pococke's Travels,[2] he will see good reason to believe that Solomon's gardens and pools in Syria were gardens of Daphne or a Meru.  Though Pococke did not in the least understand the subject, he could not help observing that " it is probable there were *hanging* " *gardens* on the side of the hill."  The plate describes a perfect Meru with its seven hills one above another, and its mount; on which Pococke observes, " probably the house stood at the top."

In Asia Minor, near Telmessus, noticed before, there were Solymean mountains, one of these of great height, called Takhta-lu by the present Turks, was called formerly by the Greeks *Mount Solyma.*  Here is, I think, the Tekte Solyma of the Hindoos of Rajapoutana.  Here is also an example of the old name returning to the place.  I think no one can refuse his assent to the identity of these two curious names, Tecte Solyma and Takhta-lu Solyma.[3]

Josephus says, that the Jews assisted the Persians against Greece.  He cites the poet Choerilus, who, he says, names a people who dwelt on the Solymean mountains of Asia Minor, and spoke Phœnician.  Bochart, not knowing what to make of this, supposes that what he alluded to was a colony of Phœnicians, who had settled in Asia Minor, near to the lake Phaselis.  The colony here spoken of, I think, were from Tekte Solymi : they were Ioudi, which is confirmed by their *sooty heads, like horses' heads dried in the smoke,* and their having the Tonsure,[4] or shaven crown, which, Bochart has shewn, was prohibited to the Jews ; and, by the fact of the prohibition, shews that it had once existed.  The Buddhists of Tibet have the tonsure.

It is observed by Mercator, that, by the poets, Jerusalem was called Solyma or Solumæ.  From Josephus, it appears, that there was a Mount Solyma, near the lake Asphaltes, in Judea.[5]

8.  About lat. 27 N. and long. 71 E. on Col. Tod's map will be found the place called JESULMER. I learn from the Colonel's work, that it is a place of very great antiquity, and in a peculiar manner sacred among the Buddhists.  In one of the temples is a very large library, and in the centre of it, suspended by a chain of gold in a golden case, is a most sacred, holy manuscript, which is expressly forbidden to be read or even looked upon.  It is believed that any person reading it would be instantly struck blind.  Some time ago the prince of the country caused it to be brought to him, in order that he might read it; but his courage failed, and he sent back the virgin unde-flowered, and thus it will probably remain till some *sacrilegious European* lays hands on it.  These circumstances shew, I think, that the city of Jesulmer is no common place : and now I beg my reader to transpose the letters of this word Jesulmer, and he will find they make Jeruselm.  Take this by itself and the fact would be of little consequence, but couple it with all the other circum-stances—with the names of the other towns which I have pointed out, and I defy the unprejudiced reader to divest his mind of a strong suspicion, that the Jerusalem of the West is the Jesulmer of the East, or vice versa.[6]  Jesulmer changed into Jeruselm, is nothing but an example of the prac-tice called *Themeru* or changing, of the tribe of Ioudi of writing words in the way called anagram-matical.[7]  It is quite surprising to what a length this foolish and childish practice was carried

---

[1] Vol. II. p. 557.                   [2] Fol. Ed. Vol. I. p. 44.

[3] Drummond's Orig. Vol. IV. pp. 90—93.          [4] Ibid. pp. 94, 95.          [5] Ibid. pp. 90, 93.

[6] A little to the south of Jesulmer, about lat. 26, is a town called Iunuh, the old name of Antioch.

[7] Ency. Britt. voce Anagram.

even in modern times. John Calvinus called himself Alcuinus. When a person observes the variety of ways in which the names of these cities and countries are written into English by our Indian travellers from the old dialects of the country, (I do not speak of the Sanscrit,) he will be willing to allow a very considerable latitude. Scarcely any two of them use the same letters, though the striking similitude to the Jewish names is apparent in them all.

9. The meaning of Jeru-salem is *the sacred ladder*, סלם *slm* in Hebrew ; סולמא *sulma* in Chaldee. The LXX.[1] render סלם *slm* solim, by κλίμαξ, and Jerom by *scala*. The Mount Climax of Strabo, in Asia Minor, was called Mount *Solim* or *Solima* by the natives ; and Climax was only a Greek translation of the oriental name.[2] I *suspect* that the name of the town of the inhabitants of Telmessus, who lived close to Mount Solyma, and who were called Solymi,[3] was a mere corruption of סלם *slm ;* that, in a similar way, the word Jesulmer of India is a corruption from the same name, like the name of the Syrian Meru, called Moriah, or Sion, or Argha or Arca, or Solyma. The city of Jerusalem is spelt with a Shin and not a Samech. The Samech being one of the new letters, if the *sixteen* letter system be true, this makes nothing against my argument ; for in all this I must be supposed to speak of a time, before the letters of the alphabets were increased, when the *Shin* must have been used. Our priests will tell me that שלם *slm*, or salem, means *peace*. But the passages of Strabo, Jerom, and the LXX., compared with the circumstances relating to the town in Asia Minor, shew pretty well what was the original meaning. But it is very likely that it took the meaning of *peace* from being the name of the mount of peace, Mount Sion.

Ἱερος, in Greek, means *sacred*, and I suspect it has come from some Asiatic word now lost, or at least unknown to me. And when I consider the form of Meru, step above step, the Madré Solyman of Persia, and the rendering of the word סלם *slm* in the LXX. by κλίμαξ, and in the Vulgate by *scala*, and the same word סלם *slm* used for Jacob's ladder, seen at Bit-al or *the house of God*, on which seventy-two angels ascended and descended, I suspect that the Hiero, ירה *ire* means sacred, the sacred ladder, or the sacred mount. It is what the Greeks called Olympus. The Bit-al, Bethel, or house of God, which Jacob's place of the ladder was called, is not unlike the Tectum of the Solymi. We must also remember that Solomon, an incarnation of wisdom, is closely connected with the wisdom of the Buddhists. The observation respecting the similarity of the Tectum of Solyman or Tucte Soleyman to the בית אל *bit al* of Genesis, is the more striking, because I learn from my friend Col. Tod, (who lived at a little distance from the Tucte-Soleyman for almost twenty years, who speaks the language of the country with ease, and who actually made a survey of it,) that, in the language of the country generally, a temple is called Beeth-el, which means Edifice or House of the Sun. He says, that though the language of the country is not Sanscrit, yet entire sentences may sometimes be found which betray the Sanscrit ; and that it has many words which must have come from some language of central Asia.

10. But of all the temples of Solomon, I consider none of more importance than the Tact Solomon or Tecte Soleiman, which is found in Cashmere. " Mr. Forster was so much struck " with the general appearance, garb, and manners, of the Cashmerians, as to think he had suddenly " been transported among a nation of Jews."[4] The same idea was impressed upon the mind of Mons. Bernier, on his visiting that country. This Cashmerian temple of Solomon will be found of great consequence. Father Georgius, who was master of the Tibetian language, quotes the story of Anobret from Sanchoniathon, and shews that the *Jeud* of Sanchoniathon is the *Jid* of the Tibetians. *Jid a Tibetanis Butta tributum.* ירה *ieid Jehid* Isaaci epithetum est, Gen. xxii. 2 ; et *Jid* Tibetanorum *idem ac Jehid* Phœnicium et Egyptium.[5] Thus we have the mount or house or

---

[1] Gen. xxviii. 12.          [2] Drummond's Origines, Vol. IV. p. 99.          [3] Ib. p. 92.

[4] Vol. II. p. 21.          [5] Val. Col. Hib. Vol. V. p. 314.

habitation of Solomon or Solyma in India, or the country of Ioud, or of Daud-poutri, or of the sons of David; in Persia, the Madré Solyma, and the same also in Palestine and in Asia Minor; and all, in some way or other, connected with the tribe of Ioudi. Can any one believe all this to be the effect of accident? Solomon was a personification or incarnation of wisdom, and the Jews of Asia Minor were a tribe or colony from India, of black Buddhists, at or about the same time with the Ioudi to Syria, under the Brahmin.

## CHAPTER IV.

MOUNT OF SOLOMON, MOUNT OF THE CABALA.—MOUNT OLYMPUS.—AFGHANS, IOUDI.—TURKS.—AFGHANS SPEAK CHALDEE, PUSHTO, AND HEBREW.—ARABIA ON THE INDUS.—THE THOUSAND CITIES OF STRABO. PECULIARITIES IN EASTERN AND WESTERN SYRIA.

1. Mr. Bryant[1] observes, that Strabo speaks of a city of the Solymi, in Mesopotamia, called Cabalis, which he explains, *the city of the God Bal.* It may have been a city of Bal, but that was not the reason of its name. It had its name *Cbl* or *Gbl* from the secret doctrine of tradition. It had the same name as the Gabala of Western Syria. Lucian, in his treatise De Deâ Syriâ, says expressly, that "Gabala was Byblos, that is, *city of* THE BOOK or Bible, famous for the worship of Adonis." In 1 Kings v. 18, the word גבלים *Gblim* has been translated *stone squarers* or MASONS; but it means in- habitants of גבל *gbl*, or Mount Gibel or Gebel. From this comes the Gabala or Cabala, or chain of traditions. It was[2] the Mountain of Tradition. It was Gabal changed into Cabal, like גמל *gml* the name of the animal changed into that of the Camel, in the western countries. But Bal was Bala-Rama, an incarnation of Buddha. Suppose Abraham or Ioud came from thence, and it was either the Mesopotamia of Eastern or Western Syria, the Cabalis would be *the city of the traditionary doctrine.* This Cabalis also looks very like Cabul. I only throw out this for consideration, with the single observation, that it is very evident the Jews do not know the meaning of the word Cabala; and whether Christians be any wiser is very doubtful.

2. Mount Olympuses are found in many places. These, I apprehend, are the high places reprobated in scripture; but they were all known under different names, the same as the Merus of India and the Tecte 'Soleimans. This is pretty well proved by the fact, that the God Jupiter, who is called Jupiter Olympus by Jason of Cyrene and Ammianus, is, by Johannes Malalas, called Jupiter *Bottius.* Bottius is equivalent to Buddæus. [3]

Salivahana was King of Pratishtana, called also *Saileyadhara,* or simply Saileyam in a derivative form.[4] An ancient treatise of authority says, that Salivahana would appear at Saileya-d'hara, or *the city firmly seated on a rock,* which compound alludes to the city of Sion, *whose* foundations are upon the holy hills; "the city of our God, even upon his holy hill." *Saileyam* would be a very appropriate name, for it is also, in a derivative form, from *Saila,* and is really the same with *Saileya-dhara:* and the whole is not improbably borrowed from the Arabic *Dar-al-salem,* or *Dar-es-salem, the house of peace,* and the name of the celestial Jerusalem, in allusion to the Hebrew

---

[1] Anal. Vol. I. p. 106.    [2] Costa, p. 49.    [3] Nimrod, Vol. III. p. 391.
[4] Asiat. Res. Vol. X. p. 44.

name of the terrestrial one. The Sanscrit names of this city of the King of *Saileyam* or *Salem* imply its being a most holy place, and consecrated apart, and that it is firmly seated upon a stony hill. [1]

3. Not very far from the country where we find the Indian Tucte Soleyman, the country of Daud-poutri, the city and kingdom of Oude or Ioudi, &c., there is a mountainous district called Afghanistan, or country of the Afghauns, who consist of many millions of people. Their traditions tell them that they are descended from the Jews; that is, I should say, from the Ioudi of Oude; for they know nothing of their descent, except that they came into their present country from a tribe of Oudi or Jews. Their similarity to the Jews of Western Syria is so striking, that it could not escape the notice of inquiring orientalists. Our priests have had no small difficulty in accounting for them, as it was impossible to deny their Israelitish character; but at last they seem to have determined that they were descendants of the *ten tribes*, who were sent thither in the time of the Captivity, and who never, as the partisan Josephus says, though directly contrary to the fact, returned into Syria. On this I shall presently say a few words.

In the traditions of the Afghauns, noticed by Mr. Elphinston, [2] the name of Saul (from whom they say they are descended,) may be found, as also many circumstances similar to those in the Jewish history; but yet, in many respects, so different, that they can scarcely be believed to be a copy of them. Mr. Elphinston concludes by shewing, in opposition to Sir W. Jones, that they cannot be descendants from the Jews of Syria; that the story, though plausible, is clouded with many inconsistencies and contradictions. Sir W. Jones found that their language was *very like the Chaldaic.* If the Jews be descended from *them*, this is easily accounted for. The emigrants must have come away before the Sanscrit was brought to its present perfection, whether they came from Afghanistan or from Oude. I suspect that originally the Afghanistans were nothing but the mountain tribes of central Judia, having the same language and religion.

4. The Turks, who conquered the Arabians or Saracens in modern times, have, in a great measure, adopted their language. When these pagans arrived from Tartary they found the countries which they over-ran chiefly occupied by two races of men—the Christians and the Mohamedans. The mortifying fact has been concealed as much as possible, but the truth is, that the conquerors adopted the religion of the latter, not of the former. Persons who have read my *Apology for the Life of Mohamed* will easily believe me when I say this was no matter of surprise to me. But, independently of many reasons, which may be found in my treatise, why the Mohamedan, under the peculiar circumstances of the two, should gain the preference, there is yet another to be found in the language. It is reasonable to expect that (if I be right and that the Ioudi and Arabians were sectaries, from Afghanistan and Rajapoutana, which comprehend what was called the Indian Tartary or Indian Scythia) the languages of the Turks and Arabians should be nearly the same, and very different from the Greek, the prevailing language of the Christians. This *was* the fact, and it remains so to this day. The Arabic, the language of the Koran, is, in some measure, a learned language to the Turks, though they probably find no great difficulty in it, as " the *Turkish contains* " *ten Arabic or Persian words for one originally Scythian.*" [3] This agrees extremely well with what we might expect to find, if I be right in my theory. I beg leave to ask my reader, why this horde of Pagan barbarians, arriving from the very distant north-eastern countries, should bring with them a language containing *ten* out of *twelve* of its words Arabic, which Arabic was undoubtedly, in ancient times, identical with Hebrew? I am now speaking of the words, not of the forms of the letters.

---

[1] Asiat. Res. Vol. X. pp. 45, 100.      [2] Hist. of Cabul, p. 248.      [3] Rev. R. Chatfield's Hist. Hind. p. 366.

In reply to the enemies of etymology I beg leave to observe, that, in the case of the Jews, my reasoning depends very little upon it, but upon the identity of the names. If those who have written the names of places and persons, had all been guided by the sixteen-letter system, I believe in almost every case the Eastern and Western names would have been the same. Though this identity might happen in a solitary instance or two, by accident, it is quite incredible that it should have happened by accident in the great number of cases which I have pointed out.

5. It is a singular and remarkable fact, that all the authors who have written respecting the Afghans, or respecting the natives of the countries near to them to the south-eastward, have noticed, not only their personal likeness to the Jews, but also the close likeness which their language bears to the Chaldaic. Michaelis[1] says, " that the dialect of Jerusalem was East Aramean, or, as " we call it, Chaldee. The Syriac New Testament is written in the same language, but in a dif- " ferent dialect." Now this language is called the Peshito, but why it has that name I know not; for I do not believe that it means *literal*.[2] But we see that the Peshito and the Chaldaic are the same. The language of the Afghans is called Pukhto or Pushto; and it seems difficult to help believing that these are the same languages. This is the language of the sacred books of the Christians of Malabar. Now it cannot for a moment be supposed that the Afghans and Raja-poutani emigrated with their Jewish similitudes (that is the Rannæ of Arrian or Ptolemy) after the time of Christ. I think, then, that these two languages, bearing names so nearly identical, must have been originally the same, however much they may have changed in the thousands of years during which those who spoke them must have been separated. Of this Pushto I shall have more to say hereafter.

6. It is very evident from the accounts of both Dr. Dorn and Mr. Elphinston, that the whole of the fine country—Doab or Mesopotamia—from the Ganges to the Indus, and the whole valley of the latter, were once possessed by a race, the unconquered mountain tribes of which alone retain much of their ancient habits. In their intractable, unconquerable character, they very much assimilate to their brethren or children in Arabia. They were all called Afghans. The present kingdom of Cabul is stated by Mr. Elphinston to contain thirteen or fourteen millions of people, of whom more than four millions are yet genuine Afghans. The countries of the Afghans and of the Rajpouts are so intermingled, that it is impossible, with any precision, to separate them. But in addition to the above, it is a most important fact, that a large district on the Indus was called Arabia, and its inhabitants Arabi.

If the country be examined where we find these extraordinary proofs of a Jewish population, it will be found to be almost *covered* with the remains of what, in very remote times, were great and flourishing cities, and of an extent so large, that, to suppose a tribe or two of captives brought into it would change the manners and the pristine character of its inhabitants, is so extraordinary an absurdity, that no man who considers it for a moment can believe it. Besides, when these Jewish or Samaritan captives came to people this country, fifty times as large as their own, and the cities of which they must have taken possession, what became of the old inhabitants?

7. A very learned man, Mr. Carteret Web, has given it as his opinion, that the country about Bactria was, in primitive times, the seat of the arts, and that thence science was propagated to Persia, Assyria, India, and even to China. Strabo says, that Bactria, adjoining to Aria, abounded almost in every thing.[3] Justin[4] says, that it had a thousand cities under the jurisdiction of the Greeks, after they had destroyed the Persian empire. Strabo[5] also says, that Encratides, one of the successors of Theodotus, had a thousand cities under his jurisdiction.

---

[1] Marsh's Mic. Ch. vii. Sect. viii. p. 41.        [2] Ib. p. 5.        [3] Lib. ii. p. 73.
[4] Hist. Lib. xli.        [5] Lib. xv. p. 686.

Bactria[1] is the same as Bucharia, and Bochara, which Abulghazi Khan[2] says, means *country of learned men*, and was a place to which persons went from all quarters to acquire learning. It was a most beautiful country, abounding in the richest productions of the animal, vegetable, and mineral kingdoms. Perhaps, upon the whole earth, a situation more proper for the birthplace of man could not have been selected.

8. Certain circumstances of natural similarity between the places of the settlement of the Ioudi in India and in Western Syria may be observed, which raise a suspicion, that the ʟimilarity was the occasion of the selection of the place where the emigrating Ioudi settled, when they came to the West. In Afghanistan or the kingdom of Cabul (query, of the Cabala?) is a river which rises in what are called the mountains of Cabul, and runs into a dead-sea, called Loukh or Zarrah. One of its heads rises in a range of hills called the Ridge of Soleyman, not far from which is the Snow-capped mount, called Tukte Soleiman or Solomon's Throne; where the people of the country believe the Ark rested after the Deluge. Here are also mountains called Solymi and others called mountains of Ioudi. There is a place on the side of the above-named sea (which is salt, and has no outlet, and is therefore a *dead sea*), called Zoor or Zoar, the name of a city on the shore of the dead sea, or Lake Asphaltes in Western Syria. " Among the heads of tribes I found one having the " name of Lot."[3] Mr. Elphinston observes of a tribe of Afghan shepherds, that the girls had Jewish features.[4] He also observes of the Rajpouts, " They are stout and handsome, with hooked noses " and Jewish features." The mountains of Soliman run north and south, from the Indian Caucasus, to lat. 29, and are possessed by the Afghans. They are only known in *old books* (books of the Hindoos) by the name of Soliman.[5] These mountains are also called *Suffaid Coh*, which Mr. Hamilton explains *white mountains*, from their snowy tops. But I suspect the proper translation is Mount Σοφια-δι, Mounts of sacred Wisdom, of Solomon. I shall return to the word Suffaid by and by. The Arabians call the Afghans Solimanee, by which name they are not commonly known in their own country. This is a singular fact, but for which the circumstance of their being named thus only in their old books easily accounts. Several histories of the Afghans have been written by Persians and other Mohamedans, but all evidently intended to serve religious purposes; and, consequently, owing to their innate and palpable absurdity, not deserving a moment's consideration. I say this of the notice of them in the fourth Art. of Vol. II. of the Asiatic Researches. I am of opinion that the Afghans were driven out from the kingdom of Oude or Juda, (probably at the same time part of their sect came Westwards,) to the mountainous country where they are found, and from which their sectarian opponents could not expel them. Thus Jews or Ioudi are found in Afghanistan; but in Oude there are only towns formerly occupied by them.

---

[1] Bactr-ia or Boch-ara, the place of learned men, is the place of Bock or the Book.
[2] Hist. Turks and Tartars, Lond. p. 108.                    [3] Tod.                    [4] Introd. p. 49.
[5] Elphinston, Vol. II. p. 148.

## CHAPTER V.

RELIGION OF AFGHANS AND RAJPOOTS. — SAUL. — FERISHTA, ACCOUNT OF INDIAN JEWS. — ARABIA, ITS SITE AND MEANING.—TOMBS OF NOAH, SETH, AND JOB.—BENTLEY.—NAMES OF PLACES IN INDIA CONTINUED. — PLACES IN GREECE. — NAMES OF OLD TOWNS NOT NOTICED. — SABA, &c. — NILE AND EGYPT, NAMES OF.

1. In Lower India, in Greece, and in some other countries, the Arabian and Turkish conquerors seem to have settled themselves; as it were, in fact, to have deserted their old countries, and to have become residents of their new conquests. But it appears that this was not the case with the country of the Rajpoots or Afghans. If they were conquered, a momentary pillage took place, and a tribute was exacted, but in other respects the natives were left in possession of their countries; which, in fact, they soon liberated from their invaders. But from the Afghans or the kingdom of Cabul, conquerors of Asia have repeatedly issued, and probably will issue again.

The natives of Oude or Rajapoutana are Hindoos, of the religion of Cristna chiefly. But the Afghans are followers of Mohamed. They claim to be contemporaneous with him in their religion, and to have been his earliest allies. Most certainly the way in which the Arabian and Afghanistan peoples appear to assimilate together, has never been accounted for with the least probability, or the similarity of the latter to the Jews. My theory, I think, will develop the mystery. A communication between wandering tribes of two very distant countries is easier to be accounted for, than between two that are settled in walled cities, which was what became characteristic of the natives of Syria, but not of the greatest part of the inhabitants of Arabia. And I think there is nothing improbable in a tribe, (like a tribe of Gypsies,) as the Mahomedans say, having come from upper India or the Indian Tartary to Arabia, in the time of Mohamed, and having carried back his new doctrines to the Ioudi of Afghanistan, their ancestors.

I suppose that the tribe of Ioudi were driven out of Rajapoutana when the religion of Cristna or Kanyia prevailed. In consequence of this we find the religion of Kanyia in this country; but it was not driven out of Afghanistan or the mountains, but remained there in the situation of the 65 tribes of black Jews without Pentateuchs, found by Dr. Buchanan, until the arrival of the Saracens, when they instantly accepted their religion, for which, in fact, they would be in a very peculiar manner prepared, by having the patriarchs' statues which were of old in the temple at Mecca. The country of Cristna has statues and remains of the same patriarchs, but they have not the least relation now to its religion; they are quite obsolete—only antiquarian curiosities.

" The province of Ajimere in general has ever been the country of the Rajpoots; that is, the
" warrior tribe among the Hindoos, and which are noticed by Arrian and Diodorus : and Cheitore
" or Oudipour, (which I consider as synonymous,) is, I believe, reckoned the first among the Raj-
" poot states. The whole consists generally of high mountains divided by narrow valleys ; or of
" plains environed by mountains, accessible only by narrow passes and defiles : in effect, one of
" the strongest countries in the world, yet having a sufficient extent of arable land : of dimensions
" equal to the support of a numerous population, and blessed with a mild climate, being between
" the 24th and 28th degrees of latitude : in short, a country likely to remain for ever in the hands
" of its present possessors, and to prove the asylum of the Hindoo religion and customs. Not-
" withstanding the attacks which have been made on it by the Gaznavide, Pattan, and Mogul
" Emperors, it has never been more than nominally reduced. Some of their fortresses with which

" the country abounds were indeed taken, but the spirits of independent nations do not reside in " fortresses, nor are they to be conquered with them. Accordingly, every war made on these " people, even by Aurengzebe, ended in a compromise or defeat on the side of the assailants."[1] How absurd to suppose that the towns called after the names of the Israelites in these countries can have been built by Mohamedan conquerors!

The Mohamedans seldom changed the names of towns, but they sometimes did change them : for instance, they substituted the name of Islam-nuggur for Jugdes-pour, that is, for Jews-pour— or, the walled town or Islam-fort for Jews-town. But if this shews any thing, it is against their giving the Jewish names, such as Jerusalem, Solomon, David, &c., to the towns of Central India—not in favour of it. Though they have always tolerated the Jews as well as the Christians, yet they were as little likely to have adopted Jewish as Christian names for their towns. No doubt, in some instances, the Mohamedans gave new names to towns which they rebuilt, which often makes it difficult to ascertain the truth; but we see above, that they did not give Jewish names, but abolished them.

It is very evident that the old accounts which we have of the Afghans were all written by Mohamedans in or about the sixteenth century, who found the same likeness between the Afghans and the Jews which we find at this day—and not knowing how to account for it, they had recourse to what they supposed probable, and squared with their sectarian ideas of religion—sectarian as Jewish in opposition to the Samaritan. Mr. Elphinston seems most clearly to be mistaken when he says their towns have been named by the Mohamedans, and that the oldest of them have not those peculiar Jewish characteristics to which our attention has been drawn. Directly the contrary is the fact. It is evident that the places had the names before the time of Mohamed. For instance, the Tecte Soloman, one of the five sacred mounts of, and so called by, the Jain Buddhists. If the modern Mohamedans had given names to these great cities, we should have had Mecca or Medina, which we no where find.

2. It has been thought that the story of the descent of the Afghans from Saul is true ; among other reasons, because there was a tribe called Khyber in the East, and one, professing the Jewish religion, in Arabia, in the time of Mohamed. Now this has a tendency directly against the head of the tribe coming from Jerusalem ; for the head of the two tribes, if his name were Khyber, could not occupy both places—he could not emigrate a thousand miles to the East, and at the same time a thousand miles to the West. To make this probable, they should both have had some well-known Jewish name, and that have been the name of some large known Jewish division, tribe, or sect. If their tribes had been called Samaritan for instance, and their country Samaria, we might have believed that one went one way, the other another way. But there is another reason against their descent from Saul. If the Jewish history is to be received, the pious David murdered *all* Saul's children by the hands of the Gibeonites.[2] From Mr. Elphinston's account, *the traditions* of the Jews of Western Syria, and those of the Afghans of Cabul, appear, though now much varied, to have been derived from a common source.[3]

3. Ferishta accounts for the likeness between the Jews and Afghans by saying, that " The " Afghans were Copts ruled by Pharaoh, many of whom were converted to the laws and religion " of Moses ; but others who were stubborn in their worship to their Gods, fled towards Hindostan, " and took possession of the country adjoining the Koh-i-Sooliman."[4] The striking likeness

[1] Rennell, Mem. p. 153.

[2] One of the most atrocious of the actions of that most profligate man. In history there is not a more horrible character than the psalm-singing David, except, indeed, it be the church-establishing Constantine the First.

[3] Elphinston, Hist. Cabul, Vol. II.          [4] Tod's Hist. Raj. p. 241.

Ferishta could not help seeing ; his mode of accounting for it is absurd enough. He says, I have read that the Afghans are Copts of the race of the Pharaohs ; and that when the prophet Moses got the better of that Infidel, who was overwhelmed in the Red Sea, many of the Copts became converts to the Jewish faith, but others, stubborn and self-willed, refusing to embrace the true faith, leaving their country, came to India, and eventually settled in the Soolimany mountains, where they bore the name of Afghans.[1]   Here is a choice specimen of reasoning ; because they would not turn Jews in Arabia, these captive slaves, without leave, I suppose, left their masters, and turned Jews in India. All that this proves is, that the identity of the natives of the Solimany mountains in India with the Jews and Ethiopians in the West, was visible to Ferishta, which he could not account for. But it is very clear that if there had been any grounds for it, he would not have failed to have pleaded that the Jewish appearances were taken from the Mohamedans. Indeed, no one, I believe, would ever think of such a thing except our priests, and even they would not think of it except from their ignorance of the nature of the case, which, in fact, they have not the means of knowing. In deriving the Afghans from the time of Moses, Ferishta admits their Jewish existence long before the time of Mohamed. Though not much in favour of my sytem can be learnt from Ferishta, yet the little which he has, is decisively in favour of the Israelitish names being in these countries before the time of Mohamed. And it appears also that they were equally common with the Moguls, when they first marched to attack Delhi.

4. Arabia means Western Country. If this name were given to the people of the tribe of Arabi who were situated on the Indus, by the Ioudi of Oude, they would be very properly called Arabians or Western people, ערבים orbim ; Arabi-ia country of the Arabi : but they had no pretensions to have this name given to them by the Jews or Greeks. Part of the peninsula of Arabia is due South, and the remainder South-east of Western Judæa, and all of it South-east of Greece. They were a tribe from the Indus, and brought with them in the mouths of the tribe of Israelites coming from Oude, the name of Western people which they had been accustomed to call them.

5. Not far from Oude, on the banks of a river called Gagra, by Colonel Wilford, are shewn the tombs of Noah, Ayub (Job), and Shis or Sish (Seth). The stories told about them are so contradictory that their history is certainly unknown. But from two of them being noticed in the Ayeen-Akberry, they are evidently very old, and the stories about them false.[2]   The idea of the Mohamedans being the authors of these monuments is quite ridiculous, as they could never bear the idea of an image. Near them there was formerly a temple dedicated to Ganesa, and a well which, in the Puranas, is called GANA-PUT CUNDA. I suspect the name of the river Gagra was formerly Argha, and the well, I suspect, is similar to the fissure in the earth at Delphi. In this country Colonel Wilford observes, rich persons or persons of consequence are called Maiter, as Maiter Solomon. Here is the French Maître and our Master, as I have already remarked.

Along with the similarity of language, of laws, of names of places and men, almost all travellers have noticed the similarity of personal character in these people to that of the Jews. The Mohamedans could not cause this. The Adim of India, which, in Sanscreet, means *the first*, is plainly the Adam of the first book of Genesis. The Nuh or Noah is Menu, who, after the flood, repeopled the renovated world ; and the history of Noah and his family are precisely the same in the Sanscreet as in theHebrew Bible.[3]

---

[1] Briggs's Ferishta, Vol. I. p. 6. The etymology of the word Afghan sets me quite at defiance. These persons are said to have been among the first converts to Mohamedism. Before I conclude, I shall treat of a sect called Sophees, when I shall revert to this question (first considering many things of which I shall treat). Is it not possible that the word Afgh-an may be a corruption of the word Σοφ, Soph ?

[2] Asiat. Res. Vol. VI. p. 482.          [3] Maur. Ind. Ant. Vol. VI. p. 42.

6. I must stop my argument here to observe, that if Mr. Bentley be correct in his idea, that the Brahmins forged their books since the sixth century, in which the circumstances of similarity to the Christian and Jewish dispensations are to be found, it seems to me that they must also not only have given names to these ruined towns, ancient people, and mountains, &c., (many of the names of which are now obsolete, and, except in very old writings and among the remote agricultural population of peasants, superseded by more modern ones,) but they must have erected these statues of Noah, Job, and Seth, in this country, distant many hundred miles from the Christian Malabar settlement of Nestorians, to prevent the propagation of whose opinions it is alleged that the forgeries were executed: and in a country where there is not the least reason to believe that there ever was a Christian before the last century.

Beyond the limits of Judæa proper, beyond the Jordan, or the river of Adonis, as I shall presently prove its name to mean, was a country called the *Decapolis*, or country of *the ten cities*. This was in imitation of a similar arrangement and naming of the country beyond the kingdom of Oude or Juda proper, of India, called the Deccan, which is Deccan-ia, and consisted of the country to the South of the river Buddha, or נהר ner-Buddha, or Ner-mada, river of the great God. By the author of the circumnavigation of the Erythræan Sea it is called Dachanos.[1]

7. In lat. 28, 29, and long. 72, will be found an extensive country called Daoudpotra, which means Country of the sons of David. In it will be seen a town called Ahmed-poor—City of Ahmed, the name of Mohamed, and by which his followers say he was foretold. But this was an Arabian name of description before Mohamed was born, or he could not have been foretold by it. Besides, the fact of some person being foretold by it in the Prophet Haggai, shews it to be an ancient and sacred name.[2] This has a tendency to confirm the histories of the Brahmins, which say, that the Temple of Mecca was founded by a colony of Brahmins from India, and that it was a sacred place *before* the time of Mohamed, and that they were permitted to make pilgrimages to it for several centuries *after* his time.[3] Its great celebrity as a sacred place long before the time of the prophet cannot be doubted.

Not far from the Indus, in Rennell's map, will be found a place in lat. 36, long. 67, called Dura-Yoosoof; also in lat. 32, long. 71, a place on the Indus called Dera-Ismael-Khan. This is the native country of the Olive. Col. Wilford has observed that the name of Abdala is not derived from the Persian word Abdal, the servant of God; but from the name of an ancient tribe of Upper India,[4] before the time of Mohamed. This again tends to confirm the idea of the Arabians' coming from Upper India, and also shews that we must not hastily conclude that every proper name found in India, which is the same as we find among the modern Mohamedans, is taken from them.

Col. Wilford says, that there are followers of Brahma in Arabia, at this time, who are supposed to be descendants of Hindoos. The greatest part of the old names of places in Arabia are either Sanscrit or Hindi; and Pliny mentions two celebrated islands on the Southern coasts of Arabia, in which there were pillars with inscriptions in characters unknown (Col. Wilford says he supposes) to the Greek merchants who traded there, and that these were probably Sanscrit, as one of these two islands was called *Isura*, or Iswara's island, and the other Rinnea, from the Sanscrit Hriniya, or the island of the Merciful Goddess.

In the Old Testament we read anathemas in almost every page against high places. These were, I apprehend, imitative Merus. Nimrod has observed, that of this character were all the different

---

[1] Hamil. Gaz. Deccan.
[3] Asiat. Res. Vol. X. p. 100.

[2] Vide my Apology for the Life of Mohamed.
[4] Ibid. Vol. IX. p. 206.

Olympuses or sacred mounts of this and other names in Greece. There is none more striking than Pindus on its western side.

8. In or near the Bay of Ambrasius, on the Western coast of Epirus and Acarnania, in the district of Chaonia or Caonia, which word I apprehend is closely allied to the Apollo Cunnius, and to the Caonim or Cakes offered to the Queen of heaven, was situated the Temple of Dodona, which Ritter says was anciently Bodona. Here was a town called Omphalium, and another called Ambrasia, and one of Cyclopean construction called Argos or Amphilochis, or Amphipolis, that is, the city of Amphi or Omphi, or the Om; and one called Nico-polis, the city Nysi or Nysus, the same name as Bacchus, and of the mount called Sinai in Arabia, and of Jehovah Nisi, and of the famous Nysa of Alexandria in India; and one called Klissura, which seems a corruption of the Clyssobora or Klissobora or Cercesura of the Indian Doab, and one called Argyro-Kastro, that is the Castrum or fortress of Agra. This is also called Arsinoe and Acræ; and one called Phœnice.[1] There was also a town called *Amphia*, otherwise *Evora*, the name of the ancient capital of the Brigantes, and of York. There was a river called Aias, and one called Inachus, the son of Noah. There was a mount called Olympus, and the famous Pindus: and a Mons Tricala, and a Mount LINGON, i. e. Linga. It has been observed that all the ancient cities of the districts called Caonia are Cyclopean, and were inhabited by Ionians. Herodotus says, that Dodona was αρχαιοτατον των εν Ἑλλησι χρησηριων: and Julian says, that John the Baptist was χρησος Ιωαννες: and here, upon a beautiful lake, supposed to be the ancient Acherusia, stands the town of Joannina. The Temple of Dodona has been thought to have been at the town of PROTOPAPAS. What is Protopapas, but chief priest? Near this is a river called Kalama. May I suspect that this is another Kalane?[2] Near this sacred place is a Voni-tza, i. e. Ioni-tza, and the island of *Santa Maura*, or the Holy Meru, or at present *Leucadia*, or the island of the Holy Grove or Garden; in which is a town called Leucas or Neritus, and one where was a temple of Apollo called *Ell-omenus*. On the Eastern side of Pindus we have Arg-issa, Ambrasius, Olympus, Parnassus, Larissa, (the same as the district of Larice in Guzzerat,) formerly and now again Yeni-seri. Tricala, Delphi, Eleusis, Dium the name of the sacred isle near Bombay, Pelagonia Tripolis, that is the three cities of Pelagonia, a sacred river named Peneus, called by Homer Αργυροδινη, on which is a town called Ioannina,[3] and many other places whose names are evidently connected with this superstition. In Macedonia we have the sacred river Strymon, with an Amphipolis, and an Eidon or Eion, and near it a town called *Dium*, at the foot of Mount Athos, or the sacred Mount or Acro-Athos, covered with monasteries, of which I shall say more hereafter.

Between the 34th and 35th degree of North latitude, and the 72d and 73d degree of East longitude, in the Hon. Mr. Elphinston's map, is a place in the mountains of Cashmere called CHUMLA. It seems to have been a pass into, or a key as it were to, the fine countries of the South. It is in Bactria or the mountains of Balk or Bactriana, or Balkan.

There is a very lofty ridge of mountains which runs from the Black Sea to the Adriatic, and defends Greece, very much in the same way as the mountains of Bactriana defend India, which the Greeks called Hæmus. It has now recovered its ancient name of BALK-AN, and the name of its chief pass its ancient name of CHUMLA. On the South of Greece we have the Peninsula of Meru or Morea, with its Mount Olympus in its centre, its Chaonian district, its Argos, its Tripolitza or Tripoly, its Nissi, &c., &c., nearly repeated.

In Asia Minor we have the district of Troy, Ter-iia, and its capital Ilium, with the sacred Ida or

---

[1] Holland's Travels, Vol. II. p. 331.          [2] Ibid. Vol. I. p. 210, 8vo.          [3] D'Anville.

the Ida-vratta of India, and its Gargarus or stone circle, Gilgal, and Tripoli, of which we have before spoken: and in Lydia we shall find the Mount of Solym, having its towns with the same remarkable names. On the coast of Africa, at the Straits of Gibraltar, we shall again find a Tripoli, a Tangiers, &c., exact copies of the Tangore, the Trichinopoly of the Carnatic on the coast of Coromandel—and the name of Mauri-tania, is probably the country or *stan* or *tan* of Meru.

It must be unnecessary to point out the Iona of Syria with its Tripoli.· In short, in the Western as in the Eastern nations, the countries were divided into districts, each having its sacred mount, its trinity of towns, &c., &c. Sir William Drummond, by shewing that almost all the ancient Hebrew names of the Holy Land had astronomical meanings, has shewn that it was like all the others. It had its high place at Gerizim in Samaria, and after a schism took place in the time of the man we and his followers call Dud or David, another was set up at Jerusalem. When the Israelites took possession of Canaan they changed all the names of the towns, and gave them names having the same or similar *astrological* meanings with those which may be perceived in every part of their temple. To their enemies' towns they gave names of opprobrium.[1] I have before observed that in the same manner the Greeks, after the time of Alexander, almost always changed the names of the towns they conquered, giving them names after the places in their old countries, or after their great men or their superstitions. All this is practised by us continually in the Americas and Australia.[2]  The above were originally religious names.

9. It is no unusual thing, both in Greece and in Asia, to meet with the ruins of old towns, the names of which are not known or noticed by the ancient authors, and which shew in their construction two distinct and probably very remote periods from each other. An example of this is noticed by Dr. Holland.[3] He says, " The last town appears to have been probably Grecian, but it " has been built on the foundations of an older city which has been Cyclopean." The country where these ruins were found was Chaonia, and I suspect all the cities which were of date coeval with the word Chaonia would be Cyclopean. It is impossible to account for the Cyclopean remains which are found in Greece, without admitting the existence of a powerful people long previous to Grecian history, and even Grecian fable; and long prior to the received date of the Trojan war. These were the Ionians, the Hellenes, the Arg-ives, the Amazons, the Cyclopes : of the two last of whom I shall presently treat.

No doubt a careful examination of the names in the Arabian peninsula would afford clear traces of the Indian ancestry. There is the town of Ζευς Αγρευς, or of Agra, as the author of the Universal History·calls it;[4] or perhaps of the Arga, the Nysa, (in fact Mount Sinai,) the birth-place of Bacchus. And again, two cities in a southern direction called Arga and Badeo,[5] that is, Deo-bud. The river Yamana[6] and its city, the same as the river Yamuna in India, with the tribe of the Saraceni or Saracens, evidently the same as the Suraseni of the Jumna. The Mount *Merwa*, another Meru, Moriah, and Meroe ;[7] the names of Hagar and Ishmael,·and many others.

If I understand Gale rightly, he and Vossius suppose that Mount Sinai was called Nyssa or Nysa. Vide Exod. xvii. 15, Jehovah Nissi.[8]

---

[1] See Book V. Chap. XI. Sect. 2. .

[2] Augustine says, " An ignoras, Asclepi, quod Ægyptus imago sit cœli, aut quod est verius, translatio aut descensio " omnium quæ gubernantur atque exercentur in cœlo, ac si discendum est verius, terra nostra mundi totius est tem- " plum ?" De Civ. Dei., Lib. viii. Cap. xxiii.

[3] Vol. II. p. 321.                    [4] Vol. XVIII. pp. 346, 355.                       [5] Ib. p. 355.·

[6] Yamuna, the name of the sacred ·river Jumna, means Daughter of the Sun. Asiat. Res. Vol. I. p. 29 ; Sir W. Jones.

[7] Ib. p. 387.                      [8] Gale, Court Gent. Vol. I. p. 180·

10. Saba with the Hindoos meant the host of heaven: it is also a most important word in the Bible, where it had the same meaning. It is the Sabaoth of our liturgies, which does not mean Lord God of men-killers, as our narrow-minded priests suppose; but Lord God of the heavenly bodies—of the countless millions of suns and worlds in orderly and perpetual motion. Various places are called after this word. As we have found Solomon in India, it is not surprising that we should find the Saba or Sheba of his Queen there. In Rennell's map it is called Shibi. It is in the kingdom of Cabul, just where we might expect to find it. This place was also called Pramathasi and Parnasa, whence the Greeks got their Parnassus.[1] There is a place in D'Anville's ancient map called Sava or Saba on each side of the Straits of Babelmandel. I can scarcely doubt that a colony of the same people with the Ioudi settled on the East side of the Red Sea, built Mecca and Jidde, Juda, (as the Brahmins say,) and crossed the sea to Ethiopia or Abyssinia. Hence we find the tradition among the Ethiopians that they are descended from the Ioudi. This accounts for the Israelitish names in Arabia, as we shall hereafter see more fully. The statues of the patriarchs were in the temple at Mecca when Mohamed commenced his reform. The dove was also worshiped along with them.[2] Against this Mohamed, in a very particular manner, made war. With the assistance of Ali he himself destroyed the dove, the emblem of the female generative power. Mecca has been said to have been founded by Ishmael, the son of the Handmaid or concubine Agar or Hagar. Thus he was a bastard to the Jews—Agar meaning *Arga*, and Ishmael *Apostacy* to the religion of the Dove, which was found in the Temple of Mecca or Isis.

11. Near the Indus is a river called Nile, one of the branches of which is called Choaspes and Cophes; this river is said to pass through an opening in the mountains, called Gopha. I think it probable that the Nile of Egypt was called Guptus, from the river Cophes or Gopha: and the Gupts or Copts from the same: and that they crossed from the neighbourhood of Mecca or Sheba or Saba to E-gupt-ia. They were, if I be right, correctly Ethiopians and Egyptians. The word Gupta in Sanscrit means Saviour. Then the country might have the Greek name of αια Γυπτος, the country of Guptus or the Saviour.[3] Its own name was Sr, or Sur, or Sir, at least its river and a district in its upper part, were so called. But what can be the etymon of Gopha or Cophes? We know how the G and C were changed for one another. May *Coph* be Σοφ, the C being the Greek Σ? In the country where the river Cophes is found, I have before observed that there is a mount among the mountains of Solymi called Suffaid, (which is evidently a corruption of Σοφ, or צוף *zup*,) and that the Sofees of Persia are called Suffarees.

The explanation that the Guptus or Coptos was derived from the Cophrenes of India, is confirmed by the singular circumstance that the Nile, on flowing into the Delta of Egypt, is said to flow from the Cow's belly. The Ganges is said to flow from a sacred place, a gorge in the mountains called Cow's Mouth—and the word Cophrenes, Mr. Rennell says, means Cow.[4] One of the rivers of the Punjab was called Nilab—this is evidently Nile-aub, river Nile. This I take to have been one of the names of the Cophrenes. On the names of those rivers, Mr. Rennell says, " There is so much confusion in the Indian histories respecting the names of the branches of the " Indus, that I cannot refer the name *Nilab to any particular river*, unless it be another name for " the Indus or Sinde."[5] On the Indian Nile above named, is a city called *Ishmaelistan*. We have just now observed, that the city of Mecca is said by the Brahmins, on the authority of their old books, to have been built by a colony from India; and its inhabitants from the earliest era have had a tradition that it was built by *Ishmael*, the son of Agar. This town, in the Indian language, would be called Ishmaelistan.

[1] See Asiat. Res. VI. p. 496.                    [2] Ib. Vol. IV. p. 370.
[3] Ib. Vol. V. p. 286; Drummond, Orig. Vol. II. p. 55.    [4] Mem. Map Hind. pp. 115, 120.        [5] Ib. p 70.

## CHAPTER VI.

ARABIANS FROM INDIA.—LAWS AND CUSTOMS OF AFGHANS AND JEWS. — RENNELL ON THE RAJPOOTS. — PARADISE. ARARAT.—COLONEL TOD ON PLACES IN INDIA.—JEHOVAH, NAME OF, IN INDIA.—COLONEL TOD ON THE INDIAN MYTHOSES.—KÆMPFER ON SIAM.—HERODOTUS DID NOT KNOW OF THE EMPIRE OF SOLOMON.

1. My reader has probably not forgotten the proofs I have adduced, that the old Hebrew, the Samaritan, and the Arabian, are the same language. From various authors it is known that when Mohamed commenced the reform of his country's religion, the statues of the old Jewish patriarchs were in the temple at Mecca; and that the Arabians deemed themselves to have descended from Abraham, or THE Brahmin, by his son Ishmael. They never had, at any time that we know of, any connexion with the Syrian Jews, and yet, in their metropolitan temple, they had statues of the Jewish patriarchs, and their languages are radically the same, and the same, Sir William Jones says, as the Afghans'. How can this be accounted for, but by supposing them, as well as the Jews, to have migrated from Tukhte Solimaun, the Indian Arabia, or the countries on the North of India? This is proved by facts innumerable, and Sir W. Jones would have had no difficulty in seeing it, if he had not been previously tied down by a dogma, which, as he *declares*, nothing should induce him to disbelieve. In the account which Mr. Elphinston [1] has given of the division of the Afghans into tribes or clans, their similarity to the ancient tribes of the Jews and of Arabia, is very apparent. This system of tribes was formed long prior to the time of Mohamed. And it may here be observed, that the moment Mohamed or his califs conquered, the clans or tribes generally disappeared: and no instance can be produced of their founding a government by tribes where it had not been before. For some time after the conquests of Mohamed, the tribes of Arabia were all confounded beneath his victorious banner. This at once answers the idle pretences of the Afghans' founding their tribes, and naming their districts and towns, from modern Mohamedans. Their governors are called *Mullik*, evidently the Hebrew and Arabic word for King; and also *Mushir*, which is a corruption of the Arabic word Mosheer *a Counsellor*, [2] or perhaps *Judge*. The salutation of the Afghans is correctly Hebrew : Assalaum Alaikoom—Peace be with you. [3] A person accustomed to the Jewish salutation will at once perceive that in quick pronunciation the sounds of the two must be identical.

2. The Afghan mode of government by tribes, bears a striking resemblance to that of the Israelites under the Judges. They are the very pictures of what the Israelites must at that time have been. The natives have a code of criminal law different from the Mohamedan, *such as one would suppose to have prevailed before the institution of civil government.* [4] The laws and customs are in a wonderful manner similar to those of the Jews, and in cases which can be accounted for in no other way than an original identity; and this is the most important of all the circumstances relating to them, which I have pointed out.

Mr. Maurice and Mr. Halhed have observed a very close similarity between many of the institutes of Menu and the Mosaic code, and that not consisting merely in precepts of morality, but in examples of artificial refinement, which could not be discovered by the principles of common sense,

---

[1] Vol. I. p. 256.      [2] Ibid. Vol. I. p. 258.      [3] Ibid. Vol. II. p. 372.
[4] Ibid. Vol. I. p. 265.

like many moral laws—for instance the law against Murder. Of this, the order to a brother to take the widow to raise up seed to his brother, is one out of vast numbers of examples from which a judgment may be formed of the remainder, without occupying more of my reader's time,[1] The similarity is much too close to be the effect of accident, and much strengthens the position which I maintain, that the tribe of Abraham was an emigrant one from India. In the appendix to a history of India written by a man, I believe a missionary, of the name of Ward, who has much more piety than either sense or charity, may be seen *above twenty pages of close print* of similar Hebrew and Hindoo coincidences. He *calls* them illustrations of Scripture : and *proves* the former close connexion of the two, if he do not even prove their identity. The similarity was so striking that even a missionary was obliged to confess it, and explain it away as well as he was able.[2]

No doubt the allegation that the old Jewish names of ancient ruined towns and of districts have been given by Mohamedan conquerors, or the names of Jewish towns by Samaritan emigrants, or Jewish laws and customs *differing from those of the Koran*, the law of Mohamed, by followers of the prophet, will satisfy many persons who have too much faith to use their reason : but our oriental travellers, who have examined into the histories of these places, treat the idea of the building of the towns since the seventh century with perfect contempt.

3. Major Rennell will not be suspected of writing to uphold my theory, and he expressly says, that the Rajpoots of Agimere, or inhabitants of Rajpootana, who possess a country equal to half of France, preserved their independence from the conquests of Mahmood, and still preserve it to the present time.[3] He is confirmed by Col. Tod.[4] This at once puts an end to the plea that the ancient towns, whose Judaite names have been noticed by Sir W. Jones, were built by the Mohamedans. Many of them are in ruins, and were probably reduced to this state when Mahmood of Ghazni swept across the country like a tornado, not creating towns, but every where when in his power destroying them; the ruins of which, having Jewish names, remain. The Mohamedans never acquired and occupied the towns of Rajapootana, as they did many of those of Southern India. In consequence of Jewish customs being found in Tartary, (the very place where the Afghan tribes are found,) several old authors have supposed that the Jews had been carried thither at the Captivity. For instance, Philip Mornay *de verit. Relig. Christ.*, Cap. xxvi., Geneb. Chronic. *Religions du Monde*, Tome II. (vide Grot. *de Origin. Gent. Amer.*). Davity relates,[5] that there was a place called THABOR in Tartary, whence a king came into France in the reign of Francis the First. Joseph Ben Gorion states, that when Alexander the Great marched towards the North, he came to a kingdom called Arzeret, which was occupied by the captive Israelites, into which he was prevented entering by a miracle! This serves to shew that the tribe was the same then as now. Benjamin de Tudela says, that after travelling to the North-east twenty-one days, he came to the country of the *Rechabites*. Calmet[6] says from the old authors above, that the Tartars eat no swines' flesh, observe the Levitical law, which requires that the brother shall marry the brother's widow if he die without children, &c., &c.; all customs now found among the nations of Central Asia, as we have seen. Dr. Giles Fletcher was envoy from Queen Elizabeth to the

---

[1] Maurice, Ind. Ant. Vol. VII. p. 834.

[2] The opinion which I formerly expressed of the disposition of the missionaries to *suppress* evidence, is justified by a proof add'ed by Col. Van Kennedy (in the Transactions of the Bombay Society of Asiatic Literature) of their gross misrepresentations in their histories of India. This is confirmed, too, by Mr. Colebrook, (in the Second Vol. of Trans. Asiat. Soc p. 9, n.,) who shews that Mr. Ward's translation of the Vedanta-sava is so unfaithful that it cannot be called a version of the original text. In the third volume of the transactions of the Society of Bombay, is a very able defence of the Hindoos against Mill, Wilberforce, &c., in which their misrepresentations are exposed.

[3] Preface to Mem. of Map. p. xlvii.     [4] See Trans. Asiat. Soc. Vol. II. p. 270.

[5] Etats du Turc en Asie, pp. 124, 168.     [6] Dict. in voce TRA.

people of Great Bucharia. He considered them to be the remainder of the *ten tribes* of Samaria, from the Hebrew names of their cities; and from the circumstance which he discovered—that their language, called Zagathai, contained Hebrew words. Here it was where Benjamin of Tudela found what he called the Hebrew-speaking Jews.[1] The Turks came from this country; it is, therefore, not surprising that in their language ten words out of the twelve, should be Arabic, which is Hebrew. I believe that thousands of years before the time of Mohamed, several pastoral tribes, natives of Upper India, were expelled, as the Brahmin books inform us, in consequence of religious feuds, and came and settled in Asia Minor, Arabia, and Syria. Such tribes as the Afghans, as they are described by Mr. Elphinston, were peculiarly well qualified for this species of emigration.

My suspicion respecting the nature of the faith of the Mohamedans, and the effects of it, is strengthened by an observation of Col. Tod's, that when they destroyed the Idols of all the other religions, they left those of the Buddhists and Jains[2] untouched. This was because, in their secret religion, as I shall presently shew, they were followers of the doctrine of Wisdom or Buddha, and of the Linga. If this were not the case, I ask, and I have a right to insist upon an answer to my question, before my doctrine is clamoured down; Why did the Mohamedan, that is the *Arabian* or *Saracen* followers of the Prophet, leave the icons of Buddha, the lingas in India, and the obelisks in Egypt, uninjured? I say *Arabian* or *Saracen,* because I have a suspicion that the barbarous hordes of Turcomans, who destroyed the fine empires of the Califs, were not initiated into the secret doctrines of Mohamedism, which I shall by and by develop.

We have in India, as already shewn, a mount of Solomon, a country of Juda, and another of the sons of David, and a Mount Moriah or Meru, and places and persons without number called Isis or Jesse. It is certain from notice of the Solymi in ancient authors, that they cannot have had these names given by Mohamedan conquerors. Then what must be the consequence of all this, if there be any truth in the history, if there were really any persons about the time usually ascribed to Solomon and David who governed Judæa by these names, but that they must have been thus named after their ancestors in the East, in the same manner as names were selected in all countries from sacred or mythological persons?

4. If the reader look back to Book VII. Chapter VI. Section 2, he will find, in the extraordinary mysticism of the history of Paradise, and in the name of one of its rivers, a pretty strong proof that the whole came from Upper India. When all the other circumstances which I have described, and the situation and character of Josephus are considered, I cannot conceive a stronger circumstantial proof that the Mythos came from India, than that he should describe one of the rivers of Paradise to be *the Ganges.* The river Oxus or Wolga is called by Rennell *Djion.* Thus we have clearly two of the rivers, and probably the other two had the names which are given in Genesis, though now lost. The circumstance of one of them running round the whole world shews it to be the Meru of India.

In my CELTIC DRUIDS, Chap. II. Sect. II. and VI., I have given a great many reasons to prove, that the Jewish Ararat was situate to the East of the Caspian Sea. The Sibyl placed Ararat in Phrygia, near a city called Celænes: this is evidently the Calani. If the Sibylline oracles had been a *Christian* forgery, they would not have placed Ararat in Asia Minor. The more I consider these oracles, the more convinced I become that they are genuine. It may be observed again, in confirmation of the fact that Ararat was not situate between the Black and Caspian seas, that the olive does not grow in Armenia, therefore the dove could hardly have found an olive-branch to pluck, when it was sent out.[3] Sir Walter Raleigh, in his Universal History, has placed Ararat

---

[1] Buchanan, Asiat. Res.          [2] Trans. Asiat. Soc. Vol. II. p. 285.          [3] Tournefort's Voyage, Lett. VII.

among the mountains between Persia, India, and Tartary,[1] and in this he is supported by Dr. Shuckford,[2] and by an author little known, called Goropius Becanus.[3] It appears from the Universal History, that this author uses nearly the same arguments as those used by me, particularly that of the impossibility of the nations having travelled from the East, if Ararat were in the present Armenia. Ben Gorion extends the mountain of Ararat to the Caucasus. And the Samaritan version calls it Serendib, the name of Ceylon, the place in which the Hindoos put Paradise. All this proves the uncertainty of the situation of this mountain.[4] All these circumstances tend to prove, that there were sacred Merus, with their appurtenances, wherever there were settlements of the emigrators.

It is probable that a considerable part of the ancient religion consisted in the performing of pilgrimages to sacred places, as it does at this day in India and Italy; and as we know it did in Western Judæa—every Jew being obliged to go up to Jerusalem at least once a year: and in order to keep the people and their wealth at home, the priests of each tribe contrived to have its sacred places, its Mount Sion, &c., for the people to visit. We know that a contest took place between the Jews and the Samaritans for possession of the national high-place, its Meru or Sion, Olympus, Parnassus, Ida or Athos: for all these are of the kind of high-places referred to so often in the Bible in terms of reprobation. I do not, however, believe that they were objected to as being *high-places* so much as for their being Lupanars, or contaminated with the Hellenic rites, except those in Judæa: for the Jewish priests wished for only one in Judæa, and that, of course, at Jerusalem. Every where we see the same things repeated nearly by the same names: the Mount, the seven hills, the Tripoly, &c. This is the reason why we have so many Troys, so many Argoses, so many Larissas, so many Solymas, so many Olympuses.

5. Col. Tod says, " With Mat'hura as a centre, and a radius of eighty miles, describe a circle: " all within it is Vrij,[5] which was the seat of whatever was refined in Hinduism, and whose lan- " guage, the Vrij-basha, was the purest dialect of India. Vrij is tantamount to the land of the " Sura-seni, derived from Sur-sen, the ancestor of Crishna, whose capital, Surpuri (i. e. Sura or " Syra-pore,) is about fifty miles South of Mat'hura on the Yamuna (Jumna): the remains of this " city the author had the pleasure of discovering."[6] The Yamana was sometimes called *black*, sometimes *blue*.[7] The river was *Yamuna*; the country would be, as in Arabia, *Yemen*. A little before, the Colonel says, " The *Yadu* B'hatti or Shama B'hatti (the Ashani of Abul Fuzil) draw " their pedigree from Crishna or Yadu-nat'h as do the Iha-riéjas of Kutch." Here the Hebrew and Greek God Ii, or I, or Jah, or IE of Delphi, is apparent enough. Cristna or Yadu is the God Iαω—the *du-ya*. Wherever we find the words *div* or *dev* or *du* thus used, we almost always find it meant *holy* or *deity*.

---

[1] B. i. Ch. vii.

[2] Connect. Vol. I. pp. 98, 103 I have been turned into ridicule by a shallow reviewer of my *Celtic Druids* for having there maintained what I have since discovered was taught by Raleigh and Shuckford—that Ararat was East of the Caspian Sea. But it has not yet been the fortune of that work to be reviewed by any person who can ever have read it, except by one really learned writer in North America, in the Southern Review, No. V. Feb. 1829, printed at Charlestown.

[3] Ino-Scythia, p. 473.

[4] Who brought the Olive-tree to Athens? Minerva, or divine *wisdom*, or Buddha: and where could it come from but from Oude, or Tucte Soleyman, or the house of Solomon or of Wisdom, in India ITS NATIVE PLACE? Thus Minerva, or Pallas, brought it. Vide Univ. Hist. Vol. I. B. i. Ch. i. p. 240.

[5] Of this country Jyadeva was a poet : this is evidently a mystic name.

[6] Trans. Asiat. Soc. Vol. II. p. 286.         [7] Ibid. p. 287, n.

Col. Tod states, that the statue of Cristna is said to have been saved from Aurengzebe, and conveyed to Nat'hdwara in Mewar, but he gives no account of the figure of the God. He calls him Kaniya, that is, Kan-or Cun-iya ; and Nath-ji, and Jy-déva. Here, again, I think it is impossible to be blind to the *יי ii* and the *יה ie* of the Israelites—the *ii* of the Targums and of Iona [1]—the God *Iao*, that is, Jove—and the IE of Apollo on the temple of Delphi. Bishop Heber adduces an instance of one of the Mahratta princes, though of the Hindoo faith, being called Ali Jah—*Exalted of the Lord*.[2] Thus the above doctrine is confirmed by the Bishop.

In p. 714, Col. Tod says, " This hierarch bore the title of divinity, or Nat'hji : his prænomen of " Deo, or Deva, was almost a repetition of his title : and both together, Deonat'h, cannot be better " rendered than by ' Lord God.' " Deo-Nath-ji would be then, Lord God Jah or Self-existent Lord God. This Nath'ji was Cristna.[3] Nath is the Neith of Egypt, which meant Wisdom, and the Chinese name of God *Tien*, which read Hebraicè, is Neit.

" Radha was the name of the chief of the *Gopis* or Nymphs of Vrij, and the beloved of Kaniya."[4] Radha (Ray-di-ie) was the Latin radius, or *ray of light*. The district around Mathura, which was peculiarly sacred, called Vrij, might be the district or country of Ji. *יי רו ur-ii*, Ur of Ii, in the regimine of the Hebrews. And here we have the Ur of the Mesopotamia, whence the tribe of Ioudi came to the West—the Ur of the Chaldees. The district of Ur-ii is also called Hurriana.[5] The Ana is the same as *stan* and *ania* in Mauritania. I want nothing to make the demonstration complete, but the origin of the name of Chaldees, which we shall find by and by.

Col. Tod[6] remarks, the annals of the *Yadus* of *Jesulmer* state, that the Yadus and Yutis,[7] whose resemblance, he says, is more than nominal, soon after the war of the *Mahabharat*,[8] held dominion from Guzni to Samarkand ; that the race of *Ioude* was still existing near the Indus in the emperor Baber's time, who describes them as occupying the mountains in the first Do-ab, the very place the annals of the *Yadus* state them to have occupied twelve centuries before Christ, and thence called *Iadu* or *Yadu-ca-dung*, the hills of *Iadu* or *Yadu*. The circumstance of *Yadu* being said to be the father of *Cristna*,[c] seems to imply that the tribe of *Yadu* or *Ioudi* arose before Cristna, or before the Sun entered Aries. This exactly agrees with the way I have accounted for the Afghans being Mohamedans, in Chapter V.

*Aod* in Irish was a name of the Sun, and also of the Goddess of Fire. *Aodh baudea teine,*[10] Aodh, the Goddess of Fire, Vesta. Gen. Vallancey says, this *Aod* is probably the same as *Yadu*.[11] I take this *Aod* and Yadu to relate to the kingdom of Oude.

6. If I be right in my idea that the religion of the Jews came from India, it is natural to expect that we should find their famous God JEHOVAH among the Hindoos, and this is, indeed, the fact. But my reader must divest his mind of the barbarous corruption of the word *Jehovah*, and restore the God to his true name,[12] יהוה *Ieue* יה *Ie,* as we call it *Jah*, and as it is called in Sanscrit, that is, in meaning, *the self-existent*, but often denominated *the God of victory*. Among the Hindoo Gods there is scarcely one who has not a name which contains, in some way or other, the elements of

---

[1] Tod, Hist. Raj. pp. 523, 524.     [4] Vol. II. p. 562.     [3] Tod, p. 523.     [4] Tod, Hist. Raj. p. 530.

[5] Malcolm.     [6] Trans. Asiat. Soc. Vol. II. p. 295.     [7] That is, the Getæ, I suppose.

[8] i. e. the battles of Cristna.     [9] Asiat. Res. Vol. III.     [10] Cormac.

[11] Ouseley's Oriental Collections, Vol. III. p. 26.

[12] The arguments which I use, founded on the true name of the Jewish God *Ieue* or *Ie*, will, of course, have no weight with such of my learned readers as have been instructed by modern Jews to neglect the Synagogue copies and to attend to the modern Mazoretic corruptions, and who continue talking about Elohim and Jehovah. As these gentlemen will not be instructed, they must remain in ignorance. I am certain that I have cast a new light upon ancient history, and if the *old* are too prejudiced to learn, the *young* are not.

the *Ie*, or God of the Jews. Col Tod,[1] in his treatise on the religion of Mewar, the very country whence the tribe of Ioudi must have come, has given a list of the eight principal Gods of the country. He gives the names and abodes of seven of them ; but the *eighth*, whose abode he does not give, except as God of the mount,[2] he says, is above all—and he calls him Nat'h-Ji, Nat'h meaning God. When the great change is considered which has taken place in the old language by the perfecting of the Sanscrit, and which must have taken place, as I shall shew, since the emigration of the tribe, and also the change in both languages which time must have produced, it will not be a matter of surprise that the perfected language should be very different from that of the emigrant tribe. But, notwithstanding, if my reader can bring himself to cast off his prejudices in favour of the Jewish corruption of the word Jehovah, and write it as it ought to be, *Ie*, or *Ii*, or *I*,[3] he will see it in the Sanscrit names, in almost every page of the Asiatic Researches. The most remarkable of his names, which perhaps may be the best understood by an unlearned reader, is that of יה *Ie*. In the Jewish notation, which, like the Greek, is done by the letters of the alphabet, the fifth letter ה E and the tenth letter י I, (the former of which stands for five, and the latter for ten,) are never used to denote fifteen ; because they are the name of God ; and the Jews are forbidden to take the name of the God, I*E*, in vain or irreverently, which it would be to use it *thus*, and therefore for *ten* and *five* they substitute *nine* and *six*.

This name IE, corrupted into *Ia, Iy, Iu, Yu, Ya;* occurs unceasingly in the Hindoo names of Gods, and often in their sacred ceremonies, where they sing or chaunt IEYE. How can any thing be more convincing than the exclamation of this word IEYE, the meaning of which they may probably have lost?

7. I suppose Col. Tod to be a believer in the actual human existence of Cristna : but I think the following passage will satisfy my reader who and what he was, as well as strongly support my theory respecting Buddha. " Crishna, Heri,[4] Vishnu, or more familiarly Kaniya,[5] was of the " celebrated tribe of Yadu, or Jadu, the founder of the fifty-six tribes who obtained the sovereignty " of India, was descended from Yayat,[6] the third son of a primeval man called Swayambhuma " Manu[7] or MANU Lord of the earth, whose daughter Ella *(Terra)* was espoused by Buddha " *(Mercury)*, son of Chandra (the Moon), whence the Yadus are called *Chandravansi* or children " of the moon. Buddha was therefore worshiped as the great ancestor *(Pitriswara* or *father God)* " of the lunar race ; and, previous to the Apotheosis of Crishna, was the common object of devo- " tion with all the Yadu tribe. The principal shrine of Buddha was at Dwarica, where he yet " receives adoration as Buddha *Trivicrama* (triple energy—the Hermes Triplex of the Egyptians)."[8] The Indian Cristna, we find, is called *Kaniya*. He is the Apollo of India. This word is *Kan-iya*, and is the same as the word *Cunnius*, his name at Athens, and the IE the word in front of his temple at Delphi. Diodorus says, Apollo's name was *Kan.*[9] From this has come the word *Khans* of Tartary. The meaning of Kan-iya will be *self-existent generating power*. Cristna is commonly called Sham-nat'h. This is שם *sm* and the word *Nath* which means God. שם *sm* is the singular of שמין *smin*, planets, or disposers. From this may have come Samanaut or Sumnaut. Col. Tod says, Cristna worshiped Buddha before his deification. This explains itself. Afterward the Colonel adds, in the cave of Gaya is the inscription[10] " Heri, who is Buddha." Heri is Cristna.

---

[1] Trans. of Asiat. Soc. Vol. II. p. 316.          [2] Mount Meru.

[3] *Ii*, the same as the Hindoo Nat'h-Ji ; it is always so written in the Jerusalem Targums.

[4] The Saviour.          [5] Kaniya the Colonel has before stated to be the same as the Greek Apollo.

[6] Query, *Japhet?*          [7] Also called *Vaiva-swata Manu*, " *The* man son of the sun."

[8] Trans. Asiat. Soc. Vol. II. p. 299.          [9] Ibid. p. 312.          [10] Ibid. p. 304.

We have just observed that Cristna and Buddha were the same, but that Buddha was called *Trivicrama* or *Triple Energy*. This was the Hermes Trismegistus or Triptolemos—the Aleim or Trinity of the Jews, called יה *IE*, or Jah. " Cristna or Kaniya lived at the conclusion of the " *brazen age*, which is calculated to have been about 1100 or 1200 years before Christ." Here I think proof enough is admitted to shew that this Apollo or Kaniya was no other than the son or successor of Buddha in one of his renewed incarnations, which of course could be no other than the Sun. It is a common practice with the natives of India, on the naming of their children, to give them the epithets of one of their minor deities, as Europeans call their children after their saints or divi (divus Augustus, divus Paulus, divus Johannes). Here we have Christian names and names of honour. From this has arisen great confusion in their histories. To remedy this, to keep up their pedigrees, and to gratify their vanity, the princes, like the old kings of Ireland, have regular Genealogists, called by the same name, Bards or Bairds, who are domestics in their families, and whose duty it is to record every thing honourable to their patrons. Of course we need not be surprised that the apparent history is clear enough, but the real, when it gets into remote periods, fabulous enough. Every prince descends from some great God, that is, from the Sun ; and all that can be made out for a certainty is, that the Sun was the first God, and the parent of the family. From this it is clear that we are not to consider every history to be false, because the actors are called by the names of God, or to consider that the first Gods were men. The first God or King is always the sun. The only difficulty is to find out where the real history ends, and the fabulous begins. This must be judged of by circumstances. The genealogies cannot be depended on. To decide with *certainty* is very difficult, because these idle genealogists, like the genealogists or bards of Ireland and Wales, have nothing to do but to forge writings and circumstances, to make the family of their patron more honourable than that of his neighbours. I suppose that the fifty-six tribes spoken of above, were the settlements or places where the religion of Kaniya had prevailed in different parts of India—in the kingdom of Panionium, or of Pandæa the daughter of Cristna, according to another history or mythos.

8. A singular and artless observation is made by Mr. Kæmpfer, in his History of Japan,[1] in his account of JUDIA, the capital of Siam : " The Gates and other avenues of the palace are crowded " with black, checquered figures, painted in the manner as they do with the images at the holy " sepulchre at Jerusalem." This observation respecting these people of JUDIA is very striking. The name of the God worshiped here is *Prah Pudi Dsiau*. But divide the last word thus, Ds-iau, and what have we ? Deus-Iau. He is also called Siaka or Saka, the Irish Sacya. The God is an exact Buddha sitting, 120 feet high. The country swarms with monks. The Idol is also called *Amida* (Om-di), a name of Buddha. He is seen standing upright on the flower Tarate, or Faba-Egyptiaca, or *Nymphæa Magna incarnata*. He is believed to be the intercessor of departed souls. The High-priest lives in JUDIA, and his authority is such, that the king is obliged to bow to him. This shews the original superiority of the priests to the kings. *Pra* in the Baly or Bali, the sacred language of *Judia* or Odiaa, the capital of the kingdom of *Sion*, signifies the Sun and *the great living God :*[2] that is, the creator or former, giver of forms. From this has come Pra ja-pati, or the *Lord of mankind*, which means *father, ja, creator*.[3] This *Pra* is evidently the Hebrew word ברא *bra*, to create or form, of the first verse of Genesis. It is singular that Parkhurst gives us the verb ברא *bra* to create, but no noun for Creator. But though it may be lost now, it cannot be doubted that the verb must have had its correspondent noun. I have before observed that this word PR or BR, is said, by Whiter,[4] always to mean Creator.

---

' Vol. I. p. 29.     ' La Loubère, pp. 6, 7.     ³ Asiat. Res. Vol. VIII. p. 255.     ⁴ Etymol. Univ.

On the south point of Siam the Malays reside. These are the people whose language, a Hebrew friend, Mr. Salome, of Bath, understood, when he went into the depôt of the India company near Wapping, in London. But if the Mohamedans carried to India their religious names, how are we to account for the other names connected with the Hindoo and Greek superstitions being found in Greece ; such as Caon or Cawnpore, Agra or Argos ? How are we to account for two Syrias and two Dagons, two Matureas, two Sions, &c., &c.? These the Mohamedans did not take. How are we to account for the Sanscrit at Eleusis and in Italy; and how for the Linga and Ioni at Pæstum ? [1] And, as I shall shew my reader, in a future book, for the Yoni and Linga at Aberdeen in Scotland ?

No doubt it is difficult to ascertain clearly what names of towns in the countries North-west of India are ancient and what modern. This is caused by the singular circumstance of the tribes which anciently left that country to colonise the West, having returned, in modern times, to their old countries as Mohamedan conquerors and propagators of their new doctrines. The difficulty is also increased by the constant endeavours of the priests of the Jews, the Christians, and the Mohamedans, to disguise the fact, which they feel they cannot account for consistently with their received notions and their erroneous mode of explaining the sacred books. But if the Jewish names of places and persons were in these countries before the time of the arrival of the Mohamedans, there is an end of the question. The names of places enow we have seen. When Mahmud, of Gazna, the first Mohamedan conqueror, attacked Lahore, he found it defended by a native Hindoo prince called Daood or David.[2] This single fact is enough to settle the question of the places not being named by Mohamedans.

As I have before observed, when my learned friend Col. Tod visited Naples and Pæstum he saw several small figures of Ceres, which had in the hand something which the antiquarians of that capital did not understand. On looking at it the Colonel discovered, in a moment, that it was the Linga and Ioni of India. He recognized also at Pompeii, on the temple of Isis, the same effigy. I suspect the ellipses and circles of the Druids, with the stone pillar in the middle, are emblems of the same thing. [3]

I beg my reader to look at the ruins of the ancient cities of India, Agra, Delhi, Oude, Mundore, &c., which have many of them been much larger than London, the last, for instance, 37 miles in circumference, built in the oldest style of architecture in the world, the Cyclopean, and I think he must at once see the absurdity of the little Jewish mountain tribe being the founders of such a mass of cities. We must also consider that we have almost all the places of India in Western Syria. Let us also consider how we have nests of Asiatic places in Greece, in several districts the Mounts, the Argoses, Tripolies, &c., and I think no one can help seeing that these circumstances are to be accounted for in no other way than by the supposition that there was in very ancient times one universal superstition, which was carried all over the world by emigrating tribes, and that they were originally from Upper India.

9. No one can deny that it is a very extraordinary, and it is to me an unaccountable, circumstance, that Herodotus, writing the History of Babylon, of Egypt, and of Syria, and travelling across these countries, should have known nothing of the magnificent empire of King Solomon, or of the emigration of two millions of Jews from Egypt, and the destruction of the hosts of Pharaoh. How was this ignorance possible, if there be a word of truth in the Jewish histories ? Did Pythagoras or Plato never hear of the glories of Solomon ? Would not their followers have told Herodotus if they had known of them ? The plagues of Egypt at once decide the character of

---

[1] See Trans. Asiat. Soc. Vol. II. p. 285.       [2] Maur. Mod. Hist. Hind. Vol. I. p. 248.

[3] See Trans. Asiat. Soc. Vol. II. p. 302.

the miscalled history of the *going out* of Moses. They do not prove it false, any more than the mythic history of Rome proves that there was no city of the seven hills; but they reduce it to the standard of credibility, by shewing that the history is a parable or mythos, the key being known only by the initiated. The Mythos, in every place, had its αποικος : in Babylon, in Thebes, in the case of Moses, in Homer, in Rome, &c. On this Nimrod may be consulted. He has shewn this, and treated it most learnedly, and at great length. There might be, as I have no doubt that there was, a *going out* of the tribe under Moses : it was like the migration of all other nomade tribes, and might indeed be rather a large tribe. But two millions of people is a story like the other Jewish stories of their millions of soldiers, chariots, horses, talents of gold for their temple, &c., &c. Probably, in passing the end of the Red Sea, Pharaoh's army was destroyed by a tempest, of which Moses took advantage.

It has the same effect upon the glories and magnificence of the empire of Solomon. He was, probably, the prosperous king of a petty tribe, and had a mystic name given to him, though he oppressed his people, an ignorant, priest-ridden race, to erect a very fine palace and temple; and it is no way wonderful that when the energies of a whole tribe, though not a very great one, are directed for a great number of years to the raising and adorning of one building, that it should be very magnificent. The very same effect followed the same cause in the states of central India, whence the Jews had emigrated, as the prints of several of the temples in Col. Tod's history clearly prove. If any thing can be deduced from the style of architecture, the Indian temples are of the same date with the temples at Pæstum : and as the most ancient and most important of the Hindoo emblems were found there by Col. Tod, it is probable that they were erected by the same race.

The Jain temples, in Col. Tod's book, are the very pictures of the ancient temples at Pæstum, the date of which was a subject of curiosity in the time of Augustus. I shall return to this again.

## CHAPTER VII.

**JEWS HATE THE FEMALE PRINCIPLE.—JEWS AND EGYPTIANS, BLACKNESS OF.—OBSERVATIONS ON THE JEWS.—SAMARITANS.—GENERAL CONCLUSIONS.**

1. The excessive hatred of the Jews to the adoration of the Queen of Heaven, Milcomb and Asteroth of the Sidonians, is visible every where in the Bible, as well as to that of the Bull Apis, under the names of Baal, Moloch, Thamas, &c., &c. Though the hypothesis that the Jews were a branch of a sect which arose in the disputes of India about the Linga and Ioni may be new, when every thing is considered, I trust it will not be thought improbable. It seems rationally to account for circumstances which, as far as I am aware, have not been explained before, and to remove many difficulties. And I think when it is well understood and duly considered, it will be found to be in favour of the Christian and Jewish religions, and not against them.

3 K

2. " Major Orme[1] reckons .eighty-four castes in India, each of which has a physiognomy " peculiar to itself. The more civilized, tribes," he says, " are more comely in their appearance. " The noble order of the Brahmins are the fairest and the most comely. The mountaineers most " resemble Negroes in their countenances and their hair. The natives of the hilly districts of " Bengal and Bahar can hardly be distinguished by their features from the modern Ethiopians."[2] All this accords very well with my theory respecting the black Buddha. Probably at the time the black Jews divided from their countrymen, they were black—and, from being always few in number and low in rank, and breeding entirely in their own caste, they have kept their ancient sable complexion. It has been observed, that the figures in all the old caves of India have the appearance of Negroes.[3] This tends to prove not only the extreme antiquity of the caves, but also the original Negro character of the natives.

Dr. Pritchard has most clearly proved, as I have stated in Book V. Chap. XIII. Sect. 2, that the ancient Egyptians were Negroes. He observes that " the Greek writers always mention the " Egyptians as being *black* in their complexions. In the Supplices of Æschylus, when the " Egyptian ship is described as approaching the land, and seen from an eminence on the shore, it " is said,

" Πρεπουσι δ' ανδρες νηιοι μελαγχιμοις
" Γυιοισι λευκον εκ πεπλωτων ιδειν—

" The sailors too I marked,
" Conspicuous in white robes their sable limbs :

" And again,

" Επλευσαν ωδ' επιτυχει κοτῳ
" Πολει μελαγχιμῳ συν ϛρατῳ.

" Herodotus, who was well acquainted with the Egyptians, mentions the blackness of their com-" plexions more-than once. After relating the fable of the foundation of the Dodonean oracle by a " black dove which had fled from Thebes in Egypt, and uttered her prophecies from the beach-tree " at Dodona, he adds his conjecture of the true meaning of the story. He supposes the oracle to " have been instituted by a female captive from the Thebaid, who was enigmatically described as a " bird, and subjoins[4] that, by representing the bird as *black*, they marked that the woman was an " Egyptian."[5]

3. I now beg my reader to, reflect upon what was said in Book IV. Chap. I. respecting Cristna and his adventures ; to cast his eye upon the plates of Cristna treading on the head of the serpent described in Genesis, and of the serpent in return biting his foot—and, as Dr. Clarke has shewn, biting it in a way which proves that the oriental author did not copy from Genesis, though the author of Genesis may have copied from him ; and then, I think, he will be obliged to admit that there must have been a mythos common to Eastern and Western Asia. Let him then consider the history of and the facts relating to circumcision, and the other particulars dilated upon by me, and he can hardly scruple to allow that the Western mythos was copied or derived from that of the East.

For the truth of the theory which I have advanced—that the Jews *did* originally come from India, in addition to the circumstantial evidence, I have as good proof as it is possible for written

---

[1] Indostan, Introd.    [2] Pritchard, Phys. Hist. p. 392.

[3] Hunter, in Archæologia, Vol. VII. ; Dr. F. Buchanan, Asiat. Res. Vol. VI.

[4] Herod. Lib. ii.    [5] Pritchard, Phys. Hist. p. 377.

records to afford. This I say roundly of the testimony of Magasthenes. He cannot be supposed to have had any prejudice against the Jews : his observation respecting their being an Indian tribe seems to have fallen from him merely as illustrative of the character of the Hindoos. The *Hindoos* were the object of the book, not the *Jews*. He had no interested motive to induce him to misre-present or to deceive ; and the priests cannot here set up even their hackneyed argument of hatred to the Jews to account for or obviate any thing which is unfavourable to them, as his assertion is merely confirmatory of Moses's narrative—that they came from the East, and is in praise of them or their system. The passage, which I have noticed before, where he observes that the Indians and the Jews were the only people who had a true idea of chronology and the nature of the crea-tion of the world, is very striking, when coupled with what I have just laid before the reader. It all tends strongly to prove the close connexion between the Indians and the Jews.

I now beg my reader to make a visit to Duke's Place, or to any settlement of Jews, and to look them in the face and deny if he can, that they have *oriental black* written on them in the clearest characters. Let him look at the long black hair and fine aquiline nose of the handsome Cristna, and then let him deny, if he can, his likeness to the tribe of Abraham. Let him look at the beau-tiful black-eyed, black-haired, half-bleached Jewish girls, and deny it, if he can. If I be right in my theory, the Jews were one of the latest emigrations from India to the West : we have no symptoms of any after them, except one of which I shall immediately treat: and this accounts for their being not so much *whitened* as the remainder of the Western nations. All this exactly agrees with the theory which I have advanced respecting the change in the features of Buddha in Book V. Ch. XIII. Sect. 2. Of course, as I suppose the Ioudi did not depart from India till about the time of the sun's entrance into Aries, or the time of Cristna, they would have the advantage of the improve-ment to his time, and though *black* would not have *curly* hair or *flat* faces.

Another reason for the continuance of the dark complexion of the Jews, and their marked national character, is to be found in their ancient law, which forbade them from marrying out of their own tribe. This law was long anterior to Moses, and was only re-enacted by him. We have, perhaps, the first appearance of it, in the esoteric history of Jacob and Esau. The idle story of *the mess of pottage* is very good as a subject for the priests to make sermons upon ; but probably the real rea-son for Jacob's conduct to Esau, may be found in the fact that Esau had forfeited his birthright by marrying out of the tribe, and *he* was excluded that his children might not inherit.[1] The same thing happened to Moses, who married an Ethiopian woman, as I have before pointed out, and therefore his children did not inherit ; but the supreme power and the priesthood descended to the sons of Aaron, his nephews. In the case of Esau and Jacob the truth is disguised under the para-ble or ænigma of a mess of pottage. It is surprising that persons do not see that almost every part of Genesis is ænigmatical or a parable. The system of concealment and of teaching by para-ble is the most marked characteristic of the religion. I suspect that there is not a sentence in Genesis which is not consistent with good sense, if its true meaning could be discovered. I feel little doubt that such passages as that of God wounding Jacob in the thigh, and his failing in his endeavours to kill Moses at an inn, are wholly misunderstood.

The Jews, as a race, are very handsome ; they take after their ancestor Cristna. Nothing is more easy than to distinguish a thorough-bred Jew or Jewess. And it is very greatly to the honour of the Jewish matrons that the family likeness or national peculiarity should have con-tinued so long. It gives me great pleasure to see this hitherto oppressed and insulted race re-

---

[1] Vide Gen. xxvi. 34, 35.

3 K 2

gaining their station in society. I hope that all distinction in civil rights will very speedily disappear.

I shall here add no more on this theory respecting Abraham and the Jews. Its probability must be left to the reader. If he do not approve it, let him account for the fact of Abraham and his wife, Sarah, being found in India; but he must not do this by telling me that the Brahmins copied from the Pentateuch, because this is an assertion which he knows he does not himself believe. Let him also account for the two Matureas, and for the *sixty-five* tribes of *Black* Jews intermixed with the tribes of *White* Jews in India, and the similarity in the names of places and identity of manners and laws : and let him shew some good reason why Megasthenes should have told a falsity. Let him also account, in a better manner, for the peculiarities which I have pointed out above, in the character and history of the Jews. But, above all, let him rebut the decisive argument which I have drawn from the circumcision of Abraham and his tribe, that the Judi of the West must have come from the East, not the Judi of the East from the West.

4. In consequence of the allegation that the Afghans were derived from the Samaritans, it becomes necessary to say a few words on the Jewish account of them; but I will compress them into as small a space as possible. The only account our priests have permitted us to have, respecting the division of the kingdom of Israel and Juda, comes from the sect of the latter. But enough transpires from the Jewish books to see that the sacred place appointed by the *Pentateuch* for the grand place of worship of the nation was Gerizim in Samaria, not Jerusalem ; and that, in order to conceal the fact, the Jews have been obliged to corrupt the text, which they have done most awkwardly—substituting *Ebal* for Gerizim, and *Gerizim* for Ebal. This corruption has been admitted by some of the first divines of the Protestant Church. I believe, myself, that the great cause of the division of the kingdom, was the removal of the sacred place from Samaria to Jerusalem.

The Samaritans were carried into captivity before the Jews, and returned a little before them. A violent contention, it appears from the Jewish books, took place between the people possessing Samaria at the time of the return of the Jews, and the latter—each wishing to have only one national temple, and that temple at its own capital. Now the Jews say, that the Samaritans never returned—but that in lieu of them, Cuthite idolaters were sent by the King of Babylon, —these idolaters, the reader will observe, being the people who were so eager to have the temple of this foreign religion in their own capital, and to prevent the rebuilding of it at Jerusalem, for the promotion of a religion *not* THEIRS *in another country !* To account for these evident absurdities, the Jews tell a story, in good keeping with many of their other stories —that in consequence of the Cuthite idolaters having been plagued with LIONS sent by God, the King of Babylon forwarded them a priest to teach them the old law of the land, and that thus they became possessors of the law of Moses. Josephus being ashamed of this story of Lions, says, it was a *plague* which God sent. But it is easy to see, as the Samaritans, on the contrary, say, that the whole story of Cuthites and Lions is an interested lie of their enemies', and that they were carried into captivity by the Assyrians, and were returned from their captivity by the Persian Monarchs precisely the same, and for the same reasons, that the Jews were. The reader will not forget that we might have had the whole Samaritan history and books, if the archpriest Usher had thought proper. For, if he did not procure the whole and suppress them, (many of which I believe he did,) he had the power to do both. This is clearly proved. The whole of what I have here said, may be found in the Prologomena of Walton, in Prideaux, and in the works of Bishop Marsh. The learned have bestowed immense labour to discover the place where the *ten tribes* went to, after their country was conquered. They have sought them in every part of the world in vain. . If they had consulted any persons except the *sectarian enemies* of the SAMARITANS and the LIONS, they might have saved themselves the trouble of travelling so far. The simple case was this : the kings of Babylon, after wasting the country, took away the *chief persons* of each nation to Babylon ; and after the Persians took that city, they, finding a number of captives of their *own sect there*, sent them home again.

But there is yet one more consideration which at once overthrows the fancy of the *ten tribes* having given names to the places in India and Rajapootana. They would never have called the city or mount by the name of David, of Solomon, or of Jerusalem, men and a place they hated ; nor countries nor districts after the name of the *tribe of Judah*, which they also hated ; but Gerizim or Samaria. This at once settles the question of the *ten tribes* having founded the places in India. It is surprising that religious prejudice should blind men like Sir W. Jones, to such obvious considerations. But though the presence of the Jewish names proves that the towns cannot have been denominated by Samaritans, the names of the Samaritans, which they bore before the division of the tribes, if they should be found, will not prove the contrary.

Thus there is an end of the ridiculous pretence of the *ten tribes* in India. The fable can deceive none but Jewish sectaries and their followers. And the story of the *ten tribes* being disposed of, I have a perfect conviction that there is no other way of accounting, rationally, for the similarity between the tribes of Upper India and the Syrians, Arabians, and Ethiopians, than that which I have pointed out, viz. emigration from the East to the West, the emigrators taking with them their religion and their laws.

5. The result of all my inquiries comes to this : that about the time of the change of the Vernal Equinox from Taurus to Aries, several emigrations took place from the Mesopotamia of India to the West, in consequence of the great civil wars which then prevailed. One of these emigrations was that of the tribe of Ioudi, who constituted the Jews, Arabians, and African Ethiopians. Another emigration about the same time, but probably a little earlier, was that of the sect of the Ionians. These, I think, also came from the Duab or Mesopotamia. Long after these succeeded the tribe of Tartars or Scythians, mentioned by Ezekiel, who came down from between the Black and Caspian seas, and overran southern Asia. These probably came from the North of the Duab spoken of above. After a long series of years, the Arabian descendants returned, under the Mohamedan Califs, and reconquered India, crossing the Duab or Mesopotamia in their progress, and partly conquering it. Here they found the rudiments of their language, and the names of towns similar to those which their ancestors had carried to the West, and a mythology in great part similar to their own—the Judahs, Jacobs, Noahs, Shems, Japhets, &c., &c. This makes it impossible, without very great care, to distinguish in the Eastern Mesopotamia the works of the ancient Mythologists from those of the modern ones ; but, with care, in most cases it may be done with certainty. Again, after the lapse of another long series of years, the descendants of the North-eastern Tartars, spoken of above as having come down from the North of the Duab under the name of Scythians, advanced towards the West—and, under the name of Turks, conquered the Saracens or Arabians in Syria, Arabia, and Greece, and took Constantinople, and Mount Hæmus, which has retaken its old name of Balk-an and Chumla. These people brought with them a language radically the same as that of the Arabians, yet, as might well be expected after a separation of so many years, considerably changed; nevertheless not so much changed, but that, with very little difficulty, they understand the Arabians. The close similarity of the Turkish and Arabian languages is a striking proof of my whole theory. The outlines of the history of the extended empires, which I have here exhibited, would have been much more conspicuous had our makers of maps and histories recorded the names of places as they must have appeared to them. But from their native religious prejudices and necessary ignorance of the nature of the history, it has seemed to them absurd to

believe, that there should be places or persons in the East having exactly the same names as places and persons in the West; and to avoid the feared ridicule of their contemporaries, which in fact (in opposition to the plainest evidence, and which they themselves could not entirely resist) they thought well-founded, they have, as much as possible, disguised the names. Thus, that which otherwise they would have called David-poutri, they call Daud-poutri ; Solomon, Soleiman ; John-guior, Jahan-guior; &c., &c. In the same way, without any wrong intention, they have been in-duced to secrete the truth, in many cases, from themselves, by hastily adopting the idea that the old Jewish names of places have been given by the modern Saracens or Turks, the erroneousness of which a moment's unprejudiced consideration would have shewn. All this, I think, I have proved ; but in the course of the following books I flatter myself I shall strengthen my proofs by a great variety of circumstances. I therefore beg my reader, on no account, to consider my argu-ment to be concluded. I shall here merely add, that in Chapter IV. Section 8, I have observed, there appears in the examples of the Dead Sea, &c., a great similarity in the countries where the tribes of Judah were settled in the East and in the West. The Western country seems, as much as possible, to have been accommodated to the Eastern ; from this it is not unfair to suppose, that when we read, in the Jewish books, of the immense armies of horsemen and chariots, of the im-mense sums expended in building their temple, &c., these were meant secretly to describe the armies, cities, and temples, of the Eastern tribe of Oude, or of the Eastern Judah and Solomon. What is perfectly ridiculous, as applied to the mountain tribe of Western Syria, is quite otherwise when applied to the armies, cities, and temples, of India. The Western temple of Solomon, exclu-sive of the squares, or courts for the residence of the officiating priests, was only of very moderate size.

---

## CHAPTER VIII.

### PANDION, PANDEUS, PANDÆA.—PANDEISM.—GYPSIES.—RECAPITULATION.

1. I MUST now make a few observations respecting a certain person called Pandion ; but whether there ever was such a person, or the stories told respecting him were mere mythoses, it is ex-tremely difficult to determine. His residence at the birthplace of Cristna, where he reigned, is very suspicious. Mr. Maurice says, " But superior to both, in grandeur and wealth, in this southern " division of India, soared the puissant sovereign, named Pandion, whose kingdom extended quite " to the southern point of Comaria or Comarin, and who was probably of the ancient race of the " renowned Pandus. He also is said, about this time, to have sent an embassy to Augustus, but " no particulars of that embassy have descended to us. The residence of this monarch was at the " city of Madura, and the extent of his power is evident from the whole of that district being de-" nominated from him Pandi-Mandalam, literally the circle or empire of Pandion. Arrian expressly " says, that the Indian Hercules (Chrisna) worshiped at Mathura, on the Jobares, (Jumna,) left " many sons, but only one daughter, Pandæa, to whom he gave a vast army and kingdom, and " ordered, that the whole of her empire should be called by her name. In this and a few other " instances do the classical confirm and illustrate the native accounts," [1] In not a few, I think, my reverend old friend Maurice. But I beg to observe that *Pan-di-Man-dalam* means, the circle or district of the *holy Pan*, or the district sacred to the Catholic God.

---

[1] Maurice, Hist. Hind. Ch. vi.

The temple of the Ionians of Asia Minor, built by the *twelve* tribes, at the place called Pan-Ionium, would mean, temple of the universal or catholic Ioni, or the Ioni-an Pan. The Indian palace of one of the great kings or Gods—Pandion, i. e. Pandu—was at Madoura, i. e. Mat'hura.[1] Here I think we have the *female* principle in Asia, and the *male* in India, at the birthplace of Cristna. Cunti or Prit'ha was the wife of Pandu, and mother of the Pandavas, and she was the daughter of Sura, king of the Surasenas. Sura, the most illustrious of the *Yadus*, was the father of Vasudeva.[2] Here is Pandu, the universal God, having for wife Cunti, the female generative power, &c. Can any one doubt the mythos here? Bishop Heber says, " King Pandoo and his four brethren " are the principal heroes of the celebrated romance f the Mahabarat; and the apparent identity of " his name with that of the *Pandion*, of whose territories in India the Greeks heard so much, is too " remarkable to be passed unnoticed."[3] Pliny says, there was a Panda—ultra Sogdianos, oppidum Panda: and Solinus ultra hos (Bactros) Panda, oppidum Sogdianorum. The same authorities mention a *gens* Panda or *Pandea gens*, whom Pliny places low down on the Indus. Ptolemy fixes the Pandions in the Punjab. There is at the South point of India a Madura Pandionis, and a Regio Pandionis.

Pandion was king of Athens,[4] whose son, by the famous Medea, was called Medus, and became king of the Medes. Perseus was the cousin of Medus, and the nephew of Pandion.[5]

When I consider all the circumstances detailed above respecting the Pans, I cannot help believing that, under a mythos, a doctrine or history of a sect is concealed. Cunti, the wife of Pandu (du or God, Pan), wife of the generative power, mother of the Pandavas or devas, daughter of Sura or Syra the Sun—Pandæa only daughter of Cristna or the Sun—Pandion, who had by Medea a son called Medus; the king of the Medes, who had a cousin, the famous Perseus—surely all this is very mythological—an historical parable !

2. I think Pandeism was a system ; and that when I say the country or kingdom of Pandæa, I express myself in a manner similar to what I should do, if I said the Popish kingdom, or the kingdoms of Popery : or, again, the Greeks have many idle ceremonies in their church, meaning the Greeks of all nations : or, the countries of the Pope are superstitious, &c. At the same time, I beg to be understood as not denying that there was such a kingdom as that of Pandæa, the daughter of Cristna, any more than I would deny that there was a kingdom of France ruled by the eldest son of the church, or the eldest son of the Pope.

The country through which the Indus runs has been called by the moderns Panjab or Panjaub. The word *Panj* means *five*, and the word *Aub* means *river*, i. e. *the country of the five rivers*. But this is, in fact, not strictly true, for the country is in reality full of rivers. Rennell says,[6] " The " river called by Europeans Indus, and by the natives generally Sinde (or Sindeh), is formed of " about *ten* principal streams." In Ptolemy this country is called *Regio Pandoniorum*—the country of the Pandus. We have seen that though Cristna was said to have left many sons, he left his immense empire, which extended from the sources of the Indus to Cape Comorin, (for we find a Regio Pandionis near this point,) to his daughter Pandæa ; but, from finding the icon of Buddha so constantly shaded with the nine Cobras, &c., I am induced to think that this Pandeism was a doctrine, which had been received both by Buddhists and Brahmins.

Col. Tod says, " But we must discard the idea that the history of Rama, the Mahabharat of " Cristna, and the five Pandua brothers, are mere allegory ; an idea supported by some, although

---

[1] Tod's Account, Trans. Asiat. Soc. Vol. I. p. 326.      [2] Wilson's History of Cashmir, p. 97.
[3] Vol. III. p. 111.      [4] Diod. Sic. Lib. iv. Cap. iii.
[5] A female Pan may be seen in the second volume of the *Monumenta Vetusta*.
[6] Memoir of Map, pp. 68, 69.

" their races, their cities, and their coins, exist." [1]  " Colossal figures cut from the mountain,
" ancient temples and caves inscribed with characters yet unknown, attributed to the Pandus,
" confirm the legendary tale."

The case, I apprehend, was this : in early times the Gods were known by their names of Bala,
Rama, Cristna, &c. : by these holy names the princes, (as we know was the fact in later times,)
were called, and the bards or family genealogists filled up the picture. Thus we have great
numbers of princes who trace their pedigrees from the same Gods.   I think there can be no doubt
that sects may be traced by their significant names.  Thus we find Ionas every where.  We
have them in India, in Syria, in Asia Minor, in Thrace, in Britain.  Can any body believe that this
peculiar and significant name is found in all these places by accident ?   Again : we have Pandions, Pan-dis, Pan-deas, Pandus, at Cape Comorin and Tanjore, in Upper India, in Asia Minor,
and at Athens.  This means Universal God—but can any one believe that this daughter or son of
Cristna, in India, means only *red*, as some orientalists would persuade us ?  Every very ancient
town has two or three names.  Every ancient person of eminence has the same.  He has one,
which is his patronymic name, another his sacred, astrological, or lucky, name ; and he has
generally a third given him from his supposed qualities or character.  This added to the frauds of
genealogists, renders all history a riddle.  The princes of Mewar, now living, trace their pedigrees
back *two thousand* years before Christ—princes of a country which, for violent revolutions, as far
as we can look back, has been exceeded by none.

Many persons have thought that this *Pan* related to what has been called Pantheism, or the
adoration of universal nature, and that Pantheism was the first system of man.  For this opinion I
cannot see a shadow of foundation.  As I have formerly said, it seems to me contrary to common
sense to believe, that the ignorant, half-savage would first worship the ground he treads upon,—
that he would raise his mind to so abstruse and so improbable a doctrine as, that the earth he
treads upon created him and created itself : for Pantheism instantly comes to this.  Against this,
all our senses revolt.  But all our senses lend their aid to forward the adoration of the glorious
Sol, with his ministers and attendants, the planetary bodies, which appear to await his commands,
and to obey his orders.  No, indeed !  Pantheism was the produce of philosophy, and excess of
refinement, of, comparatively speaking, a recent date.  I suspect that the old Pantheism is first
found in the history of Pan-dæa, the only daughter of Cristna, and in Pan-dion, the first king of
Athens ; and these histories, like many others of the same kind, are only mystical representations
of a sect of devotees, or of philosophers.  An Oriental friend doubts this ; he says, because Pandu
means *red*, and has no relation, in meaning, to any of the Pans above noticed.  I think no one
who has attended to the surprising change which must have taken place in the Sanscrit language,
in bringing it to its present perfection, will consider this of much consequence, particularly when
he attends to a remark which he will find made by Col. Van Kennedy, in the next chapter, that
the Sanscrit roots have been formed solely by grammarians, and of course artificially ; and that
they have in themselves no signification.  But this, to the extent to which he goes, is evidently
not true.  Had he said *many* or *most* Sanscrit roots, I should not have disputed his authority ; but
my eyes tell me every moment that when he speaks of *all*, he goes much too far.  However, I
think his observation is enough to account for the change in the meaning of a word having taken
place, without such present meaning being sufficient to obviate the arguments advanced above.
The question seems likely to remain in doubt—for I do not pretend to decide it.  Had Col. Van
Kennedy excepted proper names of Deities, Persons, and Places, his observation would have been
more correct.  But this matter will be discussed in the next book.

---

[1] Hist. Raj. p. 44.

It is the received opinion, I believe, of all the first professors of comparative anatomy, that the human race originally consisted of only one genus and one species. Were it not for this received opinion, the marked distinction which may be observed in the different colours in the pictures of the Hindoos, and of the ancient Egyptians, might induce a suspicion that it was meant to indicate different species. At any rate, the distinction must be held to mark varieties—varieties readily accounted for, by the examples of peculiarity exhibited by the Jews and some other tribes, which have been, in a great degree, confined to propagating the species within their own little nation. Now I suggest, for the consideration of the learned, whether it may not be probable that the Pandus may have formed a Northern sect, which at length became *fair*-complexioned, by the same cause, whatever it might be, which made the Athenian Pandions *fair ;* and whether from this yellowish-white complexion, the word Pandu may not have come to mean *red* or *yellow*. Thus a thing might be said to be of the Pandu colour, as we say a thing is of the Negro colour.[1]

If my reader will cast back his imagination over what he has read in this and the last chapter, he will find that the doctrines which I have laid down respecting the origin of the Ionians and Jews, are supported almost entirely by *evidence* and not by *theory*. The system may be said to be formed out of a great number of loose, detached parcels of a whole, brought together and fitted to their respective places, thus forming them anew into a whole again—the parts, while scattered about, offering nothing but a chaotic mass of odd materials, or the leaves of the Sibyls blown about by the winds. I shall not add any thing more here relating to the ænigma or parable : but one thing is clear—the Mythos of the Hindoos, the Mythos of the Jews, and the Mythos of the Greeks, are all, at the bottom, the same ; and what are called their early histories are not the histories of man, but are contrivances under the appearance of histories, to perpetuate doctrines, or perhaps the history of certain religious opinions, in a manner understood by those only who had a key to the ænigma. Of this we shall see many additional proofs hereafter. The histories of Brahma, of Genesis, and of Troy, cannot properly be called *frauds*, because they were not originally held out as histories ; but as the covers for a secret system. But in later times they were mistaken for history, and lamentable have been the effects of the mistake. The history of Lazarus in the Gospel is not true, but it is not a fraud.

Though I have said that the Ionians were the Buddhists, traced by me in my Celtic Druids, this is not perhaps quite correct ; for I think it probable that, in the 2160 years which the worship of Buddha or the Bull preceded that of Cristna, the Buddhists had actually in part settled the Western countries. The modified religion of the Ioni or Jains would not find much difficulty in making its way among them, as it was virtually the same—and perhaps it might be the religion only, and not the tribes of people, which latterly came. But this can never be known. From the expressions in the old Greek writers it seems probable, that when the Ionians arrived they found Buddhists—shepherds perhaps—peaceable, unarmed people, called aborigines, whom they easily conquered.

3. A few pages back, I said that the Jews were the latest emigrants from India, with one exception, of which I should presently treat. I shall now fulfil my promise. The subject to which I alluded was that of the Gypsies. Numbers of persons have treated of the Gypsies ; but as yet nothing has been written respecting them that is quite satisfactory. It is now acknowledged by all, that they are of oriental origin. I have been told by two gentlemen who had returned from

---

[1] *Pan* linguâ Ægypt. est Osiris. (Diod. Sic.) *Phan* or *Phaneus* was one of the names of Apollo, (Macrob.) *Phaneus* Deus Sol. (Alex. ab Alex.) *Sam, Bulim, Talaca,* CRISHNA, *Arun,* are common names of the sun with the Irish Druids. The Sanscrit *Vahni* FIRE, is probably the root of *Fen* or the Phœnician פ (pn) *phen,* a cycle. From this word the Druids made up their Phenniche, or Phœnix. Phœnis Ægyptiis astrologiæ symbolum, was clear to B chart. (Ouseley's Orient. Collect. Vol. III.)

India, that they understood the language of the Gypsies when they spoke it, and that it was the Hindostannee. A strong circumstance of corroboration of this is given by a German called Grellman, [1] who has written the best account of them which I have seen, though mixed with much nonsense. Mr. Marsden has proved the language of the Gypsies to be mostly Hindostannee and Bengalee. [2]

Thus I think there cannot be a doubt that the language of the Gypsies is one of the vulgar dialects of Hindostan. Grellman states the Hindoo languages to be ALL radically the same, which is what we might reasonably expect, and gives a vocabulary of words in both the Hindostannee and the Gypsy languages. Among other similar circumstances he observes, that they have each only two genders, that the cases of their nouns are made by the addition of an article, &c. This the reader will recollect is exactly like the Synagogue Hebrew. A learned German, called Wagenseil, has quoted near fifty of their words, which he maintains are pure Hebrew. Other Germans have shewn that many of their words are those of the Mongol Tartars, with whose language theirs has a great affinity. This is the language of the Afghans, which Sir W. Jones found so like the Chaldee. These facts tend strongly to prove that they have a language in fact originally the same as all those languages, and that those languages have all originally been the same.

Their complexion, like that of the Jews, proves the Gypsies also to be oriental. When they first appeared in Europe, or by what route they came, is quite unknown. I consider them to be a tribe, like that of the Jews, from India. The difference in the fortunes of the two tribes is this : one continued together till it became strong enough to create jealousy, which caused its expulsion from Egypt, and it continued united, having fortunately a leader skilled, by accident, in all the learning of the Egyptians, who took the command, and under whom it conquered and became a nation. The other was not so fortunate. It had no child accidentally adopted and educated by a princess, or other circumstances favouring it as they did the Jewish tribe ; it has, therefore, continued miserable and dispersed. The Christian will say the one was a favoured tribe for peculiar reasons. Very well. This makes nothing against my argument, or against the facts. That the Gypsies were a Buddhist tribe is proved, in part at least, by one singular remnant of the religion of Buddha, which they yet retain. It is contrary to their faith to kill animals to eat, but if they find them dead, they are permitted to eat them. Thus a dead ox or sheep is a grand feast to them. For though, as there are Mohamedans who drink wine, there are always among them some who kill and eat, yet they prefer the feast that is free from sin. Like the Jews, they couple only in their own tribe, and thus their national cast of countenance continues.

The Jews were originally believed to have a peculiar power of extinguishing fire : this is continued to the Gypsies. [3] The Jews were believed to eat children : this was formerly also believed of the Gypsies. The oldest accounts which we have of them, given by themselves, state them to be emigrants on account of religion. [4] If ever their history shall be sought into diligently by a philosopher, which has never yet been done, I think they will be found to be a tribe from Upper India—Afghans perhaps. [5] When I first began to study the Hebrew language, I received instruction from a Jewish gentleman, of the name of Salome, at Bath. I never had the least reason to entertain a doubt of his veracity. He told me that passing the depôt of the Malays, near our India House, his attention was called to it by an affray, and on going into it he found people speaking a language which, from his knowledge of Hebrew, he understood. This was an Indian or Malay language, which must have been a close dialect of the Hebrew ; to this I shall return.

---

[1] P. 171, Eng. Ed.       [2] Archæol. Vol. VII. p. 252 ; Vall. Col. Hib. Vol. V. p. 310.

[3] Grel. p. 87.       [4] Ib. p. 121.       [5] For more information see Asiat. Res. Vol. VII. p. 476.

In the Morning Herald for the 16th or 17th of April, 1827, is a paragraph stating, that the Bible societies were giving Hebrew Bibles to the native Irish, as it was found that they were better understood than the English. This, in a very remarkable manner, supports what General Vallancey has maintained, but which has been much ridiculed by weak people, that Ireland was colonised by a tribe from the East, and particularly from Phœnicia. All this seems to confirm the very close connexion which there must have been in some former time, between Siam, Afghanistan, Western Syria, and Ireland. Indeed I cannot doubt that there has been really one grand empire, or one Universal, one Pandæan, or one Catholic religion, with one language, which has extended over the whole of the old world; uniting or governing at the same time, Columbo in the island of Serendive, and Columbo in the West of Scotland. This must have been Buddhist, whether it ever really existed as one empire, or was divided into different states. A friend has observed that "The priests will have a great triumph over you, for they will endeavour to revive the almost obsolete doctrine that the Hebrew was the language of Adam." I reply, they will have no triumph over me here, for if they do triumph, it will not be *over me*, but *with me*. For I maintain, and believe that I shall prove, that the Arabian-Hebrew, as it may be called, has of all languages the best pretensions to be the first.[1] But in my next book, when I shall treat of Sanscrit and the Hieroglyphics, I shall discuss this more at large.

## RECAPITULATION.

I think it now expedient to recall to my reader's recollection a few of the subjects which I have discussed, and to consider the progress which I have made in my work; but I shall not at present notice the Preliminary Observations, because I have not yet come to that part, for the use of which they were made. After a few remarks on the cosmogony of the ancients and the abuse of his faculties by man, I commence my work with stating the doctrine of the existence of the Oriental Triune God of the ancients, and with explaining his supposed nature; and then endeavour to shew the way in which the refined system of emanations or abstractions must have arisen out of the natural perceptions of the human mind. At the same time I shew that several of the most important of the ancient doctrines were intimately connected with it, and naturally arose out of it; viz. the Androgynous nature of the Deity, the Metempsychosis, and the Immortality of the Soul, by its final absorption into the substance of the Supreme First Cause.

I next shortly point out the circumstance, that Genesis consists of three distinct works, the 1st called *the book of Wisdom ;* the 2nd (B. I. Ch. II. Sect. 12) *the book of the generations* or *regenerations* of the *planetary bodies ;* and the 3rd *the book of the generations* or *regenerations of the human race.* After this I proceed to shew that the sun either as God himself or as the Shekinah of the higher triune principle, (which is only known to us by its attributes, and which, when attempted to be subjected to a closer examination, vanishes from our grasp like a dream or illusion,) was the object of adoration of all nations—that all the Gods and Goddesses of idolatry resolve at last into this one principle.

In the fourth chapter of the first book I shew that there were two Ethiopias, and that the doctrine of Sir William Jones is probably true, that a great *black* nation once had power and pre-eminence in Asia, and that it is also probable that this was the empire of the black curly-headed Buddha.

In the beginning of the second book I endeavour to prove that the religion of Abraham was the same as that of the Persians, and that he held, like all other nations of the earth, the existence of the triune God : and that the word Aleim used in the first verse of Genesis is a noun in the plural number, and used in that number for the express purpose of describing this Being. In the third

---

[1] I speak not of the *from top to bottom written* Chinese, because I know nothing about it.

3 L 2

444 RECAPITULATION.

chapter this leads to an examination of the secret meaning of Genesis, and of course to the meaning of the first word, Berasit : when I come to the development of the sublime esoteric doctrine of WISDOM, and an exposure of the dishonest means adopted by the priests to conceal it from modern Christians : and in these assertions I shew that I am supported by almost all the most eminent men of antiquity. I also prove, that the oriental doctrine of Emanations is clearly maintained in the Pentateuch. The remainder of this book is chiefly taken up with shewing the identity, with some few exceptions made for particular purposes, of the religions of the Israelites, the Persians, and other nations, neighbours to the Jews—with the origin of Sacrifices—the reason of the restoration of the Jews to Palestine by Cyrus—the allegorical nature of the Old Testament, and the history of the Jewish Cabala—so far all tending to prove that the secret doctrine of the Jews was the secret doctrine of all nations, which was, in fact, the system of the celebrated Christian eclectic philosopher, Ammonius Saccas.

The third book discusses the origin of the famous word *Om* of India and Greece—the systems of Pythagoras, of Orpheus, and of the Greeks ; and I there shew that the doctrine of the Orphic or Platonic trinity differed in no important respect from that of the Christians : and I feel confident that I have proved it to have been universally held by all nations, Jew and Gentile, from the earliest period. The proofs of its existence before the time of Christ are numerous and incontrovertible. The observation of Mr. Maurice, that Plutarch and the Gentile authors drew their information from old writers before the Christian æra, is conclusive evidence that the doctrines were not copied from the Christians ; but that they were taken from the records of the philosophy of Orpheus and Zoroaster. The substantial identity of the two trinities I consider so clear, that I shall not waste a moment upon the subject. It is too late now to renew the nonsensical controversy between the *homoiu*sians and *homoou*sians.

When in the fourth book we come to the God of the Hindoos, the celebrated Cristna, we are drawn to the consideration of the question of the priority of the Indian or of the Egyptian mythology : and I here think the great mass of small circumstances, as well as of direct written evidence, amount to as good a proof as the nature of the case will admit, that India was the *parent* and not the *child* of Egypt. I then observe, that such facts as that of the discovery of the Cobra Capella, on almost every monument in Egypt,—as that of the discovery and adoration by the Seapoys of their God Cristna in the ruins of Thebes, are decisive of the question—and are infinitely more valuable than any written evidence whatever. The notice taken by Mr. Maurice of the descent of Cristna into Hell and his return to his proper paradise, in Book IV. Ch. I. Sect. 3, is striking : it can scarcely be believed that he did not know of the crucifixion noticed by M. Creuzer. To the crucifixion of the Avatar of Cristna, called Balajii or Wittoba, I shall return hereafter. What shall I say of the *black Christ* among the *white* Italians, Swiss, Germans, and French ? Is it necessary to say any thing ? Does it not speak for itself ? Can any thing more be wanted to shew whence the corruptions, in the religion of the Ktētōsopher[1] of Nazareth were derived ? I shall not recapitulate the particulars of the life of the most amiable and interesting of the Gods of antiquity, the playful Cristna ; my reader must remember them ; they are much too striking to be forgotten.

The lives of Buddha and Cristna are so similar, that to tell the story of *one* is to tell the story of the other. The publication of the plate of the *crucifixion* and *resurrection* of INDRA or BUDDHA, by the learned Jesuit, with the permission of the Roman Censor, is, however attempted to be explained away by him, a credit to both.

The history of Buddha, in the Fifth Book, supplies to the list of the corruptions of Christianity

---

[1] Κτητωρ-Σοφιας, *Possessor of Wisdom*. Will my reader pardon my coining this designation—admissible, perhaps, from its appropriateness ?

what was wanting in the history of Cristna. There I have shewn that from Buddha came the immaculate conception of Maia or Maria,—immaculate conception being first, in the West, ascribed to the mother of Pythagoras, and from him, perhaps, handed over to the Christian devotees. A miraculous birth, having been attributed to Pythagoras and Plato, shews that it was no *new thing* when Papias and Irenæus laid hands upon it.

In this book, the history of Buddha introduces us to perhaps the most important part of the system, and to the origin of the whole—the ancient cycles: and I think that the arithmetical proofs which I have given of their meaning, leave nothing wanting to the proof of the truth of my theory. The ancient doctrine of the millenium of the Jews, the secret meaning of the cross, the mysterious numbers of the stones at Stonehenge, Abury, &c., the prophecies of Isaiah, Zoroaster, Virgil, and the Druid of Ireland, all connect and bind together, as with a chain, the mythoses of antiquity.

The evidence to the truth of my theory, afforded by La Loubère and Cassini, is more than could have been expected : and the reality of the system of cycles, arising from the arithmetical proofs, I apprehend, is clear and satisfactory as far as we have gone ; but they are only *trifling* compared with the proofs which I shall bring, when I come to the chronological finale of the system.

I could scarcely wish for any thing more opportune for my theory, than the mode in which the two monograms, the ΥΗΣ and the ΧΗ which stand for Christ, for the ancient sacred number of the East, and for one of the cycles, viz, 608,—and the X alone standing for 600, the other cycle, connect together the two systems. No pretended accident can account for such a coincidence. The circles at Abury, the monograms at Rome, the prophecies, the ten Avatars, eight of which I have already explained, and the expected Millenium, prove the existence of an universal system— and that, as far as it has yet been stated, I have developed it.

The theory which I have formed for the origin of the sacred numbers of the ancients, 600, 608, 650, is, I think, more than plausibly supported in Book V. Ch. IV. by the monograms. And the records supplied by the number of pillars in the temples, and particularly by the number of 650 pillars in Abury, the number sacred to Bacchus, unknown to me when I published the CELTIC DRUIDS, is a striking circumstance, confirmatory of its truth. At first, when my attention was drawn to the ancient cycles, I by no means observed their great importance to the early generations of man. In fact, in the whole circle of science, there is not, perhaps, one object which must have been of equal importance. They were not only of consequence to mankind in all their temporal affairs, their seed-times and their harvests, but as the first religion consisted, as much of religion does yet, almost entirely of ceremonies and festivals, the cycles became of the greatest consequence as points of faith. Even within a short period of the present time, the question whether the devotees were to keep Easter on the fourteenth day after the full moon, or the Sunday afterward, caused terrible and bloody wars. In short, almost all the spiritual and temporal concerns of life were implicated in the cycles—and to this must be added their paramount importance in the nonsensical science of judicial astrology. To all these matters I request particular attention.

Most of my readers will be surprised at the explanation of the *Om* of Isaiah. The proofs I have yet to produce in its justification are almost innumerable. The passage from Martianus Capella, Book V. Chap. II. Sect. 8, rescues the Gentiles from the charge of worshiping many Gods, but my reader will be kind enough in the first line for the word *calls* to read *invokes*. The universal prevalence of the adoration of the Cross cannot be denied. The generality of my readers, I believe, will begin to be much surprised at finding in the Lama of Tibet, nearly an exact counterpart of the Pope of Rome—in whose fisherman's *poitrine* we shall find many things little suspected.

The identity of Hercules and Samson cannot, I think, be disputed, or that Bacchus was Buddha and the sun in Taurus, and that Hercules was Cristna and the sun in Aries.

Mr. Bentley's discoveries, finished by his recantation to Dr. Marsham, have taken from under the priests their last strong support; but much relating to this matter is yet to come. The Jewish *passover* found in the *Yajna sacrifice* of the Hindoos, is surely very interesting.

I flatter myself that I have explained the ænigma of the Negro God, and that the curly-head of Buddha, the Triune God of Wisdom, will no more be a reproach and disgrace to his followers. The resolution of numbers of Indian names into Hebrew roots, must begin to operate on the mind of my reader, to make him think it not so great a paradox to say, that the Hebrew is the *oldest* of languages. The wars of the Maha-barat are explained in the *fifth* book. It is not easy to refer to a proof of the truth of that part of my system, (which depends upon the change of the equinox from Taurus to Aries,) as scarcely a page can be pointed out in which some proof of it may not be found; but perhaps there is nothing more striking than the fact stated in Book V. Chap. XI. Sect. 3, that at a certain period, all the heads of the Gods and Goddesses changed from that of the Bos or Beeve, to that of the Agnus or Sheep.

When all the curious circumstances which have been developed are considered, an unprejudiced person will, I think, be obliged to admit that the ancient epic poems are oriental allegories, all allusive to the same mythos, and that many of those works which we have been accustomed to call histories, are but allegorical representations of mythologies, of the secret doctrines of which I am in pursuit, and which have been endeavoured to be concealed and perpetuated for the use of the elect, the initiated, under the veil of history—to which, as the first object was the doctrine or mythos, *the history* in every case was sacrificed or made subservient, and that Herodotus, from being the first historian was, in fact, as well as in name, the father of history. Thus we find in the East, as well as in the West, whenever an attempt was made to discover the meaning of any of the ancient ceremonies by the uninitiated, the inquirer was always put off with a story or history; and the great doctrine of the Creator, the Preserver, and the Destroyer, which was the foundation of the mythos, from incapacity or unwillingness in the priest, was never explained.

In the concluding chapter of Book V., I flatter myself that I have done an act of justice to the Gentile nations, and shewn that, however their different religions in time became corrupted, a very fine and beautiful system of morality, the morality in fact of the philosopher of Nazareth, was at the bottom of them all. I also flatter myself that, in the same chapter, I have only done an act of justice to Mons. Volney. The first chapter of the *sixth* book on the flood or floods, the Pyramids, the Delta of Egypt, the theory of Mr. Gab, and the Geological fact in Yorkshire, will suggest room for many queries. The history of the Virgin of the Sphere will, I fear, make many of my Catholic friends angry.

I think the history of *Bacchus* and *Iao*, in Book VI., will leave no room for doubting about who they were.

This book will have opened to my reader some new views of the origin of the ancient inhabitants of Greece, and the mythical meaning of the beautiful Lotus. The passage in the note on Chapter III. respecting Roger Bacon and his knowledge of the *modern* inventions or discoveries, as we call them, will surprise my reader, as the fact surprised me.

In this book also, the origin of the Hellenes or Ionians, and of the ancient Greeks, is traced— and their fable of the Argonauts is shewn to have come from India. The circumstance of the two Moriahs or Merus, two Sions, &c., prepares the way for the complete proof of the origin of the ancient Jews in the next book. The Gods Janus and Ganesa are also shewn to be the same; and what has been said before respecting the allegorical poems and histories, is confirmed by many observations respecting Homer, Troy, the hanging gardens of Babylon, &c., &c.—the whole tending to prove one universal system to have been at the bottom of all the ancient mythologies.

In the *eighth* Book I have made an attempt to explain the hitherto inexplicable peculiarity of the

Jewish nation, and I flatter myself with success. Here comes into great use the system of the *sixteen* letters, which I have established in my *Celtic Druids*, as the original system of all nations that had the use of letters. The authorities on which my explanation of the history of the Jews is founded I think cannot be impugned; they are chiefly unwilling witnesses,—the admissions of such men as Eusebius, Bryant, Faber, &c., all very learned, but most unwilling supporters to my cause. But their admissions are *confirmed by circumstances which admit of no other explanation.* Can any one doubt the existence of the Jewish mythos in India? The same names of God, of men, and of places? The two Ararats, the two Moriahs, two Sions? And, above all, the various Soleimans or Solomons—the mountains of Solomon—the Tucti Solumi of Cashmere and of Northern India—and of Persia, and of Syria, and of Telmessus? What I have said on all these subjects, will receive almost innumerable additional proofs hereafter. But I think that, at last, the origin of this singular and interesting people has been shewn in a way which a philosopher need not feel ashamed to receive. Indeed I contend, that the existence of Judaism before the time of Abraham, proved by Eusebius, and the Israelitish names found in the names of the countries, the mountains, the cities—like *Ioud-ia*, the capital of a mighty empire, in North or Central India, amount to as good proof as the nature of the case will admit, that the Judæan history is a mythos brought to the West by a tribe of Afghan Shepherds, probably conquered or driven out of India, from the country of Oude or Juda, in the wars of the Mahabarat. In a future page I shall shew, that when the same people established themselves, not as conquered emigrants, but as conquerors, in other foreign countries, they in a similar manner established their mythos and their religion.

I think my reader will now begin to perceive in the general prevalence of the Trinitarian doctrine, and the renewal of cycles, and in many other circumstances, an approximation to proof that what the Eclectic philosopher, Ammonius Saccas, said, was true, viz. that one universal and very refined system originally pervaded the whole world; which only required to be divested of the meretricious ornaments, or the corruptions with which the craft of priests, or the infirmities of men, had loaded it in different countries, to be every where found; that, in fact, in the Christian and Gentile systems, there was fundamentally no difference. I feel little doubt that in the remainder of this work I shall abundantly prove the truth of this doctrine of Ammonius, and upon this object, in fact the great object of my work, I must beg my reader to keep his eye steadily fixed.

---

NOTE. During the time that the part of this work which the reader has seen has been printing, I have met with several matters which would have much elucidated different points on which it has treated, only part of which I can conveniently insert hereafter, and indeed the insertion of such part will be rather misplaced. It is therefore my present intention, if health and circumstances permit, to publish a volume, or perhaps more than one, occasionally, called *Commentaries on the Anacalypsis and on Ancient History*. This will give me an opportunity of further elucidating the subjects which I have discussed, and of following up the important discoveries made by General Vallancey, which the priests have contrived to consign almost to oblivion, but which, I am of opinion, are of inestimable value for the discovery of ancient science. In this work I shall be able to answer objections of opponents, and to correct oversights and mistakes, which, as I have not the gift of infallibility, must necessarily occur.

*Nov.* 1831.

---

# BOOK IX.

## CHAPTER I.

SANSCRIT, ORIGIN OF.—VAN KENNEDY ON SANSCRIT.—LANGUAGE CHANGEABLE.—MAZORETIC HEBREW A NEW LANGUAGE. — GRAMMATICAL CONSTRUCTION NO CRITERION. — PHŒNICIAN, GREEK, AND COPTIC, THE SAME.—YADAVAS FROM INDIA.— ABYSSINIAN JEWS. — ABRAHAM FROM INDIA. — ARABIC AND ETHIOPIAN THE SAME.—DR. MURRAY ON SANSCRIT. — PROFESSOR DUNBAR, H. E. BARKER, ESQ. — HERMAN, ANTHOM, HAUGHTON, WILSON, HAGAR. — DR. PRITCHARD. — HAGAR. — DIRECTION OF WRITING.—PRONUNCIATION OF LANGUAGES.—PROFESSOR BOP.—ADAM, MEANING OF THE WORD.—GREEK AND LATIN. —NO COLONY GOES OUT WITHOUT TAKING ALL ITS LETTERS.—CONCLUDING OBSERVATIONS.

BEFORE I proceed, I think it necessary to examine the history of the celebrated written sacred language of the Brahmins of India, called the Sanscrit. It will not be denied that this is the most perfect and beautiful language which has ever been known. It is in my opinion certain that, in its present state, it is not like most, perhaps all, other languages, the child of accident or circumstance ; but that, on the contrary, it is entirely the produce of very great and systematic labour of learned and highly-civilized men. I believe it is not at present, and that probably it has never been, the vernacular language of any nation, but has been confined to one, or at most two, elevated or learned classes of the Brahmin religion in India.

1. The origin of the Sanscrit is unknown, but it is said to have been invented by the ancient Richees.[1] It is called Sanscort, or Sanskroutan ; that is, clearly, the *Sanctum Scriptum*. A person called Anoubhout or Sarasvat, Goddess of speech, is said to have made the first grammar. This is evidently the nymph Anobret of Sanchoniathon and of Western Syria, or Sarah, the wife of Abraham or the Brahmin. See John Cleland's attempt at the revival of Celtic Literature.[2] This seems to point to the Chaldæans,[3] from whose country Abraham came, as the inventors of it.

2. A gentleman of the army, of the name of Van Kennedy, has lately written a long treatise respecting it. If what he says be true, that " the roots of this language have not any meaning," I think I may venture to say that, in this respect, it probably differs from every other, and in this will be found what will be nearly a proof, that it is artificial. In what languages or where the Colonel sought without success for the meaning of the roots, I do not know. But it is evident that if it be founded on several other tongues, where the roots of the words of the respective tongues are found, in each particular case will the root of the Sanscrit word be found. But it will make little or no difference whether it be founded on *several* tongues, or on only *one*, if the several tongues be founded on one original language.

In every written language, (unless I except the Chinese,) however varied in shape its letters

---

[1] i. e. Rasees, *wise men.*    [2] P. 91.

[3] By Chaldæans, of course, Assyrians or Babylonians are not meant.

may be, the Cadmæan must be admitted to be its system; in the same manner as the Greek was the Cadmæan, although each letter had two or three forms.

There is not one written language in which several words of every written language may not be found; and they are at least so numerous as, upon Dr. Young's doctrine of chances, to reduce the fact that they are all originally one language to so high a probability, as to amount, in effect, to certainty. Then surely, under these circumstances, when I find a word in two ancient languages having the same letters and the same meaning, I am justified in considering them to be the same : for example—ערך *ord* and the English *order*—both having the same meaning, i. e. *placing methodically*.

Van Kennedy[1] gives a list of nine hundred Sanscrit words which are found in Greek, Latin, Persian, German, and English, and which are thus divided. There are 339 Sanscrit words in Greek, 319 in Latin, 263 in Persian, 163 in German, 251 in English, and 31 *common to all of them*. From this he infers, that they are all deduced from a common origin. But how came the German and English words here ? How, but because German, i. e. Saxon, (from which old English is chiefly descended,) and English are both Hebrew ?—which Hebrew is Chaldean, and Arabic, and Syriac, and Pushto, the language of the Sacæ or Saxæ of North India, as I shall presently prove.

I think, as I have before remarked, that it is evident the Colonel must go too far when he speaks of the roots generally having *no meaning :* for if there be near a thousand words now Sanscrit, which are the same nearly in form and sense as words in the languages above-named, it cannot be denied that they have meanings. I suppose, however, he means to say, their roots have no meaning in the Sanscrit language : but if they have roots in other languages, they will still have meanings ; and if the language be artificial, and formed upon a variety of other languages, in every case the root will shew where the word has come from : and if they be all founded on one, the course will be shewn by which it has descended through the medium of each language. For an example take the word *Nau-banda*, noticed in a former book. The word *Nau* will be from the Latin or Greek, the word *band* from the Saxon. Again ; take the word *Nerbuddha*, the name of a river. The word Ner is clearly the Hebrew word for *river*, and the word Bud is Sanscrit, and means *wise*, or wisdom, the River Buddha, or River of the God of Wisdom.—Again ; the word Choda. This is Choder in Arabic, and God in Saxon and English. Again ; limestones called *Shall-gramu*, containing the sacred shells. The first is evidently our shell ; the *gramu* I do not understand. In page 201, the Colonel says, " An examination of the vernacular dialects of India " will render it evident that Sanscrit is *a foreign* language, which has been superinduced on them, " and not they on Sanscrit." He then proceeds to shew that this was the opinion of the late Mr. Ellis, of Madras. Whether foreign or not, this goes to prove that, *quoad* India and all its mythoses, it is comparatively modern. The Brahmins are said to be foreigners to South India. All that this amounts to is, that the sect using this language arose in the North of India, (as stated in Eastern histories,) came down upon the Buddhists in the South, and drove them out.

3. To the arguments which I am about to use, it is not of the least consequence whether Sanscrit in its refined state was ever spoken by the mass of people in any nation or not.

Col. Van Kennedy, out of the 339 Sanscrit words which he found in the Greek, has detected three hundred of them in the poems of Homer. Indeed, it is now admitted that there are great numbers of its words in the Latin, the Greek, and other Western languages. But it is not the universal sacred language of the Buddhists or Jains. From this circumstance, I think, an impor-

---

[1] Page 232.

tant consequence will follow. The Buddhist religion having been proved to have been universally disseminated, the ancient language on which the Sanscrit was founded, for there can be little doubt that it would in some degree be founded on the vernacular language of its builders, must have been in use by the Buddhists before the division of the religions. I need not point out to my reader that the number of years required to effect a complete change in any spoken language is often very small. The language of Chaucer has become scarcely intelligible in the lapse of only about *three hundred* years. The Sanscrit, after being brought to perfection, has remained almost unchanged, because it was not a commonly-spoken language, and because it was tied down by strict and unvarying grammatical rules.

Supposing the Sanscrit to have been brought to perfection, or completed to its present state by the Brahmins after their division from the Buddhists, (which if it had not, the Buddhists would have generally used it, but this they do not,) and to have been founded upon the language at the time of the division common to both, this would be a sufficient reason why numbers of the roots of Sanscrit words should be found in all the Western nations, where Buddhism has prevailed. The vernacular language of the Brahmins before the division would probably, if the new language were founded upon it, have been constantly improving, until it arrived at a very considerable degree of perfection—but yet not to such a high degree as would serve to render it *almost* a dead language, and entirely a dead language in a few years, as it actually became when it was improved into Sanscrit. The sacred and dead language of books in the temples which admitted no change, it being in this respect like the Hebrew of the Synagogue, would remain as it was, but the language of the numerous countries into which the country of the Brahmins became divided, would be perpetually changing, until the parent language would be in them almost entirely lost, and numbers of new ones would be formed. But in all those new ones, some traces of the parent would remain, as we find them. Now, except the Sanscrit, we have only one known unspoken SACRED language in the world ; and that is the Synagogue Hebrew.[1]  From the time of the Ba-

---

[1] The corruption of old works by emendators, though actuated by the best intentions possible, is grievously to be deplored. By these emendations there is not now a *single ancient author* which can be depended on. But the sacred writings have suffered the most of all ; till *now* they are actually so corrupt, that there is not a single text, of any consequence, on which a rational faith can be placed. For if the actual corruption of any selected text cannot be shewn, it is the easiest thing imaginable to shew that it may have been corrupted for any thing which we know to the contrary. The corruption of our Bible was *doubtless* begun by the ancient Jews, in opposition to the Samaritans ; and has been continued, in a greater or a less degree, in every new version which has been published. In the last century, the University of Oxford employed the learned Dr. Grabe to publish a version of the famous Alexandrian Manuscript, and the following is the description of this work, given by the Encyclopædia Britannica : (in voce *Bible :)* " In this (version) the Alex-" andrian manuscript is not printed such as it is, but such as it was thought it should be ; i. e. it is *altered* wherever " there appeared any fault of the copyists, or *any word inserted from any particular dialect*." Thus every new version has been mended. The Jews mend the Samaritan ; Origen mends the Jews ; Jerom mends Origen ; Mohamed mends Jerom ; Luther mends Mohamed ; Calvin mends Luther ; and Dr. Grabe mends them all. Such being the case, what is to be done? The remedy to a rational person, is very simple. The evil, by its excess, as most evils do, has, in a theological view of the matter, cured itself. The man of sense must throw out every text which contains any thing derogatory to the character, or contrary to the moral attributes, of God—and also every text which has any doubt at all respecting its meaning. I shall be told that when I have performed this operation, there will be nothing of the religion of Jesus left. If this be true, I say the more the pity that the priestly emendators should have brought the matter to such a pass. But I deny the fact—much will be left.  I maintain that all will be left which is necessary for the good of man, either in this world or the next. We shall find that a good and benevolent person taught, *among other excellent doctrines,* THAT IF WE PLACE A FIRM RELIANCE ON THE BENEFICENCE OF OUR CREATOR, RETURN GOOD FOR EVIL, AND IN SHORT DO TO OUR NEIGHBOUR AS WE WISH OUR NEIGHBOUR TO DO TO US, WE SHALL INHERIT ETERNAL LIFE. Here, then, is the religion of Jesus. This religion, the religion κατ' εξοχην of the poor and ignorant man, requires no bishops in coaches-and-six, and no learned universities to explain it ; but in this consists its heresy. If persons choose to read and compare the four gospel histories, (with their thirty thousand various

bylonish captivity there is no reason to believe, that the SYNAGOGUE Hebrew has, AS a LANGUAGE, materially changed. I speak not of several wilful corruptions of the text by the Jews, which may be perceived in the Pentateuch ; for, if they interpolated, they would imitate the *old style* as much as possible. Then, under these circumstances, the great age of the Hebrew Pentateuch, viz. since the time when Ezra changed its letters from the Samaritan to the Hebrew, or Chaldee ; or, since it was, after being destroyed, remanufactured by Ezra, (whom our priests disguise by the name of Esdras,) being considered, we ought to find the Hebrew *spoken* language possessing many striking marks of similarity to the Sanscrit, if this theory be true : and these we do find.

4. The Mazoretic or pointed Hebrew is, in fact, a new language ; and if, instead of forming the letters by substituting points for the Chaldæan vowel letters, the Jews had adopted a new form of letter entirely, I believe it would have passed, like the Sanscrit, for a new language. It would, then, not have been called Hebrew, but would have been only supposed to have been formed upon it nearly ; as much of the Greek is formed on Hebrew, and of the Latin on Greek. It would have been to the ancient Synagogue Hebrew, what the Arabic is to it. It would have been infinitely more full and copious. As in the case of the Arabic, all the Hebrew roots would have been contained in it; but probably the roots of all its words would not have been found in the Hebrew.

The Synagogue Hebrew language has vowels like all other languages ; but, like the Celtic dialects, it has many words written with very few vowels, and many without any. I shall explain the reason of this in a future part of my work. In this explanation will be found, if I mistake not, a proof of a theory respecting the origin of written language, which will at first be thought paradoxical, but which is, at all events, quite new. It will not be denied that the deficiency of vowels in the Hebrew,[1] in the Welsh, and in the other Celtic dialects, is very remarkable, and has never received even a shadow of an explanation. If the Hebrew and the Celtic languages be the oldest written languages of the world ; if the theory which, in a future page, I shall explain, be well founded, they could in respect to the vowels be no other than as they are. I think, to go no farther, the fact that the names of the ancient sixteen letters of the Jews and Celts had originally meanings, and the same meanings, and that the names of the letters of no other language had meanings, is nearly sufficient to prove their priority to all others. Let it be recollected that, in the Preliminary Observations, Chap. I. Sect. 63, I have proved that both the ancient Irish and the Hebrew letters had the same meanings of trees. I think there can be no doubt that when the Brahmins made their fine Sanscrit, they generally retained the proper names, only writing them in Sanscrit letter. This accounts for many names being only part of them Sanscrit : for instance Maha-Barata ; that is Maha בראאתא *brata* Great Creator : בראת *brat* being the noun of the Hebrew verb ברא *bra* to create or form. Then the wars of the Mahabarat will be, the wars of the Great Creator, or of God, or, as we should say, holy wars.

I will here stop to observe, that I believe the wars just now spoken of were the first great wars of the world ; that in all former times, though there may have been disputes like those between the servants of Abraham and Lot, about their pastures or springs of water, yet, that there was

---

readings, many of them of vital importance to the religion,) with one another, or with the other thirty or forty gospel histories, which are now, in this country, out of fashion, and which of course will have various readings also, and with the Epistles in scores, I would not attempt to prevent them : but respecting such persons I would make only one observation ; it is totally incredible that they should be able to form an opinion on any rational ground, upon almost any one of the controversial points of the priests, all which are, in fact, of no consequence to any but themselves, without they be, in a considerable degree, conversant with Greek, Latin, and Hebrew. This brings ninety-nine out of every hundred persons to the creed which I have given above. But this is no doubt a *horrible heresy*, because it verifies the words of Jesus Christ, that his was the poor man's religion : and it instantly does away with the necessity of priests and their coaches-and-six superiors, the bishops.

[1] On the modern invention of the Mazoretic points, see my Essay in Classical Journal, Vol. XXXIII. p. 145.

3 M 2

nothing like general wars ; that before this time all the world was governed by an order of priesthood, and was like the vast domains of China, in a comparative state of peace ; that gold was the
common metal, the use of iron not being known ; and that, for these *two* reasons, the time was
called the golden age—the age of XPΣ. These subjects will, however, come into careful discussion in a future book.

But to return from this digression ; Col. Van Kennedy has quoted a very judicious observation of
Mr. Klaproth's : " It is a singular idea to suppose that languages, like animals, have sprung and
" been procreated from one another ; but it is to be wished that the notion of derivation should be
" given up, and that all languages related to each other should be considered as sisters whose
" parent is unknown." [1] Mr. Klaproth has observed, that the Sanscrit betrays in itself every appearance of recent formation, and is in his opinion a very modern language, the newness of which
is concealed and disguised by its roots. [2]

I confess I am astonished when I hear learned men declare, that there is no similarity between
the Hebrew and the Sanscrit. But my surprise, in some degree, ceases when I find them listening
to the corruptions of the modern Rabbies, that is to the modern language of the Mazorites, called,
by an old name, Hebrew. After much consideration I think I perceive several other reasons for a
circumstance which, at first view, appears so astonishing : one is, that they give into the absurd
system of the modern Jews in their mode of representing the Hebrew letters by the English. As
an example of which, among many others, I have only to instance the vowel O, which they render
NG, [3] and thus of such a simple word as בעבר *bobr* they make *begneeber*, &c. The next is, that
they never consider or make allowance for the very extraordinary and unnatural change which
must have taken place between the old language and the artificial Sanscrit that was built upon it,
or formed out of it, which would evidently tend to render the new language dissimilar to the
Hebrew. But notwithstanding this change, when we compare the Sanscrit words, as given in
our letters by Sanscrit scholars, particularly proper names and names of Gods, with the unso-
phisticated, uncorrupted Hebrew of the Synagogue, the likeness is very strong. As I have
observed in my last book, for one example take Jaya-deva. The first word here is clearly יהיה *ieie*
or יהוי *ieue*—the second, the Latin *deva*, deity, I need not notice. How striking is the likeness,
but how unlike the corrupt Jewish *Jehovah !* How unlike is the word of *four* letters, all vowels,
to the word of *seven*, three of which are consonants ! Again for another example : the Hindoos
chaunt in their ceremonies the word YEVE, YEVE. Here we have the same word repeated ; and
there are many others, as we shall occasionally observe.

5. Another cause is to be found in a mistake respecting the grammatical construction of languages. All languages are in some respects the same. Language is the produce of unpreme-
ditated circumstances, arising out of the wants of man ; and all men having the same wants, a
certain similarity arises out of the supply of them by different men. I think there is evident
proof that all men set out with one spoken language, (I do not treat of the Chinese, because I
know nothing about it,) and all men of the old world, [4] who wrote at all, with one written
language. When they branched off in tribes, they took it with them. I think there are clear
proofs that this language was in a very rude state ; that it was written, and that it had *sixteen*
letters. When men began to be civilized, and not before, they began to improve their language and

---

[1] Asiat. Polyglotta, p. 43; Van Kennedy, p. 196.          [2] Asiat. Polyglotta, p. 45.
[3] Perhaps I shall have quoted to me some Oriental example of the O having become *ng*, and, perhaps, even from
my own book. Because it has been corrupted in the East, is that any reason why it should be also corrupted in the
West ? The corruption of it in the East will no more change the ancient nature of the letter, than the corruption in
the West will do it.
[4] In opposition to the new America.

to make grammars, and of course they would, in some measure, adopt different plans or grammatize differently. Thus the Greeks made *three* numbers, the Latins were content with *two*. But still all men having nearly the same wants, all men would equally have recourse to remedies to supply them, and it seems to me that in many cases it is almost a necessary consequence, that they should have recourse to nearly the same remedies, because no other remedies would meet the evil, supply the want. We will take an example. A man wishes to communicate the idea of speaking: he would say, I spoke, or I will speak, and all men will have the wish to communicate the two ideas; and therefore all men will have these two *tenses* in their grammars. The same argument will apply to all nations, and thus to other cases; thus all grammars or the grammatical construction of all languages will have a certain fundamental likeness, but will vary in some respect according to the degree of refinement to which men have risen when their grammar is formed or completed. But their grammar would become more complicated, as they increased in refinement; and thus the grammatical construction of language among nations would come to vary, and that, in process of time, very greatly. The Hebrew language is a striking exemplification of this. When its sacred book was written, it had formed no present tense: and it still continues in the old language to have none; because its dogma prevents any addition to its sacred writing, locked up in the temple: as the present tense may be very easily dispensed with by using, in the very few instances where it is wanted, a periphrasis, as I spoke *just now*, instead of I speak. Thus we see how the grammars of the different languages of the world, or the different modes of speaking, came to vary very greatly, though there may have been only one spoken or written language at first. The existence of this grammatical difference, and the want of consideration as to the cause of it, have induced learned men to imagine that *languages* have been different. These are the reasons why languages cannot be decided to be different, from the difference of grammatical construction. If two nations, at great distance, who have had little or no connexion, give to a great and a sufficient number of ideas the *same* names, the original identity will be proved; but the difference of names, for the same ideas, will scarcely, in any case, prove the contrary. We see nations adopt new names for ideas every day, forgetting their old ones, even going to the extent of giving to the same words meanings diametrically opposite. For instance, hostis a *host* or *friend*, and hostis an *enemy*. This variation of meaning takes place much more frequently in civilized than in uncivilized nations. Thus I consider all the deductions of learned men against the identity of languages from the grammatical construction of them to be inconclusive, and that my plan of going to the meaning of the names of the letters, to their order and their numerical power, and the identity or similarity of words, is a much more rational and probable mode of proceeding. The fact that all the written languages had the same number of letters, sixteen,—and a certain number of similar words for similar ideas, a numeral meaning, and nearly the *same* numeral meaning attached to each letter, and, in all, the letters arranged in nearly the same order—*proves* that all the languages were the same, and that the division into Semitic and not Semitic is nonsense. Sir W. Jones would never have thought of any such division, if it had not flattered a religious prejudice, viz., as he fancied, the literal meaning of Genesis, which he had declared nothing should induce him to abandon,—therefore he adopted this to bolster it up. After the Hebrews became highly civilized in the schools of Alexandria, &c., they found it necessary to improve their language, and they adopted the points, added a dual, &c., &c., as other nations had done before; but fortunately the dogma preserved the old language and letter in the Synagogue untouched, which assists us greatly in our endeavours to discover the origin of languages.

To return to the identity of written language—what can prove identity? Originally all written languages had the same number of letters. There is every reason to believe that they had originally the same vocal sounds attached to the same letters. They all had the same powers of notation. They were all arranged in the same order; and a careful consideration of Mr. Astle's table will shew, that at one time they all had the same forms. And there is reason to believe that, originally, they were written from the top to the bottom. If these facts do not prove identity, I know nothing that will do it.

I have just now said, that if two nations give to a sufficient number of ideas the same names, identity of language will be proved. In cases of this kind mathematical proof can never be expected; all producible proof resolves itself at last into strong probability. On this subject Dr. Young, in his essay on *Probabilities*, has said, " Nothing whatever could be inferred, with respect " to the relation of two languages, from the coincidence of the sense of any single word in both of " them: that is, supposing the same simple and limited combination of sounds to occur in both, " but to be applied accidentally to the same number of objects without any common links of " connexion: that the odds would only be three to one against the agreement of two words; but " if three words appeared to be identical, it would be more than ten to one that they must be " derived, in both cases, from some parent language, or introduced in some other manner, from a " common source. Six words would give near 1700 chances to one, and *eight* near 100,000: so " that in these last cases the evidence would be little short of absolute certainty." [1]. If this reasoning be applied to the fact stated by Van Kennedy, that 900 Sanscrit words are to be found in Greek, Latin, Persian, German, and English, it surely proves their common descent; and if I prove the descent of one of them from the Hebrew, I prove *it*, also, to have had the same common origin. Now the numbers of English[2] and Greek words which are identical with Hebrew are quite surprising. They are sufficient in each case to prove, according to Dr. Young, absolute identity or common origin. I am quite convinced that all the old languages are the same where-ever the sixteen-letter system is found, unless I except the Sanscrit. *That*, no doubt, is an exception to them all, whether it were formed upon one original, or, as is the more probable, upon a number of languages indiscriminately, those languages having been formed upon *one*— the ancient language of the Buddhists —which I shall shew was probably Hebrew.

In order to form a judgment between the Hebrew and the Sanscrit, learned men must reduce the Hebrew and the Sanscrit to the sixteen *Greek*, or PELASGIC, or *Cadmæan* letters, as nearly as possible, and represent them in English by the similar letters, according to the powers of notation, as pointed out in my table, Prel. Obs. Chap. I. Sect. 47. Having done this, they will be surprised at the number of Sanscrit proper names which are partly or entirely composed of Hebrew words.

The Hebrew and the Greek are admitted to be *radically* the same : then, if Col. Van Kennedy be right in asserting that there are upwards of three hundred Sanscrit words in the poems of Homer, I surely need go no further. If the Sanscrit be the same as the Greek, and the Greek be the same as the Hebrew, the Sanscrit must be the same as the Hebrew. For several reasons it seems to me to be perfectly clear that these Sanscrit words must have come to the West, if they really came from that language, before the Sanscrit was brought to its present perfection. If they had come with the Sanscrit after it was perfected, there can be no doubt that they would have been accompanied by its *fifty* letters, and probably its entire grammar. This consideration seems

---

[1] Kennedy, p. 232.

[2] The following is an example of Hebrew words in the English language, similar to which a list of about 300 may be seen in the Appendix to Roland's Mona Antiqua :

He *is* ישׁ *is*; to draw out דרע *dro*; camel גמל *gml*; heat חח *ht*; sap שׁאף *sap*; fracture פרק *prq*; muck, i. e. manure מק *mk*; myrh מור *mur*; murmur מורמור *murmur*; rear or raw meat רר *rr*; wine יין *iin*; to howl ילל *ill*; bole of a tree בול *bul*; to settle שׁתל *stl*; to shout שׁועת *suot*; many מני *mni*; idea ידע *ido*; mixing, mix מזן *mzn*; mixing, mix מסן *msn*; race רץ *rz*.—Cluverius says, (ap. Casaubon,) that almost a thousand words may be collected in the Hebrew, which may be found in other languages.

to confirm my whole system. For, as the Greek has the Sanscrit words but has not the number of letters, they must have come before its sixteen Cadmæan or Pelasgic letters were increased to *fifty*; that is, they were words of the old language of both countries, before the Sanscrit was invented. I have before shewn, in my Preliminary Observations, that the Hieroglyphics must have been invented by the persons occupying Egypt, after the arrival of the Indians in that country; and I have now shewn that the Sanscrit must have been completed in India, after it had been carried to the West, in its rude state; for I cannot separate its coming to Egypt from its coming to Europe.

I think it expedient, in passing, to avow my firm persuasion, that the remark of Kircher, however he and it may have been, and may be again, ridiculed, will at length be found not to have been made without reasonable grounds, namely, that the Greek system of letters or language was formed in a great measure from the ancient Coptic, or from the parent of the Coptic. We must recollect that Cadmus brought the *sixteen* letters from Phœnicia to Greece; and the Greek authors, as I have formerly shewn, say their Gods had their names from Egypt, the Coptic land; and the Egyptians had theirs from Ethiopia. We shall also find that the Ethiopians had their language from Phœnicia, and it is natural to suppose that they had their Gods and their written language from the same country.

6. A learned writer in the Edinburgh Encyclopedia [1] says, "The Phœnicians, as is generally known, " wrote from right to left, and the old Grecian characters inverted EXACTLY RESEMBLE THE OTHER." Astle's Table, No. I. p. 64, proves the truth of this observation, which being admitted, as it must be, we have the Phœnician, (which was the same with Hebrew and Samaritan,) Hebrew, Coptic, and Greek system of letters, all identical. The histories tell us that the Greek letters came from Phœnicia; that the Greek mythology came from Egypt, the Coptic land—but who tells us, that either Syria or Africa, in *ancient times*, ever took any thing from Greece? But if the reader will attentively consider Mr. Astle's Table, and allow for the different directions of the writing, he will be convinced that ALL the *ancient* sixteen-letter alphabets in that table, have probably been the same. And we shall presently see that the Ethiopian, which is but a dialect of the Coptic, came from Syria, i. e. Phœnicia. But it is not impossible that the Coptic may have been orignally the same as the most ancient right-lined Greek and Etruscan, and have been corrupted or improved by the intermixture of modern Greeks with the Copts, when the former possessed Egypt under the Ptolemies.

The learned Jesuit Kircher, [2] not being able to blind himself to the singular affinity of the Coptic and Greek, supposed that the Greek had been derived from it. This sufficiently proves the affinity; the cause of which is at once satisfactorily explained, by the supposal of a common original. And it is very evident, as the oldest Greek and Etruscan are proved to be the same, that this original must have been the Sanscrit *or the language on which the highly-finished Sanscrit* was principally built; but as I have shewn that it cannot have been the former, it must have been the latter.

Sir W. Drummond has shewn that the Coptic has a close affinity, and is radically allied, to the Hebrew, Chaldee, Arabic, and Ethiopic. He has found seventy examples of Ethiopic terms which have a strict affinity to the Hebrew, and which express articles of the first necessity in common life. He affirms also that the Egyptian deities can be better explained in Hebrew than by modern Coptic. He also says, [3] that most Coptic words, which are not Arabic or Greek, bear a strong affinity to the ancient Syriac, and that the ancient Ethiopian language was very nearly

---

[1] Art. Philology, Sect. 132.　　　[2] See Drummond on a Punic Inscription, p. 45.　　　[3] Ibid. p. 111.

Chaldaic. I am quite certain, from my own observation, that many Egyptian proper names are in reality Hebrew.

All these facts tend strongly, on Dr. Young's system, to prove, that in a very early day, but after these countries were fully peopled, they had a language which was intelligible to them all, as the language of all the counties of England is intelligible to all the inhabitants of Britain.

There certainly appears to be something extraordinary in the well-known fact, that the African Ethiopians should have a style and manner of writing different from that of all other Eastern nations except the Indians—between whose language and theirs Sir William Jones has pointed out several very striking marks of similarity. They both write from the left hand to the right, in the manner of modern Europeans, instead of from right to left, the practice of the Phœnicians, Samaritans, Chaldeans, and other Asiatics. And they annex all the vowels to the consonants, forming a full syllabic system, like ours, but different from that of the nations named above.[1] These facts seem to shew that they have the same origin as the Indians; but yet their language is really Hebrew.

Pliny the Elder says, that the Ionian letters were the oldest of Greece, and that the most ancient Grecian letters were the same as the Etruscan: and he produces the example of an ancient inscription to prove the truth of his assertion. In consequence of this circumstance, the assertion seems more worthy of attention than most of the gossiping stories which that old gentleman collected together. That the Sanscrit or *the language on which that most beautiful system was erected* was the same as the old Latin or Etruscan[2] cannot be doubted. In my CELTIC DRUIDS, Ch. II. Sect. XXV. XXVI. App. p. 304, it is most clearly proved. This traces the written language of the Hellenians, or Ionians, or Athenians, to India, and confirms the assertion which I have made in Book VII., that they were the Indian Yavanas. The Ionians, who came by sea to Argos or Apia, were called Ionian Pelasgi,[3] that is Ionian SAILORS. We have seen that Arcadia[4] was peopled by Ionians; and the Arcadian alphabet is said to have been carried to Tuscany. This is another example of Greek vanity; but it serves to shew, that the same alphabet was to be found in both countries. It was the right-lined alphabet of *sixteen* letters. It is certainly not impossible that Greek sailors may have brought it to Italy, but it most probably came to Greece and Italy from the North-east about the same time.

Dr. Jamieson, in his Hermes Scythicus, says it is an admitted fact that the Latin language is merely the Æolic dialect of the Greek. In the following words[5] he adds what seems to me at once to overturn this " admitted fact :" " This position, however, must be received with the " following limitations : that in many instances it is considerably varied, and that it exhibits some " terms in a more rude form than that in which they appear in Greek, as indicating immediate " derivation from a cognate language far less refined." There can be no doubt of the fact, and this common language must have been that which was spoken by the Ombrici, in Italy; by the Oscans, who had only sixteen letters—reading from right to left—by the people who brought the Sanscrit ceremonies to the temple of Ceres, at Eleusis; and by the people whose groups of figures, on what are called Etruscan vases, exhibit the simplicity of nature in as high a degree as even the simple, unadorned icon of the sable Buddha of India.

Colonel Wilford's observation, that the Sanscrit alphabet, when stripped of its double letters

---

[1] Jones's 8th An. Disc. Asiat. Res.

[2] I consider the Latin language only as an improved Etruscan.

[3] Nimrod, Vol. IV. p. 24.

[4] Arca-di-ia, country of the Diva or Holy Arca, or Agra.

[5] P. 148.

and those peculiar to that language, is the Pelasgic,[1] justifies me in endeavouring to explain by, or in tracing many Sanscrit words to, the cognate old languages, or to that language which must have been the origin of them all; particularly by the Hebrew, which though, even in its present state in the synagogue, not the oldest, probably must be nearly allied to it. Thus, for example, when I find the word *Yapati*, and I learn from Mr. Turner that *pati* means *father* in the Pali or Bali language, I cannot help suspecting this word to mean FATHER IA or IE,[2] more especially as this is confirmed by the use of the word.

The surprising and close affinity between the Sanscrit, Greek, and Latin, cannot for a moment be doubted. Is it not, then, almost a necessary consequence, that the Greeks and Latins would have had the Sanscrit number of letters or some signs of them if the Sanscrit system had been perfected before the connexion between the two countries ceased? The most striking mark of similarity between the two that I know of, and it is very striking and decisive, is that before noticed, as having been pointed out by Col. Wilford, that when the Sanscrit system of letters or alphabet is stripped of the double letters and those peculiar to that language, it is reducible to the sixteen letters of the Pelasgi or of Cadmus. The example which I have produced in my CELTIC DRUIDS shews, that the two (or rather the one or united) systems must have been brought as languages to considerable perfection when they came to Italy.

Sir W. Jones has observed,[3] that the inscriptions of Canarah, in the island of Salcette, are compounded of Nagari and Æthiopic characters, which bear a close analogy to one another, not only in the singular manner of connecting the vowels with the consonants, but in the very striking fact that they are both written from the left hand to the right. Thus, in fact, the ancient system of letters of India and Ethiopia may be considered the same, notwithstanding their great distance and the intervention of so many other nations lying between them.[4]

Bardisanes Syrus[5] gives this account of the Indians: " Among the Indians and Bactrians " there are many thousand men called Brachmanes. These, as well from the tradition of their " fathers as from laws, neither worship images nor eat what is animate: they never drink wine or " beer: they are far from all malignity, attending wholly on God." Philostratus[6] says, " that in " his time the chief of the Brahmins was called Iarch, and Jerom *contra Jovin* says, the head of " the Gymnosophists was called Buddas."[7] Mr. Bryant says, " Nilus the Egyptian tells Apollo- " nius Tyannæus, that the Indi of all people in the world were the most knowing, and that the " Ethiopians were a colony from them, and resembled them greatly. Philostratus says, the Indi " are the WISEST of all mankind. The Ethiopians are a colony from them, and they inherit the " *wisdom* of their forefathers."[8]

Gale[9] observes, on the authority of Philostratus, in the life of Apollonius and of Jerom,[10] that the philosophers of Ethiopia were called Gymnosophists, and that they received their name and philo-sophy from India.

Arrian says,[11] the inhabitants upon the Indus are in their looks and appearance not unlike the Ethiopians. Those upon the southern coast resemble them the most; for they are very black; and their hair is also black; but they are not so flat-nosed, nor have they woolly hair. They, who are more to the North, have a greater resemblance to the Egyptians.[12] I learn from travellers that the Afghans have black hair, and a dark Jewish cast of countenance.

---

[1] Asiat. Res. Vol. VIII. p. 265.  [2] Ibid. p. 255.  [3] Ibid. Vol. I. p. 424.
[4] Vide Maur. Ant. Ind. Vol. IV. pp. 414—417.  [5] In Euseb. Præpar. Evang. Lib. vi. Cap. viii.
[6] Lib. iii. in vitâ Apol. Tyan.  [7] Gale, Court of Gent. Book II. p. 74.
[8] Anal. Anc. Myth. Vol. III. p. 219.  [9] Court of Gent. Vol. II. p. 75.
[10] Lib. iv. in Ezech. Cap. xiii.  [11] Hist. Indica, p. 320.  [12] Bryant, Vol. III. p. 211.

Diodorus Siculus says, that the rites in Egypt and Ethiopia had a great resemblance, so as to be nearly the same.[1] But they were also very similar to the Indian. The priests in each were recluse, and given to celibacy. Here we have the Buddhist monks. They alike used the tonsure, and wore a garment of linen; and they carried in their hands a sceptre or staff, which, at the top, had τυπον αϱοτϱοειδη, *the representation of a plough.*[2] This plough-shaped staff was clearly the same as that now borne by Bala-Rama, near Maturea in Indian. It is the old, first-invented plough; it was, in form, not unlike the pastoral crook, and I have little doubt that at last it grew into the crozier, which, with the rosary and cross, is seen over the triple-faced God in the cave of Elephanta.

The use of the tonsure, by both Indian Buddhists of Tibet, and African Ethiopians, is a striking circumstance; and the prohibition of it, by Moses, as one contrivance to separate his people from their neighbours or ancestors,—as it proves that they once had it, tends to prove the original identity of the three nations. Quintus Curtius, in his account of Alexander's march into Upper India, says, Gens, ut Barbari credunt, sapientiâ excellit, bonisque moribus regitur.

7. "The most venerable emigrants from India were the Yadavas; they were the blameless and " pious Ethiopians, whom Homer mentions and calls the remotest of mankind. Part of them, say " the old Hindoo writers, remained in this country, and hence we read of two Ethiopian nations, " the Western and the Oriental: some of them lived far to the East, and they are the Yadavas " who stayed in India; while others resided far to the West, and they are the sacred race who " settled on the shores of the Atlantic.[?] We are positively assured by Herodotus, that the Orien- " tal Ethiopians were Indians, and hence we may infer, that India was known to the Greeks, in " the age of Homer, by the name of Eastern Ethiopia."[3] I request my reader to refer to Book I. Ch. IV. Col. Wilford has stated that there are many traditions in India, that the Iadavas emi- grated to Abyssinia.[4] " *About this time,*" says Eusebius,[5] " *some Ethiopians, taking leave of their* " *country upon the river Indus, came and settled in Egypt.* Hence it is that Bacchus[6] has been " represented as the son of the river Indus. Hence arose also the true notion that the Indian " Dionusos was the most ancient: Διονυσον αϱχαιοτατον ΙΝΔΟΝ γεγονεναι." Plutarch[7] tells us, that Phylarchus said, that Bacchus first brought the worship of the two Boves called Apis and Osiris, from India into Egypt. Πϱωτος εις Αιγυπτον εξ Ινδων Διονυσος ηγαγε δυω Βυς, τω μεν Απις ονομα, τω δε Οσιϱις.[8] I entertain a strong suspicion that these Boves were the horned male and female Osiris and Isis, not Apis, for Apis was nothing but another name for Osiris.

Sir William Drummond[9] says, " We find in the language of the Copts, of which I have already " spoken, that many words, I might say most, which are not Arabic or Greek, bear a strong affi- " nity to the ancient Syriac, and consequently they may be supposed to have belonged to the " ancient Egyptian. The ancient Ethiopian language was *very nearly Chaldaic,* as we have " already seen." Ludolf says, that the African Ethiopic has a close affinity to the Chaldee, Syriac, and Arabic, and that the roots of many Hebrew words are only to be found in it. We have seen that Sir W. Jones confirmed this,[10] which is a very important observation. This is also confirmed by Mr. Bruce, who has made the very just remark respecting the Hebrew and African Ethiopic languages, " that a very great number of words are found throughout the Old " Testament, that have really no root, nor can be derived from any Hebrew origin, and yet all " have in the Ethiopic a plain, clear, unequivocal origin, to and from which they can be traced

---

[1] Lib. iii. Cap. i.      [5] Bryant, Anal. Vol. III. p. 246.      [3] Maur. Hist. Hind. II. p. 262.
[4] Asiat. Res. Vol. III. pp. 328, &c.      [5] Chron. p. 26.      [6] Philostrat. vita Apollonii, Lib. i. p. 64.
[7] Isis et Osiris, Vol. II. p. 362.      [8] Bryant, Anal. Anc Myth. Vol. III. p. 213.
[9] On Punic Inscrip. p. 111.      [10] Townsend, Veracity of Moses, p. 421.

" without force or difficulty."[1]   Mr. Bruce afterward observes, that the Geez or Ethiopic has a close affinity to the Arabic.

8. There is something very contradictory and unaccountable in the description given by Mr. Bruce of the Falasha, a tribe of Abyssinian Jews, who are stated by him to be sufficiently numerous to bring 100,000 men into the field. They have no copy of the Pentateuch in their language, or in the Hebrew or Samaritan ; but only one borrowed from the Geez, and probably translated from the LXX. by Christians in modern times. Although they have many Jewish customs, yet there are some wanting among them, the want of which is difficult to be accounted for, on the supposition that they are Mosaic Jews. They have no scribes, nor fringes, nor ribbands, on their garments, which they must have had if they had descended from the Jews of Moses.[2] They do not speak the present Jewish language, nor that of the Synagogue. They are desirous of being thought to be descended from Solomon and the Queen of Sheba ; but they are called by the other tribes Bet-Israel, which may mean to allude to the ancestors of Solomon, even to the grandson of Abraham. From the whole of the accounts of Ludolf and Bruce,[3] it seems probable that, like the Jews of India, they had no Pentateuch till they received it from modern Jews or Christians, in the time of Frumentius, a Christian bishop.

The ancients constantly called the country above the Egyptian cataracts *India*, and its inhabitants *Indians*. This is strikingly confirmatory of my hypothesis, that they came from India.[4] No one can suppose the Greek authors, from whom we have this account, to have made a mistake, and to have believed the country *South* of Thebes, was the country *East* of the Euphrates. It therefore follows that they must have been called *Indians* because they were known or believed to have come from India. The words in the Hebrew language we must recollect are not always syllabic ; but yet it is the same language as the Arabic, the near neighbour of the African Ethiopians.

### ETHIOPIC LETTERS.

It is impossible to read the names of the Ethiopic letters in *Astle*[5] as they stand in order, and not to see that though varied in shape they are really Hebrew. They have nearly the same names and stand in the same order. The following are the letters with their names, taken from Astle and the Universal History, as nearly the same in form as can be had in London.

| | | |
|---|---|---|
| አ Alpf....A. | ጠ Tait....Teth. Heb. | ፈ Af....F. |
| በ Bet ....B. | የ Jaman ..J. | ጸ Tzadi..Heb. |
| ገ Geml ..G. | ኸ Caf ....Ch. | ቀ Kopp..K. |
| ደ Dent ..D. | ለ Lawy ..L. | ረ Rees ..R. |
| ሐ Haut ..H. | መ Mai ....M. | ሠ Saut ..S. |
| ወ Waw ..W. | ነ Nahas ..N. | ተ Tawi..T. |
| ዘ Zai ....Z. | ሰ Saat ....S. C. | |
| ሐ Hharm ..H. H. | ዐ Ain ....Heb. | |

But it is necessary to observe, that there is a clerical error in the seventh and eighth letters being substituted for each other, but I have copied them exactly.

---

[1] Book ii. Ch. iii.     [2] See Numb. xv. 38, 39 ; Deut. xxii. 12.     [3] B. ii. Ch. vi.
[4] Univers. Hist. Vol. XVIII. p. 252.     [5] Origin and Progress of Writing, Ch. V. p. 90.

Ludolfus spent sixty years in the study of the Hebrew, Syriac, Arabic, and African Ethiopic languages; and he declares that their affinity is so close, that whoever understands *one* may, without difficulty, make himself master of the other; but, that the African Ethiopic is the nearest, as we might reasonably expect, to the Arabic. [1]

I think a moment's consideration must shew that the alphabet which I have given is, in reality, the same as the Hebrew and Samaritan. I speak not of the shapes of the letters, because their dissimilarity of shape in my mind does very little affect the question—the reason for which I shall give hereafter. The English written language has only one alphabet, but that alphabet has three different forms—GAD, gad, *gad*. This alphabet, as I have before observed, is not used always syllabically by the Hebrews; but it is so used by the African Ethiopians, the same as the Sanscrit. This proves the truth of what I have published in my Celtic Druids, and in the Classical Journal, Vol. XXXIII., viz. that the vowels are in the Hebrew, as really as in our language, though omitted in many words; where I refute the nonsense about their antiquity, contended for by the Mazorets, who generally render them mute, and often convert them into consonants, thereby forming, in fact, a new alphabet. With respect to the *vowels* the Celtic and Hebrew are both the same, as I have also observed in the Celtic Druids. The learned though prejudiced writer in the Encyclopædia Britannica, art. Philology, noticed a little time ago, says, " The Phœnicians wrote from " right to left, *and the old Grecian characters inverted exactly resemble the other.* [2] Besides, the " names of the Cadmean characters are Syrian, (Scaliger,) which shews the near resemblance be- " tween that language and the Phœnician. They stand thus : alpha, betha, gamla, delta, &c. " The Syrians used to add *a* to the Hebrew vocables : hence *alph* becomes *alpha*, *beth betha* or " *beta*, &c. In the Cadmean alphabet we find the vowel letters, which is an infallible proof that " this was the practice of the Phœnicians in the time of Cadmus : and this very circumstance " furnishes a presumption that the Jews did the same thing at the same period." [3]

But Mr. Mitford, in his History, has made a very important observation; namely, that the vowels were originally often omitted in the Greek, [4] as well as in the Hebrew, language, and this entirely does away with the point of Scaliger's observation. But the Hebrew system of letters, which answered to the Cadmæan *sixteen*, had vowels—Aleph, He, Vau, Iod, and Oin, though not used in very many words and syllables. The vowels were really always in use both in the Hebrew and the Greek, though only partially. In the Ethiopic they were used fully, as with us. This was an improvement upon the first system. The author of the Encyclopædia runs away with the old fancy, that they had no vowels at first, and then he infers because the language had vowels in the time of Cadmus, the full syllabic system must have been once in use, and afterward laid aside, which is by no means a necessary consequence. The contrary was the fact; they were at first seldom used, (for a reason which I shall explain hereafter in a future book,) and added as written language improved. The written language was defective without them. Mr. Bosworth, in his Saxon Grammar,[5] has proved the ancient Greek written from right to left to be nothing but the ancient Phœnician. And Dr. O'Connor in the same book [6] has proved the Phœnician to be Samaritan and Canaanitish.

---

[1] Univers. Hist. Vol. XVIII. p. 286.

[2] Cadmus was the name of a nation. (See Montfaucon, Paleog. Gr. Lib. ii. 117, Ed. fol.) The Thebans were called Καδμειος by Homer. By Joshua a nation of Phœnicians was called קדמוני *Qdmuni*, Cadmonii. The Hebrew name of *Cadmus* was קדם *Qdm*.

[3] Sect. 133, p. 536. The strongest presumption is also raised, that the numeral powers of the Cadmean or Greek letters must have been the same as the Hebrew : then the P would have stood for 200, which completely justifies my explanation of the staff of Osiris :  Ρ Ρ =600 and 608.

[4] See end of Section 4—Χρυς, Χρης, ΧΡΕ.                    [5] P. 11.                    [6] P. 23.

This, added to what I have said above, easily accounts for Kircher's deriving his Greek from Coptic. It is evident both having drawn from the Phœnician, whence must also have come the African Ethiopian. In all my speculations I consider the Hebrew and the Celtic to be but dialects of a common language, or of one another. General Vallancey has completely proved that the old Irish or Celtic is Phœnician—that is, in fact, Hebrew, for they cannot as languages be separated. The same learned writer in the Encyclopædia Britannica, on Philology, [1] says, " We have seen a ma-" nuscript in the hands of a private person, where the first twelve verses of the Iliad are carefully " analyzed; and it appears, to our satisfaction, that almost every word may be, and actually is, " traced back to a Hebrew, Phenician, Chaldean, or Egyptian original ; and we are convinced the " same process will hold good in the like manner in verses taken from any of the most celebrated " poets of Greece." This goes to prove all the languages the same. There was one original, from which they all diverged like the spokes of a wheel. The farther you go back from the circle, the nearer they come together. The following judicious observation is made by the same author : " Abraham, the Hebrew, travelled among the Chaldeans, the Canaanites, the Philistines, and the " Egyptians, and seemed to converse with them all with ease." Now this is what may easily have happened according to my theory. The dialects may not have varied enough in his time to have rendered them totally unintelligible to him. If they were *nearly* unintelligible to him and his tribe—in 400 years more, in the time of Moses, they may have become *totally* unintelligible. This is quite time enough to effect the change. Judging from what the learned Ludolf has said respecting the ease with which a person would acquire all the remainder of these languages after having learnt one of them ; I cannot doubt that the observation in the Encyclopædia is well-founded. If the example of Joseph's speaking to his brethren by means of an *interpreter* be pleaded against me, I reply, some very learned persons have maintained that by that text merely a mediator—a sort of chamberlain or introducer to the presence of the great man, but not an inter-preter—was meant. See Mr. Bellamy's Bible, and the notes. In the African Ethiopic language, we have the Synagogue Hebrew, reading syllabically and from left to right. When we couple this with the practice of the Sanscrit, and the history of its owners the African Ethiopians as coming from India, I cannot entertain much doubt that it was the ancient language before they left India. Then they must have come away before the Sanscrit was completed, to fifty letters, unless it was a secret language. It is a most important observation made [2] by Ludolfus, that the roots of many Arabic and Hebrew words are only to be found in the African Ethiopic language. All this tends to render it probable that the Gymnosophists brought it by way of Arabia, to Meroe, or the Mount Meru of African Ethiopia ; formerly the capital of the country, where the Greek authors say all the learning of the Egyptians came from, where it now remains, in some respects less changed than in Asia, owing probably to its secluded situation.

If the African Ethiopian had become known, and the Sanscrit were invented by the priests to conceal their mythos from the common people, a reason may be found for the Sanscrit to have been formed before the Ethiopians came away. The Universal History has clearly proved the identity of the African Ethiopic and the Arabic.

9. But the Arabians might readily be a tribe from the nation of that name which are found to have been seated in India on the coast between the river Indus and the river Arabus. [3] This easily accounts for their places and rivers having the same names as the sacred rivers and places in India : for example, Suraseni or Saracens ; and the existence of an Indian Arabia in this particular

---

[1] Sect. VII. p. 547.    [2] Univers. Hist. Vol. XVIII. p. 287.
[3] Arrian, Hist. Hind. Cap. xxi.; Nimrod, Vol. I. p. 116.

latitude and longitude is a most important fact, on which I shall have much to say hereafter, [1] It is in the country where the Ioudi came from, of which Oude, or Ioud-ia, was the capital. The kingdom of Ioudia extended to the Indus. From the name of the Arabians and other circumstances which an attentive reader must perceive, I suppose they were a separate tribe from the Jews, who came from nearly the same country : because their name ערב-אי orb-ia, means *country of the West*. Their first home was on the Indus, and I think they have had their name given them by the natives of Oude or Youdia or by the Eastern Jews, to whom in their native country they were Westerns ; and when both tribes migrated, they kept their name. Our Jews were one tribe, the Arabians were another, of the same nation. If I be right in my idea that the Arabians were a tribe, like the Jews, from Afghanistan or Central India, they might be expected, even before the time of Mohamed, to have received the mythos which we have found in India ; and it is manifest that they *had*, because they had statues of Abraham, Noe, &c., in their temple of Mecca. Thus their mythos is in keeping with the other circumstances. But this is strengthened by what has been observed by Stukeley,[2] that there were *two Arabias*—the Egyptian and the Asiatic, as even appears from Homer, Strabo, and Pliny. The *Egyptian* were nothing but the *peninsular* Arabians. They were originally the same, and had the same language.

The Western Arabians had the same mythos as the other nations, which may be perceived in their pretended history. Their principal kingdom was called Hamyar—the natives were called, by the Greeks, Om-erites. Ham-yar is Omaria. Aria is the Arabic or Hebrew word ארץ arz, softened into aretsia, aressia, aria, ia. This is the origin of the title Al Hareth of the Arabian kings. [3] It meant *of the country of*. Many of their kings were said to be Jews, and they had Judæan names, that is, names arising among the Jews after the time of Abraham, therefore probably names of the tribe of Ioudi from India. It is said by them that Solomon's Sheba was from their country. [4] " That SAMARKAND was built by one of the Hamyaritic kings, surnamed Tobba, seems to be " agreed upon by the best of the Eastern writers."[5] In old Samarkand, coins are constantly dug up with Cufic letters on them.[6] The Jerusalem Targum states the Ishmaelites and the Saracens to be the same people : and Pococke states the word Saraceni to mean *oriental.*[7] There was a town called Ishmael, near the Indus. The earliest tribes of Arabia, who are called the *lost ones*, had the names of AD, Thamûd, Tasm, JADIS.[8] These are Indian names. To the natives of Oude *Ishmaelistan* would be properly called ערב orb or Western. The Arabic sea is called *Suph* and *Edom*. The first is *sea of* Σοφ, צוף zup, *sea of wisdom ;* the second, *Ad-om*. Ad was די di dis, and Om, the Holy Om.

No doubt there are many persons who will think the story of the Queen of Sheba's journey to Jerusalem, and her return with the Jewish religion, satisfactory. But yet there are several circumstances which this story does not account for ; and, therefore, however true this story may be, yet some other cause must be looked for to account for the Jews in Abyssinia; and one is, their Hebrew language being syllabic, and its reading, like the Sanscrit, from left to right. Another is, their descendants' ruling the country but having no Pentateuch. To account for this, I can imagine no cause except that which, at great length, I assigned in the last book, viz. a colony from the Judæa or Oude of Central India. Oude is spelt *Ajewdheya* by Gladwin in the Ayeen Akbery, [9] and in the Mahabarat it is called *Adjudea ;* [10] that is, Holy Judea.

The state of the Temple at Mecca in the time of Mohamed, as handed down to us on the best

---

[1] They are supposed by Nimrod to have been Omerites, that is, followers of *the sacred* OM.
[2] Palœg. Sac. No. I. p. 10.     [3] Univ. Hist. Vol. XVIII. p. 436.     [4] Ibid. p. 421.     [5] Ib.
[6] Ib.     [7] Ib. p. 369.     [8] Ib. p. 370.     [9] Vol. III. p. 255.
[10] Hodges' Travels in India, p. 105.

authorities, strongly tends to support my theory. It was not Mosaic Jewish, it was not Christian, but it contained, as I have before remarked, images of the patriarchs of the Israelites. These probably came from India with the tribe.[1]

Col. Van Kennedy has noticed the affinity between the Hebrew and Arabic. I have never met with any person who understood the two languages who denied it. He says, " that Hebrew, both " in its words and its grammatical structure, bears so intimate an affinity to Arabic, as to render " it highly probable that they are both merely dialects of that language which was spoken by the " race of men by whom Arabia and Syria were originally peopled."[2]

No doubt in adducing proofs of my theory from so remote a country, I shall be accused of travelling too far; but the circumstances I leave to my reader. Near the source of the Nile, there is a valley called St. George. (For this *Saint* I have never been able satisfactorily to account, though I think I have read most of what has been said about him.) Through the middle of this valley runs the river Jemna, (*query*, the Jumna or Jamuna of India, or the Yamuna of Arabia?) which loses itself near the town of *Samseen*, (*query*, or Sams-on, the generative power of the Sun?) after crossing a district called *Ma-itsha*. It rises in hills called *Amid-amid*. Mr. Bruce thinks these hills were the Montes Lunæ. In this he is probably right, but I suspect that they were also Montes Solumi, like those of India;—Mounts of the אמד *amd* prophesied of by Haggai, and the united terms meaning *Mounts of Salvation*, Mount Sions. Near this is another river called *Iworra*. There is also a hill called *Sacale*.[3] The singularity of the names did not escape Mr. Bruce. On those of the *rivers*, he says, "We crossed a clear river called *Dee-ohha* or the river Dee. It is " singular to observe the agreement of the names of rivers in different parts of the world that have " never had communication together. The Dee is a river in the North of Scotland; the Dee runs " through Cheshire; and the Dee is a river here in Abyssinia! Kelti is the name of a river in " Monteith; Kelti, too, we find in Maitsha. Arno is a river in Tuscany, and the name of a " river below Emfras, falling into the Lake *Tzana*." (Qy. Zoan?)[4] In the first of the names, Dee-ohha, the *ohha* is found in the old English name for a piece of water, *e. g.* the old *œea* near Doncaster. Here we have mixed etymologies again. Near the source of the river is a church called *Eion Mariamo*. We shall be told, it is so called after the Virgin, as churches in Greece, which were formerly temples of the God Ἥλιος, are now called after the prophet Elias. The Eion, the same name as the town formerly Iona, at the mouth of the sacred river Strymon, in Thrace, satisfies me where the name came from. There is also a district, of

---

[1] Mr. Saylé gives the following account of the worship of large stones by the Arabians: "Several of their idols, as " Manah in particular, were no more than large rude stones, the worship of which the posterity of Ismael first intro- " duced; for as they multiplied, and the territory of Mecca grew too strait for them, great numbers were obliged to " seek new abodes; and on such migrations it was usual for them to take with them some of the stones of that reputed " holy land, and set them up in the places where they fixed; and these stones they at first only compassed out of " devotion, as they had accustomed to do the Caaba. But this at last ended in rank idolatry, the Ismaelites forgetting " the religion left them by their father so far as to pay divine worship to any fine stone they met with." Al Mostatraf, al Jannabi. Sayle Kor. Prel. Dis. p 27. When my reader recollects that the stones at Mecca, round the Caaba, were 360 in number, the same as those at Iona; the practice of the Druids, in the Deisul, and all the other strong traits of similarity between their rites, &c., and those of the children of Israel, he can hardly fail to be much surprised. There is a tradition that the *green* inner and smaller stones of Stonehenge, came from Africa. Is this possible? Those which are the smaller stones, are not of a size to preclude removal with moderate labour. I can entertain little doubt that the *first* temple at Mecca was of very great antiquity, and consisted, like the temple of Joshua on Gerizim, of a circle of rude stones.

[2] P. 32.          [3] Qy. Scala, or Xaca, or Saca? On this word much will be said hereafter.

[4] Vol. V. Ch. XII. The Editor of Bruce's work, Dr. Murray, makes a note PROFOUNDLY WISE upon this passage, that his reader may not be misled, for which he can never be too thankful, and gravely informs him, that the identity of names arises from accident!

large extent, called Bah-Iouda. No doubt all these names came from Arabia, brought by the Gymnosophists, when they brought the names of Wed Baal-anagga,[1] the town of Mandera (the cycle), the river Astaboras,[2] the Jumna or Yamuna, &c., &c., to the sacred island of MEROE, the ancient capital of Ethiopia, which, Mr. Bruce observes, has once been the fountain whence the learning and science of Egypt flowed. In this I quite agree with him; for I think Egypt was peopled from Abyssinia, and the latter from Arabia; and that it was, in part, by this circuitous route, the customs were derived which are found to be similar to those of the Ioudi of Syria: and they came by this route, because I believe at that time the Delta of Egypt did not exist above water, and the Isthmus of Suez was a morass: the reasons for this opinion may be seen in Book VI. Ch. I. On the East coast of Arabia there are a city and a river called Ommanum or Ammon. In the island of Meroe, Pliny says, there was a *temple* to Ammon; in Syria, also, there was a *town* called Ammon; in Syria, too, was the well-known Mount Libanus; and near to the Amon or Oman of the East, was the Libano-tophoros of Ptolemy.[3] The Eastern Ommanum is now *Nissuwa*, in the district of Oman. The *Nissi* is its old name of Bacchus. Not far from Meroe, (that is, a Meru, or an il-a-vratta, or[4] Ararat,) to the south is a plain called Senaar. This I call Shinar. These places I apprehend received their names when names were given to the temples of Solumi or Solomon. In Egypt, to Gize or Gaza, once the sea-port of Memphis—and to Thebes, or the city of תבה *The* or the cow, or Tibet, also in Egypt—and to TROY or Ter-ia, and Mount Troicus, and Tripoly, and to the Memnon, the same as the Memnon of the city of Susa in Persia; and to Çusa that is Susa—and to Babylon—and to Cercasura, Cercesura, or Clissobora.

Great numbers of towns in India are called Abad. This seems to be the same word as that used in the name of the fourteen Mahabads, who, we are told, lived before the flood: but I suppose it means the *abode* of, as Moorshed-abad, the abode or residence of Moorshed; or Amid-abad, the abode of Amid. I can scarcely doubt that the *abad*, when meaning *town*, is the English word *abode*. The recesses in the temples in which the icons of their Gods are placed are called Stalla: these are the stalls of our stables, and of the canons or prebendaries in our cathedrals. The towns at the mouths of rivers are often called *patam*, as Masulipatam or Kistna-patam: this means *town of Potamos* or *the river* Masuli or Kistna. Thus we find the Sanscrit names consist of words from all languages. All these places received their names before the great catastrophe took place in the valley of Sodom,[5] which is described in its own peculiar way, by parable, in Genesis. This catastrophe, it is probable, destroyed the communication between the Dead Sea and the Red Sea, by means of what Mr. Burckhardt has shewn was formerly a river or arm of the sea, but which is now a fertile valley.[6] At the time here spoken of, the Delta of Egypt did not exist; or it was probably a swamp, together with the country between the Western branch of the Red Sea, the Lacus Amari, and the Pelusiac branch of the Nile; or they might be like the Sunderbunds of India, whether covered or not with wood; but, in fact, *almost* if not *entirely* impassable. In these times were made or built the Pyramids of Egypt, the caves of Ellora, the walls of Argos and Tyrins, the Cloaca Maxima of Rome, and the temples of Stonehenge and Iona. These were the times of the Pandæan empire or sacred or golden age. The buildings were Cyclo-pæan, and the builders Cyclopes, but not one-eyed Cyclops. Of the Cyclopes I shall soon treat.

I beg my reader to turn to Book V. Ch. VI. Sect. 3, and to reconsider the Hercules or Bala Rama; and to Book V. Ch. XI. Sect. 7, and to reconsider Divine Wisdom or Minerva, with the

---

[1] Qy. Snake-headed Baal?     [2] Qy. Clyssabora?     [3] Τοπος, district of, Libanus.

[4] Mount of *il* or *al*-a-vratta, *i. e. of God the Creator*, בראת *brat*.     [5] שד *sd*, עם *om*, Plain of OM.

[6] This was the residence of the tribe of Ioudi, after it left Egypt, for perhaps *forty* years; it is now well peopled, though called, in Genesis, *a desert*—probably meaning merely a country of pasturage.

tree loaded with fruit, and the serpent. He will at once see that this is but a slightly-varied version of the history or allegory of the second book of Genesis; but he must see that it is the same story: he must also perceive that it is not a copy. Let him then consider, in Book V. Chap. XI. Sect. 6, the account of the Tree of Life, as reported by Wilson, in Nubia; and a similar example in South India, noticed in Book VIII. Chap. II. Sect. 7.

Sir William Jones has noticed several inscriptions in India, in characters very similar to those of the ancient African Ethiopian. I have said that I think the Arabian-Ethiopic Hebrew the oldest language. There is yet another reason to be assigned in support of this opinion, which is, the amazing extent of country over which this language is spread. It seems an unquestionable fact, arise from what cause it may, that all *nomade* tribes of the earth have used and do yet use the Arabic language, or one which has evidently been corrupted from it, and which is so near it that a person speaking Arabic is understood by them, although with difficulty. What can be more striking than the fact, already noticed, but which I shall discuss more fully by and by, that the Turks, coming from the North-east of the Caspian Sea, brought with them to Europe and Arabia, a language containing *ten* out of *twelve* of its words Arabic? How is it that almost all the wandering tribes of Africa have always spoken Arabic, the language of Moses and of Job? In the character of *nomade tribes* there seems something favourable to the retention of language, which it is difficult to account for.

It appears from Neuman's Chronicle of Armenia,[1] (note 31 on page 34,) that the Turks and Arabians had both originally the same name of Tadjik, which is also the name of the people of Bochara. This shews us where the tribe of Arabia came from, and the reason why ten out of twelve of the words in the Turkish language are Arabic. I apprehend the word Tad is Tat, the name of Buddha.

From all these considerations I draw the conclusion, that the Synagogue Hebrew and Sanscrit are both children of a common sixteen-letter parent, (vide CELTIC DRUIDS, Chap. II. Sect. XXV. XXVI.,) and that this is the reason why so many of the Sanscrit proper names are so obviously similar to the Hebrew names. It follows from all this, that the emigration of the tribe of Juda from India, must have taken place before the Sanscrit was completed. This will place it so early as to startle the prejudices of many persons. I know nothing of chronology except, *first*, that before the æra of about the Babylonish captivity, it cannot be depended on; and, *secondly*, except with respect to about the *supposed* times of the entrance of the sun at the vernal equinox into Taurus and Aries. The Brahmin tribe, called the tribe of Iouda, may have dwelt several, perhaps many, centuries in the central parts of Asia, before it came into Western Syria.[2] In short, it is very certain that the Ethiopians received their language from India. The two facts—that it reads from *left* to *right*, and that it is always syllabic, so different from all the other Western Asiatic languages, absolutely and independently of the written documents I have adduced to the same effect, prove it. It might be about the time of the Cali Yug when the Brahmins suppose that the equinox first fell in Aries, that they formed their language—perhaps for the sake of separating themselves from the Buddhists. The Pali is the language of many of the Buddhists, but they do not seem, like the Brahmins, to have had an exclusively sacred and unspoken language. And therefore their languages must be expected to have changed like all others; like that of our sacred book,

---

[1] A work published in 1831, by the Oriental Translation Society.

[2] In Syria it found its own sectaries—the Syriæ or Soors—under Melchizedek, who had not then been corrupted by the heresy of the Assyriæ or Assoors. It may have dwelt many hundred years among the people of the Assoor religion, the Assyrians, as it did among the Egyptians afterward, before it quitted Egypt. Syria and Assyria might be, as I have before intimated, only *sectarian* terms.

the Bible; read it in the English of 300 years ago, and read it now; and how is it already changed!

If the real Sanscrit be the language of the earliest of the Vedas, it seems not to have escaped the effects of time, to which all other spoken languages have been subjected; for, it is asserted by various learned men, that the first Vedas are very different from those of later date, and from the Puranas; and, that it is, in fact, very difficult even for very learned Brahmins to make out their meaning. But it was probably perfected by degrees, like all other languages. The Brahmin priests may have formed their sacred language to separate themselves from the caste of the kings or soldiers, (who were first their generals and afterward their masters,) as well as from the Buddhists.

It is very generally believed by both the Indians and Persians, that the earliest Vedas were handed down by tradition till a certain time; that they were then collected together and put into writing, but in a language which is now lost. Yet some say they were not handed down by tradition—though first written in a language now lost.[1] This would prove the Sanscrit a more recently-formed language than the originals of the Hindoo books. However persons who are prejudiced against oriental literature may run down the learned and honest Wilford, because he was once the dupe of a knavish priest, (an accident to which every individual at one time or other of his life may have been subject,) yet I believe no one will doubt his knowledge of the Sanscrit language, and it was his matured and deliberate opinion that it was reducible to the sixteen original Pelasgic or Cadmæan letters. This fact operates with the greatest weight upon my mind. The unprejudiced reader must see, I think, that all these facts and reasonings powerfully corroborate my opinion, that the Hebrew, or some cognate dialect very closely allied to it, was the original language. If the Samaritan or Hebrew were the system of writing used by the tribe of Ioudi or emigrants from *Oude*, its having become a sacred language, secured in the adytum of the temple, will account for its remaining similar to the old Sanscrit, as described above, and for its having undergone little or no change.

After much reflection and examination of the scattered circumstances of antiquity, I think there is reason to believe, that the art of writing was at first kept as a secret, or Masonic mystery, by the priests for many generations, and that after it once became known, various contrivances were adopted to restore its character of secrecy. Hieroglyphics was one of them : a second, probably, was the artificial Sanscrit—which was, in great part, founded on the Hebrew, or was its son or brother; (vide CELTIC DRUIDS, Chap. II. Sect. XXVI.;) and being intended by the priests for their own caste alone, they made its common words deviate as much as possible from the original, if they do so deviate, so that the Hebrew can now only be discovered in the names of places, and rivers, and Gods : but *there* it is very perceptible. All the roots of Hebrew and of the ancient natural languages have meanings; but on the Sanscrit, Col. Van Kennedy[2] says, as I mentioned in the last book, ".The roots of the Sanscrit have in themselves no signification, and " require several changes before they can be conjugated even as verbs: and the derivation from " ther of other words is often so forced and unsatisfactory, as to render it evident that the roots " could not have been a constituent part of the original language." Again, " It is, therefore, the " structure of Sanscrit which so peculiarly distinguishes it from other languages, and which " impresses on it a character of originality which cannot be disputed; for it contains no exotic " terms, and, though I have before observed that its roots are evidently the work of grammarians " and not a constituent part of the language, still its words shew that they have been all formed " solely by the people who spoke it, according to some well-known principle."[3]

---

[1] Key to Chron. Vol. I. pp. 6, 261; Vol. II. pp. 120, 127, 128.  [2] Res. p. 30.  [3] Ibid. p. 193.

In the above extracts there is quite enough to account for the paucity of Hebrew words in the Sanscrit. And if gentlemen do not strip their Hebrew of its modern corruptions, and reduce it to the Synagogue standard, and also as near as possible to the sixteen original letters, it is not wonderful that they find few or no marks of similarity. Reduce the Hebrew to the simple system laid down in my Table, and in the names of God and other proper names, and many more marks of similarity will be seen than could be expected—such as the YEYE, &c., &c. The fact noticed by Col. Van Kennedy, that the roots of Sanscrit are almost all artificial, the work of grammarians, but formed upon an old *spoken* language, leaves ample room for the old language, probably the old African Ethiopian with its deva-nagari letters in the cave at Salcette, to have had many Hebrew roots. It may be, on this account, that we now meet with few Hebrew words in the Sanscrit, except in proper names of persons and places. But when I meet with different persons, evidently mythological, bearing the same name, I must believe that there has been a connexion between the nations by whom that *same* designation was assigned.

10. It is clear that the African Ethiopic and Arabic have originally been identical. But, as might be expected, in process of time, both have undergone some change—one in one way, the other in another. I take the African Ethiopic to furnish an example of the old language of the Indian Mesopotamia, after it had increased to twenty-two letters, and in this state it probably came to Western Asia, brought by a tribe of Ioudi. Here the Ioudi would find the Arabian, used by former emigrants, nearly similar to their own language, but consisting of the original twenty-eight letters which we now find. Out of these the sixteen letters had been selected by the tribes who came from India before the letters were increased to twenty-two. In refutation of this theory I cannot attend to any nonsensical fancies of chronologists.

If the circular temples be ascertained to be, as Reuben Burrow and I think they were, *Buddhist*, the number of the stones in cycles and sacred numbers shews, that the early Buddhists had the same system of notation as we have. Mr. Colebrook thinks the Sanscrit became refined by degrees. He says, " It evidently draws *its origin from a primeval tongue*, which was gradually " refined in various climates, and became Sanscrit in India, Pahlavi (i. e. Pali or Bali) in Persia, " and Greek on the shores of the Mediterranean."[1] It is extraordinary that Mr. Colebrook should have leaped over the Hebrew and its cognate languages, the Chaldee and Arabic.

The following account of the Sanscrit is given by Sir William Drummond : " Many changes must " have been made upon it, even before the Vedas were written. The Pandits reckon above 1700 " radicals in the language. These form the elements of verbs and nouns ; are all monosyllables ; " and to their multiform combinations may be traced all existing words of pollysyllabic conforma- " tion. But while the language was yet in its infancy, these radicals must often have stood single ; " and when two or more were united in one word, must have exhibited combinations of easy com- " prehension. In the sequel the Sanscrit certainly assumed a very different aspect ; and has finally " become the most perplexed and intricate of the oriental idioms." Again he says, " It is vain to " argue, in this state of the language, that a meaning cannot be attached to certain radicals, because " that meaning is expressed by other words, and because the radical is no longer in use."[2]

No one will dispute the oriental learning of Mr. Ellis, who says, " it is the intent of the follow- " ing observations to shew that the statements contained in the preceding quotations are not cor- " rect ; that neither the Tamul, the Teluga, nor any of their cognate dialects, are derivations from " the Sanscrit ; that the latter, however it may contribute to their polish, is not necessary for their " existence, and that they form a distinct family of languages, with which the Sanscrit has, in later

---

[1] Asiat. Res. Vol. VII. p. 201.    [2] Origines, Vol. IV. p. 171.

" times especially, intermixed, but with which it has no radical connexion."[1]   This nearly accords with my theory, and the family to which he refers may be represented by the Hebrew.  Of the truth of this I shall have many proofs to give in the following part of my work.

My philanthropic and excellent friend Col. Tod, in his introduction to the History of Rajah-stan,[2] has spoken " of the familiar dialects which are formed *from* the Sanscrit."  Now the Sanscrit having never been a vernacular dialect any where, and having been confined, at least while its professors had any authority, that is, till the Mohamedan invasion, to the two highest classes, if not to the Brahmins alone, it seems altogether incredible that any such dialects should have been formed by the lower classes : and I think I can venture to say none ever were formed. A few colloquial expressions or proverbs may have become intermixed with the vulgar dialects in later times, but nothing more.   I observe that Sanscrit scholars have no certain rule, at least they follow none, for rendering Sanscrit words into English: for instance ; one half of them call the language Sanscrit, the other Sunscrit.  Sir W. Jones calls the God *Cristna* Crishna ; others call him Krishnu, others Crishna, others Creeshna, &c., &c.   I learn from a German professor, (whose name I have not authority to give,) very learned in both the Hebrew and the Sanscrit languages, that he is of my opinion—forming his opinion from the roots themselves.  After the violent revo-lution which the Sanscrit has undergone while the Synagogue Hebrew has been stationary, very little similarity can be expected, except in proper names; and in these I contend that the simi-larity will be found to be extremely striking, when the languages are reduced to their first princi-ples, in the manner which I have recommended—when, in fact, Lord Bacon's advice is followed : *Reduce things to their first institution, and observe wherein, and how, they have degenerated.*  When I find a man said to be the son of Erechtheus called *Pandion*, the first king of Athens ; when I find a female, the only daughter of CRISTNA, ruling almost all the Indian nations from the Him-maleh mountains to Ceylon, called *Pandæa ;* and a race called *Pandus ;* and a temple called Pan-dionium and the Pandivas or Pandivus, I cannot help believing that the same mythos is at the bottom of all, though one is evidently formed from the Greek words Παν and διος, or Θεος, and the other, I am told, in the Sanscrit, means *red*  I contend that in this case the meaning of the root has been lost in the Sanscrit, and is only to be found in the Greek ; while in many other cases, the meaning has been lost in the Greek, and can only be found in the Sanscrit.  Again, in the former example, the word Iaya-deva : in the Sanscrit, I am told, the first word means *victory,* while in the Hebrew, it means *self-existent,* both being names of a deity.  IE is almost always called the *God of victory* in the Bible : but may not the word have several meanings ?  No one can doubt, I think, that they have been derived from the same original, call it *root*, or whatever else my reader chooses : and they both are the Aja or Jah or Self-existent of Genesis.  It is in the most ancient books of the Israelites, viz. the books of Genesis, where I should expect to find the closest simi-larity in names ; and there we do find it.

It is impossible to look over Parkhurst's Hebrew Lexicon, and not to be struck with the great number of Greek words which appear to be derived from the Hebrew.  All these languages evi-dently came from one original—and, unless the Ethiopian be excepted, I think the Synagogue Hebrew is the nearest to that original ; probably, as I have before remarked, in consequence of its having been locked up in the recesses of the Jewish temple, and thus remaining unchanged from an earlier period than any other book with which we are acquainted.   But that period must have been after the *sixteen* letters were increased to *twenty-two*, because it is written with *twenty-two* letters.

---

Mr. Townsend observes, " I shall, however, shortly take occasion to demonstrate that Greek " and Hebrew are radically *one*, as I have adduced sufficient evidence to prove that a similar iden- " tity subsists between Sanscrit and Greek. It will then, I trust, be clear to every one, that " Sanscrit and Hebrew have a radical affinity, and may claim descent from the same progenitor, " existing at a given time, when the whole earth was of one language. This conclusion is per- " fectly agreeable to the axiom, that if two things are equal to a third, they are equal to each " other. The argument will then stand thus : Sanscrit and Greek are radically one, therefore " Sanscrit and Hebrew are radically one, q. e. d."[1]

In a paper of the first volume of the Madras Transactions, the names of the planets from the Sanscrit are given, with the Greek and English names. The author says, " The scholar will im- " mediately perceive that the Greek names of the planets are distinctly to be traced in Varaha's " enumeration thus :

" The Sun....Heli......'Ηλιος.....Helius
Mercury....Hema ....'Ερμης ....Hermes
Mars ......Arah......Αρης ......Mars
Jupiter ....Jyok.....·Ζευς ......Jupiter
Saturn......Konah ....Κρονος ....Saturn
Venus......Asphujit ..Αφροδιτη ..Venus.

" This arrangement is far from fanciful. Moreover Idya, a name of Jupiter, is the Idæus, a title " of that God with the Latins : Angiras seems to be Anxurus, another title of the same. Even " Jupiter and Diespiter appear the same with Dyupatih and Divaspatih formed on true gramma- " tical principles, from Dyō, the atmosphere, diūm, and diva, which has the same meaning, united " with patih, a Lord or Ruler : the compound being the ' Lord of the atmosphere.' "[2]

11. Dr. Murray[3] says, " Ocular inspection, assisted by such knowledge as the comparison re- quires, demonstrates the ancient identity of the Sanscrit and Chaldee letters.[4] It is a fact, not admitting a moment's dispute, that there is a surprising similarity or affinity of the Sanscrit to the Greek and Latin languages, and I believe to these languages in nearly their most improved and refined state—a state to which it is well known that they did not arrive till a time approxi- mating to the Christian æra. One example of improvement is found in the Greek *augment*, which is the signicative of past time. The learned Professor Dunbar, of Glasgow,[5] has shewn that it

[1] Van Kennedy's Researches, p. 20, note; Townsend's Character of Moses, Vol. II. p. 330.

[2] The absolute identity of the Sanscrit and the Greek cannot be doubted. To account for this the author says, *Shall not the investigator of Yavaniswara's sayings discover the golden verses of Pythagoras ?* And then he proceeds to argue, in the teeth of all ancient Grecian history, that Pythagoras went from Greece and taught the Indians the Grecian doctrines and names of the planets, &c., in opposition to the notorious fact, that the most important of the doctrines which Pythagoras held, namely, the true solar system, was not known in Greece until Pythagoras taught it ; and *this* he professed to have received from the East. And so far were the Europeans from holding it, that they ac- tually laughed at and persecuted Pythagoras for teaching what they thought such gross absurdities as, among other things, that the planets and earth moved round the sun. From an expression respecting the Atheism of Varaha, I think I can perceive that the gentleman who is the author of the paper is one of those, whose excessive zeal does not permit him to have the free use of his understanding on these subjects. However, if the identity of the names of the planets in Greece and India was so apparent as to be seen by this gentleman, it must be clear indeed ; and furnishes a very strong argument to prove that the Greek came from Indian Sanscrit, or from its parent. But from the Sanscrit it cannot have come ; for if it had, it would have had its *fifty* letters : therefore, it must have come from the parent of the Sanscrit.

[3] Hist. Europ. Lang. Vol. II. p. 227.          [4] Van Kennedy's Res. Pref. p. vi.

[5] Greek and Latin Lang., Append. p. 275.

was not in general use before the time of Homer, but that it was beginning in his time, and was sometimes, but only seldom, used by him. Now we find this improved practice of the Greeks in the Sanscrit. Professor Dunbar says, " I have been the more particular in these observations " respecting the augment of the verbs, because upon them I found a principal argument, *that the* " *Sanscrit was borrowed from the Greek, and not the Greek from the Sanscrit.* If the Greek lan- " guage was merely a dialect of the Sanscrit, as has been generally asserted, and if this latter " tongue possessed the augment of verbs, when the former was separated from it by a kindred " race, how comes it that, for a long period of time, they seem to have either totally neglected, or " only partially used it, and afterward, without any known communication with the Indians, uni- " formly prefixed it to their verbs ? The inference seems to be, that the Brahmins, when forming " their sacred language, adopted it from the Greeks, when it was in general use among them, and " only changed the character of the vowel." Of course this must have been after the time of Homer ; and when we consider that it still more nearly resembles the Latin than the Greek, it must, if it have copied from both Latin and Greek, have been *long* after the time of Homer. It may have been between the conquests in India by Alexander, and the birth of Christ. I cannot help suspecting that the Sanscrit was founded principally on the two languages—a little differing from both, but so contrived as to be unintelligible to the vulgar equally in Greece, Italy, and India. This may account for the *a* being used for the augment in the Sanscrit, instead of the *e* as in the Greek. It is well known that after the time of Alexander, the connexion between Europe and India was very intimate ; Gymnosophists and Samaneans were passing and repassing every day. Mr. Dunbar has noticed a letter, said by Strabo to be written by an Indian prince himself to Augustus, in the Greek language. Dr. Murray, we have seen, is decidedly of opinion that the Sanscrit *character* is formed from the Chaldee. Then, I ask, may not the Chaldee or lost Tamul, have been the base, improved by all the assistance which could be derived from the Latin and Greek ;—the Chaldee found by Sir W. Jones in the Carnatic and also in Afghanisthan ? The de- scription given of the Sanscrit by Sir W. Jones and Col. Van Kennedy,[1] leaves me no room to doubt that the Sanscrit is artificial.

12. The argument of Mr. Dunbar, just adduced, in favour of the Sanscrit being derived from the Greek, drawn from the Greek *augment*, is very striking.[2] If the Sanscrit were copied from the Greek and the Latin, the difference in the number of the letters forms no material objection ; for, it seems by no means improbable that one language should be formed out of two, perhaps by Sa- maneans or Gymnosophists, who returned to the East from Western journeys. This is much more likely than that those two languages should both have been copied from the Sanscrit. Many of the places in Italy, I shall shew by and by, such as Saturnia, Pallitana, &c., have their names from the vulgar dialects of India, and not from the Sanscrit : this again raises a presumption that the Sanscrit is comparatively modern. Dr. Babington says the Sanscrit of South India is written in characters derived from the Tamul, and as they are much more complicated, they are probably of later date.[3] But we have just read, that the Sanscrit is derived from Chaldee. This is because the Chaldee and first Tamul are or have been the same, or nearly the same.

My learned friend Edmund Henry Barker, Esq., has observed to me, that the similarity of the Sanscrit to the *Latin* is much more striking and close than it is to the *Greek*, and that Professor Dunbar's theory requires the contrary. This remark is very just, and increases the difficulty; but it does not tend in the least degree to prove the Greek and Latin to have been derived from the Sanscrit. I confess, I consider the fact that the Sanscrit has so many more letters than the

---

[1] Pp. 193 and 201.  [2] Vide Dunbar, pp. 276—279.  [3] Trans. Asiat. Soc. Part I. Vol. II. p. 264.

languages of Western nations as a decisive proof that they *cannot* have come from it, after it was completed. They never would have taken one half of the letters with the refinements of the language and left the other half of the letters; they never would have taken the exact sixteen Cadmean letters, the same as the Irish Celtic, the Phœnician, the Arabic, the Persian, and have left the others. There is no nation of the East among whom the Sanscrit is spoken as a vernacular tongue; nor can any one be fixed on as having probably had it as a vernacular tongue. It has been always kept by the priests (at least as strictly as it was in their power) confined to their own order. Under these circumstances it is not credible that two tribes, like the Greeks and Latins, emigrating from India in really almost a state of barbarism, as they both were at first, if their histories can be believed, should have brought this refined language with them. How is it possible to believe that if they had brought this fine *fifty*-letter language with them from India, they would have so completely lost all knowledge of it as, instead of it, to have had the tradition, and a false tradition, of letters at first having been brought to them by Cadmus from Phœnicia? Had they brought this language, it must have secured its own perpetuation, in very nearly all its pristine excellence. It must have come before the time of Homer, Hesiod, Pindar. Will any one believe, who knows the least of the Sanscrit, that, beautiful as their language is, the Greeks would have abandoned the Sanscrit to form it?

Mr. E. H. Barker says, "Can you ever prove to my satisfaction that the word *vir* (which is not " a Greek word) passed into the Sanscrit language from the Latin in the sense of a *man* and a " *husband?* It is idle to say that Alexander carried the word to India. How did the Sanscrit " language catch hold of *jivame*, ' to live,' which is merely the verb *jiv*, with the personal pronoun " *ame* subjoined? This is not in the Greek, and therefore Alexander did not convey the word into " India. But it is identical with the Latin *vivo*, i. e. viv-ego. Hence the analogies between the " three languages prove a common descent from some unknown tongue; or else that the Greek " and Latin are derived from the Sanscrit." I think all this tends strongly to support my idea that the Sanscrit was artificially founded on the Hebrew, Latin, and Greek, jointly, by the Brahmins. Had there been anciently any language from which the three could have drawn their common peculiarities, it could not have been entirely lost to us. Had the Latin and Greek been formed on the Sanscrit, they would have had all the Sanscrit refinements. The Sanscrit being formed on the Latin and Greek has all their refinements, and a great many more.

13. "The learned Hermann has the following as the scheme of the Saturnian measure.[1]

$$- \smallsmile \, | \, \smallsmile \, - | \, \smallsmile \, - \, \smallsmile \, | - \, \smallsmile \, | - \, \smallsmile \, | - \, \smallsmile$$

" A dactyl, however, is occasionally admitted in place of the first and second trochee, and a spon- " dee is sometimes introduced indiscriminately. Now if we compare this measure with those of " the Sanscrit poetry, that are given by Schlegel, [2] we cannot fail being struck by their great simi- " larity. One of their measures alluded to is as follows :

$$\smallsmile - | \, \smallsmile - | - \smallsmile \smallsmile | - \smallsmile | -- \smallsmile | --$$

" Schlegel states at the same time, that this scheme admits of variations. These may probably " bring it into full accordance with the Saturnian. All this, together with the Sanscrit derivation

---

[1] *Elem. Doctr. Metr.* p. 398.　　　　　　　[2] *Sprache und Weicheit der Indier*, p. 227.

" of the very name of Saturn, (Satouranouno,) furnishes another link in that curious chain, which
" connects the early Greeks and Romans with the primitive inhabitants of Northern India." [1]

The learned Greaves Haughton, Esq., the late professor of Sanscrit, has contended that there are
such great numbers of Sanscrit words in the Greek, as to prove that it must have come direct from
India. But I am quite certain no one can look into any half dozen pages of Parkhurst's Hebrew
or Greek Lexicon, and not be convinced that many Greek and Hebrew roots are the same : then
will not this confirm what I have said, that there must have been one common language ? I am
sure no one will maintain that the perfected Sanscrit was the parent of the Synagogue Hebrew,
for if it had been, the latter would have had *fifty* letters. It is not credible that the Sanscrit, in
the state in which it is found in any of the Vedas, ever had less than fifty letters, nor is there the
least reason to believe that it ever had less since it could be called Sanscrit, or Sanctum Scriotum,
or the *sacred language* or *writ*. Had either the Greek or Hebrew come from the fifty-letter Sanscrit, it would also have had *fifty* letters. All this goes to prove that an ancient language must
have been common to the three, on which, in their rude state, they were formed ; but after all, the
Sanscrit must have been perfected from the Greek and Latin, though for all their *roots* there may
have been a common origin.

The following observation, respecting the nature of the Sanscrit language, by Wilson, in the
preface to his Sanscrit dictionary, I think confirms, in a very remarkable manner, my opinion that
the Sanscrit was an artificial language, formed by the priests ; and, if so formed, it would scarcely
be so formed for any purpose but that of secrecy, and must have been confined to their own caste ;
as indeed it is, as far as it is in their power, at this day. I believe concealment was their object,
as was the formation of Hieroglyphics in Egypt. " The Sanscrit root or Dha'tu, appears to differ
" from the primitives of other languages in its fulfilling no other office, and being incapable of en-
" tering into any form of speech : to fit it for this purpose, it must undergo many preparatory
" modifications, and it is then evolved, with the aid of additional particles, into a noun or verb at
" pleasure." [2] The Synagogue or Pentateuch Hebrew language was latterly confined to one little
temple of one little country; the Sanscrit was dispersed and spoken among Brahmins scattered
over countries more extensive than Europe, and widely divided : this is enough to account for the
variation which exists between the first Veda and modern books. It grew into a spoken language
among a very numerous class, and this caused it, like all other languages, to change ; and, being
the language of a learned society, the members of which were connected by colleges corresponding
with each other, its change was for the better, till it arrived at perfection.

Dr. Hagar has traced the Samaritan to the Deva-nagari, the oldest form of the Sanscrit, or the
Sanscrit to the Samaritan : but the ancient Samaritan had really, at the most, only *sixteen* letters, [3]
as appears from coins, &c. Now, this being admitted, it is very evident that the Sanscrit must
have copied from the Samaritan ; because if the latter had been the copyist, it would have had fifty
letters. It would not have taken part of the letters only. Sir W. Jones says, " The square Chal-
" daic letters, a few of which are found on the Persian ruins, appear to have been originally the
" same with the Deva-nagari, before the latter were enclosed, as we now see them, in angular
" frames." [4] Of course the latter sentence must apply to the Sanscrit before it was perfected.

If these two learned men be right, my hypothesis of the identity of the Hebrew, or African
Ethiopic language, with the Sanscrit in its rude state, is proved. Need I wish for any thing more
in my favour than the matured opinion of these two learned men ?

---

[1] Professor Anthom's Ed. of Horace, published at New York, 1830, p. xlix.          [2] Pref. p. xliv.
[3] Vall. Collect. Heb. Vol. V. p. 210.                    [4] Asiat. Res. Sixth Discourse.

Col. Wilford[1] makes a remark which strongly supports my theory, and what is said above: " The Greek language has certainly borrowed largely from the Sanscrit, *but it always affects the* " *broken dialects of India;* the language of the Latins, in particular, *does,* which is acknowledged " to have been an ancient dialect of the Greek." . The fact of the Latin and Greek affecting the broken dialects is precisely what they ought to do, if they came from India, as I suppose, before the Sanscrit was perfected. Facts of this kind transpiring from such persons as Wilford and Jones, from enemies or strangers to my system, are much more valuable as evidence than any thing that I could say.

Dr. Buchanan gives his opinion that the Pali language of the Burmas is radically the same as the Sanscrit.[2] This similarity arises from their all being from one common stock. Col. Tod says, the Pali character yet exists, and appears the same as ancient fragments of the Buddha inscriptions in my possession : many *letters assimilate with the* Coptic.[3]

14. Dr. Pritchard says, " It has been discovered by Sir W. Jones, and confirmed by later re- " searches, that the Zend, the old language of the Magi, bears a close affinity to the Sanscrit, " differing from each other and from the common parent only in trifling modifications. The " Zendish alphabet was believed, by the late Dr. Leyden, to be derived from the Deva Nagari, to " which that learned orientalist supposed even the arrow-headed characters of the Persepolitan " inscriptions to be allied. The Pahlavi, in which the Pazend, a commentary on the works of " Zoroaster, was written at a time when the idiom of the works themselves was becoming obsolete, " *is a branch of the Chaldaic stock.* A dialect of Chaldee had, therefore, at some period, gained so " far the ascendancy in Persia, as to become the language of the priesthood."[4] Here I think my reader will see that the Chaldee, which is almost as near Hebrew as common Scotch is to English, is traced to have been the vernacular tongue in India: for, in what part is the Bali, that is the Pahlavi, not found ? Again, he says, " It is a curious fact that the language of the Magi was a " dialect of the Sanscrit." Again, " The modern Persic is formed by a mixture of Arabic with the " genuine Parsi, which was the common idiom of the Persians at the æra of the Mahomedan con- " quest, and is preserved nearly pure in the works of Firdausi and others of the older poets. It " is known that the Parsi has, for its basis, the Sanscrit—differing from it much in the same man- " ner as the several dialects of the Indian provinces. Therefore the Zend, the ancient written " language of Persia, being a modification of the Sanscrit, of which the Parsi is a dialect, the for- " mer may be considered as the parent of the latter, just as the Latin is of the Italian. The Parsi " is the national speech of the Persians, and therefore the Zend cannot have been introduced into " that country as a learned language. It must have been at some remote period the universal " idiom of the people." This period, I think, must have been before the Sanscrit was brought to its highest perfection. All these gentlemen seem to forget that the difference in the style of the Vedas proves, that there must have been a time when the Sanscrit was comparatively in a rude state, and very different from what it is now.

Dr. Pritchard adds,[5] " The affinity between the Greek language and the old Parsi and Sanscrit " is certain and essential. The use of cognate idioms proves the nations who used them to have " descended from one stock."—" That the religion of Greece emanated from an Eastern source, " no one will deny. Nor will the superstitions from Egypt account for the fact, since the nations " of Asia Minor, as the Phrygians and Lydians who had no connexion, partook of old of the same " rites and mythologies, and approached still more nearly to the Eastern character. And the " Greek superstitions more closely resemble the Indian than the Egyptian fictions. . We must,

---

[1] Asiat. Res. Vol. V. p. 301.     [2] Ibid. Vol. VI. p. 305.     [3] Hist. Raj. Pent. p. 58.
[4] Physical Hist. of Man, p. 461.        [5] P. 522.

" therefore, suppose the religion, as well as the language, of Greece to have been derived, in great " part, immediately from the East." [1] If my reader will consider the above attentively, he will see that, in fact, it admits all for which I contend. It directly connects the Chaldee to the Parsi, Pali, Sanscrit, and to the Greek, as the facts of the sixteen-letter system might give us reason to expect. The reader will not forget that the *old* Arabic is nearly the same with the old Hebrew, Samaritan, and Chaldee. Indeed, the identity of Arabic and Chaldee or Hebrew, I am quite certain cannot be disputed. How should it, when every Hebrew root is to be found in Arabic? Thus, they are all connected like the links of a chain. And the fanciful division into the languages of Shem, Ham, and Japhet, must be abandoned—a division, let it be observed, directly at variance with the Bible, if there be a word of truth in the confusion of tongues, as given in the tenth and eleventh chapters of Genesis: for the seventy-two nations, of the descendants of Noah, were said to be formed before the confusion of tongues. And there is not a single word to justify the supposition that the confusion confused the languages of the seventy-two nations into three only. Therefore I hope we shall hear no more of the threefold division of Sir W. Jones, for there is not a shadow of a foundation for it. At least there is reason to believe, that the Bali, Pracrit, Persian, Chaldee, Phœnician, Arabic, Hebrew, Coptic, Ethiopic, Greek, Latin, Etruscan, and Celtic, were all one language, and had the same system of letters—sixteen in number—with the same powers of notation, which fixes their identity. They were, in fact, all one nation, with one religion, that of Buddha; and they were originally Negroes, and the use of letters, if known, was known only to the priests. The king or chief ruler was always a priest, the head of the priesthood. All this I have proved or will prove.

As I have just now observed, Dr. Pritchard shews, that the Zend, the old language of the Magi, bears a close affinity to the Sanscrit; [2] that the Zend, the Pali, and the Pracrit, are three cognate dialects of the Sanscrit; that Dr. Leyden also, on careful examination, believed the Zendish alphabet to be derived from the Deva-nagari, to which the arrow-headed inscriptions of Persepolis were nearly allied; that the Pali or Pahlavi, in which the work of Zoroaster was written, was a branch of the Chaldaic stock, and that, therefore, a branch of the Chaldaic stock had at one time been used by the priests of Persia; that the Zend being a modification of the Sanscrit, of which the Parsi or modern language of Persia is a dialect, the former may be considered as the parent of the latter. I think from the above observation of the Chaldaic or Hebrew and Arabic (for the three are all one) being in use in Persia, we are brought to about the time in which I suppose the Jews may have come from India. [3] In fact, Dr. Pritchard makes the Zend—the same as the Pracrit or old Sanscrit—to have been the common language of Persia, and to have been a branch of Chaldaic. [4] This brings the Chaldaic to India, to which, by other arguments, I have traced it. Indeed, I cannot doubt that all these languages were nearly the same at the time to which Dr. Pritchard alludes; but this was before the perfecting of the Sanscrit. I know I shall have all the philosophers against me, because they will not condescend to look at the old Jewish books: for they are in those respects almost as prejudiced as the devotees. But I think the *Chaldee-Hebrew-Arabic-Ethiopic-Pali-Pahlavi-Pracrit-Zend* language was the oldest language of Asia which we know of, and that they were all one. After the time when this was the case, the Sanscrit was formed. This I think may be fairly deduced from what Drs. Pritchard and Leyden, and Sir W. Jones have shewn. To this, however, the philosophers will not listen, because the priests will be pleased with it, and triumphantly make a handle of it, in order to shew that the Hebrew is the oldest language of the world, as a means of supporting their dogmas. But I do not

---

Physical Hist. of Man, p. 525.        [2] P. 461.        [3] See Pritchard, p. 463.        [4] Ibid.

trouble myself whether they be pleased or grieved. Truth is my object; and there is evidently sufficient reason to be assigned why the Hebrew language should be the oldest, (without having recourse to the nonsense of priests,) in the circumstances which I have detailed respecting the Pentateuch, and the migration of the tribe of Ioudi from India.

In addition to what I have just shewn, that Dr. Pritchard says, "the affinity between the "Greek language and the old Parsi and Sanscrit is certain and essential, and that the use of cognate "idioms proves the nations who used them to have descended from one stock," he says, that "the "religion of Greece also came from India, not Egypt; and that the proof of this fact is even "more clear than the affinity of the languages."[1]

Conon says, that the Phœnicians once possessed the empire of Asia; that they made Egyptian Thebes their capital; and that Cadmus, migrating thence into Europe, built Bœotian Thebes,[2] and called it after his native town. Mr. Faber says rightly, I think, that the Phœnicians, the Anakim, the Philistines, the Palli, and the Egyptian shepherd-kings, were all one people. The Palli were the Phœnicians who came from the Persian Gulf, according to Herodotus, the people who spoke the Pali, Bali, or Pahali tongue. "As touching the *Baly* tongue, *M. Harbelot* "(D' Herbelot) informed me, that the ancient *Persian* is called *Pahalevi, Pahali,* and that between "*Pahali* and *Bahali* the *Persians* make no difference. And that the word *Pout,* which in *Persian* "signifies an idol, or false God, and which doubtless signified *Mercury,* when the *Persians* were "idolaters, signifies *Mercury* amongst the *Siameses.*"[3] Sommona-Codom is also called *Pout,*[4] which is a Bali word. "The sacred language of the Jains or Buddhists is Pracrit or Pali."[5] Jones, in his Dissertation on the Persians, says, that the Pehlevi was a dialect of the Chaldaic, or, in other words, that they were the same language originally. But, in another place he says, that the Pali, *i. e.* Bali or Pahali or Pehleve, are all the same. This accounts for the God Baal being found in Syria or Assyria. Bayer also maintains that the Pehlevi, which he calls Parthic, is derived from the Assyrian alphabet, called *Estrangelo.*[6] And Vallancey[7] has shewn, that the Estrangelo is the same as the Chaldean and Syrian.[8] Sir William Drummond says, "No one "can compare the Pehlvi with the Hebrew and Chaldaic, without tracing many words in the first of "these two languages to the two last."[9] This is perfectly true, but he must take them without points.

15. The Rev. Dr. Hagar thinks that before words were divided in writing into syllables, arbitrary figures were used, which he calls monograms. In this I certainly nearly agree with him, because the nail-headed monogram I would stand for one, and V for five, and X for two fives. But it seems to me to be probable that after man made these signs for the ideas of numbers, he next made use of similar signs to express other ideas. But of this more hereafter. In his Dissertation on the Babylonian Bricks, he has shewn with much learning, and I think I may say with somewhat more than a slight degree of probability, that most of the ancient alphabets were originally formed of right-lined and nail-headed characters, and in this respect he particularly points

---

[1] P. 525.

[2] Thebes in both countries probably took its name from the word Theba, a Cow, the female of the Bull of the Zodiac. Cadmus or the oriental person who built Thebes was conducted by a heifer, a virgin of course: on her side was marked a lunar crescent, emblem of Isis, the virgin mother of all nature, whose veil no mortal ever removed. The meaning of this is, that a person came from the East, under the auspices of the female Taurus or Bos of the Zodiac. Thebes was also called the city of On, and Ammon, and No, and Diospolis, the same as Tibet was called Baaltistan.

[3] La Loubère, Siam. Hist. Part III.   [4] Ibid. Life of *Thevetat,* p. 145.

[5] Colebrooke, Asiat. Soc. p. 550.   [6] Act. Erudit. Jul. 1731.   [7] Coll. de Reb. Hib. Vol. V. p. 201.

[8] Vide Kircher's Prodronus Copticus, p. 279.   [9] Origines, Vol. I. p. 334.

3 P 2

out the similarity between the Nagari, [1] one of the most ancient Indian letters said to have come from heaven, [2] and the Samaritan letters; and, as this opinion cannot be suspected of being unduly influenced by a wish to support my system, which it so evidently does, I am induced to pay much attention to it. It is clear that something very like the Samaritan must have been the old Indian letters before the Sanscrit was perfected. I think the tracing of them to the simple right-lined characters adds to the probability of his deductions. He connects them with the nails driven in the Roman temple, and in the Etruscan temple of Nurtia, to mark the passing years. But wonderful to tell, he overlooks the calculi of the Romans, and the nail-headed Roman and Etruscan[3] numerals, all which are evidently so closely allied. I think the right-lined, nail-headed, old Nagari and the Roman or Etruscan and Greek are not far from the same date. This is strikingly confirmed by the Latin words found in the Sanscrit, or the Sanscrit in the Latin language.

From finding so many Latin words in the Sanscrit, I am not surprised at meeting in the East with the mode of reckoning by calculi. The Chinese use an instrument called Abacus, as the Greeks and Romans did in ancient times; and the Brahmins in India calculate eclipses, &c., by means of little shells used as calculi, called *cauris*. And this they continue notwithstanding their skill in Arabian arithmetic and letters. [4]　Most of my readers, I suspect, will here instantly recollect the *Cowries* of the Africans, by which they count, and which they use as money. Here is the Indian practice in Africa, and the Indian name also. When did they come to Africa, and who brought them?

16. For a very long time nothing appeared to me more difficult than to account for the different direction in the style of writing by the nations of antiquity. In some it was from right to left; in others, from left to right. I think Dr. Hagar has removed the difficulty. He has shewn that it was the practice of most of the nations of antiquity and particularly of the Babylonians and the Egyptians, like the Chinese, to write from the top to the bottom.[5] The Greeks knew it by the name of Tapocon: and Eustathius informs us, that they originally used it. Diodorus Siculus says,[6] that the Ethiopians wrote perpendicularly from the top to the bottom. Dr. Hagar says that the Romans also were acquainted with it. Of the Syrians he adds, " The Syrians still write " perpendicularly, like the Babylonians, their ancestors. They turn the paper, indeed, when they " have done, so as to read horizontally : but in writing they begin at the top, and write straight " down to the bottom."

A vertical inscription was found by Dr. Clarke in Greece. The letters were formed from right to left, but the words read from top to bottom, as I understand him. [7]　Now I think that if all nations originally used this style, mere accident is quite adequate to account for one nation turning their upright line one way, and another another way. On this I shall have much to say when I proceed to discuss *again* the origin of letters.

The following is an extract taken from the letter of a literary gentleman in India, whose name I am not at liberty to use : " Of course you know how many Hebrew words are in the Arabic : " again, those very words are *common Hindostannee*. I absolutely use Hebrew words every day. " I do not know the alphabet at present, but shall positively *go the length* of doing so, at least as I " use the letters in my dictionary (he means the Hind. Dict.) every day, and without being able " to read them. (Here follow some examples, the Arabic of which I cannot write.) I could give

---

[1] P. 41.　　　　　　　[2] That is, its origin is unknown.

[3] The Etruscans had the Roman nail-headed numerals. Mr. Kenrick.

[4] Hagar, p. 48.　　　　　[5] Diss. on Babyl. Bricks, p. 5.　　　　　[6] Lib. i.

[7] Trav. Pref. to Vol. VII. ed. 8vo. p. xii.

" you many more examples, but have only represented some lying before me, without knowing " any thing of the alphabet." Though this is rather confusedly written, here is what I might expect—not the perfected Sanscrit found to be the same as the Hebrew and Arabic, but—the the Hindostannee, the vulgar language, one of the broken dialects on which the Sanscrit was built, identical with them. But what is the learned Professor Haughton doing at this moment? Printing a Sanscrit and Hindostannee dictionary as *one* into English, like Parkhurst's Chaldee and Hebrew and English Lexicon.

17. When I discuss matters of this kind with learned men, I find them perpetually raising objections from the pronunciation of the languages. I cannot admit any such considerations to come into the argument. The mode of spelling (except in some sacred codes, and even they change—witness the Keri and Cetib of the Jews, and the word אן *an* sometimes spelt און *aun*, &c., &c.), unfortunately, is too liable to vary ; but what is the pronunciation? It varies every year, between every two provinces—witness the word spoken in Stamford *Window*, and in Kent *Vinder*. If any gentleman think proper to search for the fountain-head of language by the way of pronunciation, I find no fault—but he must excuse me for not travelling his road. I will go my own, by the written words, and written words only. And when I have reduced the different systems of letters to one, which I think I have done, I will then try to find what words have roots of one or two consonants common to all the written languages ; and I must maintain that, if I find a word whose root is the same in all the systems, it is a word of the primeval language. For instance, *Ma* or *Am* for Mother ; or *Pa*, or *Ab*, or *Ap*, for Father. But though the pronunciation of words is so very uncertain, I do not maintain that it is absolutely, in all cases, of no use. It may often aid the use of letters : but I maintain that it cannot be admitted to destroy the force of any fact or consequence elicited by it. It may strengthen an argument, but it cannot overthrow it. Upon the mischievous absurdity of the common mode of rendering words out of one language into another, Sir W. Drummond has made some very pertinent observations. [1]

My reader must never forget (unless all the learned men who, without any connexion with one another, made out the Western Asiatic and European systems of letters to be *sixteen* in number, be not mistaken), that, before any comparison can be made between the Hebrew and the Indian written languages, they must be both reduced, as far as possible, to what they were before they were changed by the makers of the Sanscrit to fifty letters, and by the increase in the number of Hebrew letters from sixteen to twenty-two. And when the very great change which has taken place in both these languages is considered, there will be no room for wonder that the similarity of the languages can be found in nothing but names of persons and of places.

18. My opinion on the Sanscrit has lately received a remarkable support in the statement of the learned Mr. Bop, of Berlin, who, in a review of a work of Professor Rosen's, of the London University, has observed, that he believes there was a time when the difference between the Sanscrit and the Semitic languages had not developed itself. [2] In this the consequence is evidently implied, that the Hebrew and its sister dialects had originally all been *one* with the old Sanscrit, or with the language on which the Sanscrit was founded.

My argument chiefly rests upon the fact, that the Western letters were originally only sixteen in number. The mode in which five or six very learned men, without any connexion with each other, made out the number to be *sixteen*, and the *same* sixteen is evidence of that fact, of a much better nature than can ordinarily be expected in inquiries of this kind. If they be *all* mistaken, it is scarcely less than a miracle.

---

[1] Orig. Vol. IV. pp. 228—233.  [2] Vienna, Annals of Lit. Vol. XLII. p. 242.

19. I think from these circumstances we may almost venture to reason on the Ethiopian lan-. guage as the root of the old Sanscrit, or as being the earliest or most ancient language of India.

In the Buddhist book of Genesis the first man, or the race of man, is called by the name of אדם *adm.* It is used as applied to the race, both in the masculine and feminine genders. It is usually derived or explained by the word אדמה *adme* earth, because earth is of a red colour. This serves to shew how easily lexicographers can be satisfied when an explanation makes for their prejudices or interest. The earth is no more *red* than *black* or *brown ;* nor is the man more *red* than *black.* The explanation is absurd, and the meaning is evidently unknown. In the Ethiopic or this old parent of the Sanscrit a more probable meaning may be found. In it, *adamah* means *beautiful, elegant, pleasant*—beauty resulting from order—the same meaning as the Κοσμος of the Greeks. Upon this supposition, Adam would receive his name, not from a certain fictitious redness, but from the beauty and perfection of his nature—being, as it were, from superiority of mind, the master-piece of the creation. My observation is confirmed by Mr. Townsend: " Admah, " the name of a city in that beautiful valley, resembling paradise, the garden of the Lord, chosen " by Lot; and Adam was the name given to our first parents. These names have commonly been " referred to a root in Hebrew which means *red,* but this epithet does not seem appropriate to a " being of superior excellence as *beautiful,* which corresponds to the same root in Ethiopic. It is " worthy of remark, that Κοσμος, the Greek expression answering to Adamah, is derived from " Κοσμεω, I adorn ; and, in Latin, Mundus, like Munditia, means, not merely cleanliness, but " *ornament* and *elegance.*" [1] I beg my reader not to forget the meaning of Κοσμεω and Mundus. It will be wanted by and by. I think their signification of *beauty* was derived from the supposed beautiful and orderly cyclical motions of the planets. In the Sanscrit books the two first persons are called Adin and Iva. " Stephanus περι Πολεων on Αδανα, tells us, that Κρονος or Saturn " was called Αδανος : and that this *Adanus* was the son of heaven and earth, Εςι δε ὁ Αδανος " γης και ϑρανϑ παις : which is a perfect description of Adam's production by God out of our " earth......And, indeed, the very name Αδανος seems to be the very same with אדם *adm* Adam. " For the Greeks having no words terminating in M, for Adam they pronounced Αδαν...... " *Adana,* an ancient city of Cilicia, built by the *Syrians,* was called in memory of the first man " *Adam.*" [2] Here we have Adam in Greece by the same name as the Adam in India. It is a singular circumstance that the Greek should have no word ending in M. This is the most mysterious of all the letters. I suspect it is sometimes left out in languages, and sometimes put before words in some languages, or inserted in words in other languages, for the same mysterious reason.

20. When I consider the nature of the Sanscrit, as I learn it from scholars, it appears to be, nearly in all respects, what might be expected of an artificially-formed learned language. It is no where found to be a vernacular tongue ; but it is found strikingly similar to two languages, (the Greek and Latin,) situated at a very great distance from its home ; in certain artificial peculiarities which can on no account be attributed to accident ; though it has occasionally such affinities to native Indian words, as for one dictionary to serve both it and a native tongue, the Hindostannee. This is just what we might expect if it were formed by Brahmins for the sake of secrecy. There is nothing improbable in supposing that learned Brahmins adopted the Greek and Latin grammars as a groundwork, both from their complete state and the distance of Greece and Italy from India. I repeat, that if it had ever been a language spoken by a mass of people, it must yet have been found among their descendants ; but it is intimately like nothing but Latin

---

[1] Townsend, Verac. of Moses, p. 42 or 421.　　　[2] Gale, Court Gent. B. ii. Ch. i.

and Greek. No doubt this scheme has its difficulties, but *the facts* which we possess leave us nothing but a choice of difficulties, of which we can only choose the least. It seems the opinion is gaining ground that the Sanscrit, the Greek, and the Latin, have been all borrowed from some lost language. But it is difficult to believe that a written language should be quite lost, after it had been brought to such a high state of refinement as it must have been, to have furnished the points of similarity in the three languages. Where did this language live? It is incredible that such a language should have existed, and no traces of it be left? It must have had books innumerable. I am every day more convinced that the Sanscrit was a secret language formed by its priests, who had travelled to the West, before the founding of Rome or the institution of the Olympiads of Greece; but still after the time of Homer,—perhaps in the seventh or eighth century before Christ,—in the Saturnian times of Italy, and when several of the most important Indian customs came to Thrace and Europe, as I shall shew, and when that language, which Plato says was lost, was still spoken in Greece. When the Christian Roman Emperors became masters of Upper Egypt, the Ethiopians were converted to Christianity, and then it would be that the temples containing such groups of mystical figures as that at Ipsambul, described in Book V. Ch. XI. Sect. 6, would be dismantled. I think it probable, that the original Christianity of Upper Egypt was correctly the Christianity of Buddha or Cristna. The Brahmins, as I have already mentioned, often tell the English to reform their religion, which they say is only corrupted Brahmanism. If we do not discover many remains of it except the style of writing, and the other examples of identity in the two languages pointed out by Sir W. Jones, &c., we need not be surprised. We must not forget that the country was for many hundred years in the hands of a ruling power, whose exertions to secrete truth never ceased, and whose successors in India and England still continue the practice to the utmost of their power. Their studied concealment of the contents of the temple of Bal-iji, at Punderpoor, proves the fact past contradiction. They may abuse me for illiberality if they please: belief is not a matter of choice but necessity, and I feel obliged to believe that they have not noticed the contents of the temple, because they knew it would let out some unpleasant truths. Why was Mr. Moore tampered with to suppress it?

In Book V. Ch. IV. Sect. 11, I have made a reflection upon our orientalists of Calcutta, which will be scouted for its illiberality. Since I printed that passage, I have discovered the following speech by Sir William Jones, their great *Alim*: " The two engravings in Giorgi's book, from sketches " by a Tibetian painter, exhibit a system of Egyptian and Indian Mythology: and a complete " explanation of them would have done the learned author more credit than his fanciful etymo- " logies, which are always ridiculous, and often grossly erroneous."[1] This refers to my figures in the plates, number 14. Georgius did not give an explanation because he could not give it, not understanding it. But he did not suppress, but published the fact, which Sir W. Jones, to all intents and purposes, suppressed. He then censured the Jesuit for his candour in having printed it. It is an exact counterpart to his disgraceful misrepresentation of the great Bailley.[2] He was not angry because the Jesuit did not explain it, but because he published it, which was done with the consent and approbation of the Roman See, as witnessed by its imprimatur. I am ashamed for my country when I am obliged to say, that when Sir W. Jones made the observation or accounted for the events in the life of Cristna, (related in Book IV.,) by their being copied from Apocryphal Gospels, he knew and concealed the fact of the crucifixion in Nepaul. Thus he stands convicted of a pious fraud. We need go no farther now for the cause of his having been bespattered with praises by the priests.

---

[1] Disc. on Mount. of Asia, Asiat. Res. Vol. III. p. 11, ed. 8vo.  [2] Vide Celtic Druids, p. 45.

I entertain a strong suspicion, that figures and arithmetic, as well as writing, were for many generations confined to the order of priests; that they were considered to be magical or judicial astrology; and that, after they became commonly known, Hieroglyphics were invented to supply their place. When the priests could no longer conceal the art of writing, which most likely came to be known in the struggles and desperate wars for empire between the swordsmen and the gownsmen in the East, various contrivances were resorted to.

Actuated by the same selfish desire of retaining in their own hands the *Key of Knowledge*, as I before stated, the Jews yet keep a solemn fast, on the day on which they believe the LXX translation was finished.[1] This is as a penance for their great national sin in having permitted it to be translated by Ptolemy, and thereby made public. This is the last proof which we possess, and a decisive proof it is, of sacred writings concealed, and also of their forced exposure. In this system of Masonic secrecy we have the reason why, on the Cyclopean or Druidical buildings, there is no inscription, although the cycles, &c., which they exhibit, most clearly prove the profound astronomical learning of their founders.

I must now make one more observation on the antiquity of the language of the tribe of Abraham. Whether or not their sixteen-letter system were that of the Samaritan or Synagogue Hebrew, (Chaldee,) it must be very ancient. It must have come from India before the Sanscrit was increased to *fifty* letters. It is the most simple of all the languages with which we are acquainted. I contend that it betrays, as I have stated, in its construction, the most unequivocal signs of almost primeval simplicity, and evident proofs of formation by *degrees*, as we should say in a great measure *accidentally*, without any preconcerted plan. Our learned men have endeavoured to reduce it to system, but, in fact, almost in vain. Among other things they have divided the letters of the Synagogue Hebrew into radical and servile, making of the latter, which ought never to form a root, ELEVEN in number. But this is merely an imaginary and arbitrary and indeed unfounded, division or rule, as it is clogged with great numbers of exceptions. I am satisfied, however, that nothing like *a rule* can be formed, nor is it likely, from the nature of the case, that it should. We may be very certain that neither the tribe of Abraham nor any other nation would increase its number of letters until it found it wanted them; and when it did add more letters, we may be very certain that it would instantly use them. The language must have deviated from its first simplicity, in the method of speaking words, which made those who used it feel a want of new letters. If they had not wanted new sounds and letters representing them, the number *sixteen* would have been abundantly sufficient; but they must have formed words or sounds for the representation of which they must have imagined that the old letters were inconvenient or inadequate. Learned men fall into a great mistake in supposing that written language was the produce of profound learning: it was, on the contrary, generally the produce of ignorance and of the necessities of, comparatively speaking, unlearned and uncivilized man, and, probably, as I have said in my Preliminary Observations, must have consisted, at first, of right lines. Of this more hereafter. I beg it may be understood that I by no means wish to throw any impediment in the way of philosophical inquiries into the origin of language or letters; but I do most unequivocally protest against the assumption, in the first instance, that language is the produce of philosophy, or indeed even of system. Letters are like language, the offspring of circumstance, not of system; and grammar is an attempt to reduce them both to system. To this the PERFECTED or the comparatively speaking *modern* Sanscrit is, of course, an exception. The existence of Sanscrit words, in the languages of the nations West of the Euphrates, although those nations have not the Sanscrit number of letters, shews that an old language must have existed common to them all before the Sanscrit was per-

---

[1] Hale's Chron. Vol. I. p. 73.

fected. It goes to prove that all the nations had at first a sixteen-letter system; the Ioudi and Hellenes increased them to *twenty-two*, and other or later orientals to *fifty*. The Buddhists in Upper India have their sacred books in the Bali or Pali, by which I mean the Pracrit language, and for the better understanding of it they interline it with the Sanscrit as an explanation. [1] This is something similar to the old practice of the Jews in their synagogue, who read their Pentateuch Hebrew a verse in the original, then the same verse in the Chaldee, alternately, for the use of the people to whom the old language was obsolete. This tends to prove the Sanscrit in Upper India, i. e. Mewar, *new*.

21. I think I may safely lay it down as an indisputable principle, that if a colony or number of emigrants come from one country to another and bring a written language, they will bring the whole number of letters they used in their old country, and that, with perhaps some very trifling exception, not fewer will ever after be used. From this it follows, that the Sanscrit words and forms of construction, which are both in the Greek and the Latin, must have come to the West before the Sanscrit was perfected to *fifty* letters. This consideration renders it highly probable that Col. Wilford's assertion, that the Sanscrit alphabet originally consisted of the Pelasgic or Cadmæan letters, is correct. It is a most important observation, and of itself almost proves the truth of my theory, of the universal dissemination of the Cadmæan system. I very much suspect that almost all the languages of India, Sanscrit excepted, are now of the nature of a Lingua Franca. India is in language very much like Europe. Each of the two is a little world to itself; every province or kingdom of which has a separate and distinct language, and, in writing, though not in printing, also a separate and distinct letter; but all having, from intermixture by conquests and other causes, a great intermixture of words; and all having a close connexion with the dead language of its learned men and priests—the Sanscrit. The Latin is now to Europe what the Sanscrit is to India; and if it were not for the art of printing, the forms of letters in Europe would be just as various as the languages. The letters in unprinted languages vary as often as the handwriting of individuals. The art of printing has given a degree of fixedness to letters unknown in ancient times, and still unknown in oriental countries. Although I dissent from much of what I find in Col. Van Kennedy's book, I quite agree with him, that he has proved the absolute uncertainty of the translations of the ancient oriental manuscripts and medals. We must always recollect that when an oriental professor claims to give us a translation, we have, in many cases, no means of judging either of his honesty or of his capacity for what he undertakes: whatever he tells us we take and must take. I mean by this no reflection on oriental scholars, farther than to place them pretty much on the same footing with translators of the Bible; only that their translations of medals and manuscripts may and ought, in most cases, to be considered somewhat more doubtful, as we have seldom the means of correcting them. A pretty good example is afforded in the translation of Ferishta, by Dow. My friend Col. Briggs declares that it bears not the most distant resemblance to the original: then which of these two translations are we to believe? The answer cannot be doubtful when all the circumstances of the two are considered. Again, Mr. Colebroke declares that the translation of another work, made by one of the missionaries, has no similarity to the original. Here again I can entertain no doubt to which of the two the credit is due. Oriental scholars are not entitled to claim exemption from human frailties, any more than Hebrew translators. They are equally liable to make mistakes; and, what is much more to be dreaded, to be influenced by religious prejudice. Of the latter, Van Kennedy is no bad example: for though

---

[1] Col. Tod's Hist.

his work is full of useful information and sound observation, yet a religious motive is evidently at the bottom of it, and throws a shade over it.

.22. The result of all my inquiries respecting the Sanscrit is, that I conclude it was invented in the kingdom of Oude or Iouda or Youdia, in North India, by a people speaking a language, the words of which were nearly Hebrew or Chaldee, perhaps improved by the addition of the vowels to the syllables, making it nearly African Ethiopic, and being in fact an improved Syriac, and Pushto, or the first Tamul; that the letter of this people was nearly the oldest Samaritan, and that it was the produce of a great number of years, and brought to its last perfection about the time of Alexander by Brahmins returning to India from the West; that its letters, the Deva-nagari, were formed on the Samaritan, and the language modelled on the Latin and Greek; that it was invented after the composing, perhaps after the committal to writing, of the Poems of Homer; and that its object was to secrete the learning and elevate its owners above the people, perhaps above the princes of their country. When I come to that part of my work where I shall explain the origin of letters and of the language of ciphers, which was the first written language, I shall return to the subject of the Sanscrit, and shall support what I have said above by some additional observations and circumstances.

## CHAPTER II.

MARQUIS SPINETO. — HIEROGLYPHICS NOT ANCIENT.—EDINBURGH REVIEW ON CHANGE OF LANGUAGE.— KNOWLEDGE OF HIEROGLYPHICS SUPPOSED LOST BY GREEK AUTHORS. —NAMES OF THE PTOLEMIES AND ROMAN EMPERORS ON MONUMENTS.—TRANSLATION FROM CLEMENS AND THE ROSETTA STONE.—JEWISH EXOD PROVED.—AN OBSERVATION OF MR SALT'S.—SIR W. DRUMMOND ON HIEROGLYPHICS. — ROSETTA STONE A FORGERY. — REWARD OFFERED BY AN EMPEROR FOR THE DISCOVERY OF THEIR MEANING. —VARIOUS PARTICULARS RESPECTING THE NATURE OF THE SUPPOSED LANGUAGE. — MARQUIS SPINETO NOT A SCEPTIC, &c.—BENTLEY: ZODIACS. ESNE. DENDERA.

BEFORE I proceed to the subject of this chapter, I shall submit to my reader a few observations upon the far-famed *discoveries*, as they are called, by Messrs. Young and Champollion.

1. Some time ago a learned foreigner, the Marquis Spineto, gave a course of lectures at Cambridge, on the discoveries of Messrs. Young and Champollion, which he has since published, and in which he has explained them at great length. To these lectures, as the most authentic account or summary of those discoveries with which I am acquainted, I shall very often apply in the course of this chapter.

Among the Western nations, in general, Egypt had the credit of being the parent of letters. This idea probably arose from the circumstance, that they were used in Egypt a considerable time before they arrived in Europe. Mon. Champollion thinks he has reduced the number of the Hieroglyphical letters, in one system, to *seventeen*, and the Marquis Spineto, in his lectures,[1]

[1] Page 95.

says he thinks that the Egyptian alphabet in the time of the Pharaohs consisted of this number of letters. These circumstances powerfully support the system of the sixteen letters advocated in the *Celtic Druids*, and in the Preliminary Observations to this work.

2. After having inquired with great care and attention into the discoveries believed to have been made of the meaning and history of the Hieroglyphics of Egypt, by Messrs. Young and Champollion, I have found nothing which satisfies me respecting either their great antiquity or their priority to the art of alphabetic writing. I still continue convinced that, the knowledge of letters preceded the invention of hieroglyphics. But I see no reason whatever for maintaining that the same process should have taken place in the invention of them, both in the old and the new world. I am equally convinced that the discoveries of Messrs. Young and Champollion are mere chimeras; that either they are deceivers, or that they have been deceived. But before I proceed, I must beg my reader to recall to mind what I have said in the first chapter of the Preliminary Observations, and the proofs I have there produced, that the Pyramids preceded the invention of Hieroglyphics.

It has been maintained, and is demanded by many of the learned to be admitted, *as a postulatum*, that in every country the first attempts towards writing consisted in a rude delineation of material or physical objects. Now this I cannot allow : and I call for proof of the assertion. I maintain that there is not only no evidence in its support, but I am quite certain that there is much evidence of the direct contrary. Plato, Cicero, Pliny, Diodorus, and others, have been quoted to prove that the Egyptians were the inventors of letters; but all they say, when their whole text and context are considered, is, that letters came from Egypt to the West, or that a certain Thoth, whom I have clearly proved to have been the Buddha of India, invented them. The very circumstance of Thoth or Buddha having invented them, proves them not of Egyptian original. The idea that the Egyptians should invent and use the complicated system on their monuments, when they knew the more simple system now practised, has been turned into ridicule. But the same arguments apply against their continued use of the complicated system to the time of the Antonines as to their first adoption of them, if they did so long use them. The argument will prove that they had not the use of alphabetic writing in the time of the Antonines. I take up the argument and say, It is proved by Messrs. Young and Co., that hieroglyphics were in use in the times of the Roman Emperors : this, therefore, is a clear proof that the Romans as well as Egyptians were ignorant of the use of alphabetic writing, *q. e. d.* This is a fair and conclusive argument against Messrs. Young and Champollion. But irony apart, I must say I can see no other way of accounting for the continuance of this system, if it did continue, to the time of the Romans, than a wish for concealment from the vulgar. What else could induce them to continue this most complicated system, when they might have used the beautiful Greek letters, well known and always common in Egypt after the time of Alexander, nearly four hundred years before Christ ? For my theory, viz. that they were used for concealment, I shew a plausible reason in addition to the support of historical evidence ; but the opponents of my opinion can give no reason for theirs. In addition to the above, many rolls of Papyri, covered with letters, have been found inclosed in mummies, of which the cases are covered with hieroglyphics.

3. It is said by a very able writer in the Edinburgh Review, who is considered the great advocate of Messrs. Young and Champollion's discovery, "That the hieroglyphic inscriptions, executed " so late as the reign of Antoninus, are read into the very same language as those which belong to " the age of Sesostris. Nor is this at all remarkable or extraordinary : for in the East, language, " LIKE EVERY THING ELSE, is immutable." Immutable in the East ! Good God ! immutable ! Yet there are hundreds of different languages, hundreds of sects, the highest refinement and skill in manufactures of all kinds, which must have been brought to perfection by degrees, great changes in Religions, and accounts of unceasing revolutions in governments ! But in the state

they now are, they must have been created thousands of years ago, *for nothing changes in the East!* Every thing is as it was originally created ! All is immutable ! This seems very extraordinary. I know no spoken language which has not greatly changed, except the sacred language of the Pentateuch, and the sacred artificial language of the Hindoos, the Sanscrit,—and even they have not been entirely exempt from the law to which every thing in this sublunary world, and probably in the whole creation, is subject. Every *constantly-used language, like every thing else,* has changed and always will change, and that greatly in long periods ; and one of the most suspicious circumstances which I know of, relating to this subject is, that the hieroglyphics of the time attributed to Sesostris should be capable of being read into the Coptic of the time of Antoninus,—the Coptic not being a sacred or secret, but a commonly-spoken, language. Notwithstanding the ingenuity displayed by Messrs. Young and Co., and the apparent reasonableness of their arguments, this simple fact seems to me to be so contrary to all experience and to all probability as to cast a shade of suspicion over their whole system in the very outset. It is quite impossible not to believe, that the Coptic, admitted to have been the commonly-spoken language of the country, (passing through the times of the Ethiopians, the Shepherd Kings, the Israelites, the Persians, the Greeks, in the whole for more than two thousand years,) must have so changed as to render it impracticable to read the symbolic or hieroglyphic writing of the Coptic language of Sesostris into the Coptic of Antoninus.

My opinion upon this point is fully confirmed by an observation of Dr. Young's, in one of his letters:[1] " In the four or five hundred years which elapsed between the date of the inscription " and that of the oldest Coptic books extant, the language appears to have changed much more " than those of Greece and Italy have changed in two thousand." Again he says, " The Egyp- " tian language must have varied considerably in the time which elapsed between the publication " of the decree, and the date of the earliest Coptic works which we possess."[2]

I think no one will deny that the Egyptian system, as explained by Messrs. Young and Champollion, is one of extreme complication ; and for this reason, if they be right, among all the others which I shall give, I think it probable that it was a secret system. This is nothing against their theories, and agrees with mine, the reasoning on which, I feel confident that they cannot refute. If their theory be admitted, they seem to have succeeded in making out the names of some of the kings; but I yet fear, even with the above admission, which I make only for the sake of argument, that, in *whole sentences,* from the great number of the Phonetic characters, their explanations cannot be depended on.

I think it has been satisfactorily proved, that Egypt was not the original birth-place of letters, that is, of science or learning; but that it came to her, as well as to Greece, from the East, and that, as it could not well come any other way, it probably came by way of Babylon. Then, if she were not the inventress of letters, how else are we to account for the hieroglyphics, except that they were a secret system ? The system of secrecy was in perfect keeping with the general practice of priests and philosophers all over the world at that time. All ancient authors agree in telling us, that their secrets were concealed under the garb of hieroglyphics.

4. Respecting the change in the Coptic language, I consider what I have stated to constitute a very formidable objection ; but there is one much more formidable in the fact that Strabo, one of the most respectable of the ancient Greek authors, believed their meaning to be lost.

Strabo[3] expressly says, that the Egyptians were mere sacrificers, without any knowledge of their ancient philosophy and religion. Mr. Payne Knight, in his essay on Symbolical Language,

---

[1] Mus. Crit. Cambridge, No. VI. p. 172.        [2] Ibid. p. 182.        [3] Lib. xvii.

after making some observations on the above-cited passage, gives a number of striking reasons to prove that the meaning of their hieroglyphics was lost by the Egyptians in the time of Strabo, as well as that of their religion.[1]  Mr. Knight observes, that "in Egypt, probably AS IN OTHER " COUNTRIES, zeal and knowledge subsisted in inverse proportions to one another." The observation is very severe, but, alas ! too true.  I believe that Diodorus Siculus may be ranked with Strabo.

It has been replied to me, that Strabo and Diodorus do not *say* the meaning of the *hieroglyphics* was unknown.  This is true : but it is as clear as the sun that they were unknown to the former, and that he thought them lost. Can it be believed that, if they had known the meaning of them, and if they had contained accounts of the mythology or history, they would not have quoted them ?  If they had been historical, they must, in some measure, have been mythological: and when Diodorus was professing to describe the mythology, and censuring his predecessors for declining to describe it on account of its difficulty,[2] it is impossible to believe that he would not in some way have referred to them.  As they were always supposed to contain the history, if they had really contained it, these authors must have told us the particulars of it.  There are two things which appear irreconcileable—the plausible accounts of Messrs. Young and Champollion, and the ignorance of the historians at the very time that the Roman Emperors and Ptolemies are alleged by Messrs. Young and Champollion to have been using them.

If the passage of Diodorus were taken by itself, it would certainly be against me : but when it is considered in connexion with the other circumstances, I think it will amount to nothing more than the idle boast of the priests, unwilling to admit their ignorance to the inquis'tive Greek ; and it most clearly proves that he did not understand these letters, said to be *applicable to the purposes of common life,* and that the priests did not explain them to him.  But the following is the passage taken from Booth's translation.  Every one must judge for himself.

 " But lest we should omit things that are ancient and remarkable, it is fit something should be " said of the Ethiopic characters, and of those which the Egyptians call Hieroglyphics.

 " The Ethiopic letters represent the shapes of divers beasts, parts and members of men's " bodies, and artificers' tools and instruments.  For, by their writing, they do not express any " thing by composition of syllables, but by the signification of images and representations, the " meaning of them being engraven and fixed in the memory by use and exercise.  For sometimes " they draw the shape of a kite, crocodile, or serpent ; sometimes the members of a man's body, " as the eye, the hand, the face, and such like.  The kite signifies all things that are quickly dis- " patched ; because this bird flies the swiftest almost of any other.  For reason presently applies " it by a suitable interpretation to every thing that is sudden and quick, or of such nature, as per- " fectly as if they had been spoken.  The crocodile is the emblem of malice : the eye the preserver " of justice, and the guard of the body.  Amongst the members of the body, the right hand, with " open fingers, signifies plenty ; the left, with the fingers close, preservation and custody of men's " goods and estates.

 " The same way of reasoning extends to all other parts of the body, and the forms of tools and " all other things ; for being that they diligently pry into the hidden signification of every thing, " and have their minds and memories daily employed with continual exercise, they exactly read " and understand every thing couched within the Hieroglyphics." Lib. iii. cap. 1.

The silence of the Marquis Spineto respecting the passages of Strabo and Diodorus,[3] seems to shew a consciousness on his part that they contained nothing in his favour.

---

[1] Vide Sect. 64—66.         [2] Vide Preface.         [3] See p. 9, Preface.

I believe the Hieroglyphics were never intended to be read, except by those who received, by tradition, the explanation of the different symbols or figures. The priests having been murdered by Cambyses, the secret was lost. (It was not the same with the Mexican Hieroglyphics. There was this important difference, that their traditionary meaning was not lost; for the Spaniards obtained it and preserved it, in Latin or Spanish, although they murdered the priests.) No doubt this traditionary knowledge of the Egyptians would constitute a great part of the learning of that day.

5. According to M. Champollion, we have not only the names of the Ptolemies and their wives on the public monuments, but we have the names of Roman Emperors, to a date long after the time of Strabo and Diodorus,—and those names, in some instances, in such situations on them, that there is no room whatever for suspecting that they have been engraved upon old names erased, or on buildings renewed. The fact of these names being found, by M. Champollion's process, will of itself prove that his plan will enable him, as I suspected, to make the hieroglyphics speak just what he pleases.

If the names of the Ptolemies, Cleopatra, the Roman Emperors, &c., are now to be found upon the buildings, obelisks, &c. in Hieroglyphics, it is very certain that in their time they must have been understood, and of course they could not have been lost in the time of Strabo and Diodorus. But upon this subject what says the very able writer, and friend of the discovery, in the Edinburgh Review? He shall speak for himself : " The fact undoubtedly is, that the classical writers " supply us with only a few vague and general notices, which, but for recent discoveries, would " be nearly unintelligible : while they at once aggravate and apologize for their ignorance by " asserting, that, as Egypt was the parent of art and science, so the Hieroglyphical inscriptions " on its public monuments contain a summary of the most important mysteries of nature, and " the most sublime inventions of man, but that the interpretation of these characters had been so " studiously concealed by the priests from the knowledge of the vulgar, and had indeed been so " imperfectly understood even by themselves, that it was soon wholly lost and forgotten." [1] Nothing can be more true than the account of this learned Reviewer. But why afterward deny that the Hieroglyphics were a sacred system? I willingly end the argument by saying, let us substitute for sacred, the Reviewer's own word, concealed or SECRET. I want no more. It was for the sake of this SECRECY or concealment that they were invented, and were continued long, very long, after the invention of alphabetic writing, and by no other means can their continuance be accounted for.

How can any one read the extract above from the Review, and not see, if it be true, that all the classical writers, many of them in the time, and in the confidence, of the masters of Egypt, the Roman Emperors, and consequently the Emperors themselves initiated in the mysteries, believed the knowledge of the Hieroglyphics to be lost ?—a fact admitted even by the Reviewer. How is it possible to believe that they were all deceived? If it were lost, it is pretty much the same as if it were concealed. How is the opinion of the classic writers given above to be reconciled with what the Reviewer says, that the Hieroglyphics *constituted a real written language applicable to the purposes of history and* COMMON LIFE ?[2] — and this written language unknown to such an inquirer as Strabo—a man professing to give the best information respecting them which he could collect ! But I shall be told that we have the authority of a father of the church, Clemens Alexandrinus, who tells us what they were. Yes, indeed, and in such language, so clear, that no two translators have yet been able to agree in opinion as to his meaning. For my own part, I

---

[1] Edin. Rev. No. LXXXIX. p. 98.          [2] P. 107.

believe he had no clear idea, but merely expressed an opinion,—in fact a suspicion, of the nature of the system, properly called Hieroglyphical.

6. The following is the translation of the passage of Clemens,[1] given by the Encyclopædia Britannica:[2] " The pupils who were instructed by the Egyptians first learned the order and the " arrangement of the Egyptian letters, which is called *epistolography*, that is, the manner of " writing letters ; next the sacred character which the sacred scribes employed; lastly, the " Hieroglyphic character, one part of which is expressed by the first elements, and is called " *cyriologic*, that is *capital*, and the other *symbolic*. Of the symbolic kind, one part explains " properly by imitation ; and the other is written tropically, that is, in tropes and figures ; and a " third by certain enigmatical expressions. Accordingly, when we intend to write the word *sun* " we describe a circle ; and when the *moon* the figure of that planet appearing horned, conformable " to the appearance of that luminary after the change." From an attentive consideration of the above passage, it must be allowed that it conveys no reason whatever to believe, that the Hiero-glyphics were understood in the time of Clemens either by him or by any one else. In reply to this it will be said, But we know that they were not lost in the time of the Ptolemies, because we have the Rosetta stone in three languages. This appears at first sight a very fair and plausible argument—an argument very difficult to answer, and a fact very difficult to reconcile to the unanimous admission of the classical writers, that they were no longer known. For, how is it possible to believe, that all these writers should be ignorant that in their time, it was the practice to write inscriptions on stones in Hieroglyphics, accompanied by translations into the Coptic and Greek languages ?

But when they were inquiring into the meaning of the Hieroglyphics, why did they not go to the triple inscription for information ?

When the Egyptians made the inscription in Greek and Coptic, what could be the object of using also the secret letter ? Was it to inform the priests ignorant of Coptic or Greek ; or, was it for fear these languages should be lost, and therefore they used the sacred character, that the valuable information should be preserved in it, when the others were gone ? It may be said, that though it seems foolish enough to use three languages, yet this kind of folly is very common. I grant that the argument seems good, for we can scarcely ever give man credit for too much folly, or for too little wisdom.

I contend that the Hieroglyphics were a system made complicated, as M. Champollion has described them, if they be so complicated, for the express purpose of preventing their discovery ; and I contend, also, that this removes all the difficulties of their history, and renders every part of it consistent with all the historical accounts, with experience, and with my theory.

7. I pretend not to fix the year of the Jewish Exod; but I believe in that Exod, and that Hieroglyphics were invented after it. The conquests of Joshua, I contend, are DECISIVELY PROVED by a species of evidence which no philosopher can deny, in the sixth chapter and thirtieth section, and the note upon it, in the last page of the Appendix to my CELTIC DRUIDS ; not by the evidence of lying priests, but by circumstance and the evidence of an unwilling witness ; and this pretty well carries with it proof of the Exod of Moses. From the Hieroglyphics being no where noticed in the Pentateuch, there arises a probability, (but not a *proof*, I admit,) that they were unknown when the Israelites left Egypt. But even if they were known in the time of Moses, my principal argument is not affected thereby. I suppose that the Pyramids were not inscribed with the names of their builders, because (notwithstanding the idle stories told to Herodotus) they

---

[1] Strom. Lib. v.  [2] Art. Philology, Sect. 72.

were, with their history, unknown; therefore, upon them, there are no hieroglyphics. If there be upon the buildings the names of kings who lived thousands of years before the time of Moses, this does not invalidate my argument. Nothing is more likely or natural than that when the priests invented their system to *record their history*, they should inscribe it on their old buildings as well as the names of the kings by whom they were believed to be built. Some foolish Scotchmen, I am told, are at this time erecting a monument to *John Knox*, the bigot, the persecutor, and the enemy of literature, the disgrace of their country, long after his death; so the Egyptians may have done to their worthies. On this supposition, it is very natural that the history and names of kings, in the time of Sesostris, should read into the Coptic of the time of the Ptolemies, as it is asserted above that they do: and thus a considerable impediment to a belief in the reality of M. Champollion's system is removed, and I would, with pleasure, remove all the difficulties if it were in my power. It seems to me to be probable that they were invented during the period, embracing many hundreds of years, which passed[1] between the Exod of Moses and the conquest of Cambyses. If they were invented much before this time, they would not read into modern Coptic. What I contend for exactly agrees with what Herodotus and Diodorus say, that there were two kinds of character—the ἱερα or sacred, and δημοτικα or the popular. This also agrees with the authority of the Rosetta stone,[2] (if we allow it any credit,) which *makes mention of only two kinds of characters—the one called* ENCHORIAL, (εγχωρια γραμματα,) *or " characters of the country," evidently identical with the demotic characters of Herodotus and Diodorus; and the other* SACRED (ἱερα).

8. Mr. Salt has observed,[3] that there is not the trace (in Hieroglyphics I suppose he means) of any monument remaining throughout Egypt or Nubia, of earlier date than Rameses Thothmosis, who, he says, the best chronologists agree was nearly contemporary with Moses. If Mr. Salt be right in this, I need not point out how much it tends to confirm my hypothesis. It is said by the Marquis Spineto,[4] that the names of the later kings of Egypt and emperors of Rome are found on the monuments of the earliest periods; and that they were so inscribed by these kings or emperors in order to obtain for themselves the honour of having erected them; that the names of all the Roman emperors, from Augustus to Antoninus Pius, except Galba, Otho, and Vitellius, are found on several of them, both in Egypt and Rome; that the several obelisks now existing at Rome, such as the obelisks of the Barbarini, the Albani, the Borgian, and Pamphilian, and a part of the public buildings at Philoe, and the temples at Esne and Dendera, are covered with legends, containing the names and titles of Hadrian, Titus, Tiberius, Nero, Claudius—in short, of almost all the Roman emperors, down to the fourth century, the whole written in Phonetic hieroglyphics[5]

Now this is monstrously absurd in the case of the obelisks brought to Rome, because they were brought as antiquarian curiosities, as a species of triumphal monument of the conquests of the Romans over the Egyptians. It would have been even more absurd for the Romans to insert their names on the obelisks, than for Mr. Banks to engrave his on the obelisk which he brought from Philoe. This seems to me to strike a deadly blow at the whole system.

Mr. Salt, in p. 31 of his Essay,[6] has given an account of an old name which, in his opinion, has been erased and a modern Ptolemy inserted in its place, but, from bad workmanship, in one instance discoverable. If a modern fraud have been executed, this must have been a part of it,

---

[1] There being in reality no system of chronology.
[2] Edin. Rev. No. LXXXIX. p. 101.
[3] Essay, p. 54          [4] P. 366.          [5] P. 100.          [6] Vide Spineto, p. 366.

and was evidently necessary.[1]   But notwithstanding the opinion of Mr. Salt, whose zeal may have blinded his judgment, I must say I have seen no satisfactory proof that the letters of this name are of more recent workmanship than the others on the same edifices ; therefore I am warranted in believing that there is no such proof, that there is no foundation for such an assertion : besides, if they be so, as I have just said, they are probably modern frauds.   I do not recollect in history any thing equal to this foolish vanity of the Ptolemies and Cæsars—the gratification of a vanity which must have rendered them contemptible in the highest degree to their subjects, who could surely never pass one of these inscriptions in this *real written language, applicable to the purposes of common life*, without a smile of contempt—even though it were the gratification of such a vanity by Marcus Aurelius or Trajan.   I hope these gentlemen do not judge of such men as Trajan and Antoninus, by themselves.

9.  Sir William Drummond has made the following very ingenious observations on this subject :
" The Greeks were no doubt curious to know all the secrets of the hieroglyphics : and the priests
" of Egypt were not willing to acknowledge to their masters, that they had lost the keys of those
" mysterious symbols.   It is very possible that they may have been acquainted with the meaning of
" the kuriologic hieroglyphics, and may also have retained the knowledge of the epistolary cha-
" racters : but of the tropical and enigmatical, and allegorical signs and symbols, I cannot easily
" believe that they knew the meaning, and it may be presumed that they often imposed on the
" easy credulity of the Greeks.   They chose symbols to denote their new monarchs and their
" queens : they enclosed between lines, or placed in circular, quadrangular, or oval frames, the
" emblems of their new divinities : and Ptolemy and Berenice, admitted to the honours of the
" apotheosis, beheld their hieroglyphics placed by the side, and perhaps sometimes in the room of
" those of Osiris and Isis.   Long and adulatory inscriptions recorded the titles and the virtues of
" the Ptolemies : and these Gods, as they were styled, promulgated their decrees not only in the
" Egyptian and Greek characters, but in hieroglyphics, symbolical and tropical.   But it is difficult
" to acquit the Egyptians of fraud on these occasions : nor is it easy to avoid suspecting the
" Greeks of sometimes lending themselves to the impostures practised by their flatterers."[2]

10.  But I must return to the triple inscription or rather inscriptions, for I am told that two more have been found in other parts of Egypt, by some of the French sçavans.  I ask why Clemens, living at Alexandria, did not go to them to remove his ignorance?  Why Strabo did not apply to them ?   To these writers there could be no difficulty in reading the Greek ; which even the best of our Greek scholars cannot now understand, and by going to the triple inscriptions they would have had all their difficulties removed in a moment.  I am not ignorant of the frauds of the infamous Fourmont, exposed by the Earl of Aberdeen.  I am not ignorant of the character of the Parian Marbles.  I have heard of Annius of Viterbo, and of M. Bonelli's dispute with Mr. Payne Knight, and the Cameo in the Museum; and I must freely declare that I believe the triple inscriptions are ingenious forgeries ; that the name of the king, ill executed, discovered on a monument by. Mr. Salt, has been placed there for the purpose of being discovered, and that the deed described in the Edinburgh Review, has been forged, and the counterpart placed purposely to be discovered—as antiques are placed every day in the ruins of Pompeii to be discovered by visitors ; I suspect that they are all parts of a great lie.  I shall be told of the difficulty of executing so great

---

[1] From Mr. Salt's Essay (p. 25), it appears that the name of the king who erected the obelisk now standing at Matarea was Misarte.  Pliny says, *Mestres* and Kircher, from a Vatican MS., *Mitres*.  This seems to connect it with the Persian *Mithra*, the name of that God taken by the person who erected it.  The Indian and Egyptian practice of kings calling themselves by the names of Gods seems to render all ancient history doubtful.

[2] Drummond on Zod. p. 23.

a lie, and that Dr. Young and Champollion must have been in a league. Without difficulty there would be no probability of successful deceit. Are we not deceived with copies from Raphael, with Etruscan Vases from Staffordshire, by Bonollis with Cameos, and with manuscripts, every day ? The difficulty is no objection. I desire an answer to the question, why the inquiring authors, Clemens and Strabo, did not inform themselves from the triple inscriptions. In the Morning Herald for June 24, 1830, is the following curious account : " At the last meeting of the London Medico-Botanical " Society, Professor Houlton mentioned the following extraordinary instance of the protraction of " vegetable life.—A bulbous root, which was found in the hand of an Egyptian mummy, in which " situation it had very probably been for more than two thousand years, germinated on being " exposed to the atmosphere, though when discovered it was apparently in a state of perfect dry- " ness. The root was subsequently put into the ground, where it grew with readiness and vigour." This seems to shew us pretty clearly that what has been for some time suspected is true, that alleged ancient mummies are now manufactured in Egypt every day. This forms a good match for the Rosetta stone.

11. But another damning fact creeps out very unwillingly from the Marquis. A reward was offered by one of the first of the Cæsars to him who should give a proper interpretation of the in-scription on the obelisk which had been carried to Rome. [1] This single fact overthrows the whole system. It is quite impossible to believe that the hieroglyphics should have been in common use, for the inscribing on them the names of Roman Emperors and other matters, (*a real written language applicable to the purposes of history and* COMMON LIFE, as the Edinburgh Reviewer says,) and yet that the Roman Emperor and his ministers should have had occasion to offer a reward to discover their meaning.

I believe it is an admitted fact, that the Romans inscribed hieroglyphics on some modern obelisks in Rome to make them imitate ancient Egyptian. [2] If this be admitted, it is totally incredible that they should erase the real names from the real ancient Egyptian obelisks in that city, to insert their own, and thus make them appear to be modern.

It appears to me that the fact of the ignorance of the Greek authors is of itself a presumptive proof, that the trilinguar stones are modern fabrications. Their existence is totally incompatible with the admitted ignorance of Strabo, Diodorus Siculus, and the inquisitive Clemens Alexan-drinus the Egyptian.

A careful attention to the history of the world for the last eighteen hundred years has shewn me, that the priests of all religions have practised fraud to forward their objects ; and that with a few exceptions in the first centuries of Christianity, when they avowed that it was meritorious to practise it, they have solemnly declared their innocence, while their guilt has been clear. The consideration of these circumstances must be my excuse for my apparent illiberality ; but when-ever a Bourbon, the élève, the protégé of the Jesuits, protects a man, I suspect him. I cannot forget that the priests in every age have protected, as ours do now protect, impostures, and that in every age numerous examples of pious fraud may be found. The Reviewer, when speaking of the deeds and counterparts, says, he suspects the age of Magic is not over. I reply, Magic is pretty nearly over, but fraud seldom throve better.

These considerations destroy my faith in the discovery. I cannot bring myself to the belief that the later princes, the Trajans, Antonines, &c., would stoop to so despicable and unavailing a fraud ; that they would, with their eyes open, expose themselves to the ridicule of all mankind. But the evidence of the deeds and counterparts exhibited in the *ninetieth* number of the Edinburgh

---

[1] Spineto, p. 48.     [2] P. 51.

Review seems conclusive against me. Then what am I to make of these inconsistencies? When I consider the respectable characters of Messrs. Young and Champollion, I cannot believe them capable of practising a fraud: but I am obliged to believe that they have been in part deceived, and partly deceive themselves; and that in consequence of their mode of proceeding and of the great number of the phonetic forms for one letter, they are able to make the hieroglyphics speak what they please.

Whether the French sçavans were the inventors or the dupes of the fraudulent Rosetta stone I know not; but I can more readily believe that the priests have been at their old game, than that Diodorus, Strabo, and Clemens, and the Roman Emperors while offering rewards,[1] have all been ignorant of the state of the simple question, whether Hieroglyphics were in common use in their time or not.

No doubt, to charge the sçavans of France with having caused the Rosetta stone to be made for fraudulent purposes, will be considered, in any man having a regard for his literary or even moral character, to be very hardy; but this, notwithstanding, I must do. I find that Dr. Young did not begin his researches till after the finding of the Rosetta stone; that they in a great measure depend upon it—are founded upon it; and that he, in fact, had nothing to do with it, but simply believed what we have been told respecting it by the French in Egypt, who made such a terrible outcry for the loss of it. If they hid the stone for the purpose of having it found, they performed their parts, as indeed they generally do every part they undertake, very well. He must know very little of the French character, who finds a difficulty in believing that such of them as were likely to undertake an adventure of this kind, would be deficient in talent to carry it into effect. And as to the other stones, having on them inscriptions in the three kinds of characters, the same as those on the Rosetta stone, those who were capable of making one, were capable of making the others, and also of placing them where they, or, what would be still better, the English, would find them. The size and nature of all these stones precludes the idea, that they were intended to be kept, or were, in fact, in ancient times, kept secret. Then I again ask, how came Clemens the Egyptian—the Alexandrian—or Strabo, or Diodorus Siculus the Antiquarian, when they were inquiring into and regretting the loss of the Hieroglyphics, not to go to these stones and remove at once all their difficulties? The Greek, at that day, could not only not form a difficulty, as at present, but it must have instantly removed every difficulty, and this is the strong point upon which I ground my charge of fraud. Let the fact be accounted for. How came they not to go to these *common* triple inscriptions scattered about the country in different places, for a solution of their difficulties, and an explanation of 'all the ancient mythologies or histories? The very great ingenuity required to give these stones the appearance of antiquity, is to me no objection, when I consider the character of the French nation, and the perfection to which the art of similating the works of the ancient masters, in the arts of painting and sculpture, has been carried—and the manufacture of Etruscan vases, and the forgeries of the works of Berosus by Ennius, of the manuscripts of Shakspeare, by Ireland, and the various well-known forgeries of ancient inscriptions on stones, &c., &c., &c.

This brings me to make one more observation on the deed and counterpart. The moment I heard of these, they struck me to be very like a modern indenture, but having no suspicion I hastily passed them by, and there may be nothing in it. But the persons who could make the Rosetta stone, I have no doubt could make these deeds, and could bury them too, where the proper persons would find them. It is well known that articles are constantly buried at Pompeii in particular

---

[1] P. 48.

places, where visitors of eminence are allowed to search. I once *saw* an Archduke of Austria uncommonly successful at Pompeii. There is so large an interest now concerned in this matter, and interest and passion are so much engaged, that I should not be surprised if the *French* and *English* between them, were to find a hundred Rosetta stones. But to save them *further trouble*, I beg leave to point out to them, that the more Rosetta ☞ triplicate stones there are found, the more the difficulty will be increased of accounting for the blindness of Clemens and Strabo.

In addition to the above, I beg to refer my reader to an article in No. VIII. of the Foreign Quarterly Review, published by Teutzel and Wurtz, p. 466. In this essay the writer maintains, that he has convicted Messrs. Champollion and Sallier, of Aix, jointly, of a gross fraud. I am unwilling to decide between these gentlemen and the Reviewer, upon hearing only one side; but I confess I do not see how they are to defend themselves; and I need not point out to my reader that, if the Reviewer should be right, no man of common sense will ever pay the slightest attention to any thing which Messrs. Champollion, and Co. may say in future.

12. I might here, perhaps, safely drop the subject; but it may be satisfactory to my reader to inspect a little more minutely the machinery by which Messrs. Champollion and Co. raise the profound learning from the well where it has so long lain buried. M. Champollion[1] teaches, that many of the consonants and almost all the vowels are often represented by the *same* hieroglyphical characters. To apologize for this he says,[2] they are to represent the different dialects of the different districts of Egypt, but where he learnt the Coptic dialects he does not tell us. The most extraordinary of all delusions is that which blinds this gentleman and his friends to the absurdity of admitting, that there are three distinct modes of writing, and that they then have recourse to the whole three *promiscuously* in their explanation of a sentence. They cull out a part of the eight or nine hundred figures on the monuments, which they divide among the letters, giving to each a number of figures, even in some instances amounting to twenty-five in number;[3] the remainder they call allegorical, and symbolic, and then, in order to expound the inscriptions, they bring all the three into play at once. Thus, if the letters will not answer to the drawings so that there is a figure unexplained, it is then called one of the other kinds of writing; it is an allegorical or a symbolic letter; by this process a meaning is, at all events, made out. The Marquis Spineto says, alphabetical signs were of three kinds—Demotic, hieratic, and hieroglyphical properly so called.[4] Hieroglyphics are divided into three classes—Hieroglyphics proper; Hieroglyphics abridged; Hieroglyphics conventional.[5] There are also symbolical or enigmatical hieroglyphics; and conventional figurative hieroglyphics; and figurative abridged hieroglyphics; and the enigmatical hieroglyphics may be again divided or used in three ways.[6] The alphabet published by M. Champollion contained 134 hieroglyphical characters, strictly speaking phonetic; yet he found out the meaning of 730 more, some symbolical, others figurative.[7] Some of the consonants, and almost all of the vowels, are often represented *by the same hieroglyphical characters;*[8] and as there are no vacancies between the words, they are divided at pleasure. They are read from top to bottom, from right to left, from left to right, and in groups, all in the same inscription. Thus, in writing, the signs or figures may be placed in four different ways, and are often found so to exist in the same monument.[9] In another place M. Spineto says, all the three kinds of writing, viz. the phonetic, figurative, and symbolic, are often found in the same inscription, mixed together, not one below another, as translations of one another,[10] but used *promiscuously* (to repeat his word) in the same sentence,[11] and the words written in the sentence are not divided. The hieroglyphical

---

[1] P. 86.    [2] P. 87.    [3] P. 88.    [?] 85.    [4] P. 116.    [6] P. 120.

[7] P. 85.    [8] Pp. 86, 88.    [9] Pp. 96—98.    [10] P. 169.    [11] Pp. 177, 179.

figures stood as letters ; for a letter which began the name of the animal, as a Dog, would stand for a D.[1] Thus the hieroglyphic as Dog standing for D, or Horse for H, it seems to follow as a necessary consequence, that letters must have preceded them ; in fact, that they must be an invention founded upon letters.[2] Thus, if we wished to write London, we might take a lion, a lamb, a lancet, or a leaf, &c. ; and a net, a negro, a north star, a nave of a church, and so on, for as many words in the language as begin with the letter L, in the first instance, or with N, in the second. I think M. Champollion has been very moderate to take no more, in any case, than twenty-five ! In addition to all the above, we have yet one more kind of hieroglyphs, called Anaglyphs.[3] I shall not attempt to describe them ; we have surely had enough.

13. The capacity of the Marquis Spineto for believing, may be judged of by his belief that a subterraneous passage was carried from Thebes to Memphis.[4] This is at least two hundred miles. As the Marquis justly observes, how contemptible does this make our Thames tunnellers appear! I believe that the reason why we cannot find this subway now, is that, *for the sake of dryness*, it was carried under the bed of the river. I hope I shall no more be accused of *scepticism*, for surely I believe as much as the Marquis ; and what is more, I believe it merely out of compliment to our learned visitor the Marquis, and I hope he will sufficiently appreciate my politeness !

It is very seldom that a fraud of any length can be successfully carried through ; the performer is almost certain to let something escape to betray it. Thus, if the Rosetta stone be a forgery, the manufacturers of it forgot that the knowledge of Hieroglyphics was proved, by the historians whom I have named, to have been lost in the time of the Ptolemies, and thus he made his inscription bear their names in the Greek. The Hieroglyphics will bear to be construed into almost any thing ; and I have little doubt, if it were wanted, William of Britain might be made out of them. I suspect that some of the French sçavans formed the stone with great ingenuity, in such a manner as would enable them to make the inscriptions speak what they pleased, and that the Jesuits discovering this, induced the Bourbons to take advantage of it to support, as they supposed, the Mosaic history.

M. Champollion was sent to Egypt, by Charles the Tenth, to search for inscriptions, and, of course, with the perfect approbation of the Jesuits. He kept up a close correspondence with the well-known Duke de Blacas, Ambassador from France at Rome, and his discoveries, as described by the Marquis Spineto, exhibit, in every part, a predetermination to support the Mosaic system ; and this also creeps out from the Marquis perpetually in his Lectures. In Chapter XI., he must pardon me for saying, rather *ridiculously*, to serve his purpose,[5] he makes the usual age for females to marry to be thirty-five years, when it ought to be, in that climate, fifteen or sixteen. In one place[6] he incautiously admits that he is not authorized to state all he knows ;[7] and in another,[8] that he does not think it *necessary to mention* what would have been of the first importance. I suppose it would have made the learned Cantabs, to whom he addressed his lectures, too learned. The moment I find a person beginning to talk of concealment and holy scriptures, I suspect him. The word *holy* involves the consequence, that every question is prejudged which relates to these scriptures. The question is begged ; particularly when this is assisted by the repetition of the old cant about philosophy being dangerous.[9]

The Marquis[10] says, that Hebrew translations of many of the consecrated rolls of papyrus are to be found in the Bible. This again, coming in the manner it does, tends to create doubt ; but, for

---

[1] P. 82.          [2] P. 91.          [3] P. 411.          [4] Pp. 212, 220.          [5] P. 376.          [6] P. 253.

[7] " The French proverb of *L'oiseau de St. Luc*, the origin and signification of which I do not feel myself authorized " to state in this place." P. 253.

[8] P. 369.          [9] P. 490.          [10] P. 6.

reasons which I shall give hereafter, of the nature of which the Marquis has not the slightest suspicion, I think it very probable, that much which is recorded in the Old Testament, may be recorded also on the Egyptian monuments.

Lecture XI., on Chronology, may be called a mistake, as I think there is scarcely a sentence which is not wrong. It is, however, rather whimsical to find this learned gentleman-hierist informing not merely the *boys* of Cambridge, but also the *wise men*, that Usher established the Chronology of the LXX.[1] I think we shall not be much longer troubled with the *modern discoveries* in the Hieroglyphical branch of learning.

14. If Frenchmen should stand convicted of a Hieroglyphical fraud, their neighbours in England will not be far behind them. Mr. Bentley, of whom I have before spoken, has given an explanation of the Zodiacs of Esne and Dendera, and undertaken to prove them Calendars, for the year 708 of Rome. But his pretended copy of the Zodiacs is false in a great number of places, and the whole exhibits a most extraordinary example either of pious fraud, or of the grossest blundering. Mr. Bentley is dead and cannot defend himself, and therefore I would willingly attribute the fact to the latter of these causes ; but the evident object being to bolster up the Mosaic chronology, it is impossible to avoid suspicion of the former. This suspicion is strengthened by what appear to me, in several instances, to be *wilful misrepresentations*, and by a recollection of the misrepresentations of which we have already seen him guilty respecting the forgeries of the Brahmins, and his determination, at all events, to run down the Indian learning.

He founds his system upon a comparison of the Zodiacs with the Roman calendar of Numa. Both the Egyptian Zodiacal Almanacs, according to his exposition of them, pretend to mark the corrections introduced into the Roman Calendar by Julius Cæsar,[2] and to commence with a conjunction of the Sun and Moon at Rome, not in Egypt,[3] in the year of Rome 708. Now at this time Antony was living with Cleopatra in Egypt.

It seems impossible to believe, that the Romans at this early period should have succeeded in having their calendar inserted into the roofs of Egyptian temples, which must have been rebuilt at the time when they were inserted. The adoption of this calendar seems necessarily to carry with it the adoption of the Roman festivals, and this, again, a complete adoption of the Roman ritual—in fact, a complete change in the religion of the Egyptians. When I consider all the circumstances of the histories of Egypt and Rome at that date, if there were no other objections, I cannot bring myself to believe this. If the date of the calendar had been placed in the times of the Antonines, or of other Emperors, who were absolute Lords of Egypt, and who, we know, took a pleasure in repairing and adorning its public edifices, the case would be very different. These considerations I think Mr. Bentley overlooked.

The following observations of the ingenious Mr. Landseer will shew the extreme absurdity of believing, that the Romans could succeed in placing their calender on the top of an Egyptian temple, so early as the time of Ptolemy and Cleopatra:—" For the whole time that the classical " nations were in possession of that interesting country, they appear to have exercised but a " conciliatory controul in any other than military and municipal matters, and to have been so far " from dictating, in what concerned the truth of science or the dogmata of faith, that they " evidently chose, or were, from prudential motives, constrained to recognize and follow, what " they found established—perhaps without comprehending its essence, or fathoming its depth : " yielding to the pontifical authorities of that ancient land, the same species of deference that the " modern Catholics, of the rest of Europe, pay to the mother Church of Rome. They erected

---

[1] P. 383.          [2] P. 274.          [3] P. 253.

" there no Greek nor Roman temples, or we should have found their ruins at least : but, if they
" built at all, (which they certainly did,) re-edified the more ancient temples of Egypt, with so
" much of strict adherence to the original designs ; or constructed others so much in the same
" style, that modern antiquaries have been fairly puzzled by them." [1]    Nothing can be more true
than these observations, as I believe all will allow ; but they place in the strongest point of view
possible the absurdity of believing that they were the builders of the temple of Dendera or Esne
*in the time of Cleopatra and Antony.*  I have a great suspicion that these Zodiacs will turn out
to be perpetual calendars for the Metonic cycles or the Neros, or of both.  And this will account
for their appearing to suit the very remote ages, as some gentlemen have supposed.  It seems
also extremely absurd that the calendar should be suitable to the climate, latitude, and longitude,
of Rome, and not of Egypt.  If it be an almanac, I think it is one to serve for the whole Soli-
Lunar cycle, for both the Zodiacs are said to begin with a conjunction of the sun and moon.

The following short passage from the Encyclopædia Britannica, completely disposes of Mr.
Bentley's Roman calendar in Egypt : " The Egyptians used no intercalations till the time of
" Augustus, when the corrected Julian year was received at Alexandria, by his order : but even
" this order was obeyed only by the Greeks and Romans who resided in that city : the supersti-
" tious natives refusing to make any addition to the length of a year which had been so long
" established among them." [2]    This order, by Augustus, for the correction of the year according
to the Julian improvement, implies that it was not previously adopted; it would not, therefore,
have been inserted into the roofs of the temples many years before, in the time of Cleopatra and
Antony.  This, I think, invalidates Mr. Bentley's explanations of the Zodiacs of Esne and
Dendera, and I think strikes a hard blow at Messrs. Young and Champollion's system—it being
manifest that any thing may be made out of the Hieroglyphics—and that thus, in fact, they can
teach us nothing.  If some of Mr. Bentley's explanations were not founded, as in reality they
are, upon *false* drawings, but even upon *true* ones, this would completely blow them into air.  I
have somewhere read that the order above given by Augustus caused an insurrection.

Mr. Bentley admits that the same letter of the alphabet may be rendered ten or a dozen different
ways, [3] and that the same number is represented by several distinct characters, as described in his
plate No. IX.  On turning to the plate, I find *nine* different characters for the *unit*, and *eight* for
the number *four*, and others in the same way.  From this great number of signs for one idea, or
letter, or number, the expounder may construe them into what he pleases.

The exposure of Mr. Bentley's frauds or mistakes, is of the very first importance, as his explanation has been taken advantage of by the priests to overthrow all the former theories respecting
these Zodiacs, and to draw conclusions inimical to all further inquiry.  It has afforded to them a
grand triumph over the philosophers, and is so plausible, that it has deceived some very learned
orientalists.  But its exposure is of very great consequence for another reason : it shews that
by Messrs. Young and Champollion's system of making many phonetic signs for one letter, they
may be made to speak whatever the expositor chooses ; for they take much greater liberties than
Mr. Bentley took in this respect, and he succeeded in making out what he wished, though totally
destitute of any foundation in truth.  But the exposure is of consequence for yet one more reason
—it proves that arbitrary figures, which are *not Hieroglyphics at all,* may be made to give out
such a meaning as the expositor wishes ; for several of Mr. Bentley's drawings are not Hieroglyphics, but merely arbitrary, unmeaning figures, not in the Zodiacs.  This fact was discovered in
the following manner ; I was told by a very learned orientalist, that he was quite convinced by

---

[1] Sabæan Res. p. 218.              [2] Art. Chron. p. 751..              [3] Pp. 257, 258.

Mr. Bentley's book that the Zodiacs were Roman calendars ; and that all questions respecting them were closed.  Judging from the dates as given above I could not believe this, and being at the time very much engaged, I requested my friend Richard Makenzie Beverley, Esq., LL.D., to examine the work for me.  In consequence of my request he wrote a paper which was read, by my desire, to the Asiatic Society, and, as I was told, for I was not present, with great applause.  But, for reasons unknown to me, the council refused to publish it in their Transactions.  When I consider all the circumstances relating to this paper,—the fact that it prevents the priests from closing the door upon any further inquiry into those curious monuments ; and, again, since IT PROVES that, by the new system, Hieroglyphics may be made to say any thing or every thing, and that it thereby overturns the whole of M. Champollion's system, I am induced to take the liberty of telling this learned body, that Mr. Beverley's paper was of more consequence than all the papers hitherto published in their Transactions put together ; many of which are notoriously nonsensical enough.  These Asiatic gentlemen are constantly complaining that the Universities treat them and their learning with neglect ; how can they expect any thing better, when they thus refuse to publish the paper, *not anonymous*, of a Cantab of high academical rank ?  For, however I may regret the line he has taken since that paper was written, read, and refused to be printed, I feel bound to say, he is a gentleman of great learning and talent.  I think the circumstance altogether strikingly confirms my observation respecting the Orientalists, in Book V. Chap. IV. Sect. 12.  However, the refusal to publish the paper will not succeed in keeping the world in ignorance.  After what I have written here, Mr. Bentley's work will be soon compared with the plates in Creuzer, and in the grand work of the French in the British Museum, and the falsity of it made public.  I shall return to Mr. Bentley, of whom I shall have something of much importance to say before I finish my work.  I have no doubt that the societies of our three Presidencies in India, may justly be called, Three Societies for the Suppression of Oriental Knowledge.  I hope the Society in Grafton Street will be more cautious in future, and will not give their enemies an opportunity to say, that *they* make a *fourth*.  To say the very least, whoever advised them not to publish Mr. Beverley's paper, did not exercise a sound discretion.

---

## CHAPTER III.

SEMIRAMIS THE SAME NAME AS HELEN.—SEMIRAMIS WORSHIPED AS A DOVE.—CAUSE OF QUARREL BE-
TWEEN THE JEWS AND SAMARITANS.—PHILO ON THIS SUBJECT.—SEMIRAMIS CRUCIFIED.—STAUROBATES.
PHOINIX.—ORION. PHOINIX CONTINUED.—CECROPS.  IXION.  DIVINE LOVE CRUCIFIED.

1. I will now add a few more observations respecting the celebrated Semiramis, or the Indian Sami-Rama-Isi.  Nimrod says, " The name of Semi-Ramis will occur to every reader ; she was " both a queen of unrivalled celebrity, and also the Goddess mother, worshiped under the form of " the Dove that accompanied Noah in the Ark.

" Her name signifies the *supreme Dove*, and is of precisely the same value as the *Peleias* or " *Pleias* of the Greeks, and the *Iona* of the Syrians, Babylonish Chaldees, and Culdees or HEBRI-

" DEAN[1] Chaldees. The learned Lycophron calls *Helen* a dove by two names of that bird,
" Peleias (which has been explained) and *Oinas* or the *Bacchic dove*. Helen[2] was born out of a
" waterfowl's egg, and that which Hyginus relates evinces fully that she was the Babylonian
" Venus and the Dea Syria."[3]  She was the daughter of Dercetis, of Ascalon, of the Philistines.
She was also said to have been nursed by the river Simois. This connects her with the Hellen
of Troy. If she were the same as Diana, like Diana, she would, of course, be black.

Helen, like Semiramis, was supposed to have been born from an egg : and she is said to have
been deceived by a phantom, substituted by Juno, in the likeness of Menelaus ; and, according to
some accounts, she must have been ninety or one hundred years old at the siege of Troy. She is
called 'Ελινα and 'ΕΛΕΝΗ.[4]  I think her identity with Semiramis will scarcely be doubted, or
the identity of their mythological characters. It is probable that the Greek name had its origin
from the Asiatic אל *al* with its dialectic variations, הל *el* על *ol* אלה *ale*, &c., and נה *nh* the *anima*.
The Holy Ghost was generally female.

In the Syrian temple of Hierapolis, where between the statues of Jupiter and Juno stood the
statue of Semiramis with the dove on her head, it was the custom of the priests to emasculate
themselves, and to wear the dress of women. The same practice prevailed in the temple of Cybele
in Phrygia. Mr. Knight knows not how to account for this. I believe it was done in honour of
the female principle, the Ionism, which prevailed in these places in a peculiar manner. Lucian
*de Deá Syriá* says, that between the statues of Jupiter and Juno in the temple of Hierapolis, in
Syria, was a statue of a God, which had not the shape of any of the other Gods, on which stood a
dove. This must have been a plain stone pillar, probably of great antiquity. He says there are
two Priapuses in front of the temple 300 fathoms high, on which devotees went at certain seasons
and remained *seven* days. From this we see that the pillar saints were not peculiar to Christianity, and that they preceded it many generations. Lucian also says, the temple at Hierapolis,
or the sacred city, resembles the temples of Ionia.

2. At Hierapolis the female statue with the dove upon its head was called Sema.[5]  This was
the Semi-ramis of the Assyrians converted into a Dove, and the Rama-Sema or Sema-Rama of
India.[6]  In a future page we shall find that the Zamorin of the promontory of India—of Cape
Comorin—where, in a very particular manner, the *Cama*, or, as it is spelt in Java, *Como*, was
adored, was a Semiramis ; on this account I am induced strongly to suspect that the *Sema* above
was a corruption of *Cama ;* but I shall return to this.

The Goddess of Dodona had a dove on her head, and was called *Dione*.[7]  This Dione was
evidently *Di-ioni* or Di-iune, that is, the holy lune—diva Iune. Noah, or Nh, or MNH, or Menu,
or Mind, sent out a raven—the emblem of darkness—which made no return, produced nothing ;
he then sent out the *dove*, the emblem of Love, which brought back the *olive*, the emblem of
wisdom, of Minerva. Εϱως, Divine Love, was the *Protogonos*, the same as wisdom.

The above observations are strikingly supported by the following passages of the Jewish writings : Jeremiah xxv. 38,—facta est terra eorum in desolationem à facie iræ columbæ. Again,
ch. xlvi. 16,—à facie gladii columbæ (Vulgate). Again, ch. l. 16,—For fear of the *oppressing*
*Iönah* יונה *(iune,)* they (the nations in captivity) shall turn every one to his people, and they shall

---

[1] Here are the Culdees of the Hebrides, of whom I have treated at large in my Celtic Druids, with their saint Iona
or saint and bishop Columba.

[2] Myrrha Mæris.  [3] Nimrod, Vol. II. p. 249.  [4] Class. Jour. Vol. XXXVII. p. 204.

[5] Faber, Origin. Pag. Idol. Vol. III. pp. 33, 34.  [6] See Asiat. Res. Vol. IV. p. 369.

[7] Herodot. Lib. ii. 54, &c., apud Payne Knight on Symb. S. 73.

3 s

flee every one to his own land.[1]  The Seventy translate this passage, as also that in ch. xlvi. 16, in a very particular manner: απο προσωπη μαχαιρας Ἑλληνικῆς.

3. In confirmation of an idea which I entertain that the division between the tribes of Juda and Israel was religious more than political, several passages may be cited.  The sin of the Samaritans was in part, no doubt, a return to the adoration of the Sun in Taurus, as the Divine manifestation.  Of this the god Apis, set up at Sinai, at Dan, and at Bethel, is the first and a decisive proof.  This is confirmed by another passage,[2] which shews, that the festivals that Moses had regulated, with regard to the precession of one month, were restored by Jeroboam.  The one month is exactly the time of the equinoctial precession between Taurus and Aries, which, of course, would regulate all the other festivals.  So " Jeroboam ordained a feast in the eighth " month, like unto the feast that is in Judah.—On the fifteenth day of the eighth month, *which he* " *had devised of his own heart.*"  The expression marked in italics seems to shew that the festival had been a matter of dispute.  And it is added, that the feast was a sacrifice *vitulis*, or to the images of Taurus, which he had set up in Bethel and Dan.  " God commanded the observation " of the feast of tabernacles on the fifteenth day of the seventh month.  Jeroboam, in order to " corrupt the established worship, appointed a feast on the fifteenth day of the eighth month." [3]

The crime of the Samaritans was a return to the adoration of Taurus and the double principle, evidenced by the setting up of the calves, doubtless both *male* and *female*, at Dan and Bethel, and by the Dove found in their temple, as reported by Rabbi Meir. .

In this dispute the priests and Levites would, of course, be very much implicated.  When the persons, called in the Jewish books David and Solomon, removed the sacred place from Gerizim to Jerusalem, they would take the priests along with it.  The king would wish to have the high priest near him, that he might have a watch upon his enormous power.  The priest would like to be near the king, to watch and controul him : for a priesthood is always, without any exception, *an imperium in imperio*, always, either more or less, struggling for power.  When Jeroboam restored the old worship, he would wish to have the old priests ; and whether he had any of them or not he would claim to have them.  This appears from 1 Kings,[4] where he is charged by the Jews with making priests out of all the people.  This is again confirmed by a speech of King Abijah (son of Rehoboam) made on mount Ephraim :. " Have ye not cast out the priests of the " Lord, the sons of Aaron, and the Levites, and have made you priests after the manner of the " nations of the other land, so that whosoever cometh to consecrate himself with a young bullock " and seven rams may be a priest ?" [5]   It may be true that Jeroboam did this, but as it is made a charge against him by his enemy, and his enemy is our only witness to the fact, we cannot receive it as a thing established, on which we can reason. .

In the time of Rabbi Meir, as I have already stated, the image of a dove was found in the temple of Mount Gerizim.[6]  This serves to shew, that one reason of the schism between the Jews and Samaritans was the return of the latter to the adoration of the Queen of Heaven.  The Μαχαιρας Ἑλληνικῆς, the Hellenic Sword, clearly proves the truth of what I have before said, that Helen and Ione had the same meaning—that of *the female generative power.*  The Septuagint often serves as a most useful gloss.

4. Philo Judæus says, that Moses learnt the rest of the sciences of the Hellenes : την δε αλλην εγκυκλιον παιδειαν Ἑλληνες εδιδασκον.[7]  And Clemens Alexandrinus says, that the Hellenes

---

[1] Bryant, Anal. Vol. II. p. 300.          [2] 1 Kings xii. 32, 33.          [3] Lewis, Ant. Heb. Vol. II. p. 602.

[4] xii. 31, 32.          [5] 2 Chron. xiii. 9.          [6] See Bochart, Vol. III. Chap. I. p. 6.

[7] In Vita Mosis, Vol. II. p. 84.

educated him in Egypt as a princely child, and instructed him in the whole circle of the sciences. [1]
Zoroaster is, by Ebn Batrick, styled Iüna-Hellen. Mr. Bryant says, "From what has been said,
" it appears plainly, that the Hellenes and Iones were the same people under different appella-
" tions. They were the descendants of Hellen and Ion, two names of the same personage;
" among whose sons idolatry first began in the region of Babylonia. He was styled Iön, Iönan,
" Ionichus, and was supposed to be the author of Magic. From him the Babylonians had the
" name of Iönim, as well as of Hellenes; for these terms were used as in some degree synony-
" mous." Mr. Bryant justly observes, this accounts for the Seventy repeatedly translating the
the Hebrew *from the Hellenic sword* απο προσωπε μαχαιρας Ἑλληνικῆς, instead of from the
sword of the Dove, יונה חרב *hrb iune*. [2] " The Iones were the leaders of this people, according to
" the best information. They were descendants of one Ion or Ionah, who was concerned in the
" building of the tower, when the language of mankind was confounded." [3] This confirms my
idea that the Babylonians were followers of the Yoni, and were emigrants from India. When Mr.
Bryant wrote, the blaze of light which has shone from the East, had not fallen upon these
subjects.

5. Thus Semiramis, or Semi-rama-isi, was the same as Helen, or, in short, Venus, or Divine
Love. Her visible form was that of the dove, as well as that of the woman, who was the Io of
the Ionites, or Ionians of Syria, who was carried on the back of the Tauri-form Jove to Europe,
where her followers were known by the name of Ionian Pelasgi, or Ionian sailors. The following
are the words of the learned devotee Nimrod : " Semiramis is said to have been slain by the last
" survivor of her sons; while others say she flew away as a bird. I believe that she perished by
" that ancient and cruel punishment, crucifixion. Helen (as we are told) was put to death by
" certain women dressed up as Furies or Erinnyes, by suspending her to a tree. [4] In honour or
" rather in expiation of her suspension, she was worshiped as Helen Dendritis. But the modern
" punishment of hanging is only a modification of the ancient crucifixion, introduced quite as
" much by the devotion as by the humanity of Christendom ; and it was an ancient custom to use
" trees [5] as gibbets for crucifixion, or, if artificial, to call the cross or furca a tree—in felici arbore
" suspendito. The Deuteronomy says, 'He that is hanged is accursed of God;' [6] upon which St.
" Paul thus comments : [7] ' *Christ hath redeemed us from the curse of the law, being made a curse for*
" *us : for it is written, Cursed is every one that hangeth on a tree.*' That (I think) explains the
" ceremony of the Erinnyes or Curses suspending Helen upon the fatal tree. The same tradition
" may be traced in the history of the bird Iynx or Venereal Dove, into which Semiramis was
" changed ; but that change was her Apotheosis, *and the crucifixion is made into a glorious mys-*
" *tery by her infatuated adorers.*" So far the pious, not the infidel, Nimrod. In reply to his last
words, which I have marked by italics, the Ionian followers of this incarnate Ερως, if we had them
here to question, would most likely indignantly deny every thing which we read of her, to her dis-
advantage, in the pages of opponent sects, her enemies, or in the poems of wicked unbelieving
poets. Again Nimrod says, [8] " The *wheel* upon which criminals were extended *was a cross,*
" although the name of the thing was dissembled among Christians ; it was a St. Andrew's cross,
" of which two spokes confined the arms and two the legs. The Dove of Venus (born on the
" banks of the Euphrates) was a mænad or fanatic bird, crucified on a wheel with four spokes,

---

[1] Strom. Lib. i. p. 413.   [2] Bryant, Anal. Vol. III. p. 160.
[3] Chron. Paschale, Eusebii Chron. p. 7; Bryant, Anal. Vol. III. p. 149.
[4] Pausan. Lib. iii. Cap. xix. Sect. 10; Ptol. Heph. Lib. iv. p. 149.   [5] See Elias Schedius de Diis Germanis, p. 511.
[6] Deut. xxi. 23.   [7] Galat. iii. 13.   [8] P. 305.

Ποικιλαν ιυγγα τε
Τρακναμον Ουλυμποθεν
Εν αλυτφ ζευξασα κυκλφ
Μαιναδ' οριν Κυπρογενεια φερεν
Πρωτον ανθρωποισι. ¹

" The δεσμος² τετρακναμος of the wheel is elsewhere described by Pindar as a punishment of
" the accursed, the eternal crucifixion of Ixion." ³

Who is the Ixion crucified, but the second person of the Hindoo Trinity, called Ixora? ⁴

6.  In both Grecian and Hindoo histories this mystical queen Semiramis is said to have fought a
battle on the bank of the Indus, with a king called Staurobates, in which she was defeated, and
from which she flew away in the form of a Dove.  On this Nimrod says, " The name *Staurobates,*
" the king by whom Semiramis was finally overpowered, alludes to the cross on which she
" perished." ⁵

But Βαινω means *to carry,* so that Staurobates might very correctly mean cross-borne.  I have
little doubt that it meant Palm-tree cross and *cross-borne ;* a very interesting reason for the latter
signification I shall give when I treat of the *ninth* Indian Avatar.  The apparent contradiction in
the account of Semiramis' *flying away* and *being crucified* is reconciled by supposing, that, on her
death, her soul flew away in the form of a dove, as was always supposed to be the case with the
souls of the Roman Emperors, who were apotheosised.  I think it is not improbable that the word
*Staurobates,* known in India and Greece, may be a contraction of two words found in Greek, viz.
Σταυρος a cross,⁶ and Βαιον a Palm or Phœnix tree.  It would then mean the Phœnix or Palm-
tree cross.  It might also mean *cross-borne* from Βημα (Jones).  It is a compound word used by
the Greeks.  But the Phœnix, as I have shewn, was identified with the cycle of 600 or 608 in
Ireland, or with the Sun or Ethereal fluid, or the still higher principle.  Here, perhaps, we may
find the origin of the mystical idea of some of the early Christians, that Jesus Christ was crucified
in the heavens ; and it may lead us to a suspicion (recondite and mystical enough I grant, in this
mystical history) as to what bird the Phœnix really was.  It was a portion of the generative principle,
the divine love, the ερως, which first moved on the waters, and which, in the form of a dove, was
incarnated every 600 or 608 years, when the Sun and Moon became in conjunction and a new
sæculum arose.  Ερως or Eros, we learn from the Orphic Argonaut, ver. 11, had the name of
Phanes ;⁷ that is, Phenn or the Phœnix, which has the meaning of 608.  Phenn is the same as
the Greek Φαινω *to shine,* and Φανος *a torch,* and Φαναι *the orgies of Bacchus.*

Dr. Clarke observed a Phœnix on an obelisk of the Sun at Heliopolis.  He thinks it was a symbol of reviving nature.  Herodotus says it was like an eagle.  Ovid says it is an Assyrian bird ;⁸

---

¹ Pindar, Pyth iv. ver. 380.          ² Idem, Pyth. ii. ver. 74.          ³ Nimrod, p. 306.
⁴ Vide Georgius Alp. Tib. p. 99.          ⁵ Nimrod, 306.          ⁶ See Matt. xxvii. 32.
⁷ Bryant, Anal. Vol. II. p. 330.          ⁸ Clarke's Travels, Vol. IV. p. 73, 4to.

I doubt not the Assyrian bird of Semiramis. " Memnon when dead was transferred into a bird, " incomparable (as he had been among men) for beauty and sagacity; the Orion of the Indians, and " Phœnix of the classical writers. Memnon was the son of Aurora, or (by another account) of " Semiramis, whose Persian name is Hom-ai or the bird of Paradise. Now Phoinix was the bird " of the morning and also of Paradise; his dwelling was in the very East, at the gate of heaven, " in the land of the spring, and the grove of the sun, upon a plain of unalloyed delights, lying " twelve cubits higher than the highest of mountains." " Phoinix was also a tree." " Upon the " highest convexity or umbo of Achilles's shield stood a palm or Phoinix tree."[1]

Diodorus Siculus had learnt something relating to the cross, but he evidently did not understan it. He says that Staurobates sent to inform Semiramis that, if he conquered her, he would na her to a cross.[2] From such scraps of traditions collected together may be found the secret mear ing of the ancient mythoses, and by no other method will they ever be discovered.

7. The Arion or Aour-Ion just named was a king, who was said to have lived among the Chal deans. He is one of the constellations. The Grecian accounts of him are absolutely ridiculou and exhibit a perfect sample of the manner in which they accounted for the traditions and supe: stitions of their country. He was known by the Assyrians by the name of Al-aur, and was sa¹ l to have taught them to worship fire. The word is a compound of the Hebrew אור aur, Aour or Ur denoting *fire*, (or that higher principle to which both belong,) and Ion, a Dove, or Ioni. No only both of these things, but both of these words, have been much concerned in the mysteries c. religion, from the days of Adam to those of Christ.[3] Orion may also be construed to mean tht *mountain Dove*, and in this exactly coincides both with Semi-ramis and with the Indian Parvati.[4] Pindar says,

Εςι δ' εοικος
Ορειαν γε Πελειαδον
Μη τηλοθεν Ωριωνα νεισθαι.

Orion was said to have been nursed in a land called Hellopia,[5] or Ia-pi-el, *country of the Sun*.

Mr. Bryant[6] has shewn that Phoinix was not the name of a country only, but was also a term of honour, applied to many places. He also observes, that it was the name of *a tree* which was always held in the highest honour, and was thought to be immortal, as, if it died, it obtained a second life by renewal. Hence it was an emblem of immortality among all nations. It is pro bably to its renovating property that the Psalmist alludes when he says, *the righteous shall flourish like the Palm tree.*[7] Its name in Hebrew is תמר *Tmr.* In John xii. 13, we find the expression, τα βαϊα των φοινιχων—*branches of palm trees.* It is mentioned in the Maccabees[8] that the Jews entered the temple upon a solemn occasion, Μετα αινεσεως και βαϊων. It was called βαι or Bai in Egypt, and from its supposed immortality the Egyptians gave the name *Bai* to the soul. Εςι μεν γαρ το βαι ψυχη.[9]

The inside of the holy of holies, in the Jewish temple, was surrounded with palm trees or Phoinici, which overshadowed the cloven or ox-footed beings which guarded the Ark. See prin of it in Walton's Prologomena to his Polyglot. In the front of the Church of Maria Maggiore ir Rome, is a very large Corinthian column, the capital of course ornamented with palm leaves. Come from where it would, it was probably placed there before the Church of the Queen of Heaver.

---

[1] Nimrod, Vol. III. p. 390.           [2] B. II. Ch. i.           [3] Nimrod, Vol. I. p. 4, Sup. Ed.
[4] Nimrod, Vol. I. p. 14.             [5] Strabo, Lib. x. p. 649, Oxon. Ibid.
[6] Anal. Heath. Mythol. Vol. I. p. 322.      [7] Psalm xcii. 12.          [8] 1 Macc. xiii. 51.
[9] Horapollo, Lib. i. Cap. vii. p. 11.

for the same reason that the obelisks were placed before the temples at Dodona, at Delphi, and in Egypt, and this I will prove before I finish my work.

When the Pharaoh of Egypt gave a title of honour to Joseph, he called him Zophnat Paneach, פענח ponh צפנת zpnt. After a long disquisition the learned Pfeiffer brings out the word צפנת zpnt to mean γνωςης or *Augur*. I think the פענח ponh is the Phen or Phoinix—used metaphorically as illustrious, grand, great, the great Augur, or prophet, or wise man—the Paragon or Phœnix of Augurs.

Justin Martyr cites the example of the Phœnix burning itself to prove the immortality of the soul. If this do not prove the wisdom of the holy father, it proves the prevalence of the super-stition and its probable connexion with Christianity. He has mistaken the number of years of its period; but authors differed about this, not understanding the nature of the cycle concealed beneath the allegory.

I apprehend the palm tree or the Phoinix tree was the sacred tree, the tree of wisdom, for another reason, viz. from the use of its leaves for the purpose of writing. It had the name of Doum tree—tree of the Oum or Om, D'Om. The Phoinix was the Om, the cycle of 600. It was the ornament of the Holy of Holies of the Jewish temple, of the Αιων των Αιωνων, the eter-nally renovating cycle, which was one of his names.[1] In ancient Egyptian Pheneh meant cyclus, periodus, ævum. SCALIGER.

> Phœnix, Egyptiis astrologiæ symbolum. BOCHART.

> Una est quæ reparat seque ipsa reseminat
> Ales Assyrii Phœnica vocant. OVID.[2]

The Meneiadæ, or the priests of Menes, were said to have been changed into doves, because, says Mr. Bryant,[3] they were Ionim. Here is a remarkable proof of the ignorance of the Greeks. They found the priests to be Ionim—that is, the Hebrew plural of Ioni—or the followers of the Ioni, which had the meaning of *dove*, as we have seen. This they understood, but not under-standing the other meaning, viz. the sectarian term, they had no alternative but to make them doves, and Doves or Peleiades they made them. The priestesses at Dodona were Ioni-ans, but not, as Hesychius calls them, Πελειαι Greek doves: nor were they, as Servius described them, CHAONIAN Doves.[1] Herodotus has informed us what this means: he says they were black women, μελαινας, who came from Egypt. Where they came from is not now the question, but I dare say they were black women, Ionim, followers of the black queen of heaven—Pythonesses, or Sibyls, perhaps—Asiatic Ionim—Ionians. But it seems that he did not understand the whole of the matter, for he says, he supposes these black women were foreigners, because they were called doves—a reason foolish enough. This explains all the difficulties about the priestesses being *doves* of the different temples.

From the Sibylline oracles I learn that the Dove sent out by Noah was black. The mysticism of this *black* dove is pretty clear. I have seen very dark-coloured but never a *raven-black* dove. The *dove* was the only bird offered in sacrifice by the Jews.

8. Cecrops was said to be the founder of Athens, and to have been the inventor of a certain

---

[1] Vide Book V. Ch. IV. Sect. 10.        [2] Book V. Ch. II. Sect. 5; Ch. XIII. Sect. 2.

[3] Anal. Anc. Myth. Vol. II. p. 290.

[4] The word Chaonian is very curious. I suspect it had the same meaning as the Apollo Cunnius; and that there never was such a town as Chaon or Caon in Greece, although there might be mountains so called by the priests.

kind of cake made of fine flour and honey, offered to the Queen of Heaven.[1] These cakes were said to be made with horns, and were called *Boun*[2] or Bες· or Bεν. A similar kind of cakes are called by Jeremiah[3] כונים *cunim*. The Seventy translate this by the word χαυωνας. Μη ανευ των ανδρων ημων εποιησαμεν αυτη χαυωνας.[4] All this relates, I think, to the joint adoration of the Beeve and the Yoni—to the Baaltis ; and I think the כונים *cunim* were the cakes alluded to by Mr. Bryant and described by Herodotus.[5] At Athens there was an Apollo Cunnius.[6] Cecrops sacrificed nothing that had life. Here we go back to the Buddhists.[7] In almost all nations when we go to their origin, we meet with some circumstance of this kind to connect them with the oriental doctrines, and particularly to the abstinence from animal food.

The following observations of the very learned and pious Nimrod cannot fail, I think, to excite some sensations of a curious kind in the mind of the reader : " Candace denotes, as I believe, " the *She Hawk of the Wheel*, that is, the Anima Mundi or Divine Spirit of the world's rotation. " We read in Pindar of the venereal bird Iynx bound to the wheel, and of the pretended punish- " ment of Ixion.[8] But this rotation was really no punishment, being, as Pindar saith, voluntary, " and prepared by himself and for himself : or if it was, it was appointed in derision of his false " pretensions whereby he gave himself OUT AS THE CRUCIFIED SPIRIT OF THE WORLD."[9]

The mystic union of the Ερως and the Ψυχη, Cupid and Psyche, is celebrated by the Greeks in a vast variety of beautiful allegories ; but we almost always find the dove and the flaming torch to be part of the ceremony. The butterfly or the chrysalis, emblematical of the metempsychosis or change of state, is generally seen.[10] Varro itaque eam definit, " Anima est aer conceptus ore,

---

[1] Bryant, Anal. Vol. I. p 299.

[2] I believe that it was from this βεν we derived our word *boon* for a service rendered by a tenant to his landlord, or a piece of work done *gratis*—and our word *bon-fire*, on days of great rejoicing. I suspect that they all came to En- gland with Cunobelinus or Apollo Cunnius, after whom our king was so called, if there were such a king.

[3] Ch. vii. 18, xliv. 18, 19.        [4] Jeremiah xliv. 19.        [5] Anal. Ant. Myth. Vol. I. p. 301.

[6] Ibid. p. 350.        [7] Pausan. Lib. viii. p. 600.

[8] Τετραχναμον επραξε δεσμον Εον ολεθρον Ογ'. Pyth. 2, v. 74. The four spokes represent St. Andrew's cross, adapted to the four limbs extended, and furnish perhaps the oldest profane allusion to the crucifixion. This same cross of St. Andrew was the THAU, which Ezekiel commands them to mark upon the foreheads of the faithful, as appears from old Israelitish coins whereon that letter is engraved. The same idea was familiar to Lucian, who calls T the letter of cru- cifixion, and seems to derive it from the word ςαυρος. (Luc. Jud. voce ad finem, et vid. Chishull, Ant. Ass. p. 21.) Certainly the veneration for the cross is very ancient. Iynx the bird of Mantic inspiration, μαινας ορνις, bound to the four-legged wheel,

Τετραχναμον Ολυμποθεν<br>Εν αλυτω ζαχθεισα κικλω,

*gives the notion of divine love crucified.* The wheel denotes the world, of which she is the spirit, and the cross the sacrifice made for that world. Iynx is used for Love, Desire, Appetition, and thence the Latin word iungo or yungo *I unite*, and our name for the age of sensual love, Young—ευκιλαν ιυγγα. Having explained thus much, I may add with Columella, Lib. x. ver. 349,

HINC Amythaonius, docuit quem plurima Cheiron,<br>Nocturnas CRUCIBUS volucres suspendit, et altis<br>Culminibus vetuit feralia carmina flere.   Thus far *Nimrod.*

I shall make no observation upon the crucifixion of *the dove of Venus, the mænad or fanatic bird*, born at Askelon and on the Euphrates, of divine love, before Christianity existed, except, 1st, that the priests for almost 2000 years have been employed in destroying every thing which they thought made against their system, and how *this* has escaped them I do not know ; and, 2dly, that Ερως, or divine love, as the reader has seen, was the first-begotten son of the Platonists.

[9] Nimrod, Vol. I. p. 278, Suppressed Edition.        [10] Vide Spon. Miss. Erad. Ant. p. 7.

" defervefactus in pulmone, tepefactus in corde, diffusus in corpore." Imo Latinè Anima à Græco ανεμος, ventus : sic Plautus, Virgilius et alii animam sæpenumero pro vento usurparunt. Inde animam efflare dixerunt, quod eam pro vento flatûve haberent, comprobaturque sequenti marmore, ubi papilio à mortuo efflatus circumvolitat. Hinc Græci animam Psychen nominarunt, vel δια τὸ ανωθεν εψυχωϑαι, quasi cœlitus inspirata, ut dit Nicetas Choniates, vel à verbo ψυχρος, quod Hesychio, levis et debilis est. Anima, inquit Poteta, par levibus ventus, volucrique simillima somno, quando scilicet à corpore divortium fecit. Addendum et ψυχην Græcis æquivocatum esse, animamque significare et papilionem : unde Hesychius, ψυχη πνευμα και ζωϋφ πτηνον. [1]

" When Agamemnon sacrificed at Aulis, in Bœotia, [2] the Gods sent no fire to consume the " victim. This fire is figured as a breeze to be sent by the Gods to speed the ships on their " imaginary voyage, but it is called by the same word which meant the sacred fire, ουρος. " Whenever the Gods sent a wind, it is called Ικμενος Ουρος, [3] and it is well known to all readers " that the Creator spirit is equally represented in holy writ by a fire or luminous glory, and by a " rushing wind. Aura, in Latin, may be used for a breeze, and the divine particula auræ in a " man is called ανεμος or animus, and anima πνευμα, spiritus. [4] Upon this occasion it is said " that the king sacrificed his daughter which pacified the Gods and procured the αυρος."

Centre de toute puissance, de toute intelligence, de toute perfection, Dieu existoit avant tous les tems, avant toutes les choses, avant tous les êtres animés. Invisible par son essence, son invisibilité fut la nuit primitive, qui précédà les tems et la lumière. Dans elle, il produisit par sa puissance, ce qu'il avoit conçu par son intelligence ; c'est pour cela, que la nuit fut appelée la Mère, la Génératrice de tout ; [5] Dieu renferma, dans un œuf immense, les principes et les germes de toutes les choses : de cet œuf, sortit un être qui possédoit les deux sexes ; c'étoit le fils, la première production de Dieu : il se servit de lui, pour séparer les élémens confondus dans cahos, et pour développer les germs des créatures vivantes. Sa vertu ou sa puissance suprême confiée à son fils, fussit à la création du monde matérial, mais pour vivifier les germs, il fallut le souffle, l'esprit qui les échauffa. Cet esprit fut appelé l'amour. Orphée lui donne le titre de πνευμα et de παντογενεϑλα. Et suivant Hésiode, il fut contemporaine du cahos. [6] Ητοι μεν πωρτισα χαος γενετ, αυταρ επειτα Η' δ' Ερος. Au moment où le monde en sortit, il n'existoit que Dieu, sa force suprème, ou sa vertu, sa sagesse, ou son esprit. Ces deux êtres Metaphysiques personifiés produisirent le Fils, ou l'être Générateur, et l'Amour, par lequel il engendra d'abord, et conserva dans la suite, toutes les créatures. [7]

---

[1] Vide Spon. Miss. Erad. Ant. p. 7.            [2] Il. II. ver. 303.

[3] From which sensè of the word comes Σευς Ουρος, whose temple near Byzantium is mentioned by Arrian, Perip. Eux. p. 137 ; and see the inscription in Chishull, Ant. Ass. p. 59. The Ourian Jove presided over the command of armies. Jupiter imperator quem Græci Urion nominant, saith Tully. In Vervem, IV. p. 410, ed. Delph.

[4] See Gen. i. 2 ; Acts ii. 2, 3 ; 1 Kings viii. 11. The priests of Rome were called blowing winds or *Flamen*. A great poet says, Πυϑωνιτ αυξης ουρον, and Virgil, the thrilling song that wakes the dead " Wind,"

atque Ixionii VENTO rota constitit axis—

for I do not scruple thus to expound this most obscure verse. The Rabbins call the Holy Ghost Sephyrah or the Zephyr, when they interpret wisdom, meaning the divine afflatus. Vide Tomline's Elem. Theol Vol. II. p. 80. With the substantive πνευμα agrees that old Homeric verb πεπνευμαι, I am gifted with knowledge, inflated or inspired. Nimrod, Vol. I. p. 300, Sup. Ed.

[5] Orph. Hymn II. v. 3, Νυξ γενεσις παντων.        [6] Théog. v. 116.        [7] D'Ancarville, Res Vol. I. p. 147.

## CHAPTER IV.

AMAZONS. GENESIS.—AMAZON, MEANING AND HISTORY OF.—INVASION OF ATHENS BY THEM.—AMAZONS
IN THE TIME OF ALEXANDER, AND NOW IN INDIA.—OBSERVATIONS ON THE RAM AND THE BULL.—
RELIGIOUS WARS AND SUCCEEDING PEACE.—LETTERS KEPT SECRET.—CHRONOLOGY.

1. WE will now inquire into the origin of the Amazons. Among the ancients, many persons thought that the book of Genesis meant to describe the man and woman as at first created, to have been *one* and an androgynous being. It is there said that God created man *in his own image*, and, PRIOR TO THE CREATION OF WOMAN, *created he him*, *male and female* created he them. Many persons formerly believed that the first man and woman were united in one body.

Mr. Faber observes that this construction put upon the passage " *God created man in his own* " *image, in the image of God created he* HIM, *male and female created he* THEM," was adopted by some of the most learned Rabbis, whose names he gives at full length, who maintained that the word rendered *rib* means *side*.[1] This we shall find has an evident tendency to prove that the mythos (as Dr. Geddes calls it) of Moses, is in reality the same as the mythos of the Hindoos. The text says man was formed after the image of God; but God himself was believed to be androgynous. The text of Genesis (ii. 21) is אחת מצלעתיו which means either, one from his *sides* or one from his *ribs*; but the latter is inconsistent with the context, which says in the 23d verse, that the woman was made not only from the bones, *but from the flesh of the man*.[2] The double being, out of which it is said God formed the man and the woman, is nothing but the Amazon of the ancients; and the Amazon is nothing but a Venus Hermaphrodite—the same as that described in plate 31, figure 8, of the Supplement to Montfaucon's *Antiquity Explained*. They appear to be both the same in one respect, being both one half *male*, the other half *female*. The Isis sitting on the lotus, with the solar glory, is another example of this kind of double being, divided in various ways—sometimes *crossways*, and sometimes *lengthways*, as shewn in Montfaucon. Speaking of the worship of Artemis, by the Amazons, Creuzer says, On l'adorait dans le royaume de Pont, avec l'épithète significative de *Priapina*.

2. The word Amazon is composed of two very ancient words. The first is *Ama* or *Ma*, which, in old languages, means Mother. Its ubiquity proves its extreme antiquity. The second is an ancient name of the Sun, which was called Zon, Zan, Zaon, and Zoan. The Suanes and Soanes, of Colchis, were sometimes called Zani, Zaïnai, Zanitæ, and also Sanitæ. There was a city on the Thracian coast called Zona, to which the trees of Pieria are said to have come and ranged themselves in order to the music of Orpheus's harp.[3] Heliopolis, of Egypt, or On, was also called

---

[1] Pagan Idol. Vol. III. p. 71.

[2] The idea of the learned Jews and others alluded to by Mr. Faber, does not seem so absurd to us, since we have seen the Siamese Boys. And if it be said that had they been male and female they could not have increased the breed, the answer is very short—had the ligature which bound them together been a few inches longer, they could have done it. There have been many instances of double persons. A double lady, the daughter of Fulk de Paganel, formerly lived, and left a large property to the town of Newport Pagnel, which it now holds from her. Vide her monument in the centre aisle of the church.

[3] Argonaut. Lib. i. ver. 29; Mela, Lib. ii. Cap. iii. p. 140; Herod. Lib. vii. Cap. lix.; Bryant, Anal. Vol. III. p. 476.

3 T

Zoan, and Taphnes, and *Fons Solis,* and Balbec, and Bahalbeth.[1]  Taphnes was probably Taph-hanes.  Bahal-beth and Balbec mean Balbit, *house of the Sun* or *Bal.*

There was a city in Africa called Zona taken by the Roman general Sestius; also a city of Zona of the Amazons in Cappadocia,[2] or Armenia, &c.  There was a temple in Thrace called Σαον.  The following facts are extracted from a long passage of Mr. Bryant's Analysis.[3]  The most considerable body that went under the name of Amazons, settled upon the Atlantic in Africa, at the extreme verge of that region.  Of their exploits a long account is given in the history of Myrina.[4]  She is supposed to have lived in the time of Orus, the son of Isis, and to have conquered Africa and the greater part of Asia: but was at last slain in Thrace.  Amazons were also found in mount Caucasus, in Albania, and near the Palus Mæotis.  Polyænus speaks of Amazons in India: and they are also mentioned by Nonnus.  They likewise occur in Ethiopia.  They at one time possessed all Ionia: and there were traditions of their being at Samos, and in Italy. Αμαζονες υπεςρεψαν αυθις εις Ιταλιαν.[5]  There was a town in Messapia, towards the lower part of Italy, named Amazonia.[6]  Even the Athenians and Bœotians were of the same family: hence it is said that Cadmus had an Amazonian wife, when he went to Thebes, and that *her name was Sphinx :* Καδμος εχων γυναικα Αμαζονιδα, ἡ ονομα Σφιγξ, ηθεν εις Θηβας.[7]  He went first to Attica.  The reader will not forget that the Sphinx was half Lion, (not Lioness,) and half woman.  There were also Amazonian Colchians, who were noticed as being peculiarly black.  The Iberians, the Cimmerians, the Mæotæ, the Atlantians of Mauritania, and all the Ionians, were Amazonians—and were called Azones, Amazones, and Alazones.  They were also called Syri, Assyrii, Chaldæi, Mauri, Chalybes.  They are said to have founded the cities of Ephesus, Smyrna, Cuma, Myrina Latorea, Anæa, Eldæa, Myrlæa, Paphos, Cuna, besides many others.  Lucian, in his dialogue between Vulcan and Jupiter, calls Minerva an Amazon.

I believe, with Mr. Faber,[8] that the statues of Amazons, said to have been worshiped at most of the places named above, were statues of the double God, or of the first man of Genesis, made after the image of God.

They are represented to us, by the Greek writers, as a most turbulent and warlike race.  Pliny says, their shield was in the form of the leaf of the Indian fig-tree: and on it they carried a lunette.  This, I think, was the Argha or boat of India, which must have been like a lunette.  Monuments were shewn in various places where they are said to have had battles, and been killed; as at Megara, Chæronea, Scotussæa, Cunoscephale, also in Ionia and Mauritania, and even *within the walls of Athens.*

3.  A very celebrated and marked invasion of Attica by them is recorded.  The Athenians shewed the place where, in this invasion, the battle was fought,—a subsequent truce made, and a stone pillar erected to record it, called Amazoneum.  The commander of the Amazons is stated to have been a foreigner from Egypt, a Thracian and an Athenian, whose name was Eumolphus.  Sacrifices were offered by the Athenians to their Manes; and a temple in Athens was said to have been built by them.  The place where the truce was made was called Ὁρκωμοσιον, Horcomo-sium.  Here we have an excellent example of Grecian history.  Here are all the particulars of the war-monuments to those slain in battle; places deriving their names from the events of the war; temples erected—treaties of peace exhibited.  And yet, taken literally, every word is false: for no one can believe that there ever was an Amazonian army of women with one breast.  This

---

¹ Raleigh's Hist. Book i. Ch. iii.          ⁴ Antoninus, p. 182.          ³ Vol. III. pp. 461, 462.

⁴ Diod. Sic. Lib. iii. p. 188, and p. 185.          ⁵ Schol. in Lycoph. ver. 1332, also ver. 995.

⁶ Steph. Bysant.          ⁷ Palæphatus, p. 26.          ⁸ Vol. III. p. 80.

serves to shew how all Grecian early history ought to be estimated. It is all mythological. I cannot help here observing, that we have no sacred HISTORICAL record better authenticated than this at Athens, and not one of the same date bearing, in its literal sense, more the character of real history.

The confusion of the history of the Amazons has hitherto set all theory at defiance. But I think a little consideration of what we have said respecting the divisions and wars between the rival sects of the Brahme-Maia in conjunction, the Yoni alone, the Linga alone, and at last the reunion of the three, will enable us to account for it all. The wars of the Amazons were those between the followers of the *male* and the *female* principles, and their alternate successes. The truce with the Athenians, is a most important circumstance; for, after it is said to have taken place, they were heard of no more. [1] The reunion of the two sects took place at the time described in this truce : this is the figurative mode of describing the reunion of the religions.

The Amazons are said to have burnt the temple of Ephesus, which they erected themselves ; [2] and which was the chief seat of the Amazonian Iönim. [3] Mr. Bryant [4] acknowledges that he knows not how to account for this, because he is satisfied that the Amazonians and Iönians were the same. The difficulty is easily explained. The first founders were worshipers of the double principle, the Brahme-Maia ; their successors fell into the Yonian heresy, and were conquered by people of the original religion, when it became restored, according to the accounts in the Hindoo histories, as it was at last almost every where, either by truce, as at Athens, or by force. But at Ephesus, though they burnt the temple, the female, in Diana, seems to have recovered its power. At first we find them founding cities and settling countries ; here was the act of the persons holding the double principle ; afterward we find them making war on the cities and countries which they had formerly founded. This was when these places had gone into the adoration of the Yoni alone, or in other cases of the Linga alone ; for the Ama-Zon must have been at equal enmity with the two taken separately ; and at last when the two reunited they all merged into the *double* worship : and the Amazons, as distinguished from the others, are heard of no more ; so that, as Lysias says, their name became extinct,—at least in Greece, or the Western world. But to the general pacification, the Persians and Jews formed an exception : in consequence, we find Cambyses restoring the temple of the *male* principle at Jerusalem, destroying the temples, and, where he could, the sphinxes, but leaving the obelisks, the emblems of the Linga, untouched in Egypt, where some, and particularly that at Heliopolis, the finest of them, remain. I consider the fact of the obelisks—the Lingas—being left by the Persians when the temples were destroyed, as very important. Why were they left ? They were much more easy to overthrow than the temples.; and they are most of them covered with hieroglyphics of Gods and Goddesses. Though the temples and their idols were odious to the iconoclasts, the figures of idols on the *sacred* obelisks, which were used only as *letters*, were spared, for the sake of the pillar, the Linga, on which they were engraved.

Something similar to the story told of the race of Amazons has been found in India, among the natives of Malabar, in a tribe called Nairs. A government actually exists there, in which the *women*, not the *men*, bear rule. But although this is singular enough, there is not in their traditions the least appearance of the breast having ever been amputated. They seem to have been in

---

[1] Lysias, Funeb. Orat. τας Κορινθιων Βοηθους. Bryant, Anal. Vol. III. pp. 478, 480.
[2] Euseb. Chron. p. 35 ; Syncellus, p. 178.    [3] Dionysius, ver. 827 ; also Pausanias, Lib. iv. p. 357.
[4] Anal. Vol. III. p. 475.

existence in the time of Alexander the Great. The account of them may be seen in the fifth volume of the Asiatic Researches. Nimrod[1] has some curious observations respecting them.

4. When we come to the time of Alexander, we arrive at a period in which we may expect something like rational history. Bryant says,[2] "Some ages after, in the time of Alexander, an "interview[3] is mentioned to have passed, wherein the Queen of the Amazons makes proposals to "that monarch about sharing for a night or two his bed : and even, in the time of Pompeius Mag-"nus, during the Mithridatic war, they are supposed to exist; for, after a victory gained by that "general, the Roman soldiers are said to have found many boots and buskins, which Dion Cassius "(in bello Mithridatico) thinks were undoubtedly Amazonian." When I consider the unquestionable fact, that there is now a powerful and civilized tribe in India where the women are the governors and choose the men they like, and where the men are held in subjection, I cannot help thinking the story relating to Alexander probable. I suspect that they have had their origin from the extremes to which devotees have run in the times of the fierce contentions which arose between the followers of the *male* and *female*, the Linga and Ioni. It is difficult to doubt the story respecting Alexander; and the fact of the existence of the present Nairs, very near to or in the country where he marched, cannot be doubted. When I consider the excesses to which party and religious zeal, about the most contemptible nonsense, will often carry people, I can believe it possible that some frantic women may have cut off their own or their children's breasts, which may have been exaggerated and applied to all the armies of the followers of the *female* sect, who may hence have been all called Amazons. Perhaps these armies of the followers of the female Solar principle may have been commanded by women like Boadicea, of Britain, and hence the fable may have arisen.

Homer states the Amazons to have come from India. There is an Amazon with only one breast in the cave of Elephanta, in India.[4] Mr. Faber says,[5] "The Amazon of the Elephanta "pagoda, and of the *wonder-loving* Greek fabulists, is manifestly no other than the compound "Hermaphroditic deity, who, by the Hindoos, is called Ardhanari, and who is formed by the "lateral conjunction of Siva with Parvati. This monster, as delineated by the mythological "painters of India, has, from the head to the feet, the right side of a man and the left side of a "woman." "Near the statue in question reposes the mysterious Bull Nandi." On the Amazon of this cave, Col. Wilford[6] says, the figure with one breast has been thought by most to represent an Amazon : it, however, appears to me a representation of the consort of Siva, exhibiting the active power of her Lord; not only as *Bavani* or courage, but as Isani, *or the Goddess of Nature considered as male and female*, and *presiding over generation*.[7] The Amazon is also found in the caves at Maha-bali-pore.[8] In all parts we read of the Amazons, but generally confounded with the Cyclopes. Perhaps the Cyclopes were husbands of the Amazons, that is, had their wives in common. This custom formerly prevailed in Thrace, in Arabia,[9] according to Strabo, and, as we have just seen, yet prevails in one part of India, among the people called Nairs. In the Institutes of Menu it is written, "Having divided his own subsistence, the Mighty Power became half "*male* and half *female*."[10] Brahma is said to have manifested himself in a human shape, when

---

[1] Volume II. p. 328.    [2] Anal. Vol. III. p. 484.
[3] Cleitarchus apud Strabonem, Lib. ii. p. 771; Diod. Sic. Lib. xvii. p. 549; Arrian, Lib. vii. p. 292.
[4] Maurice, Hind. Ant. Vol. II. p. 152, ed. 8vo. 1800.
[5] Vol. III. pp. 63, 71, 82; Asiat. Res. Vol. VI. p. 523.    [6] Asiat. Res. Vol. IV. p. 414.
[7] For the Amazon *Ardhanari ishwar*, see Bombay Transactions, Vol. I. p. 220.    [8] Pritchard, p. 405.
[9] Vide Univ. Hist. Vol. XVIII. p. 413.    [10] Asiat. Res. Vol. V. p. viii. advertisement.

one half of his body sprang from the other, which yet experienced no diminution; and out of the severed moiety he framed a woman, denominated Iva or Satarupa. After some time the other half of his body sprang from him and became Swayambhuva or Adima.[1] From their embrace were born three sons.

In this wild mythos it is impossible to be blind to the account of the creation in the second book of Genesis, as expounded by the Jewish Rabbis, in the *double being* out of which man and woman were formed. At the same time I conceive it absolutely impossible to believe it to have been simply a copy of our Genesis, as we have it, unexplained, by the Rabbis. This proves that the Hindoo cannot have copied from the Hebrew. The Hebrew is a part of the Hindoo: the Hindoo cannot have copied what is not there, but only understood. There is no way of getting over the difficulty except by supposing the modern Rabbis have learnt the exposition from the Hindoo. This is hardly credible, though possible.

The same doctrine as that of the Jews respecting the union of the male and female—of whom one with four hands, four legs, two faces, was formed—may be found in Plato, as detailed by Mr. Faber.[2]

This subject affords a direct proof that the true esoteric religions of Homer, the Hindoos, and the Jews, were all the same. It is impossible to believe that the coincidence of all three could be the effect of accident in an idea or doctrine outwardly so absurd as the Amazon, and the man and woman conjoined in one body. The mode in which the learned Rabbis, enumerated by Mr. Faber, treat the subject, shews, that though they knew very well there was a secret meaning, yet they did not understand it. I once more warn my reader to recollect, that I cannot be expected to account for ALL the fooleries which the cunning of priests, and the fanaticism of devotees, in long periods of time—several thousand years—have engrafted into the ancient doctrines, which, without these assistances, would vary from the original, in consequence of the law of change alone always acting. The sacrifice of Melchizedek is an example, so beautiful in its primeval simplicity, (admitted by the Roman Church to be the origin of their Mass,) and so horrible in the *body and blood verily and indeed taken*, into which, in modern times, it has grown.

5. When I say that Moses substituted the Ram for the Bull, it does not necessarily follow that he designed to make the Ram an object of adoration or idolatry. To all idolatry he had an utter repugnance. But it seems certain, though I can perceive no reason for it, that wherever the worship of the Yoni prevailed, there was also idolatry. The prayers to the god Bull, which may be seen both in Faber and Bryant, are expressed as being offered to him merely as the emblem of a Superior Being. If Moses meant to keep his festivals in order, when the signs changed, he must of course provide against that change. The Ram never became an object of idolatry with any of the followers of Abraham, until the Yoni was again joined to the Linga. The change of the commencement of the year from the first of May to the first of April, from Taurus to Aries, was the most probable way to abolish the adoration of the former. It is generally much more difficult to destroy an old superstition than to prevent a new one; and the new festival of the Yajna or Passover, was altogether of a very different character from the old one of the Bull.

The view which I take of this subject is strikingly confirmed by the fact, that the Beeve or Urus was constantly of both sexes; but in no instance can the least appearance be discovered among the followers of the Sheep, except of the *male*; for when the Sheep succeeded among the Assyrians to the Beeve, Astarte, &c., had the head of a ram, not of an ewe. In the adoration of the Beeve, the Heifer or Cow is continually found; but in that of the Ram or Lamb of God, no in-

---

[1] Asiat. Res. Vol. VIII. p. 376; Faber, Vol. I. p. 318.        [2] Orig. Pag. Idol. Vol. III. p. 70.

stance of a female is, I believe, known. In the worship of Cristna, I also believe that no female will be found, except what existed in the previous system. All the allegories of his nine Gopies, Milkmaids, or Muses, the radii or rays of the sun with which he danced, do not amount to any thing like the female power; and this, in a striking manner, confirms my idea of his close connexion with the Jewish system. The Jews must have emigrated, when his enemies are said to have prevailed; for the alternate successes of the sects are described in his wars with the evil demons.

The image of " the Lamb of God, which taketh away the sins of the world," never was an object of adoration with the Jewish sectaries, till it was adopted by the Christians, among whom it is yet to be found in the temple of St. John Lateran, and in many other places, both Romish and Protestant, and particularly about Florence, of all which I shall treat hereafter. The Jews were correctly followers of the God *Iao* alone. The Romish Christians have, along with the God Iao, adopted the Queen of Heaven, the Mother of God, the Regina Cœli, as they call her. They are followers of the double principle, and with it they adopt the adoration or use of images. These two have always gone together. The Protestants refusing the *feminine* principle, refuse also, as usual, the use of Images. Such is the fact. Are we to attribute this to accident or design ? The female and the image do not seem to have any necessary connexion.

6. If we examine carefully, without preconceived system or dogma, into the origin of the affairs of the world, I apprehend that we should find proofs of their having been in ancient exactly or very nearly what they have been in modern times. There were great wars about religious opinions of the most trifling and unimportant nature, which extended to all countries, and lasted many hundreds, nay thousands, of years. At last the world grew tired of these wars, or had become sufficiently enlightened to see their absurdity, and for many hundred years before Christ they appear to have so completely ceased in the West that in fact the recollection of them was almost lost. Europe is now following the same route. Religious animosity is every where subsiding, and we have reason to believe that the world, on this subject, will be at peace, that is, *religious* peace, as it was before,—verifying Solomon's adage, that " there is nothing new under the sun."

In the Greek and Roman writers we find an extraordinary confusion of Hellenes, and Ionians, and Argives, and Pelasgi, &c., &c. All this arises from their not knowing, that nearly all these were sectarian terms. If the press do not prevent it, posterity, two or three thousand years hence, will be in exactly the same situation with respect to us. They will find Greeks in Turkey, Greeks in Asia, Greeks in Russia, Greeks in Rome. This is like the Ionians in Athens, in Asia Minor, at Dodona, in Egypt teaching Moses, and in the islands of the Mediterranean. They will find Papists in Rome, in France, in Russia, in Syria, in Ireland. They will find Protestants also, having their temples in all these places. What, if they do not carefully attend to the secret meaning and history of these terms, will they make of them ? They will be lost as we have been. I could, if I would, fill fifty pages in elucidating this part of my subject, but I wish to diminish, not to enlarge my book. I cannot afford to waste the paper. My book is not to raise money; a dead loss it is certain to be. It is to *instruct* my countrymen, not to *amuse* them. If I wanted to make money I would attempt to write some pretty, amusing but really worthless novels. Thus, perhaps, I might not only make money, but be made a baronet into the bargain. For my reward I look elsewhere. But why should I say worthless ? If the novels amuse idle people, and keep them out of mischief, they are not worthless : and we are much obliged to the gentleman who has written them. But, had he attended a little more to the instruction of his countrymen, without making his works less amusing he might have made them more useful ; and, in the eyes of the great and good of future ages, he would have occupied a higher place.

7. When I had advanced thus far in my work an opinion began to gain strength with me, that

the reason why all these ancient superstitions were not understood by the nations after about the time of the Trojan war, arose from the use of letters either not having been known or having been kept as a masonic secret among a class of initiated persons, and that the histories, such as they were, in reality were mere traditions. I think every step we take we shall find new reason to believe this to be true. It exactly accords with the history of the Indian Vedas. We have found in them proofs that the Indians had the mythos of the Jews, but it is very evident that it is with them mixed up with a great mass of nonsense, from which the Mosaic Judæan mythos is free. It appears that in all nations religions have advanced in complication along with time. Now, is it not possible that the art of writing may have been known to the Chaldeans only, and that Abraham may have brought it with him, and along with it the historical part of Genesis, &c. ; that after his tribe left India the mythos was not committed to writing or communicated to the people there, till it became much more corrupted or complicated than that of the Iudi ; and is not this enough to account for the difference of the style of the two ? Certainly the style of the Judæan mythos bespeaks superior antiquity ; and if with the Indians the peculiar dogma of the Iudi did not prevail, viz. that not an iota should be changed, we may readily account for the simplicity of the one, and the complication of the other. The Judæans were latterly both followers of the male and Iconoclasts, and this may furnish a reason for their superiority. Whether they corrupted their sacred books when they were idolaters, worshipers of the *female*, and cannibals, and afterward restored them to purity, I know not. That they were all three, we learn from their Prophets. Their cannibalism has been proved by Lord Kingsborough, in his fine work on the antiquities of Mexico.

8. Chronology. We will now stop to make a few observations on this subject; but they will not detain *us* long ; though it *has* occupied the pens of innumerable persons, and served to waste millions of reams of paper. To pretend to fix the dates of the earlier events with which we are acquainted, except in respect to their order of succession, would be as absurd as to adopt as *literal* histories the plagues of Egypt or the labours of Hercules. A probable theory, perhaps, may be formed as to their succession, but there is no dating events to years till about the time of Cyrus, when the famous eclipse of Thales took place. M. Volney, in his researches into ancient history, has settled this question.

I apprehend the first race of people with whom we are acquainted, we know only from the Tauric worship, the Zodiacal division into 360 parts, and the book of the deluge, which fixes the year to 360 days. We have an obscure view of this doctrine existing almost every where over the globe. Its professors lived after the time that the sun entered the sign of the Bull at the Vernal Equinox, more than 4500 years before Christ. After these people came the Amazons and Cyclops, who invented *arithmetic* and perhaps *letters*, who worshiped upon the tops of mountains, in stone circles which they invented, and which they erected in accordance with the fine cycles with which those buildings clearly prove that their fabricators were acquainted. They were the race supposed by M. Baillie to have been highly civilized. These people may have flourished for a thousand or fifteen hundred years before the sun entered Aries. They were Negroes. They were Buddhists— by degrees adopting the Linga and Yoni as emblems, and the protecting Cobra. The first book of Genesis, the *rasit* or *book of wisdom*, is probably a work of these people. It contains enough to prove that its authors possessed great science, and a knowledge of the nature of the world, and of natural philosophy. Of this, a moment's consideration of Chap. IV. and Sect. XVI. XVII. of my CELTIC DRUIDS, will convince any one. M. Cuvier has settled this question. If in some parts it be obscure or not intelligible, this may be attributed to the numerous translations of ignorant persons, through which we have it, and in fact to the language in which it is contained being in great part lost, particularly the *esoteric meaning* of words, which Jews and Christians in late years have equally endeavoured to keep out of sight; of this the word *rasit* is an example.

At the latter part of the time when these Cyclopes lived, arose the disputes and wars about the two principles. For a time, the Amazonian doctrines, or the adoration of the female principle, seems to have prevailed among them. This elucidates the account that both they and the Amazons were the builders of Argos, Ephesus, and many other towns. This is supported by the Indian histories, from which we learn that, about 3000 years before Christ, great and dreadful civil wars raged every where respecting religion, during which, as happened in the times since Christ, the world rapidly sunk into a state of ignorance, and the fine science of the makers of the Cycles was lost. This accounts for many hitherto unaccountable facts or traditions. For instance : Ephesus was built by Amazons, and destroyed by them. The histories state the wars to have been attended with alternate successes—sometimes one party prevailed, sometimes another. The wars about the *male* and *female* principles were accompanied by wars about the change from Taurus to Aries. Men seem to have been as absurd in ancient times, and to have destroyed each other and their fine works, for dogmas as trifling and childish as those contended for by Homoiusians and Homoousians, Papists and Protestants, in modern times ; proving, as observed before, the truth of what Solomon said, that there was " nothing new under the sun." It is evident that the theory here proposed is capable of being worked up into a system, and might afford room for much talent and ingenuity. It is founded on the facts which we know, and the most rational historical statements which we possess, but it is at the best but a theory, and I see not that to spend more time upon it would be of any use. It, in a word, contains all we know and all it is probable that we ever shall know. If my reader be not satisfied, he may go to the priests, and they will give him an apple of knowledge, and tell him the year, the day, the hour, the minute, and the second, in which the world was created, Abraham left the land of Vr-ii, each of the plagues of Egypt happened, or Elijah went in a chariot to heaven. On chronology I shall say no more, but shall proceed to the consideration of many facts which are extremely interesting, and which will support and elucidate what I have proposed.

---

## CHAPTER V.

CYCLOPES. — CYCLOPÆAN BUILDINGS. — ALL ANCIENT HISTORY FABLE OR ÆNIGMA. — MUNDORE, &c.— THE CYCLOPES IN MUNDORE.—ABURY AND SERPENT WORSHIP.—FREEMASONS IN MUNDORE. ALMUG.— FOURMONT. THE TEMPLE OF ONGAR.

1. The explanation which I have given of the Argives, the Hellenes, the Ionians, and the Amazons, seems to me to be satisfactory, but I cannot say quite as much of the Cyclopes ; though certainly the fact of their building Argos, &c., seems to connect them with the Ionic superstition. But this is not enough. The consideration of the prodigious number of buildings attributed to them, seems to demand something more. The French Institute, in 1804, made out that there were 127 towns in Europe, which had anciently been, at least in part, built in the Cyclopæan style. The Cyclopes must have been as general as the Amazons.

Dr. Clarke supposes the Cyclopæan style to have been cradled in the caves of India. The Cyclopæan Gallery at Tyrins is curious on account of the *lancet arch*, which is common in very old buildings, in India.

In the works of the later Greeks, the Cyclops are represented with only one eye. I suppose this arose from their absolute ignorance of what they were and who they were, or indeed of any thing about them ; and, there being merely a tradition that such persons did once live, the Greeks were obliged to have recourse to etymology, and from the word κυκλος, it is said that they made *round eye* or *one eye*. Round eye is easily accounted for, but I do not see how the Cyclops hence came to be supposed to have have had only one eye.[1] Winkleman, in his *Monumenta Antiqua inedita*, observes, that in the earliest periods the Cyclops were represented with *two* natural eyes, and a *third* in the middle of the forehead. This seems to connect them with Jupiter, who, before the Trojan war, was called Trioptolemos—Trilochan : and this again with the Hindoo Gods, some of whom are described in pictures in the cabinet of the Asiatic Society, with *three* eyes. Thus when we really get to the bottom of the Greek mythologies, we always find ourselves in India. This reminds me that Jupiter appeared at Lacedæmon, in very early times, with four heads or faces—thus identifying him with Janus of Italy and Brahma of India.

2. The Cyclopæan buildings, including the Druidical circles of large stones and tumuli, were common in Greece : but the Greeks knew not by whom they were fabricated, nor does it appear that they ever entered into a rational inquiry either whence their fabricators came, or who they were. The ignorance of the Greeks I believe arose from the buildings having been constructed long previous to the knowledge of letters, unless the use of letters was kept a secret by a few individuals or an initiated class of society, which I think it was : and I think *that* initiated society were themselves the persons called Cyclopes. The buildings were executed under the direction of a great, powerful, and dominant priesthood. The remains of buildings which we call Cyclopæan, and with which I include those called Druidical, are of so peculiar a character, that they can be compared to no others in existence. If we did not see them, but only knew of them by report, we should believe the stories of them to be no better than fairy tales. It is evident that they were in existence before the time of known history, and that their fabricators must have possessed considerable knowledge of astronomy and skill in the mechanical arts. The former is proved by the cycles exhibited in their construction, as I have shewn in my Celtic Druids, and in Book V. of this work ; and the latter is proved by the size of the stones which are so large, that without much mechanical skill they never could have been moved.[2] As the Buddhists are the oldest religionists with whom we are acquainted, we are naturally led to appropriate them to this sect, which many circumstances tend to confirm.

Mr. Bryant has proved that the Cyclopes were supposed to have been once established in Argolis, and that they were said to have built Argos, Mycænæ, and Tiryns.[3] These circumstances seem to connect or identify them with the Ionians and Amazons : and I think it will ultimately turn out that they were the same people under different names. The Cyclopes were ὡς ΕΠΤΑ μεν ιναι εκαλεισθαι δε γαςεροχειρας. They were called γαςεροχειρας and εχχειρογαςερας. These evidently allude to the womb or the female organ of generation.[4] " The " Cyclops, Cocles, or Arimasp, is any Theocrator of universal dominion, and the ten Arimasps of " Mount Riphæus,

> —— decem coclites quæ montibus alteis
> Riphæis sedere,

---

[1] Pliny, Nat. Hist. VII., has something about them. Balbec is Cyclopæan.

[2] For example—the stones in the walls at Balbec, in Western Syria, and at Mahabalipore, in India, and at Abury, &c., in Britain.

[3] Class. Jour. Vol. V. p. 294.     [4] Strabo, Lib. viii. p. 540.

3 U

" are the ten Antediluvian kings," " These are the Cyclopes who perished at the time when " Apollo was banished from heaven for a year, that is to say, in the long night of the Catoulas." [1]

Might not the kings named above, allude to the seven millenaries and the ten Neroses, and the Catoulas to the state of nature when Brahma reposes on the great deep, previous to a new creation, after the millenium ? Might not the επτα γαςεροχειρας be the *seven* circular planetary bodies, each sacred to a millenium ; and the *ten* Coclites sacred to the ten Neroses ? This is very mystical : but the Cyclopes are almost always found along with the Amazons : and the γαςερας and the peculiarity of the numbers seem to connect them in some way or other.

3. I have several times before used the expression, that a matter was *sufficiently mystical*. But, in fact, we can never give the ancient mythoses credit for too much mysticism. It was evidently almost the only employment of the idle priests to convert every historical account into a riddle, and again to give their doctrines and riddles the appearance of history. Sacred and profane history are both the same, from the ænigmas of Samson, that given by the Queen of Sheba to Solomon, and the beautiful fables of Æsop (of which I shall treat by and by) to the parables of Jesus Christ. And the reason why all our learned men have totally failed in their endeavours to discover the meaning of the ancient mythologies, is to be found in their obstinate perseverance, in attempting to construe all the mythoses meant for ænigmas to the very letter. I have no doubt that anciently every kind of ingenuity, which can be imagined, was exerted from time to time, to invent and compose new riddles, till all history became, in fact, a great ænigma. In modern times as much ingenuity has been exercised to conceal the ænigma, and, by explanation, to shew that it was meant for reality. Under these circumstances, how was it likely that the riddles should be understood ? Before the time of Herodotus every ancient history is a mythic performance, in short a gospel—a work written to enforce virtue and morality, and to conceal the mythos—and every temple had one. This was the case with most of the Jewish writings, the Works and Days, the Iliad and Odyssey, the plays of Æschylus, the Cyropædia, the Æneid, the early history of Rome, the Sagas of Scandinavia, the Sophis of Abraham, the secret book of the Athenians, the Delphic verses of Olen, the 20,000 verses repeated by heart, (Q. *art ?* artificially learnt,) of the Druids, the Vedas or Bedahs, which is a collection of hymns or psalms.

The absurd superstition, as exhibited in the verses of Virgil, that the transactions of the lives of mankind came over and over in short periods, perhaps every 600 years, of course prevented any history from being written, as long as it had influence : and it was not until that superstition began to be despised, that we have any thing of the nature of real history. To have written a real history would have been to have overturned the religion. The first history written in Europe, which was independent of the Mythos, is that of Herodotus. But I think it probable, that some of the tracts in the Bible were the same.

It cannot be denied that to most inquirers, the early history of the world presents nothing but a scene of incredible absurdities. There is scarcely a page of it which can satisfy any reasonable mind. Take what history you please, it is the same. This is carried to such an excess, that previous to about six hundred years before Christ we can be said to have no history at all. Then what is to be done ? Are we to give up all inquiry into the early transactions of mankind ? It is a difficult question. At all events, we must have recourse to some other plan than retailing the labours of Bacchus, or the loves of Venus. In this work I am making an attempt to separate religion from history, at least to shew what religion is. This will conduce to shew afterward what history is. The only fault I have to find with the histories of India by Col. Tod and others is,

---

[1] Nimrod, Vol. III. p. 85 ; Ennii Fragmenta, Zenobius, I. Prov. 18.

that they do not sufficiently mark the lines of separation between the real and fabulous æras. It is allowed that Cristna is the sun, and yet they talk of him as of a man. He is like Hercules, Bacchus, &c., always the sun; and every great family traces its origin either to him as Cristna, or to him in some other avatar—as Rama, Bali, or some other. I know the difficulty of marking the line is great; but of this we may be perfectly assured, that these adored mythological personages, and their miraculous adventures, are nothing but inventions, added by the genealogists to the pedigrees of their employers, when they could go no higher—when, perhaps, they found the ancestor to have been some bandit, or ministerial traitor, or upstart soldier of fortune.

To return to our subject.

It is remarkable that in the Latin, the famous Cyclopes have no singular number. From this I think it probable, that they were *Latin* before they were *Greek* personages. Their grand abode was the island of Sicily. Virgil says, Sicilides Musæ; but why, in his mystic poem, does he invoke the Sicilian Muses, in preference to any other muses? May the original word for one of these persons have been *Cyclo*—making in its genitive Cyclopis—and meaning, the cycle of Clo? We must remember that Sicily is the peculiar land of the Cyclopes. Clo is the same word as that which ends the Agni-cula, the Jani-cula, the Hera-cula, and many other mystic words. No doubt every profound classical scholar will laugh at me for supposing it possible, that when Virgil was celebrating the renewal of Cycles, and particularly the sacred cycle of 600, he should invoke the Muses of Cycles instead of pastoral Muses, with whom his subject has little or no connexion. I shall pursue this inquiry by and by.

4. If my reader will look to the map and back to the last book, he will find it stated, that close to Jodpoor were the ruins of a very ancient city, called Mundore. Respecting this city, in the following passage of Col. Tod's beautiful book, we have what I think will lead us to the origin of the Cyclopes : " Whoever has seen Cortona, Volterra, or others of the Tuscan cities,[1] can form " a correct idea of the walls of Mundore, which are precisely of the same ponderous character. It " is singular that the ancient races of India, as well as of Europe, (and whose name of *Pali* is the " Synonym of *Galati* or *Keltoi*,) should, in equal ignorance of the mechanical arts, have piled up " these stupendous monuments, which might induce their posterity to imagine ' *there were giants* "' *in those days.*' This Western region, in which I include nearly all Rajapootana and Saurashtra, " has been the peculiar abode of these ' *pastor kings*,' who have left their names, their monu- " ments, their religion and sacred character, as the best records of their supremacy. The *Raj-* " *Pali*, or Royal Pastors, are enumerated as one of the thirty-six royal races of ancient days : the " city of *Palithana*, ' the abode of the Pali,' in Saurashtra (built at the foot of mount SATRUNJA, " sacred to Buddha) and Palli in Godwar, are at once evidences of their political consequence and " the religion they brought with them, while the different nail-headed characters[2] are claimed by " their descendants, the sectarian Jains of the present day."[3]

Again, the Colonel says,[4]

---

[1] We constantly read of the Tusci being one of the names of the progenitors of the Romans, or, at least, of the people before the Romans, occupying a large part of their country. The word Tusci has no singular number. I believe in this word we have an example of another unobserved emphatic article, and that Tusci is THE *Osci*, the same as the English emphatic article. In like manner, I think the De of France was also used by the ancients. *The* and *De* both mean God. It is remarkable that, in almost every case, the emphatic article means God. Θυοσκοος, a seer ; Θυος, a thing offered in sacrifice; hence Thusci: Θεος-osci, *The Osci.* The language of the Osci was the Latin. Pezron, p. 241. The Etruscans wrote from right to left. Astle, p. 183.

[2] *Nail-head*, the characteristic of the Etruscan numerals.　　　[3] Tod's Hist. Raj. p. 726.　　　[4] Ibid.

" As I looked up to the stupendous walls,

> " ' Where time hath lent his hand, but broke his scythe,'

" I felt the full force of the sentiment of our heart-stricken Byron,

> " ' There is a power
> " ' And magic in the ruined battlement,
> " ' For which the palace of the present hour
> " ' Must yield its pomp, and wait till ages are its dower.'

" Ages have rolled away since these were raised, and ages will yet roll on, and find them immove-" able, unchanged. The immense blocks are piled upon, and closely fitted to, each other, without " any cement, the characteristic of all the Etruscan cities termed Cyclopean. We might, indeed, " smuggle a portion of Mundore, into the pages of Micali, amongst those of Todi or Volterra " without fear of detection."

This extract, from the work of my friend Col. Tod, will, I think, enable me to shew, at least with some probability, who were the Cyclopes, the builders of our Cyclopæan cities, and circular temples, and whence they had their strange name. In the first place, if the Palli be Celts, this exactly accords with every thing which I have said, in my CELTIC DRUIDS, respecting the Celts' coming from North India, and building Stonehenge, Abury, Iona, &c.

In the next place, their religion and name of Jain or Janus, and their Nail-headed letters, connect them with the ancient Italians—Etruscans.

Colonel Tod very justly considers the Palli or Raj-pali, or the country of Pali-stan, to extend over all Rajapootana and Guzerat, or Syrastrene or Saurastra. But we have the Pali, or Pallestini, on the Hellespont; the Pallestini, at the mouth of the Padus, of Italy; and the mount Palatinus of Rome, and Palestræna, or the Sacrum Præneste, and the celebrated Pali-Raj or Royal pastors of Egypt, the builders, probably, of the Pyramids. In the term Roy-al we see an example of the utility, and even necessity, of having recourse to mixed etymology. This Raj is the Roi of Gaul. I think the word Raj is the same as *ray*, or *radha*, or *radius*, an emanation from the Sun, and pro-bably the kings, monarchs,[1] affected to be emanations from the Supreme, or from the Sun, or, as they called themselves, sons of God.[2] The coincidence more important than all the others is, that we have here the Pallestini or Philistines (as our *book* has it for the sake of disguise) of Western Syria—the capital of which was GAZA. In the country of the Palli, above described by Col. Tod, on the summit of a hill, close to an artificial lake, in about lat. 26, 20, long. 40, (noticed before,) is the very ancient city called Ajmere or Ajimere or Ajemere. This was existing in the time of Ptolemy, and was called by him Gaza-mera.[3] Here is Gaza on the border of a mere or piece of water, an artificial sea, in India, and Gaza on the sea-shore, in the Western Syria. There was a Gaza also in Egypt; and when Memphis was near the sea, before the emergence of the Delta, Gaza was its port.

In this district we find a town (Govindgurh) founded by a person called *Oodi*, and the tribe is called *Joda*; and, in the neighbourhood, is a river called Sarasvati—(Sara-iswati ?)—which runs into the artificial, elliptic-formed lake or mere above-named, called Poshkur—one excepted, the most sacred of the lakes of India. On its banks stands the only temple now in India, solely

---

[1] Monarch Mn—Αρχη.

[2] At the side of a mountain scooped out of the solid rock, Col. Tod says, p. 726, " is a noble *Bowli* or reservoir." What will the enemies of mixed etymology say to this? Will they be so obstinate as not to see the English *Bowl* in the Indian *Bowli?* Most likely this was a Piscina.

[3] Tod, Hist. p. 772.

dedicated to Bramha, containing a quadriform image. It is surmounted with *a cross*.[1] At a little distance rises a shrine to THE MOTHER, Mama-deva.[2] Not far distant, on a rock called the *Nag*-pahar or serpent rock, are ruins said to be those of the palace of a monarch who formerly ruled the tribe of the Chohans, called Aja Pal, or the Shepherd King, or Goatherd Aja.[3] This Aja Pal was the ancestor of a famous chief called Beesildeva or Visala-deva, and was the builder of Aji-mere, the Gaza-mera of Ptolemy. He was the contemporary of a celebrated person of Rajaht'-han called *Ulysses*. The Chohans of Aji-mere were existing 1000 years before Christ, as the histories say that a certain Udya-Dit, who died about that time, served under them. In my CELTIC DRUIDS may be found an account of a circular temple of very large stones in Persia, which, the tradition of the country says, was built by a tribe called Coans, who were. pigmies, but who were persons of supernatural strength, a species of fairy. Here I think we have the tribe of Chohans of Aji-mere. There was a tribe of them near Egbatana, and we have them again in Greece, in the several towns called Caon, in the different Argolises. These Coans or Pigmies were the builders of the monument described by the learned Physiologist Sir Anthony Carlisle, in Book V. Ch. VI. Sect. 6. From the mount on which Ajimere stands, runs the river, one branch of which is called Saraswati, which joins, near a town called Doon-ara, a river on which stands a town named Palee or Pali, and another river on which stands Mundore, in lat. 26, 20— long. 73, 5—which was formerly the capital of the present Marwar; its immense cyclopæan ruins, thirty-seven miles in circumference, alone remain. But a new capital has been built about six miles from Mundore, called Jod-poor. Of the date of Jodpoor I have no information; but it no doubt had its name from a reference to the old name of the tribe Iodi or Yuda. The date of the building of the cyclopæan Mund-ore, or even of its destruction, is, I believe, unknown even to tradition.

5. In the word Mundore, I think we may find the origin of the Cyclops the fabricators of these buildings. The words Munda and κυκλος, *circulus*, are synonymes—κυκλος is a mere translation of Munda, and they mean cycle. The Greeks, through profound ignorance, from κυκλος made cyclops, or *round* or *one* eye.

It is probable that the Cyclops were named in allusion to κυκλος a cycle, and οφις or the Hebrew אוב *aub* a serpent, the circular serpent, or the serpentine circle. There cannot be devised a more proper emblem of an eternally-renovating cycle, than the Cobra Serpent, with its tail in its mouth, periodically renewing itself by casting its skin. The deadly poison of the Cobra is an emblem of the *destroying* power; and the Hood which, in thousands of instances, we see him extending, sometimes over the sleeping Kanyia, and sometimes over the conjoined Yoni and Linga, and sometimes over the figure of Buddha, is, under this peculiar circumstance, a beautiful emblem of the *preserving* power. Then might not the people of Mundore be *Ophites*—followers or inventors of the serpentine cycle?[4] The word Cyclopes, then, will mean *the founders of cycles*. Munda correctly means cycle, as well as circle and the mundane revolution. Col. Tod has observed that the Palli and Keltoi are synonymous. I need not remind my reader of the very

---

[1] Hist. Raj. pp. 772, 774. Col. Tod says it was only built four years ago by a minister of Scindia. That it was built I do not doubt, but I think the legend and tradition prove that this building must have been a rebuilding: if it were not a rebuilding, here is the old superstition revived or kept alive.

[2] Ibid. p. 773.

[3] Aja we see means goat; Gaza has the same meaning. I shall resume the subject of Ajemere, and the Rayjah and Palli, in my next book.

[4] Οτις *divine vengeance*; Οψ *a voice*; φαω *to bring to light*; Οφις *a snake*.

extraordinary manner in which the ancient Druidical or Celtic monuments are constructed in reference to the different ancient cycles, of the oriental nations—the 3, the 7, the 12, the 19, the 30, the 60, the 144, the 188, the 600, the 608, the 650,—all in the serpentine temple at Abury ; and, I have no doubt, the famous Carnac, for the age of the world.  We must recollect, that Mundus means κοσμος, which means *beauty* arising from the orderly disposition of the heavenly bodies, moving in their cyclic revolutions.

Thus the Royal Shepherds were the founders of the system of cycles, *perhaps* expelled from India ; afterward *certainly* expelled from Egypt.  In the *Saturn-ja*, sacred to Buddha, and the Saturnia Urbs of Virgil, the ancient city on which Rome was built, may be found the father of Jove, Buddha,—also the Bal or Pal, or Palli in Godwar, the fathers of the Heri-culas or Hericlo-es, (found on the coast of Malabar,) and the Agni-culas or Agni-clo-es, a race who might first adopt the adoration of the ram, or unite it with that of the Zur-aster, or the fire or solar orb.  The Heri-culas and Agni-culas [1] are very like the Jani-cula of Rome, and from the Palli might come the Mons Palatinus.

The mixture of the Naga or Serpent worship, with the traditions relating to Mundore and the Pali and Ioudi, often noticed by Col. Tod, is very striking ; and, notwithstanding the brevity of the records of Western Syria or Judæa, the Nehusthan of Moses shews it was as really common to the religion in the Western as in the Eastern Syria.  And the Serpent temple at Abury, with its Hakpen or Nag-pen, shews the union of the two in Britain.

6. The Head of the Serpent Temple at Abury is called Hackpen.  This is evidently the Pen *head*, and Hag, the old English word for Serpent.  In Hebrew חג *hg* means circle or circular motion.  Job, xxii. 14, says, חוג-שמים *hug* samim, *the circle of the planets*, or heavens ; and in Syriac חגלות *hglut* means *a circuit*.  Now, I think the נחש *nhs* or serpent was called Hag from its circular, and, of all the beasts, solely circular, form, from its likeness to eternity—to the renovation αιων των αιωνων—joined to its eternally renewing itself by casting its old skin or residence when decayed, and putting on a new one—added to its most deadly power as destroyer—thus uniting it, in every thing, with the Logos, the wisdom, the self-existent, the cycle, the creator, preserver, and destroyer.  The serpent laid eggs, which, like those the offspring of the selected human female, were impregnated with the solar ray. (This will be explained presently.)  As the emblem of the nursing mother of all, the earth, when its young are alarmed, they flee, or were believed to flee, for refuge, into the bosom of their parent.  I am not surprised that the most refined of philosophers should have invented so beautiful an allegory.

It is a bold speculation, but I cannot help suspecting that the חג *hg* and חך *hk* of the word חכם *hkm* and the αρχη had all a close connexion ; that they were all corruptions or formations of each other.  הגה *hge* meditari, eloqui.  In Irish Eag-gnaisi, a philosopher, [2] *i. e.* in the singular, חג *hg* snake—with M. *Mag-us*.  Magi appellantur quod patria sua lingua idem sonat, quod apud nos *sapientes ;* Gn. by Metathesis *ng* nega Gonesa—Irish and Indian God of Wisdom : Naga the Cobra : Druids' Eggs. Q. Eag of the Eag-gnaisi Γνωσις knowledge, wisdom, wisdom of the serpent, when in the state of a circular animal, and also of its Egg,—Egg of Wisdom, *i. e.* Egg from which the world sprung ?  The world came from Wisdom.  I shall return to this etymon in a future page.

In these countries are many towns called, either wholly or in part, Munda, the same as the Munda of Spain ; and also many Oodipoors, and towns and rivers, which bespeak corruptions of names relating to the Jewish history, as well as the very early mythologies of the Gentiles.  Such

---

[1] Yaj-niculas ?                    [2] Ouseley, Coll. Vol. II. pp. 325, 345.

are the words Noah, Japhet, Shem, Lot, Ulysses, Achilles, Cæsar. No doubt the observation respecting such names as Lot would be very trifling if it were not connected with very many other circumstances. And we must always bear in mind, that we are endeavouring to recover the view of objects just vanishing from our sight. The words Ulysses and Achilles are of the same family of words with Ileyiam, and Prometheus, and Baghis, and Hercules, and Nysa, and Meru. The word Cæsar, is the Æsar of the Kelts or Gauls, and was adopted by Julius in honour of his conquest of Gaul, as Scipio took the name of Africanus, but he took the name of Cæsar also to encourage the superstition, that he was the divine incarnation promised by the Sibyls, which we shall fully explain in a future Book.

7. On the ruins of Mundore may be seen various mystic emblems, as the quatre-feuille, the cross, the mystic triangle, the triangle within a triangle ⧆, &c. Col. Tod says, " Among " ancient coins and medals, excavated from the ruins of Oojein and other ancient cities, I possess " a perfect series with all the symbolic emblems of the *twenty-four* Jain Apostles. The compound " equilateral triangle is among them ; perhaps there were masons in those days among the Pali " (i. e. the PHILISTINES of the Indian GAZA—and of Gaza, a few miles from Solomon's temple in " Western Syria). It is hardly necessary to state that this Trinitarian symbol (the double " triangle) occurs on our (so called) Gothic edifices, e. g. the beautiful Abbey-gate of Bury St. " Edmund's, Suffolk, erected about A.D. 1377." [1] So, my good friend, Col. Tod, you are surprised that there should be masonic emblems upon the ruins of Mundore, the capital of the Ioudi, or Juds of Yuda, in the country of the Palli, or Philistines of Gaza-mera, where Jessulmer was, and unquestionably the earliest of the Mounts of *Solyma*—of Bit-Solumi or temples of Solomon. But though this may surprise you, it will not surprise his Royal Highness the Duke of Sussex, or any Mason of high degree. But the author is himself a Mason, and that of high degree ; HE MAY SAY NO MORE. Yet he will venture to add, that though much of the learning of that ancient order remains, much is lost, and much may yet be recovered. But it is not every apprentice or fellowcraft who knows all the secrets of the order.

The following observation is made by Col. Tod : [2] " The wood of Solomon's temple is called " *al-mug* : אלמג *almg*, 1 Kings x. 11 : the prefix *al* is merely the article. This is the wood also " mentioned in the annals of Guzzerat, of which the temple to ' Adnath' [3] was constructed. It is " said to be indestructible by fire. It has been surmised that the fleets of Tyre frequented the " Indian coast ; could they thence have carried Al-Mug for the temple of Solomon ?" [4] I suppose I need scarcely point out how strongly this casual observation of Col. Tod's tends to support my doctrine, of the intimate connexion of the tribe of Western Ioudi with the religion of India ? We have seen the Guzzerat God *Ad* of Western Syria, in Adad, Hadadezer, &c. A few verses afterward, in 1 Kings, ch. x., shields of gold are said to have been made. Of what use could shields be in the temple ? These shields were salvers or waiters, after the custom of Central India, where, when a person is treated with high respect, every thing is handed to him on a shield or buckler. [5]

8 The infamous Fourmont who destroyed the inscriptions on the marbles in the Morea, discovered the temple of a God or Goddess called Ongar, i. e. Minerva. The shrine of this deity is

---

[1] Hist. Raj. p. 729.   [2] Ibid. 282.   [3] i. e. God-ad, di, dis.

[4] Brother mason, what do you know of Solomon's temple ? Here are the word Almug, in Syrastrene, and the masonic emblems in Mundore,—the town of Cycles or Cyclopes. Be assured the wood was carried for certain sacred parts of the building, and by Free-Masons too. Probably all the fourteen temples of Solomon, of which we read, were partly constructed of this sacred wood, and by Free-Masons too.

[5] Vide Tod, Hist. Raj.

one of the twelve most sacred places in India. It is in the sacred island of Mundana or Mundatta, (i. e. Munda-datta,) peculiarly sacred to the God OM or M, i. e. 600,[1] on the Nerbudda in Lat. 22, 16—Long. 76, 20—called by Sir John Malcolm Ongkar. It is not far from Burg-oonda and Maundoo, and not very far from the great Mundore, which was once thirty-seven miles in circumference, whose ruins bespeak a most magnificent city in *very ancient* times.[2] Munda-datta means correctly the cycle or circle of Buddha, Datta being one of his names—Book V. Chapter I. The ruins of the ancient cities of the Buddhists, in this country, shew them to have been a race of people of prodigious power and magnificence. The Mundas are all Buddhist and I doubt not Cyclopæan. If the Buddhist Cyclops of the West, were any thing like what the ruins of their cities in the East shew them to have been, we need not be surprised at the vastness or grandeur of their temples and buildings which remain to us. These cities, in North India, were the thousand cities alluded to by Strabo, the existence of which is treated of with great talent in the unpublished manuscripts of the learned Mr. Moyle, of Southampton, now in the possession of his descendant, Sir Joseph Copley, Baronet, of Sprotsborough.

A few pages back I observed that the Palli were called Raj-Palli or royal shepherds. I have often wondered why the shepherd tribe who conquered Egypt were called *royal* shepherds. We here see the reason : they were the Raj-Palli or Roi-Palli. They were Rajah-poutans, or Rajah-palitan, or Rajah-poutan shepherds. These are beautiful coincidences. I shall return to this by and by.

I must now beg my reader to recall to his recollection that the discovery of the origins of ancient nations and religions, the object of our research, is the most difficult undertaking that can be imagined—that it has been the subject of anxious pursuit by the learned in all the ages to which by writing or tradition we have access ; that to Pythagoras, to Plato, to Cicero, to Pliny, to Bacon, to Newton, to Bryant, and to Faber, the common or acknowledged literal accounts have been unsatisfactory, and that, by the successors of each, in turn, the failure or the unsatisfactory nature of the results of the inquiries of their predecessors has been admitted; that a state of society of a very superior kind existed long previous to any Grecian historians or traditions, I think no one who meditates upon the remains of Druidical and Cyclopæan buildings can entertain any doubt. How is it possible to doubt that an uniform system must have prevailed, which gave rise to the same style of building, the same names of towns, rivers, and districts, in all quarters of the globe ? The same superstition is apparent every where, and it is very clear, that the superstitions of the ancients with which we are acquainted, are only the remains or corruptions of a previous and universal system of which we have no history, but part of which I am now rescuing from oblivion. I beg to remind my reader that originally in Rome, Greece, and Egypt, which conveys with it India, there was no idolatry, except it was simply the *Linga*, as the emblem of the creative power. This was the religion of Buddha, the ראשית *rasit* of Moses, the religion of Melchizedek, which, in the second preface to my *Celtic Druids*, I said I should unveil.

---

[1] Malcolm's Cent. Ind. Vol. II. p. 505.          [2] Ibid. p. 13.

## CHAPTER VI.

1. THE reason why the serpent became the emblem of the *destroying power*, in Genesis, has never been satisfactory or clear to me. It is said that, according to that mythos, he is made, by the Ophites, the emblem of the Creator, because, by persuading Eve to eat the apple, he was the immediate cause of the propagation of the species—that without the opening of the eyes, by which expression is meant, in fact, the exciting of the desire of procreation, the race of man would not have been multiplied—and that, without its influence in making man in this respect wise, he would have for ever continued in a state of unprolific though innocent ignorance. According to the allegory in Genesis, little as it is understood, we may certainly conclude, that the serpent put in motion the human formative power, and was at the same time the cause of the death, or at least apparent destruction, of man—of his decomposition or return to dust.[1] But I think the Cobra was emblematic of something more than *the destroying power*. Buddha was the protogonos or first-begotten, the first emanation of divine power, wisdom, *by* whom and *for* whom all things were created. But the creator of all things was also the destroyer; and the Naga being the emblem of the destroyer, and the destroyer being divine wisdom, it became also the emblem of divine wisdom; *the serpent was more subtil than any beast of the creation.* Gen. iii. 1.

Few persons, I believe, have read Genesis, without having had their curiosity excited to discover why the serpent was the *wisest* of the animal creation. The Elephant, the Dog, or the Monkey, might have had some pretension to this honour; but I think the serpent has, from its natural properties, just as little pretension to it, as the frog or the lizard. But from the refined deductions above, it might have become the emblem of wisdom. It might be the emblem of eternity for another reason—for the same reason which made the Phoinix or Palm-tree the emblem of eternal life. It possessed the faculty of renewing itself without the process of generation or fructification, as to outward appearance, by annually casting its skin. This annual renewal made it emblematical of the sun or the year. Thus we see how all these refined allegories rise out of one another, almost without end; generally to outward appearance absurd, but, when understood, often beautiful. I think no unprejudiced person reading Genesis would ever suspect that the serpent there named was the evil principle or the Devil. The literal meaning both of the text and context in fact falsifies any such idea : and yet almost all Christian priests (choosing to have recourse to allegory to serve their own purpose,[2] though they never cease abusing those who teach that

---

[1] I think if I can shew that the literal meaning of Genesis contains an absolute impossibility in itself, we must, for that reason alone, have recourse to an allegorical meaning, after the example of all the ancient Jews and Christian fathers. Adam and Eve are ordered to increase and multiply ; and had not the serpent brought death into the world, before the end of the first four thousand years the number of persons on the earth would have been so great, that they must have devoured every animal, and have been obliged to feed on one another. Long before the expiration of this period of time, the surface of the earth would have been so covered with people, that they could not have stood for want of space to stand on.

[2] The Devil is the grand ally of priests. In these days certainly, no Devil no Priests.

3 x

the book is an allegory) maintain, that a real devil or evil principle is meant; and that by the text merely a common serpent is not literally to be understood. The fact is, they have among them the tradition of its true oriental meaning, but how to explain it they know not. I beg my reader to refer to Cruden's Concordance on the word Serpent, and there he will see both the difficulties of the learned, and an extraordinary example of the meanness of understanding in a very learned, pious, and good man, produced by the thing miscalled religion.

2. It is very certain that, in ancient times, the serpent was an object of adoration in almost all nations. The Indians, the Egyptians, the Greeks, and the Romans, kept serpents in their temples alive; and treated them with the highest respect. From this superstition, I do not doubt that the Ophites, of whom we know very little, took their rise. I can pay no attention to the calum- nies of Origen and other fathers whose evidence our modern writers are so weak as to receive— the evidence of men who professed to believe fraud to be meritorious, if used against the opponents of their religion. Nothing which appears to be told by the orthodox fathers, in a regular and systematic manner, against the heretics, is *credible*. Nor are they to be believed even when they profess only to refute doctrines, for it was not uncommon with them to charge their opponents with absurd opinions which they never held, for the double purpose of disgracing those opponents and gaining credit to themselves. This has always been considered, by priests, a mere allowable *ruse* in religious controversy. It is yet had recourse to every day. For these reasons I can pay little attention to the accounts of the Ophites retailed from Origen, by Matter. I can only receive a few insulated facts, which are confirmed by other evidence. They seem to have placed at the head, or nearly at the head, of all things, and most intimately connected with the serpent, a certain *Sophia*. This is clearly a translation of the word Buddha into Greek, and strongly reminds me that the old Buddhas are always under the care of the Cobra Capella. I think we may conclude from this, that they honoured the Serpent as the emblem of the God of wisdom. Their enemies tell us, that they professed to derive their veneration for the serpent from Genesis.

The famous Brazen Serpent set up by Moses in the wilderness, called Nehustan, is called in the Targum *a Saviour*. It was probably a serpentine crucifix, as it is called a *cross* by Justin Martyr.

Mr. Bentley says that in India the serpent is the emblem of *wisdom*. He cites no authority, but I do not dispute his assertion. [1]

As I have just now stated, I do not doubt that the sect of Ophites had its origin from the consi- deration, that the *destroyer* was the *creator*, that *destruction* was *regeneration*: and the Cobra, as being the most deadly of the serpent tribe, which annually renewed itself, with its tail in its mouth, was considered the most appropriate emblem of the *destroyer* and *regenerator*, in fact, of the *saviour*. Thus we see Buddha, the creating power, constantly protected by the destroying power. The Cobra, the Ioni, and Linga, seem to be the only emblems admitted in the early Buddhist monuments, while I have no doubt that the *earliest* had no emblem. The God was represented seated, naked, contemplative, and unornamented. By degrees emblems increased in long periods of time. If we suppose only *one* emblem to have been admitted in a generation, in thirty genera- tions or one thousand years there would be *thirty* emblems. A single new emblem in a generation would not alarm the worshipers, and thus the abuse might creep on till it arrived at the state in which we find it both in India and in the Romish Church at this day. The Protestants are doing the same thing; the last generation introduced pictures into churches: the cross is now following in order. They go on slowly at first: at length the minds of men becoming accustomed to inno-

---

[1] Hist. Ant. Hind. p. 60.

vations they proceed in geometrical progression. Thus, figments of nonsense go on increasing, till some intrepid fanatic takes offence at them, and preaches against them—a bloody civil war then arises about nothing, and the emblems and the beautiful temples which contain them are destroyed.

This is their history in India, in Egypt, and in ancient and modern Europe. A high state of civilization, and skill in the fine arts and sciences, do not prevent, but seem rather to encourage, the increase of this foolery. Let us look at Rome and Greece. There we see a few philosophers crying out against the abuse; but the mass of the people, with their deceiving and flattering priests who live on their folly, running into the greatest extravagancies. When Socrates exposed the follies of the priests, what was his reward? When Numa forbade the use of *images*, who attended to him ?—his uncivilized followers. When they became civilized, his commands were forgotten.

3. The Ophites are said to have maintained, that the serpent of Genesis was the Λογος and Jesus Christ. This confirms what I have said above. The Logos was *divine wisdom*, and was the Buddha of India. The Brazen Serpent was called Λογος or the WORD by the Chaldee Paraphrast, [1] and for this word they use the Chaldee ממרא *mmra*.[2] Thus the Cross, or Linga, or Phallus, with the serpent upon it, was called by the letters which conveyed the idea of word, or voice, or lingua, or language. Hence came the phallus, the emblem of the generative power in India, to be called linga. The serpent was the emblem of the evil principle or destroyer, but, as before stated, the destroyer was the creator, hence he had the name of ΟΦΙΣ ; (in Hebrew אוב *aub ;*) and as he was the Logos or Linga, he was also Οψ *a voice*, and in Hebrew ממרא *mmra*. Query, hence Συφαρ *a seraph* or *serpent*,[3] and Σοφος *wise*? The Συφ and Σοφ are both the same root. Besides considering the Serpent as the emblem of the Logos or of Jesus Christ, the Ophites are said to have revered it as the cause of all the arts of civilized life. But still the question recurs why this animal should have been selected as the emblem of the giver of the information, except as the emblem of the creator and destroyer, and therefore of wisdom.

In Exod. iii. 14, God is called אהיה *aeie*. This word is formed from the root היה *eie* or הוה *eue*, which signifies *to live, exist*, or *be*.[4] But הוה *eue* or היוא *hiua*, or, as we miscal it, Hevah, but correctly Hiva, was the name of Eve and of a serpent. The Bacchantes invoked Eve by name, in their ceremonies.[5] Mr. Bryant has shewn, that both the Phœnicians and the Egyptians adored the serpent; that two were kept alive at Thebes ; that it was adored at Eleusis, also at Epidaurus; that one was kept in the Acropolis at Athens; and that the Deities Cneph, Hermes, and Agathodæmon, were described by this emblem. It was, says Mr. Bryant, an emblem of DIVINE WISDOM *and of the creative energy by which all things were formed*: Divine Wisdom, that is, of Buddha. Maximus Tyrius states, that when Alexander entered India, he found a prince who kept an enormous snake as the image of Bacchus.[6] Arrian also informs us, that when Alexander advanced into India he met with one of the princes who adored a large serpent, which he kept confined. This is exactly what we are informed was done by the Christian Ophites. In a future page we shall find that several illustrious females were believed to have been selected and impregnated by the Holy Ghost. In these cases, a serpent was always supposed to be the form which it assumed. This was the incarnation of the Logos; this was what I alluded to when I spoke of a *selected female*, in Chap. V. Sect. 6, of this book.

[1] Basnage, Liv. iv. Ch. xxv.    [2] Ib. xxiv.    [3] See Jones's Lexicon in voce.
[4] Bryant on Plag. of Egypt, p. 203.    [5] Parkhurst, in voce נחש *nhs*, IV.
[6] Class. Journ. Vol. XXIII. p. 14.

In almost all the emblematical groups of the Indians, we meet with the serpent in one shape or other. When it has its tail in its mouth, no doubt it is the emblem of eternity. But though it is admirable for this purpose, that is but a small part of its meaning. It is worthy of observation that it is found on very nearly the oldest of the Buddhist monuments. And the serpent most particularly chosen in India, and often found in Egypt, where it is not a native, is the Cobra or Naga, or hooded snake. This Buddhist foreigner, in Egypt, sufficiently shews that the Buddhist worship came to Egypt before the invention of Hieroglyphics. I apprehend, as I have already intimated, that the serpent, which was thought to be more deadly in its bite than all others, was selected as the most perfect emblem of the *destroying power*: and it is always found with the united Yoni and Linga, as the emblem of the *creating power*, the doctrine seen every where, that *destruction* was *creation* or *formation*. I suppose it was a brazen Cobra which Moses set up on a cross in the Wilderness. The Cobra, with its tail in its mouth, would denote eternal formation and destruction, the eternal renewal of worlds. It is very clear that a great variety of beautiful allegories present themselves where the Cobra may be used.

It is said that the word נחשתן *nhstn* nehusthan cannot be understood by the Hebrew or Arabic scholar, because, though one part be Hebrew, the other is pure Persian. The נחש *nhs* is Hebrew, the תן *tn* is Persian or Oriental. The first means serpent, the second means place.[1] But this may have a very different meaning; it may mean נה *nh* or mind, and *stan* a place, the place of the Divine Mind, of the Holy Ghost.

4. I think the different æras of Buddhism may be observed in its monuments. Its first æra is shewn, by Budda, as a Negro, seated cross-legged, perfectly naked, without any ornament whatever. This is the first stage of idolatry, unless it were preceded by the stone pillar anointed with oil. In the next, he is slightly ornamented or clothed, and accompanied with the Naga or Cobra Capella. In the next, he is accompanied with vast numbers of figures, of men, women, children, and animals: but he is never himself a monster, with several heads or hands, nor are his attendants monsters. In the next stage, he is accompanied with the Cobra with many heads—but with no other monster. After this comes Cristna with every absurdity that can be conceived. In this manner I think may be shewn the relative dates of the Buddhist monuments; and, in the second and VERY EARLY stage, a degree of skill and elegance in the workmanship may be observed, to which the later works can make no pretension. These were the works of the primeval, learned race spoken of by Baillie, the inventors of the Neros, supposed to have lived before the flood.

After a most careful comparison of the large specimen of the Cobra Capella, in the Museum of the Royal College of Surgeons, with the monuments in the British Museum, I am quite satisfied that the serpent or protuberance on the foreheads of the Memnon, and of many other figures, are cobras.

" As far as these Egyptian remains lead us into unknown ages, the symbols they contain appear " not to have been invented in that country, but to have been copied from those of some other " people still anterior, who dwelt on the other side of the Eythræan ocean. One of the most " obvious of them is the hooded snake, which is a reptile peculiar to the South-eastern parts of " ASIA, but which I found represented, with great accuracy, upon the obelisk of Rameses, " and have observed also frequently on the Isiac table."[2] The Aspic, called Thermutis, was believed to be immortal by the Egyptians.[3] Mr. Payne Knight has repeated an observation of Stukeley's, that the original name of the temple of Abury was the *snake's head*: and he adds, it

---

[1] Gerrans in Ouseley's Coll. Orient. p. 28!.    [2] Payne Knight, Wors. Pr. p. 90.

[3] See Jurien, Vol. II. p. 225.

is remarkable that the remains of a similar circle of stones in Bœotia had the same name, in the time of Pausanias. Κατα δε την ες Γλισαντα ευθειαν εκ Θηϐων λιθοις χωριον περιεχομενον λογασην Οφεως καλουσιν οἱ Θηϐαιοι κεφαλην. [1]

The three most celebrated emblems carried in the Greek mysteries, were the Phallus, the Egg, and the Serpent; or, otherwise, the Phallus, the Ioni or Umbilicus, and the Serpent. The first in each case was the emblem of the Sun, of fire, as the male or active generative power; the second, of the passive, and the third of the destroyer, the re-former, and thus of the preserver;— the preserver eternally renewing itself. The universality of the Serpentine worship or adoration no one can deny. It is not only found every where, but it every where occupies an important station; and the farther back we go, the more universally it is found, and the more important it appears to have been considered.

5. About thirty years ago, a very learned Frenchman, of the name of Dupuis, published a work[2] called The History of all Religions, in which he undertook to shew, that the labours of Hercules, and almost all ancient mythology, were astronomical allegories, applicable to a state of the sphere corrected or thrown back to a very remote period. His success, as to many parts, cannot for a moment be doubted, and particularly as to the labours of Hercules. That those labours which we read of in Diodorus Siculus and other authors, are all depicted in the heavens cannot be denied. Those labours are so closely connected with the signs and divisions of the Zodiac, as not to be separable from them. They must, I think, be contemporaneous or nearly so. Now, when my reader considers what has been said respecting the Indian origin of the Ionians, the Argives, the Hellenes, and the Amazons,—that, in fact, they were sectaries driven out from upper India, is it not possible that these labours had their origin in the wars which then took place, all over the world, between the different sects; and, consequently, that it was about that time that the sphere was invented by Chiron the Centaur?—Κεν-ταυρ-ος. Let my reader recollect that he has found the same towns in India, Asia, and in Europe; the same Gods, intelligible in India, but not in Europe; and all the other marks of simultaneous identity, and then doubt, if he can, that these constellations must have had a common origin, and probably at a common time. Let him consider the wars of Hercules with the Amazons, and he will agree with me, that all, or nearly all, the mythoses have reference to the wars of the different sects of the Ioni and the Linga—of the Hellenes and Trojans, the Argives and the Amazons. The battles of Hercules and the Titans, &c., &c., are only the European counterpart of the Indian battles of Cristna described in the Mahabarat; they are the same thing painted according to the peculiar taste of the two nations.

---

[1] Pausan. Bœot. Cap. xix. S. 2.

[2] This book, I am told, is now becoming extremely scarce, the devotees every where having made desperate war upon it, particularly the Jesuits of France. The globes which were made on purpose for it I have never been able to obtain either in Paris or elsewhere. Persons who have not perused this work, have no right to give an opinion on the subject of ancient mythology.

## CHAPTER VII.

MOON RESUMED. WATER. ISIS.—PRITCHARD ON THE MOON.—PLUTARCH ON THE MOON AND ISIS.—
ISIS UNKNOWN TO GREEKS AND ROMANS.—CRESCENT, ORIGIN AND ADORATION OF IT.—BAPTISMS.—
ICE. PAYNE KNIGHT'S EXPLANATION OF ITS NAME.—INFLUENCE OF THE MOON.

1. Among the attempted explanations of the immense mass of confusion which the ancient mythologies exhibit, there is nothing much less satisfactory than those relating to the rank and character which they ascribe to the moon. As I have before observed, in Book VI. Chapter II., to me they are indeed any thing but satisfactory. She is represented as Isis, the wife of Osiris, that is, of the sun. And if she were barely this, and nothing more, we might be contented to consider it as merely a nonsensical local superstition, or perhaps a figure of speech. But the moon was masculine as well as feminine. This raises an awkward obstacle to his being the wife of Osiris. And yet Osiris is said to enter into the moon and impregnate her. On the 17th of the month Athyr, Osiris entered into the moon. On this day Noah entered into the ark. This alone, if every thing else were wanting, would be sufficient to prove the identity of the two mythoses.

In reply to what I have just observed about the moon's being masculine, it may be said, that this only arose from the superstitions of different countries. But this is not satisfactory to me; because I am convinced that the system of the trinitarian nature of the foundation of the ancient mythology which the reader has seen, with its metempsychosis, its revolving cycles, renewal of worlds, and abstinence from animal food, pervaded all countries. A beautiful and sublime system was the foundation of all the nonsense which ignorance and selfish craft at last engendered, and engrafted upon it.

I am quite certain that by the word ‎שמים‎ smim in Genesis, the planets were meant, and they were always called the erratic stars. Speaking of these, Porphyry makes a marked distinction between them and the moon, for the *purposes of divination.* He says, " In order, therefore, to " effect this, they made use of the Gods within the heavens, both the erratic and the non-erratic, " of all of whom it is requisite to consider the sun as the leader: *but to rank the moon in the* " *second place.*" [1]

2. Dr. Pritchard observes of the moon, " The name Isis seems only to have been applied to the " moon, in the same manner in which Virgil gives the appellation of Ceres to that celestial body. " The general acceptation of both these names is much more extensive." [2]   " Plutarch generalises " all the attributes or characters of Isis, and considers her as representing the female qualities or " powers of nature, which are the passive principles of generation in all productions ; whence (he " says) she is called, by nature, the *nurse* and the *all-receiving,* and is commonly termed Myriony- " mus or possessing ten thousand names. [3]   The same idea is more diffusely expressed by Apu- " leius, in a passage in which Isis calls herself, ' Natura, rerum parens, elementorum omnium do- " ' mina.'" [4]   Again, " On the whole, we may conclude that Isis represented the Φυσις παναιολος, " the *natura multiformis,* of the Greek and Roman mythologists." [5]   This is proved by several engravings in Montfaucon, where we find her with the inscription Φυσις παναιολος under her figure, in one of which she may be seen rising from the lotus.

[1] De Abs. Taylor, Book ii. p. 71.   [2] Pritchard, Egyp. Myth. p. 132.   [3] Plut. de Iside, Cap. liii.
[4] Apul. Lib. xi.; Prit. ib. p. 133.   [5] Ib. p. 134.

After this, in p. 145, Dr. Pritchard observes that, according to Apuleius, Isis was called in Egypt *triformis* or the *triform* Goddess, and was worshiped both as a malignant and benignant Deity. Here we have most distinctly the Indian Trinity, the creator, or preserver, and the destroy* er. The Doctor warns his reader to " beware in making researches into the fictions of mythology, " not to discover more wisdom or *more* contrivance than ever really existed." [1]   We must also, I think, beware not to discover *less*. But sure I am that if nothing more was to be discovered than the unconnected collection of statements (nonsensical enough if taken by themselves) on which the learned Doctor has wasted his time, much too valuable to be thus thrown away, the pursuit would be of very little use. The Doctor observes, that it is strange and absurd to suppose (as the devotees did) that the moon exercises an influence over women in childbirth. This is an example of the mistakes of the moderns. It arose from mistaking the moon for Isis, the *female* generative power of nature. The moon was only the planet dedicated to Isis. But the supposition that the moon influenced women, is not more absurd than to suppose that it influences lunatics.

It cannot be doubted that the word Isis often means the moon. But what is there that she does not mean ?  Jablonski says, " Præter ISIDEM cœleetem quæ Luna est, religiose quoque colebant " (Ægyptii) terrestrem, ipsam scilicet Terram, quæ proinde ISIDIS nomine designabatur." [2]   Macrobius says, " Isis est vel *Terra* vel NATURA RERUM subjacens Soli.—Isis nihil aliud est, quam terra, NATURAVE rerum. [3]  Very true—natura-VE rerum, either one or the other. When we read of the moon as the wife of the sun, and of the sun entering into the moon and impregnating her, their conjunction, at the beginning of each new cycle, was probably alluded to. The produce of their conjunction was the new cycle—the renovation of nature.

3. Plutarch says, the moon was called Μητηρ Σελην τ κοσμ. But Selene was the same as Cybele, Da-Mater—in fact, the Great Mother. [4]  Cybele was called the *Idean Mother*, or *Mother Ida*. This is the title of the mother of Meru, called *Ida*-vratta or *the circle of Ida*. On the highest part of Ida was a Gargarus or stone circle, called, from the Sanscrit, Cor-Ghari. [5]

The sun was the emblem of the male, the moon of the female, generative power. They appear to be, as they are called, the two greater lights, and from this the moon came to be perpetually confounded, as an object of adoration, with the female generative power, and her crescent with the Omphalos, the Argha, or the Ioni. Her crescent, from its shape, in a very peculiar manner favours the mistake—for we never see a half moon or a full moon. The emblem became the object of adoration ; the object of the emblem was often forgotten. Nothing of this kind could so easily happen to the sun. Isis, as identified with the moon, is said to have all the attributes of the mother of God. I apprehend that, chiefly among the later Egyptians and Greeks, after they had lost the meaning of their mysteries, by mistake the crescent was taken for the Argha, which had the form of a crescent. Isis, the female generative power represented by the Lunette or crescent-shaped Argha, was mistaken for the crescent-formed moon, to whom, among astrologers, the second day of the week or Monday was dedicated. When we see the Beeve or Bos or Urus, called Taurus, marked on the side with a Lunette or Lunar crescent, this, though in honour of Isis, was not in honour of the moon, but in honour of that higher principle, the principle of generation, whence the moon herself, along with all nature, proceeded. The Theba or Tibe, תבה *Tbe,* or Cow, with a crescent on her side, which founded Thebes, was not the moon—but it was that which the Ioni represented. In this manner, in almost innumerable instances, mistakes have

---

[1] P. 156.          [2] De Iside, Sect. iii.          [3] Whiter, Etymologicum Univ. Vol. I. p. 265.
[4] Bryant, Anal. Vol. II. p. 442.          [5] Faber, Anal. Vol. III. pp. 31, 229.

arisen. I repeat, it is worthy of observation, that we never meet with a half moon or a full moon as an object of adoration : it is always a crescent ; always that which was called an umbilicus, at Delphi, which at that place was of stone, of great size, as it was also in Egypt, and carried by seventy-two men, in their sacred processions—a navis-biprora. If it be said that the moon was used as an emblem of the female generative power ; then I reply, I will not dispute about a word. If the moon, by the lunar crescent on the side of the Bos, Theba, or Io, was meant, it was not so meant as an honour to the moon as *the* moon, but to it as an emblem only. And if these distinctions be carefully attended to, all the difficulties will be removed.

Plutarch, as stated above, says, that the Egyptians called the moon *the mother of the world.* Sir William Drummond, after shewing that the Greeks and Romans did not understand the Egyptian mythology, says of Plutarch, " This author would have adhered more exactly to the " Egyptian mythology, if he had written Minerva or Neitha, instead of the Moon, and Pthah or " Vulcan instead of the Sun."[1]    Proclus makes Neitha say, The fruit which I have brought forth is the sun :[2] then how can she be the moon ?    Neitha was also divine wisdom.

4. But, as I have said before, the Greeks and Romans knew as little of the real oriental doctrines, indeed, I may say less, than we do at this day, therefore it is not surprising to find them making mistakes. Thus Plutarch says, that the Egyptian statues of Osiris had the phallus to signify his procreative and prolific power : Πανταχου δε και ανθρωπομορφον Οσιριδος αγαλμα δεικνυουσιν, εξορθιαζον τω αιδοιω, δια τογονιμον και τροφιμον.[3]    The extension of which, through the three elements of air, earth, and water, they expressed by another kind of statue, which was occasionally carried in procession, having a triple symbol of the same attribute : Αγαλμα προτιθενται και περιφερουσιν, ου το αιδοιον τριπλασιον εςιν.[4]    From these and other expressions of the same kind, I conclude with Sir William Drummond, that Plutarch had no idea of the real sublime nature of the oriental and original Trinity, or if he knew it, he did not choose to disclose it.

Apuleius calls Isis QUEEN, the Greek word for which is Βασιλεια.    Diodorus Siculus[5] informs us that Uranus and Titea had two daughters, one called Basilea. He says, " Basilea being the " eldest, brought up her brothers with the care and affection of a mother, whence she was called " the GREAT MOTHER." She married Hyperion, one of her brothers, by whom she had Helio and Selene. Her other brothers assassinated Hyperion, and drowned Helio, then a tender infant, in Eridanus. He then shews how Cybele, who was descended from Basilea, was called *Mother of the Mount,* and joined Bacchus at Nysa.[6]    The Indian mythos of Bacchus, Mount Meru, &c., &c., is evident in all this,—a tradition of the true meaning of which Diodorus was probably perfectly ignorant. The whole was taken from the East, and located in a part of Phrygia.[7]

The famous inscription on the Temple of Isis, quoted at length in Book VI. Chapter II. Sect. 8, proves that Isis was not the moon, and that, in fact, the moon was only a planet dedicated to the Goddess. In addition to the evidence afforded by that inscription, we learn from Proclus, that it had originally the following words, ον εγω καρπον ετεκον, ηλιος εγενετο, that is, " The fruit which I have brought forth is the Sun ;" the same as Neitha. I should think this at once proves that Isis cannot be the Earth or the Moon. How can any imagination invent.a mythos, allegory, or history, which shall make the sun the produce of either of these bodies ?

---

[1] Class. Journ. No. XLI.    [2] Ibid.    [3] De Is. et Osir.    [4] Ibid. p. 365.
[5] Lib. iii. Cap. iv.    [6] P. 201.
[7] Vide Lempriere ; also Drummond on a Punic Inscription, pp. 86—88.

5. Although what I have stated may be sufficient to prove that the consideration of the moon, as the wife of Osiris and the female generative principle, must have been, comparatively speaking, of modern date, yet I think the origin of the Crescent, as the emblem of the female generative power, may be found in another quarter. The Crescent is no more applicable to the moon, than the circle or semicircle; nor, indeed, so much. But if the ancients knew the nature of the planet Venus, the Alma Venus, the Mother—we have a reason for the adoption of the Crescent. She is *always* gibbous, *always* a crescent. This they would know, if they had the telescope: but I have been told that there are some persons, in very clear northern oriental climates, who can distinguish her gibbous form with the naked eye. Here, then, I think we have the reason why we always see the Crescent as the emblem of the female generative power. And hence, when the meaning of it was quite lost in the Western countries, the ignorant devotees converted the Lunus, because it was sometimes gibbous, into the female Luna.

6. Among all nations, and from the very earliest period, water has been used as a species of religious sacrament. This, like most of the other rites of the ancients when examined to the bottom, turns out to be founded on very recondite and philosophical principles, equally common in all countries. We have seen that the sun, light, or fire, was the first preserver, at the same time that he was the creator and the destroyer. But though he was the preserver and the regenerator, it is evident that he alone, without an assistant element, could regenerate nothing, though that element itself was indebted to him for its existence. That element was water. Water was the agent by means of which every thing was regenerated or born again. Water was in a peculiar manner the agent of the sun: without the Sun, either as light, heat, or fire, water would be an adamantine mass. Without water, the power of the sun would produce no living existence, animal or vegetable. Hence, in all nations, we find the Ερως, the Dove, or Divine Love, operating by means of its agent water, and all nations using the ceremony of plunging, or, as we call it, baptizing for the remission of sins, to introduce the hierophant to a regeneration, to a new birth unto righteousness. In like manner, in almost all nations we find sacred rivers. The priests of all countries wished to have the river which run through their territory sacred; from this it is that we find so many rivers dedicated to the sun, and called in the different languages by a name answering to the word sun. At present I shall not particularize them: they must be in the remembrance of every reader—the Ganges, the Nile, the Po, &c., &c. This is the origin of the different baptizings or baptisms of the followers of Mithra and of Christ. The Greek word Βαπτιζω means to plunge into any thing, or be immersed in any thing, not *to sprinkle* merely with water. From these principles arose the custom in their ceremonies of constantly baptizing the Ioni and Linga with water. And it is on the same principle that, when in a state of union, they generally float on the water in the Arga. Sometimes an artificial fountain is contrived to throw water upon them, as may be seen in two exemplars in the India-House.

Meru, with its concentric circles of land and water, surrounded by the ocean, is an emblem of the creating and destroying powers. When this system was established, the north-pole was believed or feigned to be surrounded with seven dwipas or concentric circles, the last surrounded by the ocean. All this, in later times, was an emblem of the sun surrounded with the planets; but probably it first arose from the belief that the earth was the centre, the north-pole arising in the middle of it, and the planets revolving around it.

Fire and water are beautifully emblematical of the creating and destroying powers of nature. Water is the opponent and destroyer of its creator, fire. In turn fire evaporates and destroys water. Yet fire, as already intimated, is the former of water, from the icy adamantine block, its natural state. Without water, fire with all its creating powers can produce nothing. Thus they are destroyers and creators in alternate succession. Hence, from not distinguishing between the first

3 Y

fine principle and its emblem, the water, fire, and earth, have been taken for the original objects of adoration.

The absolute necessity of the presence of water with the solar ray, to produce fructification, is obvious. The apparent effect of the moon in producing dew and water, and its connexion with the tides, were probably one cause of its being feigned to be the spouse of the sun, and also of its dedication to the female generative power, or Isis. As the second of the planets the moon was thus feigned to be the wife of the sun. *Jointly* they produced; without her, as water, the sun produced nothing.

7. Having seen the close connexion between the creating, the preserving, and the destroying powers, we shall not be surprised to find that the mystical baptism extended to them all. Thus there were baptisms by water, by fire, and by air. The baptism by air is in perfect keeping with the baptism by fire and water. We have before seen that air, the breath or spirit of God, the AIR IN MOTION, the ἅγιον πνευμα, the רוח קדיש *qdis ruh*, or Holy Ghost, was emblematical of the regenerative power—the spirit of God brooding (as Bishop Patrick says) on the face of the waters. All the three are found, both in the doctrines of the Gentiles,[1] and in the secret doctrines of the gospel of Jesus. John says, *He shall baptize you with the Holy Ghost and with fire.*[2] When Jesus was plunged in the Jordan, or the river of the sun, as I shall presently prove it to have been called, Divine Love descended upon him in the form of a dove, and a fire was kindled in the water.[3] All this will be called mystical. Indeed, it will be *truly* so called. But it is an intelligible mysticism, easy to be understood by those who give their minds to it. It contains nothing above or beyond the grasp of the human understanding. It is founded upon principles of sound philosophy and truth. It is no small proof of the good sense and sound philosophy of the professors of the Buddhist religion, that when they come to the boundary line beyond which they cannot go, they stop and call it illusion. The very idea of illusion, thus used, is beautiful. And now we begin to have a distant yet obscure view of an universal system of philosophy and truth, connected, by this baptismal ceremony, with the religion of Jesus—a really *universal* system; and, perhaps, in the end, we may find, that the followers of the Pope have a better reason, if they chose to give it, for their assumption of the name of Catholic, than the ridiculous one which they generally assign, viz. the universal dissemination of their church : an assumption, in the sense in which it is received by their followers, *false* and *absurd.*

I fear my reader will think I have gone to sources sufficiently recondite and abstruse for my doctrines, but I must yet take him a little farther. Buffon and Bailly have been most unmercifully ridiculed and grossly misrepresented, (by those who ought, consistently with their pretended great piety, to have acted otherwise,) for going to a high latitude for the birthplace or origin of man. But at the risk of being ridiculed like them, I must go thither for the origin of my doctrine. Among a people residing under a vertical, or an intensely hot sun, we are apt to forget that *cold* must be as great a luxury as *heat* is to us ; that their season of happiness, of health, of comfort, is the *winter*, not, like ours, the *summer*. It should be recollected that, during the summer, in Egypt and in India, the country is covered with water—in winter with vegetation. For these reasons the inhabitants of those countries would not have the same objections to cold, or to any thing connected with it, which we have. The reader has seen that I have derived the name of Isis from the Hebrew יׁשׁע *iso* and the Greek ζωω *to save;* and I think this very probable: but Mr. Payne Knight, first premising that he thinks the *Io* of the Syrians to be the same as Isis, says, " Her name seems to have come from the north : there is no obvious etymology for it in the Greek

---

[1] Nimrod, Vol. I. p. 119.          [2] Luke iii. 16.          [3] Justin against Apion.

" tongue : but in the ancient Gothic and Scandinavian, *Io* and *Gio* signify the earth : as *Isi* and
" *Isa* signified ICE, or water in its primordial state : and both were equally titles of the Goddess
" that represented the productive and nutritive power of the earth : and, therefore, may afford a
" more probable etymology for the name Isis, than any that has hitherto been given."[1]    I give
no opinion on Mr. Knight's theory ; but before my reader decides against him, I beg him to
recollect that water was considered as the emblem of the passive principle, in opposition to fire,
the active principle ; that water, in a *purer* state, is actually Ice, the emblem of the passive principle : when compounded with fire, the active principle, it is the emblem of the two—the rege-
nator—the Linga and Ioni—the Isa and Isi, from יש *iso* to save ; and, by the water of baptism,
to be saved.    I should think this ridiculously abstruse if I did not know that nothing can be too
abstruse for the philosophers of India and Egypt.    On this subject I shall have much more to say
when I treat of the Christian baptism.

I think no one will deny, that the explanation of Mr. Knight is ingenious and probable ; but
how is this to be reconciled with the theory stated in Book I. Chapter II. Sect. 1, that Isis was
the Bona Dea or Mother of the Gods, and with the statement lately made that her name was
derived from the Hebrew word יש *iso* to save, or the Greek word ζωω?    Are there to be two
derivations to the word Isis ?    In Book I., cited above, I have shewn that the sun came to be
considered the Saviour, in consequence of the mode in which he appears to preserve and renovate
the face of nature.    Now, if we consider a little, we shall find that without the assistance of water
in the form of rain or dew he can produce nothing : hence the name of his wife, Isis, came to be
applied to water.    In India Is-wara and Isa, or Brahma and Sara-iswati, in Egypt Osiris and Isis.
Osi-ris was often written Isi-ris ; and Plutarch says also, Usiris and Asiris.[2]    This shews that
the two words are only the same in the different genders.    In numerous Egyptian monuments we
see Isis seated on, or rising from, the lotos or water lily, as in my plates, fig. 10.

8. We all know, independently of theory, that a general belief prevails in the world, that the
moon exercises an influence on the weather, particularly in respect to the production of rain.
From this belief might she not come to be considered as presiding over water, to be called by the
name of the saviour Isis, to be converted into a female, and made the wife of Iswara, or Osiris ;
and water, when entirely by itself, free from solar influence or in its congealed shape, to be called
Ice ?    This seems to have been comparatively speaking a modern refinement, as we find the moon in
Tartary, in India with the Rajpoots,[3] in Arabia, in Egypt, in Germany, and in Etruria, to have
originally been of the masculine gender.    Here we see why she was called Helena and Theba, and
why she is every where connected with the generative principle.    In her lunette form she is
peculiarly calculated to represent the Arga, or vehicle, or medium in which the germ of animated
nature was carried, the united Linga and Yoni.    In the prayer of the Persians to the God Taurus,
water is also invoked, joined with him by the name of rain, which seems to be introduced in an
awkward way, but which is thus accounted for.    I think there can be no doubt that if Plato ever
taught, that the trinity of Orpheus or Zoroaster consisted of the sun, the moon, and the earth, it
must have been to conceal the higher theory from public view.    As we have the origin of the word
Ice in Isis, so, in similar manner, we have the origin of the name of water in the Is-wati or Iswara, Ise-יאר *iar* to flow ; יד-יאר-ש *is-iar-di*.

Is it possible that the word Sarah may be found in the Greek word χαρα *laughter ?*    She was
the mother of Isaac, which name Cruden says means *laughter,* and that he was so called from his
mother's laughing.    Before I conclude, I have no doubt I shall prove that there is no instance in

[1] Payne Knight on Symb. Lang. of Anc. Myth. S. 54.        [2] Ed. Squire.        [3] Tod, Hist. Raj. p. 538.

which the name of a God or Goddess, when uncorrupted, is without some meaning; or who had not his or her name given for a specific reason.

I apprehend the word IS to be a word of the most ancient language: in English is, in Hebrew *w* *is*. It means existens or perhaps hypostasis. As *existens*, it meant self-existent or the formative power; and as this power or creator was the preserver, the words *yw* *iso* the saviour, and Isis, came to be formed from it. In the Hebrew language it has exactly the same meaning it has in English. It is also found in the Mexican language, which bespeaks its great antiquity. The Mexicans, to mark the time of the day, point to the sun, and say, *Is Teott, there God will be.* [1] But the expression manifestly means (there) *is* God—Teott meaning God. [2] Mr. Crawfurd evidently adopted an incorrect mode of expression, to indulge his (pardonable because not ill-meaning) prejudice against the English expression or language in Mexico. But this kind of prejudice has been exceedingly detrimental to the discovery of the truth. Here we have the English word, in sound, in sense, and even in letters.—In a former section I said that I should explain the word Eridanus. Having shewn the importance of water in the mysteries of the ancients, I shall now perform my promise, and it will be seen that the meaning of the name of this river is closely connected with the sacred character of water. It is for this reason that I have made some observations upon the baptism of the ancients, which would otherwise have been better delayed till I treated of the Christian baptism.

---

## CHAPTER VIII.

RIVERS OF SAME NAME.—JORDAN.—VARIOUS RIVERS CALLED DON.—DONCASTER, &c.—PHILISTINES OR PALLI.

1. A LEARNED friend has observed to the author, that, in his opinion, all names of rivers and of places have taken their origin from accidental local circumstances, arising in the very earliest stages of society; that the man wholly or half savage, for instance, who happened to ramble to the confluence of the Rhone and Arve, would not think of distinguishing the Rhone from the Arve by calling one of them the river of the sun; but would most likely call one the *blue* river, and the other the *muddy* river, names arising out of their accidental peculiarities; that the giving such a name as the sun, is much too artificial and refined a motive for the half savage, who must have given the first names to rivers and places. This remark seems reasonable enough in many cases; but it does not apply where colonies are settled by civilized nations, as every day's experience in the Americas, New Holland, &c., proves. That rivers have been called *rivers of the sun* cannot be doubted, as the Nile proves. This was first called *Sir* after the name of the sun, and Greecized into Osiris.

When I find widely-separated countries, towns, and rivers, called by the same names, I cannot consent to attribute so striking a coincidence to the effect of accident or of unconnected causes.

---

[1] Crawfurd, Hist. Ind. Arch. Vol. I. p. 288.          [2] Teott-Teut-Tat-Θиит-ΘΕΟΣ.

I feel myself obliged to believe that some common cause must have operated to produce a common effect. I find rivers by the name of Don in many different countries, and under very peculiar circumstances, and on these I must now make some observations.

Almost all great rivers have been called rivers of the sun. May not the origin of this be found in the abstruse consideration, that they appear to be directly the produce of the sun ; and may they not originally have been thus called as a sacred name ? In all the Asiatic countries they are the fullest in the summer, when the sun causes their floods by melting the mountain snows. When he is in his glory, they are at their full ; as he withdraws, they decline. At the same time that he causes them to increase, he thereby fertilizes the plains of India, and the valley of the Nile. The name of the rivers, the Nile for instance, is said to mean *sun*—not that it means the river *of the sun*, but *the river sun*. If I be right, that a first language existed like the Hebrew in its formation, this misnomer might arise from inattention to the system (formerly named) of what in the Hebrew language is called being *in regimine.* For example : we say *house* OF *God ;* the Hebrews say, בא *al* בית *bit*—*bit al, house God*, wanting the particle ; and then the word *bit* or *house* is said to be *in regimine*, the particle OF being understood. The Nile was said to be both the gift and the emblem of Osiris, and an emanation from him—Οσιριδος Απορροη.[1] The Ganges was said to have flowed from the head or the foot of Seva. The Eridanus of the sphere flowed from the foot of Orion or Orus, as any one may see by casting his eye upon the sphere of Dupuis, Plate No. 10. It is there called also the Nile. In No. 9 it flows from the foot of Prometheus. In No. 8 it flows from the foot of Amalthea, and also of Orus and Orion.

Dr. Hyde informs us, that the constellation Eridanus was called ποταμε αςεϱισμος, the asterism of the river, by Ptolemy ; and, by the Persians, ποταμος Ωϱιωνος, *the river of Orion.*[2] I will now examine the rivers on the globe and try if we can find any of this celestial name there.

2. The first river I shall notice is the Jordan, called in Genesis xiii. 11, הירדן *e-irdn*, that is, as our translators say, *the Jordan.* The word הירדן *e-irdn* consists of, in fact, three words. The first is the emphatic article, ה *e* THE ; the second the word יר *ir* which, in the Hebrew language, means RIVER,[3] from the Hebrew word יאר *iar* to flow, a vowel (א *a*) being dropped, as is very common in the Hebrew language. For example, in the word תור *tur* a turtledove, often written תר *tr.*[4] I believe that the rendering by Mr. Bellamy of the word יר *ir* river, will not be disputed. It is proved to be correct by the striking circumstance, that although the Jordan is named in the Old Testament many times, it never, in any case, has the word river prefixed to it. The reason is, that if it were, it would create a rank tautology, and would read the *river river Dn.* From this Hebrew word Iar or Ir, the name of different rivers has been derived ; for instance, one in Norfolk, called Yar, (the town *Yarmouth,*) and the Jaar in Flanders. Respecting the word דן *dn,* Parkhurst gives as the meaning of it, *to judge* or *rule ;* as a noun, with י *i* דין *din, a judge,* and, with a formative *a* אדן *Adn, a ruler, director,* Lord—spoken of God. " Hence the word ADONIS " had his name," and the Welsh *Adon* a Lord. I have no doubt that it had, in the form דון *dun,*[5] the meaning of judgment, discretion, understanding, and, in fine, wisdom. But of course Parkhurst would keep this last offensive word out of sight, as much as possible. If Adonai or Adonis were the second person of the Trinity, of course he would be Wisdom. Hence we have the meaning of this river—the river of Adonis. I suppose I need not remind my reader, that Adonis

---

[1] Plut. de Isid.      [2] Maurice, Hist. Hind. Vol. I, p. 355.

[3] Bellamy's Anti-Deist and Translation of Bible, Gen. xiv. 14.

[4] Vide Downs's Grammar, p. 27.      [5] Vide Frey's Lex.

was the sun;[1] therefore, the Jordan ought to be, or might be, translated *the river of the sun*. When Moses gives an historical account of Abraham's success in driving his enemies to the bank of the river, or of the name of the river on which Lot chose to settle, it is out of all question to suppose that he would, as Mr. Bellamy thinks, give it a new name and call it *judgment*, because Abraham had driven his enemies to judgment. But it was called Jordan before Abraham fought his enemies, when Lot chose its borders for his residence ; thus *that* question seems settled.

In the Επεα Πτεροεντα[2] may be seen the attempts of Mr. Tooke, as well as of great numbers of other learned men, to explain the word *dun* or *don ;* in all of which I think my reader must agree with me, that there is a complete failure. This is one of the proofs how vain the attempt is to explain the English language, without going to the Hebrew. The Hebrew is of much more importance than the Saxon, because the Saxon is itself, in great part, derived from the Hebrew. So that if in many cases you pass over the Saxon and go to the Hebrew no bad consequence arises ; for, though you miss a step, you get to the real root : but in few cases, perhaps, will you get to the real root by stopping at the Saxon. If Tooke had understood Hebrew, he would have made a very different book. The observations of Mr. Taylor, the editor of the new edition of Tooke, on many words, as well as on that of *don* or *dun*, though learned and ingenious, confirm what I say. All that can be made out from these learned men is, that this name of so many rivers means HILL, a very singular name it must be allowed for river. But it is exactly like the Mere of India. This universally means Hill, (though generally a hill with a piece of water on the top of it,) but in our country it also commonly means *lake*, and I think it has become appropriated to lakes from the hill lakes of India.[3] I shall return to this subject in the next book.

From Burckhardt's Travels in Nubia,[4] it appears that the river Jordan is now called El Dhan. I found this authority after I had finished my article on this celebrated river. I think I could not have desired a more decisive proof of the truth of my theory than this. *El* is the Arabic emphatic article THE.

3. The word *duna* was the Median name for a river, and was carried into Europe by the tribes migrating from upper Asia. Thus it makes its appearance in the names Tanais, or Don, D'nieper, Rha-danus, Rho-danus, and Eri-danus.[5] In North India the Don is called *Dena* and *Dond*,[6] that is Don-di, or Dis, or Divus, *holy*.

The celebrated river called by the ancients *Ister*, is now called Danube. It was also called Don-eau, as appears from old local authorities. Dan-ube and Don-eau, both mean *water of the Don*. The Danube or Ister was known also by the name of Danusius or Tanais : in which the Puranas coincide with Horus, Apollo, Eustathius, and Strabo.[7] Tanais is evidently a corruption of Dan-usius,—I-ster : I, the Celtic emphatic article ; Ster, star, astrum, THE planet.

In Russia there is a river which flows into the Sea of Azof or the Palus Mæotis, (but whose true name Ritter makes to be Palus Maietis,) now called Don but anciently Tanais ; and about one hundred and fifty years back, as appears, by old voyages, it was called Tane. Dr. Lempriere says, " Don is a corrupt appellation of the ancient *Tanais*. There is a city at its mouth now

---

[1] Drummond, Œd. Jud. p. 231.                    [2] Part I. Chap. ix.

[3] The hill lakes in India were dedicated to Buddha, and in succession to Cristna or Kaniya. The hill lakes in England are called Tarns : *e. g.* Mallum-Tarn, a lake on the top of a hill in Yorkshire. May they not have been called from the *Buddha* or *Teut* or *Hermes* of Britain, *Taran-is ?* The Meres of India were all mothers from whom the sacred rivers descended. They were Merus, each of which was both hill and lake.

[4] Mem. p. xxxvii.                    [5] Cab. Enc. Vol. I. p. 41.                    [6] Rennell, Mem. p 88.

[7] Eustath. on Dionys. Perieg. V. 298 ; Wilford, Asiat. Res. Vol. III. p. 453.

" called *Azof*, but the Sclavonian traditions say it was anciently called *Aas-grad* or city of *Aas*."
This shews the meaning Tan-ais, was Don-ais or Don-aas—and I think meant *outlet of the Don* :
and *aas-zof* is *aas-sophia*, or *eau-σοφ*, Sea of Wisdom. The Don is called Donnez, Danaetz,
Tdnaetz, Tanaets, and Tanais.[1]  In Sogdiana, not far from the Jaxartes, was a city called Gaza,
and the river Jaxartes itself was called Tanais.[2]  According to Rennell it was at first called Sirr—
the same name as that of the ancient Nile. The Tanais we have seen was also the same as the
Don. Rennell makes the Jaxartes to be bounded by the mountains called Tag Arga. " In our
" modern maps it appears as the Don : but this word is a palpable corruption of Tanais, by which
" appellation it was known to the Greeks."[3]  In the Eastern golden Chersonesus or Siam, is a
district called, in ancient times, Daonæ, which is now called Tanasserim. This is evidently the
name of its river Don, corrupted into Tanasserim.[4]  Beyond the Ganges, again, we find a
river called Daona.[5]  I believe it was Constantine Porphyrogenitus, in the tenth century, who
first called the river Dnieper, Danapreos. Contrarini, who travelled in 1473, says, " La fiumara
" che si chiama Danambre nella loro lingua, e nella nosra Leresse." It is worthy of observation,
and can scarcely be accidental, that the Don of Yorkshire flows into the Umber, or Umbre.
There must have been some connexion between the Don and Umber, and Dan-ambre.

4. In the North of Scotland we have a river, which flows through the town of Aberdeen, called
Don. This is the same as the river Don or Dn in Syria, and the *town* of Aber-deen is עבר *obr*
the *far* or *distant deen*, whatever the word *deen* may mean : but probably the *far don* or *dun*. The
river at Whitby in Yorkshire is called Dunum or Don.[6]  In Yorkshire is another river called
Don, on which the Romans had a station, or castrum, whence a beautiful town took the name of
Don-caster. It is celebrated for its beauty. I have known it well for more than fifty years, and
I think I am qualified to say, it does not deserve more praise for the beauty of its buildings and
the cleanness of its streets, than for the moral qualities of its inhabitants.

In my CELTIC DRUIDS, plate 24, will be found a view of a fire-tower at Brechin, in Scotland. This town is on the east coast, not very far from Aberdeen or עבר דן *obr dn*, or Aberdeen
on the river רן *Dn* Don ; and near it is a small town called Dun. On this tower is a man crucified, with a lamb on one side of him, and an ELEPHANT on the other. When I published my
CELTIC DRUIDS, I thought this proved that the tower was not very ancient ; but I now begin to
doubt of this matter. In the estate of Lady Castles near Aberdeen, about forty years ago was
dug up the large ring, of which the print, No. 27 A, is a very close representation. The
figures are not mere outlines or alto-relievos, but they are of full-raised form, and well executed.
The pious, and also the learned of the priests say, it may have been brought from the East by
Crusaders. No doubt they consider this to be satisfactory. For my own part, I think it equally
satisfactory to be told, that the river and town of Aberdeen had their names given by the crusaders, and that the fire-tower and the ELEPHANT were placed upon it by them also. I dare say
these valiant heroes would be said to have given names to the Umber, Northumberland, Brigantia,
&c., if they had not been known from Roman authors to have had them long before the Christian
æra, and even before the arrival of the Romans. For example, Brigantia the country of Queen
Boadicea.

In Lombardy, in Cisalpine Gaul, there is a celebrated river called Eridanus. This is evidently
Eri-dan or E-ir-dan, with a latin termination *us*, which being left out we have ה *e* THE יר *ir* RIVER
רן *Dn*, DON or Adonis. Into this river Phaëton was supposed to have fallen, when he drove the

---

[1] Clarke's Travels.  [2] Arrian, B. iv.  [3] Fab. Orig. Pag. Idol.
[4] Vide Butler's Atlas.  [5] Drum. Orig. Vol. IV. p. 174.  [6] Young's History.

chariot of the sun. The country about the mouth of it was inhabited by the Om-bri, and there was a town at its mouth called Palestinos. This river is now called Padus or Po, which is one of the names of the Ganges and of Buddha. The country was also called Pagus Tro-ianus, and at the vertex of the Delta formed by the river, the city of Padua was built.

> Ille urbem Patavi sedesque locavit
> Teucrorum, et genti nomen dedit, armaque fixit
> Troia.[1]

The river in the sphere proceeding from Orion is called Eridanus, but Eratosthenes maintains that it is the Nile. " The river flowing from Orion's foot, graphically illustrates Homer's Διιπετεος " ποταμοιο, or the river flowing from Dis. But in truth there is no difference between the Nile " or dark blue river of hell and the fabled Eridanus : in the fortunate groves of Hades, so Virgil " sings,

> " Plurimus Eridani per sylvam volvitur amnis."[2]

The Roman poets feign, that Amber arose from the tears shed by the sisters of Phaëton for his misfortune, but the Po never produced Amber.

Nimrod again says, " But the river Ganges bore the same name (being that of the God Buddha " or Batta) as the Eridanus of Italy ; Ganges qui et *Padus* dicitur : and as the Nile was fabled to " be the Euphrates, renascent in Ethiopia, so again, it was pretended, that the Euphrates and " Tigris did not really rise from their apparent source in Armenia, but after travelling one thousand " miles from the East, juxta[3] Armeniæ montes manifestantur, or in other words, that, as Paradise " was at the source of the Indian river, by fabulous tradition, and of the Euphrates by Scripture " authority, the Euphrates must be the Ganges Eridanus prolonged."[4] A Coptic name of the Euphrates is *eu* water, and φρη=608—River of the Sun as usual. See Ouseley, Transactions of the Society of Literature,[5] where it appears that Phrat was not the Persian name, but Fala or Flad or Fulat. Is Flad *flood* or fleuve-ad, river of Ad ? Has *fleuve al* become Fala or Fulat ?

5. " Next to the emigration of the *Yadavas* the most celebrated was that of the Palis, or Pali- " putras : many of whose settlements were named Pálist'hán, which the Greeks changed into " Palaistine. A country so called was on the banks of the Tigris, and another in Syria. The " river *Strymon* had the epithet Palaistinos. In Italy we find the Palestini : and at the mouth of " the Po, a town called Philistini : to which may be added the Philistinæ fossiones, and the Philis- " tinæ arenæ in Epirus. As the Greeks wrote Palai for Pali, they rendered the word Paliputra, " by Palaigonos, which also means the offspring of Pali : but they sometimes retained the Sanscrit " word for son : and the town of Palaipatrai to this day called Paliputra by the natives, stood on " the shore of the Hellespont."[6] Here the two Palibothras are sufficiently clear. And the Pal- lestini or Philistines, as we call them, in India, on the Tigris, in Syria, on the Hellespont, on the Strymon, and on the Po, are very striking. They are all derived from the Indian name Palli, and Stan, a *stone* or *place*.

Pliny says,[7] Inde ostia plena Carbonaria ac fossiones Philistinæ, quod alii Tartarum vocant. That is, the fossiones of the Palli, or Pallestini the shepherds or nomades. Here we have the first example of the name of Tartars, but it beautifully supports all my opinions of the arrival of the Palli from the East ;[8] it also shews, that we must not conclude that names are necessarily modern,

---

[1] Nimrod, Vol. III. p. 115.     [2] Nimrod, Sup. Ed. p. 25.
[3] Aethic. Cosmog. p. 548; Lugd. Bat. 1646.    [4] Nimrod, Vol. I. p. 56.    [5] Vol. I. p. 110.
[6] Asiat. Res. Vol. III. p. 369.     [7] Lib. iii. p. 173.     [8] Bryant, Anal. Vol. I. p. 376.

because we do not meet with them in ancient Greek or Latin authors. We shall find that these Tartars were probably Sacæ or Saxons.

Mr. Bryant observes, " It is said, that the Eridanus was so called first by Pherecydes Syrus." [1] And Plutarch [2] says, that the Strymon is a river of Thrace, which runs by the city of Edonis (Ἡδωνιδα) : it was of old called the river of Palæstinus. [3] The town he calls Edonis, is called also Ειον. I have before observed, that I take this to be a corruption of Yoni or Ione ; and this Edonis I suspect was Adonis, and in this, again, connects it with the Syrian Ionian superstition. The Strymon in the North of Greece was originally called Ioneus, as Conon (Narr. iv.) tells us. [4] There was, according to Pausanias, also a river in Attica called Eridanos. Mr. Dodwell thinks the channel which joined the Ilissos near Ampelo-Kepous was the Eridanos. [5]

Another river Don is found in the Rhodaun, now called the Vistula, falling into the Baltic near Dantzig. This was anciently a celebrated place for amber. To this river the Phœnicians and Carthaginians resorted for the purchase of amber, with which they supplied the Roman empire. It had the name of Eridanus, and by its name Rhodaun, it evidently connects the Rhone with all these Dons. The Rho-daun is the River-Daun. It is said that Herodotus mistook a river for the Tanais which he called Rha, now the Wolga or Volga. The reader will not fail to perceive, that the name of the river at Dantzig consists of the river of Herodotus, and the river Don. The Rha is the ῥεω and the יאר iar. The Wolga is called the Oarus by Rennell: this is only a corruption of יאר iar, with the Latin termination. When Herodotus was told that the Wolga was called Rha, if he had had the least knowledge of etymology he would at once have seen that Rha merely meant river—the same as the Greek ῥεω to flow, or the Hebrew עיר ir river. The Dwina also is probably a Don.

That I am not singular in the opinion that the Rodaun is the same as the Eridanus, I copy the following from Lempriere : " The most curious circumstance connected with the story of Phaëton " is the fact, that the name Eridanus, into which he is said to have fallen, belongs properly to the " Rodaun, a small stream in the north of Europe, running near Dantzic."

The word Lar or Laura is still used in Gaelic, (Loar or Lomhar,) and in the dialect of the Cymri, Llueru signifies resplendence. Laurus is the Laurel, sacred to the sun. Daphne, another name for the Laurus, is derived from the Sanscrit Tapana, a name of the sun, as the author of heat ; for that place in Egypt called Tapana in the Puranas, is called Taphnai by the LXX : and Daphanæ or Daphne by Greek and Roman authors. [6] I suspect in Lomhar there is the origin of Lombardy, and in Tapana, of India, the name of Daphne, always connected with the story of Phaëton. Nimrod says, " Phaëton was not only prince of the Ethiopians but son of " Tithonus, [7] and his fall from heaven is indisputably the same event as the death of Memnon. " ' How art thou fallen from heaven, Lucifer, son of the morning ! Thou art cut down to the " ' ground, which didst weaken the nations. For thou hadst said in thine heart, I will ascend into " ' heaven, I will exalt my throne above the stars of God, I will sit upon the mount of the congre- " ' gation in the sides of the North.' " [8] The above extract from the religious Nimrod is very striking. [9]

---

[1] 'Ετεροι δε φασι δικαιετατον αυτων ειναι Νειλον. Eratosthenes, Catasterism, 37.

[2] De Fluminibus, Vol. II. p. 1154.     [3] Bryant, Anal. Vol. I. p. 377.

[4] Cumb. Orig. Gen. p. 265.     [5] Vol. I. 477.     [6] Wilford, Asiat. Res. Vol. VI. p. 500.

[7] Apollod. Biblioth. p. 354, Heyne, 1803.     [8] Nimrod, Vol. II. p. 156.

[9] Don and Douno pro Domino utuntur Hispanica Picardi 168.

I think most persons will agree with me in opinion that the following extracts, from an essay of Col. Wilford's, which I found after I had written the foregoing, confirm my theory in a remarkable manner. It does not appear that Col. Wilford had any idea when he wrote them of the connexion between the two rivers of India and Italy. The Eridanus in India, in Greece, in Italy, and in the sphere, flowing from the foot of Orion, all prove the mythological nature of the connexion between the Eastern and Western countries. " The *Brahma-putra* is also called *Hrádini*, as I " observed in a former essay, on the geography of the Puránás. This word, sometimes pro- " nounced *Hládini*, signifies in Sanscrit a deep and large river, from *Hrida*, to be pronounced " *Hrada*, or nearly so, and from which comes *Hradána* and *Hrádini*. In the list of rivers in the " *Padma-puràna*, it is called *Hrádya* or *Hrádyn*, and its mouth is called by Ptolemy the *Airradon* " *Ostium*, or the mouth of the river *Hrádan :* and according to him, another name for it was " *Antiboli*, from a town of that name, called also by Pliny *Antomela*, in Sanscrit, *Hasti-malla*, in " the spoken dialects *Hátti-malla*, now Fermgy-bazar, to the S. E. of D'haccá." [1]

My reader will please to observe in the above extract, the *Hradána* and *Hrádyn*. I then beg him to pronounce them aloud, and immediately afterward pronounce the name of the Wolga as given by Herodotus *Rha*, and also the river Rhodanum or Rhone, which runs past Lyons, and doubt if he can, that all theᴜe rivers had once the same name ; that the connexion was mythological, and that the mythological system extended to the Vistula, to Doncaster, and to Aberdeen, or עבר *obr* רון *dun*. Hrádyn is the word Rádun, and with the Hebrew emphatic article would be the Rádyn or *the river dyn*. Col. Wilford observes [2] that Ptolemy called the river Brahma-putra Daonas. This is evidently Don or Dwina. This is the same as the Dwina of Russia.

The observation respecting the Rhone, is confirmed by the name of Lyons, which was *Lug*— which means *high*—and *dun*-um, the town of the upper *Dun*. [3]  In Gibelin may be seen some very curious examples of the names of rivers, being Var or Ver—all which I suspect are derived from the Hebrew IAR.

Lyons is situated at the confluence of the Rhone and the Soane. In India also there is a river called the *Soan*, which takes its source from the same lake as the *Ner-budda*, that is (the word נהר *ner* being correctly Hebrew) *the river Buddha*. But in my observation on the river Jordan I have shewn how the Rhone is connected or identified with the Padus or Po, or, in other words, Bud.

Let us reflect a little upon what I have said relating to the emigation of the tribe of Ioudi from the kingdom of Oude, in which is the river Burrampouter or Brahma-putra, and we must be struck with the singularity of its having the same name as the famous Jordan or river Don of Western Syria. It was also called, as we have seen, Padus, one of the names of Buddha. We have seen that the Rhone or Rhadaun is the Ir, or Rha, or river *Daun*—bringing it to the same name, only translated, as the Padus of Italy. We have also the Dan-aub, i. e. the Aub-dan, or river Dan. Doab, or Duo-ab, or Mesopotamia of India, shews the meaning of the *aub* to be *river*. If the word Soan be read *Zoan* we have the two rivers of the Sun *united* in India, at their source, as we have in Europe, at their confluence. A third river, which takes its rise in the same mount as the Soan and Nerbudda, is called Mandáha, or the river of the cycle ; for I take Manda to be our Munda. On, or not far from, this river is a town called Sone-pour, and near it one of the towns is called Odey-pour or Ioudi-pour ; there is also a town called Pada, and at its mouth, in the Brahmin country, is the famous temple of Jaggernaut, [4] or of the Great Creator ; where

---

[1] Col. Wilford, Asiat. Res. Vol. XIV. p. 426.      [2] Ibid. p. 420.      [3] Gibelin, Monde Prim. Vol. VIII. p. 453.

[4] If Jaggernaut mean Great Creator, may it not be thus dissected—*Ie* self-existent ; *Ger* great, or circle, or cycle ;

the Bull projects, and where there is no distinction of castes, or, I believe, of sects, but pilgrims of all religions eat together. This is because it is a Buddhist temple. How it has escaped the fury of the Brahmins is not known. Ougein is the capital of Malwa, through which the Nerbuddha flows. It is one of the most ancient cities of India, noticed both in the Periplus of the Erythræan sea, and by Ptolemy.[1] On or near the Nerbuddha is a town called Munda and one called Mundala, and one called Mundatta.[2] I feel little doubt that the mount whence the three rivers flowed was in very ancient times the high-place of Malwa, as Moriah was of Syria.

In India will be found Dana-poor, (poor means city or town,) whence the names of all our towns which end in bury. The burghs come from the Saxon, and Dana-poor probably from the same source. This city is on the Soan, which name we have seen, is the same as the river Rhone, the Danube, the Po, &c. In the same neighbourhood will be found also Cawn-poor, or the city of Caon, and Bet-ourah, (or in Hebrew, the house or temple of Aur,) and near Agra, on the Jumna, a Betaisor, house or temple of Æsar.

I think no one can believe that all these circumstances of curious coincidence could be the effect of accident. I will not undertake to put them together, but be must see that there are the links of a chain. I have no doubt that the whole is connected with a Buddhist mythos, and that the story of Phaëton is of Oriental extraction. Lucian has given a witty description of a voyage up the Po, in search of amber, poplars, and musical swans, respecting any of which the sailors could give him no information, but for which they only laughed at him. I think this will now be a proper place to point out some strong marks of identity in the mythologies of India and Italy, which are perceptible in the names of their respective places.

## CHAPTER IX.

### LORETTO.—OBSERVATIONS ON HOMER, THE ILIAD, AND THE ÆNEID.

In Book V. Chapter X. Section 2, I said I should shew that the philosophers of India, not only brought the *black* mother and her child to Italy, but that they brought her house also. I now proceed to redeem my pledge.

In lat. 25, 50—and long. 73, 10, on the road from Pali or Palee to Jod-poor, is a hill called Poono Gir, or Poona.[3] (Now Col. Tod says, Poono means *virtue* and Gir *hill.)* It has on the

---

*New Wisdom.* The Brahmins only know that it means *great creator ;* its *etymon* they do not pretend to understand. Neith, not Nepthe, with the Egyptians, meant wisdom. Of Neith it is said, " I am what is, what was, what shall be ; " mortal has not raised my veil. The sun is the fruit of my womb." (Savary's Letters on Egypt.) Phtha is the supreme God of Egypt. (Id.) This Neith is the Nath described in Col. Tod's Hist. Raj. pp. 545—546. It is the Rasit of Genesis, and correctly means the same as Jehovah Aleim, i. e. the self-existent God.

[1] Malcolm's Hist. of Malwa, Central India, p. 23.
[2] Mundul-ooe and Mundul-eeh, in Sanscrit, mean a circle or tract of country. (Elphinston's Cabul.)
[3] Tod, Hist. p. 702.

3 z 2

top of it a small Jain temple, which was conveyed by supernatural power, by a Buddhist magician, *as is said by the Brahmins, the enemies of the Jains,* to the place where it now stands, from a certain mount called Saturn-ja, in a district now called Guzzerat, and the kingdom of Balli-caroes, or Balcarra, or Saura-stra, or Syra-strene, or Saura, but most anciently Larice,[1] that is, evidently, Larissa. This country is also called Palli-thana,[2] that is, Pallestan or Pallestine, or country of the Pali. Poono-Gir is now called *the hill* or *temple of virtue.* What this temple contains Col. Tod has not told us, but it was a temple of the Jains, that is, of Janus, the name of the great God of the Italians. It was brought by the power of magic to the neighbourhood of the ancient city now called Mundore, the ruins of which, as already noticed, are *thirty-seven* miles in circumference: but the present name of the new city, close to it, is Jod-pore, that is, town of Juda. In this part of the world, there yet exists a sect of religionists called Nazoreens, or Nazoureans, or Mundaites, or Christians of St. John—a sect of which I shall treat at large by and by. But it is evident that the Munda of these people is the same as the Munda of this great ancient Cyclopæan city. In the country of Larice or Palli-thana, the adoration of the mother of God seems much to have prevailed. The river near Pallithana is named Mahie, that is, Maia or Maria, and, by Ptolemy, called *Mais.* This is the country whose shores are washed by the Erythræan Sea, and it is therefore probably an Erythræan country. In this country is the city of *Aje-mere,* not far from which is a temple of Mama-Deva, *the holy mother.* The peculiar object of adoration in this part of India now, is Kanyia, the son of Maia, otherwise called Cristna: but Maia herself is often called Kanya. At no great distance, in this country, is the Jessulmer, formerly noticed, or Jerusalem, anagrammatically written : as Cupid, the Greek God of Love, read Hebraicè, in this country, is the same name as their God of Love, Dipuc.[3]

The Casa Santa of Loretto, every one knows, according to the Romanists, is the real house in which the mother of Jesus Christ lived at Nazareth, or the city of the Natzir, or the hermit, or the flower, whence he was called a Nazarene and his followers Nazarenes. This house was removed by angels, from Syria, to its present situation. It was first conveyed to Dalmatia ; but it having been discovered by the angels, that they had placed it among thieves, they took it up again and brought it to where it now stands, a place called Loretto, on the Italian shore of the Adriatic Sea. Here sits the mother of God, the Mama-deva, the Regina Cœli, with her infant in her arms, both as black as jet, loaded with diamonds, and every other kind of precious stone. Her humble cottage is covered with a casing of beautifully worked stone, to skreen both it and herself from impertinent curiosity, and over the door, to guard it or to ornament it, stands the statue of the Erythræan Sibyl. In Syria, whence she came, there was a town, on the Orontes, called Larissa : this word, it is evident, has been softened down in the Italian fashion into Loretto. Thus she was brought from one Lar-issa to another. In Syria were Juda and Palestine. Italy, where she is now placed, is the country of Saturn-ja, where also is the Urbs Saturnia of Virgil. It is in the district of Palitana, the district of the Palli or Palestini, which has been before noticed, at the mouth of the river which has the same name as the great river of the country whence she came, Padus, or Buddha, or Po, or Fo. This country was also called Ombria or the country of Om.

When Jesus was on the cross, he ordered John to take charge of his mother, and he, from that time, took her to his own home. Was this the city of Munda where the Mundaites, or Nasoureans, or Nazarenes of St. John come from ?

I have little or no doubt that the fable of the Virgin's house was taken from the fable of Poona

---

[1] D'Anville.    [2] Col. Tod.    [3] Query, the Puck of Shakspeare ?

Gir. Poonah or Punah is the Mexican term for woman. It is, I strongly suspect, the Greek Γυνη. Here we have in the hill of virtue the first idea of virtue, as applied to a chaste female. This will be better understood when I treat of Mexico.[1]

There was also near to the Saturn-ja Pali-thana of India, a place called Diu, and near it, in the sea which washes the shore of Syra-strene, called the Erythræan Sea, (the name of the Erythræan Sibyl, which stands in the screen of the Casa Santa at Loretto,) a sacred island of Diu, the same as the name of Diu in the mount Athos in Europe, which is on an isthmus, the very picture of Syra-strene or Guzzerat. The mount Athos is called Monte Santo, and the mount Palithana of India is also called a sacred mount, or a Monte Santo. There is another Diu now called Stan-dia, which is probably a corruption of Stambul-diu. It is in the Thermatic Gulf, near to the tomb of Orpheus and Olympus; and a second Larissa.[2] Near Athos was a city called Pallene. If a person will only view the respective countries, in the East and West, where the remains of the mythos are found, he will see that in the choice of localities, a similarity of shape and circumstance has been selected to make the two mythoses agree. The peninsula of Athos and Surastra afford a very good example. The river in India, close to Surastra, called by the ancients Mais, I should have thought nothing of, if I had not found it called in Col. Tod's map Mayhie, evidently Maia or Maria; and, not far from it, as I have just now observed, the temple to THE MOTHER, as I conceive, Queen Isi or Isha.

Thus we have the ruins of the sacred, and most ancient, Cyclopæan city, called Mund-ore, in India, and Munda in Spain, and Mundus having the same mystical meaning as Kosmos. We have Virgil's city of Saturnia, and the Palli at the mouth of the Eridanus, or Padus, or Buddha, of Italy. In India we have the mount of Satrun-ja, in or near to Pali-thana, the same as the Roman mount Palatine, at the mouth of the Ner, or river Buddha, the same as Padus in Sura or Syra-strene, whence the sacred temple was carried: which Syra-strene was also called by the ancients[3] Larice, that is, Larissa, which I beg may not be forgotten, as I shall have to make an observation upon it and its meaning hereafter. Not far from the Satrun-ja Palithana is a place called by Ptolemy Byzantium. The old name of Constantinople was Byzantium, but this was changed by Constantine to Constantinople, and it is now called by the Turks Estambul, or Stambul, which has been thought a corruption of Constantinople; but this opinion Mr. Bryant has refuted. When I find several places in India called Stambul, I then come to the conclusion that Stambul has been the first name corrupted by the Greeks into Byzantium. Stambul in India is not far from the river Chumbul, called by D'Anville Sanbal, and I believe they have both had the same name. There was a second place called Stambul, close to the Balkan mountain, not far from Chumla, in Europe: was this also a corruption of Constantinople? The city of Roma, is the city of Rama, equally found in India, Western Syria, Italy, and by its other synonym Valencia, in Spain and Ireland. Not far from Rome is the Indian town of Viturba,[4] now Viterbo. There is also, Palæstrina, now Præneste Sacrum.

When a person reflects upon the histories of the Old and New Testament, found in India and the ancient temples of Egypt; the adventures of Cristna in India, and of Joseph and his family in Nubia; he will not be surprised to find the legend of Loretto in Syrastrene, or Jodpoor, or Yadu-pora. However, surprised or not, here it is in high preservation, and it cannot be denied. The temple belonging to the Jains connects it with the Janus and Janiculum, and the Palitini

---

[1] David Malcolm's Essay on Ant. of Britain.

[2] Larissa, Thebe, and Argos, were synonymous. Bryant, Anal. Vol. II. p. 451.

[3] D'Anville.                   [4] Tod, p. 216.

with Mons Palatinus. I regret exceedingly that Col. Tod has been so concise in his description; but he does not seem to have the least suspicion of its connexion with the Lady of Loretto.

2. I consider the Æneid to be a sacred epic poem, and to contain a complete description of the ancient mysteries, as far as they were known, but conveyed in language which should only be understood by the initiated. [1]  In the following lines, Virgil declares that Rome was built on the ruins of two successive cities, which had both gone to destruction; one called Janiculum, the other Saturnia, i. e. Satrun-ja:

> Hæc duo præteria disjectis oppida muris,
> Reliquias veterumque vides monumenta virorum,
> Hanc JANUS pater, hanc SATURNUS condidit urbem :
> JANICULUM huic, ille fuerat SATURNIA nomen.

We all know that Rome was built on seven hills. Its mysterious character I have sufficiently proved. Constantinople, Nova Roma, we know had the same sacred peculiarity. Troy has been shewn by Nimrod to have been the same. Many authors have thought the Iliad to be copied from the Jewish books. Certain marks of identity may be discovered in them. In the Jewish and Gentile mythoses, we have Samson and Hercules, Jonas and Janus, Jephtha's daughter and Iphigenia. We have an Ileyan or Illium at mount Meru, in India; Pergamos, the capital of Troy, is Perg-om or Berg-om, the mountain of Om, one of the names of Meru. We have a tribe of Hericulas, on the coast of Malabar. We have the names of Ulysses and Cæsar : and, in addition, Achilles and the Hero of the Mahabarat, of Valmic, are each invulnerable in every part but the heel, and by a wound in the heel of each hero he is killed—as Cristna was, or ought to have been, when bitten by the serpent—as the serpent bit the heel of the seed of the woman of Genesis.

The poems of Homer I consider to have been originally sacred Asiatic songs or poems, adopted by the Greeks, and that, for perhaps many generations, they were unwritten; and, as they related to the cyclic Mythos, they would, in the principal part, suit every cycle,—new Argonauts and new Troys. They were like the plays of Æschylus, each an epic, but all combining to form the history of the cycle, to those who were initiated, and they were the origin of the cyclic poems. I consider, also, that it was on the religious account that Alexander had them in the casket, under his pillow, when he slept, as our devotees now use their Bible; and I think it very likely that Ossian's poems might have been moulded to produce a similar effect, if Macpherson, like Aristotle and his coadjutors, had understood the mythos. Had we the whole of the plays of Æschylus, as we have the crucifixion of Prometheus, uncorrupted by our modern emendators, I think it probable that, with our knowledge derived from India, we should find in them the development of the system. When the poems of Homer were composed, the art of writing, if known, was a magical and masonic secret. At that time the digamma or VAU was in use. When they were committed to writing by Pisistratus, it had gone out of use. This is the reason why they are without it. Poetry was not invented for its beauty, but for the purpose of aiding the memory; and it was applied to music for the same reason. A song in verse can scarcely be forgotten.

The learned Basnage says, " Several authors have attempted to make Homer consistent with the " sacred writers in four things; 1. In the style; for there are so many Hebraisms in his verses, [2] " that one can't avoid perceiving that he had read Moses, and the one may be often explained by

---

[1] All our translations of Virgil's works, in consequence of the translators' not knowing or not attending to the mythos, are absolutely ridiculous.

[2] Vide Bogani Homerus Hebraizans, in which he would prove that there is no poet comes so near the sacred writers ; *neminem poetam tantopere referre sacros scriptores.*

" the other. 2. This poet relates many rites that have an evident relation to those of the Old
" Testament. 3. His two poems, which may be justly called the two eminences of Parnassus, are
" full of admirable sentences, and therefore they are compared to those of Solomon, and a parallel [1]
" is drawn betwixt this king's thoughts, and this ancient poet's. Scaliger went too far in saying
" that Homer was divinely inspired; but at least he entered into a kind of *enthusiasm, which in-*
" *spired him,* and rendered his genius next-kin to divine.

> " Est Deus in nobis; agitante celescimus illo :
> " Impetus his sacræ semina mentis habet.

" The ancients have said, that Homer travelled into Egypt, and the Egyptians asserted that he
" was born there.[2]  No wonder then that he was acquainted with the books of Moses, and in-
" structed in the Jewish religion in this country. If the Egyptian pretence be false, it can't how-
" ever be disputed, but that this poet lived long at Samos, and had a correspondence with the
" Phœnicians for a great while, who had taught him the history of the Jews. 'Twas the notion
" of Justin Martyr, ' that Homer had taken a great deal from the writings of the Old Testament ;
" but without insisting upon this discussion, it suffices that the sentences, which are innumerable
" in this poet's verses, are like those dispersed in the books of David, Solomon, and sacred au-
" thors.'  A modern author has filled a great volume with this parallel of sentences and maxims,
" because if St. Paul has sanctified a saying of the poet Menander, he might likewise sanctify the
" maxims of Homer. But amongst a thousand examples, we'll content ourselves with one :

> Βελομ' εγω λαον σοον εμμεναι η απολεσθαι.

" Homer here introduces a prince saying, *He had rather have his people safe than see them perish.*
" 'Tis first observed, that this is not the true meaning of this maxim. The king meant, no doubt,
" that he would die in order to save his people. However, take the words as you please, they
" have a great resemblance with those of scripture. The fourth article of conformity is much
" more important than the rest, since Homer, under pretence of recounting the adventures of
" Ulysses, is PROVED to have related those of *Abraham, Isaac,* the Judges, and heroes of ancient
" *Israel.* To give the greater authority to this conjecture, 'tis observed, that the ancients have
" given this testimony to Homer, that he generally made use of allegories. Heraclides made a
" collection of this poet's allegories." [3]  There is quite discrepancy enough between the poems of
Homer and the Jewish writings to shew, that they were not copies of one another ; but when all
the other circumstances are considered, which I shall lay before my reader, I feel confident I shall
convince him, that they are but different versions of the same mythic history. Homer, as remarked
by Basnage, is said to have resided a long time in Samos. Not far from this island, on the continent, are the Mount of Solomon or of the Solumi, and the Holy Ladder, &c., described in the last
book, chapter III. sect. 7. Near this place there are a river Indus, a mount of Carmel, and a town
of Jasus, evidently Jesus, and near it also was Miletus, where there was a shrine of Apollo, celebrated for his prophecies ; among which is the following, which may be added to those of Virgil,
of Plato, of the Apollo of Delphi, of the Sibyls of Cuma and Erythræa, of the infant of the Virgo
Paritura of Gaul, of the prophecy noticed by Tacitus, and that of Figulus, of Zeradust, and of the

---

[1] " Homeri Gnomologia duplici parallelismo illustrata, uno ex locis sacræ scripturæ, quibus *Gnomæ Homericæ,* aut
" prope affines, aut non prorsus absimiles ; altero ex gentium scriptoribus, per Jacobum Duportum Cantabrigiensem,
in 4to. 1660, Cantabrigiæ, p. 4. There are 291 of them.

[2] The Greek poet Naucrates accuses Homer of having copied his poem from a book in the library of the God Ptha,
at Memphis. Spineto's Lect. p. 330. It is probable that poems of *Om-eer existed both in Egypt and India.*

[3] Basnage, Book iii. Ch. xx.

Druid of Bochara in Ireland. Lactantius makes the Apollo of Miletus say, " He was a mortal ac-
" cording to the flesh; wise in miraculous works; but, being arrested by an armed force by com-
" mand of the CHALDEAN judges, he suffered a death made bitter with nails and stakes." [1]  In
this, of course, devotees will see nothing but a Gentile prophecy of Christ. Perhaps they may be
right. But at all events we have a crucified God in North India, in South India, at Miletus, and
in Syria. In the above we have most clearly the mythos of the Indians and of the tribe of Juda
united. The scene of it lies in Phrygia, where the City of Ilion in Troy was placed, whence the
Romans got their Pessinuncian stone, and which the natives of India to this day call Roum, in
which they include the whole peninsula of Asia Minor. The reference to the Chaldean judges
shews, that this can have no reference to the crucified saviour of our Bible. Who this crucified
person of Roum or Roma was, I shall shew in a future page.

## CHAPTER X.

ENOCH. LAURENCE.—MOUNT MERU.—THE DELUGE.—CHANGE FROM TAURUS TO ARIES. — PROPHECY OF
A SAVIOUR.—PROPHECY OF TEN CYCLES.—THE ELECT ONE SLAIN.—CHANGE IN EARTH'S AXIS.—GENE-
RAL OBSERVATIONS.

1. MR. BRUCE, on his return from Abyssinia, brought with him three manuscripts which pur-
ported to be exemplars of the Ethiopian version of the long-lost and much-desired book of Enoch.
I did not examine or pay any attention to them, till after the whole of what the reader has seen
respecting the cycles was written; and, after much consideration, I have judged it better that my
observations on this curious work should be placed here by themselves, though it may perhaps be
thought that they ought to have appeared in the fifth book.

This celebrated and very interesting remnant of antiquity has been translated into English, by
Bishop Laurence, a professor of Oxford, who maintains that he has succeeded in shewing, from
internal evidence, that it was written after the Babylonish captivity, but before the reign of Herod.
I am of opinion, if I understand the Bishop, that it contains internal evidence of a much earlier
date. A learned writer in the Monthly Magazine, No. 385, August 1823, Vol. LVI. pp. 18—20,
denies that Bishop Laurence has shewn that there are marks of more recent date than Ezra in the
book of Enoch, and observes that it is alluded to in the last chapter of Malachi. I do not
profess to be certain that I understand either the seventy-first chapter, or the Bishop's note upon
it; but if I am right in my supposition that the writer makes the Equinox fall, in his time,
at the beginning of Aries, then the date of the work must have been above 2400 years before
Christ, at the latest. The Bishop says, " The *fourth* gate in his description is that which is
situated due East at sun rising, and due West at sun setting, and which, answering to the sign
Aries, the sun enters at the Vernal Equinox. It is very clear that if the sun, at the Vernal

---

[1] Propterea Milesius Apollo consultus utrumque Deus an Homo fuerit, hoc modo respondit : Θνητος ην κατα σαρκα,
σοφος τερατωδεσιν εργοις.  Αλλ' υπο Χαλδαιων κριτων υπλοις συναλωθεις, Γομφοις κατα σκολοπισσι πικρην αυτμησει τελεσσιν.
Lactant. Inst. Div. iv. Cap. xiii.  See also Euseb. Demons. Ev. iii. Cap. viii. p. 134.

Equinox, was at the beginning of Aries, the book must have been written as early as I have stated above. Though Bishop Laurence limits the period, before which it must have been written, to the end of Herod, the fact noticed by Maurice,[1] that it is quoted by Eupolemus, shews that it was well known in Greece previous to the year B. C. 200.

Bishop Laurence, in his Preliminary Dissertations, p. xxxiv., endeavours to disguise the fact of the quotation of this book by Eupolemus; but I think he fails. Mr. Maurice states it broadly and honestly as he generally quotes, and, as I think, every one who carefully examines what Laurence has said may see reason to believe, correctly too. After observing several *wilful mistranslations* of Bishop Laurence's, if there were any doubt of the two, I would much prefer the respectable old Maurice.

The following are the passages which I contend are wilful mistranslations, pious frauds of the Bishop's: Εν ταις εκκλησιαις ου πανυ φερεται ως θεια—*The church considers it not an inspired production.*[2]

Again. Non recepi a quibusdam—*Not universally rejected.*[3]

No doubt I shall be accused, as I have been before, of a rage against priests, and for illiberality in what I say against them in many passages of this work. How can I do otherwise than speak against an order, against whose frauds and usurpations on the rights of mankind this work is expressly levelled—this work whose leading object is to undeceive mankind, now the slaves of its arts? I trust I am not insensible to the private virtues of great numbers of priests the dupes of their order—of their chiefs; but what am I to say or to think when I find a reverend doctor of Oxford, in the nineteenth century, guilty of such baseness, as that which I have exhibited above, and as a consequence, instead of being disgraced for such an act, made an archbishop? Since his promotion he has, I am told, suppressed his translation. If the suppression of it be an act of remorse, let him say so. I hope it is so. But I believe it is suppressed for a very different reason.

Of course it is held by our priests, who have already more sacred books than they can manage, to be a forgery; but Bishop Laurence admits that it is noticed by Clemens Alexandrinus and Ireneus, and *that neither of them alludes to its spurious character.*[4] The truth is, that it is quoted by them precisely like any other canonical sacred scripture.

It allegorically foretells the coming of Samuel, Saul, David, Solomon, the captivity, &c.," so clearly, as to leave no room for doubt; and this clearness of completed prophecy is, in Bishop Laurence's opinion, a proof that it is spurious; while it is remarkable that supposed clearness of the same kind is a proof that Isaiah is genuine. The argument of Bishop Laurence is good in every case. Unless the genuineness of a book purporting to be prophetic be taken for granted, the proof of the verification of a prophecy is rather a proof of spuriousness than the contrary.

Faustus quoted the book of Enoch against Augustine,[5] who, instead of denying its genuineness, admits it, and I do not think it appears that this admission is granted by way of *argumentum ad hominem.* In short, I have no hesitation in saying that it is, in my opinion, to the full as well established as a work existing before the time of Christ, as Isaiah is; for Isaiah is not quoted by any author that I remember before the time of Christ. Josephus says that the Pentateuch only was translated by the LXX: and by whom, or when the remainder of the Jewish books were translated, no one knows. Every argument which applies against Enoch as stated above, applies against Isaiah; and I am much mistaken if the argument does not go farther. The argument from fulfilled prophecy is as fair for one as for the other. I think there can be no doubt, though direct authority

---

' In his Hist. Hind. Vol. I. p. 438.      ² Prel. Dis. p. xiv.      ³ Ibid. pp. xvi. xvii.
⁴ Ibid. p. xiv.                          ⁵ IX. 3

be wanting, that both the works were written after the Babylonish captivity, but before the time of Christ: and in defiance of Bishop Laurence's misrepresentations, I think there is evidence to prove that they were both *generally* admitted since the time of Christ; that is, as much admitted as any other books of the canon, by the generality of Christians. But there were no books, against which some Christians did not make objections; and the class of books called ὁμολογουμενα by Eusebius, never did exist—as that word cannot be restricted in its meaning to his own sect, a very small one indeed, compared with the great mass of Christians. His sect might be greater than any other, but it is ridiculous to believe it more numerous than all the other sects united.

Bishop Laurence has *astronomically proved* the book of Enoch to have been composed between 45 and 50 degrees of north latitude. (This is not far from the north of India, central Asia, the kingdom of Ioudia, where I have shewn that the first great nation flourished, and where I have placed Shinar. See my Map. It must not be supposed that this great nation did not spread over a considerable space of land. I have been accused of ignorance and blundering in placing Samarkand half a degree wrong. How can I be expected to answer such critics?) He has shewn also, that its original language was the Hebrew, which was formerly proved by Scaliger, from the fragments preserved by Syncellus, which are found in the present book. Now I beg my reader to tell me, whether he would wish for a stronger circumstantial proof of what I have been saying of the Hebrews or foreigners being a race of emigrants from Upper India, bringing with them the Arabic and Hebrew languages to Ethiopia? I think the evidence must be pretty strong to compel the Bishop to admit the two facts. Since he became *a bishop*, this learned Orientalist, perhaps, has discovered that it contained proofs of disagreeable circumstances, and these may have caused its suppression.

We have seen that in northern India we have the Jewish history of Solomon, David, &c., and that the Arabians had the same history. There is also in each of these countries the story of Saul; but it is very remarkable that, in both of them, he is called by a name unknown to the Western Jews, viz. Talut. Under all the circumstances I cannot conceive a stronger proof that the Arabians came from India, and not from the Mosaic Jews of Judæa.

Every page exhibits the Judæan mythos, which we have seen to have existed both in Eastern and Western Syria; but there is quite difference enough between the two mythoses to shew that they cannot be copies of each other. Of the sacred book or mythos of Eastern Syria, we have not particulars enough to form an accurate opinion. The name given to Saul, in North India, of *Talut*, a name unknown in the Bible, is a very strong circumstance in favour of its oriental extraction.

The language in which we find the book of Enoch, the African Ethiopic, when combined with the variety of circumstances relating to this language in Ethiopia, which I have laid before the reader, furnishes ground for much curious observation, and supports, in a very remarkable manner, what I have said respecting the migration of the Jewish tribe from Upper India.

If it be said that the latitude of 45 or 50 will suit Armenia as well as the East of the Caspian, I reply, this is not supported by any circumstances like the other, for there are no traditions, except what are very trifling and evidently the invention of Christians. There are no remains of great cities, no Jewish similarities, no statues of the patriarchs, no Jewish names, no Temple of Solomon, like that in Cashmere; and the fact is directly contrary to the history of Genesis, which makes the descendants of Noah to have left the hilly country and come down from the East into the plains: that they did thus migrate has been proved by both Sir Walter Raleigh and Dr. Shuckford, whose testimony strikingly confirms the hypothesis as maintained in my CELTIC DRUIDS.

2. The following passage of the book of Enoch, ch. xxiv., is so clearly descriptive of Mount Meru, that it cannot be mistaken, and proves the author to have been intimately acquainted with the Hindoo doctrines.

" 1. I went thence to another place and saw a mountain of fire flashing both by day and night. " I proceeded towards it : and perceived seven splendid mountains, which were all different from " each other.

" 2. Their stones were brilliant and beautiful ; all were brilliant and splendid to behold : and " beautiful was their surface. Three mountains were towards the East, and strengthened by " being placed one upon another ; and three were towards the South, strengthened in a similar " manner. There were likewise deep valleys, which did not approach each other. And the " seventh mountain was in the midst of them. In length they all resembled the seat of a throne, " and odoriferous trees surrounded them.

" 3. And among these there was a tree of an unceasing smell : nor of those which were in " Eden was there one of all the fragrant trees which smelt like this. Its leaf, its flower, and its " bark, never withered, and its fruit was beautiful.

" 4. Its fruit resembled the cluster of the palm. I exclaimed, Behold! this tree is goodly in " aspect, pleasing in its leaf, and the sight of its fruit is delightful to the eye. Then Michael, one " of the holy and glorious angels who were with me, and one who presided over them answered,

" 5. And said, Enoch, why dost thou inquire respecting the odour of this tree ?

" 6. Why art thou inquisitive to know it ?

" 7. Then I replied to him and said, Concerning every thing I am desirous of instruction, but " particularly concerning this tree.

" 8. He answered me saying, That mountain which thou beholdest, the extent of whose head " resembles the seat of the Lord, will be the seat on which shall sit the holy and great Lord of " glory, the everlasting King, when he shall come and descend to visit the earth with goodness.

" 9. And that tree of an agreeable smell, not one of carnal odour, *(of flesh,)* there shall be no " power to touch, until the period of the great judgment. When all shall be punished, and con- " sumed for ever, this shall be bestowed on the righteous and humble. The fruit of this *tree* shall " be given to the elect. *For towards the North life* shall be planted in the holy place, towards " *the habitation of the everlasting King.*

" 10. Then shall they greatly rejoice and exult in the holy one. The sweet odour shall enter " into their bones : and they shall live a long life as their forefathers have lived : and neither in " their days shall sorrow, distress, trouble, and punishment, afflict them.

" 11. And I blessed the Lord of glory, the everlasting King, because he had prepared *this tree* " for the saints, formed it, and declared that he would give it to them."

I think the reader must see in verse 4, in the *Palm* the *Phoinix tree* of Meru ; and in ver. 9, the mount of God in the sides of the North mentioned by Isaiah, ch. xiv. 13.

When I reflect upon this tree, I cannot help suspecting it is connected with the allegory of the trees of *life* and of *knowledge* in Eden, whose branches are words, whose leaves are letters, &c., &c.

In chap. xxxi. he again gives a description of seven mountains *of the North* with odoriferous trees.

There are many passages which have a close resemblance both to the Hindoo books and to the Jewish prophets. Of the former is the allegory of the mountains of various metals ;[1] of the latter, the comparison of the heavens to a book. The lunar period of 28 days days is distinctly named, chapter lxxvii.

3. In chapters lxxxvii. and lxxxviii. is a very clear allegorical description of the deluge : and a

---

[1] P. 166.

star is said to have fallen from heaven. This is all closely connected with animals of the Beeve race in which a cow is distinctly marked as of the masculine gender. The allegory is carried on through several chapters, in which the personages named in the Pentateuch are supposed by Bishop Laurence to be described—till it comes to a being who is called a *white cow*, and who, in ch. lxxxviii. ver. 18, is said to have brought forth a *black wild sow* and a *white sheep*. With the production of the sheep, the allegory of the bull or beeve ends : and although many other animals are named continually, the beeve is never once named afterward, till the conclusion, when the bull is said to return ; but the sheep, which was never once named before, takes the lead. The *white cow*, supposed by the Bishop to be Abraham, introduces it, although almost every other domestic animal is named distinctly many times. The distinction between the beeve and the sheep is marked in a way that is most extraordinary, and cannot possibly have been so marked without a clear and distinct meaning. The change from the Bull *Taurus* to the Ram *Aries*, is so clear that it cannot be mistaken.

The Bishop, in notes, shews or gives the names of the Jewish worthies as far as Solomon, to whom he supposes the allegory applies. And in many cases his observations seem very probable ; but there are many circumstances which do not apply to those worthies, which seem to shew that the allegory cannot be founded upon them, but rather that it is a mythos common to both. For instance, the Bishop, in his translation and note, states a cow, Abraham, to have brought forth a sheep, Isaac, and the sheep, Isaac, to have brought forth twelve sheep. Now I think with the Bishop, that this alludes to the story of the Israelites ; but if it had been a copy, it would not have omitted Jacob, who changed his name to Israel. Other similar instances might be pointed out, where the mythoses are the same, but the variation is so great, that they cannot be copies. Let it not be forgotten that almost all the histories of Genesis have been long known to be in the Vedas ; and when the places in India called after David and Solomon are considered, it will not be thought surprising, that their histories should be found there also.

4. It is not possible to give an idea of the nature of the marked distinction between the Beeve and the Ram, unless I copied several long chapters, much of which could no way interest the reader ; I must therefore refer him to the book itself. There is also something very remarkable in the way in which the Cow or Heifer is constantly spoken of in the *masculine* gender. I suspect that the studied confusion of the *colours* of the kine, and of their genders, has a reference, which I do not understand, to the different sects, and to the wars about the Linga and Ioni. When the allegory changes from the Beeve to the Sheep, one of the sheep is said to become a man, and to build a house for the Lord. In short, when I couple the wild but still methodical mysticism of this book with what the reader has seen, I can feel no doubt but that it contains a concealed history of the change of the religion from Taurus to Aries. The house to the Lord, the Bishop thinks, is the temple of Solomon. Of this there can be no doubt : but it may have been the temple in Cashmere ; and, considering it *proved* that this work was written in the North of India, it is most probable that it *was* the temple of Solomon in Cashmere.

The deluge of Noah and Noah himself are distinctly noticed by name ; but I think in such a way as to shew that it cannot have been copied from the Jewish book. The Trinity is also most distinctly named, under the appellation, as Bishop Laurence translates it, of Lords—*two of whom*, together *with the Lord of spirits*, are said to have been engaged in the formation of the world. Here is again the Oriental doctrine. What words are in the original for Noah and Lord cannot be known from the translation. They may or may not be Menu and Iswara. On the meaning of such words as these no dependence can be placed on Bishop Laurence's translation. Without we had the words represented to us, as I do now in the word Jehovah, יהוה *ieue*, no conclusion can be come to.

5. The forty-eighth chapter contains the prophecy of some one to come, of a new incarnation, of a saviour, which cannot be disputed, in the following words :

" 1. In that place I beheld a fountain of righteousness which never failed, encircled by many " springs of WISDOM. Of these all the thirsty drank, and were filled with WISDOM, having their " habitation with the righteous, the elect, and the holy.

" 2. In that hour was this son of man invoked before *(ad, apud)* the Lord of spirits, and his " name in the presence of the ancient of days.

" 3. Before the sun and the *signs* [1] were created, before the stars of heaven were formed, his " name was invoked in the presence of the Lord of spirits. A report shall be for the righteous " and the holy to lean upon, without falling, and he shall be the light of nations.

" 4. He shall be the hope of those whose hearts are troubled. All who dwell upon the earth " shall fall down and worship before him : shall bless and glorify him, and sing praises to the " name of the Lord of spirits.

" 5. Therefore the elect and the concealed one existed in his presence before the world was " created, and for ever.

" 6. In his presence *he existed,* and has revealed to the saints and to the righteous the WISDOM " of the Lord of spirits : for he has preserved the lot of the righteous, because they have hated " and rejected the world of iniquity, and have detested all its works and ways, in the name of the " Lord of spirits."

In several other places this incarnation is named ; he is said to be present with the *ancient of days,* whose head was like *white wool.* It is said that he shall raise up kings and hurl mighty ones from their thrones, because they will not praise him, or humble themselves before him. He is identified with the Lord of spirits. He is called WISDOM [2] — the ELECT ONE, THE MESSIAH. It is said that he shall sit upon a throne of glory, and shall judge sinners. [3] And finally it is said, that the saints shall rejoice because the Lord of spirits has executed judgment, for the *blood of the righteous* WHICH HAS BEEN SHED ; alluding to the blood of the elect one.

How can this be accounted for ? Does the prophet not here allude to the crucified Buddha, Cristna, or Balajii ? Here we see long before the death of Christ, the righteous blood of the elect one had been shed. At all events, at the death of Christ the doctrine of the death of *the elect one* was not new.

This passage respecting the blood of the elect one HAVING BEEN shed, clearly PROVES that this can be no forgery after the death of Christ. It is impossible to attribute such absurdity to any fabricator of such a work, professing to have been written before the time of Christ.

6. But to me the most interesting of all the passages is one which clearly makes out the cycles which I have been contending for among the Jews. The book says,

" Chap. xcii. ver. 4, Enoch then began to speak from a book and said : I have been born the " seventh in the first week, while judgment and righteousness wait with patience."

Here is evidently the first cycle ending with the translation of Enoch. See Book V. Chap. III. Sect. 2.

" 5. But after me, in the second week, great wickedness shall arise, and fraud shall spring " forth.

" 6. In that week [4] the end of the first shall take place, in which mankind shall be safe."

This is curiously contrived to describe the eight years of the Cycle of 608 running into the next or seventh century.

---

[1] Signs of the Zodiac.     [2] Ch. xlii.     [3] Ch. xlv. Sect. vii.     [4] *In it.*

" 7. But when the first is completed, iniquity shall grow up: and he shall execute judgment
" upon sinners.

" 8. Afterward, in the third week, *during its completion,* a man of the plant of righteous judg-
" ment shall be selected : and after him the plant of righteousness shall come for ever."

Here are the three cycles, ending with the birth of Noah the righteous.

" 9. Subsequently, in the fourth week, during its completion, the visions of the holy and the
" righteous shall be seen, the *order of generation after generation shall take place,* and an habita-
" tion shall be made for them. Then, in the fifth week, during its completion, the house of glory
" and of dominion shall be erected for ever."

Here in the fourth, probably, is meant what answers to the ark coming to Gerizim or Shilo,
as the Samaritans say, and in the fifth is the temple of Solomon.

" 10. After that, in the sixth week, all those who are in it shall be darkened, the hearts of all
" of them be forgetful *of wisdom,* and in it shall a man ascend.   (Elijah.)

" 11. During its completion also the house of dominion shall be burnt with fire, and all the race
" of the elect root be dispersed.   (Babylonish Captivity.)

" 12. Afterward, in the seventh week, a perverse generation shall arise: abundant shall be its
" deeds, and all its powers perverse. During its completion, the righteous, selected from the
" plant of everlasting righteousness, shall be rewarded : and to them shall be given seven-fold
" instruction, respecting every part of his creation."

Though the allusions, as explained by Bishop Laurence in the words in parentheses, are sufficiently clear, I think it is evidently not copied from the Jewish Bible as we have it.

" 13. Afterward there shall be another week, the eighth of righteousness, to which shall be
" given a sword to execute judgment and justice upon all oppressors.

" 14. Sinners shall be delivered up into the hands of the righteous, who during its completion
" shall acquire habitations by their righteousness : and the house of the great king shall be built
" up for ever. After that, in the ninth week, shall the judgment of righteousness be revealed to
" the whole world.

" 15. Every work of the ungodly shall disappear from the whole earth: the world shall be
" marked for destruction : and all men shall be on the *look out* for the path of integrity.

" 16. And after this, on the seventh day of the tenth week, there shall be an everlasting judg-
" ment, which shall be executed upon the watchers : and a spacious, eternal heaven shall spring
" forth in the midst of the angels.

" 17. The former heaven shall depart and pass away : a new heaven shall appear: and all the
" celestial powers shine with seven-fold splendour, for ever."

Thus ends the numbering of the weeks ; and I think the reader must confess, that I could
scarcely have wished for a confirmation of my theory of the ten cycles more decisive. And I think
we may fairly infer, that if the arrangement of the former part shew, that it is not a copy from the
Jewish Scriptures, the absence of a more particular prophecy in reference to JESUS, shews, that it
must have been written both before the Gospels and before his birth: for most assuredly the
writer would have imitated the prophecy relating to the Messiah, Cyrus, in Isaiah, and have named
him by his name if it had been in his power.

7. I cannot well conceive any thing more corroborative of my theory than that this curious work
should be written in the Hebrew language, be located in the mountains of Afghanistan, and be
found in the country of the African Ethiopians. That all these facts should be made out for me
by the learned Bishop, for very learned he most unquestionably is, without having the least
suspicion of the nature of my theory, which, if he had had, he would have been most violently

opposed to it, and without having any theory of his own—what can be more striking than that it should so clearly describe my *ten cycles*!—what more curious than its prophecy of the *Saviour*! In this book we find a clear description of a future Messiah or incarnate Saviour. It is also foretold that he is to be put to death. Most of the Jewish history, as well as the Pentateuchian history, is found here, as are also some of the most striking of the doctrines of the Hindoos—particularly their mount Meru and their Trinity—so that the close connexion between India and its author, cannot be disputed. The Christian professor of Oxford maintains that it is not genuine; but he proves that it was written before Christ. Then how is the prophecy to be explained,—the fulfilled prophecy? The fact is, there have been two Messiahs, or elects, or sons of man; two Jewish mythoses; two Noahs; two tribes of Juda. On this subject I shall have much more to say hereafter. However this may be, the whole serves to shew the absolute uncertainty of a religion founded on documents of this kind. It is much more clear than Isaiah, and has, to say the least, as much evidence in favour of its genuineness. When was the prophecy of Isaiah first known? Josephus proves that it was not translated with the Pentateuch; and though he pretends to shew that Isaiah was known to Ptolemy, and gives a letter of Ptolemy's respecting him, this is not contemporary evidence, but the mere assertion of a partisan, hundreds of years after Isaiah's death. In its prophecy of a Saviour, the book of Enoch is much clearer than Isaiah, though it does not (as Isaiah does in the case of Cyrus) give him by name. But from its whole character I cannot doubt, that if it had been written after the Christian religion had made any progress, it would have followed the example of Isaiah, and have given the Saviour's name. I therefore conclude that it was written before the time of Christ. The book is of great consequence to me, because it proves the truth of the system of renewed incarnations in renewed cycles.

It is impossible to read the book of Enoch, and not to be struck with the similarity of style to that of the Jewish prophets, particularly Isaiah and Jeremiah: the same expressions are perpetually recurring. The same may be said of the celebrated Desatir (which was so highly prized by Sir William Jones) in the account therein given of the *fourteen* Maha-bads or Great Buddhas or Prophets who had appeared, or were to appear, to enlighten the world: the first of whom, Hushang, divided mankind into four classes—the religious, the military, the commercial, and the agricutural. Of the genuineness of the Desatir, Sir W. Jones had no doubt. I am not so easily satisfied: though it may be true that it was translated by Moshani from a language now not in use. It clearly alludes to the Christian and Mohamedan systems, or to two systems which answer to them. By and by my reader will see that this is no proof either of its spuriousness or its corruption.

I suppose at this day *no one* will be weak enough to maintain that this book of Enoch is *divinely inspired*, as it is rejected by our conscience-keepers the bishops. Then what are we to make of it? Here are all the leading doctrines which I have been contending for clearly maintained. The residence or birth-place of the theology, Upper India; the signs of the Zodiac; the change of the Equinox from Taurus to Aries; (of which no one can judge who has not read the whole work;) the Hindoo Trinity, than which nothing can be more clear; the description of Mount Meru, with its paradise or hanging gardens, surrounded by its seven mounts, where the Gods sat on the sides of the North; the sacred Phoinix tree, and a history similar to the Jewish, but not copied from it; the prophecy of an *elect one* as described by all the prophets, including the prophecy of Virgil, and the elect one put to death, noticed by me in the cases of Buddha, Cristna, and him of the Apollo of Miletus; and lastly, the clear elucidation of the ten ages, alluded to by Virgil, and taught by the Buddhists and Brahmins. It has been the object of this work to shew that an universal system extended over the whole of the old world; and the principal facts for which I have contended are supported by this curious and unquestionably genuine document: for no one can doubt that it is the actual manuscript brought from Ethiopia by Mr. Bruce. When all these things are considered, it surely affords very extraordinary evidence. I have shewn that the history in Genesis is, in all its leading particulars, to be found in the East; and, in several of the most important points, that it is a copy from the oriental one, if either be a copy. The fact shewn by Dr. A. Clarke that the serpent bites the *foot* not the *heel*, is one example—and the Doctor's observation is decisive and invaluable: for, when the Brahmin *icon* or *picture* makes the reptile bite the *foot* he does not bite the *heel;* and, therefore, it cannot have been copied from Genesis. But when the writer of Genesis makes the serpent bite the heel, he may have copied from the East, for he does bite the foot. It will not be denied, that it is very extraordinary that this book, written in the Hebrew language, between 40 and 50 degrees of North latitude, should be found to be part of the SACRED CANON of the Ethiopians of Africa—the people who, as we have seen, have such striking marks of affinity in their language with the Hindoos; and, that the oldest copy we have of it, is in the language of this country. Bishop Laurence admits, that it was written before the time of Christ, but he does not attempt to account for the expression of the blood of the righteous being shed. The circumstance most remarkable in this book, is the mixture of the different doctrines of countries so widely separated from each other. When I consider that, in many countries, these doctrines had become forgotten or were lost, that in no one country in the times of the Romans, were they all known, and that they are the doctrines or rather the fragments of the doctrines, of different ages, and of widely separated countries, which doctrines, as I have contended, constituted those of a primeval nation, I cannot help looking to a very remote æra for its existence. When I find the account of David and Solomon alluded to in this Indian book, I am almost induced to consider them like the heroes of Troy. For, when they are alluded to, it is not by name, and their names given by the bishop, in parentheses, are not in the original, but are only inferences of his own, but which inferences are so clear that I think they cannot be doubted. Then do we at last come to this, that the whole is a mythos concealed under an apparent history; or, is it blended with true history in order the better to conceal it?—like the poem of Homer, a true *basis* and an allegorical or fabulous *superstructure.* But we must not forget that the history of Solomon, his temple, &c., may all refer to the Eastern as easily, and indeed much more easily, as to the Western Syria. I must once more remind my reader, that all attempts hitherto made to account for the anomalies of ancient history and mythology, have utterly failed to satisfy any persons, except mere devotees, who, in every nation, are the same, and are always satisfied with what their priests tell them; and that my exertions to discover the truth are in opposition to the frauds of the priests of all religions, as well as the effects of time, which is always aiding them in their system of suppressing evidence and in keeping mankind in ignorance.

8. I must not omit to notice a very extraordinary part of the prophecy relating to Noah and the flood. It says, Ch. lxiv. Sect. xi. ver. 1, p. 163, " In those days Noah saw that the earth became inclined, and that destruction approached."

This is a most extraordinary assertion, that the flood was caused by the disturbance of the axis of the earth, and is so totally original and unexpected that Bishop Laurence has placed it at the end of the book, because, he says, it is an evident interpolation; but he gives no reason for this, and has none, I suppose, except that he cannot give the author credit for the astronomical doctrine of the change of the earth's axis. I look upon it as a very curious and ancient tradition respecting the cause of the flood, which has been considered to have been its real cause by many both of the ancient and modern philosophers. I shall return to this subject hereafter.

But who was referred to in the blood of the *elect one* put to death ? Was it Prometheus crucified on Mount Caucasus ? Was it Ixion ? Was it the mystic dove or Divine Love under the form or the name of Semiramis ? Was it Bal-ji, the *Lord Ji* ? Was it Cristna, or was it Buddha? Or, was it the person foretold, or said to be crucified, by the Apollo of Miletus ?

9. I flatter myself my reader will begin to perceive that my object is to prove, that an universal language and philosophy, in very remote times, pervaded the whole of the old world; that it was a philosophy, beautiful and fundamentally true ; that it had for its basement the existence of one God, to whom were ascribed the attributes of creating, preserving, and destroying; that its professors were *black* in colour, and PROBABLY *negro* in form ; that it was a race of Herbaceous beings, killing no harmless animal, perhaps no animal whatever. Whether it were as learned as Mons. Bailly supposed his antediluvian race to have been, may be matter of doubt, or whether it may not have been the original race itself. But the Neros must have been invented by some persons, and we can trace it no farther back than the race of which I now speak, and it is found in their possession. After a certain time we find historical accounts in India, of the followers of the first principle having become split into parties, or, in other words, of its professors having fallen into differences of opinion, succeeded by wars of great length and cruelty ; in the course of which, various tribes were driven out to the West : whence, by degrees, arose the number of variations of the mythos, with which the world has been tormented or amused. Though these were different mythoses in some respects, yet in the fundamental principle they were all the same, and bore, through all their different ramifications, one universal family character—viz. the Trinity, the metempsychosis, the renewal or regeneration of worlds, at the end of every cycle of 600 and 6000 years, the absence of idols, and, as I have just now said, the abstinence from animal food. These were the Cyclopæan Buddhists, the builders of Stonehenge, of Abury, and of Carnac. They were succeeded by the founders of Oxford, Cambridge, and Iona, upon the Cyclopæan ruins. They were the Atlantides or sons of the earth ; they were the sons of the ethereal fire or of Vulcan, whose Cyclopæan buildings yet serve to astonish our mechanists, and excite the wonder and despair of our antiquarians.

I think my reader will have no difficulty now in perceiving the general characteristic marks of one system every where prevailing. It has been the great misfortune of the world, that its professors, its Vyasas, Pythagorases, and Platos, have all been deluded with the idea that the doctrine was too sublime for the mass of mankind : this imagination inducing them to conceal it in various ways, afforded an opportunity to their successors to form priesthoods, in fact corporations and corresponding societies, whose interest it became to take care, by keeping the people in ignorance, that the doctrine should always remain too sublime for them. Thus from the days of Bishop Vyasa to the days of Bishop Laurence, the same course has always been pursued ; and, with as much zeal and as much system as the improved state of mankind will permit, it is yet continued. Before I conclude this work, I hope I shall be able nearly to strip off the tawdry disguises which have been piled upon both Gentilism and Christianity, and to restore them to the identical system practised in the sacrifice of bread and wine or water, at the shrine of the ጥ *ie*, IE or Jah, at Delphi, by Pythagoras, and by Abraham, in the same rite, at the altar of the priest Melchisedek, the King of Justice—of the Dherma Rajah, of the same religion of which Jesus Christ is said to have been declared a priest. I shall shew that the religions of Melchisedek, of Jesus, and of Pythagoras, were the same, and that the celebrated Christian father, Justin the Martyr, spoke nothing but the truth, when he declared that Socrates was a Christian. I am not the first person who broached this doctrine. Sixteen hundred years ago a very celebrated, and probably, all things considered, the most learned of all the Christian fathers, Ammonius Saccas, taught this doctrine—that all the Gentile religions as well as the Christian, were to be illustrated and explained by the principles of an *universal philosophy*, but that in order to do this, the fables of the priests were to be removed from Paganism, and the comments and interpretations of the disciples of Jesus from Christianity. This philosopher might well be called, as he has been, the ornament of the Christian cause in the second century. But the seed which he sowed fell on rocky places, and brought forth no fruit. He threw his pearls before swine. Alas ! his doctrine was much too sublime for the wretched and miserable race which succeeded him. For such men as Irenæus, who saw the statue of Lot's wife,[1] and as the learned Origen, his pupil, (really in languages learned,) who castrated himself for the glory of God, and Augustine the *glory* of Africa, who says he saw men in Ethiopia without heads, but with one eye in the breast. Fabricius and Lardner, as if fearful lest something really good and respectable should be found among their predecessors the fathers of the Christian Church, wish to exclude Ammonius from the list; but Mosheim, who was originally of their opinion, saw cause, on further examination, to change it, and, in such change, as Mr. Taylor truly says, shewed the marks of a master mind.[2] But Mosheim had what has been seldom found in the Christian cause, he had sincerity, as well as learning. Although for my system I go not to the support of great names, yet I am not insensible to the value of the opinion of such a man as Saccas, who, in addition to his learning, united the advantage of being nearer to the fountain-head, the origin of things, by no contemptible period—sixteen hundred years.

---

[1] The story of Lot's wife is the best proved miracle which we have on record. If persons will not believe this, they will believe nothing. If ever I have the happiness to go to Syria, the first thing I shall do will be to visit Lot's wife. The history of the fate of this unhappy woman is first told in Genesis, xix. 26. This was about two thousand years before Christ. It is next noticed in the Wisdom of Solomon, supposed to have been written by Philo, or about his time. This author says, ch. x. 7, *a standing pillar of salt* is *a monument of an unbelieving soul.* The next witness is the Jewish historian, *so universally celebrated for his veracity,* Josephus, Antiq. Lib. i. Cap. xi., who says, *I have seen it, and it remains at this day.* The next witness is Clement, of Rome, who attests that it was standing in his day. (Whiston's note in loco, in his translation of Josephus.) But the most perfect and complete evidence, with *particulars* which are really surprising, is given about 150 years afterward, by the Christian bishop, saint, and martyr, of Gaul, Irenæus. I shall give the passage from his work at full, in the *original*, for various reasons. He says, " Quemadmodum et Lot, " qui eduxit de Sodomis filias suas, quæ conceperunt de patre suo, qui reliquit in confinio uxorem suam statuam salis " usque in hodiernum diem. . . . . . . Et cum hæc fierent, uxor remansit in Sodomis, jam non caro corrup- " tabilis, sed statua salis semper manens,[1] et per naturalia,[2] ea quæ sunt consuetudinis hominis, ostendens, quoniam " et ecclesia, quæ est sal terræ, sub relicta est in confinio terræ, patiens quæ sunt humana : et dum sæpe auferuntur " ab ea membra integra, perseverat statua salis, quod est firmamentum fidei, firmans et præmittens filios ad patrem " ipsorum" Iren. Cap. li. p. 354, ed. Oxon. 1702. And in the eleventh century it was still existing. Benj. de Tudela (Ch. ix.) says, " From this mount you have a prospec. of the sea of Sodom ; from which sea it is about two " parasangs to the pillar of salt, into which Lot's wife was metamorphosed. The pillar or statue is indeed daily wasted " by the cattle, who are perpetually licking, *or rather rubbing against,* it, but it is likewise daily restored, and becomes " as it was before." I only regret that I cannot indulge my reader with an account of its present state, from the travels of Mons. Chateaubriand ; for, of course, he would not go to the Jordan to fetch water to baptize the Duke of Bourdeaux, without examining this very interesting pillar.

[2] Mosheim, Vol. I. p. 170, note.

---

[1] " Statua salis semper manens.] Ita et Clemens Rom. in Epist. ad Corinth. Memorat, ϛηλην ἁλος ἑως της ἡμερας " ταυτης. S. xi. Atque ex Judæis, Josephus. Antiq. Lib. i. Cap. xi."

[2] " Per naturalia, ea quæ sunt consuetudinis hominis.] Menstruum fluxum muliebri sexui naturalem indigitare " videtur, utpote quem uxori Loti, licet jam in statuam salis versæ, quosquam adscripsisse, vel affinxisse, docet auctor " Carminis de Sodoma, quod inter Tertulliani atque Cypriani opera extat, post medium ita de uxore Loti canens : " Dicitur et vivens alio jam corpore sexus munificos solito dispungere sanguine menses."

# BOOK X.

## CHAPTER I.

1. In all our speculations we must never forget, that the whole Mythos, of which I have been
treating, was not known, but in great part lost, by the ancient Greeks and Romans, in their day,
and also by the Brahmins when the modern Europeans arrived in India. The only difference between them and us is, that they really believed the mythos, little as it was known to them, to be
true, and thus made every thing bend and fit to it, as far as was in their power. We have been
equally ignorant, but have endeavoured to disguise to ourselves the reality—the existence of
it ;—philosophers and inquirers in general have done this from incredulity, arising from what
appeared to them the improbability of the nature of it : for one example, that there should
be a nation of Jews or kingdom of Judah in central Asia. Another example may be found in the
name *Solomon*, disguised into Soleiman, Solyman, &c. It is inconceivable what an influence this
feeling has had on philosophers and inquirers generally in disguising and concealing the truth.
These are facts which cannot be denied ; and these are facts which we must not lose sight of for a
moment ; for, without them, we cannot form a correct idea of the real state of the case. They
will enable us to account for many circumstances : they particularly support me in shewing, that
the ancients had recourse to expedients and contrivances to remove difficulties, and by this means
to make the prophetic part of the mythos come true.

The system had its origin from the discovery and adoption of the Cycles, which I have explained
in the fifth book ;—a system which arose out of the first necessities of civilized man. With the
beginning of his civilization they must have begun. How this took place I shall shew by and by.
Upon these, by an union of cunning and credulity, the religion was by degrees formed. Circumstances were so favourable to it, that I cannot conceive any thing more natural. It was the regular course of events. There never has been a religion invented *de novo.* In fact, before I
finish I shall prove that, in the civilized world, there never was but one religion. What we have
called different religions, because we did not understand them, were but modifications of one religion. All these considerations we must bear in mind, in our future speculations.

2. It is a very extraordinary circumstance that though every one of the ancient rabbis, and
perhaps every one of the ancient fathers of the church, who must necessarily have known the
truth, have admitted that the Jewish and Christian religions contained secret and mysterious doctrines not known to the vulgar, and although great numbers of the most eminent moderns, such
as Thomas Burnet, &c., &c., have professed their belief that the religion did contain such secret
doctrines, yet that no one of them has set himself seriously to the task of unveiling them—of dis-

4 B 2

covering what was their nature. The ancient Gentiles, also, always professed the same thing of their religion, and Ammonius Saccas and his few Christian and philosophical followers always held that, at the bottom, the Christian and Gentile mysteries were the same. Writers against the modern or the exoteric Christianity we have had in abundance, but never have we had a Hobbes, a Herbert, or a Bolingbroke, to endeavour to discover this secret. Thus their attempts to expose the error and nonsense of the vulgar exoterism, have been successful enough. But the real and proper question for these philanthropists and philosophers ought first to have been, not whether it were credible that God made Eve from the side of Adam : but whether there were a *secret* religion for the Conclave—the Lateran [1]—and a *public one* for the senate and people : and if there were such secret religion, what was its nature ? En passant, I may observe, that if there be a secret religion, all the objections of Mons. Voltaire and other philosophers to such passages as that relating to the side of Adam, which never have been removed, are at once answered, and the religion relieved from a mighty mass of obloquy. For though it may be very wrong to have a secret and a public religion, this does not make it foolish or absurd.

Suppose I were to inquire into the nature of the earliest Mohamedism, and I were to find that all its followers, of different and inimical sects, maintained the existence of four Gods; however absurd, or weak, or dishonest I might believe these votaries were, should I not be compelled to believe that they did admit four Gods ; and that four Gods constituted the ground-work of their religion ? Thus it is with the very early Christians: all their writers admitted an esoteric religion, however much they might differ on other points. If there were any exceptions, they were perfectly contemptible in number or talent. I know of none. Then how is it possible to doubt that this was the principle of the religion; more particularly when we find the Gospel histories teaching in parables or allegories, and teeming with numerous mystical expressions, unintelligible in common language, and Jesus himself declaring that he taught in these very parables that he might not be understood, (as of course he must mean,) by the people who listened to him.

I am firmly persuaded that in the following books of this work, the foundation at least, indeed the principal part, of the esoteric doctrines of the Christians, Jews, and Gentiles, will be unfolded, and at last justice will be done to the Pythagorasses, Platos, Philos, Clemenses, and Ammoniuses of antiquity ; and, however false my philosophical or religious reader may think their doctrines, he will no longer think them base or contemptible.

3. In the affairs of religion, the world has always been in one respect the same as it is now. From the most remote period there has been the esoteric religion, of which I have just spoken, the existence of which the vulgar rabble of low priests have denied, but which has always been well known and admitted by a select number, who wore the mitre. This was anciently observed

---

[1] The Papal decrees always issue from the church of St. John Lateran. I suspect this is mystic, and means *secret place*. The root of Lateran is the Hebrew לאט *lat*, secret; Latin, *Lateo* ; joined to the word *ana*—place of. It is the place of the Λατρεια or *secret religion*. The Lateran is both a domus and a templum—the palace and the church adjoin. The decrees which issue from this place are called Bulls, from the Greek word Βѕλη consilium, counsel. Children anciently wore a sacred emblem, in the form of a heart, called a Bulla, as Macrobius says, to teach them *wisdom*. (Littleton's Dict. in voce.) This heart was the emblem of divine love, which was *wisdom*. It is almost always accompanied with a dove. The heart may be seen in the Vatican, upon innumerable ancient inscriptions, which the Romans call Christian. I have little doubt that anciently every person had his signet, which was some holy device, adopted probably *ad libitum*, or families might pass it by descent. This was the family Bulla, and with it the sign was made on the wax or metal, when deeds came into use ; thus the seals appended to deeds were called bulls; but more recondilely, the whole probably came from the name of God, *Bal*, the God of *Wisdom*.

I suspect that the word Vatican has come from the word vates, which is Veda, Beda, Vati-cania.

by a few philosophers, who occasionally shewed some knowledge of it, and endeavoured to explain its nature to the people. For this endeavour they were persecuted. They would never have been persecuted merely for discovering the secret; they were in reality persecuted for making their discovery known. In like manner in modern times, a Romish bishop will not refuse absolution even to an Atheist, but then he must keep his opinion secret. He is punished for telling— not for knowing, believing, or disbelieving. This knowledge applies chiefly to the Romish and Greek priests; the Protestant bigots, the Luthers, Calvins, and Knoxes, never knew any thing of the philosophy of Christianity; they were in reality insane with fanaticism. The Romish Church would have been very glad to have let them into the secret, if it had then the secret, in order to have stopped their proceedings; but how could she trust persons in their unfortunate state of mind, whom it was evident no oath would bind?[1] This is one of the great inconveniences of a double religion, but by no means the greatest. But the people will no longer be kept in the dark: on the very day[2] on which I am writing these prefatory observations to my *tenth* Book, a great nation, which has had the good fortune to have been for thirty years out of the trammels of the priests, and therefore is more enlightened than any of its neighbours, is striking the last blow at their rule. Their authority will be gone, but the French will not abolish the order—priests and excisemen will probably always be necessary. Let it be so! Only let them keep their proper place.

4. I think my reader will have begun to form a pretty correct idea of the nature of the Christian esoteric religion. I think he must see that Jesus, at least the *Romish* Jesus, was believed to be no other than a renewed incarnation of divine wisdom, of the Logos, called, in India, Buddha, or Saca, a revival or rather a continuation of an old system. In this book I shall discuss several detached points which will clear up this matter, if there be any remaining doubt, and proceed further to unveil the esoteric doctrine of Isis, and of ETERNAL Rome.

In my fifth Book I traced the history of the Avatars and Cycles in India and Judæa up to the ninth, the time of the birth of Jesus. I there said that I should return to that subject, and for the sake of clearness I have hitherto studiously avoided noticing any thing on this side of that epoch. If my theory be right, I ought to find traces of the ninth Avatar in a late day; and as, in all the other earlier Avatars, we have seen a certain similarity take place in the mythoses of the East and West, so we ought to find the same in the ninth. I flatter myself my reader will not be disappointed in this *expectation.* Like the renewal of the Argonautic expedition, the renewal of the Trojan war, &c., prophesied of by the Sibyl, we shall find in the latter Avatars a certain degree of similarity to the former; as we have seen, in many particulars, Buddha to be imitated by his successor Cristna. In fact, the theory of the system was, that every thing should be renewed at the end of certain periods, and that a new incarnation should take place. What periods these were may have been matter of doubt. This is proved very clearly by the passage in Virgil, and this it was which caused the history of the divine person in every age to resemble that of his predecessors. The fact of the imitation cannot be denied; it is clearly seen in the instance of Cristna, Buddha, and Bala-Rama, and, again, in Cyrus and Cristna, and, as I shall shew, in many others. I repeat, if my reader feel any doubt that it was the doctrine, let him read again the passage in Virgil. In the ninth Avatar, we shall find this proved still more clearly, and in a very remarkable manner.

---

[1] Luther's breach of vows, and his marriage, as he called it, with a nun, prove that if the Pope had trusted him with a secret under the most solemn obligation, though he might have kept it to-day, however innocent in its nature, he might have thought it right to divulge it to-morrow.     [2] July, 1830.

After we have discussed the ninth Avatar in the East and in the West, the next object of this book will be the tenth and last, and perhaps the most important of all.

In India, in consequence of the Mohamedan and other invasions from the North, which totally destroyed the Brahmin system of government, and overturned their seminaries of learning, not much can be found relating to the *tenth* Avatar; but this will be amply compensated in the West.

5. If my reader have attended closely to the argument, he will have perceived that there were always two classes of Avatars running at the same time : and yet, though *two* they were but *one*. This was because the Avatars were identical with the cycles, and the two cycles united formed a *third.* These were the ten presiding Geniuses of the Neroses, and the ten presiding Geniuses of the signs of the Zodiac—and the Neroses and signs revolving over and over, and crossing each other, until all, at the end of the ten signs, ended at the same moment, after a period of 21,600 years; or, if larger cycles be taken, 43,200 years, or 432,000 years. I suspect that the Vulgar were taught to expect a new divine person every six hundred years, and a millenium every 6000; but that the higher classes were taught to look to the year of Brahm 432,000 years, or, perhaps, to 4,320,000 years.

One more observation I must make on the renewed incarnations, which took place previous to the Christian æra before I proceed.

A singular admission is made by the learned Nimrod [1] in the following words : " The legend " of the birth of that bloody Cyrus, (he of the Gorgon's head,) concerning whom the Babylonians " informed Herodotus, is, though a strange and complicated one, precisely the same as that of " Romulus, and they are but one man." In another place [2] he says, speaking of a certain Habides, " In other particulars the reader will perceive the adventures of Perseus, Cyrus, Quirinus, " Hercules, Buzyges, and Triptolemus." Here we see the renewal of the incarnation just spoken of, in the fact of identity in the history of most of the ancient hero Gods, which has been fully demonstrated by Creuzer in his second volume. The case was, that all the hero Gods were incarnations—Genii of cycles, either several of the same cycle in different countries at the same time, or successive cycles—for the same series of adventures was supposed to recur again and again. This accounts for the striking similitudes in all their histories. Some persons will not easily believe that the ancients could be so weak as to suppose that the same things were renewed every six hundred years. Superstition never reasons. Let such persons as find a difficulty in this, read the work of the learned person who calls himself Nimrod, or a page or two of the work of the elder Pliny, on the cure of diseases, and they will no longer be surprised at absurd credulity. But I shall account for this satisfactorily hereafter.

The ancients of the West had not only the renewed cycle of the 600 years, but they had also that of the 6000,—at the end of which, ignorant devotees, who did not understand it, supposed that what was called the millenium, for 1000 years previous to the renewal of the world, would come. This proves the truth of the foregoing calculations. It completes the Hindoo system. In India, two systems may be perceived; one of the philosophers—merely the renewal of cycles ; the other of divines, at the end of the 6000 years, expecting a day of judgment and a millenium. The latter is a branch grafted on the former, by weakness and credulity.

If my theory be well-founded, two kinds of Avatars ought to be exhibited about the time of Christ. We have found an Avatar in the form of the celestial Taurus, and also one in the form

---

[1] Vol. I. p. 122.                          [2] Ibid. p. 218.

of the celestial Agnus or Aries, and we ought to find, in course, a third in the form of the succeeding Zodiacal sign, the celestial Pisces, the FISHES. This will be the next principal object of this book. In the performance of this part of my task, I shall have occasion to discuss several subjects which may at first appear irrelevant, but they will all be found necessary, more particularly for the purpose of elucidating the minor parts or the detail of the Romish system. In the course of this book I shall very often return to the secret religion which in the early ages of Christianity was held in the Roman conclave, and is probably yet held there.

If the identity of the modern Roman religion with the ancient be admitted, it does not appear surprising that the Pope should endeavour to revive all the ancient superstitions, which were not in themselves detrimental to public morals, but were in any way conducive to the increase of their own power, or that of the priesthood. In fact, we shall see that the *modern* Roman religion was only a reformed *ancient* Roman religion. This is not said with the least wish to insult the followers of the Romish Church, though no doubt it will offend, because it is unveiling what the church wishes to conceal. I will not say positively of the Roman Church at this time, but until about the time of the Crusades, I believe it was its faith, that the millenium foretold by the Sibyls would come. Whether they understand the length of the ages may be very doubtful ; and it is very possible that the experience of the non-arrival of the millenium in the last 600 years, may have caused them to lose the esoteric religion : for it would throw all their doctrines into confusion and uncertainty, and apparently falsify all their calculations.

It is very certain that the earliest Christians, of whom we have any account, depending upon the reported words of Jesus, that the final end and millenium should come before the people present at his speech should die, continued to entertain the expectation of it as long as possible ; and, in the same way, I have no doubt that the Popes entertained the hope, at the end of the 600 years, as long as possible, supposing when the end did not come that their calculations were wrong a few months or years, or that they had calculated by a wrong year; and at the last, when their hopes were quite extinguished, they concluded that another period was to pass away before its arrival. [1]

Soon after the time of Christ this astrological superstition prevailed, both among Christians and Gentiles. Nero was thought to be, or pretended to be, a divine person, and to open a new cycle. Again the same thing was thought of Pope Gregory the Great, and again of a Saracen called Hakim Bemrillah. [2] I have called it astrological superstition, and so, in reality, it was ; but astrology was so connected with religion that it was impossible to separate them. This superstition prevailed very much in the early ages of Christianity, but has been kept out of sight as much as possible by the priests in later ages. It was never the policy of the popes to instruct the people in the mystery—in that which the ancients kept concealed—even if they knew it. The popes wished for a gross religion for the people, such as, in their opinion, suited them—a refined one for the episcopal palace ; their Jesus was an incarnation of divine wisdom, of Iao, of ΥΗΣ. He was the

---

[1] For proofs that the end of the world was prophesied of in the Gospels, &c., see Matt. xxiii. 36, xxiv. 34, xxviii. 20 ; Mark xiii. 30 ; Luke xxi. 8, 9, 32 ; John v. 25 ; Philip. iv. 5 ; 1 Thess. iv. 15—17 ; 1 Tim. vi. 14 ; James v. 8 ; 1 Pet. iv. 7 ; Rev. xxii. 12, 20—and many other places, where *last time, latter days,* and *end of the world,* are named. So clear is this that such Christian writers as have any regard to decency have been obliged to allow, that the apostles in these matters were mistaken. Vide Baron. Tom. I. p. 656, Edit. Rom. Spondan. Epit. An. 57, S. 54 ; Mill's Prolog. to the New Test. p. 146, col. 2, apud Chishul's Sermon on Proph. When it was found that the end did *not* come almost immediately on the death of Jesus Christ, some of the latter Epistles were evidently written to account for and explain away the mistake which had taken place, probably arising from the doubtful meaning of the words Γενεα, Αιων, Παρεσια, and Τελος.

[2] Nimrod, Vol. III. p. 493.

ninth incarnation; and in the gospel history of St. John, he is made to promise another, and a last, i. e. *a tenth.* See John xiv. 16, 17, 26.

The charge against Socrates of Atheism long appeared to me quite incomprehensible, but the cause was this : he held one unmade, self-existent Deity, but denied the generated or created Gods, the produce of the first Deity. Onatus, the Pythagorean, declared that they who asserted one only God and not many *understood not what the majesty of the divine transcendency consisted in, namely in ruling over other Gods.* And Plotinus conceived, that the Supreme God was most of all glorified not by being contracted into one, but by having multitudes of Gods *derived from him* and dependent on him. [1] This, most clearly, is nothing but the doctrine of the Christians, in which the word *angels* is used for *Gods.* Every step which I take serves to convince me of the truth of what Ammonius Saccas taught, that the Gentile and Christian doctrines were identical, and that the quarrels of their professors were mere logomachy.

6. A very singular circumstance may be observed in the conduct of the Romish missionaries in the oriental nations. Where they find the doctrine of the renovating Avatars or incarnations already understood, and where of course concealment of their own doctrine is of no use, they avow and proclaim it, and announce themselves as messengers of Buddha, Cristna, &c., and that Jesus was only a renewed incarnation of the Divine mind. To the Brahmins who already know it they unveil the mystery. This enrages the Protestant missionaries to the highest degree. They accuse the Papists of the basest motives, never having the slightest suspicion of the truth. Some of the Jesuits actually turned, [2] or pretended to turn, or to be Brahmins, and preached the union of Papism and Brahmanism; maintaining that the religions of the city of Rāma in the East, and of Rōma in the West, were the same, with the single exception *that the head of the religion was then existing in the West ;* and that the Avatars were continued for ever by succession in the Popes. They may have said to the Indians, " We are all agreed except as to one point, and in-" deed we do not disagree in that in substance, but merely in name. Your Cristna is our " Jesus Christ, only he appeared or was incarnated in the West 1830 years ago. We do not " dispute what you say, that he was incarnated in a much earlier period, or at different periods for " *your* salvation ; on this we give no opinion, but he also appeared again at the time above named, " in the West, both for *your* and for *our* salvation, thus completing the salvation of the whole " world. You know very well that you are split into hundreds of sects; all this arises from the " want of a head, or hierarch. Your Cristna did not give you this head, because he foresaw that " he should return : he did return in our Cristna or Christ in Judæa, and he then completed for " ever his mission, his last Avatar, and he left all power on earth immediately transmitted by the " hand of St. Peter to the Pope, his Vicramaditya. [3] If your Cristna were the *ninth* Avatar, as you " allege, Jesus of Judæa was the *tenth*—the tenth who, you all acknowledge, was to come after " Cristna. That he was *that* person, he proved by his miracles, which were universally known to " be true throughout all the Western world, still witnessed by the continuance of the Papal power, " which is acknowledged by all its princes and rulers."—The speciousness of this mode of address no one will deny. I shall return to it presently.

7. Among the ancients there seems to have been a very general idea, that the arrival of the great person who was expected to come would be announced by a star. The births of Abraham, Moses, Cæsar, &c., &c., were all foretold by a star. [4] Calmet says, " I wish we could ascertain the ideas " annexed to the rising of the star said to occur at the birth of Abraham."

---

[1] Cudworth, Bk. i. Ch. iv. p. 544.

[2] For instance, Robertus de Nobilibus.

[3] Vicramaditya, explained by and by.

[4] Vide Calmet, Hist. Bible, Vol. I. add. art. Abraham.

The author of the Supplement to Calmet says, " I wish we could trace enough to ascertain the " ideas annexed in that country to the ' rising of the star,' said to occur at the birth of Abraham: " perhaps it might explain the prophecy of Balaam,[1] or might elucidate the ready apprehension " of the Eastern Magi, who, when they, in the East, saw a certain star rise in a certain manner, " and in a certain portion, &c., of the heavens, inferred that a remarkable child was born: " indeed, no less than the lineal King of Judea: and they journeyed many miles to visit him. " How came the rising of a star thus connected in idea with the birth of a child ? Was the idea " ancient ? And what might be its origin ? This alludes to the birth of Abraham having been " expected, and reported to Nimrod, as the Easterns say, by the Magi at his court. The same is " said in respect to the king of Egypt at the birth of Moses : we read also of a king, who dreamed " that immense splendour from the pregnant womb of his daughter illumined his kingdom. The " classic reader will recollect instances of other stars connected with great men : as the star Venus " with Julius Cæsar, and his family, Augustus, &c., in Ovid and Virgil."[2] Here we see this gentleman as near to the discovery of the mythos as possible. I have no doubt that if we had the full histories of the Herculeses and Bacchuses, we should find them all said to have stars at their births, like Moses, Christ, &c. As the conceptions were immaculate, the gestation ten months, the father of the child a holy spirit or other supernatural being, so they were all announced by a star. I flatter myself I shall convince my reader, that this story of the star was no fiction, but only a mythological or allegorical method of representing the conjunction of the sun and moon, and the conclusion of the cycle, at the end of every six hundred years, and the periodical restoration of some star or planet to its old place, or to its periodical rising in a place relative to the sun and moon, at the end of the time. Thus, whenever that star arrived at its proper place, they knew that a new cycle commenced—a new saviour would be born ; and for every Avatar, a star was said to have appeared. It was the astrological expectation of an incarnation on the renewal of every cycle : and the irregularities of the planetary motions, the precession of the equinoxes, and the neglect of making the necessary intercalations, rendered the times of the arrival of the periods and of the consequent incarnation doubtful. The time of the renewal of the cycle the astrologers could always nearly foretell, and we find they did foretell it at the same time, both in the East and West, as accurately as could be expected, when it is considered that, in later times, the principle was lost in both : but the fact that it was foretold in the East, is proved by Cassini and Abulfaragius, and in the West by Virgil, and the prophecies which I have detailed in Book V., the eighth Avatar of India, and the eighth Seculum of Virgil ending with the birth of Christ. The cycle, without regard to astrologers, would regularly renew itself. The changes in the heavens they could regularly foretell, but it was not thus with the Messiahs or the incarnations ; so that they scarcely ever exactly agree with the beginning of the cycle. Thus the astrologers foretold some one before he came, but who he would be they could not foretell. This is so marked that some of our divines set down the passage about Cyrus to be an interpolation, because he is named. And yet as his name is of so peculiar a nature, viz. a solar title, the word Cyrus meaning Sun, the prophet might give him this name in the prophecy, and, in consequence, the epithet might be given to him afterward as a title of honour. The true character of Cyrus כורש curs, is apparent from the fragment of his history, which Herodotus got hold of, and which has been thought to be a part of the history of Cristna. This speaks for itself, and strongly supports all my system. It binds the parts together beautifully. The prophets or astrologers might very safely foretell an incarnation for every next cycle or sacred period, in the period before it took

---

[1] Numb. xxiv. 17.     [2] Taylor's Sup. to Calmet, Dict. in voce Abraham.

place. If by the prophecy he incited his countrymen to such a thing as an insurrection or to do any other then desired act, his object would be obtained. If he failed, when he was in his grave, what evil would come to him ? He would be like our modern prophesiers of the Millenium, *forgotten*, that was all. If he succeeded, he then was a great prophet. A hundred persons—Dr. Mede, Mr. Faber, Mr. Irving, &c., have fixed the time of the completion of Daniel's 1260 years. If some great event should happen to support Mr. Irving, he will be a prophet—all the rest forgotten ; they are nearly so already. Is it not evident that if the art of printing had not been known, unless a mere accident had prevented it, Dr. Mede's explanation of the prophecies would have been lost ? *I* may thus speak of the celebrated prophecy of Isaiah, because the Rev. Doctor ADAM CLARKE has declared it to be no prophecy at all.

8. When all the circumstances relating to Pythagoras, and to his doctrines, both in moral and natural philosophy, are considered, nothing can be more striking than the exact conformity of the latter to the received opinions of the moderns ; and of the former to the moral doctrines of Jesus Christ. Had the moral doctrines of Pythagoras been adopted by the Western nations, in his day, there can be no doubt that the same good effects and improvement would have followed, which we know from experience followed the adoption of the same doctrines when taught by his successor Jesus Christ. In both cases, as usual, the philosophers were persecuted by the priests : in the case of *Jesus* they are said to have succeeded in crucifying him. In the case of Pythagoras, it is said, they succeeded in burning him and suppressing his doctrines. The mass of mankind were not in so improved a state of understanding as to be able to appreciate their worth : the success of the priests was owing to the ignorance of their followers. Yet notwithstanding the fate of the illustrious Nazarite, of Samaria, the state of things was widely different in his day : the human mind between the death of the Samian and the birth of the Samaritan had wonderfully improved. With the absolute loss of the secret meaning of the mythoses had sprung up a general contempt for their literal meaning, and thus the world had become prepared for the restoration or the revival of the salutary doctrines which before, under the discipline of the priests, it had despised. If it be admitted that the priest Caiaphas murdered the teacher, the philosopher, in spite of the remonstrance of the too easy Gentile Pilate, he could not suppress the doctrines. Thus the fine moral philosophy of Jesus, the Nazarite, flourished ; but it is curious to observe how soon philosophy and philosophers became reprobated by his followers : nor it was not till his beautiful system had been spoiled by fanaticism, and at the same time had begun to be loaded by artful priests with the trash, the corruptions, of the ancient mythology, fragments of which when they acquired power they never ceased adding to it, until at last, as I have shewn, or shall shew, it became nothing else but a commixture of the mysteries of the Magna Mater and of Eleusis with the nonsense of the vulgar Paganism. The whole of the ancient mythology was adopted and re-enacted and continued till new sects arose under the command of the insane persons Luther and Calvin, about the time of Leo the Tenth. These men in many countries struck off a great part of the abuses, but they were *fanatics*, not *philosophers :* another pruning knife must be applied.

Of the learned ancients of the West, Pythagoras was assuredly the greatest ; and as he was some ages in advance of his ignorant countrymen, he was laughed at and persecuted. Some persons without any good reason have doubted his existence. The superiority of his doctrines to those of his contemporaries, affords to me a convincing proof that he actually lived. The beauty of his morals, the novelty but truth of his astronomy and geometry, all which he professed to bring from the East, are of so superior a nature to those of his Western contemporaries, that it is really not credible that they should have created an imaginary being, to whom they could attribute these obnoxious, unheard-of doctrines : for instance, the 47th proposition of Euclid, the elliptic orbits of the comets. These considerations prove his existence, and the state of Eastern learning in his day, for it was only among the Brahmins of India that he could have learnt them. We know little certain of his doctrines : for, as they were not left in writing, his followers attributed to him all their own follies, but they were in perpetual contradiction to one another. Certain facts, however, they agree in, the truth of which is now admitted, and others the reason of which we may now discover. The golden thigh which he exhibited, no doubt was a golden Meru—probably a Linga and Arga, or Yoni, several of which are in the India-House, not explained to the vulgar, and therefore turned into ridicule, and taken literally by the priests of the day, in Greece, who had lost the meaning of the same emblems in their own mysteries. The same emblems are found among the ruins of the temples at Pæstum, the meaning of which was totally unknown at Naples, till my friend Col. Tod explained them.

In Herodotus there is an account of a certain Zalmoxis, a Scythian. Mr. Upham, in his History, has observed,[1] that the story of this person evidently shews, that Buddhism was the religion of the inhabitants of the banks of the Ister previous to the time of Herodotus, and thence he infers that Buddhism was the religion of the Celtic tribes. Now it is a very remarkable thing that Pythagoras was called Zalmoxis. In all this there is evidently some mystery concealed. Assuredly the particulars told of Zalmoxis have every appearance of being oriental.

9. We have seen in a former book, that Virgil in his poem alluded to certain prophecies of females called Sibyls. I think it necessary now to make my reader a little more acquainted with those persons. By the expression the Sibyls was generally meant a collection of books, written partly in very early and partly in later times by female prophetesses bearing that name. In the earliest time of Christianity they were considered by the fathers of the church as of the very first importance, in fact, of such very great importance, that the Christian religion might be considered to be almost founded upon them, and by most of the early fathers their genuineness was not only never disputed, but it was expressly admitted. They are now despised. The reason for this it will not be difficult to discover. I shall make a careful inquiry into the genuineness of these books, in the course of which we shall see various proofs as to who was the ninth Avatar in the West; after which I shall proceed to point him out in the East.

I repeat, if that, which all Christians professed, was not Christianity, I should be glad to know what was. They all expected the Millenium. The expectation is as clearly expressed in the Gospel histories as it is possible for any language to express any thing. Jesus, in some places, is made to say that another person would come after him, at a future period, while in others he is made by the compilers of those histories to say, that the world should end before the generation then living should pass away—even that some then present, standing by, should not die till the event took place.[2] All this proves, what is proved by a thousand other circumstances, that the principle of the Millenium was admitted universally, but that the detail, the particulars, were so far lost as to be a matter of very general doubt and dispute. The great difficulty seems to have been between two æras. Most of the Christian devotees imagined the consummation was to take place at the termination of the age then about to end, or just ended, and this the words of the Gospel tracts prove. Others of the Christians, judging from other expressions in the same collection of tracts, but probably in different tracts, which say that another person should come before the grand consummation, looked forwards to a more distant day. The most learned of the Gentiles supposed only that a happy æra was commencing, that some great and good man, some most excellent king, or great philosopher, or second Pythygoras—in short, they could not tell what—would arrive, only that a happy arrival would take place. This expectation the FACTS which remain to us clearly

---

[1] Hist. Buddhism, p. 27.       [2] Matt. xvi. 28 ; Luke ix. 27.

prove. The various Heathen and Jewish prophecies all clearly prove this; and the Heathen Sibyls much more clearly than the Jewish Prophets. All these prophecies, and the circumstances attending them, have long been a stumbling-block, a mystery equally to philosophers and to Christians. All explanations by either party have been alike unsatisfactory, and *this* both parties very well know, whatever they may pretend to the contrary. The mystery, I am perfectly satisfied, I have in part developed. At all events I am quite certain that the theory which I have unfolded and shall unfold, has accounted or will account for all the difficulties attending these prophecies, in a manner consistent with common sense, which none has ever done before. My scheme requires no miracles or interpositions of divine power. It requires nothing but the application of common sense, and that we should pay a little attention to the lessons of experience, and avail ourselves of the circumstances and scattered rays of light which have penetrated to us through the mist of antiquity. My theory only requires that we should believe man to have been in former times what we find him now, and reason upon him accordingly. Solomon's adage *that there is nothing new under the sun* is neglected because it is trite; but it is true: and I believe it was meant to convey a meaning much more recondite and learned than has been suspected.

10. It is an undisputed fact, that the ancient Jews founded their Cabala, although they held it to be unwritten and only handed down by tradition, on the book of Genesis, and particularly on the first verse. In this verse I have been endeavouring to shew may be found the oriental doctrines. Persons who attend to authority more than reason may be better disposed to attend to my reasoning, when they find it supported by the opinion of one of the most learned of our priests. Bishop Laurence says, speaking of the Jewish Cabala, "That singular, and to those, perhaps, "who penetrate its exterior surface, fascinating system of allegorical subtleties, has no doubt its "brighter as well as its darker parts; its true as well as its false allusions: but instead of re- "ducing its wild combinations of opinion to the standard of Scripture, we shall, I am persuaded, "be less likely to err, if we refer them to the ancient and predominant philosophy of the East: "from which they seem to have originally sprung, and from which they are as inseparable, as the "shadow is from its substance."[1] Indeed, the Bishop is quite right in what he says of the secret Jewish doctrines having come from the East. And if he be right, my reader will not be surprised that I should be able to point out in the Jewish books the oriental doctrines. That I am not able to make them *more clear* may be attributed to the fact, that I have no lexicons or other books to refer to except those of Christians, who exert all their ingenuity to disguise the truth, as I have shewn in the case of Parkhurst, in voce ראשית *rasit.*

The early Christians, in general, were fanatics, in the highest state of excitement: and most of them in that state became Monks or Carmelites, (all Monks being then in one order,) and thus under their head or superior they formed a secret, corresponding society, spreading over the whole world; and, directly in the teeth of the laws, holding their love-feasts and meetings in the night. They were not secret because they were persecuted; but they were persecuted because they were secret. Their meetings were directly in defiance of other laws as well as the law of the *twelve* tables. There can be no doubt that in the fourth or fifth century, the head of the order of Carmelites had power enough to correct or destroy, at pleasure, every gospel in the whole world, which was not preserved by heretics, and *they* were not likely to preserve them, as they did not admit their authority: and this is the reason why we have no manuscripts older than the sixth century. For one reason, when the Millenium did not arrive at the end of the sixth century, they were corrected or corrupted, as the Mohamedans say, to spiritualize the Paraclete. Although

[1] Pref. to Enoch, p. xlvi.

the seculars and the regulars often quarreled for power, and sometimes about opinions, yet there were various points in which they always agreed, and one point, and a most important one it was to the world, was the reprobation of the learning of the ancients. This object began to shew itself first in the burning of books at Antioch, as described in the Acts of the Apostles, and was continued by a succession of councils till the last canon of the Council of Trent against Heathen learning. All the manuscripts, which they preserved in the monasteries, were thus preserved for the sake of the vellum or skin. They were in fact preserved for the purpose of destruction. Here we have the cause, and almost the sole cause, which effected the darkness of the world for many generations. This is remarkably confirmed by the multitudes of Panimceste manuscripts which are found. Exceptions no doubt there were to this rule, but yet it almost universally prevailed.

St. Gregory is said by John of Salisbury, to have burnt the imperial library of the Apollo.[1]

11. There is one very important circumstance which is overlooked by writers on these subjects, which is, the change which was continually taking place in all religions. It is out of the question to suppose, that any of the systems or sects in the time of Strabo or Diodorus were exactly like what they were 2000 years before. No doubt every sect claimed to be *unchanged*, as all sects do at this day. But the whole which can be admitted is, that the original principles remain. On these accounts it is absolutely absurd to expect the Avatars to be found exactly the same, in successive periods, but they will be found more nearly so than, all things considered, could be expected.

Among all nations of the Western parts of the world, the prophetesses called Sibyls were anciently known. There were eight of them who were celebrated in a very peculiar manner, and a work is extant in eight books,[2] which purports to contain their prophecies. This work in several places is supposed to foretell the coming of Jesus Christ. They have been in all times admitted to be genuine by the Romish church, and I believe also by that of the Greeks ; in fact, they have been literally a part of the religion ; but in consequence of events in very late years not answering to the predictions, the Romish priesthood wishes to get quit of them, if it knew how ; several of its learned men (Bellarmine for instance) having called them forgeries. It is the renewed case of the ladder: being no longer useful, it is kicked down. The Protestant churches deny them altogether, as Romish forgeries. These Sibyls were held in the highest esteem by the ancient Gentiles. And it appears from the unquestionable text of Virgil, that they did certainly foretell a future Saviour, or something very like it. We find, on examination of the present copy of them, that they actually foretell in an *acrostic* the person called Jesus Christ by name. The most early fathers of the Greek and Roman churches plead them as genuine, authentic, and unanswerable proofs of the truth of their religion, against the Gentile philosophers, who, in reply, say, that they have been interpolated by the Christians. This, when merely asserted by them in argument, is not evidence ; nor is that which is asserted by modern Protestants. But when I reflect upon the prophecies which the reader has seen in the preceding chapters, I cannot help thinking that the acrostic prophecy is in good keeping with the others. I saw pictures of the supposed authoresses of these prophetic books in several places in Italy. Their figures are beautifully inlaid in the marble floor of the cathedral church at Sienna, and their statues are placed in a fine church at Venice, formerly belonging to the barefooted Carmelites ; they are also found placed round the famous Casa Santa at Loretto.

Dr. Hyde[3] says, "Chaldæis et Phœnicibus שבולא seu שבולה, Σιβυλλα, est cœlestis virginis

---

[1] Forsyth's Travels, p. 134.      [2] Published by Gallæus.      [3] De Rel. Cap. xxxii.

" signum: unde (cuique hoc perpendenti) fabula Sibyllarum tam obvia est, ut quisque fortè " dolebit quod, sine me monente, haud citius rem perceperit." He shews also that this is the same word (litterâ mutatâ after the Hebrew custom in certain cases) as the word שבולת *shult*, shibboleth. He then proceeds to shew how this celestial virgin was adopted by the Greeks and Romans, and became their famous Sibyl. This famous Sibyl became afterward the Queen of heaven, Maria.

12. Many authors, as well as Dr. Hyde, have endeavoured in vain to ascertain the meaning of the word Sibyl. Vallancey has observed, that in the *old Irish* the word means cycle; and he goes on to say, that as the Sibyls were beloved by Apollo, he supposes the cycle must have been that of the sun. Here I believe we have the truth. There was supposed to be a prophetess of each Sibyl or Cycle. We have the prophecies of eight. There was one for each cycle as it passed. At the time of Christ one was to come. For it may be observed, that as there could not be one for the first, that is, before the creation, there could in all be only nine to the consummation of all things.

The location of these Sibyls around the Casa Santa at Loretto clearly proves, that the Roman church privately maintained the mythological character of the Virgin Mary, and her close connexion with these celebrated ladies. It is absurd to suppose that they were placed in this very remarkable place by accident, or in ignorance. Then why should they be connected with the Virgin?

13. The Apostolic Constitutions quote the Sibylline oracles, and say, " When all things shall " be reduced to dust and ashes, and the immortal God, who kindled the fire, shall have quenched " it, God shall form those bones and ashes into man again, and shall place mortal men as they " were before: and then shall be the judgment, wherein God shall do justice." Here is, I think, in this very early work (for early it certainly was) an admission of the doctrine of a renewal of worlds.

Josephus quotes the Sibylline oracles concerning the tower at Babylon.

The earliest undisputed Christian writer, of whom any entire works remain, is Justin, and he pointedly says, that the Cumæan Sibyl prophesied the advent of Christ in express words.[1] Justin's first Apology was published not later than about A. D. 160. If the Sibyls were then forged, they shew how early the Christians began these practices. Justin tells the Greeks that they may find the true religion in the ancient Babylonian Sibyl, who came to Cuma and there gave her oracles, which Plato admired as divine. Clemens Romanus also quotes the Sibyls in his Epistle to the Corinthians.[2] They are also quoted by Theophilus Antiochenus, Athenagoras, Firmianus, Lactantius, Eusebius, St. Augustine, &c.

Clemens Alexandrinus quotes these words from St. Paul: Libros Græcos sumite, agnoscite Sibyllam quomodo unum Deum indicet, et ea quæ sunt futura. Clemens Alexandrinus also quotes Heraclitus as an authority that the Sibyls were inspired by God. St. Austin says the Sibyls, Orpheus, and Homer, all spoke truly of God and of his Son.[3]

There are several works extant, purporting to be the writings of Peter, Paul, and other early Christians, in which the Sibylline oracles are quoted as authorities in support of the Christian religion. These writings, for instance the preaching of Peter, are quoted as the works of the persons whose names they bear, by Clemens Alexandrinus, and, in fact, are as well supported in point of genuineness as the orthodox gospel histories themselves, though rejected by modern Christians.[4] Jeremiah Jones has laid down some rules of criticism by which he pretends to try the genuineness of ancient works. These rules or canons are false, to a ridiculous degree.

---

[1] Floyer's Sibyls, p. 225.      [2] Ibid. p. 329.      [3] Sir John Floyer on the Sibyls, p. ix.
[4] Vide Jones on Can. Pt. II. Ch. XXXIII. XXXIV., Vol. I. pp. 348—350.

Dr. Lardner admits that the old fathers call the Sibyls *prophetesses* in the strictest sense of the word.[1] The Sibyls were known as prophetesses to Plato, to Aristotle, Diodorus Siculus, Strabo, Plutarch, Pausanias, Cicero, Varro, Virgil, Ovid, Tacitus, Juvenal, and Pliny. Under all the circumstances it is absolutely impossible to deny that certain written prophecies did anciently exist; and the only question will be, whether we have the real originals, and if the originals, whether uncorrupted or not. It is evident that in the time of Plato they must, at least part of them, have been written; and the question arises, what can they have foretold? I think I am entitled to answer, The same as Isaiah, as Enoch, as Zoroaster, as the Vedas, as the Irish Druid from Bocchara, and as the Sibyl of Virgil—a renewed cycle, with its hero or divine incarnation, its presiding genius; but this I think will appear more clearly presently.

The Sibyls which we now have are of two or three dates or authors, and though, without exception, they all admit the *ten* ages, yet they are not agreed as to the time when the ages commence; some making them begin with the creation, some with the flood. This again proves that the system was lost. The first book makes five ages or generations before the flood. But whatever they may be, this want of connexion and system proves them to be unconnected works of different times and different persons. It clearly proves that they are not the produce of ONE fraudulent system, moment, or person. It adds greatly to the probability that they are, at least part of them, the produce of the cheats, or self-deluded fanatics, called Sibyls—dupes of judicial astrology.

It seems that by the word age or generation different things were meant by different persons, from which confusion has arisen. But the Sibyls *all* agree that there were to be what are called *ten* generations or ages of the world in all; but the Erythræan Sibyl is the only one who correctly states them to begin from Adam. Erythra was the name of a town in Ionia and also of the oriental ocean, at least as far as Ceylon or Taprobana. In a former book I have shewn, how the Jews and other nations expected the six millenaries: here is a clear admission of the ten periods which could be nothing but the Neroses, or periods of 600 years, as in 6000 there are ten six hundreds.

It has been said that the Erythræan Sibyl is the same as the Sibyl of Cuma.[2] I can admit this in the sense only of renewed incarnation. The Sibyl was said to have lived from the flood of Noah. Indeed, it was supposed, that she would live through ten γενεας *generations*, i. e. ten Sæcula, Neroses—which was the secret meaning, in the sense of Cycle, of 600 years. The Sibyls differ in their accounts in many respects from our present Bible, though evidently alluding to the same facts. This is a proof that they were not copied from it. For example, one of them says, that the ark rested on the top of a mountain in Phrygia. If the book of the Sibyl had been merely a Jewish or a Christian forgery, she would not have placed Ararat in Phrygia. The Sibylline oracles, in foretelling[3] that Joshua should rise again and re-establish the Jews, plainly allude to the renewal of incarnations. Indeed, this is clearly recognized in the Psalms: " Thou " takest away their breath. They die and return to their dust; thou sendest forth thy spirit and " they are created.[4] Thus thou renewest the face of the earth."[5] This was the Hindoo doctrine, and Judaism was virtually Protestant Brahminism.

14. The most important part of these oracles, is a very celebrated collection of verses in the *eighth* book, or the prophecy of the ERYTHRÆAN Sibyl, which in the first words forms the following Acrostic in the Greek language: ΙΗΣΟΥΣ ΧΡΕΙΣΤΟΣ ΘΕΟΥ ΥΙΟΣ ΣΩΤΗΡ

---

[1] Cred. Hist. Gosp. Bk. i. Ch. xxii.      [2] Gallæus, Cap. vi.
[3] Bk. v. p. 41, Blundell.      [4] i. e. renewed.      [5] Psalm civ.

ΣΤΑΥΡΟΣ. It will not be denied that this is among the very earliest of the records of Jesus Christ, whether it be a forgery or not, and it is very important, as it proves to every Greek scholar that the name of Christ does not necessarily come from the Greek word χριω *to anoint*, but may come from the word χρησος *benignus, mitis ;* for it is here written in the manner which was common in very ancient times, but in the later times disused, when the ει became changed into the η—as in σωτειρα, which became σωτηρια.[1] Thus χρεισος became χρησος. The η constantly changed into the ι, but I believe seldom or ever did the ι change into the η. This I say with diffidence, not professing to be learned enough in the Greek language to give a decided opinion on so nice a point, or to say that in all the Greek writers the change never occurs. However, no Greek scholar will deny that it *may* as readily have changed from the ει to the η as to the ι, and that any word which was written in ancient times with the ει, like σωτειρα, may have changed, like it, into σωτηρια.

The first name of Jesus may have been χρεισος, the second χρησος, and the third χρισος. The word χρεισος was used before the H was in use in the language.

If the name of Jesus were to be correctly represented in the Latin language from the Greek, it ought to have been Chreestus, because the Greek EI changed into the H—for the EI corresponds with the long E in Latin as Nimrod[2] observes. Of the mode in which the H in proper names changed into the I, M. Beausobre[3] has given a striking example in the name of Manes. He says, " Premièrement St. Augustin témoigne, que notre hérésiarque s'appelloit MANIN, c'est-" à-dire *Manen,* Μάνην, parceque les Latins substituent souvent un i à l'é long des Grecs." Thus Χρης became Cris or Chris. All this tends to prove, that the original name must have been spelt with the EI or the η, and not with the ι.

On the change in the letter H to I, Mr. Taylor[4] says, " The complimentary epithet " CHREST, (from which by what is called the Ioticism, or change of the long E into I, a term of " respect grew into one of worship,) signified nothing more than a good man. Clemens Alexan- " drinus, in the second century, founds a serious argument on this paronomasia, that[5] all who " believed in Chrest (i. e. in *a good man*) both are, and are called, *Chrestians,* that is, *good* " *men.*"[6]

15. There certainly at first sight is nothing improbable in deriving the word Christ from the word χριω *to anoint ;* but yet, on more consideration, it seems absurd to apply this to Jesus, who certainly could not with any truth be called either crowned or anointed, if the four gospel histories be correct ; as he never was either one or the other. It is true that kings and prophets were called by the name of Messiah or Anointed ; but unless a prophet had undergone the cere- mony of anointing, he could not properly be called anointed. For these reasons it is not unlikely, that the pretended derivation of the Latin word Christus from the Greek word χριω was an after- thought, adopted to serve some particular purpose.

There is unquestionably great difficulty respecting the name of Christ and the Christians. At first they certainly went by a great variety of names, and among others, by a very extraordinary one, namely Pisciculi or *little fishes.* But for *the present* we will pass this over. Dr. Heuman Witsius and Usher think, that the name of Christians was given them first by the Heathen Ro-

---

[1] See Payne Knight's Hist. of the Greek Alphabet, p. 105.      [2] Vol. III. p. 499.

[3] Hist. Manich. Vol. I. p. 72.      [4] Answer to Pye Smith, p. 113.

[5] Lib. iii. Cap. xvii. p. 53, et circa—Psal. 55, D.      [6] Strommata, Lib. ii.

mans, because, among other reasons, they shew this name has a *Latin*, not a *Greek termination.* This is a very important remark. Some observations on this subject may be found in the Palæo-romaico, Disq. iv. The name Christ may be fairly derived from the word Cristna, and the traits of similarity in the lives of Cristna and Jesus, which have been pointed out, will probably compel the reader to believe, that the *black* God of Italy was called in some way or other from the black God of India, or both from some common source, and not from the anointing of a man who *never* was anointed. We will now try to find how this arose.

The first unquestionably genuine *heathen* evidence we have respecting the name of Jesus Christ and the Christians, is found in Suetonius.[1] Here he is cited by the name of Chrēstus, not Christus. Suetonius, if he speak of the Christians, and that he does so speak I conceive no impartial person can doubt, must be allowed to be, in this case, a perfectly competent and unimpeachable witness, according to every principle of fair reasoning. The following are his words:

Judæos, impulsore Chresto assidue tumultuantes Roma expulit.

Tacitus speaks of *these same persons*, but calls them Christians, and their master Christus. This, on first view of it, seems probably a corruption, because one of the two must be a corruption, and who in later times could ever think of corrupting Suetonius into the Chrestus from Christus ?

Lactantius ascribes the name of Chrestus to the ignorance of the Greeks,[2] and says, Qui propter ignorantium errorem cum immutata litera Chrestum solent dicere.[3] Here is a most clear admission of an unimpeachable witness in this case, that the Greeks were *accustomed, solent,* to call Christ by the name of Chrestus, and not Christus.

Justin Martyr is the earliest Christian author of whom we have any undisputed works entire, and the very best authority in the Christian Church. In his first Apology he calls the Christians Χρηστιανοι. On that passage Ben David (that is, Dr. John Jones) says,[4] " To this meaning of " χριστος, Justin Martyr in his first Apology thus alludes, ὁσον τε εκ του κατηγορουμενου ἡμων " ονοματος χρηστοτατοι ὑπαρχομεν· i. e. from the mere name which is imputed to us as a crime, " we are the most excellent." On this passage Thirlby has the following note: χρηστοτατοι, Allusio est ad *vulgatam eo tempore consuetudinem*, quâ Christus ignorata nominis ratione nominabitur Chrestus. (Sylburgius.) Here is another decisive proof that in the time of Justin the Christians were commonly called Chrēstians. In the next page Justin calls the Christians χριστιανοι, and he adds, το δε χρηστον μισεισθαι ου δικαιον·—" To hate what is *good, chreston*, is not just." On this Thirlby in a note says (χριστιανοι) χρηστιανοι legendum haud immerito conjectavit Sylburgius, ex mente scilicet seu potius voce adversariorum. (Grabe.) And certain it is, that Sylburgius conjectured very truly. For it cannot be doubted that the χριστιανοι of Justin is a corruption, and a very absurd corruption. If he have been corrupted in one place he may in others.

Again Justin Martyr says,[5] " For we are indicted by the name of Christians, but now χρηστος " is a word for *kind* or *good ;* and such a word cannot surely be a just foundation for hatred."[6] It is impossible not to see that here the word Χριστιανοι or Christians is a corruption, and that it ought to be Χρηστιανοι or Chrēstians. Without this emendation the passage is nonsense, as every Greek scholar must see. In many other places, where Justin Martyr is made to speak in

---

[1] In Vita Claud. Cap. xxv.

[2] Ben David's refutation of the book called " Not Paul, but Jesus," pp. 277, 278.

[3] Lib. iv. Cap. vii. [4] Pp. 84, 103, 104. [5] Sect. iv. [6] Reeves's Justin.

the Greek of Christ and Christians, his page is evidently corrupted; but an attentive observation of the above passage will shew the reader why the word χρησος is excepted in it, namely, because it was *impossible*, consistently with the sense of the context, to do it. Therefore it is *half* corrupted; the word χϱησος could not be corrupted. Certainly Justin would not have called them Χϱησιανοι if Χϱησος had not been the common name by which Christ was known; and when, in other places, he calls him Χϱισος, this being in opposition or contradiction to the former, one of the passages. must have been corrupted. But it is absurd to suppose the χϱησος to be the corrupted orthography, because the corruption must have been made by the advocates for the ι not for the η—the work of Justin having always been in possession of the followers of the ι.

Tertullian says,[1] Christianus quantum interpretatio est, de unctione deducitur. Sed et cum perperam Chrestianus pronunciatur à vobis (nam nec nominis certa est notitia penes vos) de suavitate vel benignitate compositum est. Oditur ergo in hominibus innocuis etiam nomen innocuum.

Bingham[2] says, the Christians were not called Christians, i. e. Christiani, till the time of St. Ambrose. I suppose this was because they were called Chrestians.

Lucian, in a book called Philopatris, makes a person called Triephon answer the question, whether the affairs of the Christians were recorded in heaven, " All nations are there recorded, " since Chrestus exists even among the Gentiles :" ει τυχοι Χϱησος και εν εθνεσι. Thus it is perfectly clear that they were called Chrestians by the Gentiles, as well as by Justin Martyr, the first of the Christians in his day.

But the following evidence is conclusive upon the subject : Dr. Jones[3] observes, that this word is found in Rom. xvi. 18. He says, " And in truth the composition of it is χρησος λογια, i. e. " λογια περι τϑ χρηστϑ, oracles concerning Chrestus, that is, oracles which certain impostors " in the church at Rome propagated concerning Christ, Χϱισος being changed by them into " Χϱησος, THE USUAL NAME GIVEN HIM BY THE GNOSTICS, AND EVEN BY UNBELIEVERS."[4] Here I think enough is admitted by Dr. Jones to shew pretty clearly that his original name was Χϱησος, and that the ι was not changed into the η. but the η into the ι.

Again, Dr. Jones says, " Now it is my object to shew that the Apostle Paul, in two places, has an " obvious reference to the above interpretation of the word Χϱισος. The first is in Philipp. i. 21 : " ' For me to live is Christ, and to die is gain,' where the parallelism requires χϱιστος in the sense " of χϱηστος to correspond to κεϱδος."[5] " Onesimus was a slave of Philemon, a friend of Paul, " and his brother in Christ. While at Rome, that person was converted to Christianity by the " Apostle, who being now in chains, and as such having occasion for his service, detained him for " some time from his master, and then sent him back with this letter as an apology to Philemon : " ' I beseech thee, in behalf of my son Onesimus, whom I have begotten in my bonds, and whom I " ' again send back to thee, receive him as my own bowels.' His argument is this: ' As Onesimus, " ' while yet a stranger to Christ, was a mere eye-servant, driven by fear and compulsion, and " ' therefore worthless to his master, so by imbibing the spirit of Christ, he is now become a " ' faithful and valuable servant—τον ποτε σοι αχϱηστον, νυνι δε σοι και εμοι ευχρηστον, i. e.

---

[1] Apol. Cap. iii.; Ben David, pp. 277, 278; Bingham, Vol. I p. 12.     [2]. Book i. Chap. i p. 7.
[3] Lex. in voce
[4] To shew how far absurdity can go, Dr. Jones says, on the word Χϱισος, " Christ, he whom even God ANOINTED " WITH DIVINE POWER." He might as well say that the man who was hanged last week, was anointed with *a rope* : or, that when the Lord Mayor gave the King a dinner, he anointed him with *beef.*
[5] Ben David, pp. 278, 279.

" 'τον ποτε ὡς αχριστον, οντα σοι αχρηστον, νυνι δ' ὡς εν Χριστῳ σοι και εμοι ευχρηστον.'
" The paronomasia is perceptible only to those who understand Greek, and cannot be translated
" into any modern language."

Julian calls the Baptist Χρησος Ιωαννης. But, as I have said before, this matter is put out of
all doubt by the doctrine being expressly called by St. Paul χρησολογια, Rom. xvi. 18: Και δια
της χρηστολογιας και ευλογιας εξαπατωσι τας καρδιας, τον ακακων. St. Paul was writing
expressly against the Gnostic Christians.

But Jesus was called χρησος by St. Peter[1] as well as by St. Paul. I shall be told that this is
a various reading. True, all the manuscripts have not been corrected. But what says the learned
Bishop Marsh on this ? " 1 Pet. ii. 3: χρηστος, others χριστος, where the preceding verb
" εγευσασθε determines the former to be the true reading."[2] The Rev. Joseph White, in his
Criseωs Griesbachianæ, has very prudently not noticed this various reading : certainly one of the
most important in the book. This is either an accident or a fraud.

If my reader will consider with attention the passages which I have given above from Dr. Jones,
he must see the Doctor has shewn most clearly, that not only the Gentiles commonly called Christ
Χρηστος, but that the Gnostic Christians, as is I believe admitted, beyond all comparison the
most numerous sect of Christians, (because many sects were comprised in the term Gnostic,) as
well as the most learned and respectable, also called him Χρηστος. The important fact that
Christ was first called Χρηστος, and the Christians Χρηστιανοι, was as nearly lost as possible.
The accidental discovery of an inscription, which I shall presently notice, given by Dr. Clarke, in
his Travels, alone saved it. The orthodox must have been very industrious. But, as we have
seen, it is also quite clear that he was so called by both St. Peter and St. Paul, and surely this will
not be disputed.

In the Chrèstologia of St. Paul and Justin Martyr we have the esoteric religion of the Vatican,
a refined Gnosticism for the cardinals, a more gross one for the people. It seems very extraordinary, that when Lardner was noticing the Chrestus of Suetonius he should pass over the most
important fact—that Jesus was commonly known by the name of Χρηστος among that sect of
Christians, which was by far the most numerous and learned in the world. There never was
born a more cunning man than Lardner, nor one who knew better when to speak, and when to be
silent. In this instance he seems to have followed the example of Eusebius, when, in the life of
Constantine, he concealed the murder of his son Crispus. I cannot believe that Lardner was
ignorant that the Christians were called Χρηστιανοι. I have examined his indexes, but can find
nothing on the subject. And, in his pretended surprise that Suetonius should call Jesus, Chrestus,
he betrays the grossest disingenuousness. It is impossible that this learned man can have been
ignorant of it. But he found that if he noticed it, even to endeavour to refute it, he would bring
into observation what was as good as lost, and what it was very desirable to keep out of sight.
I cannot help suspecting that the conduct of both Lardner and White proceeded from the same
source—a wish to conceal the fact, a small part of the importance of which they saw.

16. The following extract from Dr. Clarke's Travels, relating to the Heathen monument just
named, furnishes a proof that the Χρηστος was known before Christ.

" Within the sanctuary, behind the altar, we saw the fragments of a marble cathedra ; upon the
" back of which we found the following inscription, exactly as it is here written, no part of it
" having been injured or obliterated; affording, perhaps, the only instance known of a sepulchral
" inscription upon a monument of this remarkable form :

---

[1] 1 Epis. ii. 3.        [2] Marsh's Mich. Various Readings of the N. T. Vol. I. Ch. vi. Sect. viii. p. 278.

ΧΡΗΣΤΟΣ (ʒ
ΠΡΩΤΟΥ ΘΕΣΣΑ
ΛΟΣ ΛΑΡΕΙΣΑΙΟΣ
ΠΕΛΑΣΓΙΩΤΗΣ
ΕΤΩΝ. ΙΗ

ΗΡΩΣ

" It is in honour of a youth of Larissa, in Thessaly, who died at eighteen years of age. As to the " words χρηστος and ηρως, it may be remarked that ALL THE EPITAPHS UPON LARISSÆANS, " which Spon has preserved, contain these words. There were many cities having the name of " Larissa ; consequently the city, whereof the youth here commemorated was a native, has the " distinction of Πελασγιωτης. It is named by Strabo. Though out of the *Pelasgiotis* it had " the name of Larissa Pelasgia." [1] I consider an ancient inscription of this kind as the very best species of evidence of any fact.

I consider the words Χρηςος at the top and Ηρως at the bottom of this inscription, to have a mystical meaning, and to be used as monograms, or as the D. M. are used on Roman monuments ; that Ηρως is a dialectic mode of writing Ερως [2] —and that both mean *the benignant being* or *Divine Love.* All the Heroes, who were properly so called, were Demigods or Incarnations of Divine Love or Wisdom. The fact of these words *being on all the monuments,* proves, that they are neither of them the name of a deceased person.

The *heart* may be seen in great numbers of the Christian monuments in the Vatican palace at Rome. The Roman Church has an office for the bleeding heart. As an emblem scarcely any thing is more common. But the way in which it is connected with the Romish Christian sepulchral monuments, and with those of the Heathens, shews a close connexion between them. The heart, being the emblem of the passion or sensation of affection of one person to another, came very naturally to be the emblem of divine love. [3] At first it may be thought that a figure of this kind is a trifling circumstance and not worth notice. I dare say it will be so considered, by persons who spend their lives in idle attempts to supply a Lacuna or two in a Greek play ; but, trifling as it may appear, I will compel the sceptic to belief, in the opinion I myself entertain. Here we have the heart upon an ancient Grecian monument before Christ, and connected with the word Χρηςος, and the name of Cupid or divine love Ηρως. We have it on an Indian monument of Bal-ii an incarnation of Vishnu crucified in the heavens, and we have it on vast numbers of modern Christian monuments in the Vatican at Rome. I defy any one to doubt the close connexion of the three. Circumstances of this kind are better than any written evidence whatever. This heart is often represented in Romish Churches with darts or spears stuck in it. Images of Christ are often seen with a spear thrust into the side. The image of Bal-ii has also a hole or wound in the side, and is described by an epithet which might be rendered into English *side-wounded.*

---

[1] Clarke's Travels, Vol. IV. p. 189, 4to.

[2] Dialectus Attica, ηδυναμην pro εδυναμην. SCAPULA.

[3] Over the altar of the Abbey-church at Tewkesbury, which is more ancient, I think, than the church, a winged heart is placed below the dove.

The Latin name of Christiani[1] was first given to the followers of Jesus at Antioch, probably as a term of reproach ; which is the reason, though they were perhaps not often insulted with it, why the Christian fathers in the earliest time never use it. And I believe it was not adopted till the doctrine of Paul was grafted into the gospel of Jesus, by the Roman or Popish Christians ; and then, for the first time, along with the *Christ crucified* of Paul, came the Latin word Christus.

Now, with respect to the word *anointed* it may be recollected, that every thing which was anointed had converted to it the quality peculiarly meant to be described by the word $\chi\rho\eta\varsigma o\varsigma$ of good, holy, sacred. To make the stone of Jacob holy and sacred it was anointed. To install a prophet into his office, he was anointed. To render kings sacred, they are yet anointed ; from this came the idea that Christ had his name from being anointed. And Cryso-polis and Christ are examples of the same confusion of language and idea. If the word Christ had its origin from the Greek word $\mathrm{X}\rho\iota\omega$ *to anoint*, in the acrostic it would not have been written $\mathrm{X}\rho\epsilon\iota\varsigma o\varsigma$ but $\mathrm{X}\rho\iota\varsigma o\varsigma$.

For all these reasons collectively, I conclude that the original name by which Christians were called was, followers of $\mathrm{X}\rho\eta\varsigma o\varsigma$ or $\mathrm{X}\rho\eta\varsigma\iota\alpha\nu o\iota$. I need not waste more words upon this point, for the fact cannot be disputed that they were thus called both by Christian fathers and Gentiles. But it is a point of very great importance. Dr. John Jones's admission, that the Gnostics and other early Heretics called Jesus by the epithet $\mathrm{X}\rho\eta\varsigma o\varsigma$, *Chrēstus*, coupled with the indisputable fact that Justin Martyr calls his followers $\mathrm{X}\rho\eta\varsigma\iota\alpha\nu o\iota$, is quite enough for me, without the authority of St. Peter and St. Paul.

17. No doubt I shall be asked the reason why this discovery which I have made of the ancient name of Christ has never been made before. To which I reply, Look to the decrees of Emperors, Popes, and Councils, almost innumerable, for the destruction of the writings of those persons who were likely to state or name the fact in ancient times, and you will see the reason. Had we the large and learned work of Porphyry or the works of Ammonius Saccas, no doubt we should have this and many other points cleared up.[2] If I be asked why Lardner did not discover it, I reply, No one is so blind as he who will not see. It is impossible that he can have been ignorant : and it is one of many examples of his disingenuousness. For the cause of truth it is a most fortunate circumstance that the priests in transcribing the works of Justin Martyr have overlooked the passage which the reader has seen. There can be no doubt that every place where he uses the word $\mathrm{X}\rho\iota\varsigma o\varsigma$ instead of the word $\mathrm{X}\rho\eta\varsigma o\varsigma$ is a corruption, and the same is probably the case with every writer before his time, *if any there were.*

Of all the Christian writers of antiquity there is no one of whose works I regret the loss so much as those of Ammonius Saccas. From him I have no doubt that we should have had the whole explained.

The word $\mathrm{X}\rho\eta\varsigma o\varsigma$ among the Gentiles, did not only mean *benignus, mitis,* but it also meant, when applied to a person, a being superior to man, of a benevolent nature ; precisely a divine incarnation. $\mathrm{H}\rho\omega\varsigma$ had the same meaning—*a demigod.* The result of the whole is, it is clearly proved that the Papal Christians changed the first name of Jesus from that of Chrēstus to that of Christus, with the Latin termination. In a future page I shall produce some very curious circumstances which will trace this Chrestos, foretold by the Sibyls, to India.

18. I will now return to the consideration of the Acrostic of the Sibyls. It is very certain from the passage in Virgil, that a great personage to renew the ancient times, to act again the Trojan

---

[1] Acts xi. 26.      [2] Vide Lardner's Works, Vol. IV. Ch. xvii. p. 111, 4to.

war, the Argonautic expedition, &c., was foretold by the Sibyl. It is very certain from the following passages of Cicero also, that a great person was foretold, and that for the purpose of this enunciation an Acrostic was used ; for though he is in violent opposition to the Sibylline prophecy, because it was used to justify the setting up of a tyranny, and asks, what man, and in what particular time the man is foretold, yet he does not deny the prophecy. And though he argues against the αχροςιχος, he does not deny its existence, but admits it.

Sibyllæ versus observamus quos illa furens fudisse dicitur. Quorum interpres nuper falsa quædam hominum fama dicturus in senatu putabatur eum, quem revera Regem habebamus, appellandum quoque esse regem, si salvi esse vellemus. Hoc si est in libris, in quem hominem, et in quod tempus est ? [1] (N. B.) Callidè enim, qui illa composuit, perfecit, ut, quodcumque accidisset prædictum videretur, hominum et temporum definitione sublatâ. Adhibuit etiam latebram obscuritatis, ut iidem versus alias in aliam rem posse accommodari viderentur. Non esse autem illud carmen furentis, cum ipsum Poema declarat (est enim magis artis, et diligentiæ, quam incitationis et motus) tum vero ea quæ αχροςιχος dicitur, cum deinceps ex primis versuum literis aliquid connectitur. [2] " We take notice of the verses of the Sibyl which she is said to have poured " out in a fury or prophetic phrenzy ; the interpreter whereof, was lately thought to have been " about to declare in the Senate-house, that if we would be safe we should acknowledge him for a " King who really was so. If there be any such thing contained in the Sibylline books, then we " demand, concerning what man is it spoken, and of what time ? For whoever framed those " Sibylline verses, he craftily contrived that whatsoever should come to pass, might seem to have " been predicted in them, by taking away all distinctions of persons and times. He also pur- " posely affected obscurity, that the same verses might be accommodated, sometimes to one " thing, sometimes to another. But that they proceeded not from fury and prophetic rage, but, " rather from art and contrivance, doth no less appear otherwise than from *the Acrostic in them*."

It is perfectly clear that in the time of Cicero there was an acrostic in the book. If that which is there at this time be not it, pray where is it ? If the Christians had forged this acrostic after the time of Justin, they would have contrived to insert Χριςος and not Χρειςος.

But I shall now produce in this case, I think, an unimpeachable witness, that the present acrostic was that in the Sibyl in the time of Cicero ; for *Eusebius* affirms, that Cicero quoted these very verses which contain the acrostic, and which he says was in the Erythræan Sibyl. If the father of ecclesiastical history may be credited, the fact of the existence of our present acrostic in the time of Cicero cannot be doubted. [3]

Justin says, " that the Sibyl not only expressly and clearly foretells the future coming of our " Saviour Jesus Christ, but also all things that should be done by him." [4] This was in the early part of the second century, and it exactly answers to our present Sibyls. It is very evident that, supposing the name of Jesus Christ to have been unknown as a man's name, which it might be in the time of Cicero, the poem might pass generally without the meaning of the acrostic being discovered, or without its being perceived that the letters formed an acrostic, except to the initiated.

The acrostic suited both the Heathens and the Christians. If it were Heathen, there was no occasion for the Christians to expunge it ; if it were Christian, there was no occasion for the

[1] See Floyer's Sibyls, last page, App. 336 ; and consult Martianus Capella, Lib. ii.
[2] De Div. Lib. ii.
[3] Vide Floyer's Sibyl, Pref. p. xx.
[4] Cohort. ad. Gr. p. 36, ib. 37, A ; Lard. Works, Ch. XXIX.

Heathens to expunge it : if the Heathens interpolated it, it served the Christian ; if the Christians, the Heathen. That the Christians should have corrupted the oracles is very likely, and even in some degree the verses which form the acrostic—but still keeping the acrostic. Indeed, after the observation in Justin, that all the things which had happened to Jesus were in the Sibyl, was noticed, I have no doubt that if there were any thing in the Gospels which was not in the Sibyl, the Christians would put it there. There is undoubted evidence that our Gospel histories underwent repeated revisions. Those who would revise the Gospels, would not scruple to revise the Sibyls.

Dr. Cudworth, in his fine fourth chapter has observed, that these oracles, though pretended to be kept locked up in the time of Cicero, were apparently well known. If this were the case, the difficulty of interpolating them was greatly increased. If the acrostic which we have were not the one alluded to by Cicero, I, again, beg those who deny it, to tell me to what the acrostic could possibly allude. It evidently alluded to the good being whose name was placed at the head of the epitaph on the youth of Larissa, who was not a hero as the learned and respectable Christian advocate of Cambridge, Mr. Hughes, [1] has expounded it. The circumstance noticed by Clarke, that it is on all the monumental inscriptions of Spon, shews that Clarke is right, and that the learned Cantab. is mistaken.

I beg my reader to recollect that if he expect ancient secrets of the kind here described—secrets guarded by the initiated with the greatest care and most solemn oaths, to be proved like a proposition of Euclid, he will expect what is very unreasonable, and what he will never find—secrets, too, endeavoured to be concealed by our modern priests. A probability, an approximation to a demonstration of the truth, is all that can be expected. Under all these circumstances, I cannot doubt that the acrostic which we have, was actually the acrostic referred to by Cicero, and that it meant ΙΗΣ ΧΡΗΣΤΟΣ the benignant Genius or new incarnation of Bacchus, or Buddha, or Divine Wisdom, the Protogonos of God, or ΘΕΟΥ ΥΙΟΣ ΣΩΤΗΡ. Although Cicero, in the passage I have quoted, does not give us the words of the acrostic, it is evident that it referred to some great person—but still it gave only a mystical name of him. In short, there is not the least evidence against either the genuineness of the book or of the passage.

How the Sibyls originally came to Rome it is difficult to say, for, to the story of their purchase, by Tarquin, I suppose no one now attends : but after they were burnt, in the time of Sylla, others were procured from Erythræa by ambassadors sent for the purpose, a fact which shews that they were well known to exist. Afterward, others were sought for by Augustus, whose measures Tacitus thus describes : [2] Quæsitis Samo, Ilio, Erythræis, per Africam etiam et Siciliam et Italicas colonias carminibus Sibyllæ, datum Sacerdotibus negotium, quantum humanâ ope potuissent, vera discernere. Here we see that these books were collected by Augustus from various places : of course the Erythræan from Erythræa, the Cumæan from Cuma, &c., &c.; and for several hundred years after his time, it may reasonably be believed, that their identity could not well be disputed. It is very certain that, though known to exist, they were not thrown open to the public, and I think it seems probable, that they were not published till the Christians got possession of them, and, for their purposes, published them, though they were quoted to support the tyranny of Augustus, and the attempted tyranny of others before him.

It is very certain that Scipio and Sylla both founded their claims to power upon the prophecy in the Sibyls—that an illustrious person or a saviour would come on the opening of some unknown, but speedily-expected, new age. This is confirmed by Virgil, and he is allowed to be

---

[1] See his Travels in Greece, Vol. I. p. 360, Ed. 4to.     [2] Annal. Lib. vi.

named in an acrostic by Cicero. In the time of Cicero Ιησες Χρης or Χρειςος was mystical, and meant, in Greek, the *good saviour* IE. Now a suspicion unavoidably arises, that *Jesus* (who was so called as we learn from Matthew, because that name meant *Saviour*) was also called Chrèst from this very oracle—*that* certainly being one of the sheet-anchors of the religion of Jesus in the earliest times. In the sense of divine incarnation, the appellation Ιησες Χρησος applies to all the pretenders to power noticed above ; and when Cicero was writing against the acrostic as a thing well known both to him, and to the persons to whom he was addressing himself, it was not a necessary consequence that he should recite the words of it. Almost every particular in the life of Christ as detailed in our Gospels, is to be found in the Sibyls, so that it can scarcely be doubted that the Sibyls were copied from the Gospel histories, or the Gospel histories from them. It is also very certain that there was an Erythræan Sibyl before the time of Christ, whatever it might contain. Where this Erythræa was, we shall presently try to discover.

No one can deny, that the Greek verses are of an inferior description : just such as might be expected from the Latin messengers sent by Augustus to translate them out of one foreign oriental language into another—neither of which, probably, they understood. Had he sent Virgil, it is likely that they would have been translated better. In order to produce the acrostic, the translator evidently worked with tied hands. The originals might be in Hebrew, or some other Eastern dialect, and might have the acrostic in that language in a word which might mean at once Saviour, Sun, and 608, (such for instance as *Mithra* in Hebrew,) and be translated at full length into Greek. We know acrostics were used by the Hebrews, from those used in the Psalms for the letters of the alphabet. Cicero could not quote thé words of the Sibyls, without being guilty of a great breach of the law.

19. The following passage of Dupuis shews that the Erythræan Sibyl might easily write the acrostic, and that in the Greek and Latin languages, for it is in both, as the reader will find in Gallæus : that is to say, that the knowledge of such a person as Χρησος the benignant Σωτηρ, or in Hebrew-Greek, ΙΗΣες, might be easily known to her, previous to the date of the birth of the Jesus Christ of the Romish Church.

" But the Virgin of the constellations, Isis, the mother of Orus, is really this famous Virgin
" mother of the God of light, as we have shewn in another part of this work, to which we refer the
" reader. We content ourselves here with saying, that the celestial virgin, of which the heaven
" offers us the picture at the equinox of the spring, with the celestial ark and the serpent, was
" effectually represented in all the ancient spheres with all the characters of that of the Apoca-
" lypse, that is to say, as a female newly laid in, and holding in her arms a young infant, which
" she suckles, and which has all the characters of Christ. Behold how the sphere of the Persians
" or of the Magi, in the first decan of the celestial Virgin is expressed : *Virgo pulchra* [1] *capillitio*
" *prolixo duas spicas manu gestans, sedens in siliquastro, educans puerulum, lactans et cibans eum.*
" *Caput Bestiæ :* and the sphere of the Barbarian adds, *pars* caudæ Draconis." " The Arabian
" Alboazar or Abulmazar goes farther. He gives, after the ancient traditions of the Persians, the
" real name of this infant. This is, according to him, he whom some persons call *Jesus* and
" others *Christ*, as we have seen in our chapter on the Christian religion, where we have reported
" this passage." [2]

One finds here, as in the Apocalypse, an infant newly born, placed on an elevated throne, and in the arms of a female lately delivered, who nurses him. And this infant is the Jesus, the Christ, the God who ought, as the child of the Apocalypse, to reign over the world. Can more marks of

---

[1] Scaliger, not. ad Manil. p 341                    [2] Tome III. p. 46.

similarity be expected? This is the young infant, the image of the sun born at the winter solstice, at midnight, the 24th of December, of which the Persians celebrated the birth, as may be seen in the ancient calendars, which fix it to the same day—*Natalis Solis invicti*—and of which the effigy was placed by them in the first degrees of the sign which, by its ascension at midnight on the 24th of December, fixed the epoch of this birth. This was as the horoscope of the God *Light*, who commenced his career with the year, and who ought, in the spring, under the sign of the Lamb, to make the day triumph over the night, and to repair the mischief done to nature by the winter [1]

That the work called the Apocalypse of St. John, just referred to, is of *very great antiquity* is clearly proved by the fact that it makes the year only 360 days long—the same length that it is made in the third book of Genesis, as Bailly has proved and Dr. Hales admitted. It assigns twelve hundred and sixty days to three years and a half. [2] The pious get over these matters by saying, that this was the prophetic year. It is impossible to help smiling at the credulity of these good people. No reason can be too absurd to be received by them.

Mosheim [3] says, they ALL *(i. e.* ALL the fathers of the second century) attributed a double sense to the words of Scripture, the one obvious and literal, the other hidden and mysterious, which lay concealed, as it were, under the veil of the outward letter. The former they treated with the utmost neglect.

" God also hath made us able ministers of the New Testament; not of the letter, but of the " spirit : for the letter killeth, but the spirit giveth life." [4]

The learned Burnet says, in his Archæologia, p. 279, " Duplex erat apud veteres, maxime " orientalis, theologiam et philosophiam tradendi modus δημωδης, και απορρητος : atque duplici " hoc stylo, in rebus naturalibus explicandis, uti mihi videtur Scriptura sacra : quandoque ad " occultiorem veritatem." Clemens Alexandrinus and Origen, the most learned of the Christian fathers, are much censured by the fashionables among the moderns for attributing a mystical sense to the Scriptures ; but it accidentally drops from Eusebius, that he, probably in secret, held the same opinion : he observes, κατα τινας απορρητες λογους Μωσεως, secundum arcanos sensus Mosis. [5]

Origen, against Celsus, distinctly admits, [6] that there are Arcana imperii in the Christian religion, which are not fit to be entrusted to the vulgar. He excuses it by saying, that there are the same in philosophy. Now I maintain, that this is evidence of the fact which cannot be impeached ; for he admits it with obvious unwillingness. And I have a right to ask, what were these arcana? It will not be sufficient to say, that they were only certain arcana concealed from catechumens : before I conclude, I shall shew that these were but a very small part of what constituted the mysteries of Christianity. Whatever fanciful meanings Origen might apply to the sacred books, it is very certain he would not publish in writings what he confessed to be the arcana. To publish these would be to confess his own infamy ; therefore, whatever he might pretend, his allegories were not the esoteric doctrines. I think I am justified in saying that, at least, part of these arcana were the doctrines connected with the millenium and the renewal of the cycles, and the secrets contained in the favourite Sibyls. Good God ! if all the authorities which I have produced, not only of learned *moderns* but of learned *ancients*, the chief persons of the religions, joined to the clear words of Jesus in the Gospels, will not prove that a *mystery* was concealed, what can be expected to do it? And surely, if there were such mystery, I have a

---

[1] Dupuis, *sur tous les Cultes*, Vol. III. p. 251, ed. 4to.

[2] Vide Rev. xi. 2, 3, xii. 6, 14, xiii. 5 ; and Calmet, in voce *Year*.   [3] Vol. I. p. 186, ap R. Taylor, Dieg. p. 52.

[4] 2 Cor. iii. 6, ap. Taylor, ib.   [5] Præp. Evang. Lib. xii. Cap. xi.   [6] Cap. viii.

right to endeavour to find it out: and I am certain that in great part, at least, I have found it out.

20. Bishop Horsley has some observations upon the Sibylline oracles, which are deserving of notice. He observes, that no *quotations* are to be found from these books in any of the Heathen authors, because to quote them was a capital offence. This seems a satisfactory reason why the acrostic was alluded to by Cicero, and no quotation of it made. But it is no reason to such of the Christians as sought the honour of martyrdom.

On this subject, it is said in a note of the Bishop's book, " It is remarkable, however, that " Celsus charged the Christians of his time with interpolating the Sibylline books. Origen " challenges him to support the accusation by specific instances of the fraud, and insinuates that " the most ancient copies of those books had the passages which Celsus esteemed insertions of the " Christians." [1]

There seems to be something very curious respecting a pretended debate between Celsus and Origen, in which I think we may find a little uncommonly well-managed priestcraft in Lardner and his coadjutors. The reader will please to observe, that it was the object of Lardner to *run down* the oracles, as it was the object of Origen to support them; and therefore he really wished to prove this famous Christian Apologist in the wrong; and, in so doing, to take the merit of candour in deciding against the Christian in favour of the Pagan—hoping that his secret reason would not be perceived. He therefore says, that Origen's answer to Celsus is not satisfactory. Now how stands the question? Celsus says, the oracles are interpolated, Origen replies that the passages in dispute are in all the copies, and that Celsus ought to have produced copies in which the alleged interpolations are not found. Now, I say this is a fair and satisfactory answer of Origen's. For, though Celsus was dead when Origen wrote, yet the answer must have been meant for the followers of Celsus, who could have answered Origen as easily as Celsus could have done, if he had been alive, by saying in what places the copies not interpolated were. And if they had not the passages called interpolated, they could at once say, Look, for instance, to the copy in the temple—which was in the custody of the friends of Celsus. Origen's answer is a challenge to produce it, or any copies not interpolated; and I say it is satisfactory, according to the received laws of modern biblical criticism. Origen could not be expected to produce copies, which he said, and his argument required him to say, did not exist; that is, copies wanting the passages. Lardner allows Origen to fail in the argument, (knowing that he did not fail according to the laws of biblical criticism,) to serve his own purpose, which was not an honest one. He used an economical argument.

In the time of Origen the manuscript of the oracles must have been in the temple under the statue of the God, and in the keeping of the Pagan high-priest, where it was totally impossible for the Christians to get access to it. And yet it seems, according to Justin, that this manuscript contained every thing which had been done by Jesus Christ. If we admit that the present copy is all corrupt, yet we must allow that the real Sibyl contained the same in substance as the one we have, at least if we can believe Justin.

The Bishop has observed, that it is to the Cumæan Sibyl that Virgil refers for the prediction, that a great person would appear. Now this is true, and it is very remarkable, that this shews a duplication of the prophecy, because it is the Erythræan Sibyl in which we have the acrostic. This proves that we have them only in a mutilated state, as well as a corrupted one, as is evident enough: but this cannot apply to the passages relating, as Justin says, to Jesus Christ, because they must have been in the copy in the temple which was not destroyed till after Justin's time.

---

[1] Contra Celsum, pp. 368, 369, E.

The Bishop repeatedly observes, that the style of the prophecy is exactly that of the Jewish prophets.[1] This justifies me in what I have said about Isaiah. He says, " The sum of the " character is the same in both : in its nature unequivocal, and such as even in the general outline " could not possibly belong to different persons in the same age." Before this, in p. 17, he has shewn from dates, that this use of the prophecy by Virgil, in foretelling a child to be born, (how like Isaiah's!) *cannot by any possibility have been meant at that time for Julius Cæsar or for any child of Pollio's.* It shews that it was of the same nature as the prophecy of Isaiah. But if we recollect that we have found all the Gentile rites and ceremonies, and many of their most recondite doctrines, with the Jews, it is not very surprising that what may be called their mythologic prophecies should be found with them also. When the *Interpretatio novi Sæculi*, Virgil's fourth Eclogue, was written (U. C. 714), Nimrod has observed, that Octavius had not laid open claim[2] to the supreme power, but I think his family always affected it. Nimrod says[3] he believes, " that the conduct of Octavius flowed from the same superstition, as the poem which Virgil wrote " the same year." This I think to be correct, and that he was believed to be the presiding Genius of the *ninth* age, as Juvenal properly marked it. The expectation of the new Iliums, new Argonauts, &c., evidently shews a knowledge of the system. It is much the fashion to abuse Virgil for baseness and servility, and he may have been both base and servile, but I think it very likely that he really believed that Augustus was the promised person. I shall, however, discuss this matter more by and by, when I examine the characters of the first two Cæsars.

The ultima Cumæi venit jam carminis ætas of Virgil, exactly agrees with the doctrine of Juvenal, for Virgil announces, that *the end* of the age sung of or celebrated by the Lady of Cuma had arrived. He says, " The last age (or time) of the Cumæan verse has now arrived." The Cumæan Sibyl might have sung of the *eighth* age, the Erythræan of the *ninth ;* but both, of the advent of an expected Saviour,—new Iliums, new Argonauts, &c. : and, in the expression of Virgil, if I rightly understand it, an equivoque is included. It is usually construed to mean, that the Cumæan Sibyl sung of the last or finishing age : but it may, and no doubt did, mean also, the last end of the cycle or age celebrated in the verses of Cuma ; but this did not necessarily mean the last of all ages, past and future. But it is not Cicero only who recognizes the acrostic, for I learn from Floyer in his Sibyls,[3] (who, however foolish, is a very useful writer for authors referred to,) that the acrostic was noticed by Dionysius of Halicarnassus, who lived more than thirty years before Christ : and by Varro, who lived more than a hundred and twenty : and, what is very important, they both admit that there were disputes about the acrostics in their day,—some persons maintaining that they were forgeries,[4] others the contrary. But the disputes prove the existence of the acrostic. The disputes are what we might expect : the followers of Scylla would maintain, that *he* was the *benignant Saviour ;* the contrary party, that the acrostic was a forgery : for, it may be observed, that the words Ιησυς Χρησος or Χρειςος are not necessarily *a proper name.* But if they constitute an honorific solar title, they would be circumstanced exactly as the name of Cyrus was—a solar title adopted by a man—and thus it might be given to Jesus Christ, or to any one else.

I now conclude what I have to say of the Sibyls, but it has naturally brought me to the consideration of Cæsar, who, I shall shew, was a *ninth* Avatar. But before I proceed to the proof, I shall, in the next chapter, discuss many preparatory matters.

---

[1] Page 22.          [2] Vol. III, p. 464.          [3] P, 463.          [4] Pref. p. xx.

580                               Χρης, Chres.


## CHAPTER II.

Χρης, CHRES.—INDIANS IN THRACE.—COLIDA.—CERES, Χρης.—SUBJECT CONTINUED.—HERALD, KERUX.—
CHALDEANS WHERE FROM.—GOSEN. — ERYTHRÆA, DIU, DIS.—COLLIDA OF SOUTH INDIA. — INDIANS IN
THRACE.—RITTER.—MEANING OF THE WORD Χρυσος. — CHERSONESUS.—MYTHOS IN AFRICA, MARCUS.—
GAZA-MERE.—BACCHUS.


1. In the first chapter of Book VII., on the Ionians, it was observed, that the city of Amphipolis, near the Strymon in Macedonia, was called by the names of Chryso-polis and Orpheus. Now I think this Chrysopolis is the same as Χρησος or Χρησος-πολις, and we have here the city of the Χρησος or *good Genius*, the Messiah Cyrus. We see here the Χρησος or Χρησος converted into the Χρισος or Χρισος.

In Polydore Virgil[1] is the following passage: Alii demum sine conjugibus degere, ut quidam Thraces, qui CTISTÆ, id est, creatores vocantur: et Esseni, tertium apud Judæos philosophorum genus. The following is the translation of Thomas Langley.[2] "Some people lived single, as cer- "tain nations called CRISTE and Esseni among the Hebrews, which did abhor the calamities and "trouble in marriage." This shews that the Ctistæ is an error of the press and ought to be Cristæ: and here we have probably the Christian monks in Thrace, ancestors of the monks of mount Athos, long before the time of Christ.

If we turn to Scapula we shall find that χρησις and χρησις have precisely the same significa- tion, and are convertible terms. In short, it is evident that they are used indiscriminately for one another. It is not to be supposed that in the very early times, perhaps before the invention of letters, when the names of places first took their rise, the same strictness in the pronunciation, or at first, after the invention of letters, the same strictness in the writing of them, took place, as was observed by the Greeks when they became, in regard to their language, the most fastidious people in the world. It has been shewn that the Tau in the ancient languages was constantly written by a cross. For reasons which will appear hereafter, I think the root of the χρης has been ΤΡΣ-ΧΡΣ. It was the constant practice of the Greeks to soften the harsh sounds of their language. Thus Pelasgos became Pelagos, Casmillos Camillos, Nesta Nessa, Cristos Crissos; where a strong con- sonant comes after the σ, it is often dropped. Αγνωστος became ignotus, the island of Χρησος Χρητος, the country of Crestonia had its capital *Crisa* and its port *Crysos*. In the Eastern lan- guages we find Hindo-stan, Chusi-stan, Turque-stan. In the West, where the Greek prevailed, we have Mauritania, Aquitania, Bri-tania. We can scarcely doubt that the *stan* and *tan* are the same. We have the town of *Cressa* in the *tan* or *stan* of *Cres*.

Cortona in Tuscany was formerly Croton,[3] from Croston, Croton; Tyrseni, Tyrrheni; Hetrusci, Hetrurii; Creste, Crete. The identity of the Cretans and the Cressæans is proved by their traditions, that the latter came from Crete.[4] The same effect is found in other languages; for instance, in the English, Fasten, Fassen; Whitsunday, Wissunday; Christening, Chrissening. With the Chal- deans the Sigma and Tau were convertible, as in Tur and Sur, and in Assyria called Aturia, as Dion Cassius has observed.[5] I suspect it was from the indiscriminate use of these two letters that

---

[1] Typis Jacobi Stoer, impensis, Nicolai Bassei, M. D. X. C. Cap. IIII. p. 21.     [2] Printed Anno 1551, fol. x.
[3] Ency Brit Vol I p. 729.            [4] See Philological Musæum, No. I. p. 143.
[5] Apud Drummond, Orig. Vol. I. p. 152.

at last the sigmatau arose. The S was not only in Chaldaic and Syriac, but also in Greek so frequently changed into the T, that Lucian composed a dialogue upon it.[1] In the Latin language, in old manuscripts, the c and the t are often written indiscriminately; as, for instance, *initiale* with a c. From this, I think, came the French ç, which is really in figure nothing but the sigmatau of the Greeks.[2] But though I have met with an assertion that the sigma and the sigmatau were used indiscriminately by early Greeks, I rather believe the change was from χρησος to χρησος, and χρισος to χρισος, conformably to the practice of softening, similar to that of Casmillos to Camillos, of Nestos to Nessos, &c. The sigma has something very particular about it; it is neither a mute, liquid, nor aspirate; therefore it has been called *solitarium*. It partakes something of the sound of the *Theta*, and, accordingly, we find that it was frequently employed by the Lacedæmonians for that aspirate. Thus Aristoph. Lysistr. 1302, Απολλω σιον—1303, Ασαναν.[3] This, I think, in part accounts for the indiscriminate use of the Sigma and the Tau, and the rise of the Sigmatau.

Col. Van Kennedy[4] says, " As long, therefore, as the etymologist confines his identifications of " words to those only which agree in sound and meaning, he proceeds on the surest grounds." Now where I cannot proceed on sound and meaning, I have proceeded on identity of letters and meaning. I have shewn that the letters are identical, or are those letters which, in the use of the alphabets, have actually, in each case, been exchanged: as C for G, as Camel for Gamel, H for Ch, or Heth for He, &c., &c.—the latter example evidently a corruption, and the former, the third letter in each alphabet—identified by its position, the third, and its power of notation, 3.

2. I have already proved that Thrace was peopled by a colony from North India ; and, that the Χρησος or Cristna or holy person appertaining to the latter country was crucified. From this, I think, there can be no doubt that on that account it was accounted χρησης in its sense of a *prophet* or an *oracular* or *benignant* person. It was a holy land; in every thing as far as possible an imitation of a holy land in India. In some maps it is written Grestonia, and a little to the North the Greæi are placed, and in the Peninsula of Mount Athus is Crossæa, often written Cryssæa.[5] Jesus was sometimes called Chrostus, that is, Chrost or Crost, and the district noticed above called Crossæa, was probably Crost-ia; both evidently corruptions. In the country where the sacred Strymon or *Palestinus* or Ioneus runs, there is a Doab or Mesopotamia, formed by the Strymon, or more largely by the Nessus, and the Haliacmon or Ioni-cora; it is called Sintica, and by Ptolemy Sindus, which is Sinde, a corruption of the Sinde or country of Indus of Asia. It had also another most important name which I take to be its first name—Crestona or Crestonia,[6] that is, Creston-ia, which means the country of Creston or the good Genius or Crestus. By D'Anville it was called Grestonia, and its capital Cryssa. My reader will recollect what I have said of Cristna having his name from the idea of good Genius. This Crestonia is a very sacred district; in it is the town called Chrysopolis or, as I have before shewn, Chrystopolis, *i. e.* Chrystos-polis. This town was also called Eion or Adon, and Iamboli or Emboli, the same name as the town of Emboli-ma on the Indus, and Ioni-keni, and Orpheus,[7] Or-phi, the voice of Aur, or of the oracle of Orus and Iona, and Amphi-polis, or city of Amphi or Omphi, or the OM, or the voice or oracle of OM. The district around it was called Edon or Ηδωνιδα, the same as the Garden of Eden ; and, as I have just said, the country in which it stands is called Crestonia[8] and Sintica. In this district stands a town called Heraclea Sintica.[9] There is also adjoining to the country of Crestonia, a Bothæa,

---

[1] Hagar, Diss. Bab. Brick. p. 49.
[4] Origin of Lang. p. 239.
[7] Bryant, Anal. VII. p. 129.

[?] Astle, p. 81.
[?] Smith's Classical Atlas.
[?] Rennell.

[?] Dunbar, Gr. and Lat. Lang. p. 22.
[6] Rennell, D'Anville.
[9] D'Anville.

that is Buddhæa. I have before noticed that all the monumental inscriptions found by Spon in this district, called Larissa Pelasgica, had, at the top of them, the mystic word Χρησος, and at the bottom the equally mystic word Ηρως. This was precisely similar to the practice of the Romans in placing the letters D. M. at the head of their sepulchral monuments. This was evidently a country sacred to the God of Delphi, the Ie or Ii or Jah of the Hebrews, which is the name we find used for the God of the Hindoos, either by itself, or compounded with some other word.

The whole country of Crestonia may be correctly called a Doab or Mesopotamia, as I have just said, formed on the West by the Axius or Oxus, or more largely by the Haliacmon, now Ionicora, and on the East by the *Nessus*, on which stands the city of Nyssus, and Nico-polis, which shew the real name of the river. These rivers, noticed by me in Book IX. Ch. V. Sect. 8, flow from a chain of mountains called Bactriana or Balk [1] or Balkan, and through them is a pass called Chumla, the very names of the mountains, and a pass through them, on the North of India, leading to the country where the above-named places are found. In this Mesopotamia of Greece are Mounts PAN-*gæus* and BAL-*beus* and TRI-CALA, all Indian names. In Mount Bal-beus was the town before noticed called Heraclea Sintica [2] (i. e. the Indian Heraclea). The promontory on which Byzantium stood was called Cryso-ceras; and the present Scutari, opposite to it, was called Chryso-polis. The circumstance of the Chryso-polis being in the district of Crestonia, proves what I have before said to be true, that Chrysopolis ought to be Chrēstopolis, and the letters i and y ought to be the η ; and, that they were not sacred to Gold or called from Gold, but that they were sacred to the good Genius, or called from the good Genius, and that, therefore, originally the name was Chrēstopolis. It was, probably, in reference to this superstition that Constantine selected this place for his city.

The tablet on which is the inscription with the Χρησος and ΗΡΩΣ, was found by Dr. Clarke in a place where I should expect to find it ; at Delphi, in the temple of the God called IE. [3] Under Parnassus, in a Gymnasium, where a monastery called Pana-ja (a name sufficiently Oriental— Hindoo I should think) now stands ; adjoining to the Castalian fountain which flowed by the ruins of CRISSA, probably the town called Crestona, into the Crissæan Bay, *i. e.* Cresta and Crestiæ bay. Dr. Clarke has observed what I should have expected to find, that the foundations of the ruins at Delphi are Cyclopæan. The spelling of the χρησος on the Tablet, and of the district Cres-tonia, clearly prove that the word Crissæan and Crista are the same.

In Dr. Clarke's map, Delphi, or a place close to it, is called Crissa ; and an ancient scholiast upon Pindar affirms, that under the name of Crissa, the city of Delphi was designated. This is a most important fact, but it is nothing but what other circumstances would lead us to expect. [4] I think I may assume that the Χρησος on the tomb of the youth of Larissa was the name of Apollo : but we have his priest called Chryses, not Chrystes. In Guzerat or Syra-strene there are a place called Iuna-stan and a district called Larice. In Thrace there were a town called Iona, and a place called Larissa, names evidently the same. In the Indian Larice the Palli were located, and there is a town called Palli-stana. Not far from the part of Thrace above-named were situated the

---

[1] It cannot be said that the Turks have given the name of Balk and Chumla to the places in Mount Hæmus, in remembrance of the places which they left in their own country, because they never possessed the Eastern places of this name. Their residence was beyond the mountains to the North.

[2] Heraclea, in Lat. 39¼, Long. 49¾, the Turks now call *Erekli*. (See D'Anville.) Another town in Long. 44¾, Lat. about 40¾, is called Heraclitza. Heraclea Sintica is now Seræ, or *qu.* Tricala ?

[3] We must not forget that all orthodox persons maintain that Jesus Christ was the Jehovah incarnated ; that is, the IE incarnated, whom they call Jah.

[4] Travels in Greece, Ch. vi. p. 183, 4to.

Palli or Pallestini; and the Strymon was called Pallestinos, and near it was Larissa. In Guzerat is a mount, a place called Satrun-ja. Here, as I have before remarked, is the Saturn of the Latins and Greeks. Not far from the Strymon is the promontory of Mount Athos, which is the very picture of Guzerat, and on each is a town of Diu or Dium, and near the latter an island of Diu, and both are sacred isles or districts. Athos is the Egyptian Goddess Athor[1] the Mother, and close to Guzerat is a river, called anciently Mais, now Myie, or Maia, or Maria. And what marks the similarity more between the Sinde or Indus of Thrace, and the Sinde or Indus of the East, and indeed puts identity out of doubt, is, that Herodotus informs us that, in his time, like the Indian wives now, the Thracian wives were sacrificed on the death of their husbands, and that it was a point of contest among the wives which should have the privilege. This I think completes the picture. The Thracians of rank were generally burnt after their death, and their ashes put in urns and buried in tumuli. This practice is noticed by Solinus[2] and Herodotus.[3] Stobæus,[4] who cites Herodotus, says, that the case of the Thracian women was exactly parallel with that of the wives in India, for they were burnt with their husbands. There is also a passage of Mela[5] which I think can mean nothing else; but the words fatum jacentis, used by him, are of doubtful import.[6] The Indian practice, I believe, was known to Diodorus, Cicero, Propertius, Strabo, and Plutarch.[7] The Jupiter Patröos at Larissa, (Ζευς Πατρωος of Pausanias,) was represented with three eyes: this is evidently Indian.

In the Arabic language of the Koran Jesus Christ is called Ischa. From this has come the word Larice or Larissa. The word Lar is in fact Lord—a word I shall explain hereafter. The whole name has arisen from the regimine style of the Hebrew, to which in fact the names of almost all cities and proper names are to be attributed. Larissa was the country of the Lar-ischa the Lord Ischa, or the Saviour Lord, from the Hebrew יש iso, to save. Thus it became the country called Lar-ischa. We only know the names of most places from the sacred books of the respective countries, and thus we only know their sacred or mythic names. There were no books before the time of Herodotus, which were not merely mythic, although called historical. And as there was an universal mythos, we find the universal mythos every where shewing itself in the names of places. I do not remember one of the Gods of the Western world, who had not the title of Saviour, as Ζευς, Σωτηρ. In the same way we find most of the Gods of India to have the word ishwara or iswati attached to their names; for instance, Sara-iswati, Buddhiswara,[8] which our Indian scholars tell us, means Lord, and, when applied to the female Sarah, a mere title of honour, as Lady. This, as I have previously remarked, is nothing but the Hebrew and Greek word for Saviour, יש iso and ζαω to save, with a local, an Indian, termination.

I think the words Venus and Cupid were often used for the same idea, and also the Indian Cama, and the word Ischa the wife of Abraham, and the Arabic name of Jesus. This almost identifies the benignus Χρης, with the saviour Isis. In the same way Kanyia was the name of the Indian Venus, but it was also the name of Cristna. From a passage in Burckhardt's Travels in Arabia[9] I think the adoration of the mother and child, the latter called Aysá, must have prevailed in the temple of Mecca before the time of Mohamed. The ancient name of the temple was Beitullah, house of God.[10] Solis et Lunæ nomina in sacrâ literali Brahminicâ linguâ omnia sunt generis masculini. Bartholomeus[11] says, Chandre seu Soma, Luna Brahmanibus masculini generis.[12]

---

[1] Drummond, Punic Inscrip.     [2] Cap. xv.     [3] Lib. v. p. 183, ed. Steph.
[4] Cap. cxx. p. 521.     [5] Lib. ii. Cap. ii.
[6] From the very valuable collection of most learned manuscript treatises of the late Mr. Moyle, now in the possession of Sir J. Copley, of Spotsborough, Bart , his descendant, to which I have before referred.
[7] I quote these names from memory.     [8] Tod, p. 519.     [9] P. 164, 4to.     [10] Ib. p. 165.
[11] Syst. Brach. p. 2.     [12] Ib. p. 7.

Neanthes Cyzicenus writing concerning the Macedonian priests says, they invoke Βεὸυ to be propitious to their children.[1]  This Βεὸυ is Buddha.

I have just now noticed a town called Heraclea : this leads me to repeat an observation on the termination, by the word *cula*. We have Jani-*cula* or the *cula* of Janus ; we have Hera-culas without end in the West; and we have the Hera-culas on the coast of Malabar, in India, where we have also Igni-culas, and Tri-çalas or Tri-culas. I have in another place derived the word Hercules from *Heri* the saviour and *clo*—the Chaldee כלה *clo :* כ *k* final=500, ל *l*—30, y *o*=70= 600. Then Mount Janicula would be, the mount of the cycle sacred to Janus; Igni or Agni-cula, the cycle of the Saviour or of the Lamb, (as I have shewn was the meaning of the Sanscrit word Agni in the Yajna sacrifice,) or of Fire, or the sacred Sol, invictus, the Saviour : and Tri-clo, or the cycle sacred to the Trimurti or Trinity. If this is accused of being very mystical, I reply, It is not more mystical than the increase and decrease of Jesus and John at the equinoxes and solstices ; or than the baptism by fire and the Holy Ghost—all parts of the same mythos.

3. Mr. Bryant shews that the Gymnosophistæ Æthiopum are mentioned by Hieronymus,[2] and that they extended from the INDUS to the GANGES under the name of Ethiopians and ERYTHRÆANS. He adds, they resided, according to Arrian, below Carmania, in the mouth of the great river, near the island Crocale.[3]

Again,[4] he says, " Arrian, Hist. Indic. p. 336, Oras tenent ab INDO ad GANGEM Palibothri : " à Gange ad COLIDA (or Colchida) atræ gentes, et quodam modo Æthiopes.  Pomp. Mela. Lib. " iii. Cap. vii.  They worshiped Zeus Ombrios.  Strabo, Lib. xv. p. 1046.  He mentions THE " PROMONTORY TAMUS, and the island Chruse.  Tamus was the name of the chief Egyptian " Deity : the same as Thamuz of Syria."

The words in parenthesis (or Colchida) are Mr. Bryant's.

Here we have the Buddhists or Gymnosophists, in the *tenent oras, they hold the coast,* and from the Indus to the Ganges. This clearly points out the Guzerat of Syrastrene, *or* Palli-tana.  Here we have also the island Cro-CALE and the island CHRUSE. The termination of the first is almost the same as the Agni-cula, and Heri-cula, whom we found on the coast of Malabar, and the Jani-cula of Rome, of the mount which had the nomen Janicula in Saturn-ia, near Palli-tana, both in Italy and in India ; and, in the *Zeus* OM-*brios* of India, we have the OM-bri of Italy.

Pliny[5] says, without the mouth of the river Indus two other islands there be called Chryse and Agyræ. These people have the same name as the Greæi in Mount Athos named in Smith's Classical Atlas.[6] Again he says, that there is a country of the Cryseans, whom he places on the East of the upper part of the Indus. The Cryseans here mentioned, are positively nothing but Crestians or Christians. The country on the North-east of the Sinus Thermaicus is called Crossæa and Chalcidiæ, and the point, the peninsula, is called Pallene, prius Phlegra. I think we have, at last, found the famous St. Thomas of the Portuguese in the promontory Tamus : and when I consider

---

[1] Georgius, Alp. Tib. p. 127.      [2] Lib. iv. in Ezekiel, Cap. xiii.

[3] But the Gymnosophistæ Æthiopum were also found in the Isle of Meroe (Maria or Meru, or perhaps the Mere of the Ethiopians) above Egypt.

[4] Vol. III. p. 211.

[5] He also says, that Rome had a secret name, and that where Rome now standeth was formerly a city called Saturnia, which is the same as the city of Surastrene, called Satrun-ja. Rome, was, correctly speaking, the Saturnian kingdom, its capital being placed on Mons Saturnia, afterward called Mons Capitolina. Niebuhr, Vol. I. p. 226. When I find this city of Roma in Saturnia in Italy, and the Saturnia of Rama in India, followed by the two histories of a black infant God, born of an immaculate conception, crucified and raised from the dead, and both bearing the same name—Crist—it is impossible not to believe in the identity of the mythoses.

[6] Chap. xxi.

many other very extraordinary circumstances which have been detailed in this work, and contemplate the ignorant mistakes of the Greeks, I am compelled to suspect that the Cro-cale and the Chruse are the same, and near the island of Diu, the same as the Diu of Mount Athos ; and that they ought to be represented by the Greek word χρης or chres-tos a Chrys-opolis. The word χρης has the same meaning as the word Div. And I think the island of Cruse is the same as the Diu of Guzerat and of the Diu of Mount Athos and Crestonia of Thrace. I know that I am taking a great liberty with the words Cro and Crus, but I only state my own feeling that I have *a suspicion*. Some persons will feel much where others feel little or nothing. I merely state facts and leave them to the reader. The word Crus changed from χρης, is by no means so great a corruption as many which we have ; and when I reconsider what has been said respecting the promontory of Taurus, the black Cristna in India, the black Crist or Crest at Loretto, &c., &c., in Italy, I cannot help concluding that the χρησος of Greece may increase the number of Mr. Van Kennedy's Sanscrit words in Greek from 300 to 301. In Siam, where we have found a mount Sian and its capital called Judia, Ptolemy gives us also a river called Fluv—Cresoana, that is, the river Creston. In some maps it is called only Soan.

The name of the Hindoo God Cristna is spelt in various ways, so that it is not in my power to discover which is the most proper; but Vallancey, in Ireland, and Sir W. Jones, have spelt it Creeshna, which Mr. Maurice says it ought to be. This has a strong tendency to identify it with the χρης of the West; indeed, it does identify it. I hope after Mr. Volney has been abused in very gross language by Mr. Maurice, for not calling him Creeshna, I shall not be turned upon and abused for calling him what these gentlemen say is his true name.

My reader will probably have anticipated an observation which I am going to make on the above ; but whether to attribute it to premeditation or not, I do not know: we have in India a *Chrēs* or *good genius* who is a man crucified, and we have in Europe a man crucified who is the χρης or *good genius*. But, respecting the crucified saviours, more hereafter.

The learned German, Ritter, has observed, that Dodona is often written Bodona, from which he makes Buddha. Herodotus says, that Dodona was Αρχαιοτατον των εν Ελλησι χρησηριων. I believe the word χρησηριων can mean nothing but *holy places* or places of the χρησος, and this connects the Buddha and the χρης. Bodona or Dodona is said by Ritter to be placed in the country of Cestrina. This must be a corruption of Crest-ina. It is a change not greater than Crestona to Cortona. ₽₽ was called χρησηριον,[1] and was the monogram both of Christ and Jupiter Ammon. Thus we find the same χρησος in Egypt, Greece, and India.

The name of Sind or India was given to the Promontory, *absurdly* called peninsula, of India, by the Greeks, because it was the name of all the part with which they were originally acquainted ; but its Sanscrit name was Bharata.[2] This is the Hebrew ברית *brit* אי *ia*, and means *pure* or *holy country* or *land*. It is derived from the Hebrew ברא *bra, creator*. Thus the country which Abraham left was called by his ancestors the Holy Land, and thus his successors, in like manner, gave the same name to their new residence—*the Holy Land*, which we call it to this day. Wars of Mahabarat mean the *wars of the great Creator*, in the Hebrew the *wars of the Lord*. ברא *bra*. Barat is the proper name ; Maha means *magnus, great*.

Authors have found great difficulty in an expression of Herodotus's. Speaking of a people of Italy, he says, " The Crestoniates (which some would read Cortoniates) and the Placians, the " remnants of that nation, although they speak one and the same language, are not intelligible to

---

[1] Apud Basnage, B. iii. Ch. xxiii., Scaliger in Euseb. Chron.  [2] Rennell, Mem. Introd. p. xx.

" those who live around them."[1]   Niebuhr thinks Creston meant Cortona.[2]   This is probably correct, and serves to account for the Indian temples at Pæstum, with the unknown Linga and Yoni found there by Lieut.-Col. Tod, as well as for their Janus, Saturnia regna, &c., &c. All this tends to prove that the same people who came to Italy, also came to Thrace.

When the striking similarity of the doctrines of Pythagoras to those of the Christians is considered, it will not be thought surprising that the place in Italy where he founded his school was called Crotona, which, as appears above, some would read χρησονα. In the south point of Italy, the town which in our map is called Cortona is called Crotona.

In their invocations the Hindoos chaunt forth the cry Rhada Krishn ! Rhada Krishn ! and Col. Broughton says, this has a much more holy meaning than the name Kunya (i. e. Col. Tod's Kanya). I feel little doubt that the Rhada is the Latin Radius. and Krishn the Greek Χϱης, benignant, and Hebrew חרם hrs the solar fire. Kun-ya or Kunieya is the Apollo Cunnius, the IE on the temple of Delphi; the word Cun having the same meaning as Rhadha[3] —jointly an androgynous Deity. Col. Broughton says, Kan is one of the numerous appellations of Krishna. Again, Kunue, ee, or Kunya " the beloved." Here is most clearly the Chaldee emphatic article.[4] Vallancey[5] has proved that the Indian Eeswar is the Irish Aosfhear, pronounced Eesvear and the. Etruscan Esar: and that " the Bramanick Kreeshna, an incarnation of the Deity, is the " Irish Crisean, holy, pure;" whence Crisean a priest. Here I think we have the origin of Cæsar, and Hesus of Gaul; and when I reflect on what has been shewn respecting the Crysos by Mr. Bryant, and the indiscriminate use of the σ and ς by early Greeks noticed before, I cannot help feeling that here is a strong confirmation of the identity of the Krishna of India and the Χρησος of Delphi.

We must not forget that the black Apollo of Delphi was called by the Hebrew word IE and also by the name Cunnius ; that we, in a neighbouring country, found the people sacrificing their wives ; that these people were called Sindi; that this black Apollo is called on the tomb of the Youth of Larissa Χρησος, and that we found a Chrys in Youdia of India. All these matters considered, I come to the belief that when the Brahmins perfected their Sanscrit, on the foundation of the old language of the country, they applied to the word Kris the meaning black or dark blue ; but that its original meaning was benignus, mitis. In the Hebrew, the word כרם krs or כרש krs has the same meaning as Δελφυς, which again brings us to to the Cun-ie-ya. Col. Broughton's assertion, that Kanya means beloved, looks very like the Greek Ηϱως, on the tomb of the .Youth of Larissa, in opposition to the Χρης at the top.[6]

4. In the CELTIC DRUIDS, Chap. V. Sect. XV., I have shewn that the Irish Ceara, the wife of Ceares, was the Goddess of Nature, and the same as Ceres. She had a daughter called Porsaib-hean, pronounced Porsaivean, the Persephone of the Greeks, and the Proserpine of the Romans. According to Schelling, Ceres is the Hebrew חרש hrs or chrs, and Kersa the Chaldæ חרשא hrsa or chrsa, from חרש hrs, aravit, sata. The meaning of this name was præstigiatrix, mago, or fabricatrix.[7] The Maja of India was the same as the Maia of the Greeks, but she was the same as Persephone,[8] and Persephone was Ceres, and Ceres was the mother of the Gods and Queen of

---

[1] Lib. i. Ch. v.                  [2] Cabinet Enc. Vol. I. p. 42.
[3] Vide Col. Broughton's Pop. Poet. of Hind. p. 83.     [4] Pp. 28—32.
[5] Col. Hib. Vol. IV. Part i. p. 81.
[6] In the minutes of the Society of Antiquarians of London, for the year 1767, is a letter from a Mr. Hollis, at Benares, in which he says, that some of the Brahmins study Chaldaic, in which, he adds, their books of physic are written. Vall. Coll. Vol. IV. Part i. p. xxiii.
[7] Lac. Epit. 68.          [8] Sir W. Jones.

heaven. From the same source came the Χρυσωρ and Chrysaor of Sanchoniathon. Cres or Κρης or כרס *krs*, was the being to whom the astrologers came on the birth of Christ, the 25th of December, to make the solar offerings at the temple of Bethlehem or Ceres, where Adonis or Adonai was worshiped, as described in Book V. Chap. II. Sect. 3. Gen. Vallancey says, Creasean, Crisean, a priest. It is the Chaldæan חרשין (*hrsin*), *i. e.* Magus, supposed by the Orientalists to be derived from חרש (*hrs*) Chrisb, siluit, whence חרשא (*hrsa*) Chrisha, incantator, magus, præstigiator. Syr. Chrasa, magus, incantator, magicam artem exercens : חרש (*hrs*) Chris, apud magistros, mutus, vulgarissimè respicitur.[1] Krishen, one of the thousand names of God in the Hindostanee dialect.[2] Creas, Creasna, Cheres, Creeshna, Cur, Cores, and Κυρος all mean the sun.[3] Jupiter was called Chrysaoreus.[4] Drummond says, " חרש *hrs* may be sounded *choras*, " *chros, chrus.* This word signifies faber, artifix, machinator."[5] He shews that this was the Chrysor or Chrus-aor, of Sanchoniathon. Our *choras* descended by the regimine from the praise of חרש *hrs*, or χρης, called Lord or Κυριος, and came to be our Κυριε, ελεησον, " Lord, have mercy " upon us," which was, as Cudworth has proved, a part of the ancient Pagan Liturgy or Litany.[6] In the *Lord, have mercy upon us*, the congregation *joined in choras.*

Volney says, " The Greeks used to express by X or the Spanish Iota, the aspirated Ha of the " Orientals, who said Haris : in Hebrew חרש (*hrs*) *heres* signifies the sun, but in Arabic the radical word means *to guard, to preserve,* and Haris *a preserver.*"[7] Again,[8] " If Chris comes " from *Harish* by a *chin,* it will signify *artificer,* an epithet belonging to the sun."[9] One of the names of the Vulcan of Phœnicia, according to Sanchoniathon, was Chrysor : of this Bochart makes חרש אור *hrs aur,* which he renders Πυριτεχνιτης, an artificer by fire. Here we have Χρης or Chrès. " The Chaldæan name of the sun is חרש (*hrs*) Chris, hinc et Persis Sol dicitur Κυρος, " teste Plutarcho;—hence עיר-חרש (*oir-ehrs*) Ghir-he Chris, Heliopolis, *i. e.* Civitas Solis. " This seems to be the Chrysor or Cearas, or (אור *aur*) of the Phœnicians."[10] The name of Cyrus is כורש *kurs ;* from this comes the κυρω *to be,* of the Greeks, and the Core of Proserpine or Persephone. In the חרם or חרש *hrs* we have assuredly the persons Ceres, Χρης, Cyrus, and Core, or Proserpine, otherwise called Persephone, which latter is only Perse-phnn, or Φνν=600, or φηνν= 608—the Phenn or Phœnix of Persia[11]— the cycle renewed every 600 years.

It is from the Ceres or Χρης, that the Christians got their custom of burning candles before their saints, and of carrying them in their processions. Ceres was called Tædifera.

> Quos cum Tædifera nunc habet ille Dea.[12]

See Jurieu[13] for many other proofs.

As we might expect, one of the sons of the *Yadu* of India was said to be *Croshta,* or Croshtdeva. Here we find the Christ as Crost, and the Cras-devas of Arrian : and here we see the mythos of

---

[1] Gittim, Cap. xxv.  [2] See conclusion of Chap. IX.; Coll. Hib. Vol. IV. Part i. p. 445.
[3] Alwood, Let. Ant. of Greece, p. 144.  [4] Ib. p. 166.  [5] Orig. Vol. III. p. 192.
[6] Int. Syst. Book i. Chap. iv. p. 454, ed. fol.
[7] See Volney's Ruins; Lord Kingsborough's Ant. Mex. p. 411.  [8] Ib.
[9] See Ouseley's Coll. III. p. 27.  [10] Vall. Coll. Vol. IV. p. 492.

[11] Cabul is called Zabul and Zabul-istan, (Rennell, Mem. p. 112) as Ceres was written Keres, and Cyrus Kyrus, and Cristna Krishna. In the same way Rennell (Mem. p. 127) has shewn, in a very satisfactory manner, that Persia was written Par THia or Par Tia, country of Pers or of Pert; and that the Parthians were but Persians. In a similar way Jen-aub is called Chunaub. Ib, p. 88.

[12] Ovid. Fast. iii.  [13] Vol. II. Treat. ix. Chap. iii. p. 253.

the χρης, or Χρηστ, or Crest, most clearly proved to have been in existence long anterior to the Christian æra.[1]    Christ was called Crost by the Ethiopians.    In Book I. Chap. IV., I have shewn that the Ethiopians were a colony from India.

The Tetragrammaton of the Pythagoreans I have shewn, in my Celtic Druids, was the word יהוה ieue : on this account they had great reverence for the Quadrangle, and said it corresponded to Ceres.  The reason of this was, because in the secret science the sacred four represented Jehovah, who was the Logos Incarnate, the Χρης.  Ceres was the Deity androgynous, the Creator from whom abundance and all blessings flow.

The earth is called the nursing mother of all creatures, the Ceres.  This was because the earth, like all other things, was an emanation from the Creator—was but a link in the chain of emanations proceeding from the highest to the lowest, or vice versâ.  Thus the mysticism of Plato, noticed in B. I. Ch. II., may be reconciled.  Thus the earth, in the sacred metaphorical language, was a Ceres; and all rivers were Adonises or Dons, or Sirs or Surs—*rivers of the sun*.  They were, in fact, Cereses, for they were the nurses of the creatures living on the lands fertilized by them, and which, without them, would be arid wastes.  I have a strong suspicion that every place had a *mystical* name for the priests', and a *common* name for the people's, use.[2]

When I consider the identity of the history of Cyrus with that of Cristna, and the mythological character of its date or birth, that he was the same as Adonis whose history was very similar to that of Perse-phone or Proserpine, who was also called by the same name as Cyrus, *Core*, in Hebrew כרש curs, I cannot help doubting his existence as a human being.  He was a Messiah foretold by name, a solar appellation, to save the Jews; and he was most assuredly the presiding Genius of the *eighth* cycle, being born on the first year of it.

In the male and female Χρης, M. Cruezer[3] might have found the Kiris or Kyris who came to Argos of Peloponnesus, and whom he shews to have been identical with Adonai or the Lord, or Adonis and Osiris, and afterward[4] with Proserpine, called also[5] Core.  All these Creuzer shews to have been identical with a God called Æon,[6] or the eternal Creator or Demiurge.[7]  I suppose I need not point out to my reader how all my system is here unconsciously confirmed by this learned German.  And further, he has shewn them all to be identical with Oannes, Anandatus, Dercęto, the Patares of Lycia, and the Hom or Omanus, called also Comœus;[8] and again with an Autochtone called *Cresus*,[9] the builder of the temple of Ephesus, and he with Semiramis, and Chersiphron;[10] and again with Omphale, daughter of Jordanus, (this shews a river Don probably in Lydia,) who had a son called Crœsus[11] by Hercules, whose name was *Here* and *clo ;*[12] *Here* being Chore, *Core*, or Cere, or Ceres; and again with Axiokersa, (another corruption of Ceres,) who was the same with De-meter; but Demeter was Bacchus, the Saviour, *as was also Ceres*.[13]  Thus Bacchus was the androgynous Saviour, ΙΗΣ—and ΙΗΣ is Jesus; and Jesus is

---

[1] Trans. Asiat. Soc. Vol. III. Part I. pp. 143, 144, Essay by Tod.

[2] Nell' antica ortografia si tralasciava qualche vocale nel mezzo della parola, ed era quella *quam syllaba nomine suo exprimit :* v. qr. B. pronunziandosi *Be :* invece di Lebero (cioè Libero) scrivevano solamente Lebro, come nell' ara di Pesaro.  Vittorino adduce questi esemplo, *Bne* per *bene*, *Cra* per *cera*, *Krus* per *carus*, *Dcimus* per *decimus* . . . . . . . . Spesso anche son popolari accorciamenti come poclum vinclum, ove non si supplice l'ausiliare, ma diversa lettera.  Saggio di Lingua Etrusca, Vol. I. p. 118.

[3] Tome II. Liv. iv. Ch. iii. p. 45.    [4] Ibid. p. 53.    [5] Vide Lempriere.    [6] Αιων, name of Cyrus.

[7] Tome II. Liv. iv. Ch. iii. p. 73.    [8] Comœus the aspirated Omaus.

[9] In pp. 82, 114, 116.    [10] Tome II. Liv. iv. Ch. iii. p. 94.    [11] Cruezer, p. 179.

[12] Ibid. p. 195.    [13] Ibid. p. 312.

the Logos and the Χρης, an incarnation of divine wisdom, the Ερως or Ηρως, or divine Love. Thus we see how, as Ammonius Saccas taught, all the vulgar plurality of the Gentiles, of the East and West, melt at last into precisely the same trinity of the Indians, the Jews, and the Christians. In the explanation of these identifications, no doubt, partly consisted the Eleusinian mysteries. [1] In the above I am supported by the Scholiast of Apollonius Rhodius, who affirms, that Axierus was Ceres. [2]

5. I think there can be no doubt that from a corruption of the חרש hrs we have the Cyrus, the Messiah of Isaiah, whose history was copied from the history of Cristna, though the letters in the Hebrew do not exactly suit ; and I think, also, that we have here the androgynous or male Ceres of the Greeks, to whose temple at Bethlehem the Magi came at the time of the birth of the new incarnation of divine love. Parkhurst says, הרם hrs, the solar fire. He also says, " חרש hrs, Machinator. " From this root the Greeks had the name of their God Ερος or Ερως, by which it is evident they " meant the material light, considered as possessed of the plastic or formative power." Surely all these quotations, from men not having the slightest idea of my theory, places its truth beyond a doubt.

It is impossible to dip into the inexhaustible treasury of Creuzer, without seeing my theory confirmed. Could we but make out the whole, no doubt a beautiful system would shew itself in every part. Probably many Christians, from the indulgence of their prejudices and, I·fear, from the bigotry and hatred instilled into their minds in youth by their priests, (who, as usual, will fear that some change of opinion may affect their emoluments,) will be much shocked to find their religion to be, at last, nothing but that which they have been accustomed to designate with every opprobrious epithet. But why should they object to the religion of the Gentiles being, when uncorrupted, the same as theirs ? Are they not always at work endeavouring to make proselytes ? Then I hope they will not be angry with me for at once bringing all the religions of antiquity, stripped of their corruptions, into their pale. I am, in fact, the greatest proselytist in the world. I proselyte those that have lived, those that live, and those that will live.

We have seen that the Thracians were Jews, Ioudi, and Orpheans, and Indians ; that their wives sacrificed themselves on the death of their husbands. Orpheus charmed the beasts with his music, and the trees of Pieria came down to listen to him. He was accompanied by the nine Muses. Kanya of India or Cristna, or Crishna, or Creeshna, or Χρησνα, charmed the beasts with his music, as Orpheus had done. He was accompanied by nine Gopys, each called Radha.[3] All the same things are told of Apollo in the neighbouring Temple of Delphi or Kanya, or of the Grecian Apollo Cunnius—Kan-ia. The last syllable is the IE on the Delphic temple, יה ie or Jah of the Jews, the Jah of the Sanscrit, and of Apollo or A-pol, or ה e בעל e-bol—the God Bol or Bal or Pal, of whom the shepherd kings of India, that is, the shepherds of Rajah-stan or Royal shepherds, Pallestini, were followers. Apollo had his nine muses; he was the God of Music, like Kanya, and he performed on the Lyre as Orpheus did, and as Kanya did on the same instrument, called Vina.[4]

Among the ancients nothing was guarded with greater care than their mysteries ; and nothing is more difficult to account for, than the apparent ignorance of many of the great men who must have been initiated—such as Cicero. If they understood the mysteries why did they pretend ignorance, and also pretend at the same time to give an account, though not an explanation, of them ? Was the meaning of them lost in the temples, the forms only remaining ? I much suspect

---

[1] Creuzer, Liv. v. Ch. iii. p. 315.

[2] Nimrod, Vol. III. p. 258.

[3] Vide Tod's Hist. Raj. and plate—Crishna on the flute.

[4] See a figure of an ancient violin in Montfaucon.

the latter. Various moderns, such as Warburton, Gebelen, &c., have undertaken to explain them, but they have all failed. The obvious reason of this is, that the mysteries being only a part of a system, these gentlemen have all failed in proposing any thing like a satisfactory explanation. I think the mysteries were like masonry; indeed, we shall soon see it is highly probable that the Masons were a branch of the initiated—Masonry a branch of the art. The Konx om pancha of the Indians, and the burning of widows, found in so remarkable a manner at Eleusis, which was, in fact, in the Sintica, at once identify the western with the eastern devotees. Eusebius, like every other author, at the same time that he confesses his ignorance, tells us, that there were four ministers in the ceremonies. The *first, whose name must not be given*, represented the Demiourgos; (was this Χρης ;) the second the Sun, the third the Moon, and the fourth Mercury. I think it is not difficult, from this incongruous nonsense, to perceive the First Cause, and the Trimurti. This is what we might naturally expect where we have found the *Konx om pax*. This was all celebrated at the temple of Ceres, at Eleusis, *i. e.* the Bit-lehem or house of Ceres, or Cyrus, or Χρησνα, which was situate not far from Delphi, or Δελφυς, or the town of Χρησα. Among their officers one was called Κηρυξ or Ceryx, or Herald, and one of them a king. The former carried the Caduceus; and the rites of the infant Saviour Æsculapius, to be treated of in the next book, were there celebrated. I have no doubt that we have here the origin of our Herald's office, introduced into the West about the time of the Crusades, and of course supposed by our learned men, because they can trace it no further back, to have then first arisen in the world. But Gebelen[1] has shewn that it existed many centuries before.

6. The word Κηρυξ or Ceryx, the Herald, was derived from the Hebrew word קרש qrs, and meant the cross or the caduceus of Mercury or of Buddha. The Herald or Ceryx, Littleton translates Caduceator, and from it Lardner derives the word crux. It is very curious to observe how every thing connected with a cross comes at last, when sought to the bottom, to be connected with Hermes, Mercury, or Buddha—the Taranis of the Druid oak. The caduceus was either a crucifix or a cross. I very much suspect that our coats of arms, and particularly our crests, came from the Crestian or Crêtian mythos. The ancients had their crests.[2]   The figure carried on the shield or banner was the emblem of the χρης or good dæmon; therefore every people who adored the χρης or good dæmon would have a crest. From the first word *emblem*, or whatever word stood in the place of emblem, being in regimine, it came to have the name of crest. This style of the first language accounts for innumerable names, and in particular for the priests having the names of their Gods: for if it were said, the priest of Apollo, it would be exactly the same as to say, priest Apollo.

The Druids of Ireland carried in their hands the Crux ansata, called a key, or in their language *kire* or *cire*.[3]   This we must recollect was carried by the Gods or priests of Egypt, and is also found in a very remarkable manner in the hands of many of the bearded Druidical-looking figures, given by Mr. Hammer, either as figures of the Templars, or as emblematical figures used by them. I cannot help suspecting that this *cire* was closely connected with the Cris and Ceres. קציר qzir גה *hg* means *solemnitas messis*.[4]   One of the Apocryphal Gospels states, that when Jesus celebrated the last supper—his last solemnitas messis—he and his apostles sang a hymn, and performed a circular dance: and גה *hg* has this meaning. I suspect also, that this *qzir* has a near relation to the word Cæsar. This key was what unlocked or opened the door of eternal and of human life. It was a *polis* or *pole* and a *tri-pole*. Ceres was often written for *wheat* or *bread*

---

[1] Vol. VIII. p. 220.          [2] See Book VIII. Chap. II. Sect. 1.

[3] Vall. Coll. Vol. VIII. p. xlix. Pref. to No. XII.          [4] Ib. p. 1.

" Sine Cerere, et Libero friget Venus." The Solemnitas Messis is the offering of bread of the Romists. This is the meaning of the mass. In the Eleusinian mysteries, the day when they were completed was said to be, to the initiated, the day of regeneration and new birth. [1]   See our baptismal service. The day when the initiation was finished was the day, to the initiated, of the Βαφε Μητις—Bafomet, to be explained by and by.

The Temple at Eleusis had a very large dome, which was of great antiquity, long before the time usually allotted to the invention of the arch, with radiated stones. [2]   Strabo and Vitruvius have given an account of this immense dome, [3] said to have been built by Ictinus, about 430 years B. C. for the celebration of the mysteries; and Chrysostom has described the ceremonies of initiation to have taken place with great magnificence under it. In the procession, the votaries called out what Gebelen calls, in his French, *Khaire Déméter, Salut, Ceres.* In the *Khaire* of Eleusis may not the *heri* of India or the Cyrus be found ? In the dome of the temple we have a duplicate of the Dome in the temple at Komulmar—described in Col. Tod's book. I request my brother Masons of the *Royal Arch,* to place themselves in the middle of the new room at Freemason's Tavern, when lighted up, and then to reflect upon all their ceremonies, on which, of course, I cannot enlarge, and I suspect they will find themselves both at Eleusis, and at Bit-lehem, and in India. Count de Gebelen says, Cerus signifies *creator,* and creo *to create.* [4]   " On voit dans Hesychius qu' en Grec Çérès s'ap-" pelloit Kyrus; ce peut-être le même mot." En Hébreu חרש *hrs* signifie *faire.* [5]   Thus I am not singular in my idea of Ceres and Cyrus being the same : the difference of sex can be easily accounted for, frrom the known fact, that every God and Goddess was androgynous. Ceres was Demeter, but Bacchus was also Demeter; thus ΙΗΣ or Bacchus was Ceres, [6]   It is a striking circumstance, that Ceres had the same name as Cæsar, viz. Ιελω. [7]   This seems to identify Cæsar, Ceres, and Χρης.

7. For the present I add no more respecting the Crest, but return to the Chaldees. In section 3 of this chapter, to which I beg to refer, Mr. Bryant has noticed a country of Colida. Here we have the original Chaldea, where was the Ur—Ur of the Chaldees.

Almost all writers respecting the Chaldeans have laboured under the mistaken idea, that they were identical with the Assyrians; hence they have used the words Assyrian and Chaldean as convertible terms. The error of this I have shewn in THE CELTIC DRUIDS, and I need not repeat it. There can be no doubt that many Assyrians might be Chaldeans, and vice versâ. But the Chaldeans, most assuredly, were a sect or order of some kind, totally independent of the Assyrian or Babylonian empire. They were no doubt numerous in Babylon, as they were afterward in Rome, but who would say that the Romans were Chaldeans, or the Chaldeans Romans ? Ancient history shews traces of them in many places besides Babylon. Zoroaster was always said to have been their founder: but who was Zoroaster? I shall not discuss this question at present, but content myself with saying, I suspect that he was merely the supposed genius of a cycle. Seven Zoroasters are recorded by different historians.

---

· Monde Prim. Tome IV. p. 322.    [2] De Architect. præfat. ad Lib. vii. Monde Prim. Vol. IV. p. 321.

[3] Moade prim. ibid.

[4] Ceres or Curus from Creo, *to create,* see Litt. Dict.    [5] Monde Prim. Vol. IV. p. 577.

[6] כורש *Ikurs* למשיחו *Imsihu,* Isaiah xlv. 1; חיה *e-msih* from משה *msh,* unxit; מושיע *musio* from ישע *iso, to save.* Hence the female incarnations of the nine cycles were the nine muses of Apollo, and the nine wives, or Rhadiæ or Rays of Kanya.

[7] Spanh. Observ. in Callim. p. 649 ; Jamieson's Herm. Scyth. p. 137.

In the Colida or Colchida of Arrian, noticed by Mr. Bryant, I think we have the origin of the Culdees or Chaldees. They are in the district of Ur-ii or Ur-iana, where Abraham or the Brahmin came from. He came from Ur of the Cullidei, or Chaldees, or Culdees, or from Colida. This completes the proof of my system.

The country of Calida or Colida in North India, between the Burrampooter and the Indus, is the country of the holy Cali—Cali-di, *i. e.* dis or divus and Cali.

Cali is the Greek καλος *beautiful.* It is remarkable that, in the Celtic, the word *Cal* means *wise* :[1] whence comes a *calling* or *vocation.* When a person was called, he was deemed wise for the purpose for which he was called. The Roman meeting for the election of priests was called Calata Comitia. From this comes our Gala-day, *Whit-sunday,* when the Druids granted the orders or functions to priests.

I believe myself that the Ariana, said by Col. Van Kennedy[2] to be bounded by the Indus, was Uriana, which extended thus far ; that *all* the Doab between the Ganges and Indus was Ariana and Ur-iana, and perhaps Ara-bia also. The word Ur in the Indian language signifies also *country* or *town*[3] —Epα of Greece. Then, when it is said that Abraham came from " Ur of the Chaldees," it may mean, that he came from the country of the Chaldees or from Colida, not from the fire of the Chaldees. The use here of the word Ur, without any word prefixed, having the meaning of town or country, is exactly like the use of the word Jordan, *the Jordan.* The persons translating did not know the meaning of the first words in each case. The words in the old Hebrew are never divided like ours—but all run together. Now I have no doubt that Bartholomæus is right : yet I think it was also the proper name of a country. As, if I be right, it will be merely a district of the country of Callida, it will make no material difference to the argument. The Hebrew regimine will account for this word meaning, both *country* and *fire.* It was the country of fire or Vesta; in the Hebrew style, *country fire.*

Ammianus Marcellinus, in the following passage, seems to imply that the Chaldees were eastward of Bactriana ; this will take them to my Colida : " Cui scientiæ (Magiæ) sæculis priscis, " multa ex Chaldæorum arcanis Bactrianus addidit Zoroastres : deinde Hystaspes rex, pruden- " tissimus Darii pater, qui cum superioris Indiæ secreta fidentius penetraret, ad nemorosam " quandam venerat solitudinem, cujus tranquillis silentiis præcelsa Brachmanorum ingenia poti- " untur,"[4] &c. The whole passage evidently alludes to a Chaldea far Eastward of Assyria. We must remember that the name of the God of the Jews, Jah, IE, was the name of Apollo of Delphi. But the Oracle of Apollo, preserved by Porphyry,[5] said, that the *Chaldeans* and Jews were the only people who honoured a God produced by himself, αυτογενεθλον. Now Abraham was a Chaldean, for he came from Ur of the country of the Chaldees. And, assuredly, they were the Chaldees of Abraham whom the Oracle meant, whose God had the same name as the God of the Oracle, not the Moloch-adoring Assyrians. The coupling of the Chaldeans and Jews was natural enough, if they were originally from the same country. The place here found for the Chaldeans fully justifies Jeremiah's assertion, that they came from the ends of the North and the sides of the earth.[6] *i. e.* from a very distant country. The fact of the Cholchians having come from India is strougly supported by Tzetzes, who says, Οἱ δε Κολχοι, ΙΝΔΙΚΟΙ Σκυθοι εισιν.[7] Hesychius says, Χαλδαιοι, γενος μαγων παντα γινωσκοντων.[8]

[1] Cleland, Spec. p. 124.   [2] P. 197.   [3] Barthol. System. Brach. p. 151.
[4] Hist. Lib. xxiii.   [5] Euseb. Evan. Præp. Lib. ix. Cap. x.   [6] Cab. Enc.
[7] Vallancey, Coll. Vol. VI. p. 66.   [8] Lex. voce Χαλδαιοι.

But there was another Colida at the south end of the Peninsula of India, not far from Cape Comorin, as well as that of the Doab of the Ganges and Indus ; thus there were two Colidas. It has been shewn by Bryant that the word Colida is the same as Colchida. This I believe was the place in South India to which the Argonauts, fifty-two in number, according to Onomacritus, were said to have gone in search of the golden fleece of a ram. A Colida, I think, I have proved to have been the place whence Abram came,—from Ur, or Uri-ana, of Colida. Every one knows that Abram was said to be a great astrologer, and no person at all conversant with the history of the Roman Emperors can be ignorant that the Chaldeans from India were their great astrologers or tellers of fortunes. [1]

Thrace, as we might expect, was called Aria, as well as Thracia. [2] This was, I have no doubt, after the Aria or Uria of Colida between the Indus and Ganges, [3] Duret says, it was called Χρησονη, and that some of its inhabitants were called Sapæ and Sapæi. These were, I feel little doubt, Sophees—of whom I shall treat hereafter. I think the most blind and credulous of devotees must allow that we have the existence of the Cristna of the Brahmins in Thrace, many hundred years before the Christian æra—the birth of Jesus Christ. Now, what could Mr. Maurice, Sir W. Jones, and Mr. Bentley, say to this ? Did the Cristna of Thrace take his name from the Apocryphal Gospels ? The Apollo ΕΙ, Χρης, in the country of Sind, with his flute or music, his nine muses or nine Rhadii, with the Brahmin custom of burning the widows cannot be doubted or evaded. How is it that this has never been seen before ? How, but because, if roguish priests *did* see it, they in every case endeavoured to suppress it; and because prejudice is so strong in devotees as to blind them even to an unclouded sun at noon! I beg my reader to refer to my observations in the first section of this book. In throwing out the acrostic from the Sibyls, the silly devotee Floyer, has shewn how his class corrupted books. A similar instance is to be found in the respectable antiquarian Mr. Davies, who has omitted to translate the last couplet of an ancient Welsh bard, because, he says, its reference to an *infant* Saviour shews it to be a Christian interpolation. This Saviour, I doubt not, had reference to the three Maries and *Virgo Paritura* of Gaul, and to the Jovi crescenti, fig. 20. Every ancient author, without exception, has come to us through the medium of Christian editors, who have, either from roguery or folly, corrupted them all. We know that, in one batch, all the fathers of the church and all the Gospels were corrected, that is, corrupted, by the united exertions of the Roman See, Lanfranc, Archbishop of Canterbury, and the Monks of St. Maur. And the conduct of Sir W. Jones, relating to the crucifixion of Indra, shews that the same system is now carrying on in India. But on all these points my reader will see much more important matter presently.

8. Colonel Tod has given an account in his History, of an order of priests called Gosaen. They now officiate in the temple of Eklinga, in Mewar. But the present religion of this temple is that of Kanyia or Cristna, and is said to have come from Matura. When I consider that I have found Maturea, Ur or Urii of the Colida, or Doab, or Mesopotamia of the Chaldees or Culdees, and Ayoudya, or Oude, or Judia, and the Joogees or Jews, all in India, nearly together, I cannot help believing that in the Gosaen of India we have the Goshen of Egypt, and of the Old Testament, called in the Hebrew גשן gsn, I leave the case to my reader, with the often-repeated observation, that it is not an individual name of this kind that is of any weight, but the number

---

[1] To these Chaldeans I attribute the invention of our dice and playing cards. The latter were clearly astrological instruments, and I have no doubt were connected with the system of cycles—for which, by accident or design, they were peculiarly adapted. I think they were probably invented expressly for the purpose: I pay no attention to the story of their invention in France.

ה *e*=8, ר *r*=200, ת *t*=400=608, Tre-ia.

[3] Vide Duret, Trésor des Lang. p. 729.

of them.   These Gossaen were priests.   The Hebrews dwelt in the land of *Goshen* or of the *Goshaen*.[1]

Vallancey says, Goseyn a magus, wise man, priest; in Irish it is Gaosna *wise*.[2]   A Hindoo religious is called *Gosine*; their chiefs are called *Omrahs*-Raj-Om.

We have seen the various signs of Hercules in the Syrastrene.   Every one has heard of his killing the Erymanthian boar in Arcadia, or I should say the country of the holy Arca, or Arga, of Greece.   In the Gulf of Cutch or Sinus Canthi, which washes the shore of Syrastrene, the river *Erymanthus*, now called the river Bunwas, empties itself, in about lat. 23, long. 71½.

9. I must now make some observations upon several very important words; and first, the word Erythræa.

All learned men will tell me that Erythræa means *red*, and thus, that the country between the Indus and Ganges, a great part of which must have a beautiful verdure, and the *green* Erythræan Sea, are so called from their *red* colour.   This is, as usual, Greek ignorance and learned credulity. I apprehend the name of the Erythræan Sea had the same meaning as the Goddess Προθυραια, or the Juno Lucina, or Diana Lucina of the Romans.[3]   I think the words have been Προθραια and Ερυθραια, and mean, the one Προ, the same as *Pra*, the Siamese name of creator, former, or giver of forms, added to the word θρε: and the other Ερι or Heri, the Saviour, added to the word θρε.   I think this is confirmed by the great similarity, in the very old alphabet, of the φ and ⊕ ⊖ Th.[4]   I consider them both of the same family with the Venus Aphrodite, the Sea Goddess, or the Goddess from the froth of the sea.   I take this lady to be A-Phre-Dite, in the Coptic language; A, emphatic, Φ=500, P=100, H=8,=608; sacrum nomen, cognomen, et omen. And the Dite is evidently the Dis, ditis, of Latium or the Etruscans, and the oriental Aditya or Dit, which is a term for the sun,[5] and which also means holy or sacred.   The Φρε, *Phre*, is also the Northern Freya, the Goddess of Friday, the day sacred to Venus, all over the world. The observation respecting the Venus Aphrodite, is confirmed by Nonnus, who says, Ινδωην ικετευσεν Ερυθραιην Αφροδιτην.[6]

The Θρη, *Thre*, is the *Tre* of the Egyptians, by which they designated the Nile, the *fleue-ocean*,[7] on which, in their ceremonies microcosmically, floated the heavenly bodies.   Every thing was a microcosm; every reptile was a microcosm of man; man of the globe; the globe of the planetary system; the planetary system of the universe; and the universe of God; and thus, in the image of God was man created—in the image of God male and female created he him.   The 'Eri was the Here (Juno), the Heri, Hera, the saviour of India—the destroyer and regenerator.   Thus the Erythræan Sea was the Sea of the Here-thræ.   In short, it was the universal sea; as we find it at the Straits of Gades washing the shores of the Atlantic, and on the other end of the Mediterranean washing the shores of Asia Minor, and again carrying on its bosom the sacred Tabrobane in India.

The word *Dius*, for God, in the old Latin, every one knows.   It makes Dii in its genitive. This is in fact Hebrew.   The Logos is constantly spoken of by the Targums, particularly that of Jerusalem, by the term ד"י מהמרא *memra dii*, the Logos of God.   This is the Diu of mount Athos and of Guzerat.[8]   It is impossible to doubt that the ד"י *Dii* is an old Latin or Etruscan word, though found in the Hebrew.   What say the opponents of *mixed etymology* to this?

---

[1] Do our Three Wise Men of Gotham, come from this?         [2] Vall. Coll. Hib. Vol. V. p. 60.
[3] See Parkhurst in voce פלט *plt*, IV.         [4] See Dr. Bosworth's Saxon Grammar, p. 10.
[5] Tod's Raj. p. 215.         [6] Dyonysiac. Lib. xxxv., Bryant, Anal. Vol. III. p. 187, 4to.
[7] Creuzer, Rel. An. Exp. des Planche, p. 90, Plate XLIX. fig. 192.
[8] Vide Parkhurst's GREEK Lexicon in voce Λογος.

Mr. Costard, in his Astronomy, derives the word Ζευς, Jupiter, "from the Arabic root Du or "Dsu, a word which signifies Lord; whence he conceives are derived the Dyu of the Welsh, "the Deu of the Cornish, Due in the Armoric, Dia in the old Irish, and the Deus of the Latins. "The words Dew and Diva, however, constantly occurring in nearly the same sense in Sanscrit, "as in Dewtah and Divatah, I cannot avoid putting in a claim for the Hindoos on this occasion, "*whose language bears a striking similitude to the old Chaldee.*—The planets are represented as "personified Dewtas; and it is remarkable that the Indians have a Divespiter, in Eeudra, their "God of the firmament, endowed with exactly the same functions as the Grecian Jove."[1] In my preliminary observations, Sect. 32, Gen. Vallancey says the ין *id* or *iod* stood for ten. We have seen the sacred character of the iota and the mysticism belonging to it, and that the Targum always calls God ״ *ii*—whence, I conclude, that the ין *id* ought to be ין *iid* the holy ׳ *i*. The Targums bear me out in this correction. Dr. Smith says, that the word mostly used by the Celts for the Supreme Being was Dia or Dhia, which, in the oblique case, has De and Dhe; that of this the Esus or Hesus, said to have been worshiped by the Druids, seems only to have been a corruption, and the Θεος and Deus of the Greeks and Latins were manifestly derived from it; that the Dhia or Dia of the Celts is the same as the Iah of the Hebrews.[2]

Bishop Marsh says,[3] "It has been thought indeed *anomalous* to insert the Digamma in such a "word as Δίι. But, to judge of the Digamma, we should not speak of insertion: for it was a "constituent part of the primitive Greek alphabet: and our present forms were occasioned by "the omission of it. Let us ask, therefore, in the first place, in what manner the nominative "Ζευς, or rather Δευς, according to the Æolic form, was originally written by the Pelasgi. "They could not *at first* have written ΔΕΥΣ: for Υ was an *addition* to the primitive Greek "alphabet, which ended with T, like the Phœnician, Samaritan, Hebrew, Chaldee, and Syriac "alphabets. F on the other hand was a constituent part of the primitive Greek alphabet; it "was the sixth letter in the Greek alphabet, as the corresponding letter was in all the alphabets "just mentioned. The word, therefore, which was afterward written ΔΕΥΣ[4] and then ΔΕΥΣ, "must at first have been written ΔΕFΣ and ΔΙFΣ. But the genitive and dative of ΔΙFΣ "could have been no other than ΔΙFΟΣ and ΔΙFΙ, which, when the Digamma was *dropt*, "because Διός, and Δίι. Hence, also, we see the *reason* why Διος and Δίι came to be the "genitive and dative of Ζευς."

10. The poet Dyonysius says, that Taprobana was placed IN THE Erythræan Sea. Bryant[5] shews, that Gades or Gadir was also called Syrus Erythreia. Thus we have the Erythræan Sea at nearly the extreme East and the extreme West. How absurd to suppose that this name was taken from a petty king of Asia Minor! The Erythræans are said to have founded colonies in Ionia, Libya, Cyprus, Ætolia, and Bœotia. Erythræa is only a translation of Ery-phrea, and means the Saviour 608: Φ=500, Ρ=100 Η=8=608: or, as it would be in Hebrew, ת *t*=400, ר *r*=200, ח *h*=8=608.

The Erythræan sea washed the island of Diu, or the holy island, and the coast of Malabar, as

---

[1] Maurice, Hist. Hin. Vol. I. p. 239, ed. 4to.     [2] P. 16, Celtic Druids, Ch. V. Sect. XXXVIII. note

[3] Horæ Pelasgicæ, Pt. i. Ch. iii. p. 64.

[4] When the Υψιλον was first introduced, it had the same form with the corresponding letter of the *Latin* alphabet, namely V. By degrees one of the sides was lengthened, and it acquired the form of Ѵ: but it was some time before the two lines, which form the angle, were bent into the present form Υ.

[5] Anal. Vol. III. pp. 187, 189, 4to.

well as that of the island of Serendive, or Taprobana, or Palæsimunda,[1] or Ceylon, on which stood Columbo, and, according to the Samaritan Pentateuch, mount Ararat; and where the mark of Adam's foot was; and it washed also the coast of Coromandel, or Colamandel, or Chiol-mandala. On this coast, according to Ptolemy, there were a river called Manda, a gulf called Colchicus-sinus,[2] and a place called *Malliarpha Emporium*, or Melliapour, where the Christian St. Thomas was said to have been martyred. But was he not the Tammuz who was killed, for whom the Jewish women made their lamentations, the God who was also called, in Western Syria, Adonis ? Of both of these we shall see more by and by.

In the Colchicus Sinus is a town now called Cochin,[3] and near it the Sinus Arga-ricus.[4] Here we have the Cholchos, to which the Argonauts went, as is proved, by what Ptolemy calls the Sinus Argo-ricus, in its neighbourhood. The meaning of Chiol or Chol is the same as Colida, Cali-di. The Manda or Munda of the coast, or of the island, or of the river, we know means cycle. Thus we have two Cholchoses and two Argonauts. But as few people will now believe the story of the Ethiopian colony with their curly hair going from Egypt to the shore of the Euxine, they will be obliged to believe the reverse—that the whole story came from India to the West, and was not understood by the Greeks. At the top of the coast of Malabar is the gulf of Cutch, which is the Cuttaia, called by Ptolemy the Sinus Canthi. And near to this gulf is a promontory of Tammuz.

Mr. Bryant has shewn that the Colchis of the West was also called Cutaia, and some of its inhabitants Sindi, that is, Indi. Some of the inhabitants of Colchis were called Iberi or Hebrews, and were said to come from Ur : that, of course, is the Urii or Uri-ana of Colida. The circumstance of these Iberi being divided into the four Indian castes,[5] proves them Indians pretty clearly. A little beyond Ceylon is the Chersonesus, called Golden, on which are found the river Creso-ana, and the mount Sian, the capital of which is called Judia, and the Jewish looking people. It is from this country that the Malays or Lascars come, whose language, in the depôt in Wapping, my respectable friend, Salome the Jew, understood.[6] It is on the coast of Malabar, near Ceylon, that the black Jews were found by Dr. Buchanan, and also the Christians of St. Thomas, whose service is yet performed in the Chaldee or Jewish language. In the Golden Chersonesus or Siam we have several of the same places as those we found on the coast of Malabar, Cambay, Cochin, &c. The circumstance of the promontory of *Tamus* being found in India, near to the settlement of the St. Thomas Christians of Malabar, as pointed out by Mr. Bryant, at once renders the story of St. Thomas in India doubtful. Then how are these persons called Christians, *using the Chaldee language*, to be accounted for except as I have stated, that they were a tribe of Afghans or Ioudi, having the doctrines of a person called Salivahana, (of whom I shall presently treat,) or of Bal-ii, named before, in Bk. IV. Ch. II. Sect. 1, who were made into Christians by the Portuguese, by means of a little blundering, a little lying, and, by what we know was the case, a good deal of persecution. The fact, of tribes of black Jews without the Pentateuch in this Chaldee-speaking country, agrees very well with and supports my theory.—They were Χρησ-ians, Creseans, as Pliny properly called them.

Servius on the Æneid says, that the Sibyl received the boon of long life on condition, that she

---

[1] Bartolomeus Systema Brachmanorum; also Bryant, Anal. Vol. III. pp. 187, 189.

[2] We recollect that Bryant has shewn that Cholchida is Colida.

[3] The king of this place was called a Zamorin. This has been shewn to be a Semiramis.

[4] Ibid.　　　　　　　　　[5] Bryant, Anal. Vol. III. p. 455, ed. 4to.

[6] Mr. Salome is the author of a Hebrew Grammar.

would quit the *Isle of Erythræa.*[1] Now I apprehend this island could be no other than Ceylon, unless, indeed, it was Diu. One of them, I think, it must have been.
Much has been said respecting the priority of the Scythians or the Celts. As I have said in my CELTIC DRUIDS, the question is of no value. The same race of men are evidently meant, who were resident to the North, between the Indus and the Ganges, extending to the North into Tartary. Gen. Vallancey has pointed out a most important passage of Dionysius :

Ινδον παρ' ποταμον Νοτιοι Σκυθαι ενναιεσιν,[2] &c., &c.

Upon the banks of the great river Ind
The *Southern Scuthæ* dwell : which river pays
Its wat'ry tribute to that mighty sea
Styled Erythræan. Far removed its source,
Amid the stormy cliffs of Caucasus :
Descending thence through many a winding vale
It separates vast nations . . . . . .
   .    .    .    .    .    .
These were the first great founders in the world—
Founders of cities and of mighty states ;
Who shewed a path through seas, before unknown :
And, when doubt reigned and dark uncertainty,
Who rendered life more certain. They first viewed
The starry lights, and formed them into schemes.

Afterward the same author says, that the people above alluded to also lived upon the Syrian Sea, and were called Φοινιχες, Phœnicians, and that they were descended from the true Erythræan stock.[3] These Scuthæ were also Sacæ.
Strabo describes one of the Greek kings or generals, in his war with the Indians, to have penetrated as far as the Συροι and Φαννοι. From this it is clear, that if the names have become lost, yet that formerly there were Syrians and Phœnicians on the East of the Indus. Surely if I wished for a confirmation of all my doctrines by a Greek author, I could not have desired any thing more to my purpose. Here, in these Φοινιχες from Central India, we have the people over whom Melchizedek was king; the people whose ancestors gave Jewish names to the cities of India, and who were afterward joined by their countrymen, driven out under Abraham ; who brought with them the Indian mythos, and who gave the same names to the places in their little mountain province of Judæa of the West, that they had left in the mighty empire of India, extending from Cashmere to Comorin, and from the Indus to Sian, or the Siones, or Sions, and Yudia of Pegu—to the Pan-dæan, that is, the Catholic kingdom.
Bartholomeus says, *Æthiopes*[4] *ab Indo* (nota bene) *flumine consurgentes juxta Ægyptum consederunt.* Idem habet Syncellus apud Marshamum.[5] Et Eupolemus apud eumdem Eusebium.[6] *Chus esse Æthiopum patrem et fratrem Mitzraim.*[7] Chus autem Bacchum Indicum esse suspicantur Calcuttenses Angli, et Reverend P. Georgius, qui etiam duplicem Æthiopiam scite distinguit, atque Indos adstipulante eidem De Guines a Chus oriundos esse existimati. Quod si verum est, alia profecto Indis antiquitas tribui debet, quam tribuat eisdem R. P. Marcus. Philostratus, (Lib. iii. Cap. vi. de vita Apollonii) scribit, *Erat aliquod tempus, quo Æthiopes consederunt hac in parte, gens Indica Æthiopia enim nondum erat* (nempe Æthiopes seu Indos portans). Et Lib. iv. Cap. vi. ait, *Æthiopes ab Indis venientes.* Et paulo infra, *Sapientissimi mortalium*

---

[1] Note on Virgil by Servius.     [2] Dion. Perieg. ver. 1088.     [3] Vall. Hib. Coll. Vol. V. pp. 17, 18.
[4] Art. Eusebius' Chronicon, Lib. post. edit. Scal. p. 72.     [5] P. 115, c.     [6] De Præp. Evan. Lib. ix.
[7] Ita legit Bochartus in suo Phaleg. Lib. iv. Cap. ii.

*Indi sunt: coloni autem eorum Æthiopes.* Profecto hæc omnia de veris Indis dici liquet, ac proinde ab iis potius religio per Africam in Ægyptum penetravit.[1]

11. Until I had written the above, respecting the Grecian towns, &c., I did not observe the following passage of Mr. Bryant's:[2] " The river *Indus* was often called *Sindus*, and nations of " the family whereof I am treating were called *Sindi*. There were people of this name and family " in Thrace, named by Hesychius: Σινδοι (της Θρακιης) εθνος Ινδικοι. The Sindi (of Thrace) " are an Indian nation. Some would alter it to Σινδικον, Sindicum : but both terms are of the " same purport. He mentions, in the same part of the world, πολις, Σινδικος λιμην λεγομενη : " a city, which was denominated the *Sindic* or INDIAN harbour." In the next page Bryant repeats what the reader has before seen, that Apollonius of Tyanea affirms, that the African Ethiopians were originally an Indian nation. After this Mr. Bryant goes on to shew,[3] *on the authority of the ancient authors,* that the Indians were divided into castes ; that their priests were formed into societies, in colleges, as recluses; that their religion was that of Ammon (Om-man)— that they worshiped the sun—that their priests were called, from the name of the sun, Chom, *Chomini Sophites,* from which the Greeks, he says, made Γυμνο-σοφοιται, and Γυμνοσοφιςαι, or Gymnosophists. The σοφος, I doubt not, was both a Greek and Indian word for wise, and I think no one can read the long dissertation of Mr. Bryant, and not see that the Gymnosophists were the wise men or Magi, or priests of Ammon, or of the ιερον Ομ-μανε.

The Sophites are the Asophs and Eusofzyes resident on the mount Suffaid, noticed by Mr. Elphinston in his Cabul.[4]    Of them I shall treat hereafter.

That a party of Judaites penetrated into Thrace cannot be doubted, after the visible marks of Judaism, which have been discovered in that country. The Odomantes, according to Aristophanes,[5] were Jews. The scholiast upon that author says, Οδοματων Θνος Θρεακικον, φασι δε αυτες Ιεδαιες ειναι—" The Odomantes are a people of Thrace; they say that they are Jews." Hermippus, in the Life of Pythagoras, observes, " Pythagoras performed and said these things in " imitation of the Jews and Thracians."[6]    The identity of the doctrine of the Trinitarian and Thracian Orpheus with the Trinity of India and of Genesis, again proves the Thracians and Jews both to have been colonies from India. The latter part of the word Odo-mantes I do not understand, but I have a suspicion that the first is a corruption of Ioudi.

In Thrace we have, in the doctrines of Orpheus, the triune God of India and of the Jews. In the names of towns, rivers, &c., a repetition of similar places in India : in the Χρης we have the Cristna ; in the widows sacrificing themselves, the widows of India burning themselves ; in the mysteries of Eleusis, the Indian *Concha om pancha,* &c., &c. How is all this ? Did the people of Thrace send a colony to India ; or did the Hindoos colonize Thrace ? It is impossible to be blind to the identity of the two : the sacrificing of the widows and the castes prove them of the tribe Yudi from Youdia, not of the nation of Moses, of Western Syria.

Curtius, speaking of the very people above noticed by Mr. Elphinston, says of Alexander, " Hinc in regnum *Sophitis*[7] perventum est Gens, ut Barbari credunt, SAPIENTIA excellit, bonisque " moribus regitur." I think I may now safely consider that every thing which I have formerly said of the Ammon being the Om of India is satisfactorily PROVED. The tomb of Orpheus was shewn in Thrace, and a perusal of what Mr. Bryant has said respecting him, I think must con-

---

[1] Bartol. Sys. Brach. p. 307.            [2] Vol. III. p. 215.            [3] Pp. 218—220.
[4] Chap. iv.          [5] Acharn. Act i. Scene iv.            [6] Benj. De Tudela, by Gerrans, Ch. xviii. note.
[7] Σοφια.

vince any person that there never was a man of this name, but that the Orpheans were a sect or tribe having the religion of the Trimurti, and were the Iudi who came from the East, and who were also called Iberi, or foreigners, or Hebrews. They were a tribe or sect, like the Jews of Syria, expelled from the East, who settled in Thrace, and gave the places the same names as the places they left in India; and they brought with them the Trinity, a little altered in the time of Plato, but evidently the same: and the female sacrifices, and the worship of the Χϱησος, as found on the monument at Delphi. They were, as we shall see, the Χϱησιανοι of St. Thomas, or Tammuz. It was from the Orpheans that Plato had his Trinity described in the early part of this work.

12. On the other side of the Grecian mountains, where I have formerly pointed out the Argos, the Ionnina, the Chaonia, Dodona, called by Ritter, as I am told, Bod or Bud-ona, &c., opposite to the head of the Haliacmon or Ionicora, is the town of Nicæa, and near it Chriso-dio: this is χρισος or χρησος the holy. Nicæa is the name of the God Bacchus, or Nysus, or ΙΗΣ, and Χρησος is his epithet. My reader will not forget that I formerly pointed out that in the sixteen-letter alphabet χρησος, must have been written χϱησος or χρεσος, the root of Crestonia.

A learned friend, the Rev. Mr. Kenrick, of York, has given me the following particulars of the German work of Ritter, which I regret that I cannot read: " He himself thus states the purpose " of it in his 8th page: ' I intend to shew, from the most ancient monuments which geography, " ' antiquity, mythology, architecture, and religious systems present, that Indian sacerdotal " ' colonies, with the old Buddha worship, proceeding from Central Asia, occupied mediately or " ' immediately, even earlier than the historical age of the Greeks, the countries on the Phasis, " ' Pontus, Thrace, the Danube, many places in Western Europe, and even Greece itself, whose ' " ' religious influence may be traced not only in Asiatic memorials, but in the old historical " ' fragments of the Greek, the people of Asia Minor, and in Herodotus' account of the Scythians " ' in his fourth book.' These Buddhic priests he finds in the Βεδιοι, whom Herodotus mentions " along with the Μάγοι, I. 101; the doctrine in Βάαυτ of Sanchoniathon: and the name of " Buddha in the Bod-her of the Wends, (a Slavonic tribe,) and the Bogh of the Slavians, in the " Odin of the Saxons and Woden of the Germans, whose day (Wednesday) is sacred to Buddha " even in the calendars of the Brahmins, in the Khoda of the Persians and Goth of the Germans; " in the Budini, among the Scythians on the Oaros, the Budiæans and Bottiæans of Macedonia " and Iapygia, the hero Bodo, founder of Dodona, (originally Bodona,) in Minerva Budia, worshiped " in Thessaly, (Lycophr. Cap. 359,) in Hercules Βεδώνης, in Hesychius, in the Budeion of " Homer, Il. 16, 572, in the festival Budoron, in Salamis, in the Butades and Eteobutades, the " most ancient priests of Minerva, in Attica, the Botachidæ of Arcadia, and the Butakidæ of " Naxos, Caria and Sicily, builders of the temple at Eryx. The Budoricum and Budorgis of the " Sudetes, Maro-boduum of the Marcomanni, Budissin, and Butinfeld, the Boden-see, (Lake of " Constance,) the Bothnian Gulf or Codanus Sinus, are proofs according to him, that the same " names were widely diffused also among the Germans to the North. In pursuing his argument " he endeavours to shew that the Colchians on the Euxine Sea were not, as Herodotus supposed, " and as has been generally considered, an Egyptian colony, left by Sesostris, but an Indian " colony, by shewing that the dark complexion, curly hair, and manufacture of linen, by which " he proved them to be Egyptian, are equally explicable of an Indian origin. The name Colchi " he considers as allied to the Κόλχοι, mentioned by Arrian, on the Southern coast of India, " (vinc. seq. to Periplus, p. 113,) and the κόλπος κολχικῶν of Plotemy, vii. 169; the Κῶλοι " on the Euxine, with the worship of Venus Colias in Attica, and the name Κώλιας, given by the

" Greeks to Ceylon and Cape Comorin; the Palus Μαιῆτις (for so he spells it) with the Maha
" Mai of the Buddhists in Nepaul; the κοραξοί and κορικοί on the Euxine, with the Κῶρυ ἄκρον,
" now Ramanan Kor, and Κῶρυ νῆσος, now Ramisur Kor, in Southern India, which Pliny calls
" (vi. 24) Solis insula; and the Σίντοι, also dwelling on the Euxine, with the Indi on the Sind.
" This word Kor, is then pursued through a variety of combinations; it is a name of the sun;
" the Kur of the Persians, whence κῦρος, whose name meant sun; Araxes or Kor as sacred to
" the sun; Chorasan the land of sun-worship, and the town of Κοροκανδάμη (Strabo xi. 1) on the
" Palus Maetis, a sanctuary of sun worship, from Kor and the Bactrian Kanda, signifying a
" fortified town; whence Maracanda and Sindocanda. (Ptol. vii. 180.) There is a Hypanis,
" one of the principal rivers of the Penjab, and a Hypanis falling into the Bosphorus, Strab. xi.;
" we have a Phasis in Colchis, another in Armenia, and another in Ceylon (Taprobane). This
" same country, thus connected with India, appears to him to be also in relation with the North
" of Europe. This is properly Asia; here are the Ἀσπεργιανοί, Strabo, xi., (Asa-burgers)
" inhabitants of Asgard; here is the Asof sea; Kauk-asos, this was the country of the As-kenaz
" of Moses; hence came Odin and his Asa into Scandinavia. He compares the Buddhist doc-
" trine, that, during the deluge, Buddha put his foot on certain places to preserve them from being
" covered by it, and left there an impression, with the account of Herodotus, iv. 82, of the
" gigantic footsteps of Hercules, said to be left in the land of the Scythians."

13. Berenice was called Πανχρυσος or Panchrysos, or *all gold*, from a mountain near it, where
the Ptolemies were said to get gold. I have some suspicion that the gold here was like the swans
and poplars in the Padus of Italy, sought for in vain, and ridiculed by Lucian. It is my firm
belief, that the doctrine of the Χρης or ΙΗΣ or sacred nomen, cognomen, et omen, was at
first a secret, and that the epithet of *golden* was applied in a double sense: then Πανχρυσος
would be *the beneficent* or *good* Παν. There were a golden age and a holy age: and a golden city
and a holy city. However, the Χρηςος and Ερως on the monument of the Crestonia Sindica
Prove that gold cannot be there meant.

In this opinion respecting the meaning of the word χρυσος I am completely borne out by Mr.
Bryant, whose learning no one will deny. He has undertaken to shew that, in many places,
where the words γενος χρυσεον, or γενος χρυσειον or χρυσειοι πατερες are used by Greek authors, such us Hesiod, Pausanias, &c., and translated *golden age* or *golden race* or *golden fathers,*
&c., those expressions are nonsense. In order to get over this difficulty, he proposes the violent
measure of expunging the Greek consonant ρ, which is not only contrary to all admissible rules of
etymology, but carries along with it the consequence that the Greeks did not understand their own
language. But if we leave the ρ as it is, and only suppose the change of the η for the υ, we have
good sense, and have *pious* or *holy* or *benevolent* race, or age, or fathers.[1] I believe that originally
the Greek χρης, meaning *excellent* or good, and also perhaps the solar *golden yellow rays* was
applied to the metal we call gold, and in time became corrupted into χρυς: it meant the precious
metal.[2]

This observation of the learned Bryant's is of the very first importance, for if he be right, he
completely justifies and bears me out in the only questionable part of my theory on the χρηςος
and χρυσος. He cannot have done this in accommodation to my system. What is here said is

---

[1] Bryant, Vol. III. pp. 164, &c.
[2] I beg my reader to refer to Book IX. Chap. I., Sect. 4, p. 452.

strengthened by an observation of Vallancey's in a note on Sir W. Jones's calling Cristna *Krishen*. Krishen, the Sun, Apollo; Hæb. *chors*, hinc Græc. Khrusos, aurum. Cast. p. 1409.[1] Here Vallancey agrees with me in identifying the χρησος and the χρυσος.

14. The natives of Siam and Ceylon are said by both to have once had the same religion. As we have seen a river Cresoana in Ceylon, so Ptolemy gives us a river Cresoana in Siam, (which is called a golden Chersonesus,) and in Ptolemy's map there is a cape a little to the east of what is written, Locus unde solvunt in Chrysen navigantes. I am of opinion that the Golden Chersonesus ought to be the Holy or Sacred Chersonesus.

Greek scholars explain Chersonesus by χερσος *land* and νησος *island*, that is, land-island. This only shews how soon they are satisfied. There were various Chersonesuses—as Chersonesus Aurea, Cimbrica, Taurica, and Thracia, which are now thought to be Malacca, Jutland, Crim Tartary, and Romania, and many others.[2] The explanation of land-island I consider ridiculous, and that it only proves the meaning unknown; and, in consequence, I go to collateral circumstances: finding several of them having no appearance of a peninsula, but having an evident connexion with the χρης-tian mythos, I consider it not improbable that it may be a corruption of the word χρης, and may have been the island of Crs, or Krs or Ceres, or holy or sacred island. It has also been explained to mean *desertus*—desert place. Although this is not foolish, like land-island, yet I think my explanation more probable, when all the collateral circumstances are taken into account. Upon the whole, I consider that the Chrisen of Ptolemy (see his map) to which people sailed, was clearly the Cherson-nesus aurea, and that Chrisen had the same meaning as Cherson.

The island of Java is called by the natives *Tana Jawa*, that is, Ieuetana, (the last syllable the same as in Mauritania, &c.,) and Nusa Iawa, that is, island Ieue; here we have the Greek νησος. A part of it is called the district of Kedu: this is nothing but Iodu aspirated and corrupted.[3] The residence of the prince is called Craton; this I have no doubt is Χρησον or Crestonia or Croton, and the town where it is, is called Yugya-carta—this is also Carta-Iudia. The minister of the king is called Ade-pati, that is, father Ad. Mataram is Matarea. Batavia is Buddha-via. They have also Cheri-bon. The king is called by a name which means head or chief *Rato:* this is Rasit. In the Greek language the national termination makes the word Χρης or Χρηστ into Χρης-ος : in the Tamul the national termination made it Χρησ-εν or Χρεστ-εν or Crisen.[4] This was evidently the Chersonesus, and it was not the golden Chersonesus, but (as Mr. Bryant's argument proves) the sacred peninsula island, or νησος. The golden cherson-nesus is a tautology, like river Jordan, arising from the Greeks not understanding the meaning of the mythos.

The word Chersonesus cannot be held to mean peninsula exclusively, as a general term, because we find it means also promontory. Besides, I repeat; the term land-island is absurd. I believe the χερσον in the case of Siam is the Chrysen which we find in Ptolemy's map, and the νησος answers to the *nasus* of the Romans, and means promontory; and, that the whole of what we call the golden Chersonesus was the golden or the holy promontory of Chrysen. I believe the νησος, nexus, nasus, and our word neck, had all the same origin, and meant any projection. On the coast of Malabar, in lat. 15 N., there is no peninsula, nor can South India be called a peninsula, though it may be denominated a cape or promontory. But there is a small promontory at the above-named latitude. All that I have said respecting the meaning of Chersonesus, is confirmed by an expression in Wilkinson's Atlas, in his map of Achaia, No. 28, in Eubœa,

---

[1] Coll. Hib. Vol. IV. Pt. i. p. 540.    [2] Enc. Brit.    [3] Hamilton's Gaz.    [4] See Ptolemy.

4 H

*Chersonesus vel Nasus.* In Hall's Atlas there.is a Cape Nose, in lat. 24, close to Emerald Isles. In the Sea of Marmora is found the island of Proconnesus.. In the Chersonesus of the Hellespont may be seen, lat. 40¼, Alopecon-nesus applied to a neck of land: thus it is plain that nesus means both. Chalcidon or Chrysopolis is evidently City of Chrysos or Chersos. In the old language, without vowels, they would be both the same. Though νησος means *island,* it is very clear that it does not mean island exclusively, but that it also means peninsula, and answers to the Hebrew אי *ai,* and the Greek αια, which my lexicon tells me means at once land, island, and country. To support the common explanation all peninsulas ought to have been Chersonesuses, which was not the case, at least we have no reason to believe that they were. I shall be told by Sanscrit scholars that *ia,* in Sanscrit, means victory ; no doubt it has several meanings, the same as the *ii* and *ie* and *ia* of the Hebrews. The God Ιαω, Jah, was always the God of the host of heaven, of armies, and of victory. Χερσος, Jones says, means a shell, and comes from the Hebrew חרש *hrs, chers.* I dare say it comes from the Hebrew *Hrs,* or Chres, or Cres, or Ceres, or Cyrus. Axiokersos was Ceres, that is, Axios worthy or good Χερσος. Nimrod[1] says, the Dii Magni of Samothrace—Axieros, Axiocersos, and Axiocersa, plainly correspond with the Indian names Asyoru, or Asyoruca, Asyotcersa, and Atcersa or Asyotcersas.

Georgius[2] says, Nam obvii sunt multi forte cum articulo Pi à Græcis dictus *Bi-cheres, Acen-cheres, Mer-cheres, Tar-cheres,* et Μοσχερις, *Mos-cheris,* ab Eratosthene, ne mihi litem moveas de significatione vocis, (quæ non minus Ægyptiaca, quam Hebraica est חרם *hrs, cheres,*) Græce versus Ηλιοδοτος sole datus, aut solis natus, quemadmodum eruditorum plures ante hac observarunt. Again,[3] *Cheres* Sol, unde Men-cheres. Here we have the Chres in Egypt, as might be expected.

I beg it may be observed, that in my explanation of the word Χρης, I have not availed myself of the usual practice of etymologists of changing letters for one another; as for instance, dentals into dentals, labials into labials, &c., because they are dentals or labials, but when I have changed a letter, it is because I have authority for it : for example, Crest-ona, Cort-ona, Crest-onia, Cris-sa. And in every case the changes which I have made are supported by collateral written or circumstantial evidence. Minerva was called Βυδεια, or Budea[4] in Thessaly. This is what we might expect to find in the country of the Sindi, and where the wives sacrificed themselves on the deaths of their husbands. It supports my system in a wonderful manner. The marks of the succession of the religions of Buddha and Cristna are every where apparent.

15. A learned Jew, of the name of Marcus, has given an extract from Philosturgius, a Greek of the fourth century, who says, that the inhabitants of the East shore of Africa, as far as Cape Guardafui, were called Συροι, and were tout-a-fait basanés par la chaleur du soleil, or nearly blacks. These Συροι I suppose to have been the same people who were called Συροι and Φαννοι in the Mesopotamia between the Indus and the Ganges. M. Marcus observes, that the Geez translate the word Συροι by *Saman,* which resembles *Samen.* Claudien calls the Abyssinians *Judæi.* Now these Judæi or Saman or Samen were the Samaneans whom we have found in Meroe, and proved to be the East Indian Gymnosophists of that state, and who were sometimes called, by the Greek and Roman writers, the people of the *nether* India, and, at other times, of *India* alone.[5]

We have seen the derivation of the Gazas, and that Ajmere was Gazimera. This is exactly like the Gaza of Syria, and Gaza of Egypt, the sea-port of Memphis. These would be Gazameres,

[1] Vol. II. p. 505. [2] Alph. Tib. p. 72. [3] Ibid. p. 84. [4] Littl. Dict.
[5] Journal Asiatique Nouveau, No. 18, 19, June, 1829.

in fact. Gaza is Goza ; for it is spelt with an *oin* not with an *aleph*. Mons. Marcus, the learned and ingenious Jew, thinks the Geez of Abyssinia, and the Philistines, meant *exiles*. I think they were not called by these names because they meant exiles ; but that ·they were called exiles, be- cause they were from Gazimera and Pallitana of India.

Juba, in the early part of the Christian æra, wrote that the country between Syene and Mero·; was occupied by Arabians, and that this country had the same names of places as Arabia : for instance, Ptolemy places in Nubia, Primis, Sacole, Nacis, Tathis, and Napata ; in Arabia, Priom, Saklé, Nascos, Thades, and the nation of the Napatei. M. Marcus allows that the Abyssinians call their country Gys, which, he says, signifies *emigration*, because they emigrated from Philis- tina in Syria. But he does not observe that these people were called by the same name in the country they left. This I have already accounted for in observing that they were called emigrants, because they were Geez—not Geez; because they were emigrants : for they and the Palli were equally emigrants or exiles in Western Syria and Nubia.

M. Marcus observes, it is astonishing that notwithstanding the high antiquity of the first esta- blishments of the Jews in Abyssinia, the industry of these people throws no light on the sojourn of their fathers in Palestine,.or of the civilization of the Phœnicians, Assyrians, &c. The reason of this is very simple—because they came at the same time with those who are called their fa- thers, and before Moses lived : and this is the reason why they had no Pentateuch till they ob- tained one from the Christians. M. Marcus also observes, that the founding as well as the decline of the kingdom of Meroe are involved in equal obscurity.

The country of the Chaldeans was Northern India ; in which there was a district called Syra, (Syra-strene), and Pallitana; and as the people were Judi or Judæi, they spoke the Chaldee or Syro-Chaldee language. The same took place in South India : Mysore is Maha-Sura or the Great Syria.[1] Here there was also a Colida or Chaldea, the people Judi or Judæi speaking the Syro-Chaldee language ; and there also were found the Samaneans.

In Abyssinia, the country was called India and *nether* India ; in a large district of which, the people were called Συροι—a sufficient proof that the country was called Sura or Suria :. there also people were called Judæi, and they likewise spoke the Chaldee or Syro-Chaldee language. In all these countries the Pallestini and Samaneans are found ; and what is more remarkable, the Phannoi or Phœnicians are found in Egypt, and in two of the Eastern Syrias, together, as the reader has seen, with several other striking coincidences. In three of them, all the Mosaic mythos is found, but without the Pentateuch, which was a later compilation of the people of the fourth country, and in all the four, Crestians or Chrestians are found, though their origins are for- gotten and variously accounted for. The persons whom Manetho calls *Royal Shepherds* he also calls *Phœnices* and *Hellenes*.[2]

The tribe of Juda was not stopped in its migration westward by the sea; or, perhaps when it was driven out from Egypt, part of it moved to the West, along the coast of the Mediterranean, till it got round to Guinea, and,.there it is yet, with its native curly head, possessing a beautiful country, full of fine rivers, among which are found a river Phrat and a Jachin.[3] It would be very curious to examine the language of this people.. Edrisi, in the twelfth century, says that Jews occupied the country on the river *Lamlem*, and that it is called *Yahandi*. This is confirmed by Mr, Bowditch, in his account of the Ashantee country. Every thing proves that they were of the tribe Judi,.though, as they have no Pentateuch, it is clear that they came not from the tribe

---

[1] Buchanan.    [2] Bryant's Anal. Vol. III. p. 250.

[3] See Mem. de Berlin, Tom. XVII. by M. de Francheville.

of the Western Asiatic Judæa, or at least that they did not emigrate from it after the time of Moses. Near lat. 10, N., will be found a country called Soolimana, and near it are places called Kisse and Boodyæa and Cambodia and Nalanbes—all Indian names.[1]

I have lately found that it is stated in the Talmud of Jerusalem, that Joshua, before he entered Canaan, sent to inform the inhabitants, that such as wished to escape might do so, and that, in consequence of this permission, great numbers, despairing of being able to defend themselves, fled into Africa.[2]  Pieces of evidence of this kind, unexpectedly occurring to support my theory, are very striking.  These Canaanites may have been the people who set up the pillars at the Straits of Gibraltar, (noticed in the last page of the Appendix to my CELTIC DRUIDS,) described by the Gentile Procopius.  They may have advanced along the coast till they came to where they are now found.

In the Melpomene of Herodotus, Sect. lxiii., will be found an account of one Sataspes who attempted to sail round Africa, by going through the Pillars of Hercules.  After sailing a long time he came to a nation in Εσθητι Φοινικηϊη.  This has much puzzled the learned.  These people were an early tribe of Ioudi, and they were dressed in Phœnician dresses.  That is all.  But this and other circumstances prove the truth of Herodotus's history.  They were probably the people just now noticed, who *fled from before the face of Joshua the robber, the son of Nun.*

16.  The Gaza of Syria is evidently the same in name as the Aj-mere of India, treated of in Book VIII., for in Ptolemy they have both the same name : one being called Gaza-mera, the other Gaza. The Western Gaza was also called Iona ; thus Iona is the same as Aj, or, read in the Hebrew style, Ja, the famous Io of Syria, both male and female ; the ח E converted into the o (in their dialect making the Io) from the Hebrew male and female Iε.  But the town of Gaza or Iona in the Hebrew is spelt עזה Oze.  This we see answers to the Aji of India ; and as the ז z is not one of the *sixteen* letters, it is probable that it has originally been like the Indian, the i or j.  Thus, again, we get at last to the יה ie or Jah of the Hebrews, which was of both genders, or perhaps more correctly we should say, of neither.  The יה ie was substituted for the שרי sdi, which Parkhurst clearly shews to have been the Dea Multimammia.  Thus it seems that the object of the change was, to get rid of the worship, *exclusively female*, of Hellenism.

Col. Tod says, that the word *Mer* means Hill.  Now, as I have already remarked, as far as I can make out, near each of these hill towns there is always a sacred lake, often upon the hill, and frequently made at very great expense.  Rivers generally flow from these hills, and the spring-head was converted into a lake, in a peculiar manner sacred.  These lakes by being used for the purposes of agriculture, were real and great blessings to the countries below them.  There was a great and sacred lake at Ajmere, Gaza of India.  A mer, the mr or artificial ocean, is found at Gaza or עזה oze of Western Syria, in the real ocean : it is found at Memphis, of Egypt, in Gize near the famous Lake Mœris, the head or bank of which was of very great length—Egypt of which Memphis or Gize was once a sea-port.  If the *sea* were not there, the *lake* was.  There is also in Ceylon a Lake or Tank, the banks faced with stone, of a size almost beyond credibility.  We have also mers or meers very common in England.  Now I cannot help observing, that these words Mr are all composed of the two letters which form the word for Maria or the female generative principle.  I apprehend the case of the *Mere* is precisely similar to that of the *Oceanus*.  The element round Mount Meru was called Oceanus, and, in imitation of Meru, no one will doubt that all the Mount Olympuses were consecrated.  In imitation of these Rome was built, and round it

---

[1] See large Map at the Oriental Club, Hanover Square, London.

[2] Talmud Hierosol apud Maimonid. Halach. Melachim, Cap. vi. Sect. v.; Sayle's Prel. Dis. to Koran, Sect. vi. p. 192.

a fosse was dug answering to the Oceanus called *Mundus* and Orbis, and Urbs (all the same) : but this Mundus is called by Plutarch, in Greek,[1] Olympus. Here is the mount most clearly used for the oceanus. Thus it was with Mere. It was a mount and a maris or sea—as, Horn-sea-mere and Wittlesea-mere and Mount Meru, and Aj-mere, and Casi-mere or Cash-mere.

It is a very curious natural phenomenon, that upon the top of almost every mountain a spring is found. This was the mere or meer : and from this the hill came to be called mere ; in like manner lakes on the tops of hills came to be called mounts. The mere or *lake* is the mother of the river ; the mere or *mount* is also the mother of the river. There was a lake in Wales called Pemble or Pendle Meer, in which was a sacred island.[2] We have also mounts of the mere : we have Sled-mere, and Pen-mawr, and Pen-maenmawr.

The word mere or meere was used for a lake by Pliny,[3] who says, " where now is the mere or lake Sale ?" This was near Erythræa on the coast of Asia Minor ; and in the next sentence he says, it was near a mount Colpe. There was an Erythræa near Gades, and Calpe, now Gibraltar, is close by it. By Mount Meru was probably meant Mount of the mere—Mount rising out of the Mere—Mother Ocean—Mother Isis.

The lake Mareotis, Moeris is called Maria,[4] and the island Meroe. It was called *island*, pro-bably, to make it assimilate to Meru, though it was not naturally an island. All these supersti-tions are evidently closely connected : and it is clear to me that the adoration of the male and female generative principle is at the bottom of them all ; and the terrible wars which took place, with alternate successes and reverses, between the sects, furnish cause enough to account for the mixture which we every where find. I think the יה ie or *Jah*, the Self-existent, was the founda-tion on which all was built ; and what could be more likely ? It was the *Aji* in India ; *Io* in Syria ; *Ei* at Delphi ; and at Gaza in Pali-stan, it was עוז oze, corrupted from *Aji*. The mer and the *Aji* we find always together ; it was the Mount Meru with its ocean surrounding it. But we have found the lakes or inland seas called Mareotis and Maretis, and in England Meres. We have found the mounts in India called Meres, on which, generally, were artificial lakes ; or the meer contained a sacred island and temple, as in Cashmere or Cashimere. We have found a Meroe in Egypt, being an island, artificially made, for the sake of making a mere round it. This was an imitation of Mount Meru surrounded with its ocean, and in imitation of the Mount of Maria, on which the Gods sat on the sides of the North, at Jerusalem, mistranslated Moriah, which was formed as nearly like the others as circumstances would permit. For, though it was impossible to make a sea round this fortress—this acropolis, yet, in lieu thereof, it had its brazen sea within. In Wales, in Ireland, in Arabia,[5] we meet with meres or lakes containing sacred islands. All these arise from the first imaginary Meru—the pole of the earth, with its star of Judé over it, in the heavens. All these mounts were mounts or islands of Meru or Maria or Maia ; and the sacred Argha, in which the linga or pole was erected, was an emblem of the Maria or the ocean, from this called Mare.

The word *Aja* means self-existing, according to Col. Wilsford.[6] How is it possible to doubt that we have here the יה ie of Genesis ? The female energy of nature is described by the word I.[7] This is the I or Ii of the Targums.

It is true that Ajmer is hill of victory, or hill of Ajya, as Col. Tod says ;[8] because Jah or IE or יה ie or אהוה aeue was the God of victory, as he is repeatedly called in the Old Testament.

---

[1] Rom. ch. x.; Nimrod, Vol. I. p. 313.  
[3] See Nat. Hist. Lib. v. Cap. xxix.  
[5] Vide Davies's Celtic Researches.  
[8] P. 11.  

[2] Davies, Celtic Myth. p. 191.  
[4] Euseb. Hist. Cap. xvi.  
[6] Asiat. Res. Vol. V. p. 247, ed. 8vo.  [7] Ibid.

Aja, in Sanscrit, means goat; and Gaza, in Hebrew, also means goat;[1] this proves the identity of the two: but Aja means both goat, and sheep, and Aries.[2] ·The goat copulates with a sheep and breeds forward; (goat in Hebrew is עז *oz* ;) being of the same class of animals, like the greyhound and pointer, and not like the horse and ass. Here we have the reason why the goat is often found instead of the ram. The bull, the ram, and the goat, are the three animals of which the sacrifices of the ancients chiefly consisted. The two last, I doubt not, were considered, as they are, of one genus.

When I reflect upon the fact, that the origin as well as, in a great part, the meaning of their mythologies were lost by the Greeks, I am inclined to go to the East for an explanation of the Gaia of Plato, and calculate upon his ignorance of his own mythology.[3] I find one of the most holy places of India called Gaya or Gaia, famous as the birthplace of Buddha. It is in lat. 24, 49; long. 85. In this case the Gaia must have been a mystical term for the generative power. Gaia would be synonymous to Chaonia or Caonia. If I be right, this case is exactly similar to that of the *konx om pax* of Eleusis noticed before; that is, it is an Indian word adopted by the Greeks. I suspect it has, in some way, come from the same source as the Aj, Aja, Agi, Aje. A city is often alluded to in the mythic histories called Aiai—that is, *place of Ai* ; the same meaning as the Aje and Gaia.

17. Of the different names of Bacchus, there was not one more common than that of Dio-nusus, or Dio-nisos, or the holy Nisus. The *Dio* means *holy*, and the *us* or *os* is merely a Latin or Greek termination. Then Nıs is the name. In Pagninus's Exodus the name of Jehovah Nisi is written two ways, one in the text, the other in the margin—נסי *nsi* and נסם *nss*. But the Samechs being new letters, if we want its meaning, we must put it in the letters of the old or Cadmean or sixteen-letter system; then it will be נשי *nsi* and נשש *nss*, and will mean

| I · · · · · | ׳ = | 10 | Again S · · · · · · | ש = | 3?0 | S · · · · · · | ש = | 3?0 |
|---|---|---|---|---|---|---|---|---|
| S · · · · · · | ש = | 300 | S · · · · · · | ש = | 3?0 | I · · · · · · · | ׳ = | 1? |
| N · · · · · · | נ = | 5? | N · · · · · · | נ = | 5? | N · · · · · · | נ = | 5? |
| | | 360 | | | 650 | | | 360 |

Can any man believe that these peculiar, sacred numbers come out by accident?—The first, the supposed length of the solar year, and the number sacred to Bacchus, or the Sun? · Let us recollect that Pythagoras's learned secrets were all founded on numbers. We have here the Jehovah Nisi. יהוה נשי *ieue nsi.* ש Sin and ס Samech are indiscriminately used, as appears from the authority of Elias in Thisbi, and the constant practice of oriental writers.[4]

It appears from the book or history of the Exod, that it was on the leaving of Egypt that Moses changed the object of adoration from Taurus to Aries. It was then that he represented God as having ordered, that he should be called Iαω, יהוה *ieue*, and not by his old name of שדי *sdi* or Multimammia. It appears that the change took place on the mountain of *Sin*, or *Nisi*, or Bacchus, which was evidently its old name before Moses arrived there. The Israelites were punished for adhering to the old worship, that of the Calf, in opposition to the paschal Lamb, which Moses had substituted—" the Lamb which taketh away the sins of the world," in place of the Bull or Calf which took away the sins of the world. See Faber for the prayer to the bull *Taurus the saviour*—and Bryant, end of his Vol. III., for the same.

I suppose the expression the *Bull* or *Calf taking away the sins of the world* will be most unmercifully ridiculed. It has been in part done by a very worthy priest, to whom I opened the

---

[1] Drum. Œd. Jud. p. 361.  [2] From Dr. Wilkins's MS. given me by Prof. Haughton.
[3] See Bk. Ch. II. Sect. 4, of this work.  [4] Gerran's note on Benj. de Tudela, Ch. xvii.

subject. But I beg to be informed by the dealers in ridicule, why a calf should not take away the sins of the world as well as a lamb? Verbum Sapienti. If it be said that the Lamb was the emblem of the second person in the Trinity, I reply that the Bull was, in a former period, the same. The word for the Sun is in Hebrew *Sur*, in Chaldee *Tur*. In the Hebrew this would be TR, the same as *Taurus*. Here we have T=400, R=200=600: but I think it would probably have been T=400 R=200 H=8, חרת *trh*. May we not in the TPH find the meaning of the *thre* in the name Ery-thre-a?

Addressez votre prière au Taureau excellent: addressez votre prière au Taureau pur: addressez votre prière à ces principes de tout bien: addressez votre prière à la pluie, source d'abundance: addressez votre prière au Taureau devenu pur, celeste, saint, qui n'as pas été engendré: qui est saint, &c.[1] When the Greeks became refined, they did not like to see their Bacchus with the horns of a bull, like Moses: but, as they could not mythologically be dispensed with, in the statues which are really old, they are there hidden under vine or ivy leaves. " Come, hero Dionusus, " to thy temple on the sea-shore: come, HEIFER-footed deity, to thy sacrifice, and bring the graces " in thy train! Hear us, Bull, worthy of our veneration; hear us, O illustrious Bull."[2]

As the Gods all carried heads appropriate to the solar sign to which they were sacred, a Bull's head to Taurus, a Sheep's head to Aries, so their games bore appropriate names, and were called Taurobolia and Criobolia. " But whence the more common Greek-name Διονυσος is derived, or " what it signifies, is not so easy to determine, or even to conjecture, with any reasonable proba- " bility. The first part of it appears to be from ΔΕΥΣ, ΔΙΟΣ or ΔΙΣ, the ancient name of " the supreme universal God: but whether the remainder is significant of the place from which " this Deity came into Greece, or of some attribute belonging to him, we cannot pretend to say: " and the conjectures of etymologists, both ancient and modern, concerning it, are not worthy " notice."[3] As we have seen before, it is said by Ausonius to be Indian, and by the mystics it was called Phananin—that is, Phen. I think this allowance by the learned Payne Knight of the general ignorance opens the door most beautifully to my explanation above: and I think in almost every case, if not in every one, where I have explained these proper names from numbers, like the name *Nisi* of Bacchus, they admit no other derivation, and this, in the end, will be found to be an observation of the first importance. This is the common case with the names of the Gods; they seldom or ever admit an etymological explanation. The reason of this I shall explain in a future book. On the identity of Bacchus and Iacchus, Mr. Payne Knight says, " They are in " fact the same name in different dialects, the ancient verb ΦΑΧΩ, in Lacaonian, ΒΑΧΩ, having " become by the accession of the augment ΦΙΦΑΧΩ. υ ιαχω."[4] The IAX is Iacchus and our Jack.

The Taranis of the Druids, noticed in my CELTIC DRUIDS,[5] as their object of worship, and, in fact, having the same name as the Scandinavian God Thor, and as the Belinus, the Hesus, and the Thau, and called their High Spirit by Vettius Valens;[6] is, in Hebrew, חרן *Trn*, T=400, R=200, N=50, total 650—the number of stones in the temple of Abury, and in the Hebrew name Mitra. The original name, probably, was *Tarn*, the *is* being a corruption of the Greek *os*.

---

[1] Bryant's Anal. Vol. III. p. 597.

[2] Quæst. Græc, p. 299; Davies's Celtic Myth. p. 174.

[3] Payne Knight, Class. Journ. 1821, p. 9.      [4] Ibid.

[5] Pp. 130 (misprinted TARAMIS) and 278.

[6] Ibid. p. 278.

In my CELTIC-DRUIDS, Chap. VI. Sect. XXV., 1 have given the following explanation of Meithras :

| No. 1. | | | | No. 2. | | | | No. 3. | |
|---|---|---|---|---|---|---|---|---|---|
| M | - - 40 | | | M | - - 40 | | | מ = | 40 |
| E | - - 5 | | | I | - - 10 | Or, in Hebrew, | | י = | 10 |
| I | - - 10 | But it would be better, | | Θ | - - 9 | thus : - - | | ת = | 400 |
| Θ | - - 9 | as more ancient, thus : | | P | - - 100 | | | ר = | 200 |
| P | - - 100 | | | A | - - 1 | | | | — |
| A | - - 1 | | | Σ | - - 200 | | | | 650 |
| Σ | - - 200 | | | | — | | | | |
| | — | | | | 360 | | | | |
| | 365 | | | | | | | | |

The word is often written Mitra, particularly in India; thus we have two sacred numbers for it, as we have for Bacchus. Is this accident? What says the enemy to double etymology to this? We learn part of the Pythagorean secret from the Greeks, and a part from the Hebrews. On this, very much hereafter.

---

## CHAPTER III.

CÆSAR THE NINTH AVATAR.—ZARINA.—CÆSAR HONOURED AS A GOD.—TWELVE CÆSARS.—ADRIATIC.—SIBYL'S PROPHECY OF CÆSAR.—ILIAD A SACRED MYTHOS.—CÆSAR'S DEATH FOLLOWED BY DARKNESS.—STAR.—ROMA.—NIEBUHR.—PALLADIUM.—HISTORY OF ITALY.—MUNDUS.—RAJAH.—PALA.—HELLEN.—ATTILA.—HIEROGLYPHICS.

1. WE are now prepared, I think, for another divine incarnation—the *Ninth*—and we shall find him in the celebrated Julius Cæsar.

In the history of Julius Cæsar, and, indeed, in that of his whole race, there is something peculiarly curious and mystical. He was of the family of the Julii, who were descended from Venus, by her son Æneas, the son of the Trojan Anchises. From Æneas and Creusa descended Ascanius, also named Julius, who lived in the mystic Alba, till that city was ruined by Tullus Hostilius, who, it is said, instead of destroying the family of his enemy as usual, removed it to Rome, where it flourished for many generations, until it achieved the sovereignty not only of Rome, but almost of the world, to which, in a very particular manner, it may be said *to have brought peace.* The greatest of the Cæsars was Caius Julius, who was born about half a century before Jesus Christ. The word Julius is the same as the ancient Yule, who was Saturn. The Quintile month, the month in which the great Julius is said to have been born, was sacred to Yule. See Nimrod,[1] who has shewn how the Saturnalia became our Christmas gambols. We must not forget, that the Mons Capitolina, the Roman capitol, where Julius established his empire, was first called Saturnia.

The Rev. Dr. Barret[2] says, " the woman of the Revelation clothed with the sun, and having on

---

[1] Vol. I. pp. 155, 156, 158.          [2] P. 143.

" her head a crown of twelve stars, brings forth a child, *which is* בעל *oull or Christ.*" This is Yule, Julius, or Iulus. In honour of this child, on the 25th of Dec., we have the Yule clog and the Christmas gambols, and on this day, in the morning, the old women go about with a child begging from door to door, singing, *to us a child is born,* &c. From this came, if it be not itself, the Huli festival, to celebrate the Vernal equinox, or the new year, with the Hindoos and Persians. Now what, at last, is the meaning of the Yule or annual games—whence comes the Julius or the Genius of the Sæculum or Cycle ? I believe that it comes from the Hebrew עלם *oulm, sæculum.* Abraham [1] invoked God in the name of Ieue the *Aleim* of the *Sæculum.* And Cyrus was called Pater futuri *sæculi.* Thus Julius means sæcular or sæculum—αιων των αιωνων. The letter *I* is prefixed to the בעל *oull,* making Julius, for the same reason that it is prefixed in the word Ιlχθευς, in the Sibylline acrostic, to be discussed presently. The passage in Genesis xxi. 33, rendered by me, in Book II. Chap. I. Sect. 4, *Ieue Deum æternum,* is rendered by Pagninus *in nomine Domini Dei sæculi.* This, I doubt not, was the true meaning. He invoked God in the name of Jehovah or Ieue, the God of the sæculum, cycle, or age; and in many other places Ieue is called the God (עלם *oulm*) of the sæculum, and from this came our word *holy.*

The similarity between the expressions in the fourth eclogue of Virgil and in the prophecy of Isaiah, is very observable ; and has been noticed by Bishop Horsley, and, as we have before said, by many other divines. The reader must now see, that as they were poems relating to the same mythos, this was almost a necessary consequence. From the peculiarly mystic character of Creusa, daughter of Priam, and wife of Æneas, (vide Lempriere,) I cannot help suspecting that she was a Latin Crees, or Crees-ta. It may be observed, that she was the *stirps* whence the Roman nation, or at least its highest branch, sprung, as I have lately observed. I do not understand the derivation of the word Æneas, from whom Julius was descended, but the mystic character of that hero, and of the history of the kingdom of King Latinus or Lateinus, may be seen in Nimrod,[2] where the Æneid is satisfactorily shewn to be a second Iliad. Respecting the name of King Latinus, Nimrod has pointed out a peculiarity which, when coupled with other circumstances, and the very common practice of giving numeral names to persons, is well worthy of attention, and will be accounted for hereafter. Nimrod says,[3] " A passage of Irenæus is as follows :[4] Sed et Latinos, *(lege,* Lateinos,) " nomen sexcentorum sexaginta sex numerum : et valde verisimile est, quoniam verissimum reg- " num hoc habet vocabulum, Latini enim sunt qui nunc regnant; sed non in hoc nos gloriabimur."

|   |   |
|---|---|
| L | 30 |
| A | 1 |
| T | 300 |
| E | 5 |
| I | 10 |
| N | 50 |
| O | 70 |
| S | 200 |
|   | 666 |

This sacred number being found equally among the Etruscans and Latins and in the *very ancient* Apocalypse, proves to me its very great antiquity. Æneas, in fact, conquered Latinus, and by force of arms obtained his kingdom. The beast 666 was overcome. This standing alone,

---

[1] In Gen. xxi. 33.          [2] Vol. III. pp. 6, &c.          [3] Ibid. p. 500.
[4] Advers Hær. Lib. v. Cap. xxv. p. 365, ed. Gallasii, 1570.

would not be worthy a moment's consideration. It is the connexion of circumstances with it, which gives it any value.

Of Æneas and Virgil Nimrod says, [1] " This poem originally called *Gesta Populi Romani*, repre-
" sents Æneas as a descendant of the Gods, himself also a God, a *necromancer*, and the High
" priest, Flamen, and Hierophant, establishing and expounding the religions of Roma-Troja, and
" unfolding its future destinies. He is not idly called *pius* Æneas, but his sanctity as a priest and
" prophet was the main object to which Virgil sought to draw his readers' admiration, his warlike
" achievements being but a menstruum in which he might convey this political poison."

If Julius were the family name, Cæsar was his title of honour, which might be taken from the God Hesus of his own conquered Gaul : and this Hes-us I cannot help suspecting will turn out to be, when examined to the bottom, a corruption of the ΙΗΣ of Bacchus. But Nimrod [2] says, " Æsar, which is the chief part of the word Cæsar, meant GOD *in Etruscan :* and no doubt the " same family which inherited the name of the Ænead Hero, and Indigete Julius, were also the " cognomen Æsar, or Deus, with an honorific prefix." Now, what could this honorific prefix be? If Cæsar took his title from the Celts of Gaul, whom he had conquered, and if their letters were, as we have reason to suppose, the letters of Greece, they would not then have the sibillant ς, but might, in lieu thereof, have the Greek Χ, and then the word would be Χæsar : and then this honorific prefix would be, what we might well expect, the sign of the 600, or ΧΗ-σαρ the Sar, 608, the sacrum nomen, cognomen, et omen. If read Hebraicè it would be Ras-ΗΧ. Of all the mystic names of antiquity, there was not one more universal than that of Æsar or Cæsar. It prevailed in all nations. If I be right in this, we see that the monogram will correctly apply to Cæsar, or Tzar. $T=300 \; \Sigma=200 \; P=100 \; H=8=608 : HX=HT\sigma\rho=608$. Hence the Tzars of Muscovy, and the Cæsar of Germany. As Cæsar was held to be an incarnation of the Χρησος, his birth was fixed to a period which we have found, by modern inquiries, was one of the sacred æras of India, when the ninth Χρης was supposed to be born, or the ninth benignant incarnation was believed to have taken place, or when the ninth sæculum began.

Suetonius relates, in his Life of Augustus, that " the letter C being struck off by lightning from " the inscription on his statue, this response was given, that he had only a hundred days to live, " which was the number pointed out by the deficient letter: but that he should be afterward reckoned " among the Gods, because *Aesar*, which forms the remaining part of the name of Caesar, is in the " Etruscan language the denomination of God. [3] In the Gothic language, As, Aes, Aesus, is the " name of Odin, or by way of distinction, that of God. In the plural, it is Asar and Aesir." Now Odin will not be denied to be the same as Woden, and Woden we have traced from the Carnatic, where we shall find the Kesari, the Χρης, &c., &c. Sol, in Hetrusca etiam lingua Esar vocatus est. [4] The Etruscans made it a law not to represent Æsar by any image : this was the Etruscan name of the invisible God, the *great Creator*. The Pagan Irish worshiped him under the same name, and made no image to him : the word Æsar or Esar, is undoubtedly Phœnician. עזר *izr, iasur* formavit. [5] " The God Esus is the Celtic Mars, where we have the " sense of destroyer ; and is a reduplication of the element S, as Es-us, in order to express the " idea more strongly." Again, " I have before produced the Hebrew עז *Oz-Uz*, very or ex- " *ceedingly* strong, and the Syriac Az-Az-os (Αζαζος) and the Arabic Az-Eez, *excellent, precious.*"

---

[1] Vol. III. p. 466.      [2] Ibid. p. 456.

[3] Æsar, id est, reliqua pars e Cæsaris nomine Etrusca lingua Deus vocatur. Vita Aug. Cap. xcvii. Jamieson's Orig. of Greeks, p. 151.

[4] El Schedius de Diis German. p. 108; Vall. Coll. Hib. Vol. V. p. 91.      [5] Vall. Coll. Vol. IV. p. 461.

He adds that, in the Arabic term Az and Azar, the idea of excellence united to strength seems to prevail; and also whatever tends to support life.[1]   Here, I think, both the good and evil principles seem to be found.   A town of Cilicia was called Cæsar-Augustini, but was anciently occupied by the Anazarbenes; these were evidently the Beni-azar, the sons of Æsar or Cæsar.[2]   These preceded Julius and Augustus Cæsar.

2. The Zarina of Russia, the name of the queens of that country, is evidently the שר sr with a feminine termination.   This is the Phœnician or Chaldæan Sar or Zar, a prince or grandee.[3] Thomyris, the Scythian queen, who was said to have conquered Cyrus, was called Zarina.   I have a strong suspicion that the despots of Russia and Germany both affect the name of Cæsar, for the same reason that the family of Cæsar kept its mythic name.   I have no doubt that the person who claims this title, claims, though secretly, to be autocrat of the world, both by right of the sword and of the book,—both as priest and king.

It is notorious that Nero was thought by the Romans to be a peculiarly sacred person, or to have opened some sacred period.   On this account he was, in more than an usual manner, hated by the Christians, who took him to be Antichrist, that is, another or opposition Christ.   The name of Nero, which he bore, looks very like the name of the Neros, a coincidence which would never have occurred to me had it not been for the other circumstances.   We very often hear of the wickedness of Nero, but we seldom hear of the wickedness of Constantine the GREAT, who murdered his son, his brother-in-law, his wife, his nephew under age, and amused himself by making the kings taken prisoners in war fight wild beasts in the circus.   Notwithstanding all this, the Rev. Dr. Lardner tells us this GREAT man *" was not a bad man,"* and his general conduct is marked with the approbation of the Christian world, by his equestrian statue being placed, at this very day, June 1832, in the porch of St. Peter's Church at Rome!!!

3. Cæsar had all the honours paid to him as to a divine person, and that particular divine person of whom we have been treating.   He was called Father of his country, that is, the Αιων των αιωνων, Pater futuri sæculi.   At the end of five years, a festival was instituted to his honour, as to a person of divine extraction.   A college of priests was established to perform the rites instituted for that occasion.   A day was dedicated to him, and he had the title also of Julian Jove: and a temple was erected to him.[4]   His temple bore the appellation of Heroum Iuleum, and contained images of Venus.   Julius was followed by his nephew Octavius, who was also called Cæsar, to which was added the mystic title of Augustus,[5] which meant *sanctity* and deification upon earth.[6]   *Augusto* auguria postquam incluta condita Roma est.   And to make the mythological circumstances complete, we have the astrological number of 12 applied to the first 12 Roman Emperors, called Cæsars, by the historians of those times.   We know that different Roman families had mythoses applicable to them, or they were in some respects sacred.   This was the case with the Fabii; the same with the family who had the care of the ceremonies on Mount Soracte, &c.   I suppose that the family of Julius had, or affected to have, some sacred character of this kind, and maintained the reality of their imaginary pedigree, from the mystic Ilium or Troy.   And this, probably, in no small degree, aided the brilliant Julius in possessing himself of the supreme power—the prophecy conducing to its own fulfilment, as was the case of another great man in a

[1]  See Whiter's Etymol. Univ. pp. 196, 717, 718.          [2]  Plin. Nat. Hist. Lib. v. Cap. xxvii.

[3]  Enc. Brit. voce Philology, p. 568.

[4]  Dion. Cassius, Lib. xliv. Cap. iv.; Ferguson's Roman History, Vol. III. Book v. p. 32.

[5]  The Nile was called Augustus by the Egyptians. They called it King Augustus.   Basnage, Hist. Jews, p. 247.

[6]  Ennius ap. Suet. Octav. Cap. vii.; Hor. Lib. iv. Cap. xii.

later day, as I shall presently shew.[1]  It is probable that when Julius was killed, some of the devotees would admit that they were mistaken in the person, but this would not in the slightest degree injure the credit of the mythos.  The superstition only transfers itself.  Evidence on experience in these cases is of no avail.  Octavius became the expected *great one;* and of *him* his followers had no doubt, at least the fools of his followers.  He was born like Bacchus, Hercules, Nimrod, Cyrus, Alexander, Scipio Africanus, Solomon, *mense decimo.*  He had Apollo, in the form of a serpent, for his father, and at his death his soul, like that of the Holy St. Polycarp, flew away to heaven in the form of a bird.  All this and much more of the same kind, may be found in different parts of Nimrod's work, but particularly in Vol. III. p. 458.  But the murder of Cæsar was his Aphanasia—his Apotheosis.  It was an imitation of that of Romulus.  In every case the founder of the Cycle seems to have suffered a violent death, in some way or other, and the earth to have been darkened; but we shall see much relating to this hereafter.

4. The observation made respecting the twelve Cæsars only applies to a part of an universal mythos.  There were twelve tribes of Israel, who all assembled to worship at one temple.  There were twelve tribes of Ionians, who all assembled in like manner at one temple.  There were twelve tribes of Etruscans, who all assembled at one temple; and who, by colonies, founded twelve tribes in Campania, and twelve more in the Apennine mountains.  There were twelve Cæsars, and twelve Imaums of Persia, followers of Ali, all believed to be foretold by Esdras, 2, ch. xii. 11—15.  When Moses built a Druidical temple near to Sinai, he set up twelve stones; at Gil-Gal again twelve unhewn stones, and on Gerizim, again, twelve stones in circles.  I need not point out the circles of twelves so often found in the remaining Druidical temples—all Pythagorean and Masonic—still intelligible in many of our chapter-houses, for the builders of these were the oldest monks (probably Carmelites) and masons.  For thousands of years there were no *stone* edifices except those for the use of the sacred order, religion, and the walls of towns; all others being of sun-burnt brick and wood of course, have disappeared.

The first information which we have of Æsus or Aosar is, I think, in the history of the celebrated Abaris, who came from the Hyperboreans to visit Pythagoras.  He is said to have struck his harp to the Delian Apollo or Aosar.  Of all titles of honour among the ancients, perhaps there was not one so common as that of Cæsar.  This will be thought extraordinary, but I shall prove it true.  A religious mythos or prophecy always has a tendency to cause its own fulfilment, or at least apparent fulfilment.  It is natural that the devotees attached to it should force every indifferent circumstance to fit to it, to suit it.  And if the prophecy were really true, numbers of trifling circumstances, indifferent in themselves, would be found to aid it or support it.  Thus the person called Cæsar took that name, and, in imitation of the Lucumones of the Etruscans, he was followed by eleven other Cæsars.  And his assassination and six hours' darkness formed his aphanasia, similar to that of Romulus and others.

We have found the Mount Ararat in South India, or, what is the same thing, in Ceylon.  (This island, I have no doubt, was formerly connected with the main land, and was probably disconnected when the city of Maha-bali-poor[2] was sunk in the sea, and when the Aral, Caspian and Euxine seas broke their banks, as noticed in Book VI., Chapter I.)  We have found it in North India, in Il-av-ratta or mount of Naubanda; and the Sibylline Oracles give us another in Phrygia, or Roum or Rome.  It had the same name as the Rama of India.  I have no doubt that the whole mythos was repeated in Asia Minor: for, Montanus, who came from Phrygia, was believed to be the *ninth* or *tenth* Avatar.  He was the Phrygian Avatar.

---

[1] On this subject, see the 4th Eclogue and the 6th book of the Æneid.
[2] For a treatise on Mahabalipoor see Trans. Asiat. Soc. Vol. II. p. 1.

5. At the first sight of that part of the Sibylline oracle which relates to the Emperors, down to Hadrian, every person will instantly say, it has been written to suit the history ; but when I consider that Julius Cæsar was named certainly after the month, the mythos, and not the mythos after him, and the circumstance of the twelve Cæsars, I cannot avoid a suspicion that the Emperors to Hadrian took their names to suit the mythos as Cæsar did. That the history is deeply tainted with judicial astrology cannot be doubted, or why should there be twelve Cæsars, and why should Nero (Q. Neros the Cycle of 600 ?) be considered the expected Messiah or tenth incarnation—the genius of the tenth cycle of the Neros ? I beg my reader to reconsider the singularity of the name, coupled with the tradition. I had written the above when I discovered that the Adriatic Sea was called the Adriates, Αδριες, by Herodotus ; and also by Horace. This at once proved that my suspicion was well-founded, and from this we may learn, that we ought not to be too hasty in determining a work to be spurious from anacronisms—not till they are very carefully examined. It is probable that the other Cæsars before Hadrian had their names from the mythos ; at all events, we can no longer conclude that the Sibyls are spurious from the names of Roman Emperors. However corrupted they may be, we cannot conclude them mere forgeries. When we consider that we have not a single book which is not corrupted, it would indeed be a miracle if the Sibyls had escaped. When I find two mystical persons called by the same name, I suspect mysticism. In the East Elias is called by Musselmans Kheser, and Khizir, which looks like Cæsar. Elias was said to be a divinely-inspired person, and so was Cæsar, and here we seem to have them by the same name.

We have heard of the death of Adonis only from the Greeks ; Mars was jealous of Venus. In Gaul Mars was called Esus, and Æsus, and Hesus, and Hesar. What was it in Chaldæa that killed Adonis ? חזר Hzr, Chesar, Cæsar. But חזיר hzir, a wild boar, was taken for חזר hzr, and thus a wild boar killed Adonis. The evil principle prevailed over the good, but the good one rose again to life and immortality.[1] But in Saurashtra, the God Bal had also the name of Cesar. We need not therefore be surprised to find a Cæsar in Italy, where are the Palli, the Saturnia, the temple of Loretto, &c., of Surastrene.[2] Jajati (Yayáti) Kesari was the name of the prince of Orissa.[3] Kanya is called Kesar and Kesu, which means imperial, royal. The Arabian historians inform us that Japhet had a son called Khazar, from whom came the Khozarians on the Wolga, North of the Caspian Sea, and that the Caspian itself was named from this person. In Arabic it is called Bahr-Khazar the Sea of Khazar.[4] Cæsar is the Iswara of India.

The Isan and Isuren of South India was the same as the Hebrew יש iso to save, or the Greek Ζωη life, and Σωζω or Σοω or Σωω to save. I think the root of the Hebrew יש iso has been the word יש so, the י i, jod, prefixed for the sake of the mystery ; then it would be י I the saviour. From the mixed nature of the Sigma and Tau it became Itzur-en and Itzar and Tzar. All these words are found in South India, having the meaning of the crucified God, the Wise, or the Saviour. From this came Isar, Hæsar, Isar-di or dev, and Isard, and Vizard, and Wisard, and Wise man ; and, by a similar process, Wit, Witz, Witzard. Æsar parait être employé, aujourd'hui encore, en islandais, comme pluriel de As, signifiant Dieu. Again, du reste, le nom générique de la divinité se disait en langue Etrusque Æsar, qui fut raproché de César ou Cæsar, mais qui rappelle beaucoup plus naturellement les Ases des Scandinaves.[5] I believe originally the word Cæsar was

[1] See Ouseley's Col. II. p. 221.
[2] Vide Col. Tod on the Temples of Ellora, Trans. Asiat. Soc. Vol. II. Pt. i. p. 329.
[3] Asiat. Res. Vol. XV. p. 265.     [4] D'Herbelot; Vallancey's Coll. Vol. VII. p. 24.
[5] Creutzer, Vol. II. p. 409.

As-sar, or in the Hebrew style of reading Ras-sa, closely connected with the Ras-sees of India. Upon these the word Cæsar or Tzar was formed.

In Irish, God is called AOSAR, pronounced AESAR. In Hisdostanee it is Eashoor, Esur, Iswur. In Sanscrit it is *Eswara.* Arabicè Usar, perlustrans Deus. (El. Scheid.) Egyptiorum plerique id nomen pronunciarunt Oishiri, Oisiri, Usiri (Jablonsky); and in Chaldee we find אוסרא *aisra* Jupiter. (D. de Pomis.)[1] I think no one can doubt why Julius took the Gallic epithet of Cæsar: and after all the vituperation which has been lavished on him for making himself a God, he applied to himself only what the Romish Church applies to its saints, the δѳλεια not the λατρεια— a distinction which very nearly (I do not recollect an exception) all orthodox Protestant writers keep carefully out of sight, when they treat on these subjects; in order that they be able to call their Romish fellow-countrymen idolaters. But scarcely any thing can be more gross than the idolatry of our Protestant bishops and nobles. For, did they not, when they anointed George the Fourth *King,* place him on the sacred black stone brought from Scotland for the purpose, and kept in the most sacred temple of the empire, Westminster Abbey, and never on any account removed—on that very stone, which, as every body knows, Jacob anointed with oil? In fact, thousands of the superstitions of the Papists, Hindoos, Greeks, and Romans, were no more idolatrous than that described above, and they are just as fairly represented by modern writers, as I have represented the above English δѳλεια or superstition.

6. The interpretatio Novi Sæculi, as the fourth eclogue was called, was à sacred mythos, and would, like all other sacred mythoses, have an esoteric and an exoteric meaning. In the same poem a new golden age is promised; but new Trojan wars are also promised. This account of Trojan wars to arrive in the Saturnian times is, in some degree, inconsistent with itself, and this would form a difficulty if we supposed the system to be true; but it agrees very well with my idea, that the system of Avatarism in renewed cycles, though in itself in the chief part false, was all believed by the mystics to be true. Then, of course, they would run into inconsistencies and contradictions to support their faith, as we see all erroneous religious system-believers do every day. Nothing is too absurd for most persons to believe, if they be only educated in the belief of it. Absurdity not being observed, raises no obstacle. It is very certain that, if the system were part of the mysteries of the religion, Virgil could not describe it in any other way than ænigmatically: so that it might be understood by the initiated, but not by the vulgar. The infant alluded to in the eclogue has been a subject of much dispute, but whoever it might be meant for, I think it is very clear to whom it was afterward accommodated by Virgil: unless it was (a thing not unlikely) interpolated by him afterward to make it suit to Octavius; when he became apotheosised, or called Augustus. The following passage of the Æneid, Lib. vi., puts this out of all doubt:

> —— Turn, turn thine eyes! see here thy race divine,
> Behold thy own imperial Roman line:
> Cæsar, with all the Julian name survey;
> See where the glorious ranks ascend to-day!—
> This—this is he!—the chief so long foretold
> To bless the land where Saturn ruled of old,
> And give the Lernean realms a second age of gold!
> The promised prince, AUGUSTUS the divine,
> Of Cæsar's race, and Jove's immortal line.

All this theory respecting Augustus Cæsar, receives no little confirmation from the fact noticed by me in Book V. Chap. II. Sect. 7, that his birth was coeval with the æra of Vicramaditya, or Buddha of Siam, which shews beyond all doubt the actual identity of the two systems.

---

[1] Vallancey, Col. Vol. VI. p. 87.

It appears from a passage in Suetonius, that the death of Julius Cæsar *was in a peculiar manner deplored by the Jews—præcipuèque Judæi.* I think from this and many other circumstances that the two Cæsars were not only held up by a few contemptible retainers, (hangers-on for bread, as they have been represented,) as the Cyrus or the Great One of the age, foretold by the ancient prophecies, but by a great and learned body of mankind, who were believers in them. The Cæsars were supposed by their followers, when they were alive, to be renewed incarnations, like the Lamas of Tibet. The Popes say that Constantine gave up Italy to them. This I think was very likely as the price of his absolution, when he received baptism on his death-bed. At the same time he probably surrendered all claim to the pallium and the other privileges of Pontifex Maximus. From that time I think the emperors ruled by the sword only, the Pontifex Maximus by the book. Cæsar ruled by both. Whenever a king is crowned, he is always made to swear that he will support the rights of the church. This is really nothing less than fealty disguised.

7. If my reader will make allowance for the credulity of the author of the Cambridge Key to the Chronology of the Hindoos, in the following passage, he may observe several very curious and interesting statements.[1] " In the Mahabharat, we are presented with a beautiful epic poem.
" So are we in the Iliad. The latter was written about two centuries after the former : and I have
" been inclined to think that each was taken from the same mythology : the Gods and Goddesses
" being no other than the patriarchs of the antediluvian world. That Vyasa was a name assumed
" by the author of the Maha-bharat, I have little doubt. That is, I believe, the heroic poem, as
" it is now extant, to have been taken from the history, as recorded by the antediluvian sage : and
" that the post-diluvian author, being a follower of Vishnu, ascribed to the black Shepherd, as
" Vishnu or Crishnu, a principal part of those events which are admitted, beyond controversy, by
" every Hindu, to have taken place in the antediluvian world. Homer, on the contrary, brings
" the ancient patriarchs, as deities, forward to the seige of Troy. It is not on either that we can
" safely rely for historic truths : although both poems, it is more than probable, were founded
" thereon. *There is a great resemblance between the Crishnu of Valmic, and the Achilles of*
" *Homer. Each of them, in mythology, is supposed invulnerable, except in the right heel : each*
" *was killed by an arrow piercing that part ; each was the son of the mother of the God of Love ;*
" *and the presence of each was indispensable, for the overthrow of the enemy."* The latter part of this passage of the ingenious Cantab, is no doubt very striking, and we must recollect that we have before found an Ili-vratta, an *Ilium*, and an *Achilles*, in India, and all the Greek Gods— Bacchus, Hercules, &c.; and that we have also found the Jews in India, Jeptha's daughter in Iphigenia, and the Jonas and Samson in Hercules. The learned Joshua Barnes thought that the Iliad was written by Solomon. This was very odd. The seed of the woman in Genesis was bitten in the heel, Crishnu and Achilles are both shot in the heel ! ! ! Respecting the close connexion between the poem of Homer and Solomon, or the Jewish mythos, Basnage, if my memory do not deceive me, has somewhere expressed the same opinion as Barnes.

The sacred books of India, from being called the books of Wisdom, were at length called *Wisdom* itself. In somewhat a similar way the Muses acquired their name. All sacred doctrines were contained in verse, which was invented for the purpose of preserving them, and every cycle had its epic, or song, or musa, to record its Saviour or משה mse. Thus Homer celebrated the Greek Avatar of the Asian Cyrus, and Virgil, the vates, sung the arrival of the Xæsar. So completely mythic is it, that the historians have made the early life of Virgil almost a close copy of that of Homer, as the modern author of his life, W. Walsh, Esq., has pointed out and detailed at length. This affords an admirable example of what I have observed in another place—that all history has been corrupted by judicial astrology. No one càn help seeing the similarity, almost the identity, of the histories of Homer and Virgil; but no one can doubt that Virgil lived; yet as true biography the account cannot be received. It is like the early history of Rome. No one can doubt that Rome existed, but its early history is a mythos. Every cycle had its muse, its song, its saviour. Virgil intimates that the Iliad is a sacred or mythical poem. The expectation of the generality of persons who treat on these subjects is extremely unreasonable. They expect the hidden secret to be so slightly veiled, that all who read it may discover its meaning; and if they have not this unreasonable expectation gratified, they cannot be brought to get the better of their early prejudices.

If my reader will now turn back and run over in recollection the early history of Greece, he will at once see, that it has no more claim to the name of *real* history than that of Tom Thumb, or Jack the Giant-killer. It is quite clear that a Brahminical nation has existed in the South part of Thrace and the North part of Greece. The proofs of the fact are complete. Then *when* did it exist?

After giving the subject all the consideration in my power, and a diligent examination of ancient documents for many years, I have become quite convinced, that almost all the ancient histories were written for the sole purpose of recording a mythos, which it was desired to transmit to posterity—but yet to conceal it from all but the initiated. The traditions of the countries were made subservient to this purpose, without any suspicion of fraud; and we only give them the appearance of fraud, when we confound them with history. This is the case with all early histories. They were all anciently composed, or, *if written*, they were written in verse for the sake of correct retention by the memory, and set to music for the same reason. They were all of the same nature as the Iliad and Æneid. The most ancient of the ancients had nothing of the nature of our real histories. Real history was not the object of their writing, any more than of Virgil's or Milton's. Herodotus was the inventor of history. If it be true, that all these epics or pretended histories are under one disguise or other, but particularly under the guise of real history, intended to conceal a secret mythos, or religious system from the vulgar, how could they be otherwise than as we find them? They are, no doubt in some respects, different, but there are striking marks of identity here and there to be perceived. The marks of identity are facts which cannot be denied. Let them be rationally accounted for otherwise than as I have accounted for them, viz. by one general system's prevailing, in secret, through all the ages. But enough of this digression.

8. When Cæsar was murdered there was a darkness over the earth. Virgil says,[1]

> Cum caput obscura nitidum ferrugine texit
> Impiaquæ æternam timuerunt sæcula noctem.

Servius in his note on this place, says, this darkness lasted ab horâ sextâ usque ad noctem, i. e. from noon till night, which at that time of year must have been six hours.[2] Here we see the history accommodated to the mythos, but are we therefore to suppose that there was no Julius Cæsar? Here we also see a confirmation of what I have said, that Cæsar, at the time of his death, was believed to be the presiding genius of the age: and as was the case at the death of Romulus and many others, the death did not change the mythic character of Cæsar. Soon after Cæsar's death, when Augustus obtained the power, *he* was believed to be the person, and the Æneid was written to celebrate him. The Death of Cæsar, so like to that of Romulus, rather tended to prove him a sacred character like Romulus. The darkness was easily invented afterward to complete the picture.[3]

---

[1] Georg. I. 467.      [2] Costard, Astron. p. 92.

[3] I much suspect that all chronology was corrupted for mythical purposes, as we are very sure history was. Sir

It is Cæsar that Virgil celebrates in all his verses. The mythos taught that there were to be twelve Cæsars, and Julius's praise will suit all or any of them. If the generation in this case were taken at *thirty* years, it brings us to the mythos of Constantine, who founded Nova Roma on the seven hills, 360 years after the first of the Cæsars. I have no doubt that the mythos was, that the Julian family should last for twelve generations—in all 360 years—till a new period arose. I think it not unlikely that the flatterers of Constantine (the son of Hellen by Coilus) might persuade him, that notwithstanding the actual number of Roman despots, yet that before him there were only twelve legal Emperors ; and that *he* was the divine or inspired or incarnated person destined to found a new cycle and a Nova Roma. The divine character of Cæsar is the continual theme of Virgil's praise. [1]

The circumstances respecting the Cæsars, when all considered, are surely very curious. In the first place, the family name of Julius seems to shew a latent claim to sovereignty, only waiting a fit opportunity for the family to display itself. It must be recollected that in those days hereditary high-priesthoods in families were very common, and with the high-priesthood a sovereign claim, similar to that of Tibet, mostly shews itself. Several families possessing something of this kind may be perceived in Rome. Augustus was pretended to be begotten by a God, in the form of a serpent, in the temple, and to be brought forth *after ten months.* However we may vary this in language, it is evidently what we should call an immaculate conception. And the ten months' pregnancy shews it to be a mythos, similar to that of Cristna, Hercules, Bacchus, SOLOMON ; and, I doubt not, that, had we all the apocryphal gospels entire, similar to another immaculate conception also. The name of the Indian, Etruscan, and Celtic God Æsar or Cæsar, followed by eleven other Cæsars, again shews the ancient mythos, and that the twelve Lucumones of the Etruscans were perhaps princes and high-priests in succession. Julius declared himself high-priest, Pontifex Maximus, and probably, though perhaps secretly, pretended to the office by hereditary or divine right. He certainly pretended to be the great one of the ninth age, who was to come, and was believed to be so, both by Jews and Romans. And though this is scarcely perceptible, yet it may be perceived in the fourth eclogue of Virgil, and in the regret of the Jews. His aphanasia and six hours' darkness at his death liken him to Romulus and to Jesus Christ. The suffering of a violent death seems a necessary part of the mythos ; and I suspect that the deaths of Calanus, of Cyrus, of Crœsus, of Hercules, of Romulus, &c., &c., &c., all had a connexion with it. The following two verses are of themselves enough to shew that the fourth eclogue refers to the mythos of which I have written so much.

---

Isaac Newton thought the founding of Rome was 120 years wrong. I suspect that the æra of Nabonassar, that of the first Olympiad, and that of the founding of Rome, were all meant to begin the eighth Sæculum, and that they were meant to be 650 years before the commencement of the ninth.

[1] Tuque adeò, quem mox quæ sint
  habitura Deorum
  Concilia, incertum est, urbisne invisere, Cæsar,
  Terrarumque velis curam, et te maximus orbis
  Auctorem frugum, tempestatumque potentem, accipiat. Virg. Georg. Lib. i. 24.

And chiefly thou, O Cæsar, concerning whom it is yet uncertain what the Gods in council may determine—whether thou wilt vouchsafe to visit cities, and undertake the care of countries, and the widely-extended globe receive thee, giver of the fruits and ruler of the seasons.
Again, in Georg. II. 503. Again, II. 170. This passage is clearly not understood.
Again, in Georg. III. 16, Virgil says, he shall place Cæsar in a Temple. He praises the boy Hylas, which is nothing but the boy *Iulus*—Yule—the infant Jupiter. See Fig. 20, the black Bambino.
Again, Æneid. I. 285—295, VI. 775, &c., and VIII. 678—714.

**4 K**

Incipe, parve puer, risu cognoscere matrem :
Matri longa decem tulerunt fastidia menses.

Here is the child laughing at its mother as soon as born, and its mother suffering a pregnancy of ten months. Zoroaster, Buddha, and Jesus Christ, are all represented to have laughed as soon as they were born.

9. Whether an angel appeared to the mother of Cæsar to warn her not to have connexion with her husband during gestation I do not know, but this is precisely what happened to Aristo the father of Plato, according to Apuleius, Plutarch, and Hesychius. So that there can be no doubt that it was a part of the mythos.[1] A star was said to foretell the birth of Cæsar. This seems to have been a necessary part of the mythos; refer to Book V. Ch. II. Sect. 7. I believe when Virgil wrote the line

Ecce Dionæi processit Cæsaris astrum,

he meant the star which appeared on the birth of Cæsar. Col. Tod says,[2] " The Chinese account " of the birth of Yu (Ayu) their first monarch,[3] (Mercury or Fo,) a star struck his mother while " travelling. She conceived and gave to the world Yu, the founder of the first dynasty which " reigned in China." Here we have the same mythos of the immaculate conception in China, and of the same God if I mistake not—יה ie.

In Basnage is a very curious account of a kingdom of Cosar or Cæsar, which has been much sought after.[4] It alludes to another kingdom of the Jews somewhere in the East. Lord Kingsborough has noticed this in his magnificent work on Mexico.[5] I believe this arose among them from meeting every where with remains of a mythic kingdom of a Cæsar which they could not understand. They learnt that there was a kingdom of Cæsar or Cosar or TZR or Tzarina ruled by Jews on the North of India, which they fondly flattered themselves must keep alive the prophecy that the sceptre should not pass from Juda till their Messiah came ; but when they examined it, it vanished from their touch. They were the remains of the kingdom of Oude which they found.

There is yet one more circumstance of the mythos of Cæsar which shews, in a very extraordinary manner, how all history, even almost to our own day, has been corrupted to conceal or record the mythos. We have seen that Buddha was born from the side of his mother, and that the Christian heretics taught the same thing of Jesus. To complete the secret doctrine, Cæsar was said to have been born by means of what we call the Cæsarean operation, *from the side of his mother*. No doubt this was told to the vulgar, but to the initiated the doctrine of Buddha was told. When all the other mystical circumstances relating to Cæsar are considered, the nature of this story cannot be doubted. The doctrine of the birth from the side, he probably learnt, with much more that has not come to us, from the *Chaldeans*[6] *whom he employed* to correct the calendar.

Dez Prez, the author of the notes on Horace in Usum Delphini, begins his dedication thus : " Ensem dextra, læva librum tenens Julius ille Divus quondam in numismate voluit effingi, cum " hac epigraphe, *Ex utroque Cæsar*. Julius Cæsar ordered his effigies to be stamped on a coin, " holding a sword in his right hand, and a book in his left, with an inscription that imported, he " was Cæsar both by the one and the other." Malcolme's Letters. By this he meant, as an incarnation of the God Mars or Hesus or Æsar, and not as conqueror of his country, and by the secret doctrines of the book. By right of the Liber, Bacc, Boc, Book, I have no doubt that he and his family always, though perhaps secretly, claimed to be Pontifex Maximus, which only

[1] Vide Taylor's Jamblicus, p. 6, note.                    [2] Hist. Raj. p. 57.
[3] De Guines sur les Dynasties des Huns, Vol. I. p. 7.
[4] Bki vii. Chap. i. Bk. viii.                    [5] Vol. VI. p. 284.                    [6] Proved hereafter.

waited a favourable opportunity to display itself. The claim by the biber, the book, is a very curious part of the mythos, which I hope to be able by and by to explain. Many circumstances might be pointed out which tend to shew that in all countries, in very early times, the office of Pontifex Maximus was hereditary in families, as in that of Aaron; and I think in that of Rome several families had pretensions to it, which were kept down by the jealousies of their countrymen. In the time of Octavius one of the priests told a noble matron of Rome, that Apollo was in love with her. In consequence of this she went to the temple and, as she believed, slept with the God, but having more vanity than prudence, she boasted of it, which caused it to come to the ears of the Emperor, who ordered the priest to be put to death. The Emperor did not approve of this intrigue : he *smelt a rat*. Our priests, not so wise as the Emperor, are shocked at the immorality carried on in the temples, and praise him for his regard for religion and morality. But they may be assured that, if there had not been some other reason, the God might have intrigued at his pleasure. The Emperor wished *for no sons of God*. It is pretty clear that but a very small part of this story has come down to us. I have no doubt that if the produce of this holy amour were a boy, Augustus took care to provide for it, only with more success than we are told Herod's plans were attended at Bethlehem.

If Pompey had defeated Cæsar he was prepared with his divine claim exactly as Cæsar was. He would have been an incarnation of Buddha or Mercury.

$$\text{—— } \varkappa \alpha \lambda \omega \text{ } \delta' \text{ } \alpha \mu \alpha$$
$$\Pi o \mu \pi \alpha i o \nu \text{ } E \rho \mu \eta \nu \text{ } \chi \theta o \nu i o \nu.[1]$$

A Ptolemy of Egypt was called Soter; this shews the claim again : and the name of the Ptolemies was often written Mptolemeus, when the M could not be emphatic : this was, for the same reason that the prefix X might be given to Cæsar. From the same principle proceeds the divine right of all our kings. The kings claim it by birth. The popes and priests pretend to give it by imposition of hands—χειροτωνια. It was to conceal the origin of this claim, that kings and priests have always been so solicitous to conceal this mythos. They wished to profit by it, but they feared that the people should understand it.

In the same way, it appears that Mark Antony was provided with *his* divine right, if he had succeeded in possessing himself of the empire. Jurieu says, Mark Antony was called M Arca Antonia, alluding to an Egyptian superstition; but he does not try to explain it. A tower in Jerusalem was called Antonia. The Arca floated from Egypt to Byblos. Was Byblos called Antonia ? Some very ingenious speculations may be found in Mr. Barker's Lempriere,[2] by Professor Anthon,[3] respecting the old Roman nobility; he supposes that they were the remains of a sacred caste. This seems to me to be extremely probable. They were hereditary landholders, legislators, and sacred persons or priests, each perhaps aiming to be the Pontifex Maximus—who was unquestionably the first man in the state—all jealous of one another, and perhaps agreeing in nothing but in the choice of the most imbecile for that situation, as Bishops of Canterbury and Popes of Rome are said to be selected.

The Avatars seem to have been very numerous. M. Creuzer, who, I suspect, from his some-

---

[1] Ajax, v. 1292; Nimrod, Vol. II. p. 479.          [2] In voce Rome.

[3] I beg leave to draw my reader's attention to this work of Mr. Anthon's. It exhibits in a very favourable point of view the literary character, and the enlargement of mind, of our former countrymen. It is a wonderful improvement upon the obsolete and contemptible priestisms of old Lempriere. It is the best book in our language for the education of youth. It might be greatly improved by making it more of an ancient Gazetteer, and I hope when a new edition is printed, Mr. Barker will add to the obligation under which he has laid his country by making this addition to it. By this means alone the size of it might be almost doubled with very great advantage.

times using the word *Avatar*, had a glimpse of the true and secret system of the ancients, shews that the same mythos was applied to great numbers of ancient Grecian heroes, such as Theseus and Hercules. This is perfectly correct. We have seen proofs from the names of towns or places in different countries, that each independent district had its system of Avatars: then, of course, there ought to have passed, in the time of Julius Cæsar, eight Avatars in each country; this accounts for their great number, and for the great numbers of persons or hero Gods of the same name. Each country had its Jupiter; and the only thing which surprises me is, that the devotees did not quarrel about them in the West, as they seem to have done in the East. That the system is not more apparent is easily accounted for. It was a secret alluded to in the celebration of the highest mysteries only, and perhaps understood merely by some of the professors of them. Time has long been at work with his all-destructive scythe, aided by the power of the Christian priests, to destroy or put out of sight all the facts that transpired respecting it in the works of the ancients, which had any relation or similarity to the facts related of Jesus Christ. How can any proof of this assertion be required more clear than that of the different crucifixions of Prometheus, Ixion, &c., so completely disguised, as they are, and which by good luck only have escaped destruction?

Much nonsense has been written concerning the heroes of antiquity being converted into Gods; but now, in the Cæsars, I think, we may see the real nature of the apotheosis. They were not supposed to be men converted into Gods, but incarnations of a portion of the Divine Spirit; at least this was the real and secret meaning of the apotheosis. They were men endowed with the Holy Ghost. They were nothing but men supposed to be filled with more than an usual portion of that spirit which our bishops profess to put into their priests, when they ordain them by the imposition of hands—by which they give them the unconditional power of remitting sins; at least so the book says. Like the Christian saints, they were not *generally* declared, till after their deaths; though during their lives they might be believed, by many of their followers to be divinely inspired, as was probably the case with St. Francis,[1] as I shall presently shew. In his case, his followers were only fools; in such cases as that of Octavius a due admixture of rogues would also be found. Octavius was a second Cyrus. On this account he was called *Augustus*, and, as the last and most holy appellation, the same as Cyrus, FATHER OF HIS COUNTRY, the Αιων των αιωνων— Deus fortis futuri sæculi.[2] I am surprised that we have not a life of Octavius by a Latin Xenophon, to match the *Heathen gospel called the Cyropædia*. I have very little doubt that the prophecies, in the case of Octavius, conduced to their own fulfilment, and I think it very probable that he really believed himself foretold, as many others, with much less pretensions, have done since; such as Brothers, Swendenborg, &c. All this was in strict keeping with what I suppose was the fact, that the early history of Rome was merely a mythos, which is strongly supported by many of its pretended events being only copies from the *heroical* history of Greece, as noticed by Lumsden and Niebuhr, which I shall immediately examine. Then, as the Argonautic expedition, the Trojan war, &c., took place at the end of the former millenary, or neros,—they would take place again at the end of that then coming. If we consider that the principal events said to have happened to the early Romans are only Grecian fables repeated, it is not unlikely that the devotees really believed that new Argonauts, &c., would arise in a few years. I suspect some Gentile mystics found that the time was shortly coming when the tragedies of Babylon, Thebes,

---

[1] And Johanna Southcote, whose religion continues to flourish, she having, to my knowledge, learned Protestant priests among her followers, in A. D. 1830—*one* of the rank of *honourable*.

[2] Isa. ix. 6, 7.

and Troy, would be repeated in Rome—Nova Troia or new Babylon. These were the Irvings and Fabers of their day, and probably this was the correct mythos.

10. Before I proceed, I beg my reader to look back to Book VII. Chap. VIII. Sect. 2, for what I have there said respecting Rome. The Targum of Jerusalem says, Rex Messias egredietur ex urbe Româ. Edit. Buxt. Lex. in Româ.[1] This confirms my suspicion, that there was much more mythologic matter appertaining to Rome, than what we have been accustomed to calculate on. I suspect that new Troys, &c., were expected every 600 years. In the case of the Romans this was a superstition, which could not be corrected by that kind of experience which we acquire from history, because they had no history. What we call their *history*, Mr. Niebuhr has shewn was mere *mythos*. This will account for a degree of superstition which would be otherwise scarcely credible, among the higher ranks of the Romans.

A great many years ago, the question of the truth or authenticity of the history of the first four hundred years of the Roman empire, was discussed in the Transactions of the French Academy of Inscription,[2] by Mons. De Pouilly and the Abbé Sallier. The former asserted the same as had been asserted by an Englishman called Lumsden, in his travels in Italy—that many of the incidents in the Roman history were identical with those in the heroical history of the Greeks, and therefore must have been copied from them. In reply to this, the Abbé shewed, from dates and circumstances, that they could not have been copied by the Romans from the Greeks, and, therefore, that if either copied, it must have been the Greeks who copied from the Romans, which was bringing the matter nearly to a proof *ad absurdum*. But that which seems probable has never been suspected,—that they were not copies of one another, but were drawn from a common source; were, in fact, an example of remaining fragments of the almost lost, but constantly renewed, mythos, which we have seen every where in the East and West,—new Argonauts, new Trojan wars, &c., &c. But these gentlemen, not having the least suspicion of any thing of this kind, were, as well as their readers, very much puzzled to know what to make of these odd things ; for both parties seemed to be right, as, in fact, in great part, they were.

The Abbé Sallier observes, that although Dionysius, of Halicarnassus, fixes the date of Rome, yet he does not determine whether it was then first founded or only repeopled. Dionysius contends, that facts have been received from father to son in families, as a sacred inheritance ; but to this is opposed an observation of Livy's, which we know from experience to be very probable— that families have inserted things in their own praise which have never happened : multa enim scripta sunt in eis, quæ facta non sunt : falsi triumphi, plures consulatus, genera etiam falsa.[3]

But there is another passage of Livy's and one of Plutarch's, which seem, taken together, to place the absolute uncertainty of the Roman history out of reach of reasonable doubt, even if its similarity to the Grecian fables did not do this : because these writers must be considered as unwilling witnesses to an unwelcome truth. Livy[4] says, Vitiatam memoriam funeribus laudibus reor, falsisque imaginum titulis, dum familia quæque ad se famam rerum gestarum, honorumque fallente mendacio trahunt. Inde certe et singulorum gesta, et publica monimenta rerum confusa. Nec quisquam æqualis temporibus illis scriptor extat, quo satis certo auctore stetur. Plutarch says, at the end of his treatise on the fortune of the Romans, speaking of the times which preceded 603 of the foundation of Rome, Τι δει περι ταυτα διατριβειν, σαφες ουδεν, ουδε ωρισμενον εχει.

11. In August, 1830, after this work was sent to press, a notice of Mr. Niebuhr's work made its appearance in the Edinburgh Review. That notice surprised me greatly, for it is not in the usual style of the Review. It consists of a loose tirade against the probability of Mr. Niebuhr's

---

[1] Nimrod, Vol. III. p. 381.    [2] For the year 1729.    [3] Liv. Lib. viii. Cap. xl.    [4] Ibid.

doctrine, that the early history of Rome is a mythos. It notices his observation of the peculiarity of the number of the years of its kings, 360, without noticing the collateral facts which confirm the mythic character of the history, viz. the circumstance that they are only copies of facts recorded of the heroes of Greece. Suspicious as the numbers are, they would not of themselves, perhaps, have been enough, but surely the collateral circumstances ought to have been noted. In direct opposition to the ingenious Reviewer, who, I complain, has not treated Mr. Niebuhr's work fairly,[1] I maintain. that it is not credible that the very singular number of 360 years should have elapsed between the fall of Troy and the building of Rome; 360 between the building of Rome and its destruction by the Gauls; 360 more to the foundation of the monarchy by the capture of Alexandria; and from the latter to the dedicating of Constantinople 360 more;[2] the whole making the sum of 1440. I contend that the numbers *connected with the other matters* do clearly prove a mythos,—a mythos which, like all other mythoses, was originally concealed in poems for aiding the memory—and, perhaps, when letters came into use, acrostic poems too. Directly against the Reviewer I also contend, that though the astrological taint of the early histories does not prove them all false, yet it does render them doubtful, wherever there is the least reason to suspect that the mythos may be concerned. And I contend that it is philosophical to *hold in suspicion* (ROGER BACON) all such histories, and unphilosophical to receive them without it. For, as I have observed, although the mythic character of the history does not prove it all false—that there was no Rome, that there were no kings—yet it places it in the same situation with the heroic history of Greece, the history of Theseus, &c., until the mythos is made out. I contend that wherever the mythos shews itself—and it appears that an historian has, like the Reviewer, not considered such mythos to be a suspicious circumstance—the whole is for that very reason to be doubted in a greater or less degree. The mythos has corrupted all history. Who can doubt that the Argonautic history is a *recurring* mythos? It is noticed by Homer, and some of its heroes are said to have lived long after his time. Now, our historians have endeavoured to concoct the history, so as to make out one probable story; which, if its cyclic character had been understood, they would instantly have seen it was impossible to do, consistently with truth. As Virgil has told us, new Argonauts would arise from time to time. The Reviewer says, that " historians draw largely upon their own and their readers' credulity in matters connected with " religion, when in recording common secular events they observe the most scrupulous fidelity." But the mischief is, that the mythos is historical, and all history is closely connected with it. I am sorry for the line which this influential review has taken, because it tends to aid the priests in their attempts to run down Niebuhr, and thus to stop *in limine* the attempts, by establishing the fact of the mythos, to remove the hitherto insuperable difficulties attending all the early history of mankind. However, I leave it to the writer of the article to believe in Romulus and the Lady Wolf, and, if he please, in Jack the Giant-killer. I shall continue to doubt their truth. The fact of the mythos is established; and whatever the Editor may think or say of my work in other respects, I hope his learned contributors will render me their very powerful assistance in making out the whole secret of the mythos.[3]

Whenever I find the serious argument of a sensible man treated with ridicule, I always suspect that the power of an opponent to refute it is weak. The hypothesis of Bailly and some others so much ridiculed, that the origin of man is to be sought far to the North of India, may, perhaps, receive some slight support from a passage of Gibbon's.[4] It will be accounted for by *ridicule*

---

[1] P. 374.       [2] Niebuhr, p. 171.

[3] Niebuhr has been ably vindicated by the Foreign Quarterly Review.       [4] Hist. Ch. xlii.

and *accident.* I confess neither of these modes of refuting is satisfactory to me. " In the midst " of these obscure calamities, Europe felt the shock of a revolution, which first revealed to the " world the name and nation of the Turks. Like Romulus, the founder of that martial people, " was suckled by a she-wolf, who afterward made him the father of a numerous progeny : and the " representation of that animal in the banners of the Turks preserved the memory, or rather " suggested the idea, of a fable, which was invented, without any mutual intercourse, by the " shepherds of Latium and those of Scythia." When I think of Cristna exposed, of Cyrus exposed, of Moses exposed, of Romulus exposed, and of the Turk exposed, and all, like Jesus, saved from the tyrants' power, I cannot attribute this similarity to accident ; and the proofs which I have given of the identity of the Latin and Sanscrit languages, and the identity of places in India and Italy, &c., &c., preclude the hasty conclusion of Gibbon, that there has been no intercourse between Italy and India. The country of Janus, of Saturnia, and Itala or the Bull, MUST have had a close intercourse in *very early time* with the country of Genesa, Satrun-ja, and the country where Taurus opened the Vernal Year with his horn. I leave these things to the reflection of my reader, quite certain of the result, if he will only employ his reflection upon them. To account for them I can find no way consistent with present Christianity, except by adopting the argument of Parkhurst, that, like Hercules, Romulus, &c., they are emblems of a future Saviour. To this, at present, I shall make no objection, whatever my private opinion may be, provided its proposers will only have candour enough not to insult my understanding, by stories of accidents, and will admit the facts which cannot be disputed.

Supposing the theory which I have developed, that is, in fact, the theory of Virgil, to be correct, the fragments ought to be found in occasional duplicates, as we *do* find them, some in one country, some in another. For example, the part of the story consisting of Cristna's escape and preservation by a cowherd from a tyrant, is the same story as Cyrus's, the same as Moses's, the same as Romulus's, and as several others. There has, no doubt, been originally one history of them all, and that history a mythos or a doctrine : and the doctrine of a divine incarnation in each age, which the priests of each country persuaded the people must belong to them, as proved by their history. Though I fear there is little hope of making out the story completely, I do not consider it entirely hopeless. The Christian will say, that the Pentateuch is the original mythos ; then I say in reply, by hopeless I mean, if that be the case, that by the discovery of a more full and particular account the whole meaning of Genesis may be discovered. For I assume, that no person can now believe, that the real meaning of the Tree of Life, &c., is known. How monstrous is the absurdity of taking a part of this mythos, the tree of knowledge, and making out of it such a doctrine as that of the atonement, a doctrine not only contrary to the moral attributes of God, but subversive of all morality !

The ancient spirit of mysticism is well exemplified in the names of Rome. Among others we are told, that it was called Ερως or Love, because its name, of Roma, spelt anagramatically, made Amor. In the same way, probably, its legislator, Numa, was called from Menu or Amun. [1] It is very extraordinary, that when it must be known to the learned, that all the writers on mystical subjects concealed them as much as possible by anagrams, and acrostics, and ænigmas, of every kind, they should be so unwise as to cast these things away, and pay no attention to them. The Jews and Gentiles were equally addicted to these practices. They almost all gave themselves false names, even down to the modern John Calvin. Lycophron called Πτολεμιοις, Ptolemy, απο μελιτος from Honey : Αρσινοη ιον ηρας, the Arrow of Venus. [2] Under these circumstances,

---

[1] Vide Creuzer, Vol. II. p. 521.      [2] Basn. Hist. Jews, Bk. iii. Ch. xxiii. Sect. ii.

how is any one who does not attend to them to be expected to find out the meaning of such works as the Cassandra?

In 1 Pet. v. 13, Rome is alluded to under the name of *Babylon*. This very much perplexed the Luthers and Calvins, who were not initiated in the Roman religion. But this was the mystic name of Rome, as is proved from a passage in the Sibylline Oracle, Lib. iii., where Rome is most clearly designated by the word Babylon. Very truly has Nimrod said,[1] that the Sibylline Oracles are Gnostic performances.

Urus is a name for the male or female beeve. *Ur* is the root. *Ur*, then, means *beeve*. *Ur-ia* or Ur-iana a district of India, then, means Country of Beeve, or Bull. Italy was called *Vitala* or *Itala*, which meant *bull*. It was called Saturnia regnum; then, regnum *Saturnia* meant the same as regnum *Urus*. Saman was the God of Italy. Saman-Nath of that part of India called Saturnja, in which God was also called Sum-naut, is evidently the same. The Indian Saturnja is found in a country of Pallitana, and the Italian Regnum Saturnia on Mount Pallatine. *Palli* occurs in both; while there is a God *Jain* in the one, and a God *Janus* in the other. God was also called Sam; and Meru meant *mere* or *mount;* then, Someru or Sameru was Mount Sam, or mount of the sun.

It is a striking circumstance that Rome should be called *Urum;* but it is not so surprising when we find Italy called Italus or Vitulus.[2] Littleton says, Quondam dicta fuit hæc urbs Valentia, Saturnia, Flora, CEPHALON,[3] επταλοφος sive septicollis urbs, Urbs Augusta, Sacra, Æterna ; TUSCIS URUM, et Christianis plerisque, hodie Babylon.[4]

Thus we have Rome called Babylon, and Babylon called Rome. We have a city of Rama and an island of Rama in India : and a point Romania.[5] We have in Phrygia Mount Ararat noticed by the Sibyl, and a Roma, &c., and a country of Roum ; and, to complete all, we have in each, for rulers, Cæsars or Kesari. Can any one doubt a common mythos ? And it may have been any of these Romes to which the Erythræan Sibyl in her prophecy alluded. Rome was Babylon, and Babylon was the city of the Dove, and Lanca or Ye-lanka[6] or Ceylon was the island of Rama, (in which were Ararat and Adam's foot-mark,) the capital of which was Columbo. Was there a city of Rama or Roma in Ceylon, or in the island of Rama ?

Creuzer shews that Rome was called an Olympus,[7] and in their ceremonies they chaunted Tri-omphe, Triomphe—that is, the triple Omphe.

12. Apollo had a daughter called Chryses ; he married her to *Dar-dan*us of the opposite coast to Thrace or Troy, and with her gave, as a marriage portion, the *Palla*dium, or icon of Pallas, the Goddess of wisdom.[8] It was carried by Æneas from Troy to Alba Longa, on the conquest of which, along with Cæsar's family, it was removed to Rome, and placed in the temple of Vesta. Cæsar's family was spared, as Æneas's had been, at Troy. History and not poetry, says that Æneas treacherously delivered up the Palladium, by which he purchased his safety and sacrificed his country. Was it the same with the ancestor of Cæsar ? There is a parallel for this in Holy

---

[1] Vol. I. pp. 228, 388.

[2] M. Creuzer, Vol. II. Liv. v. Ch. v. p. 518, shews how the word Itala comes from th word vitulus.

[3] Is this a translation of Ras or Αρχη ?

[4] Tarquin the ancient is said to have built the Cloacæ Maximæ, but it is forgotten, when this is said, that the famous statue of Venus Cloacina was found in them by Romulus ; (see Nimrod, Vol. I. p. 320 ;) so that one part of the tradition nullifies the other.

[5] Hamilton's Gaz. p. 184.　　　　　　　　　　[6] Called Yelanki by Wilson

[7] Liv. v. Ch. v. p. 524.　　　　　　　　　　[8] Sandy's Travels, p. 23.

Writ. The case is suspicious. As long as a city possessed this Palladium or icon of WISDOM it was impregnable. It was carried from Rome to Constantinople the new capital of Thrace, by Constantine the First. I much suspect that it was placed by him in the church of Sancta Sophia, and that for this reason it was called Sophia. Constantine is said to have given the name of Nova Roma to Byzantium, and to the district, the name of Romelia: but I imagine from its propinquity to Antiquissima Roma, as it might be called, or Troy, that he only restored the ancient names, if he did give them those names. I rather conclude, it was like the Roum of Phrygia and the Rama of Ceylon, and that he found the old names when he found the seven hills. The country of Ilium was called Mysia, (ia-רתסמ *mstr*, μυϛηριον,) like the part of Thrace called Romelia. This strengthens the ground for suspicion. Ptolemy knew nothing of the name of Romelia. He only knew the Greek names; and Romelia, if I be right, would be the name which preceded that of the Greeks. It was the country of Rama.

Let us cast our eyes on ancient Thrace, and what do we find?—the district first called *Thrace* and then *Macedonia*, restored to its ancient name, a little corrupted, Rome-lia; that is, the country of Rama, with the L inserted from a natural tendency to improve the Euphony of the word. Thus we have Rome in the country of Saturn-ja and Pallitana, and in the country of Rama where the Trimurti reigned and the widows were sacrificed. It was probably when it first bore the name of Rama, that the gold mines were worked, the vestiges of which were observed by the Greeks. When the Turks, ignorant of Greek, conquered the country, they naturally gave places the names used by the country people—the old names.

In Phrygia, with the Turks, a district has recovered its ancient name of Roum (Wilkinson's Atlas). There may be seen also a *Djanik*-IILI, that is *Iuli ;* and a *Kaisarieh ;* a town of Sivas; a Gulf of Samson; a river Euphrates, &c., &c. From this country the Romans got their Pessinuncian stone. We must remember that Troy was in Phrygia, and that Roma was Nova Troia. In Lat. 39¾, Long. 45⅓,[1] we have Hadrianotheræ; and in Lat. 39¾, Long. 47, we have Hadriani ad Olympum, now called *Edrenos* by the Turks. Here I think no one can deny the Udrinos, or the Ὑδριης. Is this the old name, or the Roman one?

13. Niebuhr says, " It appears that, in clearing away the ruins of the Colossæum, below the for-" mer pavement which they had dug, they discovered remains of a Cyclopæan wall. Unfortunately " their direction has not been stated. It will probably appear that they belonged to *Roma Qua-* " *drata.* It is rather singular that they should have carried it through this deep valley. This " mode of building vouches for an age of the city far beyond our chronology, and for a nation of " early inhabitants which had utterly disappeared."[2] It is an extraordinary thing, that Mr. Niebuhr should content himself with this observation, without making the slightest attempt to follow it up, by inquiring what this nation was which had disappeared, or whence it came. The history of Rome and Italy, previous to about three hundred and fifty years before Christ, may be given in very few words—as far as with any certainty it is known. It was probably at first occupied by Nomade tribes from the North of India, who gradually settled themselves in its delightful climate and soil; and. under a patriarchal or priestly government,[3] it increased to great population and enjoyed a state of peace for many generations, till the law of change operated and destroyed this golden age, this Pandæan state, this empire of Pandæa.[4] Quarrels and separate states arose

---

[1] D'Anville.                    [2] Vol. II. p. 530.                    [3] Treated of hereafter.

[4] This was the time when the city of Sybaris flourished, which had a population so great, that it could send an army of three hundred thousand men into the field. Posidonia or Pæstum, whose temples and walls yet remain to prove its Indian origin and its magnificence, was one of the towns of this state. The time when it enjoyed the advantages of the peaceable, patriarchal government, before the Cyclopæan walls were necessary, was probably that in which its beautiful temples of Neptune and Ceres were built, which yet remain.

by degrees, and their towns became surrounded with Cyclopæan walls. It remained in this situation, sometimes one state preponderating, sometimes another, till the famous tribe of Gauls, under Brennus, arrived, who overran the country, pillaging the open towns, but not equal to contend with hill fortresses like the Roman Capitolium, the Cyclopæan walls of Pæstum, Cortona, and other cities, or the natural defences of Civita Castellana or Veii, if it were Veii. After a short course of victory and success, a great part of the Gauls were probably destroyed by the perpetual irruptions of the natives from their walled towns, and from their fastnesses in the Apenines upon their rear; aided by a most powerful ally, the Autumn Malaria; and, the remaining part weakened and dispirited, like a late retreating army from Moscow, were expelled. When this hurricane had blown over, favourable circumstances of which we are ignorant gave a preponderance to the Roman state, and, after a series of wars for a considerable number of years, united the population of Italy under her command. The fortunate circumstance of having a Napoleon arise in her state, in the person of a Camillus, was quite enough to account for Rome acquiring the supremacy. Perhaps some superstition, respecting the ancient Cyclopæan city just alluded to, might lend its aid. How this might be, we know not, but probably the population of Italy, from the previous state of warfare in which it had been, might be much more warlike than that of the Eastern and civilized states, or the trading Carthaginian; and thus Italy might be qualified to achieve the conquest of the world. I think this is nearly all that can safely be said of Rome previous to its destruction by Brennus, in the fourth century before Christ. The histories of Livy, Polybius, Appian, &c., &c., are scarcely worthy a moment's consideration. Niebuhr has sufficiently exposed their falsities and contradictions.

We have formerly made an observation on the forged Vedah of Robert de Nobilibus. The case may have been simply this. As Ammonius Saccas, in former times, had found the Christian and Gentile religions to be radically the same, so Robertus found the Brahmin and Christian in the times of the moderns; and he endeavoured so to contrive a Vedah, that, by leaving out part of the nonsense of each religion, he might bring them to an agreement, under his master, the Grand Lama of the Western Roum or city of Rama. He may have found, what was real fact, that the mythos of modern and Western Rome was at the bottom precisely the same as that of ancient and Eastern Rome. The Rama of Ceylon proves the possibility of this theory. I shall return again to the name of the Eternal city.

Infinite almost in number are the places in the writings of the ancients, and in their ceremonies, where the sacred Argha or Ark is noticed or alluded to. Every mythos of antiquity is represented or disguised in the form of a history. We have the Trojan war, the adventures of Bacchus, Hercules, Theseus, Osiris, Cristna. The early history of Rome is like all the others; and of the same character is the history of Noah—an allegory concealed under the garb of history—Buddha, Jain, or Menu, floating on the ocean in a boat; that is, the principle of generation or the generative power reduced to its simplest elements : the Linga, in the form of Menu floating in the Yoni, in the form of a boat. In Genesis it is Noah and his three sons. These great incarnations always affected a similitude to those which had preceded, the nature of which is best described in the prophecy of Virgil, and examples of which may be seen in all the Indian Avatars, particularly in those of Buddha and Cristna. They are visible also in the accounts which we have seen of the repetitions of the ten years' sieges, of towns, &c., &c., of the Western nations. All these histories were probably repetitions of mythoses, on the same principle as the Indian Avatars. Precisely like all the others was the Mosaic history. There are Adam and his three sons, from whom all mankind descended in the first yug, age, or world. These are succeeded by Noah and his three sons, at the second yug, age, or world. Though they be not the same any more than the histories of Buddha and Cristna, they do not differ from one another more than the two latter differ. The theory was, that a renewal of every thing should take place in every mundane revolution—new Argonauts, new sieges of Troy, &c. This nature prevented, but the priests carried the practice as near to the theory as they were able. Similar adventures were attributed to every new incarnation. This is not a theory, it is a fact; and if my method of accounting for it be not satisfactory, I beg that one more probable may be proposed. My theory has this peculiar recommendation, that it requires no miracles or admissions of incredible facts, but only what is probable and consistent with the course of nature, which we learn from experience.

14. As I have just now said, it was at the end of a MUNDANE revolution that a renewal of nature was to take place ; but we may reasonably ask, what was meant by the word *mundane ?* In our dictionaries we are told, that Mundus means world; but it also means a Cycle, which implies the same as the Greek word Κοσμος. It should always be recollected that I am describing a system which would, by being constantly at variance with nature and circumstances, oblige the priest to have recourse to such expedients as chance afforded him, whether entirely satisfactory or not.

Plutarch says, that it was Pythagoras who first named all the parts of the universe Κοσμος, on account of its order. Πυθαγορας πρωτος ωνομασε την των ὁλων περιοχην, κοσμον, εκ της εν αυτω ταξεως.[1] Pliny[2] says also, Quem κοσμον Græci nomine ornamenti appellavere, eum nos a perfecta absolutaque elegantia, MUNDUM.

15. Cristna is called Can-ya. This, when all other circumstances are considered, is evidently the epithet of.the Apollo of Athens, Cun-ni-us,[3] and Ya the IE on the Delphic temple. Each of the nine wives of Can-ya is called Radha, and answers to one of the nine Muses of Apollo ; and Radha is the Latin Radius or English Ray. Each Radha or Muse or משה mse or משה msh or female Saviour or Messiah, was an emanation from the Solar Deity, incarnate in the presiding genius of each age or cycle. Each was a Ray, and thus each king-priest was a Ray-jah or Ra-ya or Ra-ja, and the Rajah was an emanation, or the Ray Jah[4] emanating from the solar power in the form of air and fire. It was, I suspect, an incarnation of wisdom, of the *Raj* or *Ras*. This Ras generally, when visible, appeared in the form of Air and Fire.[5] Thus came the Ray of light, the Ras, and the Rajah or Jah *the Wise*. All kings or Rajahs were priests, thus all inspired, all incarnations of the Ray-Jah. From these came the Rex, Regis, the Roi of France, and the females of these were the Reine of France, and the Rana of North India.

Parkhurst[6] says, " The personality in Jehovah is in Scripture represented by the *material Tri-* " *nity of Nature :* which also, like their divine antitype, are of one substance ; that the primary " scriptural type of the *Father* is *fire :* of the *Word light :* and of the *Holy Ghost, Spirit,* or *Air* " *in motion.*" This material Trinity as a type is similar to the material trinity of Plato—as a *type* to conceal the secret Trinity.

*And the* LORD *God breathed into him the breath of life ; and man became a living soul.* That

---

[1] Lib. viii.; De Placit. Phil. Lib. ii. Cap. i.          [2] Lib. ii. Cap. iv.

[3] Cuno-Belinus, the admitted Apollo of Britain, was of both genders. There are cóins yet existing where he is so described. But many learned medalists have thought, that these were not pieces of money, but medals struck by the astrologers.

[4] Col. Briggs says, Ray and Raja are found to be synonymous. Vol. I. p. 7. May not the word Raj be the same as the Greek Ρεω *to flow*, and the Hebrew ראר iar or rai, *to flow* ?

[5] When the Holy Spirit descended upon the apostles, on the day of Pentecost, it was in the form of a tongue of fire, accompanied by a rushing wind.

[6] In voce כרב *krb*, II.

is, he instilled into him the רוח *ruh*, as Parkhurst calls it, *air*, breath, without which a person cannot exist.

When God has appeared to man, he is often described as having assumed the appearance of fire. Thus he appeared to Moses in the bush, and thus on the mercy-seat in the Temple at Jerusalem. But when he appeared as the *third* person to the apostles, at the feast of Pentecost, he assumed not the appearance only but the reality of cloven tongues of fire, and the reality seems clearly to be meant, by the accompanying rushing wind. That, the fire was a real, material substance, is proved by the sound of the rushing wind evidently caused by the fire displacing the air, the usual way a rushing noise is caused. This seems fully to justify Parkhurst, in his explanation of the קדיש רוח *qdis ruh* of the first book of Genesis, by the words *air in motion*. In this he was supported by all the early fathers, who held God the Creator to consist of a subtile fire. Here we come to the true theory of the solar worship, and as usual we find the ancient Philosophers and the Fathers, their imitators or pupils, to be much nearer the truth than we have imagined. If the subtile fire were not the solar fire, I beg to be told what fire it was ? We know but of one fire or genus of fire, however varied may be its appearance, under different circumstances. In the tongues of fire we have unquestionably a portion of the Holy Ghost becoming visible and incarnate in the twelve apostles. How can any one make of these *twelve* tongues *one* Comforter or *Resoul ?* There were twelve comforters or there were none. If I endeavoured to make explanations in such a manner, I know what would be said of me. When all these things are considered, I think much of the vituperation against *fire-worshipers* might have been spared. All the holy Christian fathers believed God to be a subtile fire.

I suppose the Shepherd Kings who conquered Egypt were Rajpouts or Buddhists, of the country of the Rajahi Bedoueens, from Rajah-stan. The Israelites as well as the Royal Shepherds, were both, in fact, Arab tribes—tribes also from Arab-ia on the Indus. From Rajah, and Pout or Buddha, came the name of the country of the Raja Pouts, or the Royal Buddhists, for Pout was a name of Buddha. The inhabitants of that country were Palli or Shepherds. They were Royal Shepherds or Raja-Pout Shepherds. They came from a country called Arabia; and as they crossed the Western Arabia in their route to the Abyssinian Ethiopia, when forced forwards by succeeding tribes, they left behind them, to the peninsula, the name of Arabia, which it still possesses. משה *mse* [1] or Muse was supposed to be inspired with the solar divinity, and this is the reason why we see Cristna, Apollo, and Jesus, surrounded with the solar halo or rays. In very early times every king was a priest, or in other words the priest possessed the power of the sword, and he was also an inspired person ; whence it came, that each was a Rai or Ra-jah. No one could offer the most sacred (sacred is only *secret*) sacrifice but a king ; whence in the republics of Athens and of Rome, they had the Rex Sacrificulus, and whence also came our sacred herald, the king at arms. The king in the ceremonies was both king and priest, like Melchizedek. He was sacred, Χρης. The God Apollo was Χρης, that is, *benignus*, and his priest Χρησεος. He was the חרש *hrs* commonly rendered *Chrs* or Ceres, and the mother of the family of the Cæsars of Rome was Creusa ; and she came from the Ter-ia (or Troy country) and the city of Ili-on, or Ili-vratta, [2] cities of the seven hills, with the trimurti or trinity in each. Creusa caused, by her descendants, the founding of the sacred city of Roma or Flora or Ερως or Amor, read in the Hebrew and Etruscan fashion *Roma*, with its seven hills, and its capital with its three Dii consortes or συγκληροι. From the belief that persons were incarnations of the solar ethereal fire, came the glories, as they

---

[1] See Parkhurst, in voce, II., where I DREW, ought to be I SAVED, him from the waters.

[2] I suspect that Il-avratta is a corruption of אלה *ale*—בראת *brat*.

are called, (or, as the learned priest Taylor has called them, clarys,) round the heads, and some-times round the bodies, of incarnated persons. We are so used to see this solar glory in pictures, that we think it of no consequence ; but a careful examination of the meaning of the word Glory will shew that it is correctly what I have described. The sycophants of Augustus Cæsar said, that his glory dazzled them when they looked upon him. I suspect the Raj ראה *rae* has not only an intimate connexion with the רה *rh*, spirit, but with the ראש *ras*, wisdom.[1] Generally, when Divine Wisdom or the Logos made itself visible to man, it was in the form of fire or a ray of light.

The nine Muses or Messiahs were the same as the nine Curetes of Crete.[2] The word Curetes is only a translation of Messiah from Κυρω *to take care* or *preserve* or *save*. This shews the utility of treating all the languages but as dialects of one original. I believe that, in both the East and West, the names of the Gods were either names from other countries,·or translations of the names out of one dialect into another, as the nine Curetes are evidently a translation of the nine Messiahs or Muses, or names formed from numbers, in a way which I shall presently explain.

" The people of Delphi had told us that there were only *five Muses*, and that the opinion of " there being nine in number was a heresy. Such disputes about the number of the Muses " existed in ancient times, and the *Arracovian Greeks* reduced their number to *three.*"[3] I think that a Muse has been in the Hebrew משה *msh.* Will not this account for a doubt in the times of the Greeks, or a little after the birth of Christ, as to whether they were eight or nine ? There was one for each cycle, like the Salivahanas of India—of whom more presently.

In India there were eight Vasus. These were Jesuses or incarnations of the Holy Spirit, one for each cycle. In the early part of the Jewish Gospel they fade away, and are not visible : but Osee, the son of Nun, was *one*, preceded by Moses, or M-Oseh, as Cristna was by Ram. Elisha was *one*, preceded by Elijah. The Vasus, the Muses, and the Jesuses, were all, or had all, so far the same signification as to mean one of the persons of the Trinity,—Triune God—three in one, and one in three ; and they all meant *Saviours.*

The title Pharaoh is probably a compound of the word *Phre*, and *roh*—Raj, Roi, Rex.[4] In Hebrew רעה *roe* means *shepherd.* The shepherds of Egypt, I have shewn, were Rajahpoutans. They also bore the name of Palli and רעה *roe*. From an union of all these circumstances they became Royal Shepherds.

The style of Nimrod is such as to render it altogether impossible to make out when he is uttering his own opinions, or merely describing the doctrines of Mythology—when he is the dupe of superstition, or when he is only describing it : but I think he has clearly proved that Babylon was a second Meru, Ilion a second Babylon, and Rome a second Ilion ; and I think we may venture to add, that Constantine, initiated into the same Gnostic and Cabalistic doctrine, meant Constantinople, with its seven hills, to be one more exemplar of the ancient Mythos of Meru and its seven mounts and Dwipas. He meant himself, the son of Helena, to be a second Cæsar. If he were really the dupe of such an hallucination, he will not have been the only lunatic sovereign who has ruled in the world. What are called his vacillations between Heathenism and Chris-tianity cannot be satisfactorily accounted for by the usual resources either of fraud, or of the common superstition.

16. I think there can be no doubt that the word פלא *pla* rendered, when applied to Cyrus, by the word *wonderful*, was the root of the epithet of Minerva—Pallas—and as such meant also *wise :* but it probably came to have the epithet of *wisdom* from the use of the regimine. In Chaldean

[1] Vide Parkhurst.  [2] Vide Diod. Sic. Cap. iv.  [3] Clarke's Travels, Vol. IV. p. 203.
[4] Drummond, Pun. Ins. p. 51.

פֿלי *pli* is dijudicare, disquirere, פֿלאה *plae,* interpretatio.[1] פֿלל *pll* is by Parkhurst rendered *to judge, to mediate,* or *to intercede.* I believe the ancient Philiahs or Fileahs of Ireland, were persons whose duty it was to preserve and expound the ancient law, which was handed down by tradition, before the art. of writing became known; and after it became known, they *filed* or handed down judgments. They were the Phileati of the Scythians and Indians.[2] They were the expounders or mediators of wisdom; thus they came to be used as expounders or mediator-wisdom. Thus the Goddess Minerva came to be called Pallas.

In Isaiah, Cyrus is called פֿלא *pla,* in our *book* translated *wonderful.* This is the holy Pala, or Palladium, of the Greeks, which the Romans got from Troy or Ter-ia. It is Pallas or Minerva; it was an idol which descended from heaven; it was, I believe, a black stone, a Cornu Ammonis, like that in Westminster Abbey, on which our kings are crowned. It was the emblem of Minerva or Wisdom. It was the King's-bench on which he sat. It was the origin of the Polis or gate, in which the judge or king sat to administer justice. Mordecai sat in the king's gate. From this came the seat of the king, or his residence, to be called Pala-ce. It was the same with the Sopha or the Divan of the Eastern nations. Divan is Div-ania *place of the Divus.* Sopha is Σοφ-ια, *place of Wisdom.* Divan is also divustania, Divus-stan-ia, *place of the holy stone,* softened, like Casmillus into Camillus, Pelasgus into Pelagus, &c., &c. The seat of justice was probably in the outer court of the palace, where the king came to administer justice, whence all porches were called gates or polises. The mention of the Sofa brings me to an inquiry, why our highest law officer, the Chancellor, is seated on a large sofa of wool. The word Σοφια is wisdom. But soph also means wool, and from this double meaning came the sofa of wool. The Pallas of the Greeks is the פֿלא *pla* of Isaiah ix. 6, mistranslated, as already noticed, *wonderful,* to conceal the Gnosticism; for it is evident from the Greek Pallas, that it ought to be *wisdom.* Here I have no hesitation in saying, we discover the lost meaning of a Hebrew word from its Greek descendant.[3] As פֿלה *ple,* it means intercessor between God and man. The Palla-dium shews that the *sigma* is only the Greek termination.

If the Pall or Pal of the Oriental Palli or Shepherds, had the same meaning as the Pallas of the Greeks, we need not be surprised that Minerva or Pallas should be worshiped in Italy, Thrace, &c., where we find settlements of the Palli or Palestini. Then the Palli will only be another form of the name for Raj-pouts. I shall be told, I have no authority for giving the meaning of *wise* to פֿלא. Indeed, this is true. Poor Mr. Parkhurst has had great difficulty in avoiding to give the meaning of *wisdom* to this root of the Greek Pallas or Minerva, and has been obliged to translate it *extraordinary, wonderful.*

17. After all the most careful researches, I have not been able to satisfy myself respecting the mythological, or rather I should, perhaps, say etymological, origin of Hellen or Ellen. But I suspect that Il-avratta, Il-ion, אל *al, el,* Ἥλιος, were all closely connected; that the Logos or Divine Wisdom was incarnate in man, and that the Palladium, the image of Minerva, deposited in the Perg-amus, or Pyrg, or fire tower of Troy, was allusive to this same mythos. Palla-dium was Pallas dius, holy Pallas, and Pallas was Wisdom, the Hebrew פֿלא *pla.* The possessors of Pallas were possessors of divine wisdom, and the possessors of divine wisdom were possessors of salvation. Thus the city possessing the talismanic *diu-Palla* was safe. All the hero Gods Theseus, Bacchus, Æsculapius, &c., were saviours and *black* saviours too. These black icons were made when man himself was black. He made his God after himself, and then said that man was made after the image of God.

---

[1] Vall. Coll. Hib. Vol. V. p. 223.          [2] Ibid.          [3] Jurieu.

Respecting the Hellenes the learned Nimrod says, "Hesychius intimates to us, that his
"countrymen were Hellenes in respect to certain *Wisdom* (that is, certain doctrines) which they
"possessed. Ἑλληνες, οἱ απο τε Διος, τε Ἑλληνος· η φρονιμοι, ητοι σοφοι. In like manner
"we hear nothing of the exploits of Hellen, but only of his profound and remotely ancient
"Cabalism. ' Hellen, the founder of the Greeks, says Cassiodorus, delivered many excellent
"'things concerning the alphabet, describing its composition and virtues, in an exceedingly
"'subtile narration : insomuch that the great importance of letters may be traced to the very
"'beginning of things.'" Again Nimrod continues, "Now, Helena is merely the feminine
"form of the name Helen, and they both serve to denote the bisexual, but, of preference, feminine
"deity :

αρρητον ανασσαν
αρσενα και θηλυν, διφυη, λυσειον Ιακχον.[1]

"If Helen were Divine Wisdom, Constantine was the son or incarnation of Divine Wisdom."[2]

I suppose I need scarcely to remind my reader that Jupiter was Iao, יהו *ieu*. But Hesychius
says, the Hellenes were named after Jupiter, who was Hellen.[3] He afterward says, that his
countrymen were Hellenes, in respect of certain *Wisdom*, as just now noticed. We all know
how Constantine was connected with Helena. He understood the secret doctrine of WISDOM
or Hellenism : for this reason, as I have intimated, he probably called his metropolitan church
*St. Sophia*. And from this we see that Hellenism was the doctrine of Wisdom. Eusebius has
formerly told us, that Hellenismus came in with Serug, which shews its great antiquity. Constantine was a Hellenist and a Gnostic, or follower of Wisdom, and also of Χρης. Cæsar, the
descendant of Venus, was the same, with his liber or book, the emblem of Wisdom, in his hand.
I have no doubt that the use of letters was for many generations secret, sacred, and cabalistic, and
used only in the mythos and the temple.

18. Gengis Khan was considered a prophet ; the Turkish emperors called Khans, are also
considered to be prophets. This is the Tibetian superstition ; hence the Khans of Tartary.[4]
Guichart derives Khan from כהן *ken*, in Greek κοης.[5] From this he derives Diaconus.

If Constantine were an incarnation of Divine Wisdom in the fourth century, Attila, the Scythian and the Hun, and a Khan of Tartary, was the same in the fifth. He professed to be the
owner of the sword God Acinaces, a kind of Palladium, which entitled him to the sovereignty of
the universe. He pretended to have been reared or educated at Engaddi, an enchanted spot in
Palestine upon the shores of the sea of Sodom ; but whether this might not be a Palestine and
Sodom in the Scythian or Eastern Syria I know not. He called his capital in the West the city
of Buda, Buddha, Babylonia, and Susa.[6] He had an invincible horse called Giana, which Nimrod
thinks was closely connected with the phrase γερανιος ἱππota Νεςωρ. Attila died in his 124th
year, almost the age of a Nestor. It is probable that he was held out to be a renewed incarnation
of Odin. The Buddhist doctrines cannot be denied. By means of the Homeridæ or Bards, such
as Damascius, patronized by him, I feel little doubt that the ancient Scandinavian mythology was
in fact renovated, and probably embellished, and thus handed down to us, which would otherwise

---

[1] Nimrod, Vol. I. p. 469.

[2] The name of Delos is דהל *dhl*, and in the plural דהלן *dhln*. See Book VII. Ch. VI. Sect. 4. I have a great
suspicion that we have here the origin of Helen—Di-Al-in. No sufficient objection will arise from the letter H, when
the common convertibility of the two letters is considered.

[3] Nimrod, Vol. I. p. 468.      [4] Sandy's Travels, p. 37.      [5] Parkhurst, in voce כהן *ken*.

[6] Wilkina Saga, Cap. ccclxxiv. p. 505, *ib*. Cap. lxiii. p. 134, Cap. ccclxxvii. p. 494 ; Nimrod, Vol. I. p. 475.

have been all lost. I think it not at all unlikely that this hardy old warrior should have been induced, by the flatteries of his bards, really to believe himself the promised one, the desire of all
nations; and I think it not unlikely also, that some superstitious fear prevented him from seizing
the holy and eternal city, when it was really in his power. This seems to be the opinion of
Nimrod. The renewal of the ancient superstition by Attila and afterward by Theodoric, may satisfactorily account for many parts of the otherwise fading mythoses of antiquity being found in
colours at first sight unaccountably brilliant in the Northern climes. Our historians erroneously
suppose all these mythoses to have been invented by learned monks in the middle ages, and thus
dismiss them without examination.

One of the most curious of all assemblies was the council of the Amphictyons, which consisted of deputies from TWELVE tribes. Its date or origin is totally unknown. And although
it did sometimes act in politics, as most bodies will encroach on other powers if they can,
yet I think it was solely religious in its object. It was unaffected by the Persian conquest,
and lasted till the time of the Antonines. It met at Delphi. It was called Κοινον των
Ἑλληνων συνεδριον. It was said to have been founded by a king of Argos, called Acrisius.
In that country they had a Minerva Acrius. When I observe the Hellenes, that it assembled
not far from the temple of Ceres at Eleusis, at the temple of El or Jah, where we have
found the Χρησος and several other particulars, I cannot help suspecting that the Acria must
have been a corruption of the חרהש ehrs the Ceres or Cres. But it might be Αχριος or the Ram,
which would be nearly the same, for the Ram was the emblem of the Χρης, and might then be
called Acrios. We have here the twelve tribes meeting in the Sanhedrim or Συνεδριον : and, I
suspect originally sending seventy-two deputies, however they varied afterward. One of the Gospels
states Jesus to have been the son of a Potter, not of a Carpenter; all this I think comes from the
Hebrew name חרש hrs, which means both Machinator in general, and Potter in particular. [1] This
is also the Greek Ερως, or plastic formative power. Ερως is but חרה hrs, and, in fact, is the
same as גרש grs, [2] which means Ceres. From this word comes the word grass. This brings to
my recollection the most ancient of the sacrifices of Egypt, still continued in India, of Grass—
Cufa Grass. The Hellenian Athenians particularly affected the worship of Ceres. They had her
at Eleusis as Ceres, and at Delphi as Χρης, and again in both as Bacchus, for he was both Χρης
and Ceres.

19. As I promised in a former page, I now return for one moment to the subject of hieroglyphics. We recollect that M. Champollion found what seemed to vitiate his whole system, the
names of Ptolemies and Roman Emperors upon the old monuments of Egypt. We know that
the word Augustus as well as Cæsar was sacred : no one can doubt that such was the case also
with the word Heliogabalus : no one can doubt the mythic or religious nature of the adoption of
the number 12, by the Romans, as the peculiar Cæsars. Might not the names of the Egyptian
kings be of the same nature ? Some of them, Ptolemy Soter and Epiphanes, certainly were so.
Then, I ask, might not the words which M. Champollion takes for the names of the sovereigns of
Egypt and of Rome be merely the names of the Gods adopted by the sovereigns of both, as the
Roman dictators adopted the names of Julius Cæsar and Augustus, the latter of which is well
known to be an Egyptian sacred title ? . Whatever we may fancy to the contrary, we cannot be
certain that the names of the Antonines and the others of the twelve may not be like the words
Cæsar and Heliogabalus, that is, mystic words, foreign Latinized words. The names of the Roman
emperors are found in the Sibyls, and I do not think it any more improbable that the emperors

---

[1] Vide Parkhurst in voce.                    [2] Vide Ibid. in voce.

should have adopted them for that reason, than that Cæsar should adopt the name of Augustus, from the Egyptians, or Hadrian his name from the Adriatic, or from that superstition which gave its name to the Adriatic, the etymology of which we do not understand. I have no doubt that up to about the time of the Cæsars, Egypt held a much *higher rank* in the world than either Greece or Italy. And I see nothing improbable in the idea, that, along with the ceremonies of Isis and Mithra, the *conquerors* of Egypt should have adopted *Latinized names* of Egyptian Gods, of a nature similar to the name of Augustus. We must not decide that it was not so, merely because we cannot shew how the words had the meaning, or how they were derived from the Egyptian. Though we cannot say that it certainly was so, we cannot say that it certainly was not so.

All this I propose in perfect friendship to the Hieroglyphists, and with a sincere wish to remove a great stumbling-block in their way—for truth is my object. In an early page I suggested, that if the letters were leaves of trees, a hieroglyphical system might be formed by adding other articles between the leaves. Several writers have asserted that the Hebrew letters had the meaning of things—for instance, Beth *a house*, Gimel *a camel*. The Marquis Spineto says, that he thinks the Egyptian language had originally only sixteen letters; then, these matters considered, I ask, may not certain things have stood for the sixteen letters, and the other pictures of things have been only inserted among them to render them unintelligible to the uninitiated? As I have formerly said, this would render them more easy to persons in the secret. Then the three languages may be first, the epistolary or common Coptic; secondly, the system formed from the first letters, as M. Champollion supposes; and, thirdly, a system formed by the symbols themselves: and, that some inscriptions may be in one system, some in another; but not in the absurd way of mixing the three in each inscription. That is a practice which is not credible. The figures for the *I* in M. Champollion's alphabet, have a great resemblance to our I and the Jod.

Upon a careful search among the ruins of antiquity, we find a large part of a Mosaic mythos in North India; another, a thousand miles distant in South India; another, a thousand miles to the West in Palestine; and minor parts of the same system in other places, as proved in the numbers of the temples of Solomon, &c. Thus, as we find the Judæan mythos scattered all over the globe, it would be a little surprising if it were not found in Egypt. On this account persons must not infer that I consider the symptoms of the Jews having been in Egypt, as throwing a doubt on the hieroglyphics. I am quite certain that if the secret be ever discovered, marks of the tribe of Abraham, or the Iudi, will be found in great numbers in Egypt. I suspect that when the tribe of wandering Arabs settled (squatted, as an American would say) in Goshen, the whole Delta, particularly the upper part, was an extensive pasture country, lately emerged from the ocean— the lower part, perhaps, only beginning to emerge. I take this emerging to have been, as Cuvier would say, somewhere about 2000 years before Christ. Why are there no Pyramids in the Delta? I wish the Marquis had told us why there are no hieroglyphics on the large Pyramids in Nubia or Egypt. Did he overlook the Pyramids, or were they unworthy of his notice? The shepherd kings of Egypt were Palli, of Raja-poutana, who first conquered, and afterward were driven out of, Egypt —and partly settled in Palestine, and might build Jerusalem, as the history tells us. The shepherds, who came as friends and were driven out, were the Jews; both like the present Arab tribes—like the present shepherd Mohamedans. As they passed the end of the Red Sea, their pursuers might have been partly drowned. How very extraordinary a thing it is, that the destruction of the hosts of Pharaoh should not have been known to Berosus, Strabo, Diodorus, or Herodotus; that they should not have heard of these stupendous events, either from the Egyptians, or from the Syrians, Arabians, or Jews! The same thing happened in India. The

4 M

Afghans or Rajapoutans, shepherd tribes as at this day, invaded South India and conquered Ceylon, and were driven out, over Adam's bridge; and the same kind of accident is said to have happened to their pursuers as happened in the West. This accounts for the mythos being substantially the same in this instance in both, *in generals*—but in *particulars* varied; and, as there was no loss by drowning in Upper India, we have the Noah, Moses, David, Solomon, &c., the same mythos of the same people, but no history of a drowning. Because the histories are made subservient to the mythoses, as the early history of Rome was, we can no more infer that in one case there were no Jews, Moses, Daniel, or Solomon, than that, in the other, there was no Rome, senate, kings, or peoples. No doubt, in this case, the two drownings throw suspicions on both. These Afghans, or Eastern Scythians, or Celtæ, came to Italy and Greece at one time or other. They were all Pallatini or Palli, that is, followers of Pallas or Wisdom, and Shepherds. Thus we have Pallatini on the Po of Italy, on the Po of India, and on the Don of Syria, and Don-ube, near the Dardanelles.

Nimrod[1] has undertaken to prove, that the Theogony of Lucian is precisely the same as that of Moses; this exactly harmonizes with all the other circumstances pointed out by me; but to his work I must refer my reader.

The violent way in which *the Mosaic system* is attempted to be supported by Champollion, and his connexion with Blacas, Lewis, Charles, and the Jesuits, justify suspicion. Why did not the Marquis Spineto give a lecture upon the difficulty with which he is perfectly acquainted, arising from the three accounts, or defective accounts, of Diodorus, Strabo, and Clemens? Was he afraid that the boys and learned men of Cambridge should know too much? His Chapter XI., to support the Mosaic chronology, may be said to be a mistake; and his tirade against philosophers at the end of the last chapter, only proves, what numerous passages had before proved, that although the Marquis may be a good scholar, and a very honourable and good man, and no way connected with the fraud, if it be a fraud, yet he must be placed with the saints, the devotees, and not with the Socrateses, Pythagorases, or philosophers.

---

## CHAPTER IV.

FISH AVATAR.—FISH ACROSTIC.—FISHES IN ITALY. — DAGON. JONAS. — VISHNU. — NAME OF VISHNU. — SACRED FISHES.—OANNES.—CYCLOPES.— BISHOP BERKELEY. — ÆSCHYLUS. — EURIPIDES. — PETER THE FISHERMAN.—JOHN.—BALA RAMA.—ZOROASTER.—JANUS.—POLIS MASONS. — IDOLS MODERN. — JOHN. — MUNDAITES.—EXPLANATION OF WORDS.—JASUS.

1. In a former part of this book I observed, that if my theory were right, the Avatar of the incarnation of Aries—of the Lamb—ought in course to be succeeded by an incarnation of Pisces or the Fishes. I shall now shew that it did succeed, and that it was foretold in the Sibylline Oracles. A question very naturally arises how, when the books of the Sibyls were locked up with such

---

[1] Vol. I. p. 420.

great care, their contents came to be known to both Gentiles and Christians. They seem to have been equally well known to Cicero and to Justin. This offers at first a difficulty; but, for some reason not known to us, it could not in their day have been a difficulty; because if it had, we may be very sure that when Cicero was arguing against them, in opposition to the followers of Cæsar, he would not have failed to have urged it: and when Celsus was, in like manner, attacking them in opposition to Origen, it would not have been overlooked. It has been said that though they were deposited in the temple, yet none of them were concealed except the Cumæan prophecy relating to the fortunes of Rome, and this does not seem to have been very secret, when Cicero knew enough about it to argue the question whether the acrostic did foretell a king to his country or not—for that certainly related to its fortunes. In favour of the genuineness of these books there seems a regular train or chain of evidence. Cicero, by not denying, admits that the books of which he spoke were actually those which were quoted by the followers of Sylla. Justin, in quoting them, gives the same description of them in substance as Cicero had done. Then comes Celsus who, in argument with Origen, endeavours to impugn them, but fails; after that comes Constantine, exhibiting, or pretending to exhibit, the originals from the temple, as they had been deposited by Augustus. All this took place in an age nearly as literary as our own: when all the questions relating to these oracles were contested with the greatest keenness, and yet in no instance does any one of the parties deny the genuineness of them. They none of them go farther than to affirm that they were corrupted, and when this is alleged by Celsus, he is successfully refuted by Origen. And when what I have said respecting the names IHΣ-ους and Χϱης-ος is considered, with all the collateral circumstances relating to them, impartial persons will be obliged to admit that a probability exists of the highest order, that the acrostic alluded to by Justin was the same as that alluded to by Cicero; and, in short, that the two works, however corrupted since, were at that time substantially the same.

I now request my reader to recollect that we have had Avatars of Taurus and of Aries, and if my theory be correct, at the time of Christ, we ought to have had an Avatar of Pisces. The Χρησος was adored under the form of Taurus, and of Aries; and if the acrostic of the Sibyl foretold the Χϱησος of the Zodiac *in its proper course*, it ought to have foretold the Pisces or Fishes to succeed to the Lamb, as an object of adoration; and so in fact it did—though it has been kept out of the sight of the vulgar as much as possible. The worshipers of the Bull or Calf of gold, we have seen, in ancient times did not like to yield to the Ram or Lamb. In the same manner the followers of the Lamb did not like to yield to the Fishes. Besides, the adoration of *two Fishes*, absurd as man is on these subjects, does appear to have been rather too absurd to overcome the old prejudices of the people for the Lamb.[1] The fishes were indeed very unseemly Gods, so that the attempt to introduce them, except as a secret system, failed. But nevertheless the attempt was made, as I will now prove. The acrostic of the Sibyl, which was a mode of concealing the secret meaning of the Χϱης—of the Lamb—had also another secret meaning. IHΣΟΥΣ ΧΡΕΙΣΤΟΣ ΘΕΟΥ ΥΙΟΣ ΣΩΤΗΡ.

2. The Acrostic itself forms an Acrostic, as the learned Beausobre has shewn.[2] The first letters of the five words of the Acrostic mean IΧΘΥΣ, *a Fish, which was a name given to Jesus Christ*. This identification of the *fish* with the IHΣ ΧΡHΣΤΟΣ and Jesus Christ, and its suc-

---

[1] In former times the Lamb was eaten at the Passover. This is still done by many Christian devotees, but it is not ordered as part of the religion. But the *fishes* have succeeded, and they are now ordered (that is, a fast-day in which meat is forbidden, but fish is ordered). This is the origin of *fish* days.

[2] Basnage, Hist. Jews, Bk. III. Ch. xxiv.

4 M 2

cession, or, I should rather say, its attempted succession, must surely appear very extraordinary, and at first incredible. But I ask, what has Jesus Christ to do with a FISH ? Why was he called a *Fish ?* Why was the Saviour IHΣ, which is the monogram of the Saviour Bacchus, called IXΘΥΣ ? Here are the Saviour, the Cycle, and the Fish, all identified. The answer is, because they were all emblems of the sun, or of that higher power spoken of by Martianus Capella, of which the sun is himself the emblem ; or, as Mr. Parkhurst would say, they were types of the Saviour. From this it was, that the Christians called themselves, *in their sacred mysteries,* by the name IIXΘΥΣ meaning I the IXΘΥΣ, and Pisciculi. The I was prefixed for a mysterious reason, which I shall explain hereafter.

I　χθυς　. .　Piscis
I　ησας　. .　Jesus
X　ρηςος　. .　Chrestus
Θ　εν　. . .　Dei
Υ　ιος　. . .　Filius
Σ　ωτηρ　. .　Salvator.

Jesus is called a fish by Augustin, who says he found the purity of Jesus Christ in the word fish : " for *he is a fish* that lives in the midst of waters." This was Augustin's mode of concealing the mystery.

The doctrine was probably alluded to in some way or other in the miracle of the *five loaves* and *two fishes,* because " Paulinus saw Jesus Christ in the miracle of the five loaves and two fishes, " *who is the fish of the living water.*" Prosper finds in it the sufferings of Jesus Christ : " *for he* " *is the fish dressed at his death.*" Tertullian finds the Christian Church in it. All the faithful were with him. · So *many fishes bred in the water and saved* BY ONE GREAT FISH. Baptism is this water, out of which there is neither life nor immortality. St. Jerom commending a man that desired baptism, tells him, that like the *son of a Fish,* he *desires to be cast into the water.* Here we come to the true, secret origin of baptism. I beg my reader to look back to Bk. IX. Ch. VII. Sect. 6, and see what I have said respecting the sacredness of water. St. Jerom no doubt understood the esoteric religion. The Lamb kept its ground against the Fishes. They never greatly prevailed, and soon, at least among the rabble, went out of fashion.[1] Yet, for a particular reason which I will now give, I have a strong suspicion, that they are known in the Adyta of St. Peter's even to this day.

In several places in Italy I have seen very expensive sepulchral monuments, not of great age, at the top of which, in the place of the D. M., *i. e.* Dis. Man., grown into the Deo Maximo, is inscribed the word Ιχθυς. They are very expensive monuments of persons of consequence, to whose relations the esoteric religion may be supposed to have been known.

Mackey,[2] in his curious work, so creditable to the shoe-making caste, called Mythological Astronomy, says, that ancient Christian monuments had two fishes on them, fastened, like those in the Zodiac, together by the tails, to shew that they were those of Christians. Where he got his information I do not know, as he gives no reference. But he is confirmed by Calmet, who says, " Among the primitive Christians the figure of a fish was adopted as a sign of Christianity : " and it is sculptured among the inscriptions on their tombstones, as a *private* indication that the " persons there interred were Christians. This hint was understood by brother Christians, while " it was an enigma to the Heathen. We find also engraved on gems and other stones an anchor,

---

[1] Basn. Bk. iii. Ch. xxiv.

[2] A very profound-thinking shoemaker, of Norwich.

" and on each side of it a fish, with the letters which compose the name of Jesus, inscribed " around them." [1]　This emblem is found in the orthodox cathedral of Ravenna, which shews that it cannot be merely an emblem of the Heretics. [2]　Besides, it is chiefly in monasteries where I have seen it.　And I suppose the letters which compose the name of Jesus compose the word Saviour, and thus they are the same as Jesus.　The idea that the fish should inform Christians that a Christian was buried, and not inform Heathens, is nonsensical enough.　But allowing this, pray why was a fish, or two fishes, selected instead of some other animal ?

It must not be supposed that I mean to deny that the Sibylline Oracles have been greatly corrupted by the Christians.　This is a fact which no critic can deny : but I only contend that the probability is, that this famous Acrostic is not one of the corruptions, judging from the circumstances of there having actually been an acrostic, as proved by Cicero, and combined with the ancient style, the *ιχθυς*, and the 4th Eclogue of Virgil, &c.　I think from this very acrostic the Christians became pisciculi, and not that the *ιχθυς* was contrived from the Christian character, by Christian interpolation.　Why should Christians make the allusion to the Zodiacal fishes ?— and such the fishes on the monuments no doubt are.

3. The adoration of the fishes may be found, as we might expect, in ancient Italy.　Janus married his sister *Camisé*, and had a son and daughter called Camasenes, a word which in Greek means *the fishes*, les poissons.　*Cam-isé* is Cama the Saviour, or Isis of India, Ε*ς·ως* divine love incarnate in the fishes.　Brahma seated on the Lotus swimming on the waters was called *Camasenes*. [3]　One of the Muses, or the persons called משה *msh* or the Saviour, was called by this name, a little corrupted. [4]　As I have lately said, I suspect the number of these muses (for the number was not fixed) depended on the number of cycles, a muse for each cycle—that Apollo, or the Sun, had a MSH or Saviour for each Soli-Lunar cycle.　Of this more presently.

Persons in England will scarcely be brought to admit that it is possible for believers in such nonsense now to be found.　But great learning and fine garments do not always produce strength of mind.　Johnson believed in *second sight*.　Erskine would not sit down at table with twelve others, making the unlucky number *thirteen*.　How many readers of Moore's Almanack have we ! Sir Isaac Newton believed in dæmons, and wrote some very surprising essays on the Revelations. Judge Hales hanged old women and children for being witches ; and Tycho Brahe was a great *astrologer* as well as astronomer.　What shall we say of Transubstantiation believed by many very learned and talented men ?　When I *closely observe* the goings on among the old ladies in red stockings at St. Peter's, I can believe any thing.　If they have a secret religion it probably does not go out of the Conclave, or *St. Jovanni Laterano*.　Besides, I do not accuse them of worshiping the fishes, in any other way than as emblems of the Supreme Being—as the prayers of the Persians to the God Bull were used, which I have before given from Mr. Faber and Mr. Bryant.　They probably only pay them the honour called Douleia.

It is chiefly on account of the acrostic, that the Sibyls have been determined by the moderns to be spurious.　But again, I ask, what Christians had to do with fishes, and why they were called *little* fishes?　In these fishes we have the Syrian Dagon, which was an attempt by devotees, who, in their secret lodges, understood the real doctrine, to introduce the Avatar of the fishes, but failed.　Although the sign of the Zodiac is called Pisces, it is remarkable that the *two* are joined into *one* by a ligature, which justifies the Chrestus, or Χ*ρησος*, or benignant incarnation of that Avatar being called ΙΧΘΥΣ in the singular number : it probably alluded to the male and

[1] Fragments, No. CXLV. p. 105.　　　　　[2] Ibid.
[3] Creuzer, Vol. II. Liv. v. Ch. iii. p. 440.　　[4] Ibid. pp. 441, 442.

female, or androgynous, Deity. As we might expect from what we have already seen, the origin of this will be found in India. In the entrance of most Romish churches, is a vase full of water. This is called Piscina. It is true that the word may merely mean a vessel for water. But few persons will doubt that it has here a more mystical meaning. This Piscina was the Bowli found in the ruins of Mundore, by Col. Tod.

As the Lamb was eaten by the Egyptians, the Hindoos, and the Jews, and is yet eaten by many Christians in honour of the Saviour Lamb, so in later times the fish is eaten by the Romish Christians. I beg of those who think this very absurd, as, because it is *new*, many will do, to give me a more probable origin of the pious eating *fish* on sacred days.

4. In the history of Jonas, we have a second notice of the Gentile Hercules, probably in a second incarnation. The story of Jonas swallowed up by a whale, near Joppa, is nothing but part of the fiction of Hercules, of the sun in its passage through the signs of the Zodiac, described in the Heracleid or the Labours of Hercules, of whom the same story was told, and who was swallowed up at the very same place, Joppa, and for the same period of time, three days.[1] Lycophron says that Hercules was three nights in the belly of a fish.[2] The sun was called Jona, as appears from Gruter's inscriptions.[3]

The Syrian God is called Dag-on. Now, the fish in which Jonah was preserved, was called in the Hebrew, sometimes in the masculine דג *dg*, sometimes in the feminine, according to the Rabbies, דגה *dge*. Calmet has observed that this word *Dag* means *preserver*, which I suppose is the same as Saviour, a word which Calmet or his translator did not like to use. Here is Jonas buried three days in the ocean, and cast up again by this preserver—raised again to-day. Jonas means *Dove*, the emblem of one of the persons of the Trinity, and the same as *Oannes* and as *John*. Dagon has been likened to the ship of Noah, by Mr. Taylor, the Editor of Calmet's Fragments. In several particulars the likeness between Jonah, and Noah, and the ship or ark, and Dagon, are pointed out. But the modern date of the time when this Dagon saved Jonah, about 600 or 700 years before Christ, at first sight appears to make it impossible that it should be Noah, except as a renewed incarnation, and the ancient date of it seems equally to militate against its being an emblem of the sun's entrance into the sign Pisces. But I shall partly remove this objection by shewing, in a future book of this work, that a very extraordinary mistake took place among mythologists, and indeed among astronomers, both in the East and the West, of more than 500 years, in their chronology or calculations of time. · Indeed the ancients, before the time of Herodotus, in the Western part of the world, had no more knowledge of chronology than they had of history. Their whole system was made up after his time, from tradition and a few observations of the planetary bodies made for the purpose of Astrology and Astronomy, not of History.

Besides, there is another way of accounting for this. We must recollect that the Neros cycle was passing in about its middle state—about half of it had passed, when the cycle of the Zodiac Taurus ended, and the cycle of 2160, of Aries began. In the same manner when the sun entered Pisces at the vernal equinox, about half of the Neros cycle had passed ; thus the incarnation of that cycle was both Aries and Pisces, as in the former case he was both Taurus and Aries. This is the reason why the word *Ram* means both Beeve and Sheep. As this Avatar-Jonas ended with Christ, he would be born about six hundred years before Christ.

5. In Taylor's Calmet there is a print given of the Indian Avatar of Vish-NUH coming forth from the Fish, which looks very much like Jonah coming from the Fish's belly. (Fig. 32.) He also

---

[1] See Dupuis, Hist. de tous les Cultes, Vol. I. pp. 335, 541.   [2] Nimrod, Vol. I. p. 211, Sup. Ed.
[3] V. Atlantic II. pp. 149, 150.

notices Jonah's likeness to the Oannes of Sanchoniathon. The whole of his very long treatise on this subject, in which he has collected and repeated a most surprising mass of nonsense, is itself a most extraordinary mass of confusion. This arises from his seeing marks of similarity between several persons, without knowing how to account for them. But he has made a sort of table, unconscious of what he was doing, which will shew the reader that this Jonah or Dagon was a renewed incarnation. It is as follows :

| NOAH | JONAS | JESUS |
|---|---|---|
| In the water, | In the water, | In the earth, |
| is preserved | is preserved | is preserved |
| by Divine power | by Divine power | by Divine power |
| in his Ark, | in his Dag, | in his tomb, |
| in which he was | in which he was | in which he was |
| 1, part of a year, | 1, part of a day, | 1, part of a first day, |
| 2, the whole of a second year, | 2, the whole of a second day, | 2, the whole of a second day, |
| 3, the beginning of a third year. | 3, the beginning of a third day. | 3, the beginning of a third day. |

He also shews that this Dagon was the Buddha Nar'ayana, or Buddha dwelling in the waters of the Hindoos.[1] *Nara* means *waters*. In Hebrew נהר *ner* means *river*.[2] Ay-ana is the Hebrew יה *ie* or God, with the termination *ana* making Nara-ayana—God floating on the waters. But the most decisive proof that this Dagon was an incarnation of Pisces, is found in fig. 31 of my plates of Dagon, *male* and *female*, copied from Calmet, where the reader will see the double fishes in one—Male and Female. The renewed incarnation removes all the difficulties.

We are informed by Mr. Finlayson, that the temples in Siam are called Pra-cha-di, and by the Buddhists of Ceylon Dagoba; the meaning of which, he says, is *roof of the Lord*. The God is generally represented *asleep*. I think this proves what I have before stated, that this God is the Dagon of Western Syria. The Dag-oba, or roof of the Lord, I suspect is *Dag-o-bit*—דג ה e בית *bit—house of the Dag*. Mr. Finlayson, probably from fear of being laughed at, calls the old capital of Siam *Yuthia* instead of *Judia*, as it is called by La Loubère and others.[3] It is from this country that the Lascars come, some of whom were found by Mr. Salome to speak Hebrew. See Book VIII. Ch. VIII. Sect. 3.

Two temples are described by Hamilton, in his account of the East Indies,[4] near a town called SYRIAN, in Pegu. One was the temple of Kiakiack or the *God of Gods*.[5] The image of the Deity is sixty feet long, in a sleeping posture ; it was supposed to have lain there 6000 years. This is evidently Buddha or Bacchus, as we see him in several exemplars in the India-house. The other temple is of the God Dagun. They would not let this God be seen, but they said he was *not of a human form*. I think he must be very blind who does not see here the Syrian God Dagon—the Syria and Dagon of the West in the Syrian of Pegu.[6]

Among his epithets, in the 18th Orphic Hymn, Bacchus is called first-born, double-natured, thrice-born or third-born, the King Bacheius, the two-horned, the double-shaped, the Αγνον and the Ωμαδιον. The αγνος may mean *chaste*, but I rather suppose it to be the object of the famous Indian sacrifice, and to mean both the Lamb and Fire ; and the ωμαδιον, I take, again, to be a Hindoo word, and to mean the *holy Om*. The word is certainly not Greek : Om-a-dios is the same as Om-nu-al. In the orgies of Dyonusus the Greeks sung out the words Υης Αττης.[7]

---

[1] Fragment, No. CCCCLXXII. p. 181.    [2] Asiat. Res. Vol. V. p. VI.

[3] Mission to Siam, pp. 156, 220, 244.    [4] Vol. II. p. 57.

[5] I refer my reader to Book VI. Ch. III. Sect. 2, for the proof, that this Kiakiack is the IHΣ or Bacchus.

[6] Vide Bryant's Anal. Vol. III. 598.    [7] Bryant, Vol. II. p. 339.

The Ϋης was the sacred nomen, cognomen, et; omen. Αττης, Αττης, was an invocation of the female principle of Generation—the Great Mother. Bishop Walton [1] says, "Chaldaicè, *mulier* אתא *ata* vel אתתא *atta* dicitur." Thus we find Bacchus called Vesta, as we have before found him called Ceres; for the word Vesta, in Chaldaic, is אתשא *asta* : this word in Persian is At-esh, both having the same meaning—that of Fire. Here we have the Anagram. [2]

In the Vishnu of India, (Fig. 32,) my reader will perceive that, as usual, the renewed incarnate person or Avatar *is treading on the head of the serpent.* Here also we see him with his four emblems : the *book* and the *sword*, to shew that, like Cæsar, he ruled both in right of the sword and of the book ; the *circle*, emblem of eternal renewal, and the *shell* with its eight convolutions, to shew the place in the number of the cycles which he occupied. His Triple Crown or Mitre, or three Tufts, shew him to be an emblem of the triple God. The shell, also, is peculiarly appropriate to the *fish* God. His foot on the Serpent's head connects him with the Jewish seed of the woman, in a manner which cannot be disputed.

6. When I consider the surprising similarity of some oriental words to words having the same meaning in the West, I cannot help suspecting that Vish-nu, is the *Fish* Nu. The Fish God, treading on the head of the serpent, is very striking.

We have said enough, perhaps, of the Trinity—the Trimurti—the Creator, Preserver, and Destroyer ; but we have never inquired into the meaning of the name of this triple Hypostasis. We find the second person called Buddha, and, in succession, Caniya or Cristna, and the Brahmins now call the *three* Brahma, Vishnu, and Seva. I cannot help suspecting that, in former times, and with Buddhists, the name has been Brahma, Buddha, and Seva, and, in succession, Brahma, Cristna or Caniya, and Seva ; [3] and that it is only since the equinox fell in Pisces, that the second person has been called Vishnu or Fishnu. It is not very absurd to suppose the modern Brahmins may have made a mistake in a case which they acknowledge they do not understand. If this be admitted, all the parts of the Mythos are in harmony. I know this will be called a very bold speculation : but I recollect that *God*, in Sanscrit, is Chod or Choder, the English *same* is Sam in Sanscrit, and Bowl the Piscina is Bowli. Van Kennedy has found many other Sanscrit words in English, and I see no reason why the word Fish or Vish may not add one more to the number. It is not denied that the God Vishnu was incarnate in a Fish.

As might be expected, the same prophecy which we have found in the West, is found in the East. Vishnu in the sacred books of the Hindoos is prophesied of, as to appear in his NINTH incarnation in the form of Buddha, son of Jina. This number exactly agrees with all my calculations and theories. [4] This is the *ninth* Avatar of the Buddhists or Jains.

Col. Tod says, " The Bull was offered to Mithras by the Persians, and opposed as it now " appears to the Hindu faith, he formerly bled on the altars of the sun God (BAL-ISWARA), on " which the Buld-dan (*offering of the bull*) was made." [5] This was the predecessor to the Yajni or Agni sacrifice of the Lamb ; which, notwithstanding the objections of the Brahmins to the shedding of blood, yet bleeds on the altars of Caniya. And, I have no doubt, if we could come at the truth, that the sacrifice of the Lamb would be found to be yet followed, or to have been followed by the sacrifice of the *Fishes*, taken from the sacred finny tribe preserved in the tanks near some of the large temples, particularly at Matura.

I think I recollect that when I have talked with Indian gentlemen respecting the tanks and the

---

[1] Prol. iii. p. 15.                    [2] Hagar, p. 10 ; see Vallancey, Coll. Hib. Vol. V. p. 223, n.
[3] Seva, I suspect, is Seba and Saba, the reason for which I shall shew hereafter.
[4] Asiat. Res. Vol. III. p. 413.                    [5] Trans. Asiat. Soc. Vol. II p. 279.

sacred fishes, they have always called them Vishnu's fishes. And we must recollect that the Brahmins are just as ignorant (and indeed in many respects more ignorant) of the meaning of their mythology as we are. The Bul-dan means the *donum of the Bull.* Our English word *bull,* in Hebrew written בעל *bol,* is constantly translated, according to the idioms, bol, bul, bal, and bel; making a case similar to that of the Vish-nu or Fish-nu just now noticed. The *dan* is the Latin *donum.,* But all this is nonsense, to those who do not understand something of the Hebrew, and also to those whose minds have been poisoned by the Mazoretic nonsense of modern Jews—to those who will render the simple Hebrew word בעל *bol* by the letters *bngl* or perhaps *bengel,* because they find modern Jews pronounce it through the nose. This example is very apposite to shew the necessity of returning to the sixteen-letter system, *to the system of the Synagogue,* if the science of the ancients is ever to be recovered.

7. In the island of Ceylon or Lanca, tanks are constructed in the Cyclopæan style of building, and of a size to be really almost incredible. These enormous basins, or Bowli,[1] or Piscinæ, were not for a *few* hundred priests to wash in, but for the enjoyment of the sacred finny tribe, successors of the Lamb.

At the temples of India, before the priest officiates, ablution always takes place in the sacred river, or tank in which the holy fishes are kept. In India every temple has a tank for the fishes of Vishnu. In humble imitation of this, we have the Piscina in every Romish church. It is not merely a vas or cisterna, it is a *piscina.* The ablution in the European climate would not always be agreeable even in Rome. Each of the Grecian temples had, at its entrance, the piscina, for the holy water of the fishes. See Potter's Antiquities, and Miss Starke's Travels.

If my memory do not deceive me, when I was at Naples I was told, that under the palace of Nero, on the bank of the gulf of Baiæ, was a very wonderful reservoir, a piscina, in which he kept the fish for his table. Now I imagine, that this was for a collection of holy fishes. Surely the Gulf of Baia and the Bay of Naples were the finest piscinæ in the world, abounding in every kind of delicious fish. It is impossible to imagine any thing more unnecessary to a Roman Emperor than an immense fishpond under his palace, close to the Bay of Naples. I cannot help suspecting that this fiddling brute, called *Nero-s,* was very pious, like David, or Solomon, the son of David by the wife of Uriah, who usurped the throne of his murdered elder brother, and like Constantine, called by Christians of all sects, *the Great,* the *not-bad man* of Lardner, and whose equestrian statue stands, as I have before stated, in the porch of St. Peter's Church at Rome, a disgrace to the civilized Christian world.

Mr. Maurice[2] has proved the identity of the Syrian Dagon and the Indian Avatar. He says, " From the foregoing and a variety of parallel circumstances, I am inclined to think that the " Chaldaic Oannes, the Phœnician and Philistian Dagon, and the Pisces of the Syrian and Egyp-" tian Zodiac, were the same Deity with the Indian Vishnu." This I think will not now be disputed.

8. With respect to the Oannes, several persons make two of them, and Berosus says that there were other animals similar to Oannes, of whom he promises to give an account in his second book. These would most likely have been shewn to be renewed incarnations, but the book does not now exist. Has it been purposely destroyed? I suspect the Johns, or Oanneses, are like the Merus, the Buddhas, the Manwantaras, the Soleimans, &c. They were renewed incarnations, and the name was given after death, and sometimes during life, to any person whom the priests thought proper to designate as the guardian genius of the age.

---

[1] N. B. Bowli a bowl! Accident as usual.      [2] Hist. Hind. Vol. I. p 566.

In the Pentateuch, which is the sacred book of the Israelites, we meet with no Dagon Fish or God. But we do meet with it in the book of Judges, written nobody knows when or where or by whom, and which was always held to be spurious by ten out of the twelve tribes of the Ioudi I believe this Dagon to be the *fish* Avatar of India—the Dagon of Syrian in Pegu; in fact, the emblem of the entrance of the sun into Pisces. The order of situation in which the *fish* Avatar is now placed among the Avatars, by the ignorant Brahmins, is of no consequence, and cannot militate against the fish Avatar being Dagon; as Mr. Maurice has shewn that their exact order, that is, which is the *second* or *third*, &c., after the first Buddha, is uncertain.[1] At first, no doubt, my reader will be very much surprised at, and perhaps treat with great contempt, the idea of the devotees having converted Jesus into the *fish* Avatar: but why was he called the Lamb? And why were his followers called his flock, and his sheep, and his lambs? It does not appear to me to be more extraordinary that his followers, *as it is admitted that they did,* should call him a *fish,* and the believers in him *pisciculi,* than that they should call him a lamb, and his followers lambs. And I beg to inform my reader that he was originally represented as a lamb until one of the Popes changed his effigy to that of a man on a cross, of which I shall treat at large by and by. Applying the astronomical emblem of Pisces to Jesus, does not seem more absurd than applying the astronomical emblem of the Lamb. They applied to him the monogram of Bacchus, IHΣ; the astrological and alchymical mark or sign of Aries, or the Ram ♈; and, in short, what was there that was Heathenish that they have not applied to him? They have actually loaded the simple and sublime religion of the priest of Melchizedek, with every absurdity of Gentilism. And this I will amply prove, if I have not already done it, before I conclude this volume: for I know not one absurdity that can be excepted.

9. In the earliest time, perhaps, of which we have any history, God the Creator was adored under the form or emblem of a Bull. After that, we read of him under the form of a calf or two calves, afterward in the form of the Ram and the Lamb, and the devotees were called lambs: then came the fish or two fishes. It is a fact, not a theory, that he was called a fish, and that the devotees were called Pisciculi or little fishes. Are these circumstances accidental; or, is a secret system of religion or superstition here to be seen? I suppose few persons will attribute these appearances of system to accident. As we have *lambs* and *little fishes* in the followers of the Ram, Aries, and the constellation Pisces, it is only in character to have the followers of the Bull (though now almost lost sight of from great lapse of time) called *calves,* and I am by no means certain that we have not them in the Cyclops.

One of the most difficult etymons which I have known, and yet to myself one of the most satisfactory, is that of the Cyclopes, which I shall now conclude from Bk. IX. Ch. V. Sect. 4, 5. We must not forget the Cyclopean buildings, and, under this term, I include all those very ancient structures which are so ancient, that even tradition does not pretend to assign owners to them—and those called Druidical, which are so wonderfully marked with the numbers of the ancient cycles, marked in this manner, I have no doubt, before the art of literal syllabic writing was discovered, or at least before it was made public.

The Hebrew word עגלות *oglut* meant both young beeves and revolvers or circulators of the ethereal fluid.[2] גל *gl* means a circle and also a young beeve, and I *suspect* the word עגל *ogl* means, Syriacè, THE circle or THE young beeve—the Hebrew emphatic article ה *e* being, in the usual Syriac dialect, the ע *o*. Now *Cycle,* the C pronounced hard, is very near the גל *gl,* both in sound and sense; and the Greek κυκλ-ος,[3] if the Greek termination be taken off; the words are very

---

[1] Hist. Hind. Vol. I. p. 440, 4to.      [2] Vide Parkhurst in voce עגל *ogl,* VI. VII.

[3] גמל *gml* became Camel or Kamel.

nearly the same. This theory must be considered in conjunction with what I have said respecting the Cyclopes and Mundore in Bk. IX. Ch. V. Sect. 4, 5.

It can hardly be denied as a *singular* coincidence, that this word should have the same meaning as the Greek κυκλ-ος, and as a young beeve, and roundness or a circle or cycle, and that all these circumstances should dovetail so curiously with what we are told of the cycles in the buildings or temples of the earliest races of people, and the mystical numbers of the cycles and the Tauric worship. All this seems to agree very well, as it does also with respect to the Greek οφις. We have seen how the serpentine worship is every where closely interwoven with the Buddhist or earliest worship. Might it not be עגלאוב *oglaub* ?

In old Irish Chuig or Jog means a cycle or period. In Chaldee חוג *hug* means a cycle. This is evidently the Hindoo Yug. An ancient Hebrew word (not in Parkhurst but in Frey) for the Asp or Serpent is עכשוב *oksub*. In the *oks* I suspect we have the Greek οφις; and, in the וב *ub*, the אוב *aub* or עב *ob*, the familiar or evil spirit, or spirit of divination—the West Indian Oub or Aubi or Obi. But when I recollect the close connexion between the serpentine worship and the cycles as exhibited in the temples, I strongly suspect that this word is ע *o* the emphatic article, כש *ks* or כס *ks* the numeration or numbering, וב *ub* or עב *ob* serpent. I think the original word has been עב *ob* ; the reason for this I shall give hereafter. Thus, then, in the Cyclopes, we have the followers of the Tauric and Serpentine worship, and the inventors of the ancient cycles.

10. I think no person will doubt the sleeping God Kiakiak above spoken of to be Bacchus; and we have seen also, a few pages ago, that Bacchus was called ωμαδιος, and was said in the hymn of Orpheus to have slept three years. Although the period during which the God Kiakiak slept, viz. 6000 years is very different from the three years of the Grecian mythos of Bacchus, yet, under all the circumstances, there is enough to excite a belief, that the same principle or mythos is at the bottom of them both. An opinion has been entertained by some metaphysicians, that the world is a mere idea, a dream of the Supreme Being, if I may use such an anthropomorphitical expression—that we are all like the figures in the magic lantern, *illusion*—that all at last resolves itself into God—the great Pan. This seems to me to be the Hindoo doctrine of illusion carried to its first principles.

This I apprehend differs not greatly from the theory of Bishop Berkeley, and is perhaps the most profound and recondite of all doctrines. It is in perfect keeping with the Hermaphroditic Trinity—the Creator, Preserver, and Destroyer. It is the fashion to turn this theory into ridicule, but I observe that it is only ridiculed by persons of weak understandings, chiefly the priests and persons who have never read what Berkeley has said respecting it : persons of understanding who refuse it, do not ridicule it. I have two very learned friends who believe in this doctrine. They are both excellent classical scholars, and, besides, they are men whose minds have escaped the enfeebling influence of the education which has, until very lately, prevailed in our universities.[1] I think in the sleeping Kiakiak, sixty feet long, of Mount Sian, of Judia, in Pegu, we have the icon of this *great Pan.* He is to sleep 6000 years : when he awakes the dream ends, and all resolves itself into illusion—all is absorbed into God—the scene in the magic lantern ends.

---

[1] I have much pleasure in giving an opinion, that at the present moment a great improvement is taking place in both our universities, particularly at Cambridge. I trust that, in a very little time, no one will be able to say, that their members are only remarkable for great scholarship and meanness of understanding. Although a most learned writer, under the name of Nimrod, I believe a Cantab, often quoted by me, has shewn us how ghosts move through the air, demonstrated by the Rev. Mr. Riddle who saw one of them—I am satisfied there is not now any member of Trinity College, Cambridge, who is afraid of them, unless it be Nimrod himself.

This sleeping God is also the *Om :* in the Greek epithets of Bacchus, ωμαδιος—the Dios-Om—the *Om* of the *Judia,* and the *Sian* of Pegu, and the Om of Isaiah.

My opinion respecting the metaphysical doctrine of the Hindoos receives a strong confirmation from the laws of Menu : " This universe existed only in the first *divine idea* yet unexpanded, as " if involved in darkness, imperceptible, undefinable, undiscoverable by reason, and undiscovered " by revelation, as if it were wholly IMMERSED IN SLEEP."[1]  All this is mere idle attempt. to describe *that* of which man can form no idea, and therefore best described by the Hindoo term illusion.

11. I think there can be no doubt that the series of the tragedies of Æschylus contained a sacred mythos.  But so many of them being lost, and those we have, being misunderstood and corrupted, it is not probable that it should be ever made out clearly.  But yet, if the foundation of the mythos should be discovered by me or by any one else, the ruins of the edifice, which this fine poet has erected, may perhaps be sufficiently united to shew that the real foundation has been discovered.  The theory may be found to fit to the mythos, and the mythos to the theory, and thus they may mutually support each other.

What is said in the play of Æschylus respecting the crucifixion of Prometheus, on Mount Caucasus, finds a parallel in the Alcestis of Euripides, which is proved by a gentleman of the name of H. S. Boyd, in the Classical Journal,[2] like the *Prometheus bound,* to be a sacred drama : and he shews that there may be found in it the whole of the Christian Atonement.  No doubt all these doctrines came from India, and are founded on Genesis.  The Trinity, the Atonement, the Crucifixion, are all from the same quarter, where they were the foundations of the universal, secret religion, long before Jesus of Nazareth was born.

Mr. Boyd observes, that Alcestis offered herself as a substitute for her husband, and yet the preposition ὑπερ is employed as often as αντι, and that the wife of Admetus is not designated by so strong an expression as αντιλυτρον, which is applied to Christ by Paul.

I know what I am going to say will be thought fanciful, and be turned into ridicule for its excessive mysticism, but when all attempts at explanation have hitherto failed, surely great latitude may be allowed.  In the Prometheus *bound* we have seen a crucified God.  It is said, that one shall come at last who shall hurl Jove from his throne.  What can all this mean ?  Can any one believe that it had no meaning ?  Io, the *female Taurus,* is told, that this shall be done by the " Third of thy race, the first numbering ten descents," that is, by the third of her kind or race, the incarnation of the Zodiacal signs, distinguished from the incarnations of the Neroses ; and after ten descents, the ten ages of Virgil, or cycles of the Neros.  In a note in Potter's Æschylus it is observed, that THETIS, *the daughter of* OCEANUS, should bring forth a son, who should perform the act of deposing Jove.  This is the fish Avatar, or the male and female, androgynous Pisces, daughter of Oceanus, when the famous 6000 years should end and the millenium begin—when Jove, the creator, should, with all things else, resolve himself into the Brahme-Maia, or Illusion of India.  I shall explain this hereafter.[3]

12. The head of the religion in which we have found the fishes in Italy, the Pope, received all his authority from a fisherman, called Peter.  We must now make a little inquiry into the history of this Peter, whom we shall find a very mysterious person.

Matt. xvi. 17—19: *And Jesus said unto him, Blessed art thou, Simon Bar-Jona.*

Again. *I say unto thee, that thou art Peter : and upon this rock I will build my church.*

[1] Chap. i. 5.  Advertisement to Vol. V. Asiat. Res. p. v.          [2] Vol. XXXVII. p. 10.
[3] The tragedies of the ancients were originally all of a sacred character, and were imitated by our plays called *mysteries,* in the time of Elizabeth.

Again. *I will give unto thee the keys of the kingdom of heaven.* What can be the meaning of this Peter or Rock, called Simon, the son of Janus or Jonas, or the son of Jain, or the son of the Dove, or the son of the Ioni—the generative principle? Does it mean, that on the union of the two principles of generation the church shall be founded? What say the opponents of *allegory* in the Scriptures to this? Dare they deny that this is figurative language? Will they tell me its literal meaning? Will they dare to say there is not a concealed meaning in these texts?

On this *stone*, which was the emblem of the male generative principle, the Linga, Jesus founded his church. This sacred stone is found throughout all the world. In India at every temple. The Jews had it in the stone of Jacob, which he anointed with oil. The Greeks, at Delphi, like Jacob, anointed it with oil. The black stone was in the Caaba, at Mecca, long before the time of Mohamed, and was preserved by him when he destroyed the Dove and the Images. He not only preserved it, but he caused it to be *built into the corner* of the sacred Caaba, where it is now kissed and adored by all Mohamedans who make the pilgrimage to Mecca. Is it the corner-stone on which the Temple or Church is built? The Romans got possession of the sacred Pessinuncian stone. When Cambyses destroyed the temples in Egypt, he left the obelisks or single stones—the Lingams untouched, and in like manner they are now left untouched by the Mohamedans. The modern Romans have one in front of almost every church in Rome, and there are few churchyards in England without one, on the top of which is fixed a dial, or formerly a cross. We have it yet in the fire towers of Ireland, and in the single stone found near every Gilgal or Druidical circle; we have it as a boundary, a terminus, at the division of all our parishes, and on our Mote hills, and in Rudstone churchyard, in Yorkshire;[1] and, to complete all, we have it in Westminster Abbey, on which our kings sit at their coronations. When I examined this stone, I greatly shocked the religious feeling of the keeper, by proposing to apply a chisel to see what was its nature: but it appeared to be a shell limestone. I thought I perceived the Cornu Ammonis or Argo Argonauta upon it. Whether the allusion in the Gospel is to this species of stone, I will not be positive, but the circumstances are surely suspicious.

I believe I am not the only person, by many thousands, who has thought that expression of Jesus's very extraordinary in which he says to *Peter, Bar-Jona—thou art Peter ; and upon* THIS *rock I will build my church.* Peter was not the common name of this apostle, but a cognomen or sirname given to him by Christ. His name appears to have been Simon. Mr. Bryant[2] says, " When the worship of the sun was almost universal, this was one name of that deity, even among " the Greeks. They called him Petor, and Petros, and his temple was styled Petra." Where the temples had this name, he shews that there was generally a sacred stone which was supposed to have descended from heaven. Peter is also called Cephas, which, in Hebrew, means a stone.

In the oriental languages, without vowels, Petor, Petra, Patera, are all the same. In the Western languages *Peter* has three significations: *Paoter*, a *pastor ;* Peter (Be-tir), a fisherman of a *Peter* boat ; and *Petra*, a Rock.[3]

Saxa vocant Itali mediis quæ in fluctibus Aras.[4]

The French Peter or Pierre is Pi-ara, and our Pier-glass comes from this. Ar in Celtic means stone ; this is the Hebrew הר *er* or Har, stone mount, rock, as Har-gerizim. This stone was the emblem of wisdom or the generative power, and I suspect from this, a stone came to be called *Sax*-um. Why *sax* I shall explain hereafter. Mithra or the sun copulated with a stone, whence came a son called Di-orphos or Light.[5] This is the Holy Orpheus. And from the fire proceed-

---

[1] See Celtic Druids, plates.   [2] Anal. Vol. I. p. 291.   [3] Cleland's Specimen, p. 62.
[4] Virgil.   [5] Maurice Ind. Ant. Vol. II. p. 207.

ing from the Flint stone, came Allegories respecting the Petros or stone, in endless variety.　Sir
W. Ouseley[1] has shewn *Mithra* to mean cycle.

The priests of the oracles of the Greeks who were called Omphi, or Delphi, or the Os Minxæ,
or the Matrix, or the Umbilicus, were called Pateræ.[2]　Bochart says, " Pateræ, Sacerdotes Apol-
" linis, oraculorum interpretes :" on which Mr. Bryant[3] observes, " Pator or Petor, was an Egyp-
" tian word; and Moses, speaking of Joseph and the dreams of Pharaoh, more than once makes
" use of it in the sense above.　It occurs Genesis xli. 8, 13, and manifestly alludes to an interpre-
" tation of that divine intercourse which the Egyptians styled Omphi.　This was communicated to
" Pharoah by a dream.　These Omphean visions were explained by Joseph : he interpreted the
" dreams of Pharaoh : wherefore the title of Pator is reckoned by the Rabbins among the names of
" Joseph.　There is thought to be the same allusion to divine interpretation in the name of the
" Apostle Peter : Πετρος, ὁ επιλυων, ὁ επιγινωσκων.　Hesych.　Petrus, Hebræo sermone, agno-
" scens notat Arator."[4]

In a former part of this work I have shewn that the golden Pateræ which were hung round the
large Umbilicus or Omphalos, when it was carried in procession at Delphi, and in Egypt in their
voyages of salvation, argonautic expeditions, were the same as the vessel called Argha in India.
They were votive offerings, emblematical of the generative powers of nature.　It was from attachment, or alleged attachment, to this superstition, in some way or other, that the Manichæans were
called Paterini, by their adversaries, as a term of reproach.　It often happens that sects are called
by a name allusive to some doctrine or person to which they have an utter aversion, by their adversaries, as a term of insult, and from this, without much care, great mistakes may arise ; and
this observation is peculiarly applicable to such sects as the Manichæans, of whom we know
scarcely any thing, except from their most bitter enemies.　An example of this we have in the
Unitarians.　Half the people of England, who believe whatever their priests tell them, suppose
them Socinians, and call them so.　They may as well call them Chinese.

13. The Baptist and the author of the Apocalypse were called John, or Joannes or Ιωαννης.
Bryant says,[5] " This name, which we render John, I have shewn to be no other than Iöna.　It
" signifies *a dove ;* but means likewise an oracular person : by whom the voice of the Most High
" is made known and his will explained."　That is, a *resoul* or *prophet.*　This was the Ionas sent
to the Ninevites as noticed before.

In Berosus and other authors the being, half man, half fish, called Oannes, is said to have come
out of the ERYTHRÆAN Sea, and to have taught the Babylonians all kinds of useful knowledge.　This
is clearly the fish Avatar of India ; whether or not it be the Ioannes or Jonas I leave to the reader.
I apprehend it is the same as the Dagun of Pegu and the fish sign of the Zodiac.　Very little is
known about it, but it exactly answers the description of an Avatar.　The extraordinary number
of extraordinary circumstances detailed above will compel my reader, I think, to believe, that the
incarnation of the fishes was once, if it be not yet, among the secret doctrines of the Vatican.　I
beg those who doubt, to tell me why the fishes tied by the tails are to be seen on the Italian monuments, of the meaning of which none of the priests could or would give me any information.

Jonah " a Dove" was an appellation deemed applicable to one sent on a divine mission; and
hence, among others, John the Baptist had his name.[6]

Anna, or the year, was the mother of Maria or Mæra or Maia, all of whom (as I have shewn or
shall shew hereafter) were the same, and Maia was the first month of the year, on which, in very

---

[1] In the Col. Orient.　　　[2] Matrix, μητρα ὑςερα δελφυς.　Littleton's Dict.　　　[3] Anal. Vol. I. p. 249.
[4] Ibid.　　　[5] Vol. II. p. 293.　　　[6] Class. Jour. Vol. VI. p. 329.

ancient times, began both the year and the Cycle of ΙΗΣ-ος, or 608. There was also a certain Anna who was supernaturally pregnant (like the wife of Abraham, who was sometimes called Maria [1] and Isha, but commonly Sarah or Sarai or Sara-iswati) in her old age ; and she was delivered of a son whose name was John, Joanes, or Johna, or Jana, or Oanes. He was born at the Midsummer solstice, exactly six months before the son of Maria. Thus he might be said, astrologically, as Matthew makes him say, to be decreasing when the son of Maria was increasing. He prepared the way for the son of Maria,—as the prophet said, he was the voice of one crying in the wilderness. Was he a previous Avatar, as the learned divine Parkhurst would say, sent as a type or symbol ?

Jesus came to his exaltation or glory on the 25th of March, the Vernal equinox. At that moment his cousin John was at the Autumnal equinox : as Jesus ascended John descended. The equinoxes and solstices equally marked the births and deaths of John the Baptist, and of Jesus. John makes the Baptist say, chapter iii. ver. 30, *He must increase, but I must decrease.* As Michaelis has justly observed, this is sufficiently mystical. How can any one doubt, that what was admitted by the fathers was true—that the Christians had an *esoteric* and an *exoteric* religion ? [2] I have nothing to do here with their pretended explanations, but only with the fact which they admitted— that there was an esoteric religion. It cannot be doubted that all the explanations pretended to be made of the esoteric religion by Jerome and the early fathers, are mere fables to deceive the vulgar. How absurd to suppose, that when these men, who were at the head of the religion, were admitting that there was a SECRET religion for the initiated only, they should explain it to all the world ! Their explanations to the vulgar are suitable to the vulgar, and were meant merely to stop their inquiries.

At the time of which I now speak, the mysteries of the Gentiles were not entirely abolished, and mankind, educated in a respect for them, felt no objection to the principle of secrets or mysteries in religion ; but now, since it has become the interest of the priests, or at least since they think it has become their interest, to disallow them, persons can see the absurdity of them. But I do not doubt that a secret system is yet in the conclave, guarded with as much or more care, or at least with more power, than the secrets of masonry. The priests know that one of the best modes of secreting them is to deny that they exist. Indeed, the heads of the church must now see very clearly, if they were to confess *what cannot be denied*, that (if the most learned and respectable of the early fathers of the church are to be believed) Christianity contained a secret religion, that the populace would not consent to be kept in the dark. But whether the secret doctrine be lost or not, IT IS A FACT that it was the faith of the first Christian fathers, admitted by themselves, that there was such a secret doctrine, and before I have done, I will prove it clearly enough.

On the mystical nature of the name *John* I am not singular in my opinion. Mr. Bryant, in another place, says, [3] " The ancient and true name of the dove was, as I have shewn, Iönah, and " Iönas. It was a very sacred emblem, and seems to have been at one time almost universally " received. For, not only the Mitzraim, and the rest of the line of Ham, esteemed it in this " light: but it was admitted as an hieroglyphic among the Hebrews: and the mystic dove was " regarded as a symbol from the days of Noah, by all those who were of the Church of God. The " prophet who was sent upon an embassy to the Ninevites, is styled Iönas : a title probably be-

---

[1] Nimrod, Vol. III.
[2] See Basnage's History of the Jews, Book iii. Ch. xxiv., for St. Jerome's account of it.
[3] Anal. Anc. Myth. Vol. II. pp. 291, 293.

" stowed upon him as a messenger of the Deity. The great Patriarch who preached righteous-
" ness to the Antediluvians, is, by Berosus and Abydenus, styled Oan and Oannes, which is the
" same as Jonah. The author of the Apocalypse is denominated in the like manner : whom the
" Greeks style Ιωαννης, Joannes. And when the great forerunner of our Saviour was to be
" named, his father industriously called him Ιωαννης, for the same reason. (The name was im-
" posed antecedent to his birth.) The circumstances, with which the imposition of this name
" was attended, are remarkable ; and the whole process, as described by the Evangelist, well
" worth our notice. Luke i. 59, &c., ' And it came to pass that on the eighth day,' &c."

Indeed, Mr. Bryant, you say very truly—the circumstances are well worth our notice : but why
have you not endeavoured to explain them ? It is perfectly clear, that the Ionas or Oanneses
were types, as Mr. Parkhurst would maintain, of the John of the gospel histories, or the gospel
histories were copied after them. On this subject every one must judge for himself. I only
state the circumstances as impartially as I am able ; my private judgment or opinion I retain, till
I come to my next volume.

When Jesus was baptized by that very mysterious character Ιωαννης in the Jordanus, the
Holy Spirit descended on to him in the form of a dove, and a fire was lighted in the river. Now
I cannot help suspecting that a mystic union was meant to be represented here between the two
principles—in fact the reunion of the sects of the Linga and the Ioni or Dove—which we yet find
in Jesus and his mother in the Romish religion. Justin says, when Christ was baptized a fire was
lighted in Jordan. The same thing is said in the Gospel of the Nazarenes and the preaching of
Paul. [1]

14. In the Indian account of Bala Rama and Cristna, a difficulty occurs. Bala Rama is evidently the same, and is said to be the same, as Cristna, and this is true upon the principle, as I
have formerly said, that they are both incarnations of the Sun. But they are the same on another
principle. As Bala Rama, this person is an incarnation of the sun in his cycle of the Neros, as
Cristna, of the sun in his character of the Zodiacal sign Aries. This is the Janus of the West,
the Bifrons, the origin of the Jains, who were Buddhists and also followers of Cristna, as far as
he existed in his character of Taurus or Aries, but had nothing to do with the separation from it
of the female power. He was Brahma with his four faces. Bala Rama was the precursor of
Cristna, and aided him in the destruction of monsters, and in the regeneration of the world and
its preparation for the day of judgment ; but still the persons who thus describe him also say, that
he was the same as Cristna. The word Ram means both Bull and male Sheep—Ram. This, as
I have before stated, is because he was an incarnation in both Taurus and Aries.

Mr. Bentley thinks he has proved that Rama was born about 1200 years before Christ. It has
been often observed that Rama was to Cristna what St. John was to Christ; particularly in assisting him in clearing the world of monsters and in preparing it for a day of judgment, and
that he was an inhabitant of the desert. The identity of the mythoses cannot be disputed; and no
doubt, with Cristna, Rama was renewed every six hundred years. But the exact meaning of the
parable I have not been able to discover.

Mr. Payne Knight, speaking of Rameses, who is probably the Egyptian Rama, says, " The age
" of Rameses is uncertain ; but the generality of chronologers suppose that he was the same
" person as Sesostris, and reigned at Thebes about 1500 years before Christ. The Egyptian
" priests had a tradition, which they pretended to confirm by their monuments, that he had con-
" quered all Asia." [2] This Rameses is evidently Rama—Isi. But, as Mr. Payne Knight observes,

---

[1] Just ag. Tryph., Sect. lxxxviii. p. 60, note.      [2] Payne Knight, Evors. Pr. p. 89.

it is pretty clear that Homer knew nothing of this king. But who was Sesostris? Now I think Sesostris was a Zoroaster, who was Zur or *Sur astra*. Hyde[1] says " Supradictus Zer- " dusht apud orientales (ut dictum) decoratur titulo ذ, Rad, i. e. Sapiens." Now here I suppose that the ذ, Rad should be ذ, Ras. Here is a confirmation of what I have said of the Ras, the Hakim, and the Sapiens. Dr. Hyde has evidently mistaken or found the ذ mistaken for the ذ. In the life of Zoroaster the common mythos is apparent. *He was born in innocence of an imma- culate conception, of a ray of the Divine Reason. As soon as he was born, the glory arising from his body enlightened the room, and he laughed at his mother.* He was called a splendid light from the tree of knowledge, and, in fine, he or his soul was *suspensus a ligno* hung upon a tree, and this was the tree of knowledge.[2] Let it be remembered, that I formerly, in Book X. Ch. II. Sect. 7, pointed out the fact, that there were probably as many Zoroasters as Cycles. Here we have the universal mythos, the immaculate conception and the crucifixion; and we find this crucifixion connected with letters and the tree of knowledge.

Among the Jews and among the Indians, Rama was also known by the name of Menu and Noah. The striking similarity of Noah to Janus has been remarked, and their identity, in fact, admitted by every person who has written upon these subjects. The proofs of it to any person of observation have been exhibited a thousand times in the course of this work. I apprehend that Bala-Rama is said to be the same as Cristna, because his cycle ran, in part, along with that of Cristna. It was probably partly before the flood or entrance of the sun into Aries, and partly after, as Shem, founder of one of the cycles, lived partly before and partly after it. Thus his cycle was on the decline when that of Cristna began. If he were the fourth Avatar, he would begin in the year of the sign Taurus 1801; and when Cristna began, in the year 2161, he would have passed the best part of his time of 600 years, viz. 360, and would be declining. We must not forget that the Brahmins say, Rama and Cristna were the same. Similar to this might be the meaning of the increase of Jesus and decrease of John, just now pointed out. He answers closely to John. He stands, as lately remarked, in the same relation to Cristna that John does to Jesus. He is now to be seen, as the reader has been informed, in a temple a few miles from Muttra in the very dress of Hercules, as described by Arrian; and yet pious people persuade themselves that John and Jesus are the originals from which Cristna and Bala-Rama are copied.[3]

When we come to the next Zodiacal incarnation, we have it in the fish Avatar of India, and the Dagon of the Syrians; and as the Romish Jesus was an Avatar in the same intermediate state, partaking of the two cycles, we ought to find him, as we have found him, mixed with the Zodiacal symbols of Pisces.

In reference to the double cycles, namely the cycles of 600 and of 2160 years, we may observe how constantly the double mythoses of the Avatars, of the Neros, and of the Zodiacal signs, keep shewing themselves. They support each other. A close attention to history and circumstance will convince any one, that, in the West at least, the knowledge of the system was becoming obscure in many countries, and doubtful in all. The conquests of the Scythians, of Cambyses, of Alexander, and many other casualties, operated against the regular transmission of the system; but still it may be found.

In addition to all the other odd circumstances relating to the Ioannes and St. Peter, I have to

---

[1] De Rel. Vet. Pers p. 312.      [2] Vide Malcolm's Hist. Pers. Vol. I. Ap. p. 494; Nimrod, Vol. II. p. 31.

[3] Eusebius mentions an idol dedicated to the sun—κεφαλην κριε κεκτημενον και βασιλειον κερατα τραγε εχον, viz. having the lordly and regal head of a Ram with Goat's horns. Sharpe on Cherubim, p. 149.

inform my reader that, in the Gospel of the Nazarenes, Peter is called *Simon filius Joannæ.*[1] This shews that Jonas and Johannes were the same.

The apostles of Jesus, I believe, were most of them fishermen. There are many stories of miraculous draughts of fish, and other matters connected with fishes, in the Gospel histories ; and Peter, the son of John, Ioannes or Oannes, the great fisherman, inherited the power of ruling the church from the Lamb of God. The fisherman succeeded to the shepherd. The Pope calls himself the great Fisherman, and boasts of the contents of his Poitrine.

Vallancey dit que *Ionn* étoit le même que Baal. En Gallois Jôn, le Seigneur, Dieu, la cause prémière. En Basque Janna, Jon, Jona, Jain, Jaincoa, Jaunqoicoa, Dieu, et Seigneur, Maître. Les Scandinaves appeloient le soleil John, pour indiquer qu'il étoit le père de l'année, ainsi que du ciel et de la terre. Une des inscriptions de Gruter montre que les Troyens adoroient le même astre sous le nom de *Jona.*[2] En Persan le soleil est appelé *Jawnah.* Tous ces noms ont un rapport evident avec le Janus des Etrusques, qui étoit considéré comme le Dieu suprême, et que les poëms saliens appeloient Deorum Deus.[3] On pourroit encore rapprocher ces dénominations de l'Arabe Janab, Majesté, pouvoir, et du Persan Jauan, un chef.[4]

15. Although it cannot be shewn exactly how it was effected, yet I think no person who considers all the circumstances can doubt that there was anciently some connexion between the Roman God Janus and St. Peter—that one is the prototype of the other. Jesus is called *the Prince of Peace,* the same as Janus, and his religion *the religion of the God of Peace.* Peter was the chief of his apostles. His name was originally only Simon, but he was surnamed Peter and Cephas by Jesus, because on him Jesus said he meant to found his church. As successor of Janus he held the keys of heaven. Matthew, as briefly quoted already, in his sixteenth chapter says, ver. 17, *And Jesus answered and said unto him, Blessed art thou, Simon Bar-Jona ; for flesh and blood hath not revealed it unto thee, but my Father which is in heaven.*

Ver. 18, *And I say unto thee, that thou art Peter ; and upon this rock I will build my church, and the gates of hell shall not prevail against it.*

Ver. 19, *And I will give unto thee the keys of the kingdom of heaven ; and whatsoever thou shalt bind on earth shall be bound in heaven ; and whatsoever thou shalt loose on earth shall be loosed in heaven.*—John says, chap. i. ver. 42,

*And when Jesus beheld him, he said, Thou art Simon, the son of Jona ; thou shalt be called Cephas, which is, by interpretation, a stone.*

There can, I think, be no doubt, that out of some tradition not understood by us now concerning Janus, Peter has been made the chief of the twelve apostles, endowed with the keys, and made keeper of the gates of heaven. In this case the process by which the effect was produced is lost, but the effect itself cannot be doubted ; and surely in all this, a parable, a figurative meaning, must be allowed.[5]

---

[1] See Jones on the Canon, Vol. I. P. ii. Ch. xxv. p. 269.      [2] Jamieson's Hermes Scythicus, p. 60.

[3] Creuz. Symb. p. 507, in Ausz.      [4] Pictet, Du Culte des Cabiri, p. 104.

[5] Many years ago a statue of the God Janus, in bronze, being found in Rome, he was perched up in St. Peter's with his keys in his hand : the very identical God—not the bronze merely melted and recast—but the identical God himself, in all his native ugliness, as is proved by his duplicate in stone, which I found in the vaults below. This the Roman priests cannot say has been *recast* from the old bronze, as they say of the Peter above-stairs. This statue sits *as St. Peter,* under the cupola of the Church of St. Peter. It is looked upon with the most profound veneration : the toes are nearly kissed away by devotees. The priests, when charged with its being a *Heathen* God, deny it ; they, however, allow that the bronze anciently formed the statue of a Heathen God, but they say it was recast into a Peter,

On the Janus I have some very curious observations from Mackenzie Beverley, Esq., LL. D.:
" Many reasons have been proposed for the position of Janus at the gates of cities, but the true
" meaning is to be found only in the Ling-yoni doctrine—than which none is more ancient. The
" arch or gate of Janus was a symbol of that mysterious gate through which all men and animals
" enter into the world, and over which the two or four-faced Janus presided, representing the sun
" rising in the East and setting in the West, or the power of the Sun in the four quarters. The
" Sun, Lord of Procreation, was in his *most ancient human* figure the quadrifront Janus or Brahma.
" The quadrifront Brahma is to be seen occasionally sitting before the Lingam-Yoni, presiding
" over *the great mystery;* and the key of Janus is but another form of the crux-ansata of Egypt,
" the key that opens the ARCH through which we all pass. The crux-ansata is the lingam, and is
" the monogram of the planet Venus, the key that opens the great door of mystery over which the
" veil of Isis was drawn. This key is in the hand of Janus-Sol, because it opens the gate of the
" mysterious arch. But as the sun was always triplified in his power, and as the TRIANGLE is
" another form of the great gate of mystery, they were fond of erecting triple gates in the East, as
" in the triple portal or Tripolia of the Rajas of India,[1] from which root also comes the word Tri-
" poli. From the Sanscrit Pola, we have the Greek πυλη *a gate;* and, as I suspect, the pole and
" phallus always inseparably connected with the mysterious gate. Pylos signifies also a pass, and
" in Sanscrit these natural barriers are called Palas, which I consider a near approach to the Greek
" Phallus.

" Ganesa, the Indian Janus, was expressly formed by Oomia (the Indian Juno, and the Goddess
" OUM) *to guard the entrance of her caverned retreat in Caucasus.* Ganesa is four-armed and car-
" ries a dirk, a club, a lotus, and a shell : the two last are emblems of the female mystery. One
" of the gates of every Hindu city is called Ganesa-pol ; clearly pointing to Janus or Ganes, Lord
" of the Pole, May-Pole, or Phallus, and therefore most appropriately made to guard the GREAT
" ARCH of mystery,[2] through which all must enter." In the cross we here see the emblem of generation, and as the instrument of death of destruction—of destruction and reproduction, regeneration,—of the Cycle of the Sun and Moon, of 600.

Jesus Christ was an incarnation of divine Wisdom. He taught that he was the *door*, or that
through him was the *entrance* to the kingdom of heaven. *He that entereth not by the door is a
thief and a robber.* Again, *I am the door of the sheep.* Again, *I am the door ; by me if any man
enter in he shall be saved.*[3] This door or gate is the πυλη—the לנפ *pll, the intercessor.* This is

---

(i. e.) Bar-Jonas. Unluckily for the veracity of these priests, the ancient stone statue, exactly the same, found[1] in
the vault under the church, shews that this is not Bar Jonas, but Jonas or Janus himself. It will be objected, that
the Peter in the Vatican Church has not two faces. True: but one may have been removed or disguised; (there is
no getting at it to examine it ;) or the Romans, in later times, may have so far improved in taste, as to drop the
Hindoo custom of making monsters of their Gods, and have returned to the good taste of their Etruscan ancestors.
I believe the present statue was a Janus, and not a Jupiter. Probably on this very spot the rites of Janus had been
formerly celebrated in a temple, and this very statue found underneath, with the relics of the God, &c., &c. In this
way, and from such ridiculous mistakes of the ignorant priests of the middle ages, few of whom could either write or
read, and all of whom considered Heathen learning as wicked, most of the legends of the Christians had their origin.
Very likely they had never heard of Janus, and as for the histories of the early popes, as given by Eusebius, or other
writers after him, they are evidently unworthy of the slightest regard. Almost the whole is a manifest forgery of
Eusebius's. There may, perhaps, have been such persons as many of those he describes, a set of obscure persons, but
not any thing like what he makes them out to have been. They may have been something like our present Methodists,
with a similar organization.

[1] Tod, Hist. Raj. p. 589.      [2] Royal-Arch—verbum sapienti.      [3] John x 1, 9.

---

[1] I saw it.

also א-לפ *pl-a*, *wisdom*, *Pallas*. This is the Ganesa Pol[1] of India, the *Gate of Wisdom*. From this, Pol comes to mean *head*. Here we have ænigma within ænigma, parable upon parable. When Jesus declares himself the door of life, surely no one will deny the allegory or figure of speech, and it is in perfect keeping with the declaration that he taught in parables—that the uninitiated might *hear* and *not understand.*

Amphipolis is Polis-om ; Am or Om-bra-sius is a town of Om-creator, ברא *bra ;* Om-phi, *voice* or *Oracle of Om ;* Om-phi-arius, *place of the oracle of Om :* Om-aiarius is Om-aria, *country* or *place of Om.* Om-phale is Om-phallus ; and what is *phallus* but a formation from פלא *pla, divine wisdom*, the former or creator ? This in the Greek is φλλ=600. Am-pulla (of Rheims) is the same. All the superstitions about the πυλις, the pole, and the gate, arise from the same source. Προπολος signifies either a male or female attendant ; αμφιπολος only a female attendant. [2] This seems to confirm what has been said of the amphi.

There are people who will call this obscene and filthy ; people whose minds are depraved by the education of monks or monachism. To *me* they are most beautiful allegories. Persons who take their ideas from monks are incapable of raising their minds above the debasing ideas entertained by the generality of persons of that description. To *them* these beautiful allegories are invisible, but they can clearly see the abuses introduced into them by filthy priests. My reader will see here, as justly observed by Col. Tod, the counterpart of the Scripture Gate, in which Haman and Mordecai sat to administer justice, and he will refer to what I have said in Bk. VII. Ch. VI. Sect. 7 and 10, respecting the various Tripolis, and will find a more probable origin for their name than I was acquainted with when I wrote those observations. But I will not alter them : it will be no inconvenience to my reader to permit the way in which, by degrees, my discoveries ripened into system, to shew itself.

Here, as Col. Tod has observed, and it is very worthy of observation, we have the origin of the Ottoman PORTE. Did the Ottomans bring this with them from North-eastern Tartary ? Or, did they find it among the Arabians ? The Porte, that is, the Latin or Etruscan word Portus, for the Greek πυλη or πυλις. Hence the origin of our *ports ;* and from the gate of Oudipoor, called Ganesa-*dwara*, comes our word *door.* The Tripolis of antiquity are generally, but not always, sea-ports. But still a *polis* always meant a *city ;* for instance, the Decapolis of Syria. This was an imitation of the Decan of India, which lay beyond the river Buddha, as the Decapolis of Syria lay beyond the sacred Jordan. But there is another Pole which the Colonel has forgotten to notice—the Pole of the globe. Why does the axis of the earth bear this name, but because it is the mundane emblem of the generative power—the sacred Meru—with the beautiful diamond at the end of it—the *Pole-star*, called by the Arabians the star of Iudè or Juda ?

I have no doubt, and I think my reader will now have no doubt, of the quarter whence came the Latin or Etruscan *Janus*—a God older than any of the Gods of Greece. He will not fail to be struck with the recollection of the way in which Janus is connected with several other matters— his connexion with Peter, with Ioannes, and with the Juno Argiva or Lucina—the two latter both *male* and *female.* The Janesa holds in his hand a shell—sometimes the Cornu Ammonis, some-times the beautiful Argo-Argonautæ—at one time setting or supposed to set its pretty sail, and scud before the wind ; but at all times safe from the stormy billows ; at another time brooding on the surface of the deep. Who can doubt that these have their names from India ?

Here also we have the mystic triangle, (Freemasons understand this,) and the triangle tripli-cated, as noticed in my CELTIC DRUIDS. When I wrote that work I was not a Mason. It is no

---

[1] Ganesa, *God of Wisdom.*      [2] Monk, in Class. Jour. Vol. XXXVII. p. 126.

secret, but it is a Masonic emblem; and, as Col. Tod has observed, is found with other Masonic emblems on probably the oldest building in the world, the Cyclopæan walls of Mund-ore. Did Masonry arise during the building of these walls? What do Masons know of the Temple of Solomon? Have we not seen that parts, at least, of this temple were built of the sacred wood אלום almg of Rajahpoutana? Have these matters any thing to do with the lodge in China;[1] with the probably much-calumniated man of the mountain, and the Saracenic Lodges, or Lodges of the Knights Templars? Why do the priest-led monarchs of the continent persecute Masonry? Is it because they are not entrusted with its secrets; or, because their priests cannot make it subservient to their base purposes? All these are questions I may ask, gentle reader; but *all* I may not answer. If you be not satisfied, ask his Royal Highness the Duke of Sussex: he can answer you IF HE CHOOSES. But this I may say, it is not every apprentice or fellow-craft who knows all the secrets of Masonry.

Masonry is not inimical to priests, or kings, or religions; but though it is not an *active* enemy, it is no friend to bad priests, or bad kings, or bad morals. Masonry is patronized by the Royal family, and by many priests in Britain. The reason of this is no Masonic secret. It is because the princes of Britain are not, and desire not, to be the tyrants of their country, and because among the priests of Britain are to be found many who are neither fanatical nor base; but, on the contrary, men possessed of every virtue, and whose misfortune it may be, but not whose fault, to belong to their pernicious order.

16. When I reflect upon the many evident proofs, already so often noticed, that the philosophers of Greece and Rome, the Herodotuses, the Ciceros, the Cornutuses, &c., were completely ignorant of the meaning of their mythologies, and yet that they had certain great mysteries in which they were all initiated, I am induced to devise some scheme or theory to account for this seeming contradiction—and I have come to an opinion that, in a late day, these mysteries consisted in part in a knowledge of the system of sacred numbers and cycles, and in the first principles of Gnosticism. These I have partially unfolded, and they were so closely connected together, that there is every reason to believe Pythagoras adopted or invented this expedient to conceal his doctrines. What else was there, in fact, of which their secret mysteries could consist? I have shewn by historical evidence, that all their Deities resolved themselves into the sun: and that every where almost within the reach of history, the nations—the Latins, the Greeks, the Egyptians,[2] the Indians, the Buddhists—had no images, and gave no names to their Gods.[3] And if the mysteries did not descend from or were not the learning of the earliest times, which must have been the times when no image nor names of Gods existed, of what could they consist? There seems to have been scarcely any other thing for them to have consisted of. However, of this I feel pretty confident, that I have shewn the principle upon which all the ancient mythology was founded, and how it arose. When the Gods had no names or images, how was it possible for them to have existed at all? How was it possible to have been any other than the Deistical Buddhism which I have developed, and, at first, in its extremest simplicity, even without the icon? This I suppose to have been about the time when the earliest Druidical or Cyclopæan buildings were erected, and it accounts for their existence—and their existence in cycles, is *fact*, not *theory*, and connects them most closely with the Cyclic system of renewed incarnations, which we have traced up to the first Indians. When I find the numbers 144, 600, 608, 650, in circles

---

[1] Vide Trans. Asiat. Soc.        [2] Larcher's note on Herodotus, Vol. I. p. 193; Beloe; Ouseley's Coll.

[3] Huet has observed that there was originally no image in the temple of Jupiter Ammon. Georg. Alph. Tib. p. 116.

of stones in Britain, I cannot doubt that they alluded to the cycles of the same numbers in India and Greece.

The affectation, indeed, of concealing their doctrines or discoveries, was among the ancients carried to an extreme that is scarcely credible; and this practice was continued down to a much later time than persons who have not inquired into these matters would suspect. Leibnitz published, in the Acta Eruditorum of Leipsic, his scheme of Differential Calculation, so as to disclose neither the method nor the object. Leibnitz, it is true, was detected by the consummate mathematical science of the brothers James and John Bernouilli. Newton, in like manner, explained his invention of Infinite Series, and yet concealed it by a transposition of the letters that make up the two fundamental propositions into an alphabetical order. So also Algebra, as far as the Arabians knew it, extending to quadratic equations, was in the hands of some Italians, and was preserved nearly 300 years as a secret.[1] With respect to Algebra I *suspect* it was known in the East thousands of years ago.

In the mysteries, the initiated swore by the sacred cycles of the sun, moon, and planets. " Omnes qui inciderint, adjuro per sacrum solis *circulum*, inæquales lunæ cursus, reliquorumque " siderum vires et signiferum circulum, ut in reconditis hæc haberent, nec indoctis aut profanis " communicent, sed præceptoris memores sint, eique honorem retribuant."[2] This surely tends strongly to confirm my hypothesis, that the knowledge of the cycles constituted a part at least of the sacred mysteries.

17. I will here shortly notice another personage, called John, who is very problematical, and has been the object of much inquiry, and of whom we shall say more presently.

" Dr. Hakewill,[3] in his ingenious ' Apologie for the Power and Providence of God,' cites good "authorities to shew, what cannot but seem passing strange, that the wandering Jew was in the " thirteenth century entitled *Johannes Butta Deus*, which I doubt not to be a piece of crusading " erudition brought from the country of the Drusian and Assassin Curds."

· Again, " The fable of the wandering Jew is, that Jesus said to the man who reviled him when " on the cross, Thou shalt remain till I come."[4]

Again, " I may farther observe, in conclusion of this topic, that the title Johannes Butta means " the same as Presbyter Johannes Asiaticus, a sort of hierarch, who was looked up to with sin- " gular awe in the 12th and 13th centuries, and who was probably the same personage as the " Senex de Montanis, whose Lieutenant was found in Phœnicia by the leaders of the third cru- " sade, and who was a[5] Curd or Cordivian.[6] When the Portuguese had visited the dominions " of the king or Negus of the Abyssines in Meroetic Æthiopia, they pronounced that he was " Presbyter Johannes, but they, as well as Mr. Bruce, assure us that the Abyssinian kings give " themselves out for an Hybrid race of Jews, and display a long pedigree of their lineal descent " from Solomon and the Queen of Sheba: which explains the reason why the Portuguese thought " the Abyssinian kingdom was that of Prestre John or the wandering Jew. The prophecies " above-cited would naturally lead the inquisitive to seek for two Prestre Johns, the one beyond " the rivers of Egypt, and the other beyond the rivers of Assyria."[7]

Again, " The Ionian expulsion was the same as the Iacchic egression: and even now, when " the causes of their connexion have been long forgotten, the name Iacch is identified with John

---

[1] Southern North American Review, February, 1829, p. 179.

[2] Selden, de Diis Syr.—from Vettius Valens.     [3] Lib. iii. Sect. 7, p. 181, Oxf. 1635.

[4] Nimrod, Vol. I. Sup. Ed.     [5] Marco Polo, Cap. xxviii.     [6] Galf Vinisauf. Lib. vi. Cap. xxi.

[7] Nimrod, Vol. III. p. 401.

" or Johan, and is said to be a diminutive thereof, though it be of exactly the same length." [1] Here we find the name John connected with, or the same as, Bacchus; the reason of this we shall discover in a future book, when we return to the word Johannes.

" But what strikes me most forcibly is, the story put about by the Portuguese, that Presbyter " John's dominions were governed by a queen named HELENA." [2] " This fatal name speaks vo- " lumes. The whole of Illion, the nurse of Romulus, the Goddess concubine of Simon the " Magian, and the mother of that baleful catechumen Constantine the Great." [3]

I have inserted the above observation to call my reader's attention to it, as I am quite certain some curious meaning lies hid under the mystical character of the Prester John. I confess I am not sure that I understand Nimrod, though the name of Helena may *speak volumes*. I wish he had been a little more explicit. Johannes or John was called Χρησος Ιωαννες by Julian. This Χρησος I believe always means the good genius of a cycle. This Ιωαννες Χρησος decreased, as the ΙΗΣ Χρησος increased.

This Joannes, whom Mr. Bryant indentifies with the Oannes of the Assyrians, whom the Portuguese call Presbyter, and John, who was descended from Solomon and the Queen of Sheba in Abyssinia, and whom Mr. Maurice has declared to be the fish Avatar of India, and the God Dagon, and who, Nimrod observes, was Johannes-Butta Deus, was in reality a renewed incarnation of Buddha; or, perhaps, rather a superstition which took its rise from the half-understood doctrine of the renewal of the Indian incarnations. Jesus is made to declare that Joannes should remain till he came; that is, that, as the fish incarnation, he would remain until the end of the six mille-naries, which, as the Equinoctial incarnation, he would do; for the fish would remain the equi-noctial incarnation, or the emblem of it, till the ten less avatars were all finished. This suggests a doubt whether all the Equinoctial Avatars were not Buddhas. Of this Oannes or John Mr. Bryant says, " Oannes appeared εν τω πρωτω ενιαυτω, [4] for time commenced from his appearance." [5]

We are now in the centre of the land of mysticism. Every thing is a parable, an ænigma, a mystery. What can be more mystical than Matthew's expression, that Jesus should increase and John decrease? What can be more mystical than what we have seen respecting the Joannes, and Butta, and Deus? What more mystical than the expression, that John should stop till Jesus came again in his glory? What more mystical than that the Baptist was Elias, that is, in plain Greek, the sun—Ἡλιος?

Jonas, the amphibious, was swallowed, and returned again in three days from the fish. He was the same person as Hercules or as Heri-clo, the saviour 608, swallowed at the same time and place with Jonas, who (vide Bk. V. Ch. VI. Sect. 6) prophesied the destruction of Nineveh about the year 600 B. C. This was the time of the famous central eclipse of Thales, [6] or conjunction of

---

[1] Nimrod, Vol. I. p. 170, Sup. Ed.      [2] Purchas, Pilg. V. pp. 744, 736, 742.

[3] Nimrod, Vol. I. p. 280, Sup. Ed.      [4] Alexand. Polyhist. apud Eus. Chron. p. 6.

[5] Anal. Vol. II. p. 357.

[6] The eclipse of Thales is said to have happened in the year 610 B. C. See Herodotus, and an Essay on it, by M. Bailly, in the Phil. Trans. for 1811; Pritchard, p. 442. There are some learned dissertations on this eclipse, in the first four volumes of the Edinburgh Philosophical Transactions; but the last dissertation which I have seen upon it, is by Sir William Drummond. In his Origines, he makes it to fall in the year 603 before Christ. Vol. IV. p. 264. See also Hales's Chronology, Vol. I. I beg my reader particularly to attend to the circumstances that this central eclipse or conjunction of the sun and moon, was the birthday of Cyrus the Messiah, whose adventures, we have before seen, were partly the same as those of Cristna of India, and whose name Cyrus is a solar title: and that this was exactly the beginning of the cycle of 600 years before Christ. Is there any man living so stupid as to attribute this coincidence to accident?

the Sun and Moon, the time when the oriental Messiah, *Cyrus*, was born, he having the solar title, [1] and who having established the Persian monarchy at Babylon, restored the Jews and abolished idolatry. He is still worshiped, under the name of Jonas, on Mount Libanus, [2] by the Curds or Culdees formerly named. He has the same appellation, according to Mr. Bryant, (vide Bk. VII. Ch. V., Bk. VIII. Ch. II.,) as the half-man, half-fish, or amphibious being called Oannes, who appeared for the instruction of mankind, &c., according to Sanchoniathon; the same as Dagon, which was the name of the fish which harboured Jonas, or SAVED him, and the meaning of which is *saviour*. This Oannes or Ioannes we find again after about 600 years, born of an aged woman, called Anna, the name of the mother of the Italian Janus, miraculously foretold by the prophet Zacharias, to whom his birth was announced by an angel. He was the forerunner of Jesus Christ, and called, as above-mentioned, by the celebrated Julian, Χρησος Ιωαννες. He was by profession a saviour of men by means of baptism or immersion, like Jonas in the water. Jonas was immersed three days in the ocean for the salvation of the Ninevites, as Jesus afterward was buried three days for the salvation of the Jews and of mankind. After this we find another person called Ioannes, a fisherman, beloved by Jesus, of whom Jesus declared from the cross that he should *not die* till his return. And after this, another Ioannes, who had revelations from God; and, at last, we have that Ioannes ordered by Jesus to remain till his return, as *Ioannes, Butta, and Deus*, or the fish, or Oannes God Buddha. It is impossible to conceive any thing altogether more mystical than the character of I-oannes, whom, it will be recollected, Mr. Bryant declared to be the same as Oannes. Now John the Baptist or the Prophet, Regenerator by means of water, who was also a revived Elias, was the immediate forerunner of Jesus—in almost every respect an exact copy of Bala-rama, the forerunner of Cristna. And John the Baptist, or Saviour of men by means of water, was the Oannes or Avatar of Pisces, as Buddha was of Taurus, and Cristna of Aries; or, according to Mr. Parkhurst's doctrine, Oannes was the type of the Baptist, if ever he appeared; and, if he did not, then, according to Mr. Parkhurst, the history must have been a figurative representation of an avatar, foretelling the Baptist.

John the Baptist was born on the 25th of June, the day of the solstice, so that he began to decline immediately. St. John the Evangelist, or the enlightener, or teacher of glad-tidings, was born at the same time of the year; (but, as it is said, two days after Jesus;) and as Osiris, and Bacchus, and Cristna, and Mithra, and Horus, and many others. This winter solstice, the 25th of December, was a favourite birth-day. The English prayer on this Saint's day is, " Merciful Lord, " we beseech thee to cast *thy bright beams of light* upon thy church, that, it being enlightened by " the doctrine of thy blessed apostle, may so walk *in the light* of thy truth," &c. This is, I presume, from the Romish church, and it is unquestionably from the Gentile Gnostics, of whom I shall presently treat.

Lightfoot [3] observes of the births of John and Jesus, " So the conceptions and births of the " Baptist and our Saviour, ennobled the four famous Tekuppas (Revolutions) of the year: one " being conceived at the summer solstice, the other at the winter: one born at the vernal equinox, " the other at the autumnal."

18. In the Eastern countries, chiefly now in the neighbourhood of Bussora, there exists a sect called Mandaites, Hemerobaptists, Nazoreans, Nazareans, Nazireans, and, among the Musselmans, Nousairiens. They are evidently all the same sect, only with some slight shades of difference, which must necessarily arise between the parts of a sect, scattered into distant coun-

---

[1] Vide Univers. Hist. Vol. XXI. p. 59.     [2] See Clarke's Travels, Vol. II. Ch. xiii.
[3] Exer. on Matt. Ch. iii. Vol. II. p. 113.

tries, and unconnected for long periods, and divided by difference of language.　No doubt they may be subdivided into sects, as our Protestants of the Church of England may be divided into Evangelicals and Non-evangelicals : but my spectacles do not magnify so much as to enable me to treat on those minute differences.　They are noticed by the learned Matter. [1]

This is a sect named by St. Epiphanius, and said by him *to have been in existence before the time of Christ, and not to have known the Saviour.*　These people have a book called the book of Adam, in which, Mons. Matter says, is the mythos of Noë and most of Genesis, but he says *they equally detest the Jews and Christians,* and put their founder, the Hemero-baptist John, in the place of the Saviour : that is, in other words, that their founder was a Saviour or incarnate person. This is very important—these people having, as Epiphanius informs us, existed as a sect before the time of Christ.　They have in their mythos a person, the *Principe de Vie, Abatour,* אבאתור *abatur, pater taurus,* which answers to the Kaiomorts of the Zendavesta, translated Taurus.　This *Abatour* had a son, the creator, called Feta-Hil or El-Phtha (noticed by Matter, Vol. II. p. 203) ; but El-Phtha is the God Phtha, or $\phi$-$\theta$-$\alpha$-$\varsigma$—$\phi$=500, $\theta$=9, $\alpha$=1, $\varsigma$=90,=600, before named.

If an impartial person will consider the history of John the Baptist, he will at once perceive, that, as an adjunct or a precursor of Jesus, he is totally unnecessary to the system.　The pretended prophecies of him are actually ridiculous, and his *baptizing* nothing peculiar to him, but a common Mithraitic rite, practised in his time by multitudes of wandering devotees of the latter religion.　That there was such a man can hardly be doubted ; and, like Jesus, he had his apostles and disciples ; of the former, twelve in number ; of the latter, *thirty,* instead of *seventy.*　His sect existed before the date ascribed to Jesus, and were called Hemero-baptists, and, as above shewn, they yet continue.　A short account of them may be found in Mosheim's Commentaries. [2] There seems to be no reason why John may not have been a relation of Jesus Christ's, or why he may not have baptized him.　He may have admitted him by the ceremony of baptism into his sect : this ceremony may have been then, as it still continues, a badge of his religion.　And from this, all we read respecting him in the gospel histories may have had its origin.

These people hold the doctrine of the eternal renewal of worlds ; they abhor all bloody sacrifices ; and they do not use the rite of circumcision.　Hence I think we may conclude that they are descendants of the ancestors of Melchizedek.　From the Jews they cannot have come ; for, if they had, they would have had the rite of circumcision : and from the Christians they cannot have come, because they existed before Christianity.　My reader will please to observe, that these Mandaites or *Nazareens* or DISCIPLES OF ST. JOHN, are found in central India, and that they are certainly not disciples of the Western Jesus of Nazareth.　He will also recollect what has been said respecting Joannes Butta Deus or Prester John, or the old man of the mountain, as he was often called.　In Lardner's Cabinet Cyclopædia, [3] it is said, by a missionary called Carpini, that the Mongol army marched into *Greater* India, and fought the king of that country, called Prester John.

M. Matter has given the meaning of *Manda,* the origin of Mandaism in the word *Gnosis.* [4] This suits very well with my belief, that all Gnosticism came originally from India, and perhaps from Mundore.　Mundus in Latin, κοσμος in Greek, we know means cycle or circle.　Αιων we know also means *a period of time* or *cycle.*　And I think Matter very correctly says, " Les עולם " *olsim, αιωνες* sont à la fois les mondes, les periodes de temps, et les intelligences, qui vivent

--------

[1] Hist. Gnostiques, Vol. II. Ch. iv. Sect. iii. p. 394.　　　[2] Int. Ch. ii.

[3] Vol. I. p. 258.　　　[4] Hist. Gnost. Vol. II. pp. 400, 407.

" dans ces periodes et dans ces mondes."[1] Again, he says, " Le nom de *Mandai* offre une cer-
" taine analogie avec celui de Gnostiques.  Manda, מנדע *mndo,* en Chaldéen, signifie *science—*
" γνωσις : le *Manda di hai,* la science de la vie, est un des génies célestes, comme la Γνωσις
" des Barbelonites."[2]  From this it is clear that Mand—or Mundore, the last syllable meaning
town or place, will be *city of wisdom.*[3]  And the Mandaites or Nazareens are no other than the
sect of Gnostics, and the extreme East the place of their birth.  We must not forget that the
word מנדע *mndo* correctly means γνωσις—Mundul-ooe, Mundul-eeh, that is, Mundul-aia (Greek)
*circle* or *tract of country—*Mando meaning *wisdom :*[4] it is probable, I think, that these Mandaites
may have been Chaldæans or followers of Cali, under another name—the word Cali having the
meaning of callidus, *wise* as well as *beautiful.*  Vide Book X. Chap. II. Sect. 7.

I quite agree with M. Matter, that their numerous sacred books deserve a much more careful
examination than they have hitherto received, and I think the sect comes from Mundore in India.

19.  In the Tibetian language John is called A'rgiun.[5]  This is Arjoon, *(Ar-John,)* the coadjutor
of Cristna.

Near the small temple at Malvalipuram, or *the City of the Great Bali,* hollowed out of a single
mass of Granite about 26 feet long and 14 feet broad, is a figure of Cristna and Arjoon, with some
inscriptions in a very ancient character and now totally unknown.[6]  The size of the stones used
in the Druidical temples is equalled by that of those in the temples of India.  Some of these, as
at Seringham, on the river Caveri, being 30 feet in length.  On these stones are inscriptions in
characters now totally unknown.[7]

As Jesus was IXΘΥΣ with the mystic monogram I, prefixed, I-IXΘΥΣ, and the Deity of
Egypt was Omtha with the mystic monogram M, prefixed, M-omtha, so may Ixion, *divine love
crucified,* have been X-ion with the mystic X prefixed ; and again, Cæsar X-æsar : and Iohn may
have been the Ione or Spiritus Mundi, the Dove, the crucified Semiramis, who flew away in the
form of a Dove.  What does the X-Ιον look like ?  Ion Ionæus or Di-Ion-eus.  It is possible
that the Χρης, mitis, benignus, may have obtained this meaning as well as the prophetic connexion evident in the χρη, from the X and P and Σ=600; and XPHΣ=608.

The remarkable use of the M, puzzled Vallancey as well as Young.  He says, M, in many
words, is only the sign of a noun denominating the instrument of the action, as in the Oriental
languages.[8]  All nonsense.  It would have been better to have said he knew nothing about it.
The word Magicus was originally written by Cicero Majicus.  He also wrote *Ajio* and *Majia.*  Is
it possible that the Mage may have been *age* or *aje* with the monogram prefixed ?

It has been repeatedly observed, that the M is often prefixed to words in a way that is quite
unaccountable.  I will try to explain it.[9]  Every one knows that the vine was sacred to Bacchus.
The final letter M stands for 600, *now* the length of the Neros ; but I have shewn in Book V.
Ch. II. Sect. 5, that the length of this cycle was at first supposed to be 666.  This was made up
of M its figure or monogram and VIN its name.  *Vin* was the name of the letter *M,* when the
letters had the names of trees in Irish and Hebrew, and jointly they made 666, the number in that
very early day sacred to Buddha, Bacchus, and Sol in Taurus,[10] thus :

---

[1] Hist. Gnost. Vol. II. p. 408.          [2] Codex Nazar., I. p. 62.

[3] See Parkhurst in voce מנד *mnd,* מדע *mdo,* and ידי *ido,* V. and VII.

[4] Parkhurst, p. 274.          [5] Georg. Alp. Tib. xcv.          [6] Ibid. Vol. II. p. 92.

[7] Crauford's Res. Vol. II. p. 85.          [8] Coll. Hib. Vol. IV. Part ii. p. 228.

[9] Refer to Book V. Ch. II. Sect. 4.          [10] Carmel was *vineyard of God.*

$$M = 600$$
$$u = 6$$
$$i = 10$$
$$n = 50$$
$$\overline{\phantom{000}}$$
$$666$$

*Muin* the name of the letter M in the old Irish.[1] After the error of the 666 was discovered,[2] and after the equinoctial sun got into Aries; when Cristna arose and Buddha became a heretic, for the double reason, 666 became the mark of the beast, of the dead cycle, and X was then substituted. But still in the arithmetic the *M* in some nations would continue to keep its power. The Irish and the Hebrews kept it, the Greeks changed it, as may be seen in the table above cited, to the X for 600.

Neilos, or the river sacred to the Sun, was thus described in my Celtic Druids :

$$N = 50$$
$$E = 5$$
$$I = 10$$
$$\Lambda = 30$$
$$O = 70$$
$$\Sigma = 200$$
$$\overline{\phantom{000}}$$
$$365$$

But it was more anciently thus, for the Egyptians at first supposed the year to consist only of 360 days :

$$N = 50$$
$$I = 10$$
$$\Lambda = 30$$
$$O = 70$$
$$\Sigma = 200$$
$$\overline{\phantom{000}}$$
$$360$$

But the Nile was called *Sir* or *Sur*, or, in Hebrew, *Sr.* It has been before observed that the Eastern people often changed the T for the S, and vice versâ, and wrote *Cutites* for *Cusites*, *Turia* for *Suria*, and vice versâ. Now נ T in Hebrew is 400, and ר R is 200, this makes TR stand for 600.

The Rev. Dr. Hales distinctly admits that a tradition of six millenary ages of the world prevailed throughout the East, and was propagated to the West, by the Sibyls and others ;[2] and he expressly founds an argument upon the fact that Christ, to use his words, the star of Jacob, the star of our salvation, the true Apollo or sun of righteousness, the prince of peace, was actually born in the sixth millenary age.

Whatever offence I may give by the assertion, it is impossible to deny that what the Rev. Robert Taylor has said, respecting the epithets of Christ being applicable to the sun, is true. They meet us at every step we take in forms innumerable, and would be seen by every one if not prevented by early prejudice. Of these assertions I need not produce a stronger proof than the glory or rays of light round the head of Christ. They mark the solar incarnation in a way which devotees may disguise to themselves, but which the prejudices of education only prevent them

---

[1] See Table, Prel. Obs. Chap. I. Sect. 47.　　　　[4] See Book V. Ch. II. Sect. 5.

[2] Chron. Vol. I. p. 44.

from seeing. But have we not seen that the second person of the Trinity was the Sun, or that higher principle of which the sun is the emblem; that higher principle which was addressed by all the higher classes of the nations of antiquity, when they addressed the Sun; precisely as Jesus Christ is addressed by an enlightened Catholic when he addresses a crucifix; and as the Persian addressed the Sun—Oh THOU from whom THOU receivest thy splendour, &c.

20. We will now inquire into the history of a person called Jasius.

Mr. Bryant says, " Justin places him (Jason) in the same light as Hercules and Dionusus, and " says, that, by most of the people in the East, he was looked up to as the founder of their na- " tions, and had divine honours paid to him. Itaque Jasoni totus ferme oriens ut conditori, " divinos honores, templaque constituit. I suspect, that Æson, Jason, Jasion, and Jasius, were " originally the same title; though at this time of day we cannot perhaps arrive at the purport." On this Mr. Bryant has the following note: " It may be worth while to see the history which the " mythologists give of these personages. Jasus was the son of Argus.[1] Jasius, Janigena, tem- " pore Deucalionis, cujus nuptiis interfecit Io. Hoffman from Berosus. Ιασιων .Δημητρος " ερασθεις. See Servius in Æneid.[2] Ιω Ιασω θυγατηρ.[3] Ιασ8 Βωμος.[4] Æson was re- " stored to second youth."[5] I think few persons who consider this will doubt that Ias-on was only the person who had the sacrum nomen, cognomen, et omen, ΙΗΣ-ος, with the Greek termi- nation, and IHS-us the same person with the Latin termination—the Hesus of Gaul and Cæsar.

Quand les Juifs furent soumis aux rois Grecs de la Syrie, le Grand prêtre Jésus, se fit appeler parmi les Grecs Jason.[6]

D'Anville, in lat. 37, long. 45, has a gulf of Issius. Pliny[7] calls this the gulf of Iasius. As both words come from the Hebrew word יש iso, to save, it may have had both names. Does this prove that Isis and Jesus were the same names? Isis was both Ceres and Bacchus, and was thus both male and female. Close to the Gulf Issius stands the town of Iassus.

There is a very singular expression in Virgil, Iasiusque pater, genus à quo principe nostrum : " And father Jasius, from which prince our race is descended :"[8] i. e. Cæsar descended.

I take Jasius or Iasion son of Abas (father) and Jupiter, to be the same as Jasus, son of Triopas : see Lempriere in voce. Iasius had a daughter called Iäsis. This was Isis. Nimrod[9] shews that this Iasius was the Babylonian Jove ; and, probably, that the titles of Yazeedis, Yas- sidis, Yezidis, or Jezidis, were corruptions of the Assyrian Iasides. Here is evidently the Yes- dan of the Desatir, the name of the sun. Nimrod observes, that Yezd, in Persian, means either Dieu tout-puissant, or the evil principle. Here is the destroyer and regenerator. But Yezd is only ΥΗΣ-di, dis, divus.

As applicable to all these cases I beg my reader to recollect what was said before, and in the Celtic Druids, of this ΥΗΣ meaning Υ=400, Σ=200, Η=8, =608, the sacred nomen, cognomen, et omen.

It is very much the fashion with certain learned men to turn into ridicule, to treat with con- tempt, the exposition of names by numbers, and Sir W. Drummond has called it buffoonery. But buffoonery or not, is not the question. The question is not whether it be or it be not foolish, but whether almost all those whom we have been accustomed to call the great men of antiquity were not the contrivers and practisers of this buffoonery, and whether they did not con- ceal their knowledge beneath it. If it be answered in the affirmative, then where can we look

---

[1] Apollod. Lib. i. pp. 59, 60.      [2] Lib. iii. ver. 168.      [3] Pausan. Lib. ii. p. 145.
[4] Ibid. p. 412.      [5] Bryant, Vol. II, p. 515.      [6] Salverte sur les Noms, Vol. I. p. 369.
[7] Lib. v. Cap. xxix.      [8] Æneid iii. 168.      [9] Vol. I. p. 70, Ed. 2.

with so much probability of success for ancient learning as under this fool's dress, if it be foolish? I promise my reader that by its means I shall by and by make a discovery which will satisfy him, that it was originally any thing but buffoonery. But before I conclude this chapter, I must give him one more example of it. Mons. Matter, speaking of the ancient Cabbala and the Adam, Kadmon, says, " Tout est lie dans l'antique Asia, et à chaque pas de plus que nous faisons dans l'histoire " de ses monuments, nous decouvrons une nouvelle preuve de ce grand fait. Il y a même, dans " l'example special qui nous occupe, une analogie de nom qui est frappante : l'image de *Seir Anpin* " se compose de 243 members, nombre exprime par les letters אברם *Abrm* Abram, Bramah."[1] A=1, B=2, R=200, M=40, total ≙ 243. Abrm, Bram, Brma. This is to me convincing evidence of what was meant by the Seir Anpin. And it is also a curious proof of what I have formerly taught, that Abraham was a Brahmin.

Again, Matter says,[2] " that there is one who watches the march of the sun, and that he has under " his command 296 armies, and is called in Hebrew *harez*, that is, *arez :*" א=1, ר=200, ה=5, צ (tzdi) =90, total=296. I cannot conceive proofs of a practice, although it may be buffoonery, more striking or convincing than these. It is surprising to me that while these gentlemen admit that all these Gnostic doctrines, found at Alexandria and in Syria, came from the East, they scarcely ever go to the East of these places to seek their origin, but seek them in the West. I call every place West which is West of the Indus. Now that we have access to all the learning of the East, this neglect is inexcusable.

Critias makes Solon say, that neither he nor any other of the Greeks had any knowledge of remote antiquity.[3] He afterward makes the Egyptian priest declare to Solon, that there have been many deluges of the earth, and that a most illustrious and excellent race of men once inhabited Greece, of whom the Grecians are perfectly ignorant, their ancestors having lost the use of letters, in consequence, he seems to mean, of the last flood.[4] Again, Plato says, For the cause of this is as follows :—Solon intending to insert this narration into his verses, investigated for this purpose the power of names, and found that those first Egyptians who committed these particulars to writing, transferred these names into their own tongue. He, therefore, again receiving the meaning of every name, introduced that meaning into our language.[5] All this tends to prove a once great people in Greece, who must have been the persons who erected the Cyclopæan buildings. Was this really the nation ruled by Pandea, like an Alexander? We know how he succeeded. What happened to him may have happened before. There is nothing new under the sun. A little time ago I noticed, from the Cambridge Key, the identity of Grecian and Eastern mythoses. The passage of Plato shews that we ought to look to the East for the meaning of proper names.

I shall now assume that the Sibylline Oracles are genuine, and that they foretell the Chrestos or the ninth Avatar, in whom also is blended the *fish* Avatar. This is exactly what took place with Cristna. In his person he was mingled both with Taurus or Buddha and with Bala Rama. And here we have mingled together Buddha, Dagon, Pisces, Jonah, and Jesus or the Lamb, and we have Cristna and Arjoon, (Ar-John,) Jesus and Iohn, I-Oannes. In every case I suspect Buddha will be found to be a name of the Zodiacal incarnation—perhaps of every incarnation. No doubt all this will surprise my reader very much, but it will not surprise him more than it has done me. But the facts cannot be denied.

---

[1] Voy. Kabbala denudata appar. ad libr. Sohar, Part iv. p. 212 ; Matter on Gnostics, Vol. I. p. 104.
[2] In p. 114.  [3] Plato by Taylor.  [4] Ibid.  [5] Ibid. p. 582.

# CHAPTER V.

SALIVAHANA.—THOMAS.—SHARON TURNER.—CHALDEE TONGUE.—TAMAS.—JESUITS.—VICRAMADITYA.—
RAMA.—DANIEL.—CRUSADES.—MOHAMED.—SUBJECT CONTINUED.—M—OM—OMD.

1. WHETHER it were originally a part of the system, that there should be only one Avatar or Saviour or genius of each cycle for the whole world, or that there should be a number for each cycle, dispersed into different countries, that is, one for each country, in each cycle—it was almost a necessary consequence that the latter supposition should have prevailed as the world became divided into nations. We will now inquire into the latter Avatars of the Eastern countries.

Some time after the history of Cristna had found its way into Europe, the learned Orientalists were surprised with what appeared to be another version of the same story, from the Southern part of the Peninsula of India. In the Asiatic Researches,[1] there is an account of a person called Salivahana, near Cape Comorin. He was a divine child, born of a virgin, and was the son of Taishaca,[2] a carpenter. He was attempted to be destroyed in infancy by a tyrant who was afterward killed by him : most of the other circumstances, with slight variations, are the same as those told of Cristna. Mr. Maurice [3] says, " The manuscripts from which the above is taken " have been carefully examined and ascertained to be genuine." Again, " Sir W. Jones has " examined the age of these manuscripts, and he undertakes to prove their date COEVAL with the " birth of Christ."

Col. Wilford, in the tenth volume of the Asiatic Researches, has given a long account of this Salivahana, who is clearly identical and synchronical with Christianity, and evidently answers to the incarnation of the ninth age, alluded to before the birth of Christ by the Sibyls, and, as most Christians, but not all, have thought, by Isaiah. There is, most clearly, the origin or the produce of Manichæism in this person, and perhaps of the sect called the Christians of St. Thomas. Salivahana's crucifixion is a very striking circumstance ; but this, we have seen, was not the first crucifixion. Balii and Semiramis, or Ερως, (Divine Love,) and Buddha, and Cristna, had before suffered in like manner.

The Brahmins maintain that Salivahana, or the Carpenter, was the ninth avatar : they say he was also (i. e. by the Buddhists) called Buddha, or divine wisdom. They affirm that another, the tenth, avatar will come or has come in the shape of a horse. The Japanese say,[4] that in the reign of Syn-mu, Budo (or Buddha) otherwise called Cobotus, came over from the Indies into Japan, and brought with him, upon a white horse, his religion and doctrine. This is the tenth avatar of the Buddhists.

Thus several ninth avatars may be perceived, without having recourse to the necessity of supposing that they copied from one another. There was Salivahana, with the Brahmins, and what they called the second Buddha with the Peguese and Buddhists, and the Teve-tat [5] who, they told La Loubère, was Jesus Christ ; and among the Western nations Cæsar and Jesus Christ. Each sect said that the ninth avatar had appeared to it, or among its ancestors ; and when they say

---

[1] Vol. IX. Preface, &c.; Maurice, Bramin. Fraud. Exp. p. 61. .

[2] Ta-ish-aca. Is this any thing but TA meaning THE, and isha, and Saca—The Saviour Saca?

[3] Bramin. Fraud. Exp. p. 59.     [4] Vide Kæmpfer's Japan, quoted by Bryant.     [5] Divus TAT.

that he had been among other sects, they only mean to admit, that he was claimed by other sects as having been among them, but that the person thus claimed was not the Avatar in reality but an impostor. The Brahmins will say that there have been nine avatars with the Buddhists, one for each cycle, but that they were all impostors. The Buddhists will say the same thing of the avatars of the Brahmins.

Justin says, that the Erythræan Sibyl tells all things which will happen to Jesus Christ. We find an island of Erythræa, Ceylon probably, unknown to Justin: and in the neighbouring country, a person, in many respects similar in character to Jesus Christ, is found, to whom almost all the things ascribed to Jesus Christ are ascribed, long before the time of Christ, viz. Cristna or Crysen—and again, in the time of Christ, to Salivahana.[1] I think my reader will now understand the nature of this mythos, which has hitherto puzzled our orientalists. I beg him to recollect, that it was held by Ammonius Saccas one of the most early and respectable of the Christian fathers, that the religion of Jesus, and that of the Gentiles, were the *same*, if cleared of the corruptions of priests : and the Brahmins constantly tell our missionaries that our religion is only corrupted Brahmanism. I must now suspend my history of Salivahana, to introduce to my reader a very celebrated person—St. Thomas of India.

When the Portuguese arrived at a place on the coast of Coromandel, called Malliapour, which was called by Ptolemy Malliarpha, they found the natives professing a religion with names, doctrines, and rites, so like those of Christians, that without much, perhaps without any, inquiry, they determined that they were Christians ; but judging from several points wherein these natives differed from themselves, they considered that they were heretics. They supposed that the ancestors of these people had been converted by the Apostle St. Thomas. It is clear that they paid their adoration to a *Thomas*, who was slain in their country, and whose tomb they shewed in the church of a monastery. The same kind of people were found by the Portuguese on the coast of Malabar, called Mandaites or Nazareans. When the Portuguese examined them they found them to acknowledge for their spiritual chief a Syrian. Of course, in their superficial and prejudiced way of examining, they concluded that he must have come from Syria of the West, not from one of the Syrias of the East, either that of Siam or Sion, (La Loubère,) or that of Syrastrene : of these Syrias, in fact, they knew nothing. The mistake, if it were one, was a very natural one for them to make. But still they ought to have examined how these people came to worship the *apostle* instead of his *master*. These Christians are said to have had for their Bishop, a Mar-Thomé, a successor of the Apostle St. Thomas, whom, to complete the story, they make to have suffered martyrdom at the place formerly called Betuma or Beit-Thoma and Calamina, and by Ptolemy Maliar-pha ; in Sanscrit, Meyur-pura or the city of Peacocks.[2] St. Thomé is near to Jay-pour, that is, I should say, town of Jah, on the Coromandel coast, where the tomb of St. Thomas is shewn. The Bithuma, Bituma, near the promontory of Tamuz, we have formerly found in the peninsula of Syrastrene, as the birthplace of Cristna and Buddha. The Portuguese state these Christians to have been *Nestorians* when they found them, and that they were originally converts made by the Apostle, but afterward corrupted, by a colony of Nestorians fleeing from the persecution of Theodosius the Second. The Papists state this to support their doctrine of the universal establishment of the Papal church, in the earliest time, and the fleeing Nestorians account for their not being of the Romish religion. Most Protestants turn into ridicule the idea

---

[1] There was also noticed by ancient authors an island of Erythræa, not in Egypt: where this was is unknown: it was thought to be near to Cades: but I believe the *island* of Erythræa was Ceylon, the place in which the Samaritan Pentateuch places Mount Ararat.

[2] Asiat. Res. Vol. X. p. 77.

of the conversion of these natives by St. Thomas, but suppose them to have been Hindoos converted by Nestorian preachers. But the story of Christians in India was known to St. Jerom (ad Marcellam Epist.) before the Nestorian heresy arose, therefore they cannot have been originally Nestorians. [1] This is not surprising, if they were people of the religion of that person concerning whom the Erythræan Sibyl had foretold all the things which should happen to Jesus Christ. They are said by their priests to have sent to Babylon for Patriarchs, and to have obtained them from there so lately as the reign of the Portuguese Queen Donna Catharina, not knowing that at that time Babylon must have been for almost a thousand years before a desert, capable of supplying nothing but a tiger or a lion. This falsity proves that no dependance can be placed on any thing which they say. In short, the whole story is full of absurdities and inconsistencies, and the truth is completely disguised. Indeed it is evident that our Indian travellers tell us respecting the religions and languages of South India a number of strange stories, which I do not doubt they believe to be true, although apparently inconsistent with one another. I think, however, they are all capable of being explained, though certainly the explanation will upset some very favourite theories.

2. In Mr. Sharon Turner's History of the Anglo Saxons, there is a very particular account of an embassy from Alfred to the Tomb of St. Thomas in India. Mr. Turner has displayed the talent of a skilful lawyer, and has collected all the evidence on the subject which later times afford; but I think he has overlooked some of the earlier; perhaps he was afraid of proving too much. No doubt the evidence for the fact is very strong, and in any common case where religion was not concerned, I think it would be conclusive to prove, that the Christians had a settlement in India. But in this case, where habitual fraud, added to the greatest prejudice in witnesses, has rendered all evidence doubtful, I cannot help thinking that even if the truth be told by them, they have alluded to the Tamuz of Western Syria and Egypt, noticed in the Bible, and of the promontory of Tamuz, which was the Thomas of the Manichæans: and that every thing in fact relating to the Thomas, was to that person of whom the history is given in the Erythræan Sibyl. I have very little doubt that the whole promontory of India was once called the promontory of Tamas or Thomas.

The Indians say that their God Narayana, (which means *moving on the waters,*) in the beginning, was wholly surrounded by Tamas, which means *darkness:* Col. Wilford says, perhaps the Thamas or Thaumaz of the ancient Egyptians. Parkhurst gives one of the meanings of םאת *tam* *dark.* [2] This I shall refer to and explain presently. He also gives the meaning of twin, or Dydimus to the word Tam. In the Hebrew םאת *tam* or םות *tum* means twins. See Parkhurst, also ib. in voce זמת *tmz,* also pp. 19, 789.

It cannot be doubted, I think, that the Tamuz of the Bible or Adonis was Buddha under a different name, that is, under the name of the *Zodiacal twins* or one of them, or was in some way closely connected with them. And it is worthy of observation, that this is the account which the native Vishnuvites of Malabar give of their Thomas—calling the Christians *Baudhenmar* or *sons of Baudhen.* [3] And the Christians of the present day always call their bishops by the name of Mar-Thomé, that is, son of Thomé, Thomé-mar. Manes, whose existence I much doubt, is said to have had for his ancestors or predecessors a Budwas and a Thomas, and he may have come from Malabar, or from the Matura of Upper India or Syrastra, from the Bituma, where there is

---

[1] This fact at once renders incredible all the other histories of Nestorian conversions East of the Indus. Asiat. Res. Vol. VII. p. 366, n.

[2] Asiat. Res. Vol. III. p. 358.     [3] Bartol. System. p. 161.

the same mythos. Bithuma is evidently בית-תעמה *bit-tomé, house of Tomé*. This Bithoma is not far from the promontory of Tamus and the island of Chryse.

3. The Portuguese state, that the St. Thomé Christians had all their sacred books in the old Chaldee tongue, but what they contained we can never know, as Menezes and the Portuguese inquisition, after having held a Synod at Odiamper, sought them out with the greatest care and destroyed them all, substituting in their places books of their own, *but yet in the Chaldee language*. This I think proves that the common vernacular language of the people of this country was the Chaldee. The sailors in the service of the India Company, whom Mr. Salome found in Wapping speaking Hebrew, must have come from the country in the neighbourhood of Calamina. It seems that the Roman Catholics in this instance broke the rule of their church, to have the service in Latin, in order to indulge these Indians with the Chaldee. Nothing can be more absurd than to suppose they should have broken their rule with respect to the Latin to have given the Indians books in a language not their own. Therefore it is pretty clear that Chaldee must have been the vernacular language of these people. Now if we grant that they were converted by St. Thomas, we cannot suppose that he who (we must allow) was endowed with the gift of tongues, would change their language, although he changed their religion. It follows, therefore, that their language must have been at that time the Chaldee. Now I think the natural inference from this is, that *one* at least of the *broken* dialects of India, as they are called, must have been the Chaldee or Hebrew. It must be observed that I am speaking both of the Chaldee letter and language.

I apprehend the Nestorians did not arise till the Chaldee was a dead language : at all events it was not their *peculiar* language. Nestorius was a native of Germany.

For various reasons which I shall give by and by, I am satisfied that the Chaldee paraphrases or Targums were not written till after the time of Origen ; how long after I will not undertake to say ; and at the same time I shall shew, that there is a very strong probability that the Chaldee letter never was in common use in Babylon. Nestorius lived in the fifth century, and I apprehend it is not credible that this German should have established a sect in that day, which would carry along with it, as it extended itself, the peculiar Chaldæan language—this language not being that of its founder—instead of extending itself in the vernacular languages of the country into which it penetrated. There is no instance known of a sect extending itself into any country, and changing the vernacular dialect of it, unless it was attended by a conquering army. I believe we have no reason to suppose that the Nestorians of the West, as a sect, ever used the Chaldee tongue.

The Christians of St. Thomas are said to have had only three sacraments, Baptism, the Eucharist, and Orders. These were all Jewish rites, for the rite of orders is nothing but the samach [1] or investment with office, or communication of the holy spirit by anointment and the imposition of hands. The two former I shall treat on at large by and by. [2] In their use of the Chaldee they are the same as the remains of the Ioudi of Rajapoutana and Afghanistan, if Sir William Jones can be credited, for he has stated them to have a language, to use his words, *very like the Chaldaic*. [3] The laws of the Chaldee-speaking Malabar Christians have a near affinity to those of the Jewish-looking, Jewish-named, Chaldee-speaking Afghans of North India and to those of the Western Jews. This affinity is far too close to be the effect of accident. Their laws of inherit-

---

[1] See CELTIC DRUIDS, Chap. IV. Sect. IX.

[2] I think there can be little doubt that copies of the rituals of the Christians of Malabar must have been sent by Menezes to Rome, and that they are preserved there. If a philosopher could get hold of them before our priests, they might yet see the light, and they would be very important indeed.

[3] I observe on the Malabar coast the district of Chercull. This is of Hercul.

ance may be specified for one instance, out of great numbers, under which the land goes to the next male cousin or uncle, instead of the daughter. Our ill-informed and prejudiced writers assert, that these Christians *have not yet lost* all their old habits, but that they still follow the Brahmin custom of abstaining from the flesh of animals : in defiance of all Portuguese persecutions, these people abstain, who were Christians before the Portuguese came among them ! The fact is, it is evident that they are Brahmin Χρησιανοι, having nothing to do either with Nestorius or the Pope. They were of the same religion as that of the Youth of Larissa, the SINDI, whose widows were burnt on the death of their husbands. They are of the same religion as the people referred to by the Erythræan Sibyl. They are of the religion of the Χ ςης at Delphi. Their churches or temples were mostly destroyed by Tippoo Saib. But some of them were very handsome, and each must have cost as much as a lack of rupees. I cannot help entertaining a suspicion that they were a tribe of the Ioudi, from Upper India, and that the town of Odiamper ought to be Ioudi-pore.

4. The town of Malliapour was never called the town or port of St. Thomas, till the Portuguese, under Vasquez de Gama, arrived there.[1] It is quite clear that, judging from the legend which they learnt from the natives that a holy Thomas had been put to death there, they instantly concluded that it must have been the place to which Alfred sent his embassy. And they distorted every tradition and circumstance to make it fit this theory.

If my reader have not a very short memory he will recollect that, in Ch. II. Sect. 9, we found the island of Erythræa in Ceylon or Diu, and that, on the coast of Malabar, we also found the Erythræan Sea, and a country of Erythræa between the Indus and Ganges. We have also found a Cristna in the island and country washed by this sea, of whom the same things are told as are told of Jesus Christ. We have also found that, according to Justin Martyr, *the Erythræan Sibyl foretold all things which should happen to Jesus Christ.* Now we have likewise seen that Adonis is the Tamuz of the Bible, and that on the coast of Malabar was a promontory of Tamus, as reported by the ancient Greek geographers, and in this country there is a town or district called Adoni. Now a Thomas is said to have been found in India, and to have been put to death, and a body of Christians are found who, it is said, were followers of this Thomas. Is there not great room for suspicion, that this Thomas was the Tamus for whom the women of Judea wept, and that his followers were not Christians, but Χρης-tians, followers of him of whom the Erythræan Sibyl prophesied ? It is a very important fact, that the city of Adoni should not be far from the place where Thomas was put to death, and that a large TEMPLE should be placed on the highest mount of the country called SALEM, of course ιερος-*Salem*[2]                    *

The Portuguese finding these Christians worshiping and bewailing a Thomas or Tamuz—put to death at the vernal equinox, and after three days rising again to life, as I shall shew in a future book—to whom were attributed all things which were attributed to Jesus Christ, settled it instantly, that there was a mistake ignorantly made between St. Thomas (who must have gone to India as they believed) and Jesus Christ—a mistake before made by Jerom : they then proceeded to destroy their sacred books in the Hebrew or Chaldee tongue, the language in which we have the account of the women weeping for Tamus, and gave them their own gospels : these they properly gave them in the Chaldee or Hebrew, that being the language which the natives of this country, the Lascars, speak at this day, and that of the Mandaites or Nazarenes, Christians of St.

---

[1]  Chatfield's Hist. Rev. Hist. of Hind. p. 331, n.

[2]  In the name of Thamas Kouli-Khan we have an example of the adoption of a sacred name after the Hindoo fashion.

John. From this quarter the Manichæans had before come to the West, bringing with them also their Apostle Thomas.

5. Now let us look at Madura on the Jumna, where we have found our Cristna, and afterward towards the South, near Cape Comorin and the island of Ceylon or Erythræa, where the Sibyl came from, and we shall find another Pandion, a Madura, a Tanjore, a Tricala, a Salem, an Adoni, a COLIDA now Cochin, and a district or place called Aur, URR, or Orissa, and a Trichinopoly. At Madura is a most magnificent temple, probably the largest in India, occupying about a square mile of ground.

The Jesuit Bouchet, in a letter to the Bishop of Avranches, about the year 1710, has given an account of the religion of the Brahmins at this temple, where the Mohamedans never had any power or influence whatever. This immense temple was the property of the government of the country, not of a sect. According to their doctrine, from the Supreme emanated the Trimurti, one of whom formed our world and man, and placed him in a garden of delight, where were two trees of Good and Evil. This story was accompanied with that of the temptation, &c., &c. There is also an account of Abraham and Sarasvedi, the attempt to sacrifice Isaac, the son, and the prevention of it. Then we have a *relation* of Crishen (Moses) exposed on a river, and saved by a princess : after that Crishen exposed on a river and the river opening to save him from a tyrant who pursued him, and which closed on the tyrant and drowned him and his followers. After this, the Jesuit goes on to describe the Veda, given from a mountain, like the law at Sinai, and many of the rites and laws of the country respecting both religion and property, as being a close copy of those of the Jews. He describes the paschal sacrifice of the Lamb ; and, what is very extra-ordinary, the head chiefs of the nation, but no others, have the right of circumcision. The sub-stance of this is repeated by Bartolomeus, Tab. XIX., who, in addition to what the Jesuit has shewn, has proved, by quotations from Arrian, Pliny, &c., that this country was anciently known by the name of Pandion, which it bears to this day. Altogether this is a most curious history of this Jesuit's, though evidently full of mistakes, and well worthy of further inquiry. All the Mosaic history, and much of the Romish Christian, is here interwoven with the oldest Indian customs, names of places, laws of property, as existing in the times before Christ, as proved by the Greek and Latin authors. I have before observed, that some of these people called Christians in India abstained from animal food, which seems to shew them to be Brahmins. This they could not be, unless they took water in the Eucharist, nor could they be Jews and Brahmins also if they ate the Passover, except on the grand occasion of the Yajni or Y-agni sacrifice.[1] At a little distance from Madura in Cochin or COLIDA, and the place called Aur, is the Ur of the Chaldees called now Uri-ya and Orissa. It is perfectly clear from the whole text and context of the letters, that these people were neither Jews nor Christians in our sense of these words, but Brahmins—but still not Sanscrit-speaking Brahmins—as I believe they used the language now called Tamul. The fact is, they were Christians, of the sect of the Youth of Larissa in Thrace.

In the centre of this country, in lat. 13° 46′, long. 79° 24′, stands the famous temple of Tripetty or Terputty or Tripati, before noticed in Bk. IV. Ch. II. Sect. 3, where is the crucified Wittoba or Bal-iji, or Rama or Tripati. Pilgrims, in great numbers, come hither from the Batties or Bat tenians of North India. No European has ever penetrated into the sanctum sanctorum of this temple.[2]

---

[1] See Travels of Jesuits, in English, 1714, Lond.

[2] Beyond the sacred river Don, or the *River of Wisdom*, was a country called Decapolis. Beyond the River Ner-buddha or the River of Buddha or *Wisdom* was a country called Decan. The topographical similarity of the holy land of India, and of that of Western Asia, is very striking. Hamilton's East-India Gaz. 2 Vols. 1828.

Upon the account of the Jesuit Goguet it may be expedient to observe, that it is evidence which cannot be impeached: and here we see very clearly that the people whom he describes as possessing the doctrines of Moses and Jesus Christ, or Cristna, are Brahmins, and neither Jews nor Christians in the usual sense of these words. These people were the governors or head class of a *great state* called Madura; therefore, if a body of refugee Jews did arrive, as a gentleman of the name of Baber, from a paper read to the Asiatic Society, in March, 1830, would have us believe, in the year of Christ 56, and *purchase the sovereignty of a country*, (the only instance of the kind in the history of the old world,) this must have been a totally separate affair. Mr. Baber produces a grant to Jews, and tells us that the Jews of the present day admit that the Christians were in the country before them. All this is easily seen through. The Christians were Crestians of Colida. The Jews were Crestians of an earlier incarnation or of Moses. The child deserted and saved, and taken by the Jesuit for Moses alone, is nothing but the story which we have before seen of Moses, Cyrus, Cristna, Romulus, part of the mythos of Virgil's new Argonauts and new Troys. Thus when the Portuguese, under Gama, arrived at Melliapour, they found a story of Tamuz, &c.; all the rest followed of course. The people of the tribe of Ioudi, and the Χρης-tians, the same as the Chreestians of Delphi, are found here by Western Jews and Christians: but, like all ancient tribes, they know little or nothing of their very early history. The new comers proceed to correct what they call the mistakes of the old inhabitants, giving them Pentateuchs and Gospels; thus sects of each are raised. The Brahmins, at the immense temple at Madura, keep the old history of Moses and Crishen, the sects take the books of the new-comers from the West. The story told to Mr. Baber, of the Jews having bought the country, is an evident lie, to account for what was to them an unaccountable fact, the Brahmins' government being Jewish. The grant of seventy-two houses to exactly seventy-two families arriving from the West, as Jacob and his seventy-two souls arrived in Egypt, proves the whole to be a mythos. So decidedly Brahmin was the country, which had in its religion all the facts stated above respecting Moses and Cristna, that the Jesuit Robertus de Nobilibus and his associates, it has been said, and as I have formerly noticed, were obliged to turn, to all appearance, Brahmins and Saniasses, which they certainly did, in order to procure attention—and that they, with a fraudulent design, pretended that they were of the same religion, only from a distant Brahmin nation, called Roum. It has been said, I believe by Voltaire, who pretended to prove it against them, that they had gone the length of forging a Veda, which actually passed for many years as genuine IN THE COUNTRY: but I have a suspicion that this Veda was not forged. He only judged it to be so from its contents, consisting of doctrines strikingly similar to those of the Christians. It seems to be as absurd to suppose that the learned Brahmins, the only readers of the Vedas, should not know their own Vedas, as it would be to assert that our priests did not know their own Pentateuch or Gospels. The Jesuit Bouchet complains that he cannot get sight of the secret books, though he learns the contents, as detailed above, from the Brahmins. The Veda afterward produced by Robertus, was probably the book containing this history, and for that very reason supposed by Voltaire to be a forgery, and for that reason alone. Mr. Baber thinks he has proved the Christians to have been in this country at Madura, in the year of Christ 56. I do not dispute his proof, as I think he might have gone back to some year of a cycle a thousand years sooner. It seems almost certain that the Brahmins of Madura, in their sacred books, must have had a history of a Moses, and an Exod, and also a history similar to that told by the Sibyl. Had they a Pentateuch? Had they any other Jewish books? Had they any books about Tobit, or Saul, David, or Daud-potri, or Solumannee, or Solomon? I do not mean the Solomon, *whose magnificent empire was invisible to Herodotus*, when searching for kingdoms in Judæa, but the Solomon who gave names to the mountains in Rajah-poutana, and who built the temple in Cashmere, near which Moses was buried, and where his tomb remains, and the other Tect-Solomons in India. I will now suspend for a little time what I have farther to say concerning St. Thomas, leaving these observations respecting him to my reader's reflections, and return to Salivahana.

6. The ninth Avatar in India, was known by the name of Vicramaditya, as well as by that of Salivahana, the carpenter. As may be reasonably expected, many events of his life bear a close resemblance to those of Cristna and other incarnations, which we have seen bore, in many respects, a close resemblance to one another.[1]　Salivahana bears date the identical year of Jesus Christ: yet it is acknowledged that there were found, as Col. Wilford says, on close examination, nine persons of his name, having nearly the same history.[2]　This is precisely as it ought to be. There is one for each of the nine cycles. This is confirmed by the fact, that the Buddhists, as well as the Brahmins,[3] claim Salivahana as belonging to them. Salivahana and Vicramaditya are only descriptive terms or epithets, mistaken for proper names.

We read in Hindoo books of nine Gems, in the court of the monarch Vicrama. This is an allegory. The Gems, like the Muses of Greece, varied.[4] They increased as the cycles increased. In the time of Christ there were nine of them. They were the same as the wise men or sages, seven of whom we read of in the writings of the old Greek authors : seven only had then passed : the Messiahs were Muses, and also Curetes—in like manner varying—the first from יש *iso, to save*, the other from *curo*.

Salivahana, Sali-vahan, Saliban, or Salban, is formed of the word *Salib* or *Salb*, which has the meaning of the Greek σταυρος, furca, or cross, or crucified, and vahana, *carried*, from the Sanscrit verb *vah*, Latin *veho, to carry*.[5]　Then Salivahana will have the meaning of *cross-borne*. Thus there were nine *cross-borne* Avatars, let them be who they may, and live where they may. And now, if we look back to the Bk. IX. Ch. III. Sect. 6, on Semiramis, we shall find that her Indian conqueror was called *Staurobates*, which is a literal translation of the word *Salivahana* into the Greek language—as if we should find a person called *Lucus* in Latin, and should call him *Grove* : or *Lignum* and should call him *Wood*.

I suspect that our Salva-tion comes from the cross-borne Sali-vahana ; and that all the following words have a close connexion either by derivation or translation :

Sali-vahana—salus-veho, *I bring health or salvation*.

Sally—the name of the wife of Abraham, Sarah, Saraiswati, called שרה *ise* or Iscah or Eve or Isis.

Salus—*health*. Salutis, of health or Salvation.

Salus-bury or Sarum or Saresburie, *i. e.* Sares-pore.

Solym—the Hebrew שלם *slm*, Salem, *peace or salvation*.

Suli-Minerva, the *Bath* Goddess *of health*.

Sol—the Saviour or Healer, whence the spring at Bath was Fons Solis or Fons Suli-Minervæ. The early Christian Monks were called Therapeutæ or *physicians of the soul*.

The words *Deo-Soli* are to be seen on numerous pictures of the black mother and child in Italy—the *black* child having *a glory*. These words I shall explain by and by, when I return to the origin of letters.

The following extract from Banier's Travels contains some striking particulars, and will confirm what has been said above.

---

[1] Asiat. Res. Vol. IX. p. 211.　　　[2] Ibid. p. 117.　　　[3] Ibid. p. 211.

[4] Another example of a Greek translation may be found in the name of the city Palaigonos which is now called Paliputra and Palibothra, (Asiat. Res. Vol. III. p. 369,) both words meaning *children of Puli or Bali*.

[5] Asiat. Res. Vol. X. p. 120.

" Moreover, I have seen the Rev. father Roa, a German Jesuit and Missionary at Agra, who it being well versed in their Hanscrit, maintained that their books did not only import there was " one God in three persons, but even the second person of their Trinity was incarnated NINE " TIMES. And that I may not be thought to ascribe to myself the writings of others, I shall " relate unto you word for word what a certain Carmelite of Chiras hath lighted on, which he " related when the above-mentioned father Roa passed that way to come back to Rome. The " Gentiles (saith he) do hold that the second person of the Trinity WAS INCARNATED NINE TIMES, " and that because of divers necessities of the world, from which he hath delivered it : but the " eighth incarnation is the most notable ; for they hold, that the world being enslaved under the " power of giants, it was redeemed by the second person, incarnated and born of a Virgin at mid-" night, the angels singing in the air, and the heavens pouring down a shower of flowers all that " night." He then goes on to say, that the incarnate God was wounded in the side by a giant, in consequence of which he is called *the wounded in the side* ; and that A TENTH incarnation is yet to come. He after this relates a story that the third person of the Trinity appeared in the form of fire.[1]

The observation that the *eighth* avatar or incarnation is the most notable, is indeed very truly so ; because it proves that the mythos or history of the *eighth* was precisely the same as the *ninth*, precisely as it ought to be, according to my theory, and according to Virgil. . The words *nine times* which I have put in capital letters prove that he clearly distinguished between the eighth and ninth time, thus giving us a proof, which we have no where else, so clear, that, in several respects, the avatars were the same.

Few things have conduced more to the confusion of history, than the mistaking of descriptive terms for proper names. Along with this may be classed the addition of the emphatic article to names, by which, in many cases, a name becomes completely disguised. The Koran and the Alkoran furnish a pretty good example. Mitzraim is probably only Osiris or Isiris in the plural, as Bishop Cumberland has observed, when the letter M (the mystical M, which he did not pretend to understand) is left out.[2]

Col. Wilford confesses, that Salivahana and Vicramaditya, whom he shews to be one and the same person, (though he afterward contradicts this, and makes Salivahana kill Vicramaditya,) *are involved in impenetrable darkness.* He was too well read in Indian history to believe that Salivahana was a copy from Jesus of the West. It was against his faith to believe that Jesus was copied from Salivahana. Thus it was very natural that Wilford should be in a state of great perplexity.

About the beginning of the æra of Salivahana, the Romans became possessed of a large part of Asia, and penetrated into India, with which they carried on a great trade ; and devotees will tell us, that they carried the doctrines of Jesus Christ to India, from which the history of Salivahana was copied. Of course this will be very satisfactory to persons of this description. But philosophers will doubt, and ask, how came there to be nine Vicramadityas or Salivahanas, or crossborne Avatars ? Every one must judge for himself. It is only necessary for my argument, to point out the well-marked Avatar or Cycle correctly in its proper place, and that, in other respects, it resembles those which preceded it. I shall therefore dwell upon it no longer. For more particulars my reader may consult the ninth and tenth volumes of the Asiatic Researches. If these histories of Col. Wilford's be credited, all the accounts of Cristna will have been taken from *Modern Rome.* Perhaps I may be told, that there would be no difficulty in getting BLACK Gods—Christs—from Italy, on my own shewing, so many of them being yet left.

---

[1] Tavernier's and Bernier's Travels, Vol. II. p. 106, Ed. fol.   [2] Orig. Gen. p. 100.

The city on the coast of Asia Minor opposite to Chios called Erythræa, is supposed to have been that to which Augustus sent for the Erythræan Sibyl, but there was at a very great distance from this an Erythræan sea, now called by the Greeks Oman or Om, which extended as far as Taprobane, Serindive, Lanca, or Ceylon, or the island of Rama, the sacred Island, where the Samaritan Pentateuch says the ark rested, where there is the mark of the foot of both Adam and Buddha, where there is also a town called Columbo, the same as is found in the sacred island of Iona, in the West, all which, with various other matters, I have before shewn. In this island the worship of Salivahana prevailed. Now I ask the question, Is it not probable that the adventures of the carpenter of Syria, which we find repeated or duplicated by the Erythræan Sibyl, may be from the carpenter the cross-borne Saliva-hana of India? And if so, the Erythræan Sibyl, who, we have seen, existed before Christ, may have come from Serindive or the holy island. In a former Section of this book, we found that the Sibyl, as Lardner truly states, is represented by Justin Martyr to have foretold not only the coming of Jesus, BUT ALL THINGS THAT SHOULD BE DONE BY HIM. Now it is evident, that the Sibyl may have copied from the gospel histories, or the gospel histories may have been copied from the Sibyl: and it is absolutely incumbent on us to enter upon a close and very careful examination into the genuineness of the gospel histories. Except the gospel histories be earlier, there is no genuine Christian author entire now existing, earlier than Justin's first Apology: (all the Apostolic fathers, Constitutions, &c., are forgeries:) and we see from the quotation from Lardner, that the events relating to Jesus must have been interpolated in the Sibyls, if they were interpolated before Justin's time. Justin's observation, that all the things which were done to Jesus were to be found in the Sibyl, almost proves that it cannot have been interpolated after his time; because, if these things were put into the Sibyl, they must rather have been copies from the old copies of the Sibyl than interpolations. People could not interpolate what was there already. It is truly very surprising that the Sibyl from the Erythræan sea before the time of Christ, should contain the history both of Jesus and of Saliva-hana. The observation of Justin Martyr that almost the whole history of Jesus Christ was to be found in the Sibyl, must not be forgotten, as hereafter I shall return to it, and it will be found to involve a consequence of the very first importance.

7. It is allowed that Rama preceded Cristna, and yet they are both said to be the same. In Hebrew ראם *ram* means *Bull;* but it is easy to see from Parkhurst, (in voce,) that it also means *Ram* or *male Lamb.* Thus as Rama is the same as Cristna, and Cristna is the same as the sun in Aries, Rama is also the same as Adonis, which was the sun in Aries. Adonis is the same as Tamuz, killed and bewailed in Western Syria. Tamuz is found to have died, or to have been killed and bewailed, on the coast of *Coromandel.* Κρ-ιος and כר *kr* mean a Lamb Ram.[1] Mandalam means *a circle* or *cycle:*[2] then, coast of *Cr-mandal* will mean *coast of cycle* of the *Ram Lamb.* In the language of the West, this is the meaning of Coromandal. The language of the West being found in an Eastern country, will radically still retain its Western meaning. The locality will make no difference.[3] The Rama, Adonis, Tamuz, was the Egyptian *Am-on* or Indian *Om,* worshiped in the form of a Lamb or Saviour at Sais and Thebes.[4]

Serindive means, in the Sanscrit, Srĕ-rama-dive, the Island of the holy Rama. When I consider that in Hebrew the word Ram means both *strong* and a Ram, and that Rome was considered and called by the Heathens a *sacred city,* I cannot help suspecting that it was the city of the holy Rama.

---

[1] And also a circle. Parkhurst, in voce כר *kr*, II. pp. 337, 667.    [2] Trans. Royal Soc. Ed. Vol. II. p. 141.
[3] It is just the same with Nerbuddha.    [4] Parkhurst, in voce כר *kr*, II.

When I recollect the farce of the Pessinuncian stone, brought from Pessinus, in Phrygia, to Rome, to ensure its safety, by Scipio, *the best man* in that city, and I contemplate the places called Roma, and the country of Asia Minor called *Roum*, I cannot doubt that there was a mythos' common to the two countries. Long before the time of Christ, or the conquest of Asia Minor by the Romans, Creuzer says,[1] the Phrygians claimed to be the most ancient people of the world, and to have been civilized by the Great Mother called Mâ, or Cybele. In the Classical Journal[2] it is said, " Nor do any remains of this language appear in the Northern countries of Asia, nor in " Roum (that is to say, in Asia Minor)." I much suspect that the Rama of India ought to be Roma, or the Roma, or Ρωμη of Greece—Rama or Ραμη. When I find the Saturnias, Pallis, Viterbos, Ladies of Loretto, &c., &c., &c., in Italy, it is not absurd to expect to discover the Ramas.

A Dynasty of Egyptian priests once reigned, called Piromis, which the ancient historian expounds *a good* or *virtuous man*. But it is evidently the emphatic article Pi and Roma or Rama.[3]

One of the Gates of Antioch was called the Romanesian by Seleucas Nicator, to whom Western Rome could be known only by distant rumour.[4]

I now request my reader to recollect what has been said before, in different parts of this work, of Roma, or Rama, or Ram. In the Indian accounts of the Salivahanas or Vicramadityas frequent mention is made of a place whence they came, called by our authors, Roum, or Rom, or Ram. That the Salivahana of India, in the time of Christ, should have copied from the Papal church, not established till three hundred years afterward, seemed impossible, but how to account for this I could not tell. At last I accidentally learnt, from an Indian scholar, that the celebrated Lanca, Serindive, Palisimunda, Ceylon, called also Taprobane, was the sacred island of Ram, which I doubt not was corrupted to Rom or Roum : this removes all the difficulties. We must remember in what a singular way the God Rama or Hercules was said to be the same with Cristna ; and here we find him connected, in a striking manner, with Salivahana ; for both Ram and Salivahana were favourite objects of adoration with the Cingalese. I beg my reader to attend to the close connexion which Mr. Parkhurst shews existed, in words and in sense, between the names of Ρωμη, Rome, Valencia, Rama of Syria, the Hebrew word ראם ram, (meaning, like the Greek Ρωμη, *strength,*) the English Ram, the male Sheep, and the Lamb Ram, both in the Romish religion and in ours, and that it also had the meaning of Bull—both Bull and Sheep. We must also recollect the double Avatar of Rama and Cristna : and here is the double Avatar of Rama and Salivahana or Cristna, for Salivahana was an incarnation of Cristna or Vishnu. Rama preceded Cristna when the sun entered Aries. Did Rama, in like manner, precede Tamus or the twins, when the sun entered Gemini ? for Tamus means *twins,* the Didymus or Thomas. Of this more presently.

8. I must now return to the cycles and the prophecies of Daniel.

Daniel is said to have lived at the court of the king of Babylon, to have been at the head of the Astrologers, Magi, and Chaldeans, and to have flourished both before and after the taking of that city by the Persians. Who and what he was seems doubtful. Several books of prophecy are extant under his name. They are patronized by the Christians, but their authority, I believe, is denied by the Jews. Few subjects have exercised the pens and wits of polemics and devotees more than

---

[1] Tome II p. 57.                [2] 1828, p. 290.                [3] Univers. Anc. Hist. Vol. XVIII. Chap. xx. p. 312.

[4] Nimrod, Vol. III. p. 302.

these prophecies. I think Daniel understood the doctrine of the renewal of Cycles, as Virgil did in a later day, and I shall now endeavour to shew, that his prophecies had a reference to them, as, in fact, the Christians say.[1]  Before I proceed I must observe, that in all the prophecies of Daniel and the Apocalypse, a day means a year, and a week seven years. In keeping with this, in the Oriental cyclical mythoses, 12,000 years are called a day of Brahm, and $12,000 \times 360 = 4,320,000$ are called a year.

I think the greater part of Daniel's prophecy may be explained. I suppose it will be allowed, that the Messiah was to appear and be cut off about the end of 69 weeks or $69 \times 7 = 483$ years, after the prediction of Daniel. The 70 weeks make 490 years. He was to be cut off in the midst of the last week, that is, about three and a half years after he had begun his ministry. So that we must find 486 years from the twentieth year of Artaxerxes (as stated by the mystics) to the death of Christ. The Heathen chronologers reckon 354 years from the death of Alexander to the nineteenth year of the reign of Tiberius; and if to this be added 132 years, the time from the twentieth year of Artaxerxes to Alexander, we have 486—the number required. I suppose that Daniel calculated the cycle, from the birth of Cyrus to the birth of Christ, at 600 years, and calculated the Messiah's life at 33 or 34 years. This might be the reason why the Christians fixed his life at 33 years. If the Messiah were to be cut off about 483 years after the prediction of Daniel, then if 483 years—33 years the duration of his life—be calculated back from the conjunction of the Sun and Moon in the third or fourth year before Christ, we shall have the year in which Daniel made his prophecy, which every astrologer in the world could have made as well as Daniel; and if we calculate back to the eclipse of Thales, it ought to make up the 600.

The Astrologers and the Chaldeans were prophets, or rather the prophets were astrologers. Daniel was at the head of them at Babylon, as is most clearly proved by the Bible. Isaiah foretold the Messiah Cyrus—Om-nual, Om-our-God. Daniel foretold Jesus, Ham-Messiah, or Om—the Saviour, and Jesus was believed, as I shall presently shew, by the Gnostics and Templars, to have foretold Mo-hamed or Om-ahmed, Om *the desire of all nations*. Hence it was, as I shall shew, that these two sects or orders of persons were both of the Christian and Mohamedan religions. I have often wondered why the word *Mo* was prefixed to the Ahmed, but here we have the reason. The reason is the same as that which causes the mysterious, inexplicable M—600—to be prefixed to so many mystic words, such as M-Omptha, M-uin, &c., &c.

It is allowed in the Dialogues on Prophecy,[2] that we are now in the *seventh* millenary of the world. This is exactly my theory. When Daniel prophesied to Nebuchadnezzar of the golden head *about* the year before. Christ 603,[3] he clearly speaks of four kingdoms, (ch. ii. 39, 40,) including that then going, for he calls Nebuchadnezzar the golden head. *After thee* (he says) *shall another rise*, (the cycle of Cyrus,) and then a third of brass (the cycle of Jesus) : and a fourth strong as iron (the cycle of Mohamed). And then (verse 44) shall a kingdom be set up which shall last for ever—the Millenium. These kingdoms are cycles of 600 years, and bring the commencement of the Millenium to about the year 1200, according to what I have proved, that the æra of the birth of Christ was the beginning of the ninth age of the Romans and Sibyls,' and the ninth Avatar of India.

If the learned Nimrod be right, that the beast of John, with ten horns, is the fourth kingdom of Daniel, which I have suggested to be the tenth Neros,[4] then the beast may be the consummation of the ten Cycles. The beast with seven heads and ten horns will be the six thousands, and the seventh will be the Millenium, and the ten Cycles will be the ten horns. The beast that was

---

[1] Vide Daniel ix. 24—27.  
[3] Univers. Hist. Vol. XXI. p. 59.  
[2] Part iv. p. 338.  
[4] Nimrod, Vol III. p. 595.

to be resuscitated under one of the heads—the beast-that was, and is not, and goes into perdition, that is, goes to destruction, revolves and passes away as the former had done. It has been observed that five heads were passed at the time of the vision, and that the sixth was going; this is as it ought to be—the sixth millenary running. This-answers to the beast with seven heads and ten horns.

In chap. viii. ver. 14, it is said, *Unto two thousand and three hundred days; then shall the sanctuary be cleansed.* The present fashionable mystics, Messrs. Irving and Frere agree in opinion that the 2300 years ought to be 2400. They are justified in this by the wording of the LXX. where it is written τετραχοσιαι. The way in which these mystics and calculators accidentally and unconsciously support my system is very striking, and more convincing than any calculations which I could make; for here it is evident that Daniel [1] alluded to the cycle then running, and to the next, viz. that of Cyrus; then to the two after Christ; in all, four cycles or 2400 years; and to the six which had preceded them; that is, to 6×600=3600+2400=6000.

His famous time, times, and half a time, or 1260, arose as follows : 2160+2160+420+1260= 6000. The 420 years we must observe are equal to better than 5 degrees, but not to six. Thus :

$$
\begin{array}{lr}
\text{30 degrees} & 2160 \\
\text{30 degrees} & 2160 \\
\text{5 degrees before Christ} & 360 \\
\text{And a fraction, viz. 60 years} & 60 \\
\hline
& 4740 \\
& 1260 \\
\hline
& 6000 \\
\end{array}
$$

It is necessary that there should be a fraction of a degree, in consequence of the two cycles of the Neros and the ten Zodiacal signs not running *pari passu,* and of course not coinciding till the end of the great cycle of 21,600 and 43,200 years.

The 490 years are to the destruction of Jerusalem ; then take off *seventy,* the space to it, from the birth of Christ, and we have 360+60=420. One mode of calculation proves the other, which, if it were true, of course it would do. It must be observed that these are loose calculations (not pretending to accuracy) in whole numbers. I shall refer to this by and by, when it will be more clearly understood.

Daniel says, xii. 12, Blessed is he that cometh to the 1335 days.

Volney remarks, " According to these principles, which are those of all astronomers, we see " that the annual precession being 50″ and a fraction of about a fourth or a fifth, the consequence " is that an entire degree is lost or displaced in seventy-one years, eight or nine months, and an " entire sign in about 2152 or 2153 years." See Bk. V. Ch. II. Sect. 5, precisely in one year 50″ 9‴ ¾.

$$
\begin{array}{ll}
2153 & 30 : 2153 :: 5 : 358\tfrac{11}{18}=\tfrac{1}{6}. \\
2153 & \\
359 & \\
\hline
4665 & \\
1335 & \\
\hline
6000 & \\
\end{array}
$$

---

[1] If the number 2400 were not the original, it must have been corrected in the LXX. by the popes, to make it suit a certain mythos which I shall explain presently.

The Messiah is said to precede the final end of all things, a time, times, and a half time, or, as generally admitted, 1260 years.

If we allow for the mistake of Usher and throw back the birth of Christ to the fifth year, making the interval between his birth and the destruction of the Temple 75 years or to the 75th year, and add the 1260 to the 75, we shall have 1335 which, + 4665=6000. If Daniel knew the time of Jesus Christ, and when the temple would be destroyed, and therefore when the Millenium would commence, counting from the first of Taurus, he would fix the sums of 1260 and 1335 without any difficulty.

If 1260 (Dan. xii. 7) be added to 70, and the 4 years of Usher allowed for, it will all but one make up the 1335. The destruction of Jerusalem ought, according to Calmet, to be 74, not 70: then, 1260+74=1334.

In the eleventh verse there seems to be a corruption, or something alluded to in the Jewish history which has not come to us, for it says, or seems to mean that, at the end of 1290 years, but before the end of the 1335 days alluded to in the next verse, the sacrifice and oblation should cease. In Calmet's Chronology the sacrifice is said not to have ceased till the year of the destruction of the temple, which was 74 years after the birth of Christ, whereas the 1290 would bring it to about 45 years after his birth, when nothing particular appears to have happened, at least the daily sacrifice does not appear to have then ceased. As we have formerly seen a various reading or corruption of the text in the 2300 and 2400 years, it is not unfair, under all the circumstances, to suspect one here also. If it be not a corruption, I do not understand it. But as it contains, in language, a contradiction to the context, I am justified in suspecting another mistake.

The number 666 is called Pseudoprophetical, or would-be prophetic. It is also called the *mark* of the beast, the *name* of the beast, and the *number* of his name,[1] and the knowledge of it wisdom. If I had used those words I should have been said to accommodate the language unfairly to my theory of the first letters being figures; of this I shall treat in a future book.

Almost all the divines now fix upon some year between 600 and 615 for the beginning of Daniel's period of 1260 years. In former times this period was supposed, and rightly supposed, to begin with Christ, which makes it end and the Millenium commence just about the times of the Crusades : a little before which, all mankind ran to Palestine to be ready for the Lord's coming. We hear nothing of this now, because the time is past and new artifices are devised to conceal the truth; but the Crusaders were right: this was the end of the tenth Neros and sixth Millenary, and we are now in the seventh Millenary. The way in which most of the modern mystics fix upon some year about 608 for the period is very striking. Superstitious persons in the beginning of Christianity first thought the Millenium would commence about the year 600, then it was adjourned to 1200, and then it came to 1800, and it will shortly be adjourned to 2400. Long before that time, like the Israel Redux, all the mystics of this day will be forgotten, and this book be burnt by the priests.

The Rev. Dr. Buchanan[2] says, " In the year 1667, Mr. Samuel Lee, a scholar of enlarged " views, who had studied the prophetical writings with great attention, published a small volume, " entitled, ' Israel Redux, or the Restoration of Israel.' He calculates the event from the Pro- " phecies of Daniel and of St. John, and commences the great period of 1260 years, not from " A. D. 608, but from A. D. 476, which brings it to 1736." He then adds, " After the great " conflicts with the papal powers in the West, will begin the stirs and commotions about the " Jews and Israel in the East. If then to 1736 we add 30 more, they reach to 1766: but the

[1] Vide Mede's Works, 792; Rev. xiii. 17, 18.   [2] Christ. Res. Ed. 1819, p. 245.

" times of perplexity are determined (by Daniel) to last 45 years longer. If then we conjoin " those 45 years more to 1766, it produces 1811, for those times of happiness to Israel." [1] I do not understand this, but it is evident from what Dr. Buchanan says, that the number 608 was the end of one of the periods to which the mystics, in their exposition of Daniel, had come. But how they had arrived at this I cannot find out. I have not been able to get the book. I beg to refer my reader to the third volume of Mons. Dupuis' work on all religions—to the essay on the Apocalypse, where he will find a great number of most interesting observations, and where he will also find the doctrines of Daniel, Ezekiel, and John, proved to be identical, and all to be drawn from the school of the oriental Magi. I am convinced that, by the theory which I have suggested, if the numbers in these books be free from corruption, I have explained the meaning of them all but one ; and with respect to it, we must not forget the various reading shewn in the numbers 2300 and 2400 ; and if there be one corruption in the versions, a fact indisputable, it is not improbable that this may be another.

A deep reflection on the origin of nations and religions has induced me to come to a conclusion, that all religions have been the children of circumstances, and those circumstances arising almost entirely out of judicial astrology. The first object, in all prophecy, was to foretell a future Saviour, or the commencement of a future cycle, when a new or young Saviour was to bring an age of happiness. Of course the astrologers would have no difficulty in nearly fixing the time, and from this arises the degree of plausibility which we find the ancient prophecies to possess. To a certain degree they fitted to every cycle. Hence has arisen the specious contrivance of a double meaning ; for the prophecy which would apply to Cyrus, would equally apply to Jesus. The sectaries of religion, in each cycle, claimed the verification of the prophecy as the cycle came round, and the sectaries of each sect of the cyclar religion also claimed it, that is, there were several eighth and several ninth avatars. These were Antichrists to each other. From this, along with the belief that the planets ruled the affairs of men, arose magic or astrology in its bad sense, and for these reasons we find prophets patronised by the Jewish law, and astrology prohibited.

9. We now come to the famous Crusades, the real origin or cause of which, in modern times, has never been understood. They will be found to occupy a prominent place in the complete development of my system, and particularly of the tenth Avatar, and will lead to a variety of matters which will greatly surprise my reader.

In the time of Richard the First, about A. D. 1189, a general belief prevailed that the end of the world drew near, a belief which, in a great measure, caused the crusades to Palestine, where the devotees expected the Saviour to appear. This is attested by St. Bernard, of Clairvaux, and was foretold by Joachim, Abbot of Curacio in Calabria, [2] a most renowned interpreter of prophecy in those days. Antichrist was to appear at ANTIOCH, and the crusade was the gathering together of the kings of the earth to the battle of the great day of God Almighty. [3] It seems from the accounts that the possession of Antioch was made a great point, almost as much so, indeed, as that of Jerusalem. It was among the first cities taken by the crusaders.

Various reasons have been given to account for the crusades, but these were the true ones. In Mosheim, a detail of the reasons generally assigned may be seen, but they are admitted by him to be insufficient to account for these wars. Indeed, every cause is assigned but the true one, [4] which seems never to have been suspected by Mosheim or his translator. I think there will be no doubt in future upon this subject.

---

[1] Israel Redux, p. 122, printed in Cornhill, Lond. 1677.

[2] Rev. xvi. 12, 14; Nimrod, Vol. III. p. 393.

[3] Roger Hoveden, ap. Script. post Bedam, p. 681.

[4] Cent. xi. Part i. pp. 446, &c.

In Baronius[1] may be seen an account that both Saint Bernard and an eminent man called Norbert, preached the speedy end of the world. The celebrated Roger Bacon was born in the year 1216, and died, aged 78, in the year 1294. He was a most extraordinary man for the time he lived. I have no doubt that he was conversant with all the secret knowledge of the ancients, which remained in his day. Gunpowder, telescopes, the art of perspective, and many other branches of philosophy and science supposed to be then unknown, he was well acquainted with. I have little doubt that he perfectly understood the prophecies of Daniel and the Revelation; but, in consequence of the millenium not coming at the time predicted and calculated on, he was induced to believe, like most others of his time, that he was mistaken. The learned Nimrod affords him no quarter, but the following account which he gives is enough for my purpose. He says,

" When Roger Bacon tells us,[2] that one *Artificius* was then living, who had already been kept " alive 1250 years by the *occult powers of nature*, and who had seen Tantalus on his golden throne, " and received homage from him, it is only another way for that man to say that Antichrist was " about to return in ten years from that time. Creditur, he says, ab omnibus sapientibus[3] quod " non sumus multum remoti à temporibus Antichristi; and in another place he says, that the " time of Antichrist might[4] be fixed *with certainty* by comparing scripture with the prophecies of " Sibylla, of Merlin,[5] and of Joachim, of Calabria, with history, with the books of philosophy, and " the courses of the stars."[6]

If we knew when the observation respecting the 1250 years was written, we might pretty nearly tell on what year he supposed the calculations made out the millenium as about-to happen. By *Artificius* he probably means the Ioannes who was to wait till Jesus returned, and who, from having seen Tantalus on his throne, was evidently a renewed incarnation, or perhaps he meant Salhivahana the *carpenter* or *artificer*, or it may be a MASON.

The persons who were initiated into the Esoteric religion of the Vatican, after being disappointed in the year of Christ 600, imagined, that the famous 6000 years would end at or about the year 1200 of Christ, when the millenium would commence, and it was this which caused the crusade against the Mohamedan Antichrist, who had arisen against the new, the tenth, and the last Messiah or Avatar, patronised by the Pope of Rome, whom I shall draw from his obscurity. If the ninth age began with Christ, then the tenth would begin with the year 600, and finish with the year 1200; and then would be the manifestation of the Lord at Jerusalem, which the devotees wished to prepare for his reception.

These circumstances premised, we now, at last, come to the *tenth* Avatar, and the facts respecting it are not less remarkable than the others. My reader will recollect that, in the Gospel of the mysterious Ioannes, Jesus, the Avatar of the Sibillyne oracles, is made to declare that he would send another person to complete his mission, called in our translation a *comforter*, and also *the spirit of truth*. The words *spirit of truth* would well justify the expectation, that this person would be an incarnation of Divine Wisdom if he appeared in human form. In consequence, we

---

[1] An. 1106, Tom. XII. p. 51.    [2] Epistola de mirabili Potestate Artis et Naturæ, Cap. vii. p. 50.
[3] Opus Majus, p. 254.
[4] Ibid. 169. Noto hic pronere os meum in cœlum, sed scio quod si ecclesia vellet revolvere textum sacrum et prophetias sacras, atque prophetias Sibyllæ, et Merlini, et Aquilæ, et Sestonis, Joachim et multorum aliorum, insuper historias et libros philosophorum, atque juberet considerari vias astronomiæ, inveniretur sufficiens suspicio vel magis certitudo de tempore Antichristi. P. 169, Ed. Bowyer, 1733, Lond
[5] It seems our British Merlin was in the secret.    [6] Nimrod, Vol. II. p. 178.

find that various teachers of doctrines were believed, by their followers, to be this person. For instance, Simon Magus, Montanus, Marcion, Manes, were all so considered, and in consequence have been grievously abused by the Romish writers for the unparalleled wickedness of giving themselves out as being *the Holy Ghost*—these writers never attempting, perhaps not being able, to explain the nature of the case. The most remarkable of these Teachers was the person called Simon Magus, called by the Romists *Magus*, probably as a term of reproach.

From the immense mass of lies and nonsense which have been written respecting him, I think we may select enough to shew the probability of his followers having believed him to be the person foretold by Jesus; and the Helene or Selene, by whom he was said to be accompanied, and with whom he was enamoured, was what Mons. Beausobre [1] calls *La Sagesse, génératrix de toutes choses*. [2] After Simon Magus, Montanus was held to be the person promised; and, after him, Mani: and this brings us to a *tenth* and *last* Avatar, the celebrated prophet of Arabia—Mohamed.

10. Mr. Faber, [3] who is the most sensible of all the mystics, makes one very striking observation, which I shall give in his own words : " Now it is an undoubted *historical fact*, whatever applica-" tion we may make of the fact itself, that in the year 608 or 609, Mohamed, dexterously availing " himself of the unscriptural demonolatry which had infested the Christian church, set on foot an " imposture, which soon overspread the whole Macedonian empire, and which performed *the very* " *actions* that are ascribed to the second predicted power, both in *the same geographical region* and " during the same chronological period." This forms, to my mind, the finest example ever known of a prophecy causing its own verification or completion. In the Gospels, Christ is made to prophesy that one should come after him to complete his mission. This was nothing but the repetition of all the Gentile prophecies of a *tenth* and *last* Avatar. Mohamed was believed by his followers to be this person, whose name they said, in the original, uncorrupted gospel, was given by Jesus, as that of Cyrus was by Isaiah. I am quite certain that the context and the concomitant circumstances are such as to induce any unprejudiced person to think, that the assertion of the Mohamedans respecting this prophecy is true. In the context, a person who was to come, is repeatedly referred to.

Then what was the fact? Jesus Christ was believed, by the followers of Mohamed, to be a divine incarnation, or a person divinely inspired, and to have foretold the next and the last Avatar, *Mohamed*, to complete the *ten* periods, and the *six* millenaries, previous to the grand Millenium,

---

[1] Liv. vii. Ch. vi. p. 511.

[2] I learn from Beausobre, that it appears, from a passage of Plato and another of Sextus Empyricus, that, according to ancient authors, the war between the Greeks and Trojans was about a statue of Selene or the Moon, (I suppose the Palladium or image of Minerva, which probably was believed to have come from heaven,) and that Simon maintained, it was for the love of the Selena or Helena, the Moon, that the Greeks and Trojans had gone to war, and that the Helene he had with him was the Trojan Helen. In all this I think it easy to see the mistake constantly made, as I have noticed, between the Moon and the Maia or Magna Mater, the female generative principle. It appears that the Queen, the Mother, of all things, the Divine Wisdom *(La Sagesse)* which produced all things, was equally called Luna, Selena, and Helena. (Beausobre, *ib.*)

By the ancient Egyptian mystics, Osiris was the male generative principle—Isis the female, his wife. In judicial astrology or magic, the Sun was sacred to Osiris, the Moon to Isis; thus it was that the mistake continually arose, and the emblems and names of the female generative principle were attributed to the Moon. This perhaps might not be from mere mistake, but from a spirit of mysticism. Thus, on the 17th of the month, the Sun or Osiris is said to enter into the Moon and impregnate her. But this notion respecting the Moon was not the original doctrine, but a corruption of it, for the Moon was often masculine.

[3] Sacred Cal. of Prop. Vol. I. p. 73.

or the reign of the Χρησος, or Christ, on earth, for the last and seventh period, of one thousand years. Irenæus and the first Christian fathers said, that, during this period, the *lion* was to lie down with the *lamb*, and the grapes were to cry out to the faithful *to come and eat them!*

I think, in the expression alluded to in the Koran,[1] if I mistake not, there is a proof that my doctrine of the renewal of the cycle was held by Mohamed, or was thought to be applicable to him ; and it seems that the writer of that book held up Mohamed as a new incarnation. Divine Love, coming in the tenth sæculum, as foretold by the Sibyls, by Jesus, and also by the Prophet Haggai, (ii. 7,) "*And the desire of all nations shall come :*" "חמד HMD, *From this root,*" (says Parkhurst,) "*the pretended prophet Mohammed, or Mahomet, had his name.*"[2] Here Mohamed is expressly foretold by Haggai, and by name ; there is no interpolation here. There is no evading this clear text and its meaning, as it appeared to the mind of the most unwilling of witnesses, Parkhurst, and a competent judge too when he happened not to be warped by prejudice. He does not suppress his opinion here, as he did in the case of the *Wisdom* of the Jerusalem Targum, because he had no object to serve ; he did not see to what this truth would lead. I beg to refer to what I have said in the last section ; there my reader will see that the end of the tenth cycle was foretold by Christian astrologers, which caused the fanatical crusaders, almost by millions, to flock to Jerusalem about the year 1200, the end of Mohamed's cycle. The observation of Mr. Faber, that Mohamed's mission began at the year 608, is important. This is the very period when the tenth Avatar ought to commence, according to one of my two Neros' systems. If this be accident, it is surely a very extraordinary accident, that, among all the numbers, the identical number of the great Neros should be fallen on ; and that number the very number required to support my system—nay, to prove the truth of it, if the system be true.

The expression which the Mohamedans say has been expunged from the Romish Gospels, is as follows :. " And when Jesus, the son of Mary, said, O children of Israel, verily I am the apostle " of God sent unto you, confirming the law which was delivered before me, and bringing good " tidings of an apostle who shall come after me, and whose name shall be AHMED." Chap. lxi. This is correctly as foretold by Haggai.

On this *Sale* says, " Whose name shall be Ahmed. For Mohammed also bore the name of " Ahmed : both names being derived from the same root, and nearly of the same signification. " The Persian paraphrast, to support what is here alleged, quotes the following words of Christ : " I go to my Father, and the Paraclete shall come :[3] the Mohamedan doctors unanimously " teaching, that by the Paraclete (or, as they choose to read it, the Periclyte or Illustrious), their " prophet is intended, and no other."[4]　Mr. Sale, in page 98 of his Preliminary Discourse, distinctly admits, that Periclyte, in Arabic, means *illustrious*, the meaning of the name of Mohamed.

Bishop Marsh has observed that this word Paraclete must have been the Syriac or Arabic[5] word פרקליט *prqlit* translated into Greek.　I apprehend the whole argument between the Mohamedans and Christians will turn upon the question, whether the word פרקליט *prqlit* ought to be, when translated into Greek, rendered by the word παρακλητος or περικλυτος. Now I maintain, that if Bishop Marsh says the word *prqlit* was the word used by Jesus, and that it means *illustrious*, it is a gross mistranslation to render it by παρακλητος, which means *comforter.*

The passages in John, ch. xiv. 16, 26, xv. 26, xvi. 7, and in Luke xxiv. 49, are those which we

---

[1] Vide Sale's preface, p. 98.　　　　[2] See Parkhurst in voce, חמד *hmd.*　　　　[3] John xvi. 7, &c.

[4] Koran, Vol. II. p. 423, note.　　　　[5] Marsh's Michaelis, Chap. iv. Sect. xiv.

translate from the Greek παρακλητος, *comforter*, and which the Mohamedans say ought to be περικλυτος *illustrious*. This Comforter is said by Christians to have come, as described in the book called the Acts of the Apostles, on the day of Pentecost, in a tongue of fire settling on each apostle. The Mohamedans say this is ridiculous as the sending of a Comforter; and it c ould not have been necessary to enable them to work *miracles*, because, if the Gospel histories can be believed, Jesus had given them this power before, as appears from the first verse of the tenth chapter of Matthew ; and that with respect to the mere endowment with the Holy Ghost, it could be as little needful, since it appears from the twenty-second verse of the twentieth chapter of John, that he had endowed them with this gift prior to his ascension, not two months before.

The Mohamedans further allege, that the book of the Acts nowhere says that these fiery tongues were the promised Comforter, which it would have done if they had been so ; and further, that the object of the miracle of the tongues of fire is evident, and admits of no dispute, namely, the endowment of the apostles, as the text clearly expresses, with the power of speaking all languages.[1] Besides, the Mohamedans may fairly ask, how came Jesus not to say he would send them the רוח קדש *qds-ruh*, the Ἁγιον Πνευμα or Sanctus Spiritus ? If he had the gift of prescience he must have known that his equivocal expression would cause infinite mischief in the world.

In reply to the demand of Christians, Why did not Mohamed perform a miracle ? the answer has been, The victory of the Crescent over the Cross is the miracle. If the cause be of God, it will succeed without other miracle. But on the victory of the Russian Cross over the Crescent, it will shortly fall.

The Mohamedans, in the defence of their doctrine of the wilful corruption of the manuscripts of the Gospel histories, call upon the Christians to produce the autographs, or very old manuscripts. But to neither of these calls can a satisfactory answer be given. There are no autographs and no manuscripts older than the sixth century. The Mohamedans say, your churches in Rome, being Roman temples, are many of them much older than this period, where the MSS. might have been preserved, along with the relics which abound of Peter, Paul, and other saints, if you had thought proper. But some Christians say, these relics are forgeries ; to which the Mohamedan replies, that this is a mere subterfuge to evade his unanswerable argument. And this is fair in the mouth of a Mohamedan, who cannot be expected to make distinctions between the Protestant and Papist sects of Christians. But independently of this argumentum ad hominem, there can be assigned no good reason why the manuscripts were not preserved in the old churches. The Goths and other conquerors of Rome intentionally destroyed neither the temples, churches, nor books. The temples are there, yet existing as churches. The church in which are deposited the most sacred things of the religion, the bodies of Peter and Paul, was never destroyed.

But though the Christians cannot produce the autographs or very old manuscripts, they say, that the quotations of certain very old authors, called *Fathers*, will prove that the word was written Paracletos and not Periclytos, long before the time of Mohamed, and therefore that they cannot have been corrupted in order to oppose the Mohamedans. To this it is replied, that the word was not corrupted to counteract the Mohamedan Paraclete, but the Paraclete generally—the various Paracletes, as they called themselves, long before the time of Mohamed—Simon Magus, Manes, Montanus, and Marcion, who were all set up as paracletes by their followers, and who

---

[1] In allusion to the idea of fire and language being connected in some way or other, we have the proverb, the fire kindled and he spake.

would all have been called the *illustrious prophets* if their heresies had prevailed instead of dying away; and, that it is the peculiar object of the *corruption* to bolster up the Trinity, in opposition to the Unitarian doctrine, by making the *pesron to be sent*, into the *Holy Ghost*.[1]

Bishop Marsh, Michaelis, and divers other learned men, have alleged, with much plausibility, the difficulty and almost impossibility of corrupting the gospels after the first few centuries. But the following passages from the pens of unwilling witnesses to the FACTS of which they inform us, will shew how little dependence can be placed on this kind of specious reasoning.

In the eleventh and twelfth centuries, the Bibles were corrected by Lanfranc, Archbishop of Canterbury, and by Nicolas, Cardinal and Librarian of the Romish Church, secundum orthodoxam fidem.[2] The learned Beausobre has the following passage: "Il se peut faire, dit M. Simon,[3] "que cette histoire ait été prise de quelque ancien livre Apocryphe, ou elle étoit commune dans "les premiers siècles du Christianisme, et peut-être croyoit-on, qu'elle venoit des Apôtres, ou de "leurs disciples. C'est pourquoi ceux *qui ont osé retoucher en tant d'endroits* les premiers ex- "emplaires du Nouveau Testament, dans la seule vue de le rendre intelligible à tout le monde, "n'auront fait aucune difficulté d'y ajouter ces sortes d'histoires, qu'ils croyoient être véritables. "Je mets au bas de la page le jugement d'un autre savant moderne, me contentant de remarquer, "que si les Hérétiques ôtent un mot du texte Sacré, ou s'ils en ajoutent un, ce sont de *sacri-* "*légés violateurs* de la sainteté des écritures. Mais, si les Catholiques le font, cela s'appelle RE- "TOUCHER les premiers exemplaires, les *réformer pour les rendre plus intelligibles*. M. Simon fait "l'honneur aux Bénédictins d'avoir réformé de même *les ouvrages des Pères*, afin de les accom- "moder à la foi de l'église. Mettons le passage de M. Simon, Dissert. p. 51. Nous lisons dans "la vie de Lanfranc, Moine Bénédictin, et ensuite Archévêque de Cantorbéri, qui a été publiée "par les Bénédictins de la congrégation de *St. Maur*, avec les ouvrages de cet archévêque, "qu'ayant trouvé *les livres de l'écriture beaucoup* corrumpus par ceux qui les avoient copiez, il "s'étoit appliqué à les CORRIGER, AUSSI-BIEN QUE LES LIVRES DES SAINTS PÈRES SELON LA FOI "ORTHODOXE—SECUNDUM FIDEM ORTHODOXAM."[4]

It is impossible to deny that the Benedictine Monks of St. Maur, as far as the Latin and Greek languages went, were a very learned and talented, as well as numerous body of men. In Cleland's life of Lanfranc, Archbishop of Canterbury, is the following passage: "Lanfranc, a Benedictine

---

[1] Soon after my Apology for the Life of Mohamed came out, my former friend, Mr. Beverley, published an answer to it, part of which (as he told me himself when writing it) was written in my breakfast room. I will not deny that it caused me some uneasiness, for I felt that my friend had not written of me, as I should have written of him. In his whole argument the Prosopopœia, which I use in my argument, is put out of sight, and he treats me as giving my own opinion, instead of giving the arguments of the Mohamedans. I requested him, at my expense, to add a short appendix, as a letter from me, to the remainder of his work which was not sold, and to give it to those of his friends to whom he had given his book, but this he declined. I considered his conduct to proceed from a little Calvinistic zeal which had got the better of his kind feelings, and which I lamented, but I took care that my feeling should not cause, nor did it cause, any suspension of the intercourse between us. But since he has announced himself to the world as a Calvinistic preacher, he has sent home the books which he had of mine, has not answered my last letter, and has dropped my acquaintance. Some time after Mr. Beverley's book was printed, I opened a volume in my bookseller's shop, and, on reading the first sentence my eye met, I found it was an answer to my Mohamed, by a learned friend, *who had not sent me a copy*. From the sentence which I read, I instantly perceived that he had taken the same line of argument with Mr. Beverley, having overlooked the Prosopopœia, and that, because I honestly gave the arguments of the Mohamedans, he concluded I adopted them for my own. I bought the book, but I read no more of it. I had before determined to read no more of the answers of my friends, and I adhere to the same determination. Polemical controversy, *with a friend*, is not to my taste.

[2] Wetstein, Prologom. pp. 84, 85; Gibbon, Chap. xxxvii. N. 118.     [3] Ap. Sim. Dissert. p. 20.

[4] Beausobre, Hist. Manich. Liv. ii. Ch. i. p. 343.

4 s

" Monk, Archbishop of Canterbury, having found the Scriptures much corrupted by copyists, ap-
" plied himself to correct them, as *also the writings of the fathers*, agreeably to the orthodox faith,
" secundum fidem orthodoxam." The same very learned Protestant divine has this remarkable
passage : " Impartiality exacts from me the confession, that the orthodox have in some places
" altered the Gospels."[1]    Lanfranc was head of the Monks of St. Maur about A. D. 1050, and
it appears that this society not only corrected the Gospel histories, but they also corrected the
fathers, in order that their gospel corrections might not be discovered : and this was probably the
reason for the publication by them of their version of the whole of the fathers.  To the observation
that they would not correct all the copies, that some must escape them, it may be replied, that
they thought otherwise, and there can be no doubt that if the Pope and the Monks thought it
worth their while to correct the Gospels, they would spare no pains to make the correction
universal.

Thus we see the fact proved, not only that the Holy Scriptures have been corrupted by the
united exertions of the Monks and the Papal see, but.that the works of the fathers have also been
corrupted to be in unison with them, and this not by one man, but by a very great and powerful
society in league with the Pope.  Surely after the proof of such a fact as this, it is only fair if a
passage be found which compromises the moral attributes of God (which a passage would do if it
established *the atonement)* to suppose that it is a passage which has been *retouché*.  I may be an
obstinate heretic for entertaining such belief, but I can sooner believe that a passage is one of
those RETOUCHÉ than that God is unjust or cruel.  From the observation of Mr. Gibbon, from
Wetstein, that the retouching was done by consentaneous movement at Rome, St. Maur, and
Canterbury, we may form a pretty fair judgment that an universal movement of the Monks of the
world then took place to effect the desired object.  There can be no doubt, I think, that the very
fine edition of the fathers which was published by the Benedictins of St. Maur was done to remove
any passages which the old books might contain opposed to the RETOUCHÉS Gospels.

But this is not the only correction the Gospels are said to have undergone.  Lardner[2] says,
" Victor Tununensis, an African Bishop, who flourished about the sixth century and wrote a
" Chronicle, ending at the year 566, says, When Messala was Consul (that is, in the year of
" Christ 506) at Constantinople, by order of.the Emperor Anastasius, the holy Gospels being
" written by illiterate Evangelists are censured and corrected."  As may be expected, great pains
have been taken to run down and depreciate this piece of evidence to a dry fact, the truth or falsity
of which the narrator must have known.  Victor *was a Christian Orthodox Bishop*.  It is not credible that he would in his Chronicle record a fact like this if it were false.  His evidence is rendered more probable by the casual way in which it is given ; and he must be considered the most
unwilling of witnesses.  If evidence *like this*, to such a simple fact, is to be refused, there is
indeed an end of all history, ancient and modern.  The charge against the ruling power of corrupting the Gospels is not that of one individual only: the same charge we see was made against
it by the Mohamedans, and it was done before by the Manichæans.  It is worthy of observation,
that there is not a manuscript of the Gospels in existence earlier than the sixth century.  A strong
probability arises that the ancient Gospels were destroyed at this time.

To the arguments of Bishop Marsh, Michaelis, &c., to which I alluded a little time ago, I reply,
that in the times both of Anastasius and Lanfranc the whole world was in a very considerable
degree, as far as concerned religion, in the power of the Emperor of Constantinople and the Pope.

---

[1] Cleland's Specimens, &c., p. 62.                          [2] Cred. Gosp. Hist. Ch. clv.

I have no doubt that there was a monastery, or priest of some sort, in every small district of Northern Africa, Egypt, Western Asia, and Europe. I cannot believe it possible that there should have been a hundred copies of the orthodox Gospels in existence which were not within the reach of the Monks and priests, and I have no doubt that in either time, an order to correct the gospels given out at Constantinople, Rome, and Canterbury, would be competent to cause every copy, probably altogether not two thousand, to be rewritten. This rationally accounts for the extraordinary fact of the destruction of all manuscripts before this period. Every inquirer knows that St. Augustine is looked up to by both Papists and Protestants as one of the first luminaries of the Christian Church; and he not only professed to teach that there were secret doctrines in the religion, but he went a step farther—for he affirmed, Multa esse vera quæ vulgo scire non sit utile, et quædam quæ tametsi falsa sunt, aliter existimare populum expediat:[1] that there were many things true in religion, which it was not convenient for the vulgar to know; and again, some things which, *though false*, yet it was expedient should be believed by them. It is not unfair to suppose that in these withheld truths we have part of the modern Christian mysteries, and I think it will hardly be denied, that the church, whose highest authorities held such doctrines, would not scruple to *retouch* the sacred writings.

11. As I have formerly said, in the early ages of Christianity the doctrine of the Millenium was the universal faith. As it did not come when expected, the consideration of the Ultima Cumæ carminis ætas, of Virgil, and the ninth age of Juvenal, and circumstances which the Romish esoteric policy and universal power have concealed from us, (but which Roger Bacon in a later age partly let out,[2] ) taught the College of Cardinals, that the tenth age would not come till about the year 600, and would, of course, not end till about the time which we have seen fixed by Bernard of Clairvaux and Joachim, viz. the year 1200. How far this knowledge might extend, or may extend, it is not possible to say, but the Linga in their temple, with its Zeus Soter, &c., seems to shew that the whole is understood.

From the Mohamedans we can learn little; we are at too much enmity with them; and it is probable that the Turks may really possess nothing of the Arabian knowledge upon these subjects. But it is a most important fact, that the Brahmins maintain that Mohamed either was or pretended to be a Vicramaditya and Avatar. This will lead us to some very important consequences.

The fact cannot be denied, and a very important fact it is, that when the Mohamedans overran India they did not destroy the images of the Buddhists. The reason was because, in the simple, unadorned, uncorrupted icon of Buddha, they found their own *Om*, and I have no doubt that they were in reality Buddhists, and Mohamed was believed by himself, (for what is too absurd for human folly not to believe? How much or how far is prosperity capable of corrupting even the strongest minds![3] ) or by his followers, to be the tenth and last Avatar—incarnation of the sacred *Om*—the Amed or *desire of all nations*. On this account it was, that the Afghans and the mountaineers of Mewar and Malwa came to be among the first of Mohamed's followers.

If we reconsider what I have said in Bk. VIII. Chap. V., respecting a tribe proceeding from India, as the Mohamedans say, and their having carried back the religion of Mohamed, the tenth

---

[1] Civ. Dei. Lib. iv. Cap. xxxi.

[2] Roger Bacon spent the greater portion of his life in prison. This was not for *knowing* too much, but for betraying the secrets of initiation, for telling the secrets out of the conclave.

[3] When I consider that Alexander was born exactly when the Sun entered Aries, and that Mohamed's name meant *Great*, in connexion with other circumstances, I am induced to suspect that they were both, as well as Constantine, called Great, because they were thought to be Avatars. I think this superstition might probably make them conquerors.

avatar, we may observe, that there was no great man in their own country to answer to *the tenth* whom they daily expected; and when they saw this Om-amed, *the desire of all nations,* conquering all Asia, and declaring that his success was the proof of his mission, it was very natural for them to receive him : it was no change, but only a necessary completion of their religion, arriving, as they would learn, to the very year in which, according to their doctrines, he ought to arrive.

In the province of Oude or Judæa, in North India, the people still flatter themselves with the hopes of a Saviour, of whom they know nothing, except that he is to be a tenth Outar or Ontar. He is to be called the " spotless," because he is to be born of a pure virgin. He is expected to appear in the province of Oude, *i. e.* Youdia. He will destroy all distinctions, and establish happiness on the earth.[1] As these people did not accept Mohamed for their last Avatar or incarnation, and all their seminaries of sacred learning were destroyed, they still, like the Jews, continue in expectation of they know not what.

Col. Tod says,[2] " The libraries of Jessulmer, in the desert of Anhulwara, the cradle of their " *(meaning the Buddhist and Jain )* faith, of Cambay and other places of minor importance, con- " sist of thousands of volumes. These are under the controul not of the priests alone, but of com- " munities of the most wealthy and respectable amongst the laity, and are preserved in the crypts " of their temples, which precaution ensured their preservation, as well as that of their deified " teachers, when the temples themselves were destroyed by the Mohamedan invaders, who paid " more deference to the images of Buddha than to those of Siva or Vishnu." Here we have a part of the secret religion of Mohamed. Among his followers, as among the Christians, when, in the thirteenth century, the stars did not fall from heaven or the sun cease to give its light, the doctrine became forgotten. But in this passage the Colonel does not display his usual acuteness of understanding. If he will reflect, he will see that the idea of large libraries or teachers being preserved in crypts unknown to conquerors is not credible. They were preserved, because the Arabians were the patrons of literature of every kind. They no more destroyed libraries in India than *they did in Egypt.*

I have before observed, that the term Vicramaditya is merely a descriptive term. This is confirmed by the mode in which the Hindoos apply it to Mohamed, whom they count a Vicramaditya, and whom they state to have made his appearance A. D. 621—and whose æra began from that year ; but he began to preach, or he appeared, as Mr. Faber has observed, in A. D. 608.[3]

The name Vicramaditya consists of these words : Vicra, which means *Vicar,* the same as Vicarius ; the word *Om,* and Ditya : the whole meaning *the holy Vicar of the God Om,* or *the Vicar of the holy Om.* Mohamed was also called *Resoul :* that is, the Ras of Al, or the *wisdom of God.* The Hebrew אמד *amd* is formed of the word OM and *di, the holy* OM. The Mohamedan sect of the Shiahs, in the language of Siam and of Malabar, is called Rafzi. This is evidently from the Hebrew *Ras*—Rashees.

The prejudices of modern Christians entirely blind them to the undeniable fact, that every Mohamedan is as really a Christian as themselves. If this be the case, it is in perfect keeping with their possession of the magnificent church or mosque of St. John, at Damascus, where his head is preserved, and so much venerated, that the Turks will not permit even one of their own religion to look at it, and never permit a Christian to go into the church or mosque.[4]

---

[1] Col. Broughton's Popular Poetry, notes, p. 152.      [3] P. 520.
[2] Asiat. Res. Vol. IX. p. 160.     [4] Maundrel's Journey, p. 170.

Vicentius Belovacensis notices the custom of two Indian nations making Carns in honour of their Gods, at the equinoxes.[1] This is still continued in Tibet, and what is very remarkable, he says the custom passed from the Indians to the Arabians, and was ordered to be continued by Mohamed. This seems to support what I have said of the Arabians' first coming from India, and to have been connected with the Mohamedans' protection of the Buddhist images in India.[2] Buddha was spared, because he was the male generative principle, as the Lingas were spared by Cambyses. Late travellers have found, as we might expect, Carns in Western Syria.

The fact is, Mohamedism was no *new* religion ; it was only a continuation of Buddhism. Mecca, the sacred city of Mohamed, was well known to the ancients by a name which had the meaning of the name of Mohamed. It was called *Maco* or *Moca Raba* by Ptolemy, or *Moca the great* or *illustrious*,[3] or in other words, the city of *Mo-hamed*. Guy Patin mentions a medal of *Antoninus Pius* with this legend MOK. IEP. AXY. AYTO. which he very properly translates Moca, sacra, inviolabilis, suis utens legibus: *Moca the holy, the inviolable, and using her own laws*. This, Wilford says, can only be applicable to the place now called by us Mecca, and in the Brahmin books Mócsha-st'han, and considered a most holy place, to which the Indians formerly made pilgrimages, and not to the little place called Mocha.[4] The medal of Antoninus serves to shew the universal nature of the Gentile religion. Col. Wilford informs us, that the Arabian writers unanimously support the doctrine, that the present Mecca is the Moca of Ptolemy. The sea-port of this Moca is the town or port of Bad-deo, regia, or the city of the holy and royal Buddha.

Mocsha means *eternal bliss ;* then the name will be *place of eternal happiness.* The indubitable fact that Mecca was a place sacred to the Amed or *desire of all nations* before Mohamed, the camel-driver, was born, opens to our view a new ænigma, which cannot be solved without supposing an esoteric religion in Mohamedism, as well as in all other religions, as held by the celebrated Avicenna and many others, and into which I shall inquire by and by. The whole history of Mohamed furnishes a most curious example of a prophecy causing its own verification.

12. The Jews well know that there is a very peculiar mystery concealed under the letter M, as M. Cassini has shewn. The Jews have the same twenty-eight letter figures as the Arabians, with the single exception that they want the *last* for the number 1000. This is contrived for the purpose of making their mystical letter M the central letter of their alphabet. They have only twenty-two letters, but they add five finals for this purpose. And similar to this they form a sacred cabalistic word אמת *amt* or אסח *amt*, which has the meaning of *truth*. It comes from the root אמן *amn*, which is the *Amen* and *Omen* of Christians ; the Om-man and Amun of Egypt corrupted, as is allowed, to *Ammón* by the moderns, and it is the OM of India. It is the first, and middle, and last—similar to the Alpha and Omega, with the sign for 600 in the middle ; as, in the Crismon Sancti Ambrogii, we have the Alpha A, and Omega Ω, with the ₱ in the middle, the emblem of 600. The figure at the top of the cross is the Samaritan Resh, which means 200, and the cross, which on Samaritan coins is put for the Tau, stands for 400. The letter Resh is

---

[1] Parkhurst in voce, רמה *rme.*

[2] The Christians accuse the Jews of blindness in believing that the promised Messiah or Saviour was to be a temporal prince. In this case, it is necessary, in justice to the Jews, to ask in what sense the word was used in their sacred writings. It had always one sense, and I believe *only* one sense, and that sense is at once seen when we look to Isaiah, where Cyrus is expressly called a Messiah.

[3] Asiat. Res. Vol. IV. p. 369.                    [4] Ibid.

read from left to right. This may be because it is used by modern Greeks, or it may be from its extreme antiquity; for it is the staff of Osiris. If letters were taken from figures, as they were always read from left to right, of course here used as a figure, it would read from left to right. It is, as just noticed, the Crismon Sancti Ambrogii, in the church of Milan—A P Ω. I have already said, it is the same as the sacred word of the Jews for *truth* אמת *amt*, but I suspect it meant both *truth* and WISDOM—for *Truth* is Wisdom—*Wisdom* is Truth. The Resh as here used might come from African Ethiopia, where the language read from left to right, and it is notoriously the staff of Osiris, the Monogram of Jupiter Ammon, and the Labarum of Constantine.

In the Syrian copy of the Apocalypse, for our Greek *Apha* and *Omega*, there are *Alpha* and *Tau*. Here we have אמת *amt*.

I believe no one disputes that the Greeks had their sixteen letters from the Phœnicians or Hebrews. Now, it cannot be supposed that they would receive the letters and not the letter numbers, though, for various reasons, they might not come into common use ; in fact, their other system was more convenient, or the Hebrew might be a secret and mystical system. If this were the case, the Rho must have been the same as the Samaritan and Chaldee, and have stood for 200. It is very possible that the Greeks abandoned the use of the Hebrew Quoth or Koph, from its great similarity to the Kappa ; and that this by degrees, made their Resh or Rho stand for 100, instead of 200, which it must have originally done. This may have arisen when a change in the language took place, which I shall explain in my book upon the origin of letters. The letter M, the MIDDLE letter, was adopted as a sacred mystery. It was the Omphalos or Δελφυς. It was the Monogram of Maia, Maria, Mary, the Regina Cœli.

The Greeks appear to have copied the Hebrews, for they have (see the first table of letters) the same Cadmean alphabet of sixteen letters, but they have twenty-seven letter figures for numbers, and the middle one has I think formerly been the M. If my reader look to the Table in the *Celtic Druids* he will observe that the Digamma expelled the Vau, which took up its place after the Tau, making a seventeenth letter, and not being one of the letters added by Palamedes or Simonides. Now when I consider the close connexion which must have once existed between the Sanscrit and the Greek, I cannot help *suspecting* that the A, U, M, has been the A, M, Ω—Alpha and Omega—taken from the Greek, when the M has been in some way, which I confess I cannot satisfactorily explain, the central letter as it was among the Hebrews. We find all the Indian nations admitting their ignorance of the etymology or meaning of their sacred AUM. We find them constantly using it as Om, which they acknowledge to be a corruption, but they know not how. Then may it not as easily have been AMΩ as AUM ? If they knew that it was the three letters corrupted into two, OM, it was natural to take the AΩM for the original, and not AMΩ. All this respecting the OM I give as a mere suspicion. It does not affect the theory that both the Greek and Hebrew have had the central M. We may observe upon this, that it connects well with the mystic Amo, I love—divine love—and Mo-ahmed ; in short, with the Om in a hundred senses and mystical relations.

But if in the end it should prove that my suspicion be well founded, have the Indians copied from the Greeks, or the Greeks from the Indians? Neither. The Greeks copied from the Hebrew, and the Hebrew was the language of South India, and Coromandel, and the Lascars, before the Sanscrit was formed : but not before their mythology was formed. The Sanscrit language must have been perfected since the sun entered Aries, as the Buddhists have it not; and great ingenuity was exerted to make it as different as possible from its parent, in order to keep it from the Buddhist heretics, as the Brahmins called them. In considering the question of the probability of my suspicion relative to the M, all the mystical particulars which we have before seen respecting this letter, and the cycle of 600, must be taken into consideration.

In the word אמת *amt* the Jews find various mysteries. They strike off the ciphers from the numbers which these letters denote, viz. 400 and 40, and they have 4, 4, 1, which make 9, which always multiplied, and then added, always make 9. Thus 9+9=81, and 8+1=9, and the מ, the middle letter is the fourteenth letter, and denotes the fourteen attributes of God, which they find somewhere in Exodus. We see in the earliest of the monuments of the Buddhists of India the number *nine* recur continually as a sacred number. This shews that my suspicion is in perfect keeping with the apparently trifling *nonsense* of figures giving names, but from which I imagine I shall in a future book evolve something very far from nonsensical.

It is very wonderful how prejudice may blind the understandings of men upon the subject of religion, though they reason well upon every other subject. M. Beausobre says, "Besides the "fulfilling of the ancient prophecies, the Messiah shines so *conspicuously* in the writings of the "New Testament, and all these so exactly centre in Jesus Christ, that it is absolutely impossible "a mind free from prejudice should not be affected with these marks of truth and sincerity."[1] The case is simply this, in the sacred books of the Jews written from time to time, a person is predicted by the name of Messiah. The meaning of this word is over and over again explained to mean a person to deliver them from bondage. If there could be any doubt of its meaning, the examples where it is applied to persons would remove it. Cyrus, for instance, is expressly called the Messiah of God. He was a temporal prince and a conqueror. How surprising that Dr. A. Clarke should not be able to see these *conspicuous* prophecies!

According to the doctrines of the Jewish Pharisees and the Christians, the works of the prophets are full of prophecies of a Messiah; but in no case whatever can any passage be pointed out where it is expressly stated that the Messiah alluded to was to be a *spiritual* not a *temporal* king. The meaning of the word Messiah was never doubted: the prophets whom God had sent had fixed its meaning by repeatedly declaring different persons to be Messiahs, such for instance as Cyrus. These prophets, it is said, were continued at different times even to the presentation of Jesus in the temple by his father and mother. How can it be reconciled to the goodness of God that even unto the very time when the last prophets, Zacharias, Simeon, and Anna, Luke i. 67, ii. 25, 38, prophesied of a Messiah, he should never have inspired one of them to explain to the Jews that a new Messiah was to come totally different in character from all the Messiahs they had had before, and that the visible child was to be a spirit! This, it has been said, was to blind the Jews, lest they should see and repent, and be saved; that is, should not be damned. Did any one ever before hear such shocking impiety? In reply to this last observation I shall be told that the passage is in the sacred book; to which I rejoin—Indeed it is, and is, like many others in the sacred books, a corruption of the gospel of Jesus, as in my next volume I will endeavour to shew. I can more readily believe that it was put into the book, by Anastasius or Lanfranc, from hatred to the Jews, than that it was put there by divine inspiration.

The difficulties which have arisen in the construction of these prophecies between a temporal and a spiritual Messiah, are all removed by the fact which I have pointed out, that the Messiah who was to deliver the Jewish nation from bondage was to be an incarnation of the Supreme Wisdom, in the flesh, like Cyrus. Thus he was both spiritual and temporal, though not exactly in the sense contended for by our divines; but in such a sense as justifies, in a great measure, many

---

[1] Int. New Test. Pt. ii. pp. 2, 3.

of the constructions put upon great numbers of the passages by the friends of both opinions. In fact, it shews that when the two parties have been opposing each other with the greatest bitterness, the real meaning of the texts justifies both of them. It is curious to see how persons permit their passions to mislead their reason, as well in India as in Europe. The followers of Cristna, never thinking that they can honour their favourite too much, maintain that he is not an incarnation, but Vishnu himself. This is exactly followed by our devotees, who contend that Jesus Christ is not an incarnation or a person divinely inspired, but that he is God himself.

Among some sects of the Jews, about the time of Christ, an opinion prevailed that there were to be two Messiahs, one of the tribe of Ephraim,[1] the other of the tribe of Judah. This opinion referred to the two cycles to come, of which these people had obtained some information—in fact, to the cycles of Jesus and Mohamed.

One of these Messiahs was to be a *suffering,* the other a *triumphant* Messiah. How curiously this dovetails into the history of Jesus and Mohamed! How curiously exhibiting, in the case of Mohamed, an example of a prophecy causing its own fulfilment! I suspect that this superstition has caused many great men to arise, and also, as I conjecture, it caused Napoleon to fall. Nimrod thinks that Brothers and Southcote were instructed by persons wiser than themselves: the time they appeared is very remarkable and suspicious. It is not impossible that vanity or priestly knavery may have whispered to Napoleon that a great one was yet to come, and vanity arising from unexpected success may have re-echoed the whisper, that *he* was the man.

CHAPTER VI.

TEMPLARS, OBSERVATIONS ON.—CHAIR OF ST. PETER.—GOSPEL OF JOACHIM.—ST. FRANCIS. ISHMAELIANS OR ASSASSINS.—GIBLIM.—CASIDEANS.—TEMPLARS RESUMED.—TEMPLARS CONTINUED.—GOOD AND EVIL. MANES.—RASIT. WISDOM. — TEMPLARS RESUMED. — MASONS.—MASONS CONTINUED.—MANES. MASONS CONTINUED.—SOPHEES.—LOCKMAN. ÆSOP.

1. In the dark and mystical learning of the middle ages we meet with many very odd circumstances which have never yet been accounted for, but which have in vain attracted the curiosity of the philosophers: until at last the inquiry seems to have been given up as hopeless. The circumstances to which I allude seem to connect the learning called Gnosticism with the Christian and Mohamedan systems: but though a connexion evidently existed, yet it was in an obscure, mystical and incomprehensible way, of which no one could make any sense. All this learning was closely connected with judicial astrology—with a famous prophetic magical demagorgon or brazen

---

[1] The Editor of Mr. Bruce's Travels has observed, that the word PHRE, which he says means the sun, occurs commonly in the composition of Egyptian names. For instance, Mephres, Uebphres, in Greek Ουαφρης, in Hebrew Hophra, priest of the sun. Vide Marshami Can. Chron. pass.; Bruce's Travels, Vol. II. p. 466.

head, and various idolatrous and Gnostic emblems—with the well-known mysterious man of the mountain or Syrian Assassins, and with the person called Johannes, Butta, and Deus, of whom we have lately treated. On charges intimately related to secrets of this kind the famous Knights Templars were destroyed. The accusations brought against them, as well as their defences, were involved in mystery. This was closely connected with the Millenium, and the Crusades in the eleventh and the twelfth centuries were the effects of that doctrine. The foundation of this was laid in the Virgilian doctrine of the renewed cycles—the expected commencement of the Millenium at the end of 1200 years, or at most in the thirteenth century, and the belief that Mohamed was either the tenth Avatar or Beast of the Revelations, or Antichrist, or the person foretold by Jesus, by Daniel and the prophets, and referred to by the Magician Virgil.[1] And thus came to be united the doctrines of Magic, Heathenism, Christianity, and Mohamedism, an union at first sight totally incomprehensible, of things to all appearance absolutely in diametrical opposition. The expectation of the Millenium was clearly entertained by the Papal See, which, on this account, encouraged the Crusades, and though the Cardinals of course could not believe that Mohamed was the hero of the tenth age or cycle, yet they believed that the seventh millenary or the Millenium was about to come, till the thirteenth century had considerably advanced, probably till after the year 1260, and till its non-arrival had proved to them, as well as to the others, their mistake. Then this dogma, from its evident falsity, was despised, and by degrees almost forgotten. Then and from this cause arose a reaction in the college of Cardinals. From this disappointed superstition, in the time of Leo X., it became Deistical or Atheistical, and how long it thus continued, or if it do yet so continue, may be matter of curious speculation. I have no doubt whatever, that the Romish secret religion was essentially magical or astrological, till about the end of the thirteenth century, when the prophecies of the Millenium failed, and proved its falsity.[2] Perhaps it might exist in a doubtful kind of way, till after the year 1260 had passed over; then, if not before, astrology became heresy.

In the prosecutions of the Knights Templars, which are known to every body, a certain mystification and secrecy may be observed, as if the whole of the charges against them were not brought publicly out. This arose from various causes. The persecuted were really very religious, and were bound by the most solemn Masonic oaths (and Masonry was intimately connected with these matters) not to divulge the secrets of the order. This caused them to recant at the stake, when all hope had fled, what they had confessed when on the wheel; and by this means they endeavoured to make amends for the secrets betrayed, and the oaths involuntarily broken on the rack. But yet it is charged upon them that although at the last they declared themselves innocent of the charges brought against them, yet they acknowledged themselves guilty and deserving of punishment; but the wickedness which they are said to have confessed is concealed from us. I have no doubt it consisted in part, at least, in having, when under the torture, accused, and thereby having brought on the ruin of, the order. The Papal See having first come at the secrets by means of confession, of persons who had gone over to the Heretics, and afterward repented

---

[1] I believe a life of Virgil is yet extant describing him as a great magician. And he is said to have been consulted by Octavius on astrology.

[2] Mr. Gibbon has some very curious and striking passages in Chap. XV. N. 64, 65; Chap. XX. N. 59; Chap. XXI. N. 19, 24, &c., on the Millenium, and on its universal reception in the early ages of the church. (See Burnet's Sacred Theory, Ch. V. p. iii., Justin ag. Trypho, pp. 177, 178, Edit. Bened.; Lact. Lib. vii.; Daillé de Usu Patrum, Lib. ii. Cap. iv.) The Trinitarian doctrines of Philo are shewn to have preceded the death, or probably the birth, of Christ, Ch. xxi. N. 17. It will be of importance to remember this.

4 T

and confessed, proceeded with the greatest certainty; but at the same time in a way which appeared very cruel, and also very mysterious : for it knew the truth, but it would not divulge the mode by which it obtained it, namely, that it acquired it by confession.

Protestants say, these persecutions were undertaken for the sake of the wealth of the order. This I think is a mistake. The ignorant devotees of that day were much more likely *to give* to holy mother church than *to rob* her, and the idea that the Pope would authorize the robbery, by the kings, merely for the sake of giving them the wealth, of the well-trained and disciplined light troops of the church, is out of all probability. That the kings might be tempted to take some of it I do not deny, but most of it was bestowed on other orders, with whom the Templars who were not murdered, after making every required confession, were incorporated. For I do not believe that the Popes put more of them to death than they thought necessary to eradicate the heresy, and to satisfy the bigoted kings. In truth, the bitterness against the Templars was with the kings more than the Pope, and this arose from the knowledge which the conclave possessed that the doctrines of the Templars were only a remnant of those doctrines which itself had professed a very few years before, as we shall soon see. But this it could not explain to the kings.

When in humble life a cobbler confesses to his priest that he has stolen a fallen apple or poisoned his parents, the secret is kept ; but not so when a person of high degree confesses such a fact, as, that an extremely rich and powerful body entertain opinions dangerous to the Roman See and to the holy father: then the case becomes very different. For the priest must confess, and from various causes he begins to entertain a doubt how far he is justified in keeping such dangerous, such sinful, knowledge from his superior, to whom at last he states the doubt which presses upon his conscience, or his superior has a scruple how far he is justified in keeping such a secret. The case goes to Rome, by a confidential messenger or by the priest himself. An order to confess in full returns or is given, and along with it a plenary absolution for betraying the secret of confession. In this way it arises, that there are very few things done, or proposed to be done, by courts professing the Romish religion, if they affect the interest of the Papacy, which are not as well known to the Pope, as if they were inserted in the Diaria di Roma. In this manner every government of the Romish religion is prostrate before the Pope and his cabinet or conclave of Cardinals, who are all bound to each other by the most solemn oaths, and these oaths strengthened by the knowledge that a breach of them would be followed by the cells of the inquisition, (still retained in Rome for the use of the priesthood,) the poisoned chalice, or the poniard. [1]

The doctrines to which I have alluded above, are visible every where in the curious mystical figures always seen upon the monuments of the Templars, in the fishes bound together by the tails, on the tombs of Italy—in the astrological emblems on many churches, such as the Zodiacs on the floor of the church of St. Irenæus at Lyons, and on a church at York, and Notre Dame at Paris, and Bacchus or the God IHΣ filling the wine-cask, formerly on the floor of the church of St. Denis. Again, in the round churches of the Templars, in imitation of the round church at Jerusalem, probably built by them in the Circlar or Cyclar or Gilgal form in allusion to various recondite subjects which I flatter myself I need not now point out to my reader, and in the monograms IHΣ and XH in thousands of places. In these mysteries, not only the Cardinals, but the heads and chapters of all the orders of knighthood, and of all the old orders of Monks, were more or

---

[1] If my memory do not deceive me, the records of Florence testify that the Eucharist, even the *sacred Eucharist*, has been made subservient to the destruction of the enemies of God and the Papacy.

less implicated; and from that part of them more intimately connected with the ancient doctrines of Ionism, arose the profound devotion of all orders of knighthood to the fair sex and the mother of God. That the Gnostic doctrines named above, that is, that Christianity was only a species, or an uncorrupted or reformed kind, of Paganism, were secretly held by the Cardinals in the Vatican, I can scarcely doubt, and I think I shall prove it by and by; and their refusal to believe Mohamed to be the Paraclete is easily accounted for.

In none of the modern histories of the church which have been written, has any attempt been made to penetrate into the secret mysteries of the religion; although every age exhibits avowals or admissions of the heads or chief persons of it, that there were such secrets, the truth of which admissions or avowals is proved by circumstances which can in no other way be accounted for. In the earlier periods we have histories of what different eminent persons have stated them to be; these our writers have handed to us, credulously believing them, and never adverting to this glaring fact, that if such men as Origen had really explained them, they would have been guilty of the blackest perfidy and perjury, and would soon have been murdered: whence it follows, that the explanations which they gave could only have been intended to mislead, or were not meant to apply to the *secret mysteries properly so called.* And with respect to the secrets themselves, they are probably like those of the Freemasons. If they were told by any traitor, so many other false stories were told along with the true ones, that their secrecy is by this means most effectually secured. It is also pretty certain, I think, that this esoteric religion must be of such a nature as to leave room for heresies and philosophical varieties of opinion to take place to a considerable extent, without much affecting it. Now I think in the Millenium and its collateral doctrines of astrology and some parts of Gnosticism these requisites may be found, and most assuredly in almost every age evident proofs of these matters shew themselves, when the history is carefully looked into. These are the causes why so many inconsistencies may be observed in all the accounts of the church, which the writers of them have been unable satisfactorily to explain. When a person reads Mosheim or other ecclesiastical writers, nothing is more easy and flowing than the history: there seem to be no difficulties. But when he examines into the documents on which it is founded, nothing is more difficult.

2. At every turn we meet with some remnants of Paganism, any one of which taken by itself would be of no consequence, but which becomes of consequence when united to many others. Some of these are ridiculous enough. The Pope boasts of being descended from St. Peter, Bar-Jonas, or Janus, *i. e.* son of Janus, and as *he* held the keys of heaven, so the Romanists maintain that their Pope holds them, and, by virtue,of this, possesses the power of granting or refusing absolution for sins—opening or shutting the gates of heaven. This is evidently a grand step to universal empire, and it is not surprising that great exertions should have been made to establish it. Various miracles are recorded of St. Peter, at Rome; and, to support the credit of the chief of the apostles, the actual chair on which this Bar-Jonas sat was formerly exhibited. As Bar-Jonas was holy, it followed that the chair on which he sat must also be holy; therefore, a festival was instituted on the 18th of January to the holy chair, which on that day was annually exposed to the adoration of the people. This continued till the year 1662, when upon cleaning it, in order to set it up in some conspicuous place of the Vatican, the *twelve labours* of Hercules unluckily appeared engraved on it. " Our worship, however," says Giacomo Bartolini, who was present at this discovery, and relates it, " was not misplaced, since it was not to the wood we paid it, but to " the prince of the apostles, St. Peter. An author of no mean character, unwilling to give up the " holy chair, even after this discovery, as having a place, and a peculiar solemnity among the " other saints, has attempted to explain the labours of Hercules in a mystical sense, as emblems " representing the future exploits of the Popes. But the ridiculous and distorted conceits of

4 т 2

" that writer are not worthy our notice, though by Clement X. they were judged not unworthy of " a reward." [1]

When the wicked French got possession of Rome, they did not fail to examine this celebrated relic, and lo! in addition to the labours of Hercules, they discovered engraved upon it, in Arabic letters, the Mohamedan confession of faith. [2] In these two facts there is a beautiful exemplification of the doctrine held by me and Ammonius Saccas, that all the varieties of religions are at the bottom the same—but including, in the collection known to Ammonius, the modern Mohamedan religion, which will be accounted for presently. I can scarcely conceive a more marked proof of the nature of the secret doctrine of the Conclave. The story goes, that this chair was brought from Constantinople by a Pilgrim, who, of course, could neither see the Zodiac, nor read, nor know, when he saw Arabic letters, that they were the letters of the country where he had been travelling. And it is also clear that the Pope and all the Cardinals who adopted this chair were equally *blind*, and could not see the Zodiacal signs, and equally *ignorant* of the Arabic letters. Besides, it is also manifest, if they did see them, that there was not at that time a carpenter in the Roman dominions by whom these offensive emblems might have been removed from the chair, or who might have simplified the matter by substituting a new one, if one must be had, and if the emblems proved the falsity of the story of its being St. Peter's.

Irony aside, the fact is, there is no doubt that, under these mysterious circumstances, something lies hid. These emblems and letters did not come there by accident : nor are they to be ascribed to the ignorance of the Pope and the whole college of Cardinals, and the priests and the Propaganda employed in educating youth in *Arabic* and other languages for the foreign missions. All these circumstances are full of interest, but I think the time is come when they may be explained. The whole tenure of this work goes to explain the labours of Hercules, the symbols, as Mr. Parkhurst calls them, of what the real Saviour was to do and suffer. For the other I will propose a theory founded on a conditional fact, which, of course, if the fact be not true, falls to the ground.

I have read, but where I cannot now recollect, and which at the time I thought of no consequence, of several missions having been sent by the Popes to convert the Caliph of the Mohamedans to Christianity. This was the ostensible reason given to the Christian world for the missions. But I am of opinion that these missions had also the secret object, if conversion were not possible, of effecting accommodation; and this was in a great measure caused by the expectation of a Millenium, a doubt whether Mohamed might not really be the person foretold by Jesus ; and a fear, whether he were so or not, that the warlike Saracen, his successor, should overrun Italy and subvert the Papal power. We must not forget that attempts at accommodation would be kept in the most profound secrecy, and if suspected or discovered most strenuously denied—perhaps never committed to writing.

In the history to which I allude, one of the Popes is said to have sent a most arrogant message to the Caliph to require him to turn Christian. This story does very well to blind ignorant people, and for Protestants to laugh at, but I believe that the truth was, that a negociation was attempted with the Caliph by the Pope, which failed, and the story of the Pope's *arrogance* was told, as we have it, to conceal the truth. I know that the idea of an inclination of the Roman See to an union with Mohamedism will be treated with ridicule. However, let the Arabic inscription be accounted for; not by a pretended accident, the *great* resource of *little* minds, but by some rational theory.

---

[1] Bower, Hist. Popes, p. 7.        [2] Lady Morgan's Italy.

If the Pope had any inclination to admit Mohamed as the person to be sent, as foretold by Jesus Christ, the Arabic inscription might be placed upon the chair as a preparation for a pretended miracle to establish the fact. Or if the Pope feared the arrival of the Caliph at Rome, he might be preparing for a march out to meet him with the keys of the Holy City and of Heaven in his hand, with a pretence that he was at last convinced by the miraculous inscription on the chair (an imitation of the inscription on the wall at Babylon) that Mohamed was the Apostle of God. The march to meet the conqueror would find an exact precedent in the conduct of the Jewish High Priest (as described in the lying account of Rollin) proceeding, *in Pontificalibus*, in compliance with a dream, (to betray the former race of Messiahs which had restored the temple,) and to deliver the keys of Jerusalem to Alexander the Great, the *new incarnation*.

We shall presently see, notwithstanding the boasted immutability of the Holy See, that at the time of which I am now speaking, it was not so determined against all change as its followers pretend, and that it had not any very great objection to a new incarnation. I think when the reader has perused the remainder of this chapter, he will not consider my theory so improbable as he may do at present. The Arabic inscription must have a meaning.

3. About the time of which I am speaking, there seems to have been something strangely unsettled in the Roman See. This is proved by the fact, now almost concealed by the priests, *that a new Gospel was preached* with its permission, and actively and energetically supported by it, as Mosheim says, for above thirty years. For various reasons, which will be detailed, it was at last suppressed, the zodiac[1] and inscription on the chair were forgotten, and the Templars were burnt.

When the Grand Lama of Tibet made advances to the Emperor of the East—the Emperor of China—informing this wise and politic prince that he would receive him as the eldest son of the church, the cunning monarch accepted the offer, acknowledged the Lama for his father, and thus he became the sovereign and protector of the sacred and holy incarnation of Divine Wisdom at Lassa. When the Grand Lama of Rome made advances, if he did make them, to the Emperor of the West—the Caliph—this prince being less politic than the Chinese, the Western Lama was less successful than his brother Lama had been in the East. Had the negociation succeeded, and a new Gospel taken place of the old ones, how different might have been the state of the world! That the world was ready for a new Gospel I will now prove.

The new Gospel of which I have spoken above was called the *Evangelium Eternum*, and, after being some time preached in the 12th century, was first published in a written book by one Joachim, Abbot of Sora or Flora, in Calabria, of whom I spoke in Chap. V. Sect. 9, from which it was called the BOOK OF JOACHIM.[2] This Gospel was called the *covenant of peace*. It was intended to supersede all the old Gospels, and by it an union was expected to take place with the Mohamedans and all the other sects, which caused it to have this last name. It had the name of EVANGELIUM ETERNUM, or the EVERLASTING GOSPEL, evidently to insinuate or intimate to those capable of understanding it, that all other gospels were only of a temporary nature. This exactly agrees with the Mohamedan doctrine of the Paraclete. This gospel, known and preached in the end of the twelfth century, was received by nearly all the monks, but particularly by the Domini-

---

[1] This Zodiac is in good keeping with the Zodiac in the church of St. Irenæus, at Lyons, with the wine cask at St. Denis, with the Zodiac on the church at York, and with many other similar matters.

[2] This was the same man spoken of before as Abbot of Curacio. Here we see that this Io-akim, that is, Io *the wise*, was also Abbot of *Flora*, the mystic, perhaps secret, name of Rome. These mystic names betray the mystic nature of the system.

cans and Franciscans, and they were most warmly supported by the Popes, who censured their opponents, and particularly one St. Amour, and caused their books to be burnt.[1]

The *Everlasting Gospel* was also called the *Gospel of the Holy Ghost*. It had its name of *Evangelium Eternum* from the fourteenth chapter and sixth verse of the Revelation of Ioannes or John, of which it was the completion, and in which, as the *tenth* Avatar, or CYCLE, or Age, which would come or be completed about the end of the twelfth century, it was of course found; for the Apocalypse is a very ancient astrological work on the Zodiacal Lamb, and the doctrine of the ten Cycles and the Millenium. Its other name, given above, of the *Holy Ghost*, or the Peri-clyte, or Para-clete, is evidently in accordance with the Mohamedan doctrine. The Roman See supported the *Evangelium Eternum* by all the means in its power. This gospel announces that there have been two *imperfect ages*, the one of the Father, the age of the Old Testament, and one of the New Testament, under the administration of the Son, and that the third or the perfect one, of the Holy Ghost, which was to be preached to all nations, was at hand. Here, most clearly, we have a doctrine which assimilates again to Mohamedism, and to the expectation of the Millenium.

The Evangelium Eternum consisted of three books. *The Liber Concordiæ Veritatis*, i. e. the Book of the *Harmony of Truth*, the *Apocalypsis Nova* or *New Revelation*, and the *Psalterium decem Chordarum, Psaltery of the ten chords*, or the TEN-*stringed Harp*. The reader will please to observe that this being a new Apocalypse[2] will, like the old one, be intelligible only to those initiated in the mysteries; and, this understood, I think I need not explain to him the meaning of the Harp with TEN strings. I think if he will now look over the old Apocalypse again, he will see that its doctrines all refer to the revolution of the different cycles.[3] And if he look to the Grecian history he will find that the Lyre of Apollo at first had only *three* strings, but they increased till they amounted to *seven*. The Muses and the Curetes also increased as time advanced, till they got to nine, when the Greek temples were destroyed. They increased as the cycles increased in number.

I believe that throughout all the Roman Christian world, the Gospel of St. Joachim was received. Various circumstances convince me of this. In the latter end of the 13th century when the end of the world was daily expected, the Monks increased in number beyond all credibility, and the most violent commotions arose among them; but, however they might hate one another,

---

[1] Mosheim, Hist. Cent. xiii. Sect. xxviii.

[2] Erasmus, Luther, and Calvin, had little esteem for the Apocalypse. St. Jerom saith, (Ep. cxxix. ad Dardanum,) that some churches of the Greeks would not accept it. Gregory Nazianzen has omitted it in his poem about authentic Scripture. The Council of Laodicea, (Can. 59,) held about 364, giving a list of canonical books, hath left it out. Amphilocus, contemporary with St. Basil, saith, that though some inserted it in the legitimate writings, yet the majority did slight it as a spurious piece. Vide Euseb. Eccl. Hist. Lib. iii. Cap. xxviii., also Eccl. Hist. Lib. vii. Cap. xxv. Dorotheus, Bishop of Tyre and a Martyr, owns that St. John writ his gospel at Patmos, but not a word of this book, though the first chapter lets us know that he was in that isle when he had his visions.—Discourse on the Lord's-day, by Rev. Thomas Morer, 1701.

[3] The candlestick in the temple had seven branches. The Lamb of the Apocalypse had seven horns and seven eyes, which are the seven spirits of God, and twenty-four elders. When the six seals are opened the stars will fall; that is, at the end of the six millenaries the Millenium will come. 144,000 persons were sealed, 12,000 of each tribe. The mystery will be finished when the seventh angel begins to sound. The number of the Beast is 666. The city is 12,000 furlongs square; the wall 144 cubits. (Rev. xxi. 16, 17.) In chap. xiv. 1, 144,000 is again named. There is a river on each side, a tree of life bearing twelve fruits, one each month, and the most remarkable thing of all is, that the Lord is said, ch. ii. ver. 8, to have been *also crucified in Egypt*. I must now request my reader to look back to Book V., and he will not then be surprised that the chronology of the tribe of Abraham or Judah should coincide with that of the Hindoos; as it is very evident the secret histories of the two nations are the same.

they all joined in supporting the *evangelium eternum*. An instance of this may be found in the works of St. Amour which I have not been able to see, for though he attacked the Mendicant orders with the greatest bitterness, he founded his proofs against them on the *everlasting gospel*; he attacked them with their own weapons.[1] The reason why we have very little left respecting this gospel is to be found in the fact of its universal reception, for all parties being equally exposed to ridicule when the failure of the Millenium took place, all were equally interested in letting the subject die and be forgotten. But I think such as retained any of the doctrines were persecuted as Manichæans.[2]

4. After the devotees and followers of the new Gospel, in the 13th century, had in vain expected the *holy one* who was to come, they at last pitched upon St. Francis as having been the expected one, and, of course, the most surprising and absurd miracles were said to have been performed by him. Some of the fanatics having an indistinct idea of the secret doctrine of renewed incarnations, or letting their knowledge of the principle of renewed incarnations escape in the heat of controversy, maintained that St. Francis was " *wholly and entirely transformed*[3] *into the person of* " *Christ*—Totum Christo configuratum."[4] Mosheim says, by some of them the Gospel of Joachim was expressly preferred to the Gospel of Christ.[5]

The Gospel of the Holy Ghost, or the Evangelium Eternum of the book of Joachim, was never censured or in any way suppressed by any act of the Pope, but only the introduction to it, which deduced from it the downfal of the Holy See. John of Parma, General of the Franciscans, who was one of the most violent of its supporters, has a place among the saints in the acta sanctorum.[6] He preferred the Gospel of Joachim to that of Christ. Nothing can be more erroneous than the representation of Dr. Maclaine, that it was only supported by a few Franciscans, called spirituals, when it was at least for more than half a century supported by the whole Romish Church; how much longer I do not know. It is necessary carefully to avoid falling into the mistake of supposing, that those who wrote against the Mendicant orders wrote against the Evangelium Eternum, which was received by them, for they had many adversaries who received the gospel as eagerly as they did.

All these matters shew, with the Popes, policy, with the *common* Monks, fanaticism. As might be expected, among the monastic fanatics, who were not entrusted with the High Secrets of the Conclave, different opinions and the most violent controversies arose, each claiming for his own order the chief merits of the new gospel. After a certain time this placed the Holy See in a most awkward dilemma. It could not condemn the gospel which it had supported, and on which it had so far relied as to believe that, at the commencement of, or some time in, the thirteenth century, the millenium and the completion of the ten cycles, or the completion of the famous 1260 years, would arrive. But after the failure of its prophecies, the Holy See could no longer support it. It could not explain to the intemperate monks the real secret, and it did not like to persecute; perhaps did not *dare* to persecute the light troops of the church—the united Dominican, Franciscan, and Augustinian Monks, all of whom supported the new gospel.

---

[1] Mosheim, Hist. Cent. xiii. p. ii. Sect. xxviii.          [2] Ibid. Sect. xxxviii.
[3] The word transformed is used here to conceal the metempsychosis and renewed incarnation. It has the same meaning as the word transfigured in the gospels.
For particulars relating to St. Francis see the works of Bartholomew Albizi or de Albizis, particularly that called Liber conformitatum Sancti Francisci cum Christo, Venice, fol.; or Antiquitates Franciscanæ sive Speculum Vitæ beati Francisci et Sociorum, &c., Cologne, 1623; also the work of Peter of Alva and Astorga, entitled Naturæ prodigium, Gratiæ portentum, &c., Maduti, 1651, fol.
[4] Vide Litera Magistrorum de Postilla Fratris P. Joh. Olivi in Baluzii Miscellan. Tom. I. p. 213; Waddingi Annal. Minor. Tom. V. p. 51; Mosh. Hist. Cent. XIII. Pt. ii. Sect. xxxvi.
[5] Ibid. Sect. xxxiv. note.          [6] Tom. III. Martii, p. 157.

The Rev. Dr. Maclaine says, that the Evangelium Eternum consists, *as productions of that na-ture generally do* (how true an observation !) of ambiguous predictions and intricate riddles. This is what we might expect. After it had been published some time, and had received the greatest support possible from the Popes and all orders of Monks, the Franciscan fanatic *Gerhard* pub-lished the work called an introduction to this Gospel, in which he censured the vices of the Church of Rome, and in set terms prophesied or deduced from the Evangelium Eternum the destruction of the Roman See. This appeared in the year 1250, close upon the last period to which the Millenium could be delayed, viz. 1260 years. As this dreaded moment approached, the passions of the different orders of Monks were excited to the greatest height. Gerhard's book was burnt and its author was persecuted, though his followers, among the Franciscans, claim for him the gift of prophecy, and place him among the saints. The followers of St. Francis generally—the great supporters of the new gospel—and Gerhard maintained, *that he, St. Francis, who was the angel mentioned in the Revelations,* ch. xiv. 6, *had promulgated to the world the true and Everlasting Gospel of God : that the Gospel of Christ was to be abrogated in the year* 1260, *and to give place to this new and everlasting gospel, which was to be substituted in its room : and that the ministers of this great reformation were to be humble and barefooted friars, destitute of all worldly emoluments.* [1] This was stripping off the veil and shewing the meaning of the eternal gospel without disguise. It excited the most lively feelings of surprise, of hope, or of indigna-tion, according as it suited or opposed the opinions of the different fanatics. The Pope did not according to the usual plan burn the author, the book only was burnt, and its author mildly cen-sured *and banished to his house in the country.* This took place in the year 1255, when the par-ties, expectants of the Millenium, must have been in the highest state of fear and anxiety.

The year 1260 arrived and passed away ; but, wonderful ! the sun did not cease to give its light ; the moon and the stars did not fall from heaven ; nothing particular happened ; the pious fools stared one at another, and the impious rogues laughed. The Pope and Cardinals at Rome, half rogues half fools, and the fools every where else, finding themselves all in the wrong, soon began to charge the folly upon one another, and as they had quarrelled before who should display the most zeal for the *new* glad-tidings, they now began to quarrel about who should bear the blame—each shuffling the odium on to some other. Dr. Maclaine, feeling the extreme degree of ridicule in which the whole thing involves the church, and not understanding the truth in the slightest degree, or not suspecting that it had any connexion with the Millenium, in endeavouring to throw the whole blame on an obscure small sect of Franciscans, only exposes his unavailing wishes and contradictions. He and Mosheim have clearly proved the *great* and, indeed, I may almost say, the *universal* reception of the Everlasting Gospel. After some time, the fanatics having, by degrees, ceased to preach, and the Popes to support, the new gospel, the old gospels recovered their credit, and the friends of the new one died away, or were burnt as they came to be considered heretics. We must not forget that the exact period when the 1260 years of Daniel were to commence was always, as it yet is, a matter of great doubt with devotees : and it seems pretty clear, that in the encouragement of St. Francis or of the Gospel of Joachim, the Pope went upon the idea that the tenth avatar was to commence at the end of 1260 years, not to end at that time. At all events, uncertainty is in the very nature of the case, and it appears very probable that the court of Rome endeavoured to guard against whatever might happen. This was exactly in character with the Arabic inscription on the chair.

It is very curious to observe, that this gospel is now so completely forgotten or concealed, that

---

[1] And, I have little doubt, along with this, the Spencean doctrine of *equality of property* among all its votaries.

there is not throughout Europe one in a thousand, of commonly well-educated persons, who knows that there ever was such a gospel; though it is very certain that if, with our present mystics, the 1260 years had been foretold to end in 1860, instead of 1260 years after Christ, the whole religion of the Christian world might have been completely changed, and a new gospel would have been received, and, in St. Joachim or St. Francis, we should have had a rival of Paul, *another apostle born out of due season.* If we look back to the history of the world in the fifth and sixth centuries, we shall find that the Monks in that day swarmed almost beyond credibility. This, like their increase in the eleventh and twelfth centuries, arose from the expectation of the Millenium about the year 600, and I have no doubt that thousands of the order, a little later, joined the armies of the prophet of Arabia. After the time fixed for the Millenium to commence had passed away, it appears that various writings, called *the Gospel of Joachim,* were handed about Italy, but each of them denied, by the Papists or Monks, to be the *real gospel.* This was done in order to enable them to parry the ridicule to which it and they were exposed, by saying, in each case, that it was not the real book. On this account it would be impossible to make out the real gospel if it were worth any person's trouble to attempt it, which I think it can hardly be.

A little time ago I observed that Mr. Mosheim had said, that the Evangelium Eternum was in fashion or was received for more than thirty years. No doubt this gospel history is as disagreeable to Mosheim as to the priests of most other sects, but he had too much principle or too much regard to his own fame to suppress the history : yet he softens and disguises where it is in his power. It is true, as he says, that it was received for more than thirty years, for it was preached (I do not speak here of its being written) before the end of the twelfth century (how long before I do not know), and the introduction to it ; and the explanation of Gerhard, though grossly libelous on the Roman See, was not burnt till the year 1256, which shews it to have been preached for more than fifty years at least; so that before the Church consented to burn Gerhard's book and inflict the dreadful punishment on him, (how different from its general treatment of heretics !) *of sending him to his family residence from Paris,* it probably made itself certain that the great expected event would not happen according to their reckoning in the year 1260.

After the expectation of the Millenium had entirely passed away, and the power of the Saracens seemed to increase, the Popes became more than ever embittered against the Mohamedans, and equally furious against all who supported any thing relating to the now become obsolete Gnostic or Cyclic doctrines, or the expectation of a Millenium. This accounts, in a very satisfactory manner, for the zeal of the Popes up to a certain time for the new gospel, and their bitterness afterward towards the Templars and the Albigenses, among whom some remnants of these superstitions remained. The peculiar circumstance that a great part of these doctrines was necessarily involved in the greatest obscurity, and kept secret with the greatest possible care, being, in fact. the esoteric doctrine, accounts for many of the apparently inconsistent circumstances which we every where meet with. It easily accounts for them all.

There can be no doubt that the adoration of the Maria, the Regina Cœli, the mother of God, existed before Christianity. But it was brought forward into more notice after a certain time in opposition to Mohamed, and I cannot much doubt that it was on this account adopted peculiarly by the orders of knighthood: for the religion of Mohamed was utterly opposed to every thing which had the least tendency to the adoration of the *female principle* or Ionism. This has given countenance to the assertion of Protestants that it did not come into the Romish Church till about the eighth century, comparatively speaking a recent period. But they have fallen into this mistake, from their zeal to make it out to be a modern corruption, fearing that if they admitted its antiquity, they would prove it to be an integral part of Christianity. The black virgins and Bambinos of Italy are far older than Christianity. For these reasons the Carmelites, the great

4 U

698 GIBLIM.

friends of the Virgin Mary, the female generative power in opposition to the male, were brought forward in a peculiar manner by the Popes, and became their favourites to so absurd a length, that those Popes countenanced the doctrine, that every person who died with the scapulary of the order on his shoulders was certain of eternal salvation. [1]

As we have seen, the grand reason which caused the Crusades was the expectation of the Millenium ; the desire to be present at Jerusalem, at the grand day when the Son of Man should come in his glory—the great day of God Almighty. Here we have the real reason of the Crusades. The wish to protect a few pilgrims, was but a very small part of the cause which moved the millions to the Holy Land.

There is a book referred to by Dr. Maclaine called the ALCORAN DES CORDELIERS, which shews, I think,[2] that St. Francis was set up by his followers as the *tenth Avatar* in opposition to Mohamed. At all events it certainly is designed to shew, that he was intended to supersede Jesus Christ. Every sect of religionists receiving the millenary system believed themselves to be the favourites of God, therefore, of course, they believed that the tenth avatar would appear among them ; they were therefore ready to catch at any extraordinary person as he whom they expected— as he who was the desire of all nations. Thus we have several ninth avatars, and several tenth avatars running at the same time in different places.

In former parts of this work we have seen that the Jewish patriarchs were said to have had their images in the temple at Mecca before the time of Mohamed, along with an effigy of a Dove, which Mohamed himself destroyed. This seems very singular. We have seen also what has been said of the Ishmaelites having brought the language, at that time the same as the Jewish or Chaldean, from the mountains of Upper India. We have also seen that the Brahmins count Mohamed among the incarnations, admit him to have been a Vicramaditya or a holy energy, (as Col. Tod would say,) and that they formerly frequented and made pilgrimages to the temple at Mecca. May not Mohamed have been merely a Deistical reformer of a mythos, the same as that of the Afghans of Upper India, corrupted by his successors ? The Koran, forged twenty years after his death, offers no impediment to this. Or may not Mohamed have been announced by himself as the tenth avatar, and the Koran a made-up article, partly invented and partly formed from the memories of his followers, of such speeches as he delivered at different times and they remembered, merely to deceive the vulgar, to whom the secret mythos was never trusted in any country, and which was never known till it got out by degrees.[3] This will be found to be in perfect keeping with the secret doctrine of his religion, which I shall explain by and by. The above theory respecting the Koran is very nearly accordant with the history which we have. That it should be forgotten since the failure of the Millenium is no way surprising.

5. In the Western part of Asia in the beginning of the twelfth century, the sect or religious tribe called Ishmaelians or Battenians or Assassins began to be noticed. Many persons have attempted, and some are now attempting, their history, which is in a high degree difficult and mysterious; but the number of these historians shews, that they have none of them yet given satisfaction. As usual in cases of this kind, the reports of the enemies of these people, almost without discrimination, have been received as historical evidence by those who have undertaken

footnotes
[1] See the work of Benedict XIV. De Festis B. Mariæ Virg. Lib. ii. Cap. vi. p. 472, Tom. X. opp. edit. Rom. Mosheim, Cent. XIII. Part ii.

[2] Tom. I. pp. 256, 266, 278, &c. ; Luc. Waddingi Annales Minor. Tom. III. p. 380 ; Mosh. Hist. Cent. XIII. Part ii Ch. xxx.

[3] It is a very singular circumstance that not one of the four great teachers of the doctrine of Wisdom in the Western world, Socrates, Pythagoras, Jesus, or Mohamed, left any memorial of his existence or of his doctrines in writing.

to give us an account of them. This renders all these histories doubtful to a philosopher who understands the value of evidence and chooses to attend to it. The case is very difficult, for we have scarcely any other documents than those reports to resort to. I flatter myself that it will be in my power to cast a ray of light on this obscure subject. But the severity of my rule in cases connected with religion of scarcely ever taking the testimony of an opponent, without it have some other support, as conclusive, will reduce our knowledge of them, as the same rule reduces the history of Mohamed, to a very small compass. I believe there is not a single written document of the Ishmaelites in existence. They were equally at war with the Mohamedan Caliphs, the Christians, and the Jews. They are now nearly extinct. I think I can shew how this all arose. They seem at one time to have been considered in Syria with the same kind of horror with which the imaginary vampires were considered in Germany formerly, and probably a horror not much better founded. If we may believe the Arabian historians the murders which they committed were innumerable. But every fire or robbery seems, without discrimination, to have been attributed to them. Of some of the crimes with which they have been charged they have been proved innocent, and it seems not improbable, that their name has been used as a very convenient cover under which the governors of the Arabian towns might revenge themselves with impunity on their enemies.

M. Quatermere, froman anonymous Persian author, says, that they called themselves *Partisans de la secte qui conduit dans le droit chemin*, and Mirkond calls them *Les Sectateurs de Babon*.

About the same time, at least in the same Cycle, when St. Francis was set up by the Cordeliers for the last manifestation of God on earth, previous to the Millenium, these Assassins were first noticed in the Western world with their chief Hakem[1] Bemrillah or Hakem-biamr-allah, who was held up in Syria for the same person. He was said BY HIS FOLLOWERS to be THE TENTH AVATAR, or, as I suppose, incarnation, and, as I have said, the founder of what his enemies called the Assassins. His ideas of God were very refined. The first of the creatures of God, the only production *immediate* of his power, was the *intelligence universelle*, which shewed itself at each of the manifestations of the Divinity on earth; that by means of this minister all creatures were made, and he was the Mediator between God and man. They called themselves *Unitarians*. This *intelligence universelle* is evidently the Logos, Rasit, or Αρχη or Buddha or Μητις of which we have seen so much. In the doctrine of the ten incarnations, and that Hakem was the tenth, and in the *intelligence universelle*, we have the complete proof of the reality of the system which I have been developing and tracing through the six thousand years from the first of them. It completes my proofs if any were wanted. It was not discovered by me till more than half this volume was printed.

I think it seems probable that the followers of Bemrillah were originally adorers of Taurus or the Calf or Calves, which they continued to mix with the other doctrines of Buddha, and that after Hakem's death they returned to the superstition of their ancestors, a very likely effect to follow among an ignorant people, when the disappointment of the expected Millenium happened. I have little doubt that the Templars were followers of this Bemrillah. Much curious matter respecting these people, under the name of Druses, may be found in the 3rd Vol. of the Transactions of the Academy of Inscriptions, An. 1818, and in my Celtic Druids.

---

[1] The word Hakem is nothing but the word חכם *hkm* which means *wise*. All physicians in the East are called Hakem. This man was believed to be the tenth incarnation of Divine Wisdom; another Solomon, who I am persuaded was an incarnation of the Rasit. If this Ishmaelite had not claimed to be something more than common, the word Hakem might have been considered merely a title of honour. It is curious to observe how constantly the incarnation of the Wisdom occurs.

4 U 2

The reason why we have such a horrible idea of the man of the mountain and of the Assassins is, as I have said before, because our informants, as usual in religious matters, take their accounts from the enemies of the persons of whom they write, from persons blinded by bigotry and hatred to their enemies to such an excess, as to think it meritorious to practise any fraud to injure them.

Of the old man of the mountain and his sect or society of Assassins, a history has lately been written by Mr. Von Hammer, of Vienna, who has from his command of books and knowledge of languages every requisite qualification, *one excepted*, to unravel the mystery which surrounds them, but unfortunately the wanting qualification is indispensable—*an enlarged and unprejudiced mind.* He was the author some years ago of a treatise, in the Mines de l'Orient, called *Mysterium Baphematis revelatum*, but which was in reality a treatise on the Knights Templars, in which the same illiberal and narrow mind is displayed as in this history. Besides, there is some reason to believe that he is merely playing a game to please his enlightened master the leaden-headed Emperor of Austria. But certain facts may be gleaned from his work which are of importance. It is very certain that the Ishmaelians or society of Assassins is a Mohamedan sect; that it was at once both a military and religious association, like the Templars and Teutonic Knights ; and that, like the Jesuits, it had its members scattered over extensive countries. It was a link which connected ancient and modern Free-masonry.

A man called Hassan Sabah is said to have first founded the dynasty of Assassins, which continued for seven or eight generations, in 1090, at Almawt or the Eagles' nest, between Cazvin and Gilan. He was called Sheikh al Jebal or chief or elder of the mountains.[1] Saba means *wisdom*, as I shall presently shew. Thus we have Hassan *the wise* and Bemrillah *the wise.*[2]

The Assassins seem to have shewn themselves to the Western writers about the same time in two places ; one party consisted of the Ishmaelians from the North-east, under Hakem Bemr-illah, and the other under Hassan Saba, Caliph of Egypt ; and I think, if there was any separation between the leaders, it is probable that their followers united. And if this were the case we should have two Mohamedan tenth avatars ; but this is not quite clear. According to the Ishmaelites of the East the incarnation descended in the same manner as it does in the Lama of Tibet. But Hassan Saba, it is expressly stated, claimed to be *the tenth* incarnation. The principal was called Sheikh-el-JEBEL, of which Mr. Hammer says, the Latin *Vetus de Monte* is a fair translation. Now this is a very curious corruption or example of a devised double meaning. The word Jebel translated *mount* is the Hebrew word גבל *gbl*, and means *Cabala* or *tradition of Wisdom*, and was the name given to a mount in Palestine, which was thus the mount of the tradition or Cabala, whence the word Gibel came to have the meaning or to be translated a mount. It is often called Giblim—*verbum sapienti*. Thus he was not the old man or the father of the mount only, but of the *tradition of Wisdom* or doctrines handed down by tradition.

גבלים *Gblim*, Drummond says, " *were master Masons, who put the finishing hand to the Temple of Solomon.*"[3] In 1 Kings v. 18, the word in our translation rendered stone squarers, is גבלים *Gblim*. This the LXX. render Βυβλιοι. This is said to mean men of Byblos. This is named Ezek. xxvii. 9.[4] Byblos was the city of the Bible or the Book ; which contained in the language of parable the Cabala, or גבל *gbl* or *cbl*. These were the Masons who lived at this town, and I dare say might be the operatives who finished the temple, of whom I have treated in Bk. VIII.

---

[1] Ouseley, Sir W., Trans. Soc. Lit. Vol. II. p. 22.

[2] See Dulaure's Hist. of Paris, Tome VIII. pp. 87, 90, &c.

[3] Orig. Vol. III. p. 192.          [4] Maundrel's Travels, p. 45.

Chap. IV. Sect. 1. We must also observe that of whatever age the principal of the Assassins might be, he always bore the name of old man, which was a title given to Buddha, in India and Scotland. In fact, it was only a Saga, Sagax or Sage. The true character of this name Christian writers disguise by the designation old man.'

Thus we have here a tenth avatar descending, like the Lama of Tibet, from the East, and a tenth avatar in like manner in Egypt, in Hassan, *from whom the Illuminati are descended.* The Ishmaelians seem to claim to be the same as the Imaums of Persia, and Mr. Hammer, I think, gives us reason to believe that the Koran was held to contain a secret doctrine, and that Mohamedism was, in this respect, like Christianity, *(" which was in its origin a secret society;"* [1]) a fact, as I have before observed, which was maintained by the Mohamedan writer Avicenna—a fact of which I have no doubt, and a doctrine which I shall presently explain.

I have no doubt whatever that Mohamed was considered, in his day, as the tenth avatar: and again in the time of Saladin and Hakem Bemrillah, that they were each so considered [2] by their followers, and as such were considered by Christians either as Antichrists, or, as Joachim of Calabria informed Richard the first, the last head of the beast, the immediate forerunner of Antichrist —and of course, as Joachim would tell him, a head to be cut off by him. [3] We will now endeavour to find the meaning of the word Assassins.

6. Duret says, Chascheddim, qui est à dire le nom de Chaldees, sous l'appellation duquel sont comprises tant en général que special toutes les sectes des sages de Babylonne, signifie proprement, et particulièrement dans iceluy Daniel au dire de S. Hierosme un genre d'hommes, que le vulgaire des Latins appelle en langue Latin Mathématicos, et Genethliacos, Mathématiciens et Genethliaques. He presently adds, Philon Juif au liv. d' Abraham en parle en ces mots. [4] We have found these Chasdins or Casideans in the country of Calida. I believe they were followers of the holy Lamb that taketh away the sins of the world, of the college of כשב ksb or שה se a lamb. Here we see, Duret says, the Chaldeans were called *Mathematici,* an observation which will presently be found of much consequence. Duret says, Chascheddim is כשדום csdum, with vowels *casedim.* [5] The Chas-chisdim were the Chaldeans or Assaceni, or Assacani named by Rennell. [6] The כש ks or כסרי ksdi, the Chasdim or רי di כם ks were holy numerators or calculators. Cicero says, that Chaldean implies Sabæan. [7] But I shall presently shew that the word Saba means *wisdom.*

The word Chaldeans is said to be a corruption of the word Chasdim, and this is most clearly the same as the Colida, and Colchida, and Colchis, of Asia, and as the Colidei, and Culdees of Scotland. Now all this, and the circumstances relating to the Chaldees, often called Mathematici, to the Assassins, the Templars, Manichæans, &c., being considered, the name of the Assassins or Hassessins or Assanites or Chasiens [8] or *Alchaschischin* will not be thought unlikely to be a corruption of Chasdim, and to mean Chaldees or Culdees—Culdees at York, a certain class noticed in my *Celtic Druids*—and that they were connected with the Templars. When the Arabic emphatic article AL is taken from this hard word Al-chaschischin it is Chas-chis-chin. The Assassins were also called Druses or Druiseans : in my *Celtic Druids* I have *proved* these Druses to be both Druids and Culdees. In all accounts of the Assassins they are said also to have existed in the East in considerable numbers. They are also stated to have been found numerous by B. De Tudela, [9] not very far from Samarcand or Balk—where he also describes many great tribes of

[1] Foreign Quarterly Review, No. II. p. 471.          [2] Nimrod, Vol. III, p. 493.
[3] Nimrod, Vol. I.          [4] Orig. des Lang. p. 329.          [5] See Duret, p. 328.
[6] Mem. p. 116.          [7] Cleland, Specimen, p. 100.
[8] Vide Benj. Tudela, Ch. vii. note.          [9] Ch. xv.

what he calls *Jews* to live, *speaking the Chaldee language*, occupying the country, and possessing the government of it. He says that among these Jews are disciples of *the wise men*. He says they occupy the mountains of *Haphton.* Here are, I think, the Afghans too clearly to be disputed. Under the word Haphton lies hid the word Afghan, and the disciples of the *wise man Hakem* frequented the temples of Solomon in Cashmere, &c., and were called Hkem-ites, Ishmaelians, and Batteniens, that is, Buddheans, of whom I shall say more presently.

In the students of the College of Cashi or Casi, who spoke Chaldee, I think it probable that we have the Kasideans or Asideans, the word only aspirated, who make a figure in the history of the Temple of Solomon, and of the Jews in the time of the Maccabees, and whose origin has never been satisfactorily accounted for. These Casideans, speaking Chaldee, were the Chaldeans called Chasdim, and it does not seem very unlikely that they may have been a branch more particularly devoted to operative architecture than others of the Chaldeans or Cali-dei. A learned writer in the Edinburgh Encyclopædia says, " The Kasideans were a religious fraternity, or an order of " the *Knights of the Temple of Jerusalem*, who bound themselves to adorn the porches of that " magnificent structure, and to preserve it from injury and decay. This association was com- " posed of the greatest men of Israel, who were distinguished for their charitable and peaceable " dispositions, and by their ardent zeal for the purity and preservation of the temple."[1]

The Cambridge Key[2] says, " He obliged Mahadeva the son of the first created to retire from " the city of Casi or the splendid, and to reside on the Mandara Hill, or Holy Mount. With this " body of evidence before us, we must either reject the Hebrew, or admit the Hindu and Chaldean " account of the Antediluvian world. For this coincidence of dates may be considered mathe- " matical demonstration." Here, I think, in this city of Casi, I have Gaza, or Gazamera or Ajmere, and here I have for the sacred city, the Cyclopæan Mundore of Mewar-Rajahpoutana. There were several Casies, as we have several towns called Universities, as we have others called Colleges.[3] The word college was probably derived from its being the place where the Colidei resided.

It is a very extraordinary thing that the Christian Templars should call themselves Templars in honour of the Temple, the destruction of which all Christians boasted of as a miraculous example of Divine wrath in their favour, as Christians. This goes to prove the Templars much older than the Crusades, and that the pretended origin of these people is totally false. I can entertain little doubt that their origin is be sought in the College of Cashi, and the Temple of Solomon in Cashmere, or the lake or mere of Cashi. I do not think the Calidei had their name from the Chasdim, but the Chasi-dim were Calidei. The Gymnosophists, the Kasideans, the Essenes, the Therapeutæ, the Dionesians, the Eleusinians, the Pythagoreans, the Chaldeans, were in reality all an order of religionists, including among them, and consisting in great part of, an order of Monks, who were, in fact, the heads of the society.

The Teutonic Knights seem to have been the first instituted, but I think it appears that they were grafted upon a class of persons—charitable devotees—who had settled themselves, as the historians say, near the temple at Jerusalem, to assist poor Christian pilgrims who visited it; although the real temple had disappeared, even to the last stone, for a thousand years. This shews how little use these historians make of their understandings. They are said to have come from Germany, from the Teutonic tribes. The word Teut is Tat, and Tat is Buddha. The name of

---

[1] Scaliger de Emend. Temp.; also Eleuch. Trihæresii Nicolai Suranii, Cap. xxii. p. 441; also 1 Maccabees vii. 13; Basnage, Bk. ii. Ch. xiii. Sect. 4; Encyclop. in voce Mason, Sect. xxx.

[2] Vol. I. p. 309.      [3] Cali-age-aji-ai.

Buddha with some of the German nations was Tuisto, and from this came the Teutones, *Teutisci,* and the Teutonic Knights, and the name of Mercury *Teuisco.* [1]

The Knights of St. John are first noticed, as a society, existing near the ancient temple of Jerusalem, when a person called Raymond Dupuis distinguished himself among them. Our superficial historians, who seldom have any taste for deep researches, suppose they arose then, but it requires but little penetration to see that there is no proof whatever that they then arose. At first they were attached to no one of the orders, but were probably (without having the name of Carmelites) of the Essenean or Therapeutic ascetics of Carmel in the West, or Tibet in the East. It is probable that they existed in Jerusalem in the time of its capture by the Saracens. They would be Χρησιανοι or Sophitæ, as were, I do not doubt, the ancient Carmelites.

All temples were surrounded with pillars recording the numbers of the constellations, the signs of the zodiac, or the cycles of the planets, and each templum was supposed in some way to be a microcosm or symbol of the temple of the universe, or of the starry vault called *Templum.* [2] It was this Templum of the universe from which the Knights Templars took their name, and not from the individual temple at Jerusalem, built probably by their predecessors, and destroyed many years before the time allotted for their rise, but which rise, I suspect, was only a revivification from a state of depression, into which they had fallen. I shall return to the explanation of the word templum in a future book.

All the temples were imitative—were microcosms of the celestial Templum—and on this account they were surrounded with pillars recording astronomical subjects, and intended both to do honour to these subjects, and to keep them in perpetual remembrance. We have records of every cycle except of that of the beast 666. We have in Abury the cycles of 650—608—600—60—40—30—19—12, &c. We have the *forty* pillars around the temple of Chilminar, in Persia; [3] the temple at Balbec, with *forty* pillars; [4] the Tucte Solomon, on the frontiers of China, in Tartary, called also the Temple of the *forty pillars.* There is the same number in each, and probably for the same reason. [5] In the Temples at Pæstum, on each side of the Temple *fourteen* pillars record the Egyptian cycle of the dark and light sides of the moon, as described by Plutarch, and the whole thirty-eight, which surround them, record the two Metonic cycles so often found in the Druidical Temples. All temples were originally open at the top; so that twelve pillars curiously described the belt of the zodiac, and the vault of heaven the roof.

Theatres were originally Temples, where the mythos was scenically represented; and, until they were abused, they were intended for nothing else: but it is evident that for this purpose a peculiar construction of the temple was necessary. When Scaurus built a Theatre in Greece he surrounded it with 360 pillars. The Temple at Mecca was surrounded with 360 stones, and in like manner with the same number the Templum at Iona in Scotland was surrounded. The Templars were nothing but one branch of Masons; perhaps a branch to which the care of some peculiar part of Temples was entrusted, and, I think, that the name of Templars was only another name for Casideans.

---

[1] Pownal on Antiquities, p. 29, says, Now Θετlαλια Θατlαλια and Θισσαλια are the same: but T'uat' dale in the Celtic means, relatively speaking, northern district. Will any one deny that Θατlαλια and T'uat'alia are the same? This Tuatalia, which is Thessaly, is *Twasta* the name of Buddha; and, with the *is* added to it, Thessalia, the country where we have found the Indian mythos described so clearly. See Book V. Ch. I. Sect. 2, and Book X. Ch. II. Sect. 11.

[2] Templum is shewn by Cleland to be a Celtic word.     [3] Chardin.     [4] Maundrell.

[5] Forty is one of the most common numbers in the Druidical temples.

In many striking particulars Mr. Von Hammer has shewn the similarity of the Assassins to the Templars, so that they might be mistaken for branches of the same order. It seems very certain too, that they had each a secret doctrine or mystery, which was guarded with the most anxious care, and with the most sacred oaths; and we shall see from circumstances, that this secret was probably the same in the two societies. We must not forget that the Templars were an order which was said to have arisen about the twelfth century,[1] when the Millenium, as we have seen, was daily expected, and that it arose in the country which was a part of that in which the old man of the mountain resided, viz. in the lofty and inaccessible forests of Lebanon, where his followers are now known by the name of Curds, or Culdees, or Druses, treated on in my Celtic Druids. There it is shewn that these Druses still retain the adoration of the golden calf, and have some other religious practices (common to the Israelites in the desert of Sinai) which they are said, in a very unaccountable manner, to mix with both the Mohamedan and Christian doctrines—an extraordinary circumstance, which our travellers, not knowing how to account for, attribute to ignorance, and thus endeavour, with such flimsy pretences, to satisfy their own minds. But though these residents of Mount Carmel (the residence of the Carmelites) may be ignorant now, their religious rites are not the produce of ignorance, but of ancient learning.

7. I will now point out a circumstance certainly true and most extraordinary. The Christian Knights Templars, the enemies of all Mohamedans to the extreme length of being sworn never to make peace with them on any conditions, entered into a conspiracy with these Mohamedan sectaries, Ishmaelites, Battaneans, or Assassins, by which they agreed to betray to them the rich city of Damascus, in return for which the city of Tyre was to have been given up to them. The attempt miscarried, but it proves the connexion between the two bands of fanatics, and fanatics do not often unite except there is something in common in their fanaticism. However, there can be no doubt that there were certain points of religion common to the Ishmaelites, or these Mohamedan sectaries, and to the Templar Christians. These I think could be no other than those for which the Templars were persecuted and destroyed. And if the doctrine of the Gnosis, the Millenium, or of the renewal of cycles, were the foundation of them, as I believe it was, we see at once why they should be of all the three religions. In the time of the illustrious Saladin,[2] the head of the Assassins was called Sinan, and claimed to be, or was said by his followers to be, an incarnation of the Deity. Here we come to the old story. As we have seen, the society, like most others of its kind, had its secret mysteries, guarded by its most solemn oaths; and Mr. Von Hammer, like all other historians of societies of this kind, gives them to us with as much precision as if they were daily proclaimed from the top of the mosque by the crier. I suppose I need not follow him. What they were we can never know: but, from the circumstances or facts which I have described above, I think we have reason to believe, they were all of the same kind as the mysteries of the Millenium, Gnosticism, &c., &c., which I have traced over such a large part of the world, and from such a remote antiquity. And I think my reader now will not be surprised to find this old man of the mountain called by the then singular names, among others, of Ioannes, Butta, and Deus. It was of the first importance to the Templars to possess Tyre instead of Damascus. They would have been separated in Damascus from all their immense estates in Europe; but in Tyre, by means of fleets, they could extend their arms every where.

---

[1] Jerusalem was taken by the Christians in 1099, and retaken by Saladin in 1188. The Knights of St. John are said to have been instituted in 1099, the Templars in 1118, the Teutones in 1164.

[2] In Reinaud's History of the Crusades, p. 320, an account is given of a negociation between Saladin and Richard, when the former demanded the surety of the Templars for the performance of the treaty, which the latter refraining to give, the treaty went off. They would trust the people who were of their own religion.

The Templars had no where possession of a city as a sovereign power, though they had armies. If they had obtained Tyre, they would then have been a sovereign power, with an army of devotees, and fanatical traitors, and immense wealth, in every country of Europe, which the governments dared not to touch. It is quite clear to me that if they had gone on till they got one of their order elected Pope, they would instantly have been sovereigns of Europe, and all the kings their vassals. The Templars possessed 9000 manors in Europe, the Knights of St. John 19,000. [1]

Just now I observed, that the old man of the mountain was called Ioannes, Butta, and Deus, and that one of the names of his people was Battenians ; this, of course, is the same as Buddæans. It is very clear that a close connexion existed between them and the Templars, and we find the Templars adopt for their emblem or distinctive badge, or coat of arms, a very peculiar cross, which is that worn by the Manichæans who were followers, as we are told, of one Buddæus, and also of Thomas of India. The doctrines of the Manichæans are also, in many respects, the same as those of the Assassins and the Templars. This cross is also found to be the emblem of the Buddhists of India. It is of a very peculiar and striking kind; it is red, and is mounted on a Calvary. It is an emblem of the tree of life ; it is the tree *Taranis* of the Druids.

I much doubt the existence of Manes. At all events, if there were such a person, he was an Indian follower of Buddha, or of the Χρης-ism, of the Tamuz, of India, a follower of the God Crisen of the Tam-uls. His sect had a book called the TREASURE or the book of perfection. This was probably an imitation of the Sophi Ibrahim of Persia.

I am not a Masonic Templar, but I have ascertained that one at least of the symbols of the Masonic Templars is the eight-pointed red cross of the Buddhists and the Manichæans. See my figures 12 and 13. This completes the proof that they are a remnant of the same sects or orders of men. When I inquired into the history of the Templars, I said to a brother of the order, If you be a remnant of the ancient oriental philosophers of India, you will have the eight-pointed red cross for your symbol; and I found they had it. I am of opinion that the Templars or Casidæans were resident in the city of Jerusalem when it was taken by the Christians. Perhaps in former times, after the destruction of the temple and the rebuilding of it, or of the present building which stands in its place, they applied their services to the new temple as they had done to the old one, and if they professed the Cabalistic doctrines which I attribute to them, and the doctrines of Sophism which I shall presently explain, there is no inconsistency in their doing so.

If the Knights Templars were converts to the belief that the leader of the Ishmaelites was the tenth Avatar, this accounts for their supporting him against the Caliphs, as well as for their treachery to the Christian cause, of which most certainly they were convicted. They are accused of Manichæism. What did the Manichæan eight-pointed red cross look like? It is an emblem which has no antitype but itself. I consider this eight-pointed red cross as decisive evidence, that Buddhism, Manichæism, and Templism, were identical : that is, Manichæism as far as Manichæism consisted of Gnosticism, for the *principles* of both were the same, though in later times, in some instances, they diverged as from a common centre, as they became corrupted.

8. Faustus is made, by Augustine, most clearly[2] to admit the Triune God in the following words, and thus he connects the Manichæans with the Hindoos : " We therefore worship one " and the same Deity, under a triple appellation of the Father, the God Almighty, and of Christ " his Son, and of the Holy Ghost. Igitur nos Patris quidem Dei omnipotentis, et Christi Filii " ejus, et Spiritûs Sancti, unum idemque sub triplici appellatione colimus numen." When it is

---

[1] Hallam, p. 38.        [2] In Chap. xx. of Oper. Aug. Ben.

4 x

considered that Augustine esteemed a belief in the Trinity to be meritorious, and that he never ceased vilifying the Manichæans, his evidence in this case is unimpeachable. The Manichæans being Trinitarians the only *important* point of heresy which they held, and a most important one it was, consisted in denying the supremacy of the holy see. Had they given up this point, there would have been an instant coalition.

I must now make a few observations, but they will be very few, upon the celebrated doctrine of the good and evil principles, Osiris and Typhon, Oromasdes and Arhimanius. This, I have no doubt, was a doctrine taken up in the countries West of the Indus, when the fine philosophy of the sages of India was beginning to be forgotten; very probably after the time of Cambyses. On this doctrine Mr. Knight says,[1] " The Ægyptians held that there were two opposite powers in " the world, perpetually acting against each other: the one generating and the other destroying: the " former of whom they called Osiris, and the latter Typhon. By the contention of these two, that " mixture of good and evil, of procreation and dissolution, which was thought to constitute the har- " mony of the world, was supposed to be produced." According to this, which was in fact a new system of the Egyptian and Persian doctrine or mythos, there was an original evil principle in na- ture, co-eternal with the good, and acting in perpetual opposition to it. I think this system did not take its rise earlier than about the time of Cyrus or Cambyses. On this Mr. Knight says,[2] " This " opinion owes its origin to a false notion which we are apt to form of good and evil, by con- " sidering them as self-existing, inherent properties, instead of relative modifications dependent " upon circumstances, causes and events: but though patronized by very learned and distinguished " individuals, it does not appear to have formed a part of the religious system of any people or " established sect." Upon the modern date (comparatively speaking) of this doctrine I think Mr. Knight is unquestionably correct; but it may be doubtful if he do not go too far in saying that it never was a part of any religious system. I think he would have been quite correct if he had said, it was never a part of the system of any people until the fine system of the Indians and of Orpheus began to be misunderstood and forgotten.[3] I am of opinion that the system of Orpheus came from or originated in Persia, if it really came from there, *before* the rise of the two principles. This subject opens a most extensive field of discussion, but I shall at the present decline it, resting upon the firm support and authority of Mr. Knight.

It clearly appears that the Manichæans did not, as Christians have asserted, hold the doctrine of two equal and co-eternal Gods. Faustus says, " Is there one God or two? Plainly one. " How then do you (Manichæans) assert two? Never was the name of two Gods heard in our " assertions. But I wish to know whence you suspect this? Because you teach the two princi- " ples of good and evil. It is indeed true that we confess two principles, but one of these we " call God, the other Hyle; or to speak in the common and usual way, the Dæmon. But if you " think that this means two Gods, you might also think that there are two sorts of health when a " physician disputes about health and sickness: and when any one names *good* and *evil* you " might think that there are two goods: and hearing of plenty and want, you will suppose there " are two plenties. But if when I am disputing about black and white, hot and cold, sweet and " bitter, you should say that I shew that there are two whites, and two hots, and two sweets, will " you not appear to be devoid of reason and of unsound head? And thus when I teach two princi- " ples, God and Hyle, I ought not therefore to appear to shew two Gods."[4] It is of no consequence whether the argument put into the mouth of Faustus be absurd or not; the fact

[1] Inq. into Anc. Sym. Lan., Sect. 105.           [2] Ib. 106.
[3] Orpheus, Hymn lxxii. ed. Gesner.              Oper. Aug. Bened. ed. Vol. VIII. Chap. xxi. p. 349.

clearly comes out, that the Manichæans did not receive two equal and opposing principles as the orthodox Christians have calumniously stated them to have done. With respect to the Pantheism of which we have heard so much, I consider that the doctrine of Emanation and Reabsorption into the Supreme, of which I shall have much to say hereafter, is so nearly connected with the Pantheistic doctrine of God in all, and all in God, in their first and most remote principles; that it is almost impossible, perhaps quite impossible, to separate them, and to shew exactly wherein they differ. When they diverge from the common centre, no doubt the difference becomes perceptible enough. But the peculiarity of the nature of the difference in many instances shews the close affinity of their origin. The existence of the early Cabalistic, Gnostic, Mandaistic, and most sublime doctrine, which I shall presently unfold, can be attributed to nothing but a divine revelation, or to a society in a state of refinement, vastly superior to the state of the generality of mankind even at this day, however vain we may be of ourselves; and unless we adopt the doctrine of revelation, in this instance unphilosophical, because unnecessary, to account for an effect, we must admit a long course of generations to have brought this doctrine to its perfection.

In the ancient collections we often meet with a person in the prime of life, sometimes male, sometimes female, killing a young bull. He is generally accompanied with a number of astrological emblems. This Bull was the mediatorial Mithra, slain to make atonement for, and to take away, the sins of the world. This was the God Bull, to whom the prayers are addressed which we find in Bryant and Faber, and in which he is expressly called the Mediator. This is the Bull of Persia, which Sir William Jones and Mr. Faber identify with Buddha or Mahabad. The sacrifice of the Bull, which taketh away the sins of the world, was succeeded by the sacrifice of the Lamb, called by the Brahmins the Yajna, or Agni, or Om-an, sacrifice, or the sacrifice of the Agni or of Fire, by our Indians. This doctrine arose among the Indians in, comparatively speaking, modern times: it was closely connected with the two principles spoken of above. While the Sun was in Taurus, the Bull was slain as the vicarious sacrifice; when it got into Aries, the Ram or Lamb was substituted. The Indian histories say that Zeradust came into India and brought his doctrines thither; but this must have been from North-eastern Persia. I know nothing which he can have brought but this; and if he existed any thing near the date usually assigned to him, though they might have the sacrifice of the Bull as well as the Ram in Persia, he would, for obvious reasons, only bring that of the former into India. Gemshid and the Ram succeeded Aboudab and the Bull. The modern Brahmins, the Cristnuvites, are well known to maintain the doctrine of the Atonement. From them and from the Persians the Christians have copied it. If this heresy cannot be found here, I know not where to look for it. I say *heresy* because I believe it is no part of the doctrine of the Romish or Greek religion. They fortunately know nothing of this *pernicious, demoralizing* dogma—a dogma than which it would be very difficult to devise one more injurious to the morality of a state,—an assertion proved by the examples of the overflowing prisons of Britain, where of late years it has prevailed more than in any former time, or in any other place.

9. The very remarkable circumstance, that Hakem Bemrillah was supposed to be the *tenth* incarnation, tends strongly to confirm my hypothesis; for why should he be the *tenth*; and who and what were the other nine, according to his system? for there must have been other nine, or he could not have been the tenth.[1] I cannot help believing that the whole doctrine was well

---

[1] Vide D'Herbelot in Hakem Bemrillah and in Dararioun, Dict. Biog. Vol. XIX. p. 321, Paris, 1817; Nimrod, Vol. III. p. 493.

known to the persons who held this of the tenth avatar or incarnation.  All this is but the mythos of the ראשית *rasit*, the Mῆτις, or, in a word, divine wisdom, l'Intelligence universelle. [1]

A little time ago I observed that the sacred book of the Manichæans was called the book of Perfection.  Thus it appears to be the same, as the חכמה *hkme* or Aχμή, or PERFECTION, or Wisdom of the Jews and Greeks.  On this word חכמה *hkme* or *Chokme* as, according to the vicious habit of the moderns, it is often written, I must make another observation, which I think very important.  We every where find the words Aρχη and ראשית *rasit* written to represent each other in the two languages ; and they both mean *head* and both mean *wisdom*.  The word חכמה *hkme* means *wisdom*, that is, the same as the two former words : but the word חכמה *hkme*, *Akme*, in the English language, means head, or upper end, or point, or top, of any thing.  In a figurative sense it also has the meaning of perfection.  Hence we see that the word חכמה *hkme*, which means wisdom, has the same meaning as the words in the Greek and Hebrew which mean *first* or *beginning*.  This Rasit or חכמה *hkme* is the בקמאותה *bqmaute* of the Samaritan Genesis, the Ras of the Ethiopians, the Sophia of the Gnostics, the Metis of the Greeks, the Logos of Plato, the Sofi of Persia, in the book of the Persians called Sofi Ibrahim, the Buddha of the Hindoos, the Saga of the Scandinavians, and the Sagax of the Latins, whence come our Sages, and the Sagas of India, alluded to by Mr. Schegel. [2]

Perhaps it may not be irrelevant, in reference to the plurality of the God in the first verse of Genesis, to observe, that the Gnostics are said to have worshiped a being called Achamoth.  This is evidently nothing but the Hebrew word חכמה *Hkme* wisdom, sapientia, in the plural number, and it is feminine.  This is the first word in Genesis, as we have seen, and as recorded by the Jerusalem Targum, and the Samaritan version ; and here I conceive these learned Orientalists, the Gnostics, worshiped the plural of the Logos for the *whole three*.  If this be not the meaning, why is not the word in the singular ?  For this Achomoth the Valentinians had a great respect.  Of this Beausobre says, " Leur *Achamoth* est la *Cochmah* des Hebreux, ou la *Sagesse*." [3]  It proves that the Valentinians explained Genesis *by wisdom*, &c., like all other early Christians, and as the Israelites formerly did.  Gnostici enim ipsam *Achamoth* spiritum sanctum arbitrabantur, et sub specie columbæ repræsentabant.

The unlearned reader must be informed that the most common word in Hebrew for wisdom is חכמה *hkme*, and for wisdoms in the feminine gender *plural* חבמות *hkmut*.  The following are the two first words in the Samaritan first verse of Genesis : ꙄꙀ꙰ꙄꙆꙊꙎꙄ.  *B—kmaute*.  Though I have no Samaritan Lexicon, I think I can see that B is the sign of the ablative case, the same as in the Hebrew language, and the last *e* the emphatic article, and *kmaut* the same as the Hebrew

---

[1] Besides this Bemrillah, in the eleventh and twelfth centuries, and indeed since that time several persons have arisen, pretending to be the *tenth* incarnation ; a curious account of whom may be found in the very learned and honest, however often mistaken, Nimrod.  Eudes of Bretagne was one ; Joan D'Arc was another ; and Brothers and Southcote were others ; intended for the year 1800, or the year 1824, or the third cycle from Christ.  In Ireland, in the year 1771, a Romish Priest, Vicar Apostolic of the Roman See in the midland district of England, of the name of Walmesley, under the feigned name of Pastorini, published an Exposition of the Apocalypse, in which he made out, by some mode of calculation which I have never been able to see, that the millenium would take place at the end of the year 1824.  Here we have exactly three great Neroses to a year, from the birth of Christ.  Some time after the year 1824 had passed, his followers found out that it was a typographical mistake, and that it ought to be 1829, and, to the credit of the Roman bishop, they say, it or he only alluded to the peace which was to be given to the Irish Romish Church by the Duke of Wellington's famous Emancipation Bill in 1829.  Thus priests deceive, and dupes are deceived.  See Times newspaper, for a letter from Dublin, dated April 24th, 1829.

[2] Quoted by Dr. Pritchard.          [3] Hist. Manich. Liv. iv. Ch. i.

word for *wisdom* in the plural feminine : then it will be *by the wisdoms* God created. Thus then the old Samaritan justifies my rendering of Rasit.

Philo calls the Logos Αρχη.[1] The Logos being proved to be *wisdom*, Αρχη must consequently mean wisdom.[2] Onkelos translates the word by אמר *amr* verbum,[3] whence comes the word מימרא *mimra*, a *word* or *voice*, which I suppose is the same as the Bathkol בחתקל *bet-ql, daughter of voice*. As the Hebrew name for God, AL, is said to have the meaning of *curse*, so QL has the meaning of *vile*. These arise from the misunderstood idea of the destroyer. The Amar,[4] Mimra, and Bathkol, have all the meaning of Logos and Ras. From this word QL *voice*, comes the Greek καλεω and English *call*, which Mr. Cleland has shewn has the meaning of *wisdom* in the Celtic language : whence comes our word calling or vocation, both evidently connected with the idea of voice, word, and wisdom.[5] The Nestorians have their service in the Chaldean tongue.[6] Nestorius was a German in the time of Theodosius. This brings to my recollection the assertion of Dr. Geddes, that he would some day prove, that the language of the Saxons (that is, the Sacæ, Buddha was Saca) was nearly pure Hebrew. Here a reason presents itself why we have so many Hebrew words in English. When the Saxons arrived in Britain they must have spoken almost the same language as the natives. I recollect nothing in history against this conclusion. I shall have much to say on this subject hereafter. QL has also, I think, the meaning of *womb* κοιλια, and thus of the female generative power, the daughter of the Logos or of Wisdom, and also of the Greek καλος, *good* or *beautiful*. *Jehovah by wisdom hath founded the earth, by* (Binah) *understanding hath he established the heavens.* Prov. iii. 19. The Targum also uses the word קדם *qdm* for the Logos or Ras, which means *first*, and Binah for the following word, which means *second*, from *bis, binus*, διδυμος.

Proclus, on the Timæus, says, that after the well-known sentence on the temple of Isis were added the words ὁν εγω καρπον ετεκον, ἡλιος εγενετο—*The fruit which I have brought forth is the sun.* This at once proves that Isis was Divine Wisdom, and that the sun was not adored as the Creator, but only as an emblem.

Athenæ is only Neithe or Neitha, written anagrammatically, or Hebraically a very little corrupted. Isis was called Neith or wisdom : she was the Goddess of Sais, which probably means Saviour, from ישע *iso* and ζαω, and also wisdom from scio *to know* or *be wise*. Wisdom was the Saviour ; thus they all dovetail into one another.

The term Sofi,[7] says Knolles, signifies among these people *a wise man*, or the interpreter of the Gods. This word is the same as the Greek Σοφια.[8] Forster afterward says, " Some classes " of the Shiahs believe that Ali was an incarnation of the Deity, who perceiving, they say, the " mission which had been delegated on Mohamed to be *incomplete*, assumed the person of this " Caliph, for the purpose of fixing the Moslem faith and power on a firmer basis." [9] Here, again, the doctrines of the tenth incarnation, the regeneration, and metempsychosis, shew themselves ;

---

[1] De Confus. Ling. p. 267. B.          [2] Maur. Ind. Ant. Vol. IV. pp. 94, 95.

[3] From the close connexion between the Logos and the Lamb, lambs came to be called אמרות *amrut*.

[4] Qy. Rama?

[5] The absolute identity of the Celtic and the Hebrew has been maintained, at great length, in the Universal History, in Vol. XVIII. p. 363, Vol. V. p. 411 ; see also Dissert. on Hist. of Ireland, Dublin, 1753, p. 48.

[6] Sandys' Travels, p. 135.

[7] Given to a man called Ishmael, who was, I think, the ancestor of the Battaneans.

[8] Forster's Travels, Vol. II. p. 127.          [9] Ibid. p. 130.

but the time of the tenth incarnation being passed, the perpetual renewal or regeneration, like those of Tibet and Rome, is beginning to arise ; and I think it very probable that the perpetual renewal of Tibet arose only since about A. D. 1200.

The mission of Mohamed was not complete, because it would not be completed till the end of his cycle, when the Millenium commenced. In the Indian books we read accounts of princes being extremely desirous of establishing æras by their names. This has been mistaken, I think. They wished to establish themselves as incarnations of the cycle in which they lived, as Cæsar and several others did. The sixty year or Vrihaspati cycle was only a decimal of the 600 year or Neros cycle, and it made no difference in calculation whether one or the other was used—ten Vrihaspatis being equal to one Neros.

Of the different dreams which have terrified the imaginations of the weaker class of mankind, there is, perhaps, no one which has played a greater game than that of the fear of Antichrist, a person whom I believe to have been pretty generally misunderstood. The word Αντιχρησος I believe does not mean a person opposed to Christ, but a substitute for Christ—another Christ, a Christ in succession. In our sacred books the disciples are constantly warned against false Christs, but no where is it said that there shall not be another Christ. This is all in unison with the prophecy in John, that Jesus would send a person to them in some capacity or other. Mohamed was believed to be this Antichrist, and so was both Hakim Bemrillah and St. Francis. It is, as I have said before, nothing but the Hindoo system, each party believing that the tenth incarnation was with them. The circumstance that an Antichrist or another Christ should be foretold is very curious, and certainly Floyer and several other Christians have shewn a striking similarity between the prophecies of the Christians and Mohamed : but they never discover that this arises, in a great measure, from Mohamedan devotees doing every thing in their power to aid the Christians, as they hold that Mohamed was the real Antichrist—the person foretold by John.

10. The Templars were accused of worshiping a being called Bahúmíd, and Bafomet, or Kharuf. Mr. Hammer[1] says that this word written in Arabic has the meaning of Calf, and is what Kircher calls *Anima Mundi*. It is difficult not to believe that this Kharuf is our Calf. Bahúmíd must be Pi the Egyptian emphatic article, and אמיד *amid* the *desire of all nations*, that is Mohamed. The Assassins, we must recollect, are said to have worshiped a calf, but our travellers who tell us this story, do not tell us that they saw the calf, and it is easy to perceive that they take the account, as well as the custom of the Assassins *of rising up to play*,[2] as our Bible would call it, from their Mohamedan enemies. If they have a calf in use as an emblem, I should consider it a proof that they are a tribe of extreme antiquity, which though holding the doctrines of the ten incarnations, yet still clings to the ancient worship of Taurus. It is of the same nature as the picture in Russia of the holy family in which the calf is found instead of the Ram.

They often name a rite or doctrine called the Baptism of Wisdom. This has been said to be the meaning of the second word Bafomet, and is from the Greek Βαφη Μητεος.

The story of the Gnostics and Templars worshiping an IDOL called Bafomet and Bahúmíd in the sense in which we commonly use the word *worship*, I look upon as totally incredible. But Protestants always forget or shut their eyes to the distinction between the Δελεια and Λατρεια. If they had a figure as an effigy of the Βαφη Μητεος, baptism of wisdom, they probably paid it the same kind of adoration as Protestants pay to the bread and wine in the Eucharist, and as our king pays to the black stone on which he sits to be crowned. It is very clear that this Bafomet is the Logos, to which they gave this name—the second person of the Trinity. However, the

---

[1] On Anc. Alp. Præf. p. xiii.          [2] Exod. xxxii. 6.

circumstances altogether raise a strong probability, that the doctrines of the Assassins and the Templars were the same.

In the fourth number of the Foreign Quarterly Review, published by Treutel and Wurtz, may be found a very interesting account of the Templars, though I think not a correct one ; for, upon their innocence of Gnosticism, there are several things totally unaccountable. But of their crimes, to the extent charged, I do not believe a single word. Their βαφη μητεος, or baptism of wisdom, I do believe, and that out of it was probably formed, by their enemies, their Bafomet, the name of the image they were calumniously said to have worshiped, and which is alleged to be a corruption of Mohamed, or meant for Mohamed, which, if true, as I allege, must have been meant for the last incarnation of divine wisdom, until the failure of the Millenium proved that he might have been an impostor or fanatic, but no incarnation of divine wisdom—of the Deity.

The truth creeps from under the veil, in the instance of the symbol of the Red-cross Knights Templars. Their badge, the red cross with EIGHT POINTS, the monogram of the Buddhists of Tibet and of the Manichæans[1] connect beautifully. This badge was a real Talisman. In peace it commanded the rights of hospitality. In battle one red cross would, of course, never strike another ; though they might, as in the case of the Ishmaelians and the Templars, from circumstances be obliged to oppose each other.

The revenues of the Templars in the twelfth century are said to have amounted to six million pounds sterling a year. Notwithstanding this immense wealth, it is very certain that *their chiefs* were repeatedly guilty of betraying the Christian cause to the Assassins, and to account for this, in one instance, a very miserable pittance of money is stated to have been the reward, 3000 pieces of gold. This I cannot believe of a man of such immense wealth as their chief. On taking the vows they took the most solemn oaths of fidelity to the Christian cause, but they took them as administered to one another, and in the sense which they alone might understand. How is all this apparent contradiction to be reconciled ? I believe they took their oaths to the cause of the Χρηςος, the Chreestian cause, and that if a small body of the Knights separated from the Hospitallers to form the order of Templars of the Temple, of the ancient *circular* or cyclar temples, not of the church, (their churches differing from all other churches in the world in being of the circular form,) they had become proselytes to or were of an opinion in its nature Manichæan, that Hakem Bemrillah was, as he was claimed by his followers to be, the tenth avatar—they were believers in some sense in the Evangelium Eternum, and thus they continued to be till the passing years proved the falsity of their system, as well as that of the Franciscans. Then, though they probably abandoned the Millenium, they retained part of their Manichæan or Gnostic doctrines. Thus with the Assassins they were enemies of the Caliphs, though in some sense Mohamedan ; and, though friends to the Mohamedan Ishmaelites, they were still Christians, but it was the Gnostic Christianity, which was in fact the oriental Buddhism of the ancient Gymnosophistæ or Samaneans, of which we shall presently see more.

The Templars were divided into orders exactly after the system of the Assassins : Knights, Esquires, and lay brethren, answering to the Refeck, Fedavee, and Laseek, of the Assassins ; as the *Prior, Grand Prior,* and *Grand Master,* of the former, correspond with the *Dai, Dai-ul-kebir,* and *Sheik* of the mountain, of the latter. As the Ishmaelite Refeck was *clad in white,* with a *red mark of distinction,* so the Knight of the Temple wore a white mantle adorned with a red mark of distinction—the red cross. It is probable that the red cross was worn by both,[2] though for *some reason* it is kept back. The author says, " As the Ishmaelite Refeck was clad in white, *with a*

---

[1] Vol. X. Asiatic Researches.     [2] Foreign Quarterly Review, No. II. p. 464.

" *red mark of distinction*, so the Knight of the Temple wore a white mantle adorned with the red " cross." It is remarkable that they were called illuminators ;[1] and I suspect *the red mark of distinction* not described was a red eight-point cross, or a red rose on a cross. Why has not the Reviewer told us what it was ?

In the very highest orders of Freemasons, viz. the Templars and Rossicrucians, as I imagine them to be, there is no emblem more sacred than the cross. Here I stop. Verbum Sapienti.

Mr. Hammer has observed, that the identity of the symbols of the Templars and of the Architectonici, by whom he means the Freemasons, are demonstrated. But he does not doubt that the Architectonici existed before the Templars : he says, Doctrinæ Architectonicæ symbola, figuræ nimirum mathematicæ et instrumenta ædificatoria, quæ in picturis ecclesiæ Templariorum et in sculpturis Baphometorum invenimus, eadem etiam in ædificiis antiquioribus, præcipue Scoticis, et in monumentis Gnosticis ut in sigillis et Abraxis conspiciuntur (vide Icones ex Macario desumptas, et in ornatum frontispicii libri sui à Nicolaio adhibitas); sed eadem jam in monumentis vetustioris adhuc ævi, nimirum Romanis deprehenduntur (vide tabula IV. fig. 9, in my figures, No. 33) ex quorum inscriptionibus nihil arguere licet, hæc monumenta ab architectis aut fabris murariis posita fuisse.[2]   Again he says, Senatus consulto (irrito) urbe pulsos, et ex his ad orientalem Philosophiam, Chaldaicam, Syriacam, et Egyptiacam, referre licebit. Here Mr. Hammer refers the Mathematicians to a Chaldaic original. In the former part of the sentence he had identified the Mathematicians and the Architecti or Freemasons. In this I think he is perfectly correct. The Chaldeans and the Mathematicians of whom we read in the Augustin age as being the fortune-tellers, or the magicians, or judicial astrologers of the great men of the day in Rome, were in fact Freemasons, and of this the emblems, above copied from his work, in plate IV., are a sufficient proof. I need not tell any one, *whether Mason or not*, how large a space the history of the building of the temple of Solomon occupies in the ceremonies of Masonry. And I think I need not remind my reader that the temple of Solomon, with its Jakim and Boaz, displays evident marks of Astrology and Astronomy in every part. All the sacred numbers, and these astronomical symbols, relate directly to the building of *the temple of the universe*. The whole temple is a microcosm or an emblem of the universe, and the history of the building of it is a Genesis : and under the allegory, a beautiful and refined cosmogony is concealed.

In the building of the temple of Solomon the most profound silence prevailed ; not a nail was driven, not a blow was struck. As the Creator built up the edifice of the world from matter previously prepared, so in like manner was every thing prepared in the temple. Wisdom, the Logos, was the Megalhistor or Grand Architect of the Universe. Solomon THE WISE was the Grand Architect of the Microcosm of the temple. The architect or builder of the universe was the Logos, the Prince of Peace. The architect or builder of the temple, was Solomon, the prince of Iero-Salem or *the holy peace*. By his Logos, word, or command, God formed the world. By his word, without a blow of hammer, Solomon formed the temple. Dominus in Sapientiâ fundavit terram; disposuit cœlos in Intelligentiâ. Prov. iii. 19.

In the Wisdom of Solomon and Ecclesiasticus the secret doctrine of the Ras, or Wisdom, or Logos, that is, of the Cabala and the Gnosis, is continually shewing itself :[3] though there can be no doubt that the intention of the *translators* is to conceal it as much as possible. Perhaps they did not understand the Cabalistic doctrine. I think I cannot well wish for a more decisive proof of the truth of my system than that Solomon should be a ten-month child like Hercules, Alexander, Cæsar, &c., &c., as is proved by Wisd. vii. 2. The knowledge of the doctrine of the cycles and of the aberrations of the planets is shewn ch. vii. vers. 18, 19.

---

[1] Foreign Quarterly Review, No. II. p. 464.          [2] P. 43.          [3] Wisdom i. 6, iv. 9, 10, &c.

In every quarter of the globe we have met with a curious repetition of names. We have numerous river Dons, Jordans, mounts Olympus, Argo, &c. ; and if we consider them attentively, I think we shall see reason to believe, that this was in consequence of each tribe, when it became fixed, having established around.it its own little mythos which it had brought from the East : its sacred mount, its Argo, its Don, its Labyrinth perhaps, &c. Thus when the Mandaites or the Nousaïreans, in comparatively-speaking modern times, arrived in Syria, they found the mount Carmel, the mount of the garden of God, the sacred Ir-don, the city of Nazareth, &c. I strongly suspect that those persons were only descendants, or a succession of the first Mandaites or Nousaïreans or Nazareans, driven out from the city of the Cyclopæan Mundore when it was destroyed, and of which there still are the immense ruins. The Ishmaelians were a succession of the same people. An attentive observer cannot fail to see the same mythos under a succession of leaders, perhaps all having the similar doctrine of incarnations, but under different names, and necessarily with some variations. When I consider all the circumstances relating to Elias—his great miracles when he overcame the priests of Baal—the numerous circumstances which tend to prove Nazareth a sacred place, and the laws respecting Nazarites, the rose of Sharon being called Nazir, the schools of the prophets which were on the mount of Carmel or the vineyard of God, I cannot help suspecting that these Nazareans were the same with the Mandaites, who were called Nousaïreans.[1] The Arabic Nuzur means prophet.

I had long sought in vain for the meaning of the word Don, which, from its universality, is evidently a word of great importance in my system, when I found it in Persia. Dr. Hagar says that the Persian name for science or knowledge, which I call wisdom, is Danush.[2] Whence comes the Persian word Behar-danush, or the garden of knowledge. This garden of Danush is the garden of Adonis.[3] The river Araxes, we have formerly seen, was called Don. This river was anciently called by the Arabians, Rosh. This is Ras or Wisdom. A translation of the word Dan.[4] Arax is probably only Ras with the emphatic article. The ancient name of the Persian Ispahan As-padana exhibits the same mythos, as that of the Padus of India and Italy. I am satisfied that Pad and Bud were the same words, and as Dón in ancient Persian meant wisdom, this seems confirmed. I have little doubt that the Druidical colleges in groves were gardens of Adonis, like our universities, intended to educate young persons in science as well as religion, and therefore represented by other sects as receptacles of vice. But they might be, like our universities, not too good. Dr. Hagar also says, " Dana in Persian signifies a " wise or learned man." [5] This, he adds, is derived; that is, it is the same as the Chaldaic אנת tna, a learned man. From this comes the word Titans. They were Tat-tans. Tat-tan is the wisdom of Buddha ; and from this word tana, wise, came the name of the laws which the Irish boast of so much for their wisdom, and which they call the laws of Tanistry. The Persians also have the word Danish-MEND which has the same meaning (this, I think, is learned mind or man). The Hindoos of Bengal and Bombay use the word Danish-MEND in the same sense.

A little consideration will serve to shew that in every case Menu has a reference to mind, to understanding, to wisdom. Here we at last come to the origin of the word Man and Homo, hominis and Nemo, neminis, i. e. ne-homo. Man is the Mn of Om homan, or human. Inhuman is the negative of human. The Mend of Persia is Mn-di holy Mn Om-mannus, mind of Om. In

---

[1] Matter, Vol. II. p. 394.  [2] Diss. on Bab. Bricks, p. 7.

[3] In Western Syria is a river of Adonis ; this is now called the river of Abraham or of Brahma. This seems to me a striking circumstance, when I recollect that there is a city of Adonis in Collida, in South India.

[4] Paxton, Illust. of Scrip. Vol. I. p. 73.  [5] P. 22.

Irish Om means *man*, Omona *human*.[1]  Vossius, Scaliger, and others, derive the Amanus or Omanos of the Persians from חום *hum* Chom, Calor; unde חמה *hme*, Sol et Ignis.[2]  There can be no doubt that they are the same words.  If we look back to Bk. V. Chap. V. Sect. 2, we shall find that Noah is called ענהמני *inhmni*.  I have never been satisfied with the etymon which I have there given.  In the first word ני *in* or *ini* we have the Greek word for a son.  A prophet in India is called a Muni or wise man.  This seems to be the same as Menu.  And hence I think has come our Nh *mind*, the son of the Muni.  Noah was an Avatar or renewed incarnation.  Mannus a man, name of Noah.[3]  Mind and Man were, in fact, the same.  Man was an incarnation of the holy mind, Mn-di=Mn=650.  The root, *Man*, think, remember, makes in the preterite Mamana corresponding with *Meminit*.  From this root comes Mana, mens, mind.  The name of the first human being Manu is obviously derived from this root, and signifies *endowed with reason*.  Mankind are hence named Manava—a man, son of Manu; this word being the regular patronymic of Manu.  From this word the Gothic word Manu is manifestly derived, but the Germans appear to have retained some tradition of Manu himself.  Tacitus says of the Germans, celebrant carminibus antiquis Tuistonem deum terra editum et filium Mannum originem gentis conditoresque.[4]

The Mandaites taught that from the throne of God flowed a *Jourdain primitif*, of the pure water of life, from which again flowed 360,000 Jourdains.  When we consider the proof which I have given that the Jordan only meant the river of wisdom or of Adonis or of the sun, the meaning of this will be sufficiently clear.  The observation above induces Mons. Matter to make the following curious observation, which shews that without my theory the facts upon which I have founded it forced themselves upon him : " Le nom de Manes, Mani ou Manitho, reçoit peut-être ici son ex-" plication.  Il s'appellait Mano, intelligence de lumière, comme Simon le magicien se disait " δυναμις ὑψιςου.  Peut-être un jour nous parviendrons à savoir si Manes a fait desemprunts " aux Mandaïtes, ou si ces derniers furent en quelque chose ses disciples :  Il est vrai que les " Mandaïtes, sont les ennemis des Manichéens ; mais ils sont également ceux des Chrétiens et des " Juifs, et ils profitent neanmoins des doctrines des uns et des autres."[5]

Carcham, so celebrated in the history of Mani, is called Syria and Mesopotamia by the Tartars.  Kar means *habitable country*  Then I think this would be Kar חכם *hkm*, country of wisdom, country of Mani or Mens. *Mind.*  Georgius says of this Carcham, Hoc est Regio μεση των τοταμων inter-amnia.[6]  He afterward[7] shews that this is the same as Cataia (now Cuthay), and says, Quidam autem Kathaiam Sophitis regionem, qui unus fuit ex nomarchis in hâc Mesopotamiâ collocarunt.  This was the Doab between the Indus and Ganges, which he calls Soph-itis or the country of Wisdom.  It was the Ioud-ia or Youdya or Oude.

The Mogul was the Irish Mog or Mogh ; and the Mogh was the head priest—chief priest.  Zoroaster or Zeradust was an incarnation, a genius of a cycle.  He was called Hakem,[8] and also Mog or Mogh, which meant Sapientia.  He predicted the Messiah[9] by the name Iosa, in Irish Eesa, in Arabic Issa.  He came from the city of Bochara or of wisdom or of learning or of the Boc or Book.  But whence comes the word Mogh?  The word *ogh* in Irish means circle, pure, holy, a hero, and *eag* wisdom ;[10] the same in the Sanscrit, and the Sanscrit Yug or Yog.  Now I think Mogh is the wisdom or cycle of *M :* then, by the regimine, it became Mogh.  The highest noble

[1] Vall. Coll. Hib. Vol. V. p. 67.                    [2] Ibid. Vol. IV. p. 508.

[3] Introd. to Webster's Dictionary, p. i. note.

[4] Edinburgh Review, of Dr. Wilkins's Arabic Dictionary.          [5] Matter sur Gnost. Vol. II. p. 405.

[6] Sect. cxvi.              [7] In Sect. cxvii.              [8] Vall. Coll. Hib. Vol. IV. Pt. i. p. 197.

[9] Vall. Coll. Hib. Vol. IV. Pt. i. pp. 199, 202.              [10] Ibid. p. 82.

and prime minister of the Mogul was made by him an Omrah, *Om-ray*.[1]  The Eesa named above
is the Etruscan Esar Æsar and Cæsar, the Brahmin Eeswar.[2]  Among the Irish[3] and Persians[4]
Mogh was equally the name of a priest, and hence Mogul-al-mogh, *the priest* κατ᾽ εξοχην. Here
we have the origin of the wood, with which the sacred part of the temple of Jerusalem was built,
Almug. It was the wood of אל מג *al mg*, the tree of wisdom, the tree of the Magus or wise man.
The Chaldæans have the word מג *mg*, whence the Greeks made Μαγος.[5]

The Ishmaelites are the same, I believe, as the Nasareens or Nasourians, or Nesseenes or Nes-
saries, and the Yezeedis or Yezidis or Yesdes. Mr. Buckingham has observed their similarity to
one another and to the Hindoo castes.[6]  The Yezdes or in fact Yes-des, that is, the followers of
the holy Yęs or IHS = 608, are said to worship Satan or Sheitan. Mr. Buckingham gives an
account of them from one Père Garzoni, who says of them, Ils n'ont ni jeûnes, ni prières ;
et disent, pour justifier l'omission de ces œuvres de religion, que le scheikh Yézid a satisfait
pour tous ceux qui feront profession de sa doctrine jusqu'à la fin du monde.[7]  The judgment
of the father and the dependance to be placed on him, may be estimated from the following
passage, which he gives a little previously : Le matin, à peine le soleil commence-t-il à
paroître, qu'ils se jettent à genoux les pieds nus, et que tournes vers cet astre, ils se mettent in
adoration, le front contre terre. These people are found at present in the Mesopotamia of the
Euphrates, near a place called RAS-EL-AIN, (the fountain of *wisdom*,) at the foot of what Mr.
Buckingham calls Mount Sinjar, and Ptolemy Mount Masius, in about lat. 37¼, on the river
Khaboor or Chaboras. Garzoni says, they hold that the devil whom they worship *has resided* in
Moses, Jesus, and Mohamed ; that the devil has no name in their language, but " Ils se servent
" tout au plus pour le désigner de cette périphrase, *scheikh mazen*, le grand chef."[8]  I have a
strong suspicion that these dwellers at the RAS-EL-AIN, call their chief Scheikh *Raz-en*, not
*Maz-en ;* and that the latter is a mistake ; or M-Raz-en has become Mazen. They are a very
large and powerful tribe. In their country a Chalchos, an Houran, or Urriana are found, and in
short the evident remains of the Chaldean mythos. In their doctrine the renewed incarnation in
Moses, Jesus, and Mohamed, is obvious ; and the creative and destructive power confounded by
them or by Garzoni. In lat. about 35¼ is a Sulimania, and near it is a Jebel Judee.[9]

In the language of the Yezeedis *Yesdan* means *God*, and it makes Yesdam in the plural.[10]  This
is evidently a Hebrew termination. The author of the Desatir calls God *Yesdan*. This raises a
presumption that he was of this tribe—Yes-dan, Wisdom, of YES, or ΥΗΣ.

11. Cleland states the adherents of Druidism to have had various names, *Guydelians*, *Pauli-
cians*, *Manichæans*, *Leogrians*, *Oughers*,[11] May's-ons, besides others. But as the word May's-on
is here the particular object of inquiry, I shall confine myself principally to it ; and even upon
that, without pushing the analysis lower, I shall only observe that, in the sense of the bough, or

---

[1] Vall. Coll. Hib. Vol. IV. Pt. i. pp. 34, 35.   [2] Ibid. p. 81.   [3] Ibid.
[4] Hyde, de Rel. Vet. Pers. p. 357.   [5] Ibid. p. 242.
[6] Travels in Mesopotamia, 8vo., Vol. I. p. 210.   [7] P. 212.   [8] Ibid.
[9] Buckingham, p. 474.   [10] Ibid. Vol. II. p. 109.

[11] The word Paganus derives from Payen : this answers to our old word Paynim ; which meant a worshiper of the
May ; a Payinhom, or as the labials P and M frequently convert, a *Maymhom*, *May's-hom*, or *Mason*, words not more
essentially different than Henriques Kenrick, Henry Harry, which are at bottom all the same name. The festival
Mauime, in Syria, near Gaza, abolished by Arcadius, and said to have taken its name from a country village, was more
likely a *May-festival*, or *Mai-chomme* instituted there by some of the Northern military in the service of Constantine.
This, however, is only a slight conjecture. Cleland's Attempt to restore Celtic Lit. p. 121.

office of justice, (the thyrsus or the wand of the Magician or Druid which Cleland shews to have been identical,) the word-May is primitive to the month of May, to Maia the Goddess of Justice, to Majestas, and to the proper name among the Romans, of *Maius*, *Mágus* or *Majus*. Considering too, that the May (May Pole) was eminently the great sign of Druidism, as the Cross was of Christianity, is there any thing forced or far-fetched in the conjecture, that the adherents of Druidism should take the name of *Men of the May*, or May's-ons? Here the *on* stands for *homme*, as it does in the very politest French to this day, *on dit* for *homme dit* ; or, as anciently, *Preudon* for Preud-homme, as may be seen on the tomb of one of the high constables of France.[1]

Free Mason is PH-RE—PH the Coptic emphatic article and *re* the sun, Mason of the sun. Re is roi, rex, rai, ray, whence Ph-aroah. Cleland observes[2] that the Druids taught the doctrines of an overruling providence, and the immortality of the soul : that they had also their Lent, their Purgatory, their Paradise, their Hell, their Sanctuaries, *and the similitude of the May Pole* IN FORM TO THE CROSS,[3] &c., &c.

From Cleland I learn that in Celtic Sab means *wise*, whence Saba and Sabaśius, no doubt wise in the stars. From this comes the Sab-bath or day dedicated to Wisdom, and the Sabbat, a species of French Masonry,[4] an account of which may be seen in Dulaure's History of Paris.[5] Sunday was the day of instruction of the Druids, whence it was called Sabs, from the preachment of the Sabs or Sages or Wise, Sagart sacerdos.[6]

The discovery of this meaning in the word Sab, supplies a link which seemed wanting in the chain. And I now beg my reader, by means of the index, to review and to reconsider the different passages where the word Sabæan or Saba is used, and he will instantly see how it supports my system in several cases. A practice in the French schools supplies a good commentary upon this. They had Theses performed for the exercise of the wisdom or understanding of the pupils, called Sabbatines : but they had nothing to do with the Sunday, they were not performed on the Sabbath, but on *any* day. The day sacred to *divine wisdom* was the day of *Sab*, and as it was a day of rest the word *Sab* came to mean *rest*. And as the planetary bodies were endowed with wisdom, the disposers of the affairs of men, they were Sab, in the plural Sabaoat, our *Sabaoth.*

Mr. Hammer, to a certain extent, does not err very much in his explanation of Gnosticism : Tota gnoseos doctrina, ut vidimus circa duo præcipue puncta versatur, Cosmogoniam nempe et Genesin, ut, quod mortalibus scire haud datum esse videtur, quomodo mundus hic genitus sit, et quomodo per Genesin continuam conservetur, indagaretur.

Of the earliest well-recorded Lodge of Freemasons which I have met with, Mr. Hammer gives the following very interesting account : Majorem merentur fidem, quæ de prima ædis architectonica seu *domus salomonicæ* institutione ex historicis arabicis referimus, et cum nullum testimonium historicum nobis innotuerit, quod melius instituto architectonico congruat, *ædem* illam *sapientiæ (Darol-hikmet)* quam *Hakemus* in fine sæculi undecimi Cahiræ fundavit, reveram primam εταιϱιαν *(Lodge)* architectonicam fuisse credimus, quam historiæ testentur. Erat autem hæc ædes sapientiæ (ut ex *Macrisio* discimus) academia quædam, in qua ad ostentum omnes Philosophiæ et Mathesios præcepta tradebantur regalibus divitiis aucta, et frequens studiosorum omnis

---

[1] Cleland's Attempt to revive Celtic Lit. p. 122.      [2] Ibid. p. 102.

L'Escalopier suggests a curious etymological conjecture. His words are these : Pro Heso, quidem Hëum, nonnulli Esum sine aspiratione substituunt, vel Jesum sub Hesi nomine cultum volunt futili commento. Cap. v. Cleland, ib p. 103. He observes that Kruys means a cross in the Celtic tongue.

[4] P. 44.      [5] Vol. VIII. p. 90.      [6] Clel. Spec. p. 95.

generis, et sexus catervis.   Præter hanc autem publicam doctrinam arcana etiam ibidem disciplina vigebat, cujus varii erant gradus, per quos candidatus deductus, in ultimo *nihil credere et omnia facere licere* docebatur. [1]   Now I beg my reader to observe, that this Lodge of Freemasons was called the Lodge of SOLOMON or of *wisdom*, and that it was founded by the Battanean (query Buddæan, Ishmaelian Hakem, *i. e.* חכם *Hkm* or the *wise*, and that it taught the mathematics, and besides this that *certain secret doctrines* were taught there, and, among other things, it was taught *nihil credere*.    Now, Mr. Hammer's object being to run down the Masons and Carbonari in every possible way, I consider a little before I construe these words, and I go to the authority of Faustus, of the Manichæan, for an explanation, as I find it was also their doctrine, according to the account of their enemies ; but I find they say it was *nihil credere, except after careful examination*, and unless it was consistent with the moral attributes of God, and the moral fitness of things ; and they severely censured the Papists for believing without inquiring or using their understandings.   The next words *omnia facere licere*, must in a similar manner be qualified.   As they are given without qualification, they are most clearly nothing but a repetition of one of the old calumnies propagated against the Gnostics 1500 years ago, and repeated by the Rev. Mr. Reeves in the last century,—such as that ALL heretics eat children. [2]

In the school of Hakem, at Cairo, (what does the word *Cairo* mean, and how ought it to be spelt ?) we readily recognise the school of Pythagoras, with its secret numbers and its mathesios, which in a later day was succeeded by the Esseniens.

The striking similarity between Masonry and Pythagoreanism has been well pointed out by Mr. Clinch in his Essays on Masonry. [3]   The best account of Masonry which I have seen is in the Encyclopædia Londinensis in voce Masonry : though, as every Mason must see, it is not correct, and particularly respecting the York Masons.

I think it may be discerned that there were formerly several lodges of Freemasons in Britain, whose origin cannot be traced : but perfectly independent of each other, though now united under one head, the Duke of Sussex—the old Lodge at York, now extinct, being clearly the oldest, as far as can be traced.

The Chaldeans are found in Scotland, under the name of Culdees or Chaldees, [4] and the last notice I have of them is about the year 900, in the Church of St. Peter's at York. [5]   My reader will not fail to observe the notice in one of the above passages of Mr. Hammer's of the emblems, &c., found *in Scoticis ;* and if he know any thing of the history of Masonry he will know that popular prejudice has supposed Freemasonry to have been invented in Scotland, and to have travelled thence to France with the Stewart refugees.   That the Scotch refugee Masons might establish lodges in France I think very probable ; but they were not then *new ;* though perhaps they might not be numerous or much known.

---

[1] Mines de l'Orient, Tome VI. p 46. — Those accounts " are entitled to greater credit concerning the. first Masonic institution of a temple or house of Solomon, which we obtain from Arabic historians—since there is no historic testimony known to us which better answers to a Masonic institution than that House of Wisdom (Darolhikmet) which Hakem, in the end of the eleventh century built at Cairo, esteemed, we believe, to have been the first Masonic brotherhood (Lodge) which histories attest. But there was a House of Wisdom, (as we learn from Macrisius,) a certain academy adorned with regal riches, full of the studious of every extraction, and of multitudes of the sex, in which all the precepts of philosophy and of the mathematics were taught.   But besides this public instruction there prevailed in the same place a *secret* doctrine, of which there were various grades, through which the pupil being led, he was ultimately taught *to believe nothing*, and that it was lawful *to do all things*."

[2] The Templars have been vindicated from the calumnies of Mr. Hammer, by Mons. Raynaard, in the Journal des Savans, for March, 1819.

[3] Vide Anthologia Hibernica, for 1794.          [4] See Celtic Druids.          [5] Notitia Mon.

I have no doubt that the Masons were Druids, Culidei, or Chaldei, and Casidæans.   The Chaldæans are traced downward to Scotland and York, and the Masons backwards from this day to meet the Culidei at York.   It has been observed that the Masons, and particularly the Templars, always held their lodges or chapters under the crypts of the Cathedrals : of this I entertain no doubt.   FROM A MASONIC DOCUMENT NOW IN MY POSSESSION, I can prove that no very long time ago the Chaldees at York were Freemasons, that they constituted the *Grand Lodge* of England, and that they held their meetings in the crypt, under the grand Cathedral of that city. The *circular* chapter house did very well for ordinary business, but the secret mysteries were carried on in the crypts.   I think it is very probable that the Gnostic doctrines were held among the select heads of all orders of monks.

Though it be very true, as Mr. Hammer says, that the Templars held their Lodges or Chapters in the crypts of the churches, it by no means follows that all the churches in which Gnostic effigies are found belonged to the Templars.   These Gnostic emblems are found in numbers of churches, of which the records are quite perfect, and shew that with them the Templars never had any concern, and which were built long before the Templars are said to have existed with us. These effigies prove the identity of Papism and Gnosticism, for I cannot for a moment credit the assertion, that they were placed on these buildings by Gnostic Freemasons *without the consent* of their employers.

12.  The Chaldees or Masons having come to Britain before the establishment of the Papal power here, of course it happened that when the Romish Church obtained the command, it found them (the monks, Χρηςιανοι. *Chrees*tians probably) in possession of monasteries, but in some respects differing from itself.   But it did not burn them as heretics, it only seized the monasteries, leaving them a corner or retired place in the church, where they continued to perform their own ceremonies and religious rites.   And they continued thus to *perpetuate their order* and religious service, for many hundred years, *along with the Romish monks.*   They had only the three *Jewish* and old *Mithraitic,* and perhaps *Buddhic* sacraments—the eucharist or sacrifice of bread and wine, the *ordination of priests.* and baptism.   They kept their vernal or paschal festival according to the Eastern or Jewish time ; and, notwithstanding all the efforts of the respectable Presbyterian Jamieson to prove to the contrary, I think that these monks, like their monkish ancestors in Tibet, had a hierarchy.   I have no doubt of it ; they were nothing but Druids.   They continued to enjoy their Druidical College of Iona or Columkil, along with the Romish monks, from the most remote antiquity, till they, their monastery, and their ancient library, were destroyed, as far as it was in the power of the disciples of John Knox, at the Reformation.

The Eucharist spoken of above was the sacrifice or feast of bread and wine ; and I apprehend the reason why the *wine* instead of *water* was taken at this sacrifice, by those who never took wine on any other occasion, was the same as that which causes the Brahmins, (who never eat flesh at any other time,) in the Paschal festival or the Yajna sacrifice, to eat the flesh of the lamb. It was to be a feast, that is, an indulgence in something more than usual—or it would not have been a feast.   All sacrifices were feasts.

" The Dionysiacs of Asia Minor were undoubtedly an association of architects and engineers, " who had the exclusive privilege of building temples, stadia, and theatres, under the mysterious " tutelage of Bacchus, and distinguished from the uninitiated or profane inhabitants by the science " which they possessed, and by many private signs and tokens, by which they recognized each " other. This association came into Ionia from Syria, into which country it had come from Persia, " along with that style of architecture which we call Grecian." [1]   The style here spoken of, I

[1] Robison's History of a Conspiracy against Government, &c., Chap. i. p. 21, 1798.

apprehend, is that of the temples at Pæstum, the Parthenon, and the temples, which may be seen in Col. Tod's History of Rajahpoutana.· These Masons were the builders of Solomon's temple, and they procured the wood Almug. from India, whence they and their art came. As Robison says, they came into Syria from Persia. They were the ancestors of our Freemasons. The temple at Jerusalem, we know from Josephus, was of the Corinthian order. This had the capitals of its columns ornamented with the Ram's horn and the eternal Phoinix tree.

Speaking of the initiation of Moses by the Egyptian priests, Schiller says,

" These ceremonies were connected with the mysterious images and hieroglyphics. And the " hidden truths so carefully concealed under them, and used in their rites, were all comprised " under the name mysteries, such as had been used in the temples of Isis and Serapis, which were " the models of the mysteries of Eleusis and Samothrace, and in more modern times gave rise " to the order of *Freemasonry.*"

I doubt not that what Mr. Schiller says is true, with one exception: the mysteries were not the origin of Masonry ; they were Masonry itself: for Masonry was a part of them, and every part, except that which my Masonic engagements prevent, I will explain before I finish this work.

We know very well that there were no arches in the temple of Jerusalem, that is, radiated arches ; but we also know that there were vaults in which there were great treasuries, (which were said to have been concealed by Solomon and his successors,) and from which, whoever placed them there, the subsidies to neighbouring States, much too large for the temporary means of Judea to have supplied, were drawn in later times. These arches, I apprehend, were of the nature of that of the treasury of Atreus at Messina, and of the Cupola of Komilmar, described by Col. Tod. If a person wanted to open such an arch, he would use a rope, putting it round the cap, and pulling it aside ; if he wanted to open a key-stoned arch, he would not use a rope, but a hammer. When the key-stoned arch was discovered it superseded the ancient one. This is one of the parts of my subject on which I do not choose to say all I know.

The form of the church of the holy Sepulchre at Jerusalem is round. Vide Adamnus de locis sanctis apud Acta Sanctorum. [1] In that work there is a cut of the old church at Jerusalem.· The old part of the round church at Cambridge is of Saxon architecture—therefore of a style older than the Templars ; in fact, a corrupted Grecian or Roman style. There was a *domus templi* at Cambridge, and it was probably St. John's College. This Saxon round church, and the adjoining College of St. John's, called in old books the house of the Templars, are exactly similar to the house of Solomon and the College of Education of Hakem at Cairo. The church at Maplestead, in Essex, and in the Temple in London, are round. In the latter there have formerly been, as is evident, only twelve arches, each containing six Stalla, or Stalls, or Cells, making seventy-two in all, and six smaller and inner arches, under each of which probably sat two knights, twelve in all, at the round table. I entertain little doubt that St. John's College is a college of the Culidei, in short, of the ancient Druids, and perhaps the only one which has descended to us, in any thing like integrity.

There is something about the circular churches of the Templars, which seems to me to be very remarkable. We have only four in England I believe ; and they are all round. This form, we are told, was adopted in imitation of the round church at Jerusalem. But how came the church at Jerusalem to be round ; and how came these Christian knights to be called by the name of the detested Jewish temple ?

---

[1] Ord. St. Bened. Sect. iii. Part ii. præf. p. 505.

The intimate connexion between the Knights of St. John of Jerusalem and the Templars is well known, and it is worthy of observation, that they are both dedicated to St. John the Baptist. Their churches are mostly round, and the baptisteries the same. The followers of St. John the Baptist are called Nazareens, Mandaites, and Iohnites. We must not forget the Iohannes, Butta, and Deus. Mr. Britton has collected every thing which is known respecting our circular churches, but still he is obliged to leave them involved in very great difficulties. I have a strong suspicion that the Templars took their name from the Gnostic doctrine, that the temple at Jerusalem was the emblem of the universe, as I have before suggested, which had a close alliance with the Jewish Cabala. Each chapter consisted of *twelve* elect, perfect, or initiated, past masters, after the twelve signs—and seventy-two initiated, after the Dodecans, the symbols of the universe.

The Templars had no objection to the Jewish temple, for the same reason that the Mohamedan, the Jew, and the Christian, all sit down together, as I have, with great pleasure experienced, at a lodge or chapter of Freemasons. And I take the liberty of telling the Rossicrucians and Templars, that if there be any thing in their ceremonies to prevent this, it is a heresy, and contrary to the spirit of their orders. Let them remember this : without Jew, that is, Judaite, there is no Christian, without both Jew and Christian there is no Mohamedan. The Christians, that is, Χρηϛιανοι of Malabar and Coromandel, are founded on the Ioudi of Trichinopoly.

I now beg my reader to recollect some curious circumstances attending the number ten. It is described in Latin by the X, which X in Greek stands for 600, and is one of the monograms of Christ. It is also one of the monograms of Buddha of India. Its name in Greek is Iota, in Hebrew Iod, and in old Irish Iodha, and gives name to the sacred tree called with us Yew, evidently the Iαω of Diodorus Siculus. The tenth letter of the Hebrew which stands for ten is ، iod, and this is commonly written for the name of God by the Hebrews. The name of the pole-star was, with the Chaldeans, אתוי iuta, and with the Arabians it is called the star of judité جدي With the Tibetians the word for *ten* was Lamb, and was described by an X; and in the West the person called Christ and described by the monogram X was also called a Lamb, the Lamb of God —and was described by a Lamb carrying a cross in his paw, and by the head of the sun or a solar glory. I beg my reader to look back to several parts of this work, and to reconsider what is said respecting the Arga, and the Nabli or navel of the earth, of the Ie of Delphi and Moses, and respecting Jason or Ies, or in Greek Ὑης-ον or Jesus in Latin, and the Hellenic worship ; to recollect how Moses was educated by the Hellenicns, both in Egypt and at Sinai, and that the church of the holy sepulchre, of the God Ies-es, who was slain and after three days rose again, was built by Hellen the daughter of Coilus. Then let him recollect that at this church, to this day, the death of the God is lamented with the same cries, and his resurrection celebrated with precisely the same ceremonies as those of Tamuz or Adonis, as I shall shew in my next book. All this considered, he will no longer be surprised to find the church of the holy sepulchre built in a circular form, nor that, in the centre of it, to this day, is the Nabli or navel of the earth, as is described by Dr. Clarke. [2]  Here we have the union of the worship of the Linga and Yoni, and the reason why the Templars built all their churches round, and why they became the defenders of unfortunate females.

I consider the fact of the superstition of the Nabli, the Navel, the Omphale, the Umbilicus, still being continued at the church of the holy sepulchre, with all its attendant circumstances, as decisive a proof as can be imagined of the continuance of the ancient superstition, and of the re-

---

[1]  Vall. Col. Vol. V. p. 196.            [2]  Travels, Ch. vi. p. 228. Ed. 8vo.

union of the worship of the Linga and Yoni. I beg my reader's attention to the Tamuz in the last page, to recollect the exclamation in the Yajna sacrifice of the Lamb, *when will it be that the Saviour will appear!* in both India and Western Syria, and the same adoration of the Lamb, the Saviour, which I shall shew was practised among the Carnutes of Gaul.

When all this mysticism has been well considered, and also the singular way in which the Templars and red-cross Knights honoured the fair sex, my reader will not be surprised, perhaps, to find, that the prophecy in Haggai of Christ and Mohamed, was delivered by a word in the feminine gender, חמדת *hmdt*, as Mr. Parkhurst[1] has observed. Surely this is mystical enough. But I consider it as allusive to the double worship, and particularly to that of the Ishmaelites.

We have seen the surprising affinity between the religions of the Indians, Jews, and Western nations. Every one has remarked in the character of Constantine the son of Helena, an extraordinary mixture of Christianism and Heathenism—a mixture hitherto quite inexplicable. One little circumstance I think lets us into the secret. His Christianity was in substance, though perhaps in secret, the ancient Gnosticism. I think the fact that he dedicated his magnificent new cathedral at Byzantium or Nova Roma built on seven hills, neither to God, nor to Christ, nor to the Trinity, but to the Sancta Sophia the *holy wisdom,* lets us into the secret. It was to the Logos, Rasit, Wisdom—the creative power, by the name of Σοφια *Sophia.*

13. Col. Wilford notices a tribe of Battenians, that is Buddhæans, a tribe named by Ptolemy long before the Hegira, and whom we have proved to be the Ishmaelians who emigrated to the West. The people of this tribe, the Colonel says, were followers of Salivahana before they turned Musselmans.[2] If my theory be well-founded, this accounts for Hakem being the tenth Avatar or Salivahana, and we may see why they would be among the first Mohamedans, as he was believed to be a Vicramaditya or the tenth incarnation. This, perhaps, accounts for the early conversion of the Afghans to Mohamedism. Col. Wilford says, " Bhats or Bhatties, who live between " Dílli (I suppose Delhi) and the Panjab, insist that they are descended from a certain king, " called Salivahana, who had three sons, Bhat, Maha, or Moye, and *Thamaz* or *Thomas.* Moye " settled at Pattyaleh, and either was a *Thanovi* or *Thawovi,* or had a son so called. When " Amir-Timur invaded India, he found at Toglocpoor, to the N.W. of Dílli, a tribe called *Soloun* " or Salivan,[3] who were Thonovis or Manichæans."[4] After this the Colonel goes on to shew that on the rocks of *Gualior* is a group of thirteen figures called, by Christians, Christ and his apostles, now very much defaced. He then states that the Hindoos consider Manes to be a Salivahana, and he observes that Manes had twelve apostles and THREE DISCIPLES, EXALTED ABOVE THE REST, CALLED BUDDHA OR ADDAS, HERMAS OR HERMIAS, AND THOMAS, whom he supposes to be the same with the sons of Salivahana, called Bhat, Maha, and Thamaz. He then goes on to say, that there was a Christian monastery at Sirhind, and monks who brought silkworms to Constantinople in the time of Justinian, in the seventh century. But the most important part of Wilford's information consists in his observation, that the Bhats existed as a tribe long before the time of Manes or probably the Christian æra, since they are noticed as a tribe by Ptolemy. When I look on the map and consider what I have written respecting the Jews, the tribe of Youde, &c., &c., I can entertain no doubt that the origin of the Manichæans is found here as well as the Battanians or Ishmaelians and Templars of Syria.[5] The Jewish Sanhedrim consisted of seventy-two

---

[1] In voce חמד *hmd*, II.

[2] Asiat. Res. Vol. IX. p. 221.

[3] I have no doubt in Soloun we have another Solomon.

[4] Asiat. Res. Vol. IX. p. 212.

[5] We have the same mythos as this which we have seen in the kingdom of Oude, in part repeated in the Carnatic at Trichinopoly.

persons. IT HAD THREE PRESIDENTS, but whether they were included in the seventy-two is not known. The first President was called נשי *nsi*, the second סגן *sgn*, or דין *din* בית *bit* אב *ab* or *Abbitdin*, that is Abbot, Father of the house of Wisdom, *din* or *don*, and the third חכם *hkm*, the wise. Calmet's Dict. in voce San, and in voce Sagan. Moses was a Sagan to Aaron. This is the Latin Sagax and Scandinavian Saga.

The three first disciples of Manes were *Thomas*, *Addas* or *Buddhas*, as Cyril writes the word *Addas*, and *Hermes*. The three shew the nature of the mythos very clearly, and the explanation of *Addas*, by Cyril, shews what was meant by the God and King, of Western Syria, and also of Rajah-poutan or Eastern Syria, being called Ad, and Adad, as Ben-adad, &c. He is said to have sent *Thomas* into Egypt, and Addas into Scythia to preach.

The word Manes has been derived by Usher from the name of a king of Israel called Menahem,[1] and by the LXX. Μαναημ, which has the meaning, as he says, of Paraclete or Comforter, or rather, I should say, *Saviour*. This at once lets us into the secret—a new incarnation of Buddha, the general mythos—born from the side of his mother, and put to a violent death—crucified by a king of Persia. The teacher with his twelve apostles on the rocks of Gualior at once shews that he was not a copyist of the Jesus of Western Syria.[2]

The mistakes of the fathers respecting Manes, or, more correctly, the Manichæan doctrine, are wonderful. One says that the doctrine was first preached by a man called Scythian in the country of the Saracens in Arabia, another says he was of the race of the Brahmins and finds him at a castle called Arabion, on a river called Stranga, in Mesopotamia. These are nothing but Indian Scythia or Indian Arabia, the Doab, the Ganges; and the Saracens are the Suraceni. Another makes him to have come from Judea. This is the Indian Judia. Another says his doctrine was first preached in Egypt by one P-apis. This is nothing but Apis with the Egyptian emphatic article Pi-apis. The work called the acts of Archelaus is generally supposed to be a gross forgery. If my reader will consult the first three chapters of Beausobre's history, bearing in mind the explanation which I have given of the mythos of Manes, the whole will unravel itself and the difficulties will explain themselves.

When a Manichæan came over to the orthodox he was required to curse his former friends in the following terms: " I curse Zarades[3] who, Manes said, had appeared as a God before his time " among the Indians and Persians, *and whom he calls the sun.* I curse those who say Christ is " the sun, and who make prayers to the sun, and to the moon, and to the stars, and pay attention " to them as if they were really Gods, and who give them titles of most lucid Gods, and who do " not pray to the true God, only towards the East, but who turn themselves round, following the " motions of the sun with their innumerable supplications. I curse those persons who say that " Zarades and Budas and Christ and Manichæus and the sun are all one and the same." By Zarades is evidently meant Zoroaster, and the whole shews us that the orthodox believed Mani to be both the sun, and, as I have said I believed him to be, Buddha of India—the tenth incarnation of Buddha, whose followers arose on the North of India, and became very numerous, but were not able to overcome the Brahmins, the followers of Salivahana.

Col. Wilford, in p. 218, gives us another account of Manes; that he was called Terebinthus and his father Scythianus, and that Manes propagated his doctrines in Tartary. We must recollect that Manes is said, by Christian authors, to have fled from the West to India; and, Col. Wilford tells us, the name of the tree called Terebinthus is not to be found any where except beyond the Indus. It is the tree sacred to Buddha, on which the Manichæans held Christ to have

---

[1] Usher's Annal. Vol. I. An. 3032, p. m. 82; 2 Kings xv. 14, 16.
[2] Beausob. Hist. Manich. Tome I. p. 71.          [3] Cotelerii, Pat. Ap. I. p. 543.

been crucified.[1] See my figures, Nos. 12, 13, 14. This story of a Terebinthus going to India, as told by Epiphanius, is like all the remainder of these stories, and can deceive none but those who are determined to be deceived. How absurd is it to suppose that a sect of Christian heretics should have fled to the East, and have returned, bearing Indian names, like those above! The fact was, the fathers found them coming from the East, and fraudulently or credulously assumed, that they must have first gone from the West. Perhaps they never suspected it possible for them to have arisen in the East.

Free-masonry is known to be founded on principles of *universal* benevolence, and not to be confined to one class or to one religion. I think I may venture to say it is so constituted, that although it would not refuse to receive a simple Deist, no test being required, yet all its forms, ceremonies, and doctrines, are so constituted, as, in a very peculiar manner, to be applicable at the same time to the doctrines of Judaism, Christianity, and Mohamedism. Christianity is founded on Judaism: Mohamedism on Christianity. Mohamedism cannot for a moment exist independent of Christianity, nor Christianity independent of Judaism. We have seen the Rosy cross with eight points of the Templars, the Cross of Christ, and of Manes, and of Buddha, and the *rose of Sharon*, symbols of the Templars and of the Rossi-(Rosy)-crucians. I am not of the two latter orders; I have abstained from becoming a member of them; that I might not have my tongue tied or my pen restrained by the engagements I must have made on entering the chapter or encampment. But I have reason to believe that they are now become in a very particular manner what is called exclusively Christian orders, and on this account are thought, by many persons, to be only a bastard kind of masons. But here are two mistakes. They are real masons, and they ought to be of that Christianity which is found in India, at Delhi and at Trichinopoly, of that universal Christianity or Creestianity, which included Jews, Buddhists, Brahmins, Mohamedans, and which, before I conclude this work, I shall shew, was a sublime and beautiful system—the secret system of the religion often alluded to by the Christian fathers. I am now only speaking of the Rossicrucians and Templars. This at once, and very naturally, accounts for the Knights Templars being Christians, and uniting with the Battanians or Ishmaelians or As-chas-dim or Assassins. These were the Chaldæi of Daniel, of the Romans, in the time of the early emperors, called Chaldæi, Mathematici, Architectonici, and who were banished and persecuted by them. They were a species of Sodalitates or a secret order, of which the government became jealous. They are the Culdees of Iona and of the Crypt of York Minster, where the grand Masonic Lodge of England was held; they are the Gnostic Manichæans, who possessed the round churches at the Temple in London, Maplestead in Essex, at Northampton and Cambridge, and who in time became the Templars. In what other way the Templars could become possessed of these churches I do not know. Perhaps they might be built or more probably rebuilt by them; but the Saxon order of architecture in the church at Cambridge shews a date before the usually supposed existence of the Order of Templars in England. The Templars in other countries did not build their churches round, but perhaps they found them here in the hands of their brethren the Culdees, and they coalesced with their brethren whom they found here, when they brought their doctrines from the crusades. Thus they are found in the crypt of the Cathedral at York. All our old establishments of collegiate churches, deans and chapters, were Culdee establishments, which accounts for the Culdees in them not being destroyed by the Romish church. The church of St. Martin, at York, was built for them or by them, and this accounts for an extraordinary pulpit cloth there to be seen, which I shall notice presently. All the round *chapter houses* of our Cathedrals were built round for the

---

[1] Asiat. Res. pp. 216—218.

same reason that the four above-named churches were round. In these chapters and the crypts, till the thirteenth century, the secret religion· was celebrated far away from the profane vulgar. From this came the bridge of Ham or Om corrupted into Cambridge, and Isis and Ox or Bull of Oxford. These buildings are, I think, the successors of the Caves of India, and afterward of the cupola-formed buildings there, which we see in Col. Tod's book,—of the Cyclopæan treasury of Atreus at Messena, and of the Labyrinths of which we read in Egypt, Crete, Italy, &c. These labyrinths could be only for the purposes of religion, and I doubt not of that religion of the Cyclopes which universally prevailed. The underground crypts of our cathedrals with their forests of pillars were labyrinths in miniature.

The round church of Jerusalem, built by Helena, the Mystic Helena, (daughter of COILUS,) Mother of Constantine, who was born at York; and the chapter-houses at York and at other cathedrals were children, grand or great-grand children, of the circular Stonehenge and Abury; and the choirs of many of the cathedrals in France and England are built crooked of the nave of the church, for the same reason, whatever that might be, that the Druidical temple is so built at Classerniss, in Scotland. Vide *Celtic Druids*, plate 28.

I think I have stated enough to raise or justify what the Jesuits would call a *probable opinion*, that the masonic ceremonies or secrets are descendants of the Eleusenian Mysteries. Every body knows the now ridiculous traditionary fancy that a mason is, in some way, marked or branded or mutilated before he can be admitted into the order. I believe this, like most other traditions, had not its origin from nothing. I believe the higher classes of Masons were originally persons who were admitted into the mysteries of Eleusis and Egypt, and that they were Chaldæans and Mathematici, and I believe that what the above tradition of the branding alluded to, was Circumcision, and that they were circumcised. Origen and Clemens Alexandrinus both affirm, that the secret learning of the Egyptians was only taught to such persons as had undergone the operation of circumcision, for which reason it was submitted to by Pythagoras.[1] *The same word in Hebrew means both initiated and circumcised.* As infants are admitted into Christianity by baptism, so they were admitted among the initiated by circumcision. If my memory do not deceive me the priests only of the Egyptians were circumcised; and the Tamul, Chaldee, or Pushto-speaking priests of Cristna, in South India, are circumcised; and we shall find the rite, by and by, in a place where we little expect it. Abraham, the Chaldæan, is called an astronomer and a mathematician by Philo.[2] In the twelfth volume of the Asiatic Researches, p. 461, may be seen an account, given by a Mr. Moorcroft, of a society in Tibet which can be no other than Free-masons.

In the beginning of the celebration of the Gentile mysteries a herald proclaimed,

      . . . . . . Procul! hinc procul este, profani !

Saint Chrysostom[3] says, when we celebrate the mysteries, we send away those who are not initiated, and shut the doors, a deacon exclaiming, " Far from hence, ye profane! close the doors, " the mysteries are about to begin. Things holy for the saints; hence all dogs." (From something allusive to this has probably been derived the custom among the Mohamedans of calling Christians *dogs*.) M. Dulaure, in his history of Paris,[4] has observed, that the explanation of the doctrines of the Trinity and the Eucharist constituted probably the Christian mysteries, and, *in part*, he is certainly right. But he might have added the Gentile mysteries also, for the Gentile

---

[1] Origen, Comment. ad 2 Ep. ad Rom.; Clemens, Lib. i. p. 130; Concordia Naturæ et Scripturæ, Caput v.

[2] Stanley's Hist. Chald. Phil. p. 796, 4to.     [3] Homelia 23, in Matt.     [4] Vol. VIII. p. 80.

Trimurti, I need not describe again, and the Charistia of the Romans was the Eucharist of the χρης, or Latin Christus—the sacrifice of Pythagoras, of which I shall say more by and by.

In M. Dulaure's 8th volume of the history of Paris may be found, a very interesting account of the union of the pagan mysteries or crafts of the ancients with those of the Christians in the seventh and eighth centuries. Any person who has read this work with attention must see that the mystery or craft of modern trades is but the Raz of India, all continuing until they became no longer mysteries. All our guilds and corporations have come from this source. Hence all their mysterious numbers—*twelve* aldermen, twenty-four common councilmen, &c., &c. It has been said[1] that the Templars, fleeing from the persecution of Philip le Bel, took refuge in Scotland, and that some apostates, at the instigation of Robert Bruce, founded the order of Templars in that country. All this may be very true, with the single exception, that it is absurd to call them *apostates*. They were evidently emigrés because they would not be apostates, and there was no apostacy in opening a lodge, and initiating Robert Bruce and others into the mysteries, and thus continuing the order in defiance of Philip.

The word Raz, in India, signified masonry or mystery or secret learning or wisdom, or a ray emanating from the sun, as I have formerly shewn. It also had the signification of King, whence came the Raj-ah, and the Rajah-pout-ans, who, when they came from the East to the West—to Syria and Egypt, were, for this reason, ROYAL-palli or Shepherds. From this came the Ras of Abyssinia; and more to the West, the Rex, à Rege, of Rome, and the Roi of France, and the person, in the Roman and the Eleusinian mysteries, called a king, or Rex; but who, in the most early times, was a Ras or person in whom was incarnate a certain portion of Divine Wisdom or the Logos. Melchizedek was a Ras, and an Archè, and priest, as I have little doubt that all kings were originally. It was the wisdom (or perhaps more properly *cunning*) that made them kings. They were supposed to be incarnations of wisdom or Sons of God. This was the case with Alexander the Great.

It is certainly worthy of observation that in the Hindostannee, the language of the country in which I believe masonry had its rise, a mason is called a *raz*, and has the meaning of *mystery*. This word has the same meaning as the שׁרׁ *ras* of Genesis, the Αρχη of St. John. The persons called Royal-Arch Masons were the Archi-tect-onici, before the invention of key-stoned or radiated Arches, the Cyclopæan builders of the only *stone* edifices, at that time, in the world, which were temples. It was not till comparatively modern times that private persons had stone houses. The immense cities of Benares, Delhi, &c., they are still chiefly built of mud or sun-dried bricks and wood. Dwelling-houses were also framed of oak timber, filled in with brick or mud, and were, as we may yet see from a few poor ones which are left in England, in a few old towns, *capable* of great magnificence. Hence the reason why, in the countries where the ruins of temples are common, and where we know that high civilization once prevailed, there are no ruins of houses. The Architectonici, the Chaldæi, the Gnostici, the Mathematici, the Dionisiaci, constituted a MYSTERY, and erected Gothic buildings, the ruins of which now remain in India, thousands of years before they existed in Europe.[2] In, I believe, the remains of Mundore, and in all very ancient towns, we find only the ruins of the temple and perhaps of the palace. We know the size of the town only from the ruins of the walls. Thus in England and Ireland we have Stonehenge and Abury, and tumuli, with *glass beads* and *gold ornaments* in plenty, but not the least appearance of a dwelling-house. Can any one suppose that the people who raised the stone lintels upon the jambs at Stonehenge, did not know how to place beams of timber, one over the other, so as to

---

[1] Ib. 126.                            [2] Vid. Hist. Dion. Artif. by Da Costa.

form roofs for houses? It is the deficiency of the remains of houses which induces persons to think, that there can have been no high civilization in these northern countries. I desire such persons to examine the Mosaic floors, three or four feet under ground, at Aldborough in York-shire, the ancient Iseur or Isurium, the capital of Brigantia, from which Boadicea led forth her 80,000 men against the Romans who defeated her, and destroyed her capital, removing it to Evora or York.

The Masons were the first priests, or a branch from them, and as they were the persons employed to provide every thing requisite for honouring the Gods, the building of temples naturally fell into their hands, and thus priests and masons were identified. This was the first practical attempt at Masonry. Thus the Masons were an order of priests, that is, of initiated. Every initiated person was a priest, though he might not exercise the functions of a priest. Thus they became identified with the most powerful and influential body of society, and though all priests were not Masons, I think that all Masons were priests in one sense, being initiated. I think they were priests originally; and, as was to be expected, they provided good houses for themselves, and, when many of them consisted of Monks, Monasteria. In many instances, from superiority of intellect, the consequence of the constant use of their faculties, they acquired the sovereign power.

14. Having shewn how the Mohamedan and various sects were connected together, it is now time to unveil the secret doctrine of Mohamed, which will be in a great measure that of them all, and will, I think, easily account for the rapid diffusion of Mohamedism, and for its adoption when first promulgated by the most learned and talented of the Arabian philosophers—a secret doctrine yet found in a state of persecution among the followers of Ali in Persia. What my reader has seen I had principally written before I made the discovery of the secret doctrine, and I think it expedient to leave what I had written, as it is, to shew how the whole, by degrees, unravelled itself—to shew that there was no preconceived system at the bottom to which every thing was to be made to bend, and the literal meaning of which I had determined nothing should ever persuade me to disbelieve. We must never forget that in every thing respecting Mohamedism we labour under the greatest difficulties. The truth is, that its real doctrine is now confined to a persecuted sect, which considers that to unveil its mysteries would be to be guilty of the greatest moral turpitude; and the pretended history, as we have it, has been received from the meanest-minded of devotees, or from zealots of another sect, the Christians, whose malice and hatred have blinded their understandings—zealots so mean in mind too, that if they had been willing to exercise any thing like criticism they were incapable of it. What are we to expect from even such men as the very great scholar, but mean-minded Prideaux!

It is well known that almost immediately on the death of Mohamed his followers divided into two sects, that of Abubeker, and that of Ali, the latter of whom had the twelve Imaums—his successors—the same in number as the apostles of Christ and as the twelve Cæsars. The faith of the latter of these sects became and still continues the religion of Persia. This I have no doubt was the original or rather, perhaps, contained the original esoteric religion of Mohamed, which is yet to be found in the sect of the Sofees as they are called by Sir John Malcolm, in his History of Persia. These are followers of the ancient Σοφοι, one of whom was Mo-amed, that is Mo or Om, the illustrious or desire of all nations. The Sophoi or Sofees are allowed by the vulgar or present orthodox Persian writers[1] to have descended from the ancient Sabæans and to have been contemporaneous with the prophet, that is to say, they find them and their doctrines to have

---

[1] Sir John Malcolm's History of Persia, Ch. xx.

:o-existed with him from his first appearance or from the beginning of his empire, but they know not how or why. Sir John judiciously observes, that "their rapturous zeal, perhaps, aided, in ' no slight degree, its first establishment."[1] I have no doubt that it did. But this acknowledgment conveys along with it the *admission* of the fact, that Mohamed was a Sofee, and his secret religion Sopheism. Sir John then adds, that they have been since considered as its most dangerous enemies. There can be no doubt that they are thus considered by all the vulgar rabble—by such persons as believe that Mohamed did really ride a horse called Borak from Mecca to Jerusalem in a minute; that is, by the followers of the literal meaning of the forged Koran. By these *enlightened persons* in modern times the Sophees have been persecuted. Whether in Persia the sect of Sofees possessed the power without intermission from the time of the twelve Imaums to the time of Nadir Shah, it may now be difficult to determine; but certainly they ruled Persia from A. D. 1500 to 1736, when the kingdom was conquered by Nadir Shah, who was himself originally a Sophee, but who, after the conquest of Persia, is said to have abandoned the Sophee doctrines, and to have compelled his followers and his new subjects to change their religion along with him. The reason of this is very perceptible. The Persians were no longer capable of appreciating the refined doctrines of *Sopheism*, of *Wisdom*, of Gnosticism. Whatever he and his twelve Imaums, if he had such a cabinet, might believe, the trash of the Koran was more suitable to the vulgar populace. Sopheism, the secret doctrine, might have become too common; it was necessary to put it down—to keep the people in ignorance. This was what the Popes did with Gnosticism—prohibit it publicly, hold it secretly. This was, perhaps, the original reason of the composition of the Koran, at all events I cannot doubt that it was the reason which caused the Caliph *Othman* to redact the Korān. For any thing we know, the first copy of it may have been an exposé of the doctrines of Sopheism or Wisdom as taught by the Great Mohamed, and if we judge of it from his high character, we may readily believe that it may have been very fine and worthy of its author; but we really can know nothing about it, nor is it likely that we ever shall know any thing unless some copy of it may remain among the Sophees of the East.

I can entertain little doubt that all the Caliphs of the Saracens were secretly or openly Sophees; and that Sopheism continued the Esoteric religion of the state till the Turkish barbarians overran their empire, and came over to the religion of the vulgar Koran from their own, whatever it might be. Whether the Sultans and the upper classes of the Turks are at this day in any respect superior to their followers upon these subjects, I have not the means of acquiring information. It is probable that, like the Christians and the Jews, they are all victims of the policy which formed or retained, when formed by accidental circumstances, a refined religion for the cabinet, the conclave —a base one for the people. Alas! what misery has this brought upon the world! But its day is nearly past.

The word Soph, in Persian, has the meaning of wool, and therefore some persons have thought the doctrines of Sopheism were named from it—overlooking what I should have thought could not well be missed, the word Σοφια, *wisdom*, from which no doubt it took its name. We are also told by Sir John Malcolm that these people had a very remarkable name, that of. *Philosaufs*, that is, philosophers.

The sovereigns of Persia have the titles of *Sophi* and *Shah*. The first explains itself; the second means, protector, preserver, saviour, from the Hebrew word יש *iso, to save*  From Eli-sha, successor of Elijah, of the *God* Jah, has come the title of all the Shas of Persia and other countries. The Pa-sha is the same; the word Pa is either Ba or Ab *father*, or the Egyptian and Coptic em-

---

[1] Sir John Malcolm's History of Persia, Ch. xx. p. 266.

phatic article Pi. As we call our king *majesty ;* and as the Romans called their emperor *Divus,* so the Asiatics call their kings *Shas.*

Om-rahs are Om-rays, judges, possessors of wisdom, rays or emanations of Om. In Tait's Edinburgh Magazine,[1] an account is given of some young Mohamedan devotees chaunting in chorus, in praise of the prophet, the word Amber-*ee.* I cannot help suspecting that he is here invoked by the title of Om, and that the name of the famous palace in Spain, Alambra, has been the house of Al-am-bra, *the holy Am*—the *bra* used like the Latin *Divus.*

I think the word for *wise* may be found in the Hebrew שׁפה *spe, religious sentiment.* See Parkhurst in voce, IV, and in שׁפט *spt, judgment,* whence came the Sufetes or judges of the Tyrians. But שׁפ *sp* will be the root, the ה mutable or omissable. Hence Sapio and Sapientia.

Sir John Malcolm takes his accounts of these persons from their enemies, therefore in every part of it an evident bias against them may be perceived; but he admits that they have had among them great numbers of the wisest and ablest men and finest poets and literary characters of Persia and the East. He says,[2] "The Mahomedan Soofees have endeavoured to connect their mystic faith " with the doctrine of their prophet, who, they assert, *was himself an accomplished Sofee.* The " Persian followers of this sect deem Ali, his sons, and all the twelve Imaums, teachers of Sofee- " ism ;"[3] *and they claim as followers of their sect almost all the great men of the world.*[4] Here, if I do not greatly mistake, we find the Esoteric religion of Mohamed, however much persecuted and endeavoured to be suppressed by his vulgar followers the present Turks.

Sopheism, we are told, is divided into four stages. In the first, a man is required to observe the rites and ceremonies of religion for the sake of the vulgar, who are incapable of looking to higher matters. In the second stage, a man is said to obtain power or force, and may leave his teacher to study by himself; he is said to enter the pale of Sopheism, and he may quit forms and ceremonies, which he exchanges for spiritual worship. This stage cannot be obtained without great piety, virtue, and fortitude : for the mind cannot be trusted in the neglect of usages and rites necessary to restrain it when weak, till it hath acquired strength from habits of mental devotion, grounded on a proper knowledge of its own dignity, and of the Divine nature. The third stage is that of knowledge, i. e. *Wisdom,* and the disciple who arrives at it is deemed to have attained supernatural knowledge; in other words, to be inspired; and when he arrives at this state, he is supposed to be equal to the angels. The fourth and last stage denotes his arrival at *truth,* which implies his complete union with the Divinity.[5]

It appears that by their teachers they " *are invited to embark on the sea of doubt ;*"[6] unquestionably this must be heresy in every religion. They hold doctrines respecting the existence of matter similar to the refined doctrines of the illusion of India, and I have no doubt, from what drops from the gallant knight,[7] also similar to the doctrines of the emanation from the το ον of Plato and of Orpheus, and of the Indians, with the latter of whom he says that these delusive and visionary doctrines have most flourished.[8] He further states that their doctrines may be "traced " in *some shape or other in every region of the world.*"[9] I dare say they may. Again, he says, " The Sofees represent themselves as devoted to the search of truth, and incessantly occupied in " adoring the Almighty, an union with whom they desire with all the fervour of divine love. The " Creator, according to their belief, is diffused over all his creation. He exists every where and " in every thing.[10] They compare the emanations of his essence or spirit to the rays of the sun,

---

| [1] No. I. p. 32. | [2] P. 279. | [3] P. 276. | [4] P. 278. |
|---|---|---|---|
| [5] P. 270. | [6] P. 268. | [7] P. 269, *n.* | |
| [8] P. 268. | [9] P. 267. | [10] Ibid. p. 269. | |

" which, they conceive, are continually darted forth and reabsorbed, and they believe that the
" soul of man, and the principle of life which exists throughout all nature, *are not from God, but*
" *of God.*" [1]    Here ·is certainly the Gnostic doctrine of emanations which I have in part explained, and of which I shall have much to say hereafter.

The Sofees are divided at this day into many sects, and, in their four stages, they have a species of Masonic or Eleusinian initiation from lower to higher degrees.   As we have just now seen,
Sir John says, the third stage is that of *knowledge*, the fourth of *truth.* . I suspect that it ought to
be, the *third* of *truth*, the *fourth* of *knowledge*, i. e. WISDOM, Σοφια.   The Sofees of Persia are
enthusiastically attached to poetry and music, both of which I have no doubt owe their origin to ·
religion, and that recitative and chaunting are not modern Italian inventions, but that they have ·
existed from the most remote antiquity.   Sir John, after stating the chief part of what the reader
has seen, admits that they involve their tenets in mystery, [2] and that they have secrets and mysteries of every stage, which are never revealed to the profane, and to reveal which would be a
crime of the deepest turpitude. [3]   One of their most learned works, called the *Musnavi, which
teaches, in the sweetest strains, that all nature abounds with divine love*, was written by a
person called the *Moollah of Room*.   I have no doubt under this mystic name more is meant than
meets the eye. [4]   Sir John says Hasan Sabah and his descendants were (as I think might be expected) a race of Sofees, [5] and that they were of the sect of Bâtteneâh, that is Buddha.   They
were Templars, or Casi-deans or Chas-di-im, or followers of Ras, or Masons.

The use of the Pallium or sacred cloak to convey the character of inspiration was practised by
the Imaums of Persia, the same as practised by Elias and Elishab, Eli-Shah; and it is continued
by their followers to this day.   When a person is admitted to the highest degree, he will receive
the investiture with the Pallium and the Samach, which is the Χειροτωνια.   When the Grand·
Seignor means to honour a person he gives him a Pellise, a Pall, a בלא *pla*, a sacred cloak, a remnant of the old superstition, the meaning probably being forgotten.

From this comes the word palls at our funerals.   One of the names of the chief of the Assassins was Old man of the mountain—Senex de montibus.   The Buddwa of Scotland was called old
man, and Buddha, in India, means *old man*.   My opinion that the Assassins were Buddhists receives confirmation in part from this.   He was the ancient of days, whose hair was wool, of a
white colour; but in Persian the word Sofee means both *wisdom* and *wool*. [6]   Long white hair
was the peculiar emblem of wisdom.

A careful consideration of what I have said will enable my reader to account for many circumstances which he has seen stated respecting Hassan Sabah and the Saracen chiefs, in the time of
the Crusades, though the subject is still not entirely without difficulty: and will furnish a satisfactory reason why, about the year of Christ 1200, when the expected completion of the period of
cycles arrived, and brought nothing with it but the usual phenomena of nature, the expectants of
the secret system lost their hopes, and gradually sunk into the vulgar mass.

The true character of the Sofees and of the Esoteric faith of pure Mohamedism may be clearly
discerned from the following concluding passage of Sir John Malcolm's respecting them : " I have
" abstained from any description of the various extraordinary shapes which this mystical faith has
" taken in India, where it has always flourished, and where it has at times been beneficial in
" uniting the opposite elements of the Hindu and Mohamedan faith : [7] nor have I ventured to

---

| | | |
|---|---|---|
| [1] Sir John Malcolm's Hist p. 269. | [2] P. 281. | [3] P. 290. |
| [4] P. 279  ..  [5] P. 293. | [6] Malcolm's Hist. Pers. Chap. xx. | |
| [7] Shewn in the case of the Sikhs. | | |

" offer any remarks on the similarity between many usages and opinions of the Soofees and those
" of the Gnostics and other Christian sects, as well as of some of the ancient Greek philosophers.
" The principal Soofee writers are familiar with the wisdom of Aristotle and Plato : their most
" celebrated works abound with quotations *from the latter*. An account of Pythagoras, if trans-
" lated into Persian, would be read as that of a Soofee saint. His initiation into the mysteries of
" the Divine nature; his deep contemplation and abstraction, his miracles, his passionate love of
" music, his mode of teaching his disciples, the persecution he suffered, and the manner of his
" death, present us with a close parallel to what is related of many eminent Soofee teachers, and
" may lead to a supposition *that there must be something similar in the state of knowledge and of*
" *society, where the same causes produce the same effects.*" [1]   Indeed, Sir John, there is something
similar, for they are all identical, with a few trifling alterations, produced by time and change of
country. Here, in the Soofees of Persia, we have the Esoterici of Buddha, of Moses, of Jesus,
and of Mohamed, however disgraced at this time by numerous sectarian divisions and mischievous
absurdities of every kind. In short, Sopheism is Gnosticism ; and, if we can discover the one,
we shall discover the other.

On the Sofees Sir William Jones says, " I will only detain you with a few remarks on that me-
" taphysical theology which has been professed immemorially by a numerous sect of Persians and
" Hindus, was carried in part into Greece, and prevails even now among the learned Musselmans,
" who sometimes avow it without reserve. The modern philosophers of this persuasion are called
" *Sufis*, either from the Greek word for a sage, or from the woollen mantle which they used to
" wear in some provinces of Persia : their fundamental tenets are, that nothing exists absolutely
" but God ; that the human soul is an emanation from his essence, and though divided for a time
" from its heavenly source, will be finally reunited with it : that the highest possible happiness
" will arise from its reunion : and that the chief good of mankind in this transitory world, consists
" in as perfect an union with the Eternal Spirit as the incumbrances of a mortal frame will allow :
" that for this purpose they should break all *connexion* ( or *taalluk*, as they call it [2] ) with ex-
" trinsic objects, and pass through life without attachments, as a swimmer in the ocean strikes
" freely without the impediment of clothes, that they should be straight and free as the cypress,
" whose fruit is hardly perceptible, and not sunk under a load, like fruit-trees attached to a trellis :
" that if mere earthly charms have power to influence the soul, the idea of celestial beauty must
" overwhelm it in ecstatic delight : that for want of apt words to express the Divine perfections
" and the ardour of devotion, we must borrow such expressions as approach the nearest to our
" ideas, and speak of beauty and love in a transcendent and mystical sense : that, like a reed torn
" from its native bank, like wax separated from its delicious honey, the son of man bewails its
" disunion with melancholy music, and sheds burning tears, like the lighted taper waiting passion-
" ately for the moment of its extinction, as a disengagement from earthly trammels, and the
" means of returning to its only beloved. Such in part (for I omit the minuter and more subtil
" metaphysics of the Sufis which are mentioned in the Dabistan) is the wild and enthusiastic re-
" ligion of the modern Persian poets, especially of the sweet Hafiz and the great Maulavi : such
" is the system of the Vedanti philosophers and best Lyric poets of India—a system of the highest
" antiquity both in Persia and India." [3]   We must not forget that the above is the figurative description of the poets, the real doctrines of the Sofees are a profound secret, untold by Hafiz or
Maulavi, and only very partially known, by guesses or inference, by Jones. But enough transpires to shew the nature of the real uncorrupted system.

---

[1] Shewn in the case of the Sikhs, p. 300.      [2] That is, hold no conversation, no talk. G. H.
[3] Asiat. Res. Vol. II. pp. 62, 63.

If the reader consider what has been said respecting the character of the Caliph, the sacred head of the Musselman religion, and respecting the religion of the Sophees, evidently the secret religion of Mohamed, and of the doctrine of Wisdom every where apparent, then carefully examine my table of alphabets and observe the way in which the Gamma or Gimel became C, and how again the C and the Σ became confounded, and that the C came to be written in very many cases by K,[1] I shall not be thought guilty of a great paradox in maintaining, that there is a strong probability that the word Khalif was formed of the word Al-soph; that the Sphahees or Sipahis had their name from the same root; that they were the cavalry of Wisdom, of the Suph. Many words might be pointed out which have undergone much greater changes. The circumstances in favour of this are peculiarly strong. But it may also come from Soph-Cali, taking Cali in the sense either of Wisdom or Logos, or Kosmos in the sense of *beauty* arising from *order.*

In addition to the Sophees, who are the same as the Persian Sophis, we have, among the Indians, the WISE men called Ras-ees or Rish-ees: these are evidently taken from the Hebrew Ras, or Rasit. The Pleiades were believed to be different from all other stars in having a motion within themselves. Perhaps it might be for some reason connected with this, that they were called Rishees or Rashees, but their epithet or quality of *wisdom* shews what they were. Arrian notices these Rashees or Sophees by the latter name: he calls them *Sophists* or *wise men*, who, he says, are few in number, but rank first in the country.[2] These Sophists are found in the neighbourhood of the temple of Solomon in Cashmere, called *Rashees.* The identity of the two cannot be doubted. They are described as follows in the Ayeen Akberry: " The most respectable people " in this country are the Reyshees, who, although they do not suffer themselves to be fettered by " traditions, are doubtless true worshipers of God. They revile not any other sect, and ask no- " thing of any one: they plant the roads with fruit-trees to furnish the traveller with refreshment: " they abstain from flesh; and have no intercourse with the other sex. There are near 2000 of " this sect in Cashmeer."[3] Cashmere is all Holy land: its capital Sirrynagur. It has a river called Latchmehkul;[4] that is, a corrupt way of writing la, or el, or al, חכמה *hkme.* These Rishees are the same as Sofees, and are the Carmelites, Nazarites, or Essenians, belonging to the temple of Solomon in this country. Cashi-college can be nothing but Cashimere, or the mere or island of Cashi, where stood the temple of Solomon, which the Mohamedans destroyed, and the tomb of Moses. We have formerly seen that at the College of Cashi the Chaldee language was spoken, which was studied by all the physicians at Delhi, Abul Fazel says, in the words just quoted, " The most respectable people of this country are the Reyshees, who, although they do not suffer " themselves to be fettered by traditions, are doubtless true worshipers of God."[5] These Reyshees I apprehend are Ras-shees or wise men, whom Diodorus calls Sophites,[6] and places at a little distance between Cashmere and the Hyphasis. The Greek word Sophites, is but a translation of Ras-shees.

In the Yogees or Fakeers of India we have dervises of Mohamedism, and the Hermits and Friars of Christianity. The dervises of Mohamedism are copies either from the Christians or Hindoos, and, in fact, corruptions of Mohamedism. Mohamed declared that he would have no monks in his religion, and it had none for the first two hundred years. It is evident from Arrian and Porphyry that these orders of men were well known in their time; and that they were found in India in the time of Alexander. They existed in different orders before the times of Jesus in Egypt, Syria, &c., as Essenes, Cœnobites, &c.; and those on Carmel, described by Pliny, became Carmelites.

---

[1] The first part of Payne Knight's treatise on the Greek alphabet may be consulted on these changes.
[2] Hist. Ind. Ch. x., xi.     [3] Gladwin's Ayeen Akberry, Vol. II. 155.
[4] Ibid. p. 156.     [5] Rennel, Mem. p. 106.     [6] Ibid. p. 94.

We may find in the schools of the prophets צופים *zupim*[1] in 1 Sam. i. 1, the city of the Sophim or learned, and again 1 Sam. x. 10, 11, and xix. 18—24. Samuel and David dwelt in the city of נוית *nuit* Naioth, that is, the city of Neith or of *wisdom*, and in the country of Rama רמה *rme*. The Raz of India is the Ras of Genesis, and means *secret wisdom*, or *knowledge*. It is the mistur of the Hebrews. The head or chief was a *ras* or ᴀ*RAISED* person; the first emanation or Raj was wisdom, therefore wisdom was the first or head or $\alpha\rho\chi\eta$. He was the first existence or hypostasis in time. The head, the seat of wisdom, was *ras*: the head ruler was the same: so the seat of the *ras* was the sofa or divan, sop-aia, place of wisdom. The Hebrew word for a sopha or oriental divan, is נטה *nte*, as often written *nthe*, the neith. The sopha is the divan in eastern countries, used solely by the Ras or prince or divine incarnation of wisdom. Divan is Div-ana, place of the holy one. Our word *raise* comes from the word Ras, in the sense of head, as head or chief of the clan. The way in which we have found the words Ras and Sophia used as a title of honour for the kings of Persia and Abyssinia is very curious, and I think it will not be thought surprising if the same system be found carried a little farther. Adonis, as I have shewn, has the meaning of Wisdom. It is א-דון *a-dun* THE wisdom.- From this come the title of the Dons of Spain and Portugal, of the Welsh Adon for *Lord*, and the title of O'Conner Don of Ireland. The Rossi, or Rosy-crucians,[2] with their emblematic red *cross* and red *rose*, probably came from the fable of Adonis (who was the Sun, whom we have seen so often crucified) being changed into a red *rose* by Venus.[3] *Rus* in Irish signifies a *tree, knowledge, science*: this is the Hebrew *Rus*. Hence the Persian *Rustan*.[4]

We have before seen, that when we pursued the word Don to the utmost point to which we could carry our researches, we found it to end in Wisdom. This is what was natural, if my system be true. It could scarcely be expected that in some one of the dialects the meaning would not be found. We have seen that Maia was considered the mother of Buddha or the Logos or the same as the Logos and divine wisdom. We have a sea called Mæotis or Maietis or Maria. It is also called the sea of A-soph or of *the* wisdom. Into it runs the river Tan-ais or Don, also called river of Asopus, the Soph, on which is a town called Asoph (or Asow in Russian) and Tanais, and it is in the district called B-achmut, or of בחכמות *b-hkmut*, or of Wisdom.[5]

The Red Sea is called the sea of סוף *sup*. This name I take to be the same as the name of the Palus Mæotis or Sea of *Asoph*, and to have been אשף *asp* in the singular, אשפים *aspim* in the plural, which is the word used in Daniel for Astrologers or *wise men*, or Magi.[6] They were the same as the Chasdim or Chaldeans. The root of this was the same as the Greek Σοφος or wise man, and this sea of Suph was the sea of wisdom, *Sophia*, the same as the Mæotis, and came from the same root. I think it may also be found in Frey, with the meaning of vertex, in סעיף *soip*, and סעפים *sopim*, thoughts, cogitationes, from the root סעף *sop*.

Dr. Stanley says,[7] "Ashaphim were rather the same as Souphoun in Arabick, wise, religious "person." Again he says,[8] "perhaps from the Hebrew root *Ashaph* comes the Greek σοφος." When I consider the propinquity of the district of Bachmut, and the town of Don, and the Sea of

---

[1] Called by Pagninus *Sophim*.

[2] The Jewel of the Rossicrucians is formed of a transparent red stone, with a red *cross* on one side, and a red *rose* on the other. Thus it is a crucified rose.

[3] See Drummond's Orig. Vol. III. p. 121.

[4] Vall. Coll. Hib. Vol. IV. Pt. I. p. 84. The ancient Sardica, in Lat. 40 deg. 50 min., is now called *Sophia*; the ancient Aquincum Buda or Buddha. These were, I believe, old names restored. Vide D'Anville's Atlas.

[5] Enc. Brit. in voce, Asow.　　　　[6] Duret, p. 329.　　　　[7] Hist. Chald. Phil. p. 764, 4to.　　　　[8] Ibid.

Asoph to Cholcos, and Sindica and the Chaldei,[1] and other circumstances, I cannot feel any doubt, that in the words Don, Asoph, Bachmut, we have the ancient mythos. When we consider that the empire of the Ras is on one side of the Red Sea, and Mecca, the capital of the Mohamedan Sophees, on the other, we cannot be surprised that it should be called the sea of wisdom.

Zoroaster had with the Parses the surname of *Sapet-man*. When I recollect that with the Northern nations *Mannus* meant *man*, I cannot help believing that Sapet-man meant *wise man*. Anquital derives it from Sapetmé, *excellent*.[2] The אשפים *aspim*, in Chaldee, mean *conjurers* or *wise men*;[3] אשף *asp*, Asophim, שפט *spt*, *judgment*; שופתים *suptim*, *judges*. These were the Carthaginian Suffetes or Judges.

In Book IX. Chap. I. Sect. 9, I have derived the name of the sea of Arabia or the Red Sea, the sea of סוף *sup*, from צוף *zup*, which means correctly, *the most secret place*, and *the Holy of Holies*. I believe it is the same as סוף *sup*, from being the peculiar place of Wisdom, which is said to shroud itself in darkness. But it is of little consequence; it may be considered an erratum, and that it comes from אשף *asp*, the *wise man* or Magus; but it is evidently the same thing. No one can doubt that the real root is שף *sp*. From the Serpent being the emblem of wisdom in Egypt it was called *Asp*, which has passed to us. It was commonly believed in Egypt, that it never died.[4]

The famous well, *Zem Zem*, at Mecca, is the well of wisdom, צמם *zmm*.[5] In the refined doctrines of Sopheism, that is, of Gnosticism, and in the doctrines of the eternal renewal of cycles, we may find the reason why the greatest men of the oriental world turned Mohamedans. No one can deny that those doctrines, chastened down to their primitive simplicity, are refined and beautiful, although capable of being carried to an excess pernicious to its professors. But if it have made self-tormentors for the love of God, it seems never to have excited its votaries to the cutting of the throats of those who did not profess its doctrines. I think when, in the latter part of this book, my reader shall have seen the whole development of the ancient doctrine of Wisdom, he will no longer be at a loss for a reason why Mohamedism prevailed in the seventh century over the base Christianism which was then taught to the vulgar by its priests.

15. When we look around us, innumerable detached circumstances prove that a former very fine and enlightened race existed, and that its theology, however false it might be, was not only not foolish, but very refined and beautiful; and this I shall prove at large presently. But look at he works given to us by Mr. Upham and others, as the Indian theology of this day, and how can any thing be meaner? It is not unlikely that the priests have corrupted even the Vedas, the ldest of their books, in the different ages through which they have passed, to make them fit to, or to raise upon them, superstitions suitable to the degraded taste of the time. But there is one fine work come down to us, extremely beautiful, the simplicity of which is in perfect keeping with the contemplative icon of divine wisdom, called Buddha (Plates, Fig. 34); with the simplicity of the circular temples of Stonehenge, Dipaldenha, and the Pyramids; with the simplicity of the doctrines of the Trimurti, and the renewal of Cycles, &c., &c., &c.; and that is the work called the Fables of Æsop or Lockman.[6]

---

[1] Vide D'Anville, Anc. At.    [2] De Salverte, Essai sur Noms, Vol. I. p. 90.    [3] See Parkhurst.

[4] The Arabians call a Serpent, Supphon. Parkhurst in voce שפה *spe*, שפף *spp.* p. 760.

[5] Vall. Coll. Hib. Vol. V. p. 42.

[6] See Univ. Hist. Vol. XVIII. p. 401; see also D'Herbelot, in the article Lokman; Nimrod, II. p. 660.

He is said to have lived in the time of Heber, of David, and of Solomon : and to have been a Jew, that is, of the tribe of Ioudi or Judah. He is claimed by the Greeks, the Jews, the Arabians, the Persians, the Ethiopians, and the Indians. Much has been written about him. I believe the fables of Æsop are the fables of *the* Σοφια and of Lockman, of L'hkm, לחכם *lhkm, the wise*. His residence, if he ever lived, probably was in Oudia. The nations are all right, because they are the fables of Wisdom, and they all had the doctrine of Wisdom. In Arabia there was a tribe of *Lochmians* whose general name was *Mondar*.[1] They were descended from *Lakhm*, the son of *Am-ru*, the son of *Saba*. *Their kingdom lasted 600 years.* The words Lochman, Mondar, Lakhm, *Am*-ru, Saba, and their 600-year kingdom, can want no explanation for any person who has read this book. They evidently bespeak the universal mythos.

Hottinger says, " Lokman, vel Lukman est hic plane παρεισακτος," (this is most clearly the Parasacti of India, which Hottenger has got hold of and misunderstood,) " quem tamen integrâ " *Suratá* commendat Muhamed quæ numero est XXX. Quis vero fuerit, à Muhamedanis " Arabibus difficulter obtinebis. Muhamed eum facit Davidi coætaneum. *Beidavi* in comment. " p. 651, refert illum fuisse filium Naora, ex filiis Azed, filii Sororis (nepotis ex sorore) Jobi, " Materteræ ejus ; vivisse autem ad tempora Davidis, à quo ille scientiam didiceret. Ex Chris- " tianis *Lokmani* hujus meminit Elmacinus diebus ejus (Josiæ, Regis Judæ) fuit *Lokman sapiens.* " Author translationis Alkorani veteris, eum Aluchmen appellat." Georgius, p. 97, says, Para- sachti, prima lux sive flamma à Deo invisibili manans. But Parasachti is Lachmi, and Lachmi is Al Acham, חכם *hkm*, אל *al*—חכמה *hkme* אל *al*, Lochman idem.

Thus Lochman was *the wise man*, a corruption of חכם *hkm* and *mannus*. He was known to be Æsop the author of the fables. The latter name is the same as the former in substance, it is the emphatic article, and שפ *sp*, which is the Hebrew root of the Greek word Σοφια, and means wisdom or the wise man. Thus Lochman לחכם *lhkm* and Luchme is לחכמה *lhkme*, the same word in the feminine form. The Parasacti one of the names of Lachmi found by Hottinger in the Greek is very curious. It means *to insinuate* the same as παρεισαγα. The σαγα is the Sagax. The Scandinavian Mercury or God of cunning, that is, in other words, wisdom, was called Loke. No one can doubt whence this comes.[2] Lughman (Lochman) is a district of the *Afghans*, between Peshawer and Cabul. It contains the mount Suffaid (*i. e.* Suf-ai-di). The language is unknown, but it has many Pushto words.[3]

---

[1] Univ. Hist. Vol. XVIII. p. 429.

[2] Vall. Coll. Hib. Vol. VI. p. 130. Lokman Al Hakim. Lokman the **wise**. Univers. Hist. Vol. XVIII. p. 401. The kings of Cochin are also called Hakim.
Soph is a common title in India, as Asoph ud Dowlah. Hamilton, p. 132.

[3] See Nimrod, Vol. II. p. 660.

---

*London, November* 12, 1832.

# CHAPTER VII.

AFGHANS.—TAMUL LANGUAGE.—SUBJECT CONTINUED.—OBSERVATIONS ON LANGUAGE.—BOEES, BAIEUX.—
THOMAS, SHARON TURNER.—TWINS, TAMAS.—CRETE, CRES.—MALABAR, MEANING OF.—CAMA, CAMA-
SENE.—TWO TOMBS OF THOMAS.—JAGGERNAUT.—VEDA.

1. WE will now return to the tribe of Afghans, of whom we noticed many circumstances in the 4th, 5th, and 6th chapters of the Eighth Book, and in which pretty good proof was given that they were the ancestors of the Jews. The author of the Cambridge Key, whose authority cannot be disputed for such a fact as this, says expressly, that the Vedas, in the Sanscrit, are now believed, both by Persians and Hindoos, to have been originally written in a CELESTIAL language, long since extinct.[1] By this celestial language the Pali is not meant, for reasons which it is unnecessary to explain, and also because it is not extinct or lost. Then what language was it so likely to be, as the old Hebrew language of the tribe of Ioudi or Yud or Western Oude, whose Samaritan nail-headed characters Dr. Hagar traced from India, and from which the Sanscrit letters descended ? What language was it so likely to be, as that which we find among the low-land tribes who, in South India, mix not with the Brahmin tribes, and whom we find also among the mountaineers of North India, whose retired situations have prevented their intermixture with the higher classes of lowlanders, the followers of the Tamul Woden ? What language can it have been but that of the tribe whose names of God we find in the Brahmin service—Ie-peti, Iaya—names of rivers explainable in their language, NER-Buddha, NER-ma-da, River of Buddha, River of Maha-deva—whose towns and kings are called after the tribe, Ioudi-pore, Tuct-Soliman—whose mountains have the same names, Montes Ioudi, Montes Solumi ? And the very oldest temples in the country and in the world, the temple of Solomon in Cashmere ? Whose language can it have been but that of the people described by the Jesuit to have all the Jewish ceremonies, at Madura, in the Carnatic, near the tomb of St. Thomas and the temple of Bal-ii or Triputty ? which we shall now find to have been a language of learned men. But we have the express authority of the sacred writ for another equally important fact. The Geta opens with informing us, that " this immutable " system of devotion was revealed to Vaivaswat, who declared it to his son Menu, who explained " it to Ishwacu. Thus the chief Reshees knew this divine doctrine delivered from one to an- " other."[2] From this we see that it was held that the doctrines were handed down for several generations by tradition, unwritten.

The translation of a history of the Afghans, made by Dr. Dorn, has been published by the Oriental Translation Society. It is like most oriental histories, a collection of nonsensical stories. On the similarity of the names to the Hebrew the learned Doctor says, " The fact, that " the Afghans make frequent use of Hebrew names, as Esau, Yacoob, Musa, &c., and that their " tribes bear Hebrew names, as Davudze, &c., is as little a proof of their Hebrew origin as the " circumstance that their nobles bear the title Melik, which title, even according to their own " assertion, was not introduced before Mohamed's time, and is undoubtedly the Arabic for a ruler, " a king."[3]

---

[1] Vol. I. p. 261, Vol. II. pp. 128, 129.
[3] Dorn, Hist. Afghans, Pref. p. viii.

[2] Camb. Key, Vol. II. p. 121.

Upon the assertion that the word *Melik* stands *for nothing*, I must observe, that I do not attempt to prove that the Afghans were descended from the Jews, therefore that style of argument does not apply to me. But the admission that their tribes *bear Hebrew names* is most important; they cannot have come from the Mohamedans. The ancient temple of Solomon in Cashmere was destroyed by the Mohamedans. It is surprising to me that the learned Doctor has not attempted to account for the identity of names, which he admits. Without going further, the names, which he admits to be Hebrew, are alone, under all the circumstances, quite enough to prove the original identity of the languages. In Dr. Dorn's work it is stated that the *eldest* son of Jacob or Yacoob was Juda. Now this clearly proves that though the mythoses are evidently the same, they are not merely copies of one another, and that the Asiatic author was, in fact, not giving an account of the Jews in Western Syria; for if he had, he would not have made Judah the eldest son of Jacob.[1]

The first attack of the Mohamedans on India was made by Mohamed of Ghezni, A. D. 1000. It does, indeed, seem surprising that any one can believe the names of mountains, tribes, cities—such as temple of Solomon in Cashmere, mountains of Solumi, tribe of the sons of David, city of Oude or Iudi in the North, and Judia and the Mosaic Mythos in Siam, Ceylon, Comorin, and Malabar, a thousand miles to the South—should have been brought by the Saracens to these countries, some of which they never possessed.[2]

Jamblicus has observed that the *real ancient* names of places are still to be found among the inhabitants. This is confirmed by the Marquess Spineto.[3] He says he could prove it of Egyptian places, but he does *not think fit to do it*. But this I very much regret. I am quite sure more true history is to be learnt from the names of places than from all other sources. They are historians which cannot deceive us. The observation of Jamblicus is most important.

Dr. Babington says, that the Sanscrit of South India is written in characters derived from the Tamul.[4] It must be extremely difficult and perhaps impossible to determine which form of letter is derived from any other, but the important fact comes out that they are all in system really the same. In a future part of this work I shall shew why the forms of the letters have varied so much, although the systems were identical.

Mr. Wilson, I suppose a very competent judge, says, the Tamul language may be considered as the most classical of the languages of the Peninsula. It was the language of the kingdom of Pandya, Madura, Regio Pandionis,[5] now comprehending South Arcot, SALEM, Coimbatur, Kumbakonam, Tanjore, Trichinopoli, MADURA, Dindigal, Tinnivelli, and great part of Mysur,[6] containing five millions of people. According to Dr. Babington and the late Mr. Ellis, it is a language not derived from the Sanscrit, but of independent origin. Wilson says, " It is not derived " from any language at present in existence, and is itself either the parent of the Teluga, MALAVA- " lam, and Canarese languages, or what is more probable, has its origin in common with these " in some ancient tongue, which is now lost or only partially preserved in its offspring." Again,

---

[1] The same kind of observation may be made on the book of Enoch; it makes Jacob the son of Abraham, passing over Isaac. The work translated Dr. Dorn was evidently written by a modern Persian, who, not knowing how to reconcile the circumstance of two Judeas, has mixed together the traditions which he met with respecting the two.

[2] For proof that the mountains of Solomon in India were so called before the Mohamedans went thither, see Elphinston, p. 245. In the Hindoo books we read of a great war carried on between the followers of Gautam or Buddha and Wiswa-Mitra, in the country called Yudha Bhumi. Is it possible to be blind here to the Latin *Humus* and the tribe of *Judah?* Nimrod, Vol. I. p. 219.

[3] Lect. on Hier p. 369.                          [4] Trans. Asiat. Soc. Vol. II. Part i. p. 264.

[5] Ptol. Geog.                          [6] Maha-sura, *Buchanan.*

in another place, he makes an observation of the very first importance to all my theories, as follows : " The higher dialect of the Tamul, on the contrary, is almost entirely free from Sanscrit " words and idioms, and the language retains an alphabet which tradition affirms to have hereto- " fore *consisted of but sixteen letters*, and which so far from resembling the very perfect alphabet " of the Sanscrit, wants nearly half its characters, and has several letters of peculiar powers." He then goes on to shew, that there is a very close affinity between the *Maharastra* and *Oddya*[1] and the Tamul ; and he observes, it is extraordinary that the uncivilized races of the North of India should bear any resemblance to the Hindus of the South. He says, " it is nevertheless the fact " that, if not of the same radical derivation, the language of the mountaineers of Rajamahal " abounds in terms common to the Tamul and Telugu." Rajah-mahal was Aja-mahal, in lat. 25, long. 87, near the towns of Daoud Nagur and Danapore Afghan. But *I* say it is not at all extraordinary, if the Tamul be either the sixteen-letter Hebrew or its first descendant, one of which I have no doubt that it is. I beg my reader to recollect the various examples which I hase given of the Hebrew language in South India, and of the Hebrew-speaking Malays. Mr. Wilson then goes on to shew that the Tamul had a number of fine writers and a regal college at Madura, and I believe he might have added another at Muttra on the Jumna, and another at Maturea on the Nile, in Egypt, all speaking or writing the language of Brahma and Saraiswati.[2] Mr. Ellis states that a contest took place between the Brahmins and inferior castes in the Tamul countries for pre-eminence in literature and knowledge.[3] No doubt it did, both in North and South India, and Abraham, the follower of Brahma and Buddha, was driven out by the Brahmins and obliged to emigrate to the West, probably bringing the book of Genesis with him.

To prove the learning of the Tamulese I beg to refer my reader to the Asiatic Researches,[4] where he may find a translation of some of their sacred poetry which will bear a comparison with, and also strongly remind him of, the books of Solomon as they are called, and perhaps properly so called. These writings are admitted by the Tamulese not to be in the old language, and therefore, of course, a translation. They recognize a divine Son[5] or Logos, and direct the adoration of Sarasbadie (or Sara-iswati, wife of Abraham). In the flower of Konnie is the Kanya of North India and the rose of Sharon. The wisdom is found in almost every line. In the adoration of Sarasbadie, I think the adoration of the female principle shews itself, which may have been the reason for Abraham's emigration.

It is a very striking circumstance that the verses in one of the poems translated by Dr. John begin with the letters of the alphabet acrostically, as is the practice with some of the Hebrew psalms : the Doctor admits that the language is very ænigmatical and difficult to understand, even in the opinion of the natives, who say that each sentence or verse may be translated five different ways. I cannot help suspecting that the Kalwioluckam, one of the Tamulese sacred works, is the wisdom of Solomon, each probably much corrupted and changed from the original.[6]

The observation that every text of the Kalwioluckam would bear several senses is a fact strikingly similar to the Pentateuch, which scarcely contains a passage of which this may not truly be said. The double sense of the word wisdom is very apparent. Nor need this be a matter of surprise, for the practice is strictly in harmony with its system of having one religion for the people, and another for the learned or initiated.

[1] Qy. Ioudia ?   [2] For Tamul language, see Transactions Orient. Soc. Vol. I. Pt. i. p. 264.
[3] P. xxxii.   [4] Vol. VII. p. 350.   [5] P. 355.
[6] Asiat. Res. Vol. VII. p. 354.

5 B

If at a future time a person should read in an author of the present day, that the English language was spoken in Australia, although at that time the language of Australia should vary greatly from the then spoken English, I think he would have no difficulty. Then why should there be any difficulty in the Pushto of Afghanistan or Eastern Syria and the Pushto of Western Syria? It cannot be forgotten that both languages must have been diverging as from a common centre. It seems extremely probable that the old Hebrew was the common centre from which the Tamul, the Afghan, and the Western Syriac diverged. It must also be remembered, that neither the Synagogue Hebrew nor the Samaritan is the original language, because it is written in twenty-two—not in sixteen letters. This forms another reason for a divergence from the Pushto or the Tamul. The two latter must have been diverging, each in one way, from the common centre, while the Hebrew was diverging in another. Sir W. Jones says, the Pushto or Pukhto language, of which I have seen a dictionary, has a *manifest resemblance* to the Chaldaic.[1] This, if correct, comes as near as can be expected. The Syriac has been thought the oldest language by some learned men.[2] From all these circumstances I am induced to believe that the Tamul language with its sixteen letters was originally the Pushto, the language in which the common people of Tamul who are Christians have their Gospels and Bible, given by the Portuguese. In not one of the books treating of the Christians of Malabar is there a single word to induce any one to suppose, that they had a language different from the other people of the country, and that we certainly know was what is called Pushto, Syriac, and Chaldee, which are in fact all the same; differing in nothing of consequence, but in the forms of their letters, and perhaps in the direction in which they are written.

Mr. Wilson, if I understand him aright, says, that the Tàmul language was known to Arrian.[3] And now we will ask what was the meaning of Tamul? Was it *Tam* the first word of *Tamuz*, of Adóni, a place near to or the same as Tripetty in the Tamul country? I believe that the old Tamul is what Buchanan and others call the Syro-Chaldee, the language of the Jews and Christians of South India and St. Thomé. It is the language of the physicians of Ayoudya noticed as being spoken at Cashi, and of the physicians of Madura.[4] There is a dialect in this country called Shen Tamizh.[5] This speaks for itself.

The word Tam-ul itself is nothing but the Hebrew L-tam, or the Syriac Ol-tam, the language of the, or the country of the, Twins; of which I shall say more presently.

In forming a judgment upon this subject, let us look at the languages of the nations of America, South of the United States, and I am informed by a very learned friend, whose attention has been in a very particular manner turned to them, that though upwards of a hundred of them are found, yet it is really impossible to discover the slightest affinity or relationship between any two of them, and that it is precisely the same in the languages of Australia and the Polynesian islands. All this arises from these languages not being written. We must also recollect that all our Asiatic writers, endeavour by every means in their power to disguise the fact of the Hebrew or Chaldee language being in these countries; and they do this not from a wish to do any thing wrong, but from a rooted persuasion that it is absolutely incredible, the very acme of absurdity, to suppose it possible that the Hebrew language should be spoken in these remote countries, in districts of India. Thus, in a similar manner, in the account of the Lama of Tibet given by a missionary in the Oriental Repertory, he calls the Mitre worn by the Grand Lama a *cap of ceremony*,

---

[1] Asiat. Res. Vol. II. p. 76.

[2] Vide Univ. Hist. Vol. I. p. 347, and Astle, p. 37. For Syriac letters, see Univers. Hist. Vol. II. p. 293.

[3] P. xxxii.          [4] P. xxxiv.          [5] P. xlvi.

and in a note he acknowledges this circumstance, but assigns no reason for it. [1]  The writer seems to have had no ill intention, but he could not bring himself to use the Christian term *mitre* though the cap of ceremony was evidently nothing else.  This feeling has operated in thousands of instances in the same manner, particularly in the names of places, which has done more than can be easily conceived to keep us in the dark.

2. Nimrod has observed, that the question, What national or local language is the least altered from the language which was spoken before the confusion, (by which I suppose is meant, what is the least changed from the primeval language,) is a question to which the greatest linguists will find it difficult to give an answer; and, he adds, " So deceitful and slippery are the paths of philo- " logy, that perhaps historical and traditional arguments, if any could be brought to bear upon it, " would enlighten the question more than those of grammar or those of etymology." [2]  The observation appears to me to be excellent and deserving of the most serious consideration.  In this work it will be seen that the plan has been almost invariably adopted, and that traditional and historical arguments almost supersede all others.  Grammar is entirely omitted.  Upon this kind of foundation it is that I contend for the very great antiquity of the Chaldee or Hebrew.  In the copy locked up in the temple of the Jews we have an example of an old language in its *old state* much prior to any other, unless the Sanscrit be excepted; and if we give the Hebrew in the Temple an age 1500 years before Christ, and the Sanscrit 2000 or 2500, yet we can never know how long before the 1500 the Buddhist Genesis may have been preserved as a sacred work; and it is presumed that numerous facts are visible to shew that the names of Chaldee gods, places, and persons, are found in the Sanscrit, so as to prove it to have arisen since the writing of the Hebrew books : this, of course, will throw back the writing of the first book, or Buddhist book of Genesis, to a very remote period, long before Moses adopted it into his compilation, as it ought to be thrown if it be really a Buddhist work.

It is impossible to say what would be the first step which would be adopted by man in the formation of language, but a probable near approximation to the truth I think may be contemplated, merely by the application of a little common sense.  His first words would consist of simple sounds, which, by our present letter system, might be represented by such words as *ba bal ;* or by our vowels, *a* or *ah.*  They would be nouns or the signs of things.  They would have only one number, one case, one gender.  After some time, probably by very slow degrees, the words which we describe by the other parts of speech would arise.  But the noun would have no inflections.  The different cases would be formed by adding words in the most simple manner ; as, *bit*, house ; *le bit*, to house ; *be-bit*, by house.  It is evident that this would be regulated, in a great measure, by caprice or accident.  I can have no doubt whatever that the written language which comes the nearest to this simplicity has the greatest probability of being nearest to the first language—and this is the Hebrew of the Synagogue.  Its cases are made, like the English, by words, and its use of the rude form instead of a genitive case, called being in regimine, is a peculiarity which marks almost primeval simplicity. [3]  The words which denote the past and future times may be used one for the other, and which is to be adopted, in any case, can only be known from the context.  They have been attempted to be subjected to rule by what is called the vau conversa, but I think in vain.  Many other marks of rudeness might be pointed out.

---

[1] Vide Orient. Repertory, Vol. II. p. 277.　　　　　　　　　[2] Vol. II. p. 493.

[3] This has been before named in Book V. Chap. V. Sect. 2, but it ought to have been more fully explained.  My reader will observe the words בית־אל *bit-al.*  They mean correctly *house God*, and when in regimine, that is, when the second is in the genitive case, they mean *house of God*, the words remaining exactly similar.  This shews how men and places came to have the names of gods.  The priest of Jove came to be *priest Jove.*

Maimonidès says, Scito, multas egregias scientias, quæ in gente nostra olim fuerunt de veritate istarum rerum, partim longitudine temporis, partim infidelium et stultorum populorum in nos dominatione, partim etiam quod non cuivis concessa erant, (sicut exposuimus,) periisse et in oblivionem devenisse (nihil enim permissum erat, nisi ea, quæ in libros sacros digesta et relata erant).[1]   I know of no written language which exhibits such marks of rudeness and simplicity as the Synagogue Hebrew or Chaldee, and on this account has such a claim to antiquity.   Probably the first language and letter of the Culdees or Chaldei or Chaldeans, when they came from India, was the Samaritan.   In the *thousand years* which passed between the time of Abraham and the return of the tribe from Babylon, the Chaldees of the East had improved the present Chaldee letter, which Ezra adopted.   The discovery of the Chaldee or Syro-Chaldee language yet in India, is, when well considered, almost a proof of the truth of my theory.   Whenever the natives of Malabar became Christians, whatever the nature of their Christianity may have been or may be, they must then have used the Syro-Chaldee language and letter.   I have a strong suspicion, arising from various circumstances, that Buchanan, who was unacquainted with Hebrew, found the people speaking that language, which was what he took for the Tamul.   I think it possible that Wilson and Mackenzie may have supposed that Buchanan was writing about the language of a few separate Jews and Christians, when, in fact, they were all writing about the same language.   That this naturally arose from none of them having the least suspicion of the real state of the case, and that the now corrupted Tamul, is the Syro-Chaldee or the parent of the Syro-Chaldee, and that it is the circumstance of the *sacred* books being written in the Chaldee that has preserved the Tamul or spoken Chaldee or Pushto language, from changing so much as to be entirely lost, though the form of its letter be entirely changed, as might be expected.   This is what has taken place with the Arabic in other countries since Mohamed's time.[2]   Sir W. Drummond says, " The Chaldaic, the " ancient Syriac, and the Phœnician, appear to have been very nearly the same; that the two first were " so will not probably be disputed : *Chaldaicæ* linguæ ita affinis est Syriaca, says Walton, ut a " plerisque pro una eademque habeantur, sola enim dialecto differunt : in Scripturis dicitur " Aramæa ab Aram, ut Syriaca a Syriâ."[3]

The natives of Cashmere as well as those of Afghanistan, pretending to be descended from the Jews, give pedigrees of their kings reigning in their present country up to the sun and moon : and along with this, they shew you Temples still standing, built by Solomon, statues of Noah, and other Jewish patriarchs.   Concerning these matters, when our travellers are told of the descent from the Jews they make no inquiry; at the same time they are occasionally obliged to allow, that the descent from the Jews is, for many reasons, totally incredible.   Then how is this to be explained ?   Simply by the fact, that the traditions of the Afghans tell them, that they are descended from the tribe of Ioudi or Yuda : and in this they are right; for it is the tribe of Joudi noticed by Eusebius to have existed before the Son of Jacob in Western Syria was born, the Joudi of Oude, and from which tribe the Western Jews with the Brahmin (Abraham) descended and migrated.   The same or some of the same people who came to Thrace burning the widows—the Orpheans who brought the Trimurti to Plato; and, to Syria and Egypt, the people of the country of Tam, *i. e.* Tamuz, of whom Ezekiel speaks.   " The Afghans call Saul, *Melic Talut.*   They are " called Solaimani, either because they were formerly the subjects of Solomon, king of the Jews, " or because they inhabit the mountain of Solomon."[4]   I quote this for the fact, the reason for it

---

[1] In More Nev. Cap. lxxi.

[2] The Afghan language is called both Pukhto and Pushto.  Asiat. Res. Vol. II. p. 68.

[3] Punic. Ins. p. 11.                                             [4] Asiat. Res. Vol II p. 73.

is very unsatisfactory. How extraordinary that it should never occur to this writer to inquire, how these subjects of Solomon and Saul should live near the temple of Solomon in Cashmere, or the mountains of Solomon in Mewar or Malwa![1] In the fragments xxxiv. xxxv., Calmet's editor shews, that a great part of the Jewish history of Samuel, Saul, David, and Solomon, is to be found in the history of the Afghans. From this I have been led to a suspicion, that the reason for the monstrous numbers of soldiers, chariots, horses, &c., of which we read in the Bible, applied not to Western, but to Eastern, Judea; and the same of the gold used in the temple. All this, as applied to *Western* Syria, is ridiculous; but not so as applied to the state and the enormous city of Oudia of India.

It is quite impossible for any unprejudiced person not to see, that the Jewish history, in matters unconnected with miracle, is full of absolute impossibilities. The use of 6,900,000,000 pounds sterling[2] in the temple, is one out of many examples. Then what are we to say, unless we choose to charge the whole as priestcraft, except that the object of the book was neither history nor chronology, but *as was the case in all other nations,* the concealment of a mythos under apparent history, as noticed before, by me, in Book VIII. Chap. VIII. Sect. 5.

So completely is the tribe of Afghans Judaite, that in the time of Mahmud of Ghaznah, the family of Saul was still remaining in the mountains, and eight of his descendants were taken into pay by Mahmud, and treated with high respect.[3] How is it possible on any principle to make the descendants of Saul, of Western Syria, all killed by the Gibeonites, to pass through the reigns of David, Solomon, &c., and the captivity, and survive to the time of Mahmud, here in India?

In Dr. Dorn's History of the Afghans[4] is an account of an embassy sent by one of the first Caliphs to the Afghans, to inform them that the last of the prophets had come, and to solicit them to turn Mohamedans. If we consider that the originals of the Jews were found in their country, and that it was called Arabia, there seems nothing improbable in this, or that this should be the reason why these mountaineers should have been among Mohamed's first proselytes. If we suppose that the Arabians in the time of Mohamed were acquainted with their descent from the Afghans, and that the latter were expecting a new incarnation to arrive, this does not seem very unlikely to have happened.

It is also worthy of recollection, that Saul in India is called by a different name, i. e. *Talut,* from that which he bears in the Bible, but it is the same name as that which he bears in Arabia. This has a strong tendency to confirm what I have said of the Arabians coming from India, and also to confirm what the Mohamedans say, that the Afghans sent Abdul Raschid to acknowledge Mohamed as the Resoul or prophet, among the first of his followers.[5] They, in short, acknowledged him for the *tenth* Avatar. This was the Talisman (from us concealed by such of our priests as knew it, with the greatest care) which gave to Mohamed the conquest of this world. It had done the same thing before for Alexander and Cæsar.[6]

Respecting the word Talut, there is something very curious and worthy of observation. In the first book of Samuel, chapter nine, and the second verse, it is said, that Saul was HIGHER than any of the people of Israel. It is evident that the word Talut is a formation of the Hebrew word ללת *tll,* which means a *tall* man. Here we have an Afghan, an Arabian, a Hebrew, and an English word all representing the same idea.

---

[1] For Solomon's temple in Cashmere see Forster's Travels, Vol. II. p. 11, also p. 17. For more respecting Talut, refer to what I have said in the chapter on Freemasons.

[2] Villapandus has proved, that Solomon's temple cost, according to the text, six thousand nine hundred millions of pounds sterling. Oliver, p. 349.

[3] See Asiat. Res Vol. II. p. 71.      [4] P. 37.      [5] Asiat. Res. Vol. II. p. 71.

[6] Saul vocatur Taluth in Alkorano Hotting, de Geneal. Moham. p. 112.

The Arabians call the people of the Afghanistan Cashmere and Kandahar, *Soleymanye*, and there is a district near Mecca called by this name also, the inhabitants of which have a tradition that they came from these Eastern countries.[1]

We find at three of the temples of Solomon—that in Upper India, that which I suppose to have been at Salem, in the Carnatic, and that in Western Syria, the same mythos of a Moses or Saviour (for the word Moses means *Saviour*). From this I think it probable that it was the same or nearly the same in the secret writings in every one of the fourteen temples of Solumi of which we have read, for fragments of this mythos are to be found every where.

3. If we reflect deeply upon the Sindi, the sacrificing of wives, and other marks of the most ancient Indian polity in Thrace, we cannot help seeing that they must have gone thither long before the march of Alexander to India. The sacrificing of their widows by these Thracian Sindi puts their Hindoo character out of all doubt. Let us reflect a little on the consequences which would arise among mankind, if, as I suppose, one original language pervaded the whole world. It seems the natural course that when colonies went out to different countries, if their language were in comparatively-speaking a rude and unimproved state, they should take their language poor and rude, and that after they were settled, and began to get rich, and to become civilized, they should improve it. And in this manner cases, genders, numbers, would come to be formed in all languages, but the means by which they would be formed would vary. For instance, in the cases of nouns : some nations would form them by changes of the terminations, like the Greeks and Latins; some by the substitution of what we call prepositions. Thus different languages would vary, but yet the principles of nature being the same in all nations, a certain general character of similarity would remain; for all nations would want different numbers, tenses, cases, &c. Though the variations are considerable, yet the similarity among most nations is so great, that it can in no other way be accounted for than by supposing that the use of the same system of letters prevailed among them all in very early times. It is very clear that at the time when a barbarous people first received the *sixteen* letters would be the first beginning of their grammatical speculations, though no doubt they would previously, perhaps unconsciously but PRACTICALLY, have formed what we call in grammar numbers, cases, &c.; for they could not have done without them : but they probably would have given them no names. I think when they received the sixteen-letter system, they must have received some information respecting the nature of the grammar of the country from which they received it : and casualties of this kind no doubt would operate in various ways. The intermixture of nations for purposes of commerce would also have considerable influence in many cases, which may be more easily supposed than described. But what would have taken place if the art of writing were at first secret and confined to one order, which extended over all the world, and that it became known by degrees as all secrets of this kind of such great importance to mankind in long periods will certainly do ? This is the theory which seems to me to be the most rational and probable, which I have been able to devise, to account for many anomalies. This fact and the supposal of a constant wish to conceal doctrines against their natural tendency to obtain publicity or to become public, will, I think,

---

[1] Burckhardt's Travels in Arabia, 4to. pp, 127, 128. He calls the Palm-tree the Dom-tree. Here we have the old name restored, the tree of *the holy Om*. Rosetta is Raschid. This is *town of di-ras*, holy wisdom. About lat. 27, in Arabia, is a mount Salma. This is probably a Soluma. Drummond's Origines, Vol. III. p. 243, map. One of the rivers which runs into the Ganges is called Solomatis. Arrian, Ind. Hist. Cap. iv. For the Solumi or Mylæans, see Creuzer, Liv. Quat. Ch. iv. p. 110; Tome II. The river called by Rennell, Selima, in the same country with the mountains of Juda and Solumi, I believe was a river of Solomon. This was anciently in the country of Oude or Ioudia. Mem. p. 74. Is not the Turris Lapidea of Ptolemy in 42½ North lat. the temple of Solomon ? The Sacæ or Saxons are just below it. The Afghans are called Rohillas. This has come from the Hebrew *Regimen*. They are followers of the Rohilla, i. e. Ray-al, or ale.

remove every difficulty with which the subject has been encumbered. I believe the art of writing was at first strictly magical and masonic, and many of the anomalies which we meet with may be accounted for by the unskilful or awkward attempts of its possessors to keep it so, or to restore it to secrecy after it had become partly known. In India, to divide themselves from the Tamulese and Buddhists, the Sanscrit was probably invented by the Brahmins. Every one knows that this language was solely confined to their order for many generations. From this view of the subject we see why we have, in great numbers of instances, the same *words* for the same *things*, in countries the most remote. I know no instance in which one language can be *properly* said to be derived from another. I know many where a language may be said to be compounded of two or three others. Our own is a compound of Hebrew, Greek, Latin, several German dialects, and French. I have not named the Celtic, because at the very early period when Britain must have been first inhabited by its Druids, there must have been little or no difference between it and the Hebrew. The rays diverging from the centre cannot at that time have had much length. I think this theory will remove all difficulties, and that my reader must see it is supported by almost innumerable facts, and by circumstances without end, which are otherwise unaccountable. The universal prevalency of the sixteen-letter system almost of itself shews, that all the written languages ought to be considered but merely as dialects of one original.

In the history of languages there is a circumstance which is well known, but which has not received the attention which it merits, and this is the universal diffusion of that of the Arabians. This language (of course with some dialectic variations) is found to be in use by the nomade tribes throughout all Africa and a very great part of Asia. We know that this is actually traceable back to Job and thus to the Hebrew. My reader cannot, I think, have forgotten the great number of cases in which different authors have stated that some dialect of the old Hebrew was found. This old Hebrew is but, in other words, Arabic; and this accounts for traces of this language where Mohamedan Saracens never had any power. It is found, I believe, in the Polynesian islands among people never conquered by the Saracens and not professing the Mohamedan faith, and among the idolaters of the interior part of Africa. The length of time which the Hebrew and Arabic, really the same language, have lasted, is easily accounted for. The sacred books, first the Jewish canon, preserved it to the time of Christ: then the Targums preserved it to the time of Mohamed: then the Koran continued its preservation. Each in its turn served as a standard of reference. The fine works of Greece and Rome operated in the same manner with their languages after *they* became *dead* ones. After the flood, probably, language was every where the same. As it deviated from the first original, nations became separated. Of course this separation would be aided by other causes. But the separation again tended to confound the languages. So far the allegory of Genesis is very clear. The confusion of language caused the separation of all mankind. Man endeavoured to build a tower to reach to heaven. Was this an observatory accompanied with an attempt in part successful to discover the secrets of the privileged caste? Did the soldiers rebel against the priests? This suspicion is strengthened by what the book of Enoch declares, that one of the greatest of the sins of the Antediluvians was the searching into and the discovering of hidden secrets. Was the story of the dispersion and confusion of tongues a local mythos? I think I have not heard of it in India. That there is an allegory cannot be doubted. That a true discovery of the whole of its meaning will ever be made, is, perhaps, not even probable. If the history of the dispersion, tower of Babel, &c., be not found in the Vedas or Puranas, I shall believe that I am correct. I have formerly given very powerful reasons for believing that hieroglyphics were comparatively speaking a modern invention. I think they must have been invented after this mythos came to the West. If they had not, we should have found traces of them somewhere. Had they been previously invented, it is impossible that the mythos should be found every where, and the hieroglyphics no where except in one country.

The more I examine ancient geography the more I become convinced that in the countries of the old world, a certain number of places in each country were called after the same names, or by names having the same meanings. For instance, mounts Olympus, Parnassus, Ida. Again towns, Argo-or Argos; again rivers, Don, &c., &c., &c. ; that certain mounts or towns or rivers, in each district, as I might say each parish or deanery or bishopric, had all the sacred places which the universally-spread mythos required ; and that the names of these places must have been at first merely religious, the places for common use having other names. After some time the sacred names in different places would come into common use by historians ; they being at first the only written names, all early writings being mythical and not historical. I believe most of the early accounts or traditions, what we call histories, such as that of Rome, were not intended for a real account of transactions of states, but were a mode of concealing under the garb of history (real facts being mostly used) the mythos which every person initiated understood, but which passed with the populace for history. The mythos was Eleusinian or Masonic. I have no doubt that for many generations the art of writing was part of it.

In the Romish church the whole history of Jesus Christ from his birth to his crucifixion was formerly and is now, I believe, annually represented or acted in their ceremonies : and it was for a similar purpose that all the places in the different countries had certain similar sacred names : and it is also in many cases because we have only the sacred stories which we take for histories, (real history not being then invented,) that we have no other names of the places than the sacred ones. If a person will pass his eye carefully and slowly over D'Anville's maps of ancient geography, I think he will be obliged to confess, that the names of towns, as we have them there, cannot have been in use for the common purposes of life. How should we do if in every parish or deanery or district the principal town or river or mountain had the same name and no other ? We do very well with a Don in Scotland, and one in Yorkshire, but how should we do if the chief river of each small district was called Don or its town Argos, and no other name ? It is evident that if all the chief towns or rivers of each district of Greece or Britain had the same name one day, they would not have it the next. Thus we have great numbers of Argoses, of Troys, of Heracleas, of Romes, or (which is the same) Ramas, of Olympuses. In the same way we have many Homers—singers of the mythos [1]—many Jupiters, many Bacchuses. In the same way we have many Sibyls, prophesying in each larger or smaller district.

An attentive person must instantly see that all countries were divided, as our country is at this day, into districts within one another, with their boundaries often crossing one another—the religious district independent of the civil or the military, or local jurisdictions, seignories or shires. [2] We have plenty of cathedral towns, we have plenty of parishes, but we have no difficulty, because these are only sacred names, and these districts have one name in England, another in Germany, another in France, besides other local names. The sacred places are called, sometimes and in

---

[1] The poems of Homer were collected by Lycurgus and Pisistratus from the different parts of Greece, when they had become dispersed and nearly lost. And this operation was again performed by Aristotle and his coadjutors for the use of Alexander. This accounts for the state in which those poems are found. It is quite enough to account satisfactorily for all the pretended interpolations, and for the difficulties with which they have been attended. In the search, part was found in one district, part in another, and thus nearly the whole was recovered when almost lost And thus we have it exhibiting the marks of the Lacunæ supplied by Aristotle and his friends, which our critical Grecists call interpolations.

[2] Plin. Nat. Hist. Lib. v. Cap. xxix.

some places, cathedrals—in others, minsters. Thus the sacred mount was Olympus, in some places, Parnassus in others. We now all have our Christian names. I believe the ancients had their Christian, χρησιαν, names precisely in the same manner, and that the towns, &c., had Christian names also. In such of the histories as are evidently mythical, it can scarcely be doubted that there are a great number of facts stated which have really taken place. The early history of Rome, for instance. If we consider the matter, we shall see that this is a necessary consequence if it were desired to describe the mythos under the disguise of a history, and that it was the very best contrivance which could be adopted to get it received by the people among whom it was to be propagated. And if, among the highest or initiated classes, it was really considered only as a fable, intended to lead the people into a belief in the renewal of worlds, of new Troys, new Argonauts, &c., the very best plan they could adopt (and it was a necessary plan) was, to make all their ancient histories, as we find them in certain respects, mere copies of one another. These histories, till within a very few centuries of the Christian æra, were, I believe, all confined to certain initiated persons, no doubt very numerous, but having different grades of initiation, precisely like the orders of Masonry—the highest grade or order, being, in fact, very few in number, and consisting of the governors of the countries.

I cannot have a doubt that a real Hierarchy, like that in Rome and in Tibet, at one time extended over the whole world. But whether I am to place its origin in Oude, or Tibet, or Babylon, or Thebes of Egypt, or Ilium in Troy, or in Rome when it consisted of the Cyclopæan buildings found beneath the Flavian Amphitheatre, I know not. Perhaps Cashi-mere, with its temple of Solomon or Wisdom, has no mean claim. But at all events the עשר Ras or Wisdom and the Trimurti were the foundations of it. Every new cycle, a renewed incarnation of divine wisdom took place,—one of the Trimurti became incarnate, was born sans souillure, after ten months,—was attempted to be killed, but miraculously escaped,—spent a life in doing good to mankind,—was ultimately put to death, and the third day rose again to life and immortality: of all which, I shall say much more by and by.

4. I will now point out a circumstance not a little curious. I need not repeat, but I beg my reader to recollect, what has lately been stated respecting the Manichæans having come from India, their connexion with the Christians of St. Thomas on the coast of Malabar, who are found every where about Goa, and also respecting the Χρησιανοι and Chryson, &c., in that country: and then, if he will look into my CELTIC DRUIDS, in Chap. III. Sect. V., he will find that the Manichæans were connected, by means of their name of Pattarini, with the people of Baieux or Baiocassæ, in Gaul, and the worship of Bel or Bal.

On the coast of Malabar, about Goa, there exists a race of people called by the natives Bhoees. They are Hindoos and refuse to eat the flesh of the Beeve, &c., &c.; but still they are called Christians. I learnt from a medical gentleman, who has dwelt long on the coast of Malabar, that they are divided into two classes by the natives; one class, consisting of modern Portuguese converts, are called Christians; the other, those who resided there before the Portuguese came, are called Crestons or Cræstons. As this gentleman had no theory and did not know mine, and had not the least suspicion that the fact was of any consequence, I pay much attention to his information; it tends strongly to confirm my theory. The Creston is exactly the same name as the Creston of Italy or Crotona. In the country called Belgaum, in which these people chiefly reside, there are remains of some very beautiful and curious Buddhist or Jain Temples, which, if not destroyed by the Brahmins, must have been destroyed by the Portuguese. The distinction made by the natives clearly marks and distinguishes the old Christianity from the new, in spite of all the unceasing, though not ill-intentioned, attempts of the missionaries, both Portuguese and

5 c

English, to confound them. The Crestons were the Christians of the three sacraments, the Culdees or Chaldees of Scotland and Ireland in fact, as distinguished from the Christians of the seven, introduced by the Portuguese. Here we have really the ancient Brahmin (flesh-refusing) followers of the χϱης—of the secret, unwritten religion of all nations; and, after all, what was this religion called? not *Christian* as a proper name, but as an appellative; it was the mitis, benignus religion, the particulars of which, in process of time had escaped from the mysteries—the Cabala by degrees becoming public. It was the religion of the Bloodless Apollo of Delos, at whose altar, called *the altar of the pious* because no blood was shed there, Pythagoras offered the sacrifice of bread and wine or water. It was the religion of the Χϱης of Delphi, of the Sindi, in Thrace where the widows were burned, and of the Youth of Larissa.

In these Bhoees, Boicassæ, and Pettyeyah or Pattarini, I think we have the origin, or a colony, of the Manichæans, followers of Menu in Gaul.[1] The Jews found by the Jesuit at Madura, in the Carnatic, are far removed from Samaritan refugees, and the country never was conquered by the Saracens; so that they can have come neither from the Samaritans nor the Arabians.

In Wilson's catalogue is an account[2] of a *Salivahana*, who was a favourer of the *Bauddhas*, being obliged to return from Trichinopoly, at that time his residence, to his own former capital of *Bhoja Rayapur* in *Ayodhya* or *Oude*, by the king of Pandya, who restored the temples of *Ekámeswara* and *Kamakshi*. Wilson says, " These transactions are placed in the Kali year 1443, or " 1659 B. C., and 1737 before Salivahana reigned, agreeably to the æra, which dates from his " reign or A. D. 78." Here is a proof of all I have said respecting the nature of the æras, i. e. that they are cycles, each æra a cycle, and of the Salivahanas. Thus, upon the evidence of the records or histories one Salivan lived long before Christ; therefore, his story cannot have been copied from the latter, but *vice versa,* if either be a copy.

Mr. Wilson places the æra of Yudhishthira at the end of the Dwapar and beginning of the Cali age, 3000 years before Christ.[3] He also shews that Bhoja (that is, I suppose, the Baieux tribe) is said to have existed before the æras of Vicrama and Salivan, who must, if ever they existed, have lived before him. The case is very plain. Their æras are all 600-year cycles, of different tribes, crossing each other—recurring over and over again, till modern times, when the millenium not coming as had been expected, the system of 600-year cycles fell into disuse. Calculations were then made from the Salivan or Vicrama who was the last in vogue about the time of Christ; and it became a fixed æra. This seems to me to be a reasonable way of accounting for the difficulty. We are told that now they calculate by cycles of *sixty* years : this is the same as the 600. It forms a cycle as well as 600, with the 21,600.

Here we cannot fail to observe, that the Bhoiæ who came to Gaul, Baieux of the Manichæans, are in Ayodhya or Juda, as I am quite certain I have proved it to be. These Baieux or Bhoiæ we find on the sea-coast, and it is very remarkable that these persons or this caste, among whom we find the Manichæans and the St. Thomé Christians, *are a tribe of fishermen.* It is impossible to forget that the first Christians were most of them *fishermen ;* and the Pope calls himself a *fisherman.* In the above we may observe the temple of the Eswara-Ekam—or, in Hebrew, *Eswara the wise.* It would have been remarkable if we had no where found an חכם *hkm* in that country where there are a district and a town of Salem, or temple of Sophia or Wisdom, among the other Chaldee words. The temple of Buddha, the other temple of Kama-kshi, is Cama, *Divine Love,*

---

[1] The father of Cristna or Kanyia, *Yadu,* had a son called *Druhya,* from whom descended a tribe. I cannot help suspecting that in this tribe we may have the origin of the Druids. Cambridge Key, Vol. I. p. 145.

[2] Vol. I. p. 184.                    [3] Pref. to Cat. of Mack. MS. p. cxxiii.

and *Isi* or *Issi* or *Ischa* the name of Eve. It is probably a different name for the same God *Ischa*. The king of Cochin, as before remarked, is called Hakim.

After I had finished the above, (March 19, 1830,) I was introduced to a gentleman, who, when resident at Madras, had frequently visited the mount of St. Thomé at Jaypour.[1] He told me that the church or temple on mount St. Thomé was built chiefly of very large stones, without any cement, in the Cyclopæan style of architecture : it has an arched roof formed not by wedge-shaped stones, but by stones projecting by battering over each other with a flat stone at the top, in the manner of the stones in the dome at Komulmar.[2] This church or temple covers an ancient CARN or heap of stones, on which, he said, in modern times, it was supposed that chunam had been thrown to make them fast, to support a flat stone which is the altar of the modern monks. This, he supposed, had probably been placed there by the Portuguese. Here we have evidently a *Carn* and CROMLEH, of the same kind as those described by Miss Graham in her book, which she found in this part of India, and which I am told are very common. Vide my figure, No. 18.

But this gentleman told me an extremely important fact—that though the Christians have got possession since the arrival of the Portuguese of the tomb, temple, or whatever it is, yet that it is considered by the natives as an ancient Buddhist temple, and that great numbers of Buddhists come to it yet in pilgrimage from all parts of India. The Brahmins hold the place in detestation as they *consider this Thomas to be a form of Buddha.* The Chaldee language is commonly spoken in the country. In consequence of the above information, I was induced to examine Mr. Sharon Turner a little more closely,[3] and I will now communicate the result of that examination.

5. Mr. Sharon Turner, in his account noticed in Chap. V. Section 2, has given all the later authorities for the history of St. Thomas in India, and passed slightly over the early ones—in this respect shewing himself a skilful advocate. He well knew how to humour the weakness of his case. There are two accounts of a mission of one Pantænus, in some degree contradictory : one by Eusebius, the other by Jerom. The latter says that, in consequence of missionaries having arrived from the East requesting instruction, Pantænus was *sent ;* the former says, he went of his own accord. Nothing can be more likely than that missionaries should have arrived in Egypt, as they had often done before ; and the fact of the pilgrimages to the tomb of St. Thomas being made by Buddhists, points out to us who these pilgrims were, viz. *Samaneans,* who, we know from Clemens and others, had before repeatedly arrived in Egypt. This I think reconciles all the different histories, both of the missions from India and the mission of St. Bartholomew, who was said to have gone to India ; but who, as Valesius, Holstenius, and others have shewn, went to the Indians, though not to the East Indians, but to the Indians of Upper Egypt—Indians as they were always called ; and who, as I have formerly shewn, spoke the Hebrew language. Mosheim says, it is perfectly clear also, that he went into Arabia. These accounts are consistent with one another. But it is very remarkable, that the East-Indian people who were Christians, were converted, according to the accounts of these early writers, not by St. Thomas but by St. Bartholomew. St. Thomas is never named by either Eusebius or Jerom, (as the Christian Protestant authors well know,) and this is the reason why Mr. Sharon Turner never names Eusebius, and only barely notices Jerom—the two authors on whose authority the whole fable rests. This at once restores the entire story to the Tamuz, of whom I have before spoken, and of whom I shall again treat presently. *En passant,* I must observe, that Pantænus is a very suspicious name of the person to be sent to the kingdom of Pandæa. We all know how medical persons affect the God Mercury or Buddha and the Caduceus and the Serpent. The Essenians were called physicians of the soul or Therapeutæ : being resident both in Judæa and Egypt, they probably spoke or had their sacred

---

[1] Printed January 1833.     [2] Vide Col. Tod, p. 671.     [3] See Asiat. Res. Vol. X. pp. 74—92.

books in Chaldee. They were Pythagoreans, as is proved by all their forms, ceremonies, and doctrines, and they called themselves sons of Jesse, that is, of *שי isi*.[1] If the Pythagoreans or Cœnobitæ, as they are called by Jamblicus, were Buddhists, the Essenians were Buddhists. The Essenians, called *Koinobii*, lived in Egypt on the lake of Parembole or Maria, in *monasteries*. These are the very places in which we formerly found the Gymnosophists or *Samaneans* or Buddhist priests to have lived, which Gymnosophistæ are placed also by Ptolemy in North-eastern India. Mr. Sharon Turner says, ' It is not of great importance to our subject to ascertain whether St. " Thomas really taught in India : we know of the circumstance only from tradition, and tradition " is a capricious sylph, which can seldom be allowed to accompany the dignified march of au- " thentic history." [2] St. Jerom never names St. Thomas, but says expressly that Bartholomæus had preached the gospel there ; however, he does not specify any place. [3] Eusebius, [4] in his Ecclesiastical History, says, that Bartholomew was said to have gone to India, and that Pantænus went thither also, but not a word, that I can find, does he say of St. Thomas.[5]

In the edition of 1823, Mr. Turner wisely leaves out nearly all he had said about St. Thomas, and apologizes for leaving it to Buchanan and others : but he is too wise to say that he had proved that St. Thomas was ever in India : he contents himself merely with saying and shewing it was believed in the middle ages. But why has not the really very learned Mr. Sharon Turner told us, that Eusebius and Jerom never name St. Thomas ? Can any one suppose *him* ignorant ? Sharon Turner ignorant ! Impossible. Alas ! Alas ! Well might Roger Bacon say, Omnia ad' Religionem in suspicione habenda. If St. Thomas had gone to India, Eusebius and St. Jerom must infallibly have known it, and, under the circumstances, must as infallibly have named it. But the fact of Eusebius and Jerom having attributed the conversion of the Indians to St. Bartholomew, and not to St. Thomas, at once proves that the whole history is a part of what had come to the West, probably with the prophecy of the Erythræan Sibyl. It is not unlikely that there may have been some place in Upper Egypt, to which Alfred may have supposed his ambassador went, and who probably never went farther than Rome, where plenty of precious stones, which he is said to have carried back, would be supplied to him. And Mosheim [6] has proved that Pantenus never went to the East Indies at all.

It may not be useless to recall attention to the fact noticed a little time ago, that we have most clearly three distinct exemplars of the same mythos, consisting of *Noe and his sons, Abraham, the Mosaic history, Saul, David, and Solomon*, &c. : first in Syria of the West, brought thither by the Brahmin Abraham and his successors ; secondly in the North-eastern Syria, the kingdom of Pandæa and Mutra, or Madura, the land of Ur or Uriana, of Colida or of the Chaldees, with Noe, Ararat, Saul, David, Solomon, substantially the same as in the West ; and thirdly in the kingdom of Madura or Pandæon, in Mysore or Maha-Sura, i. e. *great Syria*,[7] as described by the Jesuit in Southern India. In these two parts of the East these mythoses are the foundation of the religion of the Brahmins : but it is a most important part of the story, that with the mythos of Moses, in India, is intimately blended, so as to form an integral part of it, the history of a person of the

---

[1] Jesus Christ, as I have before stated, is called by the Arabians *Issa*. This is nothing but a form of Isis, *שי iso*, to save Vall. Coll. Hib. Vol. IV. Pt. i. p. 199.
[2] Ed. 1802.
[3] Cat. Scrip. Eccles. Cap. xxxvi. ; see Epist. lxxxiii. p. 656, Op. Tom. IV. Pt. ii. ed. Benedict. Fabric.
[4] Lib. v. Cap. v. or x.
[5] The Saxon Chronicle, Florence of Worcester, Radulph, Brompton, Sinthelm, Huntingdon, Matthew of Westminster, Malmesbury, have treated on this subject the fullest. Fabricius remarks, that Vulgo India Thomæ tribuitur, and cites Ambrosius, in Ps. xlv., Hieronymi Epist. 148, and Nicetas, with others, Codex Apocryph. I. 7, 687, note 22 of Turner on Book V. p. 354. Ed. 1802.
[6] Com. Cent. II.          [7] Buchanan, Index Mysore.

same name, *Cristna,* and containing the same facts, in substance, as are related of Jesus Christ. All this is ridiculously attempted to be accounted for by the lost tribes of Samaria, who, to the last known of them, spoke a language though a dialect of the old first language, yet not intelligible to the Chaldee-speaking people of the three settlements at Youdia, Madura, and Jerusalem, who all spoke the Syriac Chaldee. Yet, on every principle of sound Biblical criticism, there is no reason to believe that these tribes were ever lost at all ; but that, till the time of John Hyrcanus, they continued in possession of their country and temple, when the latter was destroyed—the Cuthite idolaters and the Lions being only a story of their enemies, and therefore, independent of its innate absurdity, not admissible as evidence.

From the Western colony having left India to avoid the idolatry which was introduced with the adoration of the Lamb or Crishen, about the time of the Maha-bharat, we have little or none of the latter part of the mythos, or of Crishen in the Western tribe, i. e. in the tribe of the Jews. This is as it ought to be if my theory be correct.

On the Christianity of the Southern part of the Peninsula, beyond all doubt the most important and interesting subject which could be imagined to an Englishman and Christian, or a philosophic inquirer, Col. Mackenzie, in his collection, is perfectly silent. On this most extraordinary silence Mr. Wilson, the Editor of the Catalogue of Col. Mackenzie's papers, has the following passage : " The collection is also silent on the subject of the native Christians of the Peninsula, and throws " no light on their ancient or modern history. These omissions resulted from the character of " Col. Mackenzie's agents, who, as Hindus and Brahmins, were not likely to feel any interest in " these subjects, nor to communicate freely with the persons from whom alone information could " be obtained." [1] The unsatisfactory nature of this excuse, and indeed its absolute absurdity, I scarcely need point out. A more probable reason I will now suggest. Perhaps Col. Mackenzie was too honest to misrepresent what he knew of the native Christians. He had no absolute tie to publish the truth, or indeed any thing respecting them. He knew it was probable, that if he did, he would thereby mar all chance of preferment and be worried to death by a pack more fierce than the hounds of Acteon. But to me it is incredible that his immense collection should not have *contained,* though he might not have published it, something relating to the Christians and Jews. The truth is evident—it has been suppressed by somebody. The excuse of Mr. Wilson shews that he felt that an excuse was wanting. But I have not the least suspicion of Mr. Wilson.

Page cv. of the Catalogue of Col. Mackenzie's collection contains the following passage : " The " collections of Col. Mackenzie do not present any satisfactory materials for tracing the ancient " history of the countries North of the Krishna, on the Western part of the Peninsula ; and the " fabulous stories of Vikramaditya, Salivahana, and Bhoja, [2] which relate to them, differ in no re- " spect from those common in other parts of Hindostan, and reflect little light upon the real his- " tory of the country or its princes." Here is evidently another suppression of all notices relating to these persons—by whom made I know not, neither do I care. Whoever made it, knew well that the story of these histories being copied from the Western gospel histories is really untenable for a moment, and, however skilfully or artfully disguised, is absolutely ridiculous in the eyes of every unprejudiced Indian European : and therefore, the same policy which induced the suppression of the meaning of the word Rasit, by Parkhurst, and of the word Χρησος, by Lardner, operated here. Now we see why our slave-trading, church-building government, which cares as little for religion, except as an engine of state, as it does for the man in the moon, sends bishops

---

[1] Mackenzie's Collection, p. lxviii.

[2] Boiæ, shewn by me to be the probable originals of the Manichæans.

to India.  They are sent to superintend the Asiatic Society and the press at Calcutta, to prevent them from falling into mistakes in what they publish.  The truth of these illiberal reflections, as they will be called, is brought to an absolute demonstration by the fact that, in the whole book, no account is to be found of the rites and ceremonies at the famous temple at Tripetty or Tripeti, of the temple of Bal-ii, of the crucified Wittoba,[1] within sixty miles of Madras, being in the very centre of Col. Mackenzie's survey and his most particular inquiries, as the book proves, a temple paying the immense sum of £15,000 a year, as Dr. Buchanan says, for the privilege of being *exempt from examination*, and in consequence of which no European has ever penetrated into its *sanctum sanctorum*.  Did this payment excite no curiosity in Col. Mackenzie?[2]

One fact escapes from Dr. Buchanan of a most important nature, and it is this, that at a TEMPLE OF JAGGERNAUT, I suppose with his car, &c., at Aughoor, between Trichinopoly and Madura, the rites of the Roman Christian church were celebrated in the Syro-Chaldaic language (that is, I suppose, the Pushto) by a priest called Joseph.[3]  Surely this speaks for itself, in spite of Buchanan's disguise, and confirms every thing which was said by the Jesuit Goguet.  (Jaggernaut means *Great Creator*.)  Here we have the worship of the tribe of Yudi, the father of Cristna.  Here is true Yuda-ism united to Χρης-ism.  This shews why the Jesuits turned Brahmins, and it accounts for the Brahmins' telling our missionaries that they were of their religion, only in a corrupted state.

In the well-established fact that the service was done in the temple or church (or whatever it was) of Jaggernaut in the Syro-Chaldee language, and in the delivery of Gospels to the people in Chaldee by the Portuguese, we have a circumstance deserving of the most serious consideration. We have the Chaldee or Hebrew language continuing as a vernacular tongue, at least a thousand years after it had ceased to be so everywhere else.  For, though certain Jews speak it in most nations, as in most nations certain people read and speak Latin, it is their vernacular tongue nowhere, and in no country, except this, do they commonly speak it among themselves.  Now I cannot help suspecting that this must have been a corrupted Chaldee, more of the nature of the Aramean Syriac—the Pushto, than the Chaldee of Daniel.  This will readily account for our travellers, not well skilled in the Hebrew, calling it Chaldee, without any intention of deceiving us.  In the Asiat. Res.,[4] Sir W. Jones, who examined the Pushto, says, it had a manifest

---

[1] The crucified God Wittoba is also called Balii, and in Sanscrit Vinkatyeish, in the Telinga country, Vincratramna-Govinda. In Guzerat, and to the Westward Ta'khur or Thakhur, and generally the same among the Maharattas. He is worshiped in a marked manner at Pander-poor or Bunderpoor, near Poonah. In the inside of the palms of the hands of almost all Indian Gods a round mark or a lotus-flower is to be seen.  Learned Indians, to whom I have spoken on this subject, say, it is the *discus* which has grown by degrees into this figure. Unfortunately for this hypothesis, the mark is on the feet as well as the hands. All the Gods, it is admitted, melt into one—the Sun.  Of course Salivahana, Wittoba, and Buddha, are all one, and consequently cross-borne.  I believe this is nothing but the nail mark, ornamented like a lotus.  If the marks on the hands and the soles of the feet of the Wittobas, and many other icons of the Hindoo Gods, were meant for ornamental Lotuses, they would *always* have the form of that flower; but it is very common to see them with the appearance of a nail-head, but not the least appearance of the flower.  This shews they are not meant for Lotuses.  Any ornament on the soles of the feet must infallibly have prevented the God walking.  It is as absurd to fix a figure on the soles of the feet of the *otherwise naked* God as an ornament, as it would be to tie his hands behind him for this purpose.  The nails were honoured in India as they are in Europe.  The nails, the hammer, pincers, &c., are constantly seen on crucifixes, as objects of adoration.  On this principle the iron crown of Lombardy has within it a nail of the true cross.  For Bal-ii see my Fig. 7.

[2] The India Company gave ten thousand pounds for Col. Mackenzie's manuscripts.  The few which are come from India are in a most disgraceful state of confusion.  *It is probable the Bishop of Calcutta has some use for the remainder.* I have no hesitation in saying, if they were all together, and had a good catalogue referring to each article, they would be the most valuable collection in existence.  The liberality of the Company has been shamefully abused.

[3] Pp. 151, 155.                                    [4] Vol. II. p. 76.

resemblance to the Chaldean. Here we have the *fact* with Sir William, the *exaggeration* with the priest. The manifest resemblance is as near identity as can be expected. The Palli (that is Philistines) were of the Tamul nation.[1]

I have formerly observed that I learnt from Mr. Salome, that the Lascars spoke Hebrew. Another Jewish friend met with two of the black Lascars from the Malabar Cochin in London, who were both Jews, and spoke the Hebrew or Chaldee language. They were quite black, and had, in every respect, the Lascar character, not at all like the Jews of the West, from whom they are easily distinguishable. They accompanied my friend, the English Jew, to his synagogue. If the black Jews were a colony from the West like the white ones, they would have been white like the white ones. It is out of the question to pretend that difference of climate can have made them black, because they are black in the country above the peninsula, where there is little or no difference between the latitude and that of Western Syria. They cannot be supposed to be *blacks* converted to Judaism, because the Jews never made proselytes: in this, as in some other matters, retaining their Brahmin habits.[2] They cannot have come from the *ten* tribes as nonsensically pretended, because they are Jews, having the Jewish or Chaldee language, and not the Samaritan. The Jews of Western Syria, in the time of Jesus Christ, were not black, but there are great numbers of *black* infant Christs and *black* crucifices in Italy, and Christ was a Jew. Was he of a *black* tribe? Indeed I believe that the Christ, whose black icon I saw in Italy, was; and I believe that he came to Italy when his black mother arrived at Loretto,[3] from Syra-strene, from Satrun-ja or Regna Saturnia or Pallitana, even before the foundation of the Rome of Romulus.[4] That a colony of white Jews, fleeing from the Romans, should take refuge among their ancient countrymen seems not improbable, nor does it seem improbable that the black Jews in some instances should have acquired pentateuchs from their white neighbours; for though, perhaps, nothing would induce them to change their religion, yet they would easily be led to suppose themselves of the same religion as the Western Jews, (which, fundamentally, they were,) in the same manner and for similar reasons as those which induced the Western Christians to believe the Christians of Malabar to be of theirs. But yet I think another cause will be found for it presently.

Christ is called יהוה *ieue* דבר *dbr the word of the Lord*,[5] and the Targums frequently substitute מימרא די *mimra dii*, the word of Jehovah, for the Hebrew יהוה *ieue*.[6] Parkhurst's proof that the Jews had the *Logos* in their doctrines is quite complete; and this I think pretty well carries with it the other persons in the Trinity, or the Trimurti of India.

6. It appears to me that soon after the entrance of the sun into Aries, according to Brahmin time, a calculation backwards to the entrance of the sun into the equinoctial Taurus must have taken place, to settle the calculation of the cycles, which gave them three cycles and the 360 years or life of Enoch before the flood, in all the 2160 years, as I have formerly shewn. I never suspected that it was possible to carry this back any farther, and I thought that the equinoctial Taurus was the beginning of the mythos. But the circumstances which my reader has lately

---

[1] Buchanan, Vol. I. p. 260; Vol. II. p. 272.    [2] Yet see Matt. xxiii. 15; Acts ii. 10.

[3] Near the Fossiones Tartarum, or Italian TARTARY.

[4] The Jews were not black when the following passage was written, which we find in the Song of Solomon, i. 5, 6: " I am *black*, but *comely*, O ye daughters of Jerusalem, as the tents of Kedar, as the curtains of Solomon. Look not " upon me, because I am black, because the sun hath looked upon me," &c. Had the Jews been *black* when this was written, the colour would not have been noticed as uncommon.

[5] Inter al. Gen. xv. 1, 4; 1 Sam. iii. 7, 21, xv. 10; Parkhurst's Gr. Lex. in voce ΛΟΓ, &c.

[6] See also Gen. xlix. 18, Jerus. Targ., מימרך *mimrk, thy word* (i. e. of the Lord) is evidently meant.

seen, and some others which I will now point out, have induced me to believe, that I can perceive a glimmering of light a little more remote in the back ground.  M. Dupuis thought he could shew *astronomically* that the mythos of the equinoctial sun could be proved backward, till the bull was in the autumnal equinox.  But I must refer my reader to Dupuis for his remarks on this matter.

We all know that the retrogradation of the sun through the Twins or Gemini, if the signs in the Zodiac were then invented, must have preceded the Bull, Taurus, and that all the common visible appearances of the heavens, must have taken place while it was passing through the sign of Gemini as those which followed under Taurus ; it will not, therefore, be any matter of surprise if some remnants of this superstition be found.[1]

We have seen that Adonis was the Sun.  We have seen that he was Thamus, or Tamus, or Tamas.  This is in Hebrew תם *tam*, which means to *connect*, to cohere, to embrace, as twins in the womb : as a noun תאומים *taumim, twins*—and sometimes תומים *tumim* without the letter א *a*, which makes of it *tumim*.  Parkhurst[2] says, " Hence the proper name *Thomas* which is inter- " preted Δίδυμος, or the twin, by St. John, ch. xi. 16, et al." But it may be said, that the word twins equally applies to the Pisces tied by the tails, as to Gemini, and this I do not deny.

The Tamulic language, I learn from Sir S. Raffles and Mr. Chalmers, in a particular manner affects the termination of its words in *En*.  From this the Pood, or Wood, became *Poden* and the *Woden* of the Goths.  The Chaldee makes its plural in *n*, and the Greeks use the *n* in the termination of their words ; but never the m.  From this practice of the Tamulese the Cres became Cresen, their name of Cristna.[3]  Thus it appears that Woden, the Northern God, is simply the Tamulic method of pronouncing Buddha.  That Woden came from the North, not the South, of India cannot be doubted.  But this serves to shew us that the Tamul language formerly prevailed in North India.

By the ancients, the whole promontory of India, from the Ganges and Guzerat to Comorin, must have been called the promontory of Tamus.[4]  We find various places called Sura or Syria, as Mysore, Maha-Sura.[5]  Coromandel is but the Manda or circle of Sur, as I have formerly shewn, often written Tur—meaning both Taurus and Sol : for Tur was Sur, and Sur was Tur.  Now the sign Gemini preceded Taurus.  The Twins were the produce of two eggs, and Taurus broke the vernal egg of Siam, well known to Virgil, with his horn.  The twins were brought up at Palli-ni. They were in the Argonautic expedition to Colchos, or the bay of Argo and Colida in India. Here we may see Virgil's theory, a new Argonautic story for every cycle.

As we have a Staurobates along with Salivahana and Semiramis in the North of India, and as

[1] Eorum Osiris, alio nomine vocatus est à Bacchus, à בכי fletu sic dictus : ut bene demonstrat clariss. Golius, ex Abul-pharagio indicans apud Sabæos (Phœniciæ religionis homines) in medio mensis Tammuz celebrari. (Festum בוכיות Bochioth seu mulierum ejaculentiam) vel ut ipse Abulpharagius ex Arabibus exponit. . . . . *Festum Boucat, erat fœminarum flentium, quod celebrabatur in gratiam Dei Tammuz.  Illum vero mulieres deflent, quomodo interfecerit eum dominus suus, et ossa ejus in mola comminuerit, et ea comminuta postea disperserit.*  Nempe nomine Tammuz intelligunt Solem : quamvis, referente Maimonide, Sabaitæ nugatores (sui ritus usum et originem obliti) putent se lugere aliquem prophetam suum dictum Tammuz, ab aliquo injusto rege occisum, &c.  Dictæ autem institutionis meminit propheta Ezechiel, Cap. viii., de fœminis plangentibus pro Tammuz, (seu sole,) cui Julius mensis erat sacer et ab eo denomi-natus Tammuz Syro Phœnicibus, utpote mensis ferventissimus et sole saturatus.  Solis vero discessum, quia tum postea declinare incipit, deflebant, fingentes eum a domino suo interfici et in partes dissipari.  Sed initio vernantis anni, ejusdem Osiridis, seu circuitoris accessus et rursus inventio, haud minimum eis gaudium parere solebat.  Et sol dictus Osir seu circuitor, propter ceremoniam deflendi eum, alio nomine dicitur quoque Bacchus, qui dicente Herodoto est Osiris, p. 165 ; Οσιρις δε ες-ι Διονυσος κατ' Ελλαδα γλωσσαν.  Hyde, Itinera Mundi, p. 46.

[2] In voce תאם, p. 782.             [3] Raffles, Emb. to Ava, p. 301, 4to.
[4] Vide Lempriere, Ed. Barker, in voce Tamos.             [5] Buchanan.

we have found most of the same mythos in the South, we need not be surprised at finding also a Semiramis. To the Rev. Mr. Faber we are indebted for the observation, that the Zamorin or Samarin is nothing but a Semiramis, which name was applied to many princes. The terminations in IN and IM are clearly the Tamul, Chaldee, and Hebrew terminations : and the rulers of Cochin, Cholcos, or Colida, where he or she ruled, were called HAKIM—חכם *hkm*, wisdom.

It is not to be expected that we should any where find the whole mythos of these remote times ; but we find all that could be expected—scraps of traditions, little bits of the mythos, for each obsolete cycle—sufficient to prove one universal system to have prevailed. We cannot expect these detached scraps to be the same in different and far distant countries. Two or three thousand years having elapsed, we cannot expect to find the story of the Argonautæ of Greece in every respect the same as that of India ; but it is enough if we see the same mythos to be substantially at the bottom.

From a careful examination of the most ancient Greek, Hebrew, and Tamul sixteen-letter alphabets, and from a comparison of them, together with the inscription exhibited in Stirling's History of Orissa, that is, Urissa or Uria, I am satisfied that they have all originally been one ; but they may all be more properly said to have descended from one alphabet, because there is not one of them which has not necessarily changed in the form of its letters, not excepting even the Hebrew before it was shut up in the temple, from what it probably was about the beginning of the Cali Yug—therefore not one of them can be called correctly the original. I have little or no doubt that the ancient sixteen-letter Tamul was once the Pushto of Upper India, or the Uddya or Juddia letter. But considering the long time since it first took the name of TAM or language of the Twins, there must be expected to have arisen much variation ; indeed, quite as much as we find. But the names of Pushto, Uddya, &c., are the fading shadows of the nearly-gone truth. The country of Orissa or Or-desa or Oresa is called the Uria nation by Stirling.[1] This must be an Ur of the Chaldees.

I think it is very evident that the terms Syrian and Chaldean have been confounded when speaking of the Malabar Christians,[2] by several authors. And when the close similarity of the two languages is considered, this is not surprising. I think also there can scarcely be a doubt that the Chaldee, the Pushto of North India, the Pushto of Western Syria, the Syrian and Chaldee of South India, and the higher Tamul, which consisted of sixteen letters only, have all been the same ; and with a reasonable allowance to be made for the change which length of time and other circumstances rendered inevitable, are yet nothing but close dialects of the same language,—perhaps, if written in the same letter, not varying more than the dialects of Greece. The matter for surprise with me is, not that the three languages should vary so much, but that they should vary so *little* as to be mistaken for each other if such be the fact.[3]

If I be right, the mythos must be expected to be found in the adjoining island of Ceylon, or Candy, of which I have so often treated. Candy is the name of the central kingdom of Ceylon. It seems pretty clear that the island formerly had this name among its others. It is said to have been conquered by Rama, king of Oude.[4] The central district consists of what are called the Corles of *Ouda*-noor,[5] and *Tata*-noor.[6] Now here we see a wonderful assimilation to the British Saxon language, for the *Corles* are nothing but German *circles* and have the same meaning, whether accidental or not: and the two *Corles* form what is called the *Conde Udda*. This is

---

[1] Asiat. Res. Vol. XV.     [2] Vide Last Days of Bishop Heber, by Robinson, p. 311, n. G., &c.
[3] Dr. Babington says, Sanscrit founded on Tamul; see Trans. Asiat. Soc. Vol. I. p. 2 ; and I doubt not both were founded on Hebrew, or this earlier language, whatever it might be called. To this I shall return.
[4] Ham. Disc. Ind.          [5] i. e. *Jouda.*          [6] i. e. *Buddha.*

nothing but *County* of *Juda*.[1] A person might mistake it for English.[2] In the island is a river *Maha-vali Gunga*, and the race which inhabits the inmost mountain are called Vaddahs and Bedahs, i. e. Buddhas. Are the Vaddahs *Yuddas*? And there is a place called *Batti-calo;* this is Buddha-*clo*,[3] and their language is the *Tam*-ul. There is a town called Pala-bina or Palatina near the mount called Adam's Peak, where we formerly found the foot of Adam and of Buddha, and Mount Ararat. The principal town is called Columbo, the name of the sacred island of Scotland.[4] As we find Tam on the coast of Coromandel, so, on the opposite coast, we find a Tam, in the kingdom of Tamala.[5]

7. Ceylon or Lanca or Serendive or Palisimunda or CANDY, was a sacred island;[6] we will try if we cannot discover it, with its corles or circles in the West. Ceres[7] is but another name for Venus Aphrodite, and the Urania of Persia. Ur-ania, of the country of Ur or Urie. Her residence was on the top of Mount Ida, in the island of Creta or Candia.[8] This is the יְרֵי *ido* which Parkhurst renders very correctly Idea or γνωσις, or Maia of India, perhaps. There was an Ida above Ilium, as well as this of Creta or Kriti or CANDIA.[9] It was thus the mountain of Knowledge, or of Manda or Mundo, of which I shall say more hereafter. In this island, as we might expect, is all *the oriental mythos*. It is called Candia, and we have places called Creta or Kriti, Ida, Erythræa, Dium, Sulia, Phœnix, Hermæum, Cnossus, Γνωσος, Omphalium, DIDYMUS or TAMUZ or THOMAS, Chersonesus, Dyonysiades, Ampelos. The Island CHRYSE is adjoining to it. But Ceres had a very remarkable name, allusive, I believe, to this mythos : she was called TAM-eios, and from her and this name a plain in Crete[10] was called TAMESA : and from this I suspect, paradoxical as it may appear, that the Tamarus, near Plymouth, and the Thames, had their names — שעי *iso* תאם *tam.*

---

[1] In India the shrines or recesses in which the God is placed are called Stalla—? c. in English language Stalls. This Sanscrit word comes from the Hebrew שתל *stl.* a settleme.

[2] These English words are here because they are, I do, it not, observe Synagogue, not Mazoretic, Hebrew words —the *old* English or *Saxon* being Hebrew Refer to Book IX. Ch. I. Sect. 6, note.

[3] Similar to the *Heri-clo.* Discussed at large hereafter.

[5] Vide Ptolemy, Geog. Lib. i. Cap. xiii. and Map.

[6] Ceylon is called by Bochart Insula Iaba-diu, id est, insulam Iaba, vel Java, probatur ex Ptolemæo, Iaßadiu pro Iabaddiu. Here, I think, we have the *Diu-Ieue* or *Baßara.* Ammiano *Serindivi.*

[7] This Ceres or Venus was Creusa, the mother of Ascanius, who was thus the son and grandson of God, as one of the Gospel Histories makes *Mary* the daughter of God thus Jesus was son and grandson of God.

[8] Candia—Can-di-ia may be holy priest of IE, or place of the holy Kan, or Kanya, or Cohen.

[9] In the Zend Khret-osh is understanding, κρατ. nom. κραι. Asiat. Journ. June, 1830. Here we come at another very important meaning of the word Cret or Reet, whence, I take it or in like manner I take it, that the word Crete came. For the word there represented *understanding* is probably *wisdom*. These words are commonly used for one another in the Bible. Χρησις and Χοησος have the same meaning. Vide Dr. Jones's Lexicon. And Nestus is written Nessus. See Wilkinson's Atlas. This completely justifies me in considering the city of Cressa in Creston-ia as the same as Creston. Lempriere calls it Creston. Crestonia was the country of Cres, Cryssa the town of Cres. Littleton says, Cres, Cretis, Cressa fœm. *one of Crete.* Again, the Crestones he represents as a people among whom the widow who had been the most favoured of his wives, was sacrificed on the death of the husband. Homer's mother was called Critheis, and one of the rivers of Troy or Ter-ia was called Cryssa. Among the French, where are to be found a surprising number of close coincidences with the doctrines of the ancients, in the word Crétiens, we have exhibited the true name of the people of Crete. My view of the origin of the island of Crete is confirmed by Hesselius, who says, In ea Cres Arionis filius, Demagorgonis nepos, regnasse fertur, eamque de suo nomine Cretam appellavisse. This Cres was the eldest son of Nimrod. Nimrod, Vol. I. p. 15.

[10] The Cretans are well known and are mostly named along with the Philistines or Pallitini in the Bible : 2 Sam. viii. 18, xv. 18, xx. 23.

Plato tells us, [1] that Thammuz was king of Egypt, before Thoth, who taught him letters. Here are the twins preceding Buddha or Mercury [2] or the Bull. And the inhabitants of Egypt are said to have descended from Thammuz. Eutychius says, that the first city was built by Noah, who called it Thamanim. [3] This is most important; I shall return to it hereafter. Indeed, in every part of the world, the remains of the worship of Tam may be found.

Tahmuras taught letters to the Persians. [4]

The Egyptians had certain secret books, called those of Ammon. The author of the Concordia [5] says, "Quicquid vero sit de Ammoneorum libris, illud certum, Platonem in Phædro commemorare "libros, artes quasdam continentes, quos ipse Tautus Regi THAMO obtulit, Egyptiis distribuendos "aut describendos." Here we have Taut or Buddha receiving his learning from Thamo. These books were called αποκρυφα Αμμενεων γϱαμματα. Here we have the Apocrypha of Ammon and Thebes. I ask my reader to look into our Apocryphal books and doubt if he can, that the doctrine of Wisdom, which I have been unfolding, is the Wisdom so often treated of by them.

The Jewish Bible contains several very fine works called Apocryphal or doubtful, and of no authority, by Paulite Christians, who fancy themselves reformed. This is because they, in a very peculiar manner, teach the doctrines of Wisdom or the Cabala, which was *heresy* to the vulgar Jews and Paulites. It is very extraordinary to see all our scholars admitting, without thought, that Apocrypha means *spurious* or *doubtful*, overlooking the real meaning, which is, *secret doctrine.* I am quite certain that no person can look into the Apocrypha, after having read this work, and not see that most of the books are ænigmatical depositories of the secret doctrine of wisdom. The Athenians had a prophetic and mysterious book called *the Testament*, which they did not permit to be seen, nor even to be named or written about; but it is alluded to in the speech of Dinarchus against Demosthenes. [6] The Romans, I believe, and, in fact, every nation had its Apocrypha.

Stanley has observed, that the Sabæans, as well as the Jews, had the custom of weeping for Tammuz. This took place in June, the month called by them *Tammuz,* and of which, in the Zodiac, the Twins are the sign. [7] Narayana [8] moving on the waters, the first male or principle of all things, was wholly surrounded by what they call Tamas or Thamas, by which they mean darkness. This is correctly one of the meanings of this word in Hebrew. [9] The system was not established till the sun got into Aries; their knowledge extended no farther back than the beginning of Taurus, when the Mythos was made to commence. Before that there were Tamus *the twins;* but here all was darkness. Hence Tam came to mean darkness. In Arabia was a nation called Thamydeni or Thamuditæ, followers of Tamus. [10] The Chinese equally adore Tamo or Thomas, from whom Buddha is said to have descended. [11]

If Mr. Ritter's observation be right, Dodona ought to be Bod- or Bud-ona, the Bud meaning wisdom. And if I be right, every incarnation of a sign of the Zodiac would be an incarnation of wisdom, as it comes to be the equinoctial sign: thus it would once have been with the incarnation of the twins. From Potter I find the inhabitants of Dodona were called Tomuri, the prophetesses Tomuræ, as Potter says, from an adjoining mount called Tomurus; but why had the mount this name? This was unknown to the Greeks who were perfectly ignorant of the origin of Dodona,

---

[1] Vol. X. pp. 379, 280, Bipont.      [2] Nimrod, Vol. II. p. 475.      [3] Ib. Vol. I. p. 230.

[4] Ouseley's Coll. Orient. Vol. I. p. 113.      [5] Naturæ et Scripturæ, Lipsiæ, 1752.

[6] Spineto's Lectures, p. 122.      [7] See Stanley's History of the Chaldaic Philosophy, p. 799, 4to.

[8] This means Ie-ana-ner, or ana-ie-ner—Ie carried on the water, נהר *ner*, Sanscrit *nar.*

[9] Vide Parkhurst in voce.      [10] Drummond's Origines, Vol. III. p. 243, Map.      [11] Georg. Alph. Tib. p. 20.

except that it was founded by two *black doves*. I think in the Tamuri we have the twins. From Potter [1] I also learn an important fact, that Dodona was placed on a river called Don by Stephanus. We have before shewn that Don, in one of the languages, meant wisdom. In the neighbourhood of Dodona are several places connected with the name of John, for instance, Joannina. Almost all the mythos shews itself in the country around Dodona. As we have the Twins in the Tamuri, so we have the Arca or Arga in Arca-dia, and in Apia, the Bull Apis, or the Bees, the Melissæ or Muses. Strabo says, the Oracle of Dodona went to Epirus from Thessaly. From its evident Indian character it might be expected to have come from the side of the country where we found the Sindi, *Thrace*.

Calmet, on the word *Tho*, thus writes : " It is said, that the first Christians of the Indies, con-" verted by St. Thomas, relapsed into their former infidelity, and so far forgot the instructions " they had received from this apostle, that they did not so much as remember there had ever been " any Christians in their country; so that a certain holy man, called Mar-Thomé, or Lord " Thomas, a Syrian by nation, went to carry the light of the Gospel into these parts." I think we have good grounds from this to suspect, that what I have said respecting the mode in which the Portuguese mistook the followers of the ancient superstition for Christians is correct.

Mons. Creuzer cites the words of Ezekiel viii. 14, [2] and observes, that the most and the best of interpreters have construed *Tammuz* to mean Adonis, [3] whose feast the Jewish women solemnized after the manner of the Phœnicians, sitting all night weeping and looking towards the north, and afterward rejoicing and calling it the death and resurrection of Tammuz. But he observes, that the festival fell in June, the month called Tammuz, and that therefore it was solstitial. The festival, however, did not fall in June, because the solstice fell, in the time of Ezekiel, or now falls in June, but because June was the month of Tammuz, or the Twins. No doubt the festival was *equinoctial* at one time ; but by the precession of the equinoxes it had become *solstitial*, as calculation shews. Creuzer observes, that the worship of Tammuz had all the characteristics of that of Adonis and Osiris, and, he might have added, of the Lamb and of Jesus ; the weeping on Good-Friday and the rejoicing on Easter-Sunday. [3]

I believe the island of Candia had its name of Crete from the word $K\rho\eta\varsigma$, *a Cretan*, all the oriental mythos being here evident from the names of places. The $K\rho\eta\varsigma$ was Ceres and the bearded Venus, the Kanya or Apollo Cunnius. The Ram or Aries was called $K\rho\iota o\varsigma$. Whence comes this name $K\rho\iota o\varsigma$ ? I suspect it had relation to the same mythos. The Lunar mansion of the Lamb in India was called Kriti-ka. But the Crit-i-ka of India was also the Bull, and we have shewn that the Cres was the Lamb. In its turn the Bull Taurus was the emblem of the $X\rho\eta\varsigma$ or the Christ ; then the Lamb ; and, lastly, the Fishes ; and the followers of the fishes were Chrestiani or Pisciculi. But before the Bull, the emblem was the Tamas, which became Adonis, and in each case it was the emblem of the Cres or benignant Deity. The Golden fleece was called Crios-le mouton ou Crysomalle, la toison d'or. The word Can-dia is divus or dis, Can or Kan. Now we must observe in Crete a Tomas or Dydimus. On the coast of Coromandal there were Male-pour or town of Male, and Salem, and Adoni, and Wittoba, [5] &c., &c. This in Greek would be town of *the fleece* or of *the apple*. We must not forget that in the Peninsula, where this town of the fleece is, we had a Colchis and Sinus Argo-ricus and an Argari, &c., &c., whither the twins, or Castor and Pollux, went for the fleece or Male. I suspect the island of Creta was nothing but Cresta a

---

[1] B. ii. Ch. viii.        [2] See Nimrod, Vol. I. pp. 215—220.        [3] Creuz. Vol. II. Ch. iii. p. 42.

[4] See Nimrod, Vol. I. pp. 219, 230, and Creuzer, last Vol. p. 210.        [5] Witta-gemote—Witto-abba ! !

little changed, like Casmillus into Camillus.[1] —a practice very common; for Χρης was the Lamb of God, which taketh away the sins of the world. The change of such words as Pelasgus into Pelagos, the dropping of the S arose from the habit which all nations acquire of dropping the rough-sounding letters for the sake of euphony, as civilization advances.

It is also extremely curious to find constantly in the temples, as objects of adoration, Gods, of whom it is said, that no one knew the history, or who or what they were. Were they *really* unknown, or were they known to the initiated, and their history kept from the vulgar? The rites of the Aruspices were brought into Cyprus, and the shrine at Paphos founded by a certain Cilician, called Tam-iras; but it was unknown who he was.[2] The priests of the isle of Cyprus were called Tamarides. After my attention was turned by examination into the evidence of St. Thomas to the question of the twins, I was surprised to find remains of them in every part of the old world.

I believe the word *Carn* is the Hebrew קרן *krn*, which Lowth construes *hill* or *single mount*.[3] Pausanias[4] says, that Apollo Carnus had his sirname from Carnus, who came from Acarnania; but the word Acarnania is *country of the Carn*. He says this Carnus Apollo was worshiped in the house of the prophet *Crius*. He also says, that not far from the temple of Carnus Apollo (in Lacedemon) was the place where the *Crotani* disputed. All this was in the kingdom of Argo, in Greece. I know not what others may do, but I cannot help seeing here the same mythos in Carnate and Lacedemon.

In an old French map I find the whole of the lower end of the Peninsula of India called Carnate. When I reflect upon the absolute identity of the Druidical circles of India and Europe, as exhibited in the drawings of Col. Mackenzie, and on the identity of the carns and of the cromlehs, as exhibited in the example copied from a plate given by Miss Graham, in her Travels, and the single stone pillars, as given by the same lady, I cannot help believing that the country had its name of Carnate from the Carns of the Twin Gods or of St. Thomas; this, then, would be the country of the sacred Carns—and that the superstition of Carnac, in Morbihan, France, came with the Bhoiæ to Baieux.

I consider the Carnac of Normandy (see plates in the Celtic Druids) to be the same as the Carnac of Egypt, and as the temple of the Sun at Kanarak,[5] or the ancient pagoda near Jaggernaut, in India. In Miss Graham's Journal of a Journey in India,[6] may be seen examples of correct cromlehs and carns near Mahabalipoor. They are identical in every respect with those of Ireland and Britain. See my plates, fig. 18, and Book V. Chap. IV. Sect. 10; also the account of the very extraordinary cromleh described by Sir A. Carlisle, Book V. Chap. VI. Sect. 6, note.

I have formerly observed it is said by my informant, that the Catholics have placed their altar on a flat slab at the top of the heap of stones. The fact, I do not doubt, is, that the altar is not only a carn but a cromleh. It is like the altar over the body of St. Peter at Rome, which is placed under the cupola, the templum—the microcosm of the world, as every temple was supposed to be, which I shall discuss much at large by and by.

In the Preliminary Observations, Sect. 28, I have stated, that the ancient method of dividing the day, was into sixty hours. It appears that this was the ancient Tamul practice, thus tending to shew an identity betwixt the East and West.[7] This subject I shall resume.

---

[1] In a note in Book V. Chap. II. Sect. 7, I have shewn that the Golden Age was called Crita, in Sanscrit: this was Χρης, age of pious, age of gold, age of Taurus.

[2] Creuzer, Liv. iv. Ch. vi. p. 211.        [3] Parkhurst in voce.        [4] Lib. iii. Cap. xiii.

[5] Asiat. Res. Vol. XV. p. 316, and Hamilton's Description, Vol. II. p. 247.        [6] P. 168, 4to.

[7] Vide Vedala Cadai, Miss. Trans., Oriental Translation Society.

In Argolis there was a temple of the Kresian Bacchus. This is the Xρης, ΙΗΣ—the 608, the nomen, cognomen, et omen—Bacchus *mitis, benignus.*

Creuzer says,[1] Sous ce point de vue Axieros devient Déméter ou Cérès, *Axiokersa* Perséphoné ou Proserpine, Axiokersos Hades ou Pluton; Casmillus reste Hermès, mais il se rapproche aussi d'Iacchus, c'est-à-dire de Bacchus comme génie attaché à Cérès. Under all the circumstances shall I be very blameable for entertaining a strong suspicion that Axieros is a Greek corruption of the Ceres—the *a* the ancient emphatic article, and the *xieros* the *ceres?* We have seen the ΙΗΣ the monogram of Bacchus; and the ΙΗΣ born at the temple of Ceres, or Bethlehem. In a few lines after the above, Creuzer says, D'abord se présente à nous un nouveau couple de frères, *Jasion* et *Dardanus.* How can Jasion be any thing but the ΙΗΣ—*ιος,* or the Latin Iasus? In old Irish the Sun is called *Creas.* There yet exists a hymn to him in that name.[2] He is called in Irish Creasan, Creasna, Crusin, Crusna, and Crios. The word Cyrus meant the Sun, but yet I think we cannot doubt that there was once such a person. Ctesias in Persicis says, Και τιθεται το ονομα αυτε απο τε 'Ηλιε.[3] Plutarch says that Cyrus was named from Cores the Sun.[4] For the way in which the Hebrew כורש *curs* became the Xρης, and Κυρος, and Cyrus, see Whiter.[5] Every thing tends to confirm my suspicion, that Crishna or Cristna, called in Sanscrit *Sri,* has been the same as Cyrus, and as the Goddess *Ceres* or *Venus* worshiped at the temple of Bethlehem, the *house of Ceres,* and that Cyrus is the male Ceres, and Ceres the Xρης of Bethlehem. The God adored at Tripeti, the temple of the crucified God Bal-ii, is called Rama, or *Om Sri Ramáya Nama.*[6] Here is the Om of Isaiah, and his Cyrus and Rama. When the way in which the S, the C, the CH, and the H, have become changed for one another is considered, this will not be thought improbable. In addition to all this, Crete was a holy island, celebrated for its Mina-taur, or Bull Mina, or Menus, who was the famous legislator equally of India, Egypt, and Europe. We have his laws, the laws of Menu, translated by the learned Professor Haughton, for the East India Company.

חרם *hrs* is the solar orb. חרש *hrs,* which, in fact, must have been the same word in the sixteen-letter alphabet, means *deep thought, secret contrivance;* I should say also *secret wisdom.* It also means machinator, megalistor, artificer, particularly in potters' ware.[7] It also means a plough. From this word the Greeks had their Ερως or Ερος, the plastic or formative power— the material light. From this come the Latin *ars* the English *artificer.*[8] Who can doubt that this was Ceres and Cyrus? We have the word Xρης-ος, *Mitis,* in Greek; but I think a careful examination will prove it *not to be Greek,* or at least very unusual or obsolete Greek. It is the Crit-i-ka of India. Ceres was the same as Isis, and if we consider Isis only as the female form of the Saviour, this will bring us again to an identity of Cres and Ceres. I am quite satisfied that we very seldom sufficiently bear in mind, in these inquiries, that in ALL the Gods the male and female are united, and that almost all that may be reasonably predicated of the one may be predicated of the other.

As might be expected in Candy or Ceylon, in ancient time, we have the centre mountain called MALE-a, the rivers Phases, the Soane, and the Padacus or Po, and an oppidum Dionysii seu Bacchi. Salem, lately alluded to, the capital of Salem, is disguised into Chelam by Hamilton,[9] and

---

[1] Vol. II. p. 313.                  [2] Maurice, Hist. Vol. II. p. 170.            [3] Bryant's Anal. Vol. I. p. 80.

[4] Maur. Hist Ind. p. 171.               [5] Vol. I. p. 154.                 [6] Wilson's Cat. p. 333.

[7] It is remarkable that Jesus was said, by some sectaries, to be not a *carpenter* but a *potter.*

[8] Parkhurst.            [9] In his Des. Hist.

placed in lat. 11° 37′ long. 78° 13′. Here is the highest mountain in this part of India—Adoni disguised from its old name into Adavani by Hamilton, situated in 15° 35′ N. lat. 77° 45′ E. long. In this district runs the river Vada Vati. Has Vada-vati been Pada-vati ?

Bethel is Bit-al, *house of* or *temple of Al.* In the same manner Beth-lehem is Bit-lehem, *house,* or *temple of Ceres.* But it was also the temple of Adonis ; thus Adonis is the masculine Ceres or Cres : and it was here where the magi came to offer gifts to the new-born Cres, or, if spelt with the Sigma-tau Crest. Ceres is Cyrus and Crisna. Ceres is the feminine of Cyrus, as Juno is of Jupiter, Jana of Janus, &c. I have, I believe, before observed, that the Sigma and the Sigma-tau were constantly substituted for one another, in the early times of Greece. Take off the terminating formatives from the words, and make a just allowance for the corruption of the ח H into the CH, and for the Sigma-tau, commonly used instead of the Sigma,—and the Crys-en of India, the Cyrus of Isaiah, re-incarnated at Bethlehem, and the Χϱης at Delphi, the temple of Jah, are all one word or name, and designate Cyrus, Cristna, and Apollo.

8. The name of the coast which we find washed by the Erythræan sea with its Diu, Chryse, Argo, and Colchis, must now be explained. It is in Greek·Μαλον Βαρις, the Hebrew ברה *bire,* (Parkhurst in בר *br)*—the place or palace of the fleece or apple—Mala-bar. It has probably been a translated term from the native language, by the Greeks, from whom it has come to us. I know I shall have much difficulty in persuading my Indian friends that the word Male-bar means any thing but *mountain coast.* I shall be told that Male means *mountain* in Upper India. I am not surprised at this, since I find two Colidas, two Urias, &c., one of each in North, and one of each in South India. But it means *mountain coast,* because the coast of the Male is mountainous, in the case of Male-bar. But what is it in the case of Male-pour, on the opposite coast, the flat or level coast ? I should not insist on this, if, on this coast, I did not find the Argo, the Chersonesus, Colchis, &c.,—in fact, the complete mythos. But suppose that the word Male should mean alike mountain, fleece, and apple. This is not more extraordinary than that the Latin word Hostis should mean both *friend* and *enemy,* and Argo, in Greek, twenty different things. If I do not find the meaning of the word fleece *now* given to the word Male in the San-scrit dictionary, I maintain it is for the same reason that I do not there find the meaning of *lamb* attached to the word Agni. Dr. Babington says, Maha-bali-poor is also called Maha-malai-pour, or *the city of the great mountain,* although there is no *great* mountain near it.[1]   The learned Doctor seems to forget that there are very few places which have not several names. Malabar, in Sanscrit, is *Kerala,* i. e. chora ; in the old language `Mala.`[2]   When I recollect that we have on this coast the Hericulas, the Agniculas, the Cres, and Crys, &c., I cannot help suspecting that this KE has originally been the same as the C, the CH, in Cyrus, &c. The Tower in Jerusalem was called *Baris :* this shews the word to be Hebrew as well as Greek. We have found Ararat and Il-avratta, and a Baris, and a mount of Naubanda, in India, and a mount Ararat, called Baris or mount of the ship, in Armenia, from which the Euphrates was supposed to flow. I suspect that the river called Euphrates, is the Eu-phrat.

The natives of Western Colchos were described to be black, with curled hair, and to be cir-cumcised. In Madura the head class are circumcised, but not the lower orders. This seems to raise a fair presumption that the rite arose here, and travelled to the Egyptians, among whom Mr. Parkhurst has shewn that it existed before the time of Abraham, *but among the priests or higher class only.*[3]   Is it possible that the search after the Golden fleece, the Ram, or the Golden

---

[1] Trans. Asiat. Soc. Vol. II. Pt. i. p. 265.          [2] Asiat. Res. Vol. VII. p. 380.

[3] Parkhurst in voce, מל *ml* III.

apples of the Hesperides, by the Argonauts, may have been nothing but one of the common mistakes of the Greeks, which arose from their ignorance of the meaning of the word Malabar in the old language. In Hebrew בר *br* means place, or residence, or house, and מל *ml* circumcision or the circumcised. Then this would be *country of the circumcised*, or *initiated*. But in Greek Μαλ means either *yellow* or *golden fleece*, or *yellow* or *golden apple*. It is not a more ridiculous mistake than their Meru for *thigh*. That the Argonautic mythos, with its golden fleece and apples is here, no one can deny: and he must be credulous indeed who believes that the South Indians copied an astronomical mythos, adapted to their own astronomy, from Greece, to whose astronomy it had no relation. If any person choose to object to my explanation of Male-bar, let him consider the Sinus Argoricus, the Colchis, &c.

9. In many Roman temples in Italy there were figures of two young men seated, armed with pikes, said to be Penates and Dioscuri; but, in fact, they were totally unknown: they were probably Dii Obscuri, Tamuses.[1] They were said to have come from Troy, whence every thing *unknown* was said to have come. I think they must have been either Gemini or Pisces.

Creuzer says, a king of Italy, called Camises, Cameses, and Camasenus, married his sister; and adds, that Camaséné was une déesse ou femme poisson comme Atergatis. In fact, Camaséné signifies, in old Greek, *the Fishes*.[2] I think it is impossible to doubt that we have here in Italy and Greece the Indian Cama; and, if in this I am right, as the Sun entered Piscis 350 years before Christ, it is quite clear that the communication between the countries must have been very intimate, even up to that very late date; so that after this time the Sanscrit may have gone from one to the other. In India we have Comari, and the Cape of Comari or Comarin, near to the tomb of Tamas; but Kumari means *the Virgin*, and the Cama-deva is *the God of love*. As divine love, Cama would belong to every incarnation: thus the Twins in India were Cama, and the Fishes in Italy were the same. Camasenus came at length to mean fishes from its being an epithet of the constellation. It was probably Cama-isi, with the Latin termination. Cama is Cupid, Cama-deva God-Cupid or divine love; then Camaséné will mean the sign Pisces, the emblem of divine love, the Saviour. In the sphere, the Virgin and Child constitute one sign, and form together Cama Deva. I suspect the forgotten mythos of Tam or the Di-oscuri, was made applicable to Pisces.

La Loubère says,[3] the promontary *Cory* (Κορυ of *Ptolemy*) could be no other than that now called *Comori* or *Comorin*. On this promontory is a large nunnery, and here, in a very marked manner, prevails the worship of the Goddess Cali. Now I take Cory to be the Greek Κορη, the name of Proserpine, and the Marin is *Marina*, the Sea Goddess. Cora-Mandel is *Coramanda*, circle of Core. The coast is called the country of Calidi, that is, of Dei Cali or Holy Cali.[4] The learned Oxford Professor of Sanscrit, Mr. Wilson, generally calls the coast of Coromandel, Chola. This is the Manda or Circle of Cali. But in p. 181, it is said that Chola is also called *Chora-manda-l*, and was anciently called Regio *Soræ*, and Soretanum. The Sura or circle (as the Germans would say) of Sura, has thus come down to us. I find that the country of Sora or Chola was ruled by a king raised to the throne, not by the neighing of a horse, like Cyrus, but by an elephant, and that his name was *Kerik'ala Chola*,[5] as written by Mr. Wilson, but which ought to be, I suspect, *Hericlo Sura*, the Syrian Hercules. In the Javanese the word Cama becomes Como and Sama Somo.[6] Thus Comorinus, the end of the promontary of India, is Cama-marina; and Cama is but Ama with the aspirate. Thus Cama-marina is the Sea Goddess Venus, who is also Cupid or Dipuc. As we find in the very oldest language S and T indiscri-

[1] Creuzer, Vol. II. Liv. v, Ch. ii. p. 416.    [2] Vol. II. Liv. v. Ch. iii. p. 440.    [3] P. 259.

[4] Cali-ja, see my Book IV. Chap. 1. Sect. 5.    [5] P. 185.    [6] Crawfurd, Hist. Ind. Arch. Vol. II. p. 4.

minately used in Asia and Greece, as Tur and Sur, and Nessus and Nestus, Cryssus and Crestus ; so we find a similar practice prevailed in Italy: their first Camasenus is constantly written Camarenus.[1]

We find the Comarin in Italy, in the plain of Camera, in Calabria—and Camerinum in Umbria— and Camarina in both Italy and Sicily.[2] Mr. Bentley says, " The constellation Gemini, may, " I think, have arisen from the story of the Aswini Kumāras."[3] The close connexion between the Twins and Comari or Kumari is important. The name of Comarin, in Sanscrit is Canya-Muri, *Cape Virgin*, said to be contracted into Comari.[4] But the Kumari was the Virgin, and her images were the Kumarim. It is said that Josiah *put away the comarim which the kings of Judah had set up ;* that is, the images of the female generative power, in opposition to the male.[5] Cama was the name of the priestess of Diana, and as the priestesses bore the names of their Deities, of course Di-ana or Di-Jana, was Cama. This is the Cama-deva of India.[6] Eusebius[7] says, that the Uria or Ur of the Chaldees is called by Eupolemus Καμαρινη, and the priests of that country כמרים *kmrim*.[8] Here we have my theory of the Ur of the Chaldees confirmed. This Kmrim is evidently Comarin. In none of the cases of etymology here noticed, should I consider my explanation sufficient if unaccompanied by the circumstances which I have pointed out. It is on the circumstances I depend, not on either the sound or the similarity of letters. We have the Argonautic mythos in the languages both of India and Greece. Did the Greeks invent a mythos which is *not* the least applicable to themselves, or the Indians invent one which in every thing (as we have before shewn) *is* applicable to them ?

I now beg to recall to my reader's recollection, that we found Culdees both in Ireland and Scotland, and, as appears in the fifth Chapter of the CELTIC DRUIDS, a great number of the Gods of India. These are so marked, that they leave no room for doubt as to the identity of the two. Now, when this is considered, it will not be thought surprising that the doctrines of the inhabitants or the Culdees, of the Colida of Comorin, should be identical with those of the Culdees of Scotland. The fact is, the three sacraments, of what are called the Christians of St. Thomas, and of the Scottish Culdees, and of the Jews, viz. Orders, Baptism, and the Eucharist, are identical. When Christianity first came to Britain is not pretended to be known ; it is only admitted that it was found here by the Romish missionaries. I suspect the Christianity of the Culdees of Ireland and of Scotland was the Χρησεν of Malabar : and was brought from the city of Columbo, in Ceylon or its neighbourhood, to the Columba of Scotland ; in the same way the Hindoo Gods were brought to Ireland, where they are now found—a fact which cannot be disputed.

A very learned author says, Quid obstat, quo minus hoc inventum (he is speaking of the Zodiac) Chaldæis tribuamus, populo antiquo, et a primis, post reparationem humani generis, in terra Sinear colonis, oriundo ? Sane Sextus Empiricus,[9] famosus ille Scepticus, qui totum hoc quod scire vocamus, disputationibus suis evertit, contra astrologiam disputaturus, hoc tanquam certum et indubium assumit, Chaldæos antiquos eandem Zodiacum, quem habent Græci, cum omnibus animalibus habuisse. *Chaldæi*, inquit, *Zodiacum circulum, ut edocti sumus*, dividunt in duodecem animalia, &c.[10]

The Ioudi were Alchymists as well as Magicians. This I take them to have been in the

---

[1] Vide Berosus ap. Annius of Vit. Lug. 1554, p. 248.   [2] Lemp. Class. Dict.

[3] Hist. Ind. Ast. p. 46.   [4] Vincent's Periplus, Vol. II. 486. Is Muri, Mary, Maria ?

[5] Jurieu, Vol. II. pp. 255, 256.   [6] Ib. pp. 257, 707.   [7] Præp. Evang. Cap. xvii.

[8] Jurieu, Vol. II. Treat. vii. Ch. ii. p. 198.   [9] Lib. i. con. Astrol. p. 339.

[10] Naturæ et Scripturæ Concordia, Cap. iv. Lipsiæ, 1752.

character of Chaldæans. We see the same character of Chaldæans continue with them from beginning to end. The Egyptian kings gave permission to the Jews alone to exercise the art of making gold.[1] I have little doubt that the word Callidus for *cunning*, i. e. *wisdom*, and Callidus *hot*, and καλος *beautiful*, το καλον, are all, in their root, the same, and all arise from the same original idea: and, I have no doubt, in the numeral or arithmic letters, which I shall explain by and by, it has been XL=650 or Kala=72. Call, in Welsh, means wise, knowing, learned. This is Cali. That which a man is learned in, is denominated his vocation or calling. Country of Ur of the Chaldees is Cali or Cali-deva or dei; Ur-ia is country of Ur or Urus or the Beeve, of the holy or Goddess Cali, or the benignant or beautiful Goddess Cali—Καλος. We have Orissa, Uriana, Uria, Ur. Mahakalee, the great Cali, is the same as Mahamya, the great Maia.[2]

Chola and Chora were two names of the same thing. Cora was Cory, the name of the Indian promontory in Ptolemy; but Cory was the Goddess Kumari and Komari, and on the promontory stands a convent of Nuns, just where it ought to be. Coro-manda was the circle of Cory, and Cola-manda was the circle of Cola, which was, I believe, nothing but the Goddess Cali, another name for Cory and Komari—Καλη or Καλος, in Greek, *mitis, benignus*, having precisely the same meaning as Χρης. Colida was the country of Calie or Cali, who was peculiarly the object of worship in that country, and Abraham or the Brahmin left Ur of the Cali-dei, or Cali-deva, or Cali-da. Abraham did not leave the *country of Ur* of the Chaldees, but *Ur* of the Chaldees. Ur is also ure or yore, and means *country*. Choro-mandel became Soro-mandel;[3] one the circle of Sur, the other of Cali. Koru[4] is also written Kolis.[5] That is, the Virgin was Cali, the origin of Cali-da. Vincent says, " Koil, Kolis, and Kolkhi, and Kalli-gicum are related, I have no doubt."[6] The Koil is Coil or Coel, meaning the same as Cun-ya, the father or mother of Helena, the mother of Constantine—the same as the A-pol-lo or A-bal-lo Cunnius, of Thrace or Athens. Calida may also be Cali-tana.[7] From Kalli-gicum came Chalcos.

10. I would now draw the attention of my readers to what is noticed by our Indian inquirers, but, in their usual style, passed without reflection. There are near Madras *two Tombs of St. Thomas*, or *Tamus*, or *the Twins*, with a CARN, a monastery, &c., at each. How came these? As might be expected the Christians are permitting one of them to go to ruin, and it is almost deserted: but it is there with its CARN. This is a fact. I wonder whether the monasteries were tied together by the tails, like the fishes of Italy. Here are two Tombs or Carns for the Twins or Gemini: one for Castor, and one for Pollux, who were both in the Argonautic expedition to Male-pour or *town of the fleece or apples*. I beg my reader to think upon this. Were the Twins slain, as the Bull was slain, and as the Ram or Lamb was slain? Did they constitute the holy Thomas or Dydymus martyred on that occasion? The Thomas of the Gospel was never in India. But might it not be Thomas, the son of Budwas, the father of MANES?

The sovereigns of Orissa, or Uriana, or Urii, or Ur of Calida, on the coast where the tomb of Thomas stands, were called Kesari or Cæsars, the successors of Salivahana or Salivan, the cross-borne, or crucified, or Vicram, who was born on the same day with the Roman Cæsar. A family of Kesari or Cæsars reigned in Orissa in the fifth century.[8] All these various circumstances, and the agreement in the pretended dates of the Salivahana of India and the Cæsar of Italy, prove the truth of the cyclic part of my theory beyond a doubt. Can any one believe the princes of these distant countries copied the title of Cæsars from one another?

---

[1] See Classical Journal, Vol. XX. p. 77.          [2] Gladwin's Ayeen Akbury, Vol. III. p. 7.

[3] Rennell, Mem. p. 185.          [4] That is the Hebrew כערה *kore, Virgo*; the Greek Proserpine.

[5] Vincent, Per. Vol. II. pp. 502, 503.          [6] Ib. p. 503.          [7] Ib. p. 508.          [8] Vide Hamilton.

I have formerly pointed out the circumstance, of which Col. Wilford informs us,—that Saliva-hana and Vicramaditya are the same, and afterward that Salivahana killed Vicramaditya. The æra of the later began when that of the former ended—56 years B. C. It has also formerly been observed, that Mohamed was considered by the Brahmins to be a Vicramaditya: then here, in the æra of the Hegira, we have another æra of a Vicrama-ditya succeeding that of Salivahana. From this it is clear that an æra of Vicramaditya means an *æra of the* 600 *years:* and that when it was originally said the tenth or twentieth year of the æra of Vicramaditya, any of the nine æras may have been meant. This, indeed, is the way in which Hindoos constantly express themselves: for instance, the tenth year of the sixth or seventh cycle. The same language applies equally to the sixth or seventh 600 of the ten six hundreds, as to the sixth or seventh 60 of the 600. What a door this opens to mistakes I need not point out. The same thing takes place with the Chinese. After the time when the Brahmin power was overturned, and their seminaries destroyed, they lost all knowledge of the nature of their cycles, along with their astronomy; and the æra of Vicramaditya now, I believe, is calculated forwards from the birth of Cæsar. Some of them have learnt the meaning of their astronomy from the English, and are beginning to pretend it was never lost, but the truth, I imagine, is too well known for them to deceive any body but their own devotees. From a consideration of these facts, I am led to a suspicion that when the Jews or tribe of Ioudi, at Cochin and Madura, whom I have lately noticed, are said to have come down from the West, bringing seventy-two families, and establishing a Sanhedrim of seventy-two persons, [1] in some year of the æra of Vicrama or of the Cycle, allusion may be made to an æra long preceding both our time, and that of the Χρης-ian æra of the Thomé Chrestians. It follows that the Cres and Colida of Tam, or the Twin, should have preceded that of the tribe of Ioudi, for Yuda was the son of Cristna.

I read in Professor Wilson, that there was in Southern Pandea a dynasty of seventy-two Pandæan kings, ending with Guna Pandya. Were these the seventy-two tribes of Jews? In the same page (lvi) Wilson says, these Pandæan kings came from Ayodhya. I believe, in spite of rules of etymology, that *Guna Pandya* is nothing but the Pandion of Athens, of Delphi, and the Apollo Cunnius: and that Guna is Kanya and the Cunnius. What is Γυνη in Greek? Kan-ya is the name of the Indian Venus, as well as of Cristna or Apollo.

And now I think we may see that there are yet some real surviving remains of the mythos of Gemini or the Twins, as well as of the three posterior constellations in the precessional cycle. We have Gemini or Tamus, Taurus, Aries, and Pisces. When I consider the drawings of the Gemini and the Pisces tied together by the tails, and the construction put on the passage of Genesis, that Adam and Eve were one, I have been induced to suspect that the Gemini were like the Siamese boys: the drawings are exactly like them. About a year before these boys were heard of, I was induced to make a visit to Newport Pagnel, to inquire into an *incredible* story which I had heard, noticed before in Book IX. Chap. IV. Sect. 1, namely, that formerly a woman had lived there with two bodies. I only got laughed at for my folly in supposing such a thing possible, BUT I found the monument of the Lady or Ladies in the church, and what the corporation considers of much greater consequence, I found that it holds large possessions under the will of this Lady or Ladies, the daughter of Fulk de Paganel.

When I meet with evidence from learned men who do not the least understand my system I value it most highly, because the probability of its truth is greatly increased, as any person who understands the value of evidence must very well know. Of this nature is the following extract,

---

[1] Buch. Christ. Res. p. 222.

from the work of my learned friend, Eusèbe de Salverte : Apres avoir célébré la naissance du Kioro, de l'enfant céleste qu'il regarde comme la tige de la dynastie manchéone, le poëte empereur Khian' Lung péint cet enfant animant de son esprit tous ses descendans, et agissant lui même dans la personne de la plupart d'entre eux.[1]  C'est une véritable Métempsychose, presque aussi nettement établie que celle du pontiffe de Buddha, et qui n'a pas du révolter davantage la crédulité de Tatars.[2]  He must be blind who does not see here the regeneration of the wisdom of Cyrus.  Here we have most undoubtedly the mythos which I have developed, existing at this day among the Chinese.  M. De Salverte correctly observes, the same principle may be seen to prevail in many sovereigns who always took the same name—for example, the Syrian kings the names of Adad; the Egyptian kings the name of Pharaoh; and many others who probably do not understand the reason of the custom.[3]  Very justly indeed has M. De Salverte observed, that there is a strong probability, that the long reigns of Djemchid, Feridoun, &c., are only dynasties of the nature of Lamas,—i. e. re-incarnations.  In the same way Mohamed was a renewed incarnation of Jesus, and of Buddha ; and this was the reason why the images of Buddha were spared in the East by the Saracens.  The Caliphs and the Sultans all professed and still profess to be the same, like the Lama of Tibet, as I shall prove.

11. It may now be useful to inquire into the meaning of the far-famed Jaggernaut, in one of whose temples we lately found the priest named Joseph celebrating what Dr. Buchanan called the rites of the Roman Catholic church.  We have found, in the district particularly known for its attachment to the superstition of Jaggernaut, a crucified Bal-ii or Lord ii; also a crucified Salivahana ; also a Crysen and a Cristna, who was a crucified God.  In Upper India, Cristna is called Can-yia and Nat-ii. [4]  The Targum of the Jews calls *Jehovah* ii, and Apollo, the God of the people of Delphi, where the Χρησος was found by Dr. Clarke, was called IE, and the Bible of the Jews calls Jehovah IE.  The first word of Ja-gernaut is evidently IA, our Jah, and the Jewish יה *ie*.  The third is the Nat of Upper India, and the Irish,[5] and Egyptian Neiths, both of which were the Deities of Wisdom, and the Chinese Tien, as before stated in Book VIII. Chap. VI. Sect. 5.  The second word is the Hebrew גר *gr*, and means *circle* or *cycle ;* and *Iuger* has the same meaning as the title of Cyrus אל-עלין *al-olium*, αιων των αιωνων. *Pater* or *Deus futuri sæculi*—the wisdom of the cyclar Ia, or the self-existent cyclar or revolving incarnation of wisdom.  The Brahmins call him the *Great Creator ;* but the Creator was Wisdom or Logos.

In Travancore, not far from Madura, a very peculiar festival is celebrated to the honour of the Trimurti, called by Mr. Colebrooke Three Persons and one God, or of the Jewish Aleim, where all distinctions of caste are laid aside, and it is in these Southern countries that the worship of the crucified Wittoba chiefly prevails.  I apprehend this was the God Jaggernaut. Colida, to the South of Tanjore,[6] where this God is often found, has become Kolram and Coleroon.  I must repeat, this God is found in a country called Uria of Colida (Ur of the Chaldees).  Ur-ia is אור-יא *aur-ia*, country of fire, or the sun, because it was also called Sur-ia or Syr-ia. Persæ Συρη Deum vocant.  Colida was the country of the Chaldees, or Coli-dei, or Culi-dei, or Culdees of Abraham, and of the Irish and Scotch nations.  It has the same names as the country of North India, described by Col. Tod, and referred to by me in Book VIII. Chapter VI. Section 5.  It is the Καλ-ος of the Greeks, mitis, benignus, and has the same meaning as the

---

[1] Eloge de Monkden, Preface, p. v. et pp. 13, 17, 47, &c.  [2] Essai sur Noms, &c., Sect. 59, p. 396.

[3] Essai sur Noms, pp. 397, 398.   [4] Tod, Hist. Raj.

[5] Celtic Druids, Ch. V. p. 183.   [6] Wilson's Cat. Vol. I. p. 194.

Greek $X\rho\eta\varsigma$. It is the Goddess Cali who has become the most cruel of deities, though the beneficent Creator, for the same reason that the city of On or the generative power, or Heliopolis the city of the Sun, was called *the city of destruction.* The country of this God was also called Carnate. This is, Carnneith, Carn-naut, and the tomb of Tamas was a carn, and was the carn of the Zodiacal Twins, the emblem of Wisdom, or of Neith, or the Logos, or the Creator. How curiously all these things dove-tail into one another! We have Kali often in the West—in Ireland, [1] and in Caly-DON-ia ; in Cally-polis, in the Thracian Chersonesus, where were the Sindi, and the wives who sacrificed themselves, and near which are numbers of tumuli, yet said by tradition to be the sepulchres of the ancient kings of Thrace. [2]

Jagan-nath temple is called Mandala Panji [3] and Sri Krishna. [4] The first name means the universal cyclar ii, or 1E, or JAH. Col. Broughton says, [5] Bodh, under which form he is now worshiped by the title Jugurnath. Not far from the old temple of Jaggernaut is an immense fire tower, now in ruins : its roof was supported by two wrought-iron bearers, 21 feet long, 8 inches square. [6] They lie under blocks of stone 16 feet long, 6 feet deep, and 2 or 3 feet thick. I think we have never seen a beam of *wrought*-iron of these dimensions in Europe.

The Brahmins of India were believed by Mons. Bailly to have been Chaldeans. In the minutes of the Society of Antiquaries, dated 19th February, 1767, is a letter from a gentleman, at Benares, to Mr. Hollis, in which he describes an university. called Cashi. In this he states that the physicians study the Chaldaic language, in which their books on that science are written. This was the Chaldaic astrology, with which we know that medicine anciently was closely connected. [7] Father Georgius, the missionary, states, that the people of Tibet, or *the Indian Scythians,* have among them the Chaldean divinities. [8] Thus we have the Chaldee language both in North and South Colida of India. Mr. Wilson, in his preface, says, the Uriya or Urissa language is spoken in Cuttack. Here we have admitted the UR in Colida, (which Mr. Wilson little suspected,) in South India. [9] Wilson says, the Hindi varies every hundred miles, and presents wide discrepancies ; but I feel little doubt, that the Chaldee or Hebrew is at the bottom of all the dialects.

12. In Book III. Chapter II. Section 9, we find the Brahmins talking of the Saman Vedas These are the Buddhas of the Smin or disposers of our system. These contain the wisdom of our system, not of the universe. In the Sanscrit the B is continually changed into the V, particularly in the dialect of Bengal ; [10] thus the Vedahs become Bedas. [11] Van Kennedy (p. 247) says, in the Sanscrit the B and V are perpetually interchanged, and the change is optional. Thus, *Ved, Bed, Bud.* In some of the earlier authors the Vedas [12] are called *Beds, Bedahs, Baids.* I have a great suspicion that Dud or David ought to be or arose from the Bud of India. In Mr. Whiter's Etymologicon Universale [13] may be seen how the forms D, w-D, v-D, b-D, or BD " pass into each other." This never occurred to me till I was told that the learned Ritter had shewn Dodona to have been originally Bod-dona ; nor should I have thought of it, if I had not found the sons of David or Dud in the country of Buddha.

Hyde, in his eighth chapter, informs us, " that the Persians had a book which is yet extant,

| | | |
|---|---|---|
| [1] Celtic Druids. | [2] Sandy's Travels, p. 21. | [3] Asiat. Res. Vol. XV. p. 268. |
| [4] Asiat. Res. Vol. XV. p. 318. | [5] Popular Poetry, notes, p. 152. | [6] Asiat. Res. Vol. XV. p. 331. |
| [7] Vall. Col. Hib. Vol. IV. p. 157. | [8] Ib. | [9] Wilson's Cat. p. xlix. |

[10] See Wilkins's Grammar.        [11] Edin. Rev. Number XXV. Vol. XIII.

[12] The Vedas have been mentioned before in Book III. Chap. I. Sect 8, and Chap. II. Sect. 9.

[13] Vol. I. p. 865.

766 VEDA.

" entitled Gjâvidân Chrad, i. e. the *eternal Wisdom*, which is older than all the writings of " Zoroaster, and ascribed to one of their kings called *Hushang*. This book proves evidently that " the people of those times worshiped the only true God."[1] I think the Gja, or perhaps Ja-Vedan is *the Wisdom of Ja*, or Je, or Jah. The Buddhists are said to have Vedahs as well as the Brahmins. The sacred books of most nations seem to have been called the books of wisdom. The Persians called their sacred book the *Sophi* Ibrahim, that is, the book of the *Wisdom* of Abraham. The Jews call their book, not as we do *Genesis*, but the ראשית *rasit*, that is, the book of Wisdom. The Scandinavians called their sacred book the Saga, (Saga is the same as the Latin *Sagax*, sagacious, wise,) that is, again, the book of Wisdom ; and the Brahmins and Buddhists call their sacred book the Veda, the word Veda being only a corruption of the word Buddha, and, like all the others, it means Wisdom, and I have little doubt that the Edda of the Northern nations is the same, being V-edda, and the Kali-ol-ukham of the Tamuls the same.

" The third order of the British Druids, was named Vates, by the Greeks *Ouateis* (Borlase). " The origin of this name is preserved in the Irish Baidh and Faith, but stronger in *Faithoir* or " *Phaithoir*. The first was written *Vaedh* by the Arabs, whence the Greek *Ouateis ;* hence " *Vaedh*, signifying a prophet, became a common name to many authors of Arabia (D' Herbelot). " Baid is the Chaldæan ברא *bda*, prædicavit. Nihil apud alias Gentes (Hebræas antiquiores, " Arabes, Ægyptios, Græcos, omnes) usitatius quam ut sacerdotes, prophetæ, divinatores, " oraculorum interpretes essent, et responsa Deorum eorum ministerio redderentur. Id moris " apud Hebræos, lege Mosis antiquiores obtinuisse probabile habeatur, quod Jobus et Prophetæ " vocem ברים *(bdim)* Badim ad divinatores et oracula notanda usurpaverint.[2] Ch. ברא *bda* " Bada, Arab *Bede* prædicavit cum Hebr. בתא *bta* congruat. The Irish Faith and Faithoir is " the Hebrew פתר *ptr*, interpretus est. Solvit ænigma, Genes. Cap. xl. פותר *putr* conjector, " unde Joseph *Poter* dicitur ; et Pateræ, Sacerdotes Apollinis oraculorum interpres.[3] Hence " the Irish Bro-faith, i. e. the ancient prophets. The Scythians or Hyperboreans, says Pausanias, " gave the first Προφηται to the temple of Delphi, and they came from beyond the seas to " settle at Parnassus.[4] Finally it is the Phœnician אפתא *apta*.[5] Again,[6] Vallancey says, " From *Feadh* or *Feodh*, a tree, proceeds *Foedh*, *Fodh*, knowledge, art, science, which in the " Sanscrit language is written *Ved ;* and from Hercules being the inventor of this *Feadh* or *Feodh* " he was called *Fidius*. In the *Bhagvat-Geeta*, translated by Mr. Wilkins, we also find the origin " of this Ved is from a *tree*."

In Col. Tod's work, we have a description of a class of persons who are kept in the houses of the great men in India, to make out their pedigrees, and to write or record the transactions of their reigns. It is not possible to conceive any thing more like the bards of Ireland and Wales. But what is the most remarkable is, that they are in Sanscrit actually called by the word Bat, the T being marked in a peculiar manner to make it sound like the RT, and the word Bard. I cannot attribute this identity of the two to accident, and this leads me towards the opinion which will be thought very bold, but of the truth of which I every day become more convinced, that most of what we call histories are nothing but effusions of this order of men : and that the early poets of Greece were, in fact, nothing but the bards of India in that country. What was the Olen, named in my Celtic Druids, said to have been the first composer of verses ?

---

[1] Biograph. Brittan. voce Hyde.    [2] Spencer de Urim, p. 1020.
[3] Buxtorf, p. 666.    [4] See Collect. No. 12, Pref. clxiii.
[5] Vall. Col. Hib. Vol. IV. Pt. I. p. 426 ; for origin of Baids, see ib. p. 424.    [6] Ib. p. 80.

Somewhere in Mr. Whiter's great work which, though printed at the Cambridge press, has neither table of contents nor index, I have found it said, that almost universally the two letters B, D, meant *to form* or *to produce*. This is confirmed by Parkhurst, who says, that in the Arabic ברא *bda* means *to begin, to produce*. The *Bda* is the *Vda*, which means both self-producer, our Genesis, and Wisdom, the personification of the first production. בדים *bdim* are conjurers or wise men, whence, says Parkhurst, *perhaps the Latin word* VATES. Of this I have no doubt.

---

# CHAPTER VIII.

FREEMASONS OF YORK AND INDIA.—SOLOMONS. KINGDOM OF SOLOMON UNKNOWN.—CHALDEANS IN BABYLON, THEIR LANGUAGE AND SANSCRIT.—SACRED NUMBERS.—SEPHIROTH, CHERUBIM, SERAPHIM.—FIRST VERSE OF GENESIS.—MANI.—FREEMASONS OF YORK, METEMPSYCHOSES.

1. I SHALL not trouble my reader at present with any more observations respecting St. Thomas. I think I have shewn pretty clearly how his history arose. It furnishes a beautiful example of the way in which religions are raised by an union of weakness and roguery.

After I had, from various sources and by various means, added to reasoning, nearly arrived at a conviction, that the ancient order of Freemasons arose in India, and was established there, as a mystery, in the earliest periods, my conviction acquired wonderful strength from a knowledge of the fact which I shall now mention. I shall be censured for stating facts in this way; but I write truly and for the truth, and for this purpose alone. The style or order in such a work as this is not worth naming. At the time that I learned from Captain ——, the gentleman who was named in my last Chapter, the particulars respecting the tomb of St. Thomas, I was also told by him that he was in the strictest intimacy with the late —— Ellis, Esq., of the Madras establishment; that Mr. Ellis told him, that the pass-word and forms used by the Master Masons in their lodge, would pass a person into the sanctum sanctorum of an Indian temple; that he, Mr. Ellis, had, by means of his knowledge as a Master Mason, actually passed himself into the sacred part or adytum of one of them. Soon after Mr. Ellis told this to my informant he was taken suddenly ill, and died, and my informant stated, that he had no doubt, notwithstanding the mistake which his friends call it in giving some medicine, that he was poisoned by his servants for having done this very act, or for being known to possess this knowledge. Now, when this is coupled with the fact of the Masonic emblems found on the Cyclopean ruins of Agra and Mundore, I think, without fear of contradiction, I may venture to assume, that the oriental origin of Free-masonry cannot be disputed—and that I may reason upon it accordingly. Every person, at all conversant with inquiries of this kind, knows that our ancient and beautiful cathedrals were built by societies or fraternities of men supposed to be monks from Spain, to which country they are said to have come, along with the Saracens, from the East. These people were monks, but probably all monks were not masons. But the two societies, if separated in some things, were very closely connected in others. They were Culdee or Calidei monks, from Calida. They were Saracens from Surasena, on the Jumna in India.

After I had been led to suspect, from various causes, that the Culdees, noticed in the Notitia Monastica and in the last chapter, and there stated to have been found in the Cathedral at York, were Masons, I searched the Masonic records in London, and I 'found a document which upon the face of it seemed to shew that that Lodge, which was the Grand Lodge of all England, had been held under the Cathedral in the crypt, at York. In consequence of this I went to York, and applied to the only survivor of the Lodge, who shewed me, from the documents which he possessed, that the Druidical Lodge, or Chapter of Royal-Arch Masons, or Templar Encampment, all of which it calls itself, was held for the last time in the crypt, on Sunday, May 27, 1778. At that time the Chapter was evidently on the decline, and it is since dead. From the books it appears to have claimed to have been founded by Edwin in the year 926. From a curious parchment document, formerly belonging to the Lodge, and restored to it by Francis Drake, author of the Eboracum, as appears by an endorsement on the back of it signed by him, stating that it came from the Castle at Pontefract, it seems probable that, according to the tradition to that effect, the ancient records of the Lodge had been sent to that place for safety in the Civil Wars, as it is well known that many of the title-deeds of Yorkshire families at that time were, and on its destruction were, like them, destroyed or dispersed.

Formerly a contest arose among the Masons of England for the supremacy,—the Lodge of Antiquity in London claiming it, and the York Lodge refusing to admit it. This was at last terminated by *an Union* of the two parties, under the authority of the present Grand Master, his Royal Highness the Duke of Sussex. The Bishops of York, in their great and similar contest for precedency with the Bishops of Canterbury, maintained their See to have been founded by Scotch Monks, (Culidei probably,) entirely independent of St. Augustine.

The documents from which I have extracted the above information respecting the York Masons, were given to me by —— Blanchard, Esq., and transferred by me to the person who now possesses them, and with whom they ought most properly to be placed, His Royal Highness the Duke of Sussex. It appears from the documents above-named, that Queen Elizabeth became jealous of the York Masons, and sent an armed force to York to put them down.

I have formerly shewn, that the Masons, or Chaldei, or Culdees, were the judicial astrologers at Rome in the time of the emperors. They could be of no small consequence when they were employed by Julius Cæsar to correct the Calendar. This I shall shew hereafter.

I do not pretend *absolutely to prove* that this Druidical Royal Arch, Chapter, Lodge, or Encampment of the Temple of St. John at Jerusalem, or of the tabernacle of the temple of the HOLY WISDOM, as it calls itself, of Jerusalem, was actually the same as that of the Culdees of the Monastica, but I think the presumption is pretty strong. What more the books contain may be only known to Masons, of high degree. But if I do not by mathematical demonstration connect the Calidei, or Chaldæans, and Masons at York—I do it in the Mathematici and Chaldæi at Rome. I will repeat here, that the Christians of St. Thomas had the three rites (according to Buchanan) of Baptism, Orders, and the Eucharist. These the Jews had; and these, according to Jamieson, the Culdees of York and Iona had. The use of the word Wisdom here for the name of the Lodge, has probably come from a very remote period. In modern times no person could have known of the doctrines of the Rasit, so as to have caused him to adopt it.

However far back I search into history I always find traces of the Chaldei, and this, not in one country only, but all over the old world. I cannot help suspecting that they were correctly Freemasons from India. What I have said in my CELTIC DRUIDS, respecting them, that they were not a people but an order of priests, is confirmed by Diodorus Siculus,[1] who says, that the

---

[1] In Lib. ii. Cap. iii.

Chaldeans held the same rank in Babylon, that the Egyptian priests did in Egypt; that they transmitted their learning from father to son; that they were exempt from all public offices and burdens; that by their constant study of the stars, they learnt to foretell future events; and that they called the planets *counselling Gods* or *Interpreters*. Here we come back to my explanation of the first verse of Genesis, of the םימש *smim*, or *the disposers* or *placers in order* of Parkhurst.

In another place Diodorus speaks, as of a matter of course, of the Chaldeans as a college : Περι δε τ8 πληθ8ς των ετων εν οις φασι την θεωριαν των κατα τον κοσμον πεποιησθαι το συστημα των Χαλδαιων, 8κ αν τις ῥαδιως πιςευσειεν : " What the Chaldeans (literally the " college of the Chaldeans) say concerning the multitude of years, which they employed in the " contemplation of the universe, no one will believe."[1] I have little doubt that they were the inventors of figures and letters, and, of course, of astrology ; and that this, in many cases at least, conducted them to the possession of sovereign power.

The Rajahpoutans, or a tribe of them, have the name of Rattores ; this I much suspect has originally been Rastores or Rashtores or Ratsores. May the word Rashtra, in Sur-ashtrene or Zor-aster, have any relation to the Ras ? I suspect the Zor is Sur—and aster-ana—and that Zo-radust is a corruption of Sur and Ras-di, the rough letter S changed or dropped as usual. We must not forget that the planets were all believed to be intelligent beings, to possess wisdom. They were all Rashees or Rishees. *Sidus* is the proper Latin for star, and *aster* for planet, and *aster* is, perhaps, formed by the common practice of the anagram from the word rast or rasit. The probability of this, like all other instances of conjectural etymology, must be left for the consideration of the reader—each case, without any general rule, depending on its own circumstances. Zoroaster in the Irish books is called *Zerdust* and surnamed *Hakim*, and he is the son of *Doghdu*. Porphyry says, he dwelt in Babylon with other *Chaldees ;* and Suidas calls him a *Chaldean.*[2] Vallancey shews, from Strabo and other authorities,[3] that the Chaldeans were the first astrologers.

To myself the truth of my theories has several times been proved in a manner the relation of which to such persons only as know me, and have a dependance on my integrity, will be of any weight. After I have, from a union of theory and reasoning and doubtful records, concluded, that certain events must have taken place, I have afterward found proofs of another kind, that such events really did happen. The discovery of the Masons at York is an example of what I mean. I concluded that the Culdees of York must have been Masons, and must have held their meetings in the crypt under the Cathedral. I examined the office in London, and I found a document which not only proved what I have said, but shewed that, as might from all circumstances be expected, it was the Grand Lodge of all England which was held there. Naming this to one of the oldest and most learned Masons in England, he told me he knew the fact very well, and that if I went to the Cathedral at York, and examined certain parts which he named, I should find proof of the truth of what I conjectured. From the circumstances, this evidence becomes to me very strong.

I request my reader to think upon the Culidei or Culdees in the crypt of the Cathedral at York and at Ripon, and in Scotland, and in Ireland,—that these Culdees or Chaldeans were Masons, Mathematici, builders of the temple of Abraham's tribe, the temple of Solomon ; and, that the country where Mr. Ellis found access to the temple in South India was called Colida and Uria; that the religion of Abraham's descendants was that of *Ras ;* that Masonry in that country is called Raj or Mystery ; that we have also found the Colida, and most other of these matters on the Jumna a thousand miles distant in North India,—and when he has considered all these

---

[1] Lib. i.     [2] Vall. Coll. Hib. IV. Pt. i. p. 197.     [3] Ib. p. 221.

matters, as it is clear that one must have borrowed from the other, let him determine the question. Did York and Scotland borrow from the Jumna and Carnatic, or the Jumna and Carnatic from them? In India, there were two kingdoms of Pandæa, one in North India and one in the Carnatic, in each of which all these matters, *in both nearly the same*, are found.

I think I may venture to assume, that I have connected the Masons, the Templars, and the Ishmaelians, and I beg leave to observe that, by means of the red eight-point cross, I connect the Templars also with the Manichæans and the Buddhists of India.

The extraordinary similitude, indeed the actual identity, of the religions of Rome and Tibet, have been constant subjects of wonder and admiration to all inquirers, and have defied all attempts at explanation. But I think my reader must now see that they were actually the same religions, only with such variation as length of time and distance might well be expected to have produced. They had the same trinity, the same incarnation of the divine wisdom, the same crucifixion and resurrection, and nearly all the same rites and ceremonies—the same monks, the same vows, the same tonsure, the same monasteries. And in my next book, if I do not shew that EVERY ONE of the remaining doctrines, rites, and ceremonies of the Romish Christians were identical with those of Tibet, I shall shew that they were identical with those of the Gentiles, I believe without one exception. The truth is, that the religion of the *Ras*, of *Buddha*, of *Metis*, of *Sophia*, of the Χρησος, of *Bafomet*, of Acamoth or the *Intelligence Universelle*, extended over the whole world, and was the universal esoteric, ancient and modern religion;—the religion of Tibet, of Sion or Siam, of the Monks of the lake of Paremboli, (Embolima of India,) of Dodona or Boduna, of Eleusis, of Ephesus, of Delphi, of Virgil, of the Gnostics, of the Manichæans, and of the Pope—for which reason he very properly calls himself a CATHOLIC, and his religion Catholic or Pantheistic, and his followers Catholics or Pandees, or Saints of Pan-ism or Catholicism.

I beg to repeat to such of my readers as are Royal-Arch Masons, that Solomon was a Ras or wise man, and that a Mason in Rajapoutana is called a Raz, which also means mystery; and now I take the liberty of observing to my brethren, that they are called ROYAL-ARCH MASONS, not because they have any thing to do with kings, but because they are *Raja-pout-an* Masons, as the persons who conquered Egypt were *Royal* Shepherds or Shepherd Kings, or *Raja-pout-an* Shepherds, from *Pallitana*. Pout is Buddha, who is Αρχη, who is Ras.

2. If my reader recollect that the Queen of Sheba came from Ethiopia, and that the African Ethiopians, the Royal Family at least, pretend to be the descendants of Solomon and this Queen, whose name was Helena, he will not be surprised to find the King of the Ethiopians taking the name of that virtue for which this prince was in a particular manner celebrated—*Wisdom*. Thus he is called, not the *king* but the RAS of Abyssinia. Why was Solomon so celebrated for this virtue? It was no doubt from being the protector, or perhaps the renovator, of the doctrine of the emanation of the *Rasit*. He removed the seat of the Western doctrine of Wisdom, from the stone circle on Gerizim to Moriah or the Western Sion, for which he has been cursed by the Samaritans, and blessed by his followers, who in consequence assumed the name of the whole tribe exclusively to themselves, that is, Juda-ites, or Yadu-ites, or Jews, sinking the other ten tribes into Schismatics. It will be said, perhaps, that the monarch of Abyssinia was called Ras, because he was the head or the first of the country. This would be fair reasoning if we had not the word explained by the other names of this personage—Johannes, and Butta, and Deus—all which we have seen, or shall presently see, mean *wise*.

Speaking of the Abyssinian Christians Scaliger[1] says, " Ipsi vocant se Chaldæos, neque

---

[1] De Emend. Temp. p. 338.

" frustra : lingua Chaldaica etiam temporibus Justiniani eos usos fuisse." [1]   Of course, if all the people spoke the Chaldee the Christians would do so likewise, as they do in Tamul.

Sir William Drummond, in his essay on a Punic Inscription, [2] has proved the Geez to be nothing but Hebrew.   Sheba's son by Solomon was called *Ibn* Hakim.   This clearly is nothing but הבן חכם *è-bn-hkm*, *the son of Wisdom*.   And it gives us a probable meaning for the word Solomon.   Zeradusht was called Hakim. [3]   Mr. Hammer says, [4] " Videntur illic pro lapidibus " angularibus ac clavibus concamerationis figuræ obscenissimæ, omnes ad Genesim seu Gnosim " ophiticam pertinentes :" and in a note he adds, " Hæc est sapientia divina, de quâ in scripturis " toties mentio occurrit et quam Eusebius, secundum Hebræorum, principium nominat. [5]   *Ego* " *sapientia* habitans in consilio. [6]   Quid autem *sapientia* et quomodo genita est ? [7]   Unde autem " *sententia* inventa est ?" [8]   Again, he adds, " Hanc sapientiam, quam Hebræi Deo in creando " ac ordinando mundo, ut principium adsociaverant, Gnostici in systema suum adoptaverunt.   Sic " Theodotus."

In the valley of Cashmere, on a hill close to the lake, are the ruins of a temple of Solomon. The history states that Solomon finding the valley all covered with water except this hill, which was an island, opened the passage in the mountains and let most of it out, thus giving to Cashmere its beautiful plains. [9]   The temple which is built on the hill is called Tucht Suliman.   Afterward Forster [10] says, " Previously to the Mahometan conquest of India, Kashmere was celebrated for " the learning of its Brahmins and the magnificent construction of its temple."   Now what am I to make of this ?   Were these Brahmins Jews, or the Jews Brahmins ?   The inadvertent way in which Forster states the fact precludes all idea of deceit.

Mr. Wilson says, it is probable that the Tartars or Scythians once governed Cashmir, and that they first gave the sanction of authority to their national religion, or that of Buddha, in India. [11]

The Tuct Soliman of Cashmere in the time of Bernier, [12] was described by him to be in ruins, and to have been a temple of the idolaters and not of the Mohamedans.   The Mohamedans reported that it was built by Solomon, in very ancient times.   All this at once does away with any pretence that it was a building of the modern Mohamedans ; and is a strong confirmation of the Jewish nature of the other names of towns—Yude-poor, Jod-pore, &c., &c.   Bernier goes on to say, [13] that the natives of Cashmere had the appearance of Jews so strongly as to be remarked by every one who saw them ; that the name of Mousa or Moses is common among the natives ; that Moses died at Cashmere, and they yet shew the ruins of his tomb near the town.   This is curious when connected with the fact, that the Jews of Western Syria say, no one ever knew where he was buried.

On the frontiers of China is a place greatly resorted to by pilgrims, called the *Stone Tower*, but of what religion does not appear.   It is in a narrow pass called *Belur-tag*, not far from where the Gihon and Yerghien approach each other.   The pass is ascended from the North West: and on the left side of the road, the face of the mountain, a massy rock is hewn into a regular form, with two rows of twenty columns each; hence it is called the tower of the forty columns or *Chasotun*, [14]

---

[1] Nicephorus, Lib. ix. p. 18; Ouseley's Coll. Orient. No. III. p. 217.                [2] P. 28.

[3] Vallan. Vol. IV. Pt. I. pp. 191, 196.                [4] Mines de l'Orient, Vol. VI. pp, 35, 100, 10J.

[5] Præp. Evang. xi. 14.                [6] Prov. xiii. 12, 22.                [7] Sap. xi. 24, xii. 22.

[8] Job xxviii. 12                [9] Forster's Travels, Vol. II. p. 11.                [10] P. 17.

[11] Hist. of Cashmir, Asiat. Res. Vol. XV. p. 24.                [12] Travels, Vol. II. p. 128, Ed. fol. 1688.                [13] P. 137.

[14] The last temple of Solomon was in the *mere* of the cashi or college; this is in the *town* of the cashi or college. The *Tun* of this Saxon country or country of the Sacæ, is our *town*.   See Webster's Dict.

and is said to be a work of the Jews. But it is more generally called the *Tuct Soliman* or Throne of Solomon.[1] Here we carry this religion over the Cashmerian mountains to Tartary.[2] Many persons will have no doubt that all the Tuct Solimans were copied from the building in Western Syria. I cannot content myself with this supposition, though others may.

I suppose my reader will have observed that, besides what I call our temple of Solomon, there were many others. One for instance in Mewar, one in Cashmere, one on the frontiers of China, and one in Asia Minor, at Telmessus. And it would be no difficult matter to shew, from circumstances, that there must have been several others, for a Tuct-Solomon could be no other than a temple or house of Solomon. I suspect that the great kingdom of Solomon in Western Syria, whose monarch filled the whole world with the fame of his glory and wisdom, was only a part of the Judean mythos. I do not mean that there was no temple, but that the history was accommodated to the mythos, as was the early part of the history of Rome to its mythos, and indeed to the same mythos. I apprehend that the temple was a type of the universe, and that all the temples were the same; all parts of the one universal mythos which extended, as is evident, from the same sacred names of places being found every where, to the farthest points of the globe.

I have a strong suspicion, but I name it as a suspicion only, that the fourteen Maha-bads of Persia, on which Sir W. Jones founds his Mahabadian dynasty, merely meant towns of the great Buddha; that the fourteen Solumi, said to have existed before the flood, were the same fourteen Buddhas or incarnations of Wisdom; that the same towns are meant; that there was a temple of Solomon at each of them, and that they are fourteen certain places where we find the local mythos visible from their names. I entertain a persuasion that the Solomonian mythos, which we have found in China, in Cashmere, in Oude, in Persia, in Asia Minor, and in Matura of the Carnatic, as described by Bouchet, in the temple of the Brahmins, with its passage of the sea, &c., &c., were all the same with that in Western Syria; that they all had at the bottom the same recorded transactions; and that this was part of the secret Jewish religion. Look back to Book X. Chap. V. Sect. 5, to what Bouchet has said of the Moses, &c., at Madura, in the Carnatic.

If I can prove only one of the Indian towns or temples having Jewish names to have existed before the time of Mohamed, it is enough, under all the peculiar circumstances, to prove my case, viz. that it is probable that the Jewish names of the other places *may* have been given before his time. It opens the door to an inquiry into the probability of each particular case; and I am quite certain in nine cases out of ten the probability will amount to certainty. The temple in ruins in Cashmere is a most complete example of what I allude to : and, in fact, the city of Oude, or Ayodia, or Iuda, is another : for no one will contend that Oude has been either built or named since the time of Mohamed.

3. I know the following question, previously alluded to, will not be answered, but will be treated with contempt and ridicule; but nevertheless I must propose it—Where is the empire of Solomon the Magnificent first read of in the works of the Gentiles ? It is not noticed by Herodotus, Plato, or Diodorus Siculus. It is a most extraordinary fact, that the Jewish nation, over whom but a few years before the mighty Solomon had reigned in all his glory, with a magnificence scarcely equalled by the greatest monarchs, spending eight thousand millions on a temple, was overlooked by the historian Herodotus, writing of Egypt on one side, and of Babylon on the other,—visiting both places, and of course almost necessarily passing within a few miles of the splendid capital of the nation, Jerusalem. How can this be accounted for ? A few generations after the reign of the mighty Solomon, the nation was conquered by the Babylonians, and its

---

[1] Cab Cyclop. Vol. I. p. 118.      [2] The sovereign of which was called *Prestre John.*

chief persons carried into captivity. Before this time we have books which purport to be a history, but it is remarkable that they are found to contain incidents belonging to a very old nation spread over all India, over immense countries, and accompanied with temples, statues, towns, and mountains, with the Jewish names, and evidently of the same mythos. The dates of the statues, towns, names of mountains, &c., here noticed, are so remote that they are totally unknown to the present inhabitants, and even to their history or traditions, though they pretend to have regular histories to times long anterior to the time of the Western Solomon. The towns, names of mountains, temples, colossal statues, &c., clearly prove, that whenever they were fabricated the people who erected them must have been masters of the country. Can any one believe that all these things can have arisen from a few captive Jews or Samaritans from the country and state, so small as to be overlooked by Herodotus, and that they, so late as less than 1200 years before Christ, can have possessed those places in India unknown to the native historians of the countries who wrote perfect, regular histories of them, supported and confirmed by astronomical observations?

In reply to this, I am asked, Why Homer or Moses never names the Pyramids? The cases are totally dissimilar. But I suppose they did not name them for the same reasons that the Roman historians never named Stonehenge, Abury, or Carnac—each of the two latter equal to the greatest Pyramid,—and for the same reasons that our early English historians never named Abury. If these monuments had possessed inscriptions, which conveyed historical information, they would probably have been named. If the historians had been in search of antiquarian curiosities, the case would have been different; but they were in search both of ancient and modern empires, and it is totally incredible that the nation of Solomon could have been overlooked, if its history, as told in the Bible, be true. Herodotus might overlook an obscure little mountain, or vassal tribe of Babylon, though possessing even a large temple, but this is all which can be admitted; and this proves that the object of a chief part of the Bible was not *history* but a *mythos*, as the Bishop and Romish Apostolic Vicar Dr. Geddes properly called it, like the early history of Rome and Troy.

Almost as unaccountable as the ignorance of the inquisitive Herodotus, is the slight knowledge or comparative ignorance of Alexander the Great. So unsatisfactory to Josephus was Alexander's neglect of this formidable fortress and sumptuous temple,—by far the richest which ever existed in the world, that he felt it expedient to forge a story to fill up the chasm or blank, and in his work it may be found. I shall not enter into the subject: the falsity of Josephus has been satisfactorily proved by Mr. J. Moyle, of Southampton, in his correspondence with Dean Prideaux, and I have no need to add to the proof. Mr. Moyle has shewn that Alexander was never at Jerusalem. I have seen the ignorance of the Grecian historians of the Jewish nation accounted for by the pretence, that they despised the Jews too much to notice them. The reason is ridiculous and childish, not worthy of a moment's consideration. If the Greeks knew any thing of them, it is probable that they knew no more of them than the name, or than they knew of any other obscure mountain tribe. If I were to write a history of Britain it is probable that I should never name the town and church of Bangor: and yet I should not despise them. For a similar reason Herodotus never named the temple or empire of Solomon.

All these circumstances combined give the lie to the glories of David and Solomon, and reduce the whole to the history of a petty mountain tribe possessing a rich temple, similar to those which were to be seen at Heliopolis, that is, Tadmor, and many other places. The whole thing amounts to this; that there was in the mountains of Syria a tribe divided, like the Ionians of Asia Minor, into twelve municipalities; that they quarrelled about their superstition, and in consequence separated; that it was a tribe which came in very early times from India; that it was, until it settled and conquered Judea, exactly like the present Afghan tribes ; indeed, there is the greatest reason in the world to believe, that it was one of them, probably a strong tribe ; that its sacred books are a mere mythos, exactly like the Mahabarat or other sacred books of the Brahmins,—the foundation of it being the same mythos as theirs, accommodated by its priests to its own peculiar history and local circumstances. And this was most likely the case of the secret books of every great temple or cathedral as it might be called,—which was, in fact, the archiepiscopal see of each arrondisement. The Jews, of whom we read at Alexandria and other places, were probably partly from Judæa and partly from the other settlements of the tribe of Yudi, wherever they might happen to be—Telmessus, Upper Egypt, Heliopolis, or other places where the Tecte Solumi prove that they were settled. No doubt the Christian sectaries of the Judæan mythos, have done all they could to destroy written evidence of the truth; but the temples of Solomon, the names of places in North India, in South India, in Siam, Ceylon, China, &c., prove the existence and the great dissemination of the mythos, which was, in fact, the basis on which was erected the Pandæan kingdom, and *that* was a Sacerdotal kingdom. That the tribe of Juda did exist almost all over the world cannot possibly be denied : the city of Judia in Siam, the mythos at Cape Comorin, the temple of Solomon in Cashmere, the Montes Solumi in Mewar, the great city of Oude or Juda, are facts which prove it, and admit of no dispute.

4. I must now call my reader's attention to another fact of very great importance. We have heard much about Daniel and the Chaldeans of Babylon, and about the rendering of the law of Moses by Ezra or Esdras into the Chaldee language, at the gate of the temple, after the captivity. But there is another book extant, said to be written by Esdras, which declares that the book of the law was burnt, and that it was rewritten by him under the influence of divine inspiration. This, for very obvious reasons, is now denied to be of divine authority, by the united sect of Jews and Christians—for in this case they must be considered one. But it seems to stand upon as good ground as the other books, and in some respects upon better. But this observation is rather from my argument, though it strikes a blow at the credibility of the fact of the explanation of the law at the gate of the temple : for how could Ezra explain the law, if it were burnt ? unless, indeed, it were the *new* law revealed to Esdras.

The fact to which I have to draw my reader's attention, and from which I have digressed, is this, that though we are told that the Jews brought the Chaldee language and letters back with them from Babylon, yet that among *the great numbers of inscriptions* of different kinds found in the ruins of that city, one in the Chaldee letter and language has never been found. This seems clearly to prove, that if the Chaldean language and letter were the language and letter of Daniel and the magi or astrologers with whom he is classed in the Bible, they were not the letter and language of the Assyrians. The letter must have been a secret of the Jewish priests, and their language, their sacred language at least, probably different from that of Assyria. This all tends to prove the tribe of Abraham a distinct tribe from India, of comparatively-speaking recent date.

On the most mature consideration I have come to the opinion, and it is very important, that the similarity between the Chaldaic, or Hebrew, and the other languages noticed by Sir W. Jones, is the nearest approximation to identity which can be expected, and indeed more than could be expected, or would have been found, if the copy of the Pentateuch in the Jewish temple had not arrested the Hebrew Chaldee in its progress of change. Under these circumstances it is evidently incredible, that the *original* from which all these languages sprung can now exist. It is pretty clear that the mythos of Moses has existed from very old time. This, I think, the numbers of temples, houses, or mounts, (all the same,) of Solymi prove. And this is confirmed by the Sibyls, each of whom refers to this mythos, though the variation among them is so great as to shew that they cannot have copied from one another. If we go to the African Ethiopians we find, in the descent from Solomon, in the Ioannes, Butta, Deus, and the use of the Chaldee language, remains of the same mythos. We find the same both in North and South India. When I consider the little, obscure, mountain tribe of Jews in Western Syria, and I again contemplate the Judæa in the mighty cities of Agra, Oude, Mundore, &c., I cannot doubt that North India must have been the birth-place of the mythos; and the mistake of all these people in supposing themselves descended from the Jews of the little tribe of Western Syria, is easily accounted for; it is the natural effect of the loss by them of their real history, and of the stories told them by proselyting Christians, that they must have come from Western Syria. To these causes of mistake may be added the account of these people retailed and misrepresented to us by the same Christians, who, from prejudice, overlook important facts, (such, for instance, as that of the existence of an old temple of Solomon in Cashmere,) and who misrepresent others to make them suitable to their own superstitions and creeds. Thus, to believe them, all the Jews or Youdi, scattered in ancient times over the world, and forming great nations, were part of the mountain tribe of Western Syria, which Herodotus did not observe, or, in his search for nations, discover; the capital of which, with its temple, would not now have been in existence, had it not been preserved by Helena and the Christians.

To return to the assertion I have so often made, that the Hebrew is the first language. This assertion I must now qualify, in order to answer a question which will be asked, viz. What I mean by the first language. It is very clear that the Hebrew, when a spoken language, must have changed like all other languages, and must have undergone this change when it advanced from *sixteen* to *twenty-two* letters, and this change must have been very considerable. We have formerly seen, from the works of various learned men, that the Afghan language, called Pushto, is very similar to the Chaldee. We have seen the same Pushto very similar to the Tamul. We have seen that the Tamul is very similar to or identical with the Aramean Syriac or Pushto of Western Syria, and that this, which is the dialect of the time of Jesus Christ, is but a dialect of the Chaldee or Hebrew in which the Synagogue Pentateuch is written. All these similarities are as near identities as can be expected, and the fact of the same original sixteen letters in all, proves their original identity. Supposing them all in the sixteen-letter state, they must necessarily all have diverged from it, and the similarity discovered by different learned men is as much as can be expected, and more than would have been ever discovered, had not the common mythos operated in a direction contrary to the tendency to change—the natural effect of time—united to the circumstance of the recluse Pentateuch in the Jewish temple having been fortuitously preserved. In fact, all the written languages are but dialects of a sixteen-letter language, as Mr. Gilchrist has judiciously observed. The language which Sir William Jones and others call Chaldee can be nothing, in fact, but the Arabic, before the change in the letter and the addition to it of points, by one of the Caliphs, took place. It is, in reality, the language of the book of Job.

After much consideration I am induced to believe, that the Sanscrit has been a language artificially formed, by the caste of priests, upon the old language of the country, and, at first, as found in the earliest Veda, in a more rude state than it afterwards arrived at; and that, as long as the Brahmins were in power and prosperity, it kept improving, till it arrived at its present perfection. As they kept copying their Vedas they kept improving the language of them, exactly as we do with our Bibles. We all along keep correcting the antiquated mode of spelling and expression, though keeping to the sense.

I think, judging from all history and from all circumstances, there can be no doubt that the farther back we go, the more nearly all the ancient languages, which had the Cadmean system of letters, will be found to assimilate; on the contrary, the more we advance to our own times, the more they will diverge from their original root. In our endeavours to discover the meanings of the old languages, this consideration will be found of the greatest importance. It accounts very satisfactorily for the great number of old Hebrew words which we find in almost all the Western languages. But how are we to account for the Sanscrit, which we also find in them? I can suggest no rational theory except that which I have before stated,—that the Sanscrit must have come to the West before it increased its sixteen to fifty-two letters, and that, in fact, it was also Hebrew or Saxon, or a dialect of Hebrew, before it was improved. I still feel that this is scarcely sufficient to account for the closeness or the similarity of the Sanscrit to the improved forms of the Latin and Greek.

I confess that sometimes I cannot help suspecting, that the opinions of Dugald Stewart and Professor Dunbar are well founded, and that the Sanscrit was formed on the Greek and Latin, after the irruption of Alexander into India. It seems to me that our Sanscrit scholars are opposed to this, chiefly, because it seems to compromise the antiquity of the Indian learning : but this is, I think, a hasty conclusion ; for their learning both in astronomy and in every other branch may have existed in the Tamul or other language long before the time of Alexander, and all their works may have been very readily translated into the Sanscrit. In the sixteen-letter Tamul we have a refined language of learning and of learned men, and in the Kaliwakam[1] we have a work which will not disgrace any learned Brahmin.

The following is an extract from the Kaliwakam.

## THE KALIWAKIM OF AYVAR.

The zealous study of sciences brings increasing happiness and honour.
From the fifth year of age learning must begin.
The more we learn the more understanding we get.
Spare no expense to learn reading and writing.
Of all treasures reading and writing are the most valuable.
Learning is really the most durable treasure.
An ignorant man ought to remain dumb.
He who is ignorant of reading and writing is indeed very poor.
Though thou shouldst be very poor learn at least something.
Of each matter endeavour to get a clear knowledge.
The true end of knowledge is to distinguish good and bad.
He who has learned nothing is a confused prattler.
The five syllables Na-ma-si-va-yah[2] contain a great mystery.
He who is without knowledge is like a blind man.
Cyphering must be learned in youth.
Be not the cause of shame to thy relations.
Fly from all that is low.
One accomplished philosopher is hardly to be met with among thousands.
A wise man will never cease to learn.
If all should be lost, what we have learned will not be lost.
He who loves instruction will never perish.
A wise man is like a supporting hand.
He who has attained learning by free self-application excels other philosophers.
Continue always in learning, though thou should do it at a great expense.
Enjoy always the company of wise men.
He who has learned most is most worthy of honour.
What we have learned in youth is like a writing cut in stone.

---

[1] Kali-Hakim, Kali-akim, Kali-ow-akim ; evidently the *wisdom of Cali* or *Kali.*

[2] This is the Roman Nama Sebadia, often found on the Mithraitic monuments in Italy. I think this cannot be doubted ; and it connects the Italian and Indian mythoses together beautifully.

False speaking causes infinite quarrels.
He who studies sophistry and deceit, turns out a wicked man.
Science is an ornament wherever we come.
He who converses with the wicked perishes with them.
Honour a moral master.
He who knoweth himself, is the wisest.
What thou hast learned teach also to others.
If one knows what sin is, he becomes wise.
Well-principled wise men approach the perfection of the Divinity.
Begin thy learning in the name of the DIVINE SON. (Pulleyar.)
Endeavour to be respected among men of learning.
All perishes except learning.
Though one is of low birth, learning will make him respected.
Religious wise men enjoy great happiness.
Wisdom is firm-grounded, even on the great ocean.
Without wisdom there is no ground to stand on.
Learning becomes old age.
Wise men will never offend any by speaking.
Behave politely to men of learning.
The unwise only flatter others.
Wisdom is the greatest treasure on earth.
The wiser, the more respected.
Learning gives great fame.
Wise men are as good as kings.
Do not deceive even thine own enemy.
In whom is much science, in him is great value.
He that knows the sciences of the ancients, is the greatest philosopher.
Truth is in learning the best.
Wise men are exalted above all others.
In proportion as one increases in learning he ought to increase in virtue.
The most prosperous good is the increase in learning.
Wisdom is a treasure valued everywhere.
The Veda teaches wisdom.
Speak and write for the public good.
If knowledge has a proper influence on the mind it makes us virtuous.[1]

The very important circumstances, noticed in Chap. VII. Sect. 9, that the same mythos of Pisces is found in the same names, Camasenes in South India, the Tamul country, and in South Italy, PROVES, I repeat PROVES, a very intimate connexion between the two countries of which we have not a hint in any Greek or Roman historian, (and the Nama Sebadia confirms it,) even later than the time of Alexander, because it must have been after the sun entered Pisces at the vernal equinox, which took place 360 years before Christ. This connexion can have been no slight or casual acquaintance of the two countries which could establish the same new system (as to the populace it would appear to be) of religion in one of them. It may be observed also, that this system was not established by Sanscrit speakers, but by the Tamul or one of the broken, that is, the old dialects of India. The names Comarin, Coromandel, &c., are all common names used by the people, and if they be found in the Sanscrit this is what might be expected. It is absurd to suppose the Brahmins would not write the old names in the Sanscrit letter. Whoever they were that brought the Indian names of the Fishes to Italy, they at the same time probably brought the art of building, and the beautiful designs of the temples at Pæstum—which are, in fact, almost copies of some of those in Col. Tod's book—and which are proved to be the same as the Indian

_____

[1] Asiat. Transactions, Vol. VII. p. 357.

also, by the Ling Ioni's, found in the ruins by Col. Tod, and particularly in the hand of Ceres, the Goddess of the temple.

Once more I repeat, that I know I shall have great difficulty in convincing Sanscrit scholars that their language is comparatively modern : but its close analogy to the Greek and Latin cannot be denied, and I feel quite satisfied that they can never refute the argument drawn from the smallness of the number of the Greek and Latin letters. If the Greek and Latin had come from the Sanscrit in its present form, they must have had *fifty-two* letters instead of *sixteen*. I have PROVED in my Celtic Druids, that at the time when the colonies came from the Indus, they each had sixteen letters only, and the same sixteen. In this alphabet the names of the Indian Gods are found, and the names of places and Gods in Greece and Italy,—Saturnia, Pallatini, &c., &c., and, in the names of the Indian Gods, the names of the God of the Hebrews, and of Syria—Jah, Adoni, Taurus, &c.

When the Chaldean tribe of Yuda, or tribe of Crestons, with its Kan-ya, or $X\rho\eta\sigma\epsilon\nu$, or IE, or Cristna, came, under its Brahmin, from Uri-ana of Colida or Chaldea to Creston and Sindus of Thrace, (bringing its custom of sacrificing widows,) and Creston or Corton of Italy, and mount Meru, or Sion, or Solyma of Syria, and the other Solymas, about 2500 or 3000 years before Christ, it brought the sixteen letters of Cadmus or the East with it; perhaps the sixteen letters of the Tamul. Its mythos of Meru, and its Arga, and its cycles of returning Saviours, Buddhas, or Cristnas, put to death and raised from the dead, &c., &c., were renewed and located under every distinct, independently-formed government. Thus we find traces of these things with the cyclar temples of Stonehenge, &c., &c., every where. Every nation had its Meru, Moriah, &c., &c. And the tribe of Jews, where it differs from the others, differs in consequence of having had a great iconoclastic leader to legislate for it, in a particular manner, different from the others.

A very learned oriental friend maintains, that the languages of the Chinese and other Eastern countries, and of the Polynesian islands, have all the most complicated and artificial forms that we meet with in the Sanscrit and Western languages ; and thence he would infer, that they are primeval or anterior to the latter, and that the Hebrew, on account of its rudeness, is what he calls a broken-down language from the others. The contrary, I contend, is the fact in the case of the Hebrew, because in its case we take it in the temple copy, from which it may be said not to have deviated for thousands of years. We catch it in its infancy, and in consequence of the curses denounced against any alteration of the law written in its dialect, it has been kept in its infant state all the days of its life. Many passages may formerly have been corrupted to serve the purposes of priests, but generally the language would not be changed. In corrupting passages the old style would be studiously affected. The younger a written language is, the more simple it will be, and it will acquire complication and refinement as it acquires age. What can be more rude than the synagogue Hebrew ? What more refined and artificial than the pointed modern Hebrew of the Mazorites ? The language of the barbarians of the Polynesian islands is complicated, because its possessors have arisen from the overflowings of the civilized states, and they took with them, when they migrated, all the complicated forms in use in the country which they left.

The important fact which I gleaned from the learned and ingenious Mr. Landseer, almost the whole of whose life has been spent in the study of Assyrian antiquities, that among all the numerous inscriptions of Babylon nothing like a Chaldaic inscription was ever found, is decisive proof that the Chaldee was not the dialect of the Assyrians, nor is it the dialect of the present natives of that country ; but it *is* the dialect of several tribes in the country of the Brahmin Uria of Colida, both of that near Ayoudya or Oude, and that at Salem, Adoni, St. Thomé, Uria (in Orissa) in Colida, near Cochin. Sir William Jones found Chaldean inscriptions in Persia, as we should expect.  See his Sixth Discourse.  The conveyance of the Chaldee language to the Afghans and the Brahmins of Madura by Nestorians of Germany is absurd enough.

Dr. Hagar believes he has traced the nail-headed characters to the Indian.  Now if this be true, the Samaritan must have come from India to Melchizedek before the time of Abraham; and when Ezra changed this character into the Chaldee letter of Daniel, or of the then Chaldees, a great change must have taken place in the letter between the time of Abraham and that of Daniel, a space of a thousand years.  Daniel appears to have been not a Western Syrian Jew, but a Persian Chaldean of the Jewish religion.  We may be certain that the Chaldei of Persia, (i. e. Cyrus,) of Assyria, and of Judea, were all the same.  In Book IX. Chap. I. Sect. 11, I have given an observation of Dr. Murray's, that ocular inspection proves the identity of the Chaldean and Sanscrit letters; then the Samaritan must have been the first letter of the Chaldeans, brought by Abraham before the Sanscrit was perfected, and the Chaldean letter, the letter of Daniel, after it.

It will be difficult to persuade many persons to agree with me that the Chaldee of Daniel was not the letter or language of Babylon; (except merely as the *sacred* and probably *secret letters* of the Chaldee order of Daniel;) but they must answer the questions, Why are there no Chaldean inscriptions in the ruins of Babylon, whilst there are such numbers of inscriptions in the arrow-headed characters ? I think Dr. O'Conor says very truly, [1] that the Chaldee had a common original with the Phœnician, and that the Chaldee was the letter and language of Abraham.  I think the Chaldee was the peculiar and probably secret letter of the Chaldeans till the time of Ezra.  The Jewish tribe were correctly Chaldeans till changed to a new system by Moses.  Abraham brought it to Egypt, the Egyptians taught it and its mysteries to Moses.  Mr. Bosworth and Dr. O'Conor both prove the Gothic and Northern letters and language to be, in fact, the same as the Phœnician or Hebrew.  Then, if the Saxon came from the Hebrew, of course when it came to Britain it would bring an increase of Hebrew words, and justify the derivation of many modern English words either from the Hebrew or the Saxon, or the Sacæ of India.  (Buddha was called Saca-sa, that is, Saca-isa, the Saviour or Isis Buddha—the DIVINE SON just named in the Kaliwakim—the NAMA SEBADIA of Italy.)  Every thing tends to draw us to North India, the country of the Pushto.

I entertain a strong suspicion that the Chaldee language and the letter of the Chaldees were the higher dialect of the Tamul, and that the Syro-Chaldee of Western Syria, called Pushto, and before noticed as a language both in Western Syria and Tibet or North India, was the lower Tamul language, and the spoken language of the tribe of Judæi both in Eastern and Western Syria.

5.  I shall now proceed to make some observations on the *sacred numbers* of the ancients, which will not only confirm what has been said in several instances, but be of service in our future researches.

Before I make any observations on the sacred numbers of the *Jews*, I must observe, that *generally* where *seventy* are named, *seventy-two* are meant.  This is most important—for, without it, we shall lose half the proofs of the mythos.  The truth of this observation will presently be sufficiently clear.  This is no new discovery of mine.  Mr. Astle [2] says, " The ancients frequently " expressed sums by even numbers, adding what was deficient to complete them, or omitting " whatever might be redundant.  This mode of reckoning is often used in sacred writings, and " was thence introduced into other monuments."

Bishop Walton, in his treatise on Hebraisms, [3] says, " The Hebrews are accustomed to use " round numbers, and neglect the two or three units which exceed them in certain cases.  They " say, for example, the Seventy Interpreters, and the Council of Seventy, although the number in

---

[1] Bosworth's Saxon Grammar.          [2] On Writing, p. 185.          [3] Sect. xiii.

"each case was seventy-two; and in the book of Judges we read, that Abimelech killed seventy
"of the children of Jerobaal, although he had but sixty-eight."

Every one has heard of the famous Septuagint, usually written LXX; but the story is, that the
translation was made by seventy-two men, six out of each tribe, though it is called *the Seventy*;
that to these men seventy-two questions were put, and they finished their work in seventy-two
days.

Peter Comestor, and Vincent of Beauvais, make seventy-two generations or nations from the
three sons of Noah. According to the recognitions of Clemens[1] the earth was divided into
seventy-two[2] parts, the number of countries specified in Genesis. This required no small
ingenuity; and mankind was divided into seventy-two families: but the same author, in the
Homilies, calls them seventy tongues and seventy nations. Here is an example of seventy put
for seventy-two.[3] The number of nations was generally stated to be seventy-two by the
Greek fathers.[4] On the confusion of tongues, Shuckford says, " From all these considerations,
"therefore, I cannot but imagine the common opinion about the dispersion of mankind to be a
"very wrong one. The confusion of tongues arose at first from small beginnings, increased
"gradually, and in time grew to such a height as to scatter mankind over the face of the earth."[5]
Again he says, " but the text does not oblige us to think it so sudden a production."[6] By a
long train of argument he endeavours to support his opinion. The fathers make the languages
seventy-two, by adding Cainan and Elishah, according to the LXX, who are not mentioned in the
Hebrew. This is thought to be supported by Deut. xxxii. 8. The text says, the Most High
set the bounds of the people according to the number of the tribes of Israel—that is, seventy-two,
the number which went down into Egypt. This is confirmed by the Targum of Ben-Uzziel.
Horapollo teaches that the world was divided into seventy-two regions.[7] Clemens Alexandrinus
and Epiphanius both say, that there were seventy-two tongues at the dispersion.[8] Josephus and
the fathers of the church fix the languages at the confusion to seventy-two.[9]

Enfield[10] says, " The Jews had seventy-two names of God."

The Rabbis maintain that the angels who ascended and descended Jacob's ladder were seventy-
two in number.[11]

Lightfoot, on the Temple Service,[12] states the dress of Aaron to have had upon it seventy-two
bells.[13] This conveys with it the consequence that it must have had seventy-two pomegranates.

If Bishop Wilkins can be depended on, there were seventy-two kinds of animals in the Ark.[14]

In Numbers xi. 16, it is said, that Moses was ordered to take seventy men of the elders of
Israel. But the number was seventy-two, six out of each tribe.

The Cabalists find seventy-two names of God in three verses—the 19, 20, and 21, of the fourteenth chapter of Exodus.[15]

In Numbers xxiii. 9, Exod. xv. 27, we read of seventy palm trees. Of course the number ought
to be seventy-two.

In the book of Enoch is an allegory, in which seventy shepherds are said to superintend the

---

[1] Lib. ii. Cap. xlii.      [2] If we count the countries we shall find seventy-two.

[3] See Bryant's Anal. Vol. III. p. 427.

[4] Clemens, Alex. Strom. Lib. i.; Euseb. in Chron. Lib. i.; Epiph. adv. Hær. i.; as also Aug. de Civ. Dei.

[5] Con. B. iii.      [6] B. ii.      [7] Ency. Britt. art. Philology, Sect. i.

[8] Clemens, Strom. Lib. i. p. 404 ; Epiph. adv. Hær. Lib. i. p. 6.      [9] Vide Ency. Britt. voce Phil. p. 486.

[10] Phil. Book iv. Ch. iii.      [11] Nimrod, Vol. II. p. 453.      [12] L. iii.      [13] Moses Lowman, p. 125.

[14] Olivier's Illustrations of Masonry, p. 96.      [15] Basn. Hist. Jud. Book iii, Ch xv. p. 202.

flock, and the seventy are divided into three classes, 37, 23, and 12; but these make seventy-two. Here is an example of the common Jewish expression of seventy for seventy-two, which cannot be disputed, except the reader be disposed, with Bishop Laurence, to throw out *two* of the kings, because they reigned only short periods; and, in addition, to have recourse to confounding the number of the shepherds with the periods of time;[1] in short, to corrupting the text in two different ways. From the account which the Jews of Cochin gave to Dr. Buchanan,[2] he infers that they were governed by a council of seventy-two persons. This is evidently meant for an imitation of the Sanhedrim of the Jews of Judea: and strongly confirms what I have said that by *seventy*, almost always seventy-*two* are meant.

Jesus is said to have sent out seventy disciples or teachers. Now it has been universally allowed that Manes, in fixing the number of his apostles, and of his disciples or bishops, intended exactly to imitate Jesus Christ; and living so near the time of Jesus, the tradition could not very well be mistaken, and there could be no reason whatever for any misrepresentation, and he fixed upon the numbers *twelve* and *seventy-two*, not *seventy*. This shews that probably the expression in Matthew must be considered the same as *the Septuagint*—seventy for seventy-two. If Manes had had any reason for doubt he would certainly have taken the seventy and not seventy-two.

These sacred numbers, every where, the same, clearly prove an esoteric religion—an oriental allegory. The fact cannot be doubted. Jesus, the God of Peace, sent out his twelve apostles to preach his gospel. The God *Iao*, the Sun, had the year divided into twelve months, into twelve signs, through which, in his annual course, he passed. The year was divided by the ancient Magi into two hemispheres of light and darkness, of six months each; during one period, the genius of good or of light prevailed, during the other, the genius of darkness or evil. Each month or part was divided into twelve parts, and this multiplied by six, gives seventy-two, the number of disciples sent out by Jesus. This number is the root of almost all the ancient cycles or periods of the Chinese, Hindoos, Egyptians, Magi, &c.; multiplied by six, it gives 432, &c. See Drummond. This relates to the microcosm to be discussed in the next volume.

The Mohamedans hold that the world was divided into seventy-two nations and seventy-two languages, and that there were seventy-two sects in their religion. I believe this related to their esoteric religion, in which they considered Mohamed as the tenth Avatar of the whole world, and I have no doubt that what is above called a *sect* ought to be *divisions*, into which the Pantheistic or Mohamedan Catholic faith was divided.

Nimrod says, "We have shewn who Georgos, God of war, was, and that he died at the royal "city of Diospolis in Iran, where a king reigned over seventy kings; this is the number of nations "who constituted the universal empire of Cush." Again, "Then did Isis go forth wandering. "One Aso, Queen of the Cushim, was his accomplice, συνεργος, in this business; but besides her, "there were seventy-two confederates, leagued by oath, συνωμοται."[3]

The mystical numbers used in the religions of the sun, are constantly found in the religion of Jesus. The number of the twelve apostles, which formed the retinue of Jesus during his mission, is that of the signs, and of the secondary genii, the tutelar gods of the Zodiacal signs which the sun passes through in his annual revolution. It is that of the twelve gods of the Romans, each of whom presided over a month. The Greeks, the Egyptians, the Persians, each had their *twelve* gods, as the Christian followers of Mithra had their *twelve* apostles. The chief of the twelve Genii of the annual revolution had the barque and the keys of time, the same as the chief of the secondary

---

[1] See Laurence's Enoch, Pref. and Ch. lxxxix. vers. 1, 7, 25.  [2] Christ. Res. p. 222.

[3] Plut. de Isid. et Osir. p. 356; Nimrod, Vol. I. p. 644, Suppressed Ed., Vol. II. pp. 448, 452.

gods of the Romans or Janus, after whom St. Peter, Bar-Jona, with his barque and keys, is modelled. At the foot of the statue of Janus were placed twelve altars, dedicated to the twelve months. As Janus was the chief of the twelve lesser gods, Peter was the chief of the apostles; and, as I have said in Book X. Chap. IV., as Janus held the keys of heaven, so does Peter. The Valentinians supposed that Christ commenced his mission at thirty years of age, because it was the number of degrees in a sign of the Zodiac, and that he was crucified in the twelfth month; so that his career had one year, like that of the sun in the Twelve Labours of Hercules. It is very evident that the Valentinians considered Jesus as a Ray or Emanation from the Sun, and that he formed a microcosm of the Solar orb, each being a microcosm of a superior being. The Romists evidently do the same in their annual scenic representation of the acts of the Saviour's life.

It is said that Christ fixed the number of his apostles at twelve, because there were twelve months in the year; and that John the Baptist fixed his at thirty, because the months have thirty days.[1] Clemens Alexandrinus, on the oriental doctrine, says, that the Valentinian Theodotus maintained that the twelve apostles held, in the church, the same place that the signs of the Zodiac held in nature; because, as the twelve constellations govern the world of generation, the twelve apostles govern the world of regeneration. In Dupuis many other striking circumstances relating to the number *twelve* may be seen.

Why did Jesus choose *twelve* apostles and *seventy-two* disciples? Why did seventy-two men come from Medina to Mohamed; and why did he retain with him *twelve* as his apostles? Why does the college of Cardinals consist of seventy-two persons? Why did Ptolemy take seventy-two men to translate the Pentateuch? All accident, as usual?

The Persians had twelve angels who presided over the twelve months. He who presided over the *first* month was called the treasurer of Paradise.[2] Probably, like Peter and Janus, he carried the keys.

The Gentiles had precisely the same astrological mythos as the Jews and Christians. The commanders of the Greeks against Troy, including Philoctetes, who, though absent, was one of them in the league—one of the confederates—were seventy-two.[3] Osiris was killed by seventy-two conspirators.[4] According to Keating, the Irish divided the languages into seventy-two. Proofs, which cannot be impeached, of the astrological character of the temple and its sacred numbers, may be seen in Josephus.[5]

The Greek mina or pound was raised by Solon, as we learn from Plutarch,[6] from seventy-two drachmæ to a *hundred*.[7]

The number *seven* is equally a sacred number in the Gentile religion as in the Christian. The number of the planets has been copied in the Christian religion in the seven sacraments, seven deadly sins, seven gifts of the holy spirit.[8]

From the number of the days of the least of the cycles, seven, being identical with the number of the planetary bodies, it can never be known with a certainty when one is alluded to separately from the other. But the constant recurrence of the numbers connected intimately with the decans, dodecans, &c., 7, 12, 72, 360 not 365, 432, &c., into which the sphere was divided, sufficiently prove their intimate connexion. They are all closely bound together, and on their union was

[1] Homil. Clement, II. No. 23, Ep. No. 26; Dupuis, Vol. III. pp. 160, 319, 4to.          [2] Hyde, p. 240.

[3] Nimrod, Vol. II. p. 453.                              [4] Plut. de Isid. et Osir. p. 356.

[5] Ant. B. iii. Ch. vi. Sect. 7, and Ch. vii. Sect. 7, ed. Whiston.          [6] In Solone.

[7] Walpole's Memoirs of Turkey, Vol. I. p. 435; also see Clarke on Coins, 94.          [8] Dupuis, Vol. III. p. 47.

founded all judicial astrology and all ancient mythology. The peculiar circumstance, *accidental* I will call it, of the number of the days of the week coinciding exactly with the number of the planetary bodies, probably procured for it its character of sanctity.

In Ireland, at Wicklow, we meet with seven churches; and again, near Athlone, with seven more. Seven churches are described in the Apocalypse to have existed in Asia Minor, to whom angels or messengers were sent; but the church at Thyatira is said to have existed only in name : and in the Peninsula of India, about thirty-eight miles south of Madras, at a place called Mahabalipoorum or the city of the great Bali, is a collection of ruins, usually called the seven Pagodas. An account, but a very defective one, is given of them in the fifth volume of the Transactions of the Asiatic Society, by a gentleman named Goldingham. It seems to me that they are the work of the Buddhists. The Bull-headed Bali is conspicuous.

There are seven sephiroths, of rank inferior to the first three, answering to the seven planets. There are seven gates of the soul; there are seven gates employed in the creation; there are seven sabbaths from the Passover to the Pentecost; and seven times seven sabbaths for the year of Jubilee; lastly, the seventh Millenium will be the grand sabbath.[1]

In the Persian mythology every thing appears to have been closely connected with the numbers described in my *Celtic Druids*, that is, with judicial astrology. M. Creuzer, on the number of the planetary bodies, has observed,[2] that the nation was distributed by its founder, Djemchid, into four classes, and into seven castes. The four *classes* I take to be allusive to the four divisions of the month, and the seven *castes* to the seven days of the week. The seven Amshaspands, the seven Enceintes of Ecbatana, with their seven colours, are all in like manner closely allied both to the planets and the sacred numbers. The body of Osiris was supposed to have been buried at Elephanta, in the Isle of Philoe, in Upper Egypt. Every day the priests offered here 360 bowls of milk at his shrine, and sung suitable litanies. An usage exactly similar obtained at the city of Acanthus.[3] The great oath of the Egyptians was, by the remains of Osiris buried at Philoe.[4] Typhon made an alliance with the Queen of Ethiopia, who supplied him with seventy-two companions.[5] Every where the sacred numbers, that is, judicial astrology, is to be found. The seven gates of Thebes were erected, as stated by Nonnus, according to the number and order of the seven planets.[6] Respecting the identity of sacred numbers among Jews, Gentiles, and Christians, enough has been said; but many additional examples might be adduced if it were necessary.

6. I think on careful inspection of the exoteric religion of each of the tribes which appears to have arrived from the East, we may see in all of them occasional proofs escaping from their mysterious adyta, sufficient to furnish ground for a rational belief that what I have asserted is correct, —that the same system pervaded them all. We must not forget to make a large allowance for the circumstance that they are the *secret* doctrines to which I allude. We cannot expect to hear them explained from the top of the Mosque, by the Muizzim; nor by the Pope, from the chair of St. Peter. In almost all nations the system of which the Millenarian is a part, prevailed; and if I be asked why we have not clearer proofs of it, I assign the same cause, since the thirteenth century, as for the Gospel of Joachim or the Holy Ghost being forgotten,—it was every person's interest to conceal it.

The reputed books of Solomon, such as Wisdom and Ecclesiasticus, are full of allusions to the doctrines of wisdom. A person who has read the preceding part of this work will perceive,

---

[1] Basnage, Hist. Jud. Liv. iii. Cb. xi. p. 190.      [2] Vol. I. p. 333, ed. Guiniaut.

[3] Diod. Sicul. I. 22; ibid. 97.      [4] Cruezer, ed. Guiniaut, Vol. I. p. 393.

[5] Creuzer, ibid. p. 397.      [6] Dionys. Lib. v.; Clarke's Travels, Vol. IV. p. 65, 4to.

in a moment, that they use the word wisdom as referring to an unexplained or mystical doctrine in almost every page. This was, to the doctrine of the Cabala, to the doctrine of the Emanation, of the Sephiroth, which the *present* Jews call the *ten emanations*, which are evidently, on the slightest inspection, *nonsense*—NONSENSE designed originally to mislead; but, perhaps, latterly believed by the ignorant. Sephiroth is ספרות *sprut*, and may mean ten attributes or qualities, but it also means the doctrine of the ten sacred numbers or cycles of India, or of Virgil. ספר *spr* is to cipher, or count, or calculate; and ספרות *sprut* is the feminine plural of ספר *spr*, and means the calculations or calculated periods. It also means a symbolical or hieroglyphical or emblematical writing.[1] This actually conveys the meaning of the ten mythic or emblematical names. The Psalmist says, lxxi. 15, he shall praise the justice of God, and depend upon it for his salvation, for he has not known the ספרות *sprut* or Sephiroth; that is, the calculations of the cycles; as Pagninus says, *numeros*. The text is rather confused; but this, though not a translation, I think is its meaning. But the Sephiroth are correctly rendered *numbers*. They are the same as the feminine forms of the Seraphim, סרפים *srpim*, alluded to in Isaiah vi. 2. The six wings of each seraph alluded to the six periods just gone, in the time of Solomon. In verse nine, the TENTH of something mystical—not *understood* and not *named*, but which, it is said, in verse thirteen, has been before, and shall return—means the *tenth* sæculum or cycle. I suspect the Seraphim and the Sepharim have been used promiscuously. The text of Isaiah, if correctly translated, means, that above the throne stood winged *serpents;* for seraph, translated, is serpent. It is only written, in our translation, in the Hebrew word *seraph* to disguise the word serpent, which our priests did not like. I need not remind my reader that the serpent is an emblem of a cycle or circle. Serpents are constantly seen on the Egyptian monuments, as described by Isaiah;[2] but with wings, and, in India, overshadowing the icons of Cristna or Buddha, in number three, four, five, six, seven, eight, or nine, according to the number of cycles, of which the being he was protecting, was the genius. One of these winged serpents may be seen in the hand of the Moses, found in St. Mary's Abbey, at York. The wings are manifest in the original icon, but in the plate published by the Society of Antiquaries *they cannot be distinguished!!!* Moses is there described as the Messiah, משה *msh* or genius of a Zodiacal sign, and that of the first sign, as is evident from the *horns of Taurus which he has upon his head.* When he had finished all his labours, *the book* tells us, he delivered up his power to the saviour Joshua, and went to the top of Pisgah to die.

The word Cherub originally meant, and yet sometimes means, serpent, but this is only because its general meaning is *emblem* or *emblematical figure.* It is a compound word, formed of כר *kr*, *circle*, and אוב *aub*, *serpent:* in short, a circled or circular serpent or serpent with its tail in its mouth—כרוב *krub*. It was probably the first sacred emblem ever used, whence all such emblematical figures came to be called Cherubs; and this accounts for learned men having made them out to be of many different figures. Hutchinson explains the word Cherubims by *similitudes,* which confirms what I have said above.[3]

The ten Jewish Sephiroth were the ten cycles, and, in honour of the Trinity, the first was called כתר *ktr* Corona, the second חכמה *hkme* Sapientia, and the third בינה *bine* Intelligentia—Father, Son, and Holy Ghost. The first *three* were also the Trinitarian Sol—the Creator, Preserver, and

---

[1] Parkhurst in voce, ספר *spr*, IV.    [2] Ib. ver. 2.

[3] General Vallancey has observed, that the Hebrew word יום *ium*, translated in our Bibles *a day*, appears to be an original word, signifying a revolution. He adds, like בר *br*, *bar*, *var*, *war*. This being admitted, here is one of the difficulties of Genesis removed at once. But this will not be liked, because it is the observation of a swordsman, not of a gownsman.

Destroyer—-and the other *seven* might be the earth, moon, and planets, the host of Heaven, forming altogether the Ever-happy Octoade of the Gnostics: the whole forming the Παν, or system of the Pan-deva, holy Pan ; not the το Παν, the Παν of the universe,—but the Παν of our system only. The first of the Sephiroth called כתר *ktr*, Corona, Circulus, is also called Arich-Anpin. This was a name given (as I have formerly shewn) to Brahma or the Brahmin Abraham. Arich is Αρχη. It is also called Ensoph, *fountain* of wisdom, fountain whence wisdom flowed. Now I suspect that both these terms ought correctly to have been applicable only to a power which I shall describe in another book. The author of the *Cabala denudata* observes, that the antiquity of the Cabala cannot be disputed, as it was known to Parmenides very near 460 years before Christ.

The second of the Sephiroth is חכמה *hkme*, Sapientia, Νꞷς, Σοφια, and Λογος, by Philo called τον πρωτογονον Θεꙙ υἱον, *primogenitum Dei.* This is also Ερος or divine love—Cama and Dipuc, of India, Cupid, of Greece, the Puck and Robin good-fellow of Shakespeare.

The third of the Sephiroth is בינה *bine*, Prudentia. This is the Anima Mundi or Psyche or την θειαν ψυχην of Plato. I believe that בינה *bine* is a feminine form of בן *bn, son,* and means daughter, and was thus the daughter of כתר *ktr,* and sister of חכמה *hkme,* or Wisdom, or Logos, or Ερως. Thus, with the Greeks, we had Jupiter, son of Saturn, married to his sister Juno, and Cupid married to his sister Psyche. The Targums often treat of a מימרא די *mimra* or *daughter of voice,* that is, daughter of the Logos : this, I think, was the בינה *bine,* not the Logos.

There was also a *Dseir Anpin.* This was the same, viz. שר *sr,* in the Hebrew, as the Arich-Anpin in the Greek. Much confusion has arisen from mistaking translations of words out of one language into another, for separate words. The fourth verse of the Revelation or Apocalypse of John, which speaks of him that *was,* that *is,* and that is *to come,* alludes to the Solar triune God, and to the seven cycles, as the author of the Cabala Denudata says ; but it also alludes to the same Trinity, and to the seven planets or spirits which stand before the Sun, the throne of God. The same author, in *libri Druschim Tractatus,* [1] says, Hic tantum inculco decem sephiroth esse ; ex se nihil aliud nisi decem aridas Numerationes, non Emanationes divinas, vacuas capsulas, non aurum margaritasve illic reponendas.

7. I must now make an observation of importance respecting the word ברא *bra,* of the first verse of Genesis. We have hitherto adopted the common reading *created* or *formed;* but I apprehend the word ברא *bra* or בר *br* has the meaning exclusively neither of creating from nothing, nor of first forming, or giving the first or the then new form to matter, but a renewal of a form ; that it means renovare, [2] regenerare. This is exactly what it ought to be, if I be right, that the first book of Genesis is a Buddhist work. It will then mean, *By Wisdom Aleim renovated, regenerated, or renewed the planetary bodies, and the earth. And the earth was ungerminated—not impregnated, unprolific—and without any beautiful* (animal or vegetable) *form.* That is, it was the Ιλυς or Mud of Sanchoniathon.

After this will come the arrangement and peopling or stocking of the world in six periods of time, as described by Moses and the Etruscans, and as Cuvier has shewn most correctly, and as I have shewn in my *Celtic Druids,* Ch. IV. Sect. XVI. All this harmonizes with the fact hitherto unexplained, of the Pentateuch containing no intimation of a Future State, with the renewal of cycles, the millenium, the prophecies of Saviours from time to time, and with the actual natural history of the earth, as laid down by Cuvier,—and proves that, whoever selected or composed

---

[1] Vol. I. p. 55.　　　[2] Parkhurst in voce ברא *bra,* IV.

Genesis was a person really possessing a profound knowledge of nature: a much more rational ground for claiming for him divine inspiration, than the vulgar anthropomorphitism with which Moses has been charged by the priests, and which perhaps has been intentional, as alike suitable (as no doubt it is) to the capacity of the vulgar, and to conceal the real meaning.

I now beg to refer my reader once more to what I have said in Book II. Chap. III. Sect. 3, respecting the word רואשית rasit or wisdom of Genesis. He will there find that in the meaning which I have given to it, I have said, that I was supported by the opinions of Clemens, Origen, &c. What I have said was true, but I find, on reconsideration of the subject, that I have not stated the whole truth. I have no doubt that by the rendering of that word by *wisdom*, which meant the Logos, the first of the Æons or Αιωνες of the Valentinians and Manichæans was meant. An Æon was an Αιων. A great or eminent Æon was an Αιων των αιωνων. Every Æon was the genius of a cycle. Thus every period in the nature of a cycle had its Æon, with its small or great portion of the Divine Spirit or Holy Ghost, in proportion to its little or great importance. The Persians had 365 Æons, one for every day. The Valentinians had the same. The Romish Church has also its 365 saints, or persons divinely inspired in a low degree, one in a peculiar manner for each day in the year, besides many others.

Wisdom was one of the persons of the first triple Æon, and the translation of the word רואשית *rasit*, by the phrase *wisdom*, was *universally* recognized by the early Christians, not, as my expression would induce a person to believe, by a few only; but it was, with one trifling excep-tion, the undisputed meaning attached to it, both by Jews and Christians, in the early times of Christianity, and, indeed, until a change, which I shall hereafter treat of, took place in the Romish Church, when it fell into the Paulite heresy. We have seen that by the Logos God formed the world. But the Logos was Christ, and Christ was the Χρησος. And this Χρησος was the first Emanation, the benignant Genius or Spirit—THE Χρησος, κατ' εξοχην.

Faustus is made, by Augustin, to say, *Christ is the wisdom of God.* [1] Now this we might infer, from what we have before observed respecting Gnosticism and Manichæism. (But the *Christ* ought to be the Chreest.) As the Χρης was the Logos, and the Logos was Wisdom, it follows that the Χρης must be Wisdom. Here, in either case, we arrive at Rasit again, and thus Jesus, or the Logos, is the Creator. Here we have a key to much of the recondite and misunderstood doctrines of the Gnostic, that is, the initiated Christians—the initiated Christians, or Gnostici, against whom St. Paul preached, of which I shall say *much* more hereafter. Here we see that the Χρησος on the monument, on the tomb, of the youth of Larissa, and all the other inscriptions, in Spon, from that country, connect the doctrine with the mythology of Plato and Greece. (What would Ammonius Saccas say to this?) They connect the doctrine also with the Larissa and the other circumstances of Syra-strene and of its Diu, and with Ceylon and its Iava Diu, &c., and the Golden Chersonesus of Siam, with its mount Sion, its Judia, &c., &c.; and bind the whole together. —The links of the chain are not only there, but they are connected. Need I repeat any thing of Abraham or the Brahmin, from the land of *Maturea* or the land of the solar *fire* or *aur*—the land of Urii or Uriana—Ur of Colchis or Colida—or of the Cal or Culdees, going to Maturea, or Heliopolis, in Egypt—of the promontory of Tamus and St. Thomas, of Bituma, of Malabar, Coromandel, &c., &c., &c. ? No ! I need say no more: if my reader be blind, I have not the power of working miracles ; I cannot restore his sight.

No doubt the assertion that the translation of the most important word רואשית *rasit* by *wisdom*,

---

[1] Faust. ap. Aug. Lib. xx. 2.

was *the admitted and undisputed construction of the word*, will be denied. And it will be denied for the same reason which operated with Parkhurst to make him suppress the knowledge that it was so translated by the early Christians and Jews. It will be denied for the same reason that Lardner suppressed his knowledge that the early Christians were called Χρησιανοι not Χριςιανοι. A learned Jew, who will shortly publish an English and Hebrew Lexicon, informs me, that the word רֹאשׁ *ras* has the meaning of *wisdom* in the Talmud.

Many readers will think it quite impossible, that all the modern Lexicographers should have wilfully concealed the meaning of the word *rasit*. This is a question of fact, not of opinion. Have they or have they not given the meaning as stated by all the eminent persons whose names I have exhibited? I affirm that, with the exception of one slight notice of Parkhurst's in his GREEK NOT HEBREW Lexicon, in order to misrepresent it, they have all suppressed it. No one surely will say, that all the learned authorities cited by me are unworthy of NOTICE!

My reader, I imagine, will not have forgotten that a place supposed to be Cortona, in Italy, was called Creston. This was the place where Pythagoras, who was the son of an *Apolloniacal Spectre*, Holy Ghost, had what was called his school of WISDOM—that Pythagoras who sacrificed at the shrine of the bloodless Apollo at Delos. No doubt the school of this great philosopher from the East—India, Carmel, Egypt, Delphi, Delos, was closely connected with the schools of the Samaneans, Essenians, Carmelites, Gnostic Christians, or Χρησιανοι, or CRESTON-ians. The Pythagoreans were Essenians, and the Rev. R. Taylor, A. M., the Deist, now in gaol, infamously persecuted by the Whigs for his religious opinions, in his learned defence of Deism, called *the Diegesis*, has clearly proved all the hierarchical institutions of the Christians to be a close copy of those of the Essenians of Egypt.

If the Christians be called by any author before Origen by the term Χριςιανοι, and not Χρησιανοι, except as a term of reproach, as at Antioch; and if there be no other way of accounting for it; considering that they are so called in the teeth of the authority of Clemens, Justin, all the Gnostics and the Gentiles, and considering also the evident policy of concealment in modern divines, I say that I am justified in maintaining it or them, to be one or more examples of the innumerable corruptions of manuscripts by Christians in a later day. They possessed the means of making the corruptions when they copied the manuscripts; all of which are descended to us from them; and their numerous forgeries prove they had the inclination, and they were not prevented by principle: for, so far from thinking it wrong to corrupt the manuscripts, they avowed that they thought it meritorious to do it. The *end* has sanctified the *means* with priests, from Bishop Vyasa in India, down to Bishop Laurence, in Ireland.[1]

I now beg my reader to look back to Book X. Chap. I. Sect. 18, and consider the circumstances attendant upon the monument of the youth of Larissa—the sacred name of Χρησος at the top, and the sacred word Ἐρως or the first-begotten, divine love, at the bottom of it: let him observe that this was in Creston-ia, at Delphi, whose God was called by the name of the God of the Jews, יה IE. Then let him remember the doctrines of the Trimurti or Trinity of Orpheus, whose country this was. Next let him observe, that it was here where we found the females sacrificing themselves on the death of their husbands, and that most of the places of this country have the same names as places in India, where Cristna or Kan-iya came from, and that the country itself is called Sindi. All this being duly considered, I think my reader will conclude with me, that the Cristna of India had the name of Crist, for at least one reason, the same as that

---

[1] Vide false translation in preface to Enoch.

which caused the sacred being at Larissa to be called Χρης—that is, *mitis, benignus,* and not solely because he was *black,* the colour of his countrymen.

We have seen that Buddha was the Logos, and the Ερως, and the son of Maia. But *Camdeo* was also the son of Maia. This was the Cupid of the Romans; and Southey[1] has shewn, that Dipuc and Cupid are the same when read Hebraicè. His history is clearly an incarnation of Buddha, his exploits or adventures in the fields of Muttra succeeded in a following age the adventures of Cristna, celebrated, with almost the same circumstances, in the same places, after the expulsion of the Buddhists. This Cama, who followed Cristna, is the Cama-sene of Italy, noticed in Book X. Chap. VII. Sect. 9, the incarnation of *the fishes.*

We have seen it held that Christ or Cristna had his name from being *black;* secondly, from being *crucified;* and, thirdly, from being *mitis, benignus.* All this is true, and I do not doubt it had its origin from the word, in ancient language, having had the *three* meanings, either all in one, or in several nations. We all know the way in which the letter ח *h* of the Hebrews has been corrupted into *ch,* in both ancient and modern times. חרש *hrs* was the *solar fire,* and like the sun it meant also *machinator.* And, as I have before shewn, from this word Parkhurst says, in voce, V., the Greeks had their Ερως, *meaning the material light or plastic formative power*—the word which we found placed under the Χρησος of the youth of Larissa. It does not seem surprising that this *chrs* or ΧΡΣ should thus become Χρης, *benignus.* But this benignant being, divine love, we have seen crucified several times; and Christ was said to be crucified in the heavens.

This crucifixion of divine love is often found among the Greeks. Iönah or Juno was bound with fetters, and suspended between heaven and earth.[2] Ixion, Prometheus, Apollo of Miletus, all were crucified. When the sun crossed the equator the last time in Taurus, was he crucified in the heavens; and did he rise again as Aries? and was he crucified again when he crossed, in like manner, from Aries, and rose again in Pisces?

Was the sun born at the winter solstice and crucified when he crossed the line at the vernal equinox? From this crucifixion did he rise, triumphing over the powers of darkness, to life and immortality? Was he thus, as Justin Martyr said, described on the universe in the form of the letter X? The word חרש *hrs,* which means *Sun,* also means the *East wind,* by which, Virgil says, the mares of Thrace were impregnated. What does this mean? The Targum of Onkelos says by קדם *qdm* or קדמין *qdmin,* the Aleim formed the world. But this word means also *East wind.* Then this Chaldee word is only a translation of the word חרש *hrs,* or the solar fire, or the generative power, or the machinator. This is all very mystical. But can any thing be more mystical than the crucified Semiramis flying away as *a dove;* than the crucified Prometheus, Ixion, Staurobates, Cristna, Salivahana; than the impregnation of the mares of Thrace, or than the crucifixion of Christ *in the heavens?* A learned devotee once said in reply to this, " I care " nothing for your Christ crucified *in the heavens;* it is not in our canon." And I reply, " I care " nothing for the canon of a sect contemptible enough, till it had power given by the sword of " Constantine. I only look for the truth in all quarters; and I know the heretical Gospel must " have had a meaning, and a mystical meaning. The whole is evidently a system of the most " profound mysticism, and profound mysticism will never be explained, or its meaning discovered, " except by means of the most profound inquiries." The extraordinary word קדמין *qdmin* was adopted, no doubt, because, it had, in some degree, both the meaning of Αρχη and Λογος,

---

[1] Notes on Curse of Kehama, p. 333, 4to.

[2] Iliad, O, ver. 20, ib. Θ, ver. 25; Bryant's Anal. Vol. II. p. 372.

or could be applied in some way to the second person of the Trinity, in imitation of the word *rasit* of the Hebrew, which had, as we have seen, a double meaning.

When I reflect upon the numerous proofs which have transpired from time to time, that the polar regions were once much warmer than they are at present, and the fact, known even to both the Greeks and Romans, that the angle of the equator and ecliptic has been constantly decreasing from the earliest time,[1] I cannot help suspecting that Justin Martyr alluded to this angle, when he declared that, according to Plato, the Son of God, or Jesus Christ, was expressed or decussated upon the universe in the form of the letter X, and, that the doctrine of Jesus Christ being crucified in the clouds, alluded to the same thing. For the cross may easily have been thought to allude to the Soli-Lunar precessional Christian cycle, which immediately depended upon this Cross or Angle.

8. It is an admitted fact, that the language of Mani and the first Manichæans was Chaldaic. After the observation that the language of Babylon was not the Chaldee, it will not surprise my reader that I should consider this fact, (of this Persian, as he is called,) as strengthening my opinion that he came from India. He had twelve disciples or followers who were called *perfect* and *elect*, himself making the *thirteenth*. This continued after his death to be the system of his followers. To these twelve only the high secrets of the order were entrusted. They ate no flesh, drank no wine. He had, besides these, seventy-two followers, disciples of a lower class, to whom all the mysteries were not entrusted. Like the Roman Cardinals some of them married, but I think it probable that, from the unmarried only, the twelve elect or perfect were taken. Of course these elect will be said to have been taken in imitation of Jesus Christ. I believe they were neither of them copies of the other : and that Mani's were taken from the system that caused the twelve figures and their president to be carved on the rocks at Oujein, in India—in the Northern India—in the country of Calida—in Ur of the Chaldees—or very near to it.

In the circular part of the church of the Templars in London, the Manichæan heresy is beautifully displayed. It has originally had twelve arches ; one on the East, for the president, a little larger than any of the others, excepting that on the West, for the door ; and they have six seats in each arch, making seventy-two in all, and within are six smaller arches, which might hold the twelve *perfecti* or the Knights of the Round Table.

Among the Chinese the same sacred numbers are found, as those among the Jews. This can be no accident. Confucius had among his thousands of disciples only seventy-two initiated :[2] the exact number of the Cardinals of Rome, of the Manwantaras of India, of the chosen or distinguished disciples of Jesus Christ, of the Jewish Sanhedrim, and of Manes. Here is the universal mythos—remains of the kingdom of Pandæa.

Between the decalogue of Moses and the rule of morality of the Buddhists of Tibet, as given by Georgius,[3] there is a wonderful similarity.

> Thou shalt not kill any human being or animal.
> Thou shalt not commit adultery.
> Thou shalt not steal.
> Thou shalt not speak ill of others.
> Thou shalt not lie.
> Thou shalt honour thy father and mother.

The law of Moses, which we translate, " Thou shalt do no murder," ought to be rendered, if rendered literally, *Thou shalt not kill.* It would thus be identical with the Buddhist rule or commandment.

---

[1] Parkhurst, pp. 730, 731.     [2] Matter on the Gnostics, Vol. II. p. 83.     [3] Alp. Tib.

Along with the God Kan-ia, or Iao, or Jah, came the oriental system of masonry or mystery; and through all ages, I have little doubt, the Gnostic doctrine has prevailed with its Masons, or Μεσυρανεον, or *Maceonry*, as it is called in the York documents, or Monachism. The Monks of Tibet, at Eleusis, in Egypt, at Jerusalem or Carmel, in our circular chapters, were the preservers of the secret Pythagorean doctrines of numbers, of the Ras, or Mystery, or Masonry, or perhaps more properly, the doctrines of the IE, the Jah,—the mesos or μεσον-ry, or the Saviour, or cross-borne—renewed in every cycle, as described in Virgil. I need scarcely remind my Masonic reader that all the secrets of Masonry are concealed in the Hebrew or Chaldee language; that is, in the language of the Brahmin of Ur and Colida, where Mr. Ellis was poisoned for being known to possess them. Solomon, the Hakem or wise, who built the temple, succeeded the Brahmin Abraham, who came from Ur of Colida.

In my Celtic Druids, Ch. V. Sect. 33, the existence of the Culdees, or, as they were then called, Colidei at Armagh, in Ireland, was shewn, as venerators of *the sacred fire*. They are known to have had a monastery in Wales; and in both cases it seems the priesthood was hereditary, descending from father to son, and they were Christians, because this hereditary custom of passing the priesthood was complained of as disgracing Christianity. There is reason to believe that they were the same in Scotland; and their continuing to possess the use of the cathedrals, along with the Romish priests, is a most curious circumstance. It is also a most striking fact, that the Christians found in the country of Colida, in India, should possess exactly the same *three* rites as the Colidei of Iona, in Scotland—Baptism, the Eucharist, and Orders—and these, the three rites of the Jews.

9. The very essence of Freemasonry is *equality*. All, let their rank in life be what it may, when in the lodge, are brothers—brethren with the Father at their head. No person can read the Evangelists and not see that this is correctly Gospel Christianity. It is the Christianity of the Chaldees, of the Patriarchs, of Abraham, and of Melchizedek. Every part of Christianity refers back to Abraham, and it is all Freemasonry. Jesus Christ at table, at the head of the twelve, offering the sacrifice of Bread and Wine, is Abraham and Melchizedek over again; such, in fact, it is acknowledged to be by the Romish Church; such is its esoteric religion; and such was the custom not only of the Chaldean Abraham and Melchizedek, but also of the Calidei and Masons at York; and, I have no doubt, of the Templars in their secret round chapter-house in London.

In all the ancient systems there prevailed one universal doctrine, now despised, the metempsychosis, or what is called in old Irish the *Nua Breithe*.[1] This became corrupted into a transmigration of souls from man to man, and from man to beast; but its original meaning was, *a new birth* in another cycle or world. This is correctly the doctrine of Moses,[2] of Philo, of Plato, of the interpretatio Novi Sæculi or the Æneid of Virgil, and of the secret doctrines of the fathers of the church. It is in many places to be seen in the Gospels, in our Liturgy, and particularly in our baptismal service.

Many attempts have been made to account for the well-ascertained fact, that, in the Pentateuch, there is not the least trace of a state of future reward or punishment: for though we have the evil spirit in the serpent we have no hell. This arises from the doctrine of the renewal of worlds having been the esoteric religion of the tribe.

If a person would think deeply upon the character of the *destroyer* or the third person of the

---

[1] Vallancey, Hib. Coll. This is really the English *new birth*, both in word and meaning.

[2] Exhibited in the word ברא *bra, renovated*.

Hindoo Trinity, he would at once see tnat it is very different from that of the later Arimanius of the Persians, as placed in opposition to the Oromasdes. I consider that the evil principle *per se* of the Persians, was a corruption of the fine Trinity of the Hindoos.[1] It betrays a degradation of the mind. It is only heard of along with the *good* principle, in opposition, in the later ages, when the Mithra or middle principle had become almost lost among the Persians. The devil or future state is never found among the Jews till their return from Babylon, and this has furnished a difficulty to our divines which they have never surmounted. It stands a glaring fact in the face of all their theories and forced explanations, that the chosen people of God were not taught in their sacred Pentateuch a single word respecting the immortality of the soul and a state of reward or punishment after death. This is a glaring, an indisputable fact, clearly proved, among others, by Bishop Warburton. My theory of revolving cycles and renewal of worlds has satisfactorily accounted for this, which has never been satisfactorily accounted for before. The proper translation, or at least the translation according to the esoteric doctrine of Genesis, explains this : *By wisdom the Trimurti renovated or regenerated the planetary bodies and the earth.* But not the stars ; for, though, no doubt, they were subject to renewals, yet they were not subject to the renewals in the *same* periods as the planetary system, and Genesis only applies to our system. Consider with attention the sixteenth verse of the first chapter, where the stars are named, and an interpolation must be admitted. This all harmonizes beautifully with my system. The way in which the stars are here interpolated shews that the interpolator admitted the meaning of *planets*, which Parkhurst has correctly given to the word שמים *smim.*

In Genesis there are no fallen angels. All these came into the Mosaic religion on the return from Babylon. The Destroyer or Serpent of Genesis is correctly the *renovator* or *preserver.* In Genesis there is a tree of knowledge and a tree of life. This tree of life evidently proves the meaning of the Mythos to be, that Adam would die at some time—that he would wear out, unless he ate of the fruit of that tree. The serpent, by persuading Eve to taste of the fruit of the tree of knowledge, &c., taught her what is meant by being naked, and thus, by inducing procreation, was the preserver of the species : the very literal meaning of the words shews, that this is one of its meanings. Here we have the origin of the Ophites, or oriental emblematical-serpent worshipers, to account for whom our antiquarians have been so much perplexed. They worshiped the saviour regenerator, but not the devil, in our vulgar meaning of the word. I have formerly given an extract from a work of Mr. Payne Knight's in which he avows his belief that the *double* principle was never the religious belief of any nation.

In figure 35, taken from Spence's Polymetis, we see the Mosaic Mythos in Greece, if the gem whence it was drawn be Grecian. Here is the serpent called Heva tempting Adam. Spence calls it a drawing of Hercules, after he has killed the serpent; but why is the serpent up in the tree, instead of lying dead on the ground? Where are the club, the lion's head and feet? The serpent is evidently whispering in Adam's ear, while he is taking an apple. This quite satisfies me, that after all the labour bestowed on the Mythos of the Ophites, we are not yet quite at the bottom of it. In its general principle we are right, but not in the detail. Parkhurst has given a passage from Clemens which proves, that the Greek Bacchanals were well acquainted with the Mythos of Eve, since they constantly invoked her, or a person under her name, in their ceremonies.[2]

I recommend my reader to peruse and think upon several observations too long for insertion

---

[1] If ever they really held this doctrine. Hyde does not allow that they did. We have seen how it was held by the Manichæans. The Persians probably held it in the same manner, that is to say, they did not hold it at all.

[2] Spence refers to Lucan, ix. 367, Polymetis, plate XVIII. and p. 120, Ed. fol.

made by Spence, on the similarity in the characters or labours of Hercules, and the character or works of Jesus Christ; the ascension; the killing of the serpent; the observation of Bacon respecting the Christian mysteries and the cup of salvation. Had the cup any thing to do with the celebrated Sangreal, so much the object of search in the middle ages? Has the refusal of the cup in the Romish sacrament, so much sought after or desired by devotees, any thing to do with this? Mr. Spence might have given us some more of the labours, not a little deserving of attention; such, for instance, as his being swallowed by a fish.

One of the Targums says, that חויא *huia*, a serpent, tempted Adam or the first man, and not חוה *hue*, *Eve* his wife. Parkhurst renders this, not a serpent, but a beast, an animal. No person will doubt what animal this was, except he who will not see. It was the serpent, and here we have it, in the drawing, speaking to Adam, not lying dead at the feet of Hercules. Here we have Eva tempting Adam, and we see what Eva was, viz. the female חויא *huia*, serpent. Here we have the object of adoration of the Ophites—the female generative power—the destroying, regenerating power. As the secret doctrine of the Creator, Preserver, and Destroyer, began to be known in the middle and Western parts of Asia, at the same time it began to be corrupted, and the absurd idea of a fallen angel to creep in, at first among the ignorant vulgar only, but at last among a higher class, like what we have in Europe; who ought to be ashamed of habouring nonsense so unworthy of the Supreme Being. The adoration is paid to Sumnaut,[1] Seva, or Cali, as the severe and impartial judge, ruling, it is true, with a rod of iron, but also with a rod of justice. The followers of Seva and Cali, of India, answer to our Calvinistic dealers in damnation of Europe. The same causes produce the same effect.

I consider that the way in which my theory of the renovation of worlds (that is, the theory of all the ancients) agrees with the Mosaic doctrine and removes its difficulty, is a very strong part of my case; for I request those who will not admit its truth to account on any probable grounds for the fact stated above, and admitted by the first divines, such as Bishop Warburton, Mr. Belsham, &c., that there is nothing about Hell or Devils in the Pentateuch.

There being nothing in Genesis or the Pentateuch of the nature of a Devil in our common acceptation of the term, we are naturally induced to inquire, What was the nature of the being which tempted Eve? This being is described in our translation as a serpent, and *properly* so described, notwithstanding the attempt of the learned and Rev. Dr. Adam Clarke, in his translation, to make it *a monkey*. The serpent is the only one of all the animals of the creation which possesses the peculiar property of renovating itself. To *all appearance*, when not destroyed by violence, it possesses eternal life. Throwing off with its skin its old character, it seems to become young again every spring. These are the peculiar reasons why the Cobra, the most deadly of the genus, with its tail in its mouth, was selected as the emblem of renovating life—of the eternal destroying regenerator. It has been said, that it was the vulgar belief in Egypt that the serpent really never died. I think nothing is more likely than that, in very early times, it was thought never to die. I dare say my reader never heard of one, in a state of nature, being ascertained to have suffered a natural death, and the annual change of skin added plausibility to the doctrine of its perpetual existence.

Among the Ophites, and indeed the Gnostics generally, the serpent was called the Megalistor or Great Builder of the Universe. Here we have, under another name, Ophites, the Cyclopes or the builders of the circular temples at Stonehenge and every where else. With the tail in the mouth, Serpents were the emblems of the eternal creator or renovator of the universe. Shrouding the Linga

---

[1] This was the evil principle or Pluto, in Ireland, Italy, and India. I shall explain its meaning hereafter.

and the Yoni it was the emblem of the preserver and destroying regenerator. He was the Megalistor or Δημι*β*ργος, because he was the emblem of the Logos, the creator or renewer of cycles, or worlds in cyclic periods.

In the Church of St. Martyn's, Coney Street, York, is a very ancient and richly golden embroidered pulpit-cloth, in the centre of which is a figure of God Almighty—a very old man with a dove in a glory on his breast, and supporting in one hand a crucified Saviour, and holding the other as the Lama and the Pope hold their hand and fingers when they give their benediction to the people. A golden sun covers the head of the old man, and lifts up and shews the human head *underneath*. I can scarcely imagine any device, except writing, better calculated to tell the *initiated*, that the Sun and the Creator were identical. I was induced to go to see this by a passage in Mr. Allen's History of Yorkshire. [1] There never were Gnostics as a sect at York, but it was the place celebrated by the mystic mother of Constantine, Helena. One of the churches in York has a Zodiac upon it. In St. Mary's Abbey there is the image, before noticed, of Moses horned, with a winged serpent in his hand. All this is evidently Romish Christianity, but without doubt it is also Gnostic. St. Mary's Abbey and the parish churches could not have been built by Gnostics, exclusive of the Romanists. This lets us into the Romish secrets.

It is impossible not to see that, at the time the Romish Church was every where declaiming against Gnosticism, it was every where privately professing it. How can any thing be more conclusive than the sun on the pulpit-cloth? How can any thing be clearer than the Lamb that taketh away the sins of the world? How, than the prayers to the Sun, Son, in Saxon and Sanscrit Sunu, both yet retained by the Protestants? The great fault of the Templars seems to have been in believing that Hakem Bemrillah was the Paraclete, instead of St. Francis. For the Cordeliers certainly believed, though perhaps secretly, that St. Francis had been, by some means, *entirely converted*, to use their own words, into Jesus Christ, and had suffered all his five wounds, called the stigmas of St. Francis. This is an exact repetition of the nine Salivahanas of India, one renewed every cycle, having the wounds, like St. Francis, and called *the wounded in the side*. He was thought to be the incarnation of the *tenth* cycle. Protestants will deny that the Lamb is Gnosticism. But it is Christianity—and Gnosticism is Christianity. They cannot separate the Lamb of the Hindoos, of Moses, of the Egyptians, of the Carnutes of Gaul, of the Zodiac, from their Lamb to which they pray, to enlighten the world. How is it possible to doubt that the stigmas of St. Francis cover the same mythos as the wounds of the side-pierced Balii, of the Staurobates, the nine Salivahanas, the Cristnas, and the Buddhas of India? The same mythological history is renewed for every cyclar incarnation. Every sect or country claims the Saviour as having favoured its sect or country with his appearance—all others of that day being impostors. Thus, in the West, St. Francis was the preacher of the true Gospel in his day, which, of course, would supersede the old ones of the preceding incarnation, and Mohamed or Hakem was an impostor. [2]

---

[1] Mr. Allen says, many similar things were destroyed at the Reformation, and regrets that this pulpit cloth was not among the number. I rejoice that it is yet safe. After this notice, probably some *pious Mr. Allen* will remove it.

[2] In these superstitions there is always apparent an attempt at a repetition, or an attempt in the latter to imitate preceding Avatars. This is in strict unison with the doctrine of renewed incarnations. All Avatars came to an untimely death. The last, who was Mohamed, was poisoned. In compliance with this superstition, some years ago several nuns at Paris submitted to be crucified; and near Berne, in the winter of 1823, 1824, several persons were crucified, and one was dead before the police interfered. The perpetrators of this horrid murder were tried and condemned; an *official account of it*, which I once possessed, *was published*. The house where it took place was razed, and a monument was (I believe) erected on its place to record the fact. I was at Geneva a few months after it happened.

## CHAPTER IX.

RASIT, Aρχη—ARGONAUTS.—NAMA AMIDA BUTH.—GNOSTICS.—GNOSTICS CONTINUED.—GNOSTICS CON-
TINUED.—VALENTINIANS.—ST. JOHN, ST. THOMAS.—YES-DAN.—MYTHOS IN ASIA MINOR.—SAMARITAN
GENESIS.—ADAM CADMON.—WISDOM IN GREECE AND EGYPT.—TIME.—Tο Οʋ.—Tο Οʋ CONTINUED.—
CHRISTIAN MYSTERIES.

1. I must now request my reader to reflect deeply upon several parts of what he has read in
the preceding books. The ראשית *rasit* is the first word to which I would wish to recall his attention. It cannot be doubted that in the word *rasit*, the meaning of which has been so studiously
concealed, we have in uninterrupted succession the Logos by which the world was created. It is
the Buddha of India. It is the Logos of the Orpheans, and of Zoroaster, and of Plato. It is the
Minerva of the Etruscans and Greeks, issuing or emanating from the head of Jove;[1] and Jove
himself is IEUE. It is their Mητις or divine wisdom, and the Sophia of the Cabalists. It is, as
Mητις or divine wisdom, the object of the mystic adoration of the Gnostics, of the middle ages;
and one of the very few things which we know of these sectaries for a certainty is, that this was,
in a peculiar manner, the name under which they represented the Creator : for we know very little
else of them, the orthodox having left us nothing of all their works which we can be certain has
come to us unadulterated. But all the circumstances which we know relating to them give us
reason to believe that they were a race of persons much superior to the *Papiuses, Irenæuses,* and
*Justins,* the founders of the modern Roman religion. All we know of them we have from the
Christian fathers, whose accounts are evidently intended to depreciate them in every way ; and
these fathers thought it meritorious either to defame them, or to propagate falsities respecting
them. Besides, if the fathers had been sincere, their hatred to the Gnostics and their bigotry
were such, that it is very unlikely even that they could have understood the refined and abstruse
doctrines of such philosophers, as we may collect from circumstances and the admissions of
enemies, that Basilides was. What can we believe on the testimony of those who asserted that
*all* these philosophers ate children in the sacrament ? It is most surprising to me that such men
as Lardner and Beausobre should receive, as credible, the histories of the fathers : very certain I
am that no judge in England, France, Germany, or America, would convict an accused person of
the lowest crime on such evidence.

It is admitted by the orthodox, that these philosophers were men in the highest grade of
society. From this and a careful consideration of all the circumstances, I think we may conclude that they held the doctrines of the orientals respecting the renewal of cycles and incarnations, and that the millenium would take place. I think the fact of their designating the
Saviour by the term Χρησος pretty well proves this. They held him to be the first of the
emanations, the logos, the mind. These people became divided into a number of minor sects ;
and it is almost certain that in such times as they lived; a great number of absurdities must have
been held by one or other of them. They were not free from the common weaknesses of

---

[1] See Figures, No. 22.

humanity : as the remainder of the species retrograded, they retrograded also. I feel confident that this is a fair and impartial view of the subject; and that very little more than this can we ever certainly KNOW, though the nonsensical stories told of them by their enemies may continue for ever to be retailed. But should some of the charges alleged against them be true, yet as we have no means of ascertaining their truth, they cannot reasonably be admitted : and so far are we from possessing proofs in justification of those charges, that we find them made by persons convicted of systematic fraud. The natural inference, therefore, is, that their charges are as false as their other allegations, proved to be falsehoods. But, under all these difficulties, when I find their opponents stating facts which combine with and dovetail into the system which I have shewn to have come from the East, the acknowledged birth-place of the Gnostics, I think, I am justified in assuming that there is a *high probability* that they are true, and in thus treating them in my reasoning. In all subjects of this kind, *demonstration* of the truth is very seldom to be had.

The ancient Jews had a collection of tracts called the Apocrypha, concerning which, in fact, very little is known. Of course they will tell you every thing is known. But, if St. Jerom may be believed, their Scriptures, both what are now called Canon and the Apocrypha, were for many years after the destruction of their temple by the Romans nearly lost, scattered in divers places, and at last were collected and preserved by the Christian fathers. What may have been the number of the tracts of the Apocrypha is doubtful; but it is easy to see that some of those now in the list have nothing to do with it. The name shews that these were the books in which the secret Cabalistic or Gnostic learning was concealed; the word Apocrypha, not meaning *doubtful*, but *concealed*. The meaning given to the word of *doubtful* was contrived for the sake of concealing from the vulgar that there was *a secret* existing. The contrivance has succeeded very well, for I do not suppose that one in a thousand, even of modern priests, ever suspected the truth. The meaning of *doubtful* or *uncertain* is not conveyed by the Greek word *Apocrypha*.

In the word Αποκρυφος the απο seems unnecessary to the meaning of *secret*. I have somewhere seen it explained to be a corruption of Abba *father*, and the whole word to mean *the secret of the father*, or אביכפרות *abikprut*. [1]

The Gospel history of John is said, by modern priests, to have been written against the Gnostics. How this can be I do not understand. Its beginning breathes the oriental doctrines in every word. Its Logos, i. e. Sophia, or Buddha, or Rasit, or Trimurti made flesh, or becoming incarnate, is strict Buddhism, Persianism, Platonism, and Philoism or Cabalism. Very justly has Mr. Matter said, " Cependant S. Jean l'apôtre jouisse d'un credit non moins éminent auprès " de plusieurs écoles Gnostiques, qui découvraient dans son évangile et dans son Apocalypse tous " les éléments, la termonologie et la symbolique de leurs croyances." [2] What can be more striking than the first fourteen verses of the first chapter, or than the promise, of the *tenth incarnation*, of a person to come afterward, *even the spirit of truth*, in several passages of the fourteenth and fifteenth chapters ? The supposition that this promise was fulfilled, that this person was meant, by the twelve tongues of fire which are said, in the Acts, to have settled on the apostles, to give them the power of speaking all languages, does not deserve a serious consideration.

---

[1] There is something very curious in the word אב *ab* or אבה *abe*. The root is said to be אבה *abe* with a mutable or omissable ה *e*; that is, it may either be אב *ab* or אבה *abe* : it may have either a masculine or feminine termination. This seems odd enough, for the word *father* ; but it is still more odd, that it *always* adopts a *feminine* termination for its plural—always אבות *abut* or אבת *abt*, but never ים *im*. Here the secret doctrine shews itself. It was feminine because the Father was feminine as well as masculine—androgynous—Jupiter Genetrix.

[2] Matter, Ch. iv. p. 305.

The object for which the book means to represent that the tongues were sent is clear, viz. *to give the apostles the power of speaking languages, to them new*. This is the plain literal meaning of the *text and context*, and on principles of common sense none *other* can be admitted.[1] The person to come, endowed with the spirit of truth, is promised by Jesus. I know not a single passage in our canon which can justify the construction, that twelve tongues of fire was this person. The prophecy of another person to come connects the whole with the system of the cycles of India,' of Virgil, and of Juvenal; it completes the system, and shews that the millenary cycles were an integral part of Gnosticism, and that Gnosticism *uncorrupted* was Christianity.

Once more I repeat, if the word Ἀρχη of John had merely meant *first*, πρωτος would have been used; but it was necessary to use some word which would convey the additional meaning which the word ראשית *rasit* conveyed, and therefore the word Ἀρχη was used, which, like ראשית *rasit*, means head, chief. Being used here as a substitute for *wisdom*, ראשית *rasit* is an authority sufficient to fix one of its meanings, and so it would be taken in any common case, by every Lexicographer in the world. Ἀρχη της κτισεως the beginning, head, or *efficient cause of the creation*.[2] Κτισεως means regeneration and renovation.[3] This meaning of the word κτισεως completely justifies the rendering by the LXX of the word ברא *bra* by εποιησεν, *fecit*. Parkhurst derives Ἀρχη from the Hebrew word ערד *ord*, to set in *order*. Here we have in the Hebrew our word *to order*. If I had an English and Hebrew dictionary, as full as Parkhurst's Hebrew and English Lexicon, I think I could make, out of the two languages, a language in which conversation might very well be carried on by a Hebrew and an Englishman, respecting all the common concerns of life.

Parkhurst, in his Greek Lexicon, (though he has entirely omitted it in the Hebrew, where it ought to be found,) says, Ἀρχη[4] in this application answers to the Hebrew ראשית *rasit*, by which name, Wisdom, i. e. the Messiah, is called. Again he says,[5] *authority, rule, power*. Ἀρχη most usually answers in the LXX to the Hebrew ראש *ras* or ראשות *rasut* or ראשית *rasit*.

The observations of a learned friend of mine respecting the word Ἀρχη are very just; but yet the mode in which it is used by the Gnostics seems to shew that it had a meaning something more than merely *beginning*. We have seen it used by the LXX as the substitute for the ראשית *rasit*. It is also used by John in the same manner, and from the argument of the Gnostics it seems to require *wisdom* and not *beginning*, at least more properly *wisdom* than *beginning*. The connexion of the Eastern and Western philosophy cannot be doubted, and the application of the word *wisdom* to Ἀρχη is wanted to complete the links of a chain which seems deficient in a link, and which, being of the same manufactory as all the remainder of the chain, it seems very well to supply. In all this speculation we must remember, that a secret, refined system is to be accounted for or unveiled, which could only have existed under a vulgar disguise, such a disguise as would direct common, every-day searchers after the secret in a wrong road, and, if possible, prevent them from suspecting even that there was a secret. If the Bud and the Rasit were only

---

[1] I do not speak here of the ridiculous Paulites named in the Epistle to the Corinthians, chap. xiv., who have been most *correctly* imitated by the followers of the Rev. Mr. Irving, and of whom our newspapers have been lately filled. Feb. 1833.

[2] Parkhurst, Lex. Gr. in voce Ἀρχη.          [3] Ib. in voce κτιζω.

[4] Until the greatest part of this volume was printed, I did not discover the meaning given to *rasit* by Parkhurst. It never occurred to me to look for the meaning of a Hebrew word in his Greek, which was not in his Hebrew Lexicon. Parkhurst's object was clear, viz. to suppress the information, and to avoid the charge of pious fraud.

[5] On the word Ἀρχη, V.

contained in an oriental secret language; in order to perpetuate them among the Western initiated, a word which would convey a meaning that would not be commonly understood, and different from such a word as πρωτος, which would convey a different meaning, but not the secret meaning, ought to be used: and what word could be so proper as that which was in the language of the Western world unknown, but which had the meaning of the emblem of the female generative power—the Arg or Arc—in which the germ of all nature was supposed to float or brood on the great abyss during the interval which took place after every mundane cycle?— the vessel in which the Linga and Yoni also floated; in short, it was the vessel which we find every where in the sacred mysteries, under different names, in Greece, Egypt, India, Judea, &c. —it was the Arc in which the Pola, Palladium, of every city is found, the emblem or imitation of Meru—the Arc of the Nautæ—the Acropolis or *Arca* of Jerusalem; indeed, of every ancient city, where, from religious motives, as well as the circumstance of its natural strength, the palladium of the state or of the religion was kept. In Rome it was the Caput-ol or Capitol. This answers to the Arabic Rasit, which means *head, chief, top.* From Pola may come a British name for head, seldom used except in connexion with a tax, a poll-tax. Thus all these things connect together in a very peculiar manner when searched to the bottom.

In mount Libanus, Venus was called Architis; and under this epithet the ceremonies which are stated to have been practised by the Israelites near mount Sinai, Exod. xxxii. 6, are said to be continued in her honour.[1] Here is the Αρχη or Arga, which, I think, can allude neither to a ship nor a citadel.[2] The Greeks had what they called the Μην Αρχαιος and Αρχαιος. This was the crescent-formed Arga, which was on the side of the Theban heifer.[3] Eusebius calls the first Menes a Thebinite: " Πρωτος εβασιλευσεν Μηνης Θηβινιτης, Θηβαιος· ὁς " ερμηνευεται Διονιος: The first, who reigned, was Menes the Thebinite, the Arkæan; which " is, by interpretation, the Iönian.[4] This Thebinite and Arkæan was, we find, the same person " of whom the Iöna, or Dove, was an emblem." That the Theba was the same as Iöna cannot be doubted; and the salacious Dove was the emblem of both, of the male and female generative power. Mr. Bryant says, that Arca and Argus signified the Ark; but as the Ark and Deluge were of the highest antiquity, and every thing was deduced from that period, Archaia hence came to signify any thing very ancient, and Archa, *a beginning.*[5] Thus, if I understand this learned gentleman right, he admits, that the meaning of FIRST for αρχα or Archa, is only a secondary meaning.

If we consider the word Αρχη, it is in every respect the same as רישאת rasit. It is the chief, the head; therefore, if we commence at the top and proceed downwards, it is the first. Here we see the reason why the highest place of every town was called the Acra of the city. It was the head, the peculiar seat of wisdom, whence Minerva sprung. As Arga, the generative power or organ, whence all things descended, it was also the first, and I think the word Arga is probably the origin of Αρχα. The χ is a new letter, and I think must have been substituted for the Γ, as Γερανος became Χρανος.[6] Col. Tod says, " The expedition of the Argonauts in search of the " Golden fleece is a version of the Arkite worship of Osiris, the Dolayatra of the Hindoos: and " Sanscrit etymology, applied to the vessel of the Argonauts, will give the Sun *(argha)* god's " (nat'ha) entrance into the sign of the Ram. The Tauric and Hydra foes, with which Jason

---

[1] Celtic Druid's, Chap. VI. Sect. XXXI.　　　[3] Bryant's Anal. Vol. II. p. 356.　　　[3] Ib. 358.

[4] Bryant's Anal. Vol. I. p. 321.　　　[4] Ib. Anal. Vol. II. p. 382.

[6] See Parkhurst's Greek Lexicon, in voce Αρχη.

" had to contend before he obtained the fleece of *Aries,* are the symbols of the sun-god, both of
" the Ganges and of the Nile; and this fable, which has occupied almost every pen of antiquity,
" is clearly astronomical, as the names alone of the Argha-Nat'h, sons of *Apollo, Mars, Mercury,*
" *Sol, Arcus* or *Argus,*[1] *Jupiter, Bacchus,* &c., sufficiently testify, whose voyage is entirely
" celestial."[2]

But Αργις is the same as the Argha of India. The Argha was not only the Yoni, but the
surrounding ether in which the Yoni and Linga floated. It was also the boat in which the male
and female generative principles, when reduced to their simplest form, floated during the sleep of
Brahma. It was the Ark of Noe, or of Mind, or Νυς, or Intelligence, in which the germ of
animated nature or the principles of generation were preserved. But it was in one sense as the
Arga, the Preserver or Saviour, viz. as the Ark. But the Saviour was Logos, or Rasit, or Αρχη,
or Wisdom, by whom the Trimurti renovated the world. It was the same as the תיבה *tibe* or *Ark*
in which the Messiah Moses was saved. It was the vessel in which the covenant of God was
carried. But the most important point is, that, as the ship of Noe, it was the Saviour.

Every one has heard of the celebrated boat of Isis among the Egyptians, Greeks, and
Romans. But the Northern nations also worshiped her in the form of a ship. This ship was
placed in the constellations and called Argo. In Egypt this was called Sothis or the Star of
Isis.[3] This very well connects the Arga and Isis the Saviour—the ship in which the seed of
nature was preserved. The Egyptians, Greeks, and Romans, all had festivals in the spring season
to the ship of Isis.[4] Ausonius thus speaks of it:

> Adjiciam cultus peregrinaque sacra
> Natalem Herculeum, vel ratis Isiacæ.

2. I have not succeeded to my mind, in unravelling the allegory of the Argonautic expedition.
I think it probable that we must look for a translation of some Eastern words into Greek : such,
for example, as Salivahan into Staurobates, or Meru into the thigh of Jupiter. Now, the ship
Argo is clearly the Arga of India, or Omphalos, in which *voyages of salvation* were made. Jas-on
the Captain is ΙΗΣ-on or the Saviour, Sun, Bacchus—and Hercules one of its passengers, (who
took the command after the death of ΙΗΣ-on or Bacchus,) is Heri-clo. Minerva or Divine
Wisdom invented the ship, the Argo, or Αρχη, or Αρχα, and supplied its pole, or mast, or Linga.
The Nautæ or sailors went to the Golden or Holy Chersonesus, to seek a golden or holy apple,
or golden fleece of a Ram, or, perhaps, fleece of a Golden Ram ; for the Greek equally means
*apple* and *fleece.* I can have no doubt that the allegory relates to the Lamb, the knowledge of
which was necessary to salvation, or to the apples of Genesis, which were desirable to make one
wise unto salvation. I do not consider it of very great antiquity, and perhaps Newton may be
right as to its date. It is the remains of a history of sacred character, like the Iliad and Gesta
Romanorum or Æneid. " All the religious institutes of the highest antiquity, of which we have
" any account, were delivered in poetry, and under the shape of history, real or fictitious."[5]
ΙΗΣ-on or Bacchus, the Sun in Taurus, was killed by the Linga falling upon him ; but Heri-clo,
or the Sun in Aries, survived the voyage and obtained the fleece. In all this there are evidently
the links of a chain—but, to complete it, some are still wanting. The plays of Æschylus and
Euripides are mystic representations connected with this history or mythos, and I much fear our

---

[1] Argha the Sun, in Sanscrit.  [2] Tod's Hist. p. 601.  [3] Hist. Acad. Ins. An. 1729, p. 87, Abbé Fontenu.
[4] Vide Apuleius.  [5] Mason Good's Job, Pref. p. lxxxvi.

learned Greek scholars are every day making the mystery more impenetrable, by endeavouring to make the plays speak the language of common life, and by not attending to their mysterious or hidden meaning. It is not to be supposed that our learned men can safely make any emendations, without understanding the meaning of the mythos, which is what they never attempt. They merely suppose that the heroes, for instance Prometheus, are men deified—or, the *seven* against Thebes, the story of a war. Not a single word ought to be changed from the old manuscripts; all corrections ought to be in the notes, but not one in the text. I have no doubt whatever that the first books of Genesis, the Maha-bharat, the Argonautic expedition, the Iliad, the plays of Æschylus, and the Æneid, are all different ways of telling the same story.—Substantially the same mythos was at the bottom of all, and of that mythos the constantly-revolving cycles are a most important part. It is a drama, in which there were to be a new siege of Troy, new Argonauts, &c., as described by Virgil: but whether these renewals were to take place every 6000, or 1000, or 600 years, cannot be known with certainty—the book does not tell us. It seems probable, I think, that it was every 1000 years, yet this is attended with great difficulty; and even if it were every 6000 years, and exactly the same things were to recur, morality would be destroyed,—such a degree of fatalism would follow as would destroy all freedom of will and moral responsibility; therefore, I think, human actions must have been left to a certain degree of discretion. But perhaps in reply to this observation it may be said, and I fear said with too much truth, that morality is not always the first object considered by the projectors of religious systems. The Mohamedan predestinarians reconcile fatalism and morality.

It is possible, I think, that these astronomical religious systems arose like all others from accident and circumstance. The astronomical basis is quite clear, and probably the astronomers or astrologers were the first priests. Every circumstance tends to confirm this. The more early we begin our investigation the more clearly we find the astrological taint in every religion. The Mosaic system forms no exception; for, if magic were forbidden to the people, like the casting out of devils among Christians, it was reserved to the priests, as the Joachin and Boaz, and the recurrence of the sacred numbers proves. This readily accounts for any little incongruities or inconsistencies; indeed, I think there inconsistencies render my account or theory the more probable; for we have certainly never yet seen or heard of any system whose origin *was*, or whose present form *is*, unaccompanied by inconsistencies. Every one knows that our favourite Protestantism was only a covenant of peace; and if I were a zealous supporter of *things as they are*, I would recommend the King, as we no longer persecute the Papists, to send to the Romish Archbishop of Dublin, and request him to place his hands on the head of his brother of Canterbury. These two Reverend Fathers in God will know what I mean; if they do not, they may examine the once famous or infamous Lambeth papers.

3. In Japan, Buddha is adored with the words NAMU AMIDA BUTH, which means *Adoration to Amida Buddha*, the word *Namu* is a corruption of Nama, meaning *adoration*, in the Japan and Sanscrit languages.[1] This Indian word, I think, will exhibit to us a very remarkable proof of the identity of the Indian and Italian religions. The learned Bartolomæus says, *Nama Sebesio Deo Soli invicto Mitræ*, adoratio Sebesio (Shibæ vel Shivæ) Deo soli invicto Mitræ, et apud Muratorum inscriptionem repertam in Villa Tiburtina Hadriani, quam mihi clarissimus vir G. Zoeta communicavit, et quæ ita se habet: *Soli invicto Mithræ, sicut ipse se in visu jussit refici, Victorinus Caes. N. verna dispensator numeni præsenti suis impendiis reficiendum curavit, dedicavitque* NAMA *cunctis......Nama adoratio* unde sensus inscriptionis est: *dedicavitque adorationem cunctis,*

---

[1] Barthol. System. Brach. p. 308.

*seu ut cuncti eum adorent.* Hæc inscriptio ac vocabulum *Nama* non solum inter Brahmanes vulgarissimum est, sed et ipsa adorationis formula, quam semper in ore habent. Sic Gannavadye nama adoratio Deo Gannavadi. Shiva Shiváya náma *Deo Shivæ seu Sebesio adoratio,* dimanat enim vocabulum *Nama* a verbo—namadi *adorat,* namasi *adoras,* namami *adoro,* &c., &c.[1] The explanation of this word confirms what I have said in my Celtic Druids respecting the Sanscrit language in Italy. It probably came along with the God Ganesa or Janus, and the Saturn-ja and the Pallistini, or Palæstrina, or Sacrum Preneste, and the name of Itala or Bull. Great numbers of very ancient pictures of the Bambino are to be seen in Italy with the inscription *Deo Soli invicto,* and also numbers of inscriptions with the words Nama Mitræ invicto.

I must now request my reader to look back to Chapter VII. Section 8, page 758, and he will there see that the name of the God worshiped at the temple of Bal-ii or Tripetti, the crucified God, called the wounded in the side, is called *Om Sri Ramăya Nama,* the word *Sri* being one of the names of Cristna, and *Om* of both Buddha and Cristna; then to look to section 4, and consider the five sacred and mysterious syllables of Avyar in the Kaliwakam, which is, in the Tamul language, *Na-ma-si-va-yah,* and he will instantly see, that they are the same as the Italian Sebadia, a most extraordinary and decisive *proof* of identity, in the Mithraitic Christian mythoses of India and Italy. The root of Sabasio is Sab, the plural of which means the Planetary bodies possessing wisdom,—the disposers. The word Sab, (see Chap. VI. Sect. 11, p. 716,) Cleland has told us, means *wisdom.*

4. Many of the Gnostics maintained that Christ only *appeared* to be crucified: in this they also varied from most, but not from all, of the Romists. But whether the faith of the Gnostics or that of the orthodox, from whom they varied, were the original faith of the Eastern Cristnas and Salivahanas I cannot discover—the *pious* or the *prudent* Orientalists of Calcutta have kept from us, or have not been able to give us, the Pouranas of Salivahana or Wittoba, from which we might have known it.

Several of the texts of the Gospel histories were quoted with great plausibility by the Gnostics in support of their doctrine. The story of Jesus passing through the midst of the Jews when they were about to cast him headlong from the brow of a hill, (Luke iv. 29, 30,) and when they were going *to stone* him, (John viii. 59, x. 31, 39,) were examples not easily refuted. These were fair argumenta ad homines of the Gnostics, even though they did not receive the four Gospel histories of the orthodox. But though they did not admit the genuineness of these histories, they did not deny the authenticity of many parts of them: in this, being exactly like the Manichæans and the Mohamedans.

It is necessary that I should notice another doctrine of the Γνωσις, which like the doctrines developed in my first book respecting the Trinity, &c., arose from the application of common sense to the objects of surrounding nature. The philosophers observed that all animals were the same in respect to animal life as man, but of the possession of reason they appeared to be void. From this they were induced to believe in two souls or animæ—one the living principle dying with the body; the other, the superior one, which first emanated from and then passed by metempsychosis through several gradations before it was finally absorbed into the essence of the Creator. That this should be found in the Bible is what we might reasonably expect, and, accordingly, it may be found in great numbers of places, under the terms ψυχη and πνευμα. This has been very satisfactorily proved by Mr. Ed. King, in the fourteenth note of Vol. III. of his Morsels of Criticism. This gave rise to a very refined part of the doctrines of some of the

---

[1] Barthol. System. Brach. p. 195.

later Gnostics—that the Χρηϛος of Jesus, or the superior anima, descended into him in the form of the Dove, when he was baptized in Jordan, and left him before his crucifixion, and that only the human part remained.  From this, I think, arose a very recondite species of mysticism. He was Χρηϛος, the being κατ' εξοχην *benignus*, the Logos, the Σοφια, the חכמה *hkme*.  He was also Χριϛος *the crucified*.  He was also Κηρυξ *the Herald, the Sent of God*.  He was also Cris, *black*, his native colour, as we find him both in India and Europe ; and, when identified with the Sun, he is, as Apollo, &c., &c., always *black*.  It is for this reason that the busts of the twelve Roman Cæsars, are often black, though the drapery is white—persons having the same divine character as the twelve successors of Jacob,[1] the twelve apostles of Jesus Christ, the twelve Imaums of Persia, the twelve apostles of Hakem Bemrillah, the twelve apostles of Mani ; but above all the twelve Lucumones of Etruria or of the country of RAZENA, who are shewn by Mons. Creuzer to have been *Prêtres de la Lumière possédés, inspirés*.[2]  Here the *Raz-ena* or *Ras-ena*[3] is very remarkable.  All these were supposed to have a certain portion of the divine spirit, or the superior anima, incarnate in them, more than other men ; or, in other words, to be divinely inspired.

Nothing can be more certain than that Julius Cæsar, born at the same time as one of the Vicramadityas of India, was thought to be a divine incarnation, and that when he was assassinated, the belief in an incarnation was transferred to Octavius.  These were not copies, but the results of astrological calculations respecting the renewed cycles, noticed by Virgil, which taught the professors when the new cycle would come—and then superstition taught its votaries to look out for some person —the Ahmed Om, the Desire of all Nations.  And the times of the Indians and Romans agreed, because Cæsar had adopted the Chaldean Calendar and Calculations ; that is, the Calendar of North and South Colida of India, which is really the *true* Calendar, as is at once apparent by calculating backwards from the equinox, as now placed in the last degree of Aquarius, $25 \times 72 = 1800$.  The circumstance of identity in the period of the Jews of Sion, or the Judaites of the Siones, as proved by Cassini, of the Chaldeans or Colidei of Cochin, of the Romans and Julius Cæsar, and of the Christians,—the 25th of December, for the solstice and birth of the God, is no bad proof of the universality of the mythos.  If this be not proof, what would constitute proof?  The subject of the Chaldean correction of the Calendar I shall discuss hereafter.

The Gnostics held that, " To deliver the soul, a captive in darkness, the Principle of Light, " the Genius of the Sun, charged with the redemption (λυτρωσις) of the intellectual world, of " which the Sun is the type, manifested itself among men ; that the light appeared in the dark- " ness, but the darkness comprehended it not ; that, in fact, light could not unite with darkness ; " it put on only the appearance of the human body : that at the crucifixion Jesus Christ only " *appeared* to suffer.  His person having disappeared, the by-standers saw in his place a cross of " light, over which a celestial voice proclaimed these words : ' The Cross of Light is called " ' Logos, Christos, the Gate, the Joy.' "  I consider that the book of John contains clear and abundant proofs, that the original doctrine, though perhaps the secret doctrine of the Romish Church, was uncorrupted Gnosticism,—the Pandæan religion of the Golden age, when no icons were used, and when the Gods had no names.  How they then were supposed to exist will be clearly explained in a future book.

---

[1] Ishmael, from whom the Arabians descended, had twelve sons, who formed twelve tribes, like Abraham, Isaac, and Jacob, and the twelve tribes.

[2] Liv. iv. p. 220, Liv. v. p. 394.    [3] I construe Raz-ena, *country of wisdom*.

The doctrine of emanations was undoubtedly the universal, though, perhaps, in very early times, the *secret* doctrine. The passage which I have given in Book II. Chapter III. Section 5, from Deuteronomy, clearly and unquestionably proves that it was equally prevalent among the Jews as among all others of the oriental nations; and, as a proof of this, and strongly confirmatory of my whole system, the passage is of the greatest importance.

The Cabalistic doctrine of the later Jews is exactly consentaneous to the construction which I have put upon Genesis. It accounts for the origin of things, by making them emanations from a First Cause, and, therefore, pre-existent. They suppose all things to be at last withdrawn into the First Being, by a revolution or restitution to their first state; as if they believed their סוף עין *oin sup,* En Soph,[1] Fountain of Wisdom, or First Being, to contain all things. This *En Soph* may also be the same as the Greek Oν and ΣοΦια, Wisdom of the generative power, Oν. From this Being all things are supposed to proceed by effluxes or emanations, like rays, and when the rays are redrawn the external world perishes, and all things again become absorbed in God. *He hideth his face; and they are troubled; he taketh away their breath, they die, and return to their dust. He sendeth forth his spirit, and they are created; and he reneweth the face of the earth.*[2] All this harmonizes perfectly with my translation of the first verse of Genesis.

The expressions in several places are decisive in my favour. *Who can find out the Wisdom of God? Wisdom hath been created before all things, and the understanding of prudence from evermore.* Ecclus. i. 4. Here is most clearly the חכמה *hkme* and בינה *bine,* the first two Sephiroths. Again, *The word of God most high is the fountain of Wisdom*—Ecclus. i. 5—the *En Soph* is here most clearly. Again, *I was set up from everlasting, from the beginning, or ever the earth was.* Prov. viii. 23. Here the word *everlasting* is clearly a mistranslation: the Hebrew word only means *a long time,* but not *for ever,* without commencement. This is an admitted fact.

I do not flatter myself that I can unveil all the secret mysteries of the Cabala of the ancient Israelites, long since buried amidst the ruins of their temples. But yet I think we may be justified in believing that such men as Moses, Zoroaster, Pythagoras, and Plato, had a religion in its fundamental principles, consistent at least with common sense, and altogether different, as they themselves always asserted, from the mythoses which they tolerated among the vulgar. If we take this view of the subject, we shall find in the *triune* doctrine nothing inconsistent with reason and sense.

The following is the form of adjuration, which Cyril and Justin Martyr give to Orpheus, but which John Malela and the author of the Paschal Chronicle ascribe to Thoth or Hermes-Trismegistus. The difference, however, is immaterial: for the Orphic and Tautic systems were fundamentally the same. In the Paschal Chronicle, the oath is exhibited in the following terms: " I adjure thee, the Heaven,[3] the wise work of the great God: be propitious. I adjure thee, " the voice[4] of the Father, which he first spake, when he established the whole world by his " counsel;[5] the voice of the Father, *which he first uttered,* HIS ONLY-BEGOTTEN WORD."[6] I think this completely proves the truth of my theory. The doctrine of Hermes-Trismegistus was

---

[1] Matter, Ch. iv. p. 403.                    [2] Psalm civ. 29, 30; Universal History, Vol. I.

[3] These are the Samin of Genesis, *the disposers* endowed with understanding or wisdom. G. H.

[4] Logos. The Targums constantly use the word ממרא *mmra* for יהוה *ieue,* for which Philo uses Λογος. I believe this *m-mra* is nothing but the Maria, with the Monogram preceding it. The books of the real Apocrypha are full of these doctrines of Wisdom and of Masonry. G. H.

[5] i. e. *wisdom.* G. H.                    [6] Logos. G. H.; Faber, Pag. Idol. Vol. I. p. 229.

precisely the same as that of the Hindoos respecting the destruction and renovation of the world —that nothing is destroyed, but only changed in form.[1]

5. In the Christian religion, as in all others, the tangible or worldly sign of the Holy Spirit or Ghost was supposed to be wind, or air in motion ; the Dove its emblem. Thus it is said in John xx. 22, *When* BREATHING ON THEM, *he said to them, Receive ye the Holy Ghost.* As air in motion was the tangible or sensible sign of the *third* person, so the solar, ethereal or spiritual fire was the sign of the *second* person of the Trinity—*Wisdom, Buddha,* Protogonos. By *Wisdom* Aleim formed the planetary system. By Ruh, רוח קדש *qdis ruh,* the Holy Ghost brooding on the waters, he communicated the generative and prolific faculty, which, without moisture, can in no case exist. And, in all cases, by the Holy Ghost or Spirit, or air in motion, regeneration was supposed to take place.

The brooding of the spirit on the face of the deep ; the brooding first explained by Bishop Patrick, has a clear and direct allusion to the Orphic Egg which the Bull opened with his horn :

Taurus cum cornibus aperit annum.

In a similar manner the Logos or Word had its rise. How did God proceed when he made the world ? (Let it not be forgotten that man has his image.) Did he use his hands ? No : he spake the *word* and it was made. He gave the *word* and the effect followed. By his *word* he made it. The *word* existed before the creation. The *word* was *first,* the world instantly followed. Thus John says, " In the beginning was the word, and the word was with God, and " the word was God." Here we have the Trinity of the Oriental, the Platonic, and the Christian mystics. The ancient mystics thought that God gave the word and formed the world from previously-existing matter ; the modern ones thought he created it from nothing. Hence the anxiety shewn in their creeds to seek for terms sufficiently clear to express this idea. Hence they have run into the nonsense of *begotten before all worlds.* What jargon ! WORD BEGOTTEN ! Let us suppose a second person of the Godhead. What should cause him to be called Word ? Why not any other arbitrary name ? That which I have described was the origin of it. When God gave the *word* it was *wisely* given. It was *wisdom* itself. Hence again, *wisdom* was the first emanation from the divine power. It was identified with the *word.* It was not a creation. It was an emanation. And what was an emanation ? No one knows. Here man gets out of his depth : and whatever he might do before, he now begins to talk nonsense, unless he avail himself of a simile, and speak of *an emanation* as a ray of the Sun.

In a former section I have said, that the doctrine of the Creator, Preserver, and Destroyer, arose from the creating, preserving, and destroying powers of the solar ray. This was, I believe, the origin of the doctrine : but when the mind of man improved, and he discovered that the sun was a *creature,* not a *creator,* he was, by a very natural process, carried up to another being, from whom all blessings flowed, the Creator of the Sun itself, and of whom he could form no idea ; and he called him, perhaps not improperly, ILLUSION ; for the moment he began to form an idea of the Creator, like a phantom, like the baseless fabric of a vision, it vanished away. It was Maia, *illusion.*[2] But to this unknown Being man gave the attributes, which, in the first instance, he had given to the solar ray, and he gave them with every appearance of truth and justice—for we all know that our Creator is our Preserver, and that destruction is creation throughout this our world, in every case to which our knowledge extends. From this sublime doctrine came

---

[1] Cudworth, Intell. Syst. p. 326.

[2] Porphyry says, a ring-dove was sacred to Maia, who is the same as Proserpine, and the Goddess Night, and is at the summit of the intelligible and intellectual order. De Abstin. Lib. iv. Sect. xvi.

first the Father; *secondly*, the first-begotten Son, the Logos, Divine Wisdom, the Saviour; and *thirdly*, the Ερως, the Divine Love, the Spirit of God, under the emblem of the mild and affectionate Dove, the type of the most interesting of all passions. The passion itself is closely allied and assimilates to the character of the Creator—the spirit of God though destroying, yet destroying only to regenerate and restore to existence.[1] Here at last open upon us views of our Creator most beneficent and profound: hitherto hidden under mythoses and incarnations, and every species of base and degrading anthropomorphism. And now I think we may perceive two creators, preservers, and destroyers, unceasingly confounded: *first*, the immaterial Trinity, *a Trinity of abstractions or attributes*. The second, the Sun, the material Trinity. First, the Father, the Logos, and the Holy Ghost; the second, Brahma, Vishnu, and Seva—the *second*, nothing but incarnations of the *first ;* the second, the Sun with his corporeal properties being the object of *vulgar*-adoration—the first, the Father, Logos, and Holy Ghost, only known and adored by *philosophers*, in the adyta of the temples.

With most of the ancient philosophers an opinion prevailed, that the soul of man was a portion of the universal mind; that from it the mind of man emanated, and that to it, ultimately, it would return. From this very refined doctrine arose all the incarnations, however degrading. A portion of the universal mind, of divine wisdom, of the protogonos, became instilled into a human being. Thus it is evident that every human being endowed with more than usual wisdom, talent, or excellence, might not inappropriately be said to exhibit an example of an incarnation of the Divine Mind, or of a portion of the Divine Mind. Thus he was of two natures—the divine and human; as the first, as Divine Wisdom, he was πρωτογονος, the first-born Son of the Father, into whom, at his death, he would return. In these refined doctrines, held by such men as Plato, I think we may discover a Trinity, neither inconsistent with reason, nor incomprehensible; like that stated by Athanasius and others.

In Book V. it was observed, that there were thousands of incarnations. This was because every soul or mind was an emanation from what Plato called the Το Ον ; thus it was the incarnation of a part of the Το Ον—an emanation from the Το Ον, incarnate. It was there observed, that Cristna was thought to be something more than a common incarnation. This opinion was merely sectarian. Every sect thought so of its favourite Avatar; though it did not deny other sects to have had Avatars,—as in the case of Mohamed.

Thus every person who possessed any striking superiority of mind or talent, would be said to be inspired, or to have a portion of the Divine Mind incarnated in him ; and this accounts for the great number of incarnations both among the Hindoos and Jews; for some of the Hindoos say that the Supreme has been incarnated vast numbers of times. This is well matched by the worthies of the Jews, who have either been born miraculously, or translated to heaven, or in some way have been preternaturally endowed. Either their history or their names among the Jews shew them ; thus Enoch, Elijah, Elisha, &c. And it was, perhaps, in this way, that Buddha and Cristna, who were merely the Sun, were confounded with the minor incarnations. Then, to what do all the incarnations of Buddha at last amount ? Evidently to a refined Metaphysis—

---

[1] Jesus Christ says, John xii. 24, " Except a corn of wheat fall into the ground and die, it abideth alone: but if it die it bringeth forth much fruit." And Paul in allusion to the esoteric religion says, " That which thou sowest is not quickened except it die ; so also is the resurrection of the dead. It is sown in corruption, it is raised in incorruption." 1 Cor. xv. 36, 42. Here is the Metempsychosis. Elias was thought to have returned again in the person of Jesus. The esoteric doctrine may be perceived constantly, but, as might be expected, it requires close attention to discover what was hidden with the greatest care. The Hindoo doctrine of the Metempsychosis was thought by ancient Rabbis of the Jews to be described in Genesis. *Dust thou art, and to dust thou shalt return.* (Maur. Hind. Ant. Vol. IV. p. 275.) Here again displaying the Hindoo origin of Genesis.

to a figure of speech, an allegory—but an allegory in its foundation true, and in its superstructure beautiful—the Barasit of the Cabala, which will be explained hereafter.

Plutarch, in the treatise, in which he shews that pleasure is not attainable, according to Epicurus, has this passage : " When, through inspiration, we appear to approach very near to a " divine nature." [1] The incarnation of the Holy Spirit was not unknown to the ancient Romans, as, by the description of it, it may be found attributed to them and the ancient Egyptians, by Plutarch, in his life of Numa. The following is the answer stated by Manetho, [2] to be given by the Oracle to Sesostris ; and whether there ever was a Sesostris or not, it proves that the doctrine existed : " On his return through Africa he entered the sanctuary of the Oracle, εν υπερηφανια, " saying, Tell me, O thou strong in fire, who before me could subjugate all things ? and who shall " after me ? But the Oracle rebuked him, saying, *First, God ;* then, *the Word ;* and with them, " *the Spirit.*" [3] Here we have distinctly enumerated God, the Logos, and the Spirit or Holy Ghost, in a very early period, long previous to the Christian æra.

I expect the spirit of bigotry will excite some of the priests to represent the Trinity here displayed as horribly wicked, because it does not come from St. Giovanni Laterano or from Lambeth. And no doubt they will put on their spectacles to discover some minute differences between it and their Trinity of Incomprehensibles. [4] But I would fain hope that the liberal part of Trinitarian Christians will pay no attention to them, as the two systems are evidently at the bottom the same. And I should have much pleasure if I could entertain hopes that it would (abandoning the modern doctrine of the Atonement) be acceded to by the Unitarians ; who are in fact a society of philosophers, endeavouring to receive as much of the orthodox Christianity as their enlightened understandings will permit them. I hope these philosophers will not, with the fanatics, endeavour to narrow the door of the mansion of eternal life, but will endeavour to throw it open as wide as possible. The mansion is large and has room for all. This is a *wish,* but I confess, I must admit, that it amounts not to an *expectation.*

6. After a very careful consideration I feel quite satisfied, that the doctrine of Plato, of Philo, and of Moses, or the first chapter of Genesis, is fundamentally identical with the doctrine of the Trimurti of India ; but, as might be expected, indeed, as it must necessarily have happened under the circumstances of the case, in some particulars and its minor details, corrupted or changed. But to point out the exact particulars in which they differed, in their minute details from the real original, I conceive to be absolutely impossible, because we have not the means of examining both sides of the arguments used in the disputes which arose about these doctrines. All our writers, and the authorities from whom they draw their materials, are partisans ; so that our *miscalled* histories, (miscalled if by a history be meant an impartial account,) are not to be relied on. I know no better example of this than Enfield's History of Philosophy. The partisan is visible in almost every page.

Mons. Matter has given an account of the Gnosticism of Philo. Though in some places rather confused, I think no one can deny its identity with the Eastern doctrines which I have unfolded, and with the first chapter of John.

L'Être Suprême est, d'après Philon, la lumière primitive, la source de toute autre lumière, l'archétype de la lumière, d'où émanent des rayons innombrables qui éclairent les ames. Il est l'ame du monde, et, comme telle, il agit dans toutes ses parties.

---

[1] Taylor's Max. Tyr. p. 271.     [2] Ap. Malal. Lib. i. Cap. lv.     [3] Nimrod, Vol. I. p. 119.
[4] The word used in the Athanasian Creed.

Il remplit et limite lui-même tout son être : ses puissances et se vertus ($\alpha\rho\epsilon\tau\alpha\acute{\iota}$) remplissent et pénétrent tout. Il est sans commencement, $\alpha\gamma\epsilon\nu\nu\eta\tau\sigma\varsigma$ ; il vit dans le prototype du temps, $\alpha\iota\omega\nu$.

Son image est le $\Lambda\sigma\gamma\sigma\varsigma$, forme plus brillante que le feu, ce dernier n'étant pas la lumière pure. Ce *Logos* demeure en Dieu ; car c'est dans son intelligence que l'Être Suprême se fait les *types* ou les *idées* de tout ce que doit s'exécuter dans le monde. Le Logos est donc le véhicule par lequel Dieu agit sur l'universe. On peut le comparer à la parole de l'homme.

Le Logos étant le monde des idées, le $\varkappa\sigma\sigma\mu\sigma\varsigma$ $\nu\sigma\eta\tau\sigma\varsigma$, au moyen duquel Dieu a créé les choses visibles, il est le $\Theta\epsilon\sigma\varsigma$ $\pi\rho\epsilon\sigma\acute{6}\upsilon\tau\epsilon\rho\sigma\varsigma$ en comparaison du monde, qui est aussi Dieu, mais un Dieu de création, $\Theta\epsilon\sigma\varsigma$ $\nu\epsilon\sigma\tau\epsilon\rho\sigma\varsigma$. Le *Logos*, comme chef des intelligences, dont il est le représentant général, est nommé archange : et comme type et représentant de tous les esprits, même de ceux des mortels, il est appelé l'homme type et l'homme primitif.

*Dieu est seul sage : toute sagesse* émane de lui, comme de sa source : *la sagesse humaine* n'est que le reflet, l'image de la sienne : ou peut appeler *sa sagesse* la mère de la création, dont Dieu est le père. Il s'est uni avec la $\sigma\sigma\phi\acute{\iota}\alpha$ ou la science ; mais non pas à la manière des hommes : il lui a communiqué le germe de la création, et elle a enfanté le monde matériel.[1]

Here, in the last paragraph is very clear the Wisdom of Genesis, the Buddha of India, and the $\mathrm{A}\rho\chi\eta$ and Logos of Plato, Orpheus, Zoroaster, and John.

After this, in page 66, Matter adds, Dieu créa le monde idéal. Ensuite il fit réaliser, d'après ce type, le monde matériel par son *Logos*, qui est sa parole—that is, by the agency of the Logos. Again, Le *Logos* est non-seulement créateur, il est encore le lieutenant de l'Être Suprême, c'est par lui qu'agissent toutes les puissances ou tous les attributs de Dieu.

My reader, I think, will have no difficulty in perceiving why Plato, whose doctrine was the same as that of Philo, was called by the early fathers the *divine* Plato. Of the monde idéal named above, I shall presently treat.

7. The following observations, unwilling observations of the learned Beausobre, support me in my opinion, that a secret and mystical meaning was intended in the use of the word $\alpha\rho\chi\eta$ instead of the word $\pi\rho\omega\tau\sigma\varsigma$, by the LXX and by JOHN, on many occasions. On this point I think we may safely conclude, that the whole of the Gnostics coincided in opinion with the Valentinians, and may thus be added to the very weighty authorities which I have before given, that the word *Rasit* of Genesis meant *Wisdom*. Les Valentiniens n'entendoient pas comme nous les premières paroles de St. Jean : selon eux l'Apôtre n'a pas dit, ($\mathrm{To}$ $\epsilon\nu$ $\alpha\rho\chi\eta$ $\eta\nu$ $\acute{o}$ $\lambda\sigma\gamma\sigma\varsigma$ . . . $\sigma\acute{\iota}$ $\alpha\pi\sigma$ $\mathrm{O}\upsilon\alpha\lambda\epsilon\nu\tau\iota\nu\vartheta$ $\vartheta\tau\omega\varsigma$ $\epsilon\varkappa\delta\epsilon\chi\sigma\nu\tau\alpha\iota$. $\alpha\rho\chi\eta\nu$ $\gamma\alpha\rho$ $\tau\sigma\nu$ $\mu\sigma\nu\sigma\gamma\epsilon\nu\eta$ $\lambda\epsilon\gamma\vartheta\sigma\iota\nu$ . . . $\tau\sigma\nu$ $\delta\epsilon$ $\lambda\sigma\gamma\sigma\nu$ $\tau\sigma\nu$ $\epsilon\nu$ $\tau\eta$ $\alpha\rho\chi\eta$ $\tau\vartheta\tau\sigma\nu$ $\tau\sigma\nu$ $\epsilon\nu$ $\tau\omega$ $\mu\sigma\nu\sigma\gamma\epsilon\nu\epsilon\iota$. Eclog. Theodot. ap. Clem. Al. No. VI.) que *la parole étoit au commencement*, mais que *la parole étoit dans le Principe*. Cette explication paroit bizarre, absurde, et elle m'a paru telle à moi-même, avant que j'en eusse reconnu l'origine. Je ne doute point, qu'elle ne soit fausse, mais on ne peut la traiter d'absurde, sans condamner celle que les pères ont donnée aux premières paroles de la Genèsis. Car si Moïse a voulu dire, que *Dieu a fait le Monde par le Principe*, qui est son Fils, pourquoi S. Jean n'auroit-il pas dit aussi, que le *Verbe étoit dans le principe*, qui est son Fils unique ? Il est évident que S. Jean imite Moïse. Si donc le *Rasit* de Moïse n'est point le *commencement*, mais le *Principe* actif de toutes choses,

---

[1] Matter sur les Gnostiques, Vol. I. p. 63.

pourquoi l'arché de S. Jean, qui a la même signification, ne seroit-il pas aussi le *Principe* et non le *commencement ?* Voila, si je ne me trompe, l'origine de l'opinion Valentinienne.[1]

Again, in another place M. Beausobre confirms my observation that $A\rho\chi\eta$ meant more than *beginning :* " La contradiction ne vient peut-être que de l'équivoque du mot $A\varrho\chi\eta$ ou *Principe*, " que les uns ont pris dans un sens que je nommerai Philosophique, et les autres dans un sens " *Politique.* Dans le sens Philosophique $A\rho\chi\eta$, Principe,[2] signifie un être éternal, qui a eu " lui-même la cause de son existence, et qui est cause que d'autres existent : mais dans le *sens* " *Politique, Principe* veut dire un être qui a du pouvoir et de l'autorité sur des sujets qu'il com- " mande."[3] Between the two meanings of $A\rho\chi\eta$ here is a fine distinction.

A very learned and excellent friend, one of the priesthood, in Yorkshire, once warned me against drawing any consequences from the word $A\rho\chi\eta$, a word, which, he said, is " quite clear " and perspicuous." But he will not deny that this word was the Greek fountain-head, from which all the streams of the Gnostics flowed—the foundation on which all their learned, abstruse, and ingenious systems were built.

The Maia of India is correctly the Maia of Greece, and means *grandmother* or *first mother*, Maia $A\rho\chi\eta$, the first mother, head mother, the fountain head—and thus it became the chief or head, Acro-polis, of the city—the seat or residence of the sacreds—the place where the Palladium and Sibylline oracles were deposited. $E\nu \, \alpha\rho\chi\eta \, \eta\nu$ ' $\lambda o\gamma o\varsigma$, $\varkappa\alpha\iota$ ' $\lambda o\gamma o\varsigma \, \eta\nu \, \pi\varrho o\varsigma \, \tau o\nu \, \Theta\varepsilon o\nu$, $\varkappa\alpha\iota \, \dot{o}$ $\Theta\varepsilon o\varsigma \, \eta\nu \, \dot{o} \, \lambda o\gamma o\varsigma$. $O\upsilon\tau o\varsigma \, \eta\nu \, \varepsilon\nu \, \alpha\rho\chi\eta \, \pi\rho o\varsigma \, \tau o\nu \, \Theta\varepsilon o\nu$. Had the word *first* or *beginning* been meant, $\pi\rho\omega\tau o\varsigma$, as I have before observed, would have been used : but this would at once have negatived and overthrown all the magnificent and beautiful (however defaced in later times) superstructure erected on this word, as meaning *divine wisdom.* Very properly was the book containing the exposition of this word called $\Gamma\varepsilon\nu\varepsilon\sigma\iota\varsigma$, from the word $\Gamma\iota\nu o\mu\alpha\iota$, *gignor, nascor.* When I use the terms beautiful and magnificent as applied to the doctrines of the Gnostics, I beg my reader to observe, that I do not include in these terms the nonsense given us by the Greek and Latin fathers for their doctrines. Very little which they say can be received. We know very little of the Gnostics ; but the little we REALLY do KNOW is beautiful.

When I find learned men believing Genesis literally, which the ancients, with all their failings, had too much sense to receive except allegorically, I am tempted to doubt the reality of the improvement of the human mind. What says the celebrated St. Augustin ? " That there is no " way of preserving the literal sense of the first chapters of Genesis, without impiety, and attri- " buting things to God unworthy of him."[4] But St. Augustin has only followed the learned Origen, who has maintained that the literal sense of the history of the creation in Genesis *is absurd and contradictory*, and in this opinion M. Beausobre has shewn he was probably supported by St. Basil and Gregory of Nyssa.[5]

8. Long had I despaired of finding the meaning of the mysterious John, Joannes, Jonas three

---

[1] Beausobre, Hist. Manich. Liv. vi. Chap. i. p. 291. $A\rho\chi\eta$ scribitur aut pro $A\rho\gamma\iota\varsigma$ : aut Hesychio corruptum. Siracides, Cap. xi. 3, exemplar imposuit. Perger. Lex. Hesychii.

[2] $A\rho\chi\alpha\varsigma \, \delta\varepsilon \, \lambda\varepsilon\gamma o\mu\varepsilon\nu \, \delta\iota\alpha \, \tau\varepsilon\tau o, \, \dot{o}\tau\iota \, o\upsilon\varkappa \, \varepsilon\varsigma\iota \, \tau\iota \, \pi\rho\omega\tau\varepsilon\rho o\nu, \, \varepsilon\xi \, \dot{\eta} \, \gamma\varepsilon\iota\nu\alpha\tau\alpha\iota.$ Plut. de Plac. Phil. Cap. ii. p. 875.

[3] Beaus. Hist. Manich. Liv. iv. Ch. vi. p. 89. In the above-cited passage, Beausobre is speaking of Marcion, who, I have no doubt whatever, maintained the same doctrine of the Maia $A\rho\chi\eta$—the Trinity and Emanations of the other Gnostics. The disputes of their opponents prove it.

[4] De Genes. cont. Manich. Lib. ii. 2, ap. Beausobre, Hist. Manich. Vol. I. p. 285.

[5] Philocal. p. 12, ibid.

days buried in a fish, the fish Avatar Vishnu, or Oannes treading on the head of the serpent—bruising the serpent's head, see Fig. 32, Janus or Jana, Iona or Columba having the same name as Jehovah, Ii, and of Jove, the Yoni, the opposite of the Linga—the sect of the Jains the successors of Buddha, John the Baptist, John who should live till Jesus came again, Joannes, Butta, Deus, the Prestre Johannes,—persons seemingly so difficult to reconcile or account for—when I discovered that the old Sanscrit word for Wisdom or Γνωσις was Jnana. This at once lets in a flood of light upon us,—gives us a clue to all the mysterious Johns. It is no difficult matter now, to see what was meant by John, thought to be a second Elias, by Baptism communicating the יונה iune or dove or divine wisdom (when the fire was kindled in the water) to Jesus, who was also thought to be a second Elias,—to Jesus the successor or (as believed by the Jews the) reincarnation of Elias, and also of the משה mse or Messiah Moses—to Oannes or Vish-nu treading on the serpent's head. Hence we may see why the Ras of Abyssinia was called not only Joannes, but also Butta and Deus; he was at once the God, Buddha, and Wisdom. Like the Lama, or Lamb of Tibet, he was a renewed incarnation of Divine Wisdom. John was the precursor or pre-possessor of Divine Wisdom; the holy inspiration was incarnate in him, and he transmitted it to Jesus. It was that inspiration which Moses transmitted to the Saviour Joshua or Jesus, the son of Nave, and which Elias transmitted to Elisha by delivery or investiture of the Pallium, and which Mohamed left with his cloak to Ali. John was an announcer of the Saviour, a preparer of the way, a foreseer or fore-knower; hence he was endowed with wisdom, and called John.

Georgius maintains that the Tibetian word, which he renders Gnios in Latin, and which means Sapientia, is the same as the Γνωσις of Greece, and Agnitio in Latin. If the Gn be written as the Hebrew letter was corrupted in Tibet, it will be ע o, the next letter will be י i or yod, and both read from right to left OI the Deity of Wisdom. In the same way the Jnana for Wisdom in the Sanscrit, is Oana. Here we have the Oanes. We must not forget that the Pushto or Syriac is the dialect of Tibet, where IE is spelt IO. The Gan-esa, God of Wisdom, of India, is Jan-esa, Jan—the Saviour. The Indian Gnia is the object of Wisdom; Gnia in Irish is Wisdom. Gnia is also a tree, synonymous to Feadh or Ved also a tree.[1] · The Gnia is evidently Gnosis. Feadh, or Fiodh, Foedh, Fodh, knowledge, a tree, in Sanscrit Ved.[2]

It is a very striking and curious circumstance that in the time of Banier the Christians of St. Thomas, of whom I have so largely treated, were so clearly known to be the descendants of the Apostle St. Thomas, that they were called the Christians of St. John![3] Thus we have those good people converted by Bartholomew, Thomas, and John. Now I believe the two last are true. They are the followers of the Χρησος or Jnana incarnate, first in the Twins or Tamuz, then in the Bull, then in the Lamb, then in the Pisces or Comasene. They are the Mandaites or Nazoureans of St. John of the East—of the coast of Cali or Core-manda-la. They were the Nazarenes or Nasoureans of Carmel of the Western Syria, and the Christians of St. John.

Nimrod, amidst an immense mass of nonsense,[4] in which he calls those silly fellows who have not all his advantages, (such, for instance, as knowing how the ghosts of the dead, at this day, move from place to place by passing instead of walking,) delivers a very striking opinion, which shews that truth will sometimes make its way to the understandings of the most devoted of devotees : " The fanatical votaries of king Attila the Hun, the Christians of St. Thomas in India, " the Stylite Simeons, the apostate Nestorians, and the personage called Presbyter Johannes,

---

[1] Vall. Coll. Hib. Vol. IV. Part i. pp. 81, 82.          [2] Ib. p. 80.

[3] Tavernier's Travels, Vol. II. p. 74, ed. fol.          [4] Volume II. p. 502.

" appear to have been Manichæan Buddhists. The worship of the cross was coupled with that " of the sword and of fire ; the fiery sword being cruciform." I do not doubt that this sword was the cross. It was the Labarum. It might be a sword for the soldiers ; it was a cross, probably a crucifix, for the initiated. That the sects above named were Manichæan Buddhists I have little doubt : but they were also Templars and Rossicrucians, or followers of the eight-point Red Cross, or Naazir, or Natzir-eans, or followers of the United Red Cross and Rose of Sharon, all the same under different names.

What could induce the learned Nimrod to suppose the Buddhists Nestorians, I do not know ; but he would scarcely have made the assertion without reason, and it agrees very well with the Buddhist missions to the tomb of St. Thomas, &c., &c. I have no doubt that he was right.

The Jains, often called Jins, are admitted to be a sect of Buddhists. I suppose they took their name from the Sanscrit word Jnana, *knowledge* or *wisdom*, or from the word Gin or Jin, which signifies *creating spirit*, and is evidently the same as the other—the Buddha or Logos. Thus they are followers of Jin or Jinistes as we should say.

The Jains have the same system of time as the Brahmins. They divide it into periods, which have been succeeding each other without interruption, as Dubois [1] says, for the sake of making them Atheists, from eternity. The periods are divided like those of the Brahmins in the proportion of 4, 3, 2, 1 ; and, as usual, disguised under millions of years. They hold the existence of one supreme, invisible Deity. His first attribute is *Ananta Gnanam*, or *wisdom infinite*. This Gnana speaks for itself, and shews us that, at the bottom, the Jains are precisely the same as all the other sects. [2]

We must never lose sight of the admitted fact, that the Indians have as many sects as the Western nations, and are as much in the dark respecting the origin of their religions. But no person can observe their fine astronomy and the occasional scraps of ancient learning which are every where met with, and doubt that they have had an ancient system, beautiful and refined, before their present gross idolatry existed. *That* was at the time when the Abbé Dubois admits that they had no images. [3] If, indeed, it were not for the hope of discovering their ancient lore, their present nonsense, such, for instance, as that lately given to the world by Mr. Akerman, on the Buddhists of Ceylon, would not be worthy the attention of any man of common sense for a single moment. Few persons, in making an estimate of the present corrupt state of religion in India, allow enough for the circumstance of the country having been for thousands of years a prey to civil war and foreign conquest.

In the Ayeen Akbery, it is said, that the first *fire temple* was built by a man very famous for the austerity of his manners, called Ma-hakmah. Here I think no one can help seeing the חכמה *hkme,* or wisdom of the Hebrews in the Sanscrit. [4] There is a country of Prester John in Indian Tartary. This is nothing but the Prestre Jnana or John. [5] The real Prestre John is probably the Grand Lama, [6] and, κατ' εξοχην, THE prestre—THE incarnation of Jnana or Wisdom.

I shall again be told that this is very mystical. Indeed, it is very mystical, just as much so as the whole character of John the Baptist ; as much so as the descent of the Dove upon Jesus, and the fire in the river ; the transfiguration ; the declaration, that while John decreased Jesus increased ; and many other passages in the Gospel histories,—secret doctrines kept by the priests from the people, and for the honest explanation of which to them, the people will be in a fury with me.

---

[1] P. 557.          [ ] Dubois, p. 552.          [3] Part iii. Chap. i.
[4] Vide Vallancey's Coll. Hib. Vol. VI. p. 135.          [ ] Marsden's Marco Paulo, Ch. liv. n. 455.          [6] Ib. p. 450
5 L

9. In the Desatir, which, though perhaps in some places corrupted, is a very ancient book of the Persians, the Creator is called *Yesdan*. Here we have the ΥΗΣ, 608, of Martianus Capella, and the word *Dan* or *dana* or *dani*, in the plural Yesdanis. In Book IX. Chap. VIII. I have shewn that all the sacred rivers had the name of *Don* or *Adonis*. This *Adonis* is the Hebrew *Adonai*. But how came Adonis to be called *Don* ? The Don is the Persian Dan of the word Yesdan, and means *Wisdom* or *Wise*. Thus Adonai is used for the Logos, by the Jews, instead of יהוה *ieue*. It is curious to observe that, generally, when the names of God in the different languages are sifted to the bottom, the Sun or the idea for *Wise-dom* is found. In Yesdan we have *Dan* the Sun *Wisdom*, and the solar Cycle Yĕs, 608.

From the meaning of the word Jnana, which is evidently the same as John, we see why the chief of Abyssinia was called by the words Johannes, Butta, Deus, and Ras. They serve admirably to explain one another. In Persia, as it has been observed, the chief of the state is called Sophi. This is evidently the Greek Σοφια, and is the same word as the name given by the Simonians to their object of worship, which they called by the two words Sophia and Achamoth. These are nothing but the same word for *wisdom* in Greek and Hebrew, and the Samaritan בקמאותה *bqmaute*, the first word of Genesis.[1]

Stanley[2] says, the Chaldæans were called *Ashaphim*. I can see in this nothing but the plural of the Sophi of Persia preceded by the emphatic article. It is the Arabic *Shaphoun*. It is an example of a Hebrew or Chaldee word to us lost. It is the plural, perhaps of the word סוף *sup*, (the name of the Red Sea, which is called sup or *weedy*, because, as I have said before, it *grows no weeds*,[3] and red or *Erythræan* because it is *green !)* Then Ashaphim will mean *the* wise men.

10. If my reader look back to Book IX. Chap. X., he will find a prophecy by Apollo, of Miletus, of a divine incarnation crucified by Chaldæan judges. They were the Chaldæans of Colida. The mythos is that described in this country by the Jesuits. It was the crucifixion of Crisen and Salivahana and St. Thomas, of the Christians of Crisen. There is opposite to Rhodes, near to Miletus, a Λιμην Χρησα, Portus Cresso : this shews the Christian mythos. After this we can scarcely doubt the meaning of the name of the town of Jasus, which is not far from Miletus. There is also a place called Calinda, which I suppose is a Colida. Not far from one of the places called Ephesus, in Asia Minor, there is a river called *Indus*, near a port called *Cressa*. Here there were a Telmessus, and a Termissus, at the foot of which was a *Solyma*, in a district called CABALLA,[4] and a Carmylessus, also a place called Callidua.[5] This is Callida. Not far distant is a Calymna or Calmina. This is clearly Calamina, the name of the Indian St. Thomé. On the same coast there are Panionium, and a mount Chalcis, and the island Chalcia ; also, a little inland, a Tripolis, and Thyatira, called Ak-Hisar—that may be, Akm-Æsar, *wisdom of Cæsar*. There are also the island of Argiæ, and Erythræa, Nyssa, Phœnix, Larissa, Malea, and, in the island of Chios, a Delphin. In short, here is all the mythos both of Thrace and Cape Comorin. And the whole of it is in the country known to the Indians by the name Roum—the country where Troy stood, and from which the Romans obtained their Pessinuncian stone. The Erythræa, the Solyma under Termissus, in PAN-IONIA of Asia Minor, its Ararat in Phrygia, the source of its river, with its twelve provinces, whose inhabitants all came to worship at one temple—(probably Di-jana, Di-iana at Ephesus—Qu. Div-Ioni, Div of Ionia?) the Pandæa of Athens, with its twelve kings, &c., which I consider as a part of Thrace, where we found the widows sacrificed, &c., and the Pandæa of North India, with its Solyma in Cashmere, &c., and

---

[1] Matter, Vol. II. p. 407.          [2] Chal. Phil. Ch. iv.                    [3] Vide Shaw's Travels.

[4] D'Anville.                [5] Plin. Nat. Hist. Lib. v. Cap. xxvii. xxviii.

the Pandæa, and Salem, and Tripoly, &c., of Cape Comorin, I consider of nearly the same date. There are also a lake of Sinda and river Indus, and a Myndus and a Palæmyndus. I can make of these nothing but the Mundus and the Palœ-si-mundus of South India. Also, a town and district called *Alabanda*, (like the Nau-banda of India,) and a river Chrysorrhoa.[1] In Asia Minor, not far from Soluma and Cabala, there are a promontory of Cholidonia and Insulæ Chalidoniæ, and, at some distance, on the same coast a Chalcis ; when I reflect upon the Cullidei or Chaldei, and the island of Columbo or Iona, &c., in Scotland, I cannot doubt whence its name of Caledonia was derived. Caledonia was the sacred name of the country of the Callidei, their common names Scots and Picts.[2] This was the country of Miletus, whence General Vallancey found from the Irish records that they and the Scots came, for stating which he only got laughed at. How can any thing be more striking than the two Caledonias ? I am surprised the General overlooked this.

11. The first word in Genesis of the Samaritans is ℈⅄⅄⅄⅄Ⴒ⅊

ב ק מ א ו ת ה

ETUAMQB

as given in Drummond and Walton. In the בקמאותה *b-qmaut-e* of the Samaritans we have most clearly the ב-חכמות *b-hkmut* or *by wisdoms* of the Jews, or the חכמה *hkme*, wisdom, in the plural number, only a little corrupted, and with the definite or emphatic article placed, as is very common in the oriental languages, at the *end* instead of the *beginning* of the word ; and herein is an additional proof, if it were wanting, of the truth of my theory of the first word of Genesis. In defiance of any quibbling about the Koph in the Samaritan instead of the Heth and Caph, I must say I cannot conceive how any candid Hebrew scholar can deny this. But this most ancient of the Versions removes all doubt, as to which of the meanings *Wisdom* or *Beginning* ought to be adopted. Simon Magus was a Samaritan, and it cannot be denied that the Gnostic doctrines are more apparent among the Samaritan heretics than among those of the Jews, which is what we might well expect, from the first word of their Genesis.

The rendering of this word by the Chaldee Targum of Onkelos is very peculiar, and deserving of a little more consideration. The word is בקרמין *b-qdmin ;* the root is קרם *qdm ;* and it is a noun in the plural number. I believe it may mean *by the solar powers,* as we should scarcely like to say *by the suns,* קרם *qdm,* meaning *East* or *Sun.* And we cannot render the term *by firsts,* if we would wish to go to the sense of *first.* Besides, if it had meant the adverb FORMERLY, it would have been קרם *qdm,* not the noun plural, קרמין *qdmin.* But why has not Parkhurst noticed this rendering of the Targum ? I answer, for the same reason that he has not noticed the meaning given to the word *Ras,* of the Jewish Genesis, by the authorities I have quoted for the consideration of the reader. Though קרם *qdm* has not the meaning of Sun given to it by Parkhurst, yet I think several examples might be shewn where it must mean *sun* and not *eastern.* At all events, we may be very certain that, if the rendering of Beginning could have been supported, Parkhurst would have given it.

12. The Jews have in their Cabala a being called Adam Cadmon. The word Cadmon they do not understand, but they make him a secondary being, formed by the Supreme Being to make the world. It is evidently the קרמין *qdmin* of the Targums just treated of, which, in the singular number, is קרם *qdm.* The Jews know as little of the meaning of the word Adam—making it to mean *red ;* but in the Sanscrit I am told that its meaning is *first ;* Adam Cadmon, then, will be

---

[1] Plin. Nat. Hist. Lib. v. Cap. xxix.        [2] Consult Lingard's History of England, Vol. I. p. 54.

the *first* FIRST, which is nonsense ; therefore we must go, I think, to my explanation for the Cadmon just now given. As the words *rasit* and *arche* had several meanings, so had the word Adam : it meant *man* and in the Sanscrit it meant *first*, and in the Ethiopic it meant *beautiful*—all applied to the Adam of Genesis—differences naturally arising from distance of place and lapse of time.

We constantly read in the Gospel histories of denunciations by Jesus Christ against the traditions of the Pharisees, by which they made the word of God of no avail. The real traditions to which he is meant by the text to have alluded, were those which were afterwards collected and made into what was called the Mishna and Gemara, and collectively the Talmud—chiefly a collection like our Term reports of adjudged cases—by which decisions and forced explanations of almost every point of their law were made, I doubt not, as Jesus Christ said, to its utter subversion. But this our *learned* divines know very well was not what was meant by the Jewish Cabala, or at least (I care not about the term) by the esoteric religion, which was, in its first principles, common both to Jews and Samaritans. The latter, however, had, of course, nothing to do with the Mishna or Gemara. But the word חכמה *hkme* of the Jerusalem Targum, and the *qmut* used in the Samaritan first verse of Genesis, serve as a key to all the esoteric religions of the world. The Samaritans, as we have seen, and as might be expected, utterly rejected what were commonly called the Traditions ; that is, the judgménts in Jewish law-suits : but they did not reject the secret meaning of the first verse of Genesis, which carries with it the Hindoo, Gnostic, and Manichæan doctrines of emanations. It was to conceal this fact, that the Lexicographers have concealed the most important of the meanings of the word Ras. This is not of little importance, because it completes the proof of the ancient nature of the Triune God, which was in reality the foundation on which all the mythoses of the world were built.

13. Perhaps my reader may think that I have introduced him to a science sufficiently recondite; but, nevertheless, I must carry him a little higher—to a mystery still more profound. When we reflect upon the identity of the Trinitarian doctrines of Plato, of Orpheus, or the Indian or Sindi Orpheans of Thrace, and on the Trimurti of the Indians, and on the Trinitarian explanation which I have given of the word Aleim, of the first verse of Genesis, we cannot deny the justness of the observation of Numenius, the Platonician, that *Plato was but Moses speaking Greek,* which will be greatly strengthened by what I shall now develop.

Although we have found in Egypt the Goddess *Neith,* or their Minerva, the *Nat* of North India ; yet we have not found the Ras or Wisdom so marked as in most other countries : but, nevertheless, it was really there, as we might expect. Plutarch says, that Isis means Wisdom ;[1] that her temple is called *Iseion* : alluding to that knowledge of the Eternal and Self-existent Being which may be there obtained. Again, in Section 3, she is said to be no other than *Wisdom,* the Σοφια and the Μητις of Greece, which is repeated in Section 60. · She is also called Athena,[2] which we have formerly seen was the same as Helena, and meant Wisdom ;—in fact, Athena is only the reverse way of reading the word Neithe a little transposed. Plutarch adds that Plato asserts, that *knowledge, wisdom, understanding,* had their names in the Greek language originally from a word having the same signification as Isis. But if Isis were Wisdom, Wisdom was the Logos or Saviour, and then my derivation of Isis from יש *iso,* to save, is very appropriate. Again[3] he observes, that *Isis* is frequently called by the Egyptians *Athena,* signifying, in their language, *I proceeded from myself.* In the same section he says, that Typho is called Seth. In

---

[1] Squire's Trans. de Is. et Osir., Sect. 2.          [2] Sect. 62.          [3] Ib.

section 9 he says, that Isis is called Minerva.[1]   We must also observe that, if Plutarch be right, the word Σοφια was not Greek.   As we have found this word in use among the Chaldeans, the Persians, and the Arabians, we need not be surprised at this remark of Plutarch's.   There can be no doubt that the names Isis of Egypt and Isi of India, were derived from the word of the ancient language יש iso, *to save,* and meant Saviour, and consequently Logos as the Saviour : yet, as the Logos, according to my system, it ought to mean Wisdom, as we have every where seen the Logos to mean Wisdom, and this it did, as I have just shewn.

14. The Brahmins maintain that time does not exist with God.[2]   Then what we call *time* must be created, or called, or produced into a new existence.   And as it is certainly a thing, an existence, or ens, of the very first importance, why have we not heard of it before ?   The ancients cannot have overlooked it.   This will never be believed : then where is it in their histories ?   I ask, is it not hidden under the רוח *ruh,* the third person of the Trinity,—the destroyer,—with its emblem, the Cobra, having its tail in its mouth ?·   Every thing which can be predicated of the destroyer, both as destroyer and regenerator, can be predicated of time, past and future.   Of this, deep reflection will satisfy any one who will use it.   Then I see no other way of accounting for the absence of all notice of Time, than by supposing it a part of the secret doctrine.   Euripides says,

Πολλα γαρ τικτει
Μοιρα τελεσσιδωτειρ'
Αιων τε Κρονυ παις.[3]

" Fate that bringeth the end of things, and Æon (or an age) the son of Saturn produce many " strange events."   Saturn was the father of Jupiter as Time.[4]   Seva, of India, the destroyer, was clearly Saturn or Time.   In the early periods of the world, man was believed to have been in a state of innocence and simplicity, and consequently of happiness.   This was the reason why those times were called Saturnian, as Saturn meant *time past* as well as *time future :* and as we have found the same mythos in Guzerat, Syrastrene, and Pallitani, as we have found in Italy, we find in each the same Satrun-ja or Saturn-ia.

From the intimate union, perhaps I might say identification, of cycles with the first igneous hydrogenous emanation, visible to us in the Sun, I think Time was not supposed to exist previous to the Sun's existence—they were supposed to be contemporaneous—and it was thought that the *past,* the *present,* and the *future,* had no existence with reference to the To Ον.   I believe that Time and Space were considered but as properties or qualities of the first emanation,—that with it they existed, and, with their absorption into the To Ον, they would cease to exist.   This doctrine is of all others the most refined.   From the narrow limits of our faculties we can form no idea of the non-existence of time or space.   I believe we can form no idea of the state of the Supreme Being except it be in a state of actual rest, or of moving to form or reform.   In like manner, in our present weakness of understanding, we can have no idea of happiness, except as compared with its correlative, misery.   God may, in some other world, cause beings to exist in some other way ; but if he cause man, he must cause him as he is, or he will not be man, and happiness and unhappiness, like substance and shadow, must go together, and go along with him.   When Mr. Schegel says that nothing can be more opposed to each other than Pantheism and Emanation, I

---

[1] For Isis, see Drummond on Punic Inscription.

[2] Asiat. Res. Vol. II. p. 115.          [3] Heraclid. 900.          [4] Cudworth, Book i. Ch. iv. p. 485.

quite disagree with him.[1] When we get to the foundation of the two, nothing can be more easy than to reconcile them. No doubt, among the theorising philosophers of 'India, doctrines of Pantheism and Emanations, like those described by Mr. Schegel, will be found; for what is there that is *absurd* or *wise* in nature, which is not to be found among them? But if the fundamental and refined principle have been lost or corrupted in the debasement which took place in later times in the human intellect in India,—if the real, secret, refined doctrine along with all the sciences, have been lost; this does not change its nature or prove that it did not exist.

15. We will now try to penetrate into the Sanctum Sanctorum of the ancient philosophers of India, Egypt, Syria, and Greece; the highest and the most important part of whose philosophy was a knowledge of the Πατηρ αγνωστος, called by Plato Το Ον, WHOM NO PERSON HAS SEEN EXCEPT THE SON[2] —the ϖαν into which at last all nature was to be resolved. The knowledge of this Being, (so clearly marked in the words of Jesus,) which I now proceed to exhibit to my reader, is named or mystically alluded to in almost every page of the Gospel histories; which might, not improperly, be called histories of the parables of Jesus Christ.

In all the histories of the early Christians, called by the Paulites of Rome or Papists heretics, we read that they held the doctrine, that the God of the Jews was not the Great God, but only a Dæmon or Angel. We shall now see the origin of this doctrine, which has always been mentioned by Lardner and others in such a manner as completely to deceive their readers—themselves, probably, not seeing the nature of it: and in the explanation will be evident the secret doctrine of the Aleim and Rasit, as I have expounded them in Book II. Chap. III. And the injustice will be apparent which has been done to the sages of antiquity, in supposing that they could entertain a belief only fit for minds enfeebled by a modern education, that the book of Genesis was to be understood literally.

The first and most profound secret of the Cabala or Gnosis was the knowledge of the real Cosmogomy of the universe, as held by these philosophers. At the head of all beings and their works, the ancient Gnostics or Sophees placed a certain person called Μια Αρχη; also called Πατηρ όλων, Πατηρ αγνωςος, Ακατονομαςος. This name, *mia arche*, Mons. Matter[3] justly says, " Nous rencontrons dans tous les systèmes Gnostiques, et en général dans *toutes les doctrines* " *de l'ancien monde, dans l'Inde comme en Perse.* Tout est émané de cet être, tout doit rentrer " un jour dans son sein."

This ϖατηρ αγνωστος has been said to dwell *en profunditate*, in the *Bythos*, or Βυθος, or Βαθος, in profound *darkness.* This was because the sun and light itself, as well as all other matter, was supposed to emanate from him. Supposing that he was thought to be light itself, yet still the light was thought to dwell in darkness. If I be asked to explain how this could be, I answer, It is *illusion*, or, in other words, it is above the human understanding—it is the Illusion of India.

But before I proceed, I must make an observation upon the ancient Pantheism. Every person, who has reflected upon this subject, knows very well the impossibility of forming an idea of the mode in which mind or spirit brings matter into existence, if ever it bring it into existence at all. The term generation is but a figurative expression, used to describe an idea which a person does not really possess, whatever he may fancy—of the destruction of matter man is equally ignorant. The result of deep and profound reflection upon these points produced the doctrine of Pantheistic emanation. Men supposed that matter emanated or flowed from the Deity, like rays from the

[1] Pritchard.  [2] Gospel History.  [3] Hist. Gnost. Vol. II. p. 266.

sun, eternally flowing from a never-failing spring, and perhaps that all matter consisted of rays of light or fire in different combinations, or under different circumstances.

When the ancient philosopher reflected deeply upon what he saw constantly going on around him in the great laboratory of nature, he could not help perceiving, that by one process or other every substance was capable of being resolved, and was in fact constantly resolving, into an invisible, impalpable fluid. As this fluid was too refined to be subject to any of his senses, of course he could form no idea of it; but yet, reasoning from analogy, he was induced to believe in its existence. The fluid here spoken of was called an ethereal or a spiritual fire, [1] and I suppose more nearly answers to the Galvanic, or Electric, or Magnetic fluid than to any thing with which I am acquainted. When matter was reduced back again by igneous purification, or, in other words, when matter was resolved into this invisible fire as it had originally flowed or emanated from the first To Ον it approximated to, perhaps arrived at, a state to be ready for re-absorption into the first To Ον again. Thus when re-absorbed, all nature was God, as God had been all nature previous to the emanation. And what was the To Ον? *A Point*, the centre of a circle whose circumference is no where, and its centre every where; Illusion of which our senses cannot lay hold.

We have here the Pantheism, *the grossness* of which, more or less misrepresented, serves to horrify those priests who teach literally what the words *literally* express, that the To Ον walked in the garden, or strove to kill Moses at an inn, but failed. This is the Indian doctrine, which its professors call *illusion*—an expression which appears to me to be beautifully characteristic: for when, step by step, we arrive at last at this point, every thing appears to slip from under us, or to pass away into nothing—because the subject is beyond the reach of our senses. And now we may see what these ancient philosophers meant by their doctrine of the eternity of matter; for when it was absorbed into the To Ον, how could it be any thing but eternal? By being absorbed, it was not supposed to be destroyed. I need not point out how admirably this elucidates the doctrines of Ammonius, that *all the sects of philosophy, including the Christian,* were at the bottom the same, and originated from one and the same source.

I think much of the objection to the doctrine that *ex nihilo nihil fit* has arisen from the meaning of the word *nihil* or *nothing* being misunderstood. According to the doctrine of emanation, I think it is not absurd. If I possess an idea of emanation, and do not deceive myself, it *follows* from that doctrine, because all existences emanate from the To Ον and re-immerge into it, and it always exists; therefore, matter or existences will always exist, and without the To Ον cannot exist. [2] As the To Ον cannot *but exist*, matter cannot *but exist;* for it will always exist, either as an emanation, or in the To Ον.

As every being was an emanation, and would ultimately be re-absorbed into the To Ον, so every being was a part of the To Ον; and on this principle the adoration of animals was attempted to be excused. On this principle, also, we find the inferior emanations, the Trinity, or its Persons, receiving epithets, in strictness applicable only to the To Ον. For instance, I am Alpha and Omega. And under the belief in the existence of the Πατηρ αγνωστος, concealed

---

[1] Unmeaning words as here applied, because applied to no idea, man having, in fact, no idea of this fire—too refined to be cognizable by his senses.

[2] This has been well explained by Thomas Burnet, in his Arch. Phil. Ch. vii., and shewn to be the doctrine of the Orientals, and of the Cabala or tradition of the Jews, and of the Essenes, who, he observes, according to Philo, had their knowledge from the Brahmins.

every where, a studied mysticism is observable, which can in no other way be accounted for. This was an effect which must necessarily have followed the concealment of the First Cause from inquiring but uninitiated philosophers, if the secret of initiation were to be preserved.

Mr. Mosheim has judiciously observed, that in Philo passages in direct contradiction to each other may be found, for the evident purpose of concealment.[1] As he was confessedly of the school of Plato, which used this practice, as I have shewn in my first Book, it is what might be expected, and serves to account for various difficulties, otherwise unintelligible. It was for the purpose of concealing his system that Plato adopted the practice of maintaining doctrines in direct contradiction to each other; and thus he furnished plausible grounds for misrepresentations by his enemies, as the initiated only could understand him. It is to a want of knowledge of this principle or practice of Plato's that many of the difficulties in his works are to be attributed. Let this be kept in remembrance by his reader, and they will instantly disappear. But the practice is admitted by his commentators. So completely confused is his Timæus, that the learned translator, Mr. Taylor, of the work upon it by Proclus, in order to make sense of it, is obliged to propose 1200 emendations of the text. Without meaning any reflection on my learned and excellent friend Mr. Taylor, I must observe, that, as we know he had a system to support, and that he is not exempt from human frailty, we cannot safely admit, as a matter of course, that his translation and amended version is not in some degree coloured by his system and his 1200 emendations. And I must further observe, that if Plato intended to write enigmatically or in parables, if the 1200 emendations have for their object the rendering of the text *clear*, I much fear that, instead of *emendations*, many of them must be classed as *corruptions*.

Plato does not profess to have been the inventor of his own doctrines, but in his epistles he says that he has taken them from ancient and sacred discourses—παλαιοι και ιεροι λογοι. Mr. Colebrooke says, that many of the tenets of the Hindoos are the same as those of the Platonists and Pythagoreans, and admits that the latter appear to be the learners, rather than the teachers of them.[2] It is, indeed, very notorious that those two men went to the East to learn, not to teach.

To return to my subject. It must not be expected that the grand secret, the knowledge of the highest and last secret of the initiated, of the illuminati, will be found clearly described in any work written by one of the initiated.

I have no doubt that the Cabalistic œconomy was similar to that of a lodge of Freemasons, and proceeded to the top by gradation,[3] and that masonry, which was a part of it, existed long

---

[1] Comm. Cent. ii. note Vidal, p. 170.      [2] Asiat. Trans. Vol. I. p. 579.

[3] No Royal-Arch Mason will find a difficulty in seeing that part of his refined secret mysteries have been in ancient times closely connected with the profound doctrines exposed to public view in this book. Whether at this time they be the same as those described in this book, whether they be changed, and if changed, how much changed, and when changed, are points of which, for very obvious reasons, I do not inform my reader; and I now warn him, that from any thing here said he will not be justified in drawing a conclusion. But he must recollect that nothing but a miracle could preserve Masonry from change in so great a number of years. If he be, however, as I hope he is, an honourable, upright, and benevolent man, and wish to know the truth by working himself up to the Royal Arch, he then will know it. More I add not here: the *uninitiated* have no business to know. To the initiated I need not tell it. But every one may rest assured, from the great number of beneficed and respectable priests, both of the Roman and Protestant Church, who are admitted to the highest degrees of Masonry, that there is nothing in it at this day which can militate in the slightest degree against the Christian religion as held either at Rome or at Lambeth.

About the middle of the last century, the Masonic societies shewed themselves in Germany in a more prominent way than they had done for many generations, and, under the guidance of several able and philanthropic men, both Catholic and Protestant priests and laymen, it is probable gave encouragement to resistance to the united despotism of

before the time of the Exod from Egypt. In the time of Moses, the three elders of what might be called the chapter, were Moses, Aholiab, and Bezaleel, the son of Uri, the son of Hur,[1] and to them only was the highest secret confided. When Jesus Christ was (what is called) transfigured or metamorphosed, (is not this mysterious and esoteric enough ?) there were present *Jesus, Moses,* and *Elias,* the three *teachers,* and the three apostles, *Peter, James,* and *John,* the three *learners,* of the Gnosis or secret knowledge, which was transmitted by them to posterity with the greatest care.

The knowledge of the High Secret could only be obtained by the uninitiated by implication ; but still from unprincipled high-priests, or high-priests afflicted with insanity, against which accident nothing can for an absolute certainty guard a secret society, it may have transpired in the course of thousands of years. The close similarity of the Jewish and Indian systems, and a comparison of them with the mysterious expressions of Philo and Plato justifies what I state to be the high mystery, and of which I shall presently finish the explanation. This ignorance of the grand secret accounts very well for the attributes of the $\pi\alpha\tau\eta\rho \ \alpha\gamma\nu\omega\varsigma\circ\varsigma$ being often given by writers to the second and third emanations—accounts for the lines of distinction not being well drawn, between the different orders. A confusion of terms is clearly perceptible, though the principle is equally clear to a person understanding the secret doctrine. This confusion arose, I do not doubt, partly from ignorance, partly from design.

The ancient Jews maintained, that their Cabala was revealed by God to Moses, and was transmitted verbally ; it being too sacred to be written. (This is very like Freemasonry.) This has been unmercifully ridiculed by Christians, but though often discussed, no *cool, philosophical, and unprejudiced* inquiry into the meaning of the tradition, has, to my knowledge, been attempted. This has arisen, in a great measure, from the mistake in the meaning of the words respecting traditions attributed to Jesus Christ in the Gospel histories : his justly-merited anathemas against the traditions of the elders, as just now described, being confounded with the traditionary Cabala. It is evident that the Cabala had not any tendency, in any way whatever, either to make the law

---

the Roman Pontiffs and the Royal tyrants of Europe, which, in France and Germany, had risen to such a pitch as to be no longer tolerable. The activity of the Masons being discovered, it produced the persecution of their order all over the continent ; and it was much increased in consequence of several publications of three persons called Zimmerman, Baruel, and Robison. The first was decidedly insane, and the other two were operated on by groundless fears, in such a manner as to be in a state very little better, and which rendered them totally incapable of distinguishing between the destruction of religion, and the destruction of the base system to which the professors of religion had made it subservient. They all admit that the British Masons had nothing to do with these hydra-headed conspiracies, and endeavour to draw a line between them and their Continental Brethren, being unable to see that the difference was not in the societies, which were the same, but in the countries—Britain being comparatively free and happy, the other countries enslaved and miserable. Although the object of Masons is not politics, I flatter myself that if our King were to disperse the Parliament by means of a body of Swiss soldiers, the Freemasons would not be the only people in England who would not lend ALL the assistance in their power to effect his overthrow.

Some years ago a treatise was written on Masonry by a gentleman of the name of Preston. It contains much useful information ; but as he had not the least suspicion of the real origin of Masonry, and as his book is merely a party performance to claim for the London Grand Lodge a priority over the Lodges of Scotland and York, to which it had originally no pretension whatever, except the possession of power, I need take no more notice of it than to observe, that it is very well done, and is very creditable to its author, who, probably, was sincere in what he wrote. The Masons of Southern England, *until amalgamated with those of York,* were, in fact, only a modern offset of some other Lodge. A few Masons of other lodges associating formed a lodge. The reason was this—the Druids of Stonehenge, Abury, &c., &c., were all killed or banished to the Northern countries or Wales by the Romans. Thus we have no Culdees in the South. For though companies of masons came to build the cathedrals, they had no hereditary settlements after the time of the Romans, like the others. The Masons or Culdees of York might have returned from Scotland after their persecution was over, probably in the time of Constantine the Pagan Christian.

[1] Exod. xxxi. 2—6, xxxv. 30—34. The Jewish Sanhedrim had three presidents.

of no avail or not, and therefore could not have been what was meant by him. Indeed, I maintain that there is not in the Gospel histories a single expression of Jesus Christ's recorded against the Cabala. But there are many which pretend to shew that he was perfectly acquainted with the existence of the Father, who dwelt in the darkness, whom NO PERSON HAS SEEN EXCEPT THE SON, and that he considered himself as an incarnation of one of the persons of the Trinity.

The Jewish Cabala, that is, the Cabala of the tribe of Ioudi—the Cabala of the numerous temples of Solomon which have been mentioned, was divided into two parts—the one consisting of the natural philosophy, called Mercavah; the other of the moral, called Barasith. We will first explain the natural philosophy of the system; and first, the *creation*. There were various creations. The first creation was effected by way of emanation; and this was the idea or plan of the *universe*, not the little globe only which we inhabit. From this proceeded the second, which was the Trimurti or Trinity which formed the שמים *smim*, our world and system, (but not herein including the *stars*)[1] by the agency of one of its own persons, who was the Λογος, or Sophia, or Metis, or Buddha. The doctrine of the divine idea is distinctly expressed in the laws of Menu.[2] It was also clearly the doctrine of Plato and Philo, i. e. of the Cabala. But of course it was not expressed in the book of Genesis, which professed to be only a book or description of the generations or cosmogony of our globe and of the planetary system with which it is connected—viz. the regeneration of the planetary system and the earth. It would clearly have been inconsistent with the object of Moses to have revealed to the vulgar Jews the sublime knowledge of the Μια Αρχη or the cosmogony of the universe,[3] the knowledge of the Πατηρ Αγνωςος, the Brahme-Maia, or, as the Hindoo philosopher called it, Illusion.

The Cabalistic secret of the πατηρ αγνωςος of the Jews and the Samaritans was identical with the first principle of Buddhism. The institutes of Menu[4] say, " This universe existed " only *in the first divine idea, yet unexpanded, as if involved* in darkness, imperceptible, unde- " finable, undiscoverable by reason, *and* undiscovered *by revelation*, as if it were wholly immersed " in sleep : then the sole self-existing power, himself undiscerned, appeared with undiminished " glory, *expanding his idea*, or dispelling the gloom." From these two beings jointly emanated the Trimurti, one of whose persons was the Sanscrit Jnana or Dschnana, which is Wisdom or the Buddha, and answers to the Γνωσις or Λογος of the Greeks. Thus the Trimurti was not the Supreme Being, but an emanation.

At the top of all existences we find the Brahme-Maya. Here I think, generally speaking, is a mistake. Maya is likened to the wife of Brahme, but still she is admitted to be what is called *illusion*. Now, I apprehend Brahme (not Brahm) is the Το Ον, the Monad, and Maya is the idea or plan of the universe, which was the first emanation from the πατηρ αγνωστος or το ον, and which answers very well to the idea of *illusion*, into which all inferior existences are supposed to resolve, and which at last resolves itself into the το ον.[5]

---

[1] I beg my reader to recollect what I have said of the interpolation of the words *the stars also* in the 16th verse of the first chapter of Genesis.

[2] Asiat. Res. Advertisement to Vol. V. p. v.; Inst. of Menu, by G. C. Haughton.

[3] And it was on this account that the stars are not named, but were, in consequence, interpolated by persons who did not understand the system.

[4] By the learned Professor Haughton.

[5] This is no doubt very abstruse, and will appear very ridiculous to such wise people as believe that the Το Ον " walked in a garden in the cool of the evening." I shall be sorry if they take the trouble to read it, for it is very unfit for them. It is food which is certain to disagree with their stomachs.

But it will be said, that the first emanation from the Trimurti was Buddha, or Rasit, or Logos. True. But Buddha or Logos was Tri-Vicramaditya or the triple energy, was the Trimurti itself, which Mr. Colebrooke, and all other oriental writers, tell us the Indians held to be three persons and one God, *three* in *one* and *one* in *three*—though *three*, yet *one*; though *one*, yet *three* : Buddha in India, Logos in Greece, Ras in Syria, each being the name in the respective countries, of the Creator or person of the three employed by the three or Aleim itself to form anew or reform the world. Thus Genesis says, by Ras, or Wisdom, or the Logos, the Aleim or Trinity regenerated[1] the world; but it does not name the Supreme Being by the word Aleim. The doctrine of the πατηρ αγνωστος, the μια αρχη, the πατηρ ολων, the ακατονομαςος,[2] the Brahme-Maia of India was never written; it was only entrusted to the Cabala—to tradition—to the גבל *gbl*, in the plural גיבלים *giblim*. It was not necessary in order to explain so much as was intended to be described to the readers of Genesis, (secret as, I am certain, Genesis was kept,) or the Persian book of Ibrahim or Sophia, to name it. This was divulged only in the highest and most secret chapter of the high or chief priests, the three past principals of the cabinet of twelve, formed from the Seventy-two, the Sanhedrim, seventy-two in number, the predecessors of the *seventy-two* (when complete) in the Romish College of Cardinals. The name of this God was like the sacred M or OM of India,—the sacred Om to be meditated on, but not to be named— M=600.

These doctrines constituted the grand article of the Cabala, and are strictly in accordance with the dark allusions or mystic expressions which we find in Philo, Plato,[3] and the Gospel histories. As no religion remains unchanged, the complication, which is found in the present Cabala, was most of it probably added afterward.

All, as far as stated above, we may, I think, safely take as the Γνωσις : whether we can take any part of what is further stated as the doctrines of the different sects of Gnostics,[4] by their enemies, at once ignorant, prejudiced, and malicious, may be greatly doubted. It is certain that numbers of subordinate sects among the Gnostics had arisen in the first centuries of the Christian æra, and, in fact, the pure oriental Γνωσις had then become complicated, corrupted, and degraded. This was a natural effect. All religions as they advance in time have this tendency. What were the opinions of the different subordinate sects is scarcely worth an inquiry, except it could be made conducive to a more perfect discovery of the ancient foundation on which the whole was built. The same corruption had crept into the Jewish Cabala. They were, indeed, the same.

Philo, in his book *de Sacrificiis Abelis et Caini*, lays down the doctrine of the Triune nature of the Deity ; at the same time he states it to be a secret or mystery not, in ALL its parts, to be revealed to the vulgar. The passage is discussed at length in Mosheim's Commentaries, Cent. ii. Sect. xxxv., and it is there shewn, that the same is taught as part of the esoteric doctrine by Philo, in many other parts of his works. How strongly, and, indeed, I may say, decisively, this supports my explanation of the Aleim and the whole of the first verse of Genesis, I need not point out.

In his book upon the creation, Philo every where supposes the prior existence of Plato's *ideal* world, and represents the Deity as constructing visible nature *after a model* which he had first

---

[1] This is what we call begotten in our creeds. This degrading word is used to conceal the secret meaning of regenerated, which, if used, would have endangered the discovery of the secret doctrine of emanations.

[2] Qui nominari non potest.                    [3] Matter, Vol. II. p. 267.

[4] The Jews named their books after the first word : thus Genesis was called Barasit. The Persians at their Tuct Soleiman, I have no doubt, called the same book *Sophia* or Ελ Σοφ, perhaps meaning BY *Wisdom*.

formed. He attributes to Moses all the metaphysical subtleties of Plato upon this subject, and maintains that the philosopher received them from the followers of the holy prophet,[1] and when we recollect that Plato studied on Mount Carmel this seems probable enough : but he might also get his doctrine from the Ægyptians. Philo maintains, that God first formed an intelligible and incorporeal model, after which he framed, *by his Logos*, the corporeal world. He supposes the order of the visible world to have been adapted to the Pythagorean system of numbers ; but how this was done is not explained, being probably considered sacred and secret; but will be explained by me in a future book. But I think my reader will have no difficulty in believing it to be connected with the system of cycles found in the capitals of the Pillars Jachin and Boaz, the priest's garment of Pomegranates and Bells, $72 \times 5 = 360$, and $72 \times 6 = 432$. The language of Philo is accused of being obscure. This must necessarily be the case, where a person is describing part of a secret system, which he must not betray. This consideration also accounts, as I have formerly said, for the studied obscurity of Plato.

On EVERY account there is no philosopher, of antiquity, who deserves to rank higher than Philo. If any man could be supposed to understand the Cabala or secret doctrine, it was Philo. He was in the first rank of society, and of unimpeachable moral character. How foolish is it to permit the priests to run him down by their ridiculous, idle assertions, that he attempted to Platonise Moses,—that he was tainted with the Platonic philosophy, &c., &c.! No doubt he was tainted with his own philosophy, with that philosophy which he had learnt in the adytum of his temple, and which we have found with the Buddhists, with the Zoroastrians or Orpheans, with the followers of Hermes, Pythagoras, and Plato, and which was the same as the secret doctrine of Moses, a fact which was never doubted, (though not publicly known,) till modern priests, whose minds were of too mean a class to understand so sublime a system, denied it, though at the same time they were obliged to allow that the Jews had really FROM THE MOST REMOTE PERIOD, *secret doctrines*.[2] Their only reason for misrepresenting the doctrines and learning of Philo is this, that his doctrines place their vulgar nonsense, only fit for such minds as their own, in the shade.

But Mr. Basnage[3] has examined this question, and has shewn, that there is very good reason to believe that Philo did not copy from Plato, but that he got his Trinity and Hypostases from Egypt and the East, as might be expected. Philosophers very seldom went from the East to Greece *to learn*, but they sometimes went *to teach*.

If we now look back to Book III. Chap. I., and carefully read what is there said respecting the Trinities of Zoroaster, Orpheus or Plato, and Philo, and what is extracted from Maurice, Michaelis, Marsh, &c., we shall see that it is evident, either that the whole doctrine was not exposed to the public, or was not understood by them. There is apparently some confusion in the accounts of these esoteric doctrines as might be expected : but they all fall short in the Brahme-Maia, the μια αρχη, the πατηϱ αγνωϛος, the ακατονομαϛτος, from which the πϱωτογονος, the λογος, the ψυχη κοσμε or Triune God, proceeded. They do not go so far as this grand secret person, the Father whom no person hath known or shall know except the Son, and those to whom the Son shall reveal him.[4] An attentive reader will not fail to perceive that the whole of this abstruse doctrine is a cosmogony, that is, a formation of the *universe*, a building of it up by the Grand Megalistor, the greatest and first of Masons. *Verbum sapienti.*

I think no person will deny that the system of emanation which I have unfolded is, whether

[1] Enfield, Phil. Ch. i.      [2] Enfield, Hist. Phil. Book iv. Ch. iii.

[3] Book iv. Ch. xxiv.      [4] Matt. xi. 27 ; Luke x. 22.

true or false, very refined and beautiful: it is much to be regretted that the later Cabalists and Gnostics should, by only half understanding it, have drawn it out into a tissue of the greatest and most childish nonsense, a very fair account of which may be seen in Basnage.[1]

The Conclaves, in which the Cabalistic doctrines here treated of were held, were, I do not doubt, of the nature of Masonic societies, and were the origins of, or the same as, the Caldæi, Colidei, Culdees, Architectonici, Mathematici, Dionysionici, Freemasons, Templars, and Rosicrucians. In these societies the most refined doctrines were known only to a few of the select or *perfecti* at the head of the others : to this elevation they rose by regular gradation, and to this small chapter only the ϖατηρ αγνωστος was known. To these Masons it was known that the temple of Solomon with its Pillars and Pomegranates,[2] was only a type of the universe, a microcosm ; and the Masons themselves were only workmen and servants of the great fabricator,—of the Jupiter Megalistor of the Universe. Masons were all servants toiling in their respective vocations, and rising by degrees to the knowledge of the ⟨ᴍᴀ⟩ ⟨ᴏɴ⟩. And, in imitation and as types of the world, all their temples of Solumi were built. These Masons were the Cyclopes, the men who first fabricated temples, and thence became Masons. Look but at their circles of stones in twelves, sevens, nineteens, six hundreds, six hundred and eights, six hundred and fifties, their emblems on the Cyclopean ruins of Mundore, Agra, &c. The inferior Masons were the builders of the stone circles or temples, the superior ones were Megalistors, Cosmogonists—builders of worlds—or planners of temples in imitation of them. Nothing can well be devised more Masonic than the name given to the Trinitarian *Creator* Δημιϵργος, of which Jesus Christ was the second person, and, therefore, the great Megalistor, or fabricator, or Δημιϵργος.

16. If a person reflect deeply upon the circumstances in which the first priests must have been placed when the earliest attempt at building a temple was made, he will perceive that it was quite natural for them to become Masons. In order to place their structures according to the cardinal points, and their large stones according to the exact number of their cycles, they must have been possessed of all the learning of the world. I have a strong suspicion that at the first the Monastic and Masonic orders were identical. Monks were priests[3] REGULARLY initiati or regulars: seculars were priests or officers of religion, *not regularly* initiati, as their name shews.

I cannot conceive how it is possible to read the Gospel histories with attention, and not to see that a secret doctrine is taught. There is scarcely a chapter without a parable. "In parables spake "he unto them, that while seeing they might not perceive, and hearing they might not understand."[4] What can be clearer than the following passages ? "He answered and said unto them, Unto you "it is given to know the *mystery* of the kingdom of God : but unto them that are *without*, all

---

[1] Book iii.

[2] The pillars Jachin and Boaz had around each of their capitals one hundred pomegranates. (1 Kings vii. 20 ; 2 Chron. iii. 16, 17.) This fruit was selected *on account of the star-like flower, with six leaves or rays at the top of the fruit.* Parkhurst, in voce, רמה *rme* VII. Thus 6 × 100 = 600. The same fruits were hung round the priest's garment, 72 in number. Thus, 72 × 6 = 432. Can it be accident that these two numbers are brought out ? They arise from Parkhurst's observations, but that is a consequence of which he had not the most distant suspicion ; for he understood the nature neither of the 600 nor of the 432. The pomegranate was as sacred among the Gentiles as among the Jews. Achilles Tatius says, that at Pelusium Zeus Casius held this MYSTERIOUS fruit in his hand : Προϵϵϐληται δϵ την χϵιρα, και ϵχϵι 'POIAN ϵπ' αυτη. Της δϵ 'Ροιας ὁ λογος μυϛικος. Ach. Tat. Lib. iii. p. 167.

[3] If Eustychius can be credited, the persons who took the lead in the building of Babylon with its tower, &c., were seventy-two in number. Eutych. Annal, p. 51, Oxon. 1658, apud Nimrod, Vol. II. p. 492.

[4] For a complete proof that there was a secret religion, both Mosaic and Christian, concealed under vulgar allegorical histories, the last chapter of Burnet's Archæologia may be consulted.

" these things are done in parables: that seeing they may see, and not perceive; and hearing,
" they may hear, and *not* understand; *lest at any time they should be converted, and their sins*
" *should be forgiven them.*" Mark iv. 11, 12; Matt. xiii. 13—15. I notice this passage, ascribed
to the essence of benevolence and charity, by our books, no further at present than to point out
the doctrine of an esoteric religion or the absolute, direct authority for the opinion, that Jesus
taught the existence of an esoteric religion. On other accounts I shall have much, very much, to
say in my next volume respecting these words ascribed to Jesus. The part which I have
marked by italics is evidently an interpolation, of ignorant, uninitiated persons, Paulites, to account
for or explain what they did not understand. Mosheim [1] being obliged to allow that the Christian
religion had its mysteries like all other religions, disguises it very ingeniously. When, perhaps,
from the miseries of the times they became lost, their previous existence would be denied, and
this was much aided by the degraded state of the human mind, at that time very fit for devil
driving and exorcising, and for such pernicious nonsense as the passage in italics, but very unfit
for such refined theories as those of Plato, Philo, or Porphyry.

Indeed no one can deny, that a certain mysticism reigns in every part of the Gospel histories, as well as through the Pentateuch. Every thing is taught in parables, that the vulgar
seeing, might not perceive; and hearing, might not understand. No one, I think, who can read,
can deny this. [2]

17. The transfiguration or metamorphosis, as the Greek word means, of Jesus Christ has puzzled
all modern divines, as might well be expected. I will now shew what it means. Surely our
divines *will* not see! Do none of them read the early fathers?

The Christian religion was divided by the early fathers, in its secret and mysterious character,
into three degrees, the same as was that of Eleusis, [3] viz. *Purification, Initiation,* and *Perfection.* [4]
This is a dry matter of fact, and this we have on the authority of, and openly declared, among others,
by Clemens Alexandrinus, who it cannot be believed would have stated this if it were false,—it
being a falsity without any object, and the falsity of which must have been known to all the world.

When Jesus was transfigured, an operation sufficiently mystical and esoteric I should think, he had
with him only three of his disciples—James, John, and Peter. At the time of this transfiguration the
secret γνωσις, which was, at least in part, the knowledge of the μια αρχη, and πατηρ αγνωστος,
WAS BELIEVED to have been conferred on the three. And this we have again *on the indisputable*
*authority of Clemens Alexandrinus.* [5]     From these three I have little or no doubt, that the Popes
yet believe that they have the above-described secret doctrine or Gnosis, handed down in the

_____

[1] Com. Sect. xiii. xiv.

[2] The word mystery, Μυϛηριον, Mr. Cleland says, comes from the Celtic word *wist* or *wise* ; which, in the sense of
knowing or knowledge, which it has, he seems to think, is rather opposed to the definition of secrecy. But in this I
cannot agree with him. He says it is the radical of History; but I think of *secret* history; for, originally, there was
no other kind of history. It is istory with the mystic monogram M prefixed, and means the *istory* of Om. He says
it answers to *Gheib*, which means, in Arabic, *Fable*. This is גב *gb*, and is the root of the word Cabala, secret or
sacred tradition or history, and of Giblim. Parable is par-habul. Habul is Cabul, Cabala. This is also the same as
the Faba, a fable; whence the Pythagorean precept, Abtain from Fabæ—idle stories. Clel. et voce, p. 1. Parabl *to*
*talk*, confabulari *to talk together*. Apologue, Habul-laigh *a fable in verse.* Ib.

[3] Fabric. Bibl. Gr. Vol. VII. p. 101. The systems were the same.

[4] The Perfection applies to the expression of Jesus in Matthew : *If thou wilt be perfect*, &c., and alludes to dividing
his substance with the poor, as the perfecti, or monks, always did—that is, to the order, who no doubt did distribute,
after supplying their own necessities, the rents to the poor, keeping the capital or estate. Nimrod, Vol. III. p. 419.

[5] Mosheim, Com. Cent. ii. Sect. xxxv. pp. 165, 167; Matt. xvii. 1, 2; Luke ix. 28, 29.

conclave. Peter was the first Pope or Principal of the sacred chapter of *twelve*, and of the lodge or conclave of seventy-two or Sanhedrim.

The Jews have among them the very interesting ceremony, (of the extreme antiquity of which I have no doubt, as traces of it may be found among the followers of Mithra, and of Pythagoras, at Delphi, and as the Roman Church so far very properly holds, it existed among the Judi in the time of Melchizedek,) of the sacrifice of Bread and Wine. When a master of a Jewish family has finished the Paschal supper, he breaks the bread, and along with the crater or cup, (or perhaps holy Sangreal refused to the laity, but much sought after and desired,) hands it round to the whole of his family, servants and all, in token of brotherly love. This is purely a Masonic institution, and was practised by Jesus Christ, at his last Paschal festival or supper, when he handed it round to the *close chapter* of *twelve*, of which he was Principal. Each chapter ought to consist of *twelve* companions, past masters of Lodges, and each Lodge of *seventy-two* Brethren.[1] Perhaps the piety of some Christians may take alarm at what is here said; but they will not readily persuade me that this is solely a Christian ceremony—as I find it in India, in Persia, at Gerizim, at Delphi, in Italy, and yet existing in its original and native beauty and simplicity among the Jews all over the world.

We will now explain the second part of the Cabala called *Barasit*; but it is very difficult entirely to separate the two parts. The second is what Clemens Alexandrinus,[2] as head of the sacred college or catechetical school of Alexandria, professed to have had delivered to him, by his predecessors; the secret doctrines which he declares were delivered by Jesus Christ himself to James, John, and Peter. Mr. Mosheim says, " What those maxims and principles were which " Clement conceived himself to be precluded from communicating to the world at large, cannot " long remain a secret to any diligent and attentive reader of his works. There cannot be the " smallest question but that they were philosophical explications of the Christian tenets respecting " the Trinity, the soul, the world, the future resurrection, Christ, the life to come, and other " things of a like abstruse nature, which had in them somewhat that admitted of their being " expounded upon philosophical principles. They also, no doubt, consisted of certain mystical " and allegorical interpretations of the divine oracles, calculated to support those philosophical " expositions of the Christian principles and tenets. For since, as we have above seen, he " expressly intimates that he would in his Stromata unfold a part of that secret wisdom which " was designed only for the few, but that in doing this he would not so far throw off all reserve " as to render himself universally intelligible, and since we find him, in the course of the above- " mentioned work, continually giving to the more excellent and important truths contained in the " sacred volume, such an interpretation as tends to open a wide field for conjecture, and also " comparing not openly, but in a concise and half obscure way, the Christian tenets with the " maxims of the philosophers, I am willing to resign every pretension to penetration if it be not " clearly to be perceived of what nature that sublime knowledge respecting divine matters must " have been, of which he makes such a mystery."[3] No doubt Mr. Mosheim is right as far as he

---

[1] On the opening of the Jubilee year, the Pope, who holds many secret things, not suspected, in his *fisherman's poitrine*, acting as Grand Master of the Masons as well as of the Fishermen, striking seven blows, with a silver hammer, knocks down the sacred door. This I saw him do; and this he did as Grand Master-Mason of the world. This he did as the head of the Ras or Mysteries of the world, as Vicar of the Grand Megalistor. If an enemy of Masonry should say that the Masons are only moderns, copying in modern times from the Christian doctrines here developed, I reply, that is impossible; for these doctrines have been unknown for the last thousand years, therefore the imitation must have taken place before that date.

[2] Mosheim, Com. Cent. II. p. 164.　　　　　[3] Ibid. p. 166.

goes; but he has overlooked or concealed the most important point of the γνωσις, and that which serves as a key to all the remainder, the knowledge of the πατηρ αγνωσος,[1] in this respect exhibiting the sagacity of Clemens and his own want of it, or his own disingenuousness.

Eusebius says, that "Our Lord had preferred Peter, James, and John, before the rest." Again, "The Lord, after his resurrection, conferred the gift of knowledge (this should be wisdom) "upon James the Just, John, and Peter, which they delivered to the REST of the Apostles, and "those to the seventy disciples, one of whom was Barnabas."[2]　On this subject Mosheim says, "Why James, and John, and Peter should have been, in particular, fixed upon as the Apostles "whom Christ selected as the most worthy of having this recondite wisdom communicated to "them by word of mouth is very easily perceived.　For these were the three disciples whom "our blessed Saviour took apart with him up into the mountain, when he was about to be "transfigured."[3]　But for what was this parable of the transfiguration adopted ?　Surely if the uncontradicted evidence of Ammonius, Clemens, and Eusebius, on the fact of the meaning of the transfiguration and the nature of the secret doctrine is not to be taken, nothing can be believed. The whole forms a rational explanation of the meaning of the transfiguration which has never even been attempted before.

The doctrine that the Christian religion contained a secret or allegorical meaning is so clearly acknowledged, laid down, and treated on as an admitted fact, by Justin, Clemens Alexandrinus, Origen, and indeed by all the very early fathers, that to attempt to give quotations from their works would be wilfully to weaken the evidence of the fact, unless I were to fill fifty pages with them : indeed, I must copy their works. I shall, therefore, say no more on the subject, for it is a point which cannot be disputed ; and so the Christian religion continued till the time of Origen, when the doctrines of Paul prevailed, and Origen was declared by the Paulites a heretic for professing it.

The following passage shews the character of Mosheim. It is given in reprobation of Ammonius, while, in the mind of every philanthropic person, it carries a panygeric on him. But the doctrine of Ammonius would bring peace, not a sword. This would, indeed, be unpriestly.　"But "Ammonius, conceiving that not only the philosophers of Greece, but also all those of the "different barbarous nations, were perfectly in unison with each other with regard to every "essential point, made it his business so to temper and expound the tenets of all these various "sects, as to make it appear that they had all of them originated from one and the same source, "and all tended to one and the same end."[4]　The fact is, Christianity was no other than the eclectic philosophy which professed to contain that portion of truth possessed by every sect of religion or system of philosophy. How is it possible, in a few words, to make of it a finer panegyric ?—a panegyric which, alas ! it did not long deserve, at least in its practical operation. In another place Mosheim says, "The favourite object with Ammonius, as appears from the "disputations and writings of his disciples, was that of not only bringing about a reconciliation "between all the different philosophical sects, Greeks as well as Barbarians, but also of producing "a harmony of all religions, even of Christianity and Heathenism, and prevailing on all the wise "and good men of every nation to lay aside their contentions and quarrels, and unite together as "one large family, the children of one common mother. With a view to the accomplishment of

---

[1] Mosheim, Com. Cent. II. p. 166.

[2] Euseb. Eccl. Hist. Lib. ii. Cap. i.　There are some words in Mark iv. 11, which might justify a suspicion that there were three besides the twelve, but the words of Eusebius above, shew that in his time the three were believed to be a part of the twelve.　Had they been an addition, the word rest would not have been used.

[3] Matt. xvii. 1, 2 ; Luke ix. 28, 29.　　　　　[4] Com. Cent. II. p. 138, N.

" this end, therefore, he maintained, that divine WISDOM had been first brought to light and
" *nurtured among the people of the East by Hermes Trismegistus, Zoroaster, and other great and*
" *sacred characters :* that it was warmly espoused and cherished by Pythagoras and Plato among
" the Greeks : from whom, although the other Grecian sages might appear to have dissented,
" yet that, with nothing more than the exercise of an ordinary degree of judgment and attention,
" it was very possible to make this discordance entirely vanish, and shew that the only points on
" which these eminent characters disagreed were but of trifling moment, and that it was chiefly
" in their manner of expressing their sentiments that they varied." [1]    In this, which is a part of
a gross attempt to vilify Ammonius, are admissions enough (which I have marked with italics) to
the truth and beauty of his system, and to the truth of mine.

Again Mosheim says, that Ammonius taught that " the religion of the multitude went hand in
" hand with philosophy, and with her had shared the fate of being by degrees corrupted and
" obscured with mere human conceits, superstition, and lies : that it ought, therefore, to be
" brought back to its original purity by purging it of this dross, and expounding it upon philoso-
" phical principles : *and that the whole which Christ had in view by coming into the world, was to*
" *reinstate, and restore to its primitive integrity, the wisdom of the ancients*—to reduce within
" bounds the universally prevailing dominion of superstition—and in part to correct, and in part
" to exterminate, the various errors that had found their way into the different popular religions."
Had the advice of Ammonius been followed, the prophecy of Christ would have been falsified, for
he would not have brought a *sword* but *peace.*

I now beg my reader to recall to his recollection what I have said respecting the Χρησος,
and I think he will have no difficulty in agreeing with me that originally the religion of Jesus was
Χϱης-ianity, and that it was not, in fact, until the Paulites got possession of the Papal chair,
by a compromise, that Paul's pernicious doctrines [2] were admitted into it,—by which its whole
character was changed, and it became Christianity, such as it was for a thousand years,—quarrelling, persecuting, and devil-driving : and very different indeed from the Chrestianity of the
first fathers, and from the secret doctrines of the temples of Eleusis and Jerusalem, of the Gentiles,
and of Jesus of Nazareth, all of which were the same.

In Mosheim's Commentaries, [3] the secret doctrines of Plato and Moses are compared, and it is
shewn *that by Clemens Alexandrinus and Philo* they were held to be the same in every respect;
and that it is also held, that they both are the same as the esoteric doctrines of the Christians, which
is indeed true, if the early fathers of the Christian Church and the plain words of the Gospels can
be admitted as evidence of what was the nature of the esoteric doctrines of Christianity. Who
can deny the ϖατηρ αγνωϛως, the Father whom *no person hath seen except the Son,* [4] to allude to
the Gnosis as above explained ?

There was no man in the first two centuries of the Christian æra to be preferred to Clemens
as an authority on this dry matter of fact, that there was a *secret* doctrine and of what nature
that secret doctrine was. He was followed by Origen, who confirmed his assertion, and was the
most learned of all the early Christians ; and he and Clemens were at the very top—they
were in fact the Patriarchs of the Christian community. Mosheim endeavours to disguise the
doctrine, but the actual existence of the Γνωσις is evident enough.

---

[1] Com. Cent. II. Sec. xxviii.

[2] Paul was really, as is evident from his letters, a well meaning but insane fanatic, in no respect superior, and very
little differing from, Brothers, Southcote, and Irving.

[3] Cent. II. Sect. xxxv. p. 167.          [4] On this passage I shall treat hereafter.

And now, if the reader reconsider what has been stated, and compare it carefully with the Gospel histories, I shall be greatly surprised if he do not find many passages in them which have a direct reference to parts or to the whole of the system which I have developed. And I think there can be no doubt, however varied the respective sects of Gnostics might be in the detailed or minor parts of their systems, that the Trimurti, the $\mu\iota\alpha$ $\alpha\varrho\chi\eta$ or unknown God, was the foundation of them all. The discovery of the Triune God with the Manichæans, in so clear and marked a manner, perfectly satisfies me that this was the doctrine of all the almost innumerable classes of mankind comprehended under the term Gnostics. The Manichæans were but a succession of Gnostics; and, in believing that their founder, Mani, was a Messiah or an Incarnation of the Divine Power, that is, in other and in their words, a person imbued with more than an usual portion of the Divine Mind, from which the minds of all men emanated, they believed nothing very inconsistent with Christianity. As far as the endowment with the Divine Mind goes, they were succeeded in later times by John Wesley and his followers, whose Christianity no one, I suppose, disputes. Perhaps it may be difficult to shew in clear and distinct terms, from the work of Faustus, that the Manichæans acknowledged the $M\iota\alpha$ $A\rho\chi\eta$; but as they were evidently nothing more than a succession of Gnostics, and as this secret doctrine, at least to my knowledge, never came into discussion or was expressly denied by them, it is perfectly fair to suppose that, like the other Gnostic doctrines, it was held by them: holding one part of the system—the Triune God—they must be believed to have held the other part—the $M\iota\alpha$ $A\rho\chi\eta$.

The whole, I repeat, formed a sublime and beautiful system. At the head of it was the $\Pi\alpha\tau\eta\rho$ $A\gamma\nu\omega\varsigma o\varsigma$, from whom emanated the *first* created being or hypostasis, the idea or plan of the universe.

The *second* emanation was the Triune God, the Creator, Preserver, and Destroyer, three persons and ONE God, the whole proceeding from the $\Pi\alpha\tau\eta\rho$ $\alpha\gamma\nu\omega\varsigma o\varsigma$—Brahme-Maia or *Illusion*.

From this ILLUSION, in some way or other, all the innumerable host of suns and worlds were supposed to have proceeded, by a gradation of emanations, and into this it was supposed that they would all ultimately return.

Thus we have a double Trinity—*first*, the $M\iota\alpha$ $A\rho\chi\eta$, the Divine Idea, and the Trimurti; and *secondly*, the Trimurti, consisting of Brahma, Vishnu, and Seva—the Creator, the Preserver, and the Destroyer—Father, Son, and Holy Ghost. We have the $M\iota\alpha$ $A\rho\chi\eta$, with its two additional hypostases, one of which was the Trimurti; and the Trimurti with its two additional hypostases; the *last* of the *first* constituting the *first* of the *last*; thus forming a chain, and in this manner all nature was a microcosmic chain.

As it was believed to be with worlds, so it was with man. He was supposed to pass from cycle to cycle, from world to world, till his period was complete, the temporary evil of one cycle remedied by the abundance of good in another, till the universal absorption was to take place. This is the reason why we have no hell in the Pentateuch, and yet that the moral character and justice of God are supposed to be vindicated. Thus through millions of ages and worlds existences were supposed to keep arising and passing away, and being renewed, until the final absorption into the Divine Essence. And the Divine Essence itself was supposed to keep on its endless course, creating new existences for ultimate happiness.

Now I think we have found the fountain from which flowed the almost innumerable sects in their minor details, as we might well expect, of an infinite variety,—each sect, wherever established, bearing a relation or being in proportion not to any principles of truth, but to the state of refinement or degradation of the human mind. As the minds of men were philosophical, or vulgar, or of inferior grade, they formed sects, or united to sects assimilating to themselves. It is just the same at this day, as every philosopher sees and knows. But I do not expect this to be admitted by a Calvinist or a Ranter. But all this proves the great importance of education to the middle class of mankind, who influence public opinion. Our priests see this clearly, and are now exerting themselves, as they cannot suppress education, to give it such a turn, that the people may not be led to doubt the necessity of bishops, priests, and tithes, in order to ensure their salvation.

In the beautiful system which I have developed, I have opened, I doubt not, the secret system of the Conclave: and we may be well assured, that when the Popes were persecuting Gnostics, it was the holders of the pernicious dogmas which in their time had arisen, as they are described by Epiphanius and others, and not the sublime and original doctrines of the oriental Djnana or רשית *Rasit*, or $A\varrho\chi\eta$, as described in the book called, and properly called, the Gospel according to Djnana or John, the doctrine of the wisdom of India,—the ancient doctrines taught by Menu of India, Menes of Egypt, Minos of Crete, Numa of Rome. [1]

I think it seems evident that the current of Gnosticism has flowed from India at various times, and in various distinct streams. We have it first, I think, in the Cyclopean builders of our Druidical temples, or in the Hellenians or Ionians. We have it again in the Exod, $a\pi oikia$, of Abraham and his tribe of Yudi. [2] We have it again in the Samaneans, Essenians, or Gnostics, about the time of Jesus Christ. We have it again in the Manichæans. We have it again in the Sophees of the Mohamedans; and, lastly, we have it in the Chaldæi, Ishmaelians, the As-chas-din, the Assassins, of the eleventh century. The last were our Chaldæi or Freemasons and Templars.

If my reader will look back to what I said in my first chapter respecting the origin of the Triune God, he will now be able to form an opinion respecting the mode in which, from principles of common sense, it had its origin.

Of the various streams from this fountain, the system of the Trimurti, the eternal generation of cycles and worlds, the Androgynous nature of the Deity, and the final absorption of all into the substance of the first principle, seems to have been the most general, indeed the subdivisions seem to have been so far almost unanimous in admitting an uniform system. The system of dualism seems to have been the first grand subdivision; and I must now make one more observation upon it. If it be carefully considered or reduced to its first principle, it will be found to arise almost necessarily from the nature of the creating and regenerating or destroying power, as described by me in the first book. For creation, in the sense applicable to the Trimurti, must always be accompanied with destruction; the Creator and Destroyer must always be in opposition and simultaneous. And though the *first* person is always successful by the agency of the *second* person in preserving the world which he has formed, the destroyer is always equally successful in effecting its destruction—which destruction is still only a renovation, or new formation. Thus we may go on in a circle for ever, or till we really arrive at the Hindoo *Illusion*. Hence arose the dualists of whom we have heard so much from Christian divines, but who, I think, never really existed, except in the modified sense in which we have seen that the doctrine was held by the Manichæans. Thus, gentle reader, I flatter myself I have laid before you the grand outlines of the history of moral man—the foundation upon which all his systems have been built; the

---

[1] It is rather remarkable that no *Christian* persecution of the Gnostics took place till the fourth century was far advanced. The existence of the Sicilian councils are more than doubtful.

[2] Called in the Desatir, p. 188, Jehudi, Yehudi.

minutiæ of the different subdivisions I leave to the minute philosophers. No doubt a good PHILOSOPHICAL AND CRITICAL HISTORY of them would be very desirable. But it is, though really a desideratum, not very likely to be supplied.

As we might well expect from the holders of so refined a theogony, as that which I have explained, we may discover, through the mist with which they have been enveloped, that they held a *morale* the most beautiful and refined, well described by Mr. Matter, in the conclusion of his Treatise on Gnosticism, in the following manner, in which, taken in its uncorrupted form, I quite agree with him : " La *morale* que la Gnose prescrivait à l'homme répond parfaitement à cette " destinée. Fournir au corps ce qu'il lui faut, lui retranchir tout ce qui est superflu : nourir " l'esprit de tout ce qui peut l'éclairer, le fortifier, le rendre semblable à Dieu, dont il est " l'image ; l'unir avec Dieu, dont il est une emanation, telle est cette morale. C'est celle du " Platonisme,[1] c'est celle du Christianisme. Sans doute le Gnosticisme offre[2] quelques dévia- " tions scandaleuses de cette sublime introduction à l'immortalité : mais le soleil aussi a des " taches : il n'en est pas moins un foyer de lumière."[3]

Such was the system of moral doctrines of the Gnostics, and such was the moral doctrine of Jesus of Nazareth ; and, in my next volume, I shall endeavour to expand it in its native beauty and simplicity, and to rescue it from the filth with which it has been loaded by the meanest-minded of human beings, who, in the dark ages succeeded, by force of their numbers, in obtaining the victory over the enlightened part of mankind, to the subversion of religion, and the exclusion from it of every thing like reason or philosophy. But Priestcraft in its worst form flourished, and the performing of miracles, and the driving out of devils, occupied the attention, and debased the understandings, of mankind for fifteen hundred years together. *In the next volume I propose to inquire into the truth of the system which I have explained.*

Gentle reader, as you have gone with me thus far, do you not think that you can travel with me one stage more ? Come, try one stage more ; and on this part of my subject I have done. You have seen the planetary cycles of the sages of India extending to millions of years. What think you of THE BEING, the Πατηρ αγνωστος, placed in the centre of countless millions of stars, suns, and worlds, circulating around it with inconceivable rapidity in boundless space and in cycles of incomprehensible duration ? Now, at last, you come to the Illusion of the sages of India, to their Illusion, but it is a true Illusion. If you doubt, raise your eyes to the stars, and think upon the Wisdom of your Creator ! I have done.

---

[1] This, of course, includes Philo-ism or the esoteric doctrines of the Israelites.

[2] He should have added, *in its corruptions.*

[3] Matter, Hist. Gnos. Vol. II. p. 489.

# APPENDIX.

In a note to Section 8, Chapter III. Book. V., I have made an observation respecting the foot of Buddha. This foot was called Phrabat. In volume III. of the Transactions of the Asiatic Society, page 57, are some curious observations on the Phrabat or foot-mark of Buddha of the Siamese. Here we have, I apprehend, two words—Phra and Bat. The last is Buddha. The first is the Pra, noticed by La Loubère as being the same as Bra—the meaning of which, I have formerly shewn, was Creator or Former, from the Hebrew word ברא *bra*. Then the meaning of foot of Bhra-bat is, foot of the creator Bud. This is $\phi\rho\eta = 608$, whence came the title of the Pharoahs of the Copts. The Phrabat, as the sacred signum or impression of Buddha, proves the truth of his having been in India. The *probat* is the deed marked with the sacred impression of the Bishop's seal, or of the seal of the Christian religion. The Bishop grants probate, when he is satisfied with the proof of the truth of a deed. Phra-bat is the impress of Buddha. This *bat* is Bad, and Pad, the name of the rivers Po and Ganges, and from being the place where his foot rested, it came to mean foot; and from this comes our *pad* for *foot :* when a man walks a journey he *pads* it. The word PRA is the foundation, the root of all the words above-cited; and it is from this that the Siamese say, the French are the same as themselves, having the same name, of which I shall say more hereafter. From the same root come the Latin *probo*, and the English *approve*.

In Book VI. Chapter I. Sect. 10, I have stated a remarkable circumstance respecting the Caspian Sea, namely, that there is a great whirlpool near the Southern end of it, by which, probably, its waters are discharged. The following account of the Père Averil, in Harris's Voyages and Travels, Vol. II. p. 248, will explain this : " But what " has puzzled the most refined naturalists is, that, notwithstanding the continual access of the waters of so many rivers, " this sea is not considerably augmented, or ever transgresses its bounds : some have been of opinion, that the Black " Sea draws a great share of those waters into its bosom : but that ridge of mountains placed betwixt these two seas " by nature, seems to separate them so far as not to admit of any probability for that assertion. On the other hand, " there are two reasons that rather incline me to believe that this lake, (the Caspian Sea,) how far remote soever from " the Persian Gulf, discharges a great part of its waters there : the first is, that on the South side of the *Persian Gulf*,[1] " opposite to the province of Kilan, are dangerous whirlpools, the noise of which, as the water is thrown into the " Gulf, is so great, occasioned by the rapidity of the waters, that in calm weather it may be heard at a great distance, " and consequently these abysses are avoided by marines. The second is, that by the constant experience of those " inhabiting near the Persian Gulf, it is confirmed, that at the end of every autumn they observe a vast quantity of " willow leaves thereabouts; and it being beyond contradiction, that this sort of tree is not so much as known in " those Southern parts of Persia, whereas the Northern part, bordering on the Caspian Lake, and especially the " province of Kilan, are stored with them near the sea-shore, it is more than probable that those leaves are not carried " by the winds from one extremity of the empire to the other, but rather with the waters that carry them through the " subterraneous channels and caverns to the before-mentioned Gulf." It will not be denied that we are here made acquainted with a circumstance in a high degree confirmatory of what I have said respecting the Caspian Sea, which is again confirmed by the following passage from Muller's Universal History.

It was the opinion of Pallas that the Euxine and Caspian Seas, as well as the Lake Aral, are the remains of an extensive sea, which covered a great part of the North of Asia.[2] This conjecture of Pallas's, which was drawn from his observations in Siberia, has been confirmed by Klaproth's Survey of the Country to the Northward of the Caucasus. Lastly, M. de Choiseul Gouffier adds, that a great part of Moldavia, Walachia, and Bessarabia, bears evident traces of having formed part of the same sea.

It has been often conjectured that the opening of the Bosphorus was the occasion of the draining of this ocean in

---

[1] This is a misprint, or rather most careless mistranslation : *Caspian Sea* must be meant.

[2] See Pallas Reise durch Siberian, Book v.

the midst of Europe and Asia. The memory of this disruptioh of the two continents was preserved in the traditions of Greece. Strabo,[1] Pliny,[2] and Diodorus,[3] have collected the ancient memorials which existed of so striking a catastrophe. The truth of the story has, however, been placed on more secure grounds by physical observations on the districts in the vicinity of the Bosphorus. See Dr. Clarke's Travels, and particularly a Memoir by M. de Choiseul Gouffier in the Mems. de l'Institut. Royal de France, 1815. The above observations of the translator of Muller's Universal History very strikingly support what I have said.

I think a careful inspection of the district of Troy must convince any unprejudiced person, either that Homer is the most incorrect of topographers, (which is directly against his general character, in other respects so remarkable for accuracy,) or that its face has been considerably changed since he made it the subject of his poem. Mr. Payne Knight attributes this to earthquakes.[4] This may be true; but I think I am justified in attributing it to the devastation caused by the breaking down of the head of the Euxine, and the opening of the passage. The breaking down of the head may have been caused by a convulsion of the earth. If my memory do not fail me, there is no *undisputed* passage in the Poem of Homer from which it can be inferred, that the Dardanelles was open either in the supposed time of the war, or in the time *when the Homeric songs were first composed.*[6] Now, when I consider the very fine field which the Euxine and its shores offer to the poet, the fact of his not having availed himself of it, raises a strong présumption that from being closed, it was not in his power.

In Book VI. Chapter II. Section 8, a black Multimammia is alluded to, and described in Figure 19. A very beautiful exemplar of this black lady may be seen in Sir John Soan's Cabinet of Antiquities, in Lincoln's Inn Fields.

In Book X. Chapter VI. Section 6, I have made some observations on the peculiarity of the circumstance that the Christian Templars should take their name from the Jewish Temple at Jerusalem, and also on the fact which Mr. Hammer has pointed out, that they have a close resemblance to the Assassins and Casideans—חסידים *hsidim*. I believe that Mohamed (as well as Hassan Sabah) was considered by his followers to be the tenth Avatar, and a renewed incarnation of Jesus Christ, or at least of the ninth Avatar; and that he was to be continued by renewed incarnation till the time when he was to come in his glory to reign at Jerusalem, which is an event which the Mohamedans expect to arrive, as Maundrell says, ·at the day of judgment;[7] but which I suspect meant, on the arrival of the Millenium. This doctrine of the renewed Avatar we see most clearly in the followers of Ali in Persia; and it was for this reason that the temple in the *holy city* (as all Turks call Jerusalem) was rebuilt with the greatest magnificence in their power at the time, and is considered most sacred. For this reason it is probable that the rival temple of Solomon, (as it would appear to the Western Arabians, or Suraseni, or Saracens,) in Cashmere, was destroyed by them when they conquered the country. Here we see the reason why the Casideans, that is, Templars or Chaldeans, came from the ruined temples of Solomon in the East, about the time of the Crusades, to the temple in the West, viz. because the temple in the West by its resurrection from its ashes, shewed that it was the true one; while the temples in the East were proved not to be the true temples in consequence of their destruction by the Mohamedans. It is probable that the persons who were the originals of our Templars were a part of the Sophitæ or Sophees of Cashmere, who were persuaded to leave their country, and to separate from their countrymen, whom we found (vide Book X. Chap. VI. Section 14, p. 731) in Cashmere or Casimere and its neighbourhood, and who could not be converted to Mohamedism, but who now remain in the East like the people of Oude or Ayoudia, (vide Book X. Chap. V. Section 12, p. 684,) expecting their promised Saviour. The reason why the Saracen and Turkish chiefs constantly take the names of Abraham, Solomon, &c., is, because they consider themselves renewed incarnations of these Patriarchs. Thus at last, I believe, I have discovered what I in vain took very great pains for a long time to discover, viz. the reason for the rebuilding of the temple of Jerusalem by the Mohamedans. Here, I think, we·may see that the Ishmaelians or Ishmalites, or Assassins from Almawt, or the eagle's nest, or Almond, as Mr. Klaproth calls it, between Cazvin and Ghilan, were a sect of the Sophees of the East, probably Cashmere, claiming to possess by right the holy city of Jerusalem, from the usurping Calif; for they were at constant war with both Christians and Saracens, though they are said to have united in their religion the religion of both. Besides, I am not quite certain that Hassan Sabah did not claim to be a descendant of Ali, and as such entitled to the Kalifat; however, it is admitted that he claimed to be a *tenth Avatar.*

These Sophitæ or Sophees belonging to the Temple of Solomon in Casimere or Cashmere, must have been the Jews, or a sect of the people called by Benjamin of Tudela, Jews, not Samaritans, as their Temple of Solomon proves, whom he found in very great numbers in the countries in the neighbourhood of Cashmere. Belonging to the worship of the temple of Solomon, and speaking the Chaldee language, they might be correctly called Jews. But they were also Samaneans

---

[1] Lib. i. p. 49.    [2] Nat. Hist. Lib. ii. Cap. xc.    [3] Lib. v. Cap. xlvii.

[4] Vol. I. p. 32.    [5] Hist. Gr. Alp. p. 34.

[6] There is not a trace of the Argonautic expedition in the GENUINE parts of either of the poems of Homer. See Barker's Lempriere on the words Argos and Cyaneæ.

[7] Travels, p. 170.

r Sophees. I have no doubt that the Jews or Ioudi of the Temple of Solomon in Western Syria, were the same as ιe Jews or Ioudi of the Temple of Solomon in Eastern Syria or Cashmere, and as the Ioudi of Adoni and Salem of ιouth India, with only some trifling differences. These differences, probably, arose from the difference of country, ) which the Western Ioudi were obliged to accommodate themselves, and to other adventitious circumstances arising ut of the different fortunes of the two, after their separation in Ayoudia.

After Abraham's tribe came from the East, we know in general, from the accident of having their sacred books reserved to us, sufficient of their history to account for their peculiarities. We know how great was the care of their conoclastic leader to preserve them from idolatry; therefore, till their destruction about the time of Christ, they did ot publicly adopt the worship of any other or new Avatar or Messiah; but certain passages, which I shall point out ι their Apocrypha in a future Book, and the Papal Fisherman, and the Fishes tied by the tails, &c., &c., shew that ιey, in part, did it privately. On the contrary, in India, or the Eastern Judæa or Ayoudia, the Avatars followed ublicly in succession. Cristna or the Ram followed Taurus or the Bull, and the use of images, for which Abraham eft India, kept increasing, till, by degrees, every kind of ridiculous emblematic idol was admitted; until at last, as in ireece and Italy, the original meaning of the religion was lost. I have no doubt that at every temple of Solomon— ι that in China,—that in the Carnatic,—that in Mewar,—that at Telmessus,—that at Eleusis,—and the five in Egypt, ιs I shall shew in a very remarkable manner, there must originally have been a system, in its foundation and great ιeading features, the same as at Jerusalem. I speak not now of the minor rites and ceremonies. In all these places ιe find some remnants of the system, which must all have been imitations of the great parent in the mighty kingdom ιf Oude, or Ayoudia, or of Pandæa, for it was all the same. Jesus Christ was set up as the ninth incarnation by those ιho understood the principle of the mythos. Mohamed patronised, and his followers restored, the temple at Jeru- ιalem, in preference to that at Telmessus or that in Casi-mere, because he, in fact, belonged to the sect of that at ιerusalem.

Dr. Clarke says,[1] that the Mosque at Jerusalem is the most magnificent piece of architecture in the Turkish domi- ιions; much more magnificent than that of St. Sophia at Constantinople.

We may be very certain that when the present magnificent Temple at Jerusalem was erected, splendid as it is, more ιvas originally intended to be done by its builder, than what we find. I think there can be very little doubt that its ιuilder intended to restore the glories of Solomon, in the former existence of which, of course, he believed, and place ιhe seat of his empire there, or at least he thought that in rebuilding the temple he was preparing Jerusalem for that ιvent. This intention was probably suspended by the divisions of the Califat into three or four states, and finally pre- ιvented by the occupation of Jerusalem by the Christians, about which time the failure of the Millenium was obvious to ιts expectants. Then were blown into air the chimeras of Christians, Ishmaelites, Sonnites, and Shiites, or followers of ιΑli. Among the whole of them the doctrine of the millenium and the renewed incarnation may be most clearly seen. ιThis doctrine, for the last six hundred years, they have all endeavoured to secrete or deny, for the same reason that the ιChristians of the West have endeavoured to secrete the Gospel of Joachim. Here we begin to perceive the reason for ιhe mission of Abdul Raschid, of which the Mohamedan historians treat,[2] who was sent by the Afghans, or Arabians, ιor Suraceni, or whatever they might be, from the countries on the North of India, to Western Arabia, in the time of ιMohamed, to inquire into the circumstances of the new Amid or Desire of all Nations, who, they were told, had ιappeared in the West;[3] and who, they might, perhaps, have heard from their Tartarian or Chinese neighbours, was ιforetold to appear in Ayoudia or Oude, which was West to them. Here we begin to perceive the reason for the ιdevotees of the Eastern temple of Solomon, the Afghans, becoming the earliest converts to Islamism. The word Islam ι shall explain hereafter.

I think it not unlikely that the Casideans, found by the Christian conquerors of Jerusalem, (and who afterward ιbecame their Knights Hospitallers and Knights Templars,) were the remains of persons brought from the Eastern ιemple of Solomon, from Casi-mere, for the express purpose of rebuilding the Western Temple, according to the ιmystic plan of the Eastern one, and that this is the reason why they were found by the Christians as an appendage to ιhe new temple.

The mosque or temple on Mount Moriah was built by the Calif Omar, the son of Caleb, about the year 16 of the ιHegira, A.D. 637. Chateaubriand says,[4] La Mosquée prit le nom de cette roche Gameat-el-Sakhra. It has a large ιdome, under the centre of which is a cave, and at the top of it the sacred stone which, in all these religions, is generally ιfound in or close to the temple or church.

This building is called by our travellers a Mosque, but whether it be considered in any other light than a common ιmosque by the Musselmans I know not. But the blindness of all our travellers in not seeing that Mohamedism is ιnothing but a branch of Christianism, as Peter Martyr long before me proved, forbids any rational dependance on any

---

[1] Trav. in the Holy Land. Chap. xvii. p. 601, ed. 4to.   [2] Vide my Apol. for the Life of Mohamed.

[3] Vide Chap. VII. Sect. II. p. 741.   [4] Travels, Vol. II. p. 115.

thing which they say. Surely, if any thing like critical acumen had existed among them, they would have inquired into the reason for the profound veneration paid at Damascus to the head of John the Baptist. This single fact proves the truth of almost all I have said respecting the Christianity of Mohamed. But people seem to me never either to think or reason. However, I am rather disposed to believe that as the Millenarian system of the Christians changed after the thirteenth century, so, in like manner, the Mohamedan changed, and the building which was begun as a temple for the whole world, has dwindled down into a mere mosque; and neither Jesus nor Mohamed is expected now to come to reign in it at the end of the 6000 years.

The followers of Ali, however, still cling to this superstition, and have various fancies about it; some saying, that the last Imaum continues, but in secret. The idea of the Imaum being somewhere in secret, furnishes food for ridicul to our travellers; who generally laugh at things they do not understand, instead of inquiring into them. I apprehend this means merely, that the lineal descendant of the last Imaum of the house of Ali is living in obscurity; that the line continues; and that the lineal descendant will some day resume the government. This I shall shew is the opinion of the Sonnites as well as of the Shiites.

In the description of the Temple given by Mons. Chateaubriand is an account of the sacred stone to which I have alluded. In this Mohamedan Temple, there are in the stone Pillar and the Cave both the Nabhi or Navel of the earth, and the Yoni and the Linga, though they may not now be understood. This and other circumstances induce me to believe, that though the Mohamedans might object to the single worship of the Dove, they had not the same objection to the double one. Here, if I understand M. Chateaubriand, the stone is placed *over* the cave. Now I do not doubt that, in the ancient temple of Solomon, there were the cave and the mysterious stone pillar, pedestal or whatever it might be, the same as at Delphi and other places; but in it the pillar or pedestal was probably not *over* the cave, but *in* it, as described by Nicephorus Callistus, Lib. x. Cap. xxxiii. in the following words : " ὅπερ εγω εν απορρητης εκγω " οιηγησομαι· εχει δε ουτω. κ. τ. λ. " At the time when the foundation was laid, one of the stones, to which the lowest " part of the foundation was attached, was removed from its place, and discovered the mouth of a cavern which had " been hollowed out of the rock. Now since they could not see to the bottom on account of its depth, the overseer " of the work, wishing to be perfectly acquainted with the place, let down one of the workmen by means of a long " rope into the cavern. When he came to the bottom he found himself in water as high as his ancles, and examining " every part of the cavern, he found it to be square as far as he could ascertain by feeling. He afterward searched " nearer the mouth of the cavern, and on examination discovered a low pillar very little higher than the water, and " having placed his hand upon it, he found lying there a book carefully folded in a piece of thin and clean linen " This book he secured, and signified by the rope his wish to be drawn up. On being drawn up he produced the " book, which struck the beholders with astonishment, particularly as it appeared perfectly fresh and untouched " though it had been brought out of so dark and dismal a place. When the book was unfolded, not only the Jews " but the Greeks also were amazed, as it declared in large letters, even at its commencement, In the beginning, &c " To speak clearly, the writing here discovered, did most evidently contain all that Gospel which was uttered by the " divine tongue of the Virgin disciple."[1] What credit my reader may give to the whole or any part of the history of Nicephorus Callistus, I do *not* know; but I *do* know, that I never saw any book in which the higher part of the ancient Jewish Cabala is more distinctly marked, than in the first chapter of the Gospel according to John. Knowing as the person who has read this book must know, the doctrine of wisdom as a key, he cannot fail to see that it is contained in every line of the first part of this Gospel. If a book were to be concealed in the Temple, from a period *long anterior to the Christian æra,* I know of no one so likely as the Gospel of John, or at least as the first part of it. My reason for this, which my reader will justly think very paradoxical, I shall give in a future book.

Jesus Christ was said by some of his followers to be a renewal of Adam. He said, *before Abraham was I am,* that is, *I was,* the old language having no present tense. From this peculiarity of the Hebrew language, in the past and future tenses being convertible, the equivoque in our translation arose, but it ought to be, before Abraham was *I was.* This I have no doubt the Popes would quote to establish a claim to universal dominion, which I shall explain in my next volume. It was held that Jesus would come to rule at Jerusalem, but I suspect the Mohamedans would say as a renewed incarnation, and I think they held Mohamed to be a renewed incarnation of Jesus, and *Ali* a renewed incarnation of Mohamed. If it be objected that Ali and Mohamed lived at the same time, a devotee will quote the example of Elias and Elisha, and say, the divine spirit did not enter Ali till after Mohamed's death. It is a common expression, that when Mohamed put off his cloak he gave it to Ali. The holy spirit did not enter Jesus till it appeared as a dove at his baptism, and till the fire was lighted in the river.[2] This looks as if the author of that book meant to describe Jesus as not a divine person till the descent of the Dove. I believe the words *totum Christo configuratum* applied to St. Francis, in Chapter VI. Sect. 4, were meant to describe a renewed incarnation, but were, perhaps, not wholly understood by the persons using them. In the possession by the Turks of the head, or the pretended head of

---

[1] I have some particular reasons for inserting this here.   [2] Justin Martyr.

John the Baptist, before noticed by me in Chap. V. Sect. 12, and again just now, there is a proof that we are in general quite ignorant of the principles of their religion.[1]

To deny that Mohamed, who admitted the existence of Jesus Christ—his *divine mission*, and that he really had the power of performing miracles, and that the doctrines which he taught were true—was a Christian, is absurd, and only worthy of the devotees who deny it; and it does not deserve to have a moment's time wasted upon it.[2]

In Book X. Chapter VI. Sections 3 and 13, I have said, it was *probable* that St. John's College, at Cambridge, was the domus Templi of the round church of the Templars there; but since that was printed, I have inquired more into the church, &c., at Cambridge, and I find that the present St. John's is only of modern foundation. There is, however, annexed to, or connected with, this church, an almshouse, called Bedes-house, the name of which has puzzled all the antiquarians. This I have little doubt was the original Domus Templi—the house of Buddha corrupted into *Bede*, and meaning *wisdom*, i. e. seminary of sound learning and religious education; and to support this religious principle, I think St. John's College was built, and the ancient Domus Templi converted into an almshouse. The Saxon style of architecture of the round church at Cambridge, and the pillars upon which the pointed arches of that at Northampton are built, prove them to be far older than the tenth or eleventh century. The College of St. John at Cambridge, close to the Temple, is a similar institution to that of Hassan Sabah at Cairo. All schools and colleges in ancient times were considered to be pious foundations for the education of the priesthood; and I have no doubt that, originally, the laity was considered as encroaching on the priesthood, by learning the arts of reading and writing.

The case of St. John's College, Cambridge, I take to be like that of the Inner Temple Church in London. When you ask for the foundation of that church and institution, your inquiries are instantly stopped by being shewn the inscription, which declares it to have been built in the year 1185; but, on close examination, it appears that it was rebuilt—brought from another place, somewhere near Holborn. This serves to shew how an inquirer is liable, unless he use great caution, to be deceived by his informants, (without any thing wrong on their part being intended,) and the real age of an institution concealed. I suspect, like the removed Temple Church, that St. John's College (which, as just noticed, was of the same character as the house of Hassan Sabah at Cairo) was *rebuilt* in the place of the house of Bede or Bedes near to it, which house acquired its title when the Buddha Trigeranon in Wales, and the Buddha of Scotland, took their names in those countries, and when one university and river were called Isis and Oxford, and the other the bridge of Cam or the aspirated Om. When the improved new house of Buddha or Wisdom, the present St. John's, was built, the old one, the Bedes house, was given to the poor. I shall return in a future page to the word Templum : I know no word more curious.

Since I printed the observations respecting St. Thomas, in Book X. Chapter VII. I have re-perused the work of the Jesuit, Faria y Sousa, on the Portuguese history of India, and I find he states, that St. Thomas built churches in China as well as India : thus proving that what Bergeron Des Guines and Mons. Paravey said was true—that the mythos was to be found there. The Jesuits found it there when they arrived.

In Book X. Chapter VII. Section 7, I have expressed a doubt, whether some remains of a period earlier than the entrance of the sun into Taurus might not be found in the *Twins*, alluded to on the coast of Coromandel. This arose from a mistake which I made in the meaning of the word תאם *tam*. I hastily ran away with the idea, that it had reference only to *two human beings*, while it really has no such exclusive meaning, but may apply to the *two fishes* of the Zodiac, or even to a pair or double of any article whatever. This removes a difficulty which, if it meant Gemini, it raised in my system, as every one must see, who has attended to it closely. The allusion is evidently to the Buddhist incarnation of *the fishes*; for the votaries at the shrine of St. Thomas are Buddhists. The Buddhists had all the Zodiacal incarnations.

Faria y Sousa says[3] that the Portuguese, when they arrived at Malliapour or St. Thomé, found near the Tomb of the saint, the burying-place of a Sibylla, whom he calls Indica. But we must not forget that in the part of Italy where we found the traces of the Camasene,[4] there lived the Sibyl of Cuma. Now the country where the Indian lady lived was the country of Cuma or Cama as well as of Cali. If we refer as above, we shall see that the same mythos of Cuma or Cama, is most clearly in both countries. The Sibyl of Italy was said to have come from Chaldea, that is Calida. I also request attention to the fact named in Book X. Chapter I. Section 20, that all the things related of Jesus Christ were related by the Cumæan Sibyl, as well as by the Sibyl of Erythræa. From these circumstances I cannot help believing, notwithstanding what I have said respecting the Gemini, that the Didymus, the Tam, meant twin *fishes*, not twin *children*. Jonas was swallowed by a whale. This fish was chosen because it brings forth only two young ones at a time, and suckles them like most animals. It seems like a connecting link between the animal and the fish creation. Cama was the male and female deity of love. Cama might be Ama aspirated, and Tam might be only Ama

---

[1] The Turks have bodies of soldiers called Segmen as well as Sphahis. These are men of Saga, those men of Sophia. They still give to the Mosque at Constantinople the name given by Constantine, St. Sophia. Maundrell, p. 171.

[2] His sect of Christians seems to have absorbed nearly all the other sects, except that of the Paulites.

[3] Vol. I. p. 272.        [4] Vide pp. *760, 777, 788, 808.*

or Amor preceded by the emphatic article, T'Ama. In this way I find a rational meaning for the word Tam, in perfect keeping with the other parts of the system.

But, upon the whole, I incline to the opinion that the Camarinus is the same as Tam-marinus, and the Cam-masenus the same as Tam-masenus.[1] In order to judge of this, my reader must refer, by means of the Index, to the places where these words are treated of. If this be admitted, a high probability will be raised, that wherever St. Thomas is found, the adoration of the Fishes or of Aries may be looked for.

Ceylon is called Lanca or Langa, or Ilam or Salàbham, and by Ptolemy, Salica. The coast opposite to Ceylon, to which you pass over Adam's bridge, is called Pescaria—evidently *the fisherman's* coast.[2] Bartolomeus[3] says, near Comorin stands the temple of Ramanacoil in which the younger Bacchus and the Lingham or Phallus of Seva is preserved. The Indians believe Ceylon to be a part of Paradise. The King of Ceylon is called a *Rachia* by Pliny.[4] Here as usual we find the *Ras.*

I suspect the fishery, which is so marked here, was the fishery of pearls; and, paradoxical as I may be thought, that the *Pearl fishing town* of Colchester (not Maldon) was called Cama-lodunum for the same reason. In the province of *Picenum*, on the shore of the Adriatic, was a town called *Camarino.* Both these names I think arose from the same superstition.

Mr. Cleland says, that the pearl was the peculiar emblem of peace.[5] The Indian Cama is crowned with pearls. They took the name of beads, from the Vedda, which meant Wisdom, and on this account the Celtic Judge's coronet was surrounded with pearls. I think the fact that the town of the Roman pearl fishery in England was called Cama, when joined to the other circumstances, raises a high probability, that the word Cama meant *pearl*; and that Cama-lodunum was town of *the fishery of the pearl.* But Cama or Kama Deva has for one of his epithets Makara-Ketu, or, *he who bears the Makara on his banner.* The word Makara means a *sea monster*, and Ketu is the Greek Κητος and the Latin Cetus, *the whale.* This completes the proof of identity between the Cama of India and Italy.

It is perfectly clear that the Hebrew text is dislocated, interpolated, and has multitudes of lacunæ in it; and it is an admitted fact, that the celebrated Urim and Thummim were lost after the captivity. From the union of these circumstances I am led to believe, that part of the text respecting these words is omitted; and when I recollect that we have found the Judæan mythos in Urii of Calida, along with the Tam-mim, I cannot help suspecting that Urim, the plural of Ur of the Chaldees, and Tammim, the plural of the Tam of the country of Ur, had a reference to some superstition of the Tamul country. I suspect that originally two of the words Tam, Cam, and Sam, were corruptions of the other of the three.

Orion was the son of Mercury, Jupiter, and Neptune. I think we have here in the three, *first,* Buddha or the Bull; *secondly,* Cristna, or the Ram; and *thirdly,* Neptune, or the sign Pisces. He was born from the salt water of these three Gods, *ab Urinâ.* He was called Aquosus. *He was carried on the back of Dolphins.* Was he Jonas swallowed by a whale, by the fish with two Mammæ, which brings forth only *two* young at a time?

In Book X. Chapter VII. Section 7, I have suggested that the different *carns* there mentioned might take their names from the *sepulchral monuments* called carns. To a certain extent this may be true; but, on more reflection, I think we may go a little farther, particularly as the cause does not seem proportionate to the effect. Every carn which I have seen, has, or has had, at least one circle of stones around it, several near Inverness two or three, and those in the favourite cycles, of twelve or twenty-four. Now I find from Mr. Cleland, that the Celtic (i. e. Hebrew, as I have proved Hebrew and Celtic the same) for a *circle* or cycle was *Kern* or *Caern.* He says this word also meant a church—that would be a temple. Here, in the *circle,* (or Temple, which I shall explain hereafter to mean circle,) we have a rational explanation of the origin of the word. From this we may have the Carnutes of Gaul, and all the mystic words which we have seen occur so often, not excepting even the circular horn of the Apollo Carneus, taking its name from the circular form, of whom the horned Aries was an emblem. He was κριοπροσωπος.

Here we may have the origin of the mystic shell in the hand of almost every God, having as many circles as cycles had run. Cleland says, " The Druids, above all figures, affected the circular. Their *Cir, Hirs, Shires, Churches,* " all took their appellation and form from the radical *Hir* or *Cir* for a circle."[6] But this *Cir* is nothing but the Hebrew גר *gr,* a circle, our Kirk and *to gird.*

But besides these, and closely connected with them, is another word before unknown to me, namely, the Greek καρ or καρνος, which signifies *a sheep.*[7] This word in Celtic is *Caora,* in Hebrew כר *hr.* The Philistines had a temple called בית-כר *bit-kr.* (1 Sam. vii. 11.) Jupiter was called Καραιος by the Bœotians. From this Caria had its name. All these words were evidently closely connected—in fact, in root the same. We have formerly seen Apollo called

[1] Cape Comorin is called both Comari and Canyamuri. Forster's translation of Bartholomeus, p. 425.

[2] From this coast came the Boies or Bobees, the tribe of Fishermen whom we have traced to Baleux, the originals of the Manichæans. See the Index.

[3] Forster's Ed. p. 427.       [4] Ib. p. 432.       [5] Spec. p. 47.       [6] Ib. p. 117.

[7] Drum. Origen. Vol. IV. Book vii. Chap. vi. p. 131 ; also Hesychius.

Χρης. Sir W. Drummond says, that some held that from the city of *Chrysaoris* the whole of *Caria* had been called. I believe that all these names came from the Greek numeral symbols X or ΤΡΣ and the Hebrew כר *kr*, when the Hebrew Resh (as I shall by and by shew) denoted both one hundred and two hundred. Though it is difficult to say, yet I think it is not difficult to understand, why all the countries came to be called Carn; nor why a sacred heap of stones, with a circle of stones in the number of a sacred cycle in it, or round it, was called by the.same name.

But this word also we have just seen meant a horn : but what horn? The horn of the Ram, which was also the shell-horn of a *fish*, which we call by a proper mythologic name Cornu-Ammonis. Here the mixture of *Aries and Pisces* shews itself : both emblems of Apollo or the Sun. Callimachus describes a temple of Apollo as having been built and paved with horns.[1] These were the kind of stones containing petrifactions of the large Cornu-Ammonis, of which we have plenty in Yorkshire, near Whitby, to build thousands of temples, which if built of these stones would be *correctly said* to be built of horns. We may now understand what is meant when we read of altars to Apollo built of horns, which at first seems so foolish. But we may be certain, that these kinds of mysteries are very seldom foolish at the bottom. They all arose from the rational wish to perpetuate doctrines, before the invention of writing. This serves as a key to almost every thing. From the songs at the death of the God, plaintive songs came to be called *Karan* in Celtic, and *Garan* in Persian.[2] These songs were in like manner invented to perpetuate the mythos. Coronach, in Scotland, is a lamentation for a deceased person.

It has been observed by Mr. Logan, author of the Scottish Gael, that Crean or Creosan was a Celtic term for Sun, and that Carnac was said to have been built by Creans. This Crean is the Irish Grian. Now I cannot help suspecting that Crean is the Χρης softened and corrupted. This is strengthened by the term Cill Chriosde being rendered by Mr. Logan, Christ's Church.[3] The word Crios is a common term for the sun in Ireland. The ancient word Crios might grow into Christ, as Elios in Greece grew into Elias. The second person in the Trinity or Trimurti is designated in the very Gnostic work called the Gospel of John, by the word *Caro* (genitive) *Carnis*, and described thereby to have become incarnate in the flesh. I am disposed to ascribe all these names to the divine incarnation. Apollo was unquestionably an incarnation, and as he (and Ammon, Bacchus, &c., &c.) wore the horns of the Ram, or was the horned Apollo, and was incarnate; the word carn might from this come to mean *a horn*, among the uninitiated, who knew nothing of the doctrine of divine incarnation. From being the monument of the incarnate God, the monuments sacred to the Gods might come to be called Carns. I think it probable that the curled weapon of offence on the head of the animal had its name of Car or Carn, and the animal was called *carned* or *horned* from the carn or horn being a distinctive badge of the incarnate God; that the God was not called from the Carn, but the Carn from the God; and that the God's name of Carn or Carneus came from his being in *carne*—incarnated. I think it is very certain that the doctrine of divine incarnation was kept a secret as long as possible. We find it, now that we understand it, every where distinctly marked, but no where publicly declared. We find it in Greece, in Syria, in India; but it will not be found in the Vedas. Perhaps it may be in the Pouranas, written after the secret became public. All these explanations of the word Carn are in better keeping with the other circumstances attending the word, than that which I formerly gave. It is not more recondite than many explanations of words which are known. It may be, like so many other words which we know, Latin-Sanscrit. And if it be not in the Sanscrit Lexicons, it may be *like other old words* omitted, probably because its meaning was not understood.

In Book X. Chapter VIII. Section 4, and in Chapter IX. Section 3, I have noticed the words Nama Amido Buth, and Nama-si-va-yah. The first, I think, will mean adoration to Buddha, (or the wisdom of) the holy OM. The second, adoration to the Veda or Wisdom. The Deity being adored, under perhaps the finest of all his attributes, WISDOM, in a pandæan or universal or Catholic religion or system, we must expect it to be found, as we do find it, in great numbers of examples in every country of the world.

I believe the Χρης-tianity on the coast of Malabar, was originally the Χρης-tianity of Delphi and of the Erythræan Sibyl of Justin, who foretold every thing that should be done by Jesus Christ, which the Portuguese Romish Christians a little moulded, and which, perhaps, some Syrian Christians might previously have a little moulded to their own tastes or superstitions. This inference will be much strengthened by the proofs which I shall give in my next Book, that every rite, ceremony, and DOCTRINE, of the Romish Church, was taken from Gentilism, without a single exception,—that, in fact, the present fashionable Christianity is nothing but reformed Gentilism,—Gentilism stripped of its grosser corruptions.

But although every part of the fashionable Christianity is Gentilism, every part of Gentilism is not Christianity— the disgusting bloody sacrifices for example. But the result of the whole draws us towards the doctrines of Ammonius Saccas,[4] or the Philalethean philosophical Christians of the first century.

---

[1] Drum. Origin. Vol. IV. Book vii. Chap. vi.    [2] Ib. p. 165.    [3] Scottish Gael, Vol. II. p. 284.

[4] I consider that the name of Ammonius Saccas, must have been adopted by this philosopher from mystic motives, and not, as it is said, because he carried sacks. It is a sacred or Χρης-ian name. The Saka or Saca and Ammon, I think, shew this.

In my next volume I shall shew that the same Jewish and X$_{ρης}$-ian mythos amalgamated, which was found in India and China, foretold by the Erythræan Sibyl, and supposed by Virgil to recur every six hundred years, existed in ever greater perfection in South America, when the Spaniards arrived there, than even in India, carried thither, as the pious monks say they suppose, by the devil. I shall shew that it must have gone to America before the fabrication of any written document now in existence.

For a very long time I inquired, and the more I inquired the more proofs I found, of the universal dissemination of the Judæan mythos in India; that is, of that mythic doctrine which we find among the Jews and their sects, for the Christian religion is that only of a Judaic sect. Then what had become of the sect professing it? For though it was every where, yet it was not found any where in such large numbers as it ought to be, if its system were, as it appeared to have been, that of the great empire of Ayoudia. At last it occurred to me, that the sect must be similar to the Essenes, who, though once common in Syria and Egypt, (and in Greece as Pythagoreans,) are no where now to be found, because they became, by a change of name, the Carmelites of the Christians. In a similar manner, when the Equinoctial Pisces arrived, the Yudaites, whatever their name might have been before that time, then became Vishnuvites. We have no sacred, or properly-called canonical, writings either of the Jews or the Brahmins, after the year 360 B. C., the time of the entrance of the equinoctial sun into Pisces. I request my reader to refer to what I have said in Book X. Chapter IV. respecting the Ιχθυς and Pisciculi of the Christians, and also to what I have said respecting the God Dagon and the Vishnu of the Indians in the same chapter. When I consider all the circumstances of the fish Avatar,· or Oannes, or Wisdom, or Dagon the Saviour, and the similarity to, or rather identity, both in the letters and sound of 'other Sanscrit or Indian words with, English; such as *sam* and *same*, *stalla* and *stalla*, *hulg* and *holy*, &c., &c., I cannot doubt that the second person of the Trimurti has taken his name of Vishnu, instead of Cristna or some other name, since the Sun entered Pisces at the vernal equinox; and, as he was feigned to have become incarnate in a fish, as we see in Figure 32, where he is treading on the serpent's head, so he took the name of Fish: and that the Vish is really our Fish.[1] And that, according to order, the Lamb or Cristna succeeded to the Bull, and the Fish or Ιχθυς, or Fishes tied together by the tails, the religion of the *Pope the great Fisherman*, succeeded to the Lamb: and that in India, as well as in Europe, the followers of the Lamb or Cristna and of the Fishes, are intimately mixed, or rather are the same—as from the crossing of the two cycles they ought to be: every Neros cycle might bear the name of the Lamb, as well as its own name, whilst the Sun was passing through the Lamb. The example of the Essenes, well known by the Roman Church to have become their Carmelites, is similar to that of the Ayoudaites becoming Vishnuvites. Thus the devotees of Cristna, under the name of Yadu the father of Cristna, might become Vishnuvites, and this may be the reason why we have few or none of the people who became Jews in Western Syria, by that name in India. But it is also probable that they never went by the name of Jews, or by any name connected with it, in India. · They would be rather Pandæans, which answers to our Roman Catholic, than Jews, as Pandæa seems to have been the sacerdotal name of the government; as Catholic is now of the government of Rome. And from finding the name in Athens, in Asia Minor or Room, in Italy, as Roma, and in North·and South India, I cannot doubt the existence of this Roman or Catholic empire. We have it endeavouring to raise itself again in Italy, at this time, and I have no doubt that many of its devotees, in ALL *ranks of society*, really believe that it will in the end succeed, and rise again from its present state of depression. From the account which I have given in Book X. and Chapter V. Section 12, p. 684, and in several other places, it appears that the mass of the people of Oude or Ayoudia hold precisely the same doctrines as those held by the Jews of Western Syria, previous to their destruction by the Romans. These must have been the Jewish people met with by Benjamin of Tudela. If my reader will take the Index and peruse all which has been said before respecting Oude he will find innumerable proofs of the Judæan mythos.

The tribe of Colida or of the Chaldeans was the tribe of Ayoudia or Yadu, the father of Cristna, so that they might by strangers be called Yaduites or Iudaites. But, as I have just said, this was not their name of religion. In a similar manner I think we may have had a tribe of the same religion, or nearly so, come to the West under the name of Druids, and to have been that tribe named by me under the name of Druhya, the son of Yadu, in note 1, page 746

---

Indeed I suspect every author assumed a sacred or mythical name. We know how common it is yet with us for authors to write under false names.

¹ ·In the old Irish, *Ischa*, which is the Eastern name of Jesus, means a Fish, and the Welsh V, is our single F; our FF is the Welsh F. Ischa with digamma is F—ischa.

In addition to what I have said in Book X. Chapter IV. Section 5, I have to observe, that Buddha was called, not only as we have seen elsewhere Fo or Po, but he was also called Dak or Dag Po—ﬧﬨ *dg*, which was literally the Fish Po, or Fish Buddha— Pisces. ˙ See Littleton in voce Piscis. The Pope was not only chief of the Shepherds, but he was chief of the Fishermen, a name which he gives himself, and on this account he carries a *Poitrine*. On this account also, the followers of Jesus were Fishermen. The name *Dag Po* was evidently Buddha in his eighth or ninth incarnation. The Buddhists, we must remember, claim to have the same number of Incarnations as the Brahmins. It is very difficult to discover in what the difference between the two sect consists.

This tribe I think came from the country of the Sacæ, and brought all our Eastern Gods and Mythology to Ireland and Scotland; [1] but I shall discuss this point at large in my next volume.

The Cali-dei or Chaldeans, who had their name from the Deity Cali, and he or she had the same name as the Καλος, Μιτις, of the Greeks, which two words, I am persuaded, had the same meaning, might be some of them. Then the Καλι-dei would be the same as the Χρης-ians.

It is quite clear to me, that those tribes whom we call Jews, and who have had no Pentateuch till modern times, cannot be *Mosaic* Jews. I think most of the Jews, whom we find scattered about the world, are the remains of the Brahmin religion, who did not fall into the adoration of the Fishes. If violent altercations took place among them on the change, I can readily conceive, that the new sect of Vishnuvites would detest and abolish most of the old rites and ceremonies of the former superstition, as we have seen Moses did the rites of the Bull, and the Protestants the rites and ceremonies of the Romish Church. Religious devotees always run into extremes, and generally hate the sect they have left, and every thing belonging to it. I consider the discovery which I have made of the Yadu in the followers of the Fishes, as of great consequence.

I suppose the tribe of a person who is called Yadu, father of Cristna, came to Western Syria, and took the name of עברי *obri*, or Jews, or strangers. But their first name, assumed by themselves, was Judah, יהודה *ieude*, (hand of God,) [2] as we learn from Eusebius, and of Samaritans, or worshipers of the sun under the name of *Sam* or, in Sanscrit, *Syâma*, like the tribe lately named in the West, who, I suppose, might take the name of Druids from the Druhya of India, the son of Yadu. Though it cannot certainly be known, it seems not unlikely that the leaders of the tribes were the sons of princes bearing those mythological names. If the Patriarchs of those early days had hundreds of children, like the Eastern monarchs of the present day, it is not unlikely that they should have sent them off with gifts, as Abraham is described to have sent off his children by Keturah, (instead of leaving them to be murdered by their elder brothers, the fashion of the present day,) and let them take such people as chose to go with them to form new tribes. There are hundreds of tribes of Bedoueens in Asia, but I never met with an account of the formation of a tribe, and how it is done I do not know. They all have, or pretend to have, long pedigrees.

I attribute the loss of the tribe of the Iadu in India by us, or its not being perceptible to us, in a considerable degree to the effect of the prejudice which we have in our minds (to which I have alluded in my Preface) to any thing of the nature of the Jewish religion in India; and this has led us both to conceal and misrepresent facts and circumstances out of number, without really having any intention to do so, or to do any thing that is wrong. It has probably only acquired the name of *Jewish* as *a religion*, because it happened to be the religion of that branch of the tribe of Yadu which, with its Brahmin, emigrated to the West. If it had a name, it called itself Israelite, or perhaps it called itself by the name of the God IE or IEUE, which was the same name by which God was called, and his praises chaunted, in the country which they had left, Yeye,—or as they call him in both Sanscrit and Hebrew *the God of victory*. I beg to refer to Book VIII. Chap. VI. Sect. 6. p. 429, and Book X. Chap. II. Sect. 14, p. 602.

The name which those people gave themselves is very difficult to find, and worthy of much consideration. If we revert to Book VIII. Chap. II. Sect. 2, p. 398, we shall find an account of great numbers of tribes of black Jews in different parts of India,—Buchanan counted upwards of fifty of them. Few of them possess Pentateuchs, except what they acknowledge that they have received from Christians or Jews of the West in modern times. These are nothing more than remains of the Ioudi or Iadu, who are to be met with, as might be expected, in almost every part of India,— and whenever any of them are observed by our travellers, they are honoured with the distinctive epithet of a tribe. It is not unlikely that, if carefully sought after, five hundred such tribes might be found. They are nothing more than remains of the people of the Pandæan kingdom—or of the Yadu, who have not become followers of Vishnu— who have not adopted the later changes of any of the various sects which have arisen from the renewed Avatars, &c., &c. The new sects, as might be expected, have over-rode them—borne them down. I have no doubt that great numbers of those whom we call Jews, and whom we find in other parts of the world, are the same.

I believe that if Ptolemy had not forced the publication of the Pentateuch in Greek, we never should have heard of the Jews of Jerusalem. Had their books continued *secret*, they, like the sacred and secret books of Athens and all other places or temples, would have been lost. For, though we find the mythos contained in Genesis almost every where, we no where find it in writing. But we have no writings of that early date. I think it not unlikely that it might be found in some of the temples of Jaggernaut or Baljii in South India, perhaps in that in which Dr. Buchanan found the Romish service in the act of being celebrated. Every large tribe coming from the East would bring with it, in substance, the same religious rites as the Brahmin brought to Jerusalem, which have all been lost. But, about the temple or the sacred mount of each tribe, we generally find some traces of the mythos.

In ancient times, we all know, that the Jews placed their sins upon a scape-goat, which they turned into the wilderness. In Tibet the same rite was practised. The goat and the sheep were of the same species, for which

---

[1] Though they brought the Gods, I think they were iconoclasts.

[2] The name Youdia means *hand of God*. The native princes of India often carry a hand as their crest, as do the followers of Ali in Persia. Parkhurst in voce. Do our Baronets carry a hand for a similar reason?

reason we constantly find them used for one another. From Lord Kingsborough's Antiquities of Mexico, Vol. VI. p. 301, I learn that the Jews at this time, instead of placing their sins on a Goat, place them on a Fish. This is a very striking fact. It induces me to believe that the true system is secretly known among some of the Jews. It dovetails into my system in so extraordinary a manner, and is of so peculiar a nature, that I can attribute it to nothing but the continuance of the mythos, which I have taken so much pains to penetrate, understand, and develop. It renders it highly probable that, as I have just observed, it is yet secreted among the Jews, and, consequently, if this be the fact, it raises the probability that I have discovered the true system to *a proof*. I can entertain no doubt of the veracity of Lord Kingsborough. Whether he has acquired his information from oral or written evidence, I know not; but be it which it may, for several reasons I can rather believe (in this peculiar case) in the truth of the POSITIVE evidence on which he has received this secreted fact, or piece of secret doctrine or ritual, than I can in the NEGATIVE *evidence* of ten thousand Jews, let them be in what rank of life, or of what country, they may. Their present denial of the Trinitarian doctrine, divulged by the greatest man of their nation who ever lived—Philo—proves that no dependence can be placed on any thing which they say, where their religious prejudice is concerned.

This apparently harsh judgment will, in a great measure, be justified, when, in my next volume, I shall shew that their apocryphal books of Wisdom and Ecclesiasticus contain some secret matters, of a most important and curious kind, of which it is absolutely impossible that their learned men can be ignorant. And it will decisively prove that their conclaves have the same Cabala as the Romish Conclave; and, indeed, the same as the conclave of every temple in the world formerly had.

Chardin, in his Travels,[1] states, that the Mingrelian Christians celebrate the paschal supper by eating *fish* instead of *lamb*. He tells a nonsensical story about the change of the *fish* into a *lamb* at Jesus Christ's last supper, in which it is evident that a mistake is made—and that the mythos originally had the story the other way, namely, the Lamb changed into the Fish.

When I find Clemens Alexandrinus, who was initiated into the mysteries of Eleusis, letting escape him, that their rites, or the doctrines taught in them, were copied from the laws of Moses, I cannot help suspecting that what they call a large book, which contains the most holy part of their doctrines, *and which was made of two stones*, and called πετρωμα, was a part of a similar history to that of the two stone tables of Mount Sinai [2] This will not be thought so paradoxical, when. in my next volume, I shall produce the learned Abbé Guerin de Rocher undertaking to prove that the whole Mosaic mythos, as well as Jephtha's daughter in Iphigenia, is to be found in the Grecian mythology.

We may observe that there are three great prevailing sects in India, which over-ride all the others, and those are the sects of the three Zodiacal signs—*first*, of Buddha symbolised by the Bull; *secondly*, of Cristna symbolised by the Lamb; and, *thirdly*, of Vishnu symbolised by the Fish. The first, I am persuaded, was originally Tur or Sur; the second, Crios, or Χρης, or Cristna; the third, the Vish or Fish. All these names, and all this mixture, seem to me to have arisen from the state of man, which we know from experience is natural to him. In the first period I believe they adored the Trimurti or Trinity, *Brahma, Turia* or *Suria* or *Buddha*, and *Seva*: in the second, Brahma, Cristna, and Seva: and now they adore Brahma, Vishnu, and Seva. If the Brahmins meet this with denials, then I tell them, it is notorious that they have long lost all knowledge of their mythology; and they have not a single book which can be expected to give the requisite information. The Vedas are not histories, as the part translated by the learned Professor Rosen shews, and are long previous to the period of the entrance of the Sun into Pisces, and perhaps of Aries also.

I am quite certain, that in all my reasonings I have not given sufficient weight to the absolute and complete ignorance of the present race of Indians in their history and mythology. They are really as ignorant of them as we are, and indeed more so. For their pretended genealogies of the line of princes up to the sun and moon, except to *a very little way back*, are all nonsense. Of *real* history, till about the Christian æra, they had none, like the Greeks before Herodotus: and their mythology or secret religion, when written, was all parable. They lost even their astronomy, only retaining the tables which were in daily use to make their calendars with, and to calculate the eclipses. I believe that it is the order of nature,—that it is one of the effects of the dissemination of superficial knowledge, to produce a tendency to the destruction of real and deep knowledge. I believe it is an order of nature not ill described by the oriental doctrine of the Metempsychosical renewal of cycles. Science comes to perfection, and then recedes, then rises again; and I cannot help suspecting that if the common use of the art of printing (a new element in all our calculations, the effect of which we cannot know, having no experience) do not prevent it, we shall run the same course again.

I believe the aspect of Indian affairs presents to our Indian travellers a complete chaos, though they do not like, each in his own case, to confess that it is so. There is nothing like a standard religion any where, so that a person may say *this is the religion*. Each Pundit tells his employer the story of his own theory or sect, which, of course, (as is found among European sectaries,) is always, according to him, the admitted and acknowledged truth, and there are scores of sects. Among the Brahmins there is no head, no individual or body to which a person can look for the locale of their religion. You may as well ask for the seat of the Protestant religion in Europe. Indeed, the Brahmins

---

are as much divided into sects as other parties. When the establishment went to pieces, each Temple or Church kept its own property, and retained its devotees. Sometimes it has continued nearly the same, sometimes it has changed, and become the religion of Jaggernaut, sometimes of Cali; the devotees have generally become Vishnuvites. In some instances they have taken a name jointly from the Lamb and the beneficent character of their God, and have become Crestons; and in others, not having fallen in with the new Avatar of Pisces, they have continued practising the old rites of Ayoudia. Our people now persuade them that they are Jews, which, as they have no tradition of their origin, and no sacred writings to guide them, or to contradict the Christians or Western Jews, may easily be done. If I understand Dr. Buchanan, they are a very low and illiterate race of people. In a similar manner, probably, most of the other numerous sects, whose names I do not know, have arisen. In five hundred years the religion of Britain would be precisely similar, if the establishment were abolished, and each church or chapel left as it is, in possession of its property. Some would be Trinitarian, some Arian, some Unitarian, some Southcotian; but still all Christian. In a similar manner all the sects of India are of the Brahmin religion, not Buddhists, as we are all Protestants, and not Papists. On the whole, it comes to this, that when our Indian scholars say, the Brahmins tell us this or tell us that, they only mean that their *Pundit* has told them this or that: and in every case, if they have asked the opinion of another Pundit, he has not denied what the other has said, though it may be quite new to him, if it have not made against his sectarian principle—if it be not against the credit of his order or country. And this will take place from a natural cause, without any wrong intention on the part of the Pundit. Not knowing any thing against it, he will suppose it true. Besides, there are a great many persons in India who despise the doctrines of all the sects, as there are philosophers in Europe who despise sectarian distinctions.

Before I conclude this volume I request my reader's attention to a peculiar system of Anthropomorphitism, and to the general anthropomorphic style of description which may be observed every where in the Jewish sacred writings, and, indeed, in those also of the Gentiles, and which has drawn down the severest censures upon them from modern philosophers, ignorant of their nature. I may instance the walking in the garden in the cool of the evening. If we are to suppose the writers meant those expressions to be taken literally, and that they did really believe that the Supreme First Cause so walked, we must take them for fools, and not, as circumstances would lead us to believe that they were, in many respects, men of the profoundest wisdom. But the case becomes very materially changed, when we find the First Cause here spoken of, to be, though a person of a very high and transcendant character, yet not the Supreme Being, but a person inferior in rank and dignity to the Most High, to the ineffable To Or. This view of the subject instantly removes much of the absurdity of the expressions alluded to. It is clear to me, that the knowledge, that the meaning of these expressions did not apply to the To Or, was a part of the *secret* system; and the doctrine that the literal meaning did apply to him was intended merely for the vulgar; and that it was fit and suitable for the understandings of the vulgar, is decisively proved, by its being yet received by hundreds of millions of them, who will be very indignant at me for letting out the secret doctrines, so much above the grasp of their faculties, and for denying that the Supreme Being did walk in the garden. But nothing can be well worse than this double system. It has not only kept the bees of the hive in ignorance, but it has ended at last, as might be expected, in the ignorance also of the drones themselves, and in the debasement of the intellect of both. This observation I consider an extremely important one, and one which might and ought to have been before noticed in my work; but it was not perceived by me till this volume was nearly printed, a blindness which I attribute to the extreme difficulty of unlearning the nonsense taught to me in my youth, of which I have so much complained in my Preface. I shall be told that my observation is not new, and that several writers have observed, that the God Jehovah of the Jews was supposed, or said by some of them, not to be the First Cause. This is true, but it, like many other things, though noticed, has been noticed only by being misrepresented and turned into ridicule; so that, for the cause of truth, it had better not have been noticed at all. As it was known only by having escaped from the mysteries, it probably was not understood by those who named it, to whom it might have appeared in the contemptible light in which they represented it. But this makes no difference as to the fact of the real misrepresentation.

The idea of the Person of whom I now speak, condescending to walk and talk with man, seems degrading in our estimation at first sight; but yet I know not how, in idea, to separate the former or reformer of our globe, and of its small, as well as large parts, from a sensation of littleness, or from anthropomorphism. We can scarcely form an idea how a world, or any matter, was to be formed, or moulded into shape, without organs. From this difficulty, I have no doubt arose the expedient of calling one of the persons of the Trinity by the term Logos,—for he spake the word—gave the word—and the world was made. From this the Logos and Lingua came to be united to the Linga— words identical, I have no doubt, in letters, in ancient, though a little varied in modern, times. The connexion between Linga and Logos, as generators of the globe or system, is evident enough. I can entertain no doubt, that the whole of the refined doctrine of Emanation, of the Trimurti, of the To Or, and Παλιγ αγγσος, was a Cabalistic secret, creeping out of the crypt by degrees. And though we often read of the Cabala about the time of the beginning of the Christian æra, yet I very much suspect, that its real existence was then denied by the initiated, as it has been since, and is now at Rome and Moscow. I believe the Protestant priests are perfectly ignorant, and that they are too vain of their little bit of Greek and Latin, to submit to be taught. And, as to their predecessors, Luther and Calvin, I believe they were as much the sufferers from *monomania* as John Wesley, who fancied he had miracles performed upon him almost every day.

*March* 10, 1833.

ON

# THE VOWEL POINTS OF THE HEBREW LANGUAGE.

---

(From THE CLASSICAL JOURNAL, XXXIII. 145—153.)

*To the Editor.*

SIR,

IN consequence of the present prevailing fashion for the study of the Hebrew language, I am induced to offer some observations respecting its celebrated vowel points. It appears that a new school of divinity is arising, which is chiefly founded on an old exploded notion of the antiquity of these points. The object for which this obsolete doctrine is revived, is, I think, sufficiently evident. However, with your permission, as concisely as is in my power, I propose to submit to your readers a few of the reasons which formerly caused it to be exploded, and which, I flatter myself, will finally consign it to its long home. The Hebrew language, as it is found in the copies of the Pentateuch used in the synagogues, consists of twenty-two letters, but is devoid of the marks which are known by the name of the vowel points. The present Jews, with the followers of the new divinity school, maintain that these points are of very great antiquity; some asserting them to be as old as Ezra, others coeval with the language. On the contrary, it has been the opinion of most learned men in modern times, that they have been not only adopted as authority, but invented, since the time of Christ; that they were invented in the dark ages by the Jews, in order to enable them to give such meaning and pro-nunciation to the text as they thought proper, and further to enable them, on once having given it that meaning and pronunciation, to keep them from all change in future. The object for which they were invented is evident from the circumstance, that they not only added a system of new vowels to the language, but they contrived to abolish the old ones, and render them silent and useless as vowels, and convert them, when joined to the new letters, into consonants. Had the object of the Jews in inventing the points been merely to fix the pronunciation, they would not have done away with the old vowels, but only added some points to them. But this would not have served their purpose; there-fore they were obliged to get quit of the sturdy old vowels, which would not be made to bend to their purposes, and to convert them into consonants.

The simple question at issue betwixt the parties is, whether these points be new or old; and this, I think, it will not be difficult to settle. If what Harris says be true, that a letter is a sign significant, the vowel points and accents or marks, upwards of twenty in number, must be letters, for they are certainly signs significant; and it is pretty evident that the addition of such a number of letters to any language must enable the person adding them, to give to the origi-nal text nearly whatever meaning he thinks proper. This is the object for which they were invented by the Jews, and this is now the object for which the new school of Christians support them.

In the beginning of the last and the end of the preceding century, the question of the antiquity of these points was discussed at great length, and with no little warmth and animation, by a great number of very learned men, until the subject appeared to be completely exhausted, and the question settled. To enter into the contest again would be use-less, and evidently would occupy too much space in your miscellany: but as Dean Prideaux has summed up the chief arguments against them in a short and compendious form, it may be useful to many of your readers who are misinformed by their Jewish and Christian instructors, to see what has been said by him against them. The following are the prin-cipal reasons which he gives against their antiquity:

1. " The sacred books made use of by the Jews in their synagogues, have ever been, and still are, without the vowel points, which would not have happened had they been placed there by Ezra, and consequently been of the same autho-rity with the letters; for, had they been so, they would certainly have been preserved in the synagogues with the same care as the rest of the text. There can scarce any other reason be given why they were not admitted thither, but that, when the Holy Scriptures began first to be publicly read to the people in their synagogues, there were no such vowel points then in being; and that when they afterwards came in use, being known to be of a human invention, they were for that reason never thought fit to be added to those sacred copies, which were looked on as the true representatives of the original; and therefore they have been ever kept with the same care in the ark or sacred chest of the synagogue, as

the original draft of the law of Moses anciently was in the ark or sacred chest of the tabernacle, which was prepared for it; and they are still so kept in the same manner among them to this day.

2. " The ancient *various readings* of the sacred text, called Keri Cetib, are all about the letters, and none about the vowel points; which seem manifestly to prove, that the vowel points were not anciently in being, or else were not looked on as an authentic part of the text; for if they had, the variations of these would certainly have been taken notice of, as well as those of the letters.

3. " The ancient cabalists draw none of their mysteries from the vowel points, but all from the letters : which is an argument either that these vowel points were not in use in their time, or else were not then looked on as an authentic part of the sacred text; for had they then been so, these triflers would certainly have drawn mysteries from the one as well as from the other, as the later cabalists have done.

4. " If we compare with the present pointed Hebrew Bibles the version of the Septuagint, the Chaldee paraphrases, the fragments of Aquila, Symmachus, and Theodotion, or the Latin version of Jerome, we shall in several places find that they did read the text otherwise than according to the present punctuation; which is a certain argument that the pointed copies, if there were any such in their times, were not then held to be of any authority; for otherwise they would certainly have followed them.

5. " Neither the Mistna, nor the Gemara, either that of Jerusalem or that of Babylon, do make any mention of these vowel points, although in several places there are such special occasions and reasons for them so to have done, that it can scarce be thought possible they could have omitted it if they had been in being when these books were written; or, if in being, had been looked on by the Jews of those times to be of any authority amongst them. Neither do we find the least hint of them in Philo-Judæus or Josephus, who are the oldest writers of the Jews, or in any of the ancient Christian writers for several hundred years after Christ. And although among them Origen and Jerome were well skilled in the Hebrew language, yet in none of their writings do they speak the least of them. Origen flourished in the third, and Jerome in the fifth century; and the latter having lived a long time in Judea, and there more especially applied himself to the study of Hebrew learning, and much conversed with the Jewish Rabbies for his improvement therein, it is not likely that he could have missed making some mention of them through all his voluminous works, if they had been either in being among the Jews in his time, or in any credit or authority with them, and that especially, since in his commentaries there were so many necessary occasions for his taking notice of them; and it cannot be denied but that this is a very strong argument against them."—Prid. Con. P. i. B. v.

The Dean has not done justice to his own observations respecting Origen; for he might have added, that numerous examples might be produced from his works, where he has quoted the Hebrew in a manner different from the present masoretic punctuation, particularly in his Heptacla, in writing Hebrew into Greek characters.

This short compendium of the Dean's seems to me to be quite sufficient to decide the question. Indeed, the well-known fact named in his first section, of the text in the synagogue copies being without the points, cannot be got over. The points are not only wanting, but

" The text of the synagogue-rolls of the Pentateuch is not divided into verses, and is also without the points of distinction (:) called Soph-pesuk. Buxtorf, in his Tiberius, Ch. ii. p. 113, quotes the following note from Elias Levitta : ' It is a certain truth, and of which there is no doubt, that this law which Moses set before the Israelites was plain, without points, and without accents, and without any distinction of verses, even as we see it at this day; and according to the opinion of the cabalistic doctors, the whole law was as one verse, yea, and there are that say as one word.' Yeates's Collation, pp. 35, 36."—Townley's Illustration, Vol. I. p. 58.

The great supporters of the antiquity of the points were the two Buxtorfs—no doubt, men of great learning and talent. But the only argument which they produced of any weight which is not answered by the preceding five paragraphs of the Dean's, is this, " that when the Hebrew language ceased to be the mother tongue of the Jews, (as it is agreed on all hands that it did after the Babylonish captivity,) it was scarce possible to teach that language without the vowel points."—Prid. Con.

This argument is completely refuted by the fact, that the Samaritan Pentateuch, as well as the Chaldee paraphrases before the time of Buxtorf, were all without the points, and the former still remains so. It seems quite absurd to suppose that, if the Hebrew had once had them, it should ever have lost them. And the argument that the language must have had them because it could not be read without them, is at once refuted by the fact of the Samaritan being yet without them, as well as several other languages. The reader will find much curious information on the question here discussed in Bishop Marsh's 10th and 12th Lectures.

On this subject Dr. Robertson says,

" For neither the obsolete Arabic characters called the Cuphic, which fell into disuse about A. D 930, nor the alphabet of the Sanscrit in India, a language that has been dead or not currently spoken these 1200 years, nor the Chaldee, Syriac, or Samaritan, nor any other ancient Eastern language that we know of, ever employed vowel points as the modern Jews and Arabs do. The Arabic vowel points came first into use at the time when the modern Arabic alphabet was adopted by order of the Kalif of the Saracens, Almuktadir, A. D. 390. The new alphabet was invented by his vizir, Ibn Mukla "

Much pains have been taken to shew that without the points the meaning of the language must be doubtful; that some words will bear as many as even hundreds of different meanings; and thence it has been inferred that the language always must have had them. This argument, the fact stated above, of several languages being still without them, sufficiently refutes. The imperfection of the language may be a subject of regret, but it cannot be admitted as a proof of the antiquity of the system of pointing against such evidence as is produced. With respect to the mode of obviating this imperfection, it is evident that there is no other way to be adopted than to consult and compare similar texts with one another, and with the old versions made when the language was still living. For this purpose, in the case of the Pentateuch, the Samaritan, and the Latin Vulgate (*a version made from the Hebrew*) may be consulted, and, above all, the Septuagint. Persons wishing for more information may consult Walton's Prolegomena, his Considerator Considered, and the works of Dr. Grabbe.

It is said that the Jews in their synagogues, in reading their law, always read first a passage in the Hebrew, and then the passage in the language of the country, that it might be understood. And in order to pronounce it correctly, the reader for the day always on the day preceding practised his lesson by reading it over from a pointed copy. From this it is inferred that the points are ancient. But I do not see how this can prove any thing of the kind; for the practice itself was not ancient nor general, as is proved by a curious passage quoted by Buxtorf in his Lexicon Talm. Rabbinicum, from the Talmud of Jerusalem.

" Rabbi Levi ivit Cæsaream, audiensque eos legentes lectionem ' audi Israel,' Deut. vi., Hellenisticè, voluit impedire ipsos." Vide Marsh, Mic.

The fact of the service of the Jews being read in the synagogues in countries foreign to Judea, and after their last dispersion, in the Greek language, cannot be doubted, and may be proved from various passages in Tertullian, Origen, Philo, &c.; but the matter is put out of dispute by a decree of Justinian, A. D. 550, (Novel. 146; Photii Nomocanon, xii. 3; also Gothofredi Corpus Juris Civilis; Novel. 146, II. i. 580,) passed for the express purpose of determining the question; for disputes had arisen amongst the Jews on the question, whether their service was to be read in the Hebrew or the Greek : and the Emperor settled it by giving them permission to read the Hebrew if they pleased, *paying a tax for so doing*.

In the synagogues in Egypt and other places, the service, ever after the time of Onias, was read in the Greek language. When the Jewish captives taken by Titus and Vespasian came to be dispersed over the empire, they were not content with this practice of the Hellenistic Jews, which they considered wrong—heretical; and after some time they endeavoured to change it, and this was the cause of the disputes; similar to what had happened before at Cæsarea, when Rabbi Levi found them reading the law HELLENISTICE.

The doctors of the new school, mirabile dictu! are actually in support of their system driven to the necessity of maintaining that the LXX. was burnt in the time of Cæsar (though Tertullian witnesses that it was at Alexandria in his time); and that Origen in his Heptacla, Jerome, Justinian, and all the Jews, were mistaken; and that all these people, quoting, editing, quarrelling, legislating, never once suspected that they had mistaken the version of Aquila for the Septuagint,—Greek being the vernacular tongue of Origen, and Hebrew of the Jews!

It would occupy too much of your Journal, or else many passages might be produced from the New Testament, and the works of Jerome, Origen, &c , to prove that their authors quoted from unpointed copies. But they may be found in Walton's Prolegomena, and in his Considerator Considered. Nothing can well be more striking than this fact; yet perhaps one example may not encroach too much on your space.

In the last verse of the 47th chapter of Genesis, Jacob is said in our Bible to have *bowed himself on the bed's head*. The Vulgate renders this passage, *conversus ad lectuli caput;* the LXX., ἐπὶ τὸ ἄκρον τῆς ῥαβδου αὐτοῦ, in summitatem *virgæ suæ, upon the top of his staff*. Now, the word in Hebrew, מטה *mte*, means both staff and bed, accordingly as it is pointed; and the makers of the LXX. have evidently made a mistake, which if they had had a pointed copy they would not have done. How absurd to suppose that the old man lying on his death-bed should bow his head on his walking-staff! The truth of this rendering of the word מטה *mte* by the word *lectum* and not *virga*, is proved from its repetition in the last verse of the 49th chapter, where it is said *collegit pedes suos super lectulum*, Vulg.; τοὺς πόδας αὐτοῦ ἐπὶ τῆν κλίνην, LXX.

This proves that there were no points when the LXX was made. St. Paul, quoting the passage, uses the word *virga*—a proof that he quoted from the LXX , or else that he made a mistake in the Hebrew; and as the latter will not be allowed, it tends to prove against the new school that the version which we have is really the LXX. The Samaritan text and version and the Targum have the same reading as the Vulgate, *lectum*. The Arabic and Syriac versions made from the LXX. of course fall into its mistake This example also furnishes one proof against the dogma of the new school *that St. Jerome did not understand Hebrew*, that he did understand it, and that he used it profitably too, in his Latin version.

I apprehend that when the Hebrew became a dead language, the points were invented by degrees to enable the masters in the schools better to instruct their pupils, and after some time they began to have authority given to them by the Rabbies. No man appears to have taken more trouble to examine the question than Dean Prideaux. From him we learn that all the Rabbinical authors were unpointed in his time, and that all their other books were originally without them; that in some new editions points were put to them, but that the best editions were without them ; that they were added to the Targums by Buxtorf; and that they were only a little before his time added to the Mistna and Machzor. (Prid. Con. B. v. pp. 422, 429, ed. 8vo. 1815.) I shall not now intrude any further on you than merely to add, that if your readers wish for any more proofs of the modern date of the masoretic points, they mày consult the works of the following persons, who all wrote in defence of that doctrine, and by whom the question was considered to be settled :

Capellus, Elias Levitta, Thomas Erpenius, Isaac Casaubon, J. J. Scaliger, Isaac Vossius, J. Drusius, Arnolde Boote, Andrew Rivet, Lewis de Dieu, Grotius, Spanheim, Festus Hommius, Theodore Beza, Selden, Walton, Sennert, Basnage, Burman, Simon, Limborch, Morinus, Vitringa, Le Clerc, Heuman, L'Advocat, Houbigant, Louth, Kennicott, and Marsh, Theol. Lec. P. ii. Lib. x. p. 75 ; also see Todd's Life of Walton, note 1, Vol. II. p. 322.

Perhaps it is unnecessary to observe, that it is not so much my object to discuss the question on which I have slightly touched, as to suggest to your readers who have lately commenced the study of the Hebrew language and its history, where they may find the best authorities on the subject, in order that they may not be misled by the specious and plausible, though unfounded, assertions of the new school.

GODFREY HIGGINS.

*Skellow Grange, near Doncaster.*

# APPENDIX II.

After my First Appendix was printed, I received Mr. Von Hammer's French History of the Assassins, published March 1833. It is exactly what a book on such a subject, written by Mr. Von Hammer under the patronage of the Emperor of Austria, might be expected to be found. It is difficult to say whether religious malice or ignorant prejudice most prevails. I shall only notice one passage which, in a very striking manner, proves the truth of what I have said, in Book X., respecting the College of St. John's, at Cambridge. When all the other circumstances are considered, it cannot for a moment be believed, that the same dresses should be adopted at Cairo and at Cambridge, without some communication or without a common origin. After describing the College, or MAISON DE SAGESSE, as he calls it, at Cairo, in page 55, he says,

"Souvent les Khalifes y présidaient des thèses savantes, dans lesquelles paroissaient, suivant l'ordre de leur facultés, " les professeurs attachés à cette académie, LOGICIENS, MATHÉMATICIENS, JURISTES, et MÉDECINS, tous revêtus dans " leurs habits de cérémonie (khalaa), ou de leur manteaux de docteurs. Les manteaux des universités Anglaises ont " encore aujourd'hui la vieille forme du khalaa ou du kaftan, qui étaient les habits d'honneur des Arabes." He shews that, to the support of this establishment, the tithes were appropriated; and in p. 58, describing the doctrines of the Assassins, he unwittingly lets the following passage escape him : " On enseignait que toute législation positivement " religieuse, devait être subordonnée à la législation générale philosophique." " Les Doctrines de Plato, de Aristote. " et de Pythagore, étaient citées comme des preuves logiques et fondamentales." I cannot refrain from expressing my pleasure at this presumptive proof of the truth of what I have said of the Assassins, Templars, &c , &c., &c. It is only by taking advantage of such, to all appearance, trifling casualties, that the secret truths of the ancients can be wrested from the hand of the destroyers.

The work of Mr. Von Hammer is probably intended to create an alarm against the orders of Carbonari, Masons, Templars, &c. I shall probably return to it.

*April 15th*, 1833.

# INDEX.

5 Q

5 s

☿ 220.

♀ 220, 222.

| Title | Author | Price |
|---|---|---|
| A Book of The Beginnings Vol I & 11 | Massey. | 49.95 |
| Afrikan Holistic Health | Afrika. | 18.95 |
| Afrikan Discovery of America | Weiner | 16.95 |
| Arab Invasion of Egypt & The First 30 Years of Roman Dominion | | 16.95 |
| Anacalypsis (Set) | Massey | 49.95 |
| Ankh: African Origin of Electromagnetism | | 10.95 |
| Aids The End of Civilization | Douglass | 10.95 |
| Altered Images | Khu Schu | 14.00 |
| Aquarian Gospel of Jesus Christ | Levi | 14.95 |
| A Taste of an African Table | Egwu | 11.95 |
| Baby Names: Real Names with Real Meanings For African Children | | 11.95 |
| Black Heroes of the Martial Arts | Van Clief | 16.95 |
| Apocrypha (Hc) | | 14.95 |
| Book Your Church Doesn't want You To Read | Leedom | 19.95 |
| British Historians and the West Indies | Eric Williams | 15.95 |
| Christopher Columbus & The African Holocaust | JohnHenrik Clark | 10.95 |
| Columbus Conspiracy | Bradley | 16.95 |
| Dawn Voyage: The Black African Discovery of America | Bradley | 16.95 |
| Documents of West Indian History | Eric Williams | 16.95 |
| Education of the Negro | Carter G. Woodson | 10.95 |
| Egyptian Book of the Dead | Budge | 12.95 |
| Egyptian Book of the Dead/Ancient Mysteries of Amenta | Massey | 9.95 |
| Ethiopian Sovreignty: African Nationhood | McPherson | 9.95 |
| Enoch, The Ethiopian | Kush | 16.95 |
| First Council of Nice: A World's Christian Convention A.D 325 | | 9.95 |
| Forbidden Books of The New Testament | | 14.95 |
| From the Black Churches | MacPherson | 12.95 |
| Gerald Massey Lectures | | 10.95 |
| Global Afrikan Presence | Edward Scobie | 15.95 |
| Gospel of Barnabas | Nu'Man | 11.95 |
| Greater Key of Solomon | | 10.00 |
| Hairlocking: Everything You Need To Know | Nekhena Evans | 9.95 |
| Harlem Voices From The Soul of Black America | John Henrik Clarke | 11.95 |
| Harlem USA | John Henrik Clarke | 11.95 |
| Healthy Foods and Spiritual Nutrition HandBook | Keith Wright | 11.95 |
| Heal Thyself For Health And Longevity | Queen Afua | 15.00 |
| Heal Thyself Natural LIving Cookbook | Diane Cicone | 10.95 |
| HIstorical Jesus and The Mythical Christ | Massey | 9.95 |
| HIstory of The People of Trinidad & Tobago | Eric Williams | 15.95 |
| Keys to Your Dreams | Soccolic | 14.95 |
| Lost Books of The Bible and The Forgotten Books of Eden | | 13.95 |
| Master Teacher | Barbara Eleanor Adams | 14.95 |
| Nutrition Made Simple at a Glance | Jordan-Joseph | 8.95 |
| Rape of Paradise: Columbus and the Birth of Racism in America | Jan Carew | 15.95 |
| Signs and Symbols of Primordal Man | | 16.95 |
| Two Babylons | | 14.95 |
| Science & Myth of Melanin | | 16.95 |
| Nutricide | Afrika | 17.95 |
| Rastafari: An Open Challenge to The Church | McPherson | 7.95 |
| The Promised Key: The Original Literary Roots of Rastafari | | 7.95 |
| The Gullah People Blessed By God | Afrika | 11.95 |
| The Holy KOran of The Moorish Science Temple of America | Drew Ali | 5.00 |
| Vitamins & Minerals A To Z | Jewel Pookrum | 10.95 |
| What They Never Told You In History Class | Kush | 17.95 |
| Freemasonry Interpreted | | 12.95 |
| Freemasony & The Vatican | | 11.95 |